Foundations of Quantum Programming

Foundations of Quantum Programming

Second Edition

Mingsheng Ying

MORGAN KAUFMANN PUBLISHERS

ELSEVIER AN IMPRINT OF ELSEVIER

ISBN: 978-0-443-15942-8

For information on all Morgan Kaufmann publications
visit our website at https://www.elsevier.com/books-and-journals

Publisher: Mara Conner
Acquisitions Editor: Chris Katsaropoulos
Editorial Project Manager: Palak Gupta
Production Project Manager: Erragounta Saibabu Rao
Cover Designer: Greg Harris

Typeset by VTeX

Contents

Biography

Prof. Mingsheng Ying (1964–)

Mingsheng Ying is a Research Professor and the Deputy Director for Research with the Institute of Software, Chinese Academy of Sciences, and Cheung Kong Professor with the Department of Computer Science and Technology, and the Director of the Research Center for Quantum Software, Tsinghua University, China. He was a Distinguished Professor and the Research Director of the Centre for Quantum Software and Information, University of Technology Sydney, Australia.

His research interests are quantum computing, programming language theory, and logics in artificial intelligence. He has authored the books *Model Checking Quantum Systems: Principles and Algorithms* (Cambridge University Press, 2021), *Foundations of Quantum Programming* (1st edition, Morgan Kaufmann, 2016), and *Topology in Process Calculus: Approximate Correctness and Infinite Evolution of Concurrent Programs* (Springer-Verlag, 2001). He currently serves as the (Co-)Editor-in-Chief of *ACM Transactions on Quantum Computing*.

Preface to the second edition

The focus and style of this second edition is the same as those of the first edition. This book addresses foundational issues in quantum programming. The main aim of this edition is to include the following new materials, which, I believe, will become important in the not too distant future:

- *Parallel and distributed quantum programming*: In the first edition, we focused on sequential quantum programming. But parallel and distributed architectures of quantum computers were introduced in the IBM Quantum roadmap announced in 2022. It is likely that the same or similar architectures will soon be adopted by other builders of quantum computers. This motivated me to write two chapters to describe programming models and methodologies for parallel and distributed quantum computers.
- *More about verification and analysis of quantum programs*: As quantum hardware becomes larger and larger, more and more sophisticated quantum programs can run on it. Then verification and analysis techniques for quantum programs will be indispensable. In the first edition, quantum Hoare logic was introduced, but we did not consider how verification techniques and tools can be built upon it. In this edition, a new chapter is added to discuss this issue. In particular, several ideas are introduced for improving scalability of the verification techniques; including (i) localisation of reasoning; and (ii) Birkhoff–von Neumann quantum logic as an assertion language. There was already a chapter for quantum program analysis in the first edition. But it mainly dealt with termination and expected runtime. After the publication of the first edition, several new analysis techniques have emerged, including invariants and abstract interpretation of quantum programs. In this edition, the chapter is expanded to expose them.

Except the above, the chapter of preliminaries in the first edition is now divided into three chapters, and two new sections for quantum *Turing machines* and *random access stored program machines* are added to give the reader a more complete picture of quantum computational models. Other chapters are also updated with some minor changes and corrections.

The biggest missing in this book is compilation and optimisation of quantum programs, but an exposition of them needs another book.

It is my great pleasure to thank Chris Katsaropoulos, Palak Gupta and Erragounta Saibabu Rao of Morgan Kaufmann for the excellent cooperation in producing this new edition. I would like to thank all colleagues and students with whom the new materials in this edition are largely based on the collaborations. Finally, I also like to thank the Institute of Software, Chinese Academy of Sciences and Department of Computer Science and Technology, Tsinghua University for giving me the freedom to pursue my research agenda.

My research on quantum programming has been supported by the National Key R&D Program of China and the National Natural Science Foundation of China.

Mingsheng Ying
Beijing, China
December 2023

Preface to the first edition

Perhaps the quantum computer will change our everyday lives in this century in the same radical way as the classical computer did in the last century.

– excerpt from Press Release, Nobel Prize in Physics 2012

Quantum computers promise dramatic advantages over current computers. Governments and industries around the globe are now investing large amounts of money with the expectation of building practical quantum computers. Recent rapid physical experimental progress has made people widely expect that large-scalable and functional quantum computer *hardware* will be built within 10–20 years. However, to realise the superpower of quantum computing, quantum hardware is obviously not enough, and quantum *software* must also play a key role. The software development techniques used today cannot be applied to quantum computers. Essential differences between the nature of the classical world and that of the quantum world mean that new technologies are required to program quantum computers.

Research on quantum programming started in as early as 1996, and rich results have been presented at various conferences or reported in various journals in the last 20 years. On the other hand, quantum programming is still a premature subject, with its knowledge base being highly fragmentary and disconnected. This book is intended to provide a systematic and detailed exposition of the subject of quantum programming.

Since quantum programming is still an area under development, the book does not focus on specific quantum programming languages or techniques, which I believe will undergo major changes in the future. Instead, the emphasis is placed on the foundational concepts, methods, and mathematical tools that can be widely used for various languages and techniques. Starting from a basic knowledge of quantum mechanics and quantum computation, the book carefully introduces various quantum program constructs and a chain of quantum programming models that can effectively exploit the unique power of quantum computers. Furthermore, semantics, logics, and verification and analysis techniques of quantum programs are systematically discussed.

With the huge investment and rapid progress in quantum computing technology, I believe that within 10 years more and more researchers will enter this exciting field of quantum programming. They will need a reference book as the starting point of their research. Also, a course on quantum programming will be taught at more and more universities. Teachers and students will need a textbook. So, I decided to write this book with the two-fold aim:

1. providing a basis for further research in the area; and
2. serving as a textbook for a graduate or advanced undergraduate level course.

Quantum programming is a highly interdisciplinary subject. A newcomer and in particular, a student is usually frustrated with the requisite knowledge from many different subjects. I have tried to keep the book as selfcontained as possible with details being explicitly presented so that it is accessible to the programming languages community.

Writing this book gave me an opportunity to systemise my views on quantum programming. On the other hand, topics included in this book were selected and the materials were organised according to my own understanding of this subject, and several important topics were omitted in the main body of the book due to my limited knowledge about them. As a remedy, some brief discussions about these topics are provided in the prospects chapter at the end of the book.

Acknowledgements

This book has been developed through my research in the last 15 years at the Quantum Computation and Quantum Information Group of the State Key Laboratory of Intelligent Technology and Systems, Tsinghua University and the Quantum Computation Laboratory of the Centre for Quantum Computation and Intelligent Systems, University of Technology Sydney. I have enjoyed very much collaborations and discussions with my colleagues and students there. I would like to thank all of them.

I am particularly indebted to Ichiro Hasuo (University of Tokyo) and Yuan Feng (University of Technology Sydney) who patiently read the draft of this book and kindly provided invaluable comments and suggestions. I am very grateful to the anonymous reviewers for the book proposal, their suggestions were very helpful for the structure of the book. I also like to sincerely thank Amy Invernizzi and Steve Elliot, my editors at Morgan Kaufmann, for their editorial advice and assistance.

Special thanks go to the Centre for Quantum Computation and Intelligent Systems, Faculty of Engineering and Information Technology, University of Technology Sydney for giving me the freedom to pursue my thoughts.

My research on quantum programming has been supported by the Australian Research Council, the National Natural Science Foundation of China, and the Overseas Team Program of the Academy of Mathematics and Systems Science, Chinese Academy of Sciences. All of them are gratefully acknowledged.

Mingsheng Ying
Sydney, NSW, Australia
November 2015

Chapter 1

Introduction

> The challenge [of quantum software engineering] is to rework and extend the whole of classical software engineering into the quantum domain so that programmers can manipulate quantum programs with the same ease and confidence that they manipulate today's classical programs.
>
> – excerpt from the 2004 Report of "UK Grand Challenges in Computing Research" [212]

Quantum programming is the study of how to program future quantum computers. This subject mainly addresses the following two problems:

- How can programming methodologies and technologies developed for current computers be extended for quantum computers?
- What kind of new programming methodologies and technologies can effectively exploit the unique power of quantum computing?

Many technologies that have been very successful in classical (traditional) programming will be broken when used to program a quantum computer due to the weird nature of quantum systems (e.g. nocloning of quantum data, entanglement between quantum processes, and noncommutativity of observables – assertions about quantum program variables). Even more important and difficult is to discover programming paradigms, models, and abstractions that can properly exploit the unique power of quantum computing – *quantum parallelism*, but cannot be sourced from knowledge of classical programming.

1.1 From classical programming to quantum programming – *"Everything old is new again!"*

The earliest proposal for quantum programming was made by Knill in 1996 [254]. He introduced the Quantum Random Access Machine (QRAM) model and proposed a set of conventions for writing quantum pseudo-code. In the almost three decades since then, research on quantum programming has been continuously conducted. In particular, a rapid progress happened in the last few years, mainly stimulated by the efforts of building quantum hardware by several IT giants.

Programming Languages and Systems is a huge field of computer science. Researchers have tried to extend various classical (traditional) programming methodologies and technologies into quantum programming. But quantum computing is a new computing technology with significant changes at the foundational level of computing models. The transition from classical programming to quantum programming can be described by *"Everything old is new again"* – the title of a song by Peter Allen – which was also used by John Hennesy in his Turing Award lecture to describe Computer Architecture at the age of AI.

In this section, we briefly discuss the history of quantum programming research and some of recent work. I should apologise for that many important researches are not mentioned here due to the limitation of space and my own knowledge. For two recent reviews of this area, we refer to [204,449]. Also, the reader can find a quantum programming bibliography (maintained by Kartik Singhal) at the webpage: https://quantumpl.github.io/bib/.

1.1.1 Quantum programming languages and compilers

Early research on quantum programming focused on the design of quantum programming languages. Several high-level quantum programming languages had been defined in the later 1990's and early 2000's; for example, the first quantum programming language, QCL, was designed by Ömer [325]; he also implemented a simulator for this language. A quantum programming language in the style of Dijkstra's guarded-command language, qGCL, was proposed by Sanders and Zuliani [361,455]. A quantum extension of C++ was proposed by Bettelli et al. [60], and implemented in the form of a C++ library. The first quantum language of the functional programming paradigm, QPL, was defined by Selinger [367] based on

Foundations of Quantum Programming. https://doi.org/10.1016/B978-0-44-315942-8.00009-5

the idea of classical control and quantum data. A quantum functional programming language QML with quantum control flows was introduced by Altenkirch and Grattage [19]. Tafliovich and Hehner [387,388] defined a quantum extension of predicative programming language that supports the program development technique in which each programming step is proven correct when it is made. These early researches played an important role in helping us to understand some basic differences between classical programming and quantum programming [168,203,360,368,418].

The second wave of research on quantum programming languages occurred in early 2010's. For example, two general-purpose, scalable quantum programming languages, Quipper and Scaffold, with compilers were developed by Green, Lumsdaine, Ross, Selinger, and Valiron [187] and Abhari, Faruque, Dousti, et al. [4], respectively. A domain-specific quantum programming language QuaFL was developed by Lapets, da Silva, Thome, Adler, Beal, and Rötteler [269]. A quantum software architecture LIQUi|> together with a quantum programming language embedded in F# was designed and implemented by Wecker and Svore [405]. A series of researches on quantum computer architecture have also been carried out in this period of time [105,298].

Stimulated by the rapid progress of building quantum hardware since the middle of 2010's, quantum programming languages and compilers have become a very active research area with the emphasis on practical applications, and many new research results have been reported, from instruction sets and intermediate representations (e.g. OpenQSAM [113], Quil [380], QIR [346]) to languages for the description of quantum circuits (e.g. QWIRE [332]), high-level programming languages and frameworks (e.g. Q# [386], Quipper [187], Silq [63], Quingo [166]) and software stacks (e.g. Qiskit [221], tket [347], Cirq [181], isQ [193]). A quantum programming language Qunity was designed in [401] in order to treat quantum computing as a natural generalisation of classical computing. Also, data structures were recently introduced into quantum programming languages by Yuan and Carbin [447].

It seems that the Noisy Intermediate-Scale Quantum (NISQ) era [342] will last for a while in the future, in which hardware is too resource-constrained to support error correction, and running long sequences of operations on them is impractical. So, a particularly important research topic is optimising quantum compilers (see e.g. [225,299,412]). A large part of a classical optimising compiler target the optimisation of high-level program constructs, e.g. loop optimisation. But the current research on optimising quantum compilers mainly considers the optimisation of quantum circuits because at this moment high-level program constructs cannot be executed on quantum hardware. Since we aim mainly at dealing with the foundational issues, the compilation techniques for quantum programs are not covered in the main body of this book but will be briefly discussed in the final prospect chapter.

1.1.2 Semantics and type systems of quantum programs

Formal semantics of a programming language gives a rigorous mathematical description of the meaning of this language, to enable a precise and deep understanding of the essence of the language beneath its syntax. The operational or denotational semantics of some early quantum programming languages were already provided when they were defined; for example qGCL, QPL, and QML mentioned in the above subsection [290].

Two approaches to predicate transformer semantics of quantum programs have been proposed. The first was adopted by Sanders and Zuliani [361] in designing qGCL, where quantum computation is reduced to probabilistic computation by the observation (measurement) procedure, and thus predicate transformer semantics developed for probabilistic programs [297] can be applied to quantum programs. The second was introduced by D'Hondt and Panangaden [131], where a quantum predicate is defined to be a physical observable represented by a Hermitian operator with eigenvalues within the unit interval. Quantum predicate transformer semantics was further developed in [424] with a special class of quantum predicates; namely projection operators. Focusing on projective predicates allows to use rich mathematical methods developed in Birkhoff–von Neumann quantum logic [66] to establish various healthiness conditions of quantum programs.

Semantic techniques for quantum computation have also been investigated in some abstract, language-independent ways. Abramsky and Coeck [6] proposed a category-theoretic formulation of the basic postulates of quantum mechanics, which can be used to give an elegant description of quantum programs and communication protocols such as teleportation. Recent progress includes: Hasuo and Hoshino [202] found a semantic model of a functional quantum programming language with recursion via Girard's Geometry of Interaction [177], categorically formulated by Abramsky, et al. [8,68]. Pagani, Selinger, and Valiron [329] discovered a denotational semantics for a functional quantum programming language with recursion and an infinite data type using constructions from quantitative semantics of linear logic. Jacobs [226] proposed a categorical axiomatisation of block constructs in quantum programming. Staton [382] presented an algebraic semantic framework for equational reasoning about quantum programs.

Now the semantic techniques developed in the above work have been widely adopted in defining various quantum programming languages. In this book, we will formally define the operational and denotational semantics of several important quantum program constructs, including sequential, parallel, and distributed quantum programs, when they are introduced.

Type systems have been widely employed in modern programming languages to specify data types and to reduce the possibility of bugs due to type errors. Several quantum programming languages are also equipped with effective type systems. For example, a linear dependent type system was defined by Fu, Kishida, and Selinger [164] for Quipper, a linear type system was provided by Paykin, Rand, and Zdancewic [332] for QWIRE, and a type system for Q# was proposed by Singhal et al. [379]; one of the main purposes for all of them is to enforce statistically the noncloning principle for quantum data.

1.1.3 Verification and analysis of quantum programs

Human intuition is much better adapted to the classical world than the quantum world. This fact implies that programmers will commit many more faults in designing programs for quantum computers than programming classical computers. Thus, it is crucial to develop verification techniques for quantum programs.

First, various program logics have been generalised to the quantum setting. For example, Baltag and Smets [41] presented a dynamic logic formalism of information flows in quantum systems. Brunet and Jorrand [79] introduced a way of applying Birkhoff–von Neumann quantum logic in reasoning about quantum programs. Chadha, Mateus, and Sernadas [85] proposed a proof system of the Floyd–Hoare style for reasoning about imperative quantum programs in which only bounded iterations are allowed. Some useful proof rules for reasoning about quantum programs were proposed by Feng et al. [146] for purely quantum programs. In particular, a (Floyd–)Hoare logic for both partial and total correctness of quantum programs with (relative) completeness was developed in [419]. In the last few years, research in this area becomes very active. For example, several quantum extensions of relational Hoare logic have been proposed by Unruh [395], Barthe et al. [48] and Unruh and Li [274] for reasoning about relational properties between two quantum programs and, in particular, for verification of the security of quantum cryptographic protocols. Separation logic has been generalised by Zhou et al. [451] and Le et al. [270] for scalable verification of quantum programs. A quantum extension of incorrectness logic was proposed by Yan, Jiang, and Yu [414] for debugging of quantum programs. For applications in the current NISQ (Noisy Intermediate-Scale Quantum) era, some proof rules were advised by Hung et al. [219], Zhou et al. [452], and Tao et al. [392] for robustness analysis of quantum programs running on noisy quantum devices.

Several lines of research on verification of quantum programs are particularly important for practical applications. The first line is verification of quantum compilers, including VOQC – a fully verified optimiser for quantum circuits written in the Coq proof assistant by Hietala et al. [206,207], and Giallar – a fully-automated verification toolkit for IBM's qiskit quantum compiler by Tao et al. [391]. The second line is theorem provers of quantum Hoare logic implemented in proof assistants Isabelle/HOL by Liu et al. [281] and Coq by Zhou et al. [450] that were able to verify correctness of some sophisticated quantum algorithms, e.g. Grover search, algorithm for hidden subgroup problem, and HHL (Harrow–Hassidim–Lloyd) algorithm for solving linear systems of equations. A formal verification environment Qbricks was developed in [87] for domain-specific circuit-building language for quantum programming Qbricks-DSL, using a logical specification language Qbricks-Spec and a hybrid quantum Hoare logic. The reader can find more discussions about quantum program verification in the two recent surveys [88,271].

Program analysis techniques are very useful in the implementation and optimisation of programs. Research on analysis of quantum programs has been conducted along the following directions:

(1) The notion of invariant for quantum programs was defined in [432], where an SDP (Semi-Definite Programming) algorithm for generating invariants of quantum programs within finite-dimensional state spaces is also presented.

(2) Termination analysis of quantum programs was initiated in [426], where a measurement-based quantum loop with a unitary transformation as the loop body was considered. Termination of a more general quantum loop with a quantum operation as the loop body was studied in [435] using the semantic model of quantum Markov chains. It was also shown in [435] that the Sharir–Pnueli–Hart method for proving properties of probabilistic programs [375] can be elegantly generalised to quantum programs by exploiting the Schrödinger–Heisenberg duality between quantum states and observables. This line of research has been continued in [275,277,439,440,444] where termination of non-deterministic and concurrent quantum programs was investigated based on reachability analysis of quantum Markov decision processes. A different approach to termination analysis through synthesis of bound (i.e. ranking) functions was generalised to quantum programs in [276].

(3) The expected runtimes of quantum while-loops was first studied in [435]. Timing analysis of quantum programs was facilitated by JavadiAbhari et al. [230] in the ScaffCC quantum compilation framework. A weakest precondition calculus for reasoning about expected runtimes of quantum programs was developed by Olmedo and Díaz-Caro [324] and Liu et al. [282]. Other resources for running quantum programs have also been considered; for example, an estimation of required qubits and quantum gates for Shor's algorithm to attack ECC (Elliptic Curve Cryptography) was given by Rötteler et al. [356]. A symbolic method for resource estimation was introduced by Meuli et al. [268,299] for accuracy-aware quantum compilation.

(4) Abstract interpretation was first used by Jorrand and Perdrix [236] in analysis of quantum programs. Recently, several interesting ideas have been introduced in this direction. To mitigate the issue of exponential explosion of the dimension of state space, it was proposed by Yu and Palsberg [443] to use a tuple of (lower-dimensional) projections as an abstraction of a (high-dimensional) quantum state. A close connection between abstract interpretation and quantum Hoare logic as well as quantum incorrectness logic was observed by Feng and Li [151].

(5) Several runtime assertion schemes have been proposed for debugging, testing and error mitigation of quantum programs, including statistical assertions by Huang and Martonosi [218], assertions using swap testing by Liu, Byrd, and Zhou [279,280], and projection-based assertions by Li et al. [273].

(6) All of the above analysis techniques are quantum generalisations of the corresponding techniques used in classical programming. But there are several unique problems in analysis of quantum programs. In particular, an analysis of entanglement between program variables was introduced by JavadiAbhari et al. [230] in quantum compiler ScaffCC. More recently, a method of entanglement analysis in quantum programs was proposed by Yuan, McNally and Carbin [446] through examining the purity of the quantum states of an entangled subsystem.

1.2 Approaches to quantum programming

Naturally, research on quantum programming started from *extending classical (traditional) programming models, methodologies and technologies into the quantum realm*. As briefly reviewed in Section 1.1, both the imperative and functional programming paradigms have been generalised for quantum computing, and various semantic models, verification and analysis techniques for classical programs have also been adapted to quantum programming.

In this section, we think about quantum programming from a different angle. The ultimate goal of quantum programming is to *exploit fully the power of quantum computers*. The question is how can we achieve this goal by developing effective quantum programming models and design appropriate quantum programming languages? To answer this question, let us start from understanding the role of programming languages. Programming languages were defined by Sethi [373] as notations that are used for specifying, organising, and reasoning about computations. He suggested that language designers need to balance:

- making computing convenient for people, with
- making efficient use of computing machines;

and emphasised that convenience comes first; without it, efficiency is irrelevant. The role of programming languages in organising and reasoning about computation can be further seen in the following excerpt from Iverson's 1979 ACM Turing Award Lecture [229]:

- Constructs that are available in a language determine how we "think" and "reason" about the implemented algorithms. Therefore, the choice of programming language affects how we conceptualise a problem.

Now let us consider how to define a programming language that can properly specify, organise and reason about quantum computation. It has been well understood that the advantage of quantum computers over current computers comes from quantum parallelism – *superposition of quantum states* – and its derivatives like entanglement. So, a key issue in quantum programming is how to incorporate quantum parallelism into classical (traditional) programming models.

1.2.1 Classical parallel programming

To address the issue raised above, let us first recall some basic ideas of classical parallel programming from a standard textbook [278]. Parallelism is a fundamental technique in classical computing, employed at different levels from instructions to systems, to accelerate computations. Classical parallelism can be generally divided into the following two classes:

- *Data parallelism*: perform the same operation, say P, to different items of data, say $d_1, ..., d_n$, at the same time;
- *Task parallelism*: perform distinct computations – or tasks, say $P_1, ..., P_n$ – at the same time.

Of course, many computations are hybrids of the above two kinds of parallelism. Accordingly, two classes of classical parallel programs are introduced:

- The *data parallelism* can be conveniently described using the `forall` statement:

$$
\begin{aligned}
&\texttt{forall } (\langle variable \rangle) \texttt{ in } (\langle range\ specification \rangle) \\
&\{ \\
&\qquad \langle body \rangle \\
&\}
\end{aligned}
\tag{1.1}
$$

with the semantics: *range specification* is evaluated as the set $D = \{d_1, ..., d_n\}$ of data. Then each $d \in D$ is corresponding to a logical thread, denoted $P[d]$, which executes a copy of the code *body* with *variable* being d.

- The *task parallelism* can be properly written as the parallel composition:

$$
P_1 \| \cdots \| P_n.
\tag{1.2}
$$

Here, $P_1, ..., P_n$ stand for n different tasks, and they can share variables (and memories).

A basic idea for introducing quantum parallelism into classical (traditional) programming models comes from a translation between data parallelism and task parallelism. To present it formally, we need some notations from Dijkstra's GCL (Guarded Command Language) [132]. Recall that a conditional statement can be written as

$$
\textbf{if } b \textbf{ then } S_1 \textbf{ else } S_0 \textbf{ fi}
\tag{1.3}
$$

where b is a Boolean expression. It means that when b is true, subprogram S_1 will be executed; otherwise, S_0 will be executed. More generally, a case statement is a collection of guarded commands:

$$
\textbf{if } (\Box i \cdot G_i \rightarrow S_i) \textbf{ fi}
\tag{1.4}
$$

where for each $1 \leq i \leq n$, the subprogram S_i is guarded by the Boolean expression G_i, and S_i will be executed only when G_i is true.

Using Dijkstra's GCL, we can formally show how data and task parallelisms can be translated into each other:

- Data parallelism (1.1) can be thought of as task parallelism (1.2) with

$$
P_i \equiv x := d_i;\ P[x]
$$

for each $i = 1, ..., n$.

- Conversely, task parallelism (1.2) can be implemented as data parallelism (1.1) by introducing index variable i:

$$
\texttt{forall } i \texttt{ in } \{1, ..., n\}\ P[i]
\tag{1.5}
$$

where:

$$
\begin{aligned}
P[i] \equiv \texttt{if } (\Box\, d \in D \cdot i = d \rightarrow\ P_d)\ \texttt{fi} \equiv \texttt{if } i = 1 \rightarrow\ &P_1 \\
\Box\ i = 2 \rightarrow\ &P_2 \\
&\cdots\cdots \\
\Box\ i = n \rightarrow\ &P_n \\
\texttt{fi}&
\end{aligned}
\tag{1.6}
$$

As we will see in the next subsection, the above simple observation can serve as a bridge from classical parallelism to quantum parallelism.

1.2.2 Superposition-of-data versus superposition-of-programs

Now we are ready to introduce two different ways of incorporating quantum parallelism into traditional programming models, namely, two paradigms of superposition:

Superposition-of-data – quantum programs with classical control: The main idea of the *superposition-of-data paradigm* is to introduce new program constructs needed to manipulate quantum data, e.g. unitary transformations, quantum measurements. However, the control flows of quantum programs in such a paradigm are similar to those of classical programs. For example, in classical programming a basic program construct that can be used to define the control flow of a program is the conditional statement (1.3), or more generally the case statement (1.4). We note that nondeterminism arises from case statement (1.4) as a consequence of the "overlapping" of the guards $G_1, G_2, ..., G_n$; that is, if more than one guards G_i are true at the same time, the case statement needs to select one from the corresponding commands S_i for execution. In particular, if $G_1 = G_2 = \cdots = G_n = \textbf{true}$, then the case statement becomes a demonic choice:

$$\square_{i=1}^n \ S_i \tag{1.7}$$

where the alternatives S_i are chosen unpredictably. In the probabilistic extension of Dijkstra's GCL – pGCL (probabilistic Guarded Command Language) [297], the nondeterminism in (1.7) is refined by a probabilistic choice:

$$\square_{i=1}^n \ S_i @ p_i \tag{1.8}$$

where $\{p_i\}$ is a probability distribution; that is, $p_i \geq 0$ for all i, and $\sum_{i=1}^n p_i = 1$. Program (1.8) randomly chooses the command S_i with probability p_i for every i. It can be thought of as a resolution of the demonic choice (1.7).

Keeping the statistical nature of quantum measurements in mind, a combination of the ideas of case statement (1.4) and probabilistic choice (1.8) yields the measurement-based case statement:

$$\textbf{if} \ (\square i \cdot M[q] = m_i \rightarrow P_i) \ \textbf{fi} \tag{1.9}$$

where q is a quantum variable and M a measurement performed on q with possible outcomes $m_1, ..., m_n$, and for each i, P_i is a (quantum) subprogram. This statement selects a command according to the outcome of measurement M: if the outcome is m_i, then the corresponding command P_i will be executed. It can be appropriately called *classical case statement in quantum programming* because the selection of commands in it is based on classical information – the outcomes of a quantum measurement. Obviously, (1.9) is a natural quantum extension of statement (1.4). Other language mechanisms used to specify the control flow of quantum programs, e.g. loop and recursion, can be defined based on this case statement.

The programming paradigm defined above is called the superposition-of-data paradigm because the data inputed to and computed by these programs are quantum data – superposition of data, but programs themselves are not allowed to be superposed. This paradigm can be even more clearly characterised by Selinger's slogan "quantum data, classical control" [367] because the data flows of the programs are quantum, but their control flows are still classical.

The majority of existing research on quantum programming has been carried out in the superposition-of-data paradigm, dealing with quantum programs with classical control. A theoretical foundation of this paradigm will be developed in Parts II and III of this book.

Superposition-of-programs – quantum programs with quantum control: The second quantum programming paradigm considered in this subsection was originally inspired by the construction of quantum walks [11,24]. It was observed in [433,434] that there is a fundamentally different way to define a case statement in quantum programming – *quantum case statement* governed by a quantum "coin":

$$\textbf{qif}[c] \ (\square i \cdot |i\rangle \rightarrow P_i) \ \textbf{fiq} \tag{1.10}$$

where $\{|i\rangle\}$ is an orthonormal basis of the state Hilbert space of an *external* "coin" system c, and the selection of subprograms P_i's is made according to the basis states $|i\rangle$ of the "coin" space that *can be superposed* and thus is quantum information rather than classical information.

Furthermore, we can define a *quantum choice*:

$$[C] \left(\bigoplus_i |i\rangle \rightarrow P_i \right) \triangleq C[c]; \ \textbf{qif}[c] \ (\square i \cdot |i\rangle \rightarrow P_i) \ \textbf{fiq} \tag{1.11}$$

Intuitively, quantum choice (1.11) runs a "coin-tossing" program C to create a superposition of the execution paths of subprograms $P_1, ..., P_n$, followed by a quantum case statement. During the execution of the quantum case statement, each P_i is running along its own path within the whole superposition of execution paths of $P_1, ..., P_n$. Based on this kind of quantum case statement and quantum choice, some new quantum program constructs like quantum recursion can be defined.

Here is the right point to observe an interesting connection between classical and quantum parallelisms. If we carefully compare (1.10) and (1.11) with (1.5) and (1.6), we can see that (1.10) and (1.11) are essentially a quantum version of task parallelism. As we will see later in the book, the notion of quantum task parallelism often provides an intuitive way of thinking and reasoning about quantum algorithms.

The approach to quantum programming described above can be termed as the *superposition-of-programs paradigm*. It is clear from the definitions of quantum case statement and quantum choice that the control flow of a quantum program in the superposition-of-programs paradigm is inherently quantum. So, this paradigm can also be characterised by the slogan "quantum data, quantum control".[1]

Theoretical issues of this paradigm will be discussed in Part V of this book. But I have to admit that this paradigm is still in its very early stage of development, and a series of fundamental problems are not well understood. On the other hand, I believe that it introduces a new way of thinking about quantum programming that can help a programmer to further exploit the unique power of quantum computing.

1.2.3 Classical and quantum parallelisms working together

We discussed classical and quantum parallelisms separately in the above two subsections. Note that quantum parallelism in Section 1.2.2 was considered in the setting of sequential programming. In this section, we further consider parallel programming problem for quantum computing – how to program a parallel or distributed system of quantum computers? In such a system, classical, and quantum parallelisms coexist and work together.

As mentioned in Section 1.2.1, one of the major aims of parallelism in classical computing is to accelerate computations. This aim is still important in quantum computing. For example, the issue of instruction parallelism has already been considered in the quantum instruction set architectures of IBM Q [113] and Rigetti [380]. But there is another important aim for introducing classical parallelism into quantum computing – using the physical resources of two or more small-capacity quantum computers to realise large-capacity quantum computing, which is out of the reach of today's technology. This is particularly vital in the current NISQ era. Indeed, several models of parallel and distributed quantum computing have been proposed; for example, a model of distributed quantum computing over noisy channels was studied in [98], and a quantum parallel RAM (Random Access Memory) model was defined in [199]. In particular, parallel, and distributed architectures of quantum computers were introduced in the 2022 IBM Quantum roadmap [222].

Quantum algorithms for solving paradigmatic parallel and distributed computing problems that are faster than the known classical algorithms have also been discovered; for example, a quantum algorithm for the leader election problem was given in [390] and a quantum protocol for the dinning philosopher problem was shown in [13]. Also, several parallel implementations of the quantum Fourier transform and Shor's quantum factoring algorithm were presented in [100,312]. In particular, Bravyi, Gosset, and König discovered a parallel quantum algorithm solving a linear algebra problem called HLF (Hidden Linear Function), which gives for the first time an unconditional proof of a computational quantum advantage [74].

Parallel quantum architectures together with parallel quantum algorithms motivate us to investigate parallel quantum programming. A theoretical model of parallel quantum programming and its semantics were defined in [437,438]. Recently, some more practical models of parallel quantum programming have been proposed; for example, QMPI [197] as a quantum extension of MPI (Message Passing Interface) and QParallel [196] as a parallel extension of Q#.

Parallel quantum programming is not a straightforward generalisation of classical parallel programming. Several theoretical challenges in parallel quantum programming that would never be present in parallel programming for classical computers were identified in [437,438], including:

- *Intertwined nondeterminism*: In a classical parallel program, nondeterminism is introduced only by the parallelism, and in a sequential quantum program, nondeterminism is caused only by the involved quantum measurements. However, in a parallel quantum program, these two kinds of nondeterminism occur simultaneously, and their intertwining is hard to deal with; in particular, when it contains loops which can have infinite computations, and when different component programs share variables (and memories).
- *Entanglement*: Entanglement is indispensable for realising the advantage of quantum computing over classical computing. However, it is often very hard to reason about the behaviour of a parallel quantum program where entanglement and global quantum measurements between different component programs happens.

Some basic theoretical models of parallel and distributed quantum programming will be described in Part IV of this book. I believe that the ideas presented there will find applications in other areas. In particular, some authors (see for example [107]) started to consider how to design an operating system for quantum computers; in particular, what new abstractions could a quantum operating system expose to the programmer? It is well-known that parallelism is a major

---

1. The slogan "quantum data, quantum control" was first used in [19] and a series of its continuations to describe a class of quantum programs with quantum control flows, of which the design idea is very different from that introduced here.

issue in operating systems for classical computers [238]. As one can imagine, it will also be a major issue in the design and implementation of future quantum operating systems.

1.3 Structure of the book

This book is a systematic exposition of the theoretical foundations of quantum programming, organised along the following two lines:

- From sequential programs to parallel and distributed programs;
- From superposition-of-data to superposition-of-programs.

The book focuses on imperative quantum programming, but most of the ideas and techniques introduced in this book can be generalised to functional quantum programming.

The remainder of the book is divided into six parts:

- Part I is the preliminary part. The prerequisites for reading this book are knowledge of quantum mechanics and quantum computation and reasonable familiarity with theory of programming languages. All prerequisites about quantum mechanics and quantum computation are provided in Chapters 2 to 4. For theory of programming languages, however, I suggest the reader to consult the standard textbooks, e.g. [28,288,292,373].
- Part II studies sequential quantum programs with classical control (case statement, loop, and recursion) in the superposition-of-data paradigm. This part contains two chapters. Chapter 5 carefully introduces the syntax and the operational and denotational semantics of a simple quantum programming language – quantum **while**-language, which is a quantum extension of the classical **while**-language. At the end of this chapter, classical recursion of quantum programs is also introduced. Chapter 6 presents quantum Hoare logic – a logical foundation for reasoning about correctness of quantum **while**-programs.
- Part III consists of two chapters devoted to verification and analysis, respectively, of sequential quantum programs with classical control. Chapter 7 presents an architecture of quantum program verifiers based on quantum Hoare logic, and provides several theoretical tools for scalable verification of quantum programs; in particular, Birkhoff–von Neumann quantum logic as an assertion language. Chapter 8 develops a series of mathematical tools and algorithmic techniques for analysis of quantum programs, including invariants, termination analysis and abstract interpretation.
- Part IV studies parallel and distributed quantum programs in two chapters. Chapter 9 introduces a parallel extension of quantum **while**-language and defines its operational and denotational semantics. Some useful proof rules for reasoning about correctness of parallel quantum programs are also provided there. In Chapter 10, a formal model of distributed quantum programming is described in terms of process algebra, and several theoretical tools for reasoning about distributed quantum programs are developed.
- Part V studies quantum programs with quantum control in the superposition-of-programs paradigm. This part consists of two chapters. Chapter 11 defines quantum case statement and quantum choice and their semantics, and establishes a set of algebraic laws for reasoning about quantum programs with the constructs of quantum case statement and quantum choice. Chapter 12 illustrates how can recursion with quantum control be naturally defined using quantum case statement and quantum choice. It further defines the semantics of this kind of quantum recursion with second quantisation – a mathematical framework for dealing with quantum systems where the number of particles may vary.
- Part VI consists of a single chapter of prospects, designed to give a brief introduction to several important topics on quantum programming that have been omitted in the main body of the book and to point out several directions for future research.
- For readability, the involved proofs of some results in Chapters 5 to 12 are omitted there. But for convenience of the reader, they are collected in Appendix A.

The dependencies of chapters are shown in Fig. 1.1.

Reading the book

From Fig. 1.1, we can see that Chapters 2 to 5 are a basis for reading other chapters of the book. Then the book is designed to be read along the following five paths:

- *Path 1*: Chapters 2–5 → Chapter 6. This path is for the reader who is mainly interested in logic for quantum programs. It can be extended with → Chapter 7 for quantum program verification.
- *Path 2*: Chapters 2–5 → Chapter 8. This path is for the reader who is interested in analysis of quantum programs.

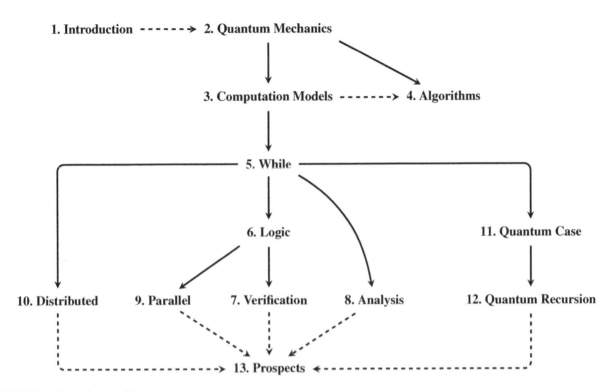

FIGURE 1.1 Dependencies of chapters.

- *Path 3*: Chapters 2–5 → Chapter 6 → Chapter 9. This path is for the reader who is interested in parallel quantum programming.
- *Path 4*: Chapters 2–5 → Chapter 10. This path is for the reader who is interested in distributed quantum programming.
- *Path 5*: Chapters 2–5 → Chapter 11 → Chapter 12. This path is for the reader who likes to learn the basic quantum program constructs in not only the superposition-of-data but also the superposition-of-programs paradigms.

Of course, only a thorough reading from the beginning to the end of the book can give the reader a full picture of the subject of quantum programming.

Teaching from the book

- Part I (Chapters 2–4) can be used for an introductory course of quantum computation.
- A short course on the basics of quantum programming can be taught based on Chapters 2 to 6.
- A one-semester advanced undergraduate or graduate course can cover each of paths 1 to 4 described above.
- Chapters 9 and 10 can be used for a more advanced course or seminar discussions.
- Since the theory of quantum programming with quantum control (in the superposition-of-programs paradigm) is still at an early stage of its development, it is better to use Chapters 11 and 12 as discussion materials for a series of seminars rather than for a course.

Exercises: The proofs of some lemmas and propositions are left as exercises. They are usually not difficult. The reader is encouraged to try all of them in order to solidify understanding of the related materials.

Research problems: A couple of problems for future research are proposed at the end of each chapter in Parts II to V.

Bibliographic notes: The last sections of Chapters 2 through 12 are Bibliographic notes, where citations and references are given, and recommendations for further reading are provided.

Errors: I would appreciate receiving any comments and suggestions about this book. In particular, if you find any errors in the book, please email them to: yingms@ios.ac.cn or yingmsh@tsinghua.edu.cn.

Part I

Preliminaries

This part introduces the basic concepts and notations from quantum mechanics and quantum computation used throughout the book.

- Of course, quantum programming theory is built based on quantum mechanics. So, Chapter 2 introduces the Hilbert space formalism of quantum mechanics, which is exactly the mathematical knowledge base of this book.
- Chapter 3 introduces several formal models of quantum computation. Historically, several major quantum algorithms appeared before any quantum programming language was defined. So, quantum circuits usually serve as the computational model in which quantum algorithms are described. Quantum circuits are introduced in Section 3.1. Then we study quantum generalisations of two more abstract computational models, namely Turing machines and random access stored-program machines in Sections 3.2 and 3.3, respectively.
- Chapter 4 introduces several basic quantum algorithms and communication protocols. The aim of this chapter is to provide examples for quantum programming rather than a systematic exposition of quantum algorithms. Thus, I decided to mainly introduce some basic ideas used in the design of various quantum algorithms but not to include more sophisticated quantum algorithms.

In order to allow the reader to enter the core of this book – quantum programming – as quick as possible, I tried to make this part minimal. Thus, the materials in this part are presented very briefly. For a total newcomer to quantum computation, she/he can start with this part, but at the same time I suggest her/him to read the corresponding parts of Chapters 2, 4, 5, 6, and 8 of book [318] for more detailed explanations and examples of the notions introduced in this part. On the other hand, for the reader who is familiar with these materials from some standard textbook like [318], I suggest her/him to directly move to the next part, using this part only for fixing notations.

Chapter 2

Quantum mechanics

Quantum mechanics is a fundamental physics subject that studies the phenomena at the atomic and subatomic scales. A general formalism of quantum mechanics can be elucidated based on several basic postulates. We choose to introduce the basic postulates of quantum mechanics via presenting the mathematical framework in which these postulates can be properly formulated. The physics interpretation of these postulates are only very briefly discussed. I hope this provides the reader a short cut towards a grasp of quantum programming. But for a better understanding, I would suggest the reader to study this chapter combined with Chapter 2 of [318].

2.1 Hilbert spaces

A Hilbert space usually serves as the state space of a quantum system. It is defined based on the notion of vector space. We write $\mathbb{C}$ for the set of complex numbers. For each complex number $\lambda = a + bi \in \mathbb{C}$, its conjugate is $\lambda^* = a - bi$. We adopt the Dirac notation which is standard in quantum mechanics: $|\varphi\rangle, |\psi\rangle, \ldots$ stand for vectors.

Definition 2.1. A (complex) vector space is a nonempty set $\mathcal{H}$ together with two operations:

- vector addition $+ : \mathcal{H} \times \mathcal{H} \to \mathcal{H}$
- scalar multiplication $\cdot : \mathbb{C} \times \mathcal{H} \to \mathcal{H}$

satisfying the following conditions:

1. $+$ is commutative: $|\varphi\rangle + |\psi\rangle = |\psi\rangle + |\varphi\rangle$ for any $|\varphi\rangle, |\psi\rangle \in \mathcal{H}$.
2. $+$ is associative: $|\varphi\rangle + (|\psi\rangle + |\chi\rangle) = (|\varphi\rangle + |\psi\rangle) + |\chi\rangle$ for any $|\varphi\rangle, |\psi\rangle, |\chi\rangle \in \mathcal{H}$.
3. $+$ has the zero element 0, called the zero vector, such that $0 + |\varphi\rangle = |\varphi\rangle$ for any $|\varphi\rangle \in \mathcal{H}$.
4. each $|\varphi\rangle \in \mathcal{H}$ has its negative vector $-|\varphi\rangle$ such that $|\varphi\rangle + (-|\varphi\rangle) = 0$.
5. $1|\varphi\rangle = |\varphi\rangle$ for any $|\varphi\rangle \in \mathcal{H}$.
6. $\lambda(\mu|\varphi\rangle) = \lambda\mu|\varphi\rangle$ for any $|\varphi\rangle \in \mathcal{H}$ and $\lambda, \mu \in \mathbb{C}$.
7. $(\lambda + \mu)|\varphi\rangle = \lambda|\varphi\rangle + \mu|\varphi\rangle$ for any $|\varphi\rangle \in \mathcal{H}$ and $\lambda, \mu \in \mathbb{C}$.
8. $\lambda(|\varphi\rangle + |\psi\rangle) = \lambda|\varphi\rangle + \lambda|\psi\rangle$ for any $|\varphi\rangle, |\psi\rangle \in \mathcal{H}$ and $\lambda \in \mathbb{C}$.

To define the notion of Hilbert space, we also need the following:

Definition 2.2. An inner product space is a vector space $\mathcal{H}$ equipped with an inner product; that is, a mapping:

$$\langle \cdot | \cdot \rangle : \mathcal{H} \times \mathcal{H} \to \mathbb{C}$$

satisfying the following properties:

1. $\langle \varphi | \varphi \rangle \geq 0$ with equality if and only if $|\varphi\rangle = 0$;
2. $\langle \varphi | \psi \rangle = \langle \psi | \varphi \rangle^*$;
3. $\langle \varphi | \lambda_1 \psi_1 + \lambda_2 \psi_2 \rangle = \lambda_1 \langle \varphi | \psi_1 \rangle + \lambda_2 \langle \varphi | \psi_2 \rangle$

for any $|\varphi\rangle, |\psi\rangle, |\psi_1\rangle, |\psi_2\rangle \in \mathcal{H}$ and for any $\lambda_1, \lambda_2 \in \mathbb{C}$.

For any vectors $|\varphi\rangle, |\psi\rangle \in \mathcal{H}$, the complex number $\langle \varphi | \psi \rangle$ is called the inner product of $|\varphi\rangle$ and $|\psi\rangle$. Sometimes, we write $(|\varphi\rangle, |\psi\rangle)$ for $\langle \varphi | \psi \rangle$. If $\langle \varphi | \psi \rangle = 0$, then we say that $|\varphi\rangle$ and $|\psi\rangle$ are orthogonal and write $|\varphi\rangle \perp |\psi\rangle$. The length of a vector $|\psi\rangle \in \mathcal{H}$ is defined to be

$$\||\psi\rangle\| = \sqrt{\langle \psi | \psi \rangle}.$$

A vector $|\psi\rangle$ is called a unit vector if $\||\psi\rangle\| = 1$. A particularly useful fact about inner product and length is the *Cauchy–Schwarz inequality*: for any vectors $|\varphi\rangle, |\psi\rangle$,

$$|\langle \varphi | \psi \rangle|^2 \leq \langle \varphi | \varphi \rangle \langle \psi | \psi \rangle = \||\varphi\rangle\|^2 \cdot \||\psi\rangle\|^2. \tag{2.1}$$

Foundations of Quantum Programming. https://doi.org/10.1016/B978-0-44-315942-8.00011-3

The notion of limit can be defined in terms of the length of a vector.

Definition 2.3. Let $\{|\psi_n\rangle\}$ be a sequence of vectors in $\mathcal{H}$ and $|\psi\rangle \in \mathcal{H}$.

1. If for any $\epsilon > 0$, there exists a positive integer N such that $||\psi_m - \psi_n|| < \epsilon$ for all $m, n \geq N$, then $\{|\psi_n\rangle\}$ is called a Cauchy sequence.
2. If for any $\epsilon > 0$, there exists a positive integer N such that $||\psi_n - \psi|| < \epsilon$ for all $n \geq N$, then $|\psi\rangle$ is called a limit of $\{|\psi_n\rangle\}$ and we write $|\psi\rangle = \lim_{n \to \infty} |\psi_n\rangle$.

Now we are ready to present the definition of Hilbert space.

Definition 2.4. A Hilbert space is a complete inner product space; that is, an inner product space in which each Cauchy sequence of vectors has a limit.

A notion that helps us to understand the structure of a Hilbert space is its basis. In this book, we only consider finite-dimensional or countably infinite-dimensional (separable) Hilbert space.

Definition 2.5. A finite or countably infinite family $\{|\psi_i\rangle\}$ of unit vectors is called an orthonormal basis of $\mathcal{H}$ if

1. $\{|\psi_i\rangle\}$ are pairwise orthogonal: $|\psi_i\rangle \perp |\psi_j\rangle$ for any i, j with $i \neq j$;
2. $\{|\psi_i\rangle\}$ span the whole space $\mathcal{H}$: each $|\psi\rangle \in \mathcal{H}$ can be written as a linear combination $|\psi\rangle = \sum_i \lambda_i |\psi_i\rangle$ for some $\lambda_i \in \mathbb{C}$ and a finite number of $|\psi_i\rangle$.

The numbers of vectors in any two orthonormal bases are the same. It is called the dimension of $\mathcal{H}$ and written as $\dim \mathcal{H}$; in particular, if an orthonormal basis contains infinitely many vectors, then $\mathcal{H}$ is infinite-dimensional and we write $\dim \mathcal{H} = \infty$.

Infinite-dimensional Hilbert spaces are required in quantum programming theory only when a data type is infinite, e.g. integers. If it is hard for the reader to understand infinite-dimensional Hilbert spaces and associated concepts (e.g. limits in Definition 2.3, closed subspaces in Definition 2.6 below), she/he can simply focus on finite-dimensional Hilbert spaces, which are exactly vector spaces that she/he learned in elementary linear algebra; in this way, the reader can still grasp an essential part of this book.

Whenever $\mathcal{H}$ is finite-dimensional, say $\dim \mathcal{H} = n$, and we consider a *fixed* orthonormal basis $\{|\psi_1\rangle, |\psi_2\rangle, ..., |\psi_n\rangle\}$, then each vector $|\psi\rangle = \sum_{i=1}^n \lambda_i |\psi_i\rangle \in \mathcal{H}$ can be represented by the vector in $\mathbb{C}^n$:

$$\begin{pmatrix} \lambda_1 \\ ... \\ \lambda_n \end{pmatrix}$$

The notion of subspace is also important for understanding the structure of a Hilbert space, and will be very useful in this book for describing properties of quantum program variables.

Definition 2.6. Let $\mathcal{H}$ be a Hilbert space.

1. If $X \subseteq \mathcal{H}$, and for any $|\varphi\rangle, |\psi\rangle \in X$ and $\lambda \in \mathbb{C}$,
   a. $|\varphi\rangle + |\psi\rangle \in X$;
   b. $\lambda|\varphi\rangle \in X$,
   then X is called a subspace of $\mathcal{H}$.
2. For each $X \subseteq \mathcal{H}$, its closure $\overline{X}$ is the set of limits $\lim_{n \to \infty} |\psi_n\rangle$ of sequences $\{|\psi_n\rangle\}$ in X.
3. A subspace X of $\mathcal{H}$ is closed if $\overline{X} = X$.

For any subset $X \subseteq \mathcal{H}$, the space spanned by X:

$$spanX = \left\{ \sum_{i=1}^n \lambda_i |\psi_i\rangle : n \geq 0, \lambda_i \in \mathbb{C} \text{ and } |\psi_i\rangle \in X \ (i = 1, ..., n) \right\} \tag{2.2}$$

is the smallest subspace of $\mathcal{H}$ containing X. In other words, $spanX$ is the subspace of $\mathcal{H}$ generated by X. Moreover, $\overline{spanX}$ is the closed subspace generated by X.

We defined orthogonality between two vectors above. It can be further defined between two sets of vectors.

Definition 2.7. Let $\mathcal{H}$ be a Hilbert space.

1. For any $X, Y \subseteq \mathcal{H}$, we say that X and Y are orthogonal, written $X \perp Y$, if $|\varphi\rangle \perp |\psi\rangle$ for all $|\varphi\rangle \in X$ and $|\psi\rangle \in Y$. In particular, we simply write $|\varphi\rangle \perp Y$ if X is the singleton $\{|\varphi\rangle\}$.
2. The orthocomplement of a closed subspace X of $\mathcal{H}$ is

$$X^\perp = \{|\varphi\rangle \in \mathcal{H} : |\varphi\rangle \perp X\}.$$

The orthocomplement $X^\perp$ is also a closed subspace of $\mathcal{H}$, and we have $(X^\perp)^\perp = X$ for every closed subspace X of $\mathcal{H}$.

Definition 2.8. Let $\mathcal{H}$ be a Hilbert space, and let X, Y be two subspaces of $\mathcal{H}$. Then

$$X \oplus Y = \{|\varphi\rangle + |\psi\rangle : |\varphi\rangle \in X \text{ and } |\psi\rangle \in Y\}$$

is called the sum of X and Y.

The above definition can be straightforwardly generalised to the sum $\bigoplus_{i=1}^n X_i$ of more than two subspaces X_i of $\mathcal{H}$. In particular, if X_i $(1 \le i \le n)$ are orthogonal to each other, then $\bigoplus_{i=1}^n X_i$ is called an orthogonal sum.

With the above preparation, we can present:

*   **Postulate of quantum mechanics 1**: The state space of a closed (i.e. an isolated) quantum system is represented by a Hilbert space, and a pure state of the system is described by a unit vector in its state space.

A linear combination $|\psi\rangle = \sum_{i=1}^n \lambda_i |\psi_i\rangle$ of states $|\psi_1\rangle, ..., |\psi_n\rangle$ is often called their *superposition*, and the complex coefficients λ_i are called probability amplitudes.

Example 2.1. A qubit – quantum bit – is the quantum counterpart of a bit. Its state space is the 2-dimensional Hilbert space:

$$\mathcal{H}_2 = \mathbb{C}^2 = \{\alpha|0\rangle + \beta|1\rangle : \alpha, \beta \in \mathbb{C}\}.$$

The inner product in $\mathcal{H}_2$ is defined by

$$(\alpha|0\rangle + \beta|1\rangle, \alpha'|0\rangle + \beta'|1\rangle) = \alpha^*\alpha' + \beta^*\beta'$$

for all $\alpha, \alpha', \beta, \beta' \in \mathbb{C}$. Then $\{|0\rangle, |1\rangle\}$ is an orthonormal basis of $\mathcal{H}_2$, called the computational basis. The vectors $|0\rangle, |1\rangle$ themselves are represented as

$$|0\rangle = \begin{pmatrix} 1 \\ 0 \end{pmatrix}, \qquad |1\rangle = \begin{pmatrix} 0 \\ 1 \end{pmatrix}$$

in this basis. A state of a qubit is described by a unit vector

$$|\psi\rangle = \alpha|0\rangle + \beta|1\rangle = \begin{pmatrix} \alpha \\ \beta \end{pmatrix}$$

with the normalisation condition $|\alpha|^2 + |\beta|^2 = 1$. The two vectors:

$$|+\rangle = \frac{|0\rangle + |1\rangle}{\sqrt{2}} = \frac{1}{\sqrt{2}} \begin{pmatrix} 1 \\ 1 \end{pmatrix}, \qquad |-\rangle = \frac{|0\rangle - |1\rangle}{\sqrt{2}} = \frac{1}{\sqrt{2}} \begin{pmatrix} 1 \\ -1 \end{pmatrix}$$

form another orthonormal basis. Both of them are superpositions of $|0\rangle$ and $|1\rangle$. The 2-dimensional Hilbert space $\mathcal{H}_2$ can also be seen as the quantum counterpart of the classical Boolean data type.

Example 2.2. Another Hilbert space often used in this book is the space of square summable sequences:

$$\mathcal{H}_\infty = \left\{ \sum_{n=-\infty}^{\infty} \alpha_n |n\rangle : \alpha_n \in \mathbb{C} \text{ for all } n \in \mathbb{Z} \text{ and } \sum_{n=-\infty}^{\infty} |\alpha_n|^2 < \infty \right\}.$$

where $\mathbb{Z}$ is the set of integers. The inner product in $\mathcal{H}_\infty$ is defined by

$$\left(\sum_{n=-\infty}^{\infty} \alpha_n |n\rangle, \sum_{n=-\infty}^{\infty} \alpha' |n\rangle \right) = \sum_{n=-\infty}^{\infty} \alpha_n^* \alpha_n'$$

for all $\alpha_n, \alpha_n' \in \mathbb{C}$ ($-\infty < n < \infty$). Then $\{|n\rangle : n \in \mathbb{Z}\}$ is an orthonormal basis, and $\mathcal{H}_\infty$ is infinite-dimensional. This Hilbert space can be seen as the quantum counterpart of the classical integer data type.

Exercise 2.1. Verify that the inner products defined in the above two examples satisfy conditions (i)–(iii) in Definition 2.2.

2.2 Linear operators

We studied the static description of a quantum system, namely its state space as a Hilbert space, in the previous subsection. Now we turn to learn how to describe the dynamics of a quantum system. The evolution of and all operations on a quantum system can be depicted by linear operators on its state Hilbert space. So, in this subsection, we study linear operators and their matrix representations.

Definition 2.9. Let $\mathcal{H}$ and $\mathcal{K}$ be Hilbert spaces. A mapping

$$A : \mathcal{H} \to \mathcal{K}$$

is called an (a linear) operator if it satisfies the following conditions:
1. $A(|\varphi\rangle + |\psi\rangle) = A|\varphi\rangle + A|\psi\rangle$;
2. $A(\lambda|\psi\rangle) = \lambda A|\psi\rangle$

for all $|\varphi\rangle, |\psi\rangle \in \mathcal{H}$ and $\lambda \in \mathbb{C}$.

An operator from $\mathcal{H}$ to itself is called an operator on $\mathcal{H}$. The identity operator on $\mathcal{H}$ that maps each vector in $\mathcal{H}$ to itself is denoted $I_\mathcal{H}$, and the zero operator on $\mathcal{H}$ that maps every vector in $\mathcal{H}$ to the zero vector is denoted $0_\mathcal{H}$. For any vectors $|\varphi\rangle, |\psi\rangle \in \mathcal{H}$, their outer product is the operator $|\varphi\rangle\langle\psi|$ on $\mathcal{H}$ defined by

$$(|\varphi\rangle\langle\psi|)|\chi\rangle = \langle\psi|\chi\rangle|\varphi\rangle$$

for every $|\chi\rangle \in \mathcal{H}$. A class of simple but useful operators are projectors. Let X be a closed subspace of $\mathcal{H}$ and $|\psi\rangle \in \mathcal{H}$. Then there exist uniquely $|\psi_0\rangle \in X$ and $|\psi_1\rangle \in X^\perp$ such that

$$|\psi\rangle = |\psi_0\rangle + |\psi_1\rangle.$$

The vector $|\psi_0\rangle$ is called the projection of $|\psi\rangle$ onto X and written $|\psi_0\rangle = P_X|\psi\rangle$.

Definition 2.10. For each closed subspace X of $\mathcal{H}$, the operator

$$P_X : \mathcal{H} \to X, \quad |\psi\rangle \mapsto P_X|\psi\rangle$$

is called the projector onto X.

Exercise 2.2. Show that $P_X = \sum_i |\psi_i\rangle\langle\psi_i|$ if $\{|\psi_i\rangle\}$ is an orthonormal basis of X.

Throughout this book, we only consider bounded operators, as defined in the following:

Definition 2.11. An operator A on $\mathcal{H}$ is said to be bounded if there is a constant $C \geq 0$ such that

$$\|A|\psi\rangle\| \leq C \cdot \|\psi\|$$

for all $|\psi\rangle \in \mathcal{H}$. The norm of A is defined to be the nonnegative number:

$$\|A\| = \inf\{C \geq 0 : \|A|\psi\rangle\| \leq C \cdot \|\psi\| \text{ for all } \psi \in \mathcal{H}\}.$$

We write $\mathcal{L}(\mathcal{H})$ for the set of bounded operators on $\mathcal{H}$.

All operators on a finite-dimensional Hilbert space are bounded.

Various operations of operators are very useful in order to combine several operators to produce a new operator. The addition, scalar multiplication and composition of operators can be defined in a natural way: for any $A, B \in \mathcal{L}(\mathcal{H})$, $\lambda \in \mathbb{C}$ and $|\psi\rangle \in \mathcal{H}$,

$$
\begin{aligned}
(A + B)|\psi\rangle &= A|\psi\rangle + B|\psi\rangle, \\
(\lambda A)|\psi\rangle &= \lambda(A|\psi\rangle), \\
(BA)|\psi\rangle &= B(A|\psi\rangle).
\end{aligned}
\tag{2.3}
$$

Exercise 2.3. Show that $\mathcal{L}(\mathcal{H})$ with addition and scalar multiplication forms a vector space.

We can also define positivity of an operator as well as an order and a distance between operators.

Definition 2.12. An operator $A \in \mathcal{L}(\mathcal{H})$ is positive if for all states $|\psi\rangle \in \mathcal{H}$, $\langle\psi|A|\psi\rangle$ is a nonnegative real number: $\langle\psi|A|\psi\rangle \geq 0$.

Definition 2.13. The Löwner order $\sqsubseteq$ is defined as follows: for any $A, B \in \mathcal{L}(\mathcal{H})$, $A \sqsubseteq B$ if and only if $B - A = B + (-1)A$ is positive.

Definition 2.14. Let $A, B \in \mathcal{L}(\mathcal{H})$. Then their norm distance is

$$
d(A, B) = \sup_{|\psi\rangle} \|A|\psi\rangle - B|\psi\rangle\|
\tag{2.4}
$$

where $|\psi\rangle$ traverses all pure states (i.e. unit vectors) in $\mathcal{H}$.

Matrix representation of operators: Operators on a finite-dimensional Hilbert space have a matrix representation, which is very convenient in applications. After reading this part, the reader should have a better understanding of those abstract notions defined above through a connection from them to the corresponding notions that she/he learned in elementary linear algebra.

If $\{|\psi_i\rangle\}$ is an orthonormal basis of $\mathcal{H}$, then an operator A is uniquely determined by the images $A|\psi_i\rangle$ of the basis vectors $|\psi_i\rangle$ under A. In particular, when $\dim \mathcal{H} = n$ is finite and we consider a *fixed* orthonormal basis $\{|\psi_1\rangle, ..., |\psi_n\rangle\}$, A can be represented by the $n \times n$ complex matrix:

$$
A = (a_{ij})_{n \times n} = \begin{pmatrix} a_{11} & ... & a_{1n} \\ & ... & \\ a_{n1} & ... & a_{nn} \end{pmatrix}
$$

where

$$
a_{ij} = \langle\psi_i|A|\psi_j\rangle = (|\psi_i\rangle, A|\psi_j\rangle)
$$

for every $i, j = 1, ..., n$. Moreover, the image of a vector $|\psi\rangle = \sum_{i=1}^n \alpha_i |\psi_i\rangle \in \mathcal{H}$ under operator A is represented by the product of matrix $A = (a_{ij})_{n \times n}$ and vector $|\psi\rangle$:

$$
A|\psi\rangle = A \begin{pmatrix} \alpha_1 \\ ... \\ \alpha_n \end{pmatrix} = \begin{pmatrix} \beta_1 \\ ... \\ \beta_n \end{pmatrix}
$$

where $\beta_i = \sum_{j=1}^n a_{ij}\alpha_j$ for every $i = 1, ..., n$. For example, $I_{\mathcal{H}}$ is the unit matrix, and $0_{\mathcal{H}}$ is the zero matrix. If

$$
|\varphi\rangle = \begin{pmatrix} \alpha_1 \\ ... \\ \alpha_n \end{pmatrix}, \qquad |\psi\rangle = \begin{pmatrix} \beta_1 \\ ... \\ \beta_n \end{pmatrix},
$$

then their outer product is the matrix $|\varphi\rangle\langle\psi| = (a_{ij})_{n \times n}$ with $a_{ij} = \alpha_i \beta_j^*$ for every $i, j = 1, ..., n$. Throughout this book, we do not distinguish an operator on a finite-dimensional Hilbert space from its matrix representation.

Exercise 2.4. Show that in a finite-dimensional Hilbert space, addition, scalar multiplication and composition of operators correspond to addition, scalar multiplication and multiplication of their matrix representations, respectively.

2.2.1 Unitary transformations

Postulate of quantum mechanics 1 introduced in Section 2.1 provides the static description of a quantum system. In this subsection, we give a description of the dynamics of a quantum system, with the mathematical tool prepared above.

The continuous-time dynamics of a quantum system is given by a differential equation, called the Schrödinger equation. But in quantum computation, we usually consider the discrete-time evolution of a system – a unitary transformation. For any operator $A \in \mathcal{L}(\mathcal{H})$, it turns out that there exists a unique (linear) operator $A^\dagger$ on $\mathcal{H}$ such that

$$(A|\varphi\rangle, |\psi\rangle) = \left(|\varphi\rangle, A^\dagger|\psi\rangle\right)$$

for all $|\varphi\rangle, |\psi\rangle \in \mathcal{H}$. The operator $A^\dagger$ is called the adjoint of A. In particular, if an operator on an n-dimensional Hilbert space is represented by the matrix $A = (a_{ij})_{n \times n}$, then its adjoint is represented by the transpose conjugate of A:

$$A^\dagger = (b_{ij})_{n \times n}$$

with $b_{ij} = a_{ji}^*$ for every $i, j = 1, ..., n$.

Definition 2.15. An (bounded) operator $U \in \mathcal{L}(\mathcal{H})$ is called a unitary transformation if the adjoint of U is its inverse:

$$U^\dagger U = U U^\dagger = I_\mathcal{H}.$$

All unitary transformations U preserve the inner product:

$$(U|\varphi\rangle, U|\psi\rangle) = \langle\varphi|\psi\rangle$$

for any $|\varphi\rangle, |\psi\rangle \in \mathcal{H}$. The condition $U^\dagger U = I_\mathcal{H}$ is equivalent to $U U^\dagger = I_\mathcal{H}$ when $\mathcal{H}$ is finite-dimensional. But this is not true for an infinite-dimensional $\mathcal{H}$. If $\dim \mathcal{H} = n$, then a unitary operator on $\mathcal{H}$ is represented by an $n \times n$ unitary matrix U; i.e. a matrix U with $U^\dagger U = I_n$, where I_n is the n-dimensional unit matrix.

A useful technique for defining a unitary operator is given in the following:

Lemma 2.1. *Suppose that $\mathcal{H}$ is a (finite-dimensional) Hilbert space and $\mathcal{K}$ is a closed subspace of $\mathcal{H}$. If linear operator $U : \mathcal{K} \to \mathcal{H}$ preserves the inner product:*

$$(U|\varphi\rangle, U|\psi\rangle) = \langle\varphi|\psi\rangle$$

for any $|\varphi\rangle, |\psi\rangle \in \mathcal{K}$, then there exists a unitary operator V on $\mathcal{H}$ which extends U; i.e. $V|\psi\rangle = U|\psi\rangle$ for all $|\psi\rangle \in \mathcal{K}$.

Exercise 2.5. Prove Lemma 2.1.

Now we are ready to present:

- **Postulate of quantum mechanics 2**: Suppose that the states of a closed quantum system (i.e. a system without interactions with its environment) at times t_0 and t are $|\psi_0\rangle$ and $|\psi\rangle$, respectively. Then they are related to each other by a unitary operator U which depends only on the times t_0 and t,

$$|\psi\rangle = U|\psi_0\rangle.$$

To help the reader to understand this postulate, let us consider two simple examples.

Example 2.3. One frequently used unitary operator on a qubit is the Hadamard transformation on the 2-dimensional Hilbert space $\mathcal{H}_2$:

$$H = \frac{1}{\sqrt{2}} \begin{pmatrix} 1 & 1 \\ 1 & -1 \end{pmatrix} \tag{2.5}$$

It transforms a qubit in the computational basis states $|0\rangle$ and $|1\rangle$ into their superpositions:

$$H|0\rangle = H\begin{pmatrix} 1 \\ 0 \end{pmatrix} = \frac{1}{\sqrt{2}}\begin{pmatrix} 1 \\ 1 \end{pmatrix} = |+\rangle,$$

$$H|1\rangle = H\begin{pmatrix} 0 \\ 1 \end{pmatrix} = \frac{1}{\sqrt{2}}\begin{pmatrix} 1 \\ -1 \end{pmatrix} = |-\rangle.$$

Example 2.4. Let k be an integer. Then the k-translation operator T_k on the infinite-dimensional Hilbert space $\mathcal{H}_\infty$ is defined by

$$T_k|n\rangle = |n + k\rangle$$

for all $n \in \mathbb{Z}$. It is easy to verify that T_k is a unitary operator. In particular, we write $T_L = T_{-1}$ and $T_R = T_1$. They move a particle on the line one position to the left and to the right, respectively.

More examples will be seen in Section 3.1, where unitary transformations are used as quantum logic gates in a quantum circuit.

2.3 Quantum measurements

Now that we understand both the static and dynamic description of a quantum system, observation of a quantum system is carried out through a quantum measurement, which is defined by:

- **Postulate of quantum mechanics 3**: A quantum measurement on a system with state Hilbert space $\mathcal{H}$ is described by a collection $\{M_m\} \subseteq \mathcal{L}(\mathcal{H})$ of operators satisfying the normalisation condition:

$$\sum_m M_m^\dagger M_m = I_{\mathcal{H}}, \tag{2.6}$$

where M_m are called measurement operators, and the index m stands for the measurement outcomes that may occur in the experiment. If the state of a quantum system is $|\psi\rangle$ immediately before the measurement, then for each m, the probability that result m occurs in the measurement is

$$p(m) = ||M_m|\psi\rangle||^2 = \langle\psi|M_m^\dagger M_m|\psi\rangle \qquad \text{(Born rule)}$$

and the state of the system after the measurement with outcome m is

$$|\psi_m\rangle = \frac{M_m|\psi\rangle}{\sqrt{p(m)}}.$$

It is easy to see that the normalisation condition (2.6) implies that the probabilities for all outcomes sum up to $\sum_m p(m) = 1$. The following simple example should help the reader to understand the above postulate.

Example 2.5. The measurement of a qubit in the computational basis $\{|0\rangle, |1\rangle\}$ has two outcomes defined by measurement operators:

$$M_0 = |0\rangle\langle0|, \qquad M_1 = |1\rangle\langle1|.$$

If the qubit was in state $|\psi\rangle = \alpha|0\rangle + \beta|1\rangle$ before the measurement, then the probability of obtaining outcome 0 is

$$p(0) = \langle\psi|M_0^\dagger M_0|\psi\rangle = \langle\psi|M_0|\psi\rangle = |\alpha|^2,$$

and in this case the state after the measurement is

$$\frac{M_0|\psi\rangle}{\sqrt{p(0)}} = |0\rangle.$$

Similarly, the probability of outcome 1 is $p(1) = |\beta|^2$ and in this case the state after the measurement is $|1\rangle$.

2.3.1 Observables and projective measurements

A specially useful class of measurements is defined in terms of Hermitian operators and their spectral decomposition.

Definition 2.16. An operator $M \in \mathcal{L}(\mathcal{H})$ is said to be Hermitian if it is self-adjoint:

$$M^\dagger = M.$$

In physics, a Hermitian operator is used to model an observable.

It turns out that an operator P is a projector; that is, $P = P_X$ for some closed subspace X of $\mathcal{H}$, if and only if P is Hermitian and $P^2 = P$.

A quantum measurement can be constructed from an observable based on the mathematical concept of spectral decomposition of a Hermitian operator. Here, we only consider spectral decomposition in a finite-dimensional Hilbert space $\mathcal{H}$. (The infinite-dimensional case requires a much heavier mathematical mechanism; see [344], Chapter III.5. In this book, it will be used only in Section A.1 as a tool for the proof of a technical lemma.)

Definition 2.17. 1. An eigenvector of an operator $A \in \mathcal{L}(\mathcal{H})$ is a nonzero vector $|\psi\rangle \in \mathcal{H}$ such that $A|\psi\rangle = \lambda|\psi\rangle$ for some $\lambda \in \mathbb{C}$, where λ is called the eigenvalue of A corresponding to $|\psi\rangle$.

2. The set of eigenvalues of A is called the (point) spectrum of A and denoted $spec(A)$.

3. For each eigenvalue $\lambda \in spec(A)$, if $A|\psi\rangle = \lambda|\psi\rangle$, then $|\psi\rangle$ is called an eigenvector of A corresponding to λ. Furthermore, the set of all eigenvectors of A corresponding to λ is a closed subspace of $\mathcal{H}$ and it is called the eigenspace of A corresponding to λ.

The eigenspaces corresponding to different eigenvalues $\lambda_1 \neq \lambda_2$ are orthogonal. All eigenvalues of an observable (i.e. a Hermitian operator) M are real numbers. Moreover, it has the spectral decomposition:

$$M = \sum_{\lambda \in spec(M)} \lambda P_\lambda$$

where P_λ is the projector onto the eigenspace corresponding to λ. Then it defines a measurement $\{P_\lambda : \lambda \in spec(M)\}$, called a projective measurement because all measurement operators P_λ are projectors. Using Postulate of quantum mechanics 3 introduced above, we obtain: upon measuring a system in state $|\psi\rangle$, the probability of getting result λ is

$$p(\lambda) = \langle\psi|P_\lambda^\dagger P_\lambda|\psi\rangle = \langle\psi|P_\lambda^2|\psi\rangle = \langle\psi|P_\lambda|\psi\rangle \tag{2.7}$$

and in this case the state of the system after the measurement is

$$\frac{P_\lambda|\psi\rangle}{\sqrt{p(\lambda)}}. \tag{2.8}$$

We observe that given the state $|\psi\rangle$, probability (2.7) and postmeasurement state (2.8) are determined only by the projectors $\{P_\lambda\}$ (rather than M itself). It is easy to see that $\{P_\lambda\}$ is a complete set of orthogonal projectors; that is, a set of operators satisfying the conditions:

1. $P_\lambda P_\delta = \begin{cases} P_\lambda & \text{if } \lambda = \delta, \\ 0_{\mathcal{H}} & \text{otherwise;} \end{cases}$

2. $\sum_\lambda P_\lambda = I_{\mathcal{H}}$.

Sometimes, we simply call a complete set of orthogonal projectors a projective measurement. A special case is the measurement in an orthonormal basis $\{|i\rangle\}$ of the state Hilbert space, where $P_i = |i\rangle\langle i|$ for every i. Example 2.5 is such a measurement for a qubit.

Expectation and standard deviation: We further examine statistical laws derived from quantum measurements. Assume that we prepare a large number of quantum systems in the same state $|\psi\rangle$, and perform the quantum measurement defined by an observable M. Then:

- Since all possible outcomes $\lambda \in spec(M)$ are real numbers, we can compute the *expectation* – average value – of M in state $|\psi\rangle$:

$$\begin{aligned} \mathbb{E}(M) = \langle M \rangle &= \sum_{\lambda \in spec(M)} p(\lambda) \cdot \lambda \\ &= \sum_{\lambda \in spec(M)} \lambda \langle\psi|P_\lambda|\psi\rangle \\ &= \langle\psi| \sum_{\lambda \in spec(M)} \lambda P_\lambda |\psi\rangle \\ &= \langle\psi|M|\psi\rangle. \end{aligned}$$

- The *variance* of M in state $|\psi\rangle$ is then defined as

$$\Delta(M) = \mathbb{E}\big[(M - \mathbb{E}(M))^2\big] = \langle(M - \langle M\rangle)^2\rangle.$$

It is easy to check that $\Delta(M) = \langle M^2\rangle - \langle M\rangle^2$. Thus, the *standard deviation* of M in state $|\psi\rangle$ is given as

$$\sigma(M) = \sqrt{\Delta(M)} = \sqrt{\langle M^2\rangle - \langle M\rangle^2}.$$

As we know from statistics, it measures the amount of dispersion of the measurement outcomes $\{\lambda\}$: a low value of $\sigma(M)$ means that these outcomes tend to be close to the expectation $\mathbb{E}(M)$, and a high value of $\sigma(M)$ indicates that outcomes $\{\lambda\}$ are spread out over a wide range.

2.3.2 Noncommutativity and uncertainty principle

With the notion of standard deviation defined above, we can introduce a fundamental principle in quantum mechanics, namely the Heisenberg uncertainty principle, which, as we will see later, has certain implications to quantum programming.

Now assume that we prepare a large number of quantum systems in the same state $|\psi\rangle$, but perform the measurement defined by an observable M_1 on some of them, and perform the measurement defined by another observable M_2 on the others. Then we have:

Theorem 2.1 (Heisenberg uncertainty principle). *For any quantum state $|\psi\rangle$, and for any two observables M_1, M_2,*

$$\sigma(M_1)\sigma(M_2) \geq \frac{1}{2}|\langle\psi|[M_1, M_2]|\psi\rangle| \tag{2.9}$$

where $[M_1, M_2] = M_1M_2 - M_2M_1$ is called the commutator of M_1 and M_2.

Proof. To simplify the presentation, let us set $N_i = M_i - \langle M_i\rangle$ for $i = 1, 2$. Then $\Delta(M_i) = \langle N_i^2\rangle$. We assume that $\langle\psi|N_1N_2|\psi\rangle = x + iy$ for some real numbers x and y. Then $\langle\psi|N_2N_1|\psi\rangle = \langle\psi|N_1N_2|\psi\rangle^\dagger = x - iy$. So, we have $\langle\psi|[N_1, N_2]|\psi\rangle = 2iy$ and $\langle\psi|\{N_1, N_2\}|\psi\rangle = 2x$, where $\{N_1, N_2\} = N_1N_2 + N_2N_1$ is called the anticommutator of N_1 and N_2. Furthermore, it holds that

$$\begin{aligned}
|\langle\psi|[N_1, N_2]|\psi\rangle|^2 + |\langle\psi|\{N_1, N_2\}|\psi\rangle|^2 &= 4(x^2 + y^2) \\
&= 4|\langle\psi|N_1N_2|\psi\rangle|^2 \leq 4\langle\psi|N_1^2|\psi\rangle\langle\psi|N_2^2|\psi\rangle \tag{2.10} \\
&= 4\langle N_1^2\rangle\langle N_2^2\rangle = 4\Delta(M_1)\Delta(M_2),
\end{aligned}$$

from which (2.9) follows. Note that the inequality in (2.10) is an application of the Cauchy–Schwarz inequality (2.1). □

Let us consider the case where two observables M_1 and M_2 do not commute; that is, $M_1M_2 \neq M_2M_1$. In this case, $[M_1, M_2] \neq 0$, and for some state $|\psi\rangle$, the right-hand side of (2.9) is greater than 0, and thus the standard deviations $\sigma(M_1)$ and $\sigma(M_2)$ cannot be arbitrarily small simultaneously. This is a phenomenon that can only happen in quantum mechanics but not in classical mechanics.

We will use observables to represent quantum predicates – assertions about quantum variables in a program – in Chapter 6. The salient difference between classical observables and quantum ones revealed by the above uncertainty principle makes that some traditional techniques for analysis and verification of classical programs no longer work for quantum programs.

2.4 Tensor products of Hilbert spaces

Up to now we only considered a single quantum system. In this section, we further show how can a large composite system be made up of two or more subsystems. The description of a composite system is based on the notion of tensor product. We mainly consider the tensor product of a finite family of Hilbert spaces.

Definition 2.18. Let $\mathcal{H}_i$ be a Hilbert spaces with $\{|\psi_{ij_i}\rangle\}$ as an orthonormal basis for $i = 1, ..., n$. We write $\mathcal{B}$ for the set of which the elements are of the form:

$$|\psi_{1j_1}, ..., \psi_{nj_n}\rangle = |\psi_{1j_1} \otimes ... \otimes \psi_{nj_n}\rangle = |\psi_{1j_1}\rangle \otimes ... \otimes |\psi_{nj_n}\rangle.$$

Then the tensor product of $\mathcal{H}_i$ ($i = 1, ..., n$) is the Hilbert space with $\mathcal{B}$ as an orthonormal basis:

$$\bigotimes_i \mathcal{H}_i = span\mathcal{B}.$$

It follows from Eq. (2.2) that each element in $\bigotimes_i \mathcal{H}_i$ can be written in the form of

$$\sum_{j_1, ..., j_n} \alpha_{j_1, ..., j_n} |\varphi_{1j_1}, ..., \varphi_{nj_n}\rangle$$

where $|\varphi_{1j_1}\rangle \in \mathcal{H}_1, ..., |\varphi_{nj_n}\rangle \in \mathcal{H}_n$ and $\alpha_{j_1, ..., j_n} \in \mathbb{C}$ for all $j_1, ..., j_n$. Furthermore, it can be shown by linearity that the choice of basis $\{|\psi_{ij_i}\rangle\}$ of each factor space $\mathcal{H}_i$ is not essential in the above definition: for example, if $|\varphi_i\rangle = \sum_{j_i} \alpha_{j_i} |\varphi_{ij_i}\rangle \in \mathcal{H}_i$ ($i = 1, ..., n$), then

$$|\varphi_1\rangle \otimes ... \otimes |\varphi_n\rangle = \sum_{j_1, ..., j_n} \alpha_{1j_1}...\alpha_{nj_n} |\varphi_{1j_1}, ..., \varphi_{nj_n}\rangle.$$

The vector addition, scalar multiplication, and inner product in $\bigotimes_i \mathcal{H}_i$ can be naturally defined based on the fact that $\mathcal{B}$ is an orthonormal basis.

We will need to consider the tensor product of a countably infinite family of Hilbert spaces occasionally in this book. Let $\{\mathcal{H}_i\}$ be a countably infinite family of Hilbert spaces, and let $\{|\psi_{ij_i}\rangle\}$ be an orthonormal basis of $\mathcal{H}_i$ for each i. We write $\mathcal{B}$ for the set of tensor products of basis vectors of all $\mathcal{H}_i$:

$$\mathcal{B} = \left\{ \bigotimes_i |\psi_{ij_i}\rangle \right\}.$$

Then $\mathcal{B}$ is a finite or countably infinite set, and it can be written in the form of a sequence of vectors: $\mathcal{B} = \{|\varphi_n\rangle : n = 0, 1, ...\}$. The tensor product of $\{\mathcal{H}_i\}$ can be properly defined to be the Hilbert space with $\mathcal{B}$ as an orthonormal basis:

$$\bigotimes_i \mathcal{H}_i = \left\{ \sum_n \alpha_n |\varphi_n\rangle : \alpha_n \in \mathbb{C} \text{ for all } n \geq 0 \text{ and } \sum_n |\alpha_n|^2 < \infty \right\}.$$

Now we are able to present:

- **Postulate of quantum mechanics 4**: The state space of a composite quantum system is the tensor product of the state spaces of its components.

Suppose that S is a quantum system composed by subsystems $S_1, ..., S_n$ with state Hilbert space $\mathcal{H}_1, ..., \mathcal{H}_n$, respectively. If for each $1 \leq i \leq n$, S_i is in state $|\psi_i\rangle \in \mathcal{H}_i$, then S is in the product state $|\psi_1, ..., \psi_n\rangle$. Furthermore, S can be in a superposition (i.e. linear combination) of several product states.

Entanglement: One of the most interesting and puzzling phenomenon in quantum mechanics – *entanglement* – occurs in a composite system: a state of the composite system is said to be entangled if it is not a product of states of its component systems. In this case, the state of a subsystem cannot be described independently of the states of the other subsystems.

Example 2.6. The state space of the system of n qubits is:

$$\mathcal{H}_2^{\otimes n} = \mathbb{C}^{2^n} = \left\{ \sum_{x \in \{0,1\}^n} \alpha_x |x\rangle : \alpha_x \in \mathbb{C} \text{ for all } x \in \{0, 1\}^n \right\}.$$

In particular, a two-qubit system can be in a product state like $|00\rangle, |1\rangle|+\rangle$ but also in an entangled state like the Bell states or the EPR (Einstein–Podolsky–Rosen) pairs:

$$|\beta_{00}\rangle = \frac{1}{\sqrt{2}}(|00\rangle + |11\rangle), \quad |\beta_{01}\rangle = \frac{1}{\sqrt{2}}(|01\rangle + |10\rangle),$$

$$|\beta_{10}\rangle = \frac{1}{\sqrt{2}}(|00\rangle - |11\rangle), \quad |\beta_{11}\rangle = \frac{1}{\sqrt{2}}(|01\rangle - |10\rangle).$$

The existence of entanglement is one of the major differences between the classical world and the quantum world. It is also indispensable resources in quantum computing for outperforming classical computing for some tasks. In Chapters 8 and 9, we will deal with entanglement between the component programs (e.g. threads or processes) of a parallel or distributed quantum program, which never occurs in classical programming.

Operators on the tensor products of Hilbert spaces: Of course, we can talk about (linear) operators, unitary transformations, and measurements on the tensor product of Hilbert spaces since it is a Hilbert space too. A special class of operators on the tensor product of Hilbert spaces are defined as follows:

Definition 2.19. Let $A_i \in \mathcal{L}(\mathcal{H}_i)$ for $i = 1, ..., n$. Then their tensor product is the operator $\bigotimes_{i=1}^{n} A_i = A_1 \otimes ... \otimes A_n \in \mathcal{L}(\bigotimes_{i=1}^{n} \mathcal{H}_i)$ defined by

$$(A_1 \otimes ... \otimes A_n)|\varphi_1, ..., \varphi_n\rangle = A_1|\varphi_1\rangle \otimes ... \otimes A_n|\varphi_n\rangle$$

for all $|\varphi_i\rangle \in \mathcal{H}_i$ $(i = 1, ..., n)$ together with linearity.

The following lemma shows that positivity and the Löwner order are preserved by tensor product of operators.

Lemma 2.2. 1. *If A_1, A_2 are positive operators in $\mathcal{H}_1$ and $\mathcal{H}_2$, respectively, then $A_1 \otimes A_2$ is a positive operator in $\mathcal{H}_1 \otimes \mathcal{H}_2$.*
2. *For any operators A_1, B_1 in $\mathcal{H}_1$ and A_2, B_2 in $\mathcal{H}_2$, $A_1 \sqsubseteq B_1$, and $A_2 \sqsubseteq B_2$ implies $A_1 \otimes A_2 \sqsubseteq B_1 \otimes B_2$.*

Using the operations defined in Eq. (2.3), more operators on $\bigotimes_{i=1}^{n} \mathcal{H}_i$ can be generated from the product operators defined in the above definition. Except these, however, some other operators are also needed in quantum mechanics. In particular, an operator that cannot be written as a tensor product of local operators represents a global quantum operation on the composite system. For example, the operator in the following example plays a key role in quantum computation because it can create entanglement.

Example 2.7. The controlled-NOT or CNOT operator C in the state Hilbert space $\mathcal{H}_2^{\otimes 2} = \mathbb{C}^4$ of a two-qubit system is defined by

$$C|00\rangle = |00\rangle, \quad C|01\rangle = |01\rangle, \quad C|10\rangle = |11\rangle, \quad C|11\rangle = |10\rangle$$

or equivalently as the 4×4 matrix

$$C = \begin{pmatrix} 1 & 0 & 0 & 0 \\ 0 & 1 & 0 & 0 \\ 0 & 0 & 0 & 1 \\ 0 & 0 & 1 & 0 \end{pmatrix}.$$

It can transform product states into entangled states:

$$C|+\rangle|0\rangle = \beta_{00}, \quad C|+\rangle|1\rangle = \beta_{01}, \quad C|-\rangle|0\rangle = \beta_{10}, \quad C|-\rangle|1\rangle = \beta_{11}.$$

Implementing a general measurement by a projective measurement: Projective measurements are introduced in Section 2.3 as a special class of quantum measurements. The notion of tensor product enables us to show that an arbitrary quantum measurement can be implemented by a projective measurement together with a unitary transformation if we are allowed to introduce an *ancilla* system. Let $M = \{M_m\}$ be a quantum measurement on Hilbert space $\mathcal{H}$.

- We introduce a new Hilbert space $\mathcal{H}_M = span\{|m\rangle\}$, which is used to record the possible outcomes of M.
- We arbitrarily choose a fixed state $|0\rangle \in \mathcal{H}_M$. Define operator

$$U_M(|0\rangle|\psi\rangle) = \sum_m |m\rangle M_m|\psi\rangle$$

for every $|\psi\rangle \in \mathcal{H}$. It is easy to check that U_M preserves the inner product, and by Lemma 2.1 it can be extended to a unitary operator on $\mathcal{H}_M \otimes \mathcal{H}$, which is denoted by U_M too.
- We define a projective measurement $\overline{M} = \{\overline{M}_m\}$ on $\mathcal{H}_M \otimes \mathcal{H}$ with $\overline{M}_m = |m\rangle\langle m| \otimes I_{\mathcal{H}}$ for every m.

Then the measurement M is realised by the projective measurement $\overline{M}$ together with the unitary operator U_M, as shown in the following:

Proposition 2.1. *Let $|\psi\rangle \in \mathcal{H}$ be a pure state.*

- *When we perform measurement M on $|\psi\rangle$, the probability of outcome m is denoted $p_M(m)$ and the postmeasurement state corresponding to m is $|\psi_m\rangle$.*
- *When we perform measurement $\overline{M}$ on $|\overline{\psi}\rangle = U_M(|0\rangle|\psi\rangle)$, the probability of outcome m is denoted $p_{\overline{M}}(m)$ and the postmeasurement state corresponding to m is $|\overline{\psi}_m\rangle$.*

Then for each m, we have: $p_{\overline{M}}(m) = p_M(m)$ and $|\overline{\psi}_m\rangle = |m\rangle|\psi_m\rangle$. A similar result holds when we consider a mixed state in $\mathcal{H}$ introduced in the next section.

Exercise 2.6. Prove Proposition 2.1.

2.4.1 Nocloning of quantum data

Now it is a right time to discuss another simple but fundamental difference between classical information and quantum information, which has implications to quantum programming. In classical computation and information processing, data are often copied from one place to another place. However, there is a so-called nocloning principle [130,410] that forbids unknown quantum states to be copied exactly. Suppose that a quantum copying machine consists of two subsystems labelled A and B, respectively. We want to copy quantum data stored in A to B. Assume that the target subsystem B is initially in state $|s\rangle$, the (unknown) state of A is $|\psi\rangle$, and the copying operation is modelled as a unitary evolution of the copying machine. Then the copying procedure can be described as:

$$U : |\psi\rangle_A |s\rangle_B \to |\psi\rangle_A |\psi\rangle_B. \tag{2.11}$$

The principle of nocloning asserts that such a quantum copying machine does not exist. Formally, it can be stated as the following:

Theorem 2.2 (Nocloning). *There does not exist any unitary U such that (2.11) holds for arbitrary $|\psi\rangle$.*

Proof. We prove this theorem by refutation. It is easy to find two states $|\psi_1\rangle, |\psi_2\rangle$ such that $\langle\psi_1|\psi_2\rangle \neq 0, 1$. On the other hand, if there is a unitary U such that (2.11) holds for arbitrary $|\psi\rangle$, then it follows that

$$|\psi_i\rangle|\psi_i\rangle = U(|\psi_i\rangle|s\rangle) \ (i = 1, 2)$$

and we have the inner products:

$$\langle\psi_1|\psi_2\rangle^2 = (|\psi_1\rangle|\psi_1\rangle, |\psi_2\rangle|\psi_2\rangle) = \big(U(|\psi_1\rangle|s\rangle), U(|\psi_2\rangle|s\rangle)\big)$$
$$= (|\psi_1\rangle|s\rangle, |\psi_2\rangle|s\rangle) = \langle\psi_1|\psi_2\rangle\langle s|s\rangle = \langle\psi_1|\psi_2\rangle$$

which implies $\langle\psi_1|\psi_2\rangle = 0$ or 1, a contradiction. $\qquad\square$

Indeed, there is even certain limitation on the ability of copying quantum states approximately [82]. Moreover, the nodeleting theorem was shown in [331], which asserts that deleting an unknown quantum state – the inverse process of (2.11) – is impossible too.

As one can imagine, the principle of nocloning puts certain constraints on the techniques of quantum programming. Thus, we should always keep it in mind so that it will not be violated in the design, testing, and analysis of quantum programs.

2.5 Density operators

We have already learned all of the four basic postulates of quantum mechanics. But they were only formulated in the case of pure states. In this section, we extend these postulates so that they can be used to deal with mixed states.

Sometimes, the state of a quantum system is not completely known, but we know that it is in one of a number of pure states $|\psi_i\rangle$, with respective probabilities p_i, where $|\psi_i\rangle \in \mathcal{H}$, $p_i \geq 0$ for each i, and $\sum_i p_i = 1$. A convenient notion for coping with this situation is density operator. We call $\{(|\psi_i\rangle, p_i)\}$ an ensemble of pure states or a mixed state, whose density operator is defined to be

$$\rho = \sum_i p_i |\psi_i\rangle\langle\psi_i|. \tag{2.12}$$

In particular, a pure state $|\psi\rangle$ may be seen as a special mixed state $\{(|\psi\rangle, 1)\}$ and its density operator is $\rho = |\psi\rangle\langle\psi|$.

Density operators can be described in a different but equivalent way.

Definition 2.20. The trace $tr(A)$ of operator $A \in \mathcal{L}(\mathcal{H})$ is defined to be

$$tr(A) = \sum_i \langle\psi_i|A|\psi_i\rangle$$

where $\{|\psi_i\rangle\}$ is an orthonormal basis of $\mathcal{H}$.

It can be shown that $tr(A)$ is independent of the choice of basis $\{|\psi_i\rangle\}$.

Definition 2.21. A density operator ρ on a Hilbert space $\mathcal{H}$ is a positive operator (see Definition 2.12) with $tr(\rho) = 1$.

It turns out that for any mixed state $\{(|\psi_i\rangle, p_i)\}$, operator ρ defined by Eq. (2.12) is a density operator according to Definition 2.21. Conversely, for any density operator ρ, there exists a (but not necessarily unique) mixed state $\{(|\psi_i\rangle, p_i)\}$ such that Eq. (2.12) holds.

The evolution of and measurement on a quantum system in mixed states can be elegantly formulated in the language of density operators:

- Suppose that the evolution of a closed quantum system from time t_0 to t is described by unitary operator U depending on t_0 and t: $|\psi\rangle = U|\psi_0\rangle$, where $|\psi_0\rangle$, $|\psi\rangle$ are the states of the system at times t_0 and t, respectively. If the system is in mixed states ρ_0, ρ at times t_0 and t, respectively, then

$$\rho = U\rho_0 U^\dagger. \tag{2.13}$$

- If the state of a quantum system was ρ immediately before measurement $\{M_m\}$ is performed on it, then the probability that result m occurs is

$$p(m) = tr\left(M_m^\dagger M_m \rho\right), \tag{2.14}$$

and in this case the state of the system after the measurement is

$$\rho_m = \frac{M_m \rho M_m^\dagger}{p(m)}. \tag{2.15}$$

Exercise 2.7. Derive Eqs. (2.13), (2.14), and (2.15) from Eq. (2.12) and Postulates of quantum mechanics 2 and 3.

Exercise 2.8. Let M be an observable (a Hermitian operator) and $\{P_\lambda : \lambda \in spec(M)\}$ the projective measurement defined by M. Show that the expectation of M in a mixed state ρ is

$$\langle M\rangle_\rho = \sum_{\lambda \in spec(M)} p(\lambda) \cdot \lambda = tr(M\rho).$$

Trace distance: A common distance between two probability distributions $p = \{p_i\}$ and $q = \{q_i\}$ is their total variation distance:

$$D(p, q) = \frac{1}{2}\sum_i |p_i - q_i|.$$

It has a natural quantum generalisation, called trace distance, for mixed states, which can be thought of as probability distributions over pure states. To define it, let us first recall that for a Hermitian operator A, if its spectral decomposition is

$$A = \sum_i \lambda_i |\psi_i\rangle\langle\psi_i|$$

where $\{|\psi_i\rangle\}$ is a family of orthonormal vectors such that for each i, $|\psi_i\rangle$ is an eigenvector of A corresponding to eigenvalue λ_i, then its square root is defined as

$$\sqrt{A} = \sum_i \sqrt{\lambda_i}|\psi_i\rangle\langle\psi_i|.$$

Furthermore, for any operator B, we define $|B| = \sqrt{B^\dagger B}$. Then for two (mixed) quantum states ρ, σ represented as density operators, its trace distance is defined as

$$D(\rho, \sigma) = \frac{1}{2}\mathrm{tr}|\rho - \sigma|. \tag{2.16}$$

The following equation presents a close connection between total variation distance and trace distance, and it also gives a physical interpretation of trace distance in terms of quantum measurements:

$$D(\rho, \sigma) = \max_{M = \{M_m\}} D(\{p_m\}, \{q_m\}).$$

In the right-hand side of the above equation, D stands for total variance distance, the maximisation is over all measurement $M = \{M_m\}$, and $p_m = \mathrm{tr}(M_m \rho M_m^\dagger)$, $q_m = \mathrm{tr}(M_m \sigma M_m^\dagger)$ are the probabilities of outcome m when measurement M is performed on quantum states ρ and σ, respectively.

Reduced density operators: Postulate of quantum mechanics 4 introduced in the last section enables us to construct composite quantum systems. Of course, we can talk about a mixed state of a composite system and its density operator because the state space of the composite system is the tensor product of the state Hilbert spaces of its subsystems, which is a Hilbert space too. Conversely, we often need to characterise the state of a subsystem of a quantum system. However, it is possible that a composite system is in a pure state, but some of its subsystems must be seen as in a mixed state. This phenomenon is another major difference between the classical world and the quantum world. Consequently, a proper description of the state of a subsystem of a composite quantum system can be achieved only after introducing the notion of density operator.

Definition 2.22. Let S and T be quantum systems whose state Hilbert spaces are $\mathcal{H}_S$ and $\mathcal{H}_T$, respectively. The partial trace over system T

$$tr_T : \mathcal{L}(\mathcal{H}_S \otimes \mathcal{H}_T) \to \mathcal{L}(\mathcal{H}_S)$$

is defined by

$$tr_T(|\varphi\rangle\langle\psi| \otimes |\theta\rangle\langle\zeta|) = \langle\zeta|\theta\rangle \cdot |\varphi\rangle\langle\psi|$$

for all $|\varphi\rangle, |\psi\rangle \in \mathcal{H}_S$ and $|\theta\rangle, |\zeta\rangle \in \mathcal{H}_T$ together with linearity.

Definition 2.23. Let ρ be a density operator on $\mathcal{H}_S \otimes \mathcal{H}_T$. Its reduced density operator for system S is

$$\rho_S = tr_T(\rho).$$

Intuitively, the reduced density operator ρ_S properly describes the state of subsystem S when the composite system ST is in state ρ. For a more detailed explanation, we refer to [318], Section 2.4.3.

Exercise 2.9. 1. When is the reduced density operator $\rho_A = tr_B(|\psi\rangle\langle\psi|)$ of a pure state $|\psi\rangle$ in $\mathcal{H}_A \otimes \mathcal{H}_B$ not a pure state?
2. Let ρ be a density operator on $\mathcal{H}_A \otimes \mathcal{H}_B \otimes \mathcal{H}_C$. Does it hold that $tr_C(tr_B(\rho)) = tr_{BC}(\rho)$?

2.6 Quantum operations

Unitary transformations defined in Section 2.2.1 are suited to describe the dynamics of closed quantum systems. For open quantum systems that interact with the outside world through, for example, measurements, we need the much more general notion of quantum operation to depict their state transformations.

A linear operator on vector space $\mathcal{L}(\mathcal{H})$ – the space of (bounded) operators on a Hilbert space $\mathcal{H}$ – is called a *superoperator* on $\mathcal{H}$. To define a quantum operation, we first introduce the notion of tensor product of superoperators.

Definition 2.24. Let $\mathcal{H}$ and $\mathcal{K}$ be Hilbert spaces. For any superoperator $\mathcal{E}$ on $\mathcal{H}$ and superoperator $\mathcal{F}$ on $\mathcal{K}$, their tensor product $\mathcal{E} \otimes \mathcal{F}$ is the superoperator on $\mathcal{H} \otimes \mathcal{K}$ defined as follows: for each $C \in \mathcal{L}(\mathcal{H} \otimes \mathcal{K})$, we can write:

$$C = \sum_k \alpha_k (A_k \otimes B_k) \tag{2.17}$$

where $A_k \in \mathcal{L}(\mathcal{H})$ and $B_k \in \mathcal{L}(\mathcal{K})$ for all k. Then we define:

$$(\mathcal{E} \otimes \mathcal{F})(C) = \sum_k \alpha_k (\mathcal{E}(A_k) \otimes \mathcal{F}(B_k)).$$

The linearity of $\mathcal{E}$ and $\mathcal{F}$ guarantees that $\mathcal{E} \otimes \mathcal{F}$ is well-defined in the sense that $(\mathcal{E} \otimes \mathcal{F})(C)$ is independent of the choice of A_k and B_k in Eq. (2.17).

Now we are ready to consider the dynamics of an open quantum system. As a generalisation of Postulate of quantum mechanics 2, suppose that the states of a system at times t_0 and t are ρ and ρ', respectively. Then they must be related to each other by a superoperator $\mathcal{E}$ which depends only on the times t_0 and t,

$$\rho' = \mathcal{E}(\rho).$$

The dynamics between times t_0 and t can be seen as a physical process: ρ is the initial state before the process, and $\rho' = \mathcal{E}(\rho)$ is the final state after the process happens. The following definition identifies those superoperators that are suited to model such a process in physics.

Definition 2.25. A quantum operation on a Hilbert space $\mathcal{H}$ is a superoperator on $\mathcal{H}$ satisfying the following conditions:

1. $tr[\mathcal{E}(\rho)] \leq tr(\rho) = 1$ for each density operator ρ on $\mathcal{H}$;
2. (Complete positivity) For any extra Hilbert space $\mathcal{H}_R$, $(\mathcal{I}_R \otimes \mathcal{E})(A)$ is positive provided A is a positive operator on $\mathcal{H}_R \otimes \mathcal{H}$, where $\mathcal{I}_R$ is the identity operator on $\mathcal{L}(\mathcal{H}_R)$; that is, $\mathcal{I}_R(A) = A$ for each operator $A \in \mathcal{L}(\mathcal{H}_R)$.

The reason for introducing an extra Hilbert space $\mathcal{H}_R$ in the above complete positivity is that a quantum operation on $\mathcal{H}$ should be considered in $\mathcal{H}_R \otimes \mathcal{H}$ with an external environment $\mathcal{H}_R$. We can show that it suffices to take $\mathcal{H}_R = \mathcal{H}$. For an argument that quantum operations are an appropriate mathematical model of state transformation of an open quantum system, we refer to [318], Section 8.2.4. Here are two examples showing how can unitary transformations and quantum measurements be treated as special quantum operations:

Example 2.8. Let U be a unitary transformation on a Hilbert space $\mathcal{H}$. We define:

$$\mathcal{E}(\rho) = U\rho U^\dagger$$

for every density operator ρ. Then $\mathcal{E}$ is a quantum operation on $\mathcal{H}$.

Example 2.9. Let $M = \{M_m\}$ be a quantum measurement on $\mathcal{H}$.

1. For each fixed measurement outcome m, if for any system state ρ before measurement, we define

$$\mathcal{E}_m(\rho) = p_m \rho_m = M_m \rho M^\dagger$$

where p_m is the probability of outcome m and ρ_m is the postmeasurement state corresponding to m, then $\mathcal{E}_m$ is a quantum operation.
2. For any system state ρ before measurement, the postmeasurement state is

$$\mathcal{E}(\rho) = \sum_m \mathcal{E}_m(\rho) = \sum_m M_m \rho M_m^\dagger$$

whenever the measurement outcomes are ignored. Then $\mathcal{E}$ is a quantum operation.

Quantum operations have been widely used in quantum information theory as a mathematical model of communication channels. In this book, quantum operations are adopted as the main mathematical tool for defining semantics of quantum programs because a quantum program may contain not only unitary transformations but also quantum measurements in order to read the middle or final computational results, and thus better be treated as an open quantum system.

The above abstract definition of quantum operations is hard to use in applications. Fortunately, the following theorem offers a helpful insight of a quantum operation as an interaction between the system and an environment as well as calculation convenience in terms of operators rather than superoperators.

Theorem 2.3. *The following statements are equivalent:*

1. *$\mathcal{E}$ is a quantum operation on a Hilbert space $\mathcal{H}$;*
2. *(System-environment model) There are an environment system E with state Hilbert space $\mathcal{H}_E$, and a unitary transformation U on $\mathcal{H}_E \otimes \mathcal{H}$ and a projector P onto some closed subspace of $\mathcal{H}_E \otimes \mathcal{H}$ such that*

$$\mathcal{E}(\rho) = tr_E\left[PU(|e_0\rangle\langle e_0| \otimes \rho)U^\dagger P\right]$$

for all density operator ρ on $\mathcal{H}$, where $|e_0\rangle$ is a fixed state in $\mathcal{H}_E$;

3. *(Kraus operator-sum representation) There exists a finite or countably infinite set of operators $\{E_i\}$ on $\mathcal{H}$ such that $\sum_i E_i^\dagger E_i \sqsubseteq I$ and*

$$\mathcal{E}(\rho) = \sum_i E_i \rho E_i^\dagger$$

for all density operators ρ on $\mathcal{H}$. In this case, we often write:

$$\mathcal{E} = \sum_i E_i \circ E_i^\dagger.$$

The proof of the above theorem is quite involved and omitted here, and the reader can find it in [318], Chapter 8.

Diamond distance: The trace distance between density operators defined in Section 2.5 has a natural generalisation for quantum operations. Let $\mathcal{E}$ and $\mathcal{F}$ be two quantum operations on Hilbert space $\mathcal{H}$. Then their diamond distance is defined as

$$D_\diamond(\mathcal{E}, \mathcal{F}) = \max_\rho D\big((\mathcal{I}_R \otimes \mathcal{E})(\rho), (\mathcal{I}_R \otimes \mathcal{F})(\rho)\big)$$

where the maximisation is over arbitrary extra Hilbert space $\mathcal{H}_R$ and all density operators ρ on $\mathcal{H}_R \otimes \mathcal{H}$, and $\mathcal{I}$ is the identity operator on $\mathcal{L}(\mathcal{H}_R)$. It is particularly worth noting that ρ can be an entangled state between $\mathcal{H}$ and an external environment $\mathcal{H}_R$. We can show that it is enough to take $\mathcal{H}_R = \mathcal{H}$. The diamond distance has been widely used in quantum information and computation theory for characterising the distinguishabilty of quantum channels and the difference between a quantum computation and its noisy implementation.

2.7   Bibliographic remarks and further readings

The materials presented in this chapter are standard and can be found in any (advanced) textbook of quantum mechanics. They are organised largely following [318]. As said before, the reader is encouraged to read the corresponding parts of [318] for more physical interpretation of the mathematical formalism introduced in this chapter. For detailed discussions about open quantum systems considered in Section 2.6, we refer to [75].

Entanglement is indispensable resource in quantum computation and quantum communication. Its studies have formed a large field in quantum information and more broadly in quantum physics. But it was only very briefly discussed in Section 2.4. Reference [341] is a nice introduction to this filed, and [216] provides a comprehensive review of it. The role of entanglement in quantum-computational speed-up was carefully examined by Jozsa and Linden [237]. In this book, entanglement will become an essential issue when we consider parallel and distributed quantum programs in Chapters 9 and 10.

Chapter 3

Models of quantum computation

A general framework of quantum mechanics was introduced in the last chapter. From this chapter on, we consider how to harness the power of quantum systems to do computation. In the more than forty years of research on quantum computing, various computational models have been generalised into the framework of quantum theory. Of course, they form a central part of the theoretical foundations of quantum programming. The aim of this chapter is to study three basic models of quantum computation, namely quantum circuits, quantum Turing machines, and quantum random access machines (QRAMs).

This chapter is organised as follows:

- We start in Section 3.1 from a lower-level model of quantum computer; namely quantum circuits.
- Quantum Turing machines are described in Section 3.2.
- We introduce the notion of quantum random access machine in Section 3.3.

Also, the relationship between the above three quantum computational models will be briefly discussed in this chapter.

3.1 Quantum circuits

Digital circuits for classical computation are made from logic gates acting on Boolean variables. Quantum circuits are the quantum counterparts of digital circuits. Roughly speaking, they are made up of quantum (logic) gates, which are modelled by unitary transformations defined in Section 2.2.1.

3.1.1 Basic definitions

We use $p, q, q_1, q_2, \ldots$ to denote qubit variables. Graphically, they can be thought of as wires in a quantum circuits. A sequence $\overline{q}$ of distinct qubit variables is called a quantum register. Sometimes, the order of variables in the register is not essential. Then the register is identified with the set of qubit variables in it. So, we can use set-theoretic notations for registers:

$$p \in \overline{q}, \quad \overline{p} \subseteq \overline{q}, \quad \overline{p} \cap \overline{q}, \quad \overline{p} \cup \overline{q}, \quad \overline{p} \setminus \overline{q}.$$

For each qubit variable q, we write $\mathcal{H}_q$ for its state Hilbert space, which is isomorphic to the two-dimensional $\mathcal{H}_2$ (see Example 2.1). Furthermore, for a set $V = \{q_1, \ldots, q_n\}$ of qubit variables or a quantum register $\overline{q} = q_1, \ldots, q_n$, we write:

$$\mathcal{H}_V = \bigotimes_{q \in V} \mathcal{H}_q = \bigotimes_{i=1}^{n} \mathcal{H}_{q_i} = \mathcal{H}_{\overline{q}}$$

for the state space of the composite system consisting of qubits $q_1, \ldots, q_n$. Obviously, $\mathcal{H}_V$ is 2^n-dimensional. Recall that an integer $0 \le x < 2^n$ can be represented by a string $x_1 \ldots x_n \in \{0, 1\}^n$ of n bits:

$$x = \sum_{i=1}^{n} x_i \cdot 2^{i-1}.$$

We shall not distinguish integer x from its binary representation. Thus, each pure state in $\mathcal{H}_V$ can be written as

$$|\psi\rangle = \sum_{x=0}^{2^n - 1} \alpha_x |x\rangle$$

where $\{|x\rangle\}$ is called the computational basis of $\mathcal{H}_2^{\otimes n}$.

Foundations of Quantum Programming. https://doi.org/10.1016/B978-0-44-315942-8.00012-5

Definition 3.1. For any positive integer n, if U is a $2^n \times 2^n$ unitary matrix; that is, $UU^\dagger = U^\dagger U = I$ (where I is the $2^n \times 2^n$ unit matrix, and $U^\dagger$ stands for the transpose conjugate of U), and $\bar{q} = q_1, ..., q_n$ is a quantum register, then

$$G \equiv U[\bar{q}], \quad \text{or} \quad G \equiv U[q_1, ..., q_n]$$

is called an n-qubit gate and we write $var(G) = \{q_1, ..., q_n\}$ for the set of quantum variables in G.

The gate $G \equiv U[\bar{q}]$ is a unitary transformation on the state Hilbert space $\mathcal{H}_{\bar{q}}$ of $\bar{q}$. We often call unitary matrix U a quantum gate without mentioning the quantum register $\bar{q}$.

Definition 3.2. A quantum circuit is a sequence of quantum gates:

$$C \equiv G_1...G_m$$

where $m \geq 1$, and $G_1, ..., G_m$ are quantum gates. The set of quantum variables of C is

$$var(C) = \bigcup_{i=1}^{m} var(G_i).$$

The presentations of quantum gates and quantum circuits in the above two definitions are somehow similar to the Boolean expressions of classical circuits and convenient for algebraic manipulations. However, they are not illustrative. Indeed, quantum circuits can be represented graphically as commonly done for classical circuits; the reader can find graphic illustrations of various quantum circuits in Chapter 4 of book [318]. There are several convenient tools for drawing quantum circuit diagrams; for example visualisation of quantum circuits in IBM qiskit (https://qiskit.org).

Let us see how does a quantum circuit $C \equiv G_1...G_m$ compute. Suppose that $var(C) = \{q_1, ..., q_n\}$, and each gate $G_i = U_i[\bar{r}_i]$, where register $\bar{r}_i$ is a subsequence of $\bar{q} = q_1, ..., q_n$, and U_i is a unitary transformation on the space $\mathcal{H}_{\bar{r}_i}$.

- If a state $|\psi\rangle \in \mathcal{H}_{var(C)}$ is inputted to the circuit C, then the output is

$$C|\psi\rangle = \overline{U}_m...\overline{U}_1|\psi\rangle \tag{3.1}$$

where for each i, $\overline{U}_i = U_i \otimes I_i$ is the cylindrical extension of U_i on $\mathcal{H}_C$, and I_i is the identity operator on the space $\mathcal{H}_{\bar{q}\backslash\bar{r}_i}$. Note that the applications of unitary operators $U_1, ..., U_m$ in Eq. (3.1) are in the reversed order of $G_1, ..., G_m$ in the circuit C.

- More generally, if $var(C) \subsetneq V$ is a set of qubit variables, then each state $|\psi\rangle \in \mathcal{H}_V$ can be written in the form of

$$|\psi\rangle = \sum_i \alpha_i |\varphi_i\rangle |\zeta_i\rangle$$

with $|\varphi_i\rangle \in \mathcal{H}_{var(C)}$ and $|\zeta_i\rangle \in \mathcal{H}_{V\backslash var(C)}$. Whenever we input $|\psi\rangle$ to the circuit C, then the output is

$$C|\psi\rangle = \sum_i \alpha_i (C|\varphi_i\rangle)|\zeta_i\rangle.$$

The linearity of C guarantees that the above output is well-defined.

Now we can define equivalence of quantum circuits whenever their outputs are the same upon the same input.

Definition 3.3. Let C_1, C_2 be quantum circuits and $V = var(C_1) \cup var(C_2)$. If for any $|\psi\rangle \in \mathcal{H}_V$, we have:

$$C_1|\psi\rangle = C_2|\psi\rangle, \tag{3.2}$$

then C_1 and C_2 are equivalent and we write $C_1 = C_2$.

A classical circuit with n input wires and m output wires is actually a Boolean function

$$f : \{0, 1\}^n \to \{0, 1\}^m.$$

Similarly, a quantum circuit C with quantum variables $var(C) = \{q_1, ..., q_n\}$ is always equivalent to a unitary transformation on $\mathcal{H}_{var(C)}$ or a $2^n \times 2^n$ unitary matrix. This can be clearly seen from Eq. (3.1).

Finally, we introduce composition of quantum circuits in order to construct a large quantum circuit from small ones.

Definition 3.4. Let $C_1 \equiv G_1...G_m$ and $C_2 \equiv H_1...H_n$ be quantum circuits, where $G_1, ..., G_m$ and $H_1, ..., H_n$ are quantum gates. Then their composition is the concatenation:

$$C_1 C_2 \equiv G_1...G_m H_1...H_n.$$

Exercise 3.1. 1. Prove that if $C_1 = C_2$ then Eq. (3.2) holds for any state $|\psi\rangle \in \mathcal{H}_V$ and for any $V \supseteq var(C_1) \cup var(C_2)$.
2. Prove that if $C_1 = C_2$ then $CC_1 = CC_2$ and $C_1 C = C_2 C$.

3.1.2 One-qubit gates

After introducing the general definitions of quantum gates and quantum circuits in the last subsection, let us look at some useful examples in this and next few subsections.

The simplest quantum gates are one-qubit gates. They are represented by 2×2 unitary matrices. One example is the Hadamard gate presented in Example 2.3. The following are some other one-qubit gates that are frequently used in quantum computation.

Example 3.1. 1. Global phase shift:

$$M(\alpha) = e^{i\alpha} I,$$

where α is a real number, and

$$I = \begin{pmatrix} 1 & 0 \\ 0 & 1 \end{pmatrix}$$

is the 2×2 unit matrix.
2. (Relative) phase shift:

$$P(\alpha) = \begin{pmatrix} 1 & 0 \\ 0 & e^{i\alpha} \end{pmatrix},$$

where α is a real number. In particular, we have:
a. Phase gate:

$$S = P(\pi/2) = \begin{pmatrix} 1 & 0 \\ 0 & i \end{pmatrix}.$$

b. $\pi/8$ gate or T gate:

$$T = P(\pi/4) = \begin{pmatrix} 1 & 0 \\ 0 & e^{i\pi/4} \end{pmatrix}.$$

Example 3.2. The Pauli matrices:

$$\sigma_x = X = \begin{pmatrix} 0 & 1 \\ 1 & 0 \end{pmatrix}, \quad \sigma_y = Y = \begin{pmatrix} 0 & -i \\ i & 0 \end{pmatrix}, \quad \sigma_z = Z = \begin{pmatrix} 1 & 0 \\ 0 & -1 \end{pmatrix}.$$

Obviously, we have $X|0\rangle = |1\rangle$ and $X|1\rangle = |0\rangle$. So, Pauli matrix X is actually the NOT gate.

Example 3.3. Rotations about the $\hat{x}, \hat{y}, \hat{z}$ axes of the Bloch sphere:

$$R_x(\theta) = \cos\frac{\theta}{2} I - i \sin\frac{\theta}{2} X = \begin{pmatrix} \cos\frac{\theta}{2} & -i\sin\frac{\theta}{2} \\ -i\sin\frac{\theta}{2} & \cos\frac{\theta}{2} \end{pmatrix},$$

$$R_y(\theta) = \cos\frac{\theta}{2} I - i \sin\frac{\theta}{2} Y = \begin{pmatrix} \cos\frac{\theta}{2} & -\sin\frac{\theta}{2} \\ \sin\frac{\theta}{2} & \cos\frac{\theta}{2} \end{pmatrix},$$

$$R_z(\theta) = \cos\frac{\theta}{2} I - i \sin\frac{\theta}{2} Z = \begin{pmatrix} e^{-i\theta/2} & 0 \\ 0 & e^{i\theta/2} \end{pmatrix},$$

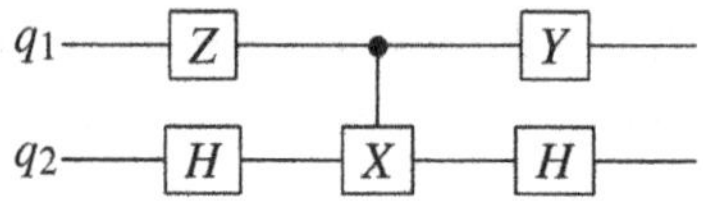

FIGURE 3.1 A quantum circuit with CNOT.

where θ is a real number.

The gates in Example 3.3 have a nice geometric interpretation: a single qubit state can be represented by a vector in the socalled Bloch sphere. The effect of $R_x(\theta)$, $R_y(\theta)$, $R_z(\theta)$ on this state is to rotate it by angle θ about the x, y, z-axis, respectively, of the Bloch sphere; for details, we refer to [318], Sections 1.3.1 and 4.2. It can be shown that any one-qubit gate can be expressed as a circuit consisting of only rotations and global phase shift.

Exercise 3.2. Prove that all the matrices in the above three examples are unitary.

3.1.3 Controlled gates

One-qubit gates are not enough for any useful quantum computation. In this subsection, we introduce an important class of multiple-qubit gates, namely the controlled gates.

The most frequently used among them is the CNOT operator C defined in Example 2.7. Here, we look at it in a different way. Let q_1, q_2 be qubit variables. Then $C[q_1, q_2]$ is a two-qubit gate with q_1 as the control qubit and q_2 as the target qubit. It acts as follows:

$$C[q_1, q_2]|i_1, i_2\rangle = |i_1, i_1 \oplus i_2\rangle$$

for $i_1, i_2 \in \{0, 1\}$, where $\oplus$ is addition modulo 2; that is, if q_1 is set to $|1\rangle$, then q_2 is flipped, otherwise q_2 is left unchanged. As a simple generalisation of the CNOT gate, we have:

Example 3.4. Let U be a 2×2 unitary matrix. Then the controlled-U is a two-qubit gate defined by

$$C(U)[q_1, q_2]|i_1, i_2\rangle = |i_1\rangle U^{i_1}|i_2\rangle$$

for $i_1, i_2 \in \{0, 1\}$. Its matrix representation is

$$C(U) = \begin{pmatrix} I & 0 \\ 0 & U \end{pmatrix}$$

where I is the 2×2 unit matrix. Obviously, $C = C(X)$; that is, CNOT is the controlled-X with X being the Pauli matrix σ_x.

Example 3.5. The quantum circuit

$$Z[q_1]H[q_2]C[q_1, q_2]Y[q_1]H[q_2]$$

using the CNOT gate $C(X)$ and the Hadamard gate H and Pauli gates Y, Z is visualised in Fig. 3.1.

Exercise 3.3. *SWAP* is a two-qubit gate defined by

$$SWAP[q_1, q_2]|i_1, i_2\rangle = |i_2, i_1\rangle$$

for $i_1, i_2 \in \{0, 1\}$. Intuitively, it swaps the states of two qubits. Show that *SWAP* can be implemented by three CNOT gates:

$$SWAP[q_1, q_2] = C[q_1, q_2]C[q_2, q_1]C[q_1, q_2].$$

Exercise 3.4. Prove the following properties of controlled gates:

1. $C[p, q] = H[q]C(Z)[p, q]H[q]$.
2. $C(Z)[p, q] = C(Z)[q, p]$.
3. $H[p]H[q]C[p, q]H[p]H[q] = C[q, p]$.
4. $C(M(\alpha))[p, q] = P(\alpha)[p]$.
5. $C[p, q]X[p]C[p, q] = X[p]X[q]$.

6. $C[p,q]Y[p]C[p,q] = Y[p]X[q]$.
7. $C[p,q]Z[p]C[p,q] = Z[p]$.
8. $C[p,q]X[q]C[p,q] = X[q]$.
9. $C[p,q]Y[q]C[p,q] = Z[p]Y[q]$.
10. $C[p,q]Z[q]C[p,q] = Z[p]Z[q]$.
11. $C[p,q]T[p] = T[p]C[p,q]$.

All the controlled gates considered above are two-qubit gates. Actually, we can define a much more general notion of controlled gate.

Definition 3.5. Let $\overline{p} = p_1, ..., p_m$ and $\overline{q}$ be registers with $\overline{p} \cap \overline{q} = \emptyset$. If $G = U[\overline{q}]$ is a quantum gate, then the controlled circuit $C^{(\overline{p})}(U)$ with control qubits $\overline{p}$ and target qubits $\overline{q}$ is the unitary transformation on the state Hilbert space $\mathcal{H}_{\overline{p} \cup \overline{q}}$ defined by

$$C^{(\overline{p})}(U)|\overline{t}\rangle|\psi\rangle = \begin{cases} |\overline{t}\rangle U|\psi\rangle & \text{if } t_1 = ... = t_m = 1, \\ |\overline{t}\rangle|\psi\rangle & \text{otherwise} \end{cases}$$

for any $\overline{t} = t_1 ... t_m \in \{0, 1\}^m$ and $|\psi\rangle \in \mathcal{H}_{\overline{q}}$.

The following example presents a class of three-qubit controlled gates.

Example 3.6. Let p_1, p_2, q be qubit variables and U a 2×2 unitary matrix. The controlled-controlled-U gate:

$$C^2(U) = C^{(p_1, p_2)}(U)$$

is the unitary transformation on $\mathcal{H}_{p_1} \otimes \mathcal{H}_{p_2} \otimes \mathcal{H}_q$:

$$C^{(2)}(U)|t_1, t_2, \psi\rangle = \begin{cases} |t_1, t_2, \psi\rangle & \text{if } t_1 = 0 \text{ or } t_2 = 0, \\ |t_1, t_2\rangle U|\psi\rangle & \text{if } t_1 = t_2 = 1 \end{cases}$$

for $t_1, t_2 \in \{0, 1\}$ and for any $|\psi\rangle \in \mathcal{H}_q$. In particular, the controlled-controlled-NOT is called the Toffoli gate.

The single Toffoli gate is universal for classical reversible computation, and it is universal for quantum computation with little extra help of single qubit gates (in the sense defined in Section 3.1.5 below). It is also very useful in quantum error-correction.

Exercise 3.5. Prove the following equalities that allow us to combine several controlled gates into a single one:
1. $C^{(\overline{p})}(C^{(\overline{q})}(U)) = C^{(\overline{p}, \overline{q})}(U)$.
2. $C^{(\overline{p})}(U_1)C^{(\overline{p})}(U_2) = C^{(\overline{p})}(U_1 U_2)$.

3.1.4 Quantum multiplexor

Controlled gates can be further generalised to multiplexors. In this subsection, we introduce the notion of quantum multiplexor and its matrix representation.

For classical computation, the simplest multiplexor is a *conditional* described by the "**if**...**then**...**else**..." construction: perform the action specified in the "**then**" clause when the condition after "**if**" is true, and perform the action specified in the "**else**" clause when it is false. The implementation of conditionals may be done by first processing the "**then**" and "**else**" clauses in parallel and then multiplexing the outputs.

Quantum conditional is a quantum analog of classical conditional. It is formed by replacing the condition (Boolean expression) after "**if**" by a qubit; that is, replacing truth values *true* and *false* by the basis states $|1\rangle$ and $|0\rangle$, respectively, of a qubit.

Example 3.7. Let p be a qubit variable and $\overline{q} = q_1, ..., q_n$ a quantum register, and let $C_0 = U_0[\overline{q}]$ and $C_1 = U_1[\overline{q}]$ be quantum gates. Then quantum conditional $C_0 \oplus C_1$ is a gate on $1 + n$ qubits $p, \overline{q}$ with the first qubit p as the select qubit and the remaining n qubits $\overline{q}$ as the data qubits, defined by:

$$(C_0 \oplus C_1)|i\rangle|\psi\rangle = |i\rangle U_i|\psi\rangle$$

for $i \in \{0, 1\}$ and for any $|\psi\rangle \in \mathcal{H}_{\overline{q}}$. Equivalently, it is defined by the matrix:

$$C_0 \oplus C_1 = \begin{pmatrix} U_0 & 0 \\ 0 & U_1 \end{pmatrix}.$$

The controlled-gate defined in Example 3.4 is a spacial case of quantum conditional: $C(U) = I \oplus U$, where I is the unit matrix.

The essential difference between classical and quantum conditionals is that the select qubit can be not only in the basis states $|0\rangle$ and $|1\rangle$ but also in their superpositions:

$$(C_0 \oplus C_1)(\alpha_0 |0\rangle |\psi_0\rangle + \alpha_1 |1\rangle |\psi_1\rangle) = \alpha_0 |0\rangle U_0 |\psi_0\rangle + \alpha_1 |1\rangle U_1 |\psi_1\rangle$$

for any states $|\psi_0\rangle, |\psi_1\rangle \in \mathcal{H}_{\overline{q}}$ and for any complex numbers α_0, α_1 with $|\alpha_0|^2 + |\alpha_1|^2 = 1$.

Multiplexor is a multi-way generalisation of conditional. Roughly speaking, a multiplexor is a switch that passes one of its data inputs through to the output, as a function of a set of select inputs. Similarly, quantum multiplexor (QMUX for short) is a multi-way generalisation of quantum conditional.

Definition 3.6. Let $\overline{p} = p_1, ..., p_m$ and $\overline{q} = q_1, ..., q_n$ be quantum registers, and for each $x \in \{0, 1\}^m$, let $C_x = U_x[\overline{q}]$ be a quantum gate. Then QMUX

$$\bigoplus_x C_x$$

is a gate on $m + n$ qubits $\overline{p}, \overline{q}$, having the first m qubits $\overline{p}$ as the select qubits and the remaining n qubits $\overline{q}$ as the data qubits. It preserves any state of the select qubits, and perform a unitary transformation on the data qubits, which is chosen according to the state of the select qubits:

$$\left(\bigoplus_x C_x \right) |t\rangle |\psi\rangle = |t\rangle U_t |\psi\rangle$$

for any $t \in \{0, 1\}^m$ and $|\psi\rangle \in \mathcal{H}_{\overline{q}}$.

The matrix representation of the QMUX is a diagonal:

$$\bigoplus_x C_x = \bigoplus_{x=0}^{2^m - 1} U_x = \begin{pmatrix} U_0 & & & & \\ & U_1 & & & \\ & & \cdot & & \\ & & & \cdot & \\ & & & & U_{2^m-1} \end{pmatrix}.$$

Here, we identify an integer $0 \le x < 2^m$ with its binary representation $x \in \{0, 1\}^m$. The difference between classical multiplexor and QMUX also comes from that the select qubits $\overline{p}$ can be in a superposition of basis states $|x\rangle$:

$$\left(\bigoplus_x C_x \right)\left(\sum_{x=0}^{2^m - 1} \alpha_x |x\rangle |\psi_x\rangle \right) = \sum_{x=0}^{2^m - 1} \alpha_x |x\rangle U_x |\psi_x\rangle$$

for any states $|\psi_x\rangle \in \mathcal{H}_{\overline{q}}$ ($0 \le x < 2^m$) and any complex numbers α_x with $\sum_x |\alpha_x|^2 = 1$. Obviously, the controlled gate introduced in Definition 3.5 is a special QMUX:

$$C^{(\overline{p})}(U) = I \oplus ... \oplus I \oplus U,$$

where the first $2^m - 1$ summands are the unit matrix of the same dimension as U.

Exercise 3.6. Prove the multiplexor extension property:

$$\left(\bigoplus_x C_x \right)\left(\bigoplus_x D_x \right) = \bigoplus_x (C_x D_x).$$

In the next chapter, we will see a simple application of QMUX in quantum walks. A close connection between QMUX and a quantum program constructs – quantum case statement – will be revealed in Chapter 11. Also, QMUXs have been successfully used for synthesis of quantum circuits (see [374]) and thus will be useful for compilation of quantum programs.

3.1.5   Universality of gates

We have already introduced several important classes of quantum gates in the last three subsections. A question naturally arises: are they sufficient for quantum computation? This section is devoted to answer this question.

To better understand the above question, let us first consider the corresponding question in classical computation. For each $n \geq 0$, there are 2^{2^n} n-ary Boolean functions. Totally, we have infinitely many Boolean functions. However, there are some small sets of logic gates that are universal: they can generate all Boolean functions; for example, {NOT, AND}, {NOT, OR}. The notion of universality can be easily generalised to the quantum case:

Definition 3.7. A set Ω of unitary matrices is universal if all unitary matrices can be generated by it; that is, for any positive integer n, and for any $2^n \times 2^n$ unitary matrix U, there exists a circuit C with quantum variables $var(C) = \{q_1, ..., q_n\}$ constructed from the gates defined by unitary matrices in Ω such that

$$U[q_1, ..., q_n] = C$$

(equivalence of circuits introduced in Definition 3.3).

One of the simplest universal sets of quantum gates is presented in the following:

Theorem 3.1. *The CNOT gate together with all one-qubit gates is universal.*

The universal sets of classical gates mentioned above are all finite. However, the universal set of quantum gates given in Theorem 3.1 is infinite. Indeed, the set of unitary operators form a continuum, which is uncountably infinite. So, it is impossible to exactly implement an arbitrary unitary operator by a finite set of quantum gates. This forces us to consider approximate universality rather than the exact universality introduced in Definition 3.7.

Definition 3.8. A set Ω of unitary matrices is approximately universal if for any positive integer n, for any $2^n \times 2^n$ unitary operator U and for any $\epsilon > 0$, there is a circuit C with $qvar(C) = \{q_1, ..., q_n\}$ constructed from the gates defined by unitary matrices in Ω such that

$$d\big(U[q_1, ..., q_n], C\big) < \epsilon,$$

where d is the norm distance defined by Eq. (2.4).

Two well-known approximately universal sets of gates are given in the following:

Theorem 3.2. *The following two sets of gates are approximately universal:*

1. *Hadamard gate H, $\pi/8$ gate T, and CNOT gate C;*
2. *Hadamard gate H, phase gate S, CNOT gate C, and the Toffoli gate (see Example 3.6).*

The proofs of Theorems 3.1 and 3.2 are quite involved and thus omitted here, but the reader can find them in book [318], Section 4.5.

3.1.6   Measurements in circuits

The universality theorems presented in the last subsection indicate that any quantum computation can be carried out by a quantum circuit constructed from the basic quantum gates described in Sections 3.1.2 and 3.1.3. But the output of a quantum circuit is usually a quantum state, which cannot be observed directly from the outside. In order to read out the outcome of computation, we have to perform a measurement at the end of the circuit. So, sometimes we need to consider a generalised notion of quantum circuit, namely circuit with quantum measurements.

As shown in Section 2.3, we only need to use projective measurements if it is allowed to introduce ancilla qubits. Furthermore, if the circuit contains n qubit variables, the measurement in the computational basis $\{|x\rangle : x \in \{0, 1\}^n\}$ is sufficient because any orthonormal basis of these qubits can be obtained from the computational basis by a unitary transformation.

Actually, quantum measurements are not only used at the end of a computation. They are also often performed as an intermediate step of a computation and the measurement outcomes are used to conditionally control subsequent steps of the computation. But Nielsen and Chuang [318] explicitly pointed out:

- **Principle of deferred measurement**: Measurements can always be moved from an intermediate stage of a quantum circuit to the end of the circuit; if the measurement results are used at any stage of the circuit then the classically controlled operations can be replaced by conditional quantum operations.

Quantum circuits with Measurements: To formally describe the above principle of deferred measurement, let first introduce the following:

Definition 3.9. Quantum circuit with measurements (mQCs for short) is defined by induction as follows:

1. Each quantum gate is an mQC;
2. If $\overline{q}$ is a quantum register, $M = \{M_m\} = \{M_{m_1}, M_{m_2}, ..., M_{m_n}\}$ is a quantum measurement in $\mathcal{H}_{\overline{q}}$, and for each m, C_m is an mQC with $\overline{q} \cap var(C_m) = \emptyset$, then

$$\mathbf{if} \left(\square m \cdot M[\overline{q}] = m \to C_m\right) \mathbf{if} \equiv \mathbf{fi} \; \begin{aligned} M[\overline{q}] &= m_1 \to C_{m_1} \\ \square \qquad & m_2 \to C_{m_2} \\ & \quad ...... \\ \square \qquad & m_n \to C_{m_n} \\ \mathbf{fi} \end{aligned} \tag{3.3}$$

is a mQC too;
3. If C_1 and C_2 are mQCs, so is $C_1 C_2$.

Intuitively, Eq. (3.3) means that we perform measurement M on $\overline{q}$, and then the subsequent computation is selected based on the measurement outcome: if the outcome is m, then the corresponding circuit C_m follows.

The notion of equivalence between quantum circuits (Definition 3.3) can be straightforwardly generalised to the case of mQCs. Then the principle of deferring measurement can be formally restated as the following:

Proposition 3.1. *For any mQC C, there is a quantum circuit C' (without measurements) and a quantum measurement $M[\overline{q}]$ such that $C = C'M[\overline{q}]$ (equivalence).*

Exercise 3.7. 1. Prove Proposition 3.1.
2. If we remove the condition $\overline{q} \cap var(C_m) = \emptyset$ from clause 2 in Definition 3.9, then the postmeasurement states of measured qubits can be used in the subsequent computation. Is the principle of deferred measurement still true for this case?

3.2 Quantum Turing machines

In this section, we turn to consider a more abstract model of quantum computation – quantum Turing machines (QTMs). QTMs are quantum analogues of classical Turing machines (TMs), which are, as is well-known, one of the most fundamental models of computation.

Turing machines: To smoothly introduce the definition of QTMs, let us recall that a (deterministic) TM is defined as a triple $\mathcal{M} = (\Sigma, Q, \delta)$, where:

- Σ is a finite alphabet with a blank symbol $\# \in \Sigma$;
- Q is a finite set of states – the states of a finite control – with an initial state $q_0 \in Q$ and a final state $q_f \in Q$ such that $(q_0 \neq q_f)$;
- $\delta : Q \times \Sigma \to Q \times \Sigma \times \{L, R\}$ is a transition function, specifying the evolution of the machine.

We assume that the machine $\mathcal{M}$ has a two-way infinite tape of cells indexed by integers $\mathbb{Z}$ and a single read/write tape head that moves along the tape. Then a configuration of $\mathcal{M}$ is a description of:

1. the state $q \in Q$ of the finite control;
2. the tape's contents. It is assumed that at any time only a finite number of tape cells contain nonblank symbols;
3. the location of the tape head.

It is worth noting that the set of configurations is countably infinite due to the condition that the tape holds only a finite number of nonblank symbols. In particular, in the initial configuration c_0, the control is in the initial state q_0, and we usually assume that the tape head is in position 0, and the tape's contents are the input $x \in (\Sigma \setminus \{\#\})^*$ arranged in positions from 0 to $|x| - 1$. Here, we use Γ^* to denote the set of all finite strings of symbols in Γ, including the empty string.

We note that the transition function δ only specifies the local action in a single step of the machine. But it actually determines the machine's global behaviour – how the machine transitions from a configuration c to another configuration c':

- if in configuration c the control is in state q, the symbol scanned by the tape head is σ, and $\delta(q, \sigma) = (q', \sigma', d)$, then the successor configuration c' is determined as follows: the control's state becomes q', the symbol in the cell under the tape head is changed from σ to σ', and the head moves one cell to the left or right according to $d = L$ or R.

Whenever the machine halts upon the input x; that is, it enters the final state q_f, then the output is the tape's contents (from the leftmost nonblank symbol to the rightmost nonblank symbol). Thus, machine $\mathcal{M}$ computes a function

$$f : \left(\Sigma \setminus \{\#\}\right)^* \to \Sigma^*,$$

which is possibly partial because $\mathcal{M}$ may never halts upon some inputs.

Quantum Turing machines: Now we can introduce the notion of quantum Turing machine. It can be naturally defined as a quantum generalisation of TMs as in the following:

Definition 3.10. A pseudo quantum Turing machine (QTM) is a triple $\mathcal{M} = (Q, \Sigma, \delta)$, where Q and Σ are the same as in a TM, and the quantum transition function is defined as

$$\delta : Q \times \Sigma \to \mathbb{C}^{Q \times \Sigma \times \{L, R\}}$$

or equivalently

$$\delta : (Q \times \Sigma) \times \left(Q \times \Sigma \times \{L, R\}\right) \to \mathbb{C}.$$

Here, for each $(q, \sigma) \in Q \times \Sigma$ and $(q', \sigma', d) \in Q \times \Sigma \times \{L, R\}$, the complex number

$$\delta(q, \sigma, q', \sigma', d) \stackrel{\triangle}{=} \delta(q, \sigma, q')(\sigma', d) \in \mathbb{C}$$

can be understood as the probability amplitude of the transition specified by (q', σ', d) from the current control state q and the symbol σ scanned by the tape head.

The configurations of a pseudo QTM are the same as those of a TM. We write $\mathcal{C}$ for the set of configurations and define $\mathcal{H}_{\mathcal{M}}$ as the Hilbert space spanned by the configurations, more precisely:

$$\mathcal{H}_{\mathcal{M}} = \text{span}\{|c\rangle : c \in \mathcal{C}\},$$

that is, $\{|c\rangle : c \in \mathcal{C}\}$ is an orthonormal basis of $\mathcal{H}_{\mathcal{M}}$. Then as in the case of classical TMs, the local transitions (specified by quantum transition function δ) determine a linear operator $U_{\mathcal{M}}$ on $\mathcal{H}_{\mathcal{M}}$, which describes the global behaviour of the machine: for each configuration $c \in \mathcal{C}$, if in c the state of the control is q and the symbol scanned by the tape head is σ, then

$$U_{\mathcal{M}}|c\rangle = \sum_{q' \in Q, \, \sigma' \in \Sigma, \, d \in \{L, R\}} \delta(q, \sigma, q', \sigma', d)|c_{q', \sigma', d}\rangle \tag{3.4}$$

where $c_{q', \sigma', d}$ is the configuration obtained from c by changing the state from q to q', replacing the scanned symbol σ by σ' and moving the tape head according to the direction d, and $\delta(q, \sigma, q', \sigma', d) \in \mathbb{C}$ is the probability amplitude with which configuration c leads to a new configuration $c_{q', \sigma', d}$ in a single step of the machine. Note that $U_{\mathcal{M}}$ is well-defined by Eq. (3.4) together with linearity.

The operator $U_{\mathcal{M}}$ describes the dynamics (or time evolution) of the machine $\mathcal{M}$. Therefore, it must be consistent with quantum physics, and we have to introduce the following:

Definition 3.11. A pseudo QTM $\mathcal{M}$ is called a QTM if $U_{\mathcal{M}}$ is a unitary operator on Hilbert space $\mathcal{H}_{\mathcal{M}}$; that is,

$$U_{\mathcal{M}}^{\dagger} U_{\mathcal{M}} = U_{\mathcal{M}} U_{\mathcal{M}}^{\dagger} = I_{\mathcal{M}},$$

where $I_{\mathcal{M}}$ is the identity operator on $\mathcal{H}_{\mathcal{M}}$.

It is usually not easy to check the unitarity of $U_{\mathcal{M}}$ directly because it is defined on the (countably) infinite-dimensional space $\mathcal{H}_{\mathcal{M}}$.

Exercise 3.8. Find a necessary and sufficient condition on the transition function δ under which $\mathcal{H}_\mathcal{M}$ is unitary.

Since the domain of δ is a finite set, such a condition found in the above exercise must be much easier to check than a direct verification of the unitarity of $U_\mathcal{M}$.

Now let us see how a QTM $\mathcal{M}$ computes. Assume that c_0 is the initial configuration with input x. Then $\mathcal{M}$ starts in the basis state $|\psi_0\rangle = |c_0\rangle$. In each step, $\mathcal{M}$ evolves according to unitary $U_\mathcal{M}$. The halting schemes for QTMs are much more subtle than their classical counterparts. For example, Deustch [128] proposed to see whether the machine enters the final state q_f by periodic measurements, and Bernstein and Vazirani [59] suggested to allow the machine to run for a predetermined number of steps. A series of papers have been devoted to discussions about the halting problem of QTMs. Here, we choose to consider a simple scheme: a measurement M_f is performed at the end of each step. The measurement is thus given as $M_f = \{P_f, P_f^\perp\}$, where measurement operators P_f are the projection onto the subspace spanned by all configurations $|c\rangle$ with the control in the final state q_f, and $P_f^\perp = I_\mathcal{M} - P_f$ is the orthocomplement of P_f in Hilbert space $\mathcal{H}_\mathcal{M}$. It should be noted that the computation of $\mathcal{M}$ is probabilistic. More precisely, for each $t \geq 1$, if at the beginning of step t, $\mathcal{M}$ is in state $|\psi_{t-1}\rangle$, then $\mathcal{M}$ halts in this step with probability

$$p(t) = \|P_f U_\mathcal{M} |\psi_{t-1}\rangle\|^2.$$

Let us write $|\varphi_t\rangle$ for the machine's (unnormalised) state after halting. On the other hand, $\mathcal{M}$ runs into next step with probability $1 - p(t)$, which starts in state

$$|\psi_t\rangle = \frac{1}{\sqrt{1-p(t)}} P_f^\perp U_\mathcal{M} |\psi_{t-1}\rangle.$$

Exercise 3.9. Prove $|\varphi_t\rangle = P_f U_\mathcal{M} (P_\mathcal{M}^\perp U_\mathcal{M})^{t-1}|c_0\rangle$ and $p(t) = \|\varphi_t\|^2$.

We can imagine that after it halts, the machine $\mathcal{M}$ is in a mixed state

$$\rho_x = \sum_t |\varphi_t\rangle\langle\varphi_t|.$$

Note that ρ_x may be a partial density operator; that if $\mathrm{tr}(\rho_x) < 1$, because $\mathcal{M}$ may not halt with a probability > 0. Then roughly speaking, the output of $\mathcal{M}$ upon input x can be obtained by measuring the tape contents of ρ_x.

There are various variants of TMs, such as those with one-way infinite tapes, multiple tapes, and multiple heads, multi-dimensional TMs and nondeterministic TMs. Most of them have been naturally generalised to the quantum setting. It has also been proved that QTMs and their variants are all equivalent to classical TMs in computability. For more details about QTMs and an excellent introduction to quantum complexity theory, we refer the reader to [59].

Problem 3.1. How can we define a quantum generalisation of nondeterministic QTMs, or how can nondeterminism and quantumness coexist in TMs?

As is well-known, Turing machines and circuits are equivalent computational models. The same relationship holds for quantum Turing machines and quantum circuits studied in Section 3.1. It was proved by Yao [415] that (up to a polynomial overhead) quantum Turing machines and (uniformly generated families of) quantum circuits can be simulated by each other.

3.3   Quantum random access stored-program machines

In the last subsection, we studied the basic model of quantum computation – quantum Turing machines (QTMs). As we know from classical computing theory, random access machines (RAMs) and random access stored-program machines (RASPs) are computational models that are closer to the architecture of real-world computers than Turing machines (TMs). So, in this subsection, we introduce quantum generalisations of RAMs and RASPs.

Most of the known quantum algorithms involve both classical computation and quantum computation. On the other hand, fully quantum machines of large scales are out of the reach of technology in the near future. So, it is widely accepted that a practical quantum computer of the first few generations should consist of a classical computer with access to quantum registers, where the classical part performs classical computations and controls the evolution of quantum registers, and the quantum part can

TABLE 3.1 QRAM instructions.

Type	Instruction	Execution time
Classical	$X_i \leftarrow C$, C any integer	1
Classical	$X_i \leftarrow X_j + X_k$	$l(X_j) + l(X_k)$
Classical	$X_i \leftarrow X_j - X_k$	$l(X_j) + l(X_k)$
Classical	$X_i \leftarrow X_{X_j}$	$l(X_j) + l(X_{X_j})$
Classical	$X_{X_i} \leftarrow X_j$	$l(X_i) + l(X_j)$
Classical	TRA m if $X_j > 0$	$l(X_j)$
Classical	READ X_i	$l(\text{input})$
Classical	WRITE X_i	$l(X_i)$
Quantum	$\text{CNOT}[Q_{X_i}, Q_{X_j}]$	$l(X_i) + l(X_j)$
Quantum	$H[Q_{X_i}]$	$l(X_i)$
Quantum	$T[Q_{X_i}]$	$l(X_i)$
Measurement	$X_i \leftarrow M[Q_{X_j}]$	$l(X_j)$

1. be initialised in certain states (e.g. basis state $|0\rangle$);
2. perform elementary unitary operations (e.g. Hadamard, $\pi/8$ and CNOT gates from an approximately universal set of basic quantum gates given in Theorem 3.2); and
3. be measured with the outcomes sent to the classical machine.

The quantum generalisations of RAMs and RASPs in this section are designed based on the above observation.

Quantum random access machines (QRAMs): Let us first consider quantum random access machines (QRAMs). The above observation leads us to define a QRAM as a RAM in the traditional sense with the ability to perform a set of quantum operations on quantum registers, including: (1) state preparation; (2) certain unitary operations; and (3) quantum measurements. Formally, we have:

Definition 3.12. A QRAM is defined as a program P, i.e. a finite sequence of QRAM instructions operating on an infinite sequence of both classical and quantum registers.

Let us further describe the ingredients of a QRAM. Each classical register holds an arbitrary integer (positive, negative, or zero), while each quantum register holds a qubit (in state $|0\rangle$, $|1\rangle$ or their superposition). The contents of the ith ($i \geq 0$) classical (resp. quantum) register are denoted by X_i (resp. Q_i). Of course, we can generalise this definition by allowing each quantum register to hold a quantum integer expressed as a state in the Hilbert space $\mathcal{H}_\infty$ in Example 2.2, but the presentation will be much more complicated.

The instructions for QRAM and their execution times are given in Table 3.1, where i, j, k are any nonnegative integers, m are integers between 0 and L (inclusive), and L is the length of the QRAM program. These QRAM instructions are divided into two types:

A. The **classical instructions** are standard (i.e. the same as those in a traditional RAM as described in textbook [12]), including:

  (a) *Direct instructions*:

- The instruction $X_i \leftarrow C$ causes X_i to hold an integer C;
- The instruction $X_i \leftarrow X_j \pm X_k$ causes X_i to hold the result of computing $X_j \pm X_k$;
- The instruction TRA m if $X_j > 0$ causes the mth instruction to be the next instruction to execute if $X_j > 0$;
- The instruction READ X_i causes X_i to hold the next input number on the input tape;
- The instruction WRITE X_i causes X_i to be printed on the output tape.

  (b) *Indirect instructions*:

- The instruction $X_i \leftarrow X_{X_j}$ causes X_i to hold X_{X_j} (provided $X_j \geq 0$);
- The instruction $X_{X_i} \leftarrow X_j$ causes X_{X_i} to hold X_j (provided $X_i \geq 0$).

As is well-known, the indirect instructions enhance the machine with indirect addressing, and thus allow a fixed program to access unbounded registers.

B. The **quantum instructions** include:

(a) *Quantum gates:* For simplicity of presentation, we choose to use a minimal but approximately universal set of quantum gates: CNOT (the Controlled-NOT gate), H (the Hadamard gate), and T (the $\pi/8$ gate) (see Theorem 3.2). Indeed, any approximately universal finite set of quantum gates is acceptable for our purpose. Thus, the instruction $U[Q_{X_i}]$ means that unitary transformation U is performed on a single qubit Q_{X_i}. Similarly, $\text{CNOT}[Q_{X_i}, Q_{X_i}]$ means that CNOT is performed on qubits Q_{X_i} and Q_{X_j}.

(b) *Measurements:* The measurement instruction $X_i \leftarrow M[Q_{X_j}]$ is a bridge between classical and quantum registers, which causes X_i to hold the measurement result of Q_{X_j} in the computational basis, provided $X_j \geq 0$.

It should be noted that in all quantum instructions, classical registers X_i, X_j are employed as classical address to indirectly access quantum registers.

For computational complexity analysis, we assume a cost function $l(n)$ with the machine, which measures the memory required to store, or the time required to load the number n. Two cost functions commonly used in studying classical RAMs are:

1. $l(n)$ is a constant, i.e. $l(n) = O(1)$; and
2. $l(n)$ is logarithmic, i.e. $l(n) = O(\log|n|)$, where $|n|$ is the absolute value of n.

We adopt these cost functions in our studies of QRAMs and QRASPs.

To describe the execution of a QRAM, we use an instruction counter (IC) to indicate which instruction to be executed next. Let $\mathbb{N}$ and $\mathbb{Z}$ stand for the sets of natural numbers and integers, respectively. Then a configuration of the QRAM is defined as a 5-tuple $(\xi, \mu, |\psi\rangle, x, y)$, where:

1. $\xi \in \mathbb{N} \cup \{\downarrow\}$ denotes the current IC, with $\downarrow$ indicating the end of execution;
2. $\mu : \mathbb{N} \to \mathbb{Z}$ is the description of all contents of classical registers;
3. $|\psi\rangle \in \bigotimes_{i \in \mathbb{N}} \mathcal{H}_2$, where $\mathcal{H}_2$ is the state space of a qubit; that is, the 2-dimensional Hilbert space;
4. $x \in \mathbb{Z}^\omega$ is a sequence of integers to read on the input tape;
5. $y \in \mathbb{Z}^*$ is a sequence of printed integers on the output tape.

Each instruction of the QRAM can be described as a probabilistic transition

$$c \xrightarrow[T]{p} c',$$

meaning that configuration c is changed to configuration c' in time T with probability p. For example, if the ξth instruction is $X_i \leftarrow M[Q_{X_j}]$, then whenever $\mu(j) \geq 0$,

$$(\xi, \mu, |\psi\rangle, x, y) \xrightarrow[l(\mu(j))]{|P_j^b|\psi\rangle|^2} \left(\xi + 1, \mu_i^b, \frac{P_j^b|\psi\rangle}{|P_j^b|\psi\rangle|^2}, x, y\right),$$

where $b = 0$ or 1, $P_j^b = (\bigotimes_{k \in \mathbb{N}\setminus\{j\}} I_2) \otimes |b\rangle\langle b|$, I_2 is the identity operator on $\mathcal{H}_2$, and μ_i^b is obtained from μ by replacing its content of the ith register with the outcome b of measurement on the jth qubit; otherwise,

$$(\xi, \mu, |\psi\rangle, x, y) \xrightarrow[l(\mu(i))]{} (\downarrow, \mu, |\psi\rangle, x, y).$$

It is worth mentioning that the transitions caused by other instructions always have probability 1. Note that the cost function $l(n)$ is used here to define the time of each execution step of the QRAM.

Now we can describe the computations of the QRAM. An execution path is a sequence of the form:

$$\pi = c_0 \xrightarrow[T_1]{p_1} c_1 \xrightarrow[T_2]{p_2} c_2 \cdots \xrightarrow[n]{p_n} c_n$$

with probability $p(\pi) = \prod_{i=1}^n p_i$ and time $T(\pi) = \sum_{i=1}^n T_i$. Given an alphabet Σ, the QRAM defines a probabilistic input-output relation $P : \Sigma^* \times \Sigma^* \to [0, 1]$ such that for any two strings $x, y \in \Sigma^*$, upon input x, the machine outputs y with probability $P(x, y)$. Roughly speaking, for any $x, y \in \Sigma^*$, we can encode them as two sequences of integers, then

$$P(x, y) = \sum_\pi p(\pi),$$

where π ranges over all paths from a configuration with x on the input tape to a terminal configuration with y on the output tape.

TABLE 3.2 QRASP instructions.

Type	Operation	Mnemonic	code	Description	Execution time
Classical	load constant	LOD, j	1	$AC \leftarrow j$; $IC \leftarrow IC + 2$	$l(IC) + l(j)$
Classical	add	ADD, j	2	$AC \leftarrow AC + X_j$; $IC \leftarrow IC + 2$	$l(IC) + l(j) + l(AC) + l(X_j)$
Classical	subtract	SUB, j	3	$AC \leftarrow AC - X_j$; $IC \leftarrow IC + 2$	$l(IC) + l(j) + l(AC) + l(X_j)$
Classical	store	STO, j	4	$X_j \leftarrow AC$; $IC \leftarrow IC + 2$	$l(IC) + l(j) + l(AC)$
Classical	branch on positive accumulator	BPA, j	5	if $AC > 0$ then $IC \leftarrow j$; otherwise $IC \leftarrow IC+2$	$l(IC) + l(j) + l(AC)$
Classical	read	RD, j	6	$X_j \leftarrow$ next input; $IC \leftarrow IC + 2$	$l(IC) + l(j) + l(input)$
Classical	print	PRI, j	7	output X_j; $IC \leftarrow IC + 2$	$l(IC) + l(j) + l(X_j)$
Quantum	CNOT	CNOT, j, k	8	$CNOT[Q_j, Q_k]$; $IC \leftarrow IC + 3$	$l(IC) + l(j) + l(k)$
Quantum	H	H, j	9	$H[Q_j]$; $IC \leftarrow IC + 2$	$l(IC) + l(j)$
Quantum	T	T, j	10	$T[Q_j]$; $IC \leftarrow IC + 2$	$l(IC) + l(j)$
Measurement	measure	MEA, j	11	$AC \leftarrow M[Q_j]$; $IC \leftarrow IC + 2$	$l(IC) + l(j)$
Termination	halt	HLT	–	stop	$l(IC) + l(X_{IC})$

Quantum random access stored-program machines (QRASPs): The idea in defining QRAMs can be used to define quantum random access stored-program machine (QRASPs) too. A QRASP is also a program P, i.e. a finite sequence of QRASP instructions operating on an infinite sequence of classical registers and an infinite sequence of quantum registers.

A. The registers of a QRASP are the same as those in a QRAM;
B. The instructions for the QRASP are presented in Table 3.2.
   (a) The classical instructions in the QRASP are standard (i.e. the same as those in a classical RASP as defined in [12]).
   (b) The quantum instructions in the QRASP are essentially the same as in QRAMs.

It should be pointed out that similar to the case of classical RASPs, each QRASP instruction is encoded as an integer – operation code (see the column "code" in Table 3.2). Therefore, the QRASP is actually a finite sequence of integers that are to be interpreted into QRASP instructions during the execution. This allows the QRASP to store its program in the (classical) registers as well as its data. As is well-known, by allowing its program stored in the registers, RASPs do not need those indirect instructions used in RAMs. Furthermore, the QRASP may modify itself during the execution and causes unpredictable interpreted QRASP instructions.

Now let us describe a computation of the QRASP. It has an accumulator (AC), which holds an arbitrary integer, an instruction counter (IC), and two infinite sequences of classical and quantum registers. Each classical register X_i holds an arbitrary integer, and each quantum register Q_i holds a qubit. An instruction is stored in two or three consecutive classical registers, where the first register contains its operation code, and the second (and the third if needed) contains the parameter of the instruction. As we can see from Table 3.2, the accumulator AC accumulates the number obtained in executing the instructions "load", "add" and "subtract". The instruction "store" causes that the number in the AC is putted into a classical register. The AC is also used in the "branch" instruction. As in a QRAM, the "measure" instruction provides a bridge between classical and quantum computing. But in the QRASP, the measurement outcome is sent to the AC rather than stored in a classical register. Whenever the operation code is beyond the range from 1 to 11, the execution terminates.

With the above intuitive description in mind, it is straightforward to formally define the computations of the QRASP in terms of a probabilistic transition system between configurations. We can further define a probabilistic input–output relation $P : \Sigma^* \times \Sigma^* \to [0, 1]$ of the QRASP for a given alphabet Σ in a way similar to the case of QRAMs.

It is well-known that TMs, RAMs, and RASPs can efficiently simulate each other. Similar results were proved in [404] for QTMs, QRAMs, and QRASPs.

The reader should be noticed that in the simple model of QRASPs described in this section, a program is stored in classical registers but not in quantum registers. Thus, it is considered as classical data rather than quantum data.

Problem 3.2. How to define a QRASP that models a fully quantum computer where a program is encoded as quantum data?

This problem is highly related to the quantum programming paradigm – superposition of quantum programs – to be discussed carefully in Part V of this book.

3.4 Bibliographic remarks and further readings

The exposition of *quantum circuits* in Section 3.1 is mainly based on [47] and Chapter 4 of book [318]. Quantum multiplexor in Section 3.6 was introduced by Shende, Bullock, and Markov [374]. The algebraic notations for quantum gates and circuits used in Section 3.1 as well as the notion of quantum circuit with measurements in Exercise 3.7 come from [425].

Section 3.1 is merely an introduction to the basics of quantum circuits. Quantum circuits have been developed into a large area since [47]. In particular, in recent years, research on quantum circuits, including synthesis (decomposition of large unitary matrices) and optimisation of quantum circuits, became very active with applications to compilation of quantum programming languages; see Section 13.2 for further discussion. It is worth mentioning that synthesis and optimisation of quantum circuits are much harder than the corresponding problems for classical circuits. Also, Section 3.1 only considers combinational quantum circuits. The model of *sequential circuits* was recently generalised to the quantum setting by Wang et al. [403].

The formal model of *quantum Turing machines (QTMs)* was first formulated by Deutsch [128]. The presentation of Section 3.2 largely follows [59], which is an excellent and detailed introduction to QTMs. For some interesting discussion about the subtle problem of halting schemes of QTMs, see [315,328]. Finite automata and pushdown automata are computational models related to but strictly weaker than Turing machines. They have play a vital role in analysis and verification of classical programs. *Quantum finite automata* were defined in [255,313] and have been systematically studied in a series of papers. But it is much trickier to define an appropriate quantum generalisation of *pushdown automata* [180,317].

The notion of *quantum random access machine* (QRAM) was first introduced in [254]. Several quantum computer architectures have been proposed based on the QRAM model with some practical quantum instruction sets, including IBM OpenQSAM [220], Rigetti's guil [355], and Delft's eQASM [165]. The formal models of QRAMs and quantum random access stored-program machines (QRASPs) presented in Section 3.3 were defined by Wang et al. in [404], where the reader can find detailed discussions about QRAMs and QRASPs as well as their relationship with QTMs.

Chapter 4

Quantum algorithms and communication protocols

Since early 1990's, various quantum algorithms that can offer speed-up over their classical counterparts have been discovered. The three quantum computational models introduced in the last chapters, namely quantum circuits, quantum Turing machines, and quantum random access machines, provide us with necessary mathematical tools for describing quantum algorithms and programs. Partially due to the historical reason and partially due to lack of convenient quantum programming languages at that time, all of them were described in the model of quantum circuits.

In this chapter, we present several interesting quantum algorithms and communication protocols. Our aim is to provide examples of the quantum program constructs introduced in the subsequent chapters but not to provide a thorough discussion of quantum algorithms. If the reader likes to enter the core of this book as quick as possible, she/he can skip this chapter for the first reading, and directly move to Chapter 5. Of course, she/he will need to come back to this point if she/he wishes to understand the examples in the subsequent chapters where the quantum algorithms presented in this chapter are programmed.

4.1 Quantum parallelism and interference

Let us start from two basic techniques for designing quantum algorithms – *quantum parallelism* and *interference*. They are two key ingredients that enable a quantum computer to outperform its classical counterpart.

Quantum parallelism: Quantum parallelism can be clearly illustrated through a simple example. Consider an n-ary Boolean function:

$$f : \{0, 1\}^n \rightarrow \{0, 1\}.$$

The task is to evaluate $f(x)$ for different values $x \in \{0, 1\}^n$ simultaneously. Classical parallelism for this task can be roughly imagined as follows: *multiple* circuits each for computing the same function f are built, and they are executed simultaneously for different inputs x. In contrast, we only need to build a *single* quantum circuit that implements the unitary transformation:

$$U_f : |x, y\rangle \rightarrow |x, y \oplus f(x)\rangle \tag{4.1}$$

for any $x \in \{0, 1\}^n$ and $y \in \{0, 1\}$. Obviously, unitary operator U_f is generated from the Boolean function f. This circuit consists of $n + 1$ qubits, the first n qubits form the "data" register, and the last is the "target" register. It can be proved that given a classical circuit for computing f we can construct a quantum circuit with comparable complexity that implements U_f.

Exercise 4.1. Show that U_f is a multiplexor (see Definition 3.6):

$$U_f = \bigoplus_x U_{f,x},$$

where the first n qubits are used as the select qubits, and for each $x \in \{0, 1\}^n$, $U_{f,x}$ is a unitary operator on the last qubit defined by

$$U_{f,x}|y\rangle = |y \oplus f(x)\rangle$$

for $y \in \{0, 1\}$; that is, $U_{f,x}$ is I (the identity operator) if $f(x) = 0$ and it is X (the NOT gate) if $f(x) = 1$.

The following procedure shows how can quantum parallelism accomplish the task of evaluating $f(x)$ simultaneously for all inputs $x \in \{0, 1\}^n$:

Foundations of Quantum Programming. https://doi.org/10.1016/B978-0-44-315942-8.00013-7

- An equal superposition of 2^n basis states of the data register is produced very efficiently by only n Hadamard gates:

$$|0\rangle^{\otimes n} \xrightarrow{H^{\otimes n}} |\psi\rangle \triangleq \frac{1}{\sqrt{2^n}} \sum_{x \in \{0,1\}^n} |x\rangle,$$

where $|0\rangle^{\otimes n} = |0\rangle \otimes \ldots \otimes |0\rangle$ (the tensor product of n $|0\rangle$'s), and $H^{\otimes n} = H \otimes \ldots \otimes H$ (the tensor product of n H's).

- Applying unitary transformation U_f to the data register in state $|\psi\rangle$ and the target register in state $|0\rangle$ yields:

$$|\psi\rangle|0\rangle = \frac{1}{\sqrt{2^n}} \sum_{x \in \{0,1\}^n} |x, 0\rangle \xrightarrow{U_f} \frac{1}{\sqrt{2^n}} \sum_{x \in \{0,1\}^n} |x, f(x)\rangle. \tag{4.2}$$

It should be noticed that the unitary transformation U_f was executed *only once* in the above equation, but the different terms in the right-hand side of the equation contain information about $f(x)$ for all $x \in \{0, 1\}^n$. In a sense, $f(x)$ was evaluated for 2^n different values of x *simultaneously*.

However, quantum parallelism is not enough for a quantum computer to outperform its classical counterpart. Indeed, to extract information from the state in the right-hand side of Eq. (4.2), a measurement must be performed on it; for example, if we perform the measurement in the computational basis $\{|x\rangle : x \in \{0, 1\}^n\}$ on the data register, then it would give $f(x)$ at the target register only for a single value of x (with probability $1/2^n$), and we cannot obtain $f(x)$ for all $x \in \{0, 1\}^n$ at the same time. Thus, a quantum computer has no advantage over a classical computer at all if such a naive way of extracting information is used.

Quantum interference: In order to be really useful, quantum parallelism has to be combined with another feature of quantum systems – quantum interference. For example, let us consider a superposition

$$\sum_x \alpha_x |x, f(x)\rangle$$

of which the right-hand side of Eq. (4.2) is a special case. As said before, if we directly measure the data register in the computational basis, we can only get *local* information about $f(x)$ for a single value of x. But if we first perform a unitary operator U on the data register, then the original superposition is transformed to

$$U\left(\sum_x \alpha_x |x, f(x)\rangle\right) = \sum_x \alpha_x \left(\sum_{x'} U_{x'x} |x', f(x)\rangle\right)$$

$$= \sum_{x'} \left[|x'\rangle \otimes \left(\sum_x \alpha_x U_{x'x} |f(x)\rangle\right)\right],$$

where $U_{x'x} = \langle x'|U|x\rangle$, and now the measurement in the computational basis will give certain *global* information about $f(x)$ for all $x \in \{0, 1\}^n$. This global information resides in

$$\sum_x \alpha_x U_{x'x} |f(x)\rangle$$

for some single value x'. In a sense, the unitary transformation U was able to merge information about $f(x)$ for different values of x. It is worth to note that the measurement in a basis after a unitary transformation is essentially the measurement in a different basis. So, an appropriate choice of a basis in which a measurement is performed is crucial in order to extract the desired global information.

4.2 Quantum algorithms based on Hadamard transforms

It is still not convincing from the general discussion in the previous section that quantum parallelism and interference can actually help us to solve some interesting computational problems. However, the power of combining quantum parallelism and interference can be clearly seen in the algorithms presented in this section.

Quantum algorithms are often classified according the main techniques employed in them. A major class of quantum algorithms are designed based on quantum Fourier transforms, which are quantum analogue of the discrete Fourier transforms. Hadamard transforms can be seen as a simple example of quantum Fourier transforms. In this section, we study several quantum algorithms using quantum Hadamard transforms.

4.2.1 Deutsch–Jozsa algorithm

The Deutsch–Jozsa algorithm [129] is a quantum algorithm that solves the following:

- **Deutsch problem:** Given a Boolean function $f : \{0, 1\}^n \to \{0, 1\}$, known to be either constant, or balanced – $f(x)$ equals 0 for exactly half of all the possible x, and 1 for the other half. Determine whether it is constant or balanced.

The Deutsch–Jozsa algorithm is described in Fig. 6.1. It should be emphasised that in this algorithm, the unitary operator U_f determined by function f according to Eq. (4.1) is supplied as an oracle.

To understand this quantum algorithm, we need to carefully look at several key ideas in its design:

- In step 2, the target register (the last qubit) is cleverly initialised in state $|-\rangle = H|1\rangle$ rather than in state $|0\rangle$ as in Eq. (4.2). This special initialisation is often referred to as the *phase kickback trick* since

$$U_f|x, -\rangle = |x\rangle \otimes (-1)^{f(x)}|-\rangle = (-1)^{f(x)}|x, -\rangle.$$

Here, only the phase of the target register is changed from 1 to $(-1)^{f(x)}$, which can be moved to the front of the data register.
- Quantum parallelism happens in step 3 when applying the oracle U_f.
- Quantum interference is used in step 4: n Hadamard gates acting on the data register (the first n qubits) yield

$$\begin{aligned}
H^{\otimes n} & \left(\frac{1}{\sqrt{2^n}} \sum_x |x\rangle \otimes (-1)^{f(x)}|-\rangle \right) \\
&= \frac{1}{\sqrt{2^n}} \sum_x \left(H^{\otimes n}|x\rangle \otimes (-1)^{f(x)}|-\rangle \right) \\
&= \frac{1}{2^n} \sum_x \left(\sum_z (-1)^{x \cdot z}|z\rangle \otimes (-1)^{f(x)}|-\rangle \right) \\
&= \frac{1}{2^n} \sum_z \left[\left(\sum_x (-1)^{x \cdot z + f(x)} \right) |z\rangle \otimes |-\rangle \right].
\end{aligned} \tag{4.3}$$

- In step 5, we measure the data register in the computational basis $\{|z\rangle : z \in \{0, 1\}^n\}$. The probability that we get outcome $z = 0$ (i.e. $|z\rangle = |0\rangle^{\otimes n}$) is

$$\frac{1}{2^n} \left| \sum_x (-1)^{f(x)} \right|^2 = \begin{cases} 1 & \text{if } f \text{ is constant}, \\ 0 & \text{if } f \text{ is balanced}. \end{cases}$$

It is interesting to note that the positive and negative contributions to the amplitude for $|0\rangle^{\otimes n}$ cancel when f is balanced.

Exercise 4.2. Prove the equality used in Eq. (4.3):

$$H^{\otimes n}|x\rangle = \frac{1}{\sqrt{2^n}} \sum_{z \in \{0,1\}^n} (-1)^{x \cdot z}|z\rangle$$

for any $x \in \{0, 1\}^n$, where

$$x \cdot z = \sum_{i=1}^n x_i z_i$$

if $x = x_1, ..., x_n$ and $z = z_1, ..., z_n$.

Finally, let us briefly compare the query complexities of the Deutsch problem in classical computing and the Deutsch–Jozsa algorithm. A deterministic classical algorithm should repeatedly select a value $x \in \{0, 1\}^n$ and calculate $f(x)$ until it can determine with certainty whether f is constant or balanced. So, a classical algorithm requires $2^{n-1} + 1$ evaluations of f. In contrast, U_f is executed only once in step 3 of the Deutsch–Jozsa algorithm.

- **Inputs:** A quantum oracle that implements the unitary operator U_f defined by Eq. (4.1).
- **Outputs:** 0 if and only if f is constant.
- **Runtime:** One application of U_f. Always succeeds.
- **Procedure:**

1. $|0\rangle^{\otimes n}|1\rangle$

2. $\xrightarrow{H^{\otimes(n+1)}} \dfrac{1}{\sqrt{2^n}} \sum_{x\in\{0,1\}^n} |x\rangle|-\rangle$

3. $\xrightarrow{U_f} \dfrac{1}{\sqrt{2^n}} \sum_x (-1)^{f(x)}|x\rangle|-\rangle$

4. $\xrightarrow{H^{\otimes n} \text{ on the first } n \text{ qubits}} \sum_z \dfrac{\sum_x (-1)^{x\cdot z+f(x)}}{2^n} |z\rangle|-\rangle$

5. $\xrightarrow{\text{measure on the first } n \text{ qubits in the computational basis}} z$

FIGURE 4.1 Deutsch–Jozsa algorithm.

4.2.2 Bernstein–Vazirani algorithm

The techniques described in the above subsection can also be used to solve the following:

- **Problem**: Given an oracle that implements a Boolean function $f : \{0, 1\}^n \to \{0, 1\}$ known to be the form of dot product:

$$f(x) = x \cdot s = \sum_{i=1}^n x_i \cdot s_i \tag{4.4}$$

for all $x = x_1, ..., x_n \in \{0, 1\}^n$, where $s \in \{0, 1\}^n$ is a secret string. Find the secret string $s =?$

It is easy to see that a classical solution to this problem needs at least n queries of the function f. But quantum computing only needs one query of U_f. Indeed, a quantum algorithm solving this problem is almost the same as Deutsch–Jozsa algorithm (see Fig. 4.1). The only difference occurs in step 5. Since for the function f considered here, it is known that $f(x) = x \cdot s$, we have $x \cdot z + f(x) = x \cdot (z \oplus s) \mod 2$ and

$$\frac{1}{2^n}\left|\sum_x (-1)^{x\cdot z+f(x)}\right|^2 = \begin{cases} 1 & \text{if } z \oplus s = 0, \\ 0 & \text{otherwise.} \end{cases}$$

Therefore, measuring the first n qubits, we obtain a string z_0 with $z_0 \oplus s = 0$ and $s = z_0$ is found.

4.2.3 Simon algorithm

Another quantum algorithm using a similar idea is the Simon algorithm solving the following:

- **Problem**: Given a Boolean function $f : \{0, 1\}^n \to \{0, 1\}^n$ known to satisfy the periodicity:

$$f(x_1) = f(x_2) \text{ iff } x_2 = x_1 \text{ or } x_2 = x_1 \oplus s$$

for some secret nonzero string $s \in \{0, 1\}^n$. Find the secret string $s =?$

The Simon algorithm is described in Fig. 4.2. It is almost the same as the Deutsch–Jozsa algorithm except that here the initial state is $|0\rangle^{\otimes n}|0\rangle^{\otimes n}$ rather than $|0\rangle^{\otimes n}|1\rangle$. We note that, in step 5 of Simon algorithm, for each $z \in \{0, 1\}^n$, we obtain z with probability

$$p_z = \left\|\frac{1}{2^n}\sum_x (-1)^{x\cdot z}|f(x)\rangle\right\|^2.$$

The periodicity (4.4) for nonzero string s implies that there exists a subset A of $\{0, 1\}^n$ such that $|A| = 2^{n-1}$ and $\{0, 1\}^n = A \cup (A \oplus s)$, where $A \oplus s = \{x \oplus s | x \in A\}$. Therefore,

- **Procedure:**

1. $|0\rangle^{\otimes n}|0\rangle^{\otimes n}$

2. $\xrightarrow{H^{\otimes n} \text{ on the first } n \text{ qubits}} \dfrac{1}{\sqrt{2^n}} \displaystyle\sum_{x\in\{0,1\}^n} |x\rangle|0\rangle^{\otimes n}$

3. $\xrightarrow{U_f} \dfrac{1}{\sqrt{2^n}} \displaystyle\sum_{x} (-1)^{f(x)}|x\rangle|f(x)\rangle$

4. $\xrightarrow{H^{\otimes n} \text{ on the first } n \text{ qubits}} \displaystyle\sum_{z} |z\rangle \left(\dfrac{1}{2^n} \sum_{x}(-1)^{x\cdot z}|f(x)\rangle \right)$

5. $\xrightarrow{\text{measure on the first } n \text{ qubits in the computational basis}} z$

FIGURE 4.2 Simon algorithm.

$$
\begin{aligned}
p_z &= \left\| \frac{1}{2^n} \sum_{x\in A}\left[(-1)^{x\cdot z} + (-1)^{(x\oplus s)\cdot z} \right] |f(x)\rangle \right\|^2 \\
&= \sum_{x\in A} \left| \frac{1}{2^n}\left[(-1)^{x\cdot z} + (-1)^{(x\oplus s)\cdot z} \right] \right|^2 \\
&= \begin{cases} \frac{1}{2^{n-1}} & \text{if } z\cdot s = 0 \ \bmod 2, \\ 0 & \text{if } z\cdot s = 1 \ \bmod 2. \end{cases}
\end{aligned}
$$

Claim: *We obtain every string in $\{z\in\{0,1\}^n | z\cdot s = 0\}$ uniformly with probability $\frac{1}{2^{n-1}}$.*

Finally, the problem of finding the secret string s can be solved by the following classical postprocessing. We can run the Simon algorithm $n-1$ times to obtain $z^{(1)}, ..., z^{(n-1)} \in \{0,1\}^n$ satisfying

$$
\begin{cases}
z^{(1)} \cdot s &= 0 \ \bmod 2, \\
& \cdots\cdots \\
z^{(n-1)} \cdot s &= 0 \ \bmod 2.
\end{cases}
\tag{4.5}
$$

Exercise 4.3. Show that the probability that $z^{(1)}, ..., z^{(n-1)}$ are linearly independent in $\mathbb{Z}_2^n$ is

$$
\prod_{k=1}^{n-1}\left(1 - \frac{1}{2^k}\right) > \prod_{k=1}^{\infty}\left(1 - \frac{1}{2^k}\right) = 0.288788... > \frac{1}{4}.
$$

Note that s in Eq. (4.5) can be uniquely solved by Gaussian elimination if $z^{(1)}, ..., z^{(n-1)}$ are linearly independent. Therefore, s can be determined with a constant probability of error by running Simon's algorithm $O(n)$ times and thus $O(n)$ queries of U_f. However, any deterministic classical algorithm for the same purpose has to run in exponential time.

4.3 Quantum Fourier transform

The Deutsch–Jozsa algorithm and others presented in the last section properly illustrate several key ideas for designing quantum algorithms, but the problems solved by them are somehow artificial. From this section on, we will introduce a series of quantum algorithms of practical importance.

The quantum algorithms studied in the last section are based on a special form of quantum Fourier transform, namely Hadamard transform. In this section, we define the general form of quantum Fourier transform and then use it to solve the problem of phase estimation.

Recall that the discrete Fourier transform takes as input a vector of complex numbers $x_0, ..., x_{N-1}$, and it outputs a vector of complex numbers $y_0, ..., y_{N-1}$:

$$
y_k = \frac{1}{\sqrt{N}} \sum_{j=0}^{N-1} e^{2\pi i jk/N} x_j
\tag{4.6}
$$

for each $0 \le j < N$. The quantum Fourier transform is a quantum counterpart of the discrete Fourier transform.

Definition 4.1. The quantum Fourier transform on an orthonormal basis $|0\rangle, ..., |N-1\rangle$ is defined by

$$FT : |j\rangle \rightarrow \frac{1}{\sqrt{N}} \sum_{k=0}^{N-1} e^{2\pi i jk/N} |k\rangle.$$

More generally, the quantum Fourier transform on a general state in the N-dimensional Hilbert space is given as follows:

$$FT : \sum_{j=0}^{N-1} x_j |j\rangle \rightarrow \sum_{k=0}^{N-1} y_k |k\rangle,$$

where the amplitudes $y_0, ..., y_{N-1}$ are obtained by the discrete Fourier (4.6) transform on amplitudes $x_0, ..., x_{N-1}$. The matrix representation of the quantum Fourier transform is given as:

$$FT = \frac{1}{\sqrt{N}} \begin{pmatrix} 1 & 1 & 1 & ... & 1 \\ 1 & \omega & \omega^2 & ... & \omega^{N-1} \\ 1 & \omega^2 & \omega^4 & ... & \omega^{2(N-1)} \\ & ... & ... & ... & \\ 1 & \omega^{N-1} & \omega^{(N-1)2} & ... & \omega^{(N-1)(N-1)} \end{pmatrix} \tag{4.7}$$

where $\omega = \exp(2\pi i/N)$.

Proposition 4.1. *The quantum Fourier transform FT is unitary.*

Exercise 4.4. Prove Proposition 4.1.

The circuit of quantum Fourier transform: An implementation of the quantum Fourier transform FT by one-qubit and two-qubit gates is presented in the following proposition and its proof.

Proposition 4.2. *Let $N = 2^n$. Then the quantum Fourier transform can be implemented by a quantum circuit consisting of n Hadamard gates and*

$$\frac{n(n-1)}{2} + 3\left\lfloor \frac{n}{2} \right\rfloor$$

controlled gates.

Proof. We prove this proposition by explicitly constructing a quantum circuit that fulfils the stated conditions. We use the binary representation:

- $j_1 j_2 ... j_n$ denotes

$$j = j_1 2^{n-1} + j_2 2^{n-2} + ... + j_n 2^0;$$

- $0.j_k j_{k+1} ... j_n$ denotes

$$j_k/2 + j_{k+1}/2^2 + ... + j_n/2^{n-k+1}$$

for any $k \ge 1$.

Then the proposition can be proved in three steps:

1. Using the notation introduced in Section 3.1, we design the circuit:

$$\begin{aligned} D \equiv \ & H[q_1]C(R_2)[q_2, q_1]...C(R_n)[q_n, q_1]H[q_2]C(R_2)[q_3, q_2] \\ & ...C(R_{n-1})[q_n, q_2]...H[q_{n-1}]C(R_2)[q_n, q_{n-1}]H[q_n] \end{aligned} \tag{4.8}$$

where R_k is the phase shift (see Example 3.1):

$$R_k = P\left(2\pi/2^k\right) = \begin{pmatrix} 1 & 0 \\ 0 & e^{2\pi i/2^k} \end{pmatrix}$$

for $k = 2, \ldots, n$. If we input $|j\rangle = |j_1 \ldots j_n\rangle$ into the circuit (4.8), then the output is:

$$\frac{1}{\sqrt{2^n}}(|0\rangle + e^{2\pi i 0.j_1 \ldots j_n}|1\rangle)\ldots(|0\rangle + e^{2\pi i 0.j_n}|1\rangle) \tag{4.9}$$

by a routine calculation.

2. We observe that whenever $N = 2^n$, the quantum Fourier transform can be rewritten as follows:

$$
\begin{aligned}
|j\rangle &\to \frac{1}{\sqrt{2^n}}\sum_{k=0}^{2^n-1} e^{2\pi i jk/2^n}|k\rangle \\
&= \frac{1}{\sqrt{2^n}}\sum_{k_1=0}^{1}\ldots\sum_{k_n=0}^{1} e^{2\pi i j(k_1 \cdot 2^{n-1} + \ldots + k_n \cdot 2^0)/2^n}|k_1 \ldots k_n\rangle \\
&= \frac{1}{\sqrt{2^n}}\left(\sum_{k_1=0}^{1} e^{2\pi i jk_1/2^1}|k_1\rangle\right)\ldots\left(\sum_{k_n=0}^{1} e^{2\pi i jk_n/2^n}|k_n\rangle\right) \\
&= \frac{1}{\sqrt{2^n}}\left(|0\rangle + e^{2\pi i 0.j_n}|1\rangle\right)\ldots\left(|0\rangle + e^{2\pi i 0.j_1 \ldots j_n}|1\rangle\right).
\end{aligned}
\tag{4.10}
$$

3. Finally, by comparing Eqs (4.10) and (4.9), we see that adding $\lfloor \frac{n}{2}\rfloor$ swap gates at the end of the circuit (4.8) will reverse the order of the qubits, and thus yield the quantum Fourier transform. It is known that each swap gate can be accomplished by using 3 CNOT gates (see Exercise 3.3). □

4.3.1 Phase estimation

Now we show how can the quantum Fourier transform defined above be used in an algorithm for phase estimation. This quantum algorithm solves the following problem:

- **Phase estimation**: A unitary operator U has an eigenvector $|u\rangle$ with eigenvalue $e^{2\pi i \varphi}$, where the value of φ is unknown. The goal is to estimate the phase φ.

The phase estimation algorithm is described in Fig. 4.3. It uses two registers:

- The first consists of t qubits $q_1, \ldots, q_t$, all of which are initialised in state $|0\rangle$;
- The second is the system p where U applies to, initialised in state $|u\rangle$.

Using the notation introduced in Section 3.1, the circuit for this algorithm can be written as follows:

$$D \equiv E \cdot FT^\dagger[q_1, \ldots, q_t] \tag{4.11}$$

where:

$$
\begin{aligned}
E \equiv{}& H[q_1]\ldots H[q_{t-2}]H[q_{t-1}]H[q_t]C\left(U^{2^0}\right)[q_t, p] \\
& C\left(U^{2^1}\right)[q_{t-1}, p]C\left(U^{2^2}\right)[q_{t-2}, p]\ldots C\left(U^{2^{t-1}}\right)[q_1, p],
\end{aligned}
\tag{4.12}
$$

$C(\cdot)$ is the controlled gate (see Definition 3.5), and $FT^\dagger$ is the inverse quantum Fourier transform FT and can be obtained by reversing the circuit of FT given in the proof of Proposition 4.2.

Obviously, circuit (4.11) consists of $O(t^2)$ Hadamard and controlled gates together with one call to oracle U^{2^j} for $j = 0, 1, \ldots, t-1$. We further observe that

$$
\begin{aligned}
E|0\rangle_{q_1}\ldots|0\rangle_{q_{t-2}}|0\rangle_{q_{t-1}}|0\rangle_{q_t}|u\rangle_p &= \frac{1}{\sqrt{2^t}}\left(|0\rangle + e^{2\pi i \varphi \cdot 2^{t-1}}|1\rangle\right) \\
&\ldots\left(|0\rangle + e^{2\pi i \varphi \cdot 2^2}|1\rangle\right)\left(|0\rangle + e^{2\pi i \varphi \cdot 2^1}|1\rangle\right)\left(|0\rangle + e^{2\pi i \varphi \cdot 2^0}|1\rangle\right)|u\rangle \\
&= \frac{1}{\sqrt{2^t}}\left(\sum_{k=0}^{2^t-1} e^{2\pi i \varphi k}|k\rangle\right)|u\rangle.
\end{aligned}
\tag{4.13}
$$

- **Inputs:**

  1. An oracle which performs controlled-U^{2^j} operators for $j = 0, 1, ..., t-1$;
  2. t qubits initialised to $|0\rangle$;
  3. An eigenvector $|u\rangle$ of U with eigenvalue $e^{2\pi i \varphi}$,

  where

  $$t = n + \left\lceil \log(2 + \frac{1}{2\epsilon}) \right\rceil.$$

- **Outputs:** An n-bit approximation $\widetilde{\varphi} = m$ to φ.
- **Runtime:** $O(t^2)$ operations and one call to each oracle. Success with probability at least $1 - \epsilon$.
- **Procedure:**

  1. $|0\rangle^{\otimes t} |u\rangle \xrightarrow{H^{\otimes t} \text{ on the first } t \text{ qubits}} \frac{1}{\sqrt{2^t}} \sum_{j=0}^{2^t-1} |j\rangle |u\rangle$

  2. $\xrightarrow{\text{oracles}} \frac{1}{\sqrt{2^t}} \sum_{j=0}^{2^t-1} |j\rangle U^j |u\rangle = \frac{1}{\sqrt{2^t}} \sum_{j=0}^{2^t-1} e^{2\pi i j \varphi} |j\rangle |u\rangle$

  3. $\xrightarrow{FT^\dagger} \frac{1}{\sqrt{2^t}} \sum_{j=0}^{2^t-1} e^{2\pi i j \varphi} \left(\frac{1}{\sqrt{2^t}} \sum_{k=0}^{2^t-1} e^{-2\pi i j k / 2^t} |k\rangle \right) |u\rangle$

     $= \sum_{k=0}^{2^t-1} \alpha_k |k\rangle |u\rangle$

  4. $\xrightarrow{\text{measure the first } t \text{ qubits}} |m\rangle |u\rangle,$

where

$$\alpha_k = \frac{1}{2^t} \sum_{j=0}^{2^t-1} e^{2\pi i j (\varphi - k/2^t)} = \frac{1}{2^t} \left[\frac{1 - e^{2\pi i (2^t \varphi - k)}}{1 - e^{2\pi i (\varphi - k/2^t)}} \right].$$

FIGURE 4.3 Phase estimation.

A special case: To understand why the algorithm works, let us first consider a special case where φ can be exactly expressed in t bits:

$$\varphi = 0.\varphi_1 \varphi_2 \varphi_3 ... \varphi_t.$$

Then Eq. (4.13) can be rewritten as:

$$E|0\rangle...|0\rangle|0\rangle|0\rangle|u\rangle = \frac{1}{\sqrt{2^t}} \left(|0\rangle + e^{2\pi i 0.\varphi_t} |1\rangle \right) ... \left(|0\rangle + e^{2\pi i 0.\varphi_3...\varphi_t} |1\rangle \right)$$
$$\left(|0\rangle + e^{2\pi i 0.\varphi_2\varphi_3...\varphi_t} |1\rangle \right) \left(|0\rangle + e^{2\pi i \varphi_1\varphi_2\varphi_3...\varphi_t} |1\rangle \right) |u\rangle.$$

(4.14)

Furthermore, by Eqs (4.11) and (4.10) we obtain:

$$C|0\rangle...|0\rangle|0\rangle|0\rangle|u\rangle = FT^\dagger (E|0\rangle...|0\rangle|0\rangle|0\rangle) |u\rangle$$
$$= |\varphi_1\varphi_2\varphi_3...\varphi_t\rangle|u\rangle.$$

Performance analysis: The above discussion about a special case should give the reader a hint why the algorithm is correct. Now we are ready to consider the general case. Let $0 \leq b < 2^t$ be such that $b/2^t = 0.b_1...b_t$ is the best t bit approximation to φ which is less than φ; i.e.

$$b/2^t \leq \varphi < b/2^t + 1/2^t.$$

We write $\delta = \varphi - b/2^t$ for the difference. It is clear that $0 \leq \delta < 1/2^t$. Note that

$$|\alpha_k| \leq \frac{1}{2^{t-1} \left| 1 - e^{2\pi i (\varphi - k)/2^t} \right|}$$

because $\left|1 - e^{i\theta}\right| \le 2$ for all θ. Put $\beta_l = \alpha_{(b+l \mod 2^t)}$ for any $-2^{t-1} < l \le 2^{t-1}$. Then

$$|\beta_l| \le \frac{1}{2^{t-1}\left|1 - e^{2\pi i(\delta - l/2^t)}\right|} \le \frac{1}{2\left|l - 2^t\delta\right|}$$

because

1. $\left|1 - e^{i\theta}\right| \ge \frac{2|\theta|}{\pi}$ if $-\pi \le \theta \le \pi$; and
2. $-\frac{1}{2} \le \delta - l/2^t \le \frac{1}{2}$.

Suppose the outcome of the final measurement is m. Then for a positive integer d, we have:

$$\begin{aligned}
P(|m - b| > d) &= \sum_{m:|m-b|>d} |\alpha_m|^2 \\
&= \sum_{-2^{t-1} < l \le -(d+1)} |\beta_l|^2 + \sum_{d+1 \le l \le 2^{t-1}} |\beta_l|^2 \\
&\le \frac{1}{4}\left[\sum_{l=-2^{t-1}+1}^{-(d+1)} \frac{1}{(l - 2^t\delta)^2} + \sum_{l=d+1}^{2^{t-1}} \frac{1}{(l - 2^t\delta)^2} \right] \\
&\le \frac{1}{4}\left[\sum_{l=-2^{t-1}+1}^{-(d+1)} \frac{1}{l^2} + \sum_{l=d+1}^{2^{t-1}} \frac{1}{(l-1)^2} \right] \quad \text{(note that } 0 \le 2^t\delta < 1\text{)} \\
&\le \frac{1}{2}\sum_{l=d}^{2^{t-1}} \frac{1}{l^2} \\
&\le \frac{1}{2}\int_{d-1}^{2^{t-1}} \frac{dl}{l^2} \le \frac{1}{2(d-1)}.
\end{aligned}$$

If we wish to approximate φ to a 2^{-n} accuracy and the success probability is at least $1 - \epsilon$, then we only need to choose $d = 2^{t-n} - 1$ and require $\frac{1}{2(d-1)} \le \epsilon$. This leads to

$$t \ge T \triangleq n + \left\lceil \log(\frac{1}{2\epsilon} + 2) \right\rceil$$

and we can make use of $t = T$ qubits in the phase estimation algorithm.

Combining the above derivation with Eq. (4.11) and Proposition 4.2 gives us the conclusion: the algorithm presented in Fig. 4.3 can compute the n-bit approximation of phase φ with at least success probability $1 - \epsilon$ within $O(t^2)$ step, using

$$n + \left\lceil \log(\frac{1}{2\epsilon} + 2) \right\rceil$$

qubits.

The phase estimation algorithm is a key procedure in a class of important quantum algorithms, including the famous Shor algorithm for factoring [377] and the Harrow–Hassidim–Lloyd algorithm for systems of linear equations [199]. A detailed presentation of these two algorithms is out of the scope of this book.

4.4 Grover search algorithm

In this section, we introduce another quantum algorithm that is very useful for a wide range of practical applications, namely the Grover algorithm that solves the following:

- **Search problem**: The task is to search through a database consisting of N elements, indexed by numbers $0, 1, ..., N - 1$. For convenience, we assume that $N = 2^n$ so that the index can be stored in n bits. We also assume that the problem has exactly M solutions with $1 \le M \le N/2$.

- **Procedure**:

  1. Apply the oracle O;

  2. Apply the Hadamard transform $H^{\otimes n}$;

  3. Perform a conditional phase shift :
     $$|0\rangle \to |0\rangle,$$
     $$|x\rangle \to -|x\rangle \text{ for all } x \neq 0;$$

  4. Apply the Hadamard transform $H^{\otimes n}$.

FIGURE 4.4 Grover rotation.

As in the Deutsch–Jozsa algorithm, we are supplied with a quantum oracle – a black box with the ability to recognise solution of the search problem. Formally, let function $f : \{0, 1, ..., N - 1\} \to \{0, 1\}$ be defined as follows:

$$f(x) = \begin{cases} 1 & \text{if } x \text{ is a solution,} \\ 0 & \text{otherwise.} \end{cases}$$

We write

$$\mathcal{H}_N = \mathcal{H}_2^{\otimes n} = span\{|0\rangle, |1\rangle, ..., |N - 1\rangle\}$$

with $\mathcal{H}_2$ being the state Hilbert space of a qubit. Then the oracle can be thought of as the unitary operator $O = U_f$ in $\mathcal{H}_N \otimes \mathcal{H}_2$ defined by

$$O|x, q\rangle = U_f|x, q\rangle = |x\rangle|q \oplus f(x)\rangle \tag{4.15}$$

for $x \in \{0, 1, ..., N - 1\}$ and $q \in \{0, 1\}$, where $|x\rangle$ is the index register, and $|q\rangle$ is the oracle qubit which is flipped if x is a solution, and is unchanged otherwise. In particular, the oracle has the phase kickback property:

$$|x, -\rangle \xrightarrow{O} (-1)^{f(x)}|x, -\rangle.$$

Thus, if the oracle qubit is initially in state $|-\rangle$, then it remains $|-\rangle$ throughout the search algorithm and can be omitted. So, we can simply write:

$$|x\rangle \xrightarrow{O} (-1)^{f(x)}|x\rangle. \tag{4.16}$$

Grover rotation: One key subroutine of the Grover algorithm is called the Grover rotation. It consists of four steps, as described in Fig. 4.4.

Let us see what the Grover rotation actually does. We write G for the unitary transformation defined by the procedure in Fig. 4.4; i.e. the composition of the operators in steps 1–4. It should be pointed out that the oracle O used in step 1 is thought of as a unitary operator on the space $\mathcal{H}_N$ (rather than $\mathcal{H}_N \otimes \mathcal{H}_2$) defined by Eq. (4.16). The conditional phase shift in step 3 is defined in the basis $\{|0\rangle, |1\rangle, ..., |N - 1\rangle\}$ of the space $\mathcal{H}_N$. The following lemma presents the unitary operator of the quantum circuit that implements the Grover rotation.

Lemma 4.1. $G = (2|\psi\rangle\langle\psi| - I)O$, where

$$|\psi\rangle = \frac{1}{\sqrt{N}} \sum_{x=0}^{N-1} |x\rangle$$

is the equal superposition in $\mathcal{H}_N$.

Exercise 4.5. Prove Lemma 4.1.

It is not easy to imagine only from the above description that the operator G represents a rotation. A geometric visualisation can help us to understand the Grover rotation better. Let us introduce two vectors in the space $\mathcal{H}_N$:

$$|\alpha\rangle = \frac{1}{\sqrt{N - M}} \sum_{x \text{ not solution}} |x\rangle,$$

- **Inputs:** A quantum oracle O defined by Eq. (4.15)
- **Outputs:** A solution x.
- **Runtime:** $O(\sqrt{N})$ operations. Succeeds with probability $\Theta(1)$.
- **Procedure:**

1. $|0\rangle^{\otimes n}|1\rangle$

2. $\xrightarrow{H^{\otimes(n+1)}} \dfrac{1}{\sqrt{2^n}} \sum_{x=0}^{2^n-1} |x\rangle|-\rangle = \left(\cos\dfrac{\theta}{2}|\alpha\rangle + \sin\dfrac{\theta}{2}|\beta\rangle \right)|-\rangle$

3. $\xrightarrow{G^k \text{ on the first } n \text{ qubits}} \left[\cos\left(\dfrac{2k+1}{2}\theta\right)|\alpha\rangle + \sin\left(\dfrac{2k+1}{2}\theta\right)|\beta\rangle \right]|-\rangle$

4. $\xrightarrow{\text{measure the first } n \text{ qubits in the computational basis}} |x\rangle$

FIGURE 4.5 Grover search algorithm.

$$|\beta\rangle = \frac{1}{\sqrt{M}} \sum_{x \text{ solution}} |x\rangle.$$

It is clear that the vectors $|\alpha\rangle$ and $|\beta\rangle$ are orthogonal. If we define angle θ by

$$\cos\frac{\theta}{2} = \sqrt{\frac{N-M}{N}} \quad \left(0 \le \frac{\theta}{2} \le \frac{\pi}{2}\right),$$

then the equal superposition in Lemma 4.1 can be expressed as follows:

$$|\psi\rangle = \cos\frac{\theta}{2}|\alpha\rangle + \sin\frac{\theta}{2}|\beta\rangle.$$

Furthermore, we have:

Lemma 4.2. $G(\cos\delta|\alpha\rangle + \sin\delta|\beta\rangle) = \cos(\theta+\delta)|\alpha\rangle + \sin(\theta+\delta)|\beta\rangle$.

Intuitively, the Grover operator G is a rotation for angle θ in the two-dimensional space spanned by $|\alpha\rangle$ and $|\beta\rangle$. For any real number δ, the vector $\cos\delta|\alpha\rangle + \sin\delta|\beta\rangle$ can be represented by a point $(\cos\delta, \sin\delta)$. Thus, Lemma 4.2 indicates that the action of G is depicted by the mapping:

$$(\cos\delta, \sin\delta) \xrightarrow{G} (\cos(\theta+\delta), \sin(\theta+\delta)).$$

Exercise 4.6. Prove Lemma 4.2.

Grover algorithm: Using the Grover rotation as a subroutine, the quantum search algorithm can be described as shown in Fig. 4.5.

It should be noted that k in Fig. 4.5 is a constant integer; the value of k will be suitably fixed in the next paragraph.

Performance analysis: It can be shown that the search problem requires approximately N/M operations by a classical computer. Let us see how many iterations of G are needed in step 3 of the Grover algorithm. Note that in step 2 the index register (i.e. the first n qubits) is prepared in the state

$$|\psi\rangle = \sqrt{\frac{N-M}{N}}|\alpha\rangle + \sqrt{\frac{M}{N}}|\beta\rangle.$$

So, rotating through $\arccos\sqrt{\frac{M}{N}}$ radians takes the index register from $|\psi\rangle$ to $|\beta\rangle$. It is asserted by Lemma 4.2 that the Grover operator G is a rotation for angle θ. Let k be the integer closest to the real number

$$\frac{\arccos\sqrt{\frac{M}{N}}}{\theta}.$$

Then we have:

$$k \leq \left\lceil \frac{\arccos \sqrt{\frac{M}{N}}}{\theta} \right\rceil \leq \left\lceil \frac{\pi}{2\theta} \right\rceil$$

because $\arccos \sqrt{\frac{M}{N}} \leq \frac{\pi}{2}$. Consequently, k is a positive integer in the interval $\left[\frac{\pi}{2\theta} - 1, \frac{\pi}{2\theta} \right]$. By the assumption $M \leq \frac{N}{2}$, we have

$$\frac{\theta}{2} \geq \sin \frac{\theta}{2} = \sqrt{\frac{M}{N}}$$

and $k \leq \left\lceil \frac{\pi}{4} \sqrt{\frac{N}{M}} \right\rceil$, i.e. $k = O(\sqrt{N})$. On the other hand, by the definition of k we obtain:

$$\left| k - \frac{\arccos \sqrt{\frac{M}{N}}}{\theta} \right| \leq \frac{1}{2}.$$

It follows that

$$\arccos \sqrt{\frac{M}{N}} \leq \frac{2k+1}{2} \theta \leq \theta + \arccos \sqrt{\frac{M}{N}}.$$

Since $\cos \frac{\theta}{2} = \sqrt{\frac{N-M}{N}}$, we have $\arccos \sqrt{\frac{M}{N}} = \frac{\pi}{2} - \frac{\theta}{2}$ and

$$\frac{\pi}{2} - \frac{\theta}{2} \leq \frac{2k+1}{2} \theta \leq \frac{\pi}{2} + \frac{\theta}{2}.$$

Thus, since $M \leq \frac{N}{2}$, it holds that the success probability

$$\Pr(\text{success}) = \sin^2 \left(\frac{2k+1}{2} \theta \right) \geq \cos^2 \frac{\theta}{2} = \frac{N-M}{N} \geq \frac{1}{2},$$

i.e. $\Pr(\text{success}) = \Theta(1)$. In particular, if $M \ll N$, then the success probability is very high.

The above derivation can be summarised as follows: The Grover algorithm can find a solution x with success probability $O(1)$ within $k = O(\sqrt{N})$ steps.

4.5   Quantum walks

In the previous sections, we saw how the power of quantum parallelism and interference can be exploited to design a series of quantum Fourier transform-based algorithms and the Grover search algorithm. We now turn to consider a class of quantum algorithms for which the design idea looks very different from that used in the previous sections. This class of algorithms were developed based on the notion of quantum walk, which is the quantum counterpart of random walk.

One-dimensional quantum walk: The simplest random walk is the one-dimensional walk where a particle moves on a discrete line whose nodes are denoted by integers $\mathbb{Z} = \{..., -2, -1, 0, 1, 2, ...\}$. At each step, the particle moves one position left or right, depending on the flip of a "coin". A quantum variant of the one-dimensional random walk is the Hadamard walk defined in the following:

Example 4.1. The state Hilbert space of the Hadamard walk is $\mathcal{H}_d \otimes \mathcal{H}_p$, where:

- $\mathcal{H}_d = span\{|L\rangle, |R\rangle\}$ is a 2-dimensional Hilbert space, called the direction space, and $|L\rangle, |R\rangle$ are used to indicate the direction Left and Right, respectively;
- $\mathcal{H}_p = span\{|n\rangle : n \in \mathbb{Z}\}$ is an infinite-dimensional Hilbert space, and $|n\rangle$ indicates the position marked by integer n,

and $span X$ is the Hilbert space spanned by a nonempty set X and defined according to Eq. (2.2). One step of the Hadamard walk is represented by the unitary operator

$$W = T(H \otimes I_{\mathcal{H}_p}),$$

where the translation T is a unitary operator in $\mathcal{H}_d \otimes \mathcal{H}_p$ defined by

$$T|L, n\rangle = |L, n-1\rangle, \quad T|R, n\rangle = |R, n+1\rangle$$

for every $n \in \mathbb{Z}$, H is the Hadamard transformation in the direction space $\mathcal{H}_d$, and $I_{\mathcal{H}_p}$ is the identity operator in the position space $\mathcal{H}_p$. The Hadamard walk is then described by repeated applications of operator W.

Exercise 4.7. We define the left and right translation operators T_L and T_R in the position space $\mathcal{H}_p$ by

$$T_L|n\rangle = |n-1\rangle, \quad T_R|n\rangle = |n+1\rangle$$

for each $n \in \mathbb{Z}$. Then the translation operator T is the quantum conditional $T_L \oplus T_R$ with the direction variable d as the select qubit (see Example 3.7).

Although the Hadamard walk was defined by mimicking the one-dimensional random walk, some of their behaviours are very different:

- The translation operator T can be explained as follows: if the direction system is in state $|L\rangle$, then the walker moves from position n to $n-1$, and if the direction is in $|R\rangle$, then the walker moves from position n to $n+1$. This looks very similar to a random walk, but in a quantum walk, the direction can be in a superposition of $|L\rangle$ and $|R\rangle$, and intuitively the walker can moves to the left and to the right simultaneously.
- In a random walk, we only need to specify the statistical behaviour of the "coin"; for example, flipping a fair "coin" gives the head and tail with the equal probability $\frac{1}{2}$. In a quantum walk, however, we have to explicitly define the dynamics of the "coin" underlying its statistical behaviour; for example, the Hadamard transformation H can be seen as a quantum realisation of the fair "coin"; but so does the following 2×2 unitary matrix (and many others):

$$C = \frac{1}{\sqrt{2}} \begin{pmatrix} 1 & i \\ i & 1 \end{pmatrix}.$$

- Quantum interference may happen in a quantum walk; for example, let the Hadamard walk starts in state $|L\rangle|0\rangle$. Then we have:

$$
\begin{aligned}
|L\rangle|0\rangle &\xrightarrow{H} \frac{1}{\sqrt{2}}(|L\rangle + |R\rangle)|0\rangle \\
&\xrightarrow{T} \frac{1}{\sqrt{2}}(|L\rangle|-1\rangle + |R\rangle|1\rangle) \\
&\xrightarrow{H} \frac{1}{2}\left[(|L\rangle + |R\rangle)|-1\rangle + (|L\rangle - |R\rangle)|1\rangle\right] \\
&\xrightarrow{T} \frac{1}{2}(|L\rangle|-2\rangle + |R\rangle|0\rangle + |L\rangle|0\rangle - |R\rangle|2\rangle) \\
&\xrightarrow{H} \frac{1}{2\sqrt{2}}[(|L\rangle + |R\rangle)|-2\rangle + (|L\rangle - |R\rangle)|0\rangle \\
&\qquad + (|L\rangle + |R\rangle)|0\rangle - (|L\rangle - |R\rangle)|2\rangle]
\end{aligned}
$$
(4.17)

Here, $-|R\rangle|0\rangle$ and $|R\rangle|0\rangle$ are out of phase and thus cancel one another.

Quantum walk on a graph: Random walks on graphs are a class of random walks widely used in the design and analysis of algorithms. Let $G = (V, E)$ be an n-regular directed graph; that is, a graph where each vertex has n neighbours. Then we can label each edge with a number between 1 and n such that for each $1 \le i \le n$, the directed edges labelled i form a permutation. In this way, for each vertex v, the ith neighbour v_i of v is defined to be the vertex linked from v by an edge labeled i. A random walk on G is defined as follows: the vertices v's of G are used to represent the states of the walk, and for each state v the walk goes from v to its every neighbour with a certain probability. Such a random walk also has a quantum counterpart, which is carefully described in the following:

Example 4.2. The state Hilbert space of a quantum walk on an n-regular graph $G = (V, E)$ is $\mathcal{H}_d \otimes \mathcal{H}_p$, where:

- $\mathcal{H}_d = span\{|i\rangle\}_{i=1}^n$ is an n-dimensional Hilbert space. We introduce an auxiliary quantum system, called the direction "coin", with the state space $\mathcal{H}_d$. For each $1 \le i \le n$, the state $|i\rangle$ is used to denote the ith direction. The space $\mathcal{H}_d$ is referred to as the "coin space";
- $\mathcal{H}_p = span\{|v\rangle\}_{v \in V}$ is the position Hilbert space. For each vertex v of the graph, there is a basis state $|v\rangle$ in $\mathcal{H}_p$.

The shift S is an operator on $\mathcal{H}_d \otimes \mathcal{H}_p$ defined as follows:

$$S|i, v\rangle = |i\rangle|v_i\rangle$$

for any $1 \le i \le n$ and $v \in V$, where v_i is the ith neighbour of v. Intuitively, for each i, if the "coin" is in state $|i\rangle$, then the walker moves in the ith direction. Of course, the "coin" can be in a superposition of states $|i\rangle$ $(1 \le i \le n)$ and the walker moves to all the directions simultaneously.

If we further choose a unitary operator C on the "coin" space $\mathcal{H}_d$, called the "coin-tossing operator", then a single step of a coined quantum walk on graph G can be modelled by the unitary operator:

$$W = S(C \otimes I_{\mathcal{H}_p}) \tag{4.18}$$

where $I_{\mathcal{H}_p}$ is the identity operator on the position space $\mathcal{H}_p$. For example, a fair "coin" can be implemented by choosing the discrete Fourier transform (4.7) (with $N = n$) as the "coin-tossing operator". The operator FT maps each direction into a superposition of directions such that after measurement each of them is obtained with the equal probability $\frac{1}{n}$. The quantum walk is then an iteration of the single-step walk operator W.

Exercise 4.8. For each $1 \le i \le n$, we can define a shift operator S_i on the position space $\mathcal{H}_p$:

$$S_i|v\rangle = |v_i\rangle$$

for any $v \in V$, where v_i stands for the ith neighbour of v. If we slightly generalise the notion of quantum multiplexor (QMUX) by allowing the select variable being any quantum variable but not only qubits, then the shift operator S in Example 4.2 is the QMUX $\bigoplus_i S_i$ with the direction d as the select variable.

It has been observed that sometimes quantum effect (e.g. interference) in a quantum walk can offer a significant speed-up; for example, it helps a quantum walk to hit a vertex from another much faster than a random walk.

4.5.1 Quantum-walk search algorithm

Is it possible to harness the quantum speed-up pointed out above to design quantum algorithms that outperform their classical counterparts? In this subsection, we present such an algorithm for solving the search problem considered in Section 4.4.

Assume that the database consists of $N = 2^n$ items, each of which is encoded as an n-bit string $x = x_1...x_n \in \{0, 1\}^n$. It was assumed in Section 4.4 that there are M solutions. Here, we only consider the special case of $M = 1$. So, the task is to find the single target item (solution) x^*. The search algorithm in this subsection is based upon a quantum walk over the n-cube – the hypercube of dimension n. The n-cube is a graph with $N = 2^n$ nodes, each of which corresponds to an item x. Two nodes x and y are connected by an edge if they have only one-bit difference: for some $1 \le d \le n$,

$$x_d \ne y_d, \text{ and } x_i = y_i \text{ for all } i \ne d;$$

that is, x and y differ by only a single-bit flip. Thus, each of the 2^n nodes of the n-cube has degree n – it is connected to n other nodes.

Quantum walk: As a special case of Example 4.2, the quantum walk over the n-cube is described as follows:

- The state Hilbert space is $\mathcal{H}_d \otimes \mathcal{H}_p$, where $\mathcal{H}_d = span\{|1\rangle, ..., |n\rangle\}$,

$$\mathcal{H}_p = \mathcal{H}_2^{\otimes n} = span\{|x\rangle : x \in \{0, 1\}^n\},$$

and $\mathcal{H}_2$ is the state space of a qubit.

- The shift operator S maps $|d, x\rangle$ to $|d, x \oplus e_d\rangle$ (the dth bit of x is flipped), where $e_d = 0...010...0$ (the dth bit is 1 and all others are 0) is the dth basis vector of the n-cube. Formally,

$$S = \sum_{d=1}^{n} \sum_{x \in \{0,1\}^n} |d, x \oplus e_d\rangle\langle d, x|$$

where $\oplus$ is component-wise addition modulo 2.
- The "coin tossing" operator C is chosen to be the Grover rotation without the oracle (see Lemma 4.1):

$$C = 2|\psi\rangle\langle\psi| - I$$

where I is the identity operator on $\mathcal{H}_d$ and $|\psi\rangle$ is the equal superposition over all n directions:

$$|\psi\rangle = \frac{1}{\sqrt{n}} \sum_{d=1}^{n} |d\rangle.$$

Search algorithm: As in the Grover algorithm, we are supplied with an oracle that can mark the target item x^*. Suppose that this oracle is implemented via a perturbation of C:

$$D = C \otimes \sum_{x \neq x^*} |x\rangle\langle x| + C' \otimes |x^*\rangle\langle x^*| \tag{4.19}$$

where C' is a unitary operator in $\mathcal{H}_d$. Intuitively, the oracle applies the original "coin tossing" operator C to the direction system whenever the position corresponds to a nontarget item, but marks the target item x^* by applying a special "coin" action C'.

Now the search algorithm works as follows:

- Initialise the quantum computer to the equal superposition over both all directions and all positions: $|\Psi_0\rangle = |\psi\rangle_d \otimes |\varphi\rangle_p$, where

$$|\varphi\rangle = \frac{1}{\sqrt{N}} \sum_{x \in \{0,1\}^n} |x\rangle.$$

- Apply the perturbed single-step walk operator

$$W' = SD = W - S\left[(C - C') \otimes |x^*\rangle\langle x^*|\right]$$

$t = \left\lceil \frac{\pi}{2}\sqrt{N} \right\rceil$ times, where W is the single-step walk operator defined by Eq. (4.18).
- Measure the state of the quantum computer in the $|d, x\rangle$ basis.

There is a remarkable difference between the "coin tossing" operator D used in this algorithm and the original "coin tossing" operator C (more precisely, $C \otimes I$) in Example 4.2: the operator C acts only in the direction space and thus is position-independent. However, D is obtained by modifying $C \otimes I$ with C' marking the target item x^*, and it is obvious from Eq. (4.19) that D is position-dependent.

For the case of $C' = -I$, it was proved that the algorithm finds the target item with probability $\frac{1}{2} - O(\frac{1}{n})$, and thus the target item can be found with an arbitrarily small probability of error by repeating the algorithm a constant number of times. The performance analysis of this algorithm is involved and not included here, but the reader can find it in the original paper [376].

The reader is invited to carefully compare this search algorithm based on quantum walk with the Grover search algorithms introduced in Section 4.4.

4.6 Basic quantum communication protocols

In this section, we turn to introduce two basic quantum communication protocols, which can be viewed as a special class of (distributed) quantum algorithms. They are surprising applications of quantum mechanics, and their tasks cannot be accomplished in the classical world. These protocols will be considered in Section 10.4.3 as examples of communicating and distributed quantum programs.

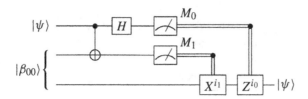

FIGURE 4.6   Quantum teleportation circuit.

4.6.1   Quantum teleportation

Quantum teleportation is a protocol for transmitting quantum information (e.g. the exact state of an atom or photon) via only classical communication but with the help of previously shared quantum entanglement between the sender and receiver. It is one of the most surprising examples where entanglement helps to accomplish a certain task that is impossible in the classical world. The *setting* is as follows. The sender, say Alice, and the receiver, say Bob, share an entanglement; more precisely, Alice is in possession of qubit q_1 and Bob in possession of qubit q_2, and q_1, q_2 are in the EPR pair

$$|\beta_{00}\rangle = \frac{1}{\sqrt{2}}(|00\rangle + |11\rangle).$$

Alice wants to send an unknown state $|\psi\rangle = \alpha|0\rangle + \beta|1\rangle$ of a qubit q_0 to Bob.

The *protocol* works in the following way. Alice interacts qubit q_0 with her half of the entanglement, i.e. q_1, by applying the CNOT gate on $q_0 q_1$ with q_0 being the control qubit and q_1 the target qubit, and Hadamard gate H on q_0. Then she measures the two qubits q_0, q_1 in her possession in the computational basis. The outcome is one of the four *two-bit* strings $00, 01, 10, 11$, written $i_0 i_1$. She sends this information to Bob. According to the received information $i_0 i_1$, Bob performs X^{i_1} and Z^{i_0} on his half of the EPR pair, i.e. q_2. Finally, he gets the state $|\psi\rangle$ at q_2. The quantum circuit teleporting a single qubit is shown in Fig. 4.6.

Exercise 4.9. Verify that the state that Bob finally gets at q_2 is $|\psi\rangle$.

4.6.2   Superdense coding

Superdense coding is another communication task that cannot be realised without the resource of entanglement. It is a protocol between two agents, conventionally called "Alice" and "Bob". The *setting* is as follows. Alice has possession of the first, say q_1, of a pair of qubits and Bob has the possession of the second, say q_2, and these two qubits are in the entangled state

$$|\beta_{00}\rangle = \frac{1}{\sqrt{2}}(|00\rangle + |11\rangle).$$

The *protocol* enables Alice to transmit *two* classical bits of information by sending a *single* qubit to Bob (so called *superdense* coding). It works in the following way: if Alice wants to send two bits $i_0 i_1$, she can first perform X^{i_0} and then Z^{i_1} on q_1, and send her qubit q_1 to Bob. Thus, Bob has the possession of both qubits $q_1 q_2$ that are in the Bell state or EPR pair:

$$|\beta_{i_0 i_1}\rangle = Z_{q_1}^{i_1} X_{q_1}^{i_0} |\beta_{00}\rangle = \begin{cases} |\beta_{00}\rangle = \frac{1}{\sqrt{2}}(|00\rangle + |11\rangle) & \text{if } i_0 i_1 = 00, \\ |\beta_{01}\rangle = \frac{1}{\sqrt{2}}(|00\rangle - |11\rangle) & \text{if } i_0 i_1 = 01, \\ |\beta_{10}\rangle = \frac{1}{\sqrt{2}}(|01\rangle + |10\rangle) & \text{if } i_0 i_1 = 10, \\ |\beta_{11}\rangle = \frac{1}{\sqrt{2}}(|01\rangle - |10\rangle) & \text{if } i_0 i_1 = 11. \end{cases}$$

Note that four Bell states $|\beta_{00}\rangle, |\beta_{01}\rangle, |\beta_{10}\rangle, |\beta_{11}\rangle$ form an orthonormal basis of the Hilbert space of two qubits. By performing the measurement in the Bell states, $M = \{M_{j_0 j_1}\}$ where measurement operators

$$M_{j_0 j_1} = |\beta_{j_0 j_1}\rangle\langle\beta_{j_0 j_1}|$$

for $j_0, j_1 \in \{0, 1\}$, Bob can determine the two bits $i_0 i_1$ that Alice wishes to transmit.

4.7 Bibliographic remarks and further readings

Quantum algorithms: The presentation of Sections 4.1 to 4.4 largely follows Sections 1.4, 5.1, 5.2, and 6.1 of the textbook [318]. The one-dimensional quantum walk and the quantum walk on a graph in Section 4.5 were defined in [11] and [24], respectively. The algorithm given in Section 4.5.1 was proposed by Shenvi, Kempe, and Whaley [376]. A different model of discrete-time quantum random walks (without quantum coins) was introduced in [291] for developing quantum algorithms solving the triangle problem. Continuous-time quantum random walks have alse been employed in designing quantum algorithms [92]. Universal models of quantum computation based on discrete- and continuous-time quantum random walks were described in [91,289], respectively.

Quantum algorithms have been one of the most active research areas in quantum computing since Shor's factoring algorithm and Grover search were discovered. For the three major quantum algorithms in the early time, namely Shor algorithm, Grover algorithm, and quantum simulation [284], and their variants, [318] is still one of the best expositions. Shor [378] proposed two explanations for why so few classes of quantum algorithms have been found and pointed out several lines of research that might lead to the discovery of new quantum algorithms. A large number of papers on quantum walks and algorithms based on them have been published in the last decade; see [23,363,400] for a thorough survey. It has also been proved that there does not exist any quantum speed-up for certain problems; see [217] for example. A recent breakthrough in quantum algorithms is the HHL (Harrow–Hassidim–Lloyd) algorithm for systems of linear equations [199]. The reader can find a comprehensive catalog of quantum algorithms at the webpage: `https://quantumalgorithmzoo.org`.

Quantum communication protocols: Quantum teleportation and superdense coding presented in Section 4.6 were proposed in [53,55], respectively. As two basic quantum communication protocols, they, together with QKD (Quantum Key Distribution) [52], have stimulated a huge amount of research on quantum communication and cryptography [178,338,339].

Part II

Sequential quantum programs

From this part on, we systematically study quantum programming methodology and its theoretical foundations. This part focuses on the simplest class of quantum programs, namely sequential quantum programs with classical control flows. It consists of two chapters:

- Chapter 5 introduces quantum **while**-language – a quantum extension of the classical **while**-language, which is a common theoretical language for sequential programming and a core of other imperative programming languages.
- Chapter 6 introduces quantum Hoare logic – a Hoare-style program logic for reasoning about correctness of quantum programs written in quantum **while**-language. It provides us with a logical foundation for verification of quantum programs.

Chapter 5

Quantum **while**-programs

In Chapter 4, several quantum algorithms were presented at the very low-level model of quantum computing – quantum circuits. How can we design and implement higher-level programming languages for quantum computers? From this chapter on, we systematically develop the theoretical foundations of quantum programming.

As the first step, let us see how can a classical programming language be directly extended for programming a quantum computer. As pointed out in Sections 1.1 and 1.2, this issue had been the main concern of early research on quantum programming. This chapter studies a class of simple quantum generalisations of classical programs – quantum programs with classical control; i.e. programs in the superposition-of-data paradigm. The design idea of this class of quantum programs was briefly introduced in Section 1.2.2. The control flow of these programs will be further discussed shortly.

More specifically, this chapter introduces a quantum extension of a very simple classical programming language, namely the **while**-language. The **while**-language constitutes the "kernel" of many classical programming languages. A familiarity of its syntax and semantics is necessary for understanding this chapter. We will briefly review its ideas in Section 5.1, but the reader should consult Chapter 3 of book [28] for an excellent introduction of the **while**-language.

The chapter is divided into three parts:

- The first part consists of Sections 5.1 to 5.3: Section 5.1 defines the syntax of the quantum **while**-language. Sections 5.2 and 5.3 present its operational and denotational semantics, respectively.
  On the road, we briefly prepare a theory of quantum domains needed for a characterisation of the denotational semantics of loops in the quantum **while**-language. For readability, the lengthy proofs of some lemmas about quantum domains are postponed to the Appendix I at the end of the book.
- The second part – Section 5.5 – extends the quantum **while**-language by adding recursive quantum programs (with classical control). The operational and denotational semantics of recursive quantum programs are defined. Here, the theory of quantum domains is also needed to deal with the denotational semantics. For a better understanding, I suggest the reader to study Chapter 4 of book [28] before reading this section. Only Chapter 12 is related to this section, the reader can also skip this section for the first reading.
- The third part – Section 5.4 – presents an illustrative example showing how can the Grover quantum search be programmed in the language defined in this chapter.

5.1 Syntax

In this section, we define the syntax of quantum **while**-language. The syntax is the rules that define how programs in the language are correctly constructed from symbols in its alphabet. As commonly practiced in classical programming theory, we will use BNF (Backus–Naur form) to describe the syntax of quantum programs.

While-programs: As said before, a quantum extension of classical **while**-language. So, for convenient of the reader, let us first briefly review the **while**-language. Using BNF, a classical **while**-program is generated by the grammar:

$$
\begin{aligned}
S ::= \ & \textbf{skip} \mid u := t \mid S_1; S_2 \\
& \mid \textbf{if } b \textbf{ then } S_1 \textbf{ else } S_2 \textbf{ fi} \\
& \mid \textbf{while } b \textbf{ do } S \textbf{ od}.
\end{aligned}
\tag{5.1}
$$

Here, S, S_1, S_2 are programs, u is a variable, t is an expression, and b is a Boolean expression. Intuitively, **while**-programs are executed as follows:

- The statement "**skip**" does nothing but terminates.
- The assignment "$u := t$" assigns the value of expression t to variable u.
- The sequential composition "$S_1; S_2$" first executes S_1, and when S_1 terminates, it executes S_2.
- The conditional statement "**if** b **then** S_1 **else** S_2 **fi**" starts from evaluating the Boolean expression b: if b is true, S_1 is executed; otherwise, S_2 is executed.

Foundations of Quantum Programming. https://doi.org/10.1016/B978-0-44-315942-8.00015-0

- The **while**-loop "**while** b **do** S **od**" starts from evaluating the loop guard b: if b is false, the loop terminates immediately; otherwise, the loop body S is executed, and when S terminates, the process is repeated.

Case statements: As already mentioned in Section 1.2, the conditional statement can be generalised to the case statement:

$$
\begin{aligned}
&\textbf{if } G_1 \to S_1 \\
&\square\ G_2 \to S_2 \\
&\quad\ \ \ldots\ldots \\
&\square\ G_n \to S_n \\
&\textbf{fi}
\end{aligned}
\tag{5.2}
$$

or more compactly written as

$$
\textbf{if } (\square i \cdot G_i \to S_i) \textbf{ fi}
$$

where $G_1, G_2, ..., G_n$ are Boolean expressions, called guards, and $S_1, S_2, ..., S_n$ are programs. The case statement starts from evaluating guards: if G_i is true, then the corresponding subprogram S_i is executed.

Quantum while-programs: Now we expand the **while**-language so that it can be used for quantum programming. We first fix the alphabet of the quantum **while**-language:

- A countably infinite set $qVar$ of quantum variables. The symbols $q, q', q_0, q_1, q_2, ...$ will be used as metavariables ranging over quantum variables.
- Each quantum variable $q \in qVar$ has a type $\mathcal{H}_q$, which is a Hilbert space – the state space of the quantum system denoted by q. For simplicity, we only consider two basic types:

$$
\textbf{Boolean} = \mathcal{H}_2, \qquad \textbf{integer} = \mathcal{H}_\infty.
$$

Note that the sets denoted by types **Boolean** and **integer** in classical computation are exactly the computational bases of $\mathcal{H}_2$ and $\mathcal{H}_\infty$, respectively (see Examples 2.1 and 2.2). The main results presented in this chapter can be easily generalised to the case with more data types.

A quantum register is a finite sequence of distinct quantum variables. (The notion of quantum register in Section 3.1 is slightly generalised here by allowing to contain other quantum variables rather than qubit variables.) The state Hilbert space of a quantum register $\overline{q} = q_1, ..., q_n$ is the tensor product of the state spaces of the quantum variables occurring in $\overline{q}$:

$$
\mathcal{H}_{\overline{q}} = \bigotimes_{i=1}^{n} \mathcal{H}_{q_i}.
$$

When necessary, we write $|\psi\rangle_{q_i}$ to indicate that $|\psi\rangle$ is a state of quantum variable q_i; that is, $|\psi\rangle$ is in $\mathcal{H}_{q_i}$. Thus, $|\psi\rangle_{q_i}\langle\varphi_i|$ denotes the outer product of states $|\psi\rangle$ and $|\varphi\rangle$ of q_i, and $|\psi_1\rangle_{q_1}...|\psi_n\rangle_{q_n}$ is a state in $\mathcal{H}_{\overline{q}}$ in which q_i is in state $|\psi_i\rangle$ for every $1 \le i \le n$.

With the above ingredients, we can define programs in the quantum **while**-language.

Definition 5.1. Using BNF, quantum programs are generated by the syntax:

$$
\begin{aligned}
S ::=\ &\textbf{skip} \mid q := |0\rangle \mid \overline{q} := U[\overline{q}] \mid S_1; S_2 \\
&\mid \textbf{if } (\square m \cdot M[\overline{q}] = m \to S_m) \textbf{ fi} \\
&\mid \textbf{while } M[\overline{q}] = 1 \textbf{ do } S \textbf{ od}.
\end{aligned}
\tag{5.3}
$$

The above definition deserves a careful explanation. We also suggest the reader to compare syntax (5.3) for quantum **while**-programs with syntax (5.1) and (5.2) for classical **while**-programs.

- As in the classical **while**-language, statement "**skip**" in (5.3) does nothing and terminates immediately.
- The initialisation statement "$q := |0\rangle$" sets quantum variable q to the basis state $|0\rangle$. For any pure state $|\psi\rangle \in \mathcal{H}_q$, there is obviously a unitary operator U in $\mathcal{H}_q$ such that $|\psi\rangle = U|0\rangle$. So, the system q can be prepared in state $|\psi\rangle$ by this initialisation and the unitary transformation $q := U[q]$.

- The statement "$\overline{q} := U[\overline{q}]$" means that unitary transformation U is performed on quantum register $\overline{q}$, leaving the states of the quantum variables not in $\overline{q}$ unchanged. The notation "$\overline{q} := U[\overline{q}]$" is a mimic of assignment in classical programming languages, and quite cumbersome. It will be often simply written as $U[\overline{q}]$.
- Sequential composition is similar to its counterpart in a classical programming language.
- The program constructs

$$
\begin{aligned}
\textbf{if } (\square m \cdot M[\overline{q}] = m \rightarrow S_m) \textbf{ fi} \equiv \textbf{ if } M[\overline{q}] = &\ m_1 \rightarrow S_{m_1} \\
\square \qquad &\ m_2 \rightarrow S_{m_2} \\
&\ \ldots\ldots \\
\square \qquad &\ m_n \rightarrow S_{m_n} \\
\textbf{fi}&
\end{aligned}
\tag{5.4}
$$

is a quantum generalisation of classical case statement (5.2). Recall that the first step of the execution of the statement (5.2) is to see which guard G_i is satisfied. However, according to Postulate of quantum mechanics 3 (see Section 2.3), the way to acquire information about a quantum system is to perform a measurement on it. So, in executing the statement (5.4), quantum measurement

$$
M = \{M_m\} = \left\{ M_{m_1}, M_{m_2}, ..., M_{m_n} \right\}
$$

will be performed on quantum register $\overline{q}$, and then a subprogram S_m will be selected to be executed next according to the outcome of measurement. An essential difference between the measurement-based case statement (5.4) and a classical case statement is that the state of program variables is changed after performing the measurement in the former, whereas it is not changed after checking the guards in the latter.

- The statement

$$
\textbf{while } M[\overline{q}] = 1 \textbf{ do } S \textbf{ od}
\tag{5.5}
$$

is a quantum generalisation of classical loop "**while** b **do** S **od**". In the latter, the loop guard b is a classical predicate. In the loop guard of the former, however, to acquire information about quantum register $\overline{q}$, a measurement M is performed on it. The measurement $M = \{M_0, M_1\}$ is a yes–no measurement with only two possible outcomes 0 ("no"), 1 ("yes"). If the outcome 0 is observed, then the program terminates, and if the outcome 1 occurs, then the program executes the subprogram S (usually called the loop body) and continues. The only difference between the quantum loop (5.5) and a classical loop is that checking the loop guard b in the classical loop does not change the state of program variables, but it is not the case in the quantum loop.

Let us consider a quantum variant of a simple probabilistic program so that the reader can better understand the difference between a probabilistic program and a quantum program.

Example 5.1 (Three quantum dials). Suppose that a slot machine has three dials d_1, d_2, d_3 and two suits $\heartsuit$ and $\diamondsuit$, and spins the dials independently so that they come to rest on each of the suits with equal probability. It can be modelled as a probabilistic program:

$$
\begin{aligned}
\textit{flip} \equiv (d_1 := \heartsuit \oplus_{\frac{1}{2}} d_1 := \diamondsuit);\ (d_2 := \heartsuit \oplus_{\frac{1}{2}} d_2 := \diamondsuit); \\
(d_3 := \heartsuit \oplus_{\frac{1}{2}} d_3 := \diamondsuit)
\end{aligned}
$$

where $P_1 \oplus_p P_2$ stands for a probabilistic choice which chooses to execute P with probability p and to execute Q with probability $1 - p$ (see [242] for more detailed description).

A quantum variant of *flip* can be defined as follows:

$$
\textit{qflip} \equiv H[d_1];\ H[d_2];\ H[d_3]
$$

where H is the Hadamard operator defined by Eq. (2.5) in the 2-dimensional Hilbert space $\mathcal{H}_2$ with $\{|\heartsuit\rangle, |\diamondsuit\rangle\}$ as an orthonormal basis. It is worth noting that the program *qflip* also spins the dials, but does it in a quantum way modelled by the Hadamard "coin-tossing" operator H.

Classical control flow: Now it is the right time to explain that the control flow of a program in the quantum **while**-language is *classical*, as indicated at the beginning of this chapter. Recall that the control flow of a program is the order of its execution. In the quantum **while**-language, there are only two statements – the case statement (5.4) and the loop (5.5) – whose execution is determined by a choice as to which of two or more paths should be followed. The case statement (5.4) selects a command to execute according to the outcome of measurement M: if the outcome is m_i, then the corresponding command S_{m_i} will be executed. Since the outcome of a quantum measurement is classical information, the control flow in statement (5.4) is classical. The same argument illustrates that the control flow in the loop (5.5) is classical too.

As pointed out in Section 1.2.2, it is also possible to define programs with quantum control flow. Quantum control flow of programs is much harder to understand, which will be the theme of Chapters 11 and 12.

Program variables: Before concluding this section, we present the following technical definition, which will be needed in the sequel.

Definition 5.2. The set $var(S)$ of quantum variables in quantum program S is recursively defined as follows:

1. If $S \equiv$ **skip**, then $var(S) = \emptyset$;
2. If $S \equiv q := |0\rangle$, then $var(S) = \{q\}$;
3. If $S \equiv \overline{q} := U[\overline{q}]$, then $var(S) = \overline{q}$;
4. If $S \equiv S_1; S_2$, then $var(S) = var(S_1) \cup var(S_2)$;
5. If $S \equiv$ **if** $(\square m \cdot M[\overline{q}] = m \to S_m)$ **fi**, then

$$var(S) = \overline{q} \cup \bigcup_m var(S_m);$$

6. If $S \equiv$ **while** $M[\overline{q}] = 1$ **do** S **od**, then $var(S) = \overline{q} \cup var(S)$.

5.2 Operational semantics

The syntax of quantum **while**-programs was defined in the last section. This section defines the operational semantics of the quantum **while**-language. It describes how a program is executed as a sequence of basic computational steps. Since it provides a formal specification of program execution, operational semantics can be used as a theoretical basis the for design of a compiler. In this book, we adopt the structural operational semantics, which defines the behaviour of a program in terms of the behaviours of its components, and thus is syntax-oriented. The structural operational semantics is usually defined as a transition system between configurations.

Configurations: To define quantum program configurations, let us first introduce several notations:

- A positive operator ρ in a Hilbert space $\mathcal{H}$ is called a *partial density operator* if $tr(\rho) \leq 1$. So, a density operator ρ (see Definition 2.21) is a partial density operator with $tr(\rho) = 1$. We write $\mathcal{D}(\mathcal{H})$ for the set of partial density operators in $\mathcal{H}$. In quantum programming theory, partial density operator is a very useful notion because a program with loops (or more generally, recursions) may not terminate with a certain probability, and its output is a partial density operator but not necessary to be a density operator.
- We write $\mathcal{H}_{all}$ for the tensor product of the state Hilbert spaces of all quantum variables:

$$\mathcal{H}_{all} = \bigotimes_{q \in qVar} \mathcal{H}_q.$$

- Let $\overline{q} = q_1, ..., q_n$ be a quantum register. An operator A in the state Hilbert space $\mathcal{H}_{\overline{q}}$ of $\overline{q}$ has a cylindrical extension $A \otimes I$ in $\mathcal{H}_{all}$, where I is the identity operator on the state Hilbert space

$$\bigotimes_{q \in qVar \setminus \overline{q}} \mathcal{H}_q$$

of the quantum variables that are not in $\overline{q}$. In the sequel, we will simply write A for its cylindrical extension, and it can be easily recognised from the context, without any risk of confusion.
- We will use $\downarrow$ to denote the empty program; i.e. termination.

Definition 5.3. A quantum configuration is a pair $\langle S, \rho \rangle$, where:

1. S is a quantum program or the empty program $\downarrow$;
2. $\rho \in \mathcal{D}(\mathcal{H}_{all})$ is a partial density operator in $\mathcal{H}_{all}$, and it is used to indicate the (global) state of quantum variables.

(SK) $\langle \mathbf{skip}, \rho \rangle \to \langle \downarrow, \rho \rangle$

(IN) $\langle q := |0\rangle, \rho \rangle \to \langle \downarrow, \rho_0^q \rangle$

$$\text{where } \rho_0^q = \begin{cases} |0\rangle_q \langle 0|\rho|0\rangle_q \langle 0| + |0\rangle_q \langle 1|\rho|1\rangle_q \langle 0| & \text{if } type(q) = \mathbf{Boolean}, \\ \sum_{n=-\infty}^{\infty} |0\rangle_q \langle n|\rho|n\rangle_q \langle 0| & \text{if } type(q) = \mathbf{integer}. \end{cases}$$

(UT) $\langle \overline{q} := U[\overline{q}], \rho \rangle \to \langle \downarrow, U\rho U^\dagger \rangle$

(SC) $$\frac{\langle S_1, \rho \rangle \to \langle S_1', \rho' \rangle}{\langle S_1; S_2, \rho \rangle \to \langle S_1'; S_2, \rho' \rangle}$$

where we make the convention that $\downarrow; S_2 = S_2$.

(IF) $\langle \mathbf{if} \, (\square m \cdot M[\overline{q}] = m \to S_m) \, \mathbf{fi}, \rho \rangle \to \langle S_m, M_m \rho M_m^\dagger \rangle$

for each possible outcome m of measurement $M = \{M_m\}$.

(L0) $\langle \mathbf{while} \, M[\overline{q}] = 1 \, \mathbf{do} \, S \, \mathbf{od}, \rho \rangle \to \langle \downarrow, M_0 \rho M_0^\dagger \rangle$

(L1) $\langle \mathbf{while} \, M[\overline{q}] = 1 \, \mathbf{do} \, S \, \mathbf{od}, \rho \rangle \to \langle S; \mathbf{while} \, M[\overline{q}] = 1 \, \mathbf{do} \, S \, \mathbf{od}, M_1 \rho M_1^\dagger \rangle$

FIGURE 5.1 Transition rules for quantum **while**-programs.

Structural operational semantics: Now we are ready to define the operational semantics of quantum programs. As in the theory of classical programming, the execution of a quantum program can be properly described in terms of transition between configurations. A transition between quantum configurations:

$$\langle S, \rho \rangle \to \langle S', \rho' \rangle$$

means that after executing quantum program S one step in state ρ, the state of quantum variables becomes ρ', and S' is the remainder of S still to be executed. In particular, if $S' = \downarrow$, then S terminates in state ρ'. The structural operational semantics is then a transition system consisting of all of the possible transitions between configurations. It is defined by a set of transition rules.

Definition 5.4. The operational semantics of quantum programs is the transition relation $\to$ between quantum configurations defined by the transition rules in Fig. 5.1.

The operational semantics (i.e. the relation $\to$) defined above should be understood as the smallest transition relation between quantum configurations that satisfies the rules in Fig. 5.1. Obviously, the transition rules (IN), (UT), (IF), (L0), and (L1) are determined by the postulates of quantum mechanics. As you saw in Section 2.3, probabilities always arise from the measurements in a quantum computation. But it should be noticed that the operational semantics of quantum programs defined above is an ordinary transition relation $\to$ rather than a probabilistic transition relation. Several remarks should help the reader to understand these transition rules:

- The symbol U in the target configuration $\langle \downarrow, U\rho U^\dagger \rangle$ of the rule (UT) stands indeed for the cylindrical extension of U in $\mathcal{H}_{all}$. A similar remark applies to the rules (IF), (L0), and (L1) for measurements and loops.
- In the rule (IF), the outcome m is observed with probability

$$p_m = tr(M_m \rho M_m^\dagger),$$

and in this case, after the measurement the state becomes

$$\rho_m = M_m \rho M_m^\dagger / p_m.$$

So, a natural presentation of the rule (IF) is the probabilistic transition:

$$\langle \mathbf{if} \, (\square m \cdot M[\overline{q}] = m \to S_m) \, \mathbf{fi}, \rho \rangle \xrightarrow{p_m} \langle S_m, \rho_m \rangle$$

However, if we encode both probability p_m and density operator ρ_m into partial density operator

$$M_m \rho M_m^\dagger = p_m \rho_m,$$

then the rule can be presented as an ordinary (a nonprobabilistic) transition.

(SK') $\langle \mathbf{skip}, |\psi\rangle \rangle \to \langle \downarrow, |\psi\rangle \rangle$

(UT') $\langle \overline{q} := U[\overline{q}], |\psi\rangle \rangle \to \langle \downarrow, U|\psi\rangle \rangle$

(SC') $$\frac{\langle S_1, |\psi\rangle \rangle \xrightarrow{p} \langle S_1', |\psi'\rangle \rangle}{\langle S_1; S_2, |\psi\rangle \rangle \xrightarrow{p} \langle S_1'; S_2, |\psi'\rangle \rangle}$$

where we make the convention that $\downarrow; S_2 = S_2$.

(IF') $\langle \mathbf{if}\ (\square m \cdot M[\overline{q}] = m \to S_m)\ \mathbf{fi}, |\psi\rangle \rangle \xrightarrow{||M_m|\psi\rangle||^2} \langle S_m, \frac{M_m|\psi\rangle}{||M_m|\psi\rangle||} \rangle$

for each outcome m of measurement $M = \{M_m\}$.

(L0') $\langle \mathbf{while}\ M[\overline{q}] = 1\ \mathbf{do}\ S\ \mathbf{od}, |\psi\rangle \rangle \xrightarrow{||M_0|\psi\rangle||^2} \langle \downarrow, \frac{M_0|\psi\rangle}{||M_0|\psi\rangle||} \rangle$

(L1') $\langle \mathbf{while}\ M[\overline{q}] = 1\ \mathbf{do}\ S\ \mathbf{od}, |\psi\rangle \rangle \xrightarrow{||M_1|\psi\rangle||^2} \langle S; \mathbf{while}\ M[\overline{q}] = 1\ \mathbf{do}\ S\ \mathbf{od}, \frac{M_1|\psi\rangle}{||M_1|\psi\rangle||} \rangle$

FIGURE 5.2   Transition rules for quantum **while**-programs in pure states.

- Likewise, in the rules (L0) and (L1) the measurement outcomes 0 and 1 occur with probabilities:

$$p_0 = tr(M_0 \rho M_0^{\dagger}), \qquad p_1 = tr(M_1 \rho M_1^{\dagger}),$$

respectively, and the state becomes $M_0 \rho M_0^{\dagger}/p_0$ from ρ when the outcome is 0, and it becomes $M_1 \rho M_1^{\dagger}/p_1$ when the outcome is 1. These probabilities and postmeasurement states are encoded into partial density operators so that the rules (L0) and (L1) can be stated as ordinary transitions instead of probabilistic transitions.

From the above discussion, we see why the convention of combining probabilities with postmeasurement states enables us to define the operational semantics $\to$ as a nonprobabilistic transition relation. The linearity of quantum mechanics warrants that such an encoding will not cause any problem. As we will see, this convention can significantly simplify our presentation and reasoning about quantum programs.

Transition rules for pure states: The transition rules in Fig. 5.1 were stated in the language of density operators. As we will see in the next section, this general setting provides us with an elegant formulation of denotational semantics. However, pure states are usually more convenient in applications. So, we display the pure state variants of these transition rules in Fig. 5.2. In the rules for pure states, a configuration is a pair

$$\langle S, |\psi\rangle \rangle$$

with S being a quantum program or the empty program E and $|\psi\rangle$ a pure state in $\mathcal{H}_{all}$. As indicated above, transitions in Fig. 5.1 are all nonprobabilistic. However, the transitions in rules (IF'), (L0'), and (L1') are probabilistic in the form of

$$\langle S, |\psi\rangle \rangle \xrightarrow{p} \langle S', |\psi'\rangle \rangle.$$

Whenever the probability $p = 1$, then the above transition is abbreviated to

$$\langle S, |\psi\rangle \rangle \to \langle S', |\psi'\rangle \rangle.$$

Of course, the rules in Fig. 5.2 are special cases of the corresponding rules in Fig. 5.1. Conversely, using the correspondence between density operators and ensembles of pure states, the rules in Fig. 5.1 can be derived from their counterparts in Fig. 5.2.

The reader might noticed that Fig. 5.2 does not include a pure state version of the initialisation rule (IN). Actually, the rule (IN) has no pure state version because it is possible that an initialisation transfers a pure state into a mixed state: although the initialisation $q := |0\rangle$ changes the state of local variable q into a pure state $|0\rangle$, its side effect on other variables may cause a transition of a global state $|\psi\rangle \in \mathcal{H}_{all}$ of all variables $qVar$ into a mixed state. To see the rule (IN) more clearly, let us look at the case of $type(q) = \mathbf{integer}$ as an example.

Example 5.2. 1. We first consider the case where ρ is a pure state; that is, $\rho = |\psi\rangle\langle\psi|$ for some $|\psi\rangle \in \mathcal{H}_{all}$. We can write $|\psi\rangle$ in the form:

$$|\psi\rangle = \sum_k \alpha_k |\psi_k\rangle,$$

where all $|\psi_k\rangle$ are product states, say

$$|\psi_k\rangle = \bigotimes_{p \in qVar} |\psi_{kp}\rangle.$$

Then

$$\rho = \sum_{k,l} \alpha_k \alpha_l^* |\psi_k\rangle\langle\psi_l|.$$

After the initialisation $q := |0\rangle$ the state becomes:

$$
\begin{aligned}
\rho_0^q &= \sum_{n=-\infty}^{\infty} |0\rangle_q \langle n|\rho|n\rangle_q \langle 0| \\
&= \sum_{k,l} \alpha_k \alpha_l^* \left(\sum_{n=-\infty}^{\infty} |0\rangle_q \langle n|\psi_k\rangle\langle\psi_l|n\rangle_q \langle 0| \right) \\
&= \sum_{k,l} \alpha_k \alpha_l^* \left(\sum_{n=-\infty}^{\infty} \langle\psi_{lq}|n\rangle\langle n|\psi_{kq}\rangle \right) \left(|0\rangle_q \langle 0| \otimes \bigotimes_{p \neq q} |\psi_{kp}\rangle\langle\psi_{lp}| \right) \\
&= \sum_{k,l} \alpha_k \alpha_l^* \langle\psi_{lq}|\psi_{kq}\rangle \left(|0\rangle_q \langle 0| \otimes \bigotimes_{p \neq q} |\psi_{kp}\rangle\langle\psi_{lp}| \right) \\
&= |0\rangle_q \langle 0| \otimes \left(\sum_{k,l} \alpha_k \alpha_l^* \langle\psi_{lq}|\psi_{kq}\rangle \bigotimes_{p \neq q} |\psi_{kp}\rangle\langle\psi_{lp}| \right).
\end{aligned}
\tag{5.6}
$$

It is obvious that ρ_0^q is not necessary to be a pure state although ρ is a pure state.

2. In general, suppose that ρ is generated by an ensemble $\{(p_i, |\psi_i\rangle)\}$ of pure states; that is,

$$\rho = \sum_i p_i |\psi_i\rangle\langle\psi_i|.$$

For each i, we write $\rho_i = |\psi_i\rangle\langle\psi_i|$ and assume that it becomes ρ_{i0}^q after the initialisation. By the above argument, we can write ρ_{i0}^q in the form:

$$\rho_{i0}^q = |0\rangle_q \langle 0| \otimes \left(\sum_k \alpha_{ik} |\varphi_{ik}\rangle\langle\varphi_{ik}| \right),$$

where $|\varphi_{ik}\rangle \in \mathcal{H}_{qVar\setminus\{q\}}$ for all k. Then the initialisation makes that ρ becomes

$$
\begin{aligned}
\rho_0^q &= \sum_{n=-\infty}^{\infty} |0\rangle_q \langle n|\rho|n\rangle_q \langle 0| \\
&= \sum_i p_i \left(\sum_{n=-\infty}^{\infty} |0\rangle_q \langle n|\rho_i|n\rangle_q \langle 0| \right) \\
&= |0\rangle_q \langle 0| \otimes \left(\sum_{i,k} p_i \alpha_{ik} |\varphi_{ik}\rangle\langle\varphi_{ik}| \right).
\end{aligned}
\tag{5.7}
$$

From Eqs (5.6) and (5.7) we see that the state of quantum variable q is set to be $|0\rangle$ and the states of the other quantum variables are unchanged.

Exercise 5.1. Find a necessary and sufficient condition under which ρ_0^q in Eq. (5.6) is a pure state. [Hint: A density operator ρ is a pure state if and only if $tr(\rho^2) = 1$; see [318], Exercise 2.71.]

Computation of a program: Now the notion of computation of a quantum program can be naturally defined in terms of its transitions.

Definition 5.5. Let S be a quantum program and $\rho \in \mathcal{D}(\mathcal{H}_{all})$.

1. A transition sequence of S starting in ρ is a finite or infinite sequence of configurations in the following form:

$$\langle S, \rho \rangle \to \langle S_1, \rho_1 \rangle \to ... \to \langle S_n, \rho_n \rangle \to \langle S_{n+1}, \rho_{n+1} \rangle \to ...$$

such that $\rho_n \neq 0$ for all n (except the last n in the case of a finite sequence).
2. If this sequence cannot be extended, then it is called a computation of S starting in ρ.
   a. If a computation is finite and its last configuration is $\langle E, \rho' \rangle$, then we say that it terminates in ρ'.
   b. If it is infinite, then we say that it diverges. Moreover, we say that S can diverge from ρ whenever it has a diverging computation starting in ρ.

To illustrate the above definition, let us see a simple example.

Example 5.3. Suppose that $type(q_1) = $ **Boolean** and $type(q_2) = $ **integer**. Consider the program

$$S \equiv q_1 := |0\rangle;\ q_2 := |0\rangle;\ q_1 := H[q_1];\ q_2 := q_2 + 7;$$
$$\mathbf{if}\ M[q_1] = 0 \to S_1$$
$$\square \qquad\qquad 1 \to S_2$$
$$\mathbf{fi}$$

where:

- H is the Hadamard transformation, $q_2 := q_2 + 7$ is a rewriting of

$$q_2 := T_7[q_2]$$

with T_7 being the translation operator defined in Example 2.4;
- M is the measurement in the computational basis $|0\rangle, |1\rangle$ of $\mathcal{H}_2$; that is, $M = \{M_0, M_1\}$, $M_0 = |0\rangle\langle0|$ and $M_1 = |1\rangle\langle1|$;
- $S_1 \equiv $ **skip**;
- $S_2 \equiv $ **while** $N[q_2] = 1$ **do** $q_1 := X[q_1]$ **od**, where X is the Pauli matrix (i.e. the NOT gate), $N = \{N_0, N_1\}$, and

$$N_0 = \sum_{n=-\infty}^{0} |n\rangle\langle n|, \qquad N_1 = \sum_{n=1}^{\infty} |n\rangle\langle n|.$$

Let $\rho = |1\rangle_{q_1}\langle1| \otimes |-1\rangle_{q_2}\langle-1| \otimes \rho_0$ and

$$\rho_0 = \bigotimes_{q \neq q_1, q_2} |0\rangle_q\langle0|.$$

Then the computations of S starting in ρ are:

$$\langle S, \rho \rangle \to \langle q_2 := |0\rangle;\ q_1 := H[q_1];\ q_2 := q_2 + 7;\ \mathbf{if...fi}, \rho_1 \rangle$$
$$\to \langle q_1 := H[q_1];\ q_2 := q_2 + 7;\ \mathbf{if...fi}, \rho_2 \rangle$$
$$\to \langle q_2 := q_2 + 7;\ \mathbf{if...fi}, \rho_3 \rangle$$
$$\to \langle \mathbf{if...fi}, \rho_4 \rangle$$
$$\to \begin{cases} \langle S_1, \rho_5 \rangle \to \langle E, \rho_5 \rangle, \\ \langle S_2, \rho_6 \rangle, \end{cases}$$

$$\langle S_2, \rho_6 \rangle \to \langle q_1 := X[q_1];\ S_2, \rho_6 \rangle$$
$$\to \langle S_2, \rho_5 \rangle$$
$$\to \dots$$
$$\to \langle q_1 := X[q_1];\ S_2, \rho_6 \rangle \quad (\textit{after } 2n - 1 \textit{ transitions})$$
$$\to \langle S_2, \rho_5 \rangle$$
$$\to \dots$$

where:

$$\rho_1 = |0\rangle_{q_1}\langle 0| \otimes |-1\rangle_{q_2}\langle -1| \otimes \rho_0,$$
$$\rho_2 = |0\rangle_{q_1}\langle 0| \otimes |0\rangle_{q_2}\langle 0| \otimes \rho_0,$$
$$\rho_3 = |+\rangle_{q_1}\langle +| \otimes |0\rangle_{q_2}\langle 0| \otimes \rho_0,$$
$$\rho_4 = |+\rangle_{q_1}\langle +| \otimes |7\rangle_{q_2}\langle 7| \otimes \rho_0,$$
$$\rho_5 = \frac{1}{2}|0\rangle_{q_1}\langle 0| \otimes |7\rangle_{q_2}\langle 7| \otimes \rho_0,$$
$$\rho_6 = \frac{1}{2}|1\rangle_{q_1}\langle 1| \otimes |7\rangle_{q_2}\langle 7| \otimes \rho_0.$$

So, S can diverge from ρ. Note that S_2 has also the transition

$$\langle S_2, \rho_6 \rangle \to \langle E, 0_{\mathcal{H}_{all}} \rangle,$$

but we always discard the transitions in which the partial density operator of the target configuration is a zero operator.

Nondeterminism: To conclude this section, let us observe an interesting difference between the operational semantics of classical and quantum **while**-programs. Classical **while**-programs are a typical class of deterministic programs that have exactly one computation starting in a given state. (Here, if not only the conditional statement "**if** ...**then** ...**else**" but also the case statement (5.2) are included, then it is assumed that the guards $G_1, G_2, ..., G_n$ do not overlap to each other.) However, the above example showed that quantum **while**-programs no longer possess such a determinism because probabilism is introduced by the measurements in the statements "**if** $(\square m \cdot M[\overline{q}] = m \to S_m)$ **fi**" and "**while** $M[\overline{q}] = 1$ **do** S **od**". Essentially, the operational semantics $\to$ of quantum programs given in Definition 5.4 is a probabilistic transition relation. However, after encoding probabilities into partial density operators, probabilism manifests as nondeterminism in the transition rules (IF), (L0), and (L2). Therefore, semantics $\to$ should be understood as a nondeterministic transition relation.

5.3 Denotational semantics

We defined the operational semantics of quantum **while**-programs in the previous section. In this section, we turn to introduce their denotational semantics. The denotational semantics defines the meaning of a program as a mathematical object; for example, a (partial) function from its inputs to its outputs. It is particularly suitable for an abstract analysis of the properties of the program.

The denotational semantics of quantum **while**-programs can be defined based on their operational semantics, or more precisely on the notion of computation introduced in Definition 5.5. The denotational semantics of a quantum program is a semantic function which maps partial density operators to themselves. Intuitively, for any quantum program S, the semantic function of S maps an input ρ to the computed result of a terminating computation starting from configuration $\langle S, \rho \rangle$. However, due to the nondeterminism discussed at the end of last section, a quantum program with the input ρ can have different execution paths. Thus, the semantic function needs to sum up the computed results of all of these execution paths. To formally define it, let us introduce some notations. If configuration $\langle S', \rho' \rangle$ can be reached from $\langle S, \rho \rangle$ in n steps through the transition relation $\to$; that is, there are configurations $\langle S_1, \rho_1 \rangle, ..., \langle S_{n-1}, \rho_{n-1} \rangle$ such that

$$\langle S, \rho \rangle \to \langle S_1, \rho_1 \rangle \to \dots \to \langle S_{n-1}, \rho_{n-1} \rangle \to \langle S', \rho' \rangle,$$

then we write:

$$\langle S, \rho \rangle \to^n \langle S', \rho' \rangle.$$

Furthermore, we write $\rightarrow^*$ for the reflexive and transitive closures of $\rightarrow$; that is,

$$\langle S, \rho \rangle \rightarrow^* \langle S', \rho' \rangle$$

if and only if $\langle S, \rho \rangle \rightarrow^n \langle S', \rho' \rangle$ for some $n \geq 0$.

Definition 5.6. Let S be a quantum program. Then its semantic function

$$[\![S]\!] : \mathcal{D}(\mathcal{H}_{all}) \rightarrow \mathcal{D}(\mathcal{H}_{all})$$

is defined by

$$[\![S]\!](\rho) = \sum \left\{ |\rho' : \langle S, \rho \rangle \rightarrow^* \langle \downarrow, \rho' \rangle | \right\} \tag{5.8}$$

for all $\rho \in \mathcal{D}(\mathcal{H}_{all})$, where $\{| \cdot |\}$ stands for multiset; that is, a (generalised) set that allows multiple instances of an element.

The reason for using a multiset rather than an ordinary set in Eq. (5.8) is that the same partial density operator may be obtained through different computational paths as we can see from the rules (IF), (L0), and (L1) in the last section. The following simple example illustrates the case more explicitly.

Example 5.4 (Semantics of three quantum dials). Consider the probabilistic program *flip* and its quantum variant *qflip* in Example 5.1. A state of *flip* is a configuration of the slot machine, i.e. a mapping from dials to suits. The semantics of *flip* are a function that maps each initial state to a uniform distribution of states in which every configuration has probability $\frac{1}{8}$. The state Hilbert space of *qflip* is then $\mathcal{H}_2^{\otimes 3}$. For instance, if we write $|+\rangle = \frac{1}{\sqrt{2}}(|\heartsuit\rangle + |\diamondsuit\rangle)$ and $|-\rangle = \frac{1}{\sqrt{2}}(|\heartsuit\rangle - |\diamondsuit\rangle)$ for the equal superpositions of $|\heartsuit\rangle$ and $|\diamondsuit\rangle$, then $[\![qflip]\!](|+, -, +\rangle) = |\heartsuit, \diamondsuit, \heartsuit\rangle$; if we write

$$|W\rangle = \frac{1}{\sqrt{3}}(|\heartsuit, \heartsuit, \diamondsuit\rangle + |\heartsuit, \diamondsuit, \heartsuit\rangle + |\diamondsuit, \heartsuit, \heartsuit\rangle)$$

for the Werner state, a typical entangled state of three qubits, then

$$[\![qflip]\!](|W\rangle) = \frac{1}{2\sqrt{6}}(3|\heartsuit, \heartsuit, \heartsuit\rangle + |\heartsuit, \heartsuit, \diamondsuit\rangle + |\heartsuit, \diamondsuit, \heartsuit\rangle -$$
$$|\heartsuit, \diamondsuit, \diamondsuit\rangle + |\diamondsuit, \heartsuit, \heartsuit\rangle - |\diamondsuit, \heartsuit, \diamondsuit\rangle - |\diamondsuit, \diamondsuit, \heartsuit\rangle - 3|\diamondsuit, \diamondsuit, \diamondsuit\rangle).$$

Here, for simplicity, a pure state $|\psi\rangle$ is identified with the corresponding density operator $\rho = |\psi\rangle\langle\psi|$.

Example 5.5. Assume that $type(q) = \mathbf{Boolean}$. Consider the program:

$$S \equiv q := |0\rangle;\ q := H[q];\ \mathbf{if}\ M[q] = 0 \rightarrow S_0$$
$$\square \qquad\qquad 1 \rightarrow S_1$$
$$\mathbf{fi}$$

where:

- M is the measurement in the computational basis $|0\rangle, |1\rangle$ of the state space $\mathcal{H}_2$ of a qubit;
- $S_0 \equiv q := I[q]$ and $S_1 \equiv q := X[q]$ with I and X being the identity operator and the NOT gate, respectively.

Let $\rho = |0\rangle_{all}\langle 0|$, where

$$|0\rangle_{all} = \bigotimes_{q \in qVar} |0\rangle_q.$$

Then the computations of S starting in ρ are:

$$\langle S, \rho \rangle \rightarrow \langle q := H[q];\ \mathbf{if}...\mathbf{fi}, \rho \rangle$$
$$\rightarrow \langle \mathbf{if}...\mathbf{fi}, |+\rangle_q\langle +| \otimes \bigotimes_{p \neq q} |0\rangle_p\langle 0| \rangle$$
$$\rightarrow \begin{cases} \langle S_0, \frac{1}{2}|0\rangle_q\langle 0| \otimes \bigotimes_{p \neq q} |0\rangle_p\langle 0| \rangle \rightarrow \langle E, \frac{1}{2}\rho \rangle, \\ \langle S_1, \frac{1}{2}|1\rangle_q\langle 1| \otimes \bigotimes_{p \neq q} |0\rangle_p\langle 0| \rangle \rightarrow \langle E, \frac{1}{2}\rho \rangle. \end{cases}$$

So, we have:

$$[\![S]\!](\rho) = \frac{1}{2}\rho + \frac{1}{2}\rho = \rho.$$

5.3.1 Basic properties

As in classical programming theory and mentioned above, operational semantics is convenient for describing the execution of quantum programs. On the other hand, denotational semantics is suitable for studying mathematical properties of quantum programs. Now we establish several basic mathematical properties of semantic functions that are useful for reasoning about quantum programs.

First of all, we observe that the semantic function of any quantum program is linear. Of course, this linearity is inherited from the linearity of quantum mechanics.

Lemma 5.1 (Linearity). *Let $\rho_1, \rho_2 \in \mathcal{D}(\mathcal{H}_{all})$ and $\lambda_1, \lambda_2 \geq 0$. If $\lambda_1\rho_1 + \lambda_2\rho_2 \in \mathcal{D}(\mathcal{H}_{all})$, then for any quantum program S, we have:*

$$[\![S]\!](\lambda_1\rho_1 + \lambda_2\rho_2) = \lambda_1[\![S]\!](\rho_1) + \lambda_2[\![S]\!](\rho_2).$$

Proof. We can prove the following fact by induction on the structure of S:

• Claim: If $\langle S, \rho_1 \rangle \rightarrow \langle S', \rho_1' \rangle$ and $\langle S, \rho_2 \rangle \rightarrow \langle S', \rho_2' \rangle$, then

$$\langle S, \lambda_1\rho_1 + \lambda_2\rho_2 \rangle \rightarrow \langle S', \lambda_1\rho_1' + \lambda_2\rho_2' \rangle.$$

Then the conclusion immediately follows. □

Exercise 5.2. Prove the claim in the proof of Lemma 5.1.

Secondly, we present a structural representation for the semantic functions of quantum programs except **while**-loops. The structural representation enables that the semantics of a program be constructed from the semantics of its subprograms. The representation of the semantic function of a quantum loop requires some mathematical tools from lattice theory. So, it is postponed to Section 5.3.3 after we prepare the necessary tools in the next subsection.

Proposition 5.1 (Structural representation). **1.** $[\![\mathbf{skip}]\!](\rho) = \rho$.
2. a. *If $type(q) = $ **Boolean**, then*

$$[\![q := |0\rangle]\!](\rho) = |0\rangle_q\langle 0|\rho|0\rangle_q\langle 0| + |0\rangle_q\langle 1|\rho|1\rangle_q\langle 0|.$$

b. *If $type(q) = $ **integer**, then*

$$[\![q := |0\rangle]\!](\rho) = \sum_{n=-\infty}^{\infty} |0\rangle_q\langle n|\rho|n\rangle_q\langle 0|.$$

3. $[\![\overline{q} := U[\overline{q}]]\!](\rho) = U\rho U^\dagger$.
4. $[\![S_1; S_2]\!](\rho) = [\![S_2]\!]([\![S_1]\!](\rho))$.
5. $[\![\mathbf{if}\,(\square m \cdot M[\overline{q}] = m \rightarrow S_m)\,\mathbf{fi}]\!](\rho) = \sum_m [\![S_m]\!](M_m\rho M_m^\dagger)$.

Proof. Clauses 1, 2, and 3 are obvious.
Clause 4: By Lemma 5.1 and the rule (SC) we obtain:

$$[\![S_2]\!]([\![S_1]\!](\rho)) = [\![S_2]\!]\left(\sum\{|\rho_1 : \langle S_1, \rho \rangle \rightarrow^* \langle E, \rho_1 \rangle|\}\right)$$
$$= \sum\{|[\![S_2]\!](\rho_1) : \langle S_1, \rho \rangle \rightarrow^* \langle E, \rho_1 \rangle|\}$$
$$= \sum\left\{\left|\sum\{|\rho' : \langle S_2, \rho_1 \rangle \rightarrow^* \langle E, \rho' \rangle|\} : \langle S_1, \rho \rangle \rightarrow^* \langle E, \rho_1 \rangle\right|\right\}$$
$$= \sum\{|\rho' : \langle S_1, \rho \rangle \rightarrow^* \langle E, \rho_1 \rangle \text{ and } \langle S_2, \rho_1 \rangle \rightarrow^* \langle E, \rho' \rangle|\}$$
$$= \sum\{|\rho' : \langle S_1; S_2, \rho \rangle \rightarrow^* \langle E, \rho' \rangle|\}$$
$$= [\![S_1; S_2]\!](\rho).$$

Clause 5 follows immediately from the rule (IF). □

5.3.2 Quantum domains

Now we turn to consider the structural representation of the semantic function of a quantum **while**-loop. Before presenting such a representation, we have to pave the road toward it. In this subsection, we examine the domains of partial density operators and quantum operations. Within these domains, we can talk about the ordering between semantic functions and limits of them, which are exactly what we need in the representation of the semantics of a loop. The notions and lemmas presented in this subsection will also be used in Section 5.5 and Chapter 12 for more general recursions.

Basic lattice theory: We first review the requisite concepts from lattice theory. For more details, the reader can consult any textbook on semantics of programming languages; for example [407], Chapter 5.

Definition 5.7. A partial order is a pair $(L, \sqsubseteq)$ where L is a nonempty set and $\sqsubseteq$ is a binary relation on L satisfying the following conditions:

1. Reflexivity: $x \sqsubseteq x$ for all $x \in L$;
2. Antisymmetry: $x \sqsubseteq y$ and $y \sqsubseteq x$ imply $x = y$ for all $x, y \in L$;
3. Transitivity: $x \sqsubseteq y$ and $y \sqsubseteq z$ imply $x \sqsubseteq z$ for all $x, y, z \in L$.

Definition 5.8. Let $(L, \sqsubseteq)$ be a partial order.

1. An element $x \in L$ is called the least element of L when $x \sqsubseteq y$ for all $y \in L$. The least element is usually denoted by 0. Dually, we can define the greatest element 1.
2. An element $x \in L$ is called an upper bound of a subset $X \subseteq L$ if $y \sqsubseteq x$ for all $x \in X$.
3. x is called the least upper bound of X, written $x = \bigsqcup X$, if
   a. x is an upper bound of X;
   b. for any upper bound y of X, it holds that $x \sqsubseteq y$.
   Dually, we can define the greatest lower bound $\bigsqcap X$ of X.

We often write $x \sqcap y$ and $x \sqcup y$ for $\sqcap X$ and $\sqcup X$, respectively, when $X = \{x, y\}$. Also, we write $\bigsqcup_{n=0}^{\infty} x_n$ or $\bigsqcup_n x_n$ for $\bigsqcup X$ when X is a sequence $\{x_n\}_{n=0}^{\infty}$.

Definition 5.9. 1. A partial order $(L, \sqsubseteq)$ is called a lattice if $x \sqcap y$ and $x \sqcup y$ exist for any $x, y \in L$.
2. It is called a complete lattice if $\sqcap X$ and $\bigsqcup X$ exist for any $X \subseteq L$.

Definition 5.10. A complete partial order (CPO for short) is a partial order $(L, \sqsubseteq)$ satisfying the following conditions:

1. it has the least element 0;
2. $\bigsqcup_{n=0}^{\infty} x_n$ exists for any increasing sequence $\{x_n\}$ in L; i.e.

$$x_0 \sqsubseteq ... \sqsubseteq x_n \sqsubseteq x_{n+1} \sqsubseteq ....$$

Definition 5.11. Let $(L, \sqsubseteq)$ be a CPO. Then a function f from L into itself is said to be continuous if

$$f\left(\bigsqcup_n x_n\right) = \bigsqcup_n f(x_n)$$

for any increasing sequence $\{x_n\}$ in L.

The following theorem has been widely used in programming theory for the description of semantics of loops and recursive programs.

Theorem 5.1 (Knaster–Tarski). *Let $(L, \sqsubseteq)$ be a CPO and function $f : L \to L$ is continuous. Then f has the least fixed point*

$$\mu f = \bigsqcup_{n=0}^{\infty} f^{(n)}(0)$$

(i.e. $f(\mu f) = \mu f$, and if $f(x) = x$ then $\mu f \sqsubseteq x$), where

$$\begin{cases} f^{(0)}(0) = 0, \\ f^{(n+1)}(0) = f(f^{(n)}(0)) & \text{for } n \geq 0. \end{cases}$$

Exercise 5.3. Prove Theorem 5.1.

Domain of partial density operators: We now consider the lattice-theoretic structures of quantum objects required in the representation of quantum **while**-loops. Actually, we need to deal with two levels of quantum objects. At the lower level are partial density operators. Let $\mathcal{H}$ be an arbitrary Hilbert space. A partial order in the set $\mathcal{D}(\mathcal{H})$ of partial density operators was already introduced in Definition 2.13. Recall that the Löwner order is defined as follows: for any operators $A, B \in \mathcal{L}(\mathcal{H})$, $A \sqsubseteq B$ if $B - A$ is a positive operator. The lattice-theoretic property of $\mathcal{D}(\mathcal{H})$ equipped with the Löwner order $\sqsubseteq$ is revealed in the following:

Lemma 5.2. $(\mathcal{D}(\mathcal{H}), \sqsubseteq)$ *is a CPO with the zero operator $0_{\mathcal{H}}$ as its least element.*

Domain of quantum operations: We further consider the lattice-theoretic structure at the higher-level, namely the structure of quantum operations (see Definition 2.25).

Lemma 5.3. *Each quantum operation on a Hilbert space $\mathcal{H}$ is a continuous function from $(\mathcal{D}(\mathcal{H}), \sqsubseteq)$ into itself.*

We write $\mathcal{QO}(\mathcal{H})$ for the set of quantum operations on Hilbert space $\mathcal{H}$. Quantum operations should be considered as a class of quantum objects at a higher lever than partial density operators because $\mathcal{D}(\mathcal{H}) \subseteq \mathcal{L}(\mathcal{H})$, whereas $\mathcal{QO}(\mathcal{H}) \subseteq \mathcal{L}(\mathcal{L}(\mathcal{H}))$. The Löwner order between operators induces a partial order between quantum operations in a natural way: for any $\mathcal{E}, \mathcal{F} \in \mathcal{QO}(\mathcal{H})$,

- $\mathcal{E} \sqsubseteq \mathcal{F} \Leftrightarrow \mathcal{E}(\rho) \sqsubseteq \mathcal{F}(\rho)$ for all $\rho \in \mathcal{D}(\mathcal{H})$.

In a sense, the Löwner order is lifted from lower-level objects $\mathcal{D}(\mathcal{H})$ to higher-level objects $\mathcal{QO}(\mathcal{H})$.

Lemma 5.4. $(\mathcal{QO}(\mathcal{H}), \sqsubseteq)$ *is a CPO.*

The proofs of Lemmas 5.2, 5.3, and 5.4 are quite involved. For readability, they are all postponed to Section A.1.

5.3.3 Semantic functions of loops

Now we are ready to show that the semantic function of a quantum **while**-loop can be represented as the limit of the semantic functions of its finite syntactic approximations. To do this, we need an auxiliary notation of **abort**. It denotes a quantum program such that

$$\llbracket \textbf{abort} \rrbracket(\rho) = 0_{\mathcal{H}_{\text{all}}}$$

for all $\rho \in \mathcal{D}(\mathcal{H})$. Intuitively, program **abort** is never guaranteed to terminate; for example, we can choose

$$\textbf{abort} \equiv \textbf{while } M_{\text{trivial}}[q] = 1 \textbf{ do skip od},$$

where q is a quantum variable, and $M_{\text{trivial}} = \{M_0 = 0_{\mathcal{H}_q}, M_1 = I_{\mathcal{H}_q}\}$ is a trivial measurement in the state space $\mathcal{H}_q$. The program **abort** will serve as the basis for inductively defining the syntactic approximations of a quantum loop.

Definition 5.12. Consider a quantum loop

$$\textbf{while} \equiv \textbf{while } M[\overline{q}] = 1 \textbf{ do } S \textbf{ od}. \tag{5.9}$$

For any integer $k \geq 0$, the kth syntactic approximation $\textbf{while}^{(k)}$ of **while** is inductively defined by

$$
\left\{
\begin{array}{lll}
\textbf{while}^{(0)} & \equiv & \textbf{abort}, \\
\textbf{while}^{(k+1)} & \equiv & \textbf{if } M[\overline{q}] = 0 \rightarrow \textbf{skip} \\
& & \square \qquad\qquad 1 \rightarrow S; \textbf{while}^{(k)} \\
& \textbf{fi} &
\end{array}
\right.
$$

Intuitively, a loop **while** denotes an unbounded number of iterations, and its kth approximations model the first k steps of **while**. This observation leads us to a representation of the semantic function of a quantum **while**-loop presented in the following:

Proposition 5.2. *Let* **while** *be the loop (5.9). Then*

$$\llbracket \textbf{while} \rrbracket = \bigsqcup_{k=0}^{\infty} \llbracket \textbf{while}^{(k)} \rrbracket, \tag{5.10}$$

where **while**$^{(k)}$ *is the kth syntactic approximation of* **while** *for every $k \geq 0$, and the symbol $\bigsqcup$ stands for the supremum of quantum operations; i.e. the least upper bound in CPO $(\mathcal{QO}(\mathcal{H}_{all}), \sqsubseteq)$.*

Proof. For $i = 0, 1$, we introduce auxiliary operators

$$\mathcal{E}_i : \mathcal{D}(\mathcal{H}_{all}) \to \mathcal{D}(\mathcal{H}_{all})$$

defined by $\mathcal{E}_i(\rho) = M_i \rho M_i^{\dagger}$ for all $\rho \in \mathcal{D}(\mathcal{H})$.

First, we prove the following semantic representation of the kth approximation:

$$\llbracket \textbf{while}^{(k)} \rrbracket (\rho) = \sum_{n=0}^{k-1} \left[\mathcal{E}_0 \circ \left(\llbracket S \rrbracket \circ \mathcal{E}_1 \right)^n \right] (\rho)$$

for all $k \geq 1$ by induction on k. The symbol $\circ$ in the above equality stands for composition of quantum operations; that is, the composition $\mathcal{F} \circ \mathcal{E}$ of quantum operations $\mathcal{E}$ and $\mathcal{F}$ is defined by $(\mathcal{F} \circ \mathcal{E})(\rho) = \mathcal{F}(\mathcal{E}(\rho))$ for every $\rho \in \mathcal{D}(\mathcal{H})$. The case of $k = 1$ is obvious. Then by Proposition 5.1 (i), (iv), and (v) and the induction hypothesis on $k - 1$ we obtain:

$$\begin{aligned} \llbracket \textbf{while}^{(k)} \rrbracket (\rho) &= \llbracket \textbf{skip} \rrbracket (\mathcal{E}_0(\rho)) + \llbracket S; \textbf{while}^{(k-1)} \rrbracket (\mathcal{E}_1(\rho)) \\ &= \mathcal{E}_0(\rho) + \llbracket \textbf{while}^{(k-1)} \rrbracket ((\llbracket S \rrbracket \circ \mathcal{E}_1)(\rho)) \\ &= \mathcal{E}_0(\rho) + \sum_{n=0}^{k-2} \left[\mathcal{E}_0 \circ (\llbracket S \rrbracket \circ \mathcal{E}_1)^n \right] ((\llbracket S \rrbracket \circ \mathcal{E}_1)(\rho)) \\ &= \sum_{n=0}^{k-1} \left[\mathcal{E}_0 \circ (\llbracket S \rrbracket \circ \mathcal{E}_1)^n \right] (\rho). \end{aligned} \tag{5.11}$$

Secondly, we have the following expansion of the semantics of loop:

$$\begin{aligned} \llbracket \textbf{while} \rrbracket (\rho) &= \sum \left\{ |\rho' : \langle \textbf{while}, \rho \rangle \to^* \langle E, \rho' \rangle| \right\} \\ &= \sum_{k=1}^{\infty} \sum \left\{ |\rho' : \langle \textbf{while}, \rho \rangle \to^k \langle E, \rho' \rangle| \right\}. \end{aligned}$$

So, it suffices to show that

$$\sum \left\{ |\rho' : \langle \textbf{while}, \rho \rangle \to^k \langle E, \rho' \rangle| \right\} = \left[\mathcal{E}_0 \circ (\llbracket S \rrbracket \circ \mathcal{E}_1)^{k-1} \right] (\rho)$$

for all $k \geq 1$. By the previous points, it is not hard to prove this equality by induction on k. $\qquad \square$

Fixed point characterisation: From Eq. (5.10) and Theorem 5.1 (Knaster–Tarski), we see that $\llbracket \textbf{while} \rrbracket$ is essentially the least fixed point of a function from quantum operations $\mathcal{QO}(\mathcal{H}_{all})$ to themselves. Indeed, the following fixed point characterisation of the semantic function of a quantum loop can be derived from the above proposition.

Corollary 5.1. *Let* **while** *be the loop (5.9). Then for any $\rho \in \mathcal{D}(\mathcal{H}_{all})$, it holds that*

$$\llbracket \textbf{while} \rrbracket (\rho) = M_0 \rho M_0^{\dagger} + \llbracket \textbf{while} \rrbracket \left(\llbracket S \rrbracket \left(M_1 \rho M_1^{\dagger} \right) \right).$$

Proof. Immediate from Proposition 5.2 and Eq. (5.11). $\qquad \square$

The above corollary can be rephrased as follows. We introduce a function $\mathcal{F}$ from $\mathcal{QO}(\mathcal{H}_{all})$ to itself: for each $\mathcal{E} \in \mathcal{QO}(\mathcal{H}_{all})$, $\mathcal{F}(\mathcal{E})$ is defined by

$$\mathcal{F}(\mathcal{E})(\rho) = M_0 \rho M_0^{\dagger} + \mathcal{E}\left(\llbracket S \rrbracket \left(M_1 \rho M_1^{\dagger}\right)\right)$$

for all $\rho \in \mathcal{D}(\mathcal{H}_{all})$. Then $\llbracket \textbf{while} \rrbracket$ is a fixed point of $\mathcal{F}$.

5.3.4 Change and access of quantum variables

One key issue in understanding the behaviour of a program is to observe how it changes the states of program variables and how it accesses program variables during its execution. As the first application of the semantic function studied above, we now address this issue for quantum programs.

To simplify the presentation, we introduce an abbreviation. Let $X \subseteq qVar$ be a set of quantum variables. For any operator $A \in \mathcal{L}(\mathcal{H}_{all})$, we write:

$$tr_X(A) = tr_{\bigotimes_{q \in X} \mathcal{H}_q}(A)$$

where $tr_{\bigotimes_{q \in X} \mathcal{H}_q}$ is the partial trace over system $\bigotimes_{q \in X} \mathcal{H}_q$ (see Definition 2.22). Then we have:

Proposition 5.3. 1. $tr_{var(S)}(\llbracket S \rrbracket(\rho)) = tr_{var(S)}(\rho)$ *whenever* $tr(\llbracket S \rrbracket(\rho)) = tr(\rho)$.
2. *If it holds that*

$$tr_{qVar \setminus var(S)}(\rho_1) = tr_{qVar \setminus var(S)}(\rho_2),$$

then we have:

$$tr_{qVar \setminus var(S)}(\llbracket S \rrbracket(\rho_1)) = tr_{qVar \setminus var(S)}(\llbracket S \rrbracket(\rho_2)).$$

Recall from Definition 2.22 that $tr_X(\rho)$ describes the state of the quantum variables not in X when the global state of all quantum variables is ρ. So, the above proposition can be intuitively explained as follows:

- Proposition 5.3.1 indicates that the state of the quantum variables not in $var(S)$ after executing program S is the same as that before executing S. This means that program S can only change the state of quantum variables in $var(S)$.
- Proposition 5.3.2 shows that if two input states ρ_1 and ρ_2 coincide on the quantum variables in $var(S)$, then the computed outcomes of S, starting in ρ_1 and ρ_2, respectively, will also coincide on these quantum variables. In other words, if the output of program S with input ρ_1 is different from that with input ρ_2, then ρ_1 and ρ_2 must be different when restricted to $var(S)$. This means that program S can access at most the quantum variables in $var(S)$.

Exercise 5.4. Prove Proposition 5.3. [Hint: use the representation of semantic functions presented in Propositions 5.1 and 5.2.]

5.3.5 Termination and divergence

Another key issue about the behaviour of a program is its termination. The first consideration about this problem for quantum programs is based on the following proposition showing that a semantic function does not increase the trace of partial density operator of quantum variables.

Proposition 5.4. *For any quantum program S and for all partial density operators $\rho \in \mathcal{D}(\mathcal{H}_{all})$, it holds that*

$$tr(\llbracket S \rrbracket(\rho)) \le tr(\rho).$$

Proof. We proceed by induction on the structure of S.

- Case 1. $S \equiv \textbf{skip}$. Obvious.

- Case 2. $S \equiv q := |0\rangle$. If $type(q) = \textbf{integer}$, then using the equality $tr(AB) = tr(BA)$ we obtain:

$$
\begin{aligned}
tr([\![S]\!](\rho)) &= \sum_{n=-\infty}^{\infty} tr(|0\rangle_q \langle n|\rho|n\rangle_q \langle 0|) \\
&= \sum_{n=-\infty}^{\infty} tr(_q\langle 0|0\rangle_q \langle n|\rho|n\rangle_q) \\
&= tr\left[\left(\sum_{n=-\infty}^{\infty} |n\rangle_q \langle n| \right) \rho \right] = tr(\rho).
\end{aligned}
$$

It can be proved in a similar way when $type(q) = \textbf{Boolean}$.
- Case 3. $S \equiv \overline{q} := U[\overline{q}]$. Then

$$
tr([\![S]\!](\rho)) = tr\left(U\rho U^{\dagger} \right) = tr\left(U^{\dagger}U\rho \right) = tr(\rho).
$$

- Case 4. $S \equiv S_1; S_2$. It follows from the induction hypothesis on S_1 and S_2 that

$$
\begin{aligned}
tr([\![S]\!](\rho)) &= tr([\![S_2]\!]([\![S_1]\!](\rho))) \\
&\leq tr([\![S_1]\!](\rho)) \\
&\leq tr(\rho).
\end{aligned}
$$

- Case 5. $S \equiv \textbf{if } (\square m \cdot M[\overline{q}] = m \rightarrow S_m) \textbf{ fi}$. Then by induction hypothesis we obtain:

$$
\begin{aligned}
tr([\![S]\!](\rho)) &= \sum_m tr\left([\![S_m]\!]\left(M_m\rho M_m^{\dagger} \right) \right) \\
&\leq \sum_m tr\left(M_m\rho M_m^{\dagger} \right) \\
&= tr\left[\left(\sum_m M_m^{\dagger}M_m \right) \rho \right] = tr(\rho).
\end{aligned}
$$

- Case 6. $S \equiv \textbf{while } M[\overline{q}] = 1 \textbf{ do } S' \textbf{ od}$. We write $(\textbf{while}')^n$ for the statement obtained through replacing S by S' in $(\textbf{while})^n$ given in Definition 5.12. With Proposition 5.2, it suffices to show that

$$
tr\left([\![(\textbf{while}')^n]\!](\rho) \right) \leq tr(\rho)
$$

for all $n \geq 0$. This can be carried out by induction on n. The case of $n = 0$ is obvious. By the induction hypothesis on n and S', we have:

$$
\begin{aligned}
tr\left([\![(\textbf{while}')^{n+1}]\!](\rho) \right) &= tr\left(M_0\rho M_0^{\dagger} \right) + tr\left([\![(\textbf{while}')^n]\!]\left([\![S']\!]\left(M_1\rho M_1^{\dagger} \right) \right) \right) \\
&\leq tr\left(M_0\rho M_0^{\dagger} \right) + tr\left([\![S']\!]\left(M_1\rho M_1^{\dagger} \right) \right) \\
&\leq tr\left(M_0\rho M_0^{\dagger} \right) + tr\left(M_1\rho M_1^{\dagger} \right) \\
&= tr\left[\left(M_0^{\dagger}M_0 + M_1^{\dagger}M_1 \right) \rho \right] \\
&= tr(\rho). \qquad \square
\end{aligned}
$$

Intuitively, $tr([\![S]\!](\rho))$ is the probability that program S terminates when starting in state ρ. From the proof of the above proposition, we can see that the only program constructs that can cause $tr([\![S]\!](\rho)) < tr(\rho)$ are the loops occurring in S. Thus,

$$
tr(\rho) - tr([\![S]\!](\rho))
$$

is the probability that program S diverges from input state ρ. This can be further illustrated by the following example.

Example 5.6. Let $type(q) = $ **integer**, and let

$$M_0 = \sum_{n=1}^{\infty} \sqrt{\frac{n-1}{2n}} (|n\rangle\langle n| + |-n\rangle\langle -n|),$$

$$M_1 = |0\rangle\langle 0| + \sum_{n=1}^{\infty} \sqrt{\frac{n+1}{2n}} (|n\rangle\langle n| + |-n\rangle\langle -n|).$$

Then $M = \{M_0, M_1\}$ is a yes–no measurement in the state Hilbert space $\mathcal{H}_q$ (note that M is not a projective measurement). Consider the program:

$$\textbf{while} \equiv \textbf{while } M[q] = 1 \textbf{ do } q := q + 1 \textbf{ od}$$

Let $\rho = |0\rangle_q \langle 0| \otimes \rho_0$ with

$$\rho_0 = \bigotimes_{p \neq q} |0\rangle_p \langle 0|.$$

Then after some calculations we have:

$$[\![(\textbf{while})^n]\!](\rho) = \begin{cases} 0_{\mathcal{H}_{all}} & \text{if } n = 0, 1, 2, \\ \frac{1}{2}\left(\sum_{k=2}^{n-1} \frac{k-1}{k!} |k\rangle_q\langle k|\right) \otimes \rho_0 & \text{if } n \geq 3, \end{cases}$$

$$[\![\textbf{while}]\!](\rho) = \frac{1}{2}\left(\sum_{n=2}^{\infty} \frac{n-1}{n!} |n\rangle_q\langle n|\right) \otimes \rho_0$$

and

$$tr([\![\textbf{while}]\!](\rho)) = \frac{1}{2}\sum_{n=2}^{\infty} \frac{n-1}{n!} = \frac{1}{2}.$$

This means that program **while** terminates on input ρ with probability $\frac{1}{2}$, and it diverges from input ρ with probability $\frac{1}{2}$.

A more systematic study of termination of quantum programs will be presented in Chapter 8.

5.3.6 Semantic functions as quantum operations

To conclude this section, we establish a connection between quantum programs and quantum operations (see Section 2.6).

First, we recall from Definition 5.6 that the semantic function of a quantum program is defined to be a mapping from partial density operators on $\mathcal{H}_{all}$ to themselves. This fact can be refined by restricting these operators to the variables appearing in the program. To this end, let V be a subset of $qVar$. Whenever a quantum operation $\mathcal{E}$ in $\mathcal{H}_{all}$ is the cylindric extension of a quantum operation $\mathcal{F}$ in $\mathcal{H}_V = \bigotimes_{q \in V} \mathcal{H}_q$; that is,

$$\mathcal{E} = \mathcal{F} \otimes \mathcal{I}_{qVar \setminus V}$$

where $\mathcal{I}_{qVar \setminus V}$ is the identity quantum operation in $\mathcal{H}_{qVar \setminus V}$, we always identify $\mathcal{E}$ with $\mathcal{F}$, and $\mathcal{E}$ can be seen as a quantum operation in $\mathcal{H}_V$. With this convention, we have:

Proposition 5.5. *For any quantum program S, its semantic function $[\![S]\!]$ is a quantum operation on $\mathcal{H}_{var(S)}$.*

Proof. It can be proved by induction on the structure of S. For the case that S is not a loop, it follows from Theorem 2.3.3 and Proposition 5.1. For the case that S is a loop, it follows from Proposition 5.2 and Lemma 5.4. □

Conversely, one may ask: is every quantum operation can be modelled by a quantum program? If so, how can we do it? The answer to the first question is yes! To answer the second question, we need to first introduce the notion of local quantum variable. This notion will be also useful in other circumstances; for example in parallel quantum programming (Chapter 9) and linking quantum choice to probabilistic choice (Section 11.5.2).

Definition 5.13. Let S be a quantum program and $\overline{q}$ a sequence of quantum variables. Then:

1. The block command defined by S with local variables $\overline{q}$ is:

$$\textbf{begin local } \overline{q} : S \textbf{ end}. \tag{5.12}$$

2. The quantum variables of the block command are:

$$var (\textbf{begin local } \overline{q} : S \textbf{ end}) = var(S) \setminus \overline{q}.$$

3. The denotational semantics of the block command is the quantum operation from $\mathcal{H}_{var(S)}$ to $\mathcal{H}_{var(S) \setminus \overline{q}}$ defined by

$$[\![\textbf{begin local } \overline{q} : S \textbf{ end}]\!] (\rho) = tr_{\mathcal{H}_{\overline{q}}}([\![S]\!](\rho)) \tag{5.13}$$

for any density operator $\rho \in \mathcal{D}(\mathcal{H}_{var(S)})$, where $tr_{\mathcal{H}_{\overline{q}}}$ stands for the partial trace over $\mathcal{H}_{\overline{q}}$ (see Definition 2.22).

The intuitive meaning of block command (5.12) is that program S is running in the environment where $\overline{q}$ are local variables that will be initialised in S. After executing S, the auxiliary system denoted by the local variables $\overline{q}$ is discarded. This is why the trace over $\mathcal{H}_{\overline{q}}$ is taken in the defining Eq. (5.13) of the semantics of block command. Note that (5.13) is a partial density operator in $\mathcal{H}_{var(S) \setminus \overline{q}}$.

Every block command will be seen as a quantum program in the sequel. Then we are able to provide an answer to the second question raised above. The following proposition is essentially a restatement of Theorem 2.3.3 in terms of quantum programs.

Proposition 5.6. *For any finite subset V of qVar, and for any quantum operation $\mathcal{E}$ in $\mathcal{H}_V$, there exists a quantum program (more precisely, a block command) S such that $[\![S]\!] = \mathcal{E}$.*

Proof. By Theorem 2.3.2, there exist:

1. quantum variables $\overline{p} \subseteq qVar \setminus \overline{q}$,
2. a unitary transformation U in $\mathcal{H}_{\overline{p} \cup \overline{q}}$,
3. a projection P onto a closed subspace of $\mathcal{H}_{\overline{p} \cup \overline{q}}$, and
4. a state $|e_0\rangle$ in $\mathcal{H}_{\overline{p}}$

such that

$$\mathcal{E}(\rho) = tr_{\mathcal{H}_{\overline{p}}} \left[PU(|e_0\rangle \langle e_0| \otimes \rho)U^{\dagger} P \right]$$

for all $\rho \in \mathcal{D}(\mathcal{H}_{\overline{q}})$. Obviously, we can find a unitary operator U_0 in $\mathcal{H}_{\overline{p}}$ such that

$$|e_0\rangle = U_0|0\rangle_{\overline{p}}$$

where $|0\rangle_{\overline{p}} = |0\rangle...|0\rangle$ (all quantum variables in $\overline{p}$ are initialised in state $|0\rangle$). On the other hand,

$$M = \{M_0 = P, M_1 = I - P\}$$

is a yes–no measurement in $\mathcal{H}_{\overline{p} \cup \overline{q}}$, where I is the identity operator in $\mathcal{H}_{\overline{p} \cup \overline{q}}$. We set

$$S \equiv \textbf{begin local } \overline{p} : \overline{p} := |0\rangle_{\overline{p}};\ \overline{p} := U_0[\overline{p}];\ \overline{p} \cup \overline{q} := U[\overline{p} \cup \overline{q}];$$
$$\textbf{if } M[\overline{p} \cup \overline{q}] = 0 \rightarrow \textbf{skip}$$
$$\square \qquad\qquad 1 \rightarrow \textbf{abort}$$
$$\textbf{fi}$$

$$\textbf{end}$$

Then it is easy to check that $[\![S]\!] = \mathcal{E}$. $\qquad\square$

It is worth noting that if only a finite set of basic quantum gates are allowed to use in the programs, then the unitary U in the above proof can only be approximated by a series of circuits (see Theorem 3.2), and accordingly $\mathcal{E}$ can only be approximated by a series of programs.

- **Procedure:**

  1. $|0\rangle^{\otimes n}|1\rangle$

  2. $\xrightarrow{H^{\otimes(n+1)}} \dfrac{1}{\sqrt{2^n}} \displaystyle\sum_{x=0}^{2^n-1} |x\rangle|-\rangle = \left(\cos\dfrac{\theta}{2}|\alpha\rangle + \sin\dfrac{\theta}{2}|\beta\rangle \right)|-\rangle,$

  3. $\xrightarrow{G^k} \left[\cos\left(\dfrac{2k+1}{2}\theta\right)|\alpha\rangle + \sin\left(\dfrac{2k+1}{2}\theta\right)|\beta\rangle \right]|-\rangle$

  4. $\xrightarrow[\text{measure the first } n \text{ qubits in the computational basis}]{} |x\rangle|-\rangle$

FIGURE 5.3 Grover search algorithm.

5.4   Illustrative example: Grover search

The quantum **while**-language has been carefully studied in the previous sections. In order to illustrate its utility, in this section we use the quantum **while**-language to program the Grover search algorithm. A particularly natural example of quantum **while**-loop, namely quantum random walks with absorbing boundaries, will be discussed later in Section 8.4.1.

For convenience of the reader, let us first briefly recall the Grover algorithm from Section 4.4. The database searched by the algorithm consists of $N = 2^n$ elements, indexed by numbers $0, 1, ..., N - 1$. It is assumed that the search problem has exactly L solutions with $1 \leq L \leq \frac{N}{2}$, and we are supplied with an oracle – a black box with the ability to recognise solutions to the search problem. We identify an integer $x \in \{0, 1, ..., N - 1\}$ with its binary representation $x \in \{0, 1\}^n$. The oracle is represented by the unitary operator O on $n + 1$ qubits:

$$|x\rangle|q\rangle \xrightarrow{O} |x\rangle|q \oplus f(x)\rangle$$

for all $x \in \{0, 1\}^n$ and $q \in \{0, 1\}$, where $f : \{0, 1\}^n \to \{0, 1\}$ defined by

$$f(x) = \begin{cases} 1 & \text{if } x \text{ is a solution,} \\ 0 & \text{otherwise} \end{cases}$$

is the characteristic function of solutions. The Grover operator G consists of the following steps:

1. Apply the oracle O;
2. Apply the Hadamard transform $H^{\otimes n}$;
3. Perform a conditional phase shift Ph:

$$|0\rangle \to |0\rangle, \quad |x\rangle \to -|x\rangle \text{ for all } x \neq 0;$$

   that is $Ph = 2|0\rangle\langle 0| - I$.
4. Apply the Hadamard transform $H^{\otimes n}$ again.

A geometric intuition of operator G as a rotation was carefully described in Section 4.4. Employing the Grover operator, the search algorithm is described in Fig. 5.3, where the number k of iterations of the Grover operator is taken to be the positive integer in the interval $[\frac{\pi}{2\theta} - 1, \frac{\pi}{2\theta}]$, and θ is the angle rotated by the Grover operator and defined by the equation:

$$\cos\frac{\theta}{2} = \sqrt{\frac{N - L}{2}} \quad (0 \leq \frac{\theta}{2} \leq \frac{\pi}{2}).$$

Now we program the Grover algorithm in the quantum **while**-language. We use $n+2$ quantum variables: $q_0, q_1, ..., q_{n-1}, q, r$.

- Their types are as follows:

$$type(q_i) = type(q) = \textbf{Boolean} \ (0 \leq i < n),$$
$$type(r) = \textbf{integer}$$

- The variable r is introduced to count the number of iterations of the Grover operator. We use quantum variable r instead of a classical variable for this purpose since, for the reason of simplicity, classical variables are not included in the quantum **while**-language.

- **Program:**

  1. $q_0 := |0\rangle; \ q_1 := |0\rangle; \ ......; \ q_{n-1} := |0\rangle;$
  2. $q := |0\rangle;$
  3. $r := |0\rangle;$
  4. $q := X[q];$
  5. $q_0 := H[q_0]; \ q_1 := H[q_1]; \ ......; \ q_{n-1} := H[q_{n-1}];$
  6. $q := H[q];$
  7. **while** $M[r] = 1$ **do** D **od**;
  8. **if** $(\Box x \cdot M'[q_0, q_1, ..., q_{n-1}] = x \rightarrow$ **skip**$)$ **fi**

FIGURE 5.4 Quantum search program *Grover*.

- **Loop Body:**

  1. $q_0, q_1, ..., q_{n-1}, q := O[q_0, q_1, ..., q_{n-1}, q];$
  2. $q_0 := H[q_0]; \ q_1 := H[q_1]; \ ......; \ q_{n-1} := H[q_{n-1}];$
  3. $q_0, q_1, ..., q_{n-1} := Ph[q_0, q_1, ..., q_{n-1}];$
  4. $q_0 := H[q_0]; \ q_1 := H[q_1]; \ ......; \ q_{n-1} := H[q_{n-1}];$
  5. $r := r + 1$

FIGURE 5.5 Loop body D.

Then the Grover algorithm can be written as the program *Grover* in Fig. 5.4. Note that the size of the searched database is $N = 2^n$, so n in the program *Grover* should be understood as a metavariable. Several ingredients in *Grover* are specified as follows:

- The measurement $M = \{M_0, M_1\}$ in the loop guard (line 7) is given as follows:

$$M_0 = \sum_{l \geq k} |l\rangle_r \langle l|, \quad M_1 = \sum_{l < k} |l\rangle_r \langle l|$$

  with k being a positive integer in the interval $\left[\frac{\pi}{2\theta} - 1, \frac{\pi}{2\theta}\right]$;
- The loop body D (line 7) is given in Fig. 5.5;
- In the **if**...**fi** statement (line 8), N is the measurement in the computational basis of n qubits; that is,

$$M' = \left\{ M'_x : x \in \{0, 1\}^n \right\}$$

with $M'_x = |x\rangle\langle x|$ for every x.

The correctness of this program will be proved in the next chapter using the program logic developed there.

5.5 Classical recursion in quantum programming

The notion of recursion allows to program repetitive tasks without a large number of similar steps to be specified individually. In the previous sections, we have studied the quantum extension of **while**-language, which provides a program construct, namely quantum **while**-loop, to implement a special kind of recursion – iteration – in quantum computation. The general form of recursive procedure has widely used in classical programming. It renders a more powerful techniques than iteration, in which a function can be defined, directly or indirectly, in terms of itself. In this section, we add the general notion of recursion into the quantum **while**-language in order to specify procedures in quantum computation that can call themselves.

Recursive quantum programs versus quantum recursive programms: The notion of recursion considered in this section should be properly termed as *classical recursion in quantum programming* because the control flow within it is still classical, or more precisely, the control is determined by the outcomes of quantum measurements. The notion of recursion with quantum control flow will be introduced in Chapter 12. To avoid confusion, a quantum program containing recursion with classical control will be called a *recursive quantum program*, whereas a quantum program containing recursion with quantum control will be referred to as a *quantum recursive program*. With the mathematical tools prepared in Section 5.3.2, the theory of recursive quantum programs presented in this section is more or less a straightforward generalisation of the theory of classical recursive programs. However, as you will see in Chapter 12, the treatment of quantum recursive programs is much more difficult, and it requires some ideas that are radically different from those used in this section.

5.5.1 Syntax

We first define the syntax of recursive quantum programs. The alphabet of recursive quantum programs is the alphabet of quantum **while**-programs expanded by adding a set of procedure identifiers, ranged over by $X, X_1, X_2, ...$

Quantum program schemes are defined as generalised quantum **while**-programs that may contain procedure identifiers. Formally, we have:

Definition 5.14. Quantum program schemes are generated by the syntax:

$$
\begin{aligned}
S ::= \ & X \mid \mathbf{skip} \mid q := |0\rangle \mid \overline{q} := U[\overline{q}] \mid S_1; S_2 \\
& \mid \mathbf{if} \ (\square m \cdot M[\overline{q}] = m \to S_m) \ \mathbf{fi} \\
& \mid \mathbf{while} \ M[\overline{q}] = 1 \ \mathbf{do} \ S \ \mathbf{od}.
\end{aligned}
\tag{5.14}
$$

The only difference between the syntax (5.3) and (5.14) is that a clause for procedure identifiers X is added in the latter. If a program scheme S contains at most the procedure identifiers $X_1, ..., X_n$, then we write

$$ S \equiv S[X_1, ..., X_n]. $$

As in classical programming, procedure identifiers in a quantum program scheme are used as subprograms, which are usually called *procedure calls*. They are specified by declarations defined in the following:

Definition 5.15. Let $X_1, ..., X_n$ be different procedure identifiers. A declaration for $X_1, ..., X_n$ is a system of equations:

$$
D: \begin{cases}
X_1 \Leftarrow S_1, \\
\quad ...... \\
X_n \Leftarrow S_n,
\end{cases}
\tag{5.15}
$$

where for every $1 \le i \le n$, $S_i \equiv S_i[X_1, ..., X_n]$ is a quantum program scheme.

Now we are ready to introduce the key notion of this section.

Definition 5.16. A recursive quantum program consists of:

1. a quantum program scheme $S \equiv S[X_1, ..., X_n]$, called the main statement; and
2. a declaration D for $X_1, ..., X_n$.

5.5.2 Operational semantics

A recursive quantum program is a quantum program scheme together with a declaration of procedure identifiers within it. So, we first define the operational semantics of quantum program schemes with respect to a given declaration. To this end, we need to generalise the notion of configuration defined in Section 5.2 to include program schemes.

Definition 5.17. A quantum configuration is a pair $\langle S, \rho \rangle$, where:

1. S is a quantum program scheme or the empty program $\downarrow$;
2. $\rho \in \mathcal{D}(\mathcal{H}_{all})$ is a partial density operator in $\mathcal{H}_{all}$.

The above definition is the same as Definition 5.3 except that S is allowed to be not only a program but also a program scheme.

Now the operational semantics of quantum programs given in Definition 5.4 can be easily generalised to the case of quantum program schemes.

Definition 5.18. Let D be a given declaration. The operational semantics of quantum program schemes with respect to D is the transition relation $\to_D$ between quantum configurations defined by the transition rules in Fig. 5.1 together with the rule (REC) in Fig. 5.6 for recursion.

$$(\text{REC}) \quad \frac{}{\langle X_i, \rho \rangle \to_D \langle S_i, \rho \rangle} \quad \text{if } X_i \Leftarrow S_i \text{ is in the declaration } D.$$

FIGURE 5.6 Transition rule for recursive quantum programs.

Of course, when used in the above definition, the rules in Fig. 5.1 are extended by allowing program schemes to appear in configurations, and the transition symbol $\to$ is replaced by $\to_D$. As in classical programming, the rule (REC) in Fig. 5.6 can be referred to as the *copy rule*, meaning that at runtime a procedure call is treated like the procedure body inserted at the place of call.

5.5.3 Denotational semantics

Based on the operational semantics described in the last subsection, the denotational semantics of quantum program schemes can be easily defined by straightforward extending Definitions 5.5 and 5.6.

Definition 5.19. Let D be a given declaration. For any quantum program scheme S, its semantic function with respect to D is the mapping:

$$[\![S|D]\!] : \mathcal{D}(\mathcal{H}_{all}) \to \mathcal{D}(\mathcal{H}_{all})$$

defined by

$$[\![S|D]\!](\rho) = \sum \left\{ |\rho' : \langle S, \rho \rangle \to_D^* \langle \downarrow, \rho' \rangle| \right\}$$

for every $\rho \in \mathcal{D}(\mathcal{H}_{all})$, where $\to_D^*$ is the reflexive and transitive closure of $\to_D$.

Suppose that a recursive quantum program consists of the main statement S and declaration D. Then its denotational semantics is defined to be $[\![S|D]\!]$. Obviously, if S is a program (i.e. a program scheme that contains no procedure identifiers), then $[\![S|D]\!]$ does not depend on D and it coincides with Definition 5.6, and thus we can simply write $[\![S]\!]$ for $[\![S|D]\!]$.

Example 5.7. Consider the declaration

$$D : \begin{cases} X_1 \Leftarrow S_1, \\ X_2 \Leftarrow S_2 \end{cases}$$

where:

$$S_1 \equiv \textbf{if } M[q] = 0 \to q := H[q]; X_2$$
$$\square \qquad 1 \to \textbf{skip}$$
$$\textbf{fi}$$
$$S_2 \equiv \textbf{if } N[q] = 0 \to q := Z[q]; X_1$$
$$\square \qquad 1 \to \textbf{skip}$$
$$\textbf{fi}$$

q is a qubit variable, M is the measurement in the computational basis $|0\rangle, |1\rangle$ and N the measurement in the basis $|+\rangle, |-\rangle$; that is,

$$M = \{ M_0 = |0\rangle\langle 0|, M_1 = |1\rangle\langle 1| \},$$
$$N = \{ N_0 = |+\rangle\langle +|, N_1 = |-\rangle\langle -| \}.$$

Then the computations of recursive quantum program X_1 with declaration D starting in $\rho = |+\rangle\langle +|$ are:

$$\langle X_1, \rho \rangle \to_D \langle S_1, \rho \rangle$$

$$\to_D \begin{cases} \langle q := H[q]; X_2, \frac{1}{2}|0\rangle\langle 0| \rangle \to_D \langle X_2, \frac{1}{2}\rho \rangle, \\ \langle \textbf{skip}, \frac{1}{2}|1\rangle\langle 1| \rangle \to_D \langle E, \frac{1}{2}|1\rangle\langle 1| \rangle \end{cases}$$

where:

$$\langle X_2, \frac{1}{2}\rho\rangle \to_D \langle S_2, \frac{1}{2}\rho\rangle \to_D \langle q := Z[q]; X_1, \frac{1}{2}\rho\rangle \to_D \langle X_1, \frac{1}{2}|-\rangle\langle -|\rangle \to_D \dots.$$

and we have:

$$[\![X_1|D]\!](\rho) = \sum_{n=1}^{\infty} \frac{1}{2^n}|1\rangle\langle 1| = |1\rangle\langle 1|.$$

Quantum while-loops as recursions: Before moving forward to study various properties of general recursive programs, let us see how can a quantum **while**-loop discussed in the previous sections be treated as a special recursive quantum program. We consider the loop:

$$\text{\textbf{while}} \equiv \text{\textbf{while}}\ M[\overline{q}] = 1\ \text{\textbf{do}}\ S\ \text{\textbf{od}}.$$

Here S is a quantum program (containing no procedure identifiers). Let X be a procedure identifier with the declaration D:

$$X \Leftarrow \text{\textbf{if}}\ M[\overline{q}] = 0 \to \text{\textbf{skip}}$$
$$\square \qquad 1 \to S; X$$
$$\text{\textbf{fi}}$$

Then the quantum loop **while** is actually equivalent to the recursive quantum program with X as its main statement.

Exercise 5.5. Show that $[\![\text{\textbf{while}}]\!] = [\![X|D]\!]$.

Basic properties of semantic functions of recursive quantum programs: We now establish some basic properties of semantic functions of recursive quantum programs. The next proposition is a generalisation of Propositions 5.1 and 5.2 to quantum program schemes with respect to a declaration.

Proposition 5.7. *Let D be the declaration given by Eq. (5.15). Then for any $\rho \in \mathcal{D}(\mathcal{H}_{all})$, we have:*

1. $[\![X|D]\!](\rho) = \begin{cases} 0_{\mathcal{H}_{all}} & \text{if } X \notin \{X_1, ..., X_n\}, \\ [\![S_i|D]\!](\rho) & \text{if } X = X_i\ (1 \le i \le n); \end{cases}$
2. *if S is* **skip***, initialisation or unitary transformation, then $[\![S|D]\!](\rho) = [\![S]\!](\rho)$;*
3. $[\![T_1; T_2|D]\!](\rho) = [\![T_2|D]\!]([\![T_1|D]\!](\rho));$
4. $[\![\text{\textbf{if}}\ (\square m \cdot M[\overline{q}] = m \to T_m)\ \text{\textbf{fi}}|D]\!](\rho) = \sum_m [\![T_m|D]\!]\left(M_m \rho M_m^\dagger\right);$
5. $[\![\text{\textbf{while}}\ M[\overline{q}] = 1\ \text{\textbf{do}}\ S\ \text{\textbf{od}}|D]\!](\rho) = \bigsqcup_{k=0}^{\infty} [\![\text{\textbf{while}}^{(k)}|D]\!](\rho)$*, where* **while**$^{(k)}$ *is the kth syntactic approximation of the loop (see Definition 5.12) for every integer $k \ge 0$.*

Proof. Similar to the proofs of Propositions 5.1 and 5.2. $\square$

Proposition 5.7.5 can be further generalised so that the denotational semantics of a general recursive quantum program can also be expressed in terms of that of its syntactic approximations.

Definition 5.20. Consider the recursive quantum program with the main statement $S \equiv S[X_1, ..., X_m]$ and the declaration D given by Eq. (5.15). For any integer $k \ge 0$, the kth syntactic approximation $S_D^{(k)}$ of S with respect to D is inductively defined as follows:

$$\begin{cases} S_D^{(0)} & \equiv \text{\textbf{abort}}, \\ S_D^{(k+1)} & \equiv S\left[S_{1D}^{(k)}/X_1, ..., S_{nD}^{(k)}/X_n\right], \end{cases} \tag{5.16}$$

where **abort** is as in Section 5.3.3, and

$$S[P_1/X_1, ..., P_n/X_n]$$

stands for the result of simultaneous substitution of $X_1, ..., X_n$ by $P_1, ..., P_n$, respectively, in S.

It should be noticed that the above definition is given by induction on k with S being an arbitrary program scheme. Thus, $S_{1D}^{(k)}, ..., S_{nD}^{(k)}$ in Eq. (5.16) are assumed to be already defined in the induction hypothesis for k. It is clear that for all $k \geq 0$, $S_D^{(k)}$ is a program (containing no procedure identifiers). The following lemma clarifies the relationship of a substitution and a declaration when used to define the semantics of a program.

Lemma 5.5. *Let D be a declaration given by Eq. (5.15). Then for any program scheme S, we have:*

1. $[\![S|D]\!] = [\![S[S_1/X_1, ..., S_n/X_n]|D]\!]$.

2. $\left[\!\left[S_D^{(k+1)}\right]\!\right] = \left[\![S|D^{(k)}]\!\right]$ *for every integer $k \geq 0$, where declaration*

$$D^{(k)} = \begin{cases} X_1 \Leftarrow S_{1D}^{(k)}, \\ \quad ...... \\ X_n \Leftarrow S_{nD}^{(k)}. \end{cases}$$

Proof. Clause 1 can be proved by induction on the structure of S together with Proposition 5.7.

Clause 2: It follows from (i) that

$$\left[\!\left[S|D^{(k)}\right]\!\right] = \left[\!\left[S\left[S_{1D}^{(k)}/X_1, ..., S_{nD}^{(k)}/X_n\right]|D^{(k)}\right]\!\right]$$
$$= \left[\!\left[S\left[S_{1D}^{(k)}/X_1, ..., S_{nD}^{(k)}/X_n\right]\right]\!\right]$$
$$= \left[\!\left[S_D^{(k+1)}\right]\!\right].$$
$\square$

Based on the above lemma, we obtain a representation of the semantic function of a recursive quantum program by its syntactic approximations.

Proposition 5.8. *For any recursive program S with declaration D, we have:*

$$[\![S|D]\!] = \bigsqcup_{k=0}^{\infty} \left[\!\left[S_D^{(k)}\right]\!\right].$$

Proof. For any $\rho \in \mathcal{D}(\mathcal{H}_{all})$, we want to show that

$$[\![S|D]\!](\rho) = \bigsqcup_{k=0}^{\infty} \left[\!\left[S_D^{(k)}\right]\!\right](\rho).$$

It suffices to prove that for any integers $r, k \geq 0$, the following claims hold:

Claim 1: $\langle S, \rho \rangle \to_D^r \langle E, \rho' \rangle \Rightarrow \exists l \geq 0$ s.t. $\langle S_D^{(l)}, \rho \rangle \to^* \langle E, \rho' \rangle$.

Claim 2: $\langle S_D^{(k)}, \rho \rangle \to^r \langle E, \rho' \rangle \Rightarrow \langle S, \rho \rangle \to_D^* \langle E, \rho' \rangle$.

This can be done by induction on r, k and the depth of inference using the transition rules. $\square$

Exercise 5.6. Complete the proof of Proposition 5.8.

5.5.4   Fixed point characterisation

Proposition 5.8 can be seen as a generalisation of Proposition 5.2 via Proposition 5.7.5. A fixed point characterisation of quantum **while**-loop was given in Section 5.3.3 as a corollary of Proposition 5.2. In this section, we give a fixed point characterisation of recursive quantum programs and thus obtain a generalisation of Corollary 5.1. In classical programming theory, recursive equations are solved in a certain domain of functions. Here, we are going to solve recursive quantum equations in the domain of quantum operations defined in Section 5.3.2. To this end, we first introduce the following:

Definition 5.21. Let $S \equiv S[X_1, ..., X_n]$ be a quantum program scheme, and let $\mathcal{QO}(\mathcal{H}_{all})$ be the set of quantum operations in $\mathcal{H}_{all}$. Then its semantic functional is the mapping:

$$[\![S]\!] : \mathcal{QO}(\mathcal{H}_{all})^n \to \mathcal{QO}(\mathcal{H}_{all})$$

defined as follows: for any $\mathcal{E}_1, ..., \mathcal{E}_n \in \mathcal{QO}(\mathcal{H}_{all})$,

$$[\![S]\!](\mathcal{E}_1, ..., \mathcal{E}_n) = [\![S|E]\!]$$

where

$$E: \begin{cases} X_1 \Leftarrow T_1, \\ ...... \\ X_n \Leftarrow T_n \end{cases}$$

is a declaration such that for each $1 \leq i \leq n$, T_i is a program (containing no procedure identifiers) with $[\![T_i]\!] = \mathcal{E}_i$.

We argue that the semantic functional $[\![S]\!]$ is well-defined. It follows from Proposition 5.6 that the programs T_i always exist. On the other hand, if

$$E': \begin{cases} X_1 \Leftarrow T_1', \\ ...... \\ X_n \Leftarrow T_n' \end{cases}$$

is another declaration with each program T_i' satisfying $[\![T_i']\!] = \mathcal{E}_i$, then we can show that

$$[\![S|E]\!] = [\![S|E']\!].$$

Now we define the domain in which we are going to find a fixed point of the semantic functional defined by a declaration for procedure identifiers $X_1, ..., X_n$. Let us consider the cartesian power $\mathcal{QO}(\mathcal{H}_{all})^n$ of the CPO (Complete Partial Order) $\mathcal{QO}(\mathcal{H}_{all})$ (see Lemma 5.4). An order $\sqsubseteq$ in $\mathcal{QO}(\mathcal{H}_{all})^n$ is naturally induced by the order $\sqsubseteq$ in $\mathcal{QO}(\mathcal{H}_{all})$: for any $\mathcal{E}_1, ..., \mathcal{E}_n$, $\mathcal{F}_1, ..., \mathcal{F}_n \in \mathcal{QO}(\mathcal{H}_{all})$,

- $(\mathcal{E}_1, ..., \mathcal{E}_n) \sqsubseteq (\mathcal{F}_1, ..., \mathcal{F}_n) \Leftrightarrow$ for every $1 \leq i \leq n$, $\mathcal{E}_i \sqsubseteq \mathcal{F}_i$.

It follows from Lemma 5.4 that $(\mathcal{QO}(\mathcal{H}_{all})^n, \sqsubseteq)$ is a CPO too. Furthermore, we have:

Proposition 5.9. *For any quantum program scheme* $S \equiv S[X_1, ..., X_n]$, *its semantic functional*

$$[\![S]\!] : \left(\mathcal{QO}(\mathcal{H}_{all})^n, \sqsubseteq\right) \to (\mathcal{QO}(\mathcal{H}_{all}), \sqsubseteq)$$

is continuous.

Proof. For each $1 \leq i \leq n$, let $\{\mathcal{E}_{ij}\}_j$ be an increasing sequence in the CPO $(\mathcal{QO}(\mathcal{H}_{all}), \sqsubseteq)$. What we need to prove is the following equality:

$$[\![S]\!] \left(\bigsqcup_j \mathcal{E}_{1j}, ..., \bigsqcup_j \mathcal{E}_{nj} \right) = \bigsqcup_j [\![S]\!] (\mathcal{E}_{1j}, ..., \mathcal{E}_{nj}).$$

Suppose that

$$D: \begin{cases} X_1 \Leftarrow P_1, \\ ...... \\ X_n \Leftarrow P_n, \end{cases} \qquad D_j: \begin{cases} X_1 \Leftarrow P_{1j}, \\ ...... \\ X_n \Leftarrow P_{nj} \end{cases}$$

are two declarations such that

$$[\![P_i]\!] = \bigsqcup_j \mathcal{E}_{ij} \text{ and } [\![P_{ij}]\!] = \mathcal{E}_{ij}$$

for any $1 \leq i \leq n$ and for any j. Then it suffices to show that

$$[\![S|D]\!] = \bigsqcup_j [\![S|D_j]\!]. \tag{5.17}$$

Using Proposition 5.7, this can be done by induction on the structure of S. $\square$

Exercise 5.7. Prove Eq. (5.17).

Let D be the declaration given by Eq. (5.15). Then D naturally induces a semantic functional:

$$[\![D]\!] : \mathcal{QO}(\mathcal{H}_{all})^n \to \mathcal{QO}(\mathcal{H}_{all})^n$$

defined by

$$[\![D]\!](\mathcal{E}_1, ..., \mathcal{E}_n) = ([\![S_1]\!](\mathcal{E}_1, ..., \mathcal{E}_n), ..., [\![S_n]\!](\mathcal{E}_1, ..., \mathcal{E}_n))$$

for any $\mathcal{E}_1, ..., \mathcal{E}_n \in \mathcal{QO}(\mathcal{H}_{all})$. It follows from Proposition 5.9 that

$$[\![D]\!] : (\mathcal{QO}(\mathcal{H}_{all})^n, \sqsubseteq) \to (\mathcal{QO}(\mathcal{H}_{all})^n, \sqsubseteq)$$

is continuous. Then by Knaster–Tarski theorem (Theorem 5.1) we assert that $[\![D]\!]$ has a fixed point:

$$\mu[\![D]\!] = (\mathcal{E}_1^*, ..., \mathcal{E}_n^*) \in \mathcal{QO}(\mathcal{H}_{all})^n.$$

We now are able to present the fixed point characterisation of recursive quantum programs:

Theorem 5.2. *For the recursive quantum program with the main statement S and the declaration D, we have:*

$$[\![S|D]\!] = [\![S]\!](\mu[\![D]\!]) = [\![S]\!](\mathcal{E}_1^*, ..., \mathcal{E}_n^*).$$

Proof. First of all, we claim that for any program scheme $T \equiv T[X_1, ..., X_n]$ and for any programs $T_1, ..., T_n$,

$$[\![T[T_1/X_1, ..., T_n/X_n]]\!] = [\![T]\!]([\![T_1]\!], ..., [\![T_n]\!]). \tag{5.18}$$

In fact, let us consider the declaration

$$E : \begin{cases} X_1 \Leftarrow T_1, \\ \qquad ...... \\ X_n \Leftarrow T_n. \end{cases}$$

Then by Definition 5.21 and Lemma 5.5 (i) we obtain:

$$\begin{aligned} [\![T]\!]([\![T_1]\!], ..., [\![T_n]\!]) &= [\![T|E]\!] = [\![T[T_1/X_1, ..., T_n/X_n]|E]\!] \\ &= [\![T[T_1/X_1, ..., T_n/X_n]]\!] \end{aligned}$$

because $T_1, ..., T_n$ are all programs (without procedure identifiers).

Secondly, we define the iteration of $[\![D]\!]$, starting from the least element $\overline{\mathbf{0}} = (\mathbf{0}, ..., \mathbf{0})$ in $\mathcal{QO}(\mathcal{H}_{all})^n$, as follows:

$$\begin{cases} [\![D]\!]^{(0)}(\overline{\mathbf{0}}) = (\mathbf{0}, ..., \mathbf{0}), \\ [\![D]\!]^{(k+1)}(\overline{\mathbf{0}}) = [\![D]\!]\left([\![D]\!]^{(k)}(\overline{\mathbf{0}})\right) \end{cases}$$

where $\mathbf{0}$ is the zero quantum operation in $\mathcal{H}_{all}$. Then it holds that

$$[\![D]\!]^{(k)}(\overline{\mathbf{0}}) = \left([\![S_{1D}^{(k)}]\!], ..., [\![S_{nD}^{(k)}]\!]\right) \tag{5.19}$$

for every integer $k \geq 0$. Eq. (5.19) can be proved by induction on k. Indeed, the case of $k = 0$ is obvious. The induction hypothesis for k together with Eq. (5.18) yields:

$$\begin{aligned} [\![D]\!]^{(k+1)}(\overline{\mathbf{0}}) &= [\![D]\!]\left([\![S_{1D}^{(k)}]\!], ..., [\![S_{nD}^{(k)}]\!]\right) \\ &= \left([\![S_1]\!]\left([\![S_{1D}^{(k)}]\!], ..., [\![S_{nD}^{(k)}]\!]\right), ..., [\![S_n]\!]\left([\![S_{1D}^{(k)}]\!], ..., [\![S_{nD}^{(k)}]\!]\right)\right) \\ &= \left([\![S_1[S_{1D}^{(k)}/X_1, ..., S_{nD}^{(k)}/X_n]]\!], ..., [\![S_n[S_{1D}^{(k)}/X_1, ..., S_{nD}^{(k)}/X_n]]\!]\right) \\ &= \left([\![S_{1D}^{(k+1)}]\!], ..., [\![S_{nD}^{(k+1)}]\!]\right). \end{aligned}$$

Finally, using Eq. (5.18), Proposition 5.9, the Knaster-Tarski Theorem and Proposition 5.5.3, we obtain:

$$[\![S]\!]\,(\mu\,[\![D]\!]) = [\![S]\!]\left(\bigsqcup_{k=0}^{\infty}[\![D]\!]^{(k)}\left(\overline{\mathbf{0}}\right)\right)$$

$$= [\![S]\!]\left(\bigsqcup_{k=0}^{\infty}\left(\left[\!\left[S_{1D}^{(k)}\right]\!\right],...,\left[\!\left[S_{nD}^{(k)}\right]\!\right]\right)\right)$$

$$= \bigsqcup_{k=0}^{\infty}[\![S]\!]\left(\left[\!\left[S_{1D}^{(k)}\right]\!\right],...,\left[\!\left[S_{nD}^{(k)}\right]\!\right]\right)$$

$$= \bigsqcup_{k=0}^{\infty}\left[\!\left[S\left[S_{1D}^{(k)},...,S_{nD}^{(k)}\right]\right]\!\right]$$

$$= \bigsqcup_{k=0}^{\infty}\left[\!\left[S_{D}^{(k+1)}\right]\!\right]$$

$$= [\![S|D]\!].\qquad\qquad\square$$

To conclude this section, we leave the following two problems for the reader. As pointed out at the beginning of this section, the materials presented in this section are similar to the theory of classical recursive programs, but I believe that research on these two problems will reveal some interesting and subtle differences between recursive quantum programs and classical recursive programs.

Problem 5.1. 1. Can a general measurement in a recursive quantum program be implemented by a projective measurement together with a unitary transformation? If the program contains no recursions (and no loops), then this question was already answered by Proposition 2.1.
2. How can a measurement in a quantum program be deferred? For the case that the program contains no recursions (and no loops), this question was answered by the principle of deferred measurement in Section 3.1.6. The interesting case is a program with recursions or loops.

Problem 5.2. Only recursive quantum programs without parameters are considered in this section. How to define recursive quantum programs with parameters and their semantics? We will have to deal with two different kinds of parameters:

1. classical parameters;
2. quantum parameters.

Problem 5.2 is widely open. Here, let us consider an interesting example of recursive quantum programs with classical parameters from physics [384]:

Example 5.8 (Lie–Trotter–Suzuki formula for simulation of Hamiltonian). The Hamiltonian of most physical systems can be written as a sum over local interactions: $H = \sum_{j=1}^{m} H_j$. It was proved in [384] that the solution $U(t) = e^{-iHt}$ of Schrödinger equation

$$\frac{d|\psi\rangle}{dt} = -iH|\psi\rangle$$

can be approximated as follows:

$$e^{-iHt} \approx S_\chi(t)$$

where product S_χ is recursively defined for integers $\chi > 0$:

$$S_1(t) = \prod_{j=1}^{m} e^{-iH_j t/2} \prod_{j=1}^{m} e^{-iH_{m-j+1}t/2}$$

$$S_\chi(t) = \left(S_{\chi-1}(\gamma_{\chi-1}t)\right)^2 S_{\chi-1}\left([1-4\gamma_{\chi-1}t]\right)\left(S_{\chi-1}(\gamma_{\chi-1}t)\right)^2$$

where $\gamma_k = \left(4 - 4^{1/(2k+1)}\right)^{-1}$ is chosen to ensure that the Taylor series of S_χ match that of $U(t)$ to $O\left(t^{2\chi+1}\right)$. Thus, the approximation of $U(t)$ by $S_\chi(t)$ can be made arbitrarily accurate for large value of χ and small value of t. Note that each

e^{iH_jt} acts on a small subsystem and thus can be easily approximated using quantum circuits. Then it is convenient to write the simulation algorithm of $U(t)$ via $S_\chi(t)$ as a recursive quantum program with classical parameters.

Bernstein–Vazirani recursive Fourier sampling [1,58,59] and Grover fixed point quantum search [190] are two more examples of recursive quantum programs with parameters.

5.6 Adding classical variables

As the reader should already noticed, all programs considered in this chapter (and indeed in the whole book, only with a few exceptions) are purely quantum in the sense that they contain only quantum variables but not any classical variables. Since any classical computation can be simulated by a quantum computation, the quantum programming language defined in this chapter is computationally universal (Turing complete). The reason for choosing to focus on purely quantum programs in this book is that it makes the presentation much simpler and more elegant. On the other hand, almost all interesting quantum algorithms involve certain classical computations. Therefore, for practical applications, it is desirable to include both classical and quantum variables in a quantum programming language. Fortunately, it is usually not difficult to extend results about purely quantum programs to classical-quantum hybrid programs, as evidenced in the literature (see for example, [125,155,367,427]).

5.7 Bibliographic remarks and further readings

First of all, it should be pointed out that this chapter is essentially the quantum generalisation of semantics of the classical **while**-programs and recursive programs as presented by Apt, de Boer, and Olderog in [28].

The quantum **while**-language presented in Section 5.1 was defined in [419], but various quantum program constructs in it were introduced in the previous works by Sanders and Zuliani [361,455,457,458] and Selinger [367] among others. A general form of quantum **while**-loops was introduced and their properties were thoroughly investigated in [426]. A discussion about the existing quantum programming languages was already given in Section 1.1.1; it is worth comparing the quantum programming language described in this chapter with the languages mentioned there. Recently, a class of interesting **while**-loops based on weak measurements were defined by Andrés-Martínez and Heunen in [26].

The presentation of operational and denotational semantics in Sections 5.2 and 5.3 is mainly based on [419]. The denotational semantics was actually first given by Feng et al. in [146], but the treatments of denotational semantics in [146] and [419] are different: in [146], the denotational semantics is directly defined, whereas in [419], the operational semantics comes first and then the denotational semantics is derived from the operational semantics. The idea of encoding a probability and a density operator into a partial density operator in the transition rules was suggested by Selinger [367]. A domain theory for quantum computation was first considered by Kashefi [241]. It was significantly extended by Rennela [351] using a category of operator algebras. Lemmas 5.2 and 5.4 were obtained by Selinger [367] in the case of finite-dimensional Hilbert spaces. The proof of Lemma 5.2 for the general case was given in [424], and it is essentially a modification of the proof of Theorem III.6.2 in [344]. A form of Proposition 5.6 was first presented by Selinger in [367]. The current statement of Proposition 5.6 is given based on the notion of local quantum variable, which was introduced in [434].

Recursion in quantum programming was first considered by Selinger in [367]. But the materials presented in Section 5.5 are slightly different from those in [367] and unpublished elsewhere.

Finally, it is worth mentioning several related works published very recently. A structured theorem for quantum programs was established by Yu [441], showing that every flowchart quantum program can be translated to a quantum **while**-program. In the last few years, variational quantum algorithms and quantum machine learning has emerged rapidly and are believed to one of the first and leading applications of quantum computing. To provide appropriate programming models for them, a parametrised extension of quantum **while**-language was defined and differential programming techniques were introduced by Zhu et al. [454] and Fang et al. [143].

Chapter 6

Quantum Hoare logic

A simple quantum programming language, namely quantum **while**-language, was defined in Chapters 5 to write sequential quantum programs with classical control. It was shown by several examples to be convenient to program some quantum algorithms.

As is well-known, programming is error-prone. It is even worse to program a quantum computer because human intuition is much better adapted to the classical world than to the quantum world. Thus, it is critical to develop methodologies and techniques for verification of quantum programs.

Hoare logic, also known as **Floyd–Hoare logic**, is a logical system for reasoning about correctness of classical **while**-programs (see (5.1) for their syntax). It was proposed by Hoare in [208], based on the idea of inductive assertions method developed by Floyd in [158] for proving correctness of flowchart programs. Hoare logic introduces a natural way for specifying correctness of classical programs, namely a Hoare triple of the form

$$\{P\}S\{Q\} \tag{6.1}$$

where P and Q are predicates or assertions about the program variables, and they are called the precondition and postcondition, respectively. Intuitively, Hoare tripe (6.1) means that when an input satisfies precondition P, executing program S upon it establishes postcondition Q. Then with a set of inference rules for proving Hoare triples, each designed for a basic program construct, Hoare logic provides a syntax-oriented, compositional technique for verifying correctness of classical programs.

In this chapter, we define a Hoare-style logic for reasoning about correctness of quantum **while**-programs and thus build a logical foundation for verification of quantum programs. This chapter consists of the following parts:

- The first step to develop a logic for quantum programs is to define the notion of quantum predicate that can properly describe properties of quantum systems and thus can serve as the precondition and postcondition of a Hoare triple for a quantum program. We introduce the notion of quantum predicate as a physical observable in Section 6.1.
- Based on Section 6.1, we define correctness formulas (i.e. Hoare triples) for quantum programs in Section 6.2. The notion of weakest precondition is further introduced for quantum programs in Section 6.3. With these preparations, we develop a logic of the Hoare style for partial and total correctness of quantum programs in Sections 6.4 and 6.5, respectively, where soundness and (relative) completeness of such a logic are proved. An example is presented in Section 6.6 to show how can quantum Hoare logic be used in verification of quantum programs.

A logic for quantum programs is not a straightforward extension of the corresponding logic for classical programs. We have to carefully consider how can various quantum features be incorporated into a logical system. It is well-known that a distinctive feature between classical and quantum systems is noncommutativity of observables about quantum systems. Section 6.1.2 is devoted to examine (non)commutativity of quantum weakest preconditions. We will see the influence of other quantum features on quantum program logics in the later chapters; for example, that of entanglement on a logic for parallel quantum programs in Chapter 9.

6.1 Quantum predicates

As said above, the central idea of Hoare logic is to use a Hoare triple of the form (6.1) for specifying the correctness of a program, with both precondition P and postcondition Q being predicates (also called assertions) about the program variables. So in this section, we define the notion of quantum predicate.

In classical logic, a predicate is used to describe a property of an individual (often called a proposition) or a relation of several individuals. Then what is a quantum predicate? This problem has been carefully considered in Birkhoff–von Neumann quantum logic [66] and its various extensions [115].

Quantum predicates as subspaces: Let us start from seeing how we can describe a proposition about a quantum system. A piece of information about a physical system is called a *state* of the system. In classical physics, a state of a

Foundations of Quantum Programming. https://doi.org/10.1016/B978-0-44-315942-8.00016-2

system is usually described by a real vector, say an n-dimensional vector $\omega = (x_1, ..., x_n)$ with all x_i being real numbers, and the *state space* Ω of the system is then the n-dimensional real vector space. A *proposition* about a classical system asserts that a physical *observable* has a certain value, and thus determines a subset $X \subseteq \Omega$ in which the proposition holds. Thus, a state $\omega \in \Omega$ satisfies a proposition X, written $\omega \models X$, if and only if $\omega \in X$.

According to the basic postulates of quantum mechanics, however, a *state* of a quantum system is represented by a complex vector $|\psi\rangle$ (in Dirac's notation), and the *state space* of the system is a Hilbert space $\mathcal{H}$, i.e. a complex vector space equipped with an inner product $\langle \cdot | \cdot \rangle$ (satisfying certain completeness in the infinite-dimensional case). Then a *proposition* asserting that a physical *observable* has a certain value is mathematically represented by a closed subspace X of $\mathcal{H}$. A basic difference between a classical proposition and a quantum proposition is that the former can be an arbitrary subset of the state space, whereas the latter must be a closed subspace; that is, those subsets of $\mathcal{H}$ closed under linear combination (and limit whenever $\mathcal{H}$ is infinite-dimensional). Moreover, different from classical physics, quantum physical laws are essentially statistical. For any $|\psi\rangle \in \mathcal{H}$ and $X \in \mathcal{P}$, the probability that the system in state $|\psi\rangle$ satisfies proposition X is computed using Born's rule:

$$\text{Prob}(|\psi\rangle \models X) = \langle \psi | P_X | \psi \rangle,$$

where P_X is the projection onto closed subspace X. In particular, $\text{Prob}(|\psi\rangle \models X) = 1$ if and only if $|\psi\rangle \in X$.

The above idea is indeed the starting point of Birkhoff–von Neumann logic, which will be further discussed in Section 7.3.

Quantum predicates as Hermitian operators: The above idea can be generalised to that a quantum predicate should be a physical observable. Recall from Section 2.3 that an observable of a quantum system is expressed by a Hermitian operator M on its state Hilbert space $\mathcal{H}$. At this moment, for simplicity, we assume that $\mathcal{H}$ is finite-dimensional. If $\lambda \in \mathbb{C}$ and a nonzero vector $|\psi\rangle \in \mathcal{H}$ satisfy

$$M|\psi\rangle = \lambda|\psi\rangle,$$

then λ is called an eigenvalue of M and $|\psi\rangle$ the eigenvector of M corresponding to λ. It turns out that all eigenvalues of M are real numbers. We write $spec(M)$ for the set of eigenvalues of M – the (point) spectrum of M. For each eigenvalue $\lambda \in spec(M)$, the eigenspace of M corresponding to λ is the (closed) subspace

$$X_\lambda = \{|\psi\rangle \in \mathcal{H} : A|\psi\rangle = \lambda|\psi\rangle\}.$$

In order to see what should be a quantum predicate, let us first consider a special class of quantum observables (Hermitian operators), namely projections. Historically, Birkhoff–von Neumann quantum logic is the first logic for reasoning about the properties of quantum systems. As discussed above, one of its basic ideas is that a proposition about a quantum system can be modelled by a (closed) subspace X of the system's state Hilbert space $\mathcal{H}$. The subspace X can be seen as the eigenspace of the projection P_X (see Definition 2.10) corresponding to eigenvalue 1, and eigenvalue 1 can be understood as the truth value of the proposition modelled by X.

Extending the above idea, whenever an observable (a Hermitian operator) M is considered as a quantum predicate, its eigenvalue λ should be understood as the truth value of the proposition described by the eigenspace X_λ. Note that the truth value of a classical proposition is either 0 (false) or 1 (true), and the truth value of a probabilistic proposition is given as a real number between 0 and 1. This observation leads to the following:

Definition 6.1. A quantum predicate in a Hilbert space $\mathcal{H}$ is a Hermitian operator M on $\mathcal{H}$ with all its eigenvalues lying within the unit interval $[0, 1]$.

Let the set of predicates in $\mathcal{H}$ be denoted $\mathcal{P}(\mathcal{H})$. The state space $\mathcal{H}$ in the above definition and the following development can be infinite-dimensional unless it is explicitly stated to be finite-dimensional, although for simplicity, we assumed it is finite-dimensional in the discussion at the beginning of this section.

Satisfaction of quantum predicates: Now we consider how can a quantum state satisfy a quantum predicate. Recall from Exercise 2.8 that $tr(M\rho)$ is the expectation value of measurement outcomes when a quantum system is in the mixed state ρ and we perform the projective measurement determined by observable M on it. Now if M is seen as a quantum predicate, then $tr(M\rho)$ may be interpreted as the degree to which quantum state ρ satisfies quantum predicate M, or more precisely the average truth value of the proposition represented by M in a quantum system of the state ρ. The reasonableness of the above definition is further indicated by the following fact:

Lemma 6.1. *Let M be a Hermitian operator on $\mathcal{H}$. Then the following statements are equivalent:*

1. $M \in \mathcal{P}(\mathcal{H})$ *is a quantum predicate.*
2. $0_{\mathcal{H}} \sqsubseteq M \sqsubseteq I_{\mathcal{H}}$, *where* $0_{\mathcal{H}}$, $I_{\mathcal{H}}$ *are the zero and identity operators on* $\mathcal{H}$, *respectively.*
3. $0 \leq tr(M\rho) \leq 1$ *for all density operators* ρ *in* $\mathcal{H}$.

Intuitively, clause 3 in the above lemma means that the satisfaction degree of a quantum predicate M by a quantum state ρ is always in the unit interval.

An operator M satisfying $0_{\mathcal{H}} \sqsubseteq M \sqsubseteq I_{\mathcal{H}}$ (and thus a quantum predicate) is commonly called an effect in the literature of quantum logic and quantum foundations. We will discuss the algebra and logic of effects in more detail in Section 7.3.4.

Exercise 6.1. Prove Lemma 6.1

The following two lemmas show some basic properties of quantum predicates that will be frequently used in this chapter. The first one gives a characterisation of the Löwner order between quantum predicates in terms of satisfaction degrees.

Lemma 6.2. *For any observables M, N, the following two statements are equivalent:*

1. $M \sqsubseteq N$;
2. *for all density operators* ρ, $tr(M\rho) \leq tr(N\rho)$.

Exercise 6.2. Prove Lemma 6.2.

Furthermore, the next lemma examines the lattice-theoretic structure of quantum predicates with respect to the Löwner partial order.

Lemma 6.3. *The set* $(\mathcal{P}(\mathcal{H}), \sqsubseteq)$ *of quantum predicates with the Löwner partial order is a complete partial order (CPO) (see Definition 5.10).*

Proof. Similar to the proof of Proposition 5.2. $\square$

It is worthy to point out that $(\mathcal{P}(\mathcal{H}), \sqsubseteq)$ is not a lattice except in the trivial case of one-dimensional state space $\mathcal{H}$; that is, the greatest lower bound and least upper bound of elements in $(\mathcal{P}(\mathcal{H}), \sqsubseteq)$ are not always defined. This fact has serious implications to logical reasoning about quantum programs where a conjunction of several propositions (i.e. predicates) is need; for example, the inference rule for parallel composition of quantum programs (i.e. the Owicki–Gries verification method for parallel quantum programs) with shared variables in Chapter 9.

Quantum relations: In classical logic, a property about a single individual is referred as a unary predicate, and an n-ary predicate is a relation among n individuals. We can classify quantum predicates in the same way. A unary quantum predicate is an observable on a single quantum system. A quantum predicate about n quantum systems q_i with state spaces $\mathcal{H}_{q_i}$ $(i = 1, ..., n)$; i.e. an observable (between the zero and identity operators) on the tensor product $\bigotimes_{i=1}^{n} \mathcal{H}_{q_i}$, can be understood as an n-ary quantum relation among $q_1, ..., q_n$. We will present some examples of quantum relations used in specifying the correctness of quantum programs in the next section.

Some important concepts in relational algebra can be generalised to the quantum case. Recall that if $R_1 \subseteq X_0 \times X_1$ and $R_2 \subseteq X_1 \times X_2$ are two binary relations, then their composition $R_1 \circ R_2 \subseteq X_0 \times X_2$ is defined by

$$x_0 (R_1 \circ R_2) x_2 \text{ iff } x_0 R_1 x_1 \text{ and } x_1 R_2 x_2 \text{ for some } x_1 \in X_1.$$

Let $R \subseteq X \times X$ be a relation between X and itself. Then its reflexive and transitive closure is defined as

$$t(R) = \bigcup_{i=0}^{\infty} R^i \qquad (6.2)$$

where R^0 is the identity relation and $R^{n+1} = R^n \circ R$ for $n \geq 0$. Likewise, if A_1, A_2 are quantum predicate in $\mathcal{H}_0 \otimes \mathcal{H}_1$ and $\mathcal{H}_1 \otimes \mathcal{H}_2$, respectively, then we can define their composition as a quantum predicate in $\mathcal{H}_0 \otimes \mathcal{H}_2$ in the following three different ways:

1. *Circle composition*:

$$A_1 \circ_\mathcal{B} A_2 = \frac{1}{d_1} \sum_i \langle ii | A_1 \otimes A_2 | ii \rangle$$

where $d_1 = \dim \mathcal{H}_1$ is the dimension and $\mathcal{B} = \{|i\rangle\}$ is an orthonormal basis of $\mathcal{H}_1$.

2. *Bullet composition*:

$$A_1 \bullet_{\mathcal{B}} A_2 = \langle \Psi | A_1 \otimes A_2 | \Psi \rangle$$

where $|\Psi\rangle_{\mathcal{B}} = \frac{1}{\sqrt{d_1}} \sum_i |ii\rangle$ is the maximal entanglement defined by an orthonormal basis $\mathcal{B} = \{|i\rangle\}$ of $\mathcal{H}_1$.

3. *Diamond composition*:

$$A_1 \diamond_v A_2 = tr_{\mathcal{H}_1^{\otimes 2}} [S_v (A_1 \otimes A_2) S_v]$$

where $v \in \{+, -\}$, $S_\pm$ are the symmetrisation and antisymmetrisation operators (see Example 6.6 below), and $tr_{\mathcal{H}_1^{\otimes 2}}$ stands for tracing out the middle two $\mathcal{H}_1$'s in $\mathcal{H}_0 \otimes \mathcal{H}_1 \otimes \mathcal{H}_1 \otimes \mathcal{H}_2$.

Accordingly, three kinds of reflexive and transitive closure of a binary quantum relation can be introduced by generalising Eq. (6.2) using the above three composition operations of quantum relations. It will be very interesting to carefully examine the algebraic structure of quantum relations equipped with the above composition operations and certain transitive closures.

Exercise 6.3. Verify $A_1 \circ_{\mathcal{B}} A_2$, $A_1 \bullet_{\mathcal{B}} A_2$ and $A_1 \diamond_v A_2$ are all Hermitian operators.

Logical connectives of quantum predicates: In classical logic, connectives are introduced for constructing more complicated predicates from basic predicates; for example, negation $\neg$, conjunction $\wedge$, disjunction $\vee$ and implication $\rightarrow$. It would be desirable if we can define corresponding connectives for quantum predicates. Here, we show some of them, but it is not the case that every classical logical connective has a meaningful quantum counterpart.

Example 6.1. 1. For each quantum predicate in Hilbert space $\mathcal{H}$, $I - A$ can be used as the negation of A. In fact, for any quantum state ρ in $\mathcal{H}$,

$$tr[(I - A)\rho] = 1 - tr(A\rho).$$

2. Conjunction in classical logic does not always have an appropriate quantum counterpart.
  a. If A_1 and A_2 are quantum predicates in $\mathcal{H}_1$, $\mathcal{H}_2$, respectively, then $A_1 \otimes A_2$ can be used as the conjunction of A_1 and A_2 (in $\mathcal{H}_1 \otimes \mathcal{H}_2$) because for any quantum states ρ_1 in $\mathcal{H}_1$ and ρ_2 in $\mathcal{H}_2$, it holds that

$$tr((A_1 \otimes A_2)(\rho_1 \otimes \rho_2)) = tr(A_1\rho_1) \cdot tr(A_2\rho_2).$$

  This kind of conjunction will be used in Chapter 9 for presenting a inference rule about disjoint parallel quantum programs.
  b. However, if the states spaces of A_1 and A_2 overlap; for example, A_1 and A_2 are in the same Hilbert space $\mathcal{H}$, or more generally, they are in $\mathcal{H} \otimes \mathcal{H}_1$ and $\mathcal{H} \otimes \mathcal{H}_2$, respectively, then their conjunction is not always definable. As will be seen in Chapter 9, the lacking of a reasonable conjunction in this case is the main difficulty in defining an inference rule for parallel quantum programs with shared variables.
3. For a family $\{A_i\}$ of quantum predicates in the same Hilbert space $\mathcal{H}$, and a probability distribution $\{p_i\}$, the convex combination $\sum_i p_i A_i$ will be often used as a connective in reasoning about quantum programs; for example, see inference rules (R.CC) and (R.Inv) in Fig. 6.9.
4. In a sense, quantum predicate $\sum_m M_m^\dagger A_m M_m$ can be understood as the disjunction of quantum predicate A_m according to the classical information that "the outcome of measurement $M = \{M_m\}$ is m". This disjunction will be used in the inference rule (R.IF) for quantum case statements in Fig. 6.3. It will be further discussed in Section 7.6 as a connective in effect calculus.

6.1.1   Quantum weakest preconditions

Quantum predicates defined above can be used to describe the properties of quantum states. The next question that we need to answer in developing a logic for reasoning about quantum programs is: how to describe the properties of quantum programs that transform a quantum state into another quantum state? One way is using the notion of Hoare triple mentioned above. In classical programming theory, weakest preconditions have also been extensively used for specifying the properties of programs. The notion of weakest precondition was introduced by Dijkstra in [133]. Let us consider a classical program S and a classical predicate Q. Intuitively, the weakest precondition of Q with respect to S is defined as a predicate P, usually written as $P = wp(S)(Q)$, that represents the least restrictive requirement needed to guarantee that Q holds for the output of S upon any input satisfying P. The weakest precondition describes a program in a backward way; that is, it determines the weakest property that the input must satisfy in order to achieve a given property of the output. Indeed, the two notions of Hoare triple and weakest precondition are closely related to each other: $Q = wp(S)(Q)$ if and only if

(a) P is a precondition of Q with respect to S in the sense that Hoare triple $\{P\}S\{Q\}$ holds; and

(b) if P' is a precondition such that Hoare triple $\{P'\}S\{Q\}$ holds, then P' implies P; that is, P' is weaker than P.

The notion of weakest precondition can be naturally generalised to the quantum case. Actually, the quantum generalisation of weakest precondition will play a crucial role in logics for quantum programs too. In this subsection, we introduce a purely semantic (syntax-independent) description of quantum weakest precondition. The weakest preconditions of quantum programs written in a concrete programming language, namely quantum **while**-language, will be discussed in Section 6.3.

We noticed that the denotational semantics of a quantum program is usually represented by a quantum operation in the last chapter. So, in this subsection, a quantum program is simply abstracted as a quantum operation. First of all, let us introduce the notion of precondition.

Definition 6.2. Let $M, N \in \mathcal{P}(\mathcal{H})$ be quantum predicates, and let $\mathcal{E} \in \mathcal{QO}(\mathcal{H})$ be a quantum operation (see Definition 2.25). Then M is called a precondition of N with respect to $\mathcal{E}$, written $\{M\}\mathcal{E}\{N\}$ (a Hoare triple for quantum operation $\mathcal{E}$), if

$$tr(M\rho) \leq tr(N\mathcal{E}(\rho)) \tag{6.3}$$

for all density operators ρ on $\mathcal{H}$.

The intuitive meaning of condition (6.3) comes immediately from the interpretation of satisfaction relation between quantum states and quantum predicates: $tr(M\rho)$ is the expectation of truth value of predicate M in state ρ. More explicitly, inequality (6.3) can be seen as a probabilistic version of the statement: if state ρ satisfies predicate M, then the state after transformation $\mathcal{E}$ from ρ satisfies predicate N.

Now quantum weakest preconditions can be defined by generalising straightforwardly the above conditions (a) and (b) for classical weakest preconditions to the quantum setting.

Definition 6.3. Let $M \in \mathcal{P}(\mathcal{H})$ be a quantum predicate and $\mathcal{E} \in \mathcal{QO}(\mathcal{H})$ a quantum operation. Then the weakest precondition of M with respect to $\mathcal{E}$ is a quantum predicate $wp(\mathcal{E})(M)$ satisfying the following conditions:

1. $\{wp(\mathcal{E})(M)\}\mathcal{E}\{M\}$;
2. for all quantum predicates N, $\{N\}\mathcal{E}\{M\}$ implies $N \sqsubseteq wp(\mathcal{E})(M)$, where $\sqsubseteq$ stands for the Löwner order.

Intuitively, condition 1 indicates that $wp(\mathcal{E})(M)$ is a precondition of M with respect to $\mathcal{E}$, and condition 2 means that whenever N is also a precondition of M, then $wp(\mathcal{E})(M)$ is weaker than N. They are the quantum counterparts of the above conditions (a) and (b), respectively.

Representations of weakest preconditions: The above abstract definition of quantum weakest precondition is often not easy to use in applications. So, it is desirable to find an explicit representation of quantum weakest precondition. We learned from Theorem 2.3 that there are two convenient representations of a quantum operation, namely the Kraus operator-sum representation and the system-environment model. If (the denotational) semantics of a quantum program is represented in one of these two forms, its weakest precondition also enjoys an elegant representation. Let us first consider the Kraus operator-sum representation.

Proposition 6.1. *Suppose that quantum operation $\mathcal{E} \in \mathcal{QO}(\mathcal{H})$ is represented by the set $\{E_i\}$ of operators; that is,*

$$\mathcal{E}(\rho) = \sum_i E_i \rho E_i^\dagger$$

for every density operator ρ. Then for each predicate $M \in \mathcal{P}(\mathcal{H})$, we have:

$$wp(\mathcal{E})(M) = \sum_i E_i^\dagger M E_i. \tag{6.4}$$

Proof. We see from condition 2 in Definition 6.3 that weakest precondition $wp(\mathcal{E})(M)$ is unique when it exists. Then we only need to check that $wp(\mathcal{E})(M)$ given by Eq. (6.4) satisfies the two conditions in Definition 6.3.

1. Since $tr(AB) = tr(BA)$ for any operators A, B in $\mathcal{H}$, we have:

$$
\begin{aligned}
tr(wp(\mathcal{E})(M)\rho) &= tr\left(\left(\sum_i E_i^\dagger M E_i\right)\rho\right) \\
&= \sum_i tr\left(E_i^\dagger M E_i \rho\right) \\
&= \sum_i tr\left(M E_i \rho E_i^\dagger\right) \\
&= tr\left(M\left(\sum_i E_i \rho E_i^\dagger\right)\right) \\
&= tr(M\mathcal{E}(\rho))
\end{aligned}
\tag{6.5}
$$

for each density operator ρ in $\mathcal{H}$. Thus, $\{wp(\mathcal{E})(M)\}\mathcal{E}\{M\}$.

2. It is known that $M \sqsubseteq N$ if and only if $tr(M\rho) \leq tr(N\rho)$ for all ρ. Thus, if $\{N\}\mathcal{E}\{M\}$, then for any density operator ρ we have:

$$
tr(N\rho) \leq tr(M\mathcal{E}(\rho)) = tr(wp(\mathcal{E})(M)\rho).
$$

Therefore, it follows immediately that $N \sqsubseteq wp(\mathcal{E})(M)$. $\qquad\square$

We can also give an intrinsic characterisation of $wp(\mathcal{E})$ in the case that the denotational semantics $\mathcal{E}$ of a quantum program is given in a system-environment model (see Theorem 2.3.2):

$$
\mathcal{E}(\rho) = tr_E\left[PU(|e_0\rangle\langle e_0| \otimes \rho)U^\dagger P\right]
\tag{6.6}
$$

for all density operator ρ on $\mathcal{H}$, where E is an environment system with state Hilbert space $\mathcal{H}_E$, U is a unitary transformation on $\mathcal{H}_E \otimes \mathcal{H}$, P is a projector onto some closed subspace of $\mathcal{H}_E \otimes \mathcal{H}$, and $|e_0\rangle$ is a fixed state in $\mathcal{H}_E$.

Proposition 6.2. *If quantum operation $\mathcal{E}$ is given by Eq. (6.6), then we have:*

$$
wp(\mathcal{E})(M) = \langle e_0|U^\dagger P(M \otimes I_E)PU|e_0\rangle
$$

for each $M \in \mathcal{P}(\mathcal{H})$, where I_E is the identity operator on the environment system's state space $\mathcal{H}_E$.

Proof. Let $\{|e_k\rangle\}$ be an orthonormal basis of $\mathcal{H}_E$. Then

$$
\mathcal{E}(\rho) = \sum_k \langle e_k|PU|e_0\rangle \, \rho \langle e_0|U^\dagger P|e_k\rangle,
$$

and using Proposition 6.1 we obtain:

$$
\begin{aligned}
wp(\mathcal{E})(M) &= \sum_k \langle e_0|U^\dagger P|e_k\rangle M\langle e_k|PU|e_0\rangle \\
&= \langle e_0|U^\dagger P\left(\sum_k |e_k\rangle M\langle e_k|\right)PU|e_0\rangle.
\end{aligned}
$$

Note that

$$
\sum_k |e_k\rangle M\langle e_k| = M \otimes \left(\sum_k |e_k\rangle\langle e_k|\right) = M \otimes I_E
$$

because $\{|e_k\rangle\}$ is an orthonormal basis of $\mathcal{H}_E$, and M is an operator on $\mathcal{H}$. This completes the proof. $\qquad\square$

$$\rho \quad \models \quad \mathcal{E}^*(M)$$

$$\mathcal{E} \downarrow \qquad \uparrow \mathcal{E}^*$$

$$\mathcal{E}(\rho) \quad \models \qquad M$$

The mapping $\rho \mapsto \mathcal{E}(\rho)$ is the Schrödinger picture, and the mapping $M \mapsto \mathcal{E}^*(M)$ is the Heisenberg picture. The symbol $\models$ stands for satisfaction relation; that is, $tr(M\rho) = \Pr\{\rho \models M\}$ (the probability that ρ satisfies M).

FIGURE 6.1 Schrödinger–Heisenberg duality.

Schrödinger–Heisenberg duality: As in the classical programming theory, the denotational semantics $\mathcal{E}$ of a quantum program with state Hilbert space $\mathcal{H}$ is a forward state transformer:

$$\mathcal{E} : \mathcal{D}(\mathcal{H}) \to \mathcal{D}(\mathcal{H}),$$
$$\rho \mapsto \mathcal{E}(\rho) \text{ for each } \rho \in \mathcal{D}(\mathcal{H}) \tag{6.7}$$

where $\mathcal{D}(\mathcal{H})$ stands for the set of partial density operators on $\mathcal{H}$; i.e. positive operators with traces ≤ 1. The mapping (6.7) is usually called the Schrödinger view in physics. On the other hand, the notion of weakest precondition defines a backward quantum predicate transformer:

$$wp(\mathcal{E}) : \mathcal{P}(\mathcal{H}) \to \mathcal{P}(\mathcal{H}),$$
$$M \mapsto wp(\mathcal{E})(M) \text{ for each } M \in \mathcal{P}(\mathcal{M}). \tag{6.8}$$

The mapping (6.8) is usually called the Heisenberg picture in physics. These two mappings provide us with two complementary ways to look at a quantum program.

The duality between forward and backward semantics has been extensively exploited to cope with classical programs. It will be equally useful for the studies of quantum programs. Moreover, the relationship between a quantum program and its weakest precondition can even be considered from a physics point of view – the Schrödinger–Heisenberg duality between quantum states (described as density operators) and quantum observables (described as Hermitian operators).

Definition 6.4. Let $\mathcal{E}$ be a quantum operation mapping (partial) density operators to (partial) density operators on a Hilbert space $\mathcal{H}$, and let $\mathcal{E}^*$ be an operator mapping Hermitian operators to Hermitian operators on $\mathcal{H}$. If we have

$$(\text{Duality}) \qquad tr[M\mathcal{E}(\rho)] = tr[\mathcal{E}^*(M)\rho] \tag{6.9}$$

for any (partial) density operator ρ, and for any Hermitian operator M on $\mathcal{H}$, then we say that $\mathcal{E}$ and $\mathcal{E}^*$ are (Schrödinger–Heisenberg) dual.

The duality defined above is visualised in Fig. 6.1. It follows from the definition that the dual $\mathcal{E}^*$ of a quantum operation $\mathcal{E}$ is unique whenever it exists. Moreover, if $\mathcal{E}$ has the Kraus operator-sum representation $\mathcal{E} = \sum_i E_i \circ E_i^\dagger$ (see Theorem 2.3), then it is easy to show that $\mathcal{E}^* = \sum_i E_i^\dagger \circ E_i$; that is, for any Hermitian operator M,

$$\mathcal{E}^*(M) = \sum_i E_i^\dagger M E_i.$$

The following proposition indicates that the notion of weakest precondition in programming theory coincides with the notion of Schrödinger–Heisenberg duality in physics.

Proposition 6.3. *Any quantum operation $\mathcal{E} \in \mathcal{QO}(\mathcal{H})$ and its weakest precondition $wp(\mathcal{E})$ are dual to each other.*

Proof. Immediate from Eq. (6.5). □

Algebraic properties of weakest preconditions: To conclude this subsection, we collect several basic algebraic properties of quantum weakest preconditions in the following proposition.

Proposition 6.4. *Let* $\lambda \geq 0$ *and* $\mathcal{E}, \mathcal{F} \in \mathcal{QO}(\mathcal{H})$, *and let* $\{\mathcal{E}_n\}$ *be an increasing sequence in* $\mathcal{QO}(\mathcal{H})$. *Then*

1. $wp(\lambda \mathcal{E}) = \lambda wp(\mathcal{E})$ *provided* $\lambda \mathcal{E} \in \mathcal{QO}(\mathcal{H})$;

2. $wp(\mathcal{E} + \mathcal{F}) = wp(\mathcal{E}) + wp(\mathcal{F})$ *provided* $\mathcal{E} + \mathcal{F} \in \mathcal{QO}(\mathcal{H})$;

3. $wp(\mathcal{E} \circ \mathcal{F}) = wp(\mathcal{F}) \circ wp(\mathcal{E})$;

4. $wp\left(\bigsqcup_{n=0}^{\infty} \mathcal{E}_n\right) = \bigsqcup_{n=0}^{\infty} wp(\mathcal{E}_n)$, *where* $\bigsqcup_{n=0}^{\infty} wp(\mathcal{E}_n)$ *is defined by*

$$\left(\bigsqcup_{n=0}^{\infty} wp(\mathcal{E}_n)\right)(M) \stackrel{\triangle}{=} \bigsqcup_{n=0}^{\infty} wp(\mathcal{E}_n)(M)$$

for any $M \in \mathcal{P}(\mathcal{H})$.

Proof. Clause 1 and 2 are immediately from Proposition 6.1.

3. It is easy to see that $\{L\}\mathcal{E}\{M\}$ and $\{M\}\mathcal{F}\{N\}$ implies $\{L\}\mathcal{E} \circ \mathcal{F}\{N\}$. Thus, we have:

$$\{wp(\mathcal{E})(wp(\mathcal{F})(M))\}\mathcal{E} \circ \mathcal{F}\{M\}.$$

On the other hand, we need to show that $N \sqsubseteq wp(\mathcal{E})(wp(\mathcal{F})(M))$ whenever $\{N\}\mathcal{E} \circ \mathcal{F}\{M\}$. In fact, for any density operator ρ, it follows from Eq. (6.5) that

$$\begin{aligned}
tr(N\rho) &\leq tr(M(\mathcal{E} \circ \mathcal{F})(\rho)) \\
&= tr(M\mathcal{F}(\mathcal{E}(\rho))) \\
&= tr(wp(\mathcal{F})(M)\mathcal{E}(\rho)) \\
&= tr(wp(\mathcal{E})(wp(\mathcal{F})(M))\rho).
\end{aligned}$$

Therefore, we obtain

$$wp(\mathcal{E} \circ \mathcal{F})(M) = wp(\mathcal{E})(wp(\mathcal{F})(M)) = (wp(\mathcal{F}) \circ wp(\mathcal{E}))(M).$$

4. First, we note that the following two equalities follow immediately from the definition of $\bigsqcup$ in CPO $(\mathcal{P}(\mathcal{H}), \sqsubseteq)$:

$$M\left(\bigsqcup_{n=0}^{\infty} M_n\right) = \lim_{n \to \infty} MM_n,$$

$$tr\left(\bigsqcup_{n=0}^{\infty} M_n\right) = \bigsqcup_{n=0}^{\infty} tr(M_n).$$

Then we can prove that

$$\left\{\bigsqcup_{n=0}^{\infty} wp(\mathcal{E}_n)(M)\right\} \bigsqcup_{n=0}^{\infty} \mathcal{E}_n\{M\}.$$

Indeed, for any $\rho \in \mathcal{D}(\mathcal{H})$, we have:

$$\begin{aligned}
tr\left(\bigsqcup_{n=0}^{\infty} wp(\mathcal{E}_n)(M)\rho\right) &= \bigsqcup_{n=0}^{\infty} tr(wp(\mathcal{E}_n)(M)\rho) \\
&\leq \bigsqcup_{n=0}^{\infty} tr(M\mathcal{E}_n(\rho)) \\
&= tr\left(\lim_{n \to \infty} M\mathcal{E}_n(\rho)\right) \\
&= tr\left(M\left(\bigsqcup_{n=0}^{\infty} \mathcal{E}_n\right)(\rho)\right).
\end{aligned}$$

Second, we show that $\{N\} \bigsqcup_{n=0}^{\infty} \mathcal{E}_n \{M\}$ implies $N \sqsubseteq \bigsqcup_{n=0}^{\infty} wp(\mathcal{E}_n)(M)$. It suffices to note that

$$
\begin{aligned}
tr(N\rho) &\leq tr\left(M\left(\bigsqcup_{n=0}^{\infty} \mathcal{E}_n\right)(\rho)\right) \\
&= tr\left(\lim_{n \to \infty} M\mathcal{E}_n(\rho)\right) \\
&= \bigsqcup_{n=0}^{\infty} tr(M\mathcal{E}_n(\rho)) \\
&= \bigsqcup_{n=0}^{\infty} tr(wp(\mathcal{E}_n)(M)\rho) \\
&= tr\left(\left(\bigsqcup_{n=0}^{\infty} wp(\mathcal{E}_n)\right)(M)\rho\right)
\end{aligned}
$$

for all density operators ρ. Thus, it holds that

$$
wp\left(\bigsqcup_{n=0}^{\infty} \mathcal{E}_n\right)(M) = \bigsqcup_{n=0}^{\infty} wp(\mathcal{E}_n)(M). \qquad \square
$$

6.1.2 Commutativity of quantum predicates

The aim of this chapter is to build a logical foundation for reasoning about correctness of quantum programs, including the quantum weakest precondition semantics and Hoare logic for quantum **while**-programs. This logical foundation is of course a generalisation of the corresponding theories for classical and probabilistic programs, but it is certainly not a simple generalisation. Indeed, it has to answer some problems that would not arise in the realm of classical and probabilistic programming. This subsection deals with one of such problems, namely (non)commutativity of quantum predicates. The influence of other fundamental differences between quantum systems and classical systems on quantum programming will be revealed in Chapters 9, 11, and 12 and discussed in Sections 13.5 and 13.6. Since this subsection deviates from the main line of this chapter, the reader can skip it on the first reading, without affecting her/his understanding of the subsequent sections.

The significance of (non)commutativity problem of quantum predicates comes from the following observation that more than one predicate may be involved in specifying and reasoning about a complicated property of a quantum program, but:

1. Quantum predicates are observables, and their physical simultaneous verifiability depends on commutativity between them according to the Heisenberg uncertainty principle (see Section 2.3.2 or [318], page 89).
2. Mathematically, a logical combination like conjunction and disjunction of two quantum predicates is well-defined only when they commute.

The above observation motivates us to consider the (non)commutativity problem of quantum weakest preconditions defined in the previous subsection. For any two operators A and B on a Hilbert space $\mathcal{H}$, it is said that A and B commute if

$$
AB = BA.
$$

So, what concerns us is the following:

- **Problem**: Given a quantum operation $\mathcal{E} \in \mathcal{QO}(\mathcal{H})$ (as the denotational semantics of a quantum program). For two quantum predicates $M, N \in \mathcal{P}(\mathcal{H})$, when do $wp(\mathcal{E})(M)$ and $wp(\mathcal{E})(N)$ commute?

This question is interesting because one may need to deal with logical combinations of quantum predicates when reasoning about complicated quantum programs. For example, one may like to know whether the conjunction "M and N" is satisfied after a quantum program $\mathcal{E}$ is executed. Then she/he would consider whether the conjunction "$wp(\mathcal{E})(M)$ and $wp(\mathcal{E})(N)$" of weakest preconditions is satisfied before the program is executed. However, as pointed out above, these conjunctions are well-defined only if the involved quantum predicates commute. (A further discussion about some related issues is left as Problem 6.2 at the end of this section.)

Now we start to carefully address the above problem. To warm up, let us first see a simple example.

Example 6.2 (Bit flip and phase flip channels). Bit flip and phase flip are quantum operations on a single qubit, and they are widely used as noise or error models in the theory of quantum error-correction. Let X, Y, Z stand for the Pauli matrices (see Example 3.2).

- The bit flip is defined by

$$\mathcal{E}(\rho) = E_0 \rho E_0^\dagger + E_1 \rho E_1^\dagger, \tag{6.10}$$

where $E_0 = \sqrt{p}I$ and $E_1 = \sqrt{1-p}X$. It is easy to see that $wp(\mathcal{E})(M)$ and $wp(\mathcal{E})(N)$ commute when $MN = NM$ and $MXN = NXM$.

- If E_1 in Eq. (6.10) is replaced by $\sqrt{1-p}Z$ (resp. $\sqrt{1-p}Y$), then $\mathcal{E}$ is the phase flip (resp. bit-phase flip), and $wp(\mathcal{E})(M)$ and $wp(\mathcal{E})(N)$ commute when $MN = NM$ and $MZN = NZM$ (resp. $MYN = NYM$).

Secondly, we consider weakest preconditions with respect to two simplest classes of quantum operations, namely unitary transformations and projective measurements.

Proposition 6.5. 1. *Let $\mathcal{E} \in \mathcal{QO}(\mathcal{H})$ be a unitary transformation; that is,*

$$\mathcal{E}(\rho) = U\rho U^\dagger$$

for any $\rho \in \mathcal{D}(\mathcal{H})$, where U is a unitary operator on $\mathcal{H}$. Then $wp(\mathcal{E})(M)$ and $wp(\mathcal{E})(N)$ commute if and only if M and N commute.

2. *Let $\{P_k\}$ be a projective measurement in $\mathcal{H}$; that is, $P_{k_1}P_{k_2} = \delta_{k_1 k_2} P_{k_1}$ and $\sum_k P_k = I_\mathcal{H}$, where*

$$\delta_{k_1 k_2} = \begin{cases} 1, & \text{if } k_1 = k_2, \\ 0, & \text{otherwise.} \end{cases}$$

If $\mathcal{E}$ is given by this measurement, with the result of the measurement unknown:

$$\mathcal{E}(\rho) = \sum_k P_k \rho P_k$$

for each $\rho \in \mathcal{D}(\mathcal{H})$, then $wp(\mathcal{E})(M)$ and $wp(\mathcal{E})(N)$ commute if and only if $P_k M P_k$ and $P_k N P_k$ commute for all indices k.

3. *In particular, let $\{|i\rangle\}$ be an orthonormal basis of $\mathcal{H}$. If $\mathcal{E}$ is given by the measurement in the basis $\{|i\rangle\}$:*

$$\mathcal{E}(\rho) = \sum_i P_i \rho P_i,$$

where $P_i = |i\rangle\langle i|$ for each basis state $|i\rangle$, then $wp(\mathcal{E})(M)$ and $wp(\mathcal{E})(N)$ commute for any $M, N \in \mathcal{P}(\mathcal{H})$.

Exercise 6.4. Prove Proposition 6.5.

After dealing with the above example and special case, we now consider the weakest preconditions with respect to a general quantum operation $\mathcal{E}$. Unfortunately, we are only able to give some useful sufficient (but not necessary) conditions for commutativity of $wp(\mathcal{E})(M)$ and $wp(\mathcal{E})(N)$.

As usual, we consider two representations of $\mathcal{E}$, namely the Kraus operator-sum representation and the system-environment model. Let us first work in the case where quantum operation $\mathcal{E}$ is given in the Kraus operator-sum form. The following proposition presents a sufficient condition for commutativity of $wp(\mathcal{E})(M)$ and $wp(\mathcal{E})(N)$ in the case where M and N already commute.

Proposition 6.6. *Suppose that $\mathcal{H}$ is finite-dimensional. Let $M, N \in \mathcal{P}(\mathcal{H})$ and they commute, i.e., there exists an orthonormal basis $\{|\psi_i\rangle\}$ of $\mathcal{H}$ such that*

$$M = \sum_i \lambda_i |\psi_i\rangle\langle\psi_i|, \quad N = \sum_i \mu_i |\psi_i\rangle\langle\psi_i|$$

where λ_i, μ_i are reals for each i (see [318], Theorem 2.2), and let quantum operation $\mathcal{E} \in \mathcal{SO}(\mathcal{H})$ be represented by the set $\{E_i\}$ of operators, i.e. $\mathcal{E} = \sum_i E_i \circ E_i^\dagger$. If for any i, j, k, l, we have either $\lambda_k \mu_l = \lambda_l \mu_k$ or

$$\sum_m \langle\psi_k|E_i|\psi_m\rangle\langle\psi_l|E_j|\psi_m\rangle = 0,$$

then $wp(\mathcal{E})(M)$ and $wp(\mathcal{E})(N)$ commute.

Exercise 6.5. Prove Proposition 6.6

To present another sufficient condition for commutativity of quantum weakest preconditions, we need to introduce commutativity between a quantum operation and a quantum predicate.

Definition 6.5. Let quantum operation $\mathcal{E} \in \mathcal{QO}(\mathcal{H})$ be represented by the set $\{E_i\}$ of operators, i.e. $\mathcal{E} = \sum_i E_i \circ E_i^\dagger$, and let quantum predicate $M \in \mathcal{P}(\mathcal{H})$. Then we say that M and $\mathcal{E}$ commute if M and E_i commute for each i.

It seems that in the above definition commutativity between quantum predicate M and quantum program $\mathcal{E}$ depends on the choice of operators E_i in the Kraus representation of $\mathcal{E}$. Thus, one may wonder if this definition is intrinsic because the Kraus operators E_i are not unique. To address this problem, we need the following:

Lemma 6.4 (Unitary freedom in the operator-sum representation; [318], Theorem 8.2). *Suppose that $\{E_i\}$ and $\{F_j\}$ are operator elements giving rise to quantum operations $\mathcal{E}$ and $\mathcal{F}$, respectively; that is,*

$$\mathcal{E} = \sum_i E_i \circ E_i^\dagger, \quad \mathcal{F} = \sum_j F_j \circ F_j^\dagger.$$

By appending zero operators to the shortest list of operation elements we may ensure that the numbers of E_i and F_j are the same. Then $\mathcal{E} = \mathcal{F}$ if and only if there exist complex numbers u_{ij} such that

$$E_i = \sum_j u_{ij} F_j$$

for all i, and $U = (u_{ij})$ is (the matrix representation of) a unitary operator.

As a simple corollary, we can see that the definition of commutativity between a quantum predicate M and a quantum operation $\mathcal{E}$ does not depend on the choice of the Kraus representation operators of $\mathcal{E}$.

Lemma 6.5. *The notion of commutativity between observables and quantum operations is well-defined. More precisely, suppose that $\mathcal{E}$ is represented by both $\{E_i\}$ and $\{F_j\}$:*

$$\mathcal{E} = \sum_i E_i \circ E_i^\dagger = \sum_j F_j \circ F_j^\dagger.$$

Then M and E_i commute for all i if and only if M and F_j commute for all j.

Furthermore, commutativity between observables and quantum operations is preserved by composition of quantum operations.

Proposition 6.7. *Let $M \in \mathcal{P}(\mathcal{H})$ be a quantum predicate, and let $\mathcal{E}_1, \mathcal{E}_2 \in \mathcal{QO}(\mathcal{H})$ be two quantum operations. If M and $\mathcal{E}_i$ commute for $i = 1, 2$, then M commutes with the composition $\mathcal{E}_1 \circ \mathcal{E}_2$ of $\mathcal{E}_1$ and $\mathcal{E}_2$.*

Exercise 6.6. Prove Proposition 6.7.

The following proposition gives another sufficient condition for commutativity of $wp(\mathcal{E})(M)$ and $wp(\mathcal{E})(N)$, also in the case where M and N commute. This condition is presented in terms of commutativity of quantum operations and quantum predicates.

Proposition 6.8. *Let $M, N \in \mathcal{P}(\mathcal{H})$ be two quantum predicates, and let $\mathcal{E} \in \mathcal{QO}(\mathcal{H})$ be a quantum operation. If M and N commute, M and $\mathcal{E}$ commute, and N and $\mathcal{E}$ commute, then $wp(\mathcal{E})(M)$ and $wp(\mathcal{E})(N)$ commute.*

Exercise 6.7. Prove Proposition 6.8.

Now we turn to consider the system-environment model of quantum operation (see Theorem 2.3.2):

$$\mathcal{E}(\rho) = tr_E \left[PU \left(|e_0\rangle\langle e_0| \otimes \rho \right) U^\dagger P \right] \tag{6.11}$$

for all density operators ρ on $\mathcal{H}$, where E is an environment system of which the state Hilbert space is $\mathcal{H}_E$, U is a unitary operator on $\mathcal{H}_E \otimes \mathcal{H}$, P is a projector onto a closed subspace of $\mathcal{H}_E \otimes \mathcal{H}$, and $|e_0\rangle$ is a given state in $\mathcal{H}_E$. To this end, we need two generalised notions of commutativity between linear operators.

Definition 6.6. Let $M, N, A, B, C \in \mathcal{L}(\mathcal{H})$ be operators on $\mathcal{H}$. Then:

1. We say that M and N (A, B, C)-commute if

$$AMBNC = ANBMC.$$

In particular, it is simply said that M and N A-commute when M and N (A, A, A)-commute;
2. We say that A and B conjugate-commute if

$$AB^\dagger = BA^\dagger.$$

Obviously, commutativity is exactly $I_\mathcal{H}$-commutativity, where $I_\mathcal{H}$ is the identity operator on $\mathcal{H}$.

The next two propositions present several sufficient conditions for commutativity of quantum weakest preconditions when quantum operation $\mathcal{E}$ is given in the system-environment model.

Proposition 6.9. *Let quantum operation $\mathcal{E}$ be given by Eq. (6.11), and we write $A = PU|e_0\rangle$. Then:*

1. $wp(\mathcal{E})(M)$ *and* $wp(\mathcal{E})(N)$ *commute if and only if* $M \otimes I_E$ *and* $N \otimes I_E$ $(A^\dagger, AA^\dagger, A)$-*commute;*
2. $wp(\mathcal{E})(M)$ *and* $wp(\mathcal{E})(N)$ *commute whenever* $(M \otimes I_E)A$ *and* $(N \otimes I_E)A$ *conjugate-commute,*

where $I_E = I_{\mathcal{H}_E}$ is the identity operator on $\mathcal{H}_E$.

Proposition 6.10. *Suppose that $\mathcal{H}$ is finite-dimensional. Let $\mathcal{E}$ be given by Eq. (6.11), and let $M, N \in \mathcal{P}(\mathcal{H})$ be quantum predicates and they commute, i.e., there exists an orthonormal basis $\{|\psi_i\rangle\}$ of $\mathcal{H}$ such that*

$$M = \sum_i \lambda_i |\psi_i\rangle\langle\psi_i|, \quad N = \sum_i \mu_i |\psi_i\rangle\langle\psi_i|$$

where λ_i, μ_i are reals for each i. If for any i, j, k, l, we have $\lambda_i \mu_j = \lambda_j \mu_i$ or

$$\langle e_0|U^\dagger P|\psi_i e_k\rangle \perp \langle e_0|U^\dagger P|\psi_j e_l\rangle,$$

then $wp(\mathcal{E})(M)$ and $wp(\mathcal{E})(N)$ commute.

Exercise 6.8. Prove Propositions 6.9 and 6.10.

Up to now, (non)commutativity of quantum weakest preconditions is still not fully understood. To conclude this subsection, we propose two problems for further studies.

Problem 6.1. The main results obtained in this subsection for commutativity of the weakest preconditions $wp(\mathcal{E})(M)$ and $wp(\mathcal{E})(N)$ (Propositions 6.6, 6.8 and 6.10) deal with the special case where M and N commute. So, an interesting problem is to find a sufficient and necessary condition for commutativity of $wp(\mathcal{E})(M)$ and $wp(\mathcal{E})(N)$ of a general quantum operation $\mathcal{E}$ in the case where M and N may not commute.

An even more general problem would be: How to characterise commutator $[wp(\mathcal{E})(M), wp(\mathcal{E})(N)]$ in terms of commutator $[M, N]$, where for any operators X and Y, their commutator $[X, Y] = XY - YX$?

Problem 6.2. Various healthiness conditions for predicate transformer semantics of classical programs were introduced by Dijkstra [133], e.g. conjunctivity and disjunctivity. These conditions were also carefully examined for probabilistic predicate transformers [297]. An interesting problem is to study healthiness conditions for quantum predicate transformers in the light of noncommutativity of quantum predicates. Note that this problem was considered in [424] for a special class of quantum predicates, namely projection operators.

6.2 Correctness formulas of quantum programs

In the last section, we introduced the notions of quantum predicate and weakest precondition with respect to a quantum program modelled by an abstract quantum operation. Now we turn to develop quantum Hoare logic for syntax-oriented reasoning about correctness of quantum programs. As briefly discussed at the beginning of this chapter, in classical Hoare logic, the correctness of a program is specified as a correctness formula represented as a Hoare triple. So, in this section, we generalise the notion of correctness formula as Hoare triple to quantum programs written in the quantum **while**-language.

Recall that a correctness formula for a classical program P is a Hoare triple of the form $\{P\}S\{Q\}$, where P is a predicate describing the input states, called the *precondition*, and Q a predicate describing the output states of the program, called the postcondition. Indeed, the notion of Hoare triple can be directly generalised into the quantum setting. Let $qVar$ be the set of quantum variables in the quantum **while**-language defined in Section 5.1. For any set $X \subseteq qVar$, we write

$$\mathcal{H}_X = \bigotimes_{q \in X} \mathcal{H}_q$$

for the state Hilbert space of the system consisting of quantum variables in X, where $\mathcal{H}_q$ is the state space of quantum variable q. In particular, we set

$$\mathcal{H}_{all} = \bigotimes_{q \in qVar} \mathcal{H}_q.$$

Recall from the last section, a quantum predicate in $\mathcal{H}_X$ is a Hermitian operator P on $\mathcal{H}_X$ such that $0_{\mathcal{H}_X} \sqsubseteq P \sqsubseteq I_{\mathcal{H}_X}$. We write $\mathcal{P}(\mathcal{H}_X)$ for the set of quantum predicates in $\mathcal{H}_X$.

Definition 6.7. A quantum correctness formula or a quantum Hoare triple is a statement of the form:

$$\{P\}S\{Q\}$$

where S is a quantum program, and both $P, Q \in \mathcal{P}(\mathcal{H}_{all})$ are quantum predicates in $\mathcal{H}_{all}$. The quantum predicate P is called the precondition of the correctness formula and Q the postcondition.

The appearance of a Hoare triple $\{P\}S\{Q\}$ in the quantum case is the same as that in the classical case, but precondition P and postcondition Q in the classical case are classical predicates (i.e. Boolean functions), and in the quantum case, they are quantum predicates (i.e. observables represented by Hermitian operators). Furthermore, it should be pointed out that a classical program logic is usually built upon an assertion logic so that preconditions and postconditions can be formally written as logical formulas in the assertion language. For example, in the Hoare logic for classical programs, the precondition P and postcondition Q in a Hoare triple $\{P\}S\{Q\}$ are two first-order logical formulas; and in separation logic [321,352], they are BI-logical formulas [224,323]. However, in the above definition, the precondition and postcondition in a quantum Hoare triple are treated simply as two operators on a Hilbert space, or matrices when the Hilbert space is finite-dimensional. The reason is that at this moment, we do not have any assertion logic that can be used to formally specify them. This issue will be partially resolved in the next chapter by introducing a first-order extension of Birkhoff–von Neumann quantum logic with quantum individual variables as an assertion language.

Partial correctness and total correctness: In classical programming theory, a Hoare logical formula $\{P\}S\{Q\}$ can be interpreted in two different ways:

- *Partial correctness*: If an input to program S satisfies the precondition P, then either S does not terminate, or it terminates in a state satisfying the postcondition Q.
- *Total correctness*: If an input to program S satisfies the precondition P, then S must terminate and it terminates in a state satisfying the postcondition Q.

Among the above two interpretations, total correctness is what we really want in practical applications. The main reason behind introducing the notion of partial correctness is that it is usually more convenient to prove the total correctness of a program by proving its partial correctness and termination separately.

Similar to the case of classical programming theory, a quantum correctness formula can also be interpreted in two different ways. Let us write $\mathcal{D}(\mathcal{H}_X)$ for the set of partial density operators, i.e. positive operators with traces ≤ 1, on $\mathcal{H}_X$. Intuitively, for any quantum predicate $P \in \mathcal{P}(\mathcal{H}_X)$ and state $\rho \in \mathcal{D}(\mathcal{H}_X)$, $tr(P\rho)$ stands for the probability that predicate P is satisfied in state ρ.

Definition 6.8. 1. The correctness formula $\{P\}S\{Q\}$ is true in the sense of total correctness, written

$$\models_{tot} \{P\}S\{Q\},$$

if we have:

$$tr(P\rho) \leq tr(Q[\![S]\!](\rho)) \tag{6.12}$$

for all $\rho \in \mathcal{D}(\mathcal{H}_{all})$, where $[\![S]\!]$ is the semantic function of S (see Definition 5.6).

2. The correctness formula $\{P\}S\{Q\}$ is true in the sense of partial correctness, written

$$\models_{par} \{P\}S\{Q\},$$

if we have:

$$tr(P\rho) \leq tr(Q[\![S]\!](\rho)) + [tr(\rho) - tr([\![S]\!](\rho))] \tag{6.13}$$

for all $\rho \in \mathcal{D}(\mathcal{H}_{all})$.

The defining inequalities (6.12) and (6.13) of quantum total correctness and partial correctness are essentially quantitative generalisations of the above interpretations of classical total correctness and partial correctness, respectively. More precisely, the intuitive meaning of inequality (6.12) for total correctness is:

- The probability that input ρ satisfies quantum predicate P is not greater than the probability that quantum program S terminates on ρ and its output $[\![S]\!](\rho)$ satisfies quantum predicate Q.

It is obvious from Definition 6.2 that $\models_{tot} \{P\}S\{Q\}$ is a restatement of the fact that P is a precondition of Q with respect to quantum operation $[\![S]\!]$, i.e.

$$\{P\}[\![S]\!]\{Q\}.$$

Recall that $tr(\rho) - tr([\![S]\!](\rho))$ is the probability that quantum program S diverges from input ρ. Thus, inequality (6.13) for partial correctness intuitively means:

- If input ρ satisfies predicate P, then either program S terminates on it and its output $[\![S]\!](\rho)$ satisfies Q, or S diverges from it.

The following proposition presents several basic properties of quantum total and partial correctness formulas.

Proposition 6.11. 1. *If* $\models_{tot} \{P\}S\{Q\}$*, then* $\models_{par} \{P\}S\{Q\}$*.*
2. *For any quantum program S, and for any $P, Q \in \mathcal{P}(\mathcal{H}_{all})$, we have:*

$$\models_{tot} \{0_{\mathcal{H}_{all}}\} S\{Q\}, \qquad \models_{par} \{P\}S \{I_{\mathcal{H}_{all}}\}.$$

3. *(Linearity) For any $P_1, P_2, Q_1, Q_2 \in \mathcal{P}((\mathcal{H}_{all})$ and $\lambda_1, \lambda_2 \geq 0$ with $\lambda_1 P_1 + \lambda_2 P_2, \lambda_1 Q_1 + \lambda_2 Q_2 \in \mathcal{P}(\mathcal{H}_{all})$, if*

$$\models_{tot} (\{P_i\} S (\{Q_i\} \ (i = 1, 2),$$

then

$$\models_{tot} (\{\lambda_1 P_1 + \lambda_2 P_2\} S (\{\lambda_1 Q_1 + \lambda_2 Q_2\}.$$

The same conclusion holds for partial correctness if $\lambda_1 + \lambda_2 = 1$.

Proof. Immediate from definition. ☐

Exercise 6.9. Prove or disprove that for any programs S_1, S_2, the following three statements are equivalent:

1. for any partial density operator ρ : $[\![S_1]\!](\rho) = [\![S_2]\!](\rho)$;
2. for any quantum predicates A, B : $\models_{par} \{A\}S_1\{B\} \Leftrightarrow \models_{par} \{A\}S_2\{B\}$;
3. for any quantum predicates A, B : $\models_{tot} \{A\}S_1\{B\} \Leftrightarrow \models_{tot} \{A\}S_2\{B\}$;

Examples of specifying correctness of quantum programs: Our experience in classical programming shows that it is highly nontrivial to properly specify the correctness of a program. It is even trickier to specify the correctness of quantum programs. Now we present a series of examples, some of which can help the reader better understand the above definition and some can serve as basic ingredients for specifying more complicated quantum programs.

Correctness with logical constants: Logical constants may appear in the precondition or postcondition of a classical program. Here, we show that their quantum counterparts are also useful in specifying the correctness of some quantum programs.

Example 6.3. The quantum predicates describing "True" and "False" are mathematically modelled by the identity and zero operators I and 0, respectively, on the state Hilbert space $\mathcal{H}_P$ of the program P under consideration. Then:

1. $\models_{par} \{I\} P \{B\}$ means that for any density operator ρ,

$$tr(B[\![P]\!](\rho)) = tr([\![P]\!](\rho));$$

that is, the probability that postcondition B is satisfied by the output is equal to the probability that the program terminates.

2. $\models_{par} \{A\} P \{I\}$ always holds, because $A \sqsubseteq I$ implies that for any partial density operator ρ,

$$tr(A\rho) \leq tr(\rho) = tr([\![P]\!](\rho)) + [tr(\rho) - tr([\![P]\!](\rho))].$$

3. $\models_{tot} \{I\} P \{B\}$ means that for any density operator ρ,

$$tr(B[\![P]\!](\rho)) = 1.$$

Since $B \sqsubseteq I$, we have $tr(B[\![P]\!](\rho)) \leq tr([\![P]\!](\rho))$ and thus $tr([\![P]\!](\rho)) = 1$; that is, program P always terminates, and output $[\![P]\!](\rho)$ satisfies postcondition B.

4. $\models_{tot} \{A\} P \{I\}$ means that for any density operator, $tr(A\rho) \leq tr([\![P]\!](\rho))$; intuitively, if precondition A is satisfied by input ρ to P, then P terminates.

Correctness with unary quantum predicates: Now let us see two examples with unary quantum predicates as the preconditions or postconditions in the correctness formulas of quantum programs.

Example 6.4. An equality like $x = c$ with x being a variable and c a constant often appears in precondition or postcondition of a classical program correctness formula, e.g.

$$\models_{tot} \{x = 1\} x := x + 1 \{x = 2\}.$$

1. Let q be a quantum variable and $|\psi\rangle$ a given (constant) state in $\mathcal{H}_q$. Then equality "$q = |\psi\rangle$" can be expressed as quantum predicate $A = |\psi\rangle\langle\psi|$ in $\mathcal{H}_q$. Clearly, we have:

$$\models_{tot} \left\{ U^\dagger |\psi\rangle\langle\psi| U \right\} q := U[q] \{A\}, \tag{6.14}$$

$$\models_{tot} \{A\} q := U[q] \left\{ U |\psi\rangle\langle\psi| U^\dagger \right\} \tag{6.15}$$

for any unitary operator U on $\mathcal{H}_q$. The precondition in (6.14) and the postcondition in (6.15) express equalities "$q = U^\dagger |\psi\rangle$", "$q = U|\psi\rangle$", respectively.

2. More generally, for any closed subspace X of $\mathcal{H}_q$, the membership "$q \in X$" can be expressed as quantum predicate P_X (the projection onto X) and we have:

$$\models_{tot} \left\{ P_{U^\dagger(X)} \right\} q := U[q] \{P_X\}, \tag{6.16}$$

$$\models_{tot} \{P_X\} q := U[q] \left\{ P_{U(X)} \right\} \tag{6.17}$$

where for any unitary V, $V(X)$ denotes the subspace $\{V|\psi\rangle \mid |\psi\rangle \in X\}$. The precondition in (6.16) and the postcondition in (6.17) express memberships "$q \in U^\dagger(X)$", "$q \in U(X)$", respectively.

The following example clearly illustrates the difference between total correctness and partial correctness.

Example 6.5. Assume that $type(q) = \mathbf{Boolean}$. Consider the program:

$$S \equiv \mathbf{while}\ M[q] = 1\ \mathbf{do}\ q := \sigma_z[q]\ \mathbf{od}$$

where $M_0 = |0\rangle\langle 0|$, $M_1 = |1\rangle\langle 1|$, and σ_z is the Pauli matrix. Let

$$P = |\psi\rangle_q \langle\psi| \otimes P'$$

where $|\psi\rangle = \alpha|0\rangle + \beta|1\rangle \in \mathcal{H}_2$, and $P' \in \mathcal{P}\left(\mathcal{H}_{qVar\setminus\{q\}}\right)$. Then

1. We see that the total correctness

$$\models_{tot} \{P\}S\left\{|0\rangle_q\langle 0| \otimes P'\right\}$$

does not hold if $\beta \neq 0$ and $P' \neq 0_{\mathcal{H}_{qVar\setminus\{q\}}}$. In fact, put

$$\rho = |\psi\rangle_q\langle \psi| \otimes I_{\mathcal{H}_{qVar\setminus\{q\}}}.$$

Note that ρ is not normalised for simplicity of presentation. Then

$$[\![S]\!](\rho) = |\alpha|^2|0\rangle_q\langle 0| \otimes I_{\mathcal{H}_{qVar\setminus\{q\}}}$$

and

$$tr(P\rho) = tr(P') > |\alpha|^2 tr(P') = tr\left(\left(|0\rangle_q\langle 0| \otimes P'\right)[\![S]\!](\rho)\right).$$

2. We have the partial correctness:

$$\models_{par} \{P\}S\left\{|0\rangle_q\langle 0| \otimes P'\right\};$$

that is, for any partial density operator ρ:

$$tr(P\rho) \leq tr\left(\left(|0\rangle_q\langle 0| \otimes P'\right)[\![S]\!](\rho)\right) + [tr(\rho) - tr([\![S]\!](\rho))]. \qquad (6.18)$$

Here, we only consider a special class of partial density operators in $\mathcal{H}_{qVar\setminus\{q\}}$:

$$\rho = |\varphi\rangle_q\langle \varphi| \otimes \rho'$$

where $|\varphi\rangle = a|0\rangle + b|1\rangle \in \mathcal{H}_2$, and $\rho' \in \mathcal{D}\left(\mathcal{H}_{qVar\setminus\{q\}}\right)$. A routine calculation yields:

$$[\![S]\!](\rho) = |a|^2|0\rangle_q\langle 0| \otimes \rho'$$

and

$$tr(P\rho) = |\langle\varphi|\varphi\rangle|^2 tr\left(P'\rho'\right)$$
$$\leq |a|^2 tr\left(P'\rho'\right) + \left[tr\left(\rho'\right) - |a|^2 tr\left(\rho'\right)\right]$$
$$= tr\left(\left(|0\rangle_q\langle 0| \otimes P'\right)[\![S]\!](\rho)\right) + [tr(\rho) - tr([\![S]\!](\rho))].$$

Exercise 6.10. Prove inequality (6.18) for all $\rho \in \mathcal{D}(\mathcal{H}_{all})$.

Correctness with quantum relations: The following three examples use some quantum relations as preconditions and postconditions in the correctness formulas of quantum programs.

Example 6.6. An equality like $x = y$ between two variables x, y also often appears in precondition or postcondition of a classical program correctness formula, e.g.

$$\models_{tot} \{x = y\}\ x := x + 1;\ y := y + 1\ \{x = y\}.$$

1. Let p, q be two quantum variables with the same state Hilbert space $\mathcal{H}$. Then equality "$p = q$" can sometimes be expressed as the symmetrisation operator:

$$S_+ = \frac{1}{2}(I + \text{SWAP})$$

where I is the identity operator on $\mathcal{H} \otimes \mathcal{H}$, and operator SWAP on $\mathcal{H} \otimes \mathcal{H}$ is defined by

$$\text{SWAP}|\varphi, \psi\rangle = |\psi, \varphi\rangle$$

for all $|\varphi\rangle, |\psi\rangle \in \mathcal{H}$, together with linearity. It is easy to see that $\text{SWAP} \cdot S_+ = S_+ \cdot \text{SWAP} = \text{SWAP} \cdot S_+ \cdot \text{SWAP} = S_+$. Furthermore, for any unitary operator U in $\mathcal{H}$, it holds that:

$$\models_{tot} \{S_+\}\ p := U[p];\ q := U[q]\ \{S_+\}.$$

It is interesting to note that a similar conclusion holds for the antisymmetrisation operator:

$$S_- = \frac{1}{2}(I - \text{SWAP})$$

that is, we have $\text{SWAP} \cdot S_- = S_- \cdot \text{SWAP} = -S_-$, $\text{SWAP} \cdot S_- \cdot \text{SWAP} = S_-$ and

$$\models_{tot} \{S_+\}\ p := U[p];\ q := U[q]\ \{S_+\}$$

2. Sometimes, equality "$p = q$" can be expressed in a different way; that is, as the operator

$$=_\mathcal{B} = |\Psi\rangle\langle\Psi|$$

on $\mathcal{H} \otimes \mathcal{H}$, where $d = \dim \mathcal{H}$ is the dimension of $\mathcal{H}$, and

$$|\Psi\rangle = \frac{1}{\sqrt{d}} \sum_i |ii\rangle$$

is the maximally entangled state defined by an orthonormal basis $\mathcal{B} = \{|i\rangle\}$ of $\mathcal{H}$. This equality $=_\mathcal{B}$ has an intuitive explanation. The Hilbert–Schmidt inner product of two operators A, B in $\mathcal{H}$:

$$\langle A|B\rangle = tr\left(A^\dagger B\right)$$

is often used to measure the similarity between A and B. For two (mixed) states ρ, σ in $\mathcal{H}$, it can be proved that

$$\langle \rho|\sigma\rangle = d \cdot \langle\Psi|\rho \otimes \sigma|\Psi\rangle = d \cdot tr(=_\mathcal{B} (\rho \otimes \sigma)).$$

The quantity $tr(=_\mathcal{B} (\rho \otimes \sigma))$ can be interpreted as the degree that ρ, σ satisfies relation $=_\mathcal{B}$. Obviously, we have:

$$\models_{tot} \left\{=_{U^\dagger(\mathcal{B})}\right\}\ p := U[p];\ q := U[q]\ \{=_\mathcal{B}\}$$
$$\models_{tot} \{=_\mathcal{B}\}\ p := U[p];\ q := U[q]\ \left\{=_{U(\mathcal{B})}\right\}$$

where $=_{U(\mathcal{B})}$, $=_{U^\dagger(\mathcal{B})}$ are the equalities defined by orthonormal bases $U(\mathcal{B}) = \{U|i\rangle\}$ and $U^\dagger(\mathcal{B}) = \left\{U^\dagger|i\rangle\right\}$, respectively.

Example 6.7. Consider the following correctness formula for classical programs:

$$\models_{tot} \{X = x \wedge Y = y\}\ R := X;\ X := Y;\ Y := R\ \{X = y \wedge Y = x\}$$

It means that after executing the program, the values of variables X and Y are exchanged. To properly specify the precondition and postcondition, auxiliary (ghost) variables x, y are introduced. In quantum computing, statements $R := X$, $X := Y$ and $Y := R$ cannot be directly realised as prohibited by the nocloning principle (see Theorem 2.2). But we can consider the following modification: let X, Y, R be three quantum variables with the same state Hilbert space $\mathcal{H}$. Then we have:

$$\models_{tot} \{A\}R, X := \text{SWAP}[R, X];\ X, Y := \text{SWAP}[X, Y]; \tag{6.19}$$
$$Y, R := \text{SWAP}[Y, R]\{(\text{SWAP} \otimes I)A(\text{SWAP} \otimes I)\}$$

for any quantum predicate A in $\mathcal{H} \otimes \mathcal{H} \otimes \mathcal{H}$, where the first, second and third $\mathcal{H}$ are the state Hilbert spaces of X, Y, R respectively, and I is the identity operator on $\mathcal{H}$. Note that we do not use any auxiliary (ghost) variable in correctness formula (6.19). If we set

$$A = |\varphi\rangle\langle\varphi| \otimes |\psi\rangle\langle\psi| \otimes I,$$

where $|\varphi\rangle, |\psi\rangle \in \mathcal{H}$, then it holds that

$$\models_{tot} \{|\varphi\rangle\langle\varphi| \otimes |\psi\rangle\langle\psi| \otimes I\}R, X := \text{SWAP}[R, X];\ Y, Y := \text{SWAP}[X, Y];$$
$$Y, R := \text{SWAP}[Y, R]\ \{|\psi\rangle\langle\psi| \otimes |\varphi\rangle\langle\varphi| \otimes I\} \tag{6.20}$$

Intuitively, the precondition and postcondition of (6.20) means "$X = |\varphi\rangle$ and $Y = |\psi\rangle$", "$X = |\psi\rangle$ and $Y = |\varphi\rangle$", respectively. Here, auxiliary variables $|\varphi\rangle, |\psi\rangle$ are employed.

Example 6.8 (Correctness of three quantum dials). Let us consider program *qflip* in Example 5.1. We write:

$$|GHZ\rangle = \frac{1}{\sqrt{2}}(|\heartsuit, \heartsuit, \heartsuit\rangle + |\diamondsuit, \diamondsuit, \diamondsuit\rangle)$$

for the GHZ (Greenberger–Horne–Zeilinger) state, a typical entangled state of three qubits,

$$|\Phi\rangle = \frac{1}{2}(|\heartsuit, \heartsuit, \heartsuit\rangle + |\heartsuit, \diamondsuit, \diamondsuit\rangle + |\diamondsuit, \heartsuit, \diamondsuit\rangle + |\diamondsuit, \diamondsuit, \heartsuit\rangle)$$

and $|\Psi\rangle = |\heartsuit, \heartsuit, \heartsuit\rangle$. Let $A = |\Phi\rangle\langle\Phi|$, $B = |\Psi\rangle\langle\Psi|$, and $C = |GHZ\rangle\langle GHZ|$. Obviously, A, B and C are all quantum predicates. It is easy to check that

$$\models_{tot} \{A\}qflip\{C\}, \qquad \models_{tot} \left\{\frac{1}{4}B\right\} qflip\{C\}.$$

This means that if the input is state $|\Phi\rangle$, then program *qflip* will certainly output the GHZ state; and if the input is state $|\Psi\rangle$, it will output a state $|\Gamma\rangle$ that is similar to the GHZ state in the sense:

$$\Pr(|\Gamma\rangle \text{ and the GHZ state cannot be discriminated}) \geq \frac{1}{4}.$$

Note that partial and total correctness are the same for *qflip* because it does not contain any loop. The quantum predicates A, B, C are very simple and defined by a particular input/output state. Of course, Definition 6.8 can be used for any quantum predicates.

6.3   Weakest preconditions of quantum programs

In Section 6.1.1, we already defined the notion of weakest precondition for a general quantum operation (thought of as the denotational semantics of a quantum program). In this subsection, we further consider its syntactic counterpart, namely weakest precondition for a quantum program written in the quantum **while**-language defined in Section 5.1. As in the case of classical Hoare logic, weakest preconditions and weakest liberal preconditions can be defined for quantum programs corresponding to total correctness and partial correctness, respectively. In practical applications, they can be used in backward analysis of quantum programs. Theoretically, they will play a key role in establishing the (relative) completeness of quantum Hoare logic.

Definition 6.9. Let S be a quantum **while**-program and $P \in \mathcal{P}(\mathcal{H}_{all})$ be a quantum predicate in $\mathcal{H}_{all}$.

1. The weakest precondition of S with respect to P is defined to be the quantum predicate $wp.S.P \in \mathcal{P}(\mathcal{H}_{all})$ satisfying the following conditions:
   a. $\models_{tot} \{wp.S.P\}S\{P\}$;
   b. if quantum predicate $Q \in \mathcal{P}(\mathcal{H}_{all})$ satisfies $\models_{tot} \{Q\}S\{P\}$ then $Q \sqsubseteq wp.S.P$.
2. The weakest liberal precondition of S with respect to P is defined to be the quantum predicate $wlp.S.P \in \mathcal{P}(\mathcal{H}_{all})$ satisfying the following conditions:
   a. $\models_{par} \{wlp.S.P\}S\{P\}$;
   b. if quantum predicate $Q \in \mathcal{P}(\mathcal{H}_{all})$ satisfies $\models_{par} \{Q\}S\{P\}$ then $Q \sqsubseteq wlp.S.P$.

By comparing the above definition and Definition 6.3, we can see that they are compatible; that is,

$$wp.S.P = wp(\llbracket S \rrbracket)(P). \tag{6.21}$$

Note that the left-hand side of this equality is given directly in terms of program S, whereas the right-hand side is given in terms of the semantics of S.

Structural representation of weakest (liberal) preconditions: Since quantum weakest (liberal) preconditions considered in this section are defined for quantum programs with syntactic structures (written in the quantum **while**-language), they have explicit representations as shown in the next two propositions. These representations will be essentially used in the proof of the (relative) completeness of quantum Hoare logic for total and partial correctness. Let us first consider weakest preconditions of quantum programs.

Proposition 6.12. 1. $wp.\textbf{skip}.P = P$.

2. a. *If* $type(q) = \textbf{Boolean}$, *then*

$$wp.q := |0\rangle.P = |0\rangle_q \langle 0|P|0\rangle_q \langle 0| + |1\rangle_q \langle 0|P|0\rangle_q \langle 1|.$$

b. *If* $type(q) = \textbf{integer}$, *then*

$$wp.q := |0\rangle.P = \sum_{n=-\infty}^{\infty} |n\rangle_q \langle 0|P|0\rangle_q \langle n|.$$

3. $wp.\overline{q} := U[\overline{q}].P = U^\dagger P U$.

4. $wp.S_1; S_2.P = wp.S_1.(wp.S_2.P)$.

5. $wp.\textbf{if } (\square m \cdot M[\overline{q}] = m \rightarrow S_m) \textbf{ fi}.P = \sum_m M_m^\dagger (wp.S_m.P) M_m$.

6. $wp.(\textbf{while } M[\overline{q}] = 1 \textbf{ do } S \textbf{ od}).P = \bigsqcup_{n=0}^{\infty} P_n$, *where*

$$\begin{cases} P_0 = 0_{\mathcal{H}_{all}}, \\ P_{n+1} = M_0^\dagger P M_0 + M_1^\dagger (wp.S.P_n) M_1 \quad \text{for all } n \geq 0. \end{cases}$$

Proof. The trick is to simultaneously prove this proposition and Corollary 6.1 below by induction on the structure of quantum program S.

Case 1. $S \equiv \textbf{skip}$. Obvious.

Case 2. $S \equiv q := |0\rangle$. We only consider the case of $type(q) = \textbf{integer}$, and the case of $type(q) = \textbf{Boolean}$ is similar. First, it holds that

$$tr\left(\left(\sum_{n=-\infty}^{\infty} |n\rangle_q \langle 0|P|0\rangle_q \langle n|\right)\rho\right) = tr\left(P\sum_{n=-\infty}^{\infty} |0\rangle_q \langle n|\rho|n\rangle_q \langle 0|\right)$$
$$= tr(P[\![q := |0\rangle]\!](\rho)).$$

On the other hand, for any quantum predicate $Q \in \mathcal{P}(\mathcal{H}_{all})$, if

$$\models_{tot} \{Q\}q := |0\rangle\{P\},$$

i.e.

$$tr(Q\rho) \leq tr(P[\![q := |0\rangle]\!](\rho))$$
$$= tr\left(\left(\sum_{n=-\infty}^{\infty} |n\rangle_q \langle 0|P|0\rangle_q \langle n|\right)\rho\right)$$

for all $\rho \in \mathcal{D}(\mathcal{H}_{all})$, then it follows from Lemma 6.2 that

$$Q \sqsubseteq \sum_{n=-\infty}^{\infty} |n\rangle_q \langle 0|P|0\rangle_q \langle n|.$$

Case 3. $S \equiv \overline{q} := U[\overline{q}]$. Similar to Case 2.

Case 4. $S \equiv S_1; S_2$. It follows from the induction hypothesis on S_1 and S_2 that

$$tr\left((wp.S_1.(wp.S_2.P))\rho\right) = tr\left((wp.S_2.P)[\![S_1]\!](\rho)\right)$$
$$= tr\left(P[\![S_2]\!]([\![S_1]\!](\rho))\right)$$
$$= tr\left(P[\![S_1; S_2]\!](\rho)\right).$$

If $\models_{tot} \{Q\}S_1; S_2\{P\}$, then for all $\rho \in \mathcal{D}(\mathcal{H}_{all})$, we have:

$$tr(QP) \leq tr\left(P[\![S_1; S_2]\!](\rho)\right) = tr((wp.S_1.(wp.S_2.P))\rho).$$

Therefore, it follows from Lemma 6.2 that $Q \sqsubseteq wp.S_1.(wp.S_2.P)$.

Case 5. $S \equiv \mathbf{if}\ (\square m \cdot M[\overline{q}] = m \rightarrow S_m)\ \mathbf{fi}$. Applying the induction hypothesis on S_m, we obtain:

$$
tr\left(\left(\sum_m M_m^\dagger (wp.S_m.P) M_m\right)\rho\right) = \sum_m tr\left((wp.S_m.P) M_m \rho M_m^\dagger\right)
$$

$$
= \sum_m tr\left(P[\![S_m]\!]\left(M_m \rho M_m^\dagger\right)\right)
$$

$$
= tr\left(P \sum_m [\![S_m]\!]\left(M_m \rho M_m^\dagger\right)\right)
$$

$$
= tr\left(P[\![\mathbf{if}\ (\square m \cdot M[\overline{q}] = m \rightarrow S_m)\ \mathbf{fi}]\!](\rho)\right).
$$

If

$$
\models_{tot} \{Q\}\mathbf{if}\ (\square m \cdot M[\overline{q}] = m \rightarrow S_m)\ \mathbf{fi}\{P\},
$$

then

$$
tr(Q\rho) \leq tr\left(\left(\sum_m M_m^\dagger (wp.S_m.P) M_m\right)\rho\right)
$$

for all ρ, and it follows from Lemma 6.2 that

$$
Q \sqsubseteq \sum_m M_m^\dagger (wlp.S_m.P) M_m.
$$

Case 6. $S \equiv \mathbf{while}\ M[\overline{q}] = 1\ \mathbf{do}\ S'\ \mathbf{od}$. For simplicity, we write $(\mathbf{while})^n$ for the nth syntactic approximation "$(\mathbf{while}\ M[\overline{q}] = 1\ \mathbf{do}\ S'\ \mathbf{od})^n$" of loop S (see Definition 5.12). First, we have:

$$
tr(P_n\rho) = tr\left(P[\![(\mathbf{while})^n]\!](\rho)\right).
$$

This claim can be proved by induction on n. The basis case of $n = 0$ is obvious. By the induction hypotheses on n and S', we obtain:

$$
tr(P_{n+1}\rho) = tr\left(M_0^\dagger P M_0 \rho\right) + tr\left(M_1^\dagger (wp.S'.P_n) M_1 \rho\right)
$$

$$
= tr\left(P M_0 \rho M_0^\dagger\right) + tr\left((wp.S'.P_n) M_1 \rho M_1^\dagger\right)
$$

$$
= tr\left(P M_0 \rho M_0^\dagger\right) + tr\left(P_n [\![S']\!]\left(M_1 \rho M_1^\dagger\right)\right)
$$

$$
= tr\left(P M_0 \rho M_0^\dagger\right) + tr\left(P[\![(\mathbf{while})^n]\!]\left([\![S']\!]\left(M_1 \rho M_1^\dagger\right)\right)\right)
$$

$$
= tr\left[P\left(M_0 \rho M_0^\dagger + [\![S'; (\mathbf{while})^n]\!]\left(M_1 \rho M_1^\dagger\right)\right)\right]
$$

$$
= tr\left(P[\![(\mathbf{while})^{n+1}]\!](\rho)\right).
$$

Now continuity of trace operator yields:

$$
tr\left(\left(\bigsqcup_{n=0}^{\infty} P_n\right)\rho\right) = \bigsqcup_{n=0}^{\infty} tr(P_n\rho)
$$

$$
= \bigsqcup_{n=0}^{\infty} tr\left(P[\![(\mathbf{while})^n]\!](\rho)\right)
$$

$$
= tr\left(P \bigsqcup_{n=0}^{\infty} [\![(\mathbf{while})^n]\!](\rho)\right)
$$

$$
= tr\left(P[\![\mathbf{while}\ M[\overline{q}] = 1\ \mathbf{do}\ S'\ \mathbf{od}]\!](\rho)\right).
$$

So, if

$$\models_{tot} \{Q\}\textbf{while } M[\overline{q}] = 1 \textbf{ do } S' \textbf{ od}\{P\},$$

then

$$tr(Q\rho) \leq tr\left(\left(\bigsqcup_{n=0}^{\infty} P_n\right)\rho\right)$$

for all ρ, and by Lemma 6.2 we obtain $Q \sqsubseteq \bigsqcup_{n=0}^{\infty} P_n$. $\qquad\qquad\square$

The following corollary shows that the probability that an initial state ρ satisfies the weakest precondition $wp.S.P$ is equal to the probability that the terminal state $[\![S]\!](\rho)$ satisfies P. It follows from the proof of the above proposition. But it can also be derived from Eqs (6.5) and (6.21).

Corollary 6.1. *For any quantum **while**-program S, for any quantum predicate $P \in \mathcal{P}(\mathcal{H}_{all})$, and for any partial density operator $\rho \in \mathcal{D}(\mathcal{H}_{all})$, we have:*

$$tr((wp.S.P)\rho) = tr(P[\![S]\!](\rho)).$$

We can also give explicit representations of weakest liberal preconditions of quantum programs according to their syntactic structures.

Proposition 6.13. **1.** $wlp.\textbf{skip}.P = P$.
2. a. *If* $type(q) = \textbf{Boolean}$, *then*

$$wlp.q := |0\rangle.P = |0\rangle_q \langle 0|P|0\rangle_q \langle 0| + |1\rangle_q \langle 0|P|0\rangle_q \langle 1|.$$

b. *If* $type(q) = \textbf{integer}$, *then*

$$wlp.q := |0\rangle.P = \sum_{n=-\infty}^{\infty} |n\rangle_q \langle 0|P|0\rangle_q \langle n|.$$

3. $wlp.\overline{q} := U[\overline{q}].P = U^{\dagger}PU$.
4. $wlp.S_1; S_2.P = wlp.S_1.(wlp.S_2.P)$.
5. $wlp.\textbf{if } (\square m \cdot M[\overline{q}] := m \rightarrow S_m) \textbf{ fi}.P = \sum_m M_m^{\dagger}(wlp.S_m.P)M_m$.
6. $wlp.(\textbf{while } M[\overline{q}] = 1 \textbf{ do } S \textbf{ od}).P = \bigsqcap_{n=0}^{\infty} P_n$, *where*

$$\begin{cases} P_0 = I_{\mathcal{H}_{all}}, \\ P_{n+1} = M_0^{\dagger}PM_0 + M_1^{\dagger}(wlp.S.P_n)M_1 & \text{for all } n \geq 0. \end{cases}$$

Proof. Similar to the case of weakest precondition, we prove this proposition and its corollary stated below simultaneously by induction on the structure of quantum program S.

Case 1. $S \equiv \textbf{skip}$, or $q := |0\rangle$, or $\overline{q} := U[\overline{q}]$. Similar to Cases 1, 2, and 3 in the proof of Proposition 6.12.

Case 2. $S \equiv S_1; S_2$. First, with the induction hypothesis on S_1 and S_2, we have:

$$\begin{aligned} tr\left(wlp.S_1.(wlp.S_2.P)\rho\right) &= tr\left(wlp.S_2.P[\![S_1]\!](\rho)\right) + \left[tr(\rho) - tr\left([\![S_1]\!](\rho)\right)\right] \\ &= tr\left(P[\![S_2]\!]\left([\![S_1]\!](\rho)\right)\right) + \left[tr\left([\![S_1]\!](\rho)\right) - tr\left([\![S_2]\!]\left([\![S_1]\!](\rho)\right)\right)\right] \\ &\quad + \left[tr(\rho) - tr\left([\![S_1]\!](\rho)\right)\right] \\ &= tr\left(P[\![S_2]\!]\left([\![S_1]\!](\rho)\right)\right) + \left[tr(\rho) - tr\left([\![S_2]\!]\left([\![S_1]\!](\rho)\right)\right)\right] \\ &= tr(P[\![S]\!](\rho)) + [tr(\rho) - tr([\![S]\!](\rho))]. \end{aligned}$$

If $\models_{par} \{Q\}S\{P\}$, then it holds that

$$\begin{aligned} tr(Q\rho) &\leq tr(P[\![S]\!](\rho)) + [tr(\rho) - tr([\![S]\!](\rho))] \\ &= tr\left(wlp.S_1.(wlp.S_2.P)\rho\right) \end{aligned}$$

for all $\rho \in \mathcal{D}(\mathcal{H}_{all})$, and by Lemma 6.2 we obtain:

$$Q \sqsubseteq wlp.S_1.(wlp.S_2.P).$$

Case 3. $S \equiv \textbf{if } (\square m \cdot M[\overline{q}] = m \rightarrow S_m) \textbf{ fi}$. It can be derived by induction hypothesis on all S_m that

$$tr\left(\sum_m M_m^\dagger (wlp.S_m.P)M_m\rho\right) = \sum_m tr\left(M_m^\dagger (wlp.S_m.P)M_m\rho\right)$$

$$= \sum_m tr\left((wlp.S_m.P)M_m\rho M_m^\dagger\right)$$

$$= \sum_m \left\{ tr\left(P[\![S_m]\!]\left(M_m\rho M_m^\dagger\right)\right) + \left[tr\left(M_m\rho M_m^\dagger\right) - tr\left([\![S_m]\!]\left(M_m\rho M_m^\dagger\right)\right)\right]\right\}$$

$$= \sum_m tr\left(P[\![S_m]\!]\left(M_m\rho M_m^\dagger\right)\right) + \left[\sum_m tr\left(M_m\rho M_m^\dagger\right) - \sum_m tr\left([\![S_m]\!]\left(M_m\rho M_m^\dagger\right)\right)\right]$$

$$= tr\left(P\sum_m [\![S_m]\!]\left(M_m\rho M_m^\dagger\right)\right)$$

$$\quad + \left[tr\left(\rho \sum_m M_m^\dagger M_m\right) - tr\left(\sum_m [\![S_m]\!]\left(M_m\rho M_m^\dagger\right)\right)\right]$$

$$= tr(P[\![S]\!](\rho)) + [tr(\rho) - tr([\![S]\!](\rho))]$$

because

$$\sum_m M_m^\dagger M_m = I_{\mathcal{H}_{\overline{q}}}.$$

If $\models_{par} \{Q\}S\{P\}$, then for all $\rho \in \mathcal{D}(\mathcal{H}_{all})$, it holds that

$$tr(Q\rho) \leq tr(P[\![S]\!](\rho)) + [tr(\rho) - tr([\![S]\!](\rho))]$$

$$= tr\left(\sum_m M_m^\dagger (wlp.S_m.P)M_m\rho\right).$$

This together with Lemma 6.2 implies

$$Q \sqsubseteq \sum_m M_m^\dagger (wlp.S_m.P)M_m.$$

Case 4. $S \equiv \textbf{while } M[\overline{q}] = 1 \textbf{ do } S' \textbf{ od}$. We first prove that

$$tr(P_n\rho) = tr\left(P[\![(\textbf{while})^n]\!](\rho)\right) + \left[tr(\rho) - tr\left([\![(\textbf{while})^n]\!](\rho)\right)\right] \qquad (6.22)$$

by induction on n, where $(\textbf{while})^n$ is an abbreviation of the syntactic approximation $(\textbf{while } M[\overline{q}] = 1 \textbf{ do } S' \textbf{ od})^n$. The case of $n = 0$ is obvious. By induction on S' and induction hypothesis on n, we observe:

$$tr(P_{n+1}\rho) = tr\left[\left(M_0^\dagger P M_0\right) + M_1^\dagger \left(wlp.S'.P_n\right) M_1\rho\right]$$

$$= tr\left(M_0^\dagger P M_0\rho\right) + tr\left(M_1^\dagger \left(wlp.S'.P_n\right) M_1\rho\right)$$

$$= tr\left(P M_0\rho M_0^\dagger\right) + tr\left(\left(wlp.S'.P_n\right) M_1\rho M_1^\dagger\right)$$

$$= tr\left(P M_0\rho M_0^\dagger\right) + tr\left(P_n[\![S']\!]\left(M_1\rho M_1^\dagger\right)\right) + \left[tr\left(M_1\rho M_1^\dagger\right) - tr\left([\![S']\!]\left(M_1\rho M_1^\dagger\right)\right)\right]$$

$$= tr\left(P M_0\rho M_0^\dagger\right) + tr\left(P[\![(\textbf{while})^n]\!]\left([\![S]\!]\left(M_1\rho M_1^\dagger\right)\right)\right)$$

$$\quad + \left[tr\left([\![S]\!]\left(M_1\rho M_1^\dagger\right)\right) - tr\left([\![(\textbf{while})^n]\!]\left([\![S]\!]\left(M_1\rho M_1^\dagger\right)\right)\right)\right] + \left[tr\left(M_1\rho M_1^\dagger\right) - tr\left([\![S']\!]\left(M_1\rho M_1^\dagger\right)\right)\right]$$

$$= tr\left(P\left[M_0\rho M_0^\dagger + [\![(\textbf{while})^n]\!]\left([\![S]\!]\left(M_1\rho M_1^\dagger\right)\right)\right]\right)$$
$$+ \left[tr(\rho) - tr\left(M_0\rho M_0^\dagger + [\![(\textbf{while})^n]\!]\left([\![S]\!]\left(M_1\rho M_1^\dagger\right)\right)\right)\right]$$
$$= tr\left(P[\![(\textbf{while})^{n+1}]\!](\rho)\right) + \left[tr(\rho) - tr\left([\![(\textbf{while})^{n+1}]\!](\rho)\right)\right].$$

This completes the proof of Eq. (6.22). Note that quantum predicate $P \sqsubseteq I$. Then $I - P$ is positive, and by continuity of trace operator we obtain:

$$tr\left(\left(\prod_{n=0}^{\infty} P_n\right)\rho\right) = \prod_{n=0}^{\infty} tr\left(P_n\rho\right)$$
$$= \prod_{n=0}^{\infty} \left\{tr\left(P[\![(\textbf{while})^n]\!](\rho)\right) + \left[tr(\rho) - tr\left([\![(\textbf{while})^n]\!](\rho)\right)\right]\right\}$$
$$= tr(\rho) + \prod_{n=0}^{\infty} tr\left[(P - I)[\![(\textbf{while})^n]\!](\rho)\right]$$
$$= tr(\rho) + tr\left[(P - I)\bigsqcup_{n=0}^{\infty}[\![(\textbf{while})^n]\!](\rho)\right]$$
$$= tr(\rho) + tr[(P - I)[\![S]\!](\rho)]$$
$$= tr(P[\![S]\!](\rho)) + [tr(\rho) - tr([\![S]\!](\rho))].$$

For any $Q \in \mathcal{P}(\mathcal{H}_{all})$, $\models_{par} \{Q\}S\{P\}$ implies:

$$tr(Q\rho) \leq tr(P[\![S]\!](\rho)) + [tr(\rho) - tr([\![S]\!](\rho))]$$
$$= tr\left(\left(\prod_{n=0}^{\infty} P_n\right)\rho\right)$$

for all $\rho \in \mathcal{D}(\mathcal{H}_{all})$. This together with Lemma 6.2 leads to $Q \sqsubseteq \prod_{n=0}^{\infty} P_n$. $\qquad\square$

Corollary 6.2. *For any quantum **while**-program S, for any quantum predicate $P \in \mathcal{P}(\mathcal{H}_{all})$, and for any partial density operator $\rho \in \mathcal{D}(\mathcal{H}_{all})$, we have:*

$$tr((wlp.S.P)\rho) = tr(P[\![S]\!](\rho)) + [tr(\rho) - tr([\![S]\!](\rho)].$$

The above lemma means that the probability that an initial state ρ satisfies the weakest liberal precondition $wlp.S.P$ is equal to the sum of the probability that the terminal state $[\![S]\!](\rho)$ satisfies P and the probability that S does not terminate when starting from ρ.

Recursive characterisations of weakest (liberal) preconditions of quantum loops: As one may expect, weakest preconditions and weakest liberal preconditions of quantum **while**-loops enjoy a recursive characterisation. This characterisation provides a key step in the proof of (relative) completeness of quantum Hoare logic.

Proposition 6.14. *We write **while** for quantum loop "**while** $M[\bar{q}] = 1$ **do** S **od**". Then for any $P \in \mathcal{P}(\mathcal{H}_{all})$, we have:*
1. $wp.\textbf{while}.P = M_0^\dagger P M_0 + M_1^\dagger(wp.S.(wp.\textbf{while}.P))M_1.$
2. $wlp.\textbf{while}.P = M_0^\dagger P M_0 + M_1^\dagger(wlp.S.(wlp.\textbf{while}.P))M_1.$

Proof. We only prove (2), and the proof of (1) is similar and easier. For every $\rho \in \mathcal{D}(\mathcal{H}_{all})$, by Proposition 6.13(2) we observe:

$$tr\left[\left(M_0^\dagger P M_0 + M_1^\dagger(wlp.S.(wlp.\textbf{while}.P))M_1\right)\rho\right]$$
$$= tr\left(P M_0\rho M_0^\dagger\right) + tr\left[(wlp.S.(wlp.\textbf{while}.P))M_1\rho M_1^\dagger\right]$$

$$= tr\left(PM_0\rho M_0^\dagger\right) + tr\left[(wlp.\textbf{while}.P)[\![S]\!]\left(M_1\rho M_1^\dagger\right)\right]$$
$$+ \left[tr\left(M_1\rho M_1^\dagger\right) - tr\left([\![S]\!]\left(M_1\rho M_1^\dagger\right)\right)\right]$$
$$= tr\left(PM_0\rho M_0^\dagger\right) + tr\left[P[\![\textbf{while}]\!]\left([\![S]\!]\left(M_1\rho M_1^\dagger\right)\right)\right]$$
$$+ \left[tr\left([\![S]\!]\left(M_1\rho M_1^\dagger\right)\right) - tr\left([\![\textbf{while}]\!]\left([\![S]\!]\left(M_1\rho M_1^\dagger\right)\right)\right)\right] + \left[tr\left(M_1\rho M_1^\dagger\right) - tr\left([\![S]\!]\left(M_1\rho M_1^\dagger\right)\right)\right]$$
$$= tr\left[P\left(M_0\rho M_0^\dagger + [\![\textbf{while}]\!]\left([\![S]\!]\left(M_1\rho M_1^\dagger\right)\right)\right)\right]$$
$$+ \left[tr\left(M_1\rho M_1^\dagger\right) - tr\left([\![\textbf{while}]\!]\left([\![S]\!]\left(M_1\rho M_1^\dagger\right)\right)\right)\right]$$
$$= tr(P[\![\textbf{while}]\!](\rho)) + \left[tr\left(\rho M_1^\dagger M_1\right) - tr\left([\![\textbf{while}]\!]\left([\![S]\!]\left(M_1\rho M_1^\dagger\right)\right)\right)\right]$$
$$= tr(P[\![\textbf{while}]\!](\rho)) + \left[tr\left(\rho\left(I - M_0^\dagger M_0\right)\right) - tr\left([\![\textbf{while}]\!]\left([\![S]\!]\left(M_1\rho M_1^\dagger\right)\right)\right)\right]$$
$$= tr(P[\![\textbf{while}]\!](\rho)) + \left[tr(\rho) - tr\left(M_0\rho M_0^\dagger + [\![\textbf{while}]\!]\left([\![S]\!]\left(M_1\rho M_1^\dagger\right)\right)\right)\right]$$
$$= tr(P[\![\textbf{while}]\!](\rho)) + [tr(\rho) - tr([\![\textbf{while}]\!](\rho))].$$

This means that

$$\left\{M_0^\dagger P M_0 + M_1^\dagger(wlp.S.(wlp.\textbf{while}.P))M_1\right\}\textbf{while}\{P\},$$

and

$$Q \sqsubseteq M_0^\dagger P M_0 + M_1^\dagger(wlp.S.(wlp.\textbf{while}.P))M_1$$

provided $\models_{par}\{Q\}\textbf{while}\{P\}$.   □

From Propositions 6.12.6 and 6.13.6 we see that the above proposition can be actually strengthened as follows:

- $wp.\textbf{while}.P$ and $wlp.\textbf{while}.P$ are the least fixed point and the greatest fixed point of functions:

$$\text{(a)} \quad X \mapsto M_0^\dagger P M_0 + M_1^\dagger(wp.S.X)M_1;$$
$$\text{(b)} \quad X \mapsto M_0^\dagger P M_0 + M_1^\dagger(wlp.S.X)M_1,$$

respectively.

To conclude this section, we suggest the reader to compare Propositions 6.12 and 6.13 with Propositions 5.1 and 5.2. She/he should observe a clear duality between them, which can be understood as a concrete embodiment of the abstract notion of Schrödinger–Heisenberg duality introduced in Definition 6.4.

6.4   Proof system for partial correctness

As said at the beginning of this chapter, the central idea of Hoare logic includes:

1. The correctness of a program is specified by a Hoare triple, with a predicate as its precondition and a predicate as its postcondition; and
2. A set of proof rules (also called inference rules) for reasoning about Hoare triples and thus proving correctness of programs, called the axiomatic system of Hoare logic. Each proof rule is given in the form of

$$\frac{\{P_1\}\,S_1\,\{Q_1\} \quad \cdots \quad \{P_n\}\,S_n\,\{Q_n\}}{\{P\}\,S\,\{Q\}} \tag{6.23}$$

The rule (6.23) means that correctness formula $\{P\}\,S\,\{Q\}$ can be inferred from correctness formulas $\{P_1\}S_1\{Q_1\}, \cdots,$ $\{P_n\}S_n\{Q_n\}$; in other words, if $\{P_1\}\,S_1\,\{Q_1\}, ..., \{P_n\}\,S_n\,\{Q_n\}$ are all true, then $\{P\}\,S\,\{Q\}$ is also true. If particular, if $n = 0$; that is, the premise is empty, then rule (6.23) is called an axiom.

We have introduced quantum predicates and quantum correctness formulas in the previous sections. Now we are ready to present an axiomatic system of quantum Hoare logic for proving correctness of quantum **while**-programs. As is well-known, the axiomatic system of Hoare logic is often presented as two proof systems, one for partial correctness and one for

$$(CAx.Sk) \quad \{P\}\mathbf{Skip}\{P\}$$

$$(CAx.Ass) \quad \{Q[t/u]\}\, u := t\{Q\}$$

$$(CR.SC) \quad \frac{\{P\}S_1\{Q\} \quad \{Q\}S_2\{R\}}{\{P\}S_1;S_2\{R\}}$$

$$(CR.IF) \quad \frac{\{P\wedge b\}S_1\{Q\} \quad \{P\wedge\neg b\}S_2\{Q\}}{\{P\}\,\mathbf{if}\ b\ S_1\ \mathbf{else}\ S_2\ \mathbf{fi}\{Q\}}$$

$$(CR.LP) \quad \frac{\{P\wedge b\}S\{P\}}{\{P\}\mathbf{while}\ b\ \mathbf{do}\ S\ \mathbf{od}\{P\wedge\neg b\}}$$

$$(CR.Im) \quad \frac{P\to P' \quad \{P'\}S\{Q'\} \quad Q'\to Q}{\{P\}S\{Q\}}$$

FIGURE 6.2 Proof system PD for partial correctness of classical programs.

$$(Ax.Sk) \quad \{P\}\mathbf{Skip}\{P\}$$

$(Ax.In)$ If $type(q) = \mathbf{Boolean}$, then

$$\left\{|0\rangle_q\langle 0|P|0\rangle_q\langle 0| + |1\rangle_q\langle 0|P|0\rangle_q\langle 1|\right\} q := |0\rangle\{P\}$$

If $type(q) = \mathbf{integer}$, then

$$\left\{\sum_{n=-\infty}^{\infty}|n\rangle_q\langle 0|P|0\rangle_q\langle n|\right\} q := |0\rangle\{P\}$$

$$(Ax.UT) \quad \{U^\dagger PU\}\,\overline{q} := U\overline{q}\{P\}$$

$$(R.SC) \quad \frac{\{P\}S_1\{Q\} \quad \{Q\}S_2\{R\}}{\{P\}S_1;S_2\{R\}}$$

$$(R.IF) \quad \frac{\{P_m\}S_m\{Q\}\ \text{for all}\ m}{\left\{\sum_m M_m^\dagger P_m M_m\right\}\mathbf{if}\ (\square m\cdot M[\overline{q}]=m\to S_m)\ \mathbf{fi}\{Q\}}$$

$$(R.LP) \quad \frac{\{Q\}S\left\{M_0^\dagger PM_0+M_1^\dagger QM_1\right\}}{\left\{M_0^\dagger PM_0+M_1^\dagger QM_1\right\}\mathbf{while}\ M[\overline{q}]=1\ \mathbf{do}\ S\ \mathbf{od}\{P\}}$$

$$(R.Or) \quad \frac{P\sqsubseteq P' \quad \{P'\}S\{Q'\} \quad Q'\sqsubseteq Q}{\{P\}S\{Q\}}$$

FIGURE 6.3 Proof system qPD of partial correctness of quantum programs.

total correctness. Accordingly, the axiomatic system of quantum Hoare logic can also be divided into two proof systems. In this section, we introduce the proof system for partial correctness of quantum **while**-programs.

Proof system of Hoare logic for partial correctness: To help the reader better understand the proof system of quantum Hoare logic for partial correctness and its relationship with classical Hoare logic, let us first briefly review the proof system PD of classical Hoare logic for partial correctness. It is designed for reasoning about classical **while**-programs defined by syntax (5.1), and consists of axioms and rules listed in Fig. 6.2.

It should be pointed out that the axioms and rules in PD are given in a syntax-oriented way. Consequently, the proof of a program in Hoare logic enjoys a structure that mirrors the syntactic structure of the program. For more details about proof system PD, the reader can consult textbook [28], Chapter 3. As one may imagine, the most difficult case is proving the correctness of a **while**-loop. The predicate P in rule (CR.LP) is usually called an *invariant* of the loop. A crucial step in proving the loop is to find an appropriate invariant.

Proof system of quantum Hoare logic for partial correctness: Now let us turn to present the proof system qPD for partial correctness of quantum **while**-programs. As its classical counterpart PD, the axioms and rules in qPD are also syntax-oriented. Essentially, qPD is obtained by properly incorporating quantum features into PD. It consists of the axioms and inference rules displayed in Fig. 6.3.

It is interesting to carefully compare the axioms and rules in Fig. 6.2 for classical programs and those in Fig. 6.3 for quantum programs. The axiom (Ax.Sk) for **Skip** and rule (R.SC) for sequential composition in quantum Hoare logic are the same as their classical counterparts. In classical Hoare logic, the precondition $Q[t/u]$ of the axiom (CAx.Ass) for assignment $u := t$ is obtained by substituting variable u with expression t in the postcondition Q. The axioms (Ax.In) for initialisation and (Ax.UT) for unitary transformation in quantum Hoare logic are designed with a similar idea. The consequence rule (CR.Im) in classical Hoare logic allows to strengthen the preconditions and weaken the postconditions.

The rule (R.Or) does the same in quantum Hoare logic. The only difference between them is that implication $\rightarrow$ in (CR.Im) is replaced by the Löwner order $\sqsubseteq$ in (R.Or). The reasonableness of (R.Or) is warranted by Lemma 6.2. The most interesting difference between classical and quantum Hoare logics lies in their inference rules for case statements and **while**-loops. At the first glances, the classical rules and quantum rules are very different. The key to understand their connection is the interpretations of logical conjunction in the classical and quantum worlds. Let us first look at the rules (CR.LP) for classical loops and (R.LP) for quantum loops. In the classical case, we start from a predicate p (the precondition) and construct its conjunctions with b (the condition in the loop guard) and $\neg b$, i.e. $p \wedge b$ and $p \wedge \neg b$, respectively. Obviously, $p \wedge b$ and $p \wedge \neg b$ can be interpreted as p under the restrictions of b and $\neg b$, respectively, and we have:

$$p = (p \wedge b) \vee (p \wedge \neg b). \tag{6.24}$$

In the quantum case, however, as mentioned in Section 6.1.2, the conjunction of two predicates is not always definable. This forces us to go in the opposite direction. Inspired by reading Eq. (6.24) from right to left, we start from quantum predicate

$$A \overset{def}{=} M_0^\dagger P M_0 + M_1^\dagger Q M_1.$$

Then P, Q can be understood as A with restriction M_0 and M_1 (the measurement operators in the loop guard), denoted $A|M_0$ and $A|M_1$, respectively. This view leads to a natural correspondence between the classical predicates in rule (CR.LP) and the quantum predicates in rule (R.PL):

$$
\begin{array}{ccc}
p & p \wedge b & p \wedge \neg b \\
\updownarrow & \updownarrow & \updownarrow \\
A = M_0^\dagger P M_0 + M_1^\dagger Q M_1 & Q = A|M_1 & P = A|M_0
\end{array}
$$

With the above correspondence, it is easy to see the connection between the two rules (CR.LP) and (R.LP). Similar to the classical case, quantum predicate $A = M_0^\dagger P M_0 + M_1^\dagger Q M_1$ is called an *invariant* of the quantum loop. This notion of invariant will be significantly extended in Section 8.2, where the issue of automatically generating invariants for quantum programs will be addressed.

Exercise 6.11. Find a connection between rule (CR.IF) for classical conditional statement and (R.IF) for quantum case statement. Hint: (R.IF) is the quantum counterpart of the generalisation of (CR.IF) for classical case statement (5.2).

An application of the proof system qPD and the proof system qTD for total correctness presented in the next section will be given in Section 6.6 below where the correctness of Grover algorithm is proved using qPD and qTD. The reader who is mainly interested in the applications of quantum Hoare logic may first leave here to learn the rule (R-LT) of the system qTD in the next section and then directly move to Section 6.6. If she/he likes, the reader can return to this point after finishing Section 6.6.

Soundness and (relative) completeness: As we know, the most important issue for any logical system is its soundness and completeness. In the remainder of this section, we study soundness and completeness of the proof system qPD. We say that a correctness formula $\{P\}S\{Q\}$ is provable in qTD, written

$$\vdash_{qPD} \{P\}S\{Q\}$$

if it can be derived by a finite number of applications of the axioms and inference rules given in Fig. 6.3.

We first prove the soundness of qPD with respect to the semantics of partial correctness:

- **Soundness**: The provability of a correctness formula in the proof system qPD implies its truth in the sense of partial correctness.

Before doing this, let us introduce an auxiliary notation. Let $M = \{M_0, M_1\}$ be a (yes/no) quantum measurement. Then for $i = 0, 1$, the quantum operation $\mathcal{E}_i$ is defined by

$$\mathcal{E}_i(\rho) = M_i \rho M_i^\dagger$$

for all $\rho \in \mathcal{D}(\mathcal{H}_{all})$. This notation was already used in the proof of Proposition 5.2. It will be frequently used in this section and the next as well as in Chapter 8.

Theorem 6.1 (Soundness). *The proof system qPD is sound for partial correctness of quantum **while**-programs; that is, for any quantum **while**-program S and quantum predicates P, Q $\in \mathcal{P}$ ($\mathcal{H}_{all}$), we have:*

$$\vdash_{qPD} \{P\}S\{Q\} \text{ implies } \models_{par} \{P\}S\{Q\}.$$

Proof. We only need to show that the axioms of *qPD* are valid in the sense of partial correctness and inference rules of *qPD* preserve partial correctness.

Case 1. (Ax.Sk): It is obvious that $\models_{par} \{P\}\mathbf{skip}\{P\}$.

Case 2. (Ax.In): We only prove the case of $type(q) = \mathbf{integer}$, and the case of $type(q) = \mathbf{Boolean}$ is similar. For any $\rho \in \mathcal{D}(\mathcal{H}_{all})$, it follows from Proposition 5.1.2 that

$$tr\left[\left(\sum_{n=-\infty}^{\infty} |n\rangle_q \langle 0| P |0\rangle_q \langle n|\right)\rho\right] = \sum_{n=-\infty}^{\infty} tr(|n\rangle_q \langle 0| P |0\rangle_q \langle n|\rho)$$

$$= \sum_{n=-\infty}^{\infty} tr(P|0\rangle_q \langle n|\rho|n\rangle_q \langle 0|)$$

$$= tr\left(P \sum_{n=-\infty}^{\infty} |0\rangle_q \langle n|\rho|n\rangle_q \langle 0|\right)$$

$$= tr(P[\![q := |0\rangle]\!](\rho)).$$

Therefore, we have:

$$\models_{par} \left\{\sum_{n=-\infty}^{\infty} |n\rangle_q \langle 0| P |0\rangle_q \langle n|\right\} q := |0\rangle\{P\}.$$

Case 3. (Ax.UT): It is easy to see that

$$\models_{par} \left\{U^{\dagger} P U\right\} \overline{q} := U[\overline{q}]\{P\}.$$

Case 4. (R.SC): If $\models_{par} \{P\}S_1\{Q\}$ and $\models_{par} \{Q\}S_2\{R\}$, then for any $\rho \in \mathcal{D}(\mathcal{H}_{all})$ we have:

$$tr(P\rho) \leq tr\left(Q[\![S_1]\!](\rho)\right) + \left[tr(\rho) - tr\left([\![S_1]\!](\rho)\right)\right]$$

$$\leq tr\left(R[\![S_2]\!]([\![S_1]\!](\rho))\right) + \left[tr\left([\![S_1]\!](\rho)\right) - tr\left([\![S_2]\!]([\![S_1]\!](\rho))\right)\right]$$

$$+ \left[tr(\rho) - tr\left([\![S_1]\!](\rho)\right)\right]$$

$$= tr\left(R[\![S_1; S_2]\!](\rho)\right) + \left[tr(\rho) - tr\left([\![S_1; S_2]\!](\rho)\right)\right].$$

Therefore, $\models_{par} \{P\}S_1; S_2\{R\}$ holds as desired.

Case 5. (R.IF): Assume that $\models_{par} \{P_m\}S_m\{Q\}$ for all possible measurement outcomes m. Then for all $\rho \in \mathcal{D}(\mathcal{H}_{all})$, since

$$\sum_m M_m^{\dagger} M_m = I_{\mathcal{H}_{\overline{q}}},$$

it holds that

$$tr\left(\sum_m M_m^{\dagger} P_m M_m \rho\right) = \sum_m tr\left(M_m^{\dagger} P_m M_m \rho\right)$$

$$= \sum_m tr\left(P_m M_m \rho M_m^{\dagger}\right)$$

$$\leq \sum_m \left\{tr\left(Q[\![S_m]\!]\left(M_m \rho M_m^{\dagger}\right)\right) + \left[tr\left(M_m \rho M_m^{\dagger}\right) - tr\left([\![S_m]\!]\left(M_m \rho M_m^{\dagger}\right)\right)\right]\right\}$$

$$\leq \sum_m tr\left(Q[\![S_m]\!]\left(M_m \rho M_m^{\dagger}\right)\right) + \left[\sum_m tr\left(M_m \rho M_m^{\dagger}\right) - \sum_m tr\left([\![S_m]\!]\left(M_m \rho M_m^{\dagger}\right)\right)\right]$$

$$= tr\left(Q\sum_m [\![S_m]\!]\left(M_m \rho M_m^\dagger\right)\right) + \left[tr\left(\sum_m \rho M_m^\dagger M_m\right) - tr\left(\sum_m [\![S_m]\!]\left(M_m \rho M_m^\dagger\right)\right)\right]$$

$$= tr(Q[\![\mathbf{if}...\mathbf{fi}]\!](\rho)) + [tr(\rho) - tr([\![\mathbf{if}...\mathbf{fi}]\!](\rho))],$$

and

$$\models_{par} \left\{\sum_m M_m^\dagger P_m M_m\right\} \mathbf{if}...\mathbf{fi}\{Q\},$$

where **if**...**fi** is an abbreviation of statement "**if** ($\Box m \cdot M[\overline{q}] = m \rightarrow S_m$) **fi**".

Case 6. (R.LP): Suppose that

$$\models_{par} \{Q\} S \left\{M_0^\dagger P M_0 + M_1^\dagger Q M_1\right\}.$$

Then for all $\rho \in \mathcal{D}(\mathcal{H}_{all})$, it holds that

$$tr(Q\rho) \leq tr\left(\left(M_0^\dagger P M_0 + M_1^\dagger Q M_1\right)[\![S]\!](\rho)\right) + [tr(\rho) - tr([\![S]\!](\rho))]. \tag{6.25}$$

Furthermore, we have:

$$tr\left[\left(M_0^\dagger P M_0 + M_1^\dagger Q M_1\right)\rho\right] \leq \sum_{k=0}^{n} tr\left(P\left(\mathcal{E}_0 \circ ([\![S]\!] \circ \mathcal{E}_1)^k\right)(\rho)\right)$$
$$+ tr\left(Q\left(\mathcal{E}_1 \circ ([\![S]\!] \circ \mathcal{E}_1)^n\right)(\rho)\right) \tag{6.26}$$
$$+ \sum_{k=0}^{n-1}\left[tr\left(\mathcal{E}_1 \circ ([\![S]\!] \circ \mathcal{E}_1)^k(\rho)\right) - tr\left(([\![S]\!] \circ \mathcal{E}_1)^{k+1}(\rho)\right)\right]$$

for all $n \geq 1$. In fact, Eq. (6.26) may be proved by induction on n. The case of $n = 1$ is obvious. Using Eq. (6.25), we obtain:

$$tr\left(Q\left(\mathcal{E}_1 \circ ([\![S]\!] \circ \mathcal{E}_1)^n\right)(\rho)\right) \leq tr\left(\left(M_0^\dagger P M_0 + M_1^\dagger Q M_1\right)([\![S]\!] \circ \mathcal{E}_1)^{n+1}(\rho)\right)$$
$$+ \left[tr\left((\mathcal{E}_1 \circ ([\![S]\!] \circ \mathcal{E}_1)^n)(\rho)\right) - tr\left(([\![S]\!] \circ \mathcal{E}_1)^{n+1}(\rho)\right)\right]$$
$$= tr\left(P\left(\mathcal{E}_0 \circ ([\![S]\!] \circ \mathcal{E}_1)^{n+1}\right)(\rho)\right) + tr\left(Q\left(\mathcal{E}_1 \circ ([\![S]\!] \circ \mathcal{E}_1)^{n+1}\right)(\rho)\right) \tag{6.27}$$
$$+ \left[tr\left((\mathcal{E}_1 \circ ([\![S]\!] \circ \mathcal{E}_1)^n)(\rho)\right) - tr\left(([\![S]\!] \circ \mathcal{E}_1)^{n+1}(\rho)\right)\right].$$

Combining Eqs (6.26) and (6.27), we assert that

$$tr\left[\left(M_0^\dagger P M_0 + M_1^\dagger Q M_1\right)\rho\right] \leq \sum_{k=0}^{n+1} tr\left(P\left(\mathcal{E}_0 \circ ([\![S]\!] \circ \mathcal{E}_1)^k\right)(\rho)\right)$$
$$+ tr\left(Q\left(\mathcal{E}_1 \circ ([\![S]\!] \circ \mathcal{E}_1)^{n+1}\right)(\rho)\right)$$
$$+ \sum_{k=0}^{n}\left[tr\left(\mathcal{E}_1 \circ ([\![S]\!] \circ \mathcal{E}_1)^k(\rho)\right) - tr\left(([\![S]\!] \circ \mathcal{E}_1)^{k+1}(\rho)\right)\right].$$

Therefore, Eq. (6.26) holds in the case of $n + 1$ provided it is true in the case of n, and we complete the proof of Eq. (6.26).

Now we note that

$$tr\left(\mathcal{E}_1 \circ ([\![S]\!] \circ \mathcal{E}_1)^k(\rho)\right) = tr\left(M_1([\![S]\!] \circ \mathcal{E}_1)^k(\rho)M_1^\dagger\right)$$
$$= tr\left(([\![S]\!] \circ \mathcal{E}_1)^k(\rho)M_1^\dagger M_1\right)$$
$$= tr\left(([\![S]\!] \circ \mathcal{E}_1)^k(\rho)\left(I - M_0^\dagger M_0\right)\right)$$
$$= tr\left(([\![S]\!] \circ \mathcal{E}_1)^k(\rho)\right) - tr\left((\mathcal{E}_0 \circ ([\![S]\!] \circ \mathcal{E}_1)^k)(\rho)\right).$$

Then it follows that

$$\sum_{k=0}^{n-1}\left[tr\left(\mathcal{E}_1 \circ ([\![S]\!] \circ \mathcal{E}_1)^k(\rho)\right) - tr\left(([\![S]\!] \circ \mathcal{E}_1)^{k+1}(\rho)\right)\right]$$
$$= \sum_{k=0}^{n-1} tr\left(([\![S]\!] \circ \mathcal{E}_1)^k(\rho)\right)$$
$$\quad - \sum_{k=0}^{n-1}\left[tr\left(\mathcal{E}_0 \circ ([\![S]\!] \circ \mathcal{E}_1)^k(\rho)\right) - \sum_{k=0}^{n-1} tr\left(([\![S]\!] \circ \mathcal{E}_1)^{k+1}(\rho)\right)\right] \tag{6.28}$$
$$= tr(\rho) - tr\left(([\![S]\!] \circ \mathcal{E}_1)^n(\rho)\right) - \sum_{k=0}^{n-1} tr\left(\mathcal{E}_0 \circ ([\![S]\!] \circ \mathcal{E}_1)^k(\rho)\right).$$

On the other hand, we have:

$$tr\left(Q\left(\mathcal{E}_1 \circ ([\![S]\!] \circ \mathcal{E}_1)^n\right)(\rho)\right) = tr\left(QM_1([\![S]\!] \circ \mathcal{E}_1)^n(\rho)M_1^\dagger\right)$$
$$\leq tr\left(M_1([\![S]\!] \circ \mathcal{E}_1)^n(\rho)M_1^\dagger\right)$$
$$= tr\left(([\![S]\!] \circ \mathcal{E}_1)^n(\rho)M_1^\dagger M_1\right) \tag{6.29}$$
$$= tr\left(([\![S]\!] \circ \mathcal{E}_1)^n(\rho)\left(I - M_0^\dagger M_0\right)\right)$$
$$= tr\left(([\![S]\!] \circ \mathcal{E}_1)^n\right)(\rho)) - tr\left((\mathcal{E}_0 \circ ([\![S]\!] \circ \mathcal{E}_1)^n)(\rho)\right).$$

Putting Eqs (6.28) and (6.29) into Eq. (6.26), we obtain:

$$tr\left[(M_0^\dagger P M_0 + M_1^\dagger Q M_1)\rho\right] \leq \sum_{k=0}^{n} tr\left(P(\mathcal{E}_0 \circ ([\![S]\!] \circ \mathcal{E}_1)^k)(\rho)\right)$$
$$+ \left[tr(\rho) - \sum_{k=0}^{n} tr\left((\mathcal{E}_0 \circ ([\![S]\!] \circ \mathcal{E}_1)^k)(\rho)\right)\right]$$
$$= tr\left(P\sum_{k=0}^{n}(\mathcal{E}_0 \circ ([\![S]\!] \circ \mathcal{E}_1)^k)(\rho)\right)$$
$$+ \left[tr(\rho) - tr\left(\sum_{k=0}^{n}(\mathcal{E}_0 \circ ([\![S]\!] \circ \mathcal{E}_1)^k)(\rho)\right)\right].$$

Let $n \to \infty$. Then it follows that

$$tr\left[\left(M_0^\dagger P M_0 + M_1^\dagger Q M_1\right)\rho\right] \leq tr(P[\![\mathbf{while}]\!](\rho) + [tr(\rho) - tr([\![\mathbf{while}]\!](\rho))]$$

and

$$\models_{par} \{M_0^\dagger P M_0 + M_1^\dagger Q M_1\}\mathbf{while}\{P\},$$

where **while** is an abbreviation of quantum loop "**while** $M[\overline{q}] = 1$ **do** S".

Case 7. (R.Or): The validity of this rule follows immediately from Lemma 6.2 and Definition 6.8.   □

Next, we turn to establish a (relative) completeness for the proof system qPD with respect to the semantics of partial correctness:

- **Completeness**: The truth of a quantum program in the sense of partial correctness implies its provability in the proof system qPD.

It should be noted that the Löwner ordering assertions between quantum predicates in the rule (R.Or) are statements about complex numbers. So, at this moment, only a completeness of qPD relative to the theory of the field of complex numbers may be anticipated; more precisely, we can add all statements that are true in the field of complex numbers into qPD in order to make it complete. The following theorem should be understood exactly in the sense of such a relative completeness. Furthermore, as discussed in Section 6.2, an assertion logic for specifying quantum predicates in the preconditions and postconditions is still missing, the relativity of this completeness cannot be formally formulated at this moment. A more precise discussion about the relativity will be given in the next chapter after introducing an appropriate assertion logic.

Theorem 6.2 (Completeness). *The proof system qPD is complete for partial correctness of quantum **while**-programs; that is, for any quantum **while**-program S and quantum predicates P, $Q \in \mathcal{P}(\mathcal{H}_{all})$, we have:*

$$\models_{par} \{P\}S\{Q\} \text{ implies } \vdash_{qPD} \{P\}S\{Q\}.$$

Proof. The key tool employed in this proof is weakest liberal preconditions developed in the last section. If $\models_{par} \{P\}S\{Q\}$, then by Definition 6.9 (2) we have $P \sqsubseteq wlp.S.Q$. Therefore, by the rule (R.Or) it suffices to prove the following:

- **Claim**:

$$\vdash_{qPD} \{wlp.S.Q\}S\{Q\}.$$

We proceed by induction on the structure of S to prove the above claim.

Case 1. $S \equiv$ **skip**: Immediate from the axiom (Ax.Sk).

Case 2. $S \equiv q := 0$: Immediate from the axiom (Ax.In).

Case 3. $S \equiv \overline{q} := U[\overline{q}]$: Immediate from the axiom (Ax.UT).

Case 4. $S \equiv S_1; S_2$: It follows from the induction hypothesis on S_1 and S_2 that

$$\vdash_{qPD} \{wlp.S_1.(wlp.S_2.Q)\} S_1\{wlp.S_2.Q\}$$

and

$$\vdash_{qPD} \{wlp.S_2.Q\} S_2\{Q\}.$$

We obtain:

$$\vdash_{qPD} \{wlp.S_1.(wlp.S_2.Q)\} S_1; S_2\{Q\}$$

by the rule (R.SC). Then with Proposition 6.13.4 we see that

$$\vdash_{qPD} \{wlp.S_1; S_2.Q\} S_1; S_2\{Q\}.$$

Case 5. $S \equiv$ **if** $(\square m \cdot M[\overline{q}] = m \rightarrow S_m)$ **fi**: For all m, by the induction hypothesis on S_m we obtain:

$$\vdash_{qPD} \{wlp.S_m.Q\} S_m\{Q\}.$$

Then applying the rule (R.IF) yields:

$$\vdash_{qPD} \left\{\sum_m M_m^{\dagger}(wlp.S_m.Q)M_m\right\} \textbf{if } (\square m \cdot M[\overline{q}] = m \rightarrow S_m) \textbf{ fi}\{Q\},$$

and using Proposition 6.13.5 we have:

$$\vdash_{qPD} \{wlp.\textbf{if } (\square m \cdot M[\overline{q}] = m \rightarrow S_m) \textbf{ fi}.Q\}\textbf{if } (\square m \cdot M[\overline{q}] = m \rightarrow S_m) \textbf{ fi}\{Q\}.$$

$$
\text{(CR-LT)} \quad \frac{
\begin{aligned}
&\bullet\ \{P \wedge b\}S\{P\}\\
&\bullet\ \{P \wedge b \wedge t = z\}S\{t < z\}\\
&\bullet\ P \rightarrow t \geq 0
\end{aligned}
}{\{P\}\textbf{while } b \textbf{ do } S \textbf{ od}\{P \wedge \neg b\}}
$$

FIGURE 6.4 Proof system *TD* of total correctness of classical programs.

Case 6. $S \equiv$ **while** $M[\overline{q}] = 1$ **do** S' **od**: For simplicity, we write **while** for quantum loop "**while** $M[\overline{q}] = 1$ **do** S' **od**". The induction hypothesis on S asserts that

$$\vdash_{qPD} \{wlp.S.(wlp.\textbf{while}.P)\}S\{wlp.\textbf{while}.P\}.$$

By Proposition 6.14.2 we have:

$$wlp.\textbf{while}.P = M_0^\dagger P M_0 + M_1^\dagger(wlp.S.(wlp.\textbf{while}.P))M_1.$$

Then by the rule (R.LP) we obtain:

$$\vdash_{qPD} \{wlp.\textbf{while}.P\}\textbf{while}\{P\}$$

as desired. $\qquad\square$

6.5 Proof system for total correctness

We studied the proof system *qPD* for partial correctness of quantum **while**-programs in the last section. In this section, we further study the proof system *qTD* for total correctness of quantum **while**-programs.

Proof system of Hoare logic for total correctness: For a better understanding of *qTD*, let us first briefly review the proof system *TD* for total correctness of classical programs. For more details of *TD*, see textbook [28], Chapter 3. Since proof system *PD* presented in Fig. 6.2 is able to prove the partial correctness of a program, we only need to strengthen it so that the termination of the program can be inferred within it in order to prove the total correctness of the program. We further notice that nontermination can only happen in **while**-loops. So, the rule (CR.LP) for loops in *PD* is refined in *TD* as the rule (CR.LT) in Fig. 6.4. The symbols t and z in rule (CR.LT) stand for an integer expression and an integer variable, respectively. Intuitively, t expresses a function from integers to themselves, called a *ranking function* of the loop. The premise $\{P \wedge b \wedge t = z\}S\{t < z\}$ means that the value of ranking function t is strictly decreased by each iteration of the loop body S, and $P \rightarrow t \geq 0$ means that t always takes nonnegative values, provided precondition P is true. They together warrant the termination of the loop. The ranking function used here is defined over nonnegative integers. Indeed, it can be defined over any well-ordered set.

Ranking functions of quantum loops: Similar to the classical case, the only difference between *qTD* for total correctness and *qPD* for partial correctness of quantum programs is the inference rule for quantum **while**-loops. In the system *qPD*, we do not need to consider termination of quantum loops. However, it is crucial in the system *qTD* to have a rule that can infer termination of quantum loops. To give the rule for total correctness of quantum loops, we also need a notion of ranking function which expresses the number of iterations of a quantum loop in its computation.

Definition 6.10. Let $P \in \mathcal{P}(\mathcal{H}_{all})$ be a quantum predicate and a real number $\epsilon > 0$. A function

$$t : \mathcal{D}(\mathcal{H}_{all}) \rightarrow \mathbb{N} \ (\textit{nonnegative integers})$$

is called a (P, ϵ)-ranking function of quantum loop "**while** $M[\overline{q}] = 1$ **do** S **od**" if it satisfies the following two conditions:

1. $t\left([\![S]\!]\left(M_1 \rho M_1^\dagger\right)\right) \leq t(\rho)$; and
2. $tr(P\rho) \geq \epsilon$ implies

$$t\left([\![S]\!]\left(M_1 \rho M_1^\dagger\right)\right) < t(\rho)$$

for all $\rho \in \mathcal{D}(\mathcal{H}_{all})$.

Like its classical counterpart, the purpose of a ranking function of a quantum loop is to warrant the termination of the loop. The basic idea is also that the value of the ranking function is always nonnegative and it is decreased with each iteration of the loop, and thus the loop should terminate after a finite number of iterations. A ranking function t of a classical loop "**while** B **do** S **od**" is required to satisfy the inequality:

$$t(\llbracket S \rrbracket(s)) < t(s)$$

for any input state s. It is interesting to compare this inequality with conditions 1 and 2 of the above definition. We see that the conditions 1 and 2 are two inequalities between

$$t\left(\llbracket S \rrbracket \left(M_1 \rho M_1^{\dagger}\right)\right)$$

and $t(\rho)$, but not between $t(\llbracket S \rrbracket(\rho))$ and $t(\rho)$. This is because in the implementation of the quantum loop "**while** $M[\overline{q}] = 1$ **do** S **od**", we need to perform the yes–no measurement M on ρ when checking the loop guard "$M[\overline{q}] = 1$", and the states of quantum variables will become $M_1 \rho M_1^{\dagger}$ from ρ whence the measurement outcome "yes" is observed.

The following lemma gives a characterisation of the existence of ranking function of a quantum loop in terms of the limit of the state of quantum variables when the number of iterations of the loop goes to infinity. It provides a key step for the proof of soundness and completeness of the proof system qTD.

Lemma 6.6. *Let $P \in \mathcal{P}(\mathcal{H}_{all})$ be a quantum predicate. Then the following two statements are equivalent:*

1. *for any $\epsilon > 0$, there exists a (P, ϵ)-ranking function t_{ϵ} of the **while**-loop "**while** $M[\overline{q}] = 1$ **do** S **od**";*
2. $\lim_{n \to \infty} tr\left(P(\llbracket S \rrbracket \circ \mathcal{E}_1)^n(\rho)\right) = 0$ *for all* $\rho \in \mathcal{D}(\mathcal{H}_{all})$.

Proof. $(1 \Rightarrow 2)$ We prove this implication by refutation. If

$$\lim_{n \to \infty} tr\left(P(\llbracket S \rrbracket \circ \mathcal{E}_1)^n(\rho)\right) \neq 0,$$

then there exist $\epsilon_0 > 0$ and strictly increasing sequence $\{n_k\}$ of nonnegative integers such that

$$tr\left(P(\llbracket S \rrbracket \circ \mathcal{E}_1)^{n_k}(\rho)\right) \geq \epsilon_0$$

for all $k \geq 0$. Thus, we have a (P, ϵ_0)-ranking function of loop "**while** $M[\overline{q}] = 1$ **do** S **od**". For each $k \geq 0$, we set

$$\rho_k = (\llbracket S \rrbracket \circ \mathcal{E}_1)^{n_k}(\rho).$$

Then it holds that $tr(P\rho_k) \geq \epsilon_0$, and by conditions 1 and 2 in Definition 6.10 we obtain:

$$
\begin{aligned}
t_{\epsilon_0}(\rho_k) &> t_{\epsilon_0}\left(\llbracket S \rrbracket(M_1 \rho_k M_1^{\dagger})\right) \\
&= t_{\epsilon_0}\left((\llbracket S \rrbracket \circ \mathcal{E}_1)(\rho_k)\right) \\
&\geq t_{\epsilon_0}\left((\llbracket S \rrbracket \circ \mathcal{E}_1)^{n_{k+1}-n_k}(\rho_k)\right) \\
&= t_{\epsilon_0}(\rho_{k+1}).
\end{aligned}
$$

Consequently, we have an infinitely descending chain $\{t_{\epsilon_0}(\rho_k)\}$ in $\mathbb{N}$. This is a contradiction because $\mathbb{N}$ is a well-founded set.

$(2 \Rightarrow 1)$ For each $\rho \in \mathcal{D}(\mathcal{H}_{all})$, if

$$\lim_{n \to \infty} tr\left(P(\llbracket S \rrbracket \circ \mathcal{E}_1)^n(\rho)\right) = 0,$$

then for any $\epsilon > 0$, there exists $N \in \mathbb{N}$ such that

$$tr\left(P(\llbracket S \rrbracket \circ \mathcal{E}_1)^n(\rho)\right) < \epsilon$$

for all $n \geq N$. We define:

$$t_{\epsilon}(\rho) = \min\left\{N \in \mathbb{N} : tr\left(P(\llbracket S \rrbracket \circ \mathcal{E}_1)^n(\rho)\right) < \epsilon \text{ for all } n \geq N\right\}.$$

- $\{Q\}S\{M_0^\dagger P M_0 + M_1^\dagger Q M_1\}$

- for any $\epsilon > 0$, t_ϵ is a $(M_1^\dagger Q M_1, \epsilon)$ − ranking function

    of loop **while** $M[\overline{q}] = 1$ **do** S **od**

(R.LT) ——————————————————————————————————

$\{M_0^\dagger P M_0 + M_1^\dagger Q M_1\}$**while** $M[\overline{q}] = 1$ **do** S **od**$\{P\}$

FIGURE 6.5 Proof system qTD of total correctness of quantum programs.

Now it suffices to show that t_ϵ is a (P, ϵ)-ranking function of loop "**while** $M[\overline{q}] = 1$ **do** S **od**". To this end, we consider the following two cases:

Case 1. $tr(P\rho) \geq \epsilon$: Suppose that $t_\epsilon(\rho) = N$. Then $tr(P\rho) \geq \epsilon$ implies $N \geq 1$. By the definition of t_ϵ, we assert that

$$tr\left(P(\llbracket S \rrbracket \circ \mathcal{E}_1)^n(\rho)\right) < \epsilon$$

for all $n \geq N$. Thus, for all $n \geq N - 1 \geq 0$,

$$tr\left(P(\llbracket S \rrbracket \circ \mathcal{E}_1)^n\left(\llbracket S \rrbracket\left(M_1^\dagger \rho M_1\right)\right)\right) = tr\left(P(\llbracket S \rrbracket \circ \mathcal{E}_1)^{n+1}(\rho)\right) < \epsilon.$$

Therefore, we have:

$$t_\epsilon\left(\llbracket S \rrbracket\left(M_1^\dagger \rho M_1\right)\right) \leq N - 1 < N = t_\epsilon(\rho).$$

Case 2. $tr(P\rho) < \epsilon$: Again, suppose that $t_\epsilon(\rho) = N$. Now we have the following two subcases:

Subcase 2.1. $N = 0$: Then for all $n \geq 0$, it holds that

$$tr\left(P(\llbracket S \rrbracket \circ \mathcal{E}_1)^n(\rho)\right) < \epsilon.$$

Furthermore, it is easy to see that

$$t_\epsilon\left(\llbracket S \rrbracket\left(M_1 \rho M_1^\dagger\right)\right) = 0 = t_\epsilon(\rho).$$

Subcase 2.2. $N \geq 1$: We can derive that

$$t_\epsilon(\rho) > t_\epsilon\left(\llbracket S \rrbracket\left(M_1 \rho M_1^\dagger\right)\right)$$

in the way of Case 1. □

The technique of termination analysis by ranking function will be further extended in Section 8.3 for a more general class of quantum programs.

Proof system of quantum Hoare logic for total correctness: Now we are ready to present the proof system qTD for total correctness of quantum **while**-programs. As mentioned before, the system qTD differs from the proof system qPD for partial correctness of quantum programs only in the inference rule for loops. More precisely, the proof system qTD consists of the axioms (Ax.Sk), (Ax.In), and (Ax.UT) and inference rules (R.SC), (R.IF), and (R.Or) in Fig. 6.3 as well as inference rule (R.LT) in Fig. 6.5.

An application of the rule (R.LT) to prove total correctness of Grover search algorithm will be presented in Section 6.6 below.

Soundness and (relative) completeness: The remainder of this subsection is devoted to establish soundness and (relative) completeness of proof system qTD for total correctness of quantum **while**-programs. Intuitively, they mean:

- **Soundness and completeness**: The provability of a correctness formula (Hoare triple) for a quantum program in the proof system qTD is equivalent to its truth in the sense of total correctness.

To formally present them, we write:

$$\vdash_{qTD} \{P\}S\{Q\}$$

whenever the correctness formula $\{P\}S\{Q\}$ can be derived by a finite number of applications of the axioms and inference rules in qTD.

Theorem 6.3 (Soundness). *The proof system qTD is sound for total correctness of quantum **while**-programs; that is, for any quantum program S and quantum predicates $P, Q \in \mathcal{P}(\mathcal{H}_{all})$, we have:*

$$\vdash_{qTD} \{P\}S\{Q\} \text{ implies } \models_{tot} \{P\}S\{Q\}.$$

Proof. It suffices to show that the axioms of *qTD* are valid in the sense of total correctness, and inference rules of *qTD* preserve total correctness.

The proof for soundness of (Ax.Sk), (Ax.In), and (Ax.UT) is similar to the case of partial correctness. The proof of the remaining inference rules is given as follows:

Case 1. (R.SC): Suppose that $\models_{tot} \{P\}S_1\{Q\}$ and $\models_{tot} \{Q\}S_2\{R\}$. Then for any $\rho \in \mathcal{D}(\mathcal{H}_{all})$, with Proposition 5.1.4 we obtain:

$$
\begin{aligned}
tr(P\rho) &\leq tr\left(Q[\![S_1]\!](\rho)\right) \\
&\leq tr\left(R[\![S_2]\!]\left([\![S_1]\!](\rho)\right)\right) \\
&= tr\left(P[\![S_1; S_2]\!](\rho)\right).
\end{aligned}
$$

Therefore, $\models_{tot} \{P\}S_1; S_2\{R\}$.

Case 2. (R-IF): Suppose that $\models_{tot} \{P_m\} S_m\{Q\}$ for all possible measurement outcomes m. Then for any $\rho \in \mathcal{D}(\mathcal{H}_{all})$, it holds that

$$tr\left(P_m M_m \rho M_m^\dagger\right) \leq tr\left(Q[\![S_m]\!]\left(M_m \rho M_m^\dagger\right)\right).$$

Therefore, we have:

$$
\begin{aligned}
tr\left(\sum_m M_m^\dagger P_m M_m \rho\right) &= \sum_m tr\left(P_m M_m \rho M_m^\dagger\right) \\
&\leq \sum_m tr\left(Q[\![S_m]\!]\left(M_m \rho M_m^\dagger\right)\right) \\
&= tr\left(Q \sum_m [\![S_m]\!]\left(M_m \rho M_m^\dagger\right)\right) \\
&= tr\left(Q[\![\mathbf{if}\,(\Box m \cdot M[\overline{q}] = m \to S_m)\,\mathbf{fi}]\!](\rho)\right),
\end{aligned}
$$

and it follows that

$$\models_{tot} \left\{\sum_m M_m^\dagger P M_m\right\} \mathbf{if}\,(\Box m \cdot M[\overline{q}] = m \to S_m)\,\mathbf{fi}\{Q\}.$$

Case 3. (R-LT): We assume that

$$\models_{tot} \{Q\}S\left\{M_0^\dagger P M_0 + M_1^\dagger Q M_1\right\}.$$

Then for any $\rho \in \mathcal{D}(\mathcal{H}_{all})$, we have:

$$tr(Q\rho) \leq tr\left((M_0^\dagger P M_0 + M_1^\dagger Q M_1)[\![S]\!](\rho)\right). \tag{6.30}$$

We first prove the following inequality:

$$
\begin{aligned}
tr&\left[\left(M_0^\dagger P M_0 + M_1^\dagger Q M_1\right)\rho\right] \\
&\leq \sum_{k=0}^{n} tr\left(P[\mathcal{E}_0 \circ ([\![S]\!] \circ \mathcal{E}_1)]^k(\rho)\right) + tr\left(Q\left[\mathcal{E}_1 \circ ([\![S]\!] \circ \mathcal{E}_1)^n\right](\rho)\right)
\end{aligned} \tag{6.31}
$$

by induction on n. Indeed, it holds that

$$
\begin{aligned}
tr\left[\left(M_0^\dagger P M_0 + M_1^\dagger Q M_1\right)\rho\right] &= tr\left(P M_0 \rho M_0^\dagger\right) + tr\left(Q M_1 \rho M_1^\dagger\right) \\
&= tr(P\mathcal{E}_0(\rho)) + tr(Q\mathcal{E}_1(\rho)).
\end{aligned}
$$

So, Eq. (6.31) is correct for the base case of $n = 0$. Assume that Eq. (6.31) is correct for the case of $n = m$. Then applying Eq. (6.30), we obtain:

$$tr\left[\left(M_0^\dagger P M_0 + M_1^\dagger Q M_1\right)\rho\right] = tr(P\mathcal{E}_0(\rho)) + tr\left(Q M_1 \rho M_1^\dagger\right)$$

$$\leq \sum_{k=0}^{m} tr\left(P[\mathcal{E}_0 \circ ([\![S]\!] \circ \mathcal{E}_1)]^k(\rho)\right) + tr\left(Q[\mathcal{E}_1 \circ ([\![S]\!] \circ \mathcal{E}_1)^m](\rho)\right)$$

$$\leq \sum_{k=0}^{m} tr\left(P[\mathcal{E}_0 \circ ([\![S]\!] \circ \mathcal{E}_1)]^k(\rho)\right)$$

$$+ tr\left(\left(M_0^\dagger P M_0 + M_1^\dagger Q M_1\right)[\![S]\!]\left([\mathcal{E}_1 \circ ([\![S]\!] \circ \mathcal{E}_1)^m](\rho)\right)\right)$$

$$= \sum_{k=0}^{m} tr\left(P[\mathcal{E}_0 \circ ([\![S]\!] \circ \mathcal{E}_1)]^k(\rho)\right) + tr\left(P M_0[\![S]\!]\left([\mathcal{E}_1 \circ ([\![S]\!] \circ \mathcal{E}_1)^m](\rho)\right)M_0^\dagger\right)$$

$$+ tr\left(Q M_1[\![S]\!]\left([\mathcal{E}_1 \circ ([\![S]\!] \circ \mathcal{E}_1)^m](\rho)\right)M_1^\dagger\right)$$

$$= \sum_{k=0}^{m+1} tr\left(P[\mathcal{E}_0 \circ ([\![S]\!] \circ \mathcal{E}_1)]^k(\rho)\right) + tr\left(Q[\mathcal{E}_1 \circ ([\![S]\!] \circ \mathcal{E}_1)^{m+1}](\rho)\right).$$

Therefore, Eq. (6.31) also holds for the case of $n = m + 1$. This completes the proof of Eq. (6.31).

Now, since for any $\epsilon > 0$, there exists $\left(M_1^\dagger Q M_1, \epsilon\right)$-ranking function t_ϵ of quantum loop "**while** $M[\overline{q}] = 1$ **do** S **od**", by Lemma 6.6 we obtain:

$$\lim_{n\to\infty} tr\left(Q[\mathcal{E}_1 \circ ([\![S]\!] \circ \mathcal{E}_1)^n(\rho)]\right) = \lim_{n\to\infty} tr\left(Q M_1([\![S]\!] \circ \mathcal{E}_1)^n(\rho)M_1^\dagger\right)$$

$$= \lim_{n\to\infty} tr\left(M_1^\dagger Q M_1([\![S]\!] \circ \mathcal{E}_1)^n(\rho)\right)$$

$$= 0.$$

Consequently, it holds that

$$tr\left[\left(M_0^\dagger P M_0 + M_1^\dagger Q M_1\right)\rho\right] \leq \lim_{n\to\infty} \sum_{k=0}^{n} tr\left(P[\mathcal{E}_0 \circ ([\![S]\!] \circ \mathcal{E}_1)]^k(\rho)\right)$$

$$+ \lim_{n\to\infty} tr\left(Q[\mathcal{E}_1 \circ ([\![S]\!] \circ \mathcal{E}_1)^n](\rho)\right)$$

$$= \sum_{n=0}^{\infty} tr\left(P[\mathcal{E}_0 \circ ([\![S]\!] \circ \mathcal{E}_1)]^n(\rho)\right)$$

$$= tr\left(P\sum_{n=0}^{\infty}[\mathcal{E}_0 \circ ([\![S]\!] \circ \mathcal{E}_1)^n](\rho)\right)$$

$$= tr\left(P[\![\textbf{while } M[\overline{q}] = 1 \textbf{ do } S \textbf{ od}]\!](\rho)\right). \qquad \square$$

Theorem 6.4 (Completeness). *The proof system qTD is complete for total correctness of quantum **while**-programs; that is, for any quantum program S and quantum predicates $P, Q \in \mathcal{P}(\mathcal{H}_{all})$, we have:*

$$\models_{tot} \{P\}S\{Q\} \text{ implies } \vdash_{qTD} \{P\}S\{Q\}.$$

Proof. Similar to the case of partial correctness, it suffices to prove the following:

- **Claim:**

$$\vdash_{qTD} \{wp.S.Q\}S\{Q\}$$

for any quantum program S and quantum predicate $P \in \mathcal{P}(\mathcal{H}_{all})$, because by Definition 6.9.1 we have $P \sqsubseteq wp.S.Q$ when $\models_{tot} \{P\}S\{Q\}$. The above claim can be proved by induction on the structure of S. We only consider the case of $S \equiv$ **while** $M[\overline{q}] = 1$ **do** S' **od**. The other cases are similar to the proof of Theorem 6.2.

We write **while** for quantum loop "**while** $M[\overline{q}] = 1$ **do** S' **od**". It follows from Proposition 6.14.1 that

$$wp.\textbf{while}.Q = M_0^\dagger Q M_0 + M_1^\dagger (wp.S'.(wp.\textbf{while}.Q))M_1.$$

So, our aim is to derive that

$$\vdash_{qTD} \left\{ M_0^\dagger Q M_0 + M_1^\dagger (wp.S'.(wp.\textbf{while}.Q))M_1 \right\} \textbf{while}\{Q\}.$$

By the induction hypothesis on S' we get:

$$\vdash_{qTD} \left\{ wp.S'.(wp.\textbf{while}.Q) \right\} S'\{wp.\textbf{while}.Q\}.$$

Then by the rule (R-LT) it suffices to show that for any $\epsilon > 0$, there exists a $\left(M_1^\dagger (wp.S'.(wp.\textbf{while}.Q))M_1, \epsilon \right)$-ranking function of the quantum loop **while**. Applying Lemma 6.6, we only need to prove:

$$\lim_{n \to \infty} tr \left(M_1^\dagger (wp.S'.(wp.\textbf{while}.Q))M_1 (\llbracket S' \rrbracket \circ \mathcal{E}_1)^n (\rho) \right) = 0. \tag{6.32}$$

The proof of Eq. (6.32) is carried out in two steps. First, by Propositions 6.12.2 and 5.1.4 we observe:

$$
\begin{aligned}
&tr \left(M_1^\dagger (wp.S'.(wp.\textbf{while}.Q))M_1 (\llbracket S' \rrbracket \circ \mathcal{E}_1)^n (\rho) \right) \\
&= tr \left(wp.S'.(wp.\textbf{while}.Q)M_1 (\llbracket S' \rrbracket \circ \mathcal{E}_1)^n (\rho) M_1^\dagger \right) \\
&= tr \left(wp.\textbf{while}.Q \llbracket S' \rrbracket \left(M_1 (\llbracket S' \rrbracket \circ \mathcal{E}_1)^n (\rho) M_1^\dagger \right) \right) \\
&= tr \left(wp.\textbf{while}.Q (\llbracket S' \rrbracket \circ \mathcal{E}_1)^{n+1} (\rho) \right) \\
&= tr \left(Q \llbracket \textbf{while} \rrbracket (\llbracket S' \rrbracket \circ \mathcal{E}_1)^{n+1} (\rho) \right) \\
&= \sum_{k=n+1}^{\infty} tr \left(Q \left[\mathcal{E}_0 \circ (\llbracket S' \rrbracket \circ \mathcal{E}_1)^k \right] (\rho) \right).
\end{aligned} \tag{6.33}
$$

Secondly, we consider the following infinite series of nonnegative real numbers:

$$\sum_{n=0}^{\infty} tr \left(Q \left[\mathcal{E}_0 \circ (\llbracket S' \rrbracket \circ \mathcal{E}_1)^k \right] (\rho) \right) = tr \left(Q \sum_{n=0}^{\infty} \left[\mathcal{E}_0 \circ (\llbracket S' \rrbracket \circ \mathcal{E}_1)^k \right] (\rho) \right). \tag{6.34}$$

Since $Q \sqsubseteq I_{\mathcal{H}_{all}}$, it follows from Propositions 5.1.4 and 5.4 that

$$
\begin{aligned}
tr \left(Q \sum_{n=0}^{\infty} \left[\mathcal{E}_0 \circ (\llbracket S' \rrbracket \circ \mathcal{E}_1)^k \right] (\rho) \right) &= tr(Q \llbracket \textbf{while} \rrbracket (\rho)) \\
&\leq tr(\llbracket \textbf{while} \rrbracket (\rho)) \\
&\leq tr(\rho) \leq 1.
\end{aligned}
$$

Therefore, the infinite series in Eq. (6.34) converges. Note that Eq. (6.33) is the sum of the remaining terms of the infinite series in Eq. (6.34) after the nth term. Then convergence of the infinite series in Eq. (6.34) implies Eq. (6.32), and we complete the proof. $\qquad \square$

It should be pointed out that as remarked for Theorem 6.2, the above theorem is also merely a relative completeness of the proof system qTD with respect to the theory of the fields of complex numbers because except that the rule (R.Or) is employed in qTD, the existence of ranking functions in the rule (R.LT) is a statement about complex numbers too.

- **Program:**

    1. $q_0 := |0\rangle;\ q_1 := |0\rangle;\ \ldots\ldots;\ q_{n-1} := |0\rangle;$
    2. $q := |0\rangle;$
    3. $r := |0\rangle;$
    4. $q := X[q];$
    5. $q_0 := H[q_0];\ q_1 := H[q_1];\ \ldots\ldots;\ q_{n-1} := H[q_{n-1}];$
    6. $q := H[q];$
    7. **while** $M[r] = 1$ **do** D **od**;
    8. **if** $(\square x \cdot M'[q_0, q_1, \ldots, q_{n-1}] = x \to$ **skip**) **fi**

FIGURE 6.6 Quantum search program *Grover*.

- **Loop Body:**

    1. $q_0, q_1, \ldots, q_{n-1}, q := O[q_0, q_1, \ldots, q_{n-1}, q];$
    2. $q_0 := H[q_0];\ q_1 := H[q_1];\ \ldots\ldots;\ q_{n-1} := H[q_{n-1}];$
    3. $q_0, q_1, \ldots, q_{n-1} := Ph[q_0, q_1, \ldots, q_{n-1}];$
    4. $q_0 := H[q_0];\ q_1 := H[q_1];\ \ldots\ldots;\ q_{n-1} := H[q_{n-1}];$
    5. $r := r + 1$

FIGURE 6.7 Loop body D.

6.6 An illustrative example: verification of Grover search

In the last two sections, we developed the proof system qPD for partial correctness and qTD for total correctness of quantum **while**-programs, and established their soundness and (relative) completeness. The purpose of this section is to show how can the proof systems qPD and qTD actually be used to verify correctness of quantum programs. We consider the Grover quantum search algorithm as an example.

Grover search as a quantum program: Recall from Sections 4.4 and 5.4 the search problem can be stated as follows. The search space consists of $N = 2^n$ elements, indexed by numbers $0, 1, \ldots, N - 1$. It is assumed that the search problem has exactly L solutions with $1 \leq L \leq \frac{N}{2}$, and we are supplied with an oracle – a black box with the ability to recognise solutions to the search problem. Each element $x \in \{0, 1, \ldots, N - 1\}$ is identified with its binary representation $x \in \{0, 1\}^n$. In the quantum **while**-language, the Grover algorithm solving this problem can be written as the program *Grover* in Fig. 6.6, where:

- $q_0, q_1, \ldots, q_{n-1}, q$ are quantum variables with type **Boolean** and r with type **integer**;
- X is the NOT gate and H the Hadamard gate;
- $M = \{M_0, M_1\}$ is a measurement with

$$M_0 = \sum_{l \geq k} |l\rangle_r \langle l|, \quad M_1 = \sum_{l < k} |l\rangle_r \langle l|,$$

and k being a positive integer in the interval $\left[\frac{\pi}{2\theta} - 1, \frac{\pi}{2\theta}\right]$ with θ being determined by the equation

$$\cos\frac{\theta}{2} = \sqrt{\frac{N - L}{2}} \quad (0 \leq \theta \leq \frac{\pi}{2});$$

- M' is the measurement in the computational basis of n qubits; that is,

$$M' = \left\{ M'_x : x \in \{0, 1\}^n \right\}$$

  with $M'_x = |x\rangle\langle x|$ for every x;
- D is the subprogram given in Fig. 6.7.

In Fig. 6.7, O is the oracle represented by the unitary operator on $n + 1$ qubits:

$$|x\rangle|q\rangle \xrightarrow{O} |x\rangle|q \oplus f(x)\rangle$$

for all $x \in \{0, 1\}^n$ and $q \in \{0, 1\}$, where $f : \{0, 1\}^n \to \{0, 1\}$ defined by

$$f(x) = \begin{cases} 1 & \text{if } x \text{ is a solution,} \\ 0 & \text{otherwise} \end{cases}$$

is the characteristic function of solutions. The gate Ph is a conditional phase shift:

$$|0\rangle \to |0\rangle, \quad |x\rangle \to -|x\rangle \text{ for all } x \neq 0;$$

that is, $Ph = 2|0\rangle\langle 0| - I$.

Correctness formula for Grover search: It was shown in Section 4.4 that the Grover algorithm can achieve success probability

$$\Pr(\text{success}) = \sin^2 \left(\frac{2k+1}{2} \theta \right) \geq \frac{N - L}{N}$$

where k is the integer closest to the real number

$$\frac{\arccos \sqrt{\frac{L}{N}}}{\theta};$$

that is, k is an integer in the interval $\left[\frac{\pi}{2\theta} - 1, \frac{\pi}{2\theta} \right]$. The success probability is at least one-half because $L \leq \frac{N}{2}$. In particular, if $L \ll N$, then it is very high. Using the ideas introduced in the previous sections, this fact can be expressed by the total correctness of the program *Grover*:

$$\models_{tot} \{p_{succ} I\} Grover\{P\},$$

where:

• the precondition is the product of the success probability $p_{succ} \triangleq \Pr(\text{success})$ and the identity operator:

$$I = \bigotimes_{i=0}^{n-1} I_{q_i} \otimes I_q \otimes I_r;$$

• the postcondition is defined by

$$P = \left(\sum_{t \text{ solution}} |t\rangle_{\overline{q}}\langle t| \right) \otimes I_q \otimes I_r;$$

• I_{q_i} ($i = 0, 1, ..., n-1$) and I_q are the identity operator on $\mathcal{H}_2$ (type **Boolean**), I_r is the identity operator on $\mathcal{H}_\infty$ (type **integer**), and $\overline{q} = q_0, q_1, ..., q_{n-1}$.

Verification of program *Grover*: Now we start to prove the correctness of Grover search. To avoid too complicated calculation, we choose to consider a very special case: $L = 1$ and $k = \frac{\pi}{2\theta} - \frac{1}{2}$ is the midpoint of the interval $\left[\frac{\pi}{2\theta} - 1, \frac{\pi}{2\theta} \right]$. In this case, there is a unique solution, say s, and the postcondition

$$P = |s\rangle_{\overline{q}}\langle s| \otimes I_q \otimes I_r.$$

Also, we have $p_{succ} = 1$. So, what we need to prove is then simply

$$\models_{tot} \{I\}Grover\{P\}.$$

By the soundness of qTD (Theorem 6.3), it suffices to show that

$$\vdash_{qTD} \{I\}Grover\{P\}. \tag{6.35}$$

We can prove it by using the proof rules presented in Figs 6.3 and 6.5. To let the reader have a better understanding, we divide the proof of Eq. (6.35) into the following three steps.

(1) Verification of loop body D: First, we verify the loop body D given in Fig. 6.7. For this purpose, the following simple lemma is useful.

Lemma 6.7. *For each $i = 1, 2, ..., n$, suppose that $\overline{q}_i$ is a quantum register and U_i is a unitary operator on $\mathcal{H}_{\overline{q}_i}$. Let $U = U_n...U_2U_1$, where U_i actually stands for its cylinder extension in $\bigotimes_{i=1}^{n} \mathcal{H}_{\overline{q}_i}$ for every $i \leq n$. Then for any quantum predicate P, we have:*

$$\vdash_{qPD} \left\{ U^{\dagger} P U \right\} \overline{q}_1 := U_1[\overline{q}_1]; \overline{q}_2 := U_2[\overline{q}_2]; ...; \overline{q}_n := U_n[\overline{q}_n]\{P\}.$$

Proof. By repeatedly using the axiom (Ax.UT). $\qquad\square$

With the above lemma, we can prove the correctness of loop body D. First, it is easy to see that

$$\sum_{t \in \{0,q\}^n} M_t'^{\dagger} P M_t' = P.$$

By the axiom (Ax.Sk) and the rule (R.IF) we obtain:

$$\vdash_{qTD} \{P\}\mathbf{if} \ (\Box x \cdot M'[q_0, q_1, ..., q_{n-1}] = x \to \mathbf{skip}) \ \mathbf{fi}\{P\} \qquad (6.36)$$

We put:

$$P' = |s\rangle_{\overline{q}}\langle s| \otimes |-\rangle_q\langle -| \otimes |k\rangle_r\langle k|,$$
$$|\psi_l\rangle = \cos\left[\frac{\pi}{2} + (l-k)\theta\right]|\alpha\rangle + \sin\left[\frac{\pi}{2} + (l-k)\theta\right]|s\rangle$$

for every integer l, and

$$Q = \sum_{l<k}(|\psi_l\rangle_{\overline{q}}\langle\psi_l| \otimes |-\rangle_q\langle -| \otimes |l\rangle_r\langle l|).$$

Then we have:

$$M_0^{\dagger} P' M_0 + M_1^{\dagger} Q M_1 = \sum_{l \leq k}(|\psi_l\rangle_{\overline{q}}\langle\psi_l| \otimes |-\rangle_q\langle -| \otimes |l\rangle_r\langle l|),$$
$$(G^{\dagger} \otimes I_q \otimes U_{+1}^{\dagger})(M_0^{\dagger} P' M_0 + M_1^{\dagger} Q M_1)(G \otimes I_q \otimes U_{+1})$$
$$= \sum_{l \leq k}(|\psi_{l-1}\rangle_{\overline{q}}\langle\psi_{l-1}| \otimes |-\rangle_q\langle -| \otimes |l-1\rangle_r\langle l-1|)$$
$$= Q$$

where G is the Grover rotation defined in Fig. 4.4 (see Section 4.4). Thus, it follows from Lemma 6.7 that

$$\vdash_{qTD} \{Q\}D\{M_0^{\dagger} P' M_0 + M_1^{\dagger} Q M_1\}.$$

(2) termination of loop while $M[r] = 1$ do D od: A key step in proving the correctness of Grover algorithm is to show termination of the loop in line 8 of Fig. 6.6. We define a ranking function

$$t : \mathcal{D}\left(\mathcal{H}_{\overline{q}} \otimes \mathcal{H}_q \otimes \mathcal{H}_r\right) \to \mathbb{N}$$

as follows: if $\rho \in \mathcal{D}\left(\mathcal{H}_{\overline{q}} \otimes \mathcal{H}_q \otimes \mathcal{H}_r\right)$ can be written as

$$\rho = \sum_{l,t=-\infty}^{\infty} \rho_{lt} \otimes |l\rangle\langle t|$$

with ρ_{lt} being an operator (but not necessarily partial density operator) on $\mathcal{H}_{\overline{q}} \otimes \mathcal{H}_q$ for all $-\infty \leq l, t \leq \infty$, then

$$t(\rho) = k - \max\{\max(l, t) | \rho_{lt} \neq 0 \text{ and } l, t \leq k\}.$$

Thus, we have:

$$\llbracket D \rrbracket (M_1 \rho M_1^\dagger) = \llbracket D \rrbracket \left(\sum_{l,t<k} \rho_{l,t} \otimes |l\rangle_r \langle t| \right)$$

$$= \sum_{l,t<k} \left[(G \otimes I_q) \rho_{lt} \left(G^\dagger \otimes I_q \right) \otimes |l+1\rangle_r \langle t+1| \right],$$

and it follows that

$$t\left(\llbracket D \rrbracket (M_1 \rho M_1^\dagger) \right) < t(\rho),$$

where G is the Grover rotation. So, t is a $\left(M_1^\dagger Q M_1, \epsilon \right)$-ranking function for any ϵ. By the rule (R.LT) we assert that

$$\vdash_{qTD} \left\{ M_0^\dagger P' M_0 + M_1^\dagger Q M_1 \right\} \textbf{ while } M[r] = 1 \textbf{ do } D \textbf{ od} \{P'\}. \tag{6.37}$$

(3) Correctness of the Grover algorithm: Finally, we can assemble all the ingredients prepared before to prove the correctness of Grover algorithm. Using the axiom (Ax.In) we obtain:

$$\left\{ \bigotimes_{i=0}^{m-1} |0\rangle_{q_i} \langle 0| \otimes \bigotimes_{i=m}^{n-1} I_{q_i} \otimes I_q \otimes I_r \right\} q_m := |0\rangle \left\{ \bigotimes_{i=0}^{m} |0\rangle_{q_i} \langle 0| \otimes \bigotimes_{i=m+1}^{n-1} I_{q_i} \otimes I_q \otimes I_r \right\}$$

for $m = 0, 1, \ldots n-1$, and they can be combined by the rule (R.SC) to yield:

$$\{I\} q_0 := |0\rangle; q_1 := |0\rangle; \ldots; q_{n-1} := |0\rangle \left\{ \bigotimes_{i=0}^{n-1} |0\rangle_{q_i} \langle 0| \otimes I_q \otimes I_r \right\}$$

$$q := |0\rangle \left\{ \bigotimes_{i=0}^{n-1} |0\rangle_{q_i} \langle 0| \otimes |0\rangle_q \langle 0| \otimes I_r \right\}$$

$$r := |0\rangle \left\{ \bigotimes_{i=0}^{n-1} |0\rangle_{q_i} \langle 0| \otimes |0\rangle_q \langle 0| \otimes |0\rangle_r \langle 0| \right\} \tag{6.38}$$

$$q := X[q]; q_0 := H[q_0]; q_1 := H[q_1]; \ldots;$$
$$q_{n-1} := H[q_{n-1}]; q := H[q] \left\{ |\psi\rangle_{\overline{q}} \langle \psi| \otimes |-\rangle_q \langle -| \otimes |0\rangle_r \langle -| \right\},$$

where

$$|\psi\rangle = \frac{1}{\sqrt{2^n}} \sum_{x \in \{0,1\}^n} |x\rangle$$

is the equal superposition. Note that the last part of Eq. (6.38) is derived by Lemma 6.7 and the following equality:

$$\left[\left(H^\dagger \right)^{\otimes n} \otimes X^\dagger H^\dagger \otimes I_r \right] \left(|\psi\rangle_{\overline{q}} \langle \psi| \otimes |-\rangle_q \langle -| \otimes |0\rangle_r \langle 0| \right) \left(H^{\otimes n} \otimes HX \otimes I_r \right)$$

$$= \bigotimes_{i=0}^{n-1} |0\rangle_{q_i} \langle 0| \otimes |0\rangle_q \langle 0| \otimes |0\rangle_r \langle 0|.$$

It is obvious that $P' \sqsubseteq P$. On the other hand, it follows from the assumption $k = \frac{\pi}{2\theta} - \frac{1}{2}$ that $|\psi\rangle = |\psi_0\rangle$. Then we obtain:

$$|\psi\rangle_{\overline{q}} \langle \psi| \otimes |-\rangle_q \langle -| \otimes |0\rangle_r \langle 0| = |\psi_0\rangle_{\overline{q}} \langle \psi_0| \otimes |-\rangle_q \langle -| \otimes |0\rangle_r \langle 0|$$

$$\sqsubseteq M_0^\dagger P' M_0 + M_1^\dagger Q M_1.$$

We complete the proof by using the rules (R.Or) and (R.SC) to combine Eqs (6.36), (6.37), and (6.38).

$$\text{(CAx.Inv)} \quad \frac{free(P) \cap change(S) = \emptyset}{\{P\}S\{P\}}$$

$$\text{(CR.Dis)} \quad \frac{\{P\}S\{Q\} \quad \{R\}S\{Q\}}{\{P \vee R\}S\{Q\}}$$

$$\text{(CR.Con)} \quad \frac{\{P_1\}S\{Q_1\} \quad \{P_2\}S\{Q_2\}}{\{P_1 \wedge P_2\}S\{Q_1 \wedge Q_2\}}$$

$$\text{(CR.Ex)} \quad \frac{x \notin var(S) \cup free(Q)}{\{(\exists x)P\}S\{Q\}}$$

$$\text{(CR.Inv)} \quad \frac{\{R\}S\{Q\} \quad free(P) \cap change(S) = \emptyset}{\{P \wedge R\}S\{P \wedge Q\}}$$

$$\text{(CR.Sub)} \quad \frac{\{P\}S\{Q\} \quad [\{\bar{z}\} \cap var(S)] \cap [var(\bar{t}) \cap change(S)] = \emptyset}{\{P[\bar{t}/\bar{z}]\}S\{Q[t/\bar{z}]\}}$$

FIGURE 6.8 Auxiliary axioms and rules for classical programs.

6.7 Auxiliary inference rules

As indicated by Theorems 6.2 and 6.4, the axioms and inference rules in proof systems qPD and qTD are complete for proving the correctness of any quantum program. However, similar to its classical counterpart, the proof of a quantum program directly from these axioms and rules is often given in a larger number of small steps and thus very hard to follow its key idea. In verification of classical programs, one way to mitigate this issue is to introduce auxiliary inference rules. Using them, one can present the correctness proofs in a more structural way by organising several smaller steps into a larger step. For a better understanding, we list several auxiliary rules for classical programs in Fig. 6.8.

In this section, we introduce several auxiliary inference rules for quantum **while**-programs. Let us first generalise the axioms and rules in Fig. 6.8 into the quantum case. To this end, we need to introduce several notations. For any quantum variables $X \subseteq Y \subseteq qVar$ and any operator A on $\mathcal{H}_X$,

$$cl_Y(A) = A \otimes I_{\mathcal{H}_{Y \setminus X}}$$

is called the cylindric extension of A in $\mathcal{H}_Y$. For any quantum variables $X, Y \subseteq qVar$ with $X \cap Y = \emptyset$, recall from Section 2.5 that the partial trace tr_Y is a mapping from operators on $\mathcal{H}_{X \cup Y}$ to operators on $\mathcal{H}_X$ defined by

$$tr_Y(|\varphi\rangle\langle\psi| \otimes |\varphi'\rangle\langle\psi'|) = \langle\psi'|\varphi'\rangle \cdot |\varphi\rangle\langle\psi|$$

for every $|\varphi\rangle, |\psi\rangle$ in $\mathcal{H}_X$ and $|\varphi'\rangle, |\psi'\rangle$ in $\mathcal{H}_Y$, together with linearity. Let $\{A_n\}$ be a sequence of operators on a Hilbert space $\mathcal{H}$. We say that $\{A_n\}$ weakly converges to an operator A, written

$$A_n \xrightarrow{w.o.t.} A,$$

if $\lim_{n \to \infty} \langle\psi|A_n|\phi\rangle = \langle\psi|A|\phi\rangle$ for all $|\psi\rangle, |\phi\rangle \in \mathcal{H}$.

Now we can present several auxiliary axioms and rules for quantum programs in Fig. 6.9. It is interesting to compare these auxiliary axioms and rules with their counterparts for classical programs in Fig. 6.8. The appearance of axiom (Ax.Inv) is the same as axiom (CAx.Inv). It is interesting to note that rule (R.TI) is a quantum generalisation of two rules (CR.Dis) and (CR.Ex), where partial trace is considered as a quantum counterpart of logical disjunction and existence quantifier. The rules (R.CC) and (R.Inv) can be thought of as quantum generalisations of rules (CR.Con) and (CR.Inv), respectively, with logical conjunction being replaced by a probabilistic (convex) combination. Obviously, rule (R.SO) is a quantum generalisation of rule (CR.Sub), with the substitution $\bar{z} := \bar{t}$ being replaced by a quantum operation $\mathcal{E}$. The rules (R.Lin) and (R.Lim) have no counterparts for classical programs.

The following lemma establishes soundness of the auxiliary axioms and rules in Fig. 6.9.

Lemma 6.8 (Soundness of auxiliary rules). **1.** *The axiom (Ax.Inv) is sound for partial correctness.*
2. *The rules (R.TI), (R.CC), (R.Inv), and (R.Lim) are sound both for partial and total correctness.*
3. *The rule (R.SO) is sound for total correctness, and it is sound for partial correctness whenever $\mathcal{E}$ is trace-preserving.*
4. *The rule (R.Lin) is sound for total correctness, and it is sound for partial correctness whenever $\lambda \leq 1$.*
5. *The rule (R.Lim) is sound for both partial and total correctness.*

For readability, the proof of Lemma 6.8.1-4 is deferred to Appendix A.2. The reader can also prove it as an exercise.

$$\text{(Ax.Inv)} \quad \frac{var(S)\cap V=\emptyset \quad A=cl_{V\cup var(S)}(B) \quad B\in\mathcal{P}(\mathcal{H}_V)}{\{A\}S\{A\}}$$

$$\text{(R.TI)} \quad \frac{\{A\otimes I_W\}S\{B\otimes I_W\} \quad V\cap W=\emptyset \quad A,B\in\mathcal{P}(\mathcal{H}_V) \quad var(S)\subseteq V}{\{A\}S\{B\}}$$

$$\text{(R.CC)} \quad \frac{\{A_i\}S\{B_i\} \ (i=1,...,m)}{\{\sum_{i=1}^m p_i A_i\}S\{\sum_{i=1}^m p_i B_i\}}$$

$$\text{(R.Inv)} \quad \frac{\{A\}S\{B\} \quad C\in\mathcal{P}(\mathcal{H}_V) \quad V\cap var(S)=\emptyset}{\{pA+qC\}S\{pB+qC\}}$$

$$\text{(R.SO)} \quad \frac{\{A\}S\{B\} \quad \mathcal{E}\in\mathcal{QO}(\mathcal{H}_V) \quad V\cap var(S)=\emptyset}{\{\mathcal{E}^*(A)\}S\{\mathcal{E}^*(B)\}}$$

$$\text{(R.Lin)} \quad \frac{\{A\}S\{B\} \quad \lambda A,\lambda B\sqsubseteq I}{\{\lambda A\}S\{\lambda B\}}$$

$$\text{(R.Lim)} \quad \frac{A_n\xrightarrow{w.o.t.}A \quad \{A_n\}S\{B_n\} \quad B_n\xrightarrow{w.o.t.}B}{\{A\}S\{B\}}$$

FIGURE 6.9 Auxiliary axioms and rules for quantum programs. In rule (R.TI), I_W is the identity operator on $\mathcal{H}_W$. In (R.CC), $p_i\geq 0$ ($i=1,...,m$) and $\sum_{i=1}^m p_j\leq 1$. In (R.Lin), $\lambda\geq 0$. In (R.Inv), $p,q\geq 0$, $p+q\leq 1$.

Let us see a simple example to show how the auxiliary axioms and rules presented above can be used to derive some new properties of a quantum program.

Example 6.9. Let q be a qubit variable. Then by axiom (Ax.UT) we obtain:

$$\{|-\rangle\langle-|\} \ q := H[q] \ \{|1\rangle\langle1|\} \tag{6.39}$$

where H is the Hadamard gate and $|-\rangle = \frac{1}{\sqrt{2}}(|0\rangle - |1\rangle)$. The auxiliary rule (R.SO) is especially useful for reasoning about quantum computation with noise. The amplitude damping channel is an important type of quantum noise where energy is lost from a quantum system with a certain probability γ. It can be modelled by quantum operation:

$$\mathcal{E}(\rho) = E_0\rho E_0 + E_1\rho E_1$$

for any density operator ρ, where

$$E_0 = \begin{pmatrix} 1 & 0 \\ 0 & \sqrt{1-\gamma} \end{pmatrix}, \qquad E_1 = \begin{pmatrix} 1 & \sqrt{\gamma} \\ 0 & 0 \end{pmatrix}.$$

Then applying (R.SO) to (6.39) yields:

$$\left\{\frac{1+\gamma}{2}|0\rangle\langle0| - \frac{\sqrt{1-\gamma}}{2}(|0\rangle\langle1| + |1\rangle\langle0|) + \frac{1-\gamma}{2}|1\rangle\langle1|\right\}$$
$$q := H[q] \ \{\gamma|0\rangle\langle0| + (1-\gamma)|1\rangle\langle1|\}.$$

The rule (R.CC) can be strengthened using the notions of termination and abortion defined in the following:

Definition 6.11. Let A be a quantum predicate and P a quantum program.

1. We say that A characterises nontermination of quantum program P, written $\models P : \text{Term}(A)$, if $\models_{tot} \{I-A\}P\{I\}$, where I is the identity operator on $\mathcal{H}_P$; that is, for all density operators ρ:

$$1 - \text{tr}(\llbracket P\rrbracket(\rho)) \leq tr(A\rho). \tag{6.40}$$

2. We say that A characterises abortion of P, written $\models P : \text{Abort}(A)$, if $\models_{par} \{A\}P\{0\}$, where 0 is the zero operator on $\mathcal{H}_P$; that is, for all density operators ρ:

$$tr(A\rho) \leq 1 - tr(\llbracket P\rrbracket(\rho)). \tag{6.41}$$

Intuitively, $tr(\llbracket P\rrbracket(\rho))$ is the probability that program P with input ρ terminates. Thus, inequality (6.40) means that its nontermination probability is upper-bounded by predicate A. On the other hand, the intuition behind inequality (6.41)

$$(R.CC1) \quad \frac{\{A_i\}P\{B_i\} \ (i=1,\cdots,m) \qquad \models P:\text{Abort}(A)}{\{\sum_{i=1}^m p_i A_i + (1 - \sum_{i=1}^m p_i)A\}P\{\sum_{i=1}^m p_i B_i\}}$$

$$(R.CC2) \quad \frac{\{A_i\}P\{B_i\} \ (i=1,\cdots,m) \qquad \models P:\text{Term}(A)}{\{\sum_{i=1}^m \lambda_i A_i - (\sum_{i=1}^m \lambda_i - 1)A\}P\{\sum_{i=1}^m \lambda_i B_i\}}$$

FIGURE 6.10 Convex combination rules for partial correctness. In rule (R.CC1), $p_i \geq 0$, $\sum_{i=1}^m p_i \leq 1$. In (R.CC2), $\lambda_i \geq 0$, $\sum_{i=1}^m \lambda_i \geq 1$ so that the precondition and post condition are quantum predicates.

is that predicate A implies nontermination. It should be noticed that by the completeness theorem, $\models P : \text{Term}(A)$ and $\models P : \text{Abort}(A)$ can be proved in qTD and qPD, respectively.

With the notations introduced in Definition 6.11, two strengthened versions of rule (R.CC) are presented in Fig. 6.10.

It is clear that with the assumptions $\sum_{i=1}^m p_i \leq 1$ and $\sum_{i=1}^m \lambda_i \geq 1$, the preconditions in the conclusions of both (R.CC1) and (R.CC2) are weaker than the precondition in the conclusion of (R.CC). We should note that a new predicate A is introduced here for weakening the precondition with the additional premises Abort(A) and Term(A) in (R.CC1) and (R.CC2), respectively. It is interesting to observe the duality between (R.CC1) and (R.CC2).

Lemma 6.9. *The rules (R.CC1) and (R.CC2) are sound for partial correctness.*

Exercise 6.12. Prove Lemma 6.9.

To conclude this section, we point out that the auxiliary rules presented in this section are not only useful for quantum **while**-programs, but also will be combined with the rule for parallel composition in Chapter 9 for reasoning about correctness of parallel quantum programs. In particular, (R.CC1) and (R.CC2) will play an important role in formulating a (relative) complete proof systems for disjoint parallel quantum programs. More auxiliary rules will be introduced in the next chapter after we prepare an assertion logic for formally expressing them.

6.8 Bibliographic remarks and further readings

Birkhoff–von Neumann quantum logic mentioned in Section 6.1 was first introduced in [66]. It will be studied more carefully in the next chapter.

The notion of quantum predicate as a Hermitian operator was conceived by D'Hondt and Panangaden in the seminal paper [131], and the notion of quantum weakest precondition was also introduced there. A special class of quantum predicates, namely those modelled by projection operators, are studied in [424] in the framework of predicate transformer semantics. In particular, a series of healthiness conditions for this class of predicate transformers are examined there. The discussion about (non)commutativity of quantum weakest preconditions given in Section 6.1.2 is based on [423]. A basis for solving Problem 6.2 is lattice-theoretic operations of quantum predicates (i.e. quantum effects), which have been widely studied in the mathematical literature since 1950s; see for example [191,239].

Several early approaches to Hoare-style logic for quantum programs were briefly discussed in Section 1.1.3. In addition, Kakutani [240] proposed an extension of Hartog's probabilistic Hoare logic [201] for reasoning about quantum programs written in Selinger's language QPL [367]. Adams [9] defined a logic QPEL (Quantum Program and Effect Language) and its categorical semantics in terms of state-and-effect triangles.

The first Hoare-style logic for quantum programs with (relative) completeness was established in [419], on which the exposition of quantum Hoare logic (QHL for short) in this chapter is based. The auxiliary rules presented in Section 6.7 are taken from [421]. In the last few years, QHL has been extended in several directions with different target applications:

- In some applications, preconditions, and postconditions can be expressed as projections rather than general Hermitian operators. A variant of QHL was derived in [452] for simplifying verification and analysis of quantum programs with projective preconditions and postconditions.
- A nonidempotent Kleene algebraic description of propositional quantum Hoare logic was given by Peng et al. [334].
- As pointed out in [250], auxiliary variables are essential for specifying the correctness of programs in Hoare logic. Unruh [396] noticed that auxiliary variables are also useful for specifying quantum programs and proposed a QHL with ghost (auxiliary) variables. Auxiliary quantum variables will be introduced in Chapter 9 for reasoning about parallel quantum programs, but in a way different from [396].
- For the purpose of scalable verification of quantum programs, the basic ideas of separation logic [321] – separation conjunction and frame rule – have been generalised by Zhou et al. [451] and Le et al. [270] to support local reasoning about quantum programs.

- Hoare logic was designed for reasoning about properties of a single program. However, some applications require to reason about relational properties between two programs; e.g. verification of compilers and cryptographic protocols. Relational Hoare logic was defined by Benton [56] for handling these applications. Several quantum extensions of relational Hoare logic have been proposed by Unruh [395], Barthe et al. [48] and Li and Unruh [274].

- Several inference rules in the style of QHL have been introduced by Hung et al. [219], Zhou et al. [452] and Tao et al. [392] for reasoning about robustness of quantum programs running on noisy quantum hardware.

- Complementary to Hoare logic of correctness, a logic for reasoning about incorrectness of programs was recently proposed by O'Hearn [322]. It as soon generalised by Yan, Jiang, and Yu [414] to quantum programs, aiming the application of static bug-catching in quantum programming.

- An extension of QHL to parallel quantum programs was given in [437,438] and it will be discussed in Chapter 9. An extension of QHL to distributed quantum programs was also proposed by Feng et. a. [152]. More recently, a QHL-style logic for nondeterministic quantum programs was developed by Feng and Xu [153].

- For simplicity of the presentation, almost all of the logics mentioned above are defined for purely quantum programs without classical variables. As briefly discussed in Section 5.6, most of practical quantum programs involve both classical and quantum variables. For more convenient applications to them, a QHL with classical variables were introduced by Feng et al. [155].

Part III

Verification and analysis

A basic theory of sequential quantum programs was presented in Part II. In this part, we develop a series of techniques and mathematical tools for verification and static analysis of this class of quantum programs. This part consists of two chapters:

- Chapter 7 introduces several ideas for turning quantum Hoare logic (QHL) into an applicable tool in verification of quantum programs, including an architecture of QHL-based verifiers, localisation for scalable verification, and symbolic verification using assertion logics.
- In Chapter 8, we extend several important techniques for analysis of classical programs to quantum programs, namely invariant generation, termination analysis and abstract interpretation.

Chapter 7

Verification of quantum programs

The importance of verification of quantum programs was already pointed out in Section 1.1.3, and current approaches to it were also briefly discussed there. In the previous two chapters, we have defined syntax and semantics of sequential quantum programs, and developed a program logic, namely quantum Hoare logic, for specifying and reasoning about their correctness. They form a basis for verification of quantum programs. In this chapter, we consider how quantum Hoare logic can actually be used for scalable and efficient verification of quantum programs. As mentioned in Section 1.1.3, several (semi)automatic tools have been built for this purpose. However, their practical applications are still facing a major hurdle in scalability:

- **The curse of dimensionality**: Pre/postconditions of quantum Hoare triples (i.e. correctness formulas) are quantum predicates, which were represented in Chapter 6 as Hermitian matrices. The dimensions of these matrices exponentially increase with the number of quantum variables; for example, a quantum predicate for n qubits is a $2^n \times 2^n$ matrix. As a result, a huge amount of vector and matrix calculations will be involved in the direct applications of quantum Hoare logic. So, a bottleneck for scalable verification of quantum programs is the manipulation of larger matrices.

  The aim of this chapter is to introduce some mathematical and logical tools needed in solving, at least mitigating, the above challenge, including:

- **Proof localisation**: Let us consider a proof of the correctness $\{A\}S\{B\}$ of a large quantum program S, where a large set of variables, say V, are involved, in precondition A, postcondition B, and program S. Usually, such a proof consists of many steps, each of them containing only a small subset of V, say V'. Then a natural idea is to make each step of the proof localised to V'. This simple idea can often help to reduce the manipulation of larger matrices to that of smaller matrices in the proof.
- **Assertion language**: An assertion for a classical program is a predicate, i.e. a Boolean-valued function, over the state space of the program. First-order logic is usually employed as an assertion language for classical programs, and thus every assertion can be represented by a logical formula constructed from atomic formulas using propositional connectives and universal and existential quantifications. A logical representation of an assertion is often much more economic than as a Boolean-valued function over the entire state space. Similarly, an assertion language is needed for compact representation of quantum predicates. On the other hand, as various classical program logics, quantum Hoare logic was designed for specifying and reasoning about the dynamic behaviours of programs. It should be used in a combination with the assertion logic for specifying and reasoning about the static properties of quantum programs.
- **Symbolic reasoning**: As we will see in Section 7.1, without using assertion logic, a verification condition for a quantum program with n qubits is derived in a quantum program verifier as an inequality between two $2^n \times 2^n$ matrices, and its proof then becomes the mathematical problem of checking the semidefinite positivity of the difference of these two matrices, which is hard when n is large. In contrast, a verification condition for a classical program can be written as a first-order logical formula and then can be symbolically inferred from validity of its subformulas structurally using logical rules for connectives and quantifiers. The assertion language defined in this chapter combined with quantum Hoare logic enables symbolic reasoning about quantum programs.

  This chapter is organised as follows:

- We start from an architecture of a quantum program verifier described in Section 7.1. Several of its key components are also discussed there. This provides us with a framework in which we can address the issues raised above.
- In Section 7.2, we define local semantics of quantum programs and show how each step of the correctness proof of a quantum program can be localised to only those variables actually involved there.
- In Section 7.3, aiming as an assertion language for quantum programs, we introduce Birkhoff–von Neumann quantum logic, including propositional quantum logic, and first-order quantum logic.
- The version of first-order quantum logic existing in the literature only deal with quantifiers over classical variables. However, it is often more convenient to use quantifiers over quantum variables for expressing static properties of quantum programs. In Section 7.4, we develop a new first-order quantum logic with quantifiers over quantum variables.

Foundations of Quantum Programming. https://doi.org/10.1016/B978-0-44-315942-8.00018-6

- In Section 7.5, quantum logic introduced in Sections 7.3 and 7.4 is employed as an assertion logic for quantum programs and combined with quantum Hoare logic for verification of quantum programs.
- Since quantum logic studied in Sections 7.3 and 7.4 is the socalled sharp quantum logic dealing with a special class of quantum predicates, namely projection operators, it was incorporated into only a simplified variant of quantum Hoare logic for the same special class of quantum predicates. To provide an assertion language that can work together with quantum Hoare logic for general quantum predicates, we develop an effect calculus, often called unsharp quantum logic, in Section 7.6.
- We briefly discuss several problems for future research in Section 7.7.

7.1 Architecture of a quantum program verifier

Many tools for verification of classical programs have been implemented based on Hoare logic and its various extensions. The basic architecture of these tools is the one proposed by King [245] in 1969. In this section, we describe a generalisation of King's architecture for quantum program verifiers.

Roughly speaking, a quantum program verifier built based on quantum Hoare logic proves partial correctness $\models_{par}$ $\{A\}S\{B\}$ of a quantum program S in the following steps:

- *Annotating the program*: The program is annotated by inserting quantum predicates at some appropriate points. Intuitively, each of these predicates denotes the quantum effect that can be observed whenever the program control reaches the point at which it is inserted.
- *Generating verification conditions*: A set of mathematical statements, called verifications (VCs for short), is generated from the annotated program. In verification of classical programs, each VC is an implication between two first-order logical formulas (and also a first-order logical formula). In contrast, each VC for a quantum program is an inequality between matrices in the form of $A \sqsubseteq B$, where A, B are Hermitian matrices, and $\sqsubseteq$ stands for the Löwner order (see Definition 2.13). This step converts a verification problem into a conventional mathematical problem.
- *Proving verification conditions*: In the verification of classical programs, the generated VCs are then proved by an automated theorem prover for first-order logic. In the quantum case, however, for each VC $A \sqsubseteq B$, the current quantum program verifies prove the mathematical statement that matrix $B - A$ is positive semidefinite, directly according to the definition of Löwner order. In Sections 7.3 to 7.6, we will define an assertion logic so that verification conditions for quantum programs can also be specified and proved in a logic system.

Total correctness $\models_{tot} \{A\}S\{B\}$ can be then proved by combining partial correctness $\models_{par} \{A\}S\{B\}$ and a proof of the termination of S. Several techniques for analysing termination of quantum programs will be introduced in next chapter.

The remaining part of this section is organised as follows. We will first elaborate the above three steps. Furthermore, we will prove the validity of the verifier; that is, if all VCs are provable, then correctness $\models_{par} \{A\}S\{B\}$ is true, by quantum Hoare logic together with an adaptation lemma.

Annotating programs: The basic idea of annotating a quantum program is the same as that for a classical program. A program is annotated by inserting an assertion at certain intermediate points so that an inserted assertion holds when the program control reaches the corresponding point. In the quantum case, an assertion is a quantum predicate mathematically modelled by a Hermitian operator between the zero and identity operators. Intuitively, the quantum effect denoted by the assertion should be observed when the control reaches the point. Usually, an assertion is assigned:

- before S_2 in a sequential composition S_1; S_2; and
- after **do** in a **while** loop.

Assigning assertions in a case statement of the form **if** $\square m \cdot M[\overline{q}] = m \rightarrow P_m$ **fi** is much tricker and will be discussed shortly. As is well-known, the choice of such an assertion is tricky and heavily depends on a good understanding of how the program works and what property of (or relation between) program variables the assertion denotes. In the classical case, the assertion itself is usually easy to understand, but in the quantum case, it is often quite hard to give an intuitive interpretation to the assertion. Moreover, a classical program S can be represented as a flowchart, and such a flowchart is very helpful in annotating program S. In next chapter, we will present a flowchart-like representation of quantum programs, and further develop an algorithm for generating assertions at the chosen points (usually called invariants) of them.

Example 7.1. Recall from Section 4.6.1 that quantum teleportation is a protocol that can send quantum states only using a classical communication channel. Suppose that Alice possesses two qubits q_0, q_1, and Bob possesses qubit q_2, and there is

$$\left\{ |\psi\rangle_p \langle\psi| \otimes |\beta_{00}\rangle_{q,r} \langle\beta_{00}| \right\}$$

$$\sqsubseteq \left\{ |\beta_{00}\rangle_{p,q} \langle\beta_{00}| \otimes |\psi\rangle_r \langle\psi| + |\beta_{10}\rangle_{p,q} \langle\beta_{10}| \otimes |\psi_1\rangle_r \langle\psi_1| \right.$$

$$\left. + |\beta_{01}\rangle_{p,q} \langle\beta_{01}| \otimes |\psi_2\rangle_r \langle\psi_2| + |\beta_{11}\rangle_{p,q} \langle\beta_{11}| \otimes |\psi_3\rangle_r \langle\psi_3| \right\}$$

$QTel \equiv p, q := \mathrm{CNOT}[p, q];$

$$\left\{ |+\rangle_p \langle+| \otimes |0\rangle_q \langle0| \otimes |\psi\rangle_r \langle\psi| + |-\rangle_p \langle-| \otimes |0\rangle_q \langle0| \otimes |\psi_1\rangle_r \langle\psi_1| \right.$$

$$\left. + |+\rangle_p \langle+| \otimes |1\rangle_q \langle1| \otimes |\psi_2\rangle_r \langle\psi_2| + |-\rangle_p \langle-| \otimes |1\rangle_q \langle1| \otimes |\psi_3\rangle_r \langle\psi_3| \right\}$$

$p := H[p];$

$$\left\{ |0\rangle_p \langle0| \otimes |0\rangle_q \langle0| \otimes |\psi\rangle_r \langle\psi| + |1\rangle_p \langle1| \otimes |0\rangle_q \langle0| \otimes |\psi_1\rangle_r \langle\psi_1| \right.$$

$$\left. + |0\rangle_p \langle0| \otimes |1\rangle_q \langle1| \otimes |\psi_2\rangle_r \langle\psi_2| + |1\rangle_p \langle1| \otimes |1\rangle_q \langle1| \otimes |\psi_3\rangle_r \langle\psi_3| \right\}$$

if $M[q] = 0 \rightarrow \left\{ |0\rangle_p \langle0| \otimes I_q \otimes |\psi\rangle_r \langle\psi| + |1\rangle_p \langle1| \otimes I_q \otimes |\psi_1\rangle_r \langle\psi_1| \right\}$ **skip**

$\square \qquad 1 \rightarrow \left\{ |0\rangle_p \langle0| \otimes I_q \otimes |\psi_2\rangle_r \langle\psi_2| + |1\rangle_p \langle1| \otimes I_q \otimes |\psi_3\rangle_r \langle\psi_3| \right\} r := X[r]$

fi;

$$\left\{ |0\rangle_p \langle0| \otimes I_q \otimes |\psi\rangle_r \langle\psi| + |1\rangle_p \langle1| \otimes I_q \otimes |\psi_1\rangle_r \langle\psi_1| \right\}$$

if $M[p] = 0 \rightarrow \left\{ I_p \otimes I_q \otimes |\psi\rangle_r \langle\psi| \right\}$ **skip**

$\square \qquad 1 \rightarrow \left\{ I_p \otimes I_q \otimes |\psi_1\rangle_r \langle\psi_1| \right\} r := Z[r]$

fi $\left\{ I_p \otimes I_q \otimes |\psi\rangle_r \langle\psi| \right\}$

FIGURE 7.1 Annotated quantum teleportation program. Here, (1) quantum states: $|\psi_1\rangle = \alpha|0\rangle - \beta|1\rangle$, $|\psi_2\rangle = \beta|0\rangle + \alpha|1\rangle$, $|\psi_3\rangle = -\beta|0\rangle + \alpha|1\rangle$; and (2) entangled states: $|\beta_{01}\rangle = \frac{1}{\sqrt{2}}(|01\rangle + |10\rangle)$, $|\beta_{10}\rangle = \frac{1}{\sqrt{2}}(|00\rangle - |11\rangle)$, $|\beta_{11}\rangle = \frac{1}{\sqrt{2}}(|01\rangle - |10\rangle)$.

entanglement, i.e. the EPR (Einstein–Podolsky–Rosen) pair:

$$|\beta_{00}\rangle = \frac{1}{\sqrt{2}}(|00\rangle + |11\rangle),$$

between q_1 and q_2. Then Alice can send a quantum state $|\psi\rangle = \alpha|0\rangle + \beta|1\rangle$ to Bob, i.e. from q_0 to q_2, by two-bit classical communication. If we ignore the communication, then this protocol can be written as quantum **while**-program:

$$QTel \equiv q_0, q_1 := \mathrm{CNOT}[q_0, q_1]; q_0 := H[q_0];$$

if $M[q_1] = 0 \rightarrow$ **skip**

$\square \qquad 1 \rightarrow q_2 := X[q_2]$

fi;

if $M[q_0] = 0 \rightarrow$ **skip**

$\square \qquad 1 \rightarrow q_2 := Z[q_2]$

fi

where $M = \{M_0, M_1\}$ is the measurement in the computational basis; that is, $M_0 = |0\rangle\langle0|$, $M_1 = |1\rangle\langle1|$. The correctness of $QTel$ can be described as the Hoare triple:

$$\left\{ |\psi\rangle_{q_0} \langle\psi| \otimes |\beta_{00}\rangle_{q_1,q_2} \langle\beta_{00}| \right\} QTel \left\{ I_{q_0} \otimes I_{q_1} \otimes |\psi\rangle_{q_2} \langle\psi| \right\}.$$

An annotated version of $QTel$ is shown in Fig. 7.1.

7.1.1 Generating verification conditions

Now suppose we are given an annotated quantum program S, and let A, B be two quantum predicates. Let us write $Spec \equiv \{A\}S\{B\}$ as a specification. In this subsection, we present a procedure that generates a set of VCs for verifying $\models_{par} \{A\}S\{B\}$.

A tricky part of our procedure is the treatment of branching introduced by a case statement. Assume that

$$\{C\}\textbf{if } \square m \cdot M[\overline{q}] = m \rightarrow P_m \textbf{ fi}$$

is a segment in *Spec*, where C is a quantum predicate inserted before the case statement. We assign a label $l = (C, M, \overline{q})$ to this segment.

Definition 7.1. Let $M = \{M_m\}$ be the measurement in a branching label $l = (C, M, \overline{q})$, and let C be a quantum predicate over variables $V \subseteq qVar$. Then a family $\mathcal{C} = \{C_m\}$ of quantum predicates over variables V is called a predecomposition for label l if

$$C \otimes I_{\overline{q} \backslash V} \sqsubseteq \sum_m (M_m^\dagger \otimes I_{V \backslash \overline{q}})(C_m \otimes I_{\overline{q} \backslash V})(M_m \otimes I_{V \backslash \overline{q}}). \tag{7.1}$$

We often choose $\mathcal{C}$ to be a minimal predecomposition; that is, a predecomposition such that for any other predecomposition $\mathcal{C}' = \{C_m'\}$, $\mathcal{C}' \sqsubseteq \mathcal{C}$ (i.e. $C_m' \sqsubseteq C_m$ for all m) implies $\mathcal{C}' = \mathcal{C}$ (i.e. $C_m' = C_m$ for all m).

With the above preparation, we are ready to describe the procedure for generating VCs. Suppose that precondition A and postcondition B in the specification $Spec \equiv \{A\}S\{B\}$ are quantum predicates over variables V and W, respectively. We further assume that for each branching segment in *Spec*, a predecomposition for it is given. Then the set of VCs for *Spec*, denoted $VC(Spec)$ is generated recursively as follows:

1. If $Spec \equiv \{A\}\textbf{skip}\{B\}$, then $VC(Spec) = \left\{ A \otimes I_{W \backslash V} \sqsubseteq B \otimes I_{V \backslash W} \right\}$.
2. If $Spec \equiv \{A\}q := |0\rangle\{B\}$, then

$$VC(Spec) = \begin{cases} \left\{ A \otimes I_{W \backslash V} \sqsubseteq B \otimes I_{V \backslash W} \right\} & \text{if } q \notin W, \\ \left\{ A \otimes I_{W \backslash V} \sqsubseteq \sum_i |i\rangle_q \langle 0|B|0\rangle_q \langle i| \otimes I_{V \backslash W} \right\} & \text{if } q \in W. \end{cases}$$

3. If $Spec \equiv \{A\}\overline{q} := U[\overline{q}]\{B\}$, then

$$VC(Spec) = \left\{ A \otimes I_{(W \cup \overline{q}) \backslash V} \sqsubseteq (U^\dagger \otimes I_{(V \cup W) \backslash \overline{q}})(B \otimes I_{(V \cup \overline{q}) \backslash W})(U \otimes I_{(V \cup W) \backslash \overline{q}}) \right\}.$$

4. If $Spec \equiv \{A\}P_1; \{C\}P_2\{B\}$, then

$$VC(Spec) = VC(\{A\}P_1\{C\}) \cup VC(\{C\}P_2\{B\}).$$

5. If $Spec \equiv \{A\}\textbf{if } \square m \cdot M[\overline{q}] = m \rightarrow P_m \textbf{ fi}\{B\}$, and the assumed predecomposition for branching label $l = (A, M, \overline{q})$ is $\mathcal{A}_l = \{A_m\}$, then

$$VC(Spec) = \bigcup_m VC\left(\{M_m^\dagger A_m M_m\}P_m\{B\} \right).$$

6. If $Spec \equiv \{A\}\textbf{while } M[\overline{q}] = 1 \textbf{ do } \{C\}P\{B\}$, then

$$VC(Spec) = \left\{ A \sqsubseteq M_0^\dagger C M_0 + M_1^\dagger B M_1 \right\} \cup VC\left(\{C\}P\{M_0^\dagger C M_0 + M_1^\dagger B M_1\} \right).$$

It should be observed that all quantum predicates in $VC(Spec)$ for specification $Spec \equiv \{A\}S\{B\}$ are defined over only the variables occurring in program S and pre/postconditions A and B rather than all quantum variables $qVar$. Our aim is to make that (the matrix representations of) these quantum predicates be much smaller than those defined over $qVar$.

7.1.2 Proving verification conditions

To verify partial correctness $\models_{par} \{A\}S\{B\}$, what remains now is to prove that all of the VCs in $VC(Spec)$ generated using the procedure presented in the previous Section are valid. Note that each VC in $VC(Spec)$ is always in the form of $A_i \sqsubseteq B_i$, where A_i and B_i are complex matrices, and $\sqsubseteq$ is the Löwner order. Usually, such a statement can be proved in one of the following three ways:

1. Check the semidefinite positivity of matrix $B_i - A_i$. This can be done by, for example, Sylvester's criterion (see [215], Theorem 7.2.5), but the computation will be huge when the dimensions of A_i and B_i are large. In Section 7.2, we will develop a localisation technique in order to make that the set of variables involved in each VC be small. Using it, the dimensions of A_i and B_i can be significantly reduced.
2. Prove $A_i \sqsubseteq B_i$ as a mathematical statement by a theorem prover for linear algebra. This idea was adopted in several quantum program verifiers, e.g. CoqQ [450] and QHLProver [281].

3. Express $A \sqsubseteq B$ as a logical formula in an assertion language and symbolically infer it in the assertion logic. We will develop the logical mechanism required for realising this idea in Sections 7.3 to 7.6.

Of course, a proof of $\models_{par} \{A\}S\{B\}$ for a large quantum program may be carried out as a combination of the above three methods. As mentioned above, total correctness $\models_{tot} \{A\}S\{B\}$ can be then derived by further proving the termination of S using some techniques in next chapter.

Exercise 7.1. A verification of Grover search was given in Section 6.6. Recast it within the architecture described in this section.

7.1.3 Validity of the verifier

To conclude this section, we show that the quantum program verifier described above is valid.

Theorem 7.1 (Validity). *For any specification Spec $\equiv \{A\}S\{B\}$, if verification conditions VC(Spec) are provable, then $\models_{par} \{A\}S\{B\}$.*

Proof. Employing the proof rules in quantum Hoare logic, this theorem can be proved by induction on the structure of program S. We omit the details of the proof, and only point out that when $S \equiv S_1; S_2$, we need to infer $\models_{par} \{A\}S\{B\}$ from premises of the form $\models_{par} \{A\}S_1\{C\}$ and $\models_{par} \{C'\}S_2\{B\}$, where quantum predicates C and C' are defined over different sets of variables. This case can be handled by using the localisation technique introduced in the next section (see Lemma 7.2 and Corollary 7.1). $\square$

Exercise 7.2. Complete the proof of Theorem 7.1.

7.2 Localisation of correctness reasoning

With the architecture described in the previous section, (semi-)automatic tools can be implemented for verifying quantum programs. However, as pointed out at the beginning of this chapter, these tools will face the issue of scalability and efficiency. From this section on, we introduce several ideas and techniques that can help to improve the scalability and efficiency.

Recall that $qVar$ is the set of all quantum variables, and for each $q \in qVar$, $\mathcal{H}_q$ is the Hilbert space of the quantum system denoted by q. For any finite subset $V \subseteq qVar$, we define $\mathcal{H}_V = \bigotimes_{q \in V} \mathcal{H}_q$ as the Hilbert space of the composite quantum system denoted by V. The zero and identity operators on $\mathcal{H}_V$ is denoted 0_V, I_V, respectively. We write $\mathcal{D}(\mathcal{H}_V)$ for the set of partial density operators, i.e. positive operators ρ with trace $tr(\rho) \leq 1$, on $\mathcal{H}_V$.

For simplifying the presentation, in Chapter 5 we defined the operational and denotational semantics of every quantum program S uniformly in the large Hilbert space $\mathcal{H}_{all} = \mathcal{H}_{qVar}$ of all quantum variables. Accordingly, partial and total correctnesses of S, i.e. $\models_{par} \{A\}S\{B\}$ and $\models_{tot} \{A\}S\{B\}$, were also defined in $\mathcal{H}_{all}$. Usually, the quantum variables involved in a single program S and its pre/postcondtions A and B are a small subset of $qVar$, say V. Note that the dimension of Hilbert space $\mathcal{H}_V$ exponentially increases in the number of variables in V, and thus $\mathcal{H}_V$ should be much smaller than $\mathcal{H}_{all}$. Therefore, if possible, verification of $\models \{A\}S\{B\}$ in $\mathcal{H}_V$ will be much more efficient than in $\mathcal{H}_{all}$. In this section, we show how the semantics and correctness of a quantum program can be localised to only those variables involved in it.

First, let $qvar(S) \subseteq V \subseteq qVar$, where $qvar(S)$ denotes the set of quantum variables occurring in S (see Definition 5.2). Then the operational semantics of S over variables V can be defined as a transition relation between configurations $\langle S', \rho \rangle$ with S' being a subprogram of S and $\rho \in \mathcal{D}(\mathcal{H}_V)$, using exactly the same transition rules as in Definition 5.4. Based on it, similar to Definition 5.6, we can define the denotational semantics of S over variables V as the mapping $[\![S]\!]_V : \mathcal{D}(\mathcal{H}_V) \to \mathcal{D}(\mathcal{H}_V)$ with

$$[\![S]\!]_V(\rho) = \sum \left\{ |\rho' \in \mathcal{D}(\mathcal{H}_V) : \langle S, \rho \rangle \to^* \langle E, \rho' \rangle | \right\}$$

for every input $\rho \in \mathcal{D}(\mathcal{H}_V)$. Furthermore, we can introduce localised correctness:

Definition 7.2. Let $qvar(S) \subseteq V$, and for some $W_1, W_2 \subseteq V$, let A, B be quantum predicates in $\mathcal{H}_{W_1}$ and $\mathcal{H}_{W_2}$, respectively. Then Hoare triple (i.e. correctness formula) $\{A\} S \{B\}$ is true over variables V in the sense of partial (respectively, total) correctness, written:

$$V \models_{par} \{A\} S \{B\} \qquad (respectively,\ V \models_{tot} \{A\} S \{B\})$$

if for all input states $\rho \in \mathcal{D}(\mathcal{H}_V)$ we have:

$$\text{tr}(A\rho) \leq \text{tr}(B[\![S]\!]_V(\rho)) + [\text{tr}(\rho) - \text{tr}([\![S]\!]_V(\rho))]$$
$$(\textit{respectively}, \text{tr}(A\rho) \leq \text{tr}(B[\![S]\!]_V(\rho))). \tag{7.2}$$

Here, all operators are understood as their cylindric extension on $\mathcal{H}_V$.

Obviously, if V, W_1, and W_2 are all taken as the set $qVar$ of all quantum variables, then the above definition degenerates to Definition 6.8.

The defining inequality (7.2) of correctness is required to hold for all inputs ρ. Using the Schrödinger–Heisenberg duality, this universal quantifier on ρ can be eliminated. This gives us a correctness condition that is easier to check.

Lemma 7.1 (Correctness conditions).

$$V \models_{par} \{A\}S\{B\} \Leftrightarrow [\![S]\!]_V^*(I_V - B) \sqsubseteq I_V - A;$$
$$V \models_{tot} \{A\}S\{B\} \Leftrightarrow A \sqsubseteq [\![S]\!]_V^*(B)$$

where $\sqsubseteq$ stands for the Löwner order, $[\![S]\!]_V^*$ is the dual of superoperator $[\![S]\!]_V$ on $\mathcal{H}_V$ (see Definition 6.4), and all operators and superoperators are understood as their cylindric extension on $\mathcal{H}_V$.

Proof. We only prove the conclusion for partial correctness. The case of total correctness is similar and easier. First, by Definition 6.4, we have:

$$\text{tr}(B[\![S]\!]_V(\rho)) + [\text{tr}(\rho) - \text{tr}([\![S]\!]_V(\rho))] = \text{tr}([\![S]\!]_V^*(B)\rho) + \text{tr}(I_V\rho) - \text{tr}([\![S]\!]_V^*(I)]\rho)$$
$$= \text{tr}[([\![S]\!]_V^*(B) + I_V - [\![S]\!]_V^*(I))\rho].$$

Then by Lemma 6.2, inequality (7.2) is equivalent to

$$A \sqsubseteq [\![S]\!]_V^*(B) + I_V - [\![S]\!]_V^*(I), \text{ i.e. } [\![S]\!]_V^*(I_V - B) \sqsubseteq I_V - A. \qquad \square$$

Now we are ready to present the main result of this section that indicates that adding extra variables has no influence on correctness, and thus correctness can be localised to those variables that are really involved.

Lemma 7.2 (Adaptation over variables). *Let $qvar(S) \subseteq V \subseteq W$. Then for any quantum predicates A, B on $\mathcal{H}_V$:*

$$V \models_{par} \{A\}S\{B\} \Leftrightarrow W \models_{par} \{A\}S\{B\};$$
$$V \models_{tot} \{A\}S\{B\} \Leftrightarrow W \models_{tot} \{A\}S\{B\}.$$

Proof. We only prove the conclusion for partial correctness because the case of total correctness is similar and simpler.
($\Rightarrow$) Assume that A and B are quantum predicates over $\overline{p}$ and $\overline{q}$, respectively. Then

$$[\![S]\!]_W^*(I_W - B) = \left([\![S]\!]_{qvar(S)}^* \otimes \mathcal{I}_{W \setminus qvar(S)}\right)\left(I_W - B \otimes I_{W \setminus \overline{q}}\right)$$
$$= \left([\![S]\!]_{qvar(S)}^* \otimes \mathcal{I}_{V \setminus qvar(S)} \otimes \mathcal{I}_{W \setminus V}\right)\left(I_V \otimes I_{W \setminus V} - B \otimes I_{V \setminus \overline{q}} \otimes I_{W \setminus V}\right)$$
$$= \left[\left([\![S]\!]_{qvar(S)}^* \otimes \mathcal{I}_{V \setminus qvar(S)}\right)\left(I_V - B \otimes I_{V \setminus \overline{q}}\right)\right] \otimes I_{W \setminus V}$$

Thus, from assumption $V \models \{A\}S\{B\}$ and Lemma 7.1, we obtain:

$$\left([\![P]\!]_{qvar(S)}^* \otimes \mathcal{I}_{V \setminus qvar(S)}\right)\left(I_V - B \otimes I_{V \setminus \overline{q}}\right) = [\![S]\!]_V^*(I_V - B)$$
$$\sqsubseteq I_V - A = I_V - A \otimes I_{V \setminus \overline{p}}$$

Then with Lemma 2.2, it follows that

$$[\![S]\!]_W^*(I_W - B) \sqsubseteq \left(I_V - A \otimes I_{V \setminus \overline{p}}\right) \otimes I_{W \setminus V}$$
$$= I_V \otimes I_{W \setminus V} - A \otimes I_{V \setminus \overline{p}} \otimes I_{W \setminus V} = I_W - A \otimes I_{W \setminus \overline{p}} = I_W - A$$

and $W \models \{A\}S\{B\}$.

($\Leftarrow$) We first note that $A \otimes I$ is positive $\Rightarrow A$ is positive. In fact, for any $|\varphi\rangle$, we choose an arbitrary pure state $|\psi\rangle$ and then it holds that

$$\langle\varphi|A|\varphi\rangle = \langle\varphi|A|\varphi\rangle \cdot \langle\psi|I|\psi\rangle = \langle\varphi \otimes \psi|A \otimes I|\varphi \otimes \psi\rangle \geq 0.$$

As a simply corollary, we have: $A \otimes I \sqsubseteq B \otimes I \Rightarrow (A - B) \otimes I = A \otimes I - B \otimes I$ is positive $\Rightarrow A - B$ is positive $\Rightarrow A \sqsubseteq B$. This fact enables us to reverse the reasoning in the above proof of $V \models_{par} \{A\}S\{B\} \Rightarrow W \models_{par} \{A\}S\{B\}$. □

The above lemma allows us to talk about partial and correctness freely without caring about the variables V in $V \models_{par} \{A\}S\{B\}$ and $V \models_{tot} \{A\}S\{B\}$, which can then be simply written as $\models_{par} \{A\}P\{B\}$ and $\models_{tot} \{A\}P\{B\}$, respectively. A simple application of this lemma is to localise verification of the premises in the following reasoning about the sequential composition of a long chain of programs:

$$\frac{\{A\}S_1\{C_1\}\cdots\{C_i\}S_i\{C_{i+1}\}\cdots\{C_{n-1}\}S_n\{B\}}{\{A\}S_1; ...; S_n\{B\}}$$

where each $qvar(S_i)$ is a small set of variables. Formally, we have:

Corollary 7.1. *The following inference rule is valid:*

$$\frac{\begin{array}{c} V_i \models \{A_i\}S_i\{B_i\} \ (i = 1, ..., n) \\ B_i \otimes I_{V_{i+1}\backslash V_i} \sqsubseteq A_{i+1} \otimes I_{V_i\backslash V_{i+1}} \ (i = 1, ..., n-1) \end{array}}{\{A_1\}S_1; ...; S_n\{B_n\}}$$

Exercise 7.3. Prove Corollary 7.1.

7.3 Birkhoff–von Neumann quantum logic

We now turn to consider symbolic reasoning for improving scalability and efficiency of a quantum program verifier. As a basis of this approach, we need an assertion logic for reasoning about static properties of quantum programs, which can be appropriately combined with quantum Hoare logic. In this section, we introduce quantum logic with the aim that it can serve as an assertion logic for quantum programs.

There are mainly two variants of quantum logic (QL for short). The original QL was proposed by Birkhoff and von Neumann [66] in 1936 to provide an appropriate logic for reasoning about quantum mechanic systems. It was defined for logical propositions interpreted as projections (or equivalently, closed subspaces of the Hilbert space of the quantum system under consideration). In Section 6.1, such propositions were called projective quantum predicates. In the QL literature, this variant of QL is often called sharp QL. Unsharp QL was introduced in the framework of effect-based formulation of quantum theory [256], where logical propositions are interpreted as effects, i.e. observables represented by Hermitian operators between the zero operator and identity operator, or (general) quantum predicates as defined in Section 6.1.

7.3.1 Orthomodular lattice of closed subspaces

Let us start from sharp QL. Recall from classical logic that a proposition about a classical system can be mathematically modelled by a subset $X \subseteq \Omega$, where Ω is the state space – the set of all possible states – of the system. For each $\omega \in \Omega$, satisfaction $\omega \models X$ (state ω satisfies proposition X) is interpreted as $\omega \in X$. As said above, in sharp QL, however, a proposition about a quantum system is mathematically represented by a closed subspace of (or equivalently, a projection operator on) the state space of the system, which is a Hilbert space $\mathcal{H}$ according to the postulates of quantum mechanics. Next, we need to find appropriate interpretations of logical connectives in this QL. For classical propositions, the logical connectives $\wedge$ (and), $\vee$ (or), $\neg$ (not) can be simply interpreted as set-theoretic operations $\cap$, $\cup$ and ^{c}, respectively:

$$\omega \models X \wedge Y \text{ iff } \omega \in X \cap Y, \qquad \omega \models X \vee Y \text{ iff } \omega \in X \cup Y, \qquad \omega \models \neg X \text{ iff } \omega \in X^c.$$

However, this interpretation of connectives cannot be directly generalised to the quantum case because although $\cap$ preserves closeness under linear combination, $\cup$ and ^{c} do not. The operations appropriate for the interpretations of logical connectives $\wedge$ (and), $\vee$ (or), $\neg$ (not) for quantum propositions are defined as follows: for any closed subspaces X, Y of $\mathcal{H}$,

- *Meet*: $X \wedge Y = X \cap Y$.

- *Join*: $X \vee Y = \overline{\text{span}(X \cup Y)}$, where for any subset $Z \subseteq \mathcal{H}$, $\overline{\text{span } Z}$ is the closed subspace of $\mathcal{H}$ generated by Z; more precisely, $\overline{Z}$ stands for the topological closure of Z, and span Z is the smallest subspace of $\mathcal{H}$ containing Z:

$$\text{span } Z = \left\{ \sum_{i=1}^{n} \alpha_i |\psi_i\rangle : n \geq 1, \alpha_i \in \mathbb{C} \text{ and } |\psi_i\rangle \in Z \text{ for all } 1 \leq i \leq n \right\}.$$

- *Orthocomplement*: $X^{\perp} = \{|\psi\rangle \in \mathcal{H} : |\psi\rangle \perp |\varphi\rangle \text{ for all } |\varphi\rangle \in X\}$, where $|\psi\rangle \perp |\varphi\rangle$ means that $|\psi\rangle$ and $|\varphi\rangle$ are orthogonal; that is, their inner product $\langle \psi | \varphi \rangle = 0$.

The early research on QL had been focusing on its algebraic aspect, namely understanding the algebraic structure of the set of closed subspaces of a Hilbert space $\mathcal{H}$. For a classical system with state space Ω, we write 2^{Ω} for the power set of Ω, i.e. the set of all subsets of Ω. It is well known that $(2^{\Omega}, \cap, \cup, {}^c)$ is a (complete) Boolean algebra. Therefore, classical (Boolean) logic is appropriate for reasoning about classical systems. Correspondingly, for a quantum system with state space $\mathcal{H}$, we write $S(\mathcal{H})$ for the set of closed subspaces of Hilbert space $\mathcal{H}$. To examine the algebraic structure of $S(\mathcal{H})$, we introduce the following:

Definition 7.3. 1. An orthomodular lattice is an algebraic structure $\mathcal{L} = (L, \vee, \wedge, \perp)$, where:
  a. $(L, \vee, \wedge, \sqsubseteq)$ is a lattice with the least element **0** and the greatest element **1**. Here, $\vee, \wedge, \sqsubseteq$ stand for the least upper bound, greatest lower bound and partial order (see Definition 5.9);
  b. $\perp : L \to L$ is a unary operation, called orthocomplement, satisfying the following conditions: for any $x, y, z \in L$,
    - *Orthomodularity*: $x \sqsubseteq y$ implies $y = x \vee (x^{\perp} \wedge y)$.
    - *Contradiction and excluded middle laws*: $x \wedge x^{\perp} = \mathbf{0}$ and $x \vee x^{\perp} = \mathbf{1}$.

2. A modular lattice is an orthomodular lattice satisfying the following condition: for any $x, y, z \in L$,
   - *Modularity*: $x \sqsubseteq y$ implies $x \vee (z \wedge y) = (x \vee z) \wedge y$

Obviously, modularity implies orthomodularity. Furthermore, a Boolean algebra satisfies the condition: for any $x, y, z \in L$,

- *Distributivity*: $x \wedge (y \vee z) = (x \wedge y) \vee (x \wedge z)$ and $x \vee (y \wedge z) = (x \vee y) \wedge (x \vee z)$

which is stronger than modularity.

Now we are able to present the following theorem that clarifies the algebraic structure of the set $S(\mathcal{H})$ of closed subspaces of a Hilbert space $\mathcal{H}$.

Theorem 7.2 (Sasaki 1954). **1.** $(S(\mathcal{H}), \wedge, \vee, \perp)$ *is a complete orthomodular lattice, in which the partial order is set inclusion $\subseteq$, and the least and greatest elements are the 0-dimensional closed subspace $\mathbf{0} = \{0\}$ and $\mathcal{H}$, respectively.*
2. $(S(\mathcal{H}), \wedge, \vee, \perp)$ *is a modular lattice if and only if $\mathcal{H}$ is finite-dimensional.*

Example 7.2. Let $\mathcal{H}$ be the Hilbert space of a quantum program variable q. For each $|\psi\rangle \in \mathcal{H}$, we write $[\psi]$ for the atomic proposition that variable q is in the 1-dimensional closed subspace of $\mathcal{H}$ generated by the single state $|\psi\rangle$. Then the proposition that q is in the closed subspace generated by a family of states $|\psi_1\rangle, ..., |\psi_m\rangle$ can be written as

$$\bigvee_{i=1}^{m} [\psi_i] = [\psi_1, ..., \psi_m].$$

Moreover, if $\{|\psi_0\rangle, |\psi_1\rangle, ..., |\psi_m\rangle\}$ is an orthonormal basis of $\mathcal{H}$, then

$$[\psi_1, ..., \psi_m] = \neg[\psi_0], \tag{7.3}$$

and more generally, for any $1 \leq k < n$,

$$[\psi_k, \psi_{k+1}, ..., \psi_m] = \neg \bigvee_{i=0}^{k-1} [\psi_i].$$

The above example indicates that the benefit of employing QL as an assertion logic for quantum programs is not limited to precise specification of quantum assertions. Indeed, it also often provides a more economic way to specify quantum assertions. For example, as pointed out at the beginning of this chapter, if q denotes an n-qubit system, then without a logical language the quantum assertion (7.3) needs to be stored as a $2^n \times 2^n$ matrix in implementation. But the logical representation given as the right-hand side of (7.3) is much more compact.

7.3.2 Propositional quantum logic

The above Section discussed the early algebraic approach to sharp QL. The later research on QL naturally turned to a more logic flavour. As is well-known, classical logic is Boolean-valued, meaning that its truth values are taken from a Boolean algebra. Motivated by the above Sasaki theorem, sharp QL is defined as orthomodular lattice-valued logic; that is, a logic with truth values as elements of $S(\mathcal{H})$, the lattice of closed subspaces of a Hilbert space $\mathcal{H}$, or even an abstract orthomodular lattice. We study propositional sharp QL in this subsection.

Syntax: We assume that the reader is familiar with classical propositional logic. The language of propositional sharp QL is the standard propositional language, but the truth value of each propositional variable is taken from a given orthomodular lattice $\mathcal{L} = (L, \vee, \wedge, \perp)$, and logical connectives $\neg$, $\wedge$ are interpreted as operations $\perp$, $\wedge$ in $\mathcal{L}$, respectively. More precisely, its alphabet consisting of:

(i) a set of propositional variables P_0, P_1, P_2, ...; and
(ii) connectives $\wedge$ (conjunction) and $\neg$ (negation).

Quantum propositional formulas can be defined in a familiar way; that is, they are generated from propositional variables using binary connective $\wedge$ and unary connective $\neg$. The disjunction is defined as a derived connective by $\beta \vee \gamma := \neg(\neg \beta \wedge \neg \gamma)$.

Semantics: The semantics of propositional sharp QL is then defined as follows. Given an orthomodular lattice $\mathcal{L} = (L, \wedge, \vee, \perp)$ with the smallest element $\mathbf{0}$ and the greatest element $\mathbf{1}$. An $\mathcal{L}$-valued interpretation is a valuation function $v : \{P_0, P_1, P_2, ...\}$ (propositional variables) $\to L$, and it can be extended to all propositional formulas by the following valuation rules:

$$v(\beta \wedge \gamma) = v(\beta) \wedge v(\gamma), \qquad v(\neg \beta) = v(\beta)^{\perp}.$$

It can be verified that $v(\beta \vee \gamma) = v(\beta) \vee v(\gamma)$. Note that symbols $\wedge$, $\vee$, $\perp$ in the right-hand sides of these rules denote the operations in $\mathcal{L}$.

Definition 7.4. For a set Σ of propositional formulas and a proposition formula β, β is called a consequence of Σ in $\mathcal{L}$, written $\Sigma \models_{\mathcal{L}} \beta$, if for any valuation function v, and for any $a \in L$: whenever $a \leq v(\gamma)$ for all $\gamma \in \Sigma$, then $a \leq v(\beta)$.

When Σ is finite, say $\Sigma = \{\gamma_1, ..., \gamma_n\}$, then $\Sigma \models_{\mathcal{L}} \beta$ if and only if in for any valuation v:

$$\bigwedge_{i=1}^{n} v(\gamma_i) \leq v(\beta).$$

In particular, $\emptyset \models_{\mathcal{L}} \beta$ if and only if $v(\beta) = \mathbf{1}$ for all valuation function v, where $\mathbf{1}$ is the greatest element of $\mathcal{L}$. In this case, β is said to be true in $\mathcal{L}$ and we write $\models_{\mathcal{L}} \beta$. If $\{\beta\} \models \gamma$ and $\{\gamma\} \models \beta$, then β and γ are equivalent, written $\beta \equiv \gamma$.

Implication in QL: Since logic is the study of reasoning, it is natural that a logical system possesses an implication connective $\to$. In classical propositional logic, it can be defined as a derived connective from negation $\neg$, conjunction $\wedge$ and disjunction:

$$\beta \equiv \neg \beta \vee \gamma \equiv \neg(\beta \wedge \neg \gamma).$$

However, all implications that can be reasonably defined in QL are anomalous to a certain extent. A minimal requirement for an operation $\to$ in an orthomodular lattice $\mathcal{L}$ that can serve as an interpretation of implication is that for all $a, b \in \mathcal{L}$,

$$a \to b = \mathbf{1} \text{ iff } a \leq b.$$

It was proved that there are only five such operations that can be defined in terms of $\wedge$, $\vee$, $\perp$. Among them, only the Sasaki implication:

$$a \to b = a^{\perp} \vee (a \wedge b)$$

satisfies the import-export condition: for all $a, b, c \in \mathcal{L}$,

$$a \wedge b \leq c \text{ iff } a \leq b \to c.$$

In this chapter, we always use the Sasaki implication.

(QL1) $\Sigma \cup \{\beta\} \vdash \beta$

(QL2) $\dfrac{\Sigma \vdash \beta \qquad \Sigma' \cup \{\beta\} \vdash \gamma}{\Sigma \cup \Sigma' \vdash \gamma}$

(QL3) $\Sigma \cup \{\beta \wedge \gamma\} \vdash \beta \quad \Sigma \cup \{\beta \wedge \gamma\} \vdash \gamma$

(QL4) $\dfrac{\Sigma \vdash \beta \qquad \Sigma \vdash \gamma}{\Sigma \vdash \beta \wedge \gamma}$

(QL5) $\dfrac{\Sigma \cup \{\beta, \gamma\} \vdash \delta}{\Sigma \cup \{\beta \wedge \gamma\} \vdash \delta}$

(QL6) $\dfrac{\beta \vdash \gamma \qquad \beta \vdash \neg \gamma}{\neg \beta}$

(QL7) $\Sigma \cup \{\beta\} \vdash \neg\neg\beta$

(QL8) $\Sigma \cup \{\neg\neg\beta\} \vdash \beta$

(QL9) $\Sigma \cup \{\beta \wedge \neg\beta\} \vdash \gamma$

(QL10) $\dfrac{\beta \vdash \gamma}{\neg\gamma \vdash \neg\beta}$

(QL11) $\beta \wedge \neg(\beta \wedge \neg(\beta \wedge \gamma)) \vdash \gamma$

FIGURE 7.2 Proof system of propositional QL.

Proof systems: Propositional sharp QL is axiomatisable. Many proof systems (i.e. axiomatisations) of it have been proposed in the literature. Here, we present one in the Gentzen-style (natural deduction or sequent calculus).

A sequent is defined as an entailment of the form $\Sigma \vdash \beta$, where Σ is a set of logical formulas and β a logical formula. Intuitively, $\Sigma \vdash \beta$ means that β is inferred from (the formulas in) Σ. A sequent calculus is then defined by a set of inference rules of the form

$$\frac{\Sigma_1 \vdash \beta_1, ..., \Sigma_n \vdash \beta_n}{\Sigma \vdash \beta}$$

meaning that if β_i is inferred from Σ_i for $i = 1, ..., n$, then β is inferred from Σ.

A proof system of propositional sharp QL can be presented as the sequent calculus consisting the rules given in Fig. 7.2. It was proved that this proof system is complete with respect to orthomular lattice-valued semantics; that is, we have:

Theorem 7.3 (Goldblatt 1974). *$\Sigma \vdash \beta$ is provable in the proof system presented in Fig. 7.2 if and only if $\Sigma \models_{\mathcal{L}} P$ for every orthomodular lattice $\mathcal{L}$.*

7.3.3 First-order quantum logic

Now let us move on to consider first-order sharp QL. The existing first-order QL in the literature is an orthomodular lattice-valued logic with classical individual variables. It has the standard first-order language with, say, individual variables $x, y, z, ...$, function symbols $f, g, ...$, predicate symbols $P, Q, ...$, connectives $\neg, \wedge$ and quantifier $\forall$. The individual variables $x, y, z, ...$ are still classical variables with values taken from a domain D. Then function symbols $f, g, ...$ are interpreted in the same way as in classical logic, and quantifier $\forall$ binds classical variables. The only difference between the quantum and classical logics is that the former is $\mathcal{L}$-valued for some orthomodular lattice $\mathcal{L} = (L, \vee, \wedge, \perp)$; that is, an n-ary predicate symbol, say P, is interpreted as a mapping $D^n \to \mathcal{L}$, and connectives $\neg, \wedge$ are interpreted as operations $\perp$ and $\wedge$ in $\mathcal{L}$, respectively.

Syntax: More precisely, first-order sharp QL has the following alphabet:

(i) a set of individual variables $x, y, z, ...$;
(ii) a set of function symbols $f, g, ...$ (including constants $c, d, ...$ as 0-ary functions);
(iii) a set of predicate symbols $P, Q, ...$;
(iv) connectives $\wedge, \neg$; and
(v) universal quantifier $\forall$.

We assume the reader is familiar with classical first-order logic. The terms and first-order logical formulas in sharp QL are defined in the same way as in the classical logic. The existential quantification can be defined as a derived formula:

$$(\exists x)\gamma := \neg(\forall x)\neg\gamma.$$

Semantics: Let $\mathcal{L} = (L, \wedge, \vee, \perp)$ be a complete orthomodular lattice. Then an $\mathcal{L}$-valued interpretation $\mathbb{I}$ of sharp QL consists of:

- a nonempty set D, called the domain of $\mathbb{I}$;

$$(\text{QL12})\quad \Sigma \cup \{(\forall x)\beta\} \vdash \beta[t/x] \qquad\qquad (\text{QL13})\quad \frac{\Sigma \vdash \beta}{\Sigma \vdash (\forall x)\beta}\ (x \text{ is not free in } \Sigma)$$

FIGURE 7.3   Proof system of first-order QL. In (QL12), $\beta[t/x]$ stands for the substitution of variable x by term t in β.

- for each n-ary function symbol f, it is interpreted as a mapping $f^{\mathbb{I}} : D^n \to D$. In particular, a constant c is interpreted as an element $c^{\mathbb{I}} \in D$;
- for each n-ary predicate symbol P, it is interpreted as an $\mathcal{L}$-valued relation, i.e., a mapping $P^{\mathbb{I}} : D^n \to L$.

Given an interpretation $\mathbb{I}$ and a valuation function $\sigma : \{x, y, z, ...\}$ (individual variables) $\to D$. They define the semantics of terms exactly in the same way as in classical first order logic. Furthermore, they define a truth valuation; that is, for a first-order logical formula β, its truth value $v(\beta)$ is inductively defined as follows:

- for an atomic formula $\beta = P(t_1, ..., t_n)$, $v(\beta) = P^{\mathbb{I}}(v(t_1), ..., v(t_n))$, where $v(t_i)$ stands for the value of term t_i;
- $v(\beta \wedge \gamma) = v(\beta) \wedge v(\gamma)$ and $v(\neg\beta) = v(\beta)^\perp$;
- $v((\forall x)\beta) = \bigwedge\{v[d/x](\beta) : d \in D\}$, where $v[d/x]$ is the truth valuation defined by the same interpretation $\mathbb{I}$ together with valuation function $\sigma[d/x]$, which coincides with σ except that $\sigma[d/x](x) = d$.

The valuation rule for existential quantifier can be derived as

$$v((\exists x)\beta) = \bigvee\{v[d/x](\beta) : d \in D\}.$$

The definition of consequence $\Sigma \models_{\mathcal{L}} \beta$ and related notions in propositional QL (see Definition 7.4) can be straightforwardly generalised to first-order QL.

It should be emphasised once again that in this first-order QL, individual variables $x, y, z, ...$ are still classical variables with values taken from an ordinary domain D. The only difference between QL and classical first order logic is that the set of truth values in QL is an orthomodular lattice $\mathcal{L}$, which is set to be the lattice $S(\mathcal{H})$ of closed subspaces of a Hilbert space $\mathcal{H}$ when QL is applied to specify and reason about a quantum system with state space $\mathcal{H}$.

Proof system: An axiomatisation of first-order sharp QL can be obtained by adding the two rules for universal quantifier presented in Fig. 7.3 to the proof system of propositional sharp QL given in Fig. 7.2. It was also proved that this proof system is complete with respect to orthomodular lattice-valued semantics; that is, Theorem 7.3 holds for first-order sharp QL too.

7.3.4 Effect algebra and unsharp quantum logic

The sharp QL considered in the previous subsections takes projection operators on a Hilbert space $\mathcal{H}$ (equivalently, closed subspaces of $\mathcal{H}$) as its truth values. It can be naturally combined with the restricted version of quantum Hoare logic with only projective quantum predicates as pre/postconditions as presented in [452]. However, quantum predicates used in the general quantum Hoare logic can be any effects, i.e. those observables represented by Hermitian operators between the zero operator and identity operator. So, in this subsection, we consider unsharp QL with effects as its truth values.

Let us start from an abstract definition of effect algebra.

Definition 7.5. An effect algebra is an algebraic structure $\mathcal{A} = (A, \oplus, \mathbf{0}, \mathbf{1})$, where:

1. $\mathbf{0}, \mathbf{1}$ are two distinct elements of A;
2. $\oplus$ is a partial binary operation on A; that is, $a \oplus b$ is defined for some (not necessarily all) a, b in A. It satisfies the following conditions:
   - Weak Commutativity: if $a \oplus b$ is defined, then $b \oplus a$ is defined too, and $a \oplus b = b \oplus a$;
   - Weak Associativity: if both $b \oplus c$ and $a \oplus (b \oplus c)$ are defined, then $a \oplus b$ and $(a \oplus b) \oplus c$ are defined, and $a \oplus (b \oplus c) = (a \oplus b) \oplus c$;
   - Excluded Middle Law: for any a, there exists an element $a^\perp$ such that $a \oplus a^\perp = \mathbf{1}$;
   - Consistency: if $a \oplus \mathbf{1}$ is defined, then $a = \mathbf{0}$.

A partial order can be defined in an effect algebra $\mathcal{A}$: for any $a, b \in A$,

$$a \leq b \text{ if and only if } b = a \oplus c \text{ for some } c \in A. \tag{7.4}$$

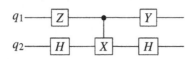

FIGURE 7.4   A quantum circuit.

A basic difference between orthomodular lattice and effect algebra is that the contradiction law $x \wedge x^{\perp} = \mathbf{0}$ is required in the former but not in the latter, with $\wedge$ in an effect algebra $\mathcal{A}$ standing for the greatest lower bound defined according to the order $\leq$ given in (7.4).

Now we construct a concrete example of effect algebra from quantum theory. Let $\mathcal{H}$ be a Hilbert space. Recall from Section 6.1 that $\mathcal{P}(\mathcal{H})$ denotes the set of quantum predicates (i.e. effects) in $\mathcal{H}$. The zero operator $0_{\mathcal{H}}$ and identity operator $I_{\mathcal{H}}$ are in $\mathcal{P}(\mathcal{H})$. For any $B, C \in \mathcal{P}(\mathcal{H})$, we define:

- $B \oplus C$ is defined if $B + C \sqsubseteq I_{\mathcal{H}}$, where $\sqsubseteq$ stands for the Löwner order. In this case, $B \oplus C \overset{def}{=} B + C$.

Then we have:

Proposition 7.1. $(\mathcal{P}(\mathcal{H}), \oplus, 0_{\mathcal{H}}, I_{\mathcal{H}})$ *is an effect algebra.*

It is easy to see that in effect algebra $\mathcal{P}(\mathcal{H})$, $B^{\perp} = I_{\mathcal{H}} - B$ for all B, and the partial order coincides with the Löwner order.

Several forms of unsharp QL have been proposed in the literature. As we saw in the previous subsections, propositional and first-order sharp QL are logics with truth values taken from an orthomodular lattice. Similarly, propositional and first-order unsharp QL are defined as logics with truth values taken from an effect algebra. Their basic aim is to provide a logical formalism of certain ambiguous feature in the effect-state characterisation of quantum systems, where the contradiction law may be violated. Up to now, the theory of unsharp QL is not very rich in the literature. In particular, the current version of unsharp QL is not suitable as an assertion logic combined with quantum Hoare logic with general quantum predicates for our purpose of quantum program verification. In Section 7.6, we will introduce some formal descriptions of effects (i.e. general quantum predicates) that have much stronger expressive power and logical reasoning ability than unsharp QL for symbolic verification of quantum programs.

7.4   Quantum logic with quantum variables

The first-order quantum logic (QL for short) described in the last section only has classical variables. It is useful in formulating various theories of quantum (orthomodular lattice-valued) mathematical structures, e.g. quantum set theory [389]. However, it is not a desirable assertion language for quantum programs (and more broadly, logical tool for formal reasoning in quantum computation and quantum information). Instead, a first-order logic with quantum variables whose values are quantum states rather than classical ones will be often more convenient, in particular in verification and analysis of quantum programs (including quantum cryptographic and communication protocols).

Informal introduction: Let us first consider a simple example that illustrates why the notions of term and logical formula in classical first-order logic should be generalised to the case with quantum variables.

Example 7.3 (Inputs/outputs of quantum circuit). The quantum circuit in Fig. 7.4 can be written as a term with quantum variables:

$$\tau = Z(q_1)H(q_2)C(q_1, q_2)Y(q_1)H(q_2) \tag{7.5}$$

where q_1, q_2 are qubit variables, operation symbols Z, Y, H, C denote Pauli gates Z, Y, Hadamard gate, and controlled-NOT, i.e. CNOT, respectively. It is easy to see that whenever in the input to the circuit, q_1 is in basis state $|0\rangle$, then the state of q_2 in the output is the same as in the input. This fact can be expressed by the first-order formula:

$$\beta = (\forall q_1)(\forall q_2)[P_0(q_1) \wedge P(q_1, q_2) \rightarrow P(\tau)] \tag{7.6}$$

where P_0 is a predicate symbol for a single qubit denoting the one-dimensional space spanned by $|0\rangle$, and P is a predicate symbol for two qubits denoting a subspace of the form $\mathcal{H}_2 \otimes X$ with $\mathcal{H}_2$ being the 2-dimensional state space of the first qubit and X an arbitrary subspace of the state space of the second qubit.

Quantum variables q_1, q_2 and universal/existential quantifications over them appear in a natural way in the above example. The statement (7.6) cannot be conveniently and meaningfully expressed in the first QL presented in the last section. In this section, we will define a new quantum logic, denoted $\mathcal{QL}$, in which logical formulas can contain quantum variables as their individual variables, and thus (7.6) is an eligible logical formula. $\mathcal{QL}$ is designed to be a first-order logic with equality $=$ so that we can use it to reason about equality of two quantum states and equivalence of two quantum circuits.

Quantifications over quantum variables: The introduction of quantum variables into a first-order logic leads us to a fundamentally new issue – quantification over quantum variables. To see this, let us consider the universal quantification. The treatment of existential quantification is similar. For any interpretation $\mathbb{I}$ of the first-order language under consideration, any valuation function v of individual variables and any logical formula β, we use $(\mathbb{I}, v) \models \beta$ to denotes that β is satisfied by $\mathbb{I}$ and v. Recall that in classical first-order logic, a universally quantified formula $(\forall x)\beta$ is interpreted as follows:

$$(\mathbb{I}, v) \models (\forall x)\beta \text{ iff } (\mathbb{I}, v[a/x]) \models \beta \text{ for any possible value } a \text{ of } x \tag{7.7}$$

where $v[a/x]$ is the valuation function that coincides with v for all variables $y \neq x$ but takes the value a for variable x. A natural quantum extension of universal quantification is a formula $(\forall \overline{q})\beta$ with a sequence $\overline{q}$ of quantum variables that is interpreted by

$$(\mathbb{I}, \rho) \models (\forall \overline{q})\beta \text{ iff } (\mathbb{I}, \mathcal{E}(\rho)) \models \beta \text{ for any } \mathcal{E} \in \mathcal{O}_{\overline{q}} \tag{7.8}$$

where $\mathcal{O}_{\overline{q}}$ is a set of quantum operations that are allowed to perform on $\overline{q}$, according to the application situations.

Quantification over quantum variables is much more intrigues than that over classical variables. We note that the quantification in (7.8) is defined over a sequence of quantum variables rather than over a single variable as usual in classical logic. The reason is that in general, a joint quantum operation on several variables cannot be implemented by a series of local operations on a single variable. Moreover, although we only consider in logic $\mathcal{QL}$ presented in this section the quantification in (7.8) defined by allowed operations, quantification over quantum variables can be defined in several other different ways that reflect some different characteristic features of quantum systems, as will be briefly discussed at the end of this chapter.

7.4.1 Syntax

Now we start to formally define first-order quantum logic $\mathcal{QL}$ with quantum variables. The syntax of $\mathcal{QL}$ is similar to that of the first-order QL defined in Section 7.3.3 except that classical individual variables in QL are replaced by quantum variables in $\mathcal{QL}$. Accordingly, function symbols in QL are replaced by symbols that denote quantum operations over (the states of) quantum variables. The predicate symbols in both QL and $\mathcal{QL}$ are interpreted as an orthomodular lattice-valued functions, but in QL they are over a domain of classical individuals and in $\mathcal{QL}$ they are over a domain of quantum states.

Alphabet: Formally, the alphabet of $\mathcal{QL}$ consists of:

1. A set $qVar$ of quantum variables $q, q_1, q_2, ...$;
2. A set of quantum operation symbols $\mathcal{E}, \mathcal{E}_1, \mathcal{E}_2, ...$, with a subset of unitary symbols $\mathcal{U}, \mathcal{U}_1, \mathcal{U}_2, ...$ and their inverses $\mathcal{U}^{-1}, \mathcal{U}_1^{-1}, \mathcal{U}_2^{-1}, ...$;
3. A set of quantum predicate symbols $P, Q, ...$;
4. Connectives $\neg, \wedge$;
5. Universal quantifier $\forall$.

To each quantum variable $q \in Var$, a nonnegative integer d or $d = \infty$ is assigned, called the dimension of q. To each quantum operation symbol $\mathcal{E}$, a nonnegative integer n and an n-tuple $\overline{d} = (d_1, ..., d_n)$ of nonnegative integers or ∞ are assigned, called the arity and signature of $\mathcal{E}$, respectively. To each quantum predicate symbol P, an arity and a signature are assigned too.

Terms: The notion of term in classical first-order logic can be straightforwardly generalised into $\mathcal{QL}$, with some formation rules specifically designed for modelling quantum operations.

Definition 7.6. Quantum terms τ and their variables $var(\tau)$ are inductively defined as follows:

1. Basic terms: If $\mathcal{E}$ is an n-ary quantum operation symbol with signature $(d_1, ..., d_n)$, and $\overline{q} = q_1, ..., q_n$ where q_i is a d_i-dimensional quantum variable for each $1 \leq i \leq n$, then $\tau = \mathcal{E}(\overline{q})$ is a quantum term and $var(\tau) = \{\overline{q}\}$;
2. Sequential composition: If τ_1, τ_2 are quantum terms, so is $\tau = \tau_1 \tau_2$ and $var(\tau) = var(\tau_1) \cup var(\tau_2)$;
3. Tensor product: If τ_1, τ_2 are quantum terms and $var(\tau_1) \cap var(\tau_2) = \emptyset$, then $\tau = \tau_1 \otimes \tau_2$ is a quantum term and $var(\tau) = var(\tau_1) \cup var(\tau_2)$;

4. Probabilistic combination: If $\{\tau_i\}$ is a family of quantum terms with the same variables $var(\tau_i) = V$, and $\{p_i\}$ is a subprobability distribution; that is, $p_i > 0$ for all i and $\sum_i p_i \leq 1$, then $\tau = \sum_i p_i \tau_i$ is a quantum term, and $var(\tau) = V$.

In particular, if τ is generated only by clauses (1)–(3) and all quantum operation symbols in τ are unitary symbols, then τ is called a unitary term, and its inverse τ^{-1} is defined as follows:

(i) If $\tau = \mathcal{U}(\overline{q})$, then $\tau^{-1} = \mathcal{U}^{-1}(\overline{q})$;
(ii) If $\tau = \tau_1 \tau_2$, then $\tau^{-1} = \tau_2^{-1} \tau_1^{-1}$;
(iii) If $\tau = \tau_1 \otimes \tau_2$, then $\tau^{-1} = \tau_1^{-1} \otimes \tau_2^{-1}$.

Clause 1 in the above definition defines the basic quantum operations. Clauses 2 and 3 are introduced for describing the sequential composition of two quantum operations and a separable operation on a composed system, respectively. The term $\tau_1 \otimes \tau_2$ can also be understood as the parallel composition of τ_1 and τ_2. Quantum terms defined by clause 4 are introduced for modelling a probabilistic combination of quantum states, in particular for merging the outcomes from different branches of a computation; i.e. a mixed state that is formed as an ensemble of output quantum states from different branches of the computation. As we will see in Definition 7.9, tensor product $\tau_1 \otimes \tau_2$ is semantically equivalent to sequential composition $\tau_1 \tau_2$ because it is required in its definition that $var(\tau_1) \cap var(\tau_2) = \emptyset$. However, a probabilistic combination $\sum_i p_i (\tau_{1i} \otimes \tau_{2i})$ of multiple tensor products cannot always be expressed by sequential composition.

Example 7.4. The term τ defined by Eq. (7.5) in Example 7.3 is a unitary term that expresses the quantum circuit in Fig. 7.4. Obviously, all (combinational) quantum circuits, including noisy quantum circuits, can be written as quantum terms. For example, if a bit-flip noise $\mathcal{E}_{bf}$ occurs immediately after the gate Z and a phase-flip noise $\mathcal{E}_{pf}$ occurs on qubit q_2 after the CNOT gate in Fig. 7.4, then the noisy circuit can be written as the following term:

$$\begin{aligned} \tau' &= Z(q_1)\mathcal{E}_{bf}(q_1)H(q_2)C(q_1,q_2)\mathcal{E}_{pf}(q_2)Y(q_1)H(q_2), \text{ or} \\ \tau' &= [Z(q_1)\mathcal{E}_{bf}(q_1) \otimes H(q_2)]C(q_1,q_2)[Y(q_1) \otimes \mathcal{E}_{pf}(q_2)H(q_2)]. \end{aligned} \tag{7.9}$$

Logical formulas: The logical formulas in $\mathcal{QL}$ are also straightforward generalisation of the standard first-order logical formulas, except those given by clause 4 in the following definition.

Definition 7.7. The formulas β of logic $\mathcal{QL}$ and their free variables $free(\beta)$ are inductively defined as follows:

1. If P is an n-ary quantum predicate symbol with signature $(d_1, ..., d_n)$, and τ a term with $var(\tau) = \overline{q} = q_1, ..., q_n$, where q_i is a d_i-dimensional quantum variable for each $1 \leq i \leq n$, then $\beta = P(\tau)$ is a formula and $free(\beta) = var(\tau)$;
2. If β' is a formula, so is $\beta = \neg\beta'$ and $free(\beta) = free(\beta')$;
3. If β_1, β_2 are formulas, so is $\beta = \beta_1 \wedge \beta_2$ and $free(\beta) = free(\beta_1) \cup free(\beta_2)$;
4. If β' is a formula and τ a term, then $\beta = \tau^*(\beta')$ is a formula and $free(\beta) = var(\tau) \cup free(\beta')$;
5. If β' is a formula and $\overline{q}$ is a sequence of quantum variables, then $\beta = (\forall\overline{q})\beta'$ is a formula and $free(\beta) = free(\beta') \setminus \overline{q}$.

In particular, if $\mathcal{I}$ is a symbol for the identity operation, then $P(\mathcal{I}(q_1)...\mathcal{I}(q_n))$ is a formula, often written as $P(q_1, ..., q_n)$ for simplicity. The existential quantification can be defined as a derived formula:

$$(\exists\overline{q})\beta = \neg(\forall\overline{q})\neg\beta.$$

Example 7.5. We use those quantum variables and quantum operation symbols in Example 7.4. Moreover, let P_0, P_1 be two quantum predicate symbols for a single qubit, and P_e a quantum predicate symbol for two qubits. The following are two logical formulas in $\mathcal{QL}$:

1. $\beta_1 = \neg P_0(Z(q_1)\mathcal{E}_{bf}(q_1)) \wedge P_2(H(q_2))$;
2. $\beta_2 = P_e(\tau') \wedge (\forall q_2)P_2(q_2)$, where τ' is the quantum term given in Eq. (7.9).

Intuitively, formula β_1 expresses that after the Pauli gate and bit-flip noise, the state of qubit q_1 is in the subspace denoted by P_0, and after the Hadamard gate, the state of q_2 is in the subspace denoted by P_2; formula β_2 says that the output of the noisy circuit (7.9) is in the subspace denoted by P_e, and after any allowed operation, the state of q_2 is still in the subspace denoted by P_2.

Clause 4 in the above definition shows a fundamental difference between classical first-order logic and our logic $\mathcal{QL}$ and deserves a careful explanation. A formula of the form $\beta = \tau^*(\beta')$ is called a *term-adjoint formula*. Essentially, whenever τ contains a single quantum variable q, i.e. $var(\tau) = \{q\}$, it is the quantum version of substitution $\beta'[t/x]$ of variable x in logical formula β' by term t. In classical logic, $\beta'[t/x]$ is obtained by substituting all free occurrences of x in β' with t.

However, in the quantum case, substitution cannot be defined in such a way due to the socalled Schrödinger–Heisenberg duality (see Section 6.1). Whence an interpretation is given, a quantum term τ denotes a quantum state, which should be considered in the Schrödinger picture. On the other hand, a $\mathcal{QL}$ formula β' denotes a closed subspace of the state Hilbert space (equivalently, a projection operator as a special form of observable) and thus should be considered in the Heisenberg picture. Consequently, when applying term τ to modify formula β', we must use the dual τ^* of τ rather than τ itself. If τ contains more than one quantum variable, say $var(\tau) = \{q_1, ..., q_n\}$, then $\tau^*(\beta')$ can be understood as a quantum analogue of simultaneous substitution $\beta'[t_1/x_1, ..., t_n.x_n]$, but we must keep in mind that τ may denote an entangled state of $q_1, ..., q_n$, and thus $q_1, ..., q_n$ cannot be separately substituted. This point will be seen more clearly from the semantics of $\beta = \tau^*(\beta')$ below. As we will see in Section 7.5.2, term-adjoint formulas are needed in defining the proof rules for some basic quantum programs.

7.4.2 Semantics

In this subsection, we define the semantics of $\mathcal{QL}$ formulas, from which we will see various differences between $\mathcal{QL}$ and first-order QL. For readability, the proofs of all results in this and the next subsections are deferred to appendices. The reader is encouraged to prove them as exercises.

Interpretations: First of all, each individual variable q in $\mathcal{QL}$ is a quantum variable, and its values are quantum states in its state space $\mathcal{H}_q$. For a d-dimensional quantum variable q, if $d < \infty$ then its state space is (isomorphic to) the Hilbert space with orthonormal basis $\{|0\rangle, ..., |d-1\rangle\}$:

$$\mathcal{H}_q = \left\{ \sum_{i=0}^{d-1} c_i |i\rangle : c_i \in \mathbb{C} \ (0 \le i < d) \right\}.$$

In this book, we only consider separable Hilbert spaces. Thus, if $d = \infty$ then we can assume:

$$\mathcal{H}_q = \left\{ \sum_{i=-\infty}^{\infty} c_i |i\rangle : c_i \in \mathbb{C} \ (0 \le i < d) \text{ with } \sum_{i=-\infty}^{\infty} |c_i|^2 < \infty \right\} \tag{7.10}$$

with orthonormal basis $\{|i\rangle : i \in \mathbb{Z} \text{ (intergers)}\}$. For any subset of quantum variables $V \subseteq Var$, we write $\mathcal{H}_V = \bigotimes_{q \in V} \mathcal{H}_q$, and the identity quantum operation on $\mathcal{H}_V$ is denoted $\mathcal{I}_V$. In particular, $\mathcal{H}_{all} = \mathcal{H}_{qVar}$ is the state space of all quantum variables assumed in our logic. Secondly, we recall from Definition 2.25 that a quantum operation on a Hilbert space $\mathcal{H}$ is defined as a completely positive and trace-non-increasing superoperator, i.e. a linear map from operators on $\mathcal{H}$ to themselves. We assume a family $\mathcal{O} = \left\{ \mathcal{O}_{\overline{d}} \right\}$, where for each signature $\overline{d} = (d_1, ..., d_n)$, $\mathcal{O}_{\overline{d}}$ is a set of quantum operations on the $\prod_{i=1}^{n} d_i$-dimensional Hilbert space, called the *allowed operations*. Thirdly, recall from Section 7.3.3 that first-order QL in Section 7.3 is interpreted in an arbitrary orthomodular lattice $\mathcal{L}$. However, logic $\mathcal{QL}$ in this section is interpreted only in a special class of $\mathcal{L} = S(\mathcal{H})$ (the orthomodular lattice of closed subspaces of $\mathcal{H}$) for certain Hilbert spaces $\mathcal{H}$. Formally, we have:

Definition 7.8. An interpretation $\mathbb{I}$ of logic $\mathcal{QL}$ is defined as follows:

1. To each d-dimensional quantum variable $q \in Var$, a d-dimensional Hilbert space $\mathcal{H}_q$ is associated, called the state space of q;
2. Each n-ary quantum operation symbol $\mathcal{E}$ with signature $(d_1, ..., d_n)$ is interpreted as an allowed quantum operation $\mathcal{E}^{\mathbb{I}} \in \mathcal{O}_{\overline{d}}$ on the $\prod_{i=1}^{n} d_i$-dimensional Hilbert space. It is required that for each unitary symbol $\mathcal{U}$, $(\mathcal{U}^{-1})^{\mathbb{I}} = (\mathcal{U}^{\mathbb{I}})^{-1}$;
3. Each n-ary quantum predicate symbol P with signature $(d_1, ..., d_n)$ is interpreted as a closed subspace $P^{\mathbb{I}}$ of the $\prod_{i=1}^{n} d_i$-dimensional Hilbert space.

The difference between an interpretation of $\mathcal{QL}$ and that of the first-order QL defined in Section 7.3.3 is obvious. Essentially, all other differences between $\mathcal{QL}$ and QL originate from it. Furthermore, the (meta)logical properties of $\mathcal{QL}$ heavily depend on the allowed quantum operations $\mathcal{O} = \left\{ \mathcal{O}_{\overline{d}} \right\}$.

Semantics of terms: Now let us define the semantics of quantum terms. As mentioned in the last subsection, a quantum term can be considered in two different ways. In the Schrödinger picture, it is interpreted as a mapping from quantum states to quantum states. Recall from Section 2.5 that a (mixed) state of a quantum system with Hilbert space $\mathcal{H}$ as its state space is described as a density operator on $\mathcal{H}$. An operator ρ on $\mathcal{H}$ is called a partial density operator if it is positive and $\text{tr}(\rho) \le 1$. In particular, if $\text{tr}(\rho) = 1$, then ρ is called a density operator. We use $\mathcal{D}(\mathcal{H})$ to denote the set of partial density operators on $\mathcal{H}$.

Definition 7.9. Given an interpretation $\mathbb{I}$. The Schrödinger semantics of a term τ is a mapping $[\![\tau]\!]_{\mathbb{I}} : \mathcal{D}(\mathcal{H}_{all}) \to \mathcal{D}(\mathcal{H}_{all})$. For each $\rho \in \mathcal{D}(\mathcal{H}_{all})$, $[\![\tau]\!]_{\mathbb{I}}(\rho)$ is defined as follows:

1. If $\tau = \mathcal{E}(\overline{q})$, then $[\![\tau]\!]_{\mathbb{I}}(\rho) = \left(\mathcal{E}^{\mathbb{I}} \otimes \mathcal{I}_{qVar\backslash\overline{q}}\right)(\rho)$;
2. If $\tau = \tau_1\tau_2$, then $[\![\tau]\!]_{\mathbb{I}}(\rho) = [\![\tau_2]\!]_{\mathbb{I}}\left([\![\tau_1]\!]_{\mathbb{I}}(\rho)\right)$;
3. If $\tau = \tau_1 \otimes \tau_2$, then $[\![\tau]\!]_{\mathbb{I}}(\rho) = [\![\tau_2]\!]_{\mathbb{I}}\left([\![\tau_1]\!]_{\mathbb{I}}(\rho)\right) = [\![\tau_1]\!]_{\mathbb{I}}\left([\![\tau_2]\!]_{\mathbb{I}}(\rho)\right)$;
4. If $\tau = \sum_i p_i\tau_i$, then $[\![\tau]\!]_{\mathbb{I}}(\rho) = \sum_i p_i[\![\tau_i]\!]_{\mathbb{I}}(\rho)$.

All of the clauses in the above definition except clause 3 are easy to understand. The idea behind clause 3 is the fact that if $\mathcal{E}_1$ and $\mathcal{E}_2$ are quantum operations on Hilbert spaces $\mathcal{H}_1$ and $\mathcal{H}_2$, respectively, then

$$(\mathcal{E}_1 \otimes \mathcal{E}_2)(\rho) = (\mathcal{E}_1 \otimes \mathcal{I}_2)((\mathcal{I}_1 \otimes \mathcal{E}_2)(\rho)) = (\mathcal{I}_1 \otimes \mathcal{E}_2)((\mathcal{E}_1 \otimes \mathcal{I}_2)(\rho))$$

for all $\rho \in \mathcal{D}(\mathcal{H}_1 \otimes \mathcal{H}_)$, where $\mathcal{I}_1, \mathcal{I}_2$ stand for the identity quantum operations on $\mathcal{H}_1$ and $\mathcal{H}_2$, respectively. It is easy to show that for any term, its Schrödinger semantics $[\![\tau]\!]_{\mathbb{I}}$ is a quantum operation (i.e. completely positive superoperator that does not increase trace) on $\mathcal{H}_{all}$.

In the Heisenberg picture, however, a quantum term should be interpreted as a mapping from observables to observables. In this section, we focus on socalled sharp quantum logic with closed subspaces (equivalently, projection operators) as logical propositions, and thus the Heisenberg interpretation of a term is defined as a mapping from subspaces to themselves. Let $\mathcal{E}$ be a quantum operation on Hilbert space $\mathcal{H}$ and $X \in \mathcal{S}(\mathcal{H})$. Then the image of X under $\mathcal{E}$ is defined as

$$\mathcal{E}(X) = \bigvee_{|\psi\rangle \in X} \text{supp}[\mathcal{E}(|\psi\rangle\langle\psi|)] \tag{7.11}$$

where $\text{supp}(\rho)$ denotes the support of ρ, i.e. the subspace spanned by the eigenvectors of ρ corresponding to nonzero eigenvalues, and for any $X_i \in S(\mathcal{H})$,

$$\bigvee_i X_i = \overline{\text{span}\left(\bigcup_i X_i\right)} \tag{7.12}$$

is the smallest closed subspace of $\mathcal{H}$ containing all X_i.

Definition 7.10. Given an interpretation $\mathbb{I}$. The Heisenberg semantics of a term τ is a mapping $[\![\tau]\!]_{\mathbb{I}}^* : S(\mathcal{H}_{all}) \to S(\mathcal{H}_{all})$. For each $X \in S(\mathcal{H}_{all})$, $[\![\tau]\!]_{\mathbb{I}}^*(X)$ is defined as follows:

1. If $\tau = \mathcal{E}(\overline{q})$, then $[\![\tau]\!]_{\mathbb{I}}^*(X) = \left((\mathcal{E}^{\mathbb{I}})^* \otimes \mathcal{I}_{qVar\backslash\overline{q}}\right)(X)$;
2. If $\tau = \tau_1\tau_2$, then $[\![\tau]\!]_{\mathbb{I}}^*(X) = [\![\tau_1]\!]_{\mathbb{I}}^*\left([\![\tau_2]\!]_{\mathbb{I}}^*(X)\right)$;
3. If $\tau = \tau_1 \otimes \tau_2$, then $[\![\tau]\!]_{\mathbb{I}}^*(X) = [\![\tau_1]\!]_{\mathbb{I}}^*\left([\![\tau_2]\!]_{\mathbb{I}}^*(X)\right) = [\![\tau_2]\!]_{\mathbb{I}}^*\left([\![\tau_1]\!]_{\mathbb{I}}^*(X)\right)$;
4. If $\tau = \sum_i p_i\tau_i$, then $[\![\tau]\!]_{\mathbb{I}}^*(X) = \bigvee_i[\![\tau_i]\!]_{\mathbb{I}}^*(X)$.

It should be noted that as usual for simplicity of presentation, both the Schrödinger and Heisenberg semantics of a term τ are defined on the state space $\mathcal{H}_{all}$ of all variables $qVar$. But we can show that only the variables $var(\tau)$ appearing in τ are essential for them. To this end, let us recall that for any density operator $\rho \in \mathcal{D}(\mathcal{H}_1 \otimes \mathcal{H}_2)$, its restriction on $\mathcal{H}_1$ is $\rho \downarrow \mathcal{H}_1 = \text{tr}_{\mathcal{H}_2}(\rho)$, where partial trace $\text{tr}_{\mathcal{H}_2}$ over $\mathcal{H}_2$ is defined by

$$\text{tr}_{\mathcal{H}_2}(|\varphi_1\rangle\langle\psi_1| \otimes |\varphi_2\rangle\langle\psi_2|) = \langle\psi_2|\varphi_2\rangle \cdot |\varphi_1\rangle\langle\psi_1|$$

for any $|\varphi_i\rangle, |\psi_i\rangle \in \mathcal{H}_i$ ($i = 1, 2$), together with linearity. In particular, if $\rho \in \mathcal{D}(\mathcal{H}_V)$ for some $V \subseteq qVar$ and $V' \subseteq V$, we simply write $\rho \downarrow V'$ for $\rho \downarrow \mathcal{H}_{V'}$. On the other hand, for any subspace $X \in \mathcal{S}(\mathcal{H}_1 \otimes \mathcal{H}_2)$, its restriction on $\mathcal{H}_1$ is defined as

$$X \downarrow \mathcal{H}_1 = \text{supp}[\text{tr}_{\mathcal{H}_2}(P_X)],$$

where P_X is the projection operator onto X. In particular, if $X \in S(\mathcal{H}_V)$ for some $V \subseteq qVar$ and $V' \subseteq V$, we simply write $X \downarrow V'$ for $X \downarrow \mathcal{H}_{V'}$. Then we have:

Lemma 7.3 (Coincidence). *Let $var(\tau) \subseteq V \subseteq qVar$. Then:*

1. $\rho \downarrow V = \rho' \downarrow V$ *implies* $[\![\tau]\!]_{\mathbb{I}}(\rho) \downarrow V = [\![\tau]\!]_{\mathbb{I}}(\rho') \downarrow V$;
2. $X \downarrow V = X' \downarrow V$ *implies* $[\![\tau]\!]_{\mathbb{I}}^*(X) \downarrow V = [\![\tau]\!]_{\mathbb{I}}^*(X') \downarrow V$.

We already mentioned that certain duality exists between the Schrödinger and Heisenberg semantics of quantum terms. It is precisely described in the following:

Lemma 7.4 (Schrödinger–Heisenberg duality). *For any term τ, density operator ρ, and closed subspace X, we have:*

$$[\![\tau]\!]_{\mathbb{I}}(\rho) \in X \Leftrightarrow \rho \in \left([\![\tau]\!]_{\mathbb{I}}^*(X^\perp)\right)^\perp.$$

In particular, if τ is unitary, or the allowed quantum operations in $\mathcal{O}_{\overline{d}}$ for the signature $\overline{d}$ of all operation symbols appearing in τ are unitary, then

$$[\![\tau]\!]_{\mathbb{I}}(\rho) \in X \Leftrightarrow \rho \in [\![\tau]\!]_{\mathbb{I}}^*(X).$$

The proofs of Lemmas 7.3 and 7.4 can be found in Apendix A.3.2.

Semantics of logical formulas: We now move on to define the semantics of logical formulas in $\mathcal{QL}$. To this end, we need the following notations:

- Let $\rho \in \mathcal{D}(\mathcal{H})$ and $X \in S(\mathcal{H})$. Then we define: $\rho \in X$ iff $\text{supp}(\rho) \subseteq X$.
- Two partial density operators $\rho_1, \rho_2 \in \mathcal{D}(\mathcal{H})$ are orthogonal, written $\rho_1 \perp \rho_2$, if $\text{supp}(\rho_1) \perp \text{supp}(\rho_2)$.

Definition 7.11. Given an interpretation $\mathbb{I}$ and a state $\rho \in \mathcal{D}(\mathcal{H}_{all})$. Let β be a formula. Then satisfaction relation $(\mathbb{I}, \rho) \models \beta$ is inductively defined as follows:

1. If $\beta = P(\tau)$, then $(\mathbb{I}, \rho) \models \beta$ iff $[\![\tau]\!]_{\mathbb{I}}(\rho) \downarrow var(\tau) \in P^{\mathbb{I}}$;
2. If $\beta = \neg\beta'$, then $(\mathbb{I}, \rho) \models \beta$ iff for all ρ', $(\mathbb{I}, \rho') \models \beta'$ implies $\rho' \perp \rho$;
3. If $\beta = \beta_1 \wedge \beta_2$, then $(\mathbb{I}, \rho) \models \beta$ iff $(\mathbb{I}, \rho) \models \beta_1$ and $(\mathbb{I}, \rho) \models \beta_2$;
4. If $\beta = \tau^*(\beta')$, then $(\mathbb{I}, \rho) \models \beta$ iff $(\mathbb{I}, [\![\tau]\!]_{\mathbb{I}}(\rho)) \models \beta'$;
5. If $\beta = (\forall \overline{q})\beta'$, then $(\mathbb{I}, \rho) \models \beta$ iff for any term τ with $var(\tau) \subseteq \overline{q}$, it holds that $(\mathbb{I}, \rho) \models \tau^*(\beta')$.

Clauses 1 and 3 are easy to understand. From clause 2 we see that if $(\mathbb{I}, \rho) \models \neg\beta'$ then $(\mathbb{I}, \rho) \models \beta'$ does not hold, but not vice versa. Indeed, $(\mathbb{I}, \rho) \models \neg\beta'$ means that $(\mathbb{I}, \rho') \models \beta'$ is not true for all ρ' that is not orthogonal to ρ. Clause 4 reflects the Schrödinger–Heisenberg duality discussed before. Clause 5 is essentially a restatement of Eq. (7.8), but here the allowed operations $\mathcal{E} \in \mathcal{O}_{\overline{q}}$ in Eq. (7.8) are syntactically expressed by quantum terms τ. In classical program logics (e.g. Hoare logic and separation logic), substitution is needed in defining the proof rules for some basic program constructs. We pointed out at the end of Section 7.9 that a term-adjoint formula of the form $\tau^*(\beta)$ is introduced for a role in our $\mathcal{QL}$ as the one of substitution in classical first-order logic. But its definition (see clause 4 of Definition 7.7) is quite different from that in the classical case: the former is defined as a primitive syntactic notion, whereas the latter is defined as a derived syntactic notion. A further discussion about the relationship between semantics of term-adjoint formulas and substitutions is given in Appendix A.3.3.

To illustrate the above definition, let us see two examples. The first one is a continuation of Example 7.3:

Example 7.6. Let $\mathbb{I}$ be the usual interpretation where H, X, Y, Z, C denotes the Hadamard gate, Pauli gates, and CNOT, respectively. We consider the logical formula in Example 7.3:

$$\beta = (\forall q_1)(\forall q_2)\beta', \text{ where } \beta' = P_0(q_1) \wedge P(q_1, q_2) \rightarrow P(\tau).$$

It is easy to show that $(\mathbb{I}, |0\rangle|0\rangle) \models \beta$. Intuitively, the two-qubit system $q_1 q_2$ is initialised in basis state $|0\rangle|0\rangle$. For $i = 1, 2$, each allowed operation on q_i can be syntactically expressed by a quantum term τ_i. After τ_i, the subsystem q_i is prepared in state $\rho_i = [\![\tau_i]\!]_{\mathbb{I}}(|0\rangle)$. Then the universal quantifications $(\forall q_1), (\forall q_2)$ mean that for any preparation operations τ_1, τ_2, the product state $\rho_1 \otimes \rho_2$ satisfies β'. Indeed, we have a stronger conclusion: $(\mathbb{I}, |0\rangle|0\rangle) \models (\forall q_1 q_2)\beta'$, which means that after any joint preparation operation on q_1 and q_2 together, denoted by a quantum term τ, the state $\rho = [\![\tau]\!]_{\mathbb{I}}(|0\rangle|0\rangle)$ satisfies β'. It should be noted that state ρ prepared by the joint operation τ can be an entanglement between q_1 and q_2.

The second example shows how some important notions in fault-tolerant quantum computation [183] can be conveniently described in our logic $\mathcal{QL}$:

Example 7.7. Let q_1, q_2 be two quantum variables. Two states $|\Phi\rangle, |\Psi\rangle \in \mathcal{H}_{q_1} \otimes \mathcal{H}_{q_2}$ are global unitary equivalent if there exists a unitary U on $\mathcal{H}_{q_1} \otimes \mathcal{H}_{q_2}$ such that $|\Psi\rangle = U|\Phi\rangle$. They are local unitary equivalent (respectively, local Clifford equivalent), if there exist unitaries (respectively, Clifford operators; i.e. those operators generated by Hadamard gate H, phase gate S, and CNOT) U_1 on $\mathcal{H}_{q_1}$ and U_2 on $\mathcal{H}_{q_2}$ such that $|\Psi\rangle = (U_1 \otimes U_2)|\Phi\rangle$. Consider an interpretation $\mathbb{I}$ where quantum predicate symbol P is interpreted as the 1-dimensional subspace of $\mathcal{H}_{q_1} \otimes \mathcal{H}_{q_2}$ spanned by state $|\Psi\rangle$, and all quantum operation symbols are interpreted as unitary operators. Then global and local unitary equivalences of $|\Phi\rangle$ and $|\Psi\rangle$ can be expressed as

$$(\mathbb{I}, |\Phi\rangle) \models (\exists q_1 q_2) P(q_1, q_2), \tag{7.13}$$

$$(\mathbb{I}, |\Phi\rangle) \models (\exists q_1)(\exists q_2) P(q_1, q_2), \tag{7.14}$$

respectively. If all quantum operation symbols are interpreted as Clifford operators, then Eq. (7.14) expresses local Clifford equivalence of $|\Phi\rangle$ and $|\Psi\rangle$. It was conjectured in [364] but disproved in [231] that local unitary equivalence and local Clifford equivalence are equivalent

The notions of logical validity and consequence in classical first-order logic can be straightforwardly generalised into $\mathcal{QL}$:

- A formula β is called valid in an interpretation $\mathbb{I}$, written $\mathbb{I} \models \beta$, if $(\mathbb{I}, \rho) \models \beta$ for all ρ.
- The set of formulas valid in $\mathbb{I}$ is denoted $Th(\mathbb{I}) = \{\beta | \mathbb{I} \models \beta\}$ (called the *theory* of $\mathbb{I}$).
- A formula β is called logical valid if it is valid in any interpretation $\mathbb{I}$.
- Let Σ be a set of formulas. A formula β is called a logical consequence of Σ, written $\Sigma \models \beta$, if for any interpretation $\mathbb{I}$ and for any state ρ, whenever $(\mathbb{I}, \rho) \models \gamma$ for all $\gamma \in \Sigma$, then $(\mathbb{I}, \rho) \models \beta$.
- Two formulas β and β' are called logically equivalent, written $\beta \equiv \beta'$, if $\beta \models \beta'$ and $\beta' \models \beta$.

To conclude this subsection, we present some useful semantic properties of logical formulas in $\mathcal{QL}$. As in classical first-order logic, we can show that the semantics of a logical formula in $\mathcal{QL}$ depends only on its free variables $free(\beta)$.

Definition 7.12. An interpretation $\mathbb{I}$ is called term-expressive if for any quantum variables $\overline{q}$ and for any $\rho, \rho' \in \mathcal{D}(\mathcal{H}_{\overline{q}})$ and for any $\epsilon > 0$, there exists a quantum term τ such that $var(\tau) \subseteq \overline{q}$ and

$$D\left([\![\tau]\!]_{\mathbb{I}}(\rho), \rho'\right) \leq \epsilon,$$

where D stands for the trace distance; that is, $D(\sigma, \sigma') = \frac{1}{2}\mathrm{tr}|\sigma - \sigma'|$ for any density operators σ, σ' (see Section 2.5).

For example, the usual interpretation $\mathbb{I}$ of $H, S, T, CNOT$ as the Hadamard, phase, $\pi/8$ and controlled-NOT gates is term-expressive.

Lemma 7.5 (Coincidence and renaming). **1.** *For any term-expressive interpretation $\mathbb{I}$, if $\rho \downarrow free(\beta) = \rho' \downarrow free(\beta)$, then:*

$$(\mathbb{I}, \rho) \models \beta \text{ iff } (\mathbb{I}, \rho') \models \beta.$$

If β is quantifier-free, then the requirement of term-expressivity is unnecessary.
2. *For any formula β, assume that $q \notin free(\beta)$, q' does not occur in β, and their dimensions are the same. If β' is obtained by replacing all bound occurrences of q in β with q', then $\beta \equiv \beta'$.*

The next lemma indicates that satisfaction relation is preserved by inclusion relation, convex combination, and limit of quantum states. Essentially, this property comes from the linearity of quantum mechanics and quantum predicates as close subspaces.

Lemma 7.6 (Monotonicity, convex combination, and limit). **1.** *If $\mathrm{supp}(\rho) \subseteq \mathrm{supp}(\sigma)$ and $(\mathbb{I}, \sigma) \models \beta$, then $(\mathbb{I}, \rho) \models \beta$.*
2. *If for each i, $(\mathbb{I}, \rho_i) \models \beta$, then for any probability distribution $\{p_i\}$, we have $\left(\mathbb{I}, \sum_i p_i \rho_i\right) \models \beta$.*
3. *If $(\mathbb{I}, \rho_n) \models \beta$ for all n, and $\lim_{n \to} \rho_n = \rho$ with the trace distance, then $(\mathbb{I}, \rho) \models \beta$.*

The proofs of Lemmas 7.5 and 7.6 are deferred to Appendix A.3.2.

Logical semantics as subspaces: As we saw in Sections 7.3.2 and 7.3.3, in the propositional quantum logic and first-order quantum logic with classical variables, the semantics of a logical formula is defined as a closed subspace of a Hilbert space (or more generally, an element of an orthomodular lattice). However, the semantics of logical formulas in logic $\mathcal{QL}$ is given in terms of satisfaction relation (see Definition 7.11). On the other hand, for a classical first-order logical formula β and an interpretation $\mathbb{I}$ with domain D, we have:

$$[\![\beta]\!]_{\mathbb{I}} = \{d \in D : (\mathbb{I}, d) \models \beta\}. \tag{7.15}$$

It is similar to the case of classical logic that we can establish a close connection between the subspace semantics and the satisfaction relation. To do so, let us first introduce the following definition as a quantum generalisation of Eq. (7.15):

Definition 7.13. Given an interpretation $\mathbb{I}$. The semantics of a formula β is defined as the closed subspace $[\![\beta]\!]_{\mathbb{I}}$ of $\mathcal{H}_{all}$:

$$[\![\beta]\!]_{\mathbb{I}} = \bigvee_{(\mathbb{I},\rho)\models\beta} \text{supp}(\rho) \in S(\mathcal{H}_{all})$$

where $\text{supp}(\rho)$ denotes the support of density operator ρ, i.e. the subspace spanned by the eigenvectors of ρ corresponding to its nonzero eigenvalues, and $\bigvee$ is defined by Eq. (7.12).

A close connection between the satisfaction in Definition 7.11 and the subspace semantics in Definition 7.13 is presented in the following:

Lemma 7.7. *For any formula β, interpretation $\mathbb{I}$ and quantum state ρ,*

$$(\mathbb{I}, \rho) \models \beta \text{ iff } \rho \in [\![\beta]\!]_{\mathbb{I}}.$$

Furthermore, the subspace semantics of $\mathcal{QL}$ formulas enjoys a structural representation:

Theorem 7.4. 1. *If $\beta = P(\tau)$, then $[\![\beta]\!]_{\mathbb{I}} = [\![\tau]\!]_{\mathbb{I}}^*(P^{\mathbb{I}}) \otimes \mathcal{H}_{qVar\setminus var(\tau)}$;*
2. *If $\beta = \neg\beta'$, then $[\![\beta]\!]_{\mathbb{I}} = ([\![\beta']\!]_{\mathbb{I}})^\perp$;*
3. *If $\beta = \beta_1 \wedge \beta_2$, then $[\![\beta]\!]_{\mathbb{I}} = [\![\beta_1]\!]_{\mathbb{I}} \cap [\![\beta_2]\!]_{\mathbb{I}}$;*
4. *If $\beta = \tau^*(\beta')$, then $[\![\beta]\!]_{\mathbb{I}} = [\![\tau]\!]_{\mathbb{I}}^*([\![\beta']\!]_{\mathbb{I}})$;*
5. *If $\beta = (\forall\overline{q})\beta'$, then $[\![\beta]\!]_{\mathbb{I}} = \bigcap_{var(\tau)\subseteq\overline{q}} ([\![\tau]\!]_{\mathbb{I}}^*([\![\beta']\!]))$.*

The proof of the above theorem can be found in Appendix A.3.2. The clauses 2 and 3 in this theorem indicate that the interpretation of propositional connectives $\neg$ and $\wedge$ in $\mathcal{QL}$ coincides with that in the original Birkhoff–von Neumann quantum logic. As a corollary of clauses 2 and 5 in the above theorem, if $\beta = (\exists\overline{q})\beta'$, then

$$[\![\beta]\!]_{\mathbb{I}} = \bigvee_{var(\tau)\subseteq\overline{q}} \left([\![\tau]\!]_{\mathbb{I}}^*([\![\beta']\!]^\perp)\right)^\perp. \tag{7.16}$$

7.4.3 Proof system

In this subsection, we present a proof system of logic $\mathcal{QL}$ with quantum variables. We promised at the beginning of this section that $\mathcal{QL}$ is a logic with equality $=$ for specifying and reasoning about equality of quantum states and equivalence of quantum circuits. But equality $=$ has not been introduced into $\mathcal{QL}$ so far. Now we introduce $=$ in the following way: the proof system of $\mathcal{QL}$ is designed as a two-layer system: the first layer is a first-order equational logic $\mathcal{QT}_=$ for quantum terms, and the second layer is built upon $\mathcal{QT}_=$ and consists of a set of inference rules for reasoning about first-order logical formulas with quantum variables.

Equational logic for quantum terms: Let us first describe logic $\mathcal{QT}_=$. The formulas in $\mathcal{QT}_=$ and their free variables are defined as follows:

1. If τ_1 and τ_2 are quantum terms, then $\tau_1 = \tau_2$ is a formula in $\mathcal{QT}_=$ and $free(\tau_1 = \tau_2) = var(\tau_1) \cup var(\tau_2)$;
2. If γ' are formulas in $\mathcal{QT}_=$, so is $\gamma = \neg\gamma'$, and $free(\gamma) = free(\gamma')$;
3. If γ_1, γ_2 are formulas in $\mathcal{QT}_=$, so is $\gamma = \gamma_1 \wedge \gamma_2$, and $free(\gamma) = free(\gamma_1) \cup free(\gamma_2)$;
4. If γ' is a formula in $\mathcal{QT}_=$, and $\overline{q}$ is a sequence of quantum variables, then $\gamma = (\forall\overline{q})\gamma'$ is a formula in $\mathcal{QT}_=$, and $free(\gamma) = free(\gamma') \setminus \overline{q}$.

For any interpretation $\mathbb{I}$, quantum state ρ, and logical formula γ in $\mathcal{QT}_=$, satisfaction relation $(\mathbb{I}, \rho) \models \gamma$ is defined as follows:

1. If $\gamma = \tau_1 = \tau_2$, then $(\mathbb{I}, \rho) \models \gamma$ iff $[\![\tau_1]\!]_{\mathbb{I}}(\rho) = [\![\tau_2]\!]_{\mathbb{I}}(\rho)$;
2. If $\gamma = \neg\gamma'$, then $(\mathbb{I}, \rho) \models \gamma$ iff it does not hold that $(\mathbb{I}, \rho) \models \gamma'$;
3. If $\gamma = \gamma_1 \wedge \gamma_2$, then $(\mathbb{I}, \rho) \models \gamma$ iff $(\mathbb{I}, \rho) \models \gamma_1$ and $(\mathbb{I}, \rho) \models \gamma_2$;
4. If $\gamma = (\forall\overline{q})\gamma'$, then $(\mathbb{I}, \rho) \models \gamma$ iff for any quantum term τ with $var(\tau) \subseteq \overline{q}$, it holds that $(\mathbb{I}, [\![\tau]\!]_{\mathbb{I}}(\rho)) \models \gamma'$.

Similar to clause 5 in Definition 7.11, the semantics of universal quantification in $\mathcal{QT}_=$ defined in clause 4 in the above definition follows the idea of Eq. (7.8).

The proof system of $\mathcal{QT}_=$ consists of the standard inference rules of the classical first-order equational logic (with quantum terms being treated in the same way as classical terms) together with the rules given in Fig. 7.5. It is easy to prove the following:

$$(\mathcal{QT}1) \quad \frac{\tau_1 = \tau_2}{\tau\tau_1 = \tau\tau_2} \qquad \frac{\tau_1 = \tau_2}{\tau_1\tau = \tau_2\tau} \qquad\qquad (\mathcal{QT}2) \quad \frac{\tau_{1i} = \tau_{i2}}{\sum_i p_i \tau_{1i} = \sum_i p_i \tau_{2i}}$$

$$(\mathcal{QT}3) \quad \frac{var(\tau_1) \cap var(\tau_2) = \emptyset}{\tau_1 \otimes \tau_2 = \tau_1\tau_2 = \tau_2\tau_1} \qquad\qquad (\mathcal{QT}4) \quad I\tau = \tau I = \tau$$

$$(\mathcal{QT}5) \quad \tau_1(\tau_2\tau_3) = (\tau_1\tau_2)\tau_3 \qquad\qquad (\mathcal{QT}6) \quad \frac{\tau \text{ is unitary}}{\tau\tau^{-1} = \tau^{-1}\tau = I}$$

FIGURE 7.5 Equational logic $\mathcal{QT}_=$ for quantum terms. Here, we assume a special quantum operation symbol I for the identity operator. In $(\mathcal{QT}4)$, $I = I(q_1, ..., q_n)$ is an identity term, with I being a quantum operation symbol denoting the identity operation acting on appropriate $q_1, ..., q_n$.

$(\mathcal{QL}1)$ Any $\Sigma \vdash \beta$ provable in propositional QL given in Fig. 7.2

$$(\mathcal{QL}2) \quad \frac{\mathcal{QT}_= \vdash \tau_1 = \tau_2}{P(\tau_1) \vdash P(\tau_2)} \qquad\qquad (\mathcal{QL}3) \quad \frac{\mathcal{QT}_= \vdash \tau_1 = \tau_2}{\tau_1^*(\beta) \vdash \tau_2^*(\beta)}$$

$$(\mathcal{QL}4) \quad \frac{P(\tau_i) \text{ for all } i}{P\left(\sum_i p_i \tau_i\right)} \qquad\qquad (\mathcal{QL}5) \quad \tau_1^*(\tau_2^*(\beta)) \equiv (\tau_2\tau_1)^*(\beta)$$

$$(\mathcal{QL}6) \quad \frac{\beta \vdash \beta'}{\tau^*(\beta) \vdash \tau^*(\beta')} \qquad\qquad (\mathcal{QL}7) \quad \tau_1^*(P(\tau_2)) \equiv P(\tau_1\tau_2)$$

$$(\mathcal{QL}8) \quad \frac{\tau \text{ is unitary}}{\tau^*(\neg\beta) \equiv \neg\tau^*(\beta)} \qquad\qquad (\mathcal{QL}9) \quad \tau^*(\beta_1 \wedge \beta_2) \equiv \tau^*(\beta_1) \wedge \tau^*(\beta_2)$$

$$(\mathcal{QL}10) \quad \frac{free(\beta_i) \subseteq var(\tau_i) \text{ for } i = 1, 2 \quad var(\tau_1) \cap var(\tau_2) = \emptyset}{(\tau_1 \otimes \tau_2)^*(\beta_1 \wedge \beta_2) \equiv \tau_1^*(\beta_1) \wedge \tau_2^*(\beta_2)}$$

$$(\mathcal{QL}11) \quad \frac{\tau^*(\beta) \vdash \gamma \quad \tau \text{ is unitary}}{\beta \vdash (\tau^{-1})^*\gamma} \qquad\qquad (\mathcal{QL}12) \quad \frac{\beta \vdash \tau^*(\gamma) \quad \tau \text{ is unitary}}{(\tau^{-1})^*(\beta) \vdash \gamma}$$

$$(\mathcal{QL}13) \quad \frac{\tau \text{ is unitary} \quad var(\tau) \subseteq free(\beta) \setminus \overline{q}}{\tau^*((\forall\overline{q})\beta) \equiv (\forall\overline{q})\tau^*(\beta)} \qquad\qquad (\mathcal{QL}14) \quad \frac{var(\tau) \subseteq \overline{q}}{\Sigma \cup \{(\forall\overline{q})\beta\} \vdash \tau^*(\beta)}$$

$$(\mathcal{QL}15) \quad \frac{\Sigma \vdash \beta \quad \overline{q} \cap free(\beta) = \emptyset \text{ or } free(\Sigma) \subseteq free(\beta) \setminus \overline{q}}{\Sigma \vdash (\forall\overline{q})\beta}$$

FIGURE 7.6 Proof system of $\mathcal{QL}$.

Lemma 7.8 (Soundness). *If $\Gamma \vdash \tau_1 = \tau_2$ is provable in the equational logic $\mathcal{QT}_=$, then $\Gamma \models \tau_1 = \tau_2$.*

Quantum predicate calculus: The second layer of the proof system of $\mathcal{QL}$ builds upon propositional quantum logic described in Section 7.3.2 and the equational logic $\mathcal{QT}_=$ for quantum terms. It consists of propositional axiom $(\mathcal{QL}1)$, equality axioms, convex combination axiom, term-adjoint axioms, and quantifier axioms presented in Fig. 7.6.

The soundness of the axiomatic system is presented as the following:

Theorem 7.5 (Soundness). *If $\Sigma \vdash \beta$ is provable in the proof system of $\mathcal{QL}$ given in Fig. 7.6, then $\Sigma \models \beta$.*

The proof of this theorem can be found in Appendix A.3.4. However, it is still an open problem to find an axiomatisation (i.e. a complete proof system) of $\mathcal{QL}$.

7.5 Quantum logic as an assertion logic

Program logics and assertion logics: Quantum Hoare logic (QHL for short) as other program logics is designed for specifying dynamic properties of programs. Usually, a classical program logic is built upon an assertion logic that is employed to describe static properties of program variables [29]. Certainly, the effectiveness of verification techniques comes from a combined power of program logics and assertion logics rather than the sole role of the former. However, this point has often not been seriously noticed. The reason is possibly that first-order logic is commonly adopted in classical program verification as an assertion logic, it is ubiquitous in mathematics, computer science, and many other fields, and thus its role is considered for granted and frequently overlooked. The important role of assertion logics in program verification became particularly clear through the great success of separation logic [321,352], which enables local reasoning by expanding assertion logic with new connectives (namely separation conjunction and the associated implication) that are not definable in first-order logic [224], especially by adopting the logic BI of bunched implications [323] as its assertion language.

Assertion languages for classical versus quantum programs: As pointed out at the beginning of this chapter, first-order logic used as an assertion language for classical programs enables that every assertion is represented by a logical formula constructed from atomic formulas using propositional connectives and universal and existential quantifications. It enhances the applicability of Hoare logic in at least two ways:

1. a logical representation of an assertion is often much more economic than as a Boolean-valued function over the entire state space;
2. first-order logic can be used to infer entailment between assertions, which can help us to apply the rules of Hoare logic more efficiently.

In contrast, a quantum predicate in QHL as presented in the last chapter is described as a Hermitian operator on the Hilbert space of quantum variables, which is, for example, a $2^n \times 2^n$ matrix for the case of n qubits. In a sense, this can be seen as a quantum counterpart of Boolean-valued function representation of a classical predicate. Then as we saw in Section 7.1, a verification condition for a quantum program with n qubits is derived as an inequality between two $2^n \times 2^n$ matrices or equivalently the semidefinite positivity of their difference, which is hard to check when dealing with large quantum algorithms because the size of the involved matrices grows up exponentially as the number of program variables.

A first-order quantum logic $\mathcal{QL}$ with quantum variables was introduced in the last section. In this section, we show how it can be incorporated into QHL for symbolic verification of quantum programs. It is expected that $\mathcal{QL}$ can play a role in scalable applications of QHL similar to that of first-order logic for classical Hoare logic.

We note that $\mathcal{QL}$ is a sharp quantum logic where propositions and predicates are modelled by projections on (or closed subspaces of) a Hilbert space. It is not strong enough for combined with QHL with general pre/postconditions. Instead, it is suitable to work together with the restricted QHL with projective quantum predicates. An assertion language for QHL with general pre/postconditions will be introduced in next section.

7.5.1 Reformulating syntax and semantics of quantum programs

Let us first recast the syntax and semantics of a quantum programming language in the context of $\mathcal{QL}$.

Syntax: A classical **while**-language usually builds upon a first order logical language, which is used to define, e.g. the term t in an assignment $x := t$ and the logical formula b in a conditional statement **if** b **then** S_1 **else** S_2 or a **while**-statement **while** b **do** S **od**. In the definition of quantum **while**-language given in Chapter 5, however, the corresponding parts were left undefined formally due to the lack of an appropriate first-order logic. Now we are able to fill in this gap by incorporating logic $\mathcal{QL}$ introduced in the previous section into the syntax of quantum **while**-language. In this vein, the alphabet of quantum **while**-language consists of:

(i) a set *Var* of quantum variables $q, q_1, q_2...$;
(ii) a set of unitary symbols $U, U_1, U_2, ...$ (for example, an approximately universal set of basic gates: Hadamard gate H, phase gate S, $\pi/8$ gate T and CNOT – controlled NOT);
(iii) a set of measurement symbols $M, M_1, M_2, ...$; and
(vi) program constructors := (for initialisation and unitary transformations), ; (sequential composition), **if...fi** (case statement), and **while...do...od** (loop).

As in the alphabet of logic $\mathcal{QL}$, each variable $q \in$ *Var* is associated with a nonnegative integer d or $d = \infty$ as its dimension, and each unitary symbol U is associated with an n-tuple $(d_1, ..., d_n)$ as its signature, where $d_1, ..., d_n$ are nonnegative integers or ∞, and n is a nonnegative integer, called the arity of U. An arity n and a signature $(d_1, ..., d_n)$ are also assigned to each measurement symbol M. In addition, a set $out(M)$ is assigned to measurement symbol M and stands for the set of all possible outcomes of the measurement denoted by M.

We now can define quantum terms over the above alphabet. To this end, let us introduce some additional quantum operation symbols:

- For any nonnegative integer d or $d = \infty$, we use $\mathbf{0}_d$ to denote the initialisation of a d-dimensional quantum variable in the basis state $|0\rangle$;
- For each measurement symbol M and for each $m \in out(M)$, we use M_m to stand for the operation that the measurement denoted by M is performed, the outcome m is observed and the state of the measured system is changed accordingly.

Then basic terms includes:

- $\mathbf{0}_d(q)$ for each d-dimensional quantum variable $q \in qVar$, meaning that q is initialised in state $|0\rangle$. It is often simply written as $\mathbf{0}(q)$;
- $U(\overline{q})$, where variables $\overline{q} = q_1...q_n$ match the signature of unitary symbol U; that is, if U has signature $(d_1, ..., d_n)$, then q_i is d_i-dimensional for each i;
- $M_m(\overline{q})$, where variables $\overline{q} = q_1, ..., q_n$ match the signature of measurement symbol M.

(Sk) $\langle \textbf{skip}, \rho \rangle \to \langle \downarrow, \rho \rangle$ (In) $\langle q := \mathbf{0}(q), \rho \rangle \to \langle \downarrow, [\![\mathbf{0}(q)]\!]_\mathbb{I}(\rho) \rangle$

(UT) $\langle \overline{q} := \tau, \rho \rangle \to \langle \downarrow, [\![\tau]\!]_\mathbb{I}(\rho) \rangle$ (SC) $\dfrac{\langle S_1, \rho \rangle \to \langle S_1', \rho' \rangle}{\langle S_1; S_2, \rho \rangle \to \langle S_1'; S_2, \rho' \rangle}$

(IF) $\langle \textbf{if } (\square m \cdot M[\overline{q}] = m \to S_m) \textbf{ fi}, \rho \rangle \to \langle S_{m'}, [\![M_{m'}(\overline{q})]\!]_\mathbb{I}(\rho) \rangle$ for every $m' \in out(M)$

(L0) $\langle \textbf{while } M[\overline{q}] = 1 \textbf{ do } S \textbf{ od}, \rho \rangle \to \langle \downarrow, [\![M_0(\overline{q})]\!]_\mathbb{I}(\rho) \rangle$

(L1) $\langle \textbf{while } M[\overline{q}] = 1 \textbf{ do } S \textbf{ od}, \rho \rangle \to \langle S; \textbf{while } M[\overline{q}] = 1 \textbf{ do } S \textbf{ od}, [\![M_1(\overline{q})]\!]_\mathbb{I}(\rho) \rangle$

FIGURE 7.7 Operational semantics of quantum programs.

Upon them, all quantum terms can be constructed by applying the formation rules 2–4 in Definition 7.6. Furthermore, using the notion of quantum term, the syntax of quantum **while**-language (i.e. Definition 5.1) can be restated in the following:

Definition 7.14. Quantum programs are defined by the syntax:

$$S ::= \textbf{skip} \mid q := \mathbf{0}(q) \mid \overline{q} := \tau \mid S_1; S_2$$
$$\mid \textbf{if } (\square m \cdot M[\overline{q}] = m \to S_m) \textbf{ fi}$$
$$\mid \textbf{while } M[\overline{q}] = 1 \textbf{ do } S \textbf{ od}$$

where τ is a unitary term with $var(\tau) \subseteq \overline{q}$, and M in the case statement (respectively, the loop) is a measurement symbol with $out(M) = \{m\}$ (respectively, $out(M) = \{0, 1\}$).

For each program S, we write $var(S)$ for the set of quantum variables in S.

Semantics: Based on the semantics of first order quantum logic $\mathcal{QL}$ defined in the last section, the semantics of quantum **while**-programs can also be formulated in a more precise way than that given in Chapter 5. An interpretation $\mathbb{I}$ of quantum **while**-language is given as follows:

- To each d-dimensional quantum variable q, a d-dimensional Hilbert space $\mathcal{H}_q$ is assigned, called the state space of q;
- Each unitary symbol U with signature $(d_1, ..., d_n)$ is interpreted as a $\prod_{i=1}^{n} d_i$-dimensional unitary operator $U^\mathbb{I}$; and
- Each measurement symbol M with signature $(d_1, ..., d_n)$ and outcomes $out(M)$ is interpreted as a *projective* measurement $M^\mathbb{I} = \{M_m^\mathbb{I} : m \in out(M)\}$ on the $\prod_{i=1}^{n} d_i$-dimensional Hilbert space, where each $M_m^\mathbb{I}$ is a projection operator.

The semantics of quantum terms in logic $\mathcal{QL}$ can be directly applied here. Given an interpretation $\mathbb{I}$, we write $\mathcal{H}_V = \bigotimes_{q \in V} \mathcal{H}_q$ for the state space of the composed system of quantum variables in V. Then each term τ is interpreted as a mapping $[\![\tau]\!]_\mathbb{I} : \mathcal{D}(\mathcal{H}_{qVar}) \to \mathcal{D}(\mathcal{H}_{qVar})$. In particular, the basic terms are interpreted as follows: for any $\rho \in \mathcal{D}(\mathcal{H}_{qVar})$,

- $[\![\mathbf{0}(q)]\!]_\mathbb{I}(\rho) = \sum_i |0\rangle_q \langle i|\rho|i\rangle_q \langle 0|$, where $\{|i\rangle\}$ is an orthonormal basis of $\mathcal{H}_q$;
- $[\![U(\overline{q})]\!]_\mathbb{I}(\rho) = (U^\mathbb{I} \otimes I)\rho((U^\mathbb{I})^\dagger \otimes I)$, where I is the identity operator on $\mathcal{H}_{qVar \setminus \overline{q}}$;
- $[\![M_m(\overline{q})]\!]_\mathbb{I}(\rho) = (M_m^\mathbb{I} \otimes I)\rho((M_m^\mathbb{I})^\dagger \otimes I)$, where I is the same as above.

For other terms τ, its semantics $[\![\tau]\!]_\mathbb{I}$ is defined using valuation rules 2–4 in Definition 7.9.

Now we can define the semantics of quantum programs based on the semantics of quantum terms. A configuration is defined as a pair $C = \langle S, \rho \rangle$, where S is a program or the termination symbol $\downarrow$, and $\rho \in \mathcal{D}(\mathcal{H}_{qVar})$ denotes a state of quantum variables. In the context of $\mathcal{QL}$, Definitions 5.4 and 5.6 can be restated as follows.

Definition 7.15. The operational semantics of quantum programs is a transition relation between configurations defined by the transition rules in Fig. 7.7.

Definition 7.16. The denotational semantics of a quantum S in interpretation $\mathbb{I}$ is a mapping $[\![S]\!]_\mathbb{I} : \mathcal{D}(\mathcal{H}_{qVar}) \to \mathcal{D}(\mathcal{H}_{qVar})$ from density operators to (partial) density operators. It is defined by

$$[\![S]\!]_\mathbb{I}(\rho) = \sum \left\{ | \rho' : \langle S, \rho \rangle \to^* \langle \downarrow, \rho' \rangle | \right\}$$

for every $\rho \in \mathcal{D}(\mathcal{H}_{Var})$, where $\to^*$ is the reflexive and transitive closure of transition relation $\to$ (operational semantics), and $\{| \cdot |\}$ denotes a multiset.

$$(\text{Ax.Sk}) \quad \{\beta\}\textbf{Skip}\{\beta\} \qquad\qquad (\text{Ax.In}) \quad \left\{\mathbf{0}(q)^*\beta\right\} q := |0\rangle\{\beta\}$$

$$(\text{Ax.UT}) \quad \left\{\tau^*(\beta)\right\}\overline{q} := \tau\{\beta\} \qquad (\text{R.SC}) \quad \frac{\{\beta\}S_1\{\gamma\} \quad \{\gamma\}S_2\{\delta\}}{\{\gamma\}S_1; S_2\{\delta\}}$$

$$(\text{R.IF}) \quad \frac{\{\beta_m\} S_m\{\gamma\} \text{ for all } m}{\left\{\bigvee_m (M_m(\overline{q}) \wedge \beta_m)\right\}\textbf{if } (\square m \cdot M[\overline{q}] = m \rightarrow S_m)\textbf{ fi}\{\gamma\}}$$

$$(\text{R.LP}) \quad \frac{\{\beta\}S\{(M_0(\overline{q}) \wedge \gamma) \vee (M_1(\overline{q}) \wedge \beta)\}}{\{(M_0(\overline{q}) \wedge \gamma) \vee (M_1(\overline{q}) \wedge \beta)\}\textbf{while } M[\overline{q}] = 1 \textbf{ do } S \textbf{ od}\{\gamma\}}$$

$$(\text{R.Con}) \quad \frac{\beta \vdash \beta' \text{ in } \mathcal{QL} \quad \{\beta'\}S\{\gamma'\} \quad \gamma' \vdash \gamma \text{ in } \mathcal{QL}}{\{\beta\}S\{\gamma\}}$$

FIGURE 7.8 Axiomatic system of quantum Hoare logic (for partial correctness).

7.5.2 Quantum Hoare logic combined with quantum logic

After redefining the syntax and semantics of quantum program upon first order logic $\mathcal{QL}$ with quantum variables, we are able to further incorporate $\mathcal{QL}$ into quantum Hoare logic (QHL) (with projective quantum predicates) so that $\mathcal{QL}$ can serve as an assertion logic of QHL. Indeed, with the help of $\mathcal{QL}$, QHL can be described in a more elegant way; in particular, its relative completeness of QHL can be precisely formulated.

Correctness formulas: Since we only consider preconditions and postconditions that are modelled as projection operators (equivalently, closed subspaces), they can be expressed by logical formulas in $\mathcal{QL}$, and thus the notion of quantum Hoare triple and the correctness of quantum programs can be precisely defined as follows.

Definition 7.17 (Quantum Hoare triple). A quantum Hoare triple (or correctness formula) is a Hoare triple, i.e. a statement of the form: $\{\beta\}S\{\gamma\}$, where S is a quantum **while**-program over the alphabet given in the previous subsection, and both β, γ are logical formulas in $\mathcal{QL}$ over the same alphabet, called the precondition and postcondition, respectively.

Let us now define the semantics of quantum Hoare triples. For simplicity, we only consider partial correctness. Total correctness can be treated by adding certain termination condition as in classical programming.

Definition 7.18. Given an interpretation $\mathbb{I}$ of the language defined in the previous subsection. A quantum Hoare triple $\{\beta\}S\{\gamma\}$ is true in the sense of partial correctness in $\mathbb{I}$, written $\models^{\mathbb{I}}_{par} \{\beta\}S\{\gamma\}$, if we have:

$$\llbracket S \rrbracket_{\mathbb{I}} (\llbracket \beta \rrbracket_{\mathbb{I}}) \subseteq \llbracket \gamma \rrbracket_{\mathbb{I}} \tag{7.17}$$

where $\llbracket S \rrbracket_{\mathbb{I}}$, $\llbracket \beta \rrbracket_{\mathbb{I}}$, and $\llbracket \gamma \rrbracket_{\mathbb{I}}$ are defined as in the previous subsection, and $\llbracket S \rrbracket_{\mathbb{I}} (\llbracket \beta \rrbracket_{\mathbb{I}})$ is the image of subspace $\llbracket \beta \rrbracket_{\mathbb{I}}$ under superoperator $\llbracket S \rrbracket_{\mathbb{I}}$ as defined by Eq. (7.11).

For any closed subspace X of $\mathcal{H}_{all}$ and $\rho \in \mathcal{D}(\mathcal{H}_{all})$, we say that ρ belongs to P, written $\rho \in P$, if $\text{supp}(\rho) \subseteq X$. Then condition (7.17) can be restated in a more intuitive way: for all ρ,

$$\rho \in \llbracket \beta \rrbracket \text{ implies } \llbracket S \rrbracket_{\mathbb{I}}(\rho) \in \llbracket \gamma \rrbracket.$$

Definition 7.19. Let Σ be a set of logical formulas in the assertion language. Then a quantum Hoare triple $\{\beta\}S\{\gamma\}$ is called a logical consequence of Σ in the sense of partial correctness, written $\Sigma \models_{par} \{\beta\}S\{\gamma\}$, if for any interpretation $\mathbb{I}$, we have:

$$\text{whenever all formulas in } \Sigma \text{ are true in } \mathbb{I}, \text{ then } \models^{\mathbb{I}}_{par} \{\beta\}S\{\gamma\}.$$

Axiomatic system: The axiomatic system of quantum Hoare logic in Chapter 6 was given for the general case where preconditions and postconditions can be any quantum predicates, i.e. Hermitian operators between the zero and identity operators. It was slightly simplified in [452] for the special case where preconditions and postconditions are restricted to projection operators. Using $\mathcal{QL}$ as the assertion language, the axiomatic system of [452] can be recast in Fig. 7.8 in a more elegant way. Note that quantum logical connectives $\wedge, \vee$ are used in the rules (R.IF) and (R.LP), and term-adjoint formulas are used in the axioms (Ax.In) and (Ax.UT). Moreover, entailment in $\mathcal{QL}$ is employed in the rule (R.Con). To do the same for general quantum Hoare logic, however, it requires a more general logical system than $\mathcal{QL}$, which will be introduced in the next section.

It should be particularly pointed out that the axioms and inference rules of quantum Hoare logic are valid in all interpretations and not designed for any specific interpretation. Therefore, to prove the correctness of a quantum program in a specific interpretation $\mathbb{I}$ using quantum Hoare logic, one may need to call upon some logical formulas from the theory $Th(\mathbb{I})$ of $\mathbb{I}$, i.e. the set of all logical formulas β in $\mathcal{QL}$ that are true in $\mathbb{I}$. For example, let q be a qubit variable, H the Hadamard gate, and X an arbitrary subspace of the 2-dimensional Hilbert space. Then the correctness

$$\models_{par} \{X\}q := H[q]; q := H[q]\{X\}$$

can be verified using the axiom (Ax.UT) together with the specific property $HH = I$ of the Hadamard gate, but not by quantum Hoare logic solely.

Soundness and relative completeness: The soundness and relative completeness of quantum Hoare logic (QHL) with general quantum predicates was established in Chapter 6. As shown in [452], the soundness and relative completeness of QHL for the special quantum predicates of projection operators can be derived through a simple reduction from the general QHL. Due to the lacking of a precisely defined assertion language, however, the soundness and relative completeness in Chapter 6 was only described in an informal way. Now with the help of assertion logic $\mathcal{QL}$, we can present them for the restricted QHL with projective predicates in a formal way. As usual, the soundness is easy to prove.

Theorem 7.6 (Soundness of QHL). *For any set Σ of logical formulas in the assertion language $\mathcal{QL}$, and for any quantum Hoare triple $\{\beta\}S\{\gamma\}$:*

$$if\ \Sigma \vdash_{par} \{\beta\}S\{\gamma\}\ then\ \Sigma \models_{par} \{\beta\}S\{\gamma\}.$$

As in the case of classical programming, it is easy to see that the inverse of the above soundness theorem is not true. To give a formal presentation of the relative completeness, let us introduce the following:

Definition 7.20. An interpretation $\mathbb{I}$ is said to be expressive if for any quantum program S and for any logical formula γ in $\mathcal{QL}$, there exists a logical formula β in $\mathcal{QL}$ that can expresses the weakest liberal precondition with respect to S; formally,

$$[\![\beta]\!]_{\mathbb{I}} = \text{wlp}.[\![S]\!]_{\mathbb{I}}.[\![\gamma]\!]_{\mathbb{I}}\ (weakest\ liberal\ precondition)$$
$$= \overline{\text{span}\left\{|\psi\rangle \in \mathcal{H}_{all} : [\![S]\!]_{\mathbb{I}}(|\psi\rangle\langle\psi|) \in [\![\gamma]\!]_{\mathbb{I}}\right\}}$$

where $\overline{\text{span}\ X}$ stands for the closed subspace generated by a set X.

With the help of the above definition, the relative completeness can be stated as the following:

Theorem 7.7 (Relative completeness of QHL). *Let $\mathbb{I}$ be an expressive interpretation. Then for any quantum Hoare triple $\{\beta\}S\{\gamma\}$:*

$$if \models_{par}^{\mathbb{I}} \{\beta\}S\{\gamma\}\ then\ Th(\mathbb{I}) \vdash_{par} \{\beta\}S\{\gamma\} \tag{7.18}$$

where $Th(\mathbb{I})$ is the theory of $\mathbb{I}$, i.e. the set of all logical formulas β in $\mathcal{QL}$ that are true in $\mathbb{I}$.

Proof. (Outline) The conclusion (7.18) can be proved by induction on the structure of program S. It is essentially a refinement of the proof of relative completeness given in Chapter 6, with first-order quantum logic $\mathcal{QL}$ defined in the last section used for formalising the reasoning about assertions; for a simple example, inference rule ($\mathcal{QL}$11) is used in the proof for the case of basic statement $S \equiv q := \tau$. The expressivity of interpretation $\mathbb{I}$ is needed so that the weakest liberal preconditions employed in the proof can be expressed in the formal logical language $\mathcal{QL}$. $\square$

Problem 7.1. An interesting problem that remains open is to determine a set of quantum operations (including unitary operators and measurement) commonly used in quantum computing (e.g. Hadamard gate, phase gate, CNOT, measurement in the computational basis) that is expressible. This problem seems not easy if we consider not only finite-dimensional quantum variables but also infinite-dimensional ones with the Hilbert space defined in (7.10).

7.5.3 Adaptation rules for quantum programs

As an application of the combination of QHL and $\mathcal{QL}$, in this subsection, we show how a series of adaptation rules can be defined and derived for more convenient applications of QHL in verification of quantum programs.

$$
\text{(Invariance)} \quad \frac{\{\beta\}S\{\gamma\} \quad free(\delta)\cap var(S)=\emptyset}{\{\beta\wedge\delta\}S\{\gamma\wedge\delta\}}
$$

$$
\text{(Substitution)} \quad \frac{\{\beta\}S\{\gamma\} \quad var(\tau)\cap var(S)=\emptyset}{\{\tau^*(\beta)\}S\{\tau^*(\gamma)\}}
$$

$$
\text{(Conjunction)} \quad \frac{\{\beta_1\}S\{\gamma_1\} \quad \{\beta_2\}S\{\gamma_2\}}{\{\beta_1\wedge\beta_2\}S\{\gamma_1\wedge\gamma_2\}}
$$

$$
\text{(Disjunction)} \quad \frac{\{\beta_1\}S\{\gamma\} \quad \{\beta_2\}S\{\gamma\}}{\{\beta_1\vee\beta_2\}S\{\gamma\}}
$$

$$
\text{(}\exists\text{-Introduction)} \quad \frac{\{\beta\}S\{\gamma\} \quad \overline{q}\cap[var(S)\cap free(\gamma)]=\emptyset \quad S \text{ terminates}}{\{(\exists q)\beta\}S\{\gamma\}}
$$

$$
\{\beta\}S\{\gamma\} \quad var(S)\subseteq\overline{p} \quad \overline{q}=free(\beta)\cup free(\gamma)\setminus[free(\delta)\cup\overline{p}]
$$

$$
\text{(Hoare Adaptation)} \quad \frac{S \text{ is term representable}}{\{(\exists\overline{q})[\beta\wedge(\forall\overline{p})(\gamma\rightarrow\delta)]\}S\{\delta\}}
$$

FIGURE 7.9 Adaptation rules for quantum programs.

Adaptation rules: As is well-know, there are usually two types of proof rules in a classical program logic (e.g. Hoare logic or separation logic), namely *construct rules* and *adaptation rules* [28,29]. A construct rule is defined for reasoning about correctness of the program construct under consideration. The construct rules make syntax-directed program verification possible. On the other hand, an adaptation rule derives a correctness formula $\{\beta'\}S\{\gamma'\}$ of a program S from an already established correctness formula $\{\beta\}S\{\gamma\}$ of the same program. Such a rule enables us to adapt correctness $\{\beta\}S\{\gamma\}$ to a new context. Adaptation rules can often help us to simplify program verification significantly.

Adaptation rules are expected to play the same role for quantum programs. So, in this subsection, we extend some classical adaptation rules to quantum programs. Indeed, one of them, namely the consequence rule can be straightforwardly generalised to the quantum case (see inference rule (R.Or) in Fig. 6.3). However, the pre/postconditions β' and γ' in the conclusions of other adaptation rules are formed from the pre/postconditions β, γ in their premises using logical connectives and quantifiers. They were not generalised to the quantum cases in Chapter 6 due to the lack of proper logical tools. Now $\mathcal{QL}$ provides with us the necessary logical tools, and we are able to present their quantum generalisations. To this end, let us first introduce:

Definition 7.21. Let $\mathbb{I}$ be an interpretation. Then:

1. We say that a quantum program S terminates in $\mathbb{I}$, written $\mathbb{I}\models S:$ Term, if $[\![S]\!]_{\mathbb{I}}(I)=I$, where I is the identity operator.
2. A quantum program S is called term representable in $\mathbb{I}$ if there exists a quantum term τ such that $var(\tau)\subseteq var(S)$ and $[\![S]\!]_{\mathbb{I}}([\![\tau]\!]_{\mathbb{I}}^*(X))=X$ for any closed subspace X of $\mathcal{H}_{var(S)}$.

A large number of adaptation rules have been introduced for classical programs in the literature. Here, we only generalise some of the most popular presented in Section 3.8 of [28] and Section 5.1 of [29] to the quantum case as examples showing the applicability of assertion logic $\mathcal{QL}$. The quantum generalisations of these rules are presented in Fig. 7.9. It should be noticed that the connectives of conjunction and disjunction in Birkhoff–von Neumann quantum logic are employed in the rules (Invariance), (Conjunction), and (Disjunction), and the term-adjoint formulas and quantifiers over quantum variables newly introduced in $\mathcal{QL}$ are used in the rules ($\exists$-Introduction) and (Hoare Adaptation). In particular, the Hoare adaptation rule is crucial for reasoning about procedure calls and recursion [209], and has been extended for reasoning about method calls in object-oriented programs [29]. We expect that its quantum generalisation given in Fig. 7.9 will play a similar role in quantum programming.

Theorem 7.8 (Soundness of adaptation rules). *All of the proof rules in Fig. 7.9 are sound in the sense of partial correctness.*

Proof. See Appendix A.3.5. □

Example 7.8. As a simple application of the adaptation rules, suppose we want to assert that the output of a quantum program S is always in a subspace Y of its state space $\mathcal{H}$ for all inputs from a subspace X of $\mathcal{H}$; that is, $\models_{par}\{X\}S\{Y\}$. We choose a basis $|\psi_1\rangle,...,|\psi_n\rangle$ of X. Then $X=\bigvee_{i=1}^{n}[\psi_i]$ (see Example 7.2), and by rule (Disjunction), it suffices to check $\models_{par}\{[\psi_i]\}S\{Y\}$ for $i=1,...,n$.

7.6 An effect calculus as assertion logic

In the last section, we incorporated logic $\mathcal{QL}$ with quantum variables into a simplified variant of quantum Hoare logic with projective predicates. This paves the way toward symbolic verification of quantum programs with respect to projective pre/postconditions. However, to realise symbolic verification of quantum programs with respect to pre/postconditions modelled by general quantum predicates (i.e. effects), a way for symbolic representation of effects is still missing. This motivates us to introduce a calculus of effects. This section is devoted to develop such a calculus, called $\mathcal{EC}$, which can be seen as a refinement of effect algebra considered in Section 7.3.4. At the end of this section, we will briefly discuss how $\mathcal{EC}$ can be properly combined with the general quantum Hoare logic.

7.6.1 A calculus of quantum effects

Syntax: We assume the same set $qVar$ of quantum variables as in Section 7.4. The alphabet of the calculus of effects $\mathcal{EC}$ consists of:

1. A set of effect symbols $E, E_1, E_2, ...$;
2. Connectives:
   a. Negation $\neg$ and tensor product $\otimes$;
   b. A set of Kraus operator symbols $K = \{K_i\}, L = \{L_j\}, ...$.

For each variable $q \in qVar$, we write $\mathcal{H}_q$ for the Hilbert space of the quantum system denoted by q. For any subset $V \subseteq qVar$, we write $\mathcal{H}_V = \bigotimes_{v \in V} \mathcal{H}_v$. To each effect symbol E, a nonnegative n and an n-tuple $\overline{d} = (d_1, ..., d_n)$ of integers or ∞ are assigned as its arity and signature, respectively. Each Kraus operator symbol K is equipped with a family $\{K_i\}$ of operator symbols. It is associated with a type of the form $type(K) = V \rightarrow V'$, where $V, V' \subseteq qVar$.

The design idea of effect calculus $\mathcal{EC}$ is as follows. Each effect symbol E will be used to denote a basic effect. It plays a role similar to that of a predicate symbol in first-order classical logic, quantum logic QL in Section 7.3.3 or $\mathcal{QL}$ in Section 7.4. Whenever associated with appropriate quantum variables, it becomes an atomic proposition of the form $E(q_1, ..., q_n)$. Based on these atomic propositions, we will build the calculus $\mathcal{EC}$ in two steps, namely *propositional calculus* and *first-order calculus*.

First, from atomic propositions, we can use connectives to construct all propositional formulas. The meanings of the connectives of negation $\neg$ and tensor product $\otimes$ are clear. Kraus operator symbols are introduced also as connectives to generate more complex propositions from simpler ones. As the name suggested, they are inspired by the Kraus operator-sum representation of quantum operations (see Theorem 2.3). Their roles will be clearlier seen after defining their semantics.

Definition 7.22 (Syntax). Effect formulas F and their variables $var(F)$ are defined inductively as follows:

1. If E is an effect symbol with signature $\overline{d} = (d_1, ..., d_n)$, and for each i, q_i is a quantum variable of dimension d_i, then $E(q_1, ..., q_n)$ is an effect formula, called an atomic formula, and $var(E(q_1, ..., q_n)) = \{q_1, ..., q_n\}$;
2. If F is an effect formula, so is $\neg F$, and $var(\neg F) = var(F)$;
3. If F and G are two effect formulas and $var(F) \cap var(G) = \emptyset$, then $F \otimes G$ is an effect formulas, and $var(F \otimes G) = var(F) \cup var(G)$.
4. If $\mathcal{F} = \{F_i\}$ is a family of effect formulas with $var(F_i) = V$ for all i, and $K = \{K_i\}$ is a Kraus operator symbol with $type(K) = V \rightarrow V'$, then

$$K(\mathcal{F}) \equiv \sum_i K_i^\dagger F_i K_i \tag{7.19}$$

is an effect formula, and $var(K(\mathcal{F})) = V'$. In particular, if $F_i = F$ for all i, then we simply write $K(F)$ for $K(\mathcal{F})$.

It is worth noting that a convex combination $\sum_i p_i F_i$ of a family $\mathcal{F} = \{F_i\}$ of effect formulas can be written as a special $K(\mathcal{F})$ with $K = \{K_i\}$ and K_i denoting constant $\sqrt{p_i}$, where $p_i \geq 0$ and $\sum_i p_i \leq 1$. We often write $F(q_1, ..., q_n)$ to indicate that F is an effect formula with $var(F) = \{q_1, ..., q_n\}$.

Semantics: An interpretation $\mathbb{I}$ of the effect calculus $\mathcal{EC}$ consists of:

- Each effect symbol E with signature $\overline{d} = (d_1, ..., d_n)$ is assigned an effect (i.e. a Hermitian operator $E^{\mathbb{I}}$ between the zero and identity operators) on the $\prod_{i=1}^n d_i$-dimensional Hilbert space;
- Each Kraus operator symbol $K = \{K_i\}$ with $type(K) = V \rightarrow V'$ is assigned a family $K^{\mathbb{I}} = \{K_i^{\mathbb{I}}\}$ of operators $K_i^{\mathbb{I}}$ from $\mathcal{H}_V$ to $\mathcal{H}_{V'}$ such that

$$\sum_i \left(K_i^{\mathbb{I}}\right)^\dagger K_i^{\mathbb{I}} \sqsubseteq I_{V'}$$

where $\sqsubseteq$ stands for the Löwner order, and $I_{V'}$ is the identity operator on $\mathcal{H}_{V'}$.

Definition 7.23 (Semantics). The semantics $[\![F]\!]_{\mathbb{I}}$ of an effect formula F in an interpretation $\mathbb{I}$ is defined inductively as follows:

1. If $F = E(q_1, ..., q_n)$ is an atomic formula, then $[\![F]\!]_{\mathbb{I}}$ is $E^{\mathbb{I}}$ as an operator on $\mathcal{H}_{var(F)} = \bigotimes_{i=1}^{n} \mathcal{H}_{q_i}$;
2. $[\![\neg F]\!] = I_{var(F)} - [\![F]\!]_{\mathbb{I}}$, where $I_{var(F)}$ is the identity operator on $\mathcal{H}_{var(F)}$;
3. $[\![F \otimes G]\!]_{\mathbb{I}} = [\![F]\!]_{\mathbb{I}} \otimes [\![G]\!]_{\mathbb{I}}$;
4. If $K = \{K_i\}$ and $\mathcal{F} = \{F_i\}$, then

$$[\![K(\mathcal{F})]\!]_{\mathbb{I}} = \sum_i \left(K_i^{\mathbb{I}}\right)^{\dagger} [\![F_i]\!]_{\mathbb{I}} K_i^{\mathbb{I}}. \tag{7.20}$$

Obviously, Eq. (7.20) is a direct interpretation of (7.19). The reader should be observed certain similarity (indeed, duality) between Eq. (7.20) and the Kraus-operator-sum representation in Theorem 2.3. It is easy to see that for any effect formula F, its semantics $[\![F]\!]_{\mathbb{I}}$ is an effect on $\mathcal{H}_{var(F)}$.

Let us consider a simple example to illustrate the above definitions.

Example 7.9. Let $Y \subseteq X \subseteq qVar$, and let A be an effect on $\mathcal{H}_X$. Recall from Definition 2.22 that the restriction of A on Y is obtained by tracing out $\mathcal{H}_{X \backslash Y}$ from A:

$$\mathrm{tr}_{\mathcal{H}_{X \backslash Y}}(A) = \sum_i \langle i|A|i \rangle$$

where $\{|i\rangle\}$ is an orthonormal basis of $\mathcal{H}_{X \backslash Y}$. We show how this restriction can be symbolically represented by an effect formula. To this end, we introduce effect symbol E and a Kraus operator symbol $K = \{K_i\}$. Let $\mathbb{I}$ be an interpretation where $E^{\mathbb{I}} = A$ and for each i, K_i is interpreted as operator $K_i^{\mathbb{I}} : \mathcal{H}_X \to \mathcal{H}_Y$ defined by

$$F_i(|\varphi\rangle|\psi\rangle) = \langle i|\psi\rangle|\varphi\rangle$$

for all $|\varphi\rangle \in \mathcal{H}_Y$ and $|\psi\rangle \in \mathcal{H}_{X \backslash Y}$, together with linearity. Let $\mathbb{F} = \{F_i\}$. Then the restriction can be represented by the effect formula $K(E)$; that is, $\mathrm{tr}_{\mathcal{H}_{X \backslash Y}} A = [\![K(A)]\!]_{\mathbb{I}}$.

As hinted by the above example, using various matrix decomposition techniques, effects (i.e. quantum predicates) of high dimensions can often be symbolically represented as an effect formula in which atomic effect formulas denote matrices of lower dimensions. On the other hand, if we introduce some effect symbols denoting basic effects (usually on Hilbert spaces of low dimensions), then complex effects on large Hilbert spaces can be constructed as effect formulas. Therefore, we can expect that symbolic techniques be applied to reason about logical relationship between these quantum predicates (represented as effect formulas) in verifying quantum programs.

Now we further define the satisfaction relation in effect calculus $\mathcal{EC}$.

Definition 7.24. Let F be an effect formula, $var(F) \subseteq V \subseteq qVar$, and $\rho \in \mathcal{H}_V$. Then the degree that quantum state ρ satisfies F in an interpretation $\mathbb{I}$ is defined as

$$[\![(\mathbb{I}, \rho) \models F]\!] = \mathrm{tr}\left([\![F]\!]_{\mathbb{I}} \rho\right). \tag{7.21}$$

The above definition is essentially a generalisation of satisfaction relation in logic $\mathcal{QL}$ studied in Section 7.4. To see this, let us consider a simple formula $P(q_1, ... q_n)$ in $\mathcal{QL}$, where P is a predicate symbol, and $q_1, ..., q_n$ are quantum variables. Recall that P is interpreted as a closed subspace X of $\bigotimes_{i=1}^n \mathcal{H}_{q_i}$ or equivalently the projection operator P_X. For any state ρ, it follows from clause 1 in Definition 7.11 that

$$(\mathbb{I}, \rho) \models P(q_1, ..., q_n) \text{ iff } \rho \in X, \text{ i.e. } \sup(\rho) \subseteq X. \tag{7.22}$$

Note that $\sup(\rho) \subseteq X$ if and only if $\mathrm{tr}(P_X \rho) = 1$ (in the case of finite dimensional state space). Thus, (7.21) can be seen as a quantitative generalisation of (7.22) since projection operator P_X is a special effect.

As usual, entailment and equivalence can be defined based on the satisfaction relation.

Definition 7.25 (Entailment and equivalence). Let F and G be two effect formulas.

1. We say that E entails F in an interpretation $\mathbb{I}$, written $\mathbb{I} \models F \Rightarrow G$, if for any ρ, it holds that $[\![(\mathbb{I}, \rho) \models F]\!] \leq [\![(\mathbb{I}, \rho) \models G]\!]$.
2. F and G are said to be equivalent in $\mathbb{I}$, written $\mathbb{I} \models F = G$, if $\mathbb{I} \models F \Rightarrow G$ and $\mathbb{I} \models G \Rightarrow F$.

$$(\text{Basis}) \quad \frac{E_1 \sqsubseteq E_2}{E(q_1, ..., q_n) \Rightarrow E_2(q_1, ..., q_n)}$$

$$(\text{Neg}) \quad \frac{F \Rightarrow G}{\neg G \Rightarrow \neg F} \qquad (\text{DP}) \quad \frac{F_1 \Rightarrow G_1 \quad F_2 \Rightarrow G_2}{F_1 \otimes F_2 \Rightarrow G_1 \otimes G_2}$$

$$(\text{Kraus}) \quad \frac{\mathcal{F} = \{F_i\} \qquad \mathcal{G} = \{G_i\} \qquad F_i \Rightarrow F_i \text{ for every } i}{K(\mathcal{F}) \Rightarrow K(\mathcal{G})}$$

FIGURE 7.10 Inference rules for effect formulas.

3. F entails G (respectively, F and G are equivalent), written $\models F \Rightarrow G$ (respectively, $\models F = G$)) if for all interpretations $\mathbb{I}$, it holds that $\mathbb{I} \models F \Rightarrow G$ (respectively, $\mathbb{I} \models F = G$).

By Lemma 6.2, it is easy to see that $\mathbb{I} \models F \Rightarrow G$ if and only if $[\![F]\!]_{\mathbb{I}} \otimes I_{var(G)\setminus var(F)} \sqsubseteq [\![G]\!]_{\mathbb{I}} \otimes I_{var(F)\setminus var(G)}$, where $\sqsubseteq$ stands for the Löwner order. For any $0 \le \lambda \le 1$, we define:

$$(\mathbb{I}, \rho) \models_\lambda F \text{ if and only if } [\![(\mathbb{I}, \rho) \models F]\!] \ge \lambda.$$

Then $\mathbb{I} \models F \Rightarrow G$ if and only if for all ρ and λ, $(\mathbb{I}, \rho) \models_\lambda F$ implies $(\mathbb{I}, \rho) \models_\lambda G$.

As is well-known, using de Morgan laws, all negations in a classical propositional logical formula can be transformed to a formula where negations only occur before propositional variables. A similar result holds for effects. To present it, we introduce:

Definition 7.26 (Negation normal form). A negation normal form of effect is an effect formula in which negations $\neg$ only occur before atomic formulas.

Theorem 7.9 (Normal form theorem). *Each effect formula F is equivalent to a negation normal form G up to a constant; that is, for some $\lambda > 0$, it holds that $[\![F]\!]_{\mathbb{I}} = \lambda [\![G]\!]_{\mathbb{I}}$ for all interpretation $\mathbb{I}$.*

Proof. See Appendix A.3.6. □

At this moment, a complete axiomatic system of the propositional part of effect calculus $\mathcal{EC}$ is still unknown. Several useful proof rules with respect to the connectives of effect formulas are presented in Fig. 7.10.

Exercise 7.4. Prove the rules in Fig. 7.10 are sound.

Quantified effect formulas: We now extend $\mathcal{EC}$ from a propositional calculus to a first-order calculus by introducing quantifiers into effect formulas. For simplicity, we only consider universally quantified effect formulas of the form:

$$A \equiv (\forall \overline{q}_1)...(\forall \overline{q}_n)F(\tau),$$

where F is an effect formula, τ a quantum term (see Definition 7.6) with $var(\tau) = var(F)$, $\overline{q}_i \subseteq var(F)$ for $1 \le i \le n$, and $\overline{q}_i \cap \overline{q}_j = \emptyset$ for $1 \le i < j \le n$. The free variables of formula A are $free(A) = var(F) \setminus \bigcup_{i=1}^n \overline{q}_i$. In particular, whence $n = 0$, then A is simply $F(\tau)$. Obviously, $F(\tau)$ can be seen as a generalisation of atomic formulas in logic $\mathcal{QL}$ (see Definition 7.7). If $A \equiv (\forall \overline{q}_1)...(\forall \overline{q}_n)F(\tau)$, $\overline{q} \subseteq var(F)$ and $\overline{q} \cap (\bigcup_{i=1}^n \overline{q}_i) = \emptyset$, then we often write $(\forall \overline{q})A$ for $(\forall \overline{q})(\forall \overline{q}_1)...(\forall \overline{q}_n)F(\tau)$. Existentially quantified effect formulas can be handled dually.

An interpretation of $A \equiv (\forall \overline{q}_1)...(\forall \overline{q}_n)F(\tau)$ is then a combination of an interpretation of effect symbols and Kraus operator symbols in F and an interpretation of quantum operation symbols in τ.

Definition 7.27 (Semantics). Let $A \equiv (\forall \overline{q}_1)...(\forall \overline{q}_n)F(\tau)$, and let $\mathbb{I}$ be an interpretation, $V \subseteq qVar$ and $\rho \in \mathcal{D}(\mathcal{H}_V)$. Then the degree that quantum state ρ satisfies A in $\mathbb{I}$ is defined as

$$[\![(\mathbb{I}, \rho) \models A]\!] = \inf_{var(\tau_i') \subseteq \overline{q}_i \ (1 \le i \le n)} \text{tr}\left[[\![F]\!]_{\mathbb{I}} [\![\tau]\!]_{\mathbb{I}} \left(\bigotimes_{i=1}^n [\![\tau_i']\!]_{\mathbb{I}}(\rho) \right) \right].$$

Definition 7.28 (Entailment and equivalence). Let A and B be two quantified effect assertions with $free(A) = free(B)$.

1. We say that A entails B in an interpretation $\mathbb{I}$, written $\mathbb{I} \models A \Rightarrow B$, if for all ρ, it holds that $[\![(\mathbb{I}, \rho) \models A]\!] \le [\![(\mathbb{I}, \rho) \models B]\!]$.

2. A and B are said to be equivalent in $\mathbb{I}$, written $\mathbb{I} \models A = B$, if $\mathbb{I} \models A \Rightarrow B$ and $\mathbb{I} \models B \Rightarrow A$.

$$(\text{Basis}) \quad \frac{F \Rightarrow G}{(\forall \overline{q})F(\tau) \Rightarrow (\forall \overline{q})G(\tau)} \qquad (\text{Eq}) \quad \frac{QT_= \vdash \tau = \eta}{F(\tau) = F(\eta)}$$

$$(\text{U1}) \quad \frac{\tau' \text{ is a quantum term}}{(\forall \overline{q})F(\tau) \Rightarrow F(\tau'\tau)} \qquad (\text{U2}) \quad \frac{A \Rightarrow B \quad \overline{q} \cap free(A) = \emptyset}{A \Rightarrow (\forall \overline{q})B}$$

FIGURE 7.11 Inference rules for quantified effect formulas.

$$(\text{R.IF.E}) \quad \frac{\{F_m\}\,S_m\,\{G\} \text{ for all } m}{\{K_M(\{F_m\})\} \text{ if } (\Box m \cdot M[\overline{q}] = m \rightarrow S_m) \text{ if } \{G\}}$$

$$(\text{R.LP.E}) \quad \frac{\{G\}S\{K_M(\{F, G\})\}}{\{K_M(\{F, G\})\} \text{ while } M[\overline{q}] = 1 \text{ do } S \text{ od } \{F\}}$$

FIGURE 7.12 Inference rules for case statements and **while**-loops.

3. A entails B (respectively, A and B are equivalent), written $\models A \Rightarrow B$ (respectively, $\models A = B$) if for all interpretations $\mathbb{I}$, it holds that $\mathbb{I} \models A \Rightarrow B$ (respectively, $\mathbb{I} \models A = B$).

Several inference rules for quantified effect algebras are presented in Fig. 7.11. It was pointed out above that it is still an open problem to find a complete axiomatic system for effect formulas. This problem is even harder for quantified effect formulas.

Exercise 7.5. Prove the rules in Fig. 7.11 are sound.

7.6.2 Quantum Hoare logic combined with effect calculus

In Section 7.5.2, first-order (sharp) quantum logic $\mathcal{QL}$ with quantum variables was employed as an assertion logic combined with a simplified variant quantum Hoare logic; namely that with only projective quantum predicates, for verification of quantum programs. Now we show how effect calculus defined in the previous Section can serve as an assertion language for quantum programs that can appropriately combined with quantum Hoare logic (QHL) for general quantum predicates.

First, recall that in the version of QHL presented in Chapter 6, pre/postconditions are represented by complex matrices. With effect calculus as assertion language, all inference rules in QHL can be reformulated such that their pre/postconditions are all symbolically represented as logical formulas. We only consider inference rules (R.IF) and (R.LP) in Fig. 6.3 for case statements and **while**-loops, respectively, as examples:

- For any quantum measurement $M = \{M_m\}$, we introduce a Kraus operator symbol $K_M = \{K_{Mm}\}$ with interpretation $K_{Mm}^{\mathbb{I}} = M_m$ for every m. Then (R.IF) can be rewritten as the rule (R.IF.E) in Fig. 7.12.
- For any binary (yes/no) measurement $M = \{M_0, M_1\}$, we introduce a Kraus operator symbol $K_M = \{K_{M0}, K_{M1}\}$ with interpretation $K_{Mi}^{\mathbb{I}} = M_i$ for $i = 0, 1$. Then (R.LP) can be rewritten as the rule (R.LP.E) in Fig. 7.12.

Second, the reformulated inference rules of QHL can work together with logical laws of the effect calculus to reason about correctness of quantum programs. In particular, the premises $P \sqsubseteq P'$ and $Q' \sqsubseteq Q$ in inference rule (R.Or) in Fig. 6.3 can be reformulated as $P \Rightarrow P'$ and $Q' \Rightarrow Q$ in the logical language of effect calculus, with P, P', Q, Q' expressed as effect formulas. Such a reformulation of rule (R.Or) serves as an interface between QHL and effect calculus $\mathcal{EC}$. Consequently, symbolic verification of quantum programs can be realised in a way similar to the case of classical programs, and a vast variety of verification techniques developed for classical programs can be translated to quantum programs.

Furthermore, in Section 7.5.2, we were able to formally formulate the relative completeness of the simplified variant of QHL with projective quantum predicates using quantum logic $\mathcal{QL}$. The same can be done for QHL with general quantum predicates in the framework of effect calculus $\mathcal{EC}$.

Exercise 7.6. Rewrite the rules for generating verification conditions $VC(Spec)$ given in Section 7.1.1 in the logical language of effect calculus $\mathcal{EC}$.

7.7 Discussion

In the last few sections, we defined two extensions of Birkhoff–von Neumann quantum logic, namely, first-order logic $\mathcal{QL}$ with quantum variables and effect calculus $\mathcal{EC}$, as an assertion language for quantum programs. In particular, $\mathcal{QL}$ and $\mathcal{EC}$

were incorporated into quantum Hoare logic (QHL) so that the relative completeness of QHL can be formulated in a more formal way than that in Chapter 6, and a series of adaptation rules can be derived to ease the verification, analysis and runtime checking of quantum programs. But several interesting problems about $\mathcal{QL}$ and $\mathcal{EC}$ themselves as well as their combination with QHL are still unsolved. For simplicity of discussion, we only consider $\mathcal{QL}$. The same or similar issues exist for $\mathcal{EC}$.

More quantifiers over quantum variables: The quantification over quantum variables in $\mathcal{QL}$ is defined by allowed quantum operations on the quantified variables (see Eq. (7.8), clause 5 in Definition 7.11 and clause 4 in the definition of the semantics of $\mathcal{QT}_=$ in Section 7.4.3). But there are some other interesting ways to introduce quantifiers in $\mathcal{QL}$. For example, a universally quantified formula $(\forall \overline{q})\beta$ with quantum variables $\overline{q}$ can be interpreted according to different levels of the correlation between $\overline{q}$ and other quantum variables:

- *Product quantification*: $(\mathbb{I}, \rho) \models (\forall_p \overline{q})\beta$ iff $(\mathbb{I}, \sigma \otimes \rho \downarrow (qVar \setminus \overline{q}) \models \beta$ for any $\sigma \in \mathcal{D}(\mathcal{H}_{\overline{q}})$.
- *Separation quantification*: $(\mathbb{I}, \rho) \models (\forall_s \overline{q})\beta$ iff $\left(\mathbb{I}, \sum_i (\sigma_i \otimes \rho_i)\right) \models \beta$ for any $\sigma_i \in \mathcal{D}(\mathcal{H}_{\overline{q}})$ and $\rho_i \in \mathcal{D}(\mathcal{H}_{qVar \setminus \overline{q}})$ with $\sum_i \rho_i = \rho \downarrow (qVar \setminus \overline{q})$.
- *Entanglement quantification*: $(\mathbb{I}, \rho) \models (\forall_e \overline{q})\beta$ iff for any ρ' with $\rho' \downarrow (free(\beta) \setminus \overline{q}) = \rho \downarrow (free(\beta) \setminus \overline{q})$, $(\mathbb{I}, \rho') \models \beta$.

Here, $qVar$ denotes the set of all quantum variables, $\otimes$ stands for tensor product, $\rho \downarrow X$ is the restriction of a quantum state on a subset $X \subseteq qVar$ of quantum variables.

Obviously, the above three quantifications over quantum variables and the one studied in Section 7.4 are useful in different circumstances, and an extension of $\mathcal{QL}$ with these new quantifiers can serve as a stronger logic tool for reasoning about quantum computation and quantum information. For example, it can help to deal with ghost (auxiliary) quantum variables considered in [396]. At the same time, a series of new problems arise in this new logic; in particular, quantifier elimination, which will be closely connected to some fundamental issues about correlation between quantum systems, we believe, one way or another.

Assertion languages for other quantum program logics: $\mathcal{QL}$ is designed as an assertion logic for quantum Hoare logic (QHL). Several extensions of QHL have been proposed in the literature, including relational quantum Hoare logic (qRHL) [48,274,395] and quantum separation logic (QSL) [270,451]. However, the assertion languages for all of these quantum program logics have not been formally defined. It seems that $\mathcal{QL}$ can be directly used as an assertion language for qRHL, but it is not the case for QSL. Some useful quantum generalisations of separation conjunction and implication were introduced in [270,451]. But we believe that more research on QSL is needed in order to find quantum separation connectives with the presence of entanglement in a more serious consideration. Furthermore, it would be nice to define them in a formal logical language so that an expansion of $\mathcal{QL}$ with them can serve as an assertion language of QSL.

Adding classical variables: For simplifying the presentation, quantum Hoare logic (QHL) was defined in Chapter 6 for purely quantum programs without classical variables. This simplification does not reduce its expressive power because classical computation can be simulated by quantum computation. In practical applications, however, it is often much more convenient to handle quantum variables and classical variables separately. The **while**-language with both classical and quantum variables was introduced in [427], where a correctness formula (Hoare triple) is defined with the pre/postcondition as a pair of a classical first-order logical formula and a quantum predicate so that the former specifies the properties of classical variables and the latter for quantum variables. Later, a QHL with both quantum and classical variables was developed in [155]. A limitation of the logic in [155] is that preconditions and postconditions are defined to be socalled classical-quantum predicates, each of which is represented as a family of Hermitian operators indexed by the states of classical variables. Such a representation is quite cumbersome, and should cause the issue of (double) explosion of the state spaces of both classical and quantum variables. In particular, the compactness offered by a logical language, even for classical variables, is totally lost. We believe that an assertion logic can significantly simplify reasoning about quantum algorithms with the program logic in [155] and thus improve its applicability. This then requires us to combine the original first-order quantum logic QL with classical variables (see Section 7.3.3) and $\mathcal{QL}$ with quantum variables introduced in Section 7.4 into a single logic system. It seems that the correctness formulas defined in [427] are more convenient that those in [155] for this purpose.

Concluding remark of the chapter: In this chapter, we have introduced various logical tools that can be used in a combination with quantum Hoare logic for verification of quantum programs. However, they are far from comprehensive. In particular, they have not been implemented in the existing quantum program verification tools mentioned in Section 1.1.3. We can reasonably expect that incorporating these logical tools into the verification tools will significantly improve the scalability and efficiency of the latter.

7.8 Bibliographic remarks and further readings

The architecture of quantum program verifiers described in Section 7.1 was very briefly discussed in Section 6 of [421], but the majority of the materials presented in Section 7.1 are new.

Birkhoff–von Neumann quantum logic studied in Section 7.3 was first introduced in [66]. After the development of 80 years, it has become a rich subject at the intersection of logic and quantum foundations. The exposition of Section 7.3 largely follows book [115].

The materials presented in Sections 7.2 and 7.6 have not been published elsewhere. The materials presented in Section 7.4 are mainly taken from the draft paper [422].

In this chapter, we focused on mathematical and logic tools useful for verification of quantum programs. But we would like to mention that several practical verification tools for quantum programs and quantum cryptographic protocols have been built; for example QHProver [281], Isabelle Marries Dirac [71], Qbricks [87], VOQC [207], EasyPQC [46], CoqQ [450], symQV [49]. Various quantum algorithms have been formally verified using these tools and others; for example, Shor's factorisation [333] and quantum phase estimation [408].

Chapter 8

Analysis of quantum programs

Chapter 7 discussed some basic issues about verification of quantum programs using quantum Hoare logic established in Chapter 6. In this chapter, we turn to algorithmic analysis of the behaviours of quantum programs. This chapter focuses on static analysis of quantum programs – program analysis method that can be performed without executing the program. In particular, we will mainly study two fundamental problems in program analysis: *invariant generation* and *termination analysis*. As is well-known, many program analysis problems are intractable or even uncomputable, including invariant generation and termination analysis. Abstract interpretation is an effective method to mitigate this issue. It computes sound and useful approximations of the program's behaviour. This method will be generalised to quantum programs at the end of this chapter.

In classical programming, the information discovered in program analysis are often very helpful in the assurance of program correctness. It can also be used in program optimisation, which improves the program's performance or reduces the resource needed in executing the program. Program analysis will play a similar role in quantum programming. In particular, the theoretical results and algorithms presented in this chapter will be useful for the following tasks among others:

1. As we saw from the architecture of a quantum program verifier presented in Section 7.1, in verification of the partial correctness of a quantum program using quantum Hoare logic, one needs to insert appropriate quantum predicates (i.e. verification conditions) at various locations in the program. The invariant generation technique developed in this chapter can be used to find these quantum predicates (i.e. invariants). Furthermore, termination analysis can be combined with the verification of partial correctness to prove total correctness of the program.
2. A fundamental difference between the modern optimising compilers and early compilers of classical programming languages is that the former can perform program optimisation using the information gathered in the static analysis of programs. One can expect that the same will happen in quantum programming. Indeed, several simple program analysis techniques have already been introduced into quantum compilation. But this line of research is still at its very early stage. We hope that the materials presented in this chapter can provide a basis for further development.

The chapter is organised as follows:

- We introduce in Section 8.1 the notion of superoperator-valued transition system as a natural representation of the control flow of a quantum program. It serves as a basis of quantum program analysis.
- The notion of invariant is introduced in Section 8.2 for quantum programs represented as superoperator-valued transition systems. We further study how to automatically generate the invariants of a quantum program.
- We will describe two different approaches to termination analysis of quantum programs. As the first approach, the notion of ranking function in Definition 6.10 will be generalised in Section 8.3 into the framework of superoperator-valued transition systems. Then we show how ranking functions can be algorithmically synthesised for assuring the termination of quantum programs.
- Our second approach to termination analysis is described in Section 8.4.
  - We start in Section 8.4.1 by examining the behaviour of quantum extension of **while**-loop defined in Section 5.1, including termination and average running time.
  - Motivated by quantum **while**-loops, we identify quantum Markov chains as the semantic model of quantum programs. Furthermore, we argue that termination analysis of quantum programs can be reduced to the reachability problem of quantum Markov chains.
  - Reachability analysis techniques for classical Markov chains heavily depend on algorithms for graph-reachability problems. Likewise, a kind of graphical structures in Hilbert spaces, called quantum graphs, play a crucial role in the reachability analysis of quantum Markov chains. So, Section 8.4.2 gives an introduction to quantum graph theory, which provides a mathematical basis of Section 8.4.4.
  - In Section 8.4.4, we study the reachability problems for quantum Markov chains. In particular, we present several (classical) algorithms for computing the reachability probabilities of quantum Markov chains.

Foundations of Quantum Programming. https://doi.org/10.1016/B978-0-44-315942-8.00019-8

- Abstract interpretation techniques for quantum programs are introduced in Section 8.5.
- For readability, the proofs of some technical lemmas in this chapter are postponed to Appendix A.4.

Assumption: Since our main aim is to develop algorithms for analysing quantum programs, the state spaces of programs – Hilbert spaces – considered in this chapter are always assumed to be finite-dimensional.

Although a few results in this chapter may also be used in an infinite-dimensional state Hilbert space, the majority cannot. Analysis of quantum programs in infinite-dimensional state spaces is a challenging problem and requires radically new ideas, and it should be a very important topic for future research.

8.1 Control flows of quantum programs

The control flow of a program is the basis for analysing the behaviour of the program. It expresses the information about which functions are called at various points of the programs's execution.

As discussed in Section 1.2.2, quantum programs can have two different kinds of control flows, namely *classical control* and *quantum control*. But the control flows of all the quantum programs that we studied up to now are classical. In this section, we introduce a way for graphically representing the control flows of these programs.

8.1.1 Superoperator-valued transition systems

In this subsection, we define the notion of superoperator-valued transition system, which can be seen as a quantum extension of a classical transition system and a probabilistic transition system. It provides us with a convenient way for modelling the control flow of quantum programs.

Let us first recall that a classical transition system is a triple $(L, \rightarrow, l_0)$, where:

- L is a (finite) set of locations;
- $\rightarrow \subseteq L \times L$ is a transition relation;
- $l_0 \in L$ is the initial location.

Intuitively, the system starts from l_0. Each pair $(l, l') \in \rightarrow$ means that the system moves from location l to l' in one step; we often write $l \rightarrow l'$. A probabilistic transition system is then a triple (L, P, l_0) where L and l_0 are the same as in a classical transition system, and

- $P : S \times S \rightarrow [0, 1]$ is the transition probability function such that for every $l \in L$:

$$\sum_{l' \in L} P(l, l') = 1. \tag{8.1}$$

Intuitively, for any $l, l' \in L$, $P(l, l')$ is the probability that the system moves from location l to l' in one step. If $p = P(l, l') > 0$, then we can write $l \xrightarrow{p} l'$.

A superoperator-valued transition system is a generalisation of a probabilistic transition system obtained from replacing probabilities $P(l, l')$ by superoperators on some Hilbert space. To present its precise definition, we need the following notation. For two quantum operations (superoperators; see Definition 2.25) $\mathcal{E}$, $\mathcal{F}$ on a Hilbert space $\mathcal{H}$, we say that they are equivalent, written $\mathcal{E} \cong \mathcal{F}$, if $\mathrm{tr}(\mathcal{E}(\rho)) = \mathrm{tr}(\mathcal{F}(\rho))$ for any density operator $\rho \in \mathcal{D}(\mathcal{H})$.

Definition 8.1 (Superoperator-valued transition systems). A superoperator-valued transition system (SVTS for short) is a 5-tuple $\mathcal{S} = \langle \mathcal{H}, L, l_0, \mathcal{T}, \Theta \rangle$, where:

1. $\mathcal{H}$ is a Hilbert space, called the state space;
2. L is a finite set of locations;
3. $l_0 \in L$ is the initial location;
4. $\mathcal{T}$ is a set of transitions. Each transition $\tau \in \mathcal{T}$ is a triple $\tau = \langle l, l', \mathcal{E} \rangle$, often written as

$$\tau = l \xrightarrow{\mathcal{E}} l'$$

where $l, l' \in L$ are the pre- and postlocations of τ, respectively, and $\mathcal{E}$ is a superoperator on $\mathcal{H}$. It is required that

$$\sum \left\{\!\!\left| \mathcal{E} : l \xrightarrow{\mathcal{E}} l' \in \mathcal{T} \right|\!\!\right\} \cong \mathcal{I} \tag{8.2}$$

for each $l \in L$, where $\{\!| \cdot |\!\}$ stands for a multiset, and $\mathcal{I}$ is the identity superoperator on $\mathcal{H}$, i.e. $\mathcal{I}(\rho) = \rho$ for all $\rho \in \mathcal{D}(\mathcal{H})$;

5. Θ is a quantum predicate in $\mathcal{H}$ denoting the initial condition.

It is easy to see the similarity between a probabilistic transition system and an SVTS. In particular, Eq. (8.2) is a generalisation of (8.1). We always assume that the transition relation $\rightarrow$ is countably branching; that is, for every $l \in L$, the set

$$\left\{ |\mathcal{E} : l \xrightarrow{\mathcal{E}} l' \text{ for some } l' | \right\}$$

is finite or countably infinite. Therefore, the summation in the left-hand side of Eq. (8.2) is well-defined. Note that in a probabilistic transition system, there is no counterpart of quantum predicate Θ. As we will see soon, Θ is added to represent a precondition when an SVTS is used to model a quantum program.

Remark 8.1. To avoid the technical problem that an SVTS may contain some terminal location l which does not satisfy Eq. (8.2), we can simply add a circle $l \xrightarrow{\mathcal{I}} l$.

For any path

$$\pi = l_1 \xrightarrow{\mathcal{E}_1} l_2 \xrightarrow{\mathcal{E}_2} \ldots \xrightarrow{\mathcal{E}_{n-1}} l_n$$

in the transition graph, we write $l_1 \xRightarrow{\pi} l_n$ and use $\mathcal{E}_\pi$ to denote the composition of the superoperators along the path, i.e.

$$\mathcal{E}_\pi = \mathcal{E}_{n-1} \circ \ldots \circ \mathcal{E}_2 \circ \mathcal{E}_1. \tag{8.3}$$

If for every transition $l \xrightarrow{\mathcal{E}} l'$ in $\mathcal{S}$, superoperator $\mathcal{E}$ is simply defined by an operator E, i.e. $\mathcal{E} = E \circ E^\dagger$, or more precisely $\mathcal{E}(\rho) = E\rho E^\dagger$ for all density operators ρ, then $\mathcal{S}$ is called an operator-valued transition system. We will write $l \xrightarrow{E} l'$ for $l \xrightarrow{\mathcal{E}} l'$ when $\mathcal{E} = E \circ E^\dagger$. In particular, we write $l \xrightarrow{I} l'$ instead of $l \xrightarrow{\mathcal{I}} l'$, where I and $\mathcal{I}$ are the identity operator and identity superoperator, respectively, on $\mathcal{H}$.

8.1.2 Quantum programs as transition systems

In this subsection, we show how the control flow graph of a quantum program can be represented by an SVTS defined in the previous subsection, and thus provide a basis for various static analyses of quantum programs.

For every quantum program P written a quantum **while**-language, we define an SVTS $\mathcal{S}_P$ in the state Hilbert space $\mathcal{H}_P$ of P by induction on the length of P. This transition system has two designated locations l_{in}^P, l_{out}^P, with the former being the initial location and the latter the exit location.

- **Case 1**: $P \equiv \textbf{skip}$. Then $\mathcal{S}_P$ has only two locations l_{in}^P, l_{out}^P and a single transition

$$l_{in}^P \xrightarrow{I} l_{out}^P;$$

- **Case 2**: $P \equiv q := |0\rangle$. Let $\{|n\rangle\}$ be an orthonormal basis of $\mathcal{H}_q$. Then $\mathcal{S}_P$ has locations l_{in}^P, l_{out}^P together with l_n for each basis state $|n\rangle$. The transitions are

$$l_{in}^P \xrightarrow{E_n} l_n \quad \text{and} \quad l_n \xrightarrow{I} l_{out}^P$$

for every basis state $|n\rangle$, where $E_n = |0\rangle\langle n|$.
- **Case 3**: $P \equiv \overline{q} := U[\overline{q}]$. Then $\mathcal{S}_P$ is simply given as

$$l_{in}^P \xrightarrow{U} l_{out}^P;$$

- **Case 4**: $P \equiv P_1; P_2$. Suppose that $\mathcal{S}_{P_1}, \mathcal{S}_{P_2}$ are the control flow graphs of subprograms P_1, P_2, respectively. Then $\mathcal{S}_P$ is constructed as follows: we identify $l_{out}^{P_1} = l_{in}^{P_2}$ and concatenate P_1 and P_2. We further set $l_{in}^P = l_{in}^{P_1}$ and $l_{out}^P = l_{out}^{P_2}$;
- **Case 5**: $P \equiv \textbf{if } (\square_m M[\overline{q}] = m \rightarrow P_m) \textbf{ fi}$. Suppose that $\mathcal{S}_{P_m}$ is the control flow graph of subprogram P_m for every m. Then $\mathcal{S}_P$ is constructed as follows: we put all $\mathcal{S}_{P_m}$'s together, and add a new location l_{in}^P and a transition

$$l_{in}^P \xrightarrow{M_m} l_{in}^{P_m}$$

for every m. Furthermore, we identify $l_{out}^P = l_{out}^{P_m}$ for all m;

- **Case 6**: $P \equiv$ **while** $M[\overline{q}] = 1$ **do** Q **od**. We construct $\mathcal{S}_P$ from the control flow graph $\mathcal{S}_Q$ of subprogram Q as follows: we add two new locations l_{in}^P, l_{out}^P and two transitions

$$l_{in}^P \overset{M_0}{\to} l_{out}^P \quad \text{and} \quad l_{in}^P \overset{M_1}{\to} l_{in}^Q.$$

We identify $l_{out}^Q = l_{in}^P$.

Note that $\mathcal{S}_P$ is an operator-valued transition system, i.e. every transition in $\mathcal{S}_P$ is of the form $l \overset{E}{\to} l'$ with E being an operator on $\mathcal{H}_P$. This is possible because we choose to depict each initialisation statement $q := |0\rangle$ in P by a family of transitions with operators $E_n = |0\rangle\langle n|$ for basis states $|n\rangle$. On the other hand, we can also use a single transition with superoperator

$$\mathcal{E}_0(\rho) = \sum_n |0\rangle\langle n|\rho|n\rangle\langle 0|$$

to model the initialisation (Case 2). Then $\mathcal{S}_P$ becomes an SVTS, but the number of locations is significantly reduced.

To illustrate the idea described above, let us consider an example of the quantum walk on an n-circle with an absorbing boundary at position 1 (see Section 4.5). Assume that $\mathcal{H}_c$ is the coin space, the 2-dimensional Hilbert space with orthonormal basis states $|L\rangle$ and $|R\rangle$, indicating directions Left and Right, respectively. Also assume that $\mathcal{H}_p$ is the n-dimensional Hilbert space with orthonormal basis states $|0\rangle, |1\rangle, ..., |n-1\rangle$, where vector $|i\rangle$ denotes position i for each $0 \le i < n$. The quantum walk is the composite system of the coin and a walker moving on these positions. Then the state space of the walk is the tensor product $\mathcal{H} = \mathcal{H}_c \otimes \mathcal{H}_p$. The initial state is $|L\rangle|0\rangle$. Each step of the walk consists of:

1. Measure the position of the system to see whether it is 1. If the outcome is "yes", then the walk terminates; otherwise, it continues. The measurement is $M = \{M_{yes}, M_{no}\}$, where

$$M_{yes} = |1\rangle\langle 1|, \ M_{no} = I_p - M_{yes} = \sum_{i \neq 1} |i\rangle\langle i|$$

and I_p is the identity operator on the position space $\mathcal{H}_p$;
2. The Hadamard "coin-tossing" operator H is applied on the coin (or direction) space $\mathcal{H}_c$;
3. The shift operator S defined by $S|L, i\rangle = |L, i \ominus 1\rangle$ and $S|R, i\rangle = |R, i \oplus 1\rangle$ for $i = 0, 1, ..., n-1$ is performed on the space $\mathcal{H}$. Intuitively, the system walks one step left or right according to the direction state. Here, $\oplus$ and $\ominus$ stand for addition and subtraction modulo n, respectively. The operator S can be equivalently written as

$$S = \sum_{i=0}^{n-1} |L\rangle\langle L| \otimes |i \ominus 1\rangle\langle i| + \sum_{i=0}^{n-1} |R\rangle\langle R| \otimes |i \oplus 1\rangle\langle i|.$$

As discussed in Section 4.5, an essential difference between the quantum walk and a classical random walk is that the coin (or direction) variable c can be in a superposition of $|L\rangle$ and $|R\rangle$ like $|+\rangle = \frac{1}{\sqrt{2}}(|L\rangle + |R\rangle)$, and thus the walker is moving left and right "simultaneously"; for example,

$$\frac{1}{\sqrt{2}}(|L\rangle + |R\rangle)|i\rangle \to \frac{1}{\sqrt{2}}(|L\rangle|i \ominus 1\rangle + |R\rangle|i \oplus 1\rangle).$$

This means that if the walker is currently at position i, then after one step she/he will be at both position $i \ominus 1$ and $i \oplus 1$.

Example 8.1 (Control flow graph of quantum walk). Using the quantum **while**-language described in Definition 5.1, the above quantum walk can be written as the quantum program:

$$QW \equiv \ c := |L\rangle; \ p := |0\rangle; \textbf{while } M[p] = no \textbf{ do } c := H[c];$$
$$c, p := S[c, p] \textbf{ od}$$

The control flow graph of the quantum program QW is given as an SVTS $\mathcal{S}_{QW} = (\mathcal{H}, L, l_0, \mathcal{T}, \Theta)$, where:

- $\mathcal{H} = \mathcal{H}_c \otimes \mathcal{H}_p$;
- $L = \{l_0 = l_{in}, l_1, l_2, l_{out}\}$;

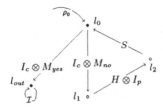

FIGURE 8.1   The SVTS of quantum walks on a cycle.

- $\mathcal{T} = \{l_0 \overset{M_{yes}}{\to} l_{out}, l_0 \overset{M_{no}}{\to} l_1, l_1 \overset{H}{\to} l_2, l_2 \overset{S}{\to} l_0\}$;
- $\Theta = |L\rangle\langle L| \otimes |0\rangle\langle 0|$.

The SVTS $\mathcal{S}_{QW}$ is visualised in Fig. 8.1.

8.2   Invariants and their generation

With the preparation of the above section, we are able to deal with the first issue of quantum program analysis; namely invariant generation. Program invariant is a fundamental notion widely used in program verification and analysis. In classical programming, an invariant is an assertion, usually formulated as a logical formula or a predicate, assigned to a certain location of a program, which holds true every time when the execution of the program reaches this location. The aim of this section is to generalise the notion of program invariant into the quantum setting and extend the invariant-based verification and analysis techniques for classical programs to quantum programs. A direct application of the techniques presented in this section is verification condition generation in a quantum program verifier (see Section 7.1.1).

8.2.1   Basic definitions

In this and next few subsections, we will generalise the notions of invariant and inductive assertion map into the quantum case.

Invariants and inductive assertions of classical programs: To motivate an appropriate definition of invariants for quantum programs, let us briefly recall the corresponding notion in classical programming. Roughly speaking, an invariant of a program at a location is an assertion that is always true when the location is reached during an execution of the program. More precisely, an invariant at a location l in the control flow graph of the program is an assertion O fulfilling the following condition:

- **Invariance**: if an input at the initial location l_0 satisfies the initial condition Θ, then for all paths π, provided π is from l_0 to l, O is always true whenever l is reached through π.

It is easy to see that this invariance is usually not easy to establish. An auxiliary notion of inductive assertion was introduced in Floyd's seminal paper [158] so that the invariance can be proved inductively. An assertion is inductive at a location of a program if it is true for the first time the location is reached, and is preserved by every cycle back to the location. A standard method for proving an assertion O to be an invariant is to find an assertion O' that is stronger than O and is inductive [158].

Formally, let $\mathcal{S}$ be a classical transition system. A cut-set of $\mathcal{S}$ is a subset $C \subseteq L$ of locations such that every cyclic path in $\mathcal{S}$ passes through some location in C. Every location $l \in C$ is called a cut-point. A basic path π between two cut-points l and l' is a path that does not pass through any cut-point other than the endpoints. An assertion map for a classical program assigns an assertion $\eta(l)$ to each cut-point $l \in C$ in its control flow graph. It is said to be inductive if it fulfils the following two conditions:

- **Initiation**: if an input satisfies the initial condition Θ, then for all basic paths π, provided π is from the initial location l_0 to some cut-point l, $\eta(l)$ is true when π reaches l;
- **Consecution**: if $\eta(l)$ is satisfied, then for all basic paths π, provided π is from l to another cut-point l', $\eta(l')$ is satisfied too, when π reaches l'.

How to define quantum invariants and inductive assertions? Now we try to find appropriate definitions of invariants and inductive assertions for quantum programs. A first thought might be that they can be defined by a straightforward generalisation from classical programs. Actually, this is not the case. First of all, of course we will deal with a superoperator-valued transition system (SVTS for short) rather than a classical transition system. As we saw in the last section, this SVTS models the semantics of a quantum program, which is determined by the principles of quantum mechanics.

Another key issue to be addressed is: in the quantum realm, how to (re-)interpret the implication as well as the quantifier "for all" appearing in the conditions **Invariance**, **Initiation**, and **Consection**? We choose to use the Łukasiewicz system of continuous-valued logic for our purpose. Different from the ordinary two-valued logic where each proposition has a truth value 0 (false) or 1 (true), a proposition in a continuous-valued logic has a real number in the unit interval $[0, 1]$ as its truth value, i.e. the degree to which the proposition is true. A characteristic feature of Łukasiewicz logic is the Łukasiewicz implication:

$$a \to_L b = \min(1, 1 - a + b) \text{ for } a, b \in [0, 1]. \tag{8.4}$$

Intuitively, if the truth values of propositions A and B are a, b, respectively, then the truth value of implication proposition $A \to B$ is given as $a \to_L b$.

We also need the following auxiliary notion in defining invariants of quantum programs: a set Π of paths is said to be prime if for each

$$\pi = l_1 \overset{\mathcal{E}_1}{\to} \ldots \overset{\mathcal{E}_{n-1}}{\to} l_n \in \Pi,$$

its proper initial segments $l_1 \overset{\mathcal{E}_1}{\to} \ldots \overset{\mathcal{E}_{k-1}}{\to} l_k \notin \Pi$ for all $k < n$. The intuitive idea behind a prime path set Π is to avoid repeatedly counting of a loop in Π.

With these design decision and preparation, we can present the following:

Definition 8.2 (Invariants). Let $\mathcal{S} = \langle \mathcal{H}, L, l_0, \mathcal{T}, \Theta \rangle$ be an SVTS and $l \in L$. An invariant at location $l \in L$ is a quantum predicate O in state Hilbert space $\mathcal{H}$ satisfying the following condition:

- **Q-Invariance**: for any density operator ρ, and for any prime set Π of paths from l_0 to l, we have:

$$\text{tr}(\Theta\rho) \leq 1 - \text{tr}(\mathcal{E}_\Pi(\rho)) + \text{tr}(O\mathcal{E}_\Pi(\rho)) \tag{8.5}$$

where $\mathcal{E}_\Pi = \sum \{|\mathcal{E}_\pi : \pi \in \Pi|\}$, and $\mathcal{E}_\pi$ is defined by Eq. (8.3).

The above definition deserves some explanations.

1. Note that if $\Pi_1 \subseteq \Pi_2$ and inequality (8.5) is true for Π_2 then it is also true for Π_1 (see Eq. (8.10) below for a more general argument). Thus, we do not need to check inequality (8.5) for all prime sets of paths from l_0 to l but only the maximal ones.

2. For each path $\pi \in \Pi$, $\mathcal{E}_\pi(\rho)$ is a partial density operator, but it can be normalised to a density operator

$$\rho_\pi = \frac{\mathcal{E}_\pi(\rho)}{p_\pi},$$

where $p_\pi = \text{tr}(\mathcal{E}_\pi(\rho))$ can be understood as the probability that path π reaches state ρ_π. Furthermore, we have:

$$\text{tr}(O\mathcal{E}_\Pi(\rho)) = \sum_{\pi \in \Pi} \text{tr}(O\mathcal{E}_\pi(\rho)) = \sum_{\pi \in \Pi} p_\pi \cdot \text{tr}(O\rho_\pi).$$

Since $\text{tr}(O\rho_\pi)$ is the (probabilistic) truth value of the proposition that state ρ_π satisfies quantum predicate O, $\text{tr}(O\mathcal{E}_\Pi(\rho))$ is the expected (or average) truth value of the proposition that for all paths $\pi \in \Pi$, O is satisfied when π reaches location l. Therefore, here, quantifier "for all" is interpreted as "the expected value according to probability (sub-)distribution $\{p_\pi\}_{\pi \in \Pi}$". This understanding can be seen as a special case of Keisler's integral quantifier in probability logic [244].

3. The quantity $\text{tr}(\mathcal{E}_\Pi(\rho)) = \sum_{\pi \in \Pi} p_\pi$ is the total probability that location l is reached through paths in Π. Here, we see that the condition that Π is prime is necessary; otherwise, a certain probability is calculated repeatedly.

4. Using the Łukasiewicz implication $\to_L$ defined in Eq. (8.4), inequality (8.5) can be rewritten as:

$$\text{tr}(\Theta\rho) \leq \text{tr}(\mathcal{E}_\Pi(\rho)) \to_L \text{tr}(O\mathcal{E}_\Pi(\rho))$$

because $0 \sqsubseteq \Theta \sqsubseteq I$ and thus $\text{tr}(\Theta\rho) \leq 1$. Combined with items 2 and 3, it shows that inequality (8.5) is indeed the reinterpretation of condition **Invariance** in the Łukasiewicz system of continuous valued logic.

8.2.2 Partial correctness

A basic reason for the usefulness of invariants in classical programming is that they can be used to establish partial correctness of programs. This is also true in quantum programming; that is, the notion of invariant defined above can be employed to establish partial correctness of quantum programs:

Theorem 8.1 (Partial correctness). *Let P be a quantum program and S_P the SVTS defined by P with initial condition Θ. If O is an invariant at l_{out}^P in S_P, then*

$$\models_{par} \{\Theta\} P\{O\}.$$

Proof. We write:

$$\Pi = \left\{ \text{paths } \pi : l_{in}^P \overset{\pi}{\Rightarrow} l_{out}^P \text{ and } \pi \text{ visits } l_{out}^P \text{ only once} \right\}.$$

It is easy to see that set Π is prime because there is not any transition outgoing from l_{out}^P. On the other hand, for any density operator ρ, we claim:

$$\llbracket P \rrbracket(\rho) = \sum \left\{ |\mathcal{E}_\pi(\rho) : l_{in}^P \overset{\pi}{\Rightarrow} l_{out}^P| \right\} = \mathcal{E}_\Pi(\rho) \tag{8.6}$$

We prove Eq. (8.6) by induction on the structure of P. We only consider the case of $P \equiv$ **while** $M[\bar{q}] = 1$ **do** Q **od** as an example, and other cases are easier (and thus omitted here). Let $\mathcal{E}_i(\rho) = M_i \rho M_i^\dagger$ for all $\rho \in \mathcal{D}(\mathcal{H}_P)$ $(i = 0, 1)$. Then it follows that

$$\llbracket P \rrbracket(\rho) = \sum_{n=0}^{\infty} \left[\mathcal{E}_0 \circ (\llbracket Q \rrbracket \circ \mathcal{E}_1)^n \right](\rho)$$

$$= \sum \left\{ | \left[\mathcal{E}_0 \circ (\mathcal{E}_{\pi_1} \circ \mathcal{E}_1)^n \right](\rho) : \left(l_{in}^P \overset{M_1}{\to} l_{in}^Q \overset{\pi_1}{\Rightarrow} l_{out}^Q \right)^n \overset{M_0}{\to} l_{out}^P | \right\}$$

$$= \sum \left\{ |\mathcal{E}_\pi(\rho) : l_{in}^P \overset{\pi}{\Rightarrow} l_{out}^P | \right\}$$

Here, the first equality comes from Proposition 5.2, the second equality from the induction hypothesis on Q as well as linearity of $\mathcal{E}_0$, $\mathcal{E}_1$ and $\mathcal{E}_\pi$, and the last from the construction of S_P for the quantum **while**-loop P.

Now we are ready to prove the conclusion $\models_{par} \{\Theta\} P\{O\}$. Since O is an invariant at l_{out}^P, it follows from Eq. (8.6) that for any density operator ρ,

$$\text{tr}(\Theta\rho) \leq 1 - \text{tr}(\mathcal{E}_\Pi(\rho)) + \text{tr}(O\mathcal{E}_\Pi(\rho))$$

$$= \text{tr}(O\mathcal{E}_\Pi(\rho)) + (\text{tr}(\rho) - \text{tr}(\mathcal{E}_\Pi(\rho))) \tag{8.7}$$

$$= \text{tr}(O\llbracket P \rrbracket(\rho)) + (\text{tr}(\rho) - \text{tr}(\llbracket P \rrbracket(\rho))).$$

We further notice that the above inequality holds for any partial density operator ρ because O, Θ, $\llbracket P \rrbracket$ and $\text{tr}(\cdot)$ are all linear. $\square$

8.2.3 Inductive assertion maps

As pointed out before, it is not easy to show by its definition that an assertion O is an invariant at a location l for a classical program because we need to check condition **Invariant** for every path π from the initial location l_0 to l. It is even harder to do the same for a quantum program directly using Definition 8.2 since we have to verify inequality (8.5) for every set of paths (rather than a single path) from l_0 to l. In classical programming, inductive assertions give us an effective way for finding and proving program invariants. In this subsection, we define a corresponding notion for quantum programs as a tool for establishing invariants.

Definition 8.3 (Assertion maps). Given an SVTS $S = \langle \mathcal{H}, L, l_0, \mathcal{T}, \Theta \rangle$ with a cut-set C (that is, every cyclic path in S passes through some location in C). An assertion map is a mapping η from each cut-point $l \in C$ to a quantum predicate $\eta(l)$ in $\mathcal{H}$.

For each cut-point $l \in C$, we write Ω_l for the set of all basic paths (i.e. those paths that does not pass through any cut-point other than the endpoints) from l to some cut-point. Moreover, the last location in a path π is denoted by l_π.

Definition 8.4 (Inductive assertion maps). Let η be an assertion map from SVTS $\mathcal{S} = \langle \mathcal{H}, L, l_0, \mathcal{T}, \Theta \rangle$ with a cut-set C. Then η is said to be inductive if it satisfies the following conditions:

- **Q-Initiation**: for any density operator ρ, we have:

$$\mathrm{tr}(\Theta\rho) \leq 1 - \mathrm{tr}\left(\mathcal{E}_{\Omega_{l_0}}(\rho)\right) + \sum_{\pi \in \Omega_{l_0}} \mathrm{tr}(\eta(l_\pi)\mathcal{E}_\pi(\rho)); \tag{8.8}$$

- **Q-Consecution**: for any density operator ρ, and for each cut-point $l \in C$, we have:

$$\mathrm{tr}(\eta(l)\rho) \leq 1 - \mathrm{tr}\left(\mathcal{E}_{\Omega_l}(\rho)\right) + \sum_{\pi \in \Omega_l} \mathrm{tr}(\eta(l_\pi)\mathcal{E}_\pi(\rho)). \tag{8.9}$$

With an argument similar to that after Definition 8.2, we can see that conditions (**Q-Initiation**) and (**Q-Consecution**) are essentially the reinterpretations of conditions (**Initiation**) and (**Consecution**), respectively, in the quantum setting using Łukasiewicz logic.

As its first application, let us see an interesting connection between the notion of inductive assertion map and the proof rule for quantum loop in quantum Hoare logic presented in Chapter 6.

Example 8.2 (Proof rule for quantum loops). Recall that the proof rule for loop **while** $M[\overline{q}] = 1$ **do** P **od** in quantum Hoare logic is given as follows:

$$\frac{\{B\}P\{M_0^\dagger A M_0 + M_1^\dagger B M_1\}}{\{M_0^\dagger A M_0 + M_1^\dagger B M_1\}\textbf{while } M[\overline{q}] = 1 \textbf{ do } P \textbf{ od}\{A\}}$$

Here, we show how this rule can be derived from an inductive assertion map. The control flow graph of the loop is given as SVTS $\mathcal{S} = (\mathcal{H}, L, l_0, \mathcal{T}, \Theta)$, where:

- $\mathcal{H}$ is the state Hilbert space of the loop;
- $L = \{l_0 = l_{in}, l_1, l_{out}\}$ are locations;
- transitions are

$$\mathcal{T} = \left\{ l_0 \overset{M_0}{\to} l_{out}, l_0 \overset{M_1}{\to} l_1, l_1 \overset{[\![P]\!]}{\to} l_0 \right\}$$

with $[\![P]\!]$ being the denotational semantics of P; and
- the initial condition is $\Theta = M_0^\dagger A M_0 + M_1^\dagger B M_1$.

We choose cut-set $C = \{l_{out}, l_1\}$, and assertion map η is defined by $\eta(l_{out}) = A$ and $\eta(l_1) = B$. It is routine to prove that η is inductive whenever

$$\models_{par} \{B\}P\{M_0^\dagger A M_0 + M_1^\dagger B M_1\}.$$

The next theorem shows that the notion of inductive assertion can be used to establish invariants of quantum programs. Combined with Theorem 8.1, it provides us with a method for verifying partial correctness of quantum programs.

Theorem 8.2 (Invariance). *Let $\mathcal{S}$ be an SVTS with cut-set C. If η is an inductive assertion map, then for every cut-point $l \in C$, $\eta(l)$ is an invariant at l.*

Proof. First of all, we observe that if $\Pi_1 \subseteq \Pi_2$, then

$$1 - \mathrm{tr}\left(\mathcal{E}_{\Pi_2}(\rho)\right) + \sum_{\pi \in \Pi_2} \mathrm{tr}(\eta(l_\pi)\mathcal{E}_\pi(\rho))$$

$$= \left[1 - \mathrm{tr}\left(\mathcal{E}_{\Pi_1}(\rho)\right) - \mathrm{tr}\left(\mathcal{E}_{\Pi_2 \backslash \Pi_1}(\rho)\right)\right]$$

$$+ \left[\sum_{\pi \in \Pi_1} \mathrm{tr}(\eta(l_\pi)\mathcal{E}_\pi(\rho)) + \sum_{\pi \in \Pi_2 \backslash \Pi_1} \mathrm{tr}(\eta(l_\pi)\mathcal{E}_\pi(\rho))\right] \tag{8.10}$$

$$= \left[1 - \mathrm{tr}\left(\mathcal{E}_{\Pi_1}(\rho)\right) + \sum_{\pi \in \Pi_1} \mathrm{tr}\left(\eta(l_\pi)\mathcal{E}_\pi(\rho)\right) \right] + \sum_{\pi \in \Pi_2 \setminus \Pi_1} \mathrm{tr}\left((\eta(l_\pi) - I)\mathcal{E}_\pi(\rho)\right)$$

$$\leq 1 - \mathrm{tr}\left(\mathcal{E}_{\Pi_1}(\rho)\right) + \sum_{\pi \in \Pi_1} \mathrm{tr}\left(\eta(l_\pi)\mathcal{E}_\pi(\rho)\right)$$

because $\eta(l_\pi)$ is a quantum predicate and thus $\eta(l_\pi) \sqsubseteq I$.

Now we are going to prove the following claim, which is stronger than Eq. (8.5): for any prime set Π of paths from l_0 to some cut-points (not necessarily a single cut-point),

$$\mathrm{tr}(\Theta\rho) \leq 1 - \mathrm{tr}\left(\mathcal{E}_\Pi(\rho)\right) + \sum_{\pi \in \Pi} \mathrm{tr}\left(\eta(l_\pi)\mathcal{E}_\pi(\rho)\right) \tag{8.11}$$

where ρ is an arbitrary density operator. Let us consider the following two cases:

Case 1: Π is finite. For any path π, its height $h(\pi)$ is defined to be the number of times that π passes through a cut-point. We further define the height of Π as $h(\Pi) = \max_{\pi \in \Pi} h(\pi)$. Then we can prove Eq. (8.11) by induction on $h(\Pi)$. For the case of $h(\Pi) = 1$, we have $\Pi \subseteq \Omega_{l_0}$, and it follows immediately from Eqs (8.8) and (8.10) that

$$\mathrm{tr}(\Theta\rho) \leq 1 - \mathrm{tr}\left(\mathcal{E}_{\Omega_{l_0}}(\rho)\right) + \sum_{\pi \in \Omega_{l_0}} \mathrm{tr}\left(\eta(l_\pi)\mathcal{E}_\pi(\rho)\right)$$

$$\leq 1 - \mathrm{tr}\left(\mathcal{E}_\Pi(\rho)\right) + \sum_{\pi \in \Pi} \mathrm{tr}\left(\eta(l_\pi)\mathcal{E}_\pi(\rho)\right).$$

In general, assume that $h(\Pi) = n \geq 2$. We can partition:

$$\Pi = \Delta \cup \left(\bigcup_j \Gamma_j \right)$$

such that

1. $h(\Delta) \leq n - 1$; and
2. for each j, there exists a path π_j such that $h(\pi_j) = n - 1$ and every path π in Γ_j can be written as $\pi = \pi_j \xrightarrow{\mathcal{E}_1} l_1 ... \xrightarrow{\mathcal{E}_k} l_k \xrightarrow{\mathcal{E}_{k+1}} l_{k+1}$ with $l_1, ..., l_k \notin C$ and $l_{k+1} \in C$. We write $tail(\pi) = l_{\pi_j} \xrightarrow{\mathcal{E}_1} l_1 ... \xrightarrow{\mathcal{E}_k} l_k \xrightarrow{\mathcal{E}_{k+1}} l_{k+1}$.

We notice that by linearity, Eq. (8.9) can be slightly generalised as follows: for any partial density operator ρ,

$$\mathrm{tr}(\eta(l)\rho) \leq \mathrm{tr}(\rho) - \mathrm{tr}\left(\mathcal{E}_{\Omega_l}(\rho)\right) + \sum_{\pi \in \Omega_l} \mathrm{tr}\left(\eta(l_\pi)\mathcal{E}_\pi(\rho)\right). \tag{8.12}$$

Thus, using Eq. (8.12) for $l = l_{\pi_j}$ and $\rho = \mathcal{E}_{\pi_j}(\rho)$ yields:

$$\mathrm{tr}\left(\mathcal{E}_{\Gamma_j}(\rho)\right) - \sum_{\pi \in \Gamma_j} \mathrm{tr}\left(\eta(l_\pi)\mathcal{E}_\pi(\rho)\right)$$

$$= \sum_{\pi \in \Gamma_j} \mathrm{tr}\left(\mathcal{E}_{tail(\pi)}\left(\mathcal{E}_{\pi_j}(\rho)\right)\right) - \sum_{\pi \in \Gamma_j} \mathrm{tr}\left(\eta(l_\pi)\mathcal{E}_{tail(\pi)}\left(\mathcal{E}_{\pi_j}(\rho)\right)\right)$$

$$\leq \sum_{\pi' \in \Omega_{l_{\pi_j}}} \mathrm{tr}\left(\mathcal{E}_{\pi'}\left(\mathcal{E}_{\pi_j}(\rho)\right)\right) - \sum_{\pi \in \Omega_{l_{\pi_j}}} \mathrm{tr}\left(\eta(l_{\pi'})\mathcal{E}_{\pi'}\left(\mathcal{E}_{\pi_j}(\rho)\right)\right) \tag{8.13}$$

$$\leq \mathrm{tr}\left(\mathcal{E}_{\pi_j}(\rho)\right) - \mathrm{tr}\left(\eta(l_{\pi_j})\mathcal{E}_{\pi_j}(\rho)\right).$$

Here, the first inequality comes from Eq. (8.10). Note that each $\pi_j \notin \Delta$ because Π is prime. Furthermore, we see that $\Pi' = \Delta \cup \{\text{all } \pi_j\}$ is prime, and $h(\Pi') = n - 1$. Then applying the induction hypothesis to Π', we obtain:

$$\mathrm{tr}(\Theta\rho) \leq 1 - \mathrm{tr}\left(\mathcal{E}_{\Pi'}(\rho)\right) + \sum_{\pi \in \Pi'} \mathrm{tr}\left(\eta(l_\pi)\mathcal{E}_\pi(\rho)\right)$$

$$
= 1 - \left[\mathrm{tr}\left(\mathcal{E}_\Delta(\rho)\right) + \sum_j \mathrm{tr}\left(\mathcal{E}_{\pi_j}(\rho)\right) \right]
$$

$$
+ \left[\sum_{\pi \in \Delta} \mathrm{tr}\left(\eta(l_\pi)\mathcal{E}_\pi(\rho)\right) + \sum_j \mathrm{tr}\left(\eta(l_{\pi_j})\mathcal{E}_{\pi_j}(\rho)\right) \right]
$$

$$
= \left[1 - \mathrm{tr}\left(\mathcal{E}_\Delta(\rho)\right) + \sum_{\pi \in \Delta} \mathrm{tr}\left(\eta(l_\pi)\mathcal{E}_\pi(\rho)\right) \right]
$$

$$
- \sum_j \left[\mathrm{tr}\left(\mathcal{E}_{\pi_j}(\rho)\right) - \mathrm{tr}\left(\eta(l_{\pi_j})\mathcal{E}_{\pi_j}(\rho)\right) \right]
$$

$$
\leq \left[1 - \mathrm{tr}\left(\mathcal{E}_\Delta(\rho)\right) + \sum_{\pi \in \Delta} \mathrm{tr}\left(\eta(l_\pi)\mathcal{E}_\pi(\rho)\right) \right]
$$

$$
- \sum_j \left[\mathrm{tr}\left(\mathcal{E}_{\Gamma_j}(\rho)\right) - \sum_{\pi \in \Gamma_j} \mathrm{tr}\left(\eta(l_\pi)\mathcal{E}_\pi(\rho)\right) \right]
$$

$$
= 1 - \left[\mathrm{tr}\left(\mathcal{E}_\Delta(\rho)\right) + \sum_j \mathrm{tr}\left(\mathcal{E}_{\Gamma_j}(\rho)\right) \right]
$$

$$
+ \left[\sum_{\pi \in \Delta} \mathrm{tr}\left(\eta(l_\pi)\mathcal{E}_\pi(\rho)\right) + \sum_j \sum_{\pi \in \Gamma_j} \mathrm{tr}\left(\eta(l_\pi)\mathcal{E}_\pi(\rho)\right) \right]
$$

$$
\leq 1 - \mathrm{tr}\left(\mathcal{E}_\Pi(\rho)\right) + \sum_{\pi \in \Pi} \mathrm{tr}\left(\eta(l_\pi)\mathcal{E}_\pi(\rho)\right).
$$

Here, the second inequality follows from Eq. (8.13). Thus, we complete the proof for finite Π.

Case 2: Π is infinite. It is clear that Π is countably infinite. So, there exists an infinite sequence $\Pi_1 \subseteq ... \subseteq \Pi_m \subseteq \Pi_{m+1} \subseteq ...$ such that Π_m is finite for all m, and $\Pi = \bigcup_m \Pi_m$. Thus, with the conclusion for Case 1, we have:

$$
\mathrm{tr}(\Theta\rho) \leq x_m \overset{\triangle}{=} 1 - \mathrm{tr}\left(\mathcal{E}_{\Pi_m}(\rho)\right) + \sum_{\pi \in \Pi_m} \mathrm{tr}\left(\eta(l_\pi)\mathcal{E}_\pi(\rho)\right).
$$

On the other hand, it follows from Eq. (8.10) that $\{x_m\}$ is a decreasing sequence. Therefore,

$$
\mathrm{tr}(\Theta\rho) \leq \lim_{m \to \infty} x_m = 1 - \mathrm{tr}\left(\mathcal{E}_\Pi(\rho)\right) + \sum_{\pi \in \Pi} \mathrm{tr}\left(\eta(l_\pi)\mathcal{E}_\pi(\rho)\right). \qquad \square
$$

8.2.4 Generation of inductive invariants

In the previous subsections, we defined the notion of invariant for quantum programs and showed how to use invariants in establishing the correctness of quantum programs. In this subsection, we further study the problem of automatically generating invariants for quantum programs.

Invariant generation for classical programs: For a better understanding of the problem of invariant generation, let us start from the case of classical programs. Discovering invariants is crucial for analysis and verification of programs, but it is a highly nontrivial task [243]. In the literature, there are mainly two approaches to invariant generation for classical programs:

- *Abstract interpretation*: This technique generates an invariant through an approximate symbolic execution of the program until an assertion is reached that remains unchanged by further execution [110,111].
- *Constraint solving*: As its name suggests, the constraint-based technique of Colón et al. [102,362] reduces invariant generation to a constraint solving problem by encoding the defining conditions of inductive assertions as constraints. Recently, the constraint-based technique was generalised by Katoen et al. [242] for generating invariants of probabilistic programs.

Several *automatic tools* for invariant generation have been developed; for example, the Stanford Invariant Generator StInG [381] implements both the abstract interpretation and constraint-based techniques; and InvGen [194] can more efficiently generate linear arithmetic invariants using the constraint-based technique.

The idea of abstract interpretation has been generalised to quantum programs in [335,443]. In Section 8.5, we will consider how abstract interpretation can be applied in quantum program analysis. But this technique has not been used in quantum invariant generation up to now.

Generating quantum invariants: In this subsection, we extend the constraint-based approach to the case of quantum programs. The problem of generating inductive assertions can be precisely stated as the following:

Problem 8.1 (Generation of inductive invariants). Given an SVTS $\mathcal{S} = \langle \mathcal{H}, L, l_0, \mathcal{T}, \Theta \rangle$ and a cut-set $C \subseteq L$. For each cut-point $l \in C$, find a quantum predicate $\eta(l)$ such that $\eta : l \mapsto \eta(l)$ is an inductive map.

The basic idea for solving this problem is to reduce the above invariant generation problem into an SDP (Semi-Definite Programming) problem by encoding the initiation and consecution conditions in Definition 8.4 for all cut-points $l \in C$ as constraints.

Formally, assume that $C = \{l_0, l_1, ..., l_m\}$. We write $O_i = \eta(l_i)$ for $i = 0, 1, ..., m$. Moreover, we write:

$$\mathcal{E}_{ij}^* = \sum \left\{ |\mathcal{E}_\pi^* : l_i \overset{\text{basic path } \pi}{\Rightarrow} l_j| \right\}$$

for $i, j = 0, 1, ..., m$; in particular, if there is no basic path from l_i to l_j, then $\mathcal{E}_{ij}^*$ is the zero superoperator. Then we have:

Theorem 8.3. *Problem 8.1 is equivalent to find complex matrices $O_0, O_1, ..., O_m$ satisfying the following constraints:*

$$0 \sqsubseteq \sum_j \mathcal{E}_{0j}^*(O_j) - \Theta, \tag{8.14}$$

$$0 \sqsubseteq \sum_{j \neq i} \mathcal{E}_{ij}^*(O_j) + (\mathcal{E}_{ii}^* - \mathcal{I})(O_i) \quad (i = 0, 1, ..., m), \tag{8.15}$$

$$0 \sqsubseteq O_i \sqsubseteq I \quad (i = 0, 1, ..., m), \tag{8.16}$$

Proof. We prove this theorem by three steps of reduction.

Step 1: We first notice that an assertion map η for an SVTS with cut-set C is inductive if and only if it is a solution to the following system of constraints:

$$0 \sqsubseteq I + \sum_{\pi \in \Omega_{l_0}} \mathcal{E}_\pi^* (\eta(l_\pi) - I) - \Theta, \tag{8.17}$$

$$0 \sqsubseteq I + \sum_{\pi \in \Omega_l} \mathcal{E}_\pi^* (\eta(l_\pi) - I) - \eta(l) \quad \text{for every } l \in C, \tag{8.18}$$

$$0 \sqsubseteq \eta(l) \sqsubseteq I \quad \text{for every } l \in C. \tag{8.19}$$

To show this, we observe that $\text{tr}(B\mathcal{E}(\rho)) = \text{tr}(\mathcal{E}^*(B)\rho)$ for all B and ρ. Indeed, if $\mathcal{E}$ has Kraus representation $\mathcal{E}(\rho) = \sum_i E_i \rho E_i^\dagger$, then we have:

$$\text{tr}(B\mathcal{E}(\rho)) = \text{tr}\left(B \left(\sum_i E_i \rho E_i^\dagger \right) \right) = \sum_i \text{tr}\left(B E_i \rho E_i^\dagger \right)$$

$$= \sum_i \text{tr}\left(E_i^\dagger B E_i \rho \right) = \text{tr}\left(\left(\sum_i E_i^\dagger B E_i \right) \rho \right) = \text{tr}(\mathcal{E}^*(B)\rho).$$

Therefore, it holds that

$$1 - \text{tr}\left(\mathcal{E}_{\Omega_l}(\rho) \right) + \sum_{\pi \in \Omega_l} \text{tr}\left(\eta(l_\pi)\mathcal{E}_\pi(\rho) \right) - \text{tr}(\eta(l)\rho)$$

$$= \operatorname{tr}(\rho) - \sum_{\pi \in \Omega_l} \operatorname{tr}(\mathcal{E}_\pi(\rho)) + \sum_{\pi \in \Omega_l} \operatorname{tr}(\eta(l_\pi)\mathcal{E}_\pi(\rho)) - \operatorname{tr}(\eta(l)\rho)$$

$$= \operatorname{tr}(\rho) + \sum_{\pi \in \Omega_l} \operatorname{tr}[(\eta(l_\pi) - I)\mathcal{E}_\pi(\rho)] - \operatorname{tr}(\eta(l)\rho)$$

$$= \operatorname{tr}(\rho) + \sum_{\pi \in \Omega_l} \operatorname{tr}[\mathcal{E}_\pi^*((\eta(l_\pi) - I))\rho] - \operatorname{tr}(\eta(l)\rho)$$

$$= \operatorname{tr}\left(\left[I + \sum_{\pi \in \Omega_l} \mathcal{E}_\pi^*(\eta(l_\pi) - I) - \eta(l)\right]\rho\right).$$

Consequently, inequality (8.9) is true for all density operators ρ if and only if (8.18) is valid. Similarly, we can prove that (8.17) is equivalent to that inequality (8.8) is true for all ρ. Finally, we notice that constraint (8.19) comes from the fact that $\eta(l)$ is a quantum predicate.

Step 2: Obviously, inequality (8.16) is equivalent to (8.19). If $l = l_i$, then by the definitions of O_j and $\mathcal{E}_{ij}^*$, we obtain:

$$\sum_{\pi \in \Omega_l} \mathcal{E}_\pi^*(\eta(l_\pi)) = \sum_j \mathcal{E}_{ij}^*(O_j),$$

$$\sum_{\pi \in \Omega_l} \mathcal{E}_\pi^*(I)) = \sum_j \mathcal{E}_{ij}^*(I).$$

Thus, we have:

$$0 \sqsubseteq \sum_j \mathcal{E}_{0j}^*(O_j) + A, \tag{8.20}$$

$$0 \sqsubseteq \sum_{j \neq i} \mathcal{E}_{ij}^*(O_j) + (\mathcal{E}_{ii}^* - \mathcal{I})(O_i) + A_i \quad (i = 0, 1, ..., m), \tag{8.21}$$

$$0 \sqsubseteq O_i \sqsubseteq I \quad (i = 0, 1, ..., m), \tag{8.22}$$

where:

$$\begin{cases} A = I - \sum_j \mathcal{E}_{0j}^*(I) - \Theta, \\ A_i = I - \sum_j \mathcal{E}_{ij}^*(I) \quad (i = 0, 1, ..., m). \end{cases} \tag{8.23}$$

Step 3: Now it suffices to show that $A = -\Theta$ and $A_i = 0$ for all i. Let Ω_i be the set of all basic paths starting from l_i. Since there is no basic path which is a prefix of another basic path, every basic path can only occur at most once in computing $\operatorname{tr}(\mathcal{E}_{\Omega_i}(\rho))$. Thus, we have $\operatorname{tr}(\mathcal{E}_{\Omega_i}(\rho)) \leq 1$ for all ρ. Actually, we assert that $\operatorname{tr}(\mathcal{E}_{\Omega_i}(\rho)) = 1$ for all density operators ρ. Otherwise, there exist a density operator σ and a (finite) path π starting form l_i such that

1. π is not a prefix of any basic path in Ω_i;
2. any basic path in Ω_i is not a prefix of π; and
3. $\operatorname{tr}(\mathcal{E}_\pi(\rho)) > 0$.

By the above fact 2, we see that there is no cut-point in π except the initial location. Suppose $\bar{\pi}$ is an infinite path with π as a prefix. By the definition of cut-set, $\bar{\pi}$ must pass cut-points infinitely many times; otherwise there must be a loop in $\bar{\pi}$ which does not pass any cut-point. This implies that π is a prefix of some basic path in Ω_i, a contradiction.

Furthermore, for all density operator ρ, it follows from $\operatorname{tr}(\mathcal{E}_{\Omega_i}(\rho)) = 1$ that

$$\sum_j \operatorname{tr}(\mathcal{E}_{ij}(\rho)) = \operatorname{tr}(\mathcal{E}_{\Omega_i}(\rho)) = 1.$$

Therefore, $\mathcal{E}_i = \sum_j \mathcal{E}_{ij}$ is trace-preserving. This implies that $\mathcal{E}_i^* = \sum_j \mathcal{E}_{ij}^*$ is unital, i.e. $\sum_j \mathcal{E}_{ij}^*(I) = I$ for every i. Consequently, we have $A = -\Theta$ and $A_i = 0$ for every i. $\qquad\square$

It is interesting to compare the constraint problem for generating invariants of quantum programs with that for classical programs. The constraint problems for generating linear and nonlinear invariants of classical programs were derived and solved in [102,362] using different techniques – Farkas's Lemma and Gröbner bases, respectively. However, stipulated by the basic postulates of quantum mechanics, all operations as well as observables involved in a quantum program must be a linear operator. The solutions to the constraint problem for classical programs are coefficients in a template of invariants, which are real numbers. But invariant generation of quantum programs is reduced to a constraint problem over linear operators on a Hilbert space, which are complex matrices when the state Hilbert space is finite-dimensional.

8.2.5 An illustrative example

In this subsection, we present an example in which the technique developed in the last subsection is employed for generating invariants of a quantum walk.

Two technical lemmas: First, we need to tailor the general results presented in the previous subsections in order to suit the problem in our example.

The quantum variables in many quantum algorithms are initialised in a special pure state $|\psi\rangle$; that is, $\rho_0 = |\psi\rangle\langle\psi|$. In this case, the initial condition can be chosen as $\Theta = |\psi\rangle\langle\psi|$ (the projection onto the one-dimensional subspace spanned by $|\psi\rangle$), and the following lemma is very useful in helping us to understand physical meaning of the generated invariants.

Lemma 8.1. *Assume that the initial state ρ_0 is a pure state, i.e. $\mathrm{tr}(\rho_0^2) = 1$, and the initial condition $\Theta = \rho_0$. If the program reaches cut-point l_i and the current state is ρ, then $\mathrm{tr}(O_i\rho) = \mathrm{tr}(\rho) = 1$.*

Proof. For the initial density operator ρ_0, any density operator ρ and $i \in \{1, ..., m\}$, from inequalities (8.8) and (8.9) we obtain:

$$\mathrm{tr}(\Theta\rho_0) \leq 1 - \mathrm{tr}\left(\sum_j \mathcal{E}_{0j}(\rho_0)\right) + \mathrm{tr}\left(\sum_j O_j\mathcal{E}_{0j}(\rho_0)\right),$$

$$\mathrm{tr}(O_i\rho) \leq 1 - \mathrm{tr}\left(\sum_j \mathcal{E}_{ij}(\rho)\right) + \mathrm{tr}\left(\sum_j O_j\mathcal{E}_{ij}(\rho)\right).$$

As shown in the proof of Theorem 8.3, $\mathrm{tr}\left(\sum_j \mathcal{E}_{ij}(\rho)\right) = 1$ for any density operator ρ. Moreover, since $\mathrm{tr}(\rho_0) = \mathrm{tr}(\rho) = 1$ and $0 \sqsubseteq O_i \sqsubseteq I$, we can derive:

$$1 \leq \mathrm{tr}\left(\sum_j O_j\mathcal{E}_{0j}(\rho_0)\right) \leq \mathrm{tr}\left(\sum_j \mathcal{E}_{0j}(\rho_0)\right) = 1,$$

$$\mathrm{tr}(O_i\rho) \leq \mathrm{tr}\left(\sum_j O_j\mathcal{E}_{ij}(\rho)\right).$$

Then, by induction, it is easy to prove that, at any time, if the system is at cut point l_i, then the current quantum state ρ satisfies $\mathrm{tr}(O_i\rho) = \mathrm{tr}(\rho) = 1$. □

In order to use an SDP solver (e.g. the CVX package of MATLAB® [185]) in quantum invariant generation, we employ a single matrix $O = \mathrm{diag}\{O_0, O_1, \cdots, O_m\}$ to represent the observables (Hermitian operators) $O_0, O_1, \cdots, O_m$ at the cut-points. Obviously, O is an $N \times N$ matrix with $N = m \times \dim\mathcal{H}$. Note that each O_i can be rewritten in terms of O; for instance, O_0 can be written as $zOz^\dagger$ where $z = [I, 0, 0, \cdots]$ is a $\dim\mathcal{H} \times N$ matrix. Then inequalities (8.14) to (8.16) can be accordingly transferred to inequalities about O.

To solve our problems using the SDP solver, we have to set a optimisation target. Let $O' = \mathrm{diag}\{O'_0, O'_1, \cdots, O'_m\}$. We write $O \sqsubseteq O'$ if $O_i \sqsubseteq O'_i$ for every $i = 0, 1, ..., m$. Note that $O_i \sqsubseteq O'_i$ means that O_i is a quantum predicate stronger than O'_i. So, what we like to do is to find the smallest O_i ($i = 0, 1, ...m$) with respect to the Löwner order $\sqsubseteq$ that satisfying (8.14) to (8.16). The following lemma shows that it only requires us to choose minimising $\mathrm{tr}(O)$ as our optimisation target.

Lemma 8.2. *Suppose that $O_{\min} = \mathrm{diag}\{O_{\min,0}, O_{\min,1}, \cdots, O_{\min,m}\}$ is the solution of constraints (8.14) to (8.16) with $[\min\mathrm{tr}(O)]$ as the objective function. Then $O_{\min} \sqsubseteq O$ for any solution $O = \mathrm{diag}\{O_0, O_1, \cdots, O_m\}$ of constraints (8.14) to (8.16).*

Proof. For each i, we write $\mathcal{H}_i$ for the subspace spanned by all possible states ρ at cut-point l_i. Moreover, let $P_{\mathcal{H}_i}$ be the projection onto $\mathcal{H}_i$. We first prove that $O_{\min,i} = P_{\mathcal{H}_i}$. By Lemma 8.1, we see that whenever the current location is cut-point l_i and the current state is ρ, then $\mathrm{tr}\left(\rho O_{\min,i}\right) = \mathrm{tr}(\rho)$. This means that $\mathrm{supp}(\rho) \subseteq \mathrm{supp}\left(O_{\min,i}\right)$. Therefore, we have $\mathcal{H}_i \subseteq \mathrm{supp}\left(O_{\min,i}\right)$, or equivalently

$$P_{\mathcal{H}_i} \sqsubseteq O_{\min,i}. \tag{8.24}$$

On the other hand, let $O_P = \mathrm{diag}\{P_{\mathcal{H}_1}, \cdots, P_{\mathcal{H}_l}\}$. Then by the definition of $P_{\mathcal{H}_i}$, we have $\mathrm{tr}\left(\rho P_{\mathcal{H}_i}\right) = \mathrm{tr}\left(\rho O_{\min,i}\right)$ for any possible state ρ at cut point l_i. Therefore, O_P is also a solution of constraints (8.14) to (8.16). Obviously, $\mathrm{tr}(O_P) \leq \mathrm{tr}(O_{\min})$, and thus $O_{\min} = O_P$. In a way similar to the proof of Eq. (8.24), we can show that $P_{\mathcal{H}_i} \sqsubseteq O_i$. Then we complete the proof by combining it with $O_{\min,i} = P_{\mathcal{H}_i}$. $\qquad\qquad\square$

Generating invariants for a quantum walk: Now we are ready to generate invariants of the quantum walk described in Example 8.1. We choose cut-set $C = \{l_0, l_3\}$ with $l_3 = l_{out}$. Then the problem is to find operators O_0 and O_3 satisfying the following constraints:

$$0 \sqsubseteq \mathcal{E}_{00}^*(O_0) + \mathcal{E}_{03}^*(O_3) - \Theta, \tag{8.25}$$

$$0 \sqsubseteq (\mathcal{E}_{00}^* - \mathcal{I})(O_0) + \mathcal{E}_{03}^*(O_3), \tag{8.26}$$

$$0 \sqsubseteq (\mathcal{E}_{33}^* - \mathcal{I})(O_3), \tag{8.27}$$

$$0 \sqsubseteq O_0, O_3 \sqsubseteq I \tag{8.28}$$

where $\mathcal{E}_{00} = E_{00} \circ E_{00}^\dagger$, $\mathcal{E}_{03} = E_{03} \circ E_{03}^\dagger$, $\mathcal{E}_{33} = \mathcal{I}$, $E_{00} = S(H \otimes I_p)(I_c \otimes M_{no})$, $E_{03} = I_c \otimes M_{yes}$, and I_c, I_p are the identity operators on the coin space $\mathcal{H}_c$ and position space $\mathcal{H}_p$, respectively.

The solution of the SDP problem with constraints (8.25) to (8.28) is as follows:

$$O_0 = |R\rangle\langle R| \otimes |0\rangle\langle 0| + |R\rangle\langle R| \otimes |1\rangle\langle 1| + |\phi\rangle\langle\phi|$$
$$+ \sum_{i=2}^{n-1} |L\rangle\langle L| \otimes |i\rangle\langle i| + \sum_{i=4}^{n-1} |R\rangle\langle R| \otimes |i\rangle\langle i|,$$
$$O_3 = I_c \otimes |1\rangle\langle 1|,$$

where:

$$|\phi\rangle = \frac{1}{\sqrt{2}}(|L\rangle\langle L| \otimes |1\rangle\langle 1| + |R\rangle\langle R| \otimes |3\rangle\langle 3|).$$

With Lemma 8.1, we see that the final state ρ_{out} satisfy $\mathrm{tr}(O_3 \rho_{out}) = 1$. This means that if the quantum walk always terminates, the final position is $|1\rangle$. Thus, we proved the partial correctness of this program.

8.3 Termination analysis – ranking functions

We now turn to consider the second issue of quantum program analysis, namely termination analysis. This issue was already touched in Section 6.5 for proving total correctness of quantum programs using quantum Hoare logic. In this and next sections, we deal with this issue in a broader way.

As usual, let us first recall how this issue was handled in classical programming. There have been mainly two approaches to termination analysis of classical programs:

- *Synthesis of ranking functions*: The idea of using ranking function in proving termination of classical programs can also be traced back to Floyd's seminal paper [158]. Recently, this idea has been generalised to probabilistic programs. Constraint-based techniques are widely used for synthesis of ranking functions. The basic idea is to use a template of ranking functions that is constrained by the desired termination properties and then to find a solution to the constraint system [103].
- *Reachability analysis*: The basic idea of this approach is that the termination condition essentially denotes a subset of the program's state space. If the program's behaviour is modelled as a transition system, then termination problem is reduced to the problem of reaching the termination subset, and can be solved using graph-theoretic techniques.

Both of the above two approaches have been extended to cope with quantum programs. In this section, we introduce the ranking function approach to termination analysis of quantum programs, and the reachability analysis will be discussed in the next section.

8.3.1 Termination problems

As a starting point, let us precisely define the termination problems for quantum programs in this subsection.

The ranking function approach works for an extension of the quantum **while**-language defined in Chapter 5. This extension includes nondeterministic quantum programs defined as angelic and demonic choices. Formally, it is obtained by adding the following clause into the syntax of quantum **while**-language given in Definition 5.1:

$$P ::= P_1 \sqcup P_2 \mid P_1 \sqcap P_2.$$

Intuitively, angelic choice (respectively, demonic choice) is the execution of a nondeterministic program that always favours a desired (respectively, undesired) result (if possible). In classical computer science, these two program constructs have been extensively applied in formulation of refinement-based development of software [37,311]. We expect that quantum generalisations of them can be used in developing refinement techniques for quantum software.

Nondeterministic quantum programs as games: Let $S = \langle \mathcal{H}, L, l_0, \mathcal{T} \rangle$ be a superoperator-valued transition system (SVTS for short). Here, we do not assume a quantum predicate Θ as the initial condition as in Definition 8.1. Instead, we assume a density operator $\rho_0 \in \mathcal{D}(\mathcal{H})$ as the initial state. To model the behaviours of angelic and demonic choices, locations L are divided into angelic locations L_A, demonic locations L_S, and standard locations L_S; that is, $L = L_A \cup L_D \cup L_S$. Since both angelic and demonic choices only select one from a set of operations but do not perform any new operation, it is reasonable to require:

- for each $l \in L_A \cup L_D$, if $l \xrightarrow{\mathcal{E}} l'$, then $\mathcal{E} = \mathcal{I}$ (the identity superoperator on $\mathcal{H}$).

A configuration of S is defined as a pair (l, ρ), where $l \in L$ is a location and $\rho \in \mathcal{D}(\mathcal{H})$ is a density operator denoting a quantum state in $\mathcal{H}$. In particular, (l_0, ρ_0) is called the initial configuration. We further introduce:

Definition 8.5 (Runs). A run of SVTS S is a finite or an infinite sequence of configurations

$$\theta = (l_0, \rho_0), (l_1, \rho_1), (l_2, \rho_2), \dots$$

(starting from the initial configuration) such that for each $i \geq 0$, we have a transition $l_i \xrightarrow{\mathcal{E}_i} l_{i+1}$ in S with $\rho_{i+1} = \mathcal{E}_i(\rho_i)$.

The SVTS S can be viewed as a game played between two players, angel and demon, according to their respective schedulers.

Definition 8.6 (Schedulers). **1.** An angelic (resp. a demonic) scheduler is a function that assigns to every finite run ending in a configuration with an angelic (resp. a demonic) location l a transition outgoing from l.
2. Let σ, τ be an angelic scheduler and a demonic scheduler, respectively. We say that a run θ satisfies σ and τ if the transitions in θ outgoing from all angelic locations are chosen according to σ, and those outgoing from all demonic locations are chosen according to τ.

SVTS's were employed in Section 8.1.2 to represent control flows of quantum **while**-programs. The idea used there can be generalised to model nondeterministic quantum programs by adding the following two cases:

- **Case 1**: $P \equiv P_1 \sqcup P_2$. The SVTS S_P for P is constructed from the respective SVTS's S_{P_1} and S_{P_2} for subprograms P_1 and P_2 as follows: we add a new angelic location l_{in}^P and a transition $l_{in}^P \xrightarrow{I} l_{in}^{P_i}$ ($i = 1, 2$), and identify $l_{out}^P = l_{out}^{P_1} = l_{out}^{P_2}$.
- **Case 2**: $P \equiv P_1 \sqcap P_2$. The same as the above item, but with l_{in}^P being demonic.

Note that angelic locations (respectively, demonic locations) in S_P are introduced only by angelic choices (respectively, demonic choices) occurring in P, and locations introduced by other program constructs are all standard locations.

Now we can formally define the termination problems for a (nondeterministic) quantum program P based on its SVTS representation S_P.

Definition 8.7. 1. A terminating run of S_P is a finite run ending at location l_{out}^P; that is, a run of the form

$$\theta = (l_{in}^P, \rho_0), (l_1, \rho_1), \dots, (l_{k-1}, \rho_{k-1}), (l_{out}^P, \rho_k)$$

with $l_1, ..., l_{k-1} \neq l_{out}^P$. The running time of θ is $T(\theta) = k$, and the probability associated to θ is $\Pr(\theta) = \text{tr}(\rho_k)$.

2. For an infinite run $\theta = (l_{in}^P, \rho_0)..., (l_k, \rho_k), ...$ of $\mathcal{S}_P$, its running time is $T(\theta) = \infty$, and the probability associated to it is:

$$\Pr(\theta) = \lim_{k \to \infty} \text{tr}(\rho_k).$$

Definition 8.8. Given an angelic scheduler σ, a demonic scheduler τ in $\mathcal{S}_P$ and a constant $x \geq 0$.

1. The termination probability of program P according to σ and τ, and the probability that the termination time of P according to σ and τ exceeds x are:

$$\Pr(P|\sigma, \tau) = \sum_{\theta} \Pr(\theta);$$

$$\Pr(P|\sigma, \tau; T > x) = \sum_{\theta \text{ s.t. } T(\theta) > x} \Pr(\theta),$$

respectively, where θ ranges over all terminating runs of $\mathcal{S}_P$ satisfying σ and τ.

2. The expected running time of program P according to σ and τ is:

$$ET(P|\sigma, \tau) = \sum_{\theta} \Pr(\theta) \cdot T(\theta),$$

where θ ranges over all runs of $\mathcal{S}_P$ satisfying σ and τ.

Definition 8.9 (Almost-sure termination, finite-termination). **1.** A program P is almost-surely terminating if there exists an angelic scheduler σ such that $\Pr(P|\sigma, \pi) = 1$ for all demonic schedulers τ.

2. A program P is finite-terminating if there exists an angelic scheduler σ such that $ET(P|\sigma, \tau) < \infty$ for all demonic schedulers τ.

Definition 8.10 (Expected running time). The expected running time of a program P is defined as:

$$ET(P) = \inf_{\sigma} \sup_{\tau} ET(P|\sigma, \tau)$$

where σ, τ ranges over all angelic and demonic schedulers of $\mathcal{S}_P$, respectively.

8.3.2 Ranking functions and termination theorems

In this subsection, we first introduce the notion of linear ranking functions for (nondeterministic) quantum programs. Then we show that existence of ranking function of a quantum program with a supporting invariant guarantees its finite termination.

Let P be a (nondeterministic) quantum program and $\mathcal{S}_P$ an SVTS representation of P. Recall from Section 8.2.1 that a set Π of paths in $\mathcal{S}_P$ is said to be prime if for each

$$\pi = l_1 \xrightarrow{\mathcal{E}_1} ... \xrightarrow{\mathcal{E}_{n-1}} l_n \in \Pi,$$

its proper initial segments $l_1 \xrightarrow{\mathcal{E}_1} ... \xrightarrow{\mathcal{E}_{k-1}} l_k \notin \Pi$ for all $k < n$. Then a set $\mathcal{O} = \{O_l\}_{l \in L}$ of quantum predicates in $\mathcal{H}_P$ is termed an invariant of program P if for every $l \in L$, for any input density operator ρ, and for any prime set Π of paths from l_0 to l, we have:

$$\text{tr}(O_{l_0}\rho) \leq 1 - \text{tr}(\mathcal{E}_\Pi(\rho)) + \text{tr}(O_l \mathcal{E}_\Pi(\rho)) \tag{8.29}$$

where $\mathcal{E}_\Pi = \sum \{|\mathcal{E}_\pi : \pi \in \Pi|\}$. The notion of ranking function will be defined with respect to a given invariant. Moreover, the following auxiliary notion of preexpectation is needed in defining ranking functions for quantum programs.

Definition 8.11 (Preexpectation). Let $\eta : L \times \mathcal{D}(\mathcal{H}_P) \to \mathbb{R}$ be a function. Then the preexpectation induced by η in game $\mathcal{G}_P$ is the function $pre_\eta : L \times \mathcal{D}(\mathcal{H}_P) \to \mathbb{R}$ defined as follows:

$$
pre_\eta(l, \rho) = \begin{cases} \min\{\eta(l', \rho) | l \xrightarrow{\mathcal{I}} l'\} & \text{if } l \in L_A; \\ \max\{\eta(l', \rho) | l \xrightarrow{\mathcal{I}} l'\} & \text{if } l \in L_D; \\ \sum\{\eta(l', \mathcal{E}(\rho)) | l \xrightarrow{\mathcal{E}} l'\} & \text{if } l \in L_S. \end{cases}
$$

With the above preparation, we are able to introduce the following:

Definition 8.12 (Ranking functions). Let $\epsilon, K \in \mathbb{R}$ be two constants with $\epsilon > 0$. A function $\eta : L \times \mathcal{D}(\mathcal{H}_P) \to \mathbb{R}$ is called a (K, ϵ)-ranking function for program P with respect to an invariant $\mathcal{O} = \{O_l\}_{l \in L}$ if:

1. for each $l \in L$, function $\eta(l, \cdot) : \mathcal{D}(\mathcal{H}_P) \to \mathbb{R}$ is linear over partial density operators on $\mathcal{H}_P$;
2. for all $l \in L$ and density operators ρ, $tr(O_l\rho) + K - 1 \leq \eta(l, \rho)$;
3. for all $l \neq l_{out}^P$ and density operators ρ, $tr(O_l\rho) + pre_\eta(l, \rho) \leq \eta(l, \rho) + 1 - \epsilon$.

Next we are going to establish a termination theorem for quantum programs with ranking functions. To this end, let us first recall the following theorem from probability theory.

Theorem 8.4 (Foster's theorem [159]). *Given a Markov chain over a finite or countably infinite space S with matrix $(P_{st})_{s,t \in S}$ of transition probabilities. Then the Markov chain almost surely reaches a subset $X \subseteq S$ with finite expected time if and only if there exist constants $\epsilon > 0$ and $K \in \mathbb{R}$ and a function $V : S \to \mathbb{R}$ satisfying the following conditions:*

1. *for all $s \in S$, $V(s) \geq K$;*
2. *for all $s \notin X$, the mean drift*

$$
\Delta V(s) = \sum_{t \in S} P_{st} \cdot V(t) - V(s) \leq -\epsilon.
$$

Moreover, for a given initial state $s_0 \in S$, we have:

$$
\text{the expected running time } \leq \frac{V(s_0) - K}{\epsilon}.
$$

Based on the concept of ranking function defined above, we can establish a quantum generalisation of the Foster's theorem, which addresses the termination problem of quantum programs in a special case.

Theorem 8.5 (Quantum generalisation of Foster's theorem). *A quantum program without angelic or demonic choices is finite-terminating for every initial configuration if and only if it has a (K, ϵ)-function η with respect to some invariant, and some constants $\epsilon > 0$ and $K \in \mathbb{R}$.*

Proof. (Sketch) We omit the proof of the "if" part, since a more general form of it will be proved as the termination theorem in the remainder of this section.

To prove the "only if" part, we assume that the program is finite-terminating. Then we can use the assumed finite expected running time $ET(\cdot)$ to define a ranking function:

$$
\eta(l, \rho) := tr(\rho) \cdot ET\left(P\left(l, \frac{\rho}{tr(\rho)}\right)\right)
$$

where $P(l, \rho)$ is the quantum program obtained from P by replacing the initial configuration (l_{in}^P, ρ_0) by (l, ρ). According to the finite-termination of the program, η is well defined. Then following immediately from the definition of expected running time, it holds that

$$
\eta(l, \rho) \geq 0 = \eta(l_{out}, \rho)
$$

for all location l and all partial density operators ρ. The fact that $pre_\eta(l, \rho) \leq \eta(l, \rho) - 1$ for all density operators ρ can be easily derived from the definition of expected running time and Eq. (8.2). Furthermore, the absence of angelic or demonic choices in P implies the linearity of $\eta(l, \cdot)$. Thus, η is actually a $(0, 1)$-ranking function with respect to the identity invariant. $\qquad\square$

For the general case where angelic and demonic choices may occur, the expected running time $ET(P(l, \cdot))$ of a quantum program may not be linear for partial density operators and thus could not be a ranking function. However, whenever a ranking function exists, termination of the program is guaranteed.

Theorem 8.6 (Termination theorem). *Suppose that quantum program P has a (K, ϵ)-ranking function η with respect to an invariant $\mathcal{O} = \{O_l\}_{l \in L}$. Then P is finite-terminating with any initial state ρ_0 satisfying $tr(\rho_0 O_{l_0}) = 1$, and the expected running time:*

$$ET(P) \le \frac{\eta(l_{in}^P, \rho_0) - K}{\epsilon}.$$

Proof. Given a (K, ϵ)-ranking function η for P with respect to invariant $\mathcal{O} = \{O_l\}_{l \in L}$, we define an angelic scheduler σ as follows: for each finite run θ ending at configuration (l, ρ) with $l \in L_A$, $\sigma(\theta)$ is the transition $l \xrightarrow{\mathcal{I}} l'$ that minimises $\eta(l', \rho)$:

$$l' = \arg\min_{l'} \{\eta(l', \rho) : l \xrightarrow{\mathcal{I}} l'\}.$$

Note that the transition relation $\rightarrow$ is finitely branching at angelic (and demonic) locations because the syntax of programs only allows finite angelic (and demonic) choice. Thus, $\sigma(\theta)$ is well-defined.

Now by definition, it suffices to show that for any demonic scheduler τ, we have:

$$ET(P|\sigma, \tau) \le \frac{\eta(l_{in}^P, \rho_0) - K}{\epsilon}.$$

We note that under the schedulers σ and τ, a transition $(l, \rho) \xrightarrow{\mathcal{I}} (l', \rho)$ from a angelic or demonic location $l \in L_A \cup L_D$ always satisfies $\eta(l', \rho) \le pre_\eta(l, \rho)$. Now, consider the paths $\pi = l_1 \xrightarrow{\mathcal{E}_1} ... \xrightarrow{\mathcal{E}_{n-1}} l_n$ under σ and τ. We write $|\pi|$ for their length n and $L(\pi)$ for their last location l_n. Let

$$\Pi_T = \left\{l_1 \xrightarrow{\mathcal{E}_1} ... \xrightarrow{\mathcal{E}_{n-1}} l_n \mid l_1 = l_{in}^P, l_n = out^P\right\},$$

$$\Pi_{NT} = \left\{l_1 \xrightarrow{\mathcal{E}_1} ... \xrightarrow{\mathcal{E}_{n-1}} l_n \mid l_1 = l_{in}^P, l_n \ne l_{out}^P\right\}$$

be the sets of terminating and nonterminating paths from the initial location, respectively. Define $\Pi_{T,n} = \{\pi \in \Pi_T \mid |\pi| \le n\}$, $\Pi_{NT,n} = \{\pi \in \Pi_{NT} \mid |\pi| = n\}$, and $\Pi_n = \Pi_{T,n} \cup \Pi_{NT,n}$. It is easy to verify that

$$\text{tr}\left(\mathcal{E}_{\Pi_n}(\rho)\right) = \text{tr}\left(\mathcal{E}_{\Pi_{T,n}}(\rho)\right) + \text{tr}\left(\mathcal{E}_{\Pi_{NT,n}}(\rho)\right) = 1,$$

for any density operator ρ and any n. Then,

$$\sum_{\pi \in \Pi_n} \eta(L(\pi), \mathcal{E}_\pi(\rho_0)) - \sum_{\pi \in \Pi_{n+1}} \eta(L(\pi), \mathcal{E}_\pi(\rho_0))$$

$$= \sum_{\pi \in \Pi_{NT,n}} \left[\eta(L(\pi), \mathcal{E}_\pi(\rho_0)) - \sum\left\{\eta(l', (\mathcal{E} \circ \mathcal{E}_\pi)(\rho)) \mid L(\pi) \xrightarrow{\mathcal{E}} l'\right\}\right]$$

$$\ge \sum_{\pi \in \Pi_{NT,n}} \left[\eta(L(\pi), \mathcal{E}_\pi(\rho_0)) - pre_\eta(L(\pi), \mathcal{E}_\pi(\rho_0))\right]$$

$$\ge \sum_{\pi \in \Pi_{NT,n}} \left(\epsilon \text{tr}(\mathcal{E}_\pi(\rho_0)) + tr(O_{L(\pi)}\mathcal{E}_\pi(\rho_0)) - tr(\mathcal{E}_\pi(\rho_0))\right)$$

$$= \epsilon \text{tr}(\mathcal{E}_{\Pi_{NT,n}}(\rho_0)) - \text{tr}(\mathcal{E}_{\Pi_{NT,n}}(\rho_0)) + \sum_{\pi \in \Pi_{NT,n}} tr(O_{L(\pi)}\mathcal{E}_\pi(\rho_0))$$

$$= \epsilon \text{tr}(\mathcal{E}_{\Pi_{NT,n}}(\rho_0)).$$

Here the last equation is due to

$$\sum_{\pi \in \Pi_{NT,n}} tr(O_{L(\pi)}\mathcal{E}_\pi(\rho_0)) = tr(\mathcal{E}_{\Pi_{NT,n}}(\rho_0)),$$

which follows from the condition $\text{tr}(\rho_0 O_{l_0}) = 1$ and Eq. (8.29). In fact, let us divide the set $\Pi_{NT,n}$ according to the last location of the paths; that is, $\Pi_{NT,n} = \bigcup_{l \in L} \Pi_l$, where $\Pi_l = \{\pi \in \Pi_{NT,n} \mid L(\pi) = l\}$. It suffices to prove that $\text{tr}(O_l \mathcal{E}_{\Pi_l}(\rho_0)) = \text{tr}(\mathcal{E}_{\Pi_l}(\rho_0))$ for all $l \in L$ due to the linearity of $\text{tr}(\cdot)$. $\text{tr}(O_l \mathcal{E}_{\Pi_l}(\rho_0)) \le \text{tr}(\mathcal{E}_{\Pi_l}(\rho_0))$ is obvious since $O_l \sqsubseteq I$. Note that all the Π_l are prime sets as $\Pi_{NT,n}$ is prime, then from Eq. (8.29),

$$\text{tr}(O_l \mathcal{E}_{\Pi_l}(\rho_0)) \ge \text{tr}(O_{l_0}\rho_0) - 1 + \text{tr}(\mathcal{E}_{\Pi_l}(\rho_0)) = \text{tr}(\mathcal{E}_{\Pi_l}(\rho_0)).$$

For convenience, we write partial density operator $\rho_n := \mathcal{E}_{\Pi_{T,n}}(\rho)$. Then $\text{tr}(\mathcal{E}_{\Pi_{NT,n}}(\rho_0)) = 1 - \text{tr}\rho_n$. We have:

$$\epsilon \sum_{k=1}^{n}(1 - tr\rho_k) = \sum_{k=1}^{n} \epsilon \text{tr}(\mathcal{E}_{\Pi_{nter,k}}(\rho_0))$$

$$\le \sum_{k=1}^{n}\left(\sum_{\pi \in \Pi_k} \eta(L(\pi), \mathcal{E}_\pi(\rho_0)) - \sum_{\pi \in \Pi_{k+1}} \eta(L(\pi), \mathcal{E}_\pi(\rho_0))\right)$$

$$= \sum_{\pi \in \Pi_1} \eta(L(\pi), \mathcal{E}_\pi(\rho_0)) - \sum_{\pi \in \Pi_n} \eta(L(\pi), \mathcal{E}_\pi(\rho_0))$$

$$= \eta(l_0, \rho_0) - \sum_{\pi \in \Pi_n} \eta(L(\pi), \mathcal{E}_\pi(\rho_0)).$$

Combining it with the fact that

$$\sum_{\pi \in \Pi_n} \eta(L(\pi), \mathcal{E}_\pi(\rho_0)) \ge \sum_{\pi \in \Pi_n}\left(K\text{tr}(\mathcal{E}_\pi(\rho_0)) + \text{tr}(O_{L(\pi)}\mathcal{E}_\pi(\rho_0)) - \text{tr}(\mathcal{E}_\pi(\rho_0))\right)$$

$$= \sum_{\pi \in \Pi_n} K\text{tr}(\mathcal{E}_\pi(\rho_0)) = K\text{tr}\mathcal{E}_{\Pi_n}(\rho_0) = K,$$

we obtain:

$$\epsilon \sum_{k=1}^{n-1}(1 - \text{tr}\rho_k) \le \eta(l_0, \rho_0) - K. \tag{8.30}$$

Note that $\sum_{k=1}^{n-1}(1 - \text{tr}\rho_k)$ has an upper bound independent of n. Thus, $\lim_{n\to\infty} \text{tr}\rho_n = 1$, which means that P is almost-surely terminating. It further implies that $ET(P) = \sum_{n=1}^{\infty}(1 - \text{tr}\rho_n)$ converges. Therefore, P is finite-terminating, and from inequality (8.29), we have:

$$ET(P) \le \frac{\eta(l_{in}^P, \rho_0) - K}{\epsilon}. \qquad \square$$

8.3.3 Realisability and synthesis of ranking functions

Theorem 8.6 shows that existence of ranking functions for a quantum program guarantees finite-termination of the program. In this subsection, we further consider the problem of realisability and synthesis of ranking functions:

Problem 8.2 (Realisability and synthesis). Given a quantum program P and an invariant $\mathcal{O} = \{O_l\}_{l \in L}$ for P, does there exist a ranking function for P with respect to $\mathcal{O}$? If so, how to construct it?

Templates and Gleason's theorem: The first step of the constraint-based approach is to choose an appropriate template of ranking functions. For both classical and probabilistic programs, the template of linear ranking functions can be straightforward taken as an affine expression over program variables. However, a reasonable template of ranking functions for quantum programs is determined by a fundamental theorem in quantum mechanics. Let $\mathcal{H}$ be a Hilbert space. We write $S(\mathcal{H})$ for the set of all closed subspaces of $\mathcal{H}$. Recall from [138,399] that a state in $S(\mathcal{H})$ is a mapping $m : S(\mathcal{H}) \to [0, 1]$ such that $m(\mathcal{H}) = 1$ and

$$m\left(\bigvee_{i=0}^{\infty} X_i\right) = \sum_{i=0}^{\infty} m(X_i)$$

for any family $\{X_i\}_{i=0}^{\infty}$ of mutually orthogonal subspaces of $\mathcal{H}$, where $\bigvee_{i=0}^{\infty} X_i$ stands for the smallest closed subspace of $\mathcal{H}$ that contains all X_i $(i \geq 0)$. The following fundamental theorem gives an elegant characterisation of states in $\mathcal{S}(\mathcal{H})$.

Theorem 8.7 (Gleason's theorem [138,179]). *If $\mathcal{H}$ is separable and $\dim \mathcal{H} > 2$, then for each state m in $\mathcal{S}(\mathcal{H})$, there exists a unique positive Hermitian matrix R with $tr(R) = 1$ such that*

$$m(X) = tr(RP_X)$$

for all $X \in \mathcal{S}(\mathcal{H})$, where P_X is the project onto X.

The conclusion of the above theorem is not true when $\dim \mathcal{H} = 2$ (see [138], page 130 for a counter-example).

As we will see in the proofs of Theorems 8.8 and 8.9, Gleason's theorem plays an essential role in determining the form of templates of ranking functions for quantum programs. The basic idea is as follows: Gleason's theorem, together with the defining conditions of an ranking function, implies that each ranking function η can be written in a trace form

$$\eta(l, \rho) = tr(R_l \rho)$$

where for any l, R_l is a Hermitian operator. For a finite-dimensional Hilbert space $\mathcal{H}$, the operator (matrix) R_l can be derived directly from the theorem: define a state m in $\mathcal{S}(\mathcal{H})$ by

$$m(X) = \eta\left(l, \frac{P_X}{\dim X}\right),$$

then let $m(X) = tr(RP_X)$ and $R_l = \dim \mathcal{H} \cdot R$. We note that m is well-defined since $\eta(l, \cdot)$ is linear. When the state Hilbert space $\mathcal{H}$ is infinite-dimensional, the projection of operator R_l onto any finite dimensional subspaces can be defined as above. Then the proof can be achieved by a reduction to the finite-dimensional case. This reduction is similar to the reduction in the proof of Gleason's theorem [179]. This argument shows that it is sufficient to use the trace form $tr(R_l \rho)$ as a template of the ranking function $\eta(l, \rho)$.

Reduction to SDP (Semi-Definite Programming) problem: Of course, for a quantum program P with a 2-dimensional state Hilbert space, Problem 8.2 can be easily solved. Using Gleason's Theorem, we are able to reduce Problem 8.2 to a constraint satisfaction problem in the case where the dimension of the state Hilbert space of program P: $\dim \mathcal{H}_P > 2$. Before doing it, we recall from Definition 6.4 that for any superoperator $\mathcal{E}$, if $\mathcal{E}$ has the Kraus operator-sum representation $\mathcal{E}(\rho) = \sum_i E_i \rho E_i^{\dagger}$, then its dual $\mathcal{E}^*$ is given by

$$\mathcal{E}^*(A) = \sum_i E_i^{\dagger} A E_i$$

for every operator A.

Let us first consider quantum programs that contains no angelic choices but may have demonic choices. In this case, the following theorem shows that Problem 8.2 can be reduced to an SDP (Semi-Definite Programming) problem.

Theorem 8.8. *Let P be a quantum program without angelic choice. Given an invariant $\mathcal{O} = \{O_l\}_{l \in L}$ for P. If $n := \dim \mathcal{H}_P > 2$, then the realisability and synthesis problem with respect to $\mathcal{O}$ is equivalent to the following constraint satisfaction problem:*

- *arbitrarily fix the value of K, then find a real number $\epsilon > 0$ and complex Hermitian matrices R_l $(l \in L)$ satisfying the constraint:*

$$\left(\bigwedge_{l \in L} \gamma_l\right) \wedge \left(\bigwedge_{l \in L \setminus \{l_{out}^P\}} \delta_l\right)$$

where:

1. *for each $l \in L$,*

$$\gamma_l := 0 \sqsubseteq R_l - O_l - (K - 1) \cdot I;$$

2. *for each $l \in L_D$,*

$$\delta_l := \bigwedge_{l \xrightarrow{l} l'} (0 \sqsubseteq R_l - R_{l'} - O_l + (1 - \epsilon) \cdot I);$$

3. *for each $l \in L_S \setminus \{l_{out}^P\}$,*

$$\delta_l := 0 \sqsubseteq R_l - \sum_{l \xrightarrow{\mathcal{E}} l'} \mathcal{E}^*(R_{l'}) - O_l + (1 - \epsilon) \cdot I.$$

Proof. We reduce the realisability and synthesis problem to the constrain satisfaction problem in two steps.

Step 1: With Definition 8.12, we see that Problem 8.2 can be equivalently stated as the following constraint satisfaction problem: for some $K > -\infty$ (which is usually chosen as $K = 0$), find a real number $\epsilon > 0$ and linear functions $\eta(l, \cdot) : \mathcal{D}(\mathcal{H}_P) \to \mathbb{R}$ $(l \in L)$ satisfying the constraint:

$$\left(\bigwedge_{l \in L} \mu_l \right) \wedge \left(\bigwedge_{l \in L \setminus \{l_{out}^P\}} \nu_l \right)$$

where

$$\mu_l := (\forall \rho \in \mathcal{D}(\mathcal{H}_P) \text{ with } tr(\rho) = 1) \, [tr(O_l \rho) + K - 1 \leq \eta(l, \rho)],$$
$$\nu_l := (\forall \rho \in \mathcal{D}(\mathcal{H}_P) \text{ with } tr(\rho) = 1) \xi(l, \rho),$$

and

$$\xi(l, \rho) := tr(O_l \rho) + pre_\eta(l, \rho) \leq \eta(l, \rho) + 1 - \epsilon.$$

Furthermore, with Definition 8.11 we have:

- if $l \in L_D$, then

$$\xi(l, \rho) \Leftrightarrow \bigwedge \left\{ tr(O_l \rho) + \eta(l', \rho) \leq \eta(l, \rho) + 1 - \epsilon : l \xrightarrow{\mathcal{I}} l' \right\}.$$

- if $l \in L_S \setminus \{l_{out}^P\}$, then

$$\xi(l, \rho) \Leftrightarrow tr(O_l \rho) + \sum \left\{ |\eta(l', \mathcal{E}(\rho)) : l \xrightarrow{\mathcal{E}} l'| \right\} \leq \eta(l, \rho) + 1 - \epsilon.$$

Step 2: For each $l \in L$, since $\dim \mathcal{H}_P > 2$, by Gleason's Theorem it is easy to see that there exists a Hermitian matrix R_l such that $\eta(l, \rho) = tr(R_l \rho)$ for all $\rho \in \mathcal{D}(\mathcal{H})$. Then we assert:

1. for each $l \in L$,

$$\mu_l \Leftrightarrow (\forall \rho \in \mathcal{D}(\mathcal{H}_P) \text{ with } tr(\rho) = 1)\{tr[(R_l - O_l - (K - 1) \cdot I) \rho] \geq 0\}$$
$$\Leftrightarrow 0 \sqsubseteq R_l - O_l - (K - 1) \cdot I.$$

2. for each $l \in L_D$,

$$\nu_l \Leftrightarrow (\forall \rho \in \mathcal{D}(\mathcal{H}_P) \text{ with } tr(\rho) = 1) \bigwedge_{l \xrightarrow{l} l'} \{tr[(R_l - R_{l'} - O_l + (1 - \epsilon) \cdot I) \rho] \geq 0\}$$
$$\Leftrightarrow \bigwedge_{l \xrightarrow{l} l'} (0 \sqsubseteq R_l - R_{l'} - O_l + (1 - \epsilon) \cdot I).$$

3. for each $l \in L_S \setminus \{l_{out}^P\}$,

$$\nu_l \Leftrightarrow (\forall \rho \in \mathcal{D}(\mathcal{H}_P) \text{ with } tr(\rho) = 1) \left\{ tr \left[\left(R_l - \sum_{l \xrightarrow{\mathcal{E}} l'} \mathcal{E}^*(R_{l'}) - O_l + (1 - \epsilon) \cdot I \right) \rho \right] \geq 0 \right\}$$
$$\Leftrightarrow 0 \sqsubseteq R_l - \sum_{l \xrightarrow{\mathcal{E}} l'} \mathcal{E}^*(R_{l'}) - O_l + (1 - \epsilon) \cdot I \qquad \square$$

For quantum programs with angelic choices, a constraint satisfaction problems can be derived in the same way as in the proof of the above theorem. However, such a constraint satisfaction problem cannot directly be solved by SDP (Semi-Definite Programming) solvers because the constraint at each location $l \in L_A$ is a disjunction of matrix positivity restrictions. In fact, a similar situation happens in termination analysis of classical programs with linear ranking functions, where the celebrated Farkas's lemma has been employed to transform it into a standard form of Linear Programming. We are going to solve our problem for quantum programs with the same strategy. But first of all, we have to establish a generalisation of Farkas's lemma in terms of observables (Hermitian operators) in quantum theory.

Lemma 8.3 (Generalised Farkas' lemma for SDP). *Let $H_1, \cdots, H_n$ be a finite number of Hermitian operators on a finite-dimensional Hilbert space $\mathcal{H}$. Then the following two statements are equivalent:*

1. *For any $\rho \in \mathcal{D}(\mathcal{H})$,*

$$\bigvee_k (tr(\rho H_k) > 0);$$

2. *There exist nonnegative numbers $p_1 \geq 0, \cdots, p_n \geq 0$, such that $p_1 + \cdots + p_n > 0$ and*

$$p_1 H_1 + p_2 H_2 + \cdots + p_n H_n \sqsupseteq 0.$$

Proof. It is obvious that statement 2 implies statement 1. We prove the converse in a similar way to the original Farkas's lemma, namely by invoking the Hyperplane Separation Theorem. Specifically, let d be the dimension of $\mathcal{H}$. We note that the set of all Hermitian operators of $\mathcal{H}$, denoted by $\mathcal{L}$, is in fact a $\frac{d(d+1)}{2}$-dimensional Hilbert space over reals, i.e.

$$\mathcal{L} \simeq \mathbb{R}^{\frac{d(d+1)}{2}}$$

where the inner product of two Hermitian operators $A, B \in \mathcal{L}$ is naturally defined as $tr(AB)$, and an orthonormal basis of $\mathcal{L}$ is

$$\{|k\rangle\langle k| \mid 0 \leq k \leq d-1\} \cup \left\{ \frac{|i\rangle\langle j| + |j\rangle\langle i|}{2} \mid 0 \leq i < j \leq d-1 \right\}.$$

Now denote by $\mathcal{P}$ the set of all positive definite operators on $\mathcal{H}$, and define

$$\mathcal{A} := \{p_1 H_1 + \cdots + p_n H_n \mid p_1 \geq 0, \cdots, p_n \geq 0, p_1 + \cdots + p_n > 0\}.$$

We assume by contradiction that $\mathcal{A} \cap \mathcal{P} = \emptyset$. Noting that both $\mathcal{P}$ and $\mathcal{A}$ are nonempty convex sets in $\mathcal{L}$. Then following the Hyperplane Separation Theorem, there exists a hyperplane to separate them; that is, there is a real number $d \in \mathbb{R}$ and a nonzero Hermitian operator $C \in \mathcal{L}$ such that:

1. $tr(CP) + d \geq 0$ for all $P \in \mathcal{P}$; and
2. $tr(CA) + d \leq 0$ for all $A \in \mathcal{A}$.

Thus, $d = 0$ follows immediately from these two conditions since the zero matrix 0 is in both of the closure of $\mathcal{P}$ and the closure of $\mathcal{A}$. Then the first condition implies that C is positive semidefinite. Consequently, the second condition implies that $C/tr(C)$ is a density matrix that makes the first statement of the lemma unsatisfied. □

Now with the help of the above lemma, we are able to find an SDP problem for realisation and synthesis of ranking functions for general quantum programs (with both angelic and demonic choices).

Theorem 8.9. *Let P be a quantum program (with angelic choice in general). Given an invariant $\mathcal{O} = \{O_l\}_{l \in L}$ for P. If $n := \dim \mathcal{H}_P > 2$, then the realisability and synthesis problem with respect to $\mathcal{O}$ is equivalent to the following constraint satisfaction problem:*

- *arbitrarily fix the value of K, then find real numbers $\epsilon > 0$, $p_{l,l'} \geq 0$ for all $l \in L_A, l \xrightarrow{l} l'$ with $\sum_{l'} p_{l,l'} = 1$ for all l, and complex Hermitian matrices R_l ($l \in L$) satisfying the constraint:*

$$\left(\bigwedge_{l \in L} \gamma_l \right) \wedge \left(\bigwedge_{l \in L \setminus \{l_{out}^P\}} \delta_l \right)$$

where:

1. *for each* $l \in L$,

$$\gamma_l := 0 \sqsubseteq R_l - O_l - (K-1) \cdot I;$$

2. *for each* $l \in L_A$,

$$\delta_l := 0 \sqsubseteq R_l - \sum_{l \xrightarrow{I} l'} p_{l,l'} R_{l'} - O_l + (1-\epsilon) \cdot I;$$

3. *for each* $l \in L_D$,

$$\delta_l := \bigwedge_{l \xrightarrow{I} l'} \left(0 \sqsubseteq R_l - R_{l'} - O_l + (1-\epsilon) \cdot I\right);$$

4. *for each* $l \in L_S \setminus \{l_{out}^P\}$,

$$\delta_l := 0 \sqsubseteq R_l - \sum_{l \xrightarrow{\mathcal{E}} l'} \mathcal{E}^* (R_{l'}) - O_l + (1-\epsilon) \cdot I.$$

Proof. The constraint for linear functions $\eta(l, \cdot)$ can be characterised by

$$\left(\bigwedge_{l \in L} \mu_l\right) \wedge \left(\bigwedge_{l \in L \setminus \{l_{out}^P\}} \nu_l\right)$$

where μ_l and ν_l are almost the same as in the proof of Theorem 8.8. The only difference comes from the treatment of $\xi(l, \rho)$. For $l \in L_A$, we have:

$$\xi(l, \rho) \Leftrightarrow \bigvee \left\{ tr(O_l \rho) + \eta(l', \rho) \leq \eta(l, \rho) + 1 - \epsilon : l \xrightarrow{I} l' \right\}.$$

Then by using Gleason's Theorem $\eta(l, \rho)$ can be replaced by $tr(R_l \rho)$ in the constraints for Hermitian matrices R_l. We particularly consider the constraint for each $l \in L_A$:

$$\nu_l \Leftrightarrow (\forall \rho \in \mathcal{D}(\mathcal{H}_P) \text{ with } tr(\rho) = 1) \bigvee_{l \xrightarrow{l} l'} [\epsilon - 1 \leq tr(\rho(T_l - O_l - T_{l'}))]$$

$$\Leftrightarrow (\forall \epsilon' \in [0, \epsilon)) \bigvee_{l \xrightarrow{l} l'} \left[0 < tr\left(\rho\left(T_l - O_l - T_{l'} + (1-\epsilon') \cdot I\right)\right)\right]$$

$$\Leftrightarrow 0 \sqsubset \sum_{l \xrightarrow{l} l'} p_{l,l'}\left(T_l - O_l - T_{l'} + (1-\epsilon') \cdot I\right) \text{ (for some } p_{l,l'} \geq 0).$$

Note that the last step is from Lemma 8.3. It actually means that if a (K, ϵ)-ranking function exists, then the constraints of γ_l and δ_l are satisfiable for (K, ϵ'), where ϵ' can be arbitrarily close to ϵ; and conversely, if the constraints of γ_l and δ_l are satisfiable for (K, ϵ), then a (K, ϵ)-ranking function exists. So, the proof is completed. $\quad\square$

8.4 Termination analysis – reachability

In the last section, we introduced ranking functions for termination analysis of quantum programs. In this section, we turn to consider the second approach to the quantum termination problem, namely reachability analysis.

8.4.1 Termination of quantum while-loops

As in classical programming, difficulty in the termination analysis of quantum programs essentially comes from loops and recursions. So, this subsection focuses on the quantum extension of **while**-loop introduced in Section 5.1. We mainly consider termination of a quantum loop, but its average running time is also briefly discussed. This subsection is divided into three parts: The first part considers a class of simple quantum loops with a unitary operator as their body, the second part further deals with quantum loops with a general quantum operation as their body, and the third part presents an example that computes the average running time of a quantum walk on an n-circle.

Quantum while-loops with unitary bodies: To ease the understanding, let us start from a special form of quantum **while**-loop:

$$S \equiv \textbf{while } M[\overline{q}] = 1 \textbf{ do } \overline{q} := U[\overline{q}] \textbf{ od} \tag{8.31}$$

where:

- $\overline{q}$ denotes quantum register $q_1, \ldots, q_n$, and its state Hilbert space is $\mathcal{H} = \bigotimes_{i=1}^{n} \mathcal{H}_{q_i}$;
- the loop body is unitary transformation $\overline{q} := U[\overline{q}]$ with U being a unitary operator on $\mathcal{H}$;
- the yes–no measurement $M = \{M_0, M_1\}$ in the loop guard is projective; that is, $M_0 = P_{X^\perp}$ and $M_1 = P_X$ with X being a subspace of $\mathcal{H}$ and $X^\perp$ being the orthocomplement of X (see Definition 2.7(ii)).

The execution of the quantum loop S in Eq. (8.31) is clearly described by its operational and denotational semantics presented in Sections 5.2 and 5.3. To help the reader further understand the behaviour of loop S, here we examine its computational process in a slightly different manner. For any input state $\rho \in \mathcal{D}(\mathcal{H})$, the behaviour of the loop S can be described in the following unwound way:

1. *Initial step*: The loop performs the projective measurement

$$M = \left\{ M_0 = P_{X^\perp}, M_1 = P_X \right\}$$

on the input state ρ. If the outcome is 1, then the program performs the unitary operation U on the postmeasurement state. Otherwise the program terminates. More precisely, we have:

- The loop terminates with probability

$$p_T^{(1)}(\rho) = tr(P_{X^\perp}\rho).$$

In this case, the output at this step is

$$\rho_{out}^{(1)} = \frac{P_{X^\perp} \rho P_{X^\perp}}{p_T^{(1)}(\rho)}.$$

- The loop continues with probability

$$p_{NT}^{(1)}(\rho) = 1 - p_T^{(1)}(\rho) = tr(P_X \rho).$$

In this case, the program state after the measurement is

$$\rho_{mid}^{(1)} = \frac{P_X \rho P_X}{p_{NT}^{(1)}(\rho)}.$$

Furthermore, $\rho_{mid}^{(1)}$ is fed to the unitary operation U and then the state

$$\rho_{in}^{(2)} = U\rho_{mid}^{(1)} U^\dagger$$

is returned. Note that $\rho_{in}^{(2)}$ will be used as the input state in the next step.

2. *Induction step*: Suppose that the loop has run n steps, and it did not terminate at the nth step; that is, $p_{NT}^{(n)} > 0$. If $\rho_{in}^{(n+1)}$ is the program state at the end of the nth step, then in the $(n+1)$th step, $\rho_{in}^{(n+1)}$ is the input, and we have:

- The termination probability is

$$p_T^{(n+1)}(\rho) = tr(P_{X^\perp}\rho_{in}^{(n+1)})$$

and the output at this step is

$$\rho_{out}^{(n+1)} = \frac{P_{X^\perp} \rho_{in}^{(n+1)} P_{X^\perp}}{p_T^{(n+1)}(\rho)}.$$

- The loop continues to perform the unitary operation U on the postmeasurement state

$$\rho_{mid}^{(n+1)} = \frac{P_X \rho_{in}^{(n+1)} P_X}{p_{NT}^{(n+1)}(\rho)}$$

with probability

$$p_{NT}^{(n+1)}(\rho) = 1 - p_T^{(n+1)}(\rho) = tr(P_X \rho_{in}^{(n+1)}),$$

and the state

$$\rho_{in}^{(n\,|\,2)} = U \rho_{mid}^{(n+1)} U^\dagger$$

will be returned. Then state $\rho_{in}^{(n+2)}$ will be the input of the $(n+2)$th step.

The reader may like to compare the above description of the execution of quantum loop S with its semantics given in Section 5.2. Based on this description, we can introduce the notion of termination.

Definition 8.13. 1. If probability $p_{NT}^{(n)}(\rho) = 0$ for some positive integer n, then we say that the loop (8.31) terminates from input ρ.

2. The nontermination probability of the loop (8.31) from input ρ is

$$p_{NT}(\rho) = \lim_{n \to \infty} p_{NT}^{(\le n)}(\rho)$$

where

$$p_{NT}^{(\le n)}(\rho) = \prod_{i=1}^{n} p_{NT}^{(i)}(\rho)$$

denotes the probability that the loop does not terminate after n steps.

3. We say that the loop (8.31) almost surely terminates from input ρ whenever nontermination probability $p_{NT}(\rho) = 0$.

Intuitively, a quantum loop almost surely terminates if for any $\epsilon > 0$, there exists a large enough positive integer $n(\epsilon)$ such that the probability that the loop terminates within $n(\epsilon)$ steps is greater than $1 - \epsilon$.

In the above definition, termination was considered for a single input. We can also define termination for all possible inputs.

Definition 8.14. A quantum loop is terminating (resp. almost surely terminating) if it terminates (resp. almost surely terminates) from all input $\rho \in \mathcal{D}(\mathcal{H})$.

In the computational process of a quantum loop, a density operator is taken as input, and a density operator is given as output with a certain probability at each step. Thus, we can obtain the overall output by synthesising these density operators returned at all steps into a single one according to the respective probabilities. Note that sometimes the loop does not terminate with a nonzero probability. So, the synthesised output may not be a density operator but only a partial density operator, and thus a quantum loop defines a function from density operators to partial density operators on $\mathcal{H}$.

Definition 8.15. The function $\mathcal{F} : \mathcal{D}(\mathcal{H}) \to \mathcal{D}(\mathcal{H})$ computed by the quantum loop (8.31) is defined by

$$\mathcal{F}(\rho) = \sum_{n=1}^{\infty} p_{NT}^{(\le n-1)}(\rho) \cdot p_T^{(n)}(\rho) \cdot \rho_{out}^{(n)}$$

for each $\rho \in \mathcal{D}(\mathcal{H})$.

It should be noted that in the defining equation of $\mathcal{F}(\rho)$ the quantity

$$p_{NT}^{(\le n-1)}(\rho) \cdot p_T^{(n)}(\rho)$$

is the probability that the loop does not terminate at steps from 1 to $n-1$ but it terminates at the nth step.

For any operator A on the Hilbert space $\mathcal{H}$ and any subspace X of $\mathcal{H}$, we write:

$$A_X = P_X A P_X$$

where P_X is the projection onto X; that is, A_X is the restriction of A on X. Then the computational process of quantum loop (8.31) can be summarised as:

Lemma 8.4. *Let ρ be an input state to the loop (8.31). Then we have:*

1.

$$p_{NT}^{(\leq n)}(\rho) = tr(U_X^{n-1} \rho_X U_X^{\dagger n-1})$$

for any positive integer n;

2.

$$\mathcal{F}(\rho) = P_{X^\perp} \rho P_{X^\perp} + P_{X^\perp} U \left(\sum_{n=0}^{\infty} U_X^n \rho_X U_X^{\dagger n} \right) U^\dagger P_{X^\perp},$$

where X is the subspace defining the projective measurement in the loop guard, and U is the unitary transformation in the loop body.

Exercise 8.1. Prove Lemma 8.4.

The following exercise further shows that the function computed by quantum loop S in Eq. (8.31) coincides with the denotational semantics of S according to Definition 5.6.

Exercise 8.2. Prove that $\mathcal{F}(\rho) = [\![S]\!](\rho)$ for any $\rho \in \mathcal{D}(\mathcal{H})$.

As shown in the following exercise, almost sure termination of a quantum loop can also be characterised in terms of the function computed by it.

Exercise 8.3. Show that for each $\rho \in \mathcal{D}(\mathcal{H})$, we have:

1. $\langle \varphi | \mathcal{F}(\rho) | \psi \rangle = 0$ if $|\varphi\rangle$ or $|\psi\rangle \in X$;
2. $tr(\mathcal{F}(\rho)) = tr(\rho) - p_{NT}(\rho)$. Thus, $tr(\mathcal{F}(\rho)) = tr(\rho)$ if and only if the loop (8.31) almost surely terminates from input state ρ.

Analysis of termination: Obviously, it is hard to decide directly by Definition 8.13 when the quantum loop (8.31) terminates. Now we try to find a necessary and sufficient condition for its termination. This can be done through several reduction steps.

First of all, the next lemma allows us to decompose an input density matrix into a sequence of simpler input density matrices when examining termination of a quantum loop.

Lemma 8.5. *Let $\rho = \sum_i p_i \rho_i$ with $p_i > 0$ for all i. Then the loop (8.31) terminates from input ρ if and only if it terminates from input ρ_i for all i.*

Exercise 8.4. Prove Lemma 8.5.

If $\{(p_i, |\psi_i\rangle)\}$ is an ensemble with $p_i > 0$ for all i, and density operator

$$\rho = \sum_i p_i |\psi_i\rangle\langle\psi_i|,$$

then the above lemma asserts that the loop (8.31) terminates from input mixed state ρ if and only if it terminates from input pure state $|\psi_i\rangle$ for all i. In particular, we have:

Corollary 8.1. *A quantum loop is terminating if and only if it terminates from all pure input states.*

Secondly, the termination problem of a quantum loop may be reduced to a corresponding problem of a classical loop in the field of complex numbers. We decompose the subspace X and its ortho-complement $X^\perp$ defining the projective measurement in the guard of quantum loop (8.31). Let $\{|m_1\rangle, \ldots, |m_l\rangle\}$ be an orthonormal basis of $\mathcal{H}$ such that

$$\sum_{i=1}^{k} |m_i\rangle\langle m_i| = P_X \quad \text{and} \quad \sum_{i=k+1}^{l} |m_i\rangle\langle m_i| = P_{X^\perp},$$

where $1 \le k \le l$. In other words, the basis $\{|m_1\rangle, \ldots, |m_l\rangle\}$ of $\mathcal{H}$ is divided into two parts $\{|m_1\rangle, \ldots, |m_k\rangle\}$ and $\{|m_{k+1}\rangle, \ldots, |m_l\rangle\}$ with the former being a basis of X and the latter a basis of $X^\perp$. Without any loss of generality, we assume in the sequel that the matrix representations of operators U (the unitary transformation in the loop body), U_X (the restriction of U in X), ρ_X (the restriction of input ρ in X), denoted also by U, U_X, ρ_X respectively for simplicity, are taken according to this basis. Also, for each pure state $|\psi\rangle$ we write $|\psi\rangle_X$ for the vector representation of projection $P_X|\psi\rangle$ in this basis.

Lemma 8.6. *The following two statements are equivalent:*

1. *The quantum loop (8.31) terminates from input $\rho \in \mathcal{D}(\mathcal{H})$;*
2. $U_X^n \rho_X U_X^{\dagger n} = \mathbf{0}_{k \times k}$ *for some nonnegative integer n, where $\mathbf{0}_{k \times k}$ is the $(k \times k)$-zero matrix.*

In particular, it terminates from pure input state $|\psi\rangle$ if and only if $U_X^n|\psi\rangle_X = \mathbf{0}$ for some nonnegative integer n, where $\mathbf{0}$ is the k-dimensional zero vector.

Proof. This result follows from Lemma 8.4.1 and the fact that $tr(A) = 0$ if and only if $A = \mathbf{0}$ when A is positive. $\square$

It should be noticed that the condition $U_X^n|\psi\rangle_X = \mathbf{0}$ in Lemma 8.6 is actually a termination condition for the following loop:

$$\textbf{while } \mathbf{v} \ne \mathbf{0} \textbf{ do } \mathbf{v} := U_X\mathbf{v} \textbf{ od} \tag{8.32}$$

This loop must be understood as a classical computation in the field of complex numbers.

Thirdly, we can show certain invariance of termination of a classical loop under a nonsingular transformation.

Lemma 8.7. *Let S be a nonsingular $(k \times k)$-complex matrix. Then the following two statements are equivalent:*

1. *The classical loop (8.32) (with $\mathbf{v} \in \mathbf{C}^k$) terminates from input $\mathbf{v}_0 \in \mathbf{C}^k$.*
2. *The classical loop:*

$$\textbf{while } \mathbf{v} \ne \mathbf{0} \textbf{ do } \mathbf{v} := (SU_X S^{-1})\mathbf{v} \textbf{ od}$$

(with $\mathbf{v} \in \mathbf{C}^k$) terminates from input $S\mathbf{v}_0$.

Proof. Note that $S\mathbf{v} \ne \mathbf{0}$ if and only if $\mathbf{v} \ne \mathbf{0}$ because S is nonsingular. Then the conclusion follows from a simple calculation. $\square$

Furthermore, we shall need the Jordan normal form theorem in the proof of the main results in this section. The proof of this normal form theorem can be found in any standard textbook on matrix theory; e.g. [61].

Lemma 8.8 (Jordan normal form theorem). *For any $(k \times k)$-complex matrix A, there is a nonsingular $(k \times k)$-complex matrix S such that*

$$A = SJ(A)S^{-1}$$

where

$$J(A) = \bigoplus_{i=1}^{l} J_{k_i}(\lambda_i)$$

$$= diag(J_{k_1}(\lambda_1), J_{k_2}(\lambda_2), \ldots, J_{k_l}(\lambda_l))$$

$$
= \begin{pmatrix}
J_{k_1}(\lambda_1) & & & & \\
& J_{k_2}(\lambda_2) & & & \\
& & \ddots & & \\
& & & \ddots & \\
& & & & J_{k_l}(\lambda_l)
\end{pmatrix}
$$

is the Jordan normal form of A, $\sum_{i=1}^{l} k_i = k$, and

$$
J_{k_i}(\lambda_i) = \begin{pmatrix}
\lambda_i & 1 & & & \\
& \lambda_i & 1 & & \\
& & \ddots & \ddots & \\
& & & \ddots & 1 \\
& & & & \lambda_i
\end{pmatrix}. \tag{8.33}
$$

is a $(k_i \times k_i)$-Jordan block for each $1 \leq i \leq l$. Furthermore, if the Jordan blocks corresponding to each distinct eigenvalue are presented in decreasing order of the block size, then the Jordan normal form is uniquely determined once the ordering of the eigenvalues is given.

The following technical lemma about the powers of Jordon blocks is also needed in the discussions below.

Lemma 8.9. *Let $J_r(\lambda)$ be a $(r \times r)$-Jordan block and $\mathbf{v}$ an r-dimensional complex vector. Then*

$$
J_r(\lambda)^n \mathbf{v} = \mathbf{0}
$$

for some nonnegative integer n if and only if $\lambda = 0$ or $\mathbf{v} = \mathbf{0}$, where $\mathbf{0}$ is the r-dimensional zero vector.

Proof. The "if" part is clear. We now prove the "only if" part. By a routine calculation we obtain:

$$
J_r(\lambda)^n = \begin{pmatrix}
\lambda^n & \binom{n}{1}\lambda^{n-1} & \binom{n}{2}\lambda^{n-2} & \cdots & \binom{n}{r-2}\lambda^{n-r+2} & \binom{n}{r-1}\lambda^{n-r+1} \\
0 & \lambda^n & \binom{n}{1}\lambda^{n-1} & \cdots & \binom{n}{r-3}\lambda^{n-r+3} & \binom{n}{r-2}\lambda^{n-r+2} \\
0 & 0 & \lambda^n & \cdots & \binom{n}{r-4}\lambda^{n-r+4} & \binom{n}{r-3}\lambda^{n-r+3} \\
& & & \cdots & & \\
0 & 0 & 0 & \cdots & \lambda^n & \binom{n}{1}\lambda^{n-1} \\
0 & 0 & 0 & \cdots & 0 & \lambda^n
\end{pmatrix}.
$$

Notice that $J_r(\lambda)^n$ is an upper triangular matrix with the diagonal entries being λ^n. So if $\lambda \neq 0$ then $J_r(\lambda)^n$ is nonsingular, and $J_r(\lambda)^n \mathbf{v} = \mathbf{0}$ implies $\mathbf{v} = \mathbf{0}$. $\square$

Now we are able to present one of the main results of this section, which gives a necessary and sufficient condition for termination of a quantum loop from a pure input state.

Theorem 8.10. *Suppose the Jordan decomposition of U_X is*

$$
U_X = S J(U_X) S^{-1}
$$

where

$$
J(U_X) = \bigoplus_{i=1}^{l} J_{k_i}(\lambda_i) = diag(J_{k_1}(\lambda_1), J_{k_2}(\lambda_2), \dots, J_{k_l}(\lambda_l)).
$$

Let $S^{-1}|\psi\rangle_X$ be divided into l subvectors $\mathbf{v}_1, \mathbf{v}_2, \dots, \mathbf{v}_l$ such that the length of $\mathbf{v}_i$ is k_i. Then the quantum loop (8.31) terminates from input $|\psi\rangle$ if and only if for each $1 \le i \le l$, $\lambda_i = 0$ or $\mathbf{v}_i = \mathbf{0}$, where $\mathbf{0}$ is the k_i-dimensional zero vector.

Proof. Using Lemmas 8.6 and 8.7 we know that the quantum loop (8.31) terminates from input $|\psi\rangle$ if and only if

$$J(U_X)^n S^{-1} |\psi\rangle_X = \mathbf{0} \tag{8.34}$$

for some nonnegative integer n. A simple calculation yields

$$J(U_X)^n S^{-1}|\psi\rangle_X = \left((J_{k_1}(\lambda_1)^n \mathbf{v}_1)^T, (J_{k_2}(\lambda_2)^n \mathbf{v}_2)^T, \dots, (J_{k_l}(\lambda_l)^n \mathbf{v}_l)^T \right)^T$$

where $\mathbf{v}^T$ stands for the transpose of vector $\mathbf{v}$; that is, if $\mathbf{v}$ is a column vector then $\mathbf{v}^T$ is a row vector, and vice versa. Therefore, Eq. (8.34) holds for some nonnegative integer n if and only if for each $1 \le i \le l$, there exists a nonnegative integer n_i such that

$$J_{k_i}(\lambda_i)^{n_i} \mathbf{v}_i = \mathbf{0}.$$

Then we complete the proof by using Lemma 8.9. □

Obviously, we can decide whether the quantum loop (8.31) terminates from any given mixed state by combining Lemma 8.5 and Theorem 8.10.

Corollary 8.2. *The quantum loop (8.31) is terminating if and only if U_X has only zero eigenvalues.*

Analysis of almost sure termination: We now turn to consider almost sure termination. A necessary and sufficient condition for almost sure termination of the quantum loop (8.31) can also be derived by several steps of reduction. We first give a lemma similar to Lemma 8.5 so that a mixed input state can be reduced to a family of pure input states.

Lemma 8.10. *Let $\rho = \sum_i p_i \rho_i$ with $p_i > 0$ for all i. Then the quantum loop (8.31) almost surely terminates from input ρ if and only if it almost surely terminates from input ρ_i for all i.*

Exercise 8.5. Prove Lemma 8.10.

Corollary 8.3. *A quantum loop is almost surely terminating if and only if it almost surely terminates from all pure input states.*

We then present a technical lemma, which forms a key step in the proof of Theorem 8.11 below.

Lemma 8.11. *The quantum loop (8.31) almost surely terminates from pure input state $|\psi\rangle$ if and only if*

$$\lim_{n \to \infty} \||U_X^n |\psi\rangle\| = 0.$$

Proof. From Lemma 8.4, we have:

$$P_{NT}^{(\le n)}(|\psi\rangle) = \|U_X^{n-1}|\psi\rangle\|^2.$$

Note that in the left hand side of the above equation, $|\psi\rangle$ actually stands for its corresponding density operator $|\psi\rangle\langle\psi|$. So $p_{NT}(|\psi\rangle) = 0$ if and only if $\lim_{n\to\infty} \||U_X^n|\psi\rangle\| = 0$. □

The following theorem gives a necessary and sufficient condition for almost sure termination of a quantum loop from a pure input state.

Theorem 8.11. *Suppose that U_X, S, $J(U_X)$, $J_{k_i}(\lambda_i)$ and $\mathbf{v}_i$ ($1 \le i \le l$) are given as in Theorem 8.10. Then the quantum loop (8.31) almost surely terminates from input $|\psi\rangle$ if and only if for each $1 \le i \le l$, $|\lambda_i| < 1$ or $\mathbf{v}_i = \mathbf{0}$, where $\mathbf{0}$ is the k_i-dimensional zero vector.*

Proof. First, for any nonnegative integer n, we have:

$$U_X^n|\psi\rangle = SJ(U_X)^n S^{-1}|\psi\rangle.$$

Then $\lim_{n\to\infty} ||U_X^n|\psi\rangle|| = 0$ if and only if

$$\lim_{n\to\infty} ||J(U_X)^n S^{-1}|\psi\rangle|| = 0 \tag{8.35}$$

since S is nonsingular. Using Lemma 8.11 we know that the loop (8.31) almost surely terminates from input $|\psi\rangle$ if and only if Eq. (8.35) holds. Note that

$$J(U_X)^n S^{-1}|\psi\rangle = \left((J_{k_1}(\lambda_1)^n \mathbf{v}_1)^T, (J_{k_2}(\lambda_2)^n \mathbf{v}_2)^T, \ldots, (J_{k_l}(\lambda_l)^n \mathbf{v}_l)^T\right)^T$$

where $\mathbf{v}^T$ stands for the transpose of vector $\mathbf{v}$. Then Eq. (8.35) holds if and only if

$$\lim_{n\to\infty} ||J_{k_i}(\lambda_i)^n \mathbf{v}_i|| = 0 \tag{8.36}$$

for all $1 \le i \le l$. Furthermore, we have:

$$J_r(\lambda)^n \mathbf{v} = \left(\sum_{i=0}^{r-1}\binom{n}{i}\lambda^{n-i}v_{i+1}, \sum_{i=0}^{r-2}\binom{n}{i}\lambda^{n-i}v_{i+2}, \cdots, \lambda^n v_{r-1} + \binom{n}{1}\lambda^{n-1}v_r, \lambda^n v_r\right)^T.$$

So, Eq. (8.36) holds if and only if the following system of k_i equations is valid:

$$\begin{cases} \lim_{n\to\infty}\sum_{j=0}^{k_i-1}\binom{n}{j}\lambda_i^{n-j}v_{i(j+1)} = 0, \\[2mm] \lim_{n\to\infty}\sum_{j=0}^{k_i-2}\binom{n}{j}\lambda_i^{n-j}v_{i(j+2)} = 0, \\[2mm] \cdots\cdots\cdots\cdots \\[2mm] \lim_{n\to\infty}\left[\lambda_i^n v_{i(k_i-1)} + \binom{n}{1}\lambda_i^{n-1}v_{ik_i}\right] = 0, \\[2mm] \lim_{n\to\infty}\lambda_i^n v_{ik_i} = 0, \end{cases} \tag{8.37}$$

where it is assumed that $\mathbf{v}_i = (v_{i1}, v_{i2}, \ldots, v_{ik_i})$.

We now consider two cases. If $|\lambda_i| < 1$, then

$$\lim_{n\to\infty}\binom{n}{j}\lambda_i^{n-j} = 0$$

for any $0 \le j \le k_i - 1$, and all of the equations in (8.37) follow. On the other hand, if $|\lambda_i| \ge 1$, then from the last equation in (8.37) we know that $v_{ik} = 0$. Putting $v_{ik} = 0$ into the second equation from bottom in (8.37) we obtain $v_{i(k-1)} = 0$. We can further move from bottom to top in the system (8.37) of equations in this way, and finally we get:

$$v_{i1} = v_{i2} = \cdots = v_{i(k_i-1)} = v_{ik_i} = 0.$$

This completes the proof.   □

Corollary 8.4. *Quantum loop (8.31) is almost surely terminating if and only if all the eigenvalues of U_X have norms less than 1.*

In the above, we only considered a special class of quantum loops with a unitary transformation as their body. It can be seen as a warming up for the termination problem of general quantum **while**-loops that we will deal with next. But the termination conditions presented above are of independent significance because they are much easier to check than the corresponding conditions for more general quantum loops.

General quantum while-loops: Termination of a special class of quantum **while**-loops with unitary bodies was carefully studied above. However, the expressive power of this kind of quantum loops is very limited; for example they cannot model the case where a measurement occurs in the loop body or a quantum loop is nested in another. Now we consider a general quantum **while**-loop as defined in Section 5.1:

$$\textbf{while } M[\overline{q}] = 1 \textbf{ do } S \textbf{ od} \tag{8.38}$$

where $M = \{M_0, M_1\}$ is a yes–no measurement, $\overline{q}$ is a quantum register, and the loop body S is a general quantum program. As we saw in Section 5.3, the denotational semantics of S is a quantum operation $[\![S]\!] = \mathcal{E}$ in the state Hilbert space of $\overline{q}$ (if the quantum variables $qvar(S) \subseteq \overline{p}$). So, the loop (8.38) can be equivalently rewritten as:

$$\textbf{while } M[\overline{q}] = 1 \textbf{ do } \overline{q} := \mathcal{E}[\overline{q}] \textbf{ od}. \tag{8.39}$$

The remainding part of this subsection focuses on the termination issue of quantum loop (8.39). Let us see how the loop (8.39) is executed. Roughly speaking, the loop consists of two parts. The loop body "$\overline{q} := \mathcal{E}[\overline{q}]$" transforms a density operator σ to density operator $\mathcal{E}(\sigma)$. The loop guard "$M[\overline{q}] = 1$" is checked at each execution step. For $i = 0, 1$, we define quantum operation $\mathcal{E}_i$ from the measurement $M = \{M_0, M_1\}$ in the loop guard as follows:

$$\mathcal{E}_i(\sigma) = M_i \sigma M_i^\dagger \tag{8.40}$$

for any density operator σ. Moreover, for any two quantum operations $\mathcal{F}_1, \mathcal{F}_2$, we write $\mathcal{F}_2 \circ \mathcal{F}_1$ for their composition; that is,

$$(\mathcal{F}_2 \circ \mathcal{F}_1)(\rho) = \mathcal{F}_2(\mathcal{F}_1(\rho))$$

for all $\rho \in \mathcal{D}(\mathcal{H})$. For a quantum operation $\mathcal{F}$, $\mathcal{F}^n$ denotes the nth power of $\mathcal{F}$, i.e. the composition of n copies of $\mathcal{F}$. Then the execution of the loop with input state ρ can be more precisely described as follows:

1. *Initial step*: We first perform the termination measurement $\{M_0, M_1\}$ on the input state ρ.

   - The probability that the program terminates; that is, the measurement outcome is 0, is

   $$p_T^{(1)}(\rho) = tr[\mathcal{E}_0(\rho)],$$

   and the program state after termination is

   $$\rho_{out}^{(1)} = \mathcal{E}_0(\rho)/p_T^{(1)}(\rho).$$

   We encode probability $p_T^{(1)}(\rho)$ and density operator $\rho_{out}^{(1)}$ into a partial density operator

   $$p_T^{(1)}(\rho)\rho_{out}^{(1)} = \mathcal{E}_0(\rho).$$

   So, $\mathcal{E}_0(\rho)$ is the partial output state at the first step.
   - The probability that the program does not terminate; that is, the measurement outcome is 1, is

   $$p_{NT}^{(1)}(\rho) = tr[\mathcal{E}_1(\rho)], \tag{8.41}$$

   and the program state after the outcome 1 is obtained is

   $$\rho_{mid}^{(1)} = \mathcal{E}_1(\rho)/p_{NT}^{(1)}(\rho).$$

   Then it is transformed by the loop body $\mathcal{E}$ to

   $$\rho_{in}^{(2)} = (\mathcal{E} \circ \mathcal{E}_1)(\rho)/p_{NT}^{(1)}(\rho),$$

   upon which the second step will be executed. We can combine $p_{NT}^{(1)}$ and $\rho_{in}^{(2)}$ into a partial density operator

   $$p_{NT}^{(1)}(\rho)\rho_{in}^{(2)} = (\mathcal{E} \circ \mathcal{E}_1)(\rho).$$

2. *Induction step*: We write

$$p_{NT}^{(\leq n)} = \prod_{i=1}^{n} p_{NT}^{(i)}$$

for the probability that the program does not terminate within n steps, where $p_{NT}^{(i)}$ is the probability that the program does not terminate at the ith step for every $1 \leq i \leq n$. The program state after the nth measurement with outcome 1 is

$$\rho_{mid}^{(n)} = \frac{\left[\mathcal{E}_1 \circ (\mathcal{E} \circ \mathcal{E}_1)^{n-1} \right](\rho)}{p_{NT}^{(\leq n)}},$$

which is then transformed by the loop body $\mathcal{E}$ into

$$\rho_{in}^{(n+1)} = \frac{(\mathcal{E} \circ \mathcal{E}_1)^n (\rho)}{p_{NT}^{(\leq n)}}.$$

We combine $p_{NT}^{(\leq n)}$ and $\rho_{in}^{(n+1)}$ into a partial density operator

$$p_{NT}^{(\leq n)}(\rho)\rho_{in}^{(n+1)} = (\mathcal{E} \circ \mathcal{E}_1)^n(\rho).$$

Now the $(n+1)$st step is executed upon $\rho_{in}^{(n+1)}$.

- The probability that the program terminates at the $(n+1)$st step is then

$$p_T^{(n+1)}(\rho) = tr \left[\mathcal{E}_0 \left(\rho_{in}^{(n+1)} \right) \right],$$

and the probability that the program does not terminate within n steps but it terminates at the $(n+1)$st step is

$$q_T^{(n+1)}(\rho) = tr \left(\left[\mathcal{E}_0 \circ (\mathcal{E} \circ \mathcal{E}_1)^n \right](\rho) \right).$$

The program state after the termination is

$$\rho_{out}^{(n+1)} = [\mathcal{E}_0 \circ (\mathcal{E} \circ \mathcal{E}_1)^n](\rho) / q_T^{(n+1)}(\rho).$$

Combining $q_T^{(n+1)}(\rho)$ and $\rho_{out}^{(n+1)}$ yields the partial output state of the program at the $(n+1)$st step:

$$q_T^{(n+1)}(\rho)\rho_{out}^{(n+1)} = [\mathcal{E}_0 \circ (\mathcal{E} \circ \mathcal{E}_1)^n](\rho).$$

- The probability that the program does not terminate within $(n+1)$ steps is then

$$p_{NT}^{(\leq n+1)}(\rho) = tr([\mathcal{E}_1 \circ (\mathcal{E} \circ \mathcal{E}_1)^n](\rho)). \tag{8.42}$$

As pointed out in Section 5.1, the major difference between a classical loop and a quantum loop comes from the checking of loop guard. During checking the guard of a classical loop, the program state is not changed. However, the quantum measurement in the guard of a quantum loop disturbs the state of the system. Thus, the quantum program state after checking the loop guard may be different from that before checking. The change of program state caused by measurement M is depicted by quantum operations $\mathcal{E}_0$ and $\mathcal{E}_1$.

The above description of the computational process of quantum loop (8.39) is a generalisation of the execution of loop (8.31) described before. Now Definitions 8.13, 8.14 and 8.15 for the special quantum loop (8.31) can be easily extended to the general quantum loop (8.39).

Definition 8.16. 1. We say that quantum loop (8.39) terminates from input state ρ if probability $p_{NT}^{(n)}(\rho) = 0$ for some positive integer n.

2. We say that loop (8.39) almost surely terminates from input state ρ if nontermination probability

$$p_{NT}(\rho) = \lim_{n\to\infty} p_{NT}^{(\leq n)}(\rho) = 0$$

where $p_{NT}^{(\leq n)}$ is the probability that the program does not terminate within n steps.

Definition 8.17. The quantum loop (8.39) is terminating (resp. almost surely terminating) if it terminates (resp. almost surely terminates) from any input ρ.

The (total) output state of a quantum loop is obtained by summing up its partial computing results obtained at all steps. Formally, we have:

Definition 8.18. The function $\mathcal{F} : \mathcal{D}(H) \to \mathcal{D}(H)$ computed by the quantum loop (8.39) is defined by

$$\mathcal{F}(\rho) = \sum_{n=1}^{\infty} q_T^{(n)}(\rho)\rho_{out}^{(n)} = \sum_{n=0}^{\infty} \left[\mathcal{E}_0 \circ (\mathcal{E} \circ \mathcal{E}_1)^n\right](\rho)$$

for each $\rho \in \mathcal{D}(\mathcal{H})$, where

$$q_T^{(n)} = p_{NT}^{(\leq n-1)} p_T^{(n)}$$

is the probability that the program does not terminate within $n-1$ steps but it terminates at the nth step.

Obviously, the above three definitions generalise the corresponding definitions given before for loops with loop bodies being unitary operators.

The following proposition gives a recursive characterisation of the function $\mathcal{F}$ computed by quantum loop (8.39). It is essentially a restatement of Corollary 5.1, and can be easily proved by the above definition.

Proposition 8.1. *The quantum operation $\mathcal{F}$ computed by loop (8.39) satisfies the following recursive equation:*

$$\mathcal{F}(\rho) = \mathcal{E}_0(\rho) + \mathcal{F}[(\mathcal{E} \circ \mathcal{E}_1)(\rho)]$$

for all density operators ρ.

Matrix representation of quantum operations: The remaindering part of this subsection is devoted to termination and running time analysis of quantum loop (8.39). Since iterations of quantum operations $\mathcal{E}, \mathcal{E}_0, \mathcal{E}_1$ are involved in the definitions of termination and the computed function $\mathcal{F}$ of loop (8.39), it is unavoidable to deal with their iterations in its analysis. However, it is usually very difficult to compute the iterations of quantum operations. To overcome this difficulty, we introduce a useful mathematical tool, namely the matrix representation of a quantum operation, which is usually much easier to manipulate than the quantum operation itself.

Definition 8.19. Suppose quantum operation $\mathcal{E}$ in a d-dimensional Hilbert space $\mathcal{H}$ has the Kraus operator-sum representation:

$$\mathcal{E}(\rho) = \sum_i E_i \rho E_i^\dagger$$

for all density operators ρ. Then the matrix representation of $\mathcal{E}$ is the $d^2 \times d^2$ matrix:

$$M = \sum_i E_i \otimes E_i^*,$$

where A^* stands for the conjugate of matrix A, i.e. $A^* = (a_{ij}^*)$ with a_{ij}^* being the conjugate of complex number a_{ij}, whenever $A = (a_{ij})$.

The effect of matrix representation of quantum operations in analysis of quantum programs is mainly based on the next lemma, which establishes a connection between the image of a matrix A under a quantum operation $\mathcal{E}$ and the multiplication of the matrix representation of $\mathcal{E}$ and the cylindrical extension of A. Actually, this lemma will play a key role in the proofs of all the main results in this subsection.

Lemma 8.12. *Suppose that* dim $\mathcal{H} = d$. *We write*

$$|\Phi\rangle = \sum_{j} |jj\rangle$$

for the (unnormalised) maximally entangled state in $\mathcal{H} \otimes \mathcal{H}$, *where* $\{|j\rangle\}$ *is an orthonormal basis of* $\mathcal{H}$. *Let M be the matrix representation of quantum operation* $\mathcal{E}$. *Then for any* $d \times d$ *matrix A, we have:*

$$(\mathcal{E}(A) \otimes I)|\Phi\rangle = M(A \otimes I)|\Phi\rangle \tag{8.43}$$

where I stands for the $d \times d$-*unit matrix.*

Proof. We first observe the matrix equality: for any matrices A, B, and C,

$$(A \otimes B)(C \otimes I)|\Phi\rangle = (ACB^T \otimes I)|\Phi\rangle,$$

where B^T stands for the transpose of matrix B. This equality can be easily proved by a routine matrix calculation. Now it follows that

$$
\begin{aligned}
M(A \otimes I)|\Phi\rangle &= \sum_{i} \left(E_i \otimes E_i^*\right)(A \otimes I)|\Phi\rangle \\
&= \sum_{i} \left(E_i A E_i^\dagger \otimes I\right)|\Phi\rangle \\
&= (\mathcal{E}(A) \otimes I)|\Phi\rangle. \qquad \square
\end{aligned}
$$

It is interesting to observe that maximally entangled state $|\Phi\rangle$ enables us to represent a $d \times d$-matrix $A = (a_{ij})$ to a d^2-dimensional vector in the following way:

$$(A \otimes I)|\Phi\rangle = (a_{11}, ..., a_{1d}, a_{21}, ..., a_{2d}, ..., a_{d1}, ..., a_{dd})^T.$$

Furthermore, it helps to translate a quantum operation $\mathcal{E}$ on a d-dimensional Hilbert space to a $d^2 \times d^2$-matrix M through Eq. (8.43).

The above lemma has an immediate application showing that the matrix representation of a quantum operation is well-defined: if

$$\mathcal{E}(\rho) = \sum_{i} E_i \rho E_i^\dagger = \sum_{j} F_j \rho F_j^\dagger$$

for all density operators ρ, then

$$\sum_{i} E_i \otimes E_i^* = \sum_{j} F_j \otimes F_j^*.$$

This conclusion can be easily seen from arbitrariness of matrix A in Eq. (8.43).

After preparing the mathematical tool of the matrix representation of a quantum operation, we now come back to consider the quantum loop (8.39). Assume that the quantum operation $\mathcal{E}$ in the loop body has the operator-sum representation:

$$\mathcal{E}(\rho) = \sum_{i} E_i \rho E_i^\dagger$$

for all density operators ρ. Let $\mathcal{E}_i$ $(i = 0, 1)$ be the quantum operations defined by the measurement operations M_0, M_1 in the loop guard according to Eq. (8.40). We write $\mathcal{G}$ for the composition of $\mathcal{E}$ and $\mathcal{E}_1$:

$$\mathcal{G} = \mathcal{E} \circ \mathcal{E}_1.$$

Then $\mathcal{G}$ has the operator-sum representation:

$$\mathcal{G}(\rho) = \sum_{i} (E_i M_1) \rho (M_1^\dagger E_i^\dagger)$$

for all density operators ρ. Furthermore, the matrix representations of $\mathcal{E}_0$ and $\mathcal{G}$ are

$$N_0 = M_0 \otimes M_0^*,$$
$$R = \sum_i (E_i M_1) \otimes (E_i M_1)^*, \tag{8.44}$$

respectively. Suppose that the Jordan decomposition of R is

$$R = SJ(R)S^{-1}$$

where S is a nonsingular matrix, and $J(R)$ is the Jordan normal form of R:

$$J(R) = \bigoplus_{i=1}^{l} J_{k_i}(\lambda_i) = diag(J_{k_1}(\lambda_1), J_{k_2}(\lambda_2), \cdots, J_{k_l}(\lambda_l))$$

with $J_{k_s}(\lambda_s)$ being a $k_s \times k_s$-Jordan block of eigenvalue λ_s ($1 \leq s \leq l$) (see Lemma 8.8).

The following is a key technical lemma that describes the structure of the matrix representation R of quantum operation $\mathcal{G}$.

Lemma 8.13. 1. $|\lambda_s| \leq 1$ *for all* $1 \leq s \leq l$.
2. *If* $|\lambda_s| = 1$ *then the sth Jordan block is 1-dimensional; that is,* $k_s = 1$.

For readability, we postpone the lengthy proof of this lemma into Section A.4.

Analysis of termination and almost sure termination: Now we are ready to study termination of the quantum loop (8.39). First of all, the following lemma gives a simple termination condition in terms of the matrix representation of quantum operations.

Lemma 8.14. *Let R be defined by Eq. (8.44), and let*

$$|\Phi\rangle = \sum_j |jj\rangle$$

be the (unnormalised) maximally entangled state in $\mathcal{H} \otimes \mathcal{H}$. Then we have:

1. *Quantum loop (8.39) terminates from input ρ if and only if*

$$R^n(\rho \otimes I)|\Phi\rangle = \mathbf{0}$$

for some integer $n \geq 0$;
2. *Quantum loop (8.39) almost surely terminates from input ρ if and only if*

$$\lim_{n \to \infty} R^n(\rho \otimes I)|\Phi\rangle = \mathbf{0},$$

Proof. We only prove part 1, the proof of part 2 is similar. First, it follows from Lemma 8.12 that

$$[\mathcal{G}(\rho) \otimes I]|\Phi\rangle = R(\rho \otimes I)|\Phi\rangle.$$

Repeated applications of the above equality yield:

$$[\mathcal{G}^n(\rho) \otimes I]|\Phi\rangle = R^n(\rho \otimes I)|\Phi\rangle.$$

On the other hand, it holds that

$$tr(A) = \langle\Phi|A \otimes I|\Phi\rangle$$

for any matrix A. Therefore, since $\mathcal{E}$ is trace-preserving, we obtain:

$$tr\left(\left[\mathcal{E}_1 \circ (\mathcal{E} \circ \mathcal{E}_1)^{n-1}\right](\rho)\right) = tr\left((\mathcal{E} \circ \mathcal{E}_1)^n(\rho)\right)$$
$$= tr(\mathcal{G}^n(\rho))$$
$$= \langle\Phi|R^n(\rho \otimes I)|\Phi\rangle.$$

Moreover, it is clear that $\langle\Phi|R^n(\rho\otimes I)|\Phi\rangle = 0$ if and only if $R^n(\rho\otimes I)|\Phi\rangle = \mathbf{0}$. $\qquad\square$

As a direct application of the above lemma, we have:

Lemma 8.15. *Let R and $|\Phi\rangle$ be as in Lemma 8.14.*

1. *Quantum loop (8.39) is terminating if and only if $R^n|\Phi\rangle = \mathbf{0}$ for some integer $n \geq 0$;*
2. *Quantum loop (8.39) is almost surely terminating if and only if $\lim_{n\to\infty} R^n|\Phi\rangle = \mathbf{0}$.*

Proof. Notice that a quantum loop is terminating if and only if it terminates from a special input (mixed) state:

$$\rho_0 = \frac{1}{d}\cdot I,$$

where $d = \dim\mathcal{H}$ and I is the identity operator on $\mathcal{H}$. Then this lemma follows immediately from Lemma 8.14. $\qquad\square$

We can now present one of the main results of this subsection, which gives a necessary and sufficient terminating condition for a quantum loop in terms of the eigenvalues of the matrix representations of the quantum operations involved in the loop.

Theorem 8.12. *Let R and $|\Phi\rangle$ be as in Lemma 8.14. Then we have:*

1. *If $R^k|\Phi\rangle = \mathbf{0}$ for some integer $k \geq 0$, then quantum loop (8.39) is terminating. Conversely, if loop (8.39) is terminating, then $R^k|\Phi\rangle = \mathbf{0}$ for all integer $k \geq k_0$, where k_0 is the maximal size of Jordan blocks of R corresponding to eigenvalue 0.*
2. *Quantum loop (8.39) is almost surely terminating if and only if $|\Phi\rangle$ is orthogonal to all eigenvectors of $R^\dagger$ corresponding to eigenvalues λ with $|\lambda| = 1$, where $R^\dagger$ is the transpose conjugate of R.*

Proof. We first prove part 1. If $R^k|\Phi\rangle = 0$ for some $k \geq 0$, then by Lemma 8.15 we conclude that loop (8.39) is terminating. Conversely, suppose that loop (8.39) is terminating. Again by Lemma 8.15, there exists some integer $n \geq 0$ such that $R^n|\Phi\rangle = 0$. For any integer $k \geq$ the maximal size of Jordan blocks of R corresponding to eigenvalue 0, we want to show that $R^k|\Phi\rangle = 0$. Without any loss of generality, we assume the Jordan decomposition of R:

$$R = SJ(R)S^{-1}$$

where

$$J(R) = \bigoplus_{i=1}^{l} J_{k_i}(\lambda_i) = diag(J_{k_1}(\lambda_1), J_{k_2}(\lambda_2), \cdots, J_{k_l}(\lambda_l))$$

with $|\lambda_1| \geq \cdots \geq |\lambda_s| > 0$ and $\lambda_{s+1} = \cdots = \lambda_l = 0$. Observe that

$$R^n = SJ(R)^n S^{-1}.$$

Since S is nonsingular, it follows immediately from $R^n|\Phi\rangle = 0$ that

$$J(R)^n S^{-1}|\Phi\rangle = \mathbf{0}.$$

We can divide both matrix $J(R)$ and vector $S^{-1}|\Phi\rangle$ into two parts:

$$J(R) = \begin{pmatrix} A & 0 \\ 0 & B \end{pmatrix}, \qquad S^{-1}|\Phi\rangle = \begin{pmatrix} |x\rangle \\ |y\rangle \end{pmatrix},$$

where

$$A = \bigoplus_{i=1}^{s} J_{k_i}(\lambda_i) = diag(J_{k_1}(\lambda_1),...,J_{k_s}(\lambda_s)),$$

$$B = \bigoplus_{i=s+1}^{l} J_{k_i}(\lambda_i) = diag(J_{k_{s+1}}(0),...,J_{k_l}(0)),$$

$|x\rangle$ is a t-dimensional vector, $|y\rangle$ is a $(d^2 - t)$-dimensional vector, and $t = \sum_{j=1}^{s} k_j$. Then it holds that

$$J(R)^n S^{-1} |\Phi\rangle = \begin{pmatrix} A^n |x\rangle \\ B^n |y\rangle \end{pmatrix}.$$

Note that $\lambda_1, ..., \lambda_s \neq 0$. So, $J_{k_1}(\lambda_1), ..., J_{k_s}(\lambda_s)$ are nonsingular, and A is nonsingular too. Thus, $J(R)^n S^{-1} |\Phi\rangle = \mathbf{0}$ implies $A^n |x\rangle = \mathbf{0}$ and furthermore $|x\rangle = \mathbf{0}$. On the other hand, for each j with $s + 1 \leq j \leq l$, since $k \geq k_j$, it holds that $J_{k_j}(0)^k = \mathbf{0}$. Consequently, $B^k = \mathbf{0}$. This together with $|x\rangle = \mathbf{0}$ implies

$$J(R)^k S^{-1} |\Phi\rangle = \mathbf{0}$$

and

$$R^k |\Phi\rangle = S J(R)^k S^{-1} |\Phi\rangle = \mathbf{0}.$$

Now we prove part 2. First, we know by Lemma 8.15 that the program (8.39) is almost terminating if and only if

$$\lim_{n \to \infty} J(R)^n S^{-1} |\Phi\rangle = \mathbf{0}.$$

We assume that

$$1 = |\lambda_1| = \cdots = |\lambda_r| > |\lambda_{r+1}| \geq \cdots \geq |\lambda_l|$$

in the Jordan decomposition of R, and we write:

$$J(R) = \begin{pmatrix} C & 0 \\ 0 & D \end{pmatrix}, \quad S^{-1} |\Phi\rangle = \begin{pmatrix} |u\rangle \\ |v\rangle \end{pmatrix}$$

where

$$C = diag(\lambda_1, ..., \lambda_r),$$
$$D = diag(J_{k_{r+1}}(\lambda_{r+1}), ..., J_{k_l}(\lambda_l)),$$

$|u\rangle$ is an r-dimensional vector, and $|v\rangle$ is a $(d^2 - r)$-dimensional vector. (Note that $J_{k_1}(\lambda_1), ..., J_{k_r}(\lambda_r)$ are all 1×1 matrices because $|\lambda_1| = ... = |\lambda_r| = 1$; see Lemma 8.13.)

If $|\Phi\rangle$ is orthogonal to all the eigenvectors of $R^\dagger$ corresponding to eigenvalue with module 1, then by definition we have $|u\rangle = \mathbf{0}$. On the other hand, for each j with $r + 1 \leq j \leq l$, since $|\lambda_j| < 1$, we have

$$\lim_{n \to \infty} J_{k_j}(\lambda_j)^n = \mathbf{0}.$$

Thus, $\lim_{n \to \infty} D^n = \mathbf{0}$. So, it follows that

$$\lim_{n \to \infty} J(R)^n S^{-1} |\Phi\rangle = \lim_{n \to \infty} \begin{pmatrix} C^n |u\rangle \\ D^n |v\rangle \end{pmatrix} = \mathbf{0}.$$

Conversely, if

$$\lim_{n \to \infty} J(R)^n S^{-1} |\Phi\rangle = \mathbf{0},$$

then $\lim_{n \to \infty} C^n |u\rangle = \mathbf{0}$. This implies $|u\rangle = \mathbf{0}$ because C is a diagonal unitary. Consequently, $|\Phi\rangle$ is orthogonal to all the eigenvectors of $R^\dagger$ corresponding to eigenvalue with module 1. $\quad\square$

Expectation of observables at the outputs: Except the program termination problem discussed, computing the expected value of a program variable is another important problem in classical program analysis. We now consider its quantum counterpart – computing the expectation of an observable at the output of a quantum program.

Recall from Exercise 2.8 that an observable is modelled by a Hermitian operator P, and the expectation (average value) of P in a state σ is $tr(P\sigma)$. In particular, whenever P is a quantum predicate, i.e. $0_{\mathcal{H}} \sqsubseteq P \sqsubseteq I_{\mathcal{H}}$, then the expectation

$tr(P\sigma)$ can be understood as the probability that predicate P is satisfied in state σ. Actually, for a given input state ρ, many interesting properties of the quantum loop (8.39) can be expressed in terms of the expectation $tr(P\mathcal{F}(\rho))$ of certain observables P in the output state $\mathcal{F}(\rho)$. Thus, analysis of quantum programs can often be reduced to the problem of computing expectation $tr(P\mathcal{F}(\rho))$.

Now we develop a method for computing the expectation $tr(P\mathcal{F}(\rho))$. As will be seen in the proof of Theorem 8.13 below, our method depends on the convergence of the following power series:

$$\sum_n R^n$$

where R is the matrix representation of $\mathcal{G} = \mathcal{E} \circ \mathcal{E}_1$ given by Eq. (8.44). But this series may not converge when some eigenvalues of R have module 1. A natural idea to overcome this objection is to modify the Jordan normal form $J(R)$ of R by vanishing the Jordan blocks corresponding to those eigenvalues with module 1, which are all 1-dimensional according to Lemma 8.13. This yields the matrix:

$$N = SJ(N)S^{-1} \tag{8.45}$$

where $J(N)$ is obtained by modifying $J(R)$ as follows:

$$J(N) = diag(J'_1, J'_2, \cdots, J'_3), \tag{8.46}$$

$$J'_s = \begin{cases} 0 & \text{if } |\lambda_s| = 1, \\ J_{k_s}(\lambda_s) & \text{otherwise,} \end{cases}$$

for each $1 \le s \le l$.

Fortunately, as shown in the following lemma, such a modification of the matrix representation R of $\mathcal{G}$ does not change the behaviour of its powers when combined with the measurement operator M_0 in the loop guard.

Lemma 8.16. *For any integer $n \ge 0$, we have:*

$$N_0 R^n = N_0 N^n,$$

where $N_0 = M_0 \otimes M_0^*$ is the matrix representation of $\mathcal{E}_0$.

The proof of this lemma is quite involved and thus also postponed to Appendix A.4.

Now we are ready to present another main result of this subsection, which gives an explicit formula for computing the expected value of an observable at the output of a quantum loop.

Theorem 8.13. *The expectation of observable P in the output state $\mathcal{F}(\rho)$ of quantum loop (8.39) with input state ρ is*

$$tr(P\mathcal{F}(\rho)) = \langle\Phi|(P \otimes I)N_0(I \otimes I - N)^{-1}(\rho \otimes I)|\Phi\rangle,$$

where symbol I stands for the identity operator on $\mathcal{H}$, and

$$|\Phi\rangle = \sum_j |jj\rangle$$

is the (unnormalised) maximally entangled state in $\mathcal{H} \otimes \mathcal{H}$, with $\{|j\rangle\}$ being an orthonormal basis of $\mathcal{H}$.

Proof. With the previous preparations, this proof is more or less a straightforward calculation based on Definition 8.18. First, it follows from Lemma 8.12 together with the defining equations of quantum operations $\mathcal{E}_0$ and $\mathcal{G}$ that

$$[\mathcal{E}_0(\rho) \otimes I]|\Phi\rangle = N_0(\rho \otimes I)|\Phi\rangle, \tag{8.47}$$

$$[\mathcal{G}(\rho) \otimes I]|\Phi\rangle = R(\rho \otimes I)|\Phi\rangle. \tag{8.48}$$

By first applying Eq. (8.47) and then repeatedly applying Eq. (8.48), we obtain:

$$[\mathcal{F}(\rho) \otimes I]|\Phi\rangle = \left[\sum_{n=0}^{\infty} \mathcal{E}_0\left(\mathcal{G}^n(\rho)\right) \otimes I\right]|\Phi\rangle$$

$$= \sum_{n=0}^{\infty}\left[\mathcal{E}_0\left(\mathcal{G}^n(\rho)\right) \otimes I\right]|\Phi\rangle$$

$$= \sum_{n=0}^{\infty} N_0\left(\mathcal{G}^n(\rho) \otimes I\right)|\Phi\rangle$$

$$= \sum_{n=0}^{\infty} N_0 R^n(\rho \otimes I)|\Phi\rangle$$

$$\overset{(a)}{=} \sum_{n=0}^{\infty} N_0 N^n(\rho \otimes I)|\Phi\rangle$$

$$= N_0\left(\sum_{n=0}^{\infty} N^n\right)(\rho \otimes I)|\Phi\rangle$$

$$= N_0(I \otimes I - N)^{-1}(\rho \otimes I)|\Phi\rangle.$$

The equality labelled by (a) follows from Lemma 8.16. Finally, a routine calculation yields $tr(\rho) = \langle\Phi|\rho \otimes I|\Phi\rangle$, and thus we have:

$$tr(P\mathcal{F}(\rho)) = \langle\Phi|P\mathcal{F}(\rho) \otimes I|\Phi\rangle$$

$$= \langle\Phi|(P \otimes I)(\mathcal{F}(\rho) \otimes I)|\Phi\rangle$$

$$= \langle\Phi|(P \otimes I)N_0(I \otimes I - N)^{-1}(\rho \otimes I)|\Phi\rangle. \qquad \square$$

Average running time: We already studied two program analysis problems, namely termination and expected value, for quantum loop (8.39) using matrix representation of quantum operations. To further illustrate the power of the method introduced above, we compute the average running time loop (8.39) with input state ρ:

$$\sum_{n=1}^{\infty} np_T^{(n)}$$

where for each $n \geq 1$,

$$p_T^{(n)} = tr\left[\left(\mathcal{E}_0 \circ (\mathcal{E} \circ \mathcal{E}_1)^{n-1}\right)(\rho)\right] = tr\left[\left(\mathcal{E}_0 \circ \mathcal{G}^{n-1}\right)(\rho)\right]$$

is the probability that the loop (8.39) terminates at the nth step. It is clear that this cannot be done by a direct application of Theorem 8.13. But a procedure similar to the proof of Theorem 8.13 leads to:

Proposition 8.2. *The average running time of quantum loop (8.39) with input state ρ is*

$$\langle\Phi|N_0(I \otimes I - N)^{-2}(\rho \otimes I)|\Phi\rangle.$$

Proof. This proof is also a straightforward calculation based on Definition 8.18. Using Eqs (8.47) and (8.48) and Lemma 8.16, we have:

$$\sum_{n=1}^{\infty} np_n = \sum_{n=1}^{\infty} n \cdot tr\left[\left(\mathcal{E}_0 \circ \mathcal{G}^{n-1}\right)(\rho)\right]$$

$$= \sum_{n=1}^{\infty} n\langle\Phi|\left(\mathcal{E}_0 \circ \mathcal{G}^{n-1}\right)(\rho) \otimes I|\Phi\rangle$$

$$= \sum_{n=1}^{\infty} n \langle \Phi | N_0 R^{n-1} (\rho \otimes I) | \Phi \rangle$$

$$= \sum_{n=1}^{\infty} n \langle \Phi | N_0 N^{n-1} (\rho \otimes I) | \Phi \rangle$$

$$= \langle \Phi | N_0 \left(\sum_{n=1}^{\infty} n N^{n-1} \right) (\rho \otimes I) | \Phi \rangle$$

$$= \langle \Phi | N_0 (I \otimes I - N)^{-2} (\rho \otimes I) | \Phi \rangle. \qquad \square$$

An illustrative example: We now give an example to show how can Proposition 8.2 be applied to quantum walks in order to compute their average running time. We consider a quantum walk on an n-circle. It can be seen as a variant of one-dimensional quantum walk, and it is also a special case of quantum walk on a graph defined in Section 4.5.

Let $\mathcal{H}_d$ be the direction space, which is a 2-dimensional Hilbert space with orthonormal basis state $|L\rangle$ and $|R\rangle$, indicating directions Left and Right, respectively. Assume that the n different positions on the n-circle are labelled by numbers $0, 1, ..., n-1$. Let $\mathcal{H}_p$ be an n-dimensional Hilbert space with orthonormal basis states $|0\rangle, |1\rangle, ..., |n-1\rangle$, where for each $0 \leq i \leq n-1$, the basis vector $|i\rangle$ is corresponding to position i on the n-circle. Thus, the state space of the quantum walk is $\mathcal{H} = \mathcal{H}_d \otimes \mathcal{H}_p$. The initial state is assumed to be $|L\rangle|0\rangle$. Different from the quantum walks considered in Section 4.5, this walk has an absorbing boundary at position 1. So, each step of the walk consists of:

1. Measure the position of the system to see whether the current position is 1. If the outcome is "yes", then the walk terminates; otherwise, it continues. This measurement is used to model the absorbing boundary. It can be described by

$$M = \{ M_{yes} = I_d \otimes |1\rangle\langle 1|, M_{no} = I - M_{yes} \},$$

where I_d and I are the identity operators in $\mathcal{H}_d$ and $\mathcal{H}$, respectively;

2. A "coin-tossing" operator

$$H = \frac{1}{\sqrt{2}} \begin{pmatrix} 1 & 1 \\ 1 & -1 \end{pmatrix}$$

is applied in the direction space $\mathcal{H}_d$. Here, the Hadamard gate is chosen to model the "coin-tossing";

3. A shift operator

$$S = \sum_{i=0}^{n-1} |L\rangle\langle L| \otimes |i \ominus 1\rangle\langle i| + \sum_{i=0}^{n-1} |R\rangle\langle R| \otimes |i \oplus 1\rangle\langle i|$$

is performed on the space $\mathcal{H}$. The intuitive meaning of the operator S is that the system walks one step left or right according to the direction state. Here, $\oplus$ and $\ominus$ stand for addition and subtraction modulo n, respectively.

Using the quantum **while**-language, this quantum walk can be properly written as the following quantum loop:

$$\textbf{while } M[d, p] = yes \textbf{ do } d, p := W[d, p] \textbf{ od}$$

where quantum variables d, p are used to denote direction and position, respectively,

$$W = S(H \otimes I_p)$$

is the single-step walk operator, and I_p is the identity operator on $\mathcal{H}_p$.

We now compute the average running time of the quantum walk. A direct application of Proposition 8.2 tells us that the average running time of this walk is given by

$$\langle \Phi | N_0 (I \otimes I - N)^{-2} (\rho \otimes I) | \Phi \rangle, \qquad (8.49)$$

where

$$N_0 = M_{no} \otimes M_{no}, \quad N = (W M_{yes}) \otimes (W M_{yes})^*,$$

I is the identity matrix on $\mathcal{H} = \mathcal{H}_d \otimes \mathcal{H}_p$, and $\rho = |L\rangle\langle L| \otimes |0\rangle\langle 0|$. Note that here we do not need to use the modification procedure given by Eqs (8.45) and (8.46). Algorithm 1 is given for computing (8.49). This algorithm was run on a laptop for $n < 30$, and the computational result showed that the average running time of the quantum walk on an n-circle is n. It was further proved in [282] that for all n, the average running time of the quantum walk on an n-circle is n; but the proof is very involved and thus omitted here.

Algorithm 1: Compute average running time of quantum walk on n-circle.

input : integer n
output: b (the average running time of quantum walk on a n-circle)
$n \times n$ **matrix** $I \leftarrow E(n)$; (*n-dimensional identity*)
integer $m \leftarrow 2n$;
$m \times m$ **matrix** $I_2 \leftarrow E(m)$; (*m-dimensional identity*)
m^2-**dimensional vector** $|\Phi\rangle \leftarrow \vec{I}_2$; (*maximally entangled state*)
$m \times m$ **matrix** $\rho \leftarrow |1\rangle\langle 1|$; (*initial state*)
2×2 **matrix** $H \leftarrow [1\ 1; 1\ -1]/\sqrt{2}$; (*Hadamard matrix*)
$m \times m$ **matrix** $M_0 \leftarrow |0\rangle\langle 0| \otimes E(2)$; (*termination test measurement*)
$m \times m$ **matrix** $M_1 \leftarrow I_2 - M_0$;
$n \times n$ **matrix** $X \leftarrow I * 0$; (*shift unitary*)
for $j = 1 : n - 1$ **do**
  $|\quad X(j, j+1) \leftarrow 1$;
end
$X(n, 1) \leftarrow 1$;
$C \leftarrow X^\dagger$;
$m \times m$ **matrix** $S \leftarrow X \otimes |0\rangle\langle 0| + C \otimes |1\rangle\langle 1|$; (*shift operator*)
$m \times m$ **matrix** $W \leftarrow S(I \otimes H)M_1$;
$m^2 \times m^2$ **matrix** $M_T \leftarrow M_0 \otimes M_0$;
$m^2 \times m^2$ **matrix** $N_T \leftarrow W_1 \otimes W_1$;
$m^2 \times m^2$ **matrix** $I_3 \leftarrow E(m^2)$; (*m^2-dimensional identity*)
real number $b \leftarrow \langle\Phi|M_T(I_3 - N_T)^{-2}(\rho \otimes I_2)|\Phi\rangle$; (*calculate the average running time*)
return b

8.4.2 Quantum graph theory

We carefully studied termination and almost termination for quantum **while**-loops in the last subsection. As we will see later in the next subsection, termination problem for quantum loops is a special case of reachability problem for quantum Markov chains. Indeed, classical Markov chains have been widely used in verification and analysis of randomised algorithms and probabilistic programs. So, this and the next subsections are devoted to develop a theoretical framework and several algorithms for reachability analysis of quantum Markov chains. Hopefully, this will pave a path toward further research on algorithmic analysis of quantum programs.

Reachability analysis techniques for classical Markov chains heavily rely on algorithms for graph-reachability problems. Similarly, a kind of graph structures in Hilbert spaces, called quantum graphs, play a crucial role in the reachability analysis of quantum Markov chains. Therefore, in this subsection, we present a brief introduction to the theory of quantum graphs.

This subsection and the next one can be seen as the quantum generalisation of reachability analysis of classical Markov chains; the reader should consult Chapter 10 of book [40] for their classical counterparts in case she/he finds some parts of these two subsections hard to understand.

Basic definitions: A quantum graph structure naturally resides in a quantum Markov chain. So, let us start from the definition of quantum Markov chain. Recall that a classical Markov chain is a pair $\langle S, P \rangle$, where S is a finite set of states, and P is a matrix of transition probabilities, i.e. a mapping $P : S \times S \to [0, 1]$ such that

$$\sum_{t \in S} P(s, t) = 1$$

for every $s \in S$, where $P(s, t)$ is the probability of the system going from s to t. There is a directed graph underlying a Markov chain $\langle S, P \rangle$. The elements of S are vertices of the graph. The adjacency relation of this graph is defined as follows: for any $s, t \in S$, if $P(s, t) > 0$, then the graph has an edge from s to t. Understanding the structure of this graph is often very helpful for analysis of Markov chain $\langle S, P \rangle$ itself.

A quantum Markov chain is a quantum generalisation of a Markov chain where the state space of a Markov chain is replaced by a Hilbert space and its transition matrix is replaced by a quantum operation which, as we saw in Section 2.6, is a mathematical formalism of the discrete-time evolution of (open) quantum systems.

Definition 8.20. A quantum Markov chain is a pair $\mathcal{C} = \langle \mathcal{H}, \mathcal{E} \rangle$, where:

1. $\mathcal{H}$ is a finite-dimensional Hilbert space;
2. $\mathcal{E}$ is a quantum operation (or superoperator) on $\mathcal{H}$.

The behaviour of a quantum Markov chain can be roughly described as follows: if currently the process is in a mixed state ρ, then it will be in state $\mathcal{E}(\rho)$ in the next step. So, a quantum Markov chain $\langle \mathcal{H}, \mathcal{E} \rangle$ is a discrete-time quantum system of which the state space is $\mathcal{H}$ and the dynamics is described by quantum operation $\mathcal{E}$. From the viewpoint of quantum programming, it can be used to model the body of quantum loop (8.39).

Now we examine the graph structure underlying a quantum Markov chain $\mathcal{C} = \langle \mathcal{H}, \mathcal{E} \rangle$. First of all, we introduce the adjacency relation between quantum states in $\mathcal{H}$ induced by the quantum operation $\mathcal{E}$. To this end, we need several auxiliary notions. Recall that $\mathcal{D}(\mathcal{H})$ denotes the set of partial density operators on $\mathcal{H}$; that is, positive operators ρ with trace $tr(\rho) \leq 1$. For any subset X of $\mathcal{H}$, we write $span X$ for the subspace of $\mathcal{H}$ spanned by X; that is, it consists of all finite linear combinations of vectors in X.

Definition 8.21. The support $supp(\rho)$ of a partial density operator $\rho \in \mathcal{D}(\mathcal{H})$ is the subspace of $\mathcal{H}$ spanned by the eigenvectors of ρ with nonzero eigenvalues.

Definition 8.22. Let $\{X_k\}$ be a family of subspaces of $\mathcal{H}$. Then the join of $\{X_k\}$ is defined by

$$\bigvee_k X_k = span \left(\bigcup_k X_k \right).$$

In particular, we write $X \vee Y$ for the join of two subspaces X and Y. It is easy to see that $\bigvee_k X_k$ is the smallest subspace of $\mathcal{H}$ that contains all X_k.

Definition 8.23. The image of a subspace X of $\mathcal{H}$ under a quantum operation $\mathcal{E}$ is

$$\mathcal{E}(X) = \bigvee_{|\psi\rangle \in X} supp(\mathcal{E}(|\psi\rangle\langle\psi|)).$$

Intuitively, $\mathcal{E}(X)$ is the subspace of $\mathcal{H}$ spanned by the images under $\mathcal{E}$ of all states in X. Note that in the defining equation of $\mathcal{E}(X)$, $|\psi\rangle\langle\psi|$ is the density operator of pure state $|\psi\rangle$.

We collect several simple properties of the supports of density operators and images of quantum operations for latter uses.

Proposition 8.3. **1.** *If $\rho = \sum_k \lambda_k |\psi_k\rangle\langle\psi_k|$ where all $\lambda_k > 0$ (but $|\psi_k\rangle$'s are not required to be pairwise orthogonal), then $supp(\rho) = span\{|\psi_k\rangle\}$;*
2. *$supp(\rho + \sigma) = supp(\rho) \vee supp(\sigma)$;*
3. *If $\mathcal{E}$ has the Kraus operator-sum representation $\mathcal{E} = \sum_{i \in I} E_i \circ E_i^\dagger$, then*

$$\mathcal{E}(X) = span\{E_i|\psi\rangle : i \in I \text{ and } |\psi\rangle \in X\};$$

4. *$\mathcal{E}(X_1 \vee X_2) = \mathcal{E}(X_1) \vee \mathcal{E}(X_2)$. Thus, $X \subseteq Y \Rightarrow \mathcal{E}(X) \subseteq \mathcal{E}(Y)$;*
5. *$\mathcal{E}(supp(\rho)) = supp(\mathcal{E}(\rho))$.*

Exercise 8.6. Prove Proposition 8.3.

Based on Definitions 8.21 and 8.23, we can define the adjacency relation between (pure and mixed) states in a quantum Markov chain.

Definition 8.24. Let $\mathcal{C} = \langle \mathcal{H}, \mathcal{E} \rangle$ be a quantum Markov chain, and let $|\varphi\rangle, |\psi\rangle \in \mathcal{H}$ be pure states and $\rho, \sigma \in \mathcal{D}(\mathcal{H})$ be mixed states in $\mathcal{H}$. Then

1. $|\varphi\rangle$ is adjacent to $|\psi\rangle$ in $\mathcal{C}$, written $|\psi\rangle \to |\varphi\rangle$, if $|\varphi\rangle \in supp(\mathcal{E}(|\psi\rangle\langle\psi|))$.
2. $|\varphi\rangle$ is adjacent to ρ, written $\rho \to |\varphi\rangle$, if $|\varphi\rangle \in \mathcal{E}(supp(\rho))$.
3. σ is adjacent to ρ, written $\rho \to \sigma$, if $supp(\sigma) \subseteq \mathcal{E}(supp(\rho))$.

Intuitively, $\langle \mathcal{H}, \to \rangle$ can be imagined as a "directed graph". However, there are two major differences between this graph and a classical graph:

- The set of vertices of a classical graph is usually finite, whereas the state Hilbert space $\mathcal{H}$ is a continuum;
- A classical graph has no other mathematical structure rather than the adjacency relation, but the space $\mathcal{H}$ possesses a linear algebraic structure that must be preserved by an algorithm searching through the graph $\langle \mathcal{H}, \to \rangle$.

As we will see below, these differences between a quantum graph and a classical graph make analysis of the former much harder than that of the latter.

We now can define the core notion of this section, namely reachability in a quantum graph, based on the adjacency relation in the same way as in the classical graph theory.

Definition 8.25. 1. A path from ρ to σ in a quantum Markov chain $\mathcal{C}$ is a sequence

$$\pi = \rho_0 \to \rho_1 \to \cdots \to \rho_n \ (n \geq 0)$$

of adjacent density operators in $\mathcal{C}$ such that $supp(\rho_0) \subseteq supp(\rho)$ and $\rho_n = \sigma$.

2. For any density operators ρ and σ, if there is a path from ρ to σ then we say that σ is reachable from ρ in $\mathcal{C}$.

Definition 8.26. Let $\mathcal{C} = \langle \mathcal{H}, \mathcal{E} \rangle$ be a quantum Markov chain. For any $\rho \in \mathcal{D}(\mathcal{H})$, its reachable space in $\mathcal{C}$ is the subspace of $\mathcal{H}$ spanned by the states reachable from ρ:

$$\mathcal{R}_{\mathcal{C}}(\rho) = span\{|\psi\rangle \in \mathcal{H} : |\psi\rangle \text{ is reachable from } \rho \text{ in } \mathcal{C}\}. \tag{8.50}$$

Note that in Eq. (8.50), $|\psi\rangle$ is identified with its density operator $|\psi\rangle\langle\psi|$.

Reachability in classical graph theory is transitive; that is, if a vertex v is reachable from u, and w is reachable from v, then w is also reachable from u. As expected, the following lemma shows that reachability in a quantum Markov chain is transitive too.

Lemma 8.17. *(Transitivity of reachability) For any $\rho, \sigma \in \mathcal{D}(\mathcal{H})$, if $supp(\rho) \subseteq \mathcal{R}_{\mathcal{C}}(\sigma)$, then $\mathcal{R}_{\mathcal{C}}(\rho) \subseteq \mathcal{R}_{\mathcal{C}}(\sigma)$.*

Exercise 8.7. Prove Lemma 8.17.

We now consider how to compute the reachable space of a state in a quantum Markov chain. To motivate our method, let us consider a classical directed graph $\langle V, E \rangle$, where V is the set of vertices and $E \subseteq V \times V$ is the adjacency relation. The transitive closure of E is defined as follows:

$$t(E) = \bigcup_{n=0}^{\infty} E^n = \{\langle v, v' \rangle : v' \text{ is reachable from } v \text{ in } \langle V, E \rangle\}.$$

It is well-known that the transitive closure can be computed as follows:

$$t(E) = \bigcup_{n=0}^{|V|-1} E^n$$

where $|V|$ is the number of vertices. As a quantum generalisation of this fact, we have:

Theorem 8.14. *Let $\mathcal{C} = \langle \mathcal{H}, \mathcal{E} \rangle$ be a quantum Markov chain. If $d = \dim \mathcal{H}$, then for any $\rho \in \mathcal{D}(\mathcal{H})$, we have*

$$\mathcal{R}_{\mathcal{C}}(\rho) = \bigvee_{i=0}^{d-1} supp\left(\mathcal{E}^i(\rho)\right) \tag{8.51}$$

where $\mathcal{E}^i$ is the ith power of $\mathcal{E}$; that is, $\mathcal{E}^0 = \mathcal{I}$ (the identity operation on $\mathcal{H}$) and

$$\mathcal{E}^{i+1} = \mathcal{E} \circ \mathcal{E}^i$$

for $i \geq 0$.

Proof. We first show that $|\psi\rangle$ is reachable from ρ if and only if $|\psi\rangle \in supp\left(\mathcal{E}^i(\rho)\right)$ for some $i \geq 0$. In fact, if $|\psi\rangle$ is reachable from ρ, then there exist $\rho_1, ..., \rho_{i-1}$ such that

$$\rho \to \rho_1 \to ... \to \rho_{i-1} \to |\psi\rangle.$$

Using Proposition 8.3.5, we obtain:

$$|\psi\rangle \in supp(\mathcal{E}(\rho_{i-1})) = \mathcal{E}(supp(\rho_{i-1}))$$
$$\subseteq \mathcal{E}(supp(\mathcal{E}(\rho_{i-2}))$$
$$= supp\left(\mathcal{E}^2(\rho_{i-2})\right) \subseteq ... \subseteq supp\left(\mathcal{E}^i(\rho)\right).$$

Conversely, if $|\psi\rangle \in supp(\mathcal{E}^i(\rho))$, then

$$\rho \to \mathcal{E}(\rho) \to ... \to \mathcal{E}^{i-1}(\rho) \to |\psi\rangle$$

and $|\psi\rangle$ is reachable from ρ. Therefore, it holds that

$$\mathcal{R}_\mathcal{C}(\rho) = span\{|\psi\rangle : |\psi\rangle \text{ is reachable from } \rho\}$$
$$= span\left[\bigcup_{i=0}^{\infty} supp\left(\mathcal{E}^i(\rho)\right)\right]$$
$$= \bigvee_{i=0}^{\infty} supp\left(\mathcal{E}^i(\rho)\right).$$

Now for each $n \geq 0$, we put

$$X_n = \bigvee_{i=0}^{n} supp\left(\mathcal{E}^i(\rho)\right).$$

Then we obtain an increasing sequence

$$X_0 \subseteq X_1 \subseteq ... \subseteq X_n \subseteq X_{n+1} \subseteq ...$$

of subspaces of $\mathcal{H}$. Let $d_n = \dim X_n$ for every $n \geq 0$. Then

$$d_0 \leq d_1 \leq ... \leq d_n \leq d_{n+1} \leq ....$$

Note that $d_n \leq d$ for all n. Thus, there must be some n such that $d_n = d_{n+1}$. Assume that N is the smallest integer n such that $d_n = d_{n+1}$. Then we have

$$0 < \dim supp(\rho) = d_0 < d_1 < ... < d_{N-1} < d_N \leq d$$

and $N \leq d - 1$. On the other hand, both X_N and X_{N+1} are subspaces of $\mathcal{H}$, $X_N \subseteq X_{N+1}$ and $\dim X_N = \dim X_{N+1}$. Thus, $X_N = X_{N+1}$. We can prove that

$$supp\left(\mathcal{E}^{N+k}(\rho)\right) \subseteq X_N$$

for all $k \geq 1$ by induction on k. So, $\mathcal{R}_\mathcal{C}(\rho) = X_N$.   □

Bottom strongly connected components: We have carefully defined the graph underlying a quantum Markov chain above. Now we move forward to examine its mathematical structure. In classical graph theory, the notion of bottom strongly connected component (BSCC) is an important tool in the studies of reachability problems. It has also been extensively applied in analysis of probabilistic programs modelled by Markov chains. Here, we extend this notion to the quantum case. The quantum version of BSCC will be a basis of the reachability analysis algorithms for quantum Markov chains given in the next subsection.

We first introduce an auxiliary notation. Let X be a subspace of $\mathcal{H}$ and $\mathcal{E}$ a quantum operation on $\mathcal{H}$. Then the restriction of $\mathcal{E}$ on X is the quantum operation $\mathcal{E}_X$ on X defined by

$$\mathcal{E}_X(\rho) = P_X \mathcal{E}(\rho) P_X$$

for all $\rho \in \mathcal{D}(X)$, where P_X is the projection onto X. With this notation, we are able to define strong connectivity in a quantum Markov chain.

Definition 8.27. Let $\mathcal{C} = \langle \mathcal{H}, \mathcal{E} \rangle$ be a quantum Markov chain. A subspace X of $\mathcal{H}$ is called strongly connected in $\mathcal{C}$ if for any $|\varphi\rangle, |\psi\rangle \in X$, we have:

$$|\varphi\rangle \in \mathcal{R}_{\mathcal{C}_X}(\psi) \ and \ |\psi\rangle \in \mathcal{R}_{\mathcal{C}_X}(\varphi) \tag{8.52}$$

where $\varphi = |\varphi\rangle\langle\varphi|$ and $\psi = |\psi\rangle\langle\psi|$ are the density operators corresponding to pure states $|\varphi\rangle$ and $\psi\rangle$, respectively, quantum Markov chain $\mathcal{C}_X = \langle X, \mathcal{E}_X \rangle$ is the restriction of $\mathcal{C}$ on X, and $\mathcal{R}_{\mathcal{C}_X}(\cdot)$ denotes a reachable subspace in $\mathcal{C}_X$.

Intuitively, condition (8.52) means that for any two states $|\varphi\rangle, |\psi\rangle$ in X, $|\varphi\rangle$ is reachable from $|\psi\rangle$ and $|\psi\rangle$ is reachable from $|\varphi\rangle$.

We write $SC(\mathcal{C})$ for the set of all strongly connected subspaces of $\mathcal{H}$ in $\mathcal{C}$. It is clear that $SC(\mathcal{C})$ with set inclusion $\subseteq$, i.e. $(SC(\mathcal{C}), \subseteq)$ is a partial order (see Definition 5.7). To further examine this partial order, we recall several concepts from lattice theory. Let $(L, \sqsubseteq)$ be a partial order. If any two elements $x, y \in L$ are comparable; that is, either $x \sqsubseteq y$ or $y \sqsubseteq x$, then we say that L is linearly ordered by $\sqsubseteq$. A partial order $(L, \sqsubseteq)$ is said to be inductive if for any subset K of L that is linearly ordered by $\sqsubseteq$, the least upper bound $\bigsqcup K$ exists in L.

Lemma 8.18. *The partial order $(SC(\mathcal{C}), \subseteq)$ is inductive.*

Exercise 8.8. Prove Lemma 8.18.

Now we further consider some special elements in the partial order $(SC(\mathcal{C}), \subseteq)$. Recall that an element x of a partial order $(L, \sqsubseteq)$ is called a maximal element of L if for any $y \in L$, $x \sqsubseteq y$ implies $x = y$. The Zorn lemma in set theory asserts that every inductive partial order has (at least one) maximal elements.

Definition 8.28. A maximal element of $(SC(\mathcal{C}), \subseteq)$ is called a strongly connected component (SCC) of $\mathcal{C}$.

To define the concept of BSCC (bottom strongly connected component) in a quantum Markov chain, we need one more auxiliary notion, namely invariant subspace.

Definition 8.29. We say that a subspace X of $\mathcal{H}$ is invariant under a quantum operation $\mathcal{E}$ if $\mathcal{E}(X) \subseteq X$.

The intuition behind the inclusion $\mathcal{E}(X) \subseteq X$ is that quantum operation $\mathcal{E}$ cannot transfer a state in X into a state outside X. Suppose that quantum operation $\mathcal{E}$ has the Kraus representation $\mathcal{E} = \sum_i E_i \circ E_i^\dagger$. Then it follows from Proposition 8.3 that X is invariant under $\mathcal{E}$ if and only if it is invariant under the Kraus operators E_i: $E_i X \subseteq X$, for all i.

The following theorem presents a useful property of invariant subspaces showing that a quantum operation does not decrease the probability of falling into an invariant subspace.

Theorem 8.15. *Let $\mathcal{C} = \langle \mathcal{H}, \mathcal{E} \rangle$ be a quantum Markov chain. If subspace X of $\mathcal{H}$ is invariant under $\mathcal{E}$, then we have:*

$$tr(P_X \mathcal{E}(\rho)) \geq tr(P_X \rho)$$

for all $\rho \in \mathcal{D}(\mathcal{H})$.

Proof. It suffices to show that

$$tr(P_X \mathcal{E}(|\psi\rangle\langle\psi|)) \geq tr(P_X |\psi\rangle\langle\psi|)$$

for each $|\psi\rangle \in \mathcal{H}$. Assume that $\mathcal{E} = \sum_i E_i \circ E_i^\dagger$, and $|\psi\rangle = |\psi_1\rangle + |\psi_2\rangle$ where $|\psi_1\rangle \in X$ and $|\psi_2\rangle \in X^\perp$. Since X is invariant under $\mathcal{E}$, we have $E_i|\psi_1\rangle \in X$ and $P_X E_i|\psi_1\rangle = E_i|\psi_1\rangle$). Then

$$a \overset{\triangle}{=} \sum_i tr\left(P_X E_i|\psi_2\rangle\langle\psi_1|E_i^\dagger\right) = \sum_i tr\left(E_i|\psi_2\rangle\langle\psi_1|E_i^\dagger P_X\right)$$

$$= \sum_i tr\left(E_i|\psi_2\rangle\langle\psi_1|E_i^\dagger\right) = \sum_i \langle\psi_1|E_i^\dagger E_i|\psi_2\rangle = \langle\psi_1|\psi_2\rangle = 0.$$

Similarly, it holds that

$$b \triangleq \sum_i tr\left(P_X E_i|\psi_1\rangle\langle\psi_2|E_i^\dagger\right) = 0.$$

Moreover, we have:

$$c \triangleq \sum_i tr\left(P_X E_i|\psi_2\rangle\langle\psi_2|E_i^\dagger\right) \geq 0.$$

Therefore,

$$tr\left(P_X \mathcal{E}(|\psi\rangle\langle\psi|)\right) = \sum_i tr\left(P_X E_i|\psi_1\rangle\langle\psi_1|E_i^\dagger\right) + a + b + c$$

$$\geq \sum_i tr\left(P_X E_i|\psi_1\rangle\langle\psi_1|E_i^\dagger\right) = \sum_i\langle\psi_1|E_i^\dagger E_i|\psi_1\rangle$$

$$= \langle\psi_1|\psi_1\rangle = tr(P_X|\psi\rangle\langle\psi|). \qquad \Box$$

Now we are ready to introduce the key notion of this subsection, namely bottom strongly connected component.

Definition 8.30. Let $\mathcal{C} = \langle\mathcal{H}, \mathcal{E}\rangle$ be a quantum Markov chain. Then a subspace X of $\mathcal{H}$ is called a bottom strongly connected component (BSCC) of $\mathcal{C}$ if it is an SCC of $\mathcal{C}$ and it is invariant under $\mathcal{E}$.

Example 8.3. Consider quantum Markov chain $\mathcal{C} = \langle\mathcal{H}, \mathcal{E}\rangle$ with state Hilbert space $\mathcal{H} = span\{|0\rangle, \cdots, |4\rangle\}$ and quantum operation $\mathcal{E} = \sum_{i=1}^5 E_i \circ E_i^\dagger$, where the Kraus operators are given by

$$E_1 = \frac{1}{\sqrt{2}}(|1\rangle\langle\theta_{01}^+| + |3\rangle\langle\theta_{23}^+|), \qquad E_2 = \frac{1}{\sqrt{2}}(|1\rangle\langle\theta_{01}^-| + |3\rangle\langle\theta_{23}^-|),$$

$$E_3 = \frac{1}{\sqrt{2}}(|0\rangle\langle\theta_{01}^+| + |2\rangle\langle\theta_{23}^+|), \qquad E_4 = \frac{1}{\sqrt{2}}(|0\rangle\langle\theta_{01}^-| + |2\rangle\langle\theta_{23}^-|),$$

$$E_5 = \frac{1}{10}(|0\rangle\langle4| + |1\rangle\langle4| + |2\rangle\langle4| + 4|3\rangle\langle4| + 9|4\rangle\langle4|),$$

and

$$|\theta_{ij}^\pm\rangle = (|i\rangle \pm |j\rangle)/\sqrt{2}. \tag{8.53}$$

It is easy to verify that $B = span\{|0\rangle, |1\rangle\}$ is a BSCC of quantum Markov chain $\mathcal{C}$. Indeed, for any $|\psi\rangle = \alpha|0\rangle + \beta|1\rangle \in B$, we have

$$\mathcal{E}(|\psi\rangle\langle\psi|) = (|0\rangle\langle0| + |1\rangle\langle1|)/2.$$

Characterisations of BSCCs: To help the reader to have a better understanding of them, we give two characterisations of BSCCs. The first characterisation is simple and it is presented in terms of reachable subspaces.

Lemma 8.19. A subspace X is a BSCC of quantum Markov chain $\mathcal{C}$ if and only if $\mathcal{R}_\mathcal{C}(|\varphi\rangle\langle\varphi|) = X$ for any $|\varphi\rangle \in X$.

Proof. We only prove the "only if" part because the "if" part is obvious. Suppose X is a BSCC. By the strong connectivity of X, we have $\mathcal{R}_\mathcal{C}(|\varphi\rangle\langle\varphi|) \supseteq X$ for all $|\varphi\rangle \in X$. On the other hand, for any vector $|\varphi\rangle$ in X, using the invariance of X, i.e. $\mathcal{E}(X) \subseteq X$, it is easy to show that if $|\psi\rangle$ is reachable from $|\varphi\rangle$ then $|\psi\rangle \in X$. So, $\mathcal{R}_\mathcal{C}(|\varphi\rangle\langle\varphi|) \subseteq X$. $\qquad \Box$

The second characterisation of BSCCs is a little bit more complicated. To present it, we need the notion of fixed point of a quantum operation.

Definition 8.31. 1. A density operator ρ in $\mathcal{H}$ is called a fixed point state of quantum operation $\mathcal{E}$ if $\mathcal{E}(\rho) = \rho$.
2. A fixed point state ρ of quantum operation $\mathcal{E}$ is called minimal if for any fixed point state σ of $\mathcal{E}$, it holds that $supp(\sigma) \subseteq supp(\rho)$ implies $\sigma = \rho$.

The following lemma shows a close connection between the invariant subspaces under a quantum operation $\mathcal{E}$ and the fixed point states of $\mathcal{E}$. It provides a key step in the proof of Theorem 8.16 below.

Lemma 8.20. *If ρ is a fixed point state of $\mathcal{E}$, then $supp(\rho)$ is invariant under $\mathcal{E}$. Conversely, if X is invariant under $\mathcal{E}$, then there exists a fixed point state ρ_X of $\mathcal{E}$ such that $supp(\rho_X) \subseteq X$.*

Exercise 8.9. Prove Lemma 8.20.

Now we are able to give the second characterisation which establishes a connection between BSCCs and minimal fixed point states.

Theorem 8.16. *A subspace X is a BSCC of quantum Markov chain $\mathcal{C} = \langle \mathcal{H}, \mathcal{E} \rangle$ if and only if there exists a minimal fixed point state ρ of $\mathcal{E}$ such that $supp(\rho) = X$.*

Proof. We first prove the "if" part. Let ρ be a minimal fixed point state such that $supp(\rho) = X$. Then by Lemma 8.20, X is invariant under $\mathcal{E}$. To show that X is a BSCC, by Lemma 8.19 it suffices to prove that for any $|\varphi\rangle \in X$, $\mathcal{R}_{\mathcal{C}}(|\varphi\rangle\langle\varphi|) = X$. Suppose conversely that there exists $|\psi\rangle \in X$ such that $\mathcal{R}_{\mathcal{C}}(|\psi\rangle\langle\psi|) \subsetneq X$. Then by Lemma 8.17 we can show that $\mathcal{R}_{\mathcal{C}}(|\psi\rangle\langle\psi|)$ is invariant under $\mathcal{E}$. By Lemma 8.20, we can find a fixed point state ρ_ψ with

$$supp(\rho_\psi) \subseteq \mathcal{R}_{\mathcal{C}}(|\psi\rangle\langle\psi|) \subsetneq X.$$

This contradicts the assumption that ρ is minimal.

For the "only if" part, suppose that X is a BSCC. Then X is invariant under $\mathcal{E}$, and by Lemma 8.20, we can find a minimal fixed point state ρ_X of $\mathcal{E}$ with $supp(\rho_X) \subseteq X$. Take $|\varphi\rangle \in supp(\rho_X)$. By Lemma 8.21 we have $\mathcal{R}_{\mathcal{C}}(|\varphi\rangle\langle\varphi|) = X$. But using Lemma 8.20 again we know that $supp(\rho_X)$ is invariant under $\mathcal{E}$, so $\mathcal{R}_{\mathcal{C}}(|\varphi\rangle\langle\varphi|) \subseteq supp(\rho_X)$. Therefore, $supp(\rho_X) = X$. □

As mentioned above, BSCCs will play a key role in analysis of quantum Markov chains. This application of BSCCs is based on not only our understanding of their structure described in Lemma 8.19 and Theorem 8.16 but also their relationship to each other. The following lemma clarifies the relationship between two different BSCCs.

Lemma 8.21. 1. *For any two different BSCCs X and Y of quantum Markov chain $\mathcal{C}$, we have $X \cap Y = \{0\}$ (0-dimensional Hilbert space).*
2. *If X and Y are two BSCCs of $\mathcal{C}$ with $\dim X \neq \dim Y$, then they are orthogonal, i.e. $X \perp Y$.*

Proof. (i) Suppose conversely that there exists a nonzero vector $|\varphi\rangle \in X \cap Y$. Then by Lemma 8.19, we have $X = \mathcal{R}_{\mathcal{C}}(|\varphi\rangle\langle\varphi|) = Y$, contradicting the assumption that $X \neq Y$. Therefore $X \cap Y = \{0\}$.

(ii) We postpone this part to Appendix A.4 because it needs to use Theorem 8.18 below. □

8.4.3 Decomposition of the state Hilbert space

In the previous subsection, a graph structure in a quantum Markov chain was defined, and the notion of BSCC was generalised to the quantum case. In this subsection, we further study such a graph structure in a quantum Markov chain through a decomposition of the state Hilbert space.

Recall that a state in a classical Markov chain is transient if there is a nonzero probability that the process will never return to it, and a state is recurrent if from it the returning probability is 1. It is well-known that in a finite-state Markov chain a state is recurrent if and only if it belongs to some BSCC, and thus the state space of the Markov chain can be decomposed into the union of some BSCCs and a transient subspace. The aim of this subsection is to prove a quantum generalisation of this result. Such a decomposition of the state Hilbert space forms a basis of our algorithms for reachability analysis of quantum Markov chains to be presented in the next subsection.

Transient subspaces: Let us first define the notion of transient subspace of a quantum Markov chain. Transient states in a finite-state classical Markov chain can be equivalently characterised as follows: a state is transient if and only if the probability that the system stays at it will eventually become 0. This observation motivates the following:

Definition 8.32. A subspace $X \subseteq \mathcal{H}$ is transient in a quantum Markov chain $\mathcal{C} = \langle \mathcal{H}, \mathcal{E} \rangle$ if

$$\lim_{k \to \infty} tr\left(P_X \mathcal{E}^k(\rho) \right) = 0 \tag{8.54}$$

for any $\rho \in \mathcal{D}(\mathcal{H})$, where P_X is the projection onto X.

Intuitively, $tr_X\left(P_X\mathcal{E}^k(\rho)\right)$ is the probability that the system's state falls into the subspace X after executing the quantum operation $\mathcal{E}$ for k times. So, the defining Eq. (8.54) means that the probability that the system stays in subspace X is eventually 0.

It is obvious from the above definition that if subspaces $X \subseteq Y$ and Y is transient, then X is transient too. So, it is sufficient to understand the structure of the largest transient subspace. Fortunately, we have an elegant characterisation of the largest transient subspace. To give such a characterisation, we need the following:

Definition 8.33. Let $\mathcal{E}$ be a quantum operation on $\mathcal{H}$. Then its asymptotic average is

$$\mathcal{E}_\infty = \lim_{N\to\infty} \frac{1}{N}\sum_{n=1}^{N}\mathcal{E}^n. \tag{8.55}$$

It follows from Lemma 5.4 that $\mathcal{E}_\infty$ is a quantum operation as well.

The following lemma points out a link between fixed point states of a quantum operation and its asymptotic average. This link will be used in the proof of Theorem 8.17 below.

Lemma 8.22. 1. *For any density operator ρ, $\mathcal{E}_\infty(\rho)$ is a fixed point state of $\mathcal{E}$;*
2. *For any fixed point state σ, it holds that $supp(\sigma) \subseteq \mathcal{E}_\infty(\mathcal{H})$.*

Exercise 8.10. Prove Lemma 8.22.

Now we can give a characterisation of the largest transient subspace in terms of asymptotic average.

Theorem 8.17. *Let $C = \langle\mathcal{H}, \mathcal{E}\rangle$ be a quantum Markov chain. Then the ortho-complement of the image of $\mathcal{H}$ under the asymptotic average of $\mathcal{E}$:*

$$T_\mathcal{E} = \mathcal{E}_\infty(\mathcal{H})^\perp$$

is the largest transient subspace in C, where $^\perp$ stands for orthocomplement (see Definition 2.7.2).

Proof. Let P be the projection onto the subspace $T_\mathcal{E}$. For any $\rho \in \mathcal{D}(\mathcal{H})$, we put $p_k = tr\left(P\mathcal{E}^k(\rho)\right)$ for every $k \geq 0$. Since $\mathcal{E}_\infty(\mathcal{H})$ is invariant under $\mathcal{E}$, by Theorem 8.15 we know that the sequence $\{p_k\}$ is nonincreasing. Thus the limit $p_\infty = \lim_{k\to\infty} p_k$ does exist. Furthermore, noting that

$$supp(\mathcal{E}_\infty(\rho)) \subseteq \mathcal{E}_\infty(\mathcal{H})$$

we have

$$\begin{aligned}
0 = tr(P\mathcal{E}_\infty(\rho)) &= tr\left(P\lim_{N\to\infty}\frac{1}{N}\sum_{n=1}^{N}\mathcal{E}^n(\rho)\right) \\
&= \lim_{N\to\infty}\frac{1}{N}\sum_{n=1}^{N}tr\left(P\mathcal{E}^n(\rho)\right) \\
&= \lim_{N\to\infty}\frac{1}{N}\sum_{n=1}^{N}p_n \\
&\geq \lim_{N\to\infty}\frac{1}{N}\sum_{n=1}^{N}p_\infty = p_\infty.
\end{aligned}$$

Thus $p_\infty = 0$, and $T_\mathcal{E}$ is transient by the arbitrariness of ρ.

To show that $T_\mathcal{E}$ is the largest transient subspace of C, we first note that

$$supp\left(\mathcal{E}_\infty(I)\right) = \mathcal{E}_\infty(\mathcal{H}).$$

Let $\sigma = \mathcal{E}_\infty(I/d)$. Then by Lemma 8.22, σ is a fixed point state with $supp(\sigma) = T_\mathcal{E}^\perp$. Suppose Y is a transient subspace. We have

$$tr(P_Y\sigma) = \lim_{i\to\infty} tr\left(P_Y\mathcal{E}^i(\sigma)\right) = 0.$$

This implies $Y \perp supp(\sigma) = T_{\mathcal{E}}^{\perp}$. So, we have $Y \subseteq T_{\mathcal{E}}$. □

BSCC decomposition: After introducing the notion of transient subspace, we now consider how to decompose the state Hilbert space of a quantum Markov chain $C = \langle \mathcal{H}, \mathcal{E} \rangle$. First, it can be simply divided into two parts:

$$\mathcal{H} = \mathcal{E}_{\infty}(\mathcal{H}) \oplus \mathcal{E}_{\infty}(\mathcal{H})^{\perp}$$

where $\oplus$ stands for (orthogonal) sum (see Definition 2.8), and $\mathcal{E}_{\infty}(\mathcal{H})$ is the image of the whole state Hilbert space under the asymptotic average. We already know from Theorem 8.17 that $\mathcal{E}_{\infty}(\mathcal{H})^{\perp}$ is the largest transient subspace. So, what we need to do next is to examine the structure of $\mathcal{E}_{\infty}(\mathcal{H})$.

Our procedure for decomposition of $\mathcal{E}_{\infty}(\mathcal{H})$ is based on the following key lemma that shows how can a fixed point state be subtracted by another.

Lemma 8.23. *Let ρ and σ be two fixed point state of $\mathcal{E}$, and $supp(\sigma) \subsetneq supp(\rho)$. Then there exists another fixed point state η such that*

1. *$supp(\eta) \perp supp(\sigma)$; and*
2. *$supp(\rho) = supp(\eta) \oplus supp(\sigma)$.*

Intuitively, state η in the above lemma can be understood as the subtraction of state ρ by σ. For better readability, the proof of this lemma is postponed to Appendix A.4.

Now the BSCC decomposition of $\mathcal{E}_{\infty}(\mathcal{H})$ can be derived simply by repeated applications of the above lemma.

Theorem 8.18. *Let $C = \langle \mathcal{H}, \mathcal{E} \rangle$ be a quantum Markov chain. Then $\mathcal{E}_{\infty}(\mathcal{H})$ can be decomposed into the direct sum of orthogonal BSCCs of C.*

Proof. We notice that $\mathcal{E}_{\infty}\left(\frac{I}{d}\right)$ is a fixed point state of $\mathcal{E}$ and

$$supp\left(\mathcal{E}_{\infty}\left(\frac{I}{d}\right)\right) = \mathcal{E}_{\infty}(\mathcal{H})$$

where $d = \dim \mathcal{H}$. Then it suffices to prove the following:

- *Claim*: Let ρ be a fixed point state of $\mathcal{E}$. Then $supp(\rho)$ can be decomposed into the direct sum of some orthogonal BSCCs.

In fact, if ρ is minimal, then by Theorem 8.16, $supp(\rho)$ is itself a BSCC and we are done. Otherwise, we apply Lemma 8.23 to obtain two fixed point states of $\mathcal{E}$ with smaller orthogonal supports. Repeating this procedure, we can get a set of minimal fixed point states $\rho_1, \cdots, \rho_k$ with mutually orthogonal supports such that

$$supp(\rho) = \bigoplus_{i=1}^{k} supp(\rho_i).$$

Finally, from Lemma 8.20 and Theorem 8.16, we know that each $supp(\rho_i)$ is a BSCC. □

Now we eventually achieve the decomposition promised at the beginning of this subsection. Combining Theorems 8.17 and 8.18, we see that the state Hilbert space of a quantum Markov chain $C = \langle \mathcal{H}, \mathcal{E} \rangle$ can be decomposed into the direct sum of a transient subspace and a family of BSCCs:

$$\mathcal{H} = B_1 \oplus \cdots \oplus B_u \oplus T_{\mathcal{E}} \tag{8.56}$$

where B_i's are orthogonal BSCCs of C, and $T_{\mathcal{E}}$ is the largest transient subspace.

The above theorem shows the existence of BSCC decomposition for quantum Markov chains. Then a question immediately arises: is such a decomposition unique? It is well known that the BSCC decomposition of a classical Markov chain is unique. However, it is not the case for quantum Markov chains as shown in the following:

Example 8.4. Let quantum Markov chain $C = \langle \mathcal{H}, \mathcal{E} \rangle$ be given as in Example 8.3. Then

$$B_1 = span\{|0\rangle, |1\rangle\}, \qquad B_2 = span\{|2\rangle, |3\rangle\},$$

$$D_1 = span\{|\theta_{02}^+\rangle, |\theta_{13}^+\rangle\}, \quad D_2 = span\{|\theta_{02}^-\rangle, |\theta_{13}^-\rangle\}$$

are all BSCCs, where the states $|\theta_{ij}^\pm\rangle$ are defined by Eq. (8.53). It is easy to see that $T_{\mathcal{E}} = span\{|4\rangle\}$ is the largest transient subspace. Furthermore, we have two different decompsitions:

$$\mathcal{H} = B_1 \oplus B_2 \oplus T_{\mathcal{E}} = D_1 \oplus D_2 \oplus T_{\mathcal{E}}.$$

Although the BSCC decomposition of a quantum Markov chain is not unique, fortunately we have the following weak uniqueness in the sense that any two decompositions have the same number of BSCCs, and the corresponding BSCCs in them must have the same dimension.

Theorem 8.19. *Let $\mathcal{C} = \langle \mathcal{H}, \mathcal{E} \rangle$ be a quantum Markov chain, and let*

$$\mathcal{H} = B_1 \oplus \cdots \oplus B_u \oplus T_{\mathcal{E}} = D_1 \oplus \cdots \oplus D_v \oplus T_{\mathcal{E}}$$

be two decompositions in the form of Eq. (8.56), and B_is and D_is are arranged, respectively, according to the increasing order of the dimensions. Then

1. *$u = v$; and*
2. *$\dim B_i = \dim D_i$ for each $1 \le i \le u$.*

Proof. For simplicity, we write $b_i = \dim B_i$ and $d_i = \dim D_i$. We prove by induction on i that $b_i = d_i$ for any $1 \le i \le \min\{u, v\}$, and thus $u = v$ as well.

First, we claim $b_1 = d_1$. Otherwise let, say, $b_1 < d_1$. Then $b_1 < d_j$ for all j. Thus by Lemma 8.21.2, we have:

$$B_1 \perp \bigoplus_{j=1}^{v} D_j.$$

But we also have $B_1 \perp T_{\mathcal{E}}$. This is a contradiction as it holds that

$$\left(\bigoplus_{j=1}^{v} D_j \right) \oplus T_{\mathcal{E}} = \mathcal{H}.$$

Now suppose we already have $b_i = d_i$ for all $i < n$. We claim $b_n = d_n$. Otherwise let, say, $b_n < d_n$. Then from Lemma 8.21.2, we have

$$\bigoplus_{i=1}^{n} B_i \perp \bigoplus_{i=n}^{v} D_i,$$

and consequently

$$\bigoplus_{i=1}^{n} B_i \subseteq \bigoplus_{i=1}^{n-1} D_i.$$

On the other hand, we have

$$\dim \left(\bigoplus_{i=1}^{n} B_i \right) = \sum_{i=1}^{n} b_i > \sum_{i=1}^{n-1} d_i = \dim \left(\bigoplus_{i=1}^{n-1} D_i \right),$$

a contradiction. $\square$

Decomposition algorithm: We have proved the existence and weak uniqueness of BSCC decomposition for quantum Markov chains. With these theoretical preparations, we can now develop an algorithm for finding a BSCC and transient subspace decomposition of a quantum Markov chain. It is presented as Algorithm 2 together with the procedure Decompose(X).

To conclude this subsection, we consider correctness and complexity of the BSCC decomposition algorithm. The following lemma is the key in settling the complexity of Algorithm 2.

Algorithm 2: Decompose($\mathcal{C}$).

---
input : A quantum Markov chain $\mathcal{C} = \langle \mathcal{H}, \mathcal{E} \rangle$
output: A set of orthogonal BSCCs $\{B_i\}$ and a transient subspace $T_{\mathcal{E}}$ such that $\mathcal{H} = \left(\bigoplus_i B_i \right) \oplus T_{\mathcal{E}}$
begin
    $\mathcal{B} \leftarrow \text{Decompose}(\mathcal{E}_\infty(\mathcal{H}))$;
    return $\mathcal{B}$, $\mathcal{E}_\infty(\mathcal{H})^\perp$;
end

Procedure Decompose(X).

---
input : A subspace X which is the support of a fixed point state of $\mathcal{E}$
output: A set of orthogonal BSCCs $\{B_i\}$ such that $X = \bigoplus B_i$
begin
    $\mathcal{E}' \leftarrow P_X \circ \mathcal{E}$;
    $\mathcal{B} \leftarrow$ a density operator basis of the set $\{\text{operators } A \text{ in } \mathcal{H} : \mathcal{E}'(A) = A\}$;
    if $|\mathcal{B}| = 1$ **then**
        $\rho \leftarrow$ the unique element of $\mathcal{B}$;
        return $\{supp(\rho)\}$;
    else
        $\rho_1, \rho_2 \leftarrow$ two arbitrary elements of $\mathcal{B}$;
        $\rho \leftarrow$ positive part of $\rho_1 - \rho_2$;
        $Y \leftarrow supp(\rho)^\perp$;   (*the ortho-complement of $supp(\rho)$ in X*)
        return Decompose($supp(\rho)$) $\cup$ Decompose(Y);
    end
end

Lemma 8.24. *Let $\langle \mathcal{H}, \mathcal{E} \rangle$ be a quantum Markov chain with $d = \dim \mathcal{H}$, and $\rho \in \mathcal{D}(\mathcal{H})$. Then*

1. *The asymptotic average state $\mathcal{E}_\infty(\rho)$ can be computed in time $O(d^8)$.*
2. *A density operator basis of the set of fixed points of $\mathcal{E}$:*

$$\{operators\ A\ in\ \mathcal{H} : \mathcal{E}(A) = A\}$$

can be computed in time $O(d^6)$.

For readability, we postpone the proof of the above lemma into Appendix A.4.

Now the correctness and complexity of Algorithm 2 are shown in the following:

Theorem 8.20. *Given a quantum Markov chain $\langle \mathcal{H}, \mathcal{E} \rangle$, Algorithm 2 decomposes the Hilbert space $\mathcal{H}$ into the direct sum of a family of orthogonal BSCCs and a transient subspace of $\mathcal{C}$ in time $O(d^8)$, where $d = \dim \mathcal{H}$.*

Proof. The correctness of Algorithm 2 is easy to prove. Actually, it follows immediately from Theorem 8.17.

For the time complexity, we first notice that the nonrecursive part of the procedure Decompose(X) runs in time $O(d^6)$. Thus total complexity of Decompose(X) is $O(d^7)$, as the procedure calls itself at most $O(d)$ times. Algorithm 2 first computes $\mathcal{E}_\infty(\mathcal{H})$, which, as indicated by Lemma 8.24.1, costs time $O(d^8)$, and then feeds it into the procedure Decompose(X). Thus the total complexity of Algorithm 2 is $O(d^8)$. □

Problem 8.3. Quantum graph theory has been developed in this section merely to provide necessary mathematical tools for reachability analysis of quantum Markov chains in the next section. It is desirable to build a richer theory of quantum graphs by generalising more results in (di-)graphs theory [45] into the quantum setting and by understanding the essential differences between classical and quantum graphs.

Problem 8.4. The notion of noncommutative graph was introduced in [135] in order to give a characterisation of channel capacity in quantum Shannon information theory. It is interesting to find some connections between noncommutative graphs and quantum graphs defined in this section.

8.4.4 Reachability analysis of quantum Markov chains

The graph structures of quantum Markov chains were carefully examined in the last subsection. This prepares necessary mathematical tools for reachability analysis of quantum Markov chains. In this subsection, we study reachability of quantum Markov chains using the quantum graph theory developed in the last subsection.

As will be shown in Exercise 8.11 below, termination of a quantum **while**-loop can be reduced to a reachability problem of a quantum Markov chain. Indeed, as in classical and probabilistic programming theory, many other behaviours of quantum programs can be described in terms of the reachability discussed in this subsection and related properties (e.g. persistence) when their semantics are modelled as quantum Markov chains. Furthermore, this subsection provides a basis for further research on analysis of more complicated quantum programs like recursive quantum programs defined in Section 5.5 as well as nondeterministic and concurrent quantum programs because various extensions of quantum Markov chains, e.g. recursive quantum Markov chains and quantum Markov decision processes can serve as their semantic models.

Reachability probability: We first consider the reachability probability in a quantum Markov chain, which is formally defined in the following:

Definition 8.34. Let $\langle \mathcal{H}, \mathcal{E} \rangle$ be a quantum Markov chain, $\rho \in \mathcal{D}(\mathcal{H})$ an initial state, and $X \subseteq \mathcal{H}$ a subspace. Then the probability of reaching X, starting from ρ, is

$$\Pr(\rho \vDash \Diamond X) = \lim_{i \to \infty} tr\left(P_X \widetilde{\mathcal{E}}^i(\rho) \right) \tag{8.57}$$

where $\widetilde{\mathcal{E}}^i$ is the composition of i copies of $\widetilde{\mathcal{E}}$, and $\widetilde{\mathcal{E}}$ is the quantum operation defined by

$$\widetilde{\mathcal{E}}(\sigma) = P_X \sigma P_X + \mathcal{E}\left(P_{X^\perp} \sigma P_{X^\perp} \right)$$

for all density operator σ.

Obviously, the limit in the above definition exists, as the probabilities $tr\left(P_X \widetilde{\mathcal{E}}^i(\rho) \right)$ are nondecreasing in number i. Intuitively, $\widetilde{\mathcal{E}}$ can be seen as a procedure that first performs the projective measurement $\{P_X, P_{X^\perp}\}$ and then applies the identity operation $\mathcal{I}$ or $\mathcal{E}$, depending on the measurement outcome.

Exercise 8.11. 1. Consider the special form of quantum **while**-loop (8.39) where the measurement in the loop guard is projective:

$$M = \{M_0 = P_X, M_1 = P_{X^\perp}\}.$$

Find a connection between the reachability probability $\Pr(\rho \vDash \Diamond X)$ in quantum Markov chain $\langle \mathcal{H}, \mathcal{E} \rangle$ and the termination probability

$$p_T(\rho) = 1 - \lim_{n \to \infty} p_{NT}^{(n)}(\rho)$$

where ρ is the initial state, $\mathcal{E}$ is the quantum operation in the loop body, and $p_{NT}^{(n)}(\rho)$ is defined by Eqs (8.41) and (8.42).

2. Note that a general measurement can be implemented by a projective measurement together with a unitary transformation (see Section 2.4). Show how can the termination problem of loop (8.39) in its full generality be reduced to the reachability problem of a quantum Markov chain.

Computation of reachability probability: Now we see how can the reachability probability (8.57) be computed using the quantum BSCC decomposition given in the last section. We first note that the subspace X in Eq. (8.57) is invariant under $\widetilde{\mathcal{E}}$. Thus $\langle X, \widetilde{\mathcal{E}} \rangle$ is a quantum Markov chain too. It is easy to verify that $\widetilde{\mathcal{E}}_\infty(X) = X$. Thus, we can decompose X into a set of orthogonal BSCCs according to $\widetilde{\mathcal{E}}$ by Theorem 8.18.

The following lemma shows a connection between the limit probability of hitting a BSCC and the probability that the asymptotic average of the initial state lies in the same BSCC.

Lemma 8.25. *Let* $\{B_i\}$ *be a BSCC decomposition of* $\mathcal{E}_\infty(\mathcal{H})$, *and* P_{B_i} *the projection onto* B_i. *Then for each* i, *we have*

$$\lim_{k \to \infty} tr\left(P_{B_i} \mathcal{E}^k(\rho) \right) = tr\left(P_{B_i} \mathcal{E}_\infty(\rho) \right) \tag{8.58}$$

for all $\rho \in \mathcal{D}(\mathcal{H})$.

Proof. We write P for the projection onto $T_{\mathcal{E}} = \mathcal{E}_\infty(\mathcal{H})^\perp$. Then similar to the proof of Theorem 8.17, we see that the limit

$$q_i \triangleq \lim_{k\to\infty} tr\left(P_{B_i}\mathcal{E}^k(\rho)\right)$$

does exist, and $tr\left(P_{B_i}\mathcal{E}_\infty(\rho)\right) \leq q_i$. Moreover, we have:

$$1 = tr((I-P)\mathcal{E}_\infty(\rho)) = \sum_i tr\left(P_{B_i}\mathcal{E}_\infty(\rho)\right)$$
$$\leq \sum_i q_i$$
$$= \lim_{k\to\infty} tr\left((I-P)\mathcal{E}^k(\rho)\right) = 1.$$

This implies $q_i = tr\left(P_{B_i}\mathcal{E}_\infty(\rho)\right)$. $\qquad\square$

The above lemma together with Theorem 8.17 gives us an elegant way to compute the reachability probability of a subspace in a quantum Markov chain.

Theorem 8.21. *Let $\langle\mathcal{H}, \mathcal{E}\rangle$ be a quantum Markov chain, $\rho \in \mathcal{D}(\mathcal{H})$, and $X \subseteq \mathcal{H}$ a subspace. Then*

$$\Pr(\rho \models \Diamond X) = tr\left(P_X\widetilde{\mathcal{E}}_\infty(\rho)\right),$$

and this probability can be computed in time $O(d^8)$ where $d = \dim(\mathcal{H})$.

Proof. The claim that

$$\Pr(\rho \models \Diamond X) = tr\left(P_X\widetilde{\mathcal{E}}_\infty(\rho)\right)$$

follows directly from Lemma 8.25 and Theorem 8.17. The time complexity of computing reachability probability follows from Lemma 8.24(i). $\qquad\square$

It should be pointed out that the reachability probability $\Pr(\rho \models \Diamond X)$ can also be computed directly by the techniques used in the proofs of Theorem 8.13 and Proposition 8.2.

We conclude this section by raising a research problem:

Problem 8.5. All algorithms for analysis of quantum programs presented in last section and this one are classical; that is, they were developed for analysis of quantum programs using classical computers. It is desirable to develop quantum algorithms for the same purpose that can improve the complexities of the corresponding algorithms given in this chapter.

8.5 Quantum abstract interpretation

In the previous sections, we studied two major problems in the analysis of quantum programs, namely invariant generation and termination analysis. The reader must be noticed that the algorithms for solving these problems described there are not very efficient. Moreover, these algorithms can only be applied to quantum programs with finite-dimensional state spaces. Indeed, many program analysis problems have no solutions that are both precise and efficient, and they are even uncomputable in infinite-dimensional state spaces. A key technique widely used to mitigate this issue for classical programs is abstract interpretation proposed by Cousot and Cousot [110]. Roughly speaking, it is a trade-off between precision and efficiency. It computes approximations of the semantics of programs to derive sound and effective program analysis. The price needed to pay for keeping the analysis automatic is that some information may be missed and thus the analysis may not be complete. In this section, we extend the ideas of abstract interpretation to quantum programs.

8.5.1 Basics of abstract interpretation

For convenience of the reader, let us first briefly review the framework of abstract interpretation. The starting point is the basic idea that the precise program semantics and its approximations can be viewed as the same object at different levels of abstraction. Then program analysis can be derived from the link between the precise semantics and the approximation at a chosen abstraction.

Formally, a minimal structural of the domain in which program semantics can be defined is often modelled as a partial order $(C, \leq)$ (see Definition 5.7) together with certain functions $f : C \to C$. This idea has been extensively used in semantics of classical programming languages. It was also used in Section 5.3 for defining denotational semantics of quantum **while**-programs.

As a mathematical framework of abstract interpretation, let us assume that the precise program semantics domain and an approximation of it are modelled as partial orders $(C, \leq)$ and $(A, \sqsubseteq)$, and called the concrete and abstract domains, respectively. Then the links between them are concretisation and abstraction functions defined in the following:

Definition 8.35 (Concretisation and abstraction). **1.** A concretisation function is a monotonic mapping $\gamma : A \to C$ from abstract domain to concrete domains: for any $a_1, a_2 \in A$, $a_1 \leq a_2$ implies $\gamma(a_1) \sqsubseteq \gamma(a_2)$.
2. An abstraction function is a monotonic mapping $\alpha : C \to A$ from concrete domain to abstract domain: for any $c_1, c_2 \in C$, $c_1 \leq c_2$ implies $\alpha(c_1) \sqsubseteq \alpha(c_2)$.

The abstractions of concrete elements can be defined based on the notion of concretisation function.

Definition 8.36 (Soundness). Given a concretisation γ. Then an element $a \in A$ is called a sound abstraction of an element $c \in C$ under γ if $c \leq \gamma(a)$. In particular, a is an exact abstraction of c if $a = \gamma(c)$.

The abstraction in the above definition was realised through a concretisation function. It can also be described in terms of an abstraction function. Indeed, there is an elegant duality between concretisation and abstraction functions as defined in the following:

Definition 8.37 (Galois connection). A pair of concretisation function γ and abstraction function α is called a Galois connection, written

$$(C, \leq) \xrightleftharpoons[\gamma]{\alpha} (A, \sqsubseteq)$$

if for any $c \in C$ and $a \in A$:

$$c \leq \gamma(a) \text{ if and only if } \alpha(c) \sqsubseteq a. \tag{8.59}$$

It is easy to check that condition (8.59) is equivalent to the following:

(i) $\gamma \circ \alpha$ is extensive: $c \leq \gamma(\alpha(c))$ for ever $c \in C$; and
(ii) $\alpha \circ \gamma$ is reductive: $\alpha(\gamma(a)) \sqsubseteq a$ for ever $a \in A$.

Some basic properties of Galois connections are presented in the following:

Lemma 8.26. *Given a Galois connection* $(C, \leq) \xrightleftharpoons[\gamma]{\alpha} (A, \sqsubseteq)$. *Then:*

1. *For any $c \in C$ and $a \in A$:*

$$\alpha(c) = \bigsqcap \{a | c \leq \gamma(a)\}; \tag{8.60}$$

$$\gamma(a) = \bigvee \{c | \alpha(c) \sqsubseteq a\}. \tag{8.61}$$

2. *α preserves least upper bounds; that is, for any $X \subseteq C$, if $\bigvee X$ exists, then*

$$\alpha \left(\bigvee X \right) = \bigsqcup \{\alpha(x) | x \in X\};$$

3. *γ preserves greatest lower bound; that is, for any $Y \subseteq A$, if $\bigsqcap Y$ exists, then*

$$\gamma \left(\bigsqcap Y \right) = \bigwedge \{\gamma(a) | a \in Y\}.$$

Intuitively, Eq. (8.60) means that $\alpha(c)$ is the best (i.e. smallest) sound abstraction of c.
Now we lift the notion of abstraction from concrete elements to concrete functions.

Definition 8.38 (Soundness). Given a concretisation γ. Then a function $g : A \to A$ is called a sound abstraction of a function $f : C \to C$ under γ if for any $a \in A$, $f(\gamma(a)) \leq \gamma(g(a))$. In particular, g is called an exact abstraction if $f \circ \gamma = \gamma \circ g$.

Lemma 8.27. **1.** *If $g_i : A \to A$ is a sound abstraction of $f_i : C \to C$ ($i = 1, 2$) under γ, and f_2 is monotonic, then $g_2 \circ g_1$ is a sound abstraction of $f_2 \circ f_1$ under γ.*
2. *If $(C, \leq) \xrightarrow[\gamma]{\alpha} (A, \sqsubseteq)$ is a Galois connection, then for any function $f : C \to C$, $\alpha \circ f \circ \gamma$ is the best (i.e. smallest) sound abstraction of f under γ.*

Exercise 8.12. Prove Lemmas 8.26 and 8.27.

Fixpoint approximation: It is often very difficult to compute the precise semantics of a loop, or more generally, a recursive program, which is usually defined as the least fixpoint $lfp\,f$ of a function $f : C \to C$ in the concrete domain. Therefore, it is desirable to find an abstraction of $lfp\,f$ in an abstract domain $(A, \sqsubseteq)$ that can serve as a useful approximation. Let us assume that a sound abstraction $g : A \to A$ of f is given. Many techniques have been proposed in the literature to compute useful approximations of fixpoint $lfp\,f$ from g. The simplest is given in the following:

Lemma 8.28. *Let C be a CPO (see Definition 5.10) and A have the least element $\perp_A$. If:*

(1) *$f : C \to C$ is continuous (see Definition 5.11); and*
(2) *g is a sound abstraction of f under concretisation function γ,*

then whenever $x = \bigsqcup_{i=0}^{n} g^i(\perp_A)$ exists, it is a sound approximation of $lfp\,f$, where:

$$\begin{cases} g^0(\perp_A) = \perp_A, \\ g^i(\perp_A) = g\left(g^{i-1}(\perp_A)\right) \text{ for } i \geq 1. \end{cases}$$

Fixpoint acceleration: We observe that if sequence $\{g^i(\perp_A)\}$ in Lemma 8.28 stabilises after a finite number n of steps; that is, $g^i(\perp_A) = g^n(\perp_A)$ for all $i \geq n$, then we can compute $\bigsqcup_{i=0}^{\infty} g^i(\perp_A) = g^n(\perp_A)$ as an overapproximation of the fixpoint $lfp\,f$. In general, however, it is not always this case. To accelerate the convergence in computing an abstract of fixpoint, the notion of widening operator is introduced:

Definition 8.39. A widening operator in an abstract domain $(A, \sqsubseteq)$ is a mapping $\nabla : A \times A \to A$ satisfying:

1. It computes upper bounds: for any $x, y \in A$, $x \sqsubseteq x \nabla y$ and $y \sqsubseteq x \nabla y$;
2. It enforces convergence: for any sequences $\{x_i\}$ in A, sequence $\nabla\{x_i\} \overset{\triangle}{=} \{y_i\}$ stabilises; that is, for some n, $y_{n+1} = y_n$, where:

$$\begin{cases} y_0 = x_0; \\ y_i = i_{i-1} \nabla x_i \quad \text{for } i \geq 1. \end{cases}$$

The following lemma describes a way in which widening operators are used to accelerate fixpoint computation.

Lemma 8.29. *Let f be a continuous function on the concrete domain and g a sound abstraction of f under concretisation function γ. We construct sequence $\{x_i\}$ by*

$$\begin{cases} x_0 = \perp_A, \\ x_i = x_{i-1} \nabla g(x_{i-1}) \quad \text{for } i \geq 1. \end{cases}$$

Then:

1. *$\{x_i\}$ converges in a finite number of steps; that is, there exists $n \geq 0$ such that $x_i = x_n \overset{\triangle}{=} x$ for all $i \geq n$; and*
2. *The limit x is a sound abstraction of $lfp\,f$.*

Exercise 8.13. Prove Lemmas 8.28 and 8.29. Hint: Use Knaster–Tarski Fixpoint Theorem 5.1.

To conclude this subsection, we would like to point out that a key to successful applications of abstract interpretation is to find appropriate abstract domains in which program semantics can be efficiently computed.

8.5.2 Restriction and extension of projections

Now we consider how to apply abstract interpretation technique introduced in the previous subsection to quantum computing. Several ways to do this have been proposed in the literature. In this section, we only describe the one introduced in [443] as an example. The basic idea of [443] is that a quantum state can be abstracted as a family of projections. More precisely, let us consider a quantum program with a large number n of qubits. A state of the program is 2^n-dimensional and usually intractable. As a tractable approximation, we can choose a family of subsets of these n qubits, with the number of qubits in each subset being $\ll n$. Then we only look at the parts of the program state over these subsets, and for each subset of qubits, the part over it is further approximated by a projection (i.e. subspace). Thus, the tuples of projections are chosen as abstraction domain.

In this subsection, we prepare several mathematical tools needed for such abstraction of quantum states. As in Birkhoff–von Neumann quantum logic (Section 7.3), we identify a closed subspace X of $\mathcal{H}$ with the projection P_X onto X. We write $S(\mathcal{H})$ for the set of closed subspaces of $\mathcal{H}$.

Definition 8.40. 1. Let $P \in S(\mathcal{H}_1 \otimes \mathcal{H}_2)$. Then its restriction of P on $\mathcal{H}_1$ is defined as

$$P \downarrow \mathcal{H}_1 = \mathrm{supp}(\mathrm{tr}_{\mathcal{H}_2} P).$$

2. Let $P \in S(\mathcal{H}_1)$. Then its cylindrical extension of P on $\mathcal{H}_1 \otimes \mathcal{H}_2$ is defined as

$$P \uparrow (\mathcal{H}_1 \otimes \mathcal{H}_2) = P \otimes I_{\mathcal{H}_2}.$$

Some basic properties of restriction and cylindrical extension are presented in the following lemmas. Recall from Section 7.3 that for any family $\{P_i\} \subseteq S(\mathcal{H})$ of subspaces of $\mathcal{H}$, their join is defined as

$$\bigvee_i P_i = span\left(\bigcup_i P_i\right).$$

The next lemma shows that restriction and cylindrical extension are (partially) preserved by join and intersection of subspaces:

Lemma 8.30. 1. *Let* $P_i \in S(\mathcal{H}_1 \otimes \mathcal{H}_2)$ *for all i. Then*

$$\left(\bigvee_i P_i\right) \downarrow \mathcal{H}_1 = \bigvee_i (P_i \downarrow \mathcal{H}_1), \tag{8.62}$$

$$\left(\bigcap_i P_i\right) \downarrow \mathcal{H}_1 \subseteq \bigcap_i (P_i \downarrow \mathcal{H}_1). \tag{8.63}$$

2. *Let* $P_i \in S(\mathcal{H}_1)$ *for all i. Then*

$$\left(\bigvee_i P_i\right) \uparrow (\mathcal{H}_1 \otimes \mathcal{H}_2) = \bigvee_i [P_i \uparrow (\mathcal{H}_1 \otimes \mathcal{H}_2)], \tag{8.64}$$

$$\left(\bigcap_i P_i\right) \uparrow (\mathcal{H}_1 \otimes \mathcal{H}_2) \subseteq \bigcap_i [P_i \uparrow (\mathcal{H}_1 \otimes \mathcal{H}_2)]. \tag{8.65}$$

3. *Let* $P \in S(\mathcal{H}_1 \otimes \mathcal{H}_2 \otimes \mathcal{H}_3)$. *Then* $[P \downarrow (\mathcal{H}_1 \otimes \mathcal{H}_2)] \downarrow \mathcal{H}_1 = P \downarrow \mathcal{H}_1$.
4. *Let* $P \in S(\mathcal{H}_1)$. *Then*

$$[P \uparrow (\mathcal{H}_1 \otimes \mathcal{H}_2)] \uparrow (\mathcal{H}_1 \otimes \mathcal{H}_2 \otimes \mathcal{H}_3) = P \uparrow (\mathcal{H}_1 \otimes \mathcal{H}_2 \otimes \mathcal{H}_3).$$

The equalities in inclusions (8.63) and (8.65) do not hold in general. For example, let $\mathcal{H}_1 = \mathcal{H}_2$ be the state space of a qubit, and $P_1 = span\{|00\rangle\}$, $P_2 = span\{|01\rangle\}$. Then $(P_1 \downarrow \mathcal{H}_1) \cap (P_2 \downarrow \mathcal{H}_1) = span\{|0\rangle\}$ and $(P_1 \cap P_2) \downarrow \mathcal{H}_1 = \{0\}$ (the 0-dimensional space).

A close connection between restriction and cylindrical extension is established in the following:

Lemma 8.31. 1. $[P \uparrow (\mathcal{H}_1 \otimes \mathcal{H}_2)] \downarrow \mathcal{H}_1 = P$ *for any* $P \in S(\mathcal{H}_1)$.
2. $P \sqsubseteq (P \downarrow \mathcal{H}_1) \uparrow (\mathcal{H}_1 \otimes \mathcal{H}_2)$ *for any* $P \in S(\mathcal{H}_1 \otimes \mathcal{H}_2)$.

3. *Let $P \in S(\mathcal{H}_1)$ and $Q \in S(\mathcal{H}_1 \otimes \mathcal{H}_2)$. Then*

$$Q \downarrow \mathcal{H}_1 \sqsubseteq P \Leftrightarrow Q \sqsubseteq P \uparrow (\mathcal{H}_1 \otimes \mathcal{H}_2).$$

Exercise 8.14. Find a necessary and sufficient condition under which $P = (P \downarrow \mathcal{H}_1) \uparrow (\mathcal{H}_1 \otimes \mathcal{H}_2)$.

Finally, we show that restriction and cylindrical extension are preserved by quantum operations. Recall from Definition 8.23 that the image of $P \in S(\mathcal{H})$ under a quantum operation $\mathcal{E}$ is defined as

$$\mathcal{E}(P) = \bigvee_{|\psi\rangle \in P} \mathrm{supp}[\mathcal{E}(|\psi\rangle\langle\psi|)].$$

Lemma 8.32. *Let $\mathcal{E}$ be a quantum operation on $\mathcal{H}_1$ and $\mathcal{I}_2$ the identity quantum operation on $\mathcal{H}_2$. Then:*
1. *For any $P \in S(\mathcal{H}_1 \otimes \mathcal{H}_2)$,*

$$\mathcal{E}(P \downarrow \mathcal{H}_1) = (\mathcal{E} \otimes \mathcal{I}_2)(P) \downarrow \mathcal{H}_1;$$

2. *For any $P \in S(\mathcal{H}_1)$,*

$$(\mathcal{E} \otimes \mathcal{I}_2)(P \uparrow (\mathcal{H}_1 \otimes \mathcal{H}_2)) = \mathcal{E}(P) \uparrow (\mathcal{H}_1 \otimes \mathcal{H}_2).$$

The proofs of Lemmas 8.30, 8.31, and 8.32 are postponed to Appendix A.4.2.

8.5.3 Abstraction of quantum states

In this subsection, we define abstract domains of quantum states and abstraction functions based on the idea described at the beginning of the last subsection.

Concrete domain of quantum states: To set the stage, let us first recall some basic facts about quantum domains from Section 5.3.2. Let $\mathcal{H}$ be a Hilbert space. We write $\mathcal{D}(\mathcal{H})$ for the set of partial density operators on $\mathcal{H}$. Then $(\mathcal{D}(\mathcal{H}), \sqsubseteq)$ is a CPO with the zero operator $0_{\mathcal{H}}$ as its least element, where $\sqsubseteq$ stands for the Löwner order (Lemma 5.2). It was proved that each quantum operation on $\mathcal{H}$ is a continuous function from $(\mathcal{D}(\mathcal{H}), \sqsubseteq)$ into itself (Lemma 5.3). These structures serve as a concrete domain and functions on it for quantum abstract interpretation.

Abstract quantum states: Now we consider how to define an abstract domain of quantum states. Given a set $qVar$ of quantum variables. For each $q \in qVar$, we assume that $\mathcal{H}_q$ is the state Hilbert space of quantum system denoted by q. Then for any subset $V \subseteq qVar$, the state space of (composed) quantum system V is

$$\mathcal{H}_V \overset{\triangle}{=} \bigotimes_{q \in V} \mathcal{H}_q.$$

Definition 8.41. **1.** A nonempty family $S \subseteq 2^{qVar}$ of subsets of quantum variables $qVar$ is called a frame.
2. The Smyth order between two frames S, T is defined by

$$S \trianglelefteq T \text{ iff } (\forall V \in S)(\exists W \in T) \text{ such that } V \subseteq W.$$

Intuitively, $S \trianglelefteq T$ means that S can be thought of as a more local view than T, and conversely, T is a more global view than S. In particular, let $\bot = \{\emptyset\}$ and $\top = \{qVar\}$ be the bottom and top frames, respectively. Then $\bot \trianglelefteq S \trianglelefteq \top$ for any frame S.

According to the idea described at the beginning of the last subsection, the notion of abstract quantum state is defined in the following:

Definition 8.42. **1.** An abstract quantum state over a frame S is a family $\mathbb{P} = (P_V)_{V \in S}$ with $P_V \in S(\mathcal{H}_V)$ for every $V \in S$.
2. $\mathbb{P}$ is called normal if it satisfies the consistency; that is, for any $V_1, V_2 \in S$:

$$P_{V_1} \downarrow (V_1 \cap V_2) = P_{V_2} \downarrow (V_1 \cap V_2).$$

We write $\mathcal{LS}(S)$ and $\mathcal{LS}_n(S)$ for the sets of abstract quantum states and normal abstract quantum states, respectively, over S. It is easy to see that if any two sets $V_1, V_2 \in S$ are disjoint, then all $\mathbb{P} \in \mathcal{LS}(S)$ are normal; that is, $\mathcal{LS}(S) = \mathcal{LS}_n(S)$.

Example 8.5. For any mixed quantum state (i.e. density operator) ρ in $\mathcal{H}_{qVar}$, we set:

$$P_V^\rho = \text{supp}\left(\text{tr}_{\mathcal{H}_{qVar\backslash V}}(\rho)\right) \tag{8.66}$$

for each $V \in S$. Then $\left(P_V^\rho\right)_{V \in S}$ is an abstract quantum state over S. It can be seen as an approximation of ρ.

Exercise 8.15. Prove that the abstract quantum state in Example 8.5 is normal.

A order between abstract quantum states can be defined as follows: for any $\mathbb{P} = (P_V)_{V \in S}$ and $\mathbb{Q} = (Q_V)_{V \in S} \in \mathcal{LS}(S)$,

$$\mathbb{P} \sqsubseteq \mathbb{Q} \text{ iff for each } V \in S : P_V \subseteq Q_V.$$

Lemma 8.33. *Both* $(\mathcal{LS}(S), \sqsubseteq)$ *and* $(\mathcal{LS}_n(S), \sqsubseteq)$ *are CPOs.*

Localisation as abstraction function: As said before, the basic idea of quantum abstraction interpretation considered in this section is that instead of dealing with a whole quantum state, we look at its localisations (i.e. parts over a small number of quantum variables). Now for a chosen frame T, this idea can be formalised as abstraction function:

$$\overline{\alpha}_T : \mathcal{D}\left(\mathcal{H}_{qVar}\right) \to \mathcal{LS}_n(T),$$
$$\rho \mapsto \left(P_W^\rho\right)_{W \in T} \text{ for every } \rho \in \mathcal{D}\left(\mathcal{H}_{qVar}\right) \tag{8.67}$$

where P_W^ρ is defined by Eq. (8.66). It is easy to see that $\overline{\alpha}_T$ is monotonic. Furthermore, if abstract quantum states over T are still intractable, we can choose another frame S that is more local than T and introduce the following:

Definition 8.43. Let $S \trianglelefteq T$. Then the localisation operator $\alpha_{T \to S} : \mathcal{LS}(T) \to \mathcal{LS}(S)$ is defined as follows: for any $\mathbb{Q} = (Q_W)_{W \in T} \in \mathcal{LS}(T)$,

$$\alpha_{T \to S}(\mathbb{Q}) \overset{\triangle}{=} \mathbb{P} = (P_V)_{V \in S} \in \mathcal{LS}(S), \text{ where} :$$
$$P_V = \bigvee_{W \in T : V \subseteq W} (Q \downarrow V) \text{ for each } V \in S.$$

Exercise 8.16. Prove or disprove $\overline{\alpha}_T \circ \alpha_{T \to S} = \overline{\alpha}_S$.

The following lemma gives a simple characterisation of the image of a normal abstract quantum state under the localisation operator.

Lemma 8.34. *For any* $\mathbb{P} = (P_V)_{V \in T} \in \mathcal{LS}_n(T)$, *if* $\alpha_{T \to S}(\mathbb{P}) = (Q_W)_{W \in S}$, *then for any* $W \in S$,

$$Q_W = P_V \downarrow W$$

for all $V \in T$ *with* $W \subseteq V$.

The next lemma further shows that the localisation of a normal abstract quantum state is normal too.

Lemma 8.35. $\alpha_{T \to S}(\mathcal{LS}_n(T)) \subseteq \mathcal{LS}_n(S)$.

For any two mappings $\mathcal{F}_1, \mathcal{F}_2 : \mathcal{LS}(S) \to \mathcal{LS}(T)$, we define:

$$\mathcal{F}_1 \sqsubseteq \mathcal{F}_2 \Leftrightarrow \mathcal{F}_1(\mathbb{P}) \sqsubseteq \mathcal{F}_2(\mathbb{P}) \text{ for all } \mathbb{P} \in \mathcal{LS}(S).$$

The following lemma shows that the localisation from T to R can be refined by the composition of the localisations from T to some S and from S to R.

Lemma 8.36. $\alpha_{S \to R} \circ \alpha_{T \to S} \sqsubseteq \alpha_{T \to R}$. *In particular, when restricted to* $\mathcal{LS}_n(T)$, *the equality holds.*

The proofs of Lemmas 8.33 to 8.36 can be found in Appendix A.4.2. But the reader is encouraged to prove these lemmas by themselves as exercises. [Hint: Use Lemmas 8.30, 8.31 and 8.32.]

Extension as concretisation function: Now we turn to define the concretisation function from abstract quantum states over a more local frame S to those over a more global frame T.

Definition 8.44. Let $S \trianglelefteq T$. Then the extension operator $\gamma_{S \to T} : \mathcal{LS}(S) \to \mathcal{LS}(T)$ is defined as follows: for any $\mathbb{P} = (P_V)_{V \in S} \in \mathcal{LS}(S)$,

$$\gamma_{S \to T}(\mathbb{P}) \overset{\triangle}{=} \mathbb{Q} = (Q_W)_{W \in T} \in \mathcal{LS}(T), \text{ where}:$$

$$Q_W = \bigcap_{V \in S : V \subseteq W} (P \uparrow V) \text{ for each } W \in T.$$

The following theorem establishes a Galois connection between the localisation and extension operators.

Theorem 8.22. *Let $S \trianglelefteq T$. Then $\mathcal{LS}(S) \xleftrightarrow[\gamma]{\alpha} \mathcal{LS}(T)$ is a Galois connection.*

Proof. For any $\mathbb{P} = (P_V)_{V \in S} \in \mathcal{LP}(S)$ and $\mathbb{Q} = (Q_W)_{W \in T} \in \mathcal{LP}(T)$, we have:

$$\alpha_{T \to S}(\mathbb{Q}) \sqsubseteq \mathbb{P} \Leftrightarrow (\forall V \in S) \left(\bigvee_{W \in T : V \subseteq W} (Q_W \downarrow V) \subseteq P_V \right)$$

$$\Leftrightarrow (\forall V \in S)(\forall W \in T)(V \subseteq W \Rightarrow Q_W \downarrow V \sqsubseteq P_V)$$

$$\Leftrightarrow (\forall V \in S)(\forall W \in T)(V \subseteq W \Rightarrow Q_W \sqsubseteq P_V \uparrow W) \qquad \text{by Lemma 8.31}$$

$$\Leftrightarrow (\forall W \in T)(\forall V \in S)(V \subseteq W \Rightarrow Q_W \sqsubseteq P_V \uparrow W)$$

$$\Leftrightarrow (\forall W \in T) \left(\mathbb{Q} \sqsubseteq \bigcap_{V \in S : V \subseteq W} (P \uparrow W) \right)$$

$$\Leftrightarrow \mathbb{Q} \sqsubseteq \gamma_{S \to T}(\mathbb{P}). \qquad \square$$

Corollary 8.5. $\gamma_{S \to T} \circ \alpha_{T \to S} \sqsupseteq I_T$ *and* $\alpha_{T \to S} \circ \gamma_{S \to T} \sqsubseteq I_S$, *where* I_S, I_T *stand for the identity mappings over $\mathcal{LS}(S)$ and $\mathcal{LS}(T)$, respectively.*

8.5.4 Abstraction of quantum operations

In the last subsection, we described abstraction of quantum states. In this subsection, we lift it to abstraction of quantum operations.

Let us start from the concrete domain of quantum operations. We write $\mathcal{QO}(\mathcal{H})$ for the set of quantum operations on a Hilbert space $\mathcal{H}$. Then recall from Lemma 5.4 that $(\mathcal{QO}(\mathcal{H}), \sqsubseteq)$ is a CPO, where $\sqsubseteq$ is the lifting of the Löwner order from operators to quantum operations; that is, for any $\mathcal{E}, \mathcal{F} \in \mathcal{QO}(\mathcal{H})$:

$$\mathcal{E} \sqsubseteq \mathcal{F} \Leftrightarrow \mathcal{E}(\rho) \sqsubseteq \mathcal{F}(\rho) \text{ for all } \rho \in \mathcal{D}(\mathcal{H}).$$

Now as in the last subsection, we assume a set $qVar$ of quantum variables. Let $\mathcal{H}_{qVar}$ be their Hilbert space. Then for any frame T, using abstraction function $\overline{\alpha}_T$ defined by Eq. (8.67), we can define an abstraction in the abstract domain $\mathcal{LS}_n(\mathcal{H}_{qVar})$ of a quantum operation in the concrete domain $\mathcal{D}(\mathcal{H}_{qVar})$. Formally, a mapping $\mathcal{E}_T : \mathcal{LS}_n(T) \to \mathcal{LS}_n(T)$ is a sound abstraction of a quantum operation $\mathcal{E} \in \mathcal{QO}(\mathcal{H}_{qVar})$ if for any $\rho \in \mathcal{D}(\mathcal{H}_{qVar})$, it holds that

$$\overline{\alpha}_T(\mathcal{E}(\rho)) \sqsubseteq \mathcal{E}_T(\overline{\alpha}_T(\rho)).$$

Next we consider how can an operation on abstract quantum states over a more global frame be restricted to one over a more local frame, and conversely, how can an operation on abstract quantum states over a more local frame be extended to one over a more global frame.

Definition 8.45. 1. Let $S_i \trianglelefteq T_i$ for $i = 1, 2$. Then for any mapping $\mathcal{E} : \mathcal{LS}(T_1) \to \mathcal{LS}(T_2)$, its restriction on S_1 is defined as

$$\mathcal{E}_\# = \alpha_{T_2 \to S_2} \circ \mathcal{E} \circ \gamma_{S_1 \to T_1}.$$

2. Let $S_i \trianglelefteq T_i$ for $i = 1, 2$. Then for any mapping $\mathcal{F} : \mathcal{LS}(S_1) \to \mathcal{LS}(S_2)$, its (cylindrical) extension on T_1 is defined as

$$\mathcal{F}^\# = \gamma_{S_2 \to T_2} \circ \mathcal{F} \circ \alpha_{T_1 \to S_1}.$$

The following lemma shows that restriction $\#$ and extension $^{\#}$ are a pseudo-inverse of each other, and presents a connection of them to abstraction and concretisation functions α and γ. In particular, for a given operation $\mathcal{E} : \mathcal{LS}(T_1) \to \mathcal{LS}(T_2)$ on abstract quantum states over more global frames T_i, it provides a useful tool for constructing a sound abstraction of $\mathcal{E}$ over more local frames S_i.

Lemma 8.37. *Let S_i, T_i $(i = 1, 2)$ and $\mathcal{E}$, $\mathcal{F}$ be the same as in Definition 8.45.*

1. *If $\mathcal{E}$ is monotonic, then:*
   a. $\mathcal{E} \sqsubseteq (\mathcal{E}_\#)^{\#}$;
   b. *for any $\mathbb{P} \in \mathcal{LS}(T_1)$ and $\mathbb{Q} \in \mathcal{LS}(S_1)$:*

$$\alpha_{T_1 \to S_2}(\mathbb{P}) \sqsubseteq \mathbb{Q} \Rightarrow \alpha_{T_2 \to S_2}(\mathcal{E}(\mathbb{P})) \sqsubseteq \mathcal{E}_\#(\mathbb{Q}).$$

2. *If $\mathcal{F}$ is monotonic, then:*
   a. $(\mathcal{F}^{\#})_\# \sqsubseteq \mathcal{F}$;
   b. *for any $\mathbb{P} \in \mathcal{LS}(T_1)$ and $\mathbb{Q} \in \mathcal{LS}(S_1)$:*

$$\mathbb{P} \sqsubseteq \gamma_{S_1 \to T_1}(\mathbb{Q}) \Rightarrow \mathcal{F}^{\#}(\mathbb{P}) \sqsubseteq \gamma_{S_2 \to T_2}(\mathcal{F}(\mathbb{Q})).$$

Proof. We only prove clause 1, and clause 2 can be proved by duality.

a. Since $\mathcal{E}$ is monotonic, it follows from Corollary 8.5 that

$$(\mathcal{E}_\#)^{\#} = \gamma_{S_2 \to T_2} \circ \mathcal{E}_\# \circ \alpha_{T_1 \to S_1}$$
$$= \gamma_{S_2 \to T_2} \circ \alpha_{T_2 \to S_2} \circ \mathcal{E} \circ \gamma_{S_1 \to T_1} \circ \alpha_{T_1 \to S_1} \sqsupseteq \mathcal{E}.$$

b. Since $\alpha_{T_1 \to S_1}(\mathbb{P}) \sqsubseteq \mathbb{Q}$, by Corollary 8.5 we have:

$$\mathcal{E}_\#(\mathbb{Q}) \sqsupseteq \mathcal{E}_\#(\alpha_{T_1 \to S_1}(\mathbb{P})) = \left(\alpha_{T_2 \to S_2} \circ \mathcal{E} \circ \gamma_{S_1 \to T_1}\right)(\alpha_{T_1 \to S_1}(\mathbb{P}))$$
$$= \alpha_{T_2 \to S_2}\left(\mathcal{E}\left(\left(\gamma_{S_1 \to T_1} \circ \alpha_{T_1 \to S_1}\right)(\mathbb{P})\right)\right)$$
$$\sqsupseteq \alpha_{T_2 \to S_2}(\mathcal{E}(\mathbb{P})). \qquad \square$$

The next lemma shows that restriction $\#$ and extension $^{\#}$ are partially preserved by the composition of quantum operations.

Lemma 8.38. $S_i \trianglelefteq T_i$ $(i = 1, 2, 3)$, *and let $\mathcal{E}_i : \mathcal{LS}(T_i) \to \mathcal{LS}(T_{i+1})$ and $\mathcal{F}_i : \mathcal{LS}(S_i) \to \mathcal{LS}(S_{i+1})$ for $i = 1, 2$. Then:*

1. $(\mathcal{E}_1 \circ \mathcal{E}_2)_\# \sqsubseteq \mathcal{E}_{1\#} \circ \mathcal{E}_{2\#}$.
2. $(\mathcal{F}_1 \circ \mathcal{F}_2)^{\#} \sqsupseteq \mathcal{F}_1^{\#} \circ \mathcal{F}_2^{\#}$.

Exercise 8.17. Prove Lemma 8.38.

Finally, we can assemble all of the mathematical tools developed in this section to construct a chain of abstraction steps:

$$\mathcal{D}\left(\mathcal{H}_{qVar}\right) \xrightarrow{\overline{\alpha}_{S_1}} \mathcal{LS}(S_1) \xrightarrow{\alpha_{S_1 \to S_2}} \mathcal{LS}(S_2) \xrightarrow{\alpha_{S_2 \to S_3}} \dots \xrightarrow{\alpha_{S_{n-1} \to S_n}} \mathcal{LS}(S_n)$$

$$\mathcal{E} \downarrow \qquad\qquad \mathcal{E}_1 \downarrow \qquad\qquad \mathcal{E}_2 \downarrow \qquad\qquad\qquad \mathcal{E}_n \downarrow$$

$$\mathcal{D}\left(\mathcal{H}_{qVar}\right) \xrightarrow{\overline{\alpha}_{S_1}} \mathcal{LS}(S_1) \xrightarrow{\alpha_{S_1 \to S_2}} \mathcal{LS}(S_2) \xrightarrow{\alpha_{S_2 \to S_3}} \dots \xrightarrow{\alpha_{S_{n-1} \to S_n}} \mathcal{LS}(S_n)$$

where $S_n \trianglelefteq S_{n-1} \trianglelefteq \dots \trianglelefteq S_2 \trianglelefteq S_1$. Imagine that the denotational semantics of a quantum program with variables $qVar$ is a quantum operation $\mathcal{E} : \mathcal{D}\left(\mathcal{H}_{qVar}\right) \to \mathcal{D}\left(\mathcal{H}_{qVar}\right)$, and it is too hard to analyse because the dimension of state space $\mathcal{H}_{qVar}$ exponentially increases as the number of quantum variables. We can choose a family S_1 of subsets of $qVar$ so that each $V \in S_1$ is much smaller than $qVar$, and inspect the local behaviour of the program over all $V \in S_1$. In this way, an operation $\mathcal{E}_1$ on $\mathcal{LS}(S_1)$ is obtained as an approximation of $\mathcal{E}$ using abstraction function $\overline{\alpha}_{S_1}$. If $\mathcal{E}_1$ is still hard to analyse, then we can repeat the procedure until a frame S_n is chosen and an approximation $\mathcal{E}_n$ of $\mathcal{E}$ on $\mathcal{LS}(S_n)$ can be efficiently analysed. Thus, information gathered in analysing abstract semantics $\mathcal{E}_n$ can be traced back through concretisation functions $\gamma_{S_n \to S_{n-1}}, \dots, \gamma_{S_2 \to S_1}$ to obtain some useful information about concrete semantics $\mathcal{E}$. This technique was employed in [443] to analyse several quantum algorithms, including Grover search, with a large number of qubits.

To conclude this section, we would like to point out that several other quantum abstraction interpretation techniques have been proposed; for example, Bichsel et al. [64] presented an abstract interpretation technique for efficient analysis of quantum circuits using abstract stabiliser simulation that merges multiple summands in the stabiliser formalism of arbitrary quantum states. On the other hand, classical abstract interpretation is widely used in analysis and verification of loops and recursive programs and approximate computation of program invariants. However, up to now, quantum abstract interpretation does not facilitate fixpoint computation and has only be applied to quantum circuits. It is an interesting topic for future research to develop abstract interpretation that can be used to compute approximations of the fixpoints of quantum operations and thus can be applied to quantum loops and recursive quantum programs.

8.6 Bibliographic remarks and further readings

Section 8.1 is presented mainly according to [432]. An SVTS is essentially a quantum Markov chain in the sense of Gudder [192] and Feng et al. [157], which is different from that studied in Section 8.4, together with an initial quantum predicate Θ. Each SVTS S can be seen as a transition graph with locations as its vertices and transitions as its edges. It is an operator-valued graph, called a quiver in representation theory [126].

Invariants: The notion of invariant for quantum programs was defined in [432] using SVTS (Superoperator Valued Transition Systems) for modelling the control flows. The results presented in Section 8.2 all come from [432]. Only a simple example of generating invariants for a quantum walk was given in Section 8.2. The reader can find a more sophisticated example in [432], where the technique described in Section 8.2 is used to generate invariants for verifying the correctness of an important quantum algorithm – quantum Metropolis sampling for simulation of quantum systems [393].

Termination through reachability: The studies on termination analysis of quantum programs were initiated in [426], where termination of a quantum **while**-loop with a unitary transformation as the loop body was considered. In [435], the verification method for probabilistic programs developed by Sharir, Pnueli, and Hart [375] was generalised to the quantum case, termination analysis of quantum programs was carried out using a quantum Markov chain as their semantic model, and thus several major results in [426] were significantly extended. The materials presented in Section 8.4.1 of this chapter are taken from [426] and [435]. This line of research is a natural quantum extension of reachability approach to classical program analysis (see [353] for example). It was further extended by S.G. Ying et al. [439] to reachability analysis of quantum Markov chains; in particular, the notion of BSCC of a quantum graph was introduced in [439]. Sections 8.4.2 to 8.4.4 are mainly based on [439]. It should be mentioned that several more complicated reachability properties, e.g. *repeated reachability* and *persistence*, were considered in [439], which further lead to the studies of model checking quantum systems [428]. More researches along this line include:

1. *Perturbation of quantum programs*: Although not discussed in this chapter, perturbation analysis is particularly interesting for quantum programs because of noise in the implementation of quantum logical gates. It was proved in [426] that a small disturbance either on the unitary transformation in the loop body or on the measurement in the loop guard can make a quantum loop to (almost surely) terminate, provided that some obvious dimension restriction is satisfied.

2. *Expected runtime of quantum programs*: A calculus of quantum weakest preconditions [131] was proposed by Olmedo and Díaz-Caro [324], Liu et al. [282], and Avanzini et al. [35] for reasoning about expected runtime of quantum programs.

3. *Analysis of recursive quantum programs*: In this chapter, we only considered analysis of quantum loop programs. In [156], Feng et al. introduced a quantum generalisation of Etessami and Yannakakis's recursive Markov chains [141], namely recursive superoperator-valued Markov chains, and developed some techniques for their reachability analysis. It is obvious that these techniques can be used to analysis of recursive quantum programs defined in Section 5.5. Another class of analysis techniques for classical recursive programs are based on pushdown automata; see for example [140]. The notion of pushdown quantum automata was introduced in [180], but it still not clear how to use pushdown quantum automata in the analysis of recursive quantum programs.

4. *Analysis of nondeterministic and concurrent quantum programs*: An analysis for termination of nondeterministic quantum programs was carried out by Li et al. [277], generalised several results by Hart, Sharir and Pnueli [200] for probabilistic programs. Termination of concurrent quantum programs with fairness conditions was studied by Yu et al. [444]. It was further discussed by S.G. Ying et al. [440] in terms of reachability of quantum Markov decision processes. On the other hand, only simplest reachability of quantum programs was examined in this chapter. Several more complicated reachability properties of quantum systems were studied by Li et al. [275].

Termination using ranking functions: Ranking functions are a standard tool for proving termination of classical programs. In Chapter 6, this approach was employed in quantum Hoare logic to prove total correctness of quantum programs.

The notion of ranking martingale was introduced in [89] as a generalisation of ranking function for termination analysis of probabilistic programs. In [276], ranking martingales are further generalised to handle quantum programs. The exposition of Section 8.3 is based on [276].

Abstract interpretation: The brief review of abstract interpretation in Section 8.5.1 is based on the tutorial [305]. The book [109] provides a comprehensive exposition of the subject. Abstract interpretation was first introduced to quantum computing by Perdrix [236,335] for entanglement analysis. The main results presented in Section 8.5 were obtained by Yu and Palsberg [443], but are presented in slightly different way; in particular, Definition 8.43 is different from its original form in [443]. An interesting link from abstraction interpretation to quantum Hoare logic and quantum incorrectness logic [414] was observed by Feng and Li [151]. As is well-known, one of the major applications of abstract interpretation is (approximately) generating invariants of classical programs. But up to now, this technique has not been applied to generating quantum invariants.

Finally, we would like to point out that in this chapter, we only considered static analysis of quantum programs. Some dynamic analysis methods performed during runtime have also been generalised to quantum programs, including runtime assertion, testing and debugging; see for example [83,90,213,218,273,279,280,402].

Part IV

Parallel and distributed quantum programs

In the previous parts from Chapter 5 to Chapter 8, we have focused on sequential quantum programs, in which one computation completes before the next starts. In this part, we study concurrent quantum programs, in which more than one computation are executed concurrently during overlapping time periods, including parallel and distributed quantum programs.

Indeed, as already briefly discussed in Section 1.2.3, parallel and distributed programming problem has already arisen in the following four areas of quantum computing:

- Firstly, several models of parallel and distributed quantum computing were proposed, mainly with the motivation of using the physical resources of two or more small-capacity quantum computers to realise large-capacity quantum computing, which is out of the reach of current technology. For example, a model of distributed quantum computing over noisy channels was considered in [98]. More recently, a quantum parallel RAM (Random Access Memory) model was defined in [199], and a formal language for defining quantum circuits in distributed quantum computing was introduced in [425].
- Secondly, quantum algorithms for solving paradigmatic parallel and distributed computing problems that are faster than the known classical algorithms have been discovered. For example, a quantum algorithm for the leader election problem was given in [390] and a quantum protocol for the dinning philosopher problem was shown in [13]. Also, several parallel implementations of the quantum Fourier transform and Shor's quantum factoring algorithm were presented in [100, 312]. In particular, Bravyi, Gosset, and König recently discovered a parallel quantum algorithm solving a linear algebra problem called HLF (Hidden Linear Function), which gives for the first time an unconditional proof of a computational quantum advantage [74].
- Thirdly, parallelism has been carefully considered in the physical level design of quantum computer architecture; see for example [308]. Furthermore, the issue of instruction parallelism has already been discussed in Rigetti's quantum instruction set architecture [380] and IBM Q [113]. Moreover, experiments of the physical implementation of parallel and distributed quantum computing have been frequently reported in the recent years.
- Fourthly, motivated by the rapid progress toward practical quantum hardware in the latest years, some authors [107] started to consider how to design an operating system for quantum computers; in particular, what new abstractions could a quantum operating system expose to the programmer? It is well-known that parallelism and concurrency are a major issue in operating systems for classical computers [238]. As one can imagine, they will also be a major issue in the design and implementation of future quantum operating systems.

As is well-known, classical concurrent programs are already difficult to understand and reason about. Concurrent quantum programs add a new dimension of difficulty, namely quantumness. In this class of programs, quantumness and concurrency are intertwined together, making a theory of them even more complicated. We will gradually develop such a theory in this part, from the simplest case of disjoint parallel quantum programs to parallel quantum programs with shared variables and then to distributed quantum programs with message passing (communication).

It must be pointed out that the theory of parallel and distributed quantum programming is still at the very early stage of development, and as we will see in this part, many problems in it are unsolved.

Chapter 9

Parallel quantum programs

In this and next chapters, we are going to systematically study a theory of parallel and distributed quantum programming. This chapter will focus on parallel quantum programs.

As in the case of classical parallel programming, a parallel quantum program consists of parallel processes that communicate through one common shared memory, i.e. whereas processes are considered as separate entities, their memory is considered as a single monolithic entity. Therefore, a theory of parallel quantum programming should be a generalisation of the theory of classical parallel programming. However, it faces the following:

Major challenges in parallel quantum programming:

1. *Intertwined nondeterminism*: As we saw in Chapter 5, in a quantum **while**-program, nondeterminism is caused only by the involved quantum measurements. On the other hand, in a classical parallel program, nondeterminism is introduced only by the parallelism. However, in a parallel quantum program, say

$$P_1 \| \cdots \| P_n,$$

a parallel composition of sequential quantum programs $P_1, ..., P_n$, these two kinds of nondeterminism occur simultaneously, and their intertwining is hard to deal with in defining the denotational semantics of the program; in particular, when it contains loops which can have infinite computations (see Definition 9.5 and Example 9.3 below).

2. *Entanglement*: The denotational semantics achieved by solving the above challenge provides us with a basis for building a proof system for reasoning about correctness of parallel quantum programs. One of the main aims of this chapter is to develop such a proof system.

   The proof system introduced by Owicki and Gries [326,327] and Lamport [267] is one of the most popular methods for reasoning about classical parallel programs. Roughly speaking, it consists of the Hoare logic for sequential programs, a rule for introducing auxiliary variables recording control flows and a key rule (R.PC) for parallel composition shown in Fig. 9.1.

   We want to establish a Owicki–Gries and Lamport-like proof system for parallel quantum programs. At the first glance, it seems easy to find a quantum generalisation of proof rule (R.PC) in the simplest case of disjoint parallel quantum programs because:

   a. interference freedom is automatically there, as what happens in classical disjoint parallel programs; and
   b. conjunctives $\bigwedge_{i=1}^{n} A_i$ and $\bigwedge_{i=1}^{n} B_i$ in rule (R.PC) have proper quantum counterparts, namely tensor products $\bigotimes_{i=1}^{n} A_i$ and $\bigotimes_{i=1}^{n} B_i$, respectively, when $P_1, ..., P_n$ are disjoint.

   But actually a difficulty that makes no sense in classical computing arises in reasoning about parallel quantum programs even in this simple case. More explicitly, entanglement is indispensable for realising the advantage of quantum computing over classical computing, but a quantum generalisation of (R.PC) is not strong enough to cope with the situation where entanglement between component programs is present.

3. *Combining quantum predicates in the overlap of state Hilbert spaces*: When we further consider a parallel quantum program $P_1 \| \cdots \| P_n$ with shared variables, another difficulty appears which never happens in classical computation: the Hilbert spaces $\mathcal{H}_{P_i}$ ($i = 1, ..., n$) of quantum predicates A_i, B_i ($i = 1, ..., n$) have overlaps. Then conjunctives $\bigwedge_{i=1}^{n} A_i$ and $\bigwedge_{i=1}^{n} B_i$ cannot be simply replaced by tensor products $\bigotimes_{i=1}^{n} A_i$ and $\bigotimes_{i=1}^{n} B_i$, respectively, because they are not well-defined in the state Hilbert space $\bigotimes_{i=1}^{n} \mathcal{H}_{P_i}$ of $P_1 \| \cdots \| P_n$.

$$(\text{R.PC}) \quad \frac{\text{Proofs of } \{A_i\}\, P_i\, \{B_i\}\ (i = 1, ..., n) \text{ are interference free}}{\left\{\bigwedge_{i=1}^{n} A_i\right\} P_1 \| \cdots \| P_n \left\{\bigwedge_{i=1}^{n} B_i\right\}}$$

FIGURE 9.1 Proof rule for parallel composition.

Foundations of Quantum Programming. https://doi.org/10.1016/B978-0-44-315942-8.00021-6

Essentially, this chapter aims at developing a theory around the central theme of how to resolve the above challenges. We introduce a programming language that can be used to program parallel quantum algorithms like those mentioned above. Its syntax is obtained by expanding the quantum **while**-language defined in Chapter 5 with the construct of parallel composition. Then we formally define its semantics and develop a series of inference rules for reasoning about correctness of parallel quantum programs. The theory of parallel quantum programs is presented in two steps:

- As the first step, we consider the class of disjoint parallel quantum programs in Sections 9.1 to 9.3. The syntax of disjoint parallel quantum programs is given in Sections 9.1.
- We define the operational and denotational semantics of disjoint parallel quantum programs in Section 9.2. The challenge of *intertwined nondeterminism* is settled there. In particular, we are able to establish a confluence property of different execution paths for disjoint parallel quantum program (see Lemmas 9.2 and 9.3).
- A series of proof rules for reasoning about correctness of disjoint parallel quantum programs are introduced step by step there. In particular, we propose two techniques to tame the difficulty of *entanglement* in Sections 9.3.2 through 9.3.6:

   (a) introducing an additional inference rule obtained by invoking a deep theorem about the relation between noise and entanglement from quantum physics [195] (see rule (R.S2E) in Fig. 9.8); and
   (b) introducing auxiliary variables (see Section 9.3.5) based on the observation in physics that entanglement may emerge when reducing a state of a composite system to its subsystems [318].

   In Sections 9.3.7 and 9.3.8, we organise the rules given in Sections 9.3.2 to 9.3.6 into two proof systems, and prove the (relative) completeness of the two systems. These proof systems are generalisations of quantum Hoare logic studied in Chapter 6.

   A reader who is mainly interested in applications can skip Sections 9.3.7 and 9.3.8 in which very heavy mathematical reasoning is involved.

- As the second step, in Sections 9.4 to 9.6, we generalise the results for disjoint parallel quantum programs to parallel quantum programs with shared variables. The syntax and semantics of parallel quantum programs with shared variables are defined in Sections 9.4 and 9.5, respectively.
- Section 9.6 is devoted to develop proof techniques for parallel quantum programs with shared variables. The notion of proof outline is required to present inference rule (R.PC) for classical parallel programs with shared variables. A corresponding notion is needed to present the quantum generalisation(s) of rule (R.PC). As a preparation, such a notion is introduced for quantum **while**-programs in Section 9.6.2.

   We only have a partial solution to the difficulty of *overlaping state Hilbert spaces*. The idea is that probabilistic (convex) combinations of A_i $(i = 1, ..., n)$ and B_i $(i = 1, ..., n)$ are well-defined in $\bigotimes_{i=1}^{n} \mathcal{H}_{P_i}$, even when $P_1, ..., P_n$ share variables, and can serve as a kind of approximations to the quantum counterparts of conjunctives $\bigwedge_{i=1}^{n} A_i$, $\bigwedge_{i=1}^{n} B_i$, respectively. Although a probabilistic combination is not a perfect quantum version of conjunctive, as a tensor product did in the case of disjoint parallel quantum programs, its reasonableness and usefulness can be clearly seen through its connection to local Hamiltonians in many-body quantum systems (see a detailed discussion in Remark 9.6). Furthermore, we can define a notion of parametrised interference freedom between the proof outlines of component quantum programs. Then a quantum variant of inference rule (R.PC) can be introduced to reason about parallel quantum programs with shared variables. A strong soundness theorem is proved for the rules showing that partial correctness is well maintained at each step of the transitions in the operational semantics of a parallel quantum program with shared variables (see Theorem 9.7).

9.1 Syntax of disjoint parallel quantum programs

In this section, we define the syntax of disjoint parallel quantum programs.

Definition 9.1 (Syntax). Parallel quantum programs are generated by the grammar given in Eq. (5.3) together with the following clause:

$$P ::= P_1 \| \cdots \| P_n \equiv \|_{i=1}^{n} P_i \tag{9.1}$$

where $n > 1$, and $P_1, ..., P_n$ are quantum **while**-programs, and $var(P_i) \cap var(P_j) = \emptyset$ for $i \neq j$.

Program P in Eq. (9.1) is called the (disjoint) parallel composition of $P_1, ..., P_n$. Let us write

$$var(P) = \bigcup_{i=1}^{n} var(P_i)$$

for the set of quantum variables in P. Then the state Hilbert space of P is

$$\mathcal{H}_P = \mathcal{H}_{var(P)} = \bigotimes_{i=1}^{n} \mathcal{H}_{P_i}.$$

Remark 9.1. There is a serious difference between disjoint parallelism in classical programming and that in quantum programming. In the classical case, disjoint parallelism allows component programs to have reading access to common variables. Formally, two programs S_1 and S_2 are disjoint if $change(S_1) \cap var(S_2) = \emptyset$ and $change(S_2) \cap var(S_1) = \emptyset$, where $change(S)$ stands for the set of variables in a program S that can be modified, and $var(S)$ is the set of all variables in S. In the quantum case, however, since measurements can change the state of variables, and the variables in the left-hand side and in the right-hand side of a unitary statement $\overline{q} := U[\overline{q}]$ are the same, we always have $change(S) = var(S)$. Consequently, two disjoint parallel quantum programs S_1 and S_2 cannot have any common variables. Instead, as we will see soon, they are linked by entanglement between them (usually starting from the inputs).

As a simple example, let us consider the fanout-based parallelisation of quantum circuits proposed by Moore and Nilsson [310].

Example 9.1 (Fanout-based parallelisation). The basic idea in [310] is that one can parallelise a quantum computation by fanning out an input into multiple copies. Note that this does not violate the nocloning principle stated in Section 2.4.1. Formally, a fanout gate can be realised by several CNOT gates as follows:

$$Fanout[q; q_1, ..., q_{n-1}] = CNOT[q, q_1]; ...; CNOT[q, q_{n-1}].$$

1. Suppose we have a quantum circuit C consisting of a series of controlled-gates, all of which are controlled by the same qubit q, but act on different qubits:

$$C := C[q, U_1[\overline{r_1}]]; ...; C[q, U_n[\overline{r_n}]]$$

where quantum registers $\overline{r_1}, ..., \overline{r_n}$ are pairwise disjoint, and $U_1, ..., U_n$ are quantum gates (i.e. unitary operators). By using $n - 1$ ancillary qubits $q_1, ..., q_{n-1}$, it can be parallelised as

$$D := Fanout[q; q_1, ..., q_{n-1}];$$
$$C[q, U_1[\overline{r_1}]] \| C[q_1, U_2[\overline{r_2}]] \| ... \| C[q_{n-1}, U_n[\overline{r_n}]];$$
$$Fanout[q; q_1, ..., q_{n-1}]$$

where symbol $\|$ stands for parallel composition, and the second fan-out for uncomputation.

2. Let $\{U_i\}_{i=1}^{n}$ be pairwise commuting gates on k qubits $\overline{r}$. Then they can be simultaneously diagonalised; that is, there exists a gate T on $\overline{r}$ such that $T U_i T^{\dagger} = V_i$ is diagonal for all $1 \leq i \leq n$. Consequently, circuit

$$C := C[q_1, U_1[\overline{r}]]; ...; C[q_n, U_n[\overline{r}]]$$

can be parallelised as

$$D := T[\overline{r}]; Fanout[\overline{r}; \overline{r_1}, ...; \overline{r_n}];$$
$$C[q_1, U_1[\overline{r}]] \| C[q_2, U_2[\overline{r_1}]] \| ... \| C[q_n, U_n[\overline{r_{n-1}}]];$$
$$Fanout[\overline{r}; \overline{r_1}, ...; \overline{r_n}]; T^{\dagger}[\overline{r}]$$

Exercise 9.1. Generalise fanout-based parallelisation in Example 9.1 from the case of controlled gates to the case of quantum multiplexors (QMUXs) (see Section 3.1.4).

9.2 Semantics of disjoint parallel quantum programs

In this section, we define the operational and denotational semantics of disjoint parallel quantum programs. Before doing it, let us first observe a fundamental difference between the classical and quantum cases. As we saw in Definition 5.4, the statistical nature of quantum measurements introduces nondeterminism even in the operational semantics of quantum **while**-programs. Such nondeterminism is much more complicated in parallel quantum programs; in particular when they contain loops and thus can have infinite computations, because it is intertwined with another kind of nondeterminism, namely nondeterminism introduced in parallelism. This will be seen more explicitly in Example 9.3.

(IF') $\langle \mathbf{if}\,(\Box m \cdot M[\overline{q}] = m \to P_m)\,\mathbf{fi}, \rho\rangle \to \left\{|\langle P_m, M_m \rho M_m^\dagger\rangle|\right\}$

(L') $\langle \mathbf{while}\,M[\overline{q}] = 1\,\mathbf{do}\,P\,\mathbf{od}, \rho\rangle \to$

$$\left\{|\langle \downarrow, M_0 \rho M_0^\dagger\rangle, \langle P;\,\mathbf{while}\,M[\overline{q}] = 1\,\mathbf{do}\,P\,\mathbf{od}, M_1 \rho M_1^\dagger\rangle|\right\}$$

(MS1) $\dfrac{C \to \mathcal{A}}{\{C\} \to \mathcal{A}}$

(MS2) $\dfrac{\{\mathcal{A}_i\}_{i \in I}\text{ is a partition of }\mathcal{A} \qquad I = I_0 \cup I_1 \\ \mathcal{A}_i \nrightarrow \text{ for every }i \in I_0 \qquad \mathcal{A}_i \to \mathcal{B}_i \text{ for every }i \in I_1}{\mathcal{A} \to \left(\bigcup_{i \in I_0} \mathcal{A}_i\right) \cup \left(\bigcup_{i \in I_1} \mathcal{B}_i\right)}$

FIGURE 9.2 Extended transition rules for quantum **while**-programs. In rule (MS1), C is a configuration and $\mathcal{A}$ is a configuration ensembles. In rule (MS2), $\mathcal{A}_i$ and $\mathcal{B}_i$ are all configuration ensembles. Note that in (MS2), $\bigcup$ stands for union of multisets.

(PC) $\dfrac{\langle P_i, \rho\rangle \to \left\{|\langle P'_{ij}, \rho'_j\rangle|\right\}}{\langle P_1\|...\|P_{i-1}\|P_i\|P_{i+1}\|...\|P_n, \rho\rangle \to \left\{|\langle P_1\|...\|P_{i-1}\|P'_{ij}\|P_{i+1}\|...\|P_n, \rho'_j\rangle|\right\}}$

FIGURE 9.3 Transition rule for (disjoint) parallel quantum programs. Here, $1 \leq i \leq n$.

9.2.1 Operational semantics

The operational semantics of quantum **while**-programs was defined as a transition relation between configurations. To accommodate the intertwined nondeterminism in parallel quantum programs introduced by quantum measurements and parallelism together, we have to first recast the operational semantics of quantum **while**-programs in a slightly different way; that is, as a transition relation between configuration ensembles.

Reformulating operational semantics of quantum while-programs: We define a configuration ensemble as a multiset

$$\mathcal{A} = \{|\langle P_i, \rho_i\rangle|\}$$

of configurations with $\sum_i tr(\rho_i) \leq 1$. For simplicity, we identify a singleton $\{|\langle P, \rho\rangle|\}$ with the configuration $\langle P, \rho\rangle$. Moreover, we need to extend the transition relation between configurations given in Definition 5.4 to a transition relation between configuration ensembles.

Definition 9.2. The operational semantics of quantum **while**-programs is the transition relation between configuration ensembles of the form:

$$\{|\langle P_i, \rho_i\rangle|\} \to \{|\langle Q_j, \sigma_j\rangle|\}$$

defined by rules (Sk), (In), (UT), (SC) in Fig. 5.1 together with the rules presented in Fig. 9.2.

The above definition is a restatement of Definition 5.4 in terms of configuration ensembles. We observe that for each possible measurement outcome m, transition rule (IF) in Fig. 5.1 gives a transition from configuration $\langle \mathbf{if} \cdots \mathbf{fi}, \rho\rangle$. So, (IF) is essentially a family of transition rules. Transition rule (IF') in Fig. 9.2 is thus a merge of these transitions by collecting all the target configurations into a configuration ensemble. Note that (IF') is a single rule. Similarly, transition rule (L') is a merge of (L0) and (L1) in Fig. 5.1. Both of transition rules (MS1) and (MS2) are introduced for manipulating configuration ensembles as *multisets* of configurations. Rule (MS1) is used simply for lifting transitions of configurations to transitions of configuration ensembles. Rule (MS2) allows us to combine several transitions from some small ensembles into a single transition from a large ensemble.

Defining operational semantics of parallel quantum programs: With the above preparation, we can define the operational semantics of disjoint parallel quantum programs in a simple way.

Definition 9.3 (Operational semantics). The operational semantics of disjoint parallel quantum programs is the transition relation between configuration ensembles defined by the rules used in Definition 9.2 together with rule (PC) in Fig. 9.3.

Transition rule (PC) defines the semantics of (disjoint) parallel composition $P_1\|...\|P_n$ of (sequential) components $P_1,...,P_n$. Intuitively, it models interleaving concurrency; more precisely, it means that for a fixed $1 \leq i \leq n$, if the ith component P_i of parallel quantum programs $P \equiv P_1 \| \cdots \| P_n$ performs a transition, then P can perform the same transition. Rule (PC) is similar to the transition rule for classical parallel programs. We will use the convention for termination that $P_1 \| \cdots \| P_n = \downarrow$ when $P_i = \downarrow$ for all i. This means that a parallel program $P_1 \| \cdots \| P_n$ terminates if and only if all of its components terminate.

To further illustrate the transition rule (PC), we consider the following simple example. To simplify the presentation, for a pure state $|\varphi\rangle$ and a complex number α with $|\alpha| \leq 1$, we use the vector $\alpha|\varphi\rangle$ to denote the corresponding partial density operator $|\alpha|^2|\varphi\rangle\langle\varphi|$.

Example 9.2. Let p, q, r be three qubit variables. We consider the following two programs:

$$P_1 \equiv p := X[p]; q := Z[q], \qquad P_2 \equiv \textbf{if } M[r] = 0 \to \textbf{skip}$$
$$\square \qquad\qquad 1 \to r := H[r]$$
$$\textbf{fi}$$

Program P_1 performs Pauli gate X on qubit p and then Pauli gate Z on qubit q. Program P_2 is a measurement-based conditional. It first performs the measurement in the computational basis, $M = \{M_0 = |0\rangle\langle 0|, M_1 = |1\rangle\langle 1|\}$, on qubit r. If the measurement outcome is 0 then the program does **skip**, and if the outcome is 1 then it performs the Hadamard gate H on qubit r. Obviously, P_1 and P_2 are disjoint. Now let us examine their execution in parallel with an input entangled between the variables p, q of P_1 and the variable r of P_2. Let

$$|\psi\rangle = \frac{1}{\sqrt{2}}(|000\rangle + |111\rangle)$$

be the GHZ (Greenberger–Horne–Zeilinger) state, a maximally entanglement of three qubits p, q, r. Then

$$\langle P_1 \| P_2, |\psi\rangle\rangle \to_1 \langle q := Z[q] \| P_2, \frac{1}{\sqrt{2}}(|100\rangle + |011\rangle)\rangle$$

$$\to_2 \begin{cases} \langle q := Z[q] \| \textbf{skip}, \frac{1}{\sqrt{2}}|100\rangle\rangle \\ \langle q := Z[q] \| r := H[r], \frac{1}{\sqrt{2}}|011\rangle\rangle \end{cases}$$

$$\to_1 \begin{cases} \langle \downarrow \| \textbf{skip}, \frac{1}{\sqrt{2}}|100\rangle\rangle \\ \langle q := Z[q] \| r := H[r], \frac{1}{\sqrt{2}}|011\rangle\rangle \end{cases} \to_2 \begin{cases} \langle \downarrow \| \textbf{skip}, \frac{1}{\sqrt{2}}|100\rangle\rangle \\ \langle q := Z[q] \| \downarrow, \frac{1}{\sqrt{2}}|01-\rangle\rangle \end{cases}$$

$$\to_1 \begin{cases} \langle \downarrow \| \textbf{skip}, \frac{1}{\sqrt{2}}|100\rangle\rangle \\ \langle \downarrow, -\frac{1}{\sqrt{2}}|01-\rangle\rangle \end{cases} \to_2 \begin{cases} \langle \downarrow, \frac{1}{\sqrt{2}}|100\rangle\rangle \\ \langle \downarrow, -\frac{1}{\sqrt{2}}|01-\rangle\rangle \end{cases}$$

is a computation of parallel program $P_1 \| P_2$ starting in state $|\psi\rangle$. Here, we use $\to_i$ to indicate that the transition is made by P_i according to rule (PC), and $|-\rangle = \frac{1}{\sqrt{2}}(|0\rangle - |1\rangle)$.

It is interesting to see that at the second step of the computation in the above example, measurement M is performed by component P_2 and thus certain nondeterminism occurs; that is, two different configurations are produced according to the two different outcomes 0, 1 of M. Then in steps 3, 4, and 5, the following kind of interleaving appears: an action of component P_2 happens between two actions of component P_1 executed on the two different configurations that come from the same measurement M. Here, in a sense, nondeterminism caused by quantum measurements is intertwined with nondeterminism introduced by parallelism. It is worth noting that for a classical parallel program $P \equiv P_1 \| \cdots \| P_n$ with P_i ($1 \leq i \leq n$) being **while**-programs, such an interleaving never happens because nondeterminism does not occur in the execution of any component P_i.

9.2.2 Denotational semantics

In this subsection, we define the denotational semantics of disjoint parallel quantum programs based on the operational semantics defined in the last subsection. As a preparation, we need to reformulate the denotational semantics of quantum **while**-programs, since the operational semantics of them was redefined in terms of the transition between configuration ensembles.

Reformulating denotational semantics of quantum while-programs: The denotational semantics (i.e. semantic function) of a quantum **while**-program given in Definition 5.6 can be represented using configuration ensembles introduced in the last subsection as follows. For any configuration ensemble $\mathcal{A}$, we define:

$$val(\mathcal{A}) = \sum \left\{ |\rho' : \langle \downarrow, \rho' \rangle \in \mathcal{A}| \right\}.$$

It is evident that if $\mathcal{A} \to \mathcal{B}$ then $val(\mathcal{A}) \sqsubseteq val(\mathcal{B})$ because $\langle \downarrow, \rho \rangle$ has no transition; that is, $\langle \downarrow, \rho \rangle \in \mathcal{A}$ implies $\langle \downarrow, \rho \rangle \in \mathcal{B}$.

Definition 9.4. 1. A computation of a quantum **while**-program P starting in a state $\rho \in \mathcal{D}(\mathcal{H}_P)$ is a maximal finite sequence $\pi = \langle P, \rho \rangle \to \mathcal{A}_1 \to \cdots \to \mathcal{A}_n \nrightarrow$ or an infinite sequence $\pi = \langle P, \rho \rangle \to \mathcal{A}_1 \to \cdots \to \mathcal{A}_n \to \cdots$.
2. The value of computation π is defined as follows:

$$val(\pi) = \begin{cases} val(\mathcal{A}_n) \text{ if } \pi \text{ is finite and } \mathcal{A}_n \text{ is the last configuration ensemble,} \\ \lim_{n \to \infty} val(\mathcal{A}_n) \text{ if } \pi \text{ is infinite.} \end{cases}$$

Note that in the case of infinite π, sequence $\{val(\mathcal{A}_n)\}$ is increasing according to the Löwner order $\sqsubseteq$. On the other hand, we know that $\mathcal{D}(\mathcal{H}_P)$ with $\sqsubseteq$ is a CPO (Complete Partial Order; see Lemma 5.2). So, $\lim_{n \to \infty} val(\mathcal{A}_n)$ exists.

The following lemma shows determinism of quantum **while**-programs.

Lemma 9.1. *For any quantum **while**-program P and $\rho \in \mathcal{D}(\mathcal{H}_P)$, there is exactly one computation π of P starting in ρ and $[\![P]\!](\rho) = val(\pi)$.*

Defining denotational semantics of parallel quantum programs: Now we are ready to introduce the denotational semantics of disjoint parallel quantum programs. But it cannot be defined by simply mimicking Definitions 5.6 and 9.4. For each parallel quantum program P, we set:

$$\mathcal{V}(P, \rho) = \{val(\pi) : \pi \text{ is a computation of } P \text{ starting in } \rho\} \tag{9.2}$$

for any $\rho \in \mathcal{D}(\mathcal{H}_P)$, where $val(\pi)$ is given as in Definition 9.4. Then we have:

Definition 9.5 (Denotational semantics). The semantic function of a disjoint parallel program P is the mapping $[\![P]\!] : \mathcal{D}(\mathcal{H}_P) \to 2^{\mathcal{D}(\mathcal{H}_P)}$ defined by

$$[\![P]\!](\rho) = \{\text{maximal elements of } (\mathcal{V}(P, \rho), \sqsubseteq)\}$$

for any $\rho \in \mathcal{D}(\mathcal{H}_P)$.

The above definition deserves a careful explanation. First, the reader may be wondering why we need to take maximal elements in the definition of $[\![P]\!](\rho)$. For a parallel quantum programs without loop, it is unnecessary to consider maximal elements; for instance, we simply have:

$$[\![P_1 \| P_2]\!](|\psi\rangle) = \left\{ \frac{1}{2}(|100\rangle\langle100| + |01-\rangle\langle01-|) \right\}$$

in Example 9.2. However, the following example clearly shows that only maximal elements are appropriate whenever infinite computations occur.

Example 9.3. Let q_0, q_1 be two qubit variables, and for $k = 0, 1$,

$$P_k \equiv \textbf{if } M[q_k] = 0 \to \textbf{skip}$$
$$\square \qquad 1 \to \textbf{skip}$$
$$\textbf{fi}; \textbf{ while}_k$$

where:

$$\textbf{while}_k \equiv \textbf{while } M[q_k] = k \textbf{ do skip od},$$

and M is the measurement in the computational basis. Then the following are three computations of parallel program $P_0 \| P_1$ starting in state $|++\rangle$ with $|+\rangle = \frac{1}{\sqrt{2}}(|0\rangle + |1\rangle)$:

1. All transitions are performed by P_0:

$$\pi_0 = \langle P_0 \| P_1, |++\rangle\rangle \to_0 \mathcal{A}_1 \to_0 \mathcal{A}_2 \to_0 \mathcal{A}_3 \to_0 \cdots \to_0 \mathcal{A}_{2n} \to_0 \mathcal{A}_{2n+1} \to_0 \cdots$$

where for every $n \geq 1$:

$$\mathcal{A}_1 = \left\{ \langle \mathbf{while}_0 \| P_1, \frac{1}{\sqrt{2}}|0+\rangle\rangle, \langle \mathbf{while}_0 \| P_1, \frac{1}{\sqrt{2}}|1+\rangle\rangle \right\},$$

$$\mathcal{A}_{2n} = \left\{ \langle \mathbf{skip}; \mathbf{while}_0 \| P_1, \frac{1}{\sqrt{2}}|0+\rangle\rangle, \langle \downarrow \| P_1, \frac{1}{\sqrt{2}}|1+\rangle\rangle \right\},$$

$$\mathcal{A}_{2n+1} = \left\{ \langle \mathbf{while}_0 \| P_1, \frac{1}{\sqrt{2}}|0+\rangle\rangle, \langle \downarrow \| P_1, \frac{1}{\sqrt{2}}|1+\rangle\rangle \right\}.$$

2. All transitions are performed by P_1:

$$\pi_1 = \langle P_0 \| P_1, |++\rangle\rangle \to_1 \mathcal{B}_1 \to_1 \mathcal{B}_2 \to_1 \mathcal{B}_3 \to_1 \cdots \to_1 \mathcal{B}_{2n} \to_1 \mathcal{B}_{2n+1} \to_1 \cdots$$

where for every $n \geq 1$:

$$\mathcal{B}_1 = \left\{ \langle P_0 \| \mathbf{while}_1, \frac{1}{\sqrt{2}}|+0\rangle\rangle, \langle P_0 \| \mathbf{while}_1, \frac{1}{\sqrt{2}}|+1\rangle\rangle \right\},$$

$$\mathcal{B}_{2n} = \left\{ \langle P_0 \| \downarrow, \frac{1}{\sqrt{2}}|+0\rangle\rangle, \langle P_0 \| \mathbf{skip}; \mathbf{while}_1, \frac{1}{\sqrt{2}}|+1\rangle\rangle \right\},$$

$$\mathcal{B}_{2n+1} = \left\{ P_0 \| \downarrow, \frac{1}{\sqrt{2}}|+0\rangle\rangle, \langle P_0 \| \mathbf{while}_1, \frac{1}{\sqrt{2}}|+1\rangle\rangle \right\}.$$

3. The transitions are fairly performed by P_0 and P_1:

$$\pi = \langle P_0 \| P_1, |++\rangle\rangle \to_0 \mathcal{A}_1 \to_0 \mathcal{A}_2 \to_0 \mathcal{A}_3 \to_1 \mathcal{C}_4 \to_1 \mathcal{C}_5 \to \cdots$$

where

$$\mathcal{C}_4 = \{ \langle \mathbf{while}_0 \| \mathbf{while}_1, \frac{1}{2}|00\rangle\rangle, \langle \mathbf{while}_0 \| \mathbf{while}_1, \frac{1}{2}|01\rangle\rangle,$$

$$\langle \downarrow \| \mathbf{while}_1, \frac{1}{2}|10\rangle\rangle, \langle \downarrow \| \mathbf{while}_1, \frac{1}{2}|11\rangle\rangle \},$$

$$\mathcal{C}_5 = \{ \langle \mathbf{while}_0 \| \downarrow, \frac{1}{2}|00\rangle\rangle, \langle \mathbf{while}_0 \| \mathbf{skip}; \mathbf{while}_1, \frac{1}{2}|01\rangle\rangle,$$

$$\langle \downarrow \| \downarrow, \frac{1}{2}|10\rangle\rangle, \langle \downarrow \| \mathbf{skip}; \mathbf{while}_1, \frac{1}{2}|11\rangle\rangle \}.$$

Obviously, $val(\pi_0) = val(\pi_1) = 0 < \frac{1}{4}|10\rangle\langle 10| = val(\pi)$, and $val(\pi)$ is a maximal element of $\mathcal{V}(P_0 \| P_1, |++\rangle)$. Furthermore, we have:

$$[\![P_0 \| P_1]\!] (|++\rangle) = \left\{ \frac{1}{4}|10\rangle\langle 10| \right\}.$$

Exercise 9.2. Work out the operational and denotational semantics of the two parallel quantum programs in Example 9.1.

Second, the output $[\![P]\!] (\rho)$ of a parallel program P with input ρ is defined as the set of maximal elements of a partially ordered set. In general, there may be no or more than one maximal element. But we will see shortly, in the case of disjoint parallelism, the structure of $[\![P]\!] (\rho)$ is simple.

Determinism and sequentialisation: As we saw in the last subsection, the operational semantics of disjoint parallel quantum programs may demonstrate a very complicated nondeterminism. But surprisingly, similar to the case of classical disjoint parallel programs, the determinism is still true for the denotational semantics of disjoint parallel quantum programs. In other words, we have a (partial) generalisation of Lemma 9.1:

$$(\text{R.Seq}) \quad \frac{\{A\}\, P_1; \cdots; P_n\, \{B\}}{\{A\}\, P_1 \| \cdots \| P_n\, \{B\}}$$

FIGURE 9.4 Sequentialisation rule for disjoint parallel programs.

Lemma 9.2 (Determinism). *For any disjoint parallel quantum program P and $\rho \in \mathcal{D}(\mathcal{H}_P)$, $[\![P]\!](\rho)$ is a singleton.*

For a disjoint parallel quantum program P and for any $\rho \in \mathcal{D}(\mathcal{H}_P)$, if singleton $[\![P]\!](\rho) = \{\rho'\}$, then we will always identify $[\![P]\!](\rho)$ with the partial density operator ρ'. Indeed, ρ' must be the greatest element of $(\mathcal{V}(P, \rho), \sqsubseteq)$.

It is well-known that every disjoint parallel composition of classical **while**-programs can be sequentialised (see for example [28], Lemma 7.7). This result can also be generalised to the quantum case. Indeed, it is a corollary of determinism presented in Lemma 9.2.

Lemma 9.3 (Sequentialisation). *Suppose that quantum **while**-programs $P_1, \cdots, P_n$ are disjoint. Then:*

1. *For any permutation $i_1, \cdots, i_n$ of $1, \cdots, n$, $[\![P_1 \| \cdots \| P_n]\!] = [\![P_{i_1} \| \cdots \| P_{i_n}]\!]$.*
2. $[\![P_1 \| \cdots \| P_n]\!] = [\![P_1; \cdots; P_n]\!]$.

For readability, the proofs of the above two lemmas are postponed to Appendix A.5.

9.3 Proof system for disjoint parallel quantum programs

In this section, we present a series of proof rules for reasoning about correctness of disjoint parallel quantum programs, which will be proved to form a (relatively) complete proof system. Some of these rules will be generalised to the general case of parallel quantum programs with shared variables in Section 9.6.

Correctness: Let us first define the notion of correctness for disjoint parallel quantum programs. As in the case of sequential quantum programs, the (partial and total) correctness of parallel quantum programs can be defined based on their denotational semantics. In particular, due to its determinism (Lemma 9.2), the correctness of a disjoint parallel quantum program P can be defined simply using Definition 6.8 provided that for each input ρ, we identify the singleton $[\![P]\!](\rho) = \{\rho'\}$ with the partial density operator ρ'.

9.3.1 Sequentialisation rule

Now let us turn to think about the question: how to define proof rules for parallel programs? First of all, all disjoint parallel programs in classical computing can be sequentialised with the same denotational semantics. Accordingly, they can be verified through sequentialisation (see for example [28], Section 7.3). For quantum computing, since we have Lemma 9.3, the sequentialisation rule (R.Seq) in Fig. 9.4 is valid too.

Lemma 9.4. *The rule (R.Seq) is sound for both partial and total correctness.*

Exercise 9.3. Prove the above lemma.

Let us give a simple example to show how rule (R.Seq) can be applied to verify disjoint parallel quantum programs by *Sequentialisation*, i.e. transforming them into equivalent sequential programs. Our example is a quantum analog of the following simple example given in [28] to show the necessity of introducing auxiliary variables:

$$\{x = y\}\, x := x + 1 \,\|\, y := y + 1 \,\{x = y\}.$$

This correctness formula for a disjoint parallel program cannot be proved by merely using the parallel composition rule (R.PC) in Fig. 9.1. However, it can be simply derived by rule (R.Seq). Similarly, we have:

Example 9.4. Let p, q be two quantum variables with the same state Hilbert space $\mathcal{H}$. For each orthonormal basis $\Phi = \{|\varphi_i\rangle\}$ of $\mathcal{H}$, we define a quantum predicate:

$$A_\Phi = \sum_i \mu_i |\varphi_i \varphi_i\rangle \langle \varphi_i \varphi_i| \tag{9.3}$$

$$(\text{R.PC.D}) \quad \frac{\{A_i\}\,P_i\,\{B_i\}\ (i=1,...,n) \qquad free(A_{i_1}, B_{i_1}) \cap change(P_{i_2})\ \text{for}\ i_1 \neq i_2}{\left\{\bigwedge_{i=1}^{n} A_i\right\} P_1 \|\cdots\| P_n \left\{\bigwedge_{i=1}^{n} B_i\right\}}$$

FIGURE 9.5   Proof rule for parallel composition. Here, $free(A_i, B_i)$ denotes the set of free variables in A_i and B_i, and $change(P_i)$ is the set of variables that can be modified by P_i.

$$(\text{R.PC.P}) \quad \frac{\{A_i\}\,P_i\,\{B_i\}\ (i=1,...,n)}{\left\{\bigotimes_{i=1}^{n} A_i\right\} P_1 \|\cdots\| P_n \left\{\bigotimes_{i=1}^{n} B_i\right\}}$$

FIGURE 9.6   Rule for tensor product of quantum predicates.

in $\mathcal{H} \otimes \mathcal{H}$, where $\mu_i > 0$ for every i. It can be viewed as a quantum counterpart of equality $x = y$. It is interesting to note that the quantum counterpart of $x = y$ is not unique because for different bases $\Phi = \{|\varphi_i\rangle\}$, A_Φ are different. For any unitary operator U in $\mathcal{H}$, we have:

$$\models_{tot} \{A_\Phi\}\,p := U[p]\|q := U[q]\{A_{U(\Phi)}\} \tag{9.4}$$

where $A_{U(\Phi)}$ is the quantum counterpart of equality defined by orthonormal basis $U(\Phi) = \{U|\varphi_i\rangle\}$. Clearly, (9.4) can be proved using rule (R.Seq) together with (Ax.UT) in Fig. 5.6.

It is worth pointing out that the quantum generalisation of a concept in a classical system usually has the flexibility arising from different choices of the basis of its state Hilbert space.

To conclude this subsection, we observe that by Lemma 9.3, in principle, the rule (R.Seq) is strong enough for reasoning about the correctness of all disjoint parallel quantum programs. But this proof rule is not instructive in understanding the behaviour of parallel quantum programs. More explicitly, it does not reflect the essence of (disjoint) parallelism where $P_1, ..., P_n$ are independent processes. Moreover, it does not allow us to combine local reasoning about each process P_i to form a global judgement about the parallel program $P_1 \|\cdots\| P_n$. Furthermore, it cannot be extended to the general parallelism with shared variables.

9.3.2   Tensor product of quantum predicates

To see how we can define more interesting proof rule for parallel quantum programs, we first notice that for a disjoint parallel quantum program $P_1 \|\cdots\| P_n$, the rule (R.PC) shown in Fig. 9.1 degenerates to rule (R.PC.D) in Fig. 9.5, which is often called the Hoare's rule for disjoint parallelism. So, let us try to find an appropriate quantum generalisation of the rule (R.PC.D). As discussed at the beginning of this chapter, we first need to identify a quantum counterpart of conjunction $\bigwedge_{i=1}^{n} A_i$ (and $\bigwedge_{i=1}^{n} B_i$) in the pre- and postconditions of the conclusion of rule (R.PC.D). For disjoint parallel quantum programs, a natural choice of, e.g. the precondition, is tensor product $\bigotimes_{i=1}^{n} A_i$. The reason for this choice is that it enjoys a nice physical interpretation:

$$tr\left(\left(\bigotimes_{i=1}^{n} A_i\right)\left(\bigotimes_{i=1}^{n} \rho_i\right)\right) = \prod_{i=1}^{n} tr(A_i \rho_i).$$

The above equation shows that the probability that a product state $\bigotimes_{i=1}^{n} \rho_i$ satisfies quantum predicate $\bigotimes_{i=1}^{n} A_i$ is the product of the probabilities that each component state ρ_i satisfies the corresponding predicate A_i. This observation motivates an inference rule with tensor products of quantum predicates presented in Fig. 9.6. It is quantum generalisation of rule (R.PC.D) and thus can be seen as the simplest quantum generalisation of rule (R.PC) in Fig. 9.1.

Remark 9.2. In the Hoare's rule (R.PC.D) for classical disjoint parallel programs, it is required that $free(A_{i_1}, B_{i_1}) \cap change(S_{i_2}) = \emptyset$ for $i_1 \neq i_2$; that is, S_{i_2} cannot modify the values of free variables in the precondition A_{i_1} and postcondition B_{i_1} of another component program S_{i_1}. In our rule (R.PC.P) in Fig. 9.6, such a condition is implicitly guaranteed by our assumption that the state spaces of A_{i_1}, B_{i_1} and that of S_{i_1} are the same, and $var(S_{i_1}) \cap var(S_{i_2}) = \emptyset$.

Lemma 9.5. *The rule (R.PC.P) is sound with respect to both partial and total correctness.*

Exercise 9.4. Prove Lemma 9.5.

$$(\text{R.PC.S}) \quad \frac{\{A_{ji}\}\, P_i\, \{B_{ji}\} \quad (i=1,...,n;\ j=1,...,m)}{\left\{\sum_{j=1}^{m} p_j \left(\bigotimes_{i=1}^{n} A_{ji}\right)\right\} P_1 \|\cdots\| P_n \left\{\sum_{j=1}^{m} p_j \left(\bigotimes_{i=1}^{n} B_{ji}\right)\right\}}$$

FIGURE 9.7 Rule for separable quantum predicates. Here, coefficients $p_j \geq 0$ and $\sum_{j=1}^{m} p_j \leq 1$; m is a positive integer or ∞.

The rule (R.PC.P) can only be used to deal with a very limited case, namely inferring correctness of disjoint parallel quantum programs with respect to (tensor) *product* quantum predicates as preconditions and postconditions. For instance, we can use (R.PC.P) to prove a very special instance of correctness (9.4) in Example 9.4 with $\{p_i\}$ being a degenerate distribution at some i_0:

$$\vdash_{tot} \{|\varphi\varphi\rangle\langle\varphi\varphi|\}\, p := U[p]\|q := U[q]\{|\psi\psi\rangle\langle\psi\psi|)|\}$$

where $|\varphi\rangle = |\varphi_{i_0}\rangle$ and $|\psi\rangle = U|\varphi\rangle$, but it is not strong enough to derive the entire correctness (9.4).

9.3.3 Separable quantum predicates

The proof rule (R.PC.P) presented in the last subsection can be straightforwardly generalised for dealing with a larger family of predicates in $\bigotimes_{i=1}^{n} \mathcal{H}_{P_i}$ than product predicates, namely separable predicates defined in the following:

Definition 9.6. Let A be a quantum predicate in $\bigotimes_{i=1}^{n} \mathcal{H}_{P_i}$. Then:

1. A is said to be separable if there exist $p_j \geq 0$ and quantum predicates A_{ji} in $\mathcal{H}_{P_i}$ ($i=1,...,n;\ j=1,...,m$) such that $\sum_{j=1}^{m} p_j \leq 1$ and

$$A = \sum_{j=1}^{m} p_j \left(\bigotimes_{i=1}^{n} A_{ji}\right)$$

where m is a positive integer or ∞.
2. A is entangled if it is not separable.

A combination of rule (R.PC.P) with the auxiliary axioms and the rules (R.CC), (Ax.Inv), (R.Inv) and (R.Lim) in Fig. 6.9 yields the rule (R.PC.S) in Fig. 9.7.

The rule (R.PC.S) can also be seen a quantum generalisation of proof rule (R.PC) for classical parallel programs given in Fig. 9.1. Obviously, it can deal with a more general case than what rule (R.PC.P) does; that is, it can reason about disjoint parallel quantum programs with *separable* quantum predicates as preconditions and postconditions; for example, correctness (9.4) in Example 9.4 can be proved using rule (R.PC.S).

9.3.4 Entangled quantum predicates

It is well-understood that entangled states are indispensable physical resources that make quantum computers outperform classical computers. Entangled quantum predicates represent quantum nonlocality in a dual setup where more information can be revealed by joint (i.e. globally entangled) measurements than can be gained by local operations and classical communications (LOCC) [54,336].

In the remainder of this section, we are going to find some proof rules that can be used for reasoning about the correctness of (disjoint) parallel quantum programs with respect to *entangled* preconditions and postconditions. In this subsection, let us first see an example that shows why the inference rule (R.PC.S) is unable to prove any correctness of the form

$$\{A\} P_1 \|\cdots\| P_n \{B\}$$

for a parallel quantum program $P_1 \|\cdots\| P_n$ where A or B is an entangled predicate.

Example 9.5. We consider a variant of Example 9.4. For each orthonormal basis $\Phi = \{|\varphi_i\rangle\}$ of $\mathcal{H}$, we write:

$$\beta_\Phi = \frac{1}{\sqrt{d}} \sum_i |\varphi_i \varphi_i\rangle$$

for the maximally entangled state in $\mathcal{H} \otimes \mathcal{H}$, where $d = \dim \mathcal{H}$. Then $E_\Phi = |\beta_\Phi\rangle\langle\beta_\Phi|$ can be seen as another quantum counterpart of equality $x = y$ (different from A_Φ defined by Eq. (9.3)). Obviously,

$$\models_{tot} \{|\beta_\Phi\rangle\langle\beta_\Phi|\} \; p := U[p] \| q := U[q] \left\{|\beta_{U(\Phi)}\rangle\langle\beta_{U(\Phi)}|\right\}; \tag{9.5}$$

that is, if the input is maximally entangled, so is the output after the same unitary operator is performed separately on two subsystems. Indeed, we can prove correctness (9.5) by using rules (R.Seq) and (Ax.UT), but (9.5) cannot be derived by directly using rule (R.PC.S).

9.3.5 Auxiliary variables

In this subsection, we present the first solution to the verification problem for disjoint parallel quantum programs with entangled preconditions and postconditions. It is a combination of (R.PC.S) and several rules in Fig. 6.9 for introducing auxiliary variables.

For easy understanding, let us introduce the method of using auxiliary variables by considering an example.

Example 9.6. We use rule (R.PC.S) together with (R.TI) and (R.SO) in Fig. 6.9 to prove correctness (9.5) in Example 9.5. The key idea is to introduce two auxiliary variables p', q' with the same state space $\mathcal{H}$. First, by (Ax.UT) we have:

$$\begin{aligned}
\vdash_{tot} \left\{(E_\Phi)_{pp'}\right\} p := U[p] \left\{|\alpha\rangle_{pp'}\langle\alpha|\right\}, \\
\vdash_{tot} \left\{(E_\Phi)_{qq'}\right\} q := U[q] \left\{|\alpha\rangle_{qq'}\langle\alpha|\right\}
\end{aligned} \tag{9.6}$$

where we use subscripts p, q, p', q' to indicate the corresponding subsystems, and $|\alpha\rangle = \sum_i (U|i\rangle) |i\rangle$. Now applying rule (R.PC.S) to (9.6) yields:

$$\vdash_{tot} \left\{(E_\Phi)_{pp'} \otimes (E_\Phi)_{qq'}\right\} p := U[p] \| q := U[q] \left\{|\alpha\rangle_{pp'}\langle\alpha| \otimes |\alpha\rangle_{qq'}\langle\alpha|\right\} \tag{9.7}$$

Finally, we define superoperator:

$$\mathcal{E}(\rho) = \sum_i \left(|\beta\rangle_{p'q'}\langle i|\right) \rho \left(|i\rangle_{p'q'}\langle\beta|\right)$$

for all mixed states ρ of p' and q', and obtain (9.5) by applying rule (R.SO) to (9.7) because

$$\begin{aligned}
E_\Phi \otimes I_{p'q'} &= \mathcal{E}^* \left((E_\Phi)_{pp'} \otimes (E_\Phi)_{qq'}\right) \\
&= \sum_i \left(|i\rangle_{p'q'}\langle\beta|\right) \left((E_\Phi)_{pp'} \otimes (E_\Phi)_{qq'}\right) \left(|\beta\rangle_{p'q'}\langle i|\right), \\
E_{U(\Phi)} \otimes I_{p'q'} &= \mathcal{E}^* \left(|\alpha\rangle_{pp'}\langle\alpha| \otimes |\alpha\rangle_{qq'}\langle\alpha|\right) \\
&= \sum_i \left(|i\rangle_{p'q'}\langle\beta|\right) \left(|\alpha\rangle_{pp'}\langle\alpha| \otimes |\alpha\rangle_{qq'}\langle\alpha|\right) \left(|\beta\rangle_{p'q'}\langle i|\right).
\end{aligned}$$

The idea employed in the above example can be summarised as a general proof technique. It consists of the following three steps:

(1) *Pushing out*: Introducing a fresh copy of each quantum variable as an auxiliary variable;
(2) *Entangling*: Establishing the maximal entanglement between each original variable and its corresponding auxiliary variable; and
(3) *Pulling back*: Pulling certain entanglement between the auxiliary variables through the entanglement between the original and auxiliary variables to generate indirectly the entanglement between the original variables in the precondition and postcondition.

Indeed, as will be shown in Section 9.3.7, this strategy of introducing auxiliary variables can be generalised to deal with all entangled preconditions and postconditions for disjoint parallel quantum programs.

9.3.6 Transferring separable predicates to entangled

It was shown in the last subsection that correctness of disjoint parallel quantum programs with entangled preconditions or postconditions can be derived by introducing auxiliary variables. Interestingly, a deep result in the theoretical analysis of

$$(\text{R.S2E}) \quad \frac{\{(1-\epsilon)I + \epsilon A\} \, P \, \{(1-\epsilon)I + \epsilon B\}}{\{A\} \, P \, \{B\}}$$

FIGURE 9.8 Rule for transforming separable predicates to entangled predicates. Here, $0 < \epsilon \le 1$.

NMR (Nuclear Magnetic Resonance) quantum computing provides us with another solution. It was discovered in [73,459] that all mixed states of n qubits in a sufficiently small neighbourhood of the *maximally mixed state* $\frac{1}{d}I$ are separable, where I is the identity operator and d is the dimension of the Hilbert space under consideration. The interpretation of this result in physics is that entanglement cannot exist in the presence of too much noise. The result was generalised in [195] to the case of any quantum systems with finite-dimensional state Hilbert spaces.

Recall that the Hilbert–Schmidt norm (or 2-norm) of operator A is defined as follows:

$$\|A\|_2 = \sqrt{tr(A^\dagger A)}.$$

In particular, if $A = \left(A_{ij}\right)$ is a matrix, then

$$\|A\|_2 = \sqrt{\sum_{i,j} |A_{ij}|^2}.$$

Then the above result can be formally stated as the following:

Theorem 9.1 (Gurvits and Barnum [195]). *Let $\mathcal{H}_1, \cdots, \mathcal{H}_n$ be finite-dimensional Hilbert spaces, and let A be a positive operator on $\bigotimes_{i=1}^{n} \mathcal{H}_n$. If*

$$\|A - I\|_2 \le \frac{1}{2^{n/2-1}}$$

where I is the identity operator on $\bigotimes_{i=1}^{n} \mathcal{H}_n$, then A is separable.

The following corollary can be easily derived from the above theorem.

Corollary 9.1. *For any two positive operators A, B on $\bigotimes_{i=1}^{n} \mathcal{H}_i$, there exists $0 < \epsilon \le 1$ such that both $(1-\epsilon)I + \epsilon A$ and $(1-\epsilon)I + \epsilon B$ are separable.*

Motivated by Corollary 9.1, we introduce a new inference rule (R.S2E) in Fig. 9.8. The name (R.S2E) of this rule is designated for the idea of transforming *separable to entangled*:

- In order to prove correctness $\{A\}P_1\|\cdots\|P_n\{B\}$ for entangled predicates A and B, we find a parameter $\epsilon > 0$ such that $(1-\epsilon)I + \epsilon A$ and $(1-\epsilon)I + \epsilon B$ are separable, and then we can prove:

$$\{(1-\epsilon)I + \epsilon A\}P_1\|\cdots\|P_n\{(1-\epsilon)I + \epsilon B\} \tag{9.8}$$

by using rule (R.PC.S). It is worth pointing out that Corollary 9.1 warrants that we can choose the same parameter ϵ in the precondition and postcondition. Therefore, $\{A\}P_1\|\cdots\|P_n\{B\}$ can be derived by rule (R.S2E) from (9.8).

For a better understanding of this proof technique, let us see a simple example.

Example 9.7. For $k = 0, 1$, consider the quantum program $\textbf{while}_k$ given in Example 4.2. We write: $|\Phi\rangle = \frac{1}{\sqrt{2}}(|01\rangle + |10\rangle)$ for a maximally entangled state of a 2-qubit system. Then it holds that

$$\models_{par} \left\{ I_4 - \frac{1}{2}|10\rangle\langle 10| \right\} \textbf{while}_0 \, \| \, \textbf{while}_1 \{|\Phi\rangle\langle\Phi|\}, \tag{9.9}$$

where I_4 is the 4×4 unit matrix. The correctness formula (9.9) has entangled precondition and postcondition, and thus cannot be proved by only using rule (R.PC.S). Here, we show that it can be proved by combining rule (R.S2E) with (R.PC.S). In fact, one can first verify that

$$\models_{par} \left\{ I_2 - |\alpha|^2|1-k\rangle\langle 1-k| \right\} \textbf{while}_k \{|\psi\rangle\langle\psi|\} \tag{9.10}$$

for $k = 0, 1$ and any state $|\psi\rangle = \alpha|k\rangle + \beta|1-k\rangle$, where I_2 is the 2×2 unit matrix. Moreover, we write:

$$|\curvearrowright\rangle = \frac{1}{\sqrt{2}}(|0\rangle + i|1\rangle), \ |\curvearrowleft\rangle = \frac{1}{\sqrt{2}}(|0\rangle - i|1\rangle).$$

Then we have the following decomposition of separable operator:

$$\left(1 - \frac{2}{3}\right)I_4 + \frac{2}{3}|\Phi\rangle\langle\Phi| = \frac{1}{3}(|01\rangle\langle01| + |10\rangle\langle10| + |++\rangle\langle++| + |--\rangle\langle--|$$
$$+ |\curvearrowright\curvearrowright\rangle\langle\curvearrowright\curvearrowright| + |\curvearrowleft\curvearrowleft\rangle\langle\curvearrowleft\curvearrowleft|),$$

and it is derived that

$$\left\{I_4 - \frac{1}{3}|10\rangle\langle10|\right\} \mathbf{while}_0 \| \mathbf{while}_1 \left\{\left(1 - \frac{2}{3}\right)I_4 + \frac{2}{3}|\Phi\rangle\langle\Phi|\right\} \tag{9.11}$$

by applying (9.10) for $|\psi\rangle = |0\rangle, |1\rangle, |+\rangle, |-\rangle, |\curvearrowright\rangle, |\curvearrowleft\rangle$ and $i = 0, 1$, respectively, and applying rule (R.PC.S). Finally, correctness (9.9) is obtained by applying rule (R.S2E) to (9.11) with $\epsilon = \frac{2}{3}$.

We conclude this subsection by presenting the soundness of inference rule R.S2E). Its proof is left for the reader as an exercise.

Lemma 9.6. *The rule (R.S2E) is sound for both partial and total correctness.*

9.3.7 Completeness of the auxiliary variables method

Two methods for verification of disjoint parallel quantum programs, namely (i) auxiliary variables and (ii) entanglement transformation, and the corresponding proof rules were introduced in the previous subsections. In this and next subsections, we organise these rules into two formal proof systems and show that both of them are (relatively) complete. It should be noted that the sequentialisation rule (R.Seq) is not included in these proof systems.

This subsection is devoted to prove completeness of the method of auxiliary variables.

Total correctness: Let us first consider total correctness. We define proof systems $qTPA$ to be the quantum Hoare logic for total correctness qTD (see Section 6.5) extended with the parallel composition rule (R.PC.P) for tensor products of quantum predicates and some appropriate auxiliary rules:

$$qTPA = qTD \cup \{(R.PC.P), (R.CC), (R.Lin), (R.SO), (R.TI), (R.Lim)\}.$$

As hinted by Example 9.6, disjoint parallel quantum programs with entangled preconditions and postconditions can be verified by introducing auxiliary variables using a combination of parallel rule (R.PC.P) and other rules in $qTPA$. Indeed, we have the following:

Theorem 9.2 (Completeness for total correctness). *The proof system $qTPA$ is (relatively) complete for total correctness of disjoint parallel quantum programs; that is, for any disjoint quantum programs $P_1, ..., P_n$ and quantum predicates A, B:*

$$\models_{tot} \{A\}P_1 \| \cdots \| P_n \{B\} \Leftrightarrow \vdash_{qTPA} \{A\}P_1 \| \cdots \| P_n \{B\}.$$

Proof. The overall idea of the proof is essentially the same as Example 9.6; that is, the proof can be carried out in the procedure from (1) pushing out to (2) entangling and then (3) pulling back (see detailed description of this procedure at the end of Example 9.6). Now let us present the proof formally. Assume that

$$\models_{tot} \{A\}P_1 \| \cdots \| P_n \{B\}.$$

We write $\mathcal{E} = [\![P_1 \| \cdots \| P_n]\!]$ for the semantic function of the parallel program and for each $i = 1, ..., n$, let $\mathcal{E}_i$ be the semantic function of P_i. Then by Lemma 7.1, we have $A \sqsubseteq \mathcal{E}^*(B)$, where $\mathcal{E}^*$ stands for the dual of $\mathcal{E}$. By rule (R.Or) it suffices to show that

$$\vdash_{qTP} \{\mathcal{E}^*(B)\}P_1 \| \cdots \| P_n \{B\}. \tag{9.12}$$

For simplicity of presentation, for each $i = 1, ..., n$, we use $\mathcal{H}_i = \mathcal{H}_{P_i}$ to denote the state Hilbert space of program P_i. We use p to indicate the system of the parallel program $P_1 \| \cdots \| P_n$, called the principal system. Thus, it has the state space $\mathcal{H}_p = \bigotimes_{i=1}^n \mathcal{H}_i$.

In what follows, we prove (9.12) in three steps, gradually from a special form of B to a general B.

Step 1: As the first step, let us consider the very special case of $B = |\beta\rangle\langle\beta|$ with some constraints on vector $|\beta\rangle$.

Claim 9.1. *For any vector $|\beta\rangle$ in $\mathcal{H}_p$, if its norm is less than or equal to 1 and its reduced density operator to each $\mathcal{H}_i$ is of finite rank, then we have:*

$$\vdash_{qTP} \{\mathcal{E}^*(|\beta\rangle\langle\beta|)\} P_1 \| \cdots \| P_n \{|\beta\rangle\langle\beta|\}.$$

Proof of Claim 9.1. For each i, as the reduced density operator of $|\beta\rangle$ to $\mathcal{H}_i$ is of finite rank, we can use $\mathcal{K}_i$ to denote the support of the reduced density operator and assume its rank is d_i:

$$\mathcal{K}_i = \mathrm{supp}\left(\mathrm{tr}_{1\cdots(i-1)(i+1)\cdots n}|\beta\rangle\langle\beta|\right).$$

Here, an index j in the subscript of tr indicates the state space of program P_j. Obviously, $\mathcal{K}_i \subseteq \mathcal{H}_i$. We assume that $\Phi_{\mathcal{K}_i} = \{|1\rangle_i, \cdots, |d_i\rangle_i\}$ is an orthonormal basis of $\mathcal{K}_i$ and its expansion $\Phi_i = \{|1\rangle_i, \cdots, |d_i\rangle_i, |d_i + 1\rangle_i, \cdots\}$ is an orthonormal basis of $\mathcal{H}_i$. Then $|\beta\rangle$ can be written as follows:

$$|\beta\rangle = \sum_{\forall i \in [n]: j_i \in [d_i]} \alpha_{j_1 \ldots j_n} \left(\bigotimes_{i=1}^n |j_i\rangle_i\right).$$

We define the conjugate vector of $|\beta\rangle$ as:

$$|\overline{\beta}\rangle = \sum_{\forall i \in [n]: j_i \in [d_i]} \alpha^*_{j_1 \ldots j_n} \left(\bigotimes_{i=1}^n |j_i\rangle_i\right).$$

Pushing out: For each i, we further introduce an auxiliary system with the state Hilbert space $\mathcal{H}_{i'}$ isomorphic to $\mathcal{H}_i$. Let $\{|j_i\rangle_{i'}\}_{j\in[d_i]}$ and $\{|j_i\rangle_{i'}\}_{j\in\Phi_i}$ be the orthonormal basis of $\mathcal{K}_{i'}$ and $\mathcal{H}_{i'}$ corresponding to $\Phi_{\mathcal{K}_i}$ and Φ_i, respectively.

Entangling: Then

$$|\Psi_i\rangle = \sum_{j_i \in [d_i]} \frac{1}{\sqrt{d_i}} |j_i\rangle_i |j_i\rangle_{i'} \tag{9.13}$$

is the maximally entangled state in $\mathcal{K}_i \otimes \mathcal{K}_{i'}$. We use p' to indicate the composed auxiliary system with state space $\mathcal{H}_{p'} = \bigotimes_{i=1}^n \mathcal{H}_{i'}$. Then putting all of the entangled states together yields:

$$E = \bigotimes_{i=1}^n (|\Psi_i\rangle\langle\Psi_i|), \tag{9.14}$$

which is a density operator on $\mathcal{H}_p \otimes \mathcal{H}_{p'}$.

Now for each program P_i, the completeness of qTD ensures that:

$$\vdash_{qTD} \left\{(\mathcal{E}_i^* \otimes \mathcal{I}_{i'})(|\Psi_i\rangle\langle\Psi_i|)\right\} P_i \{|\Psi_i\rangle\langle\Psi_i|\},$$

where $\mathcal{I}_{i'}$ is the identity superoperator on $\mathcal{H}_{i'}$. Applying rule (R.PC.P), we obtain:

$$\vdash_{qTD} \left\{\bigotimes_{i=1}^n (\mathcal{E}_i^* \otimes \mathcal{I}_{i'})(|\Psi_i\rangle\langle\Psi_i|)\right\} P_i \left\{\bigotimes_{i=1}^n |\Psi_i\rangle\langle\Psi_i|\right\},$$

or simply,

$$\vdash_{qTP} \{D\} P_1 \| \cdots \| P_n \{E\} \tag{9.15}$$

where:

$$D = \bigotimes_{i=1}^{n} \left[\left(\mathcal{E}_i^* \otimes \mathcal{I}_{i'} \right) \left(|\Psi_i\rangle \langle \Psi_i| \right) \right]. \tag{9.16}$$

We further define a superoperator $\mathcal{F}_\beta$ on $\mathcal{H}_{p'}$ as follows:

$$\mathcal{F}_\beta(\rho) = \sum_{\forall i \in [n]: k_i \in \mathcal{J}_i} |\bar{\beta}\rangle_{p'} \left(\bigotimes_{i=1}^{n} {}_{i'}\langle k_i| \right) \rho \left(\bigotimes_{i=1}^{n} |k_i\rangle_{i'} \right) {}_{p'}\langle\bar{\beta}| \tag{9.17}$$

for every density operator ρ on $\mathcal{H}_{p'}$. It is easy to see that $\mathcal{F}_\beta$ is well-defined and is completely positive and trace nonincreasing. Moreover, we observe:

Fact 9.1.

$$(\mathcal{I}_p \otimes \mathcal{F}_\beta^*)(E) = \frac{1}{\prod_i d_i} |\beta\rangle_p \langle\beta| \otimes I_{p'} \tag{9.18}$$

$$\left(\mathcal{I}_p \otimes \mathcal{F}_\beta^* \right)(D) = \frac{1}{\prod_i d_i} \left(\bigotimes_{i=1}^{n} \mathcal{E}_i^* \right) (|\beta\rangle_p \langle\beta|) \otimes I_{p'}, \tag{9.19}$$

where $\mathcal{I}_p$ is the identity superoperator on $\mathcal{H}_p$ and $I_{p'}$ the identity operator on $\mathcal{H}_{p'}$.

The proof of this fact involves some tedious calculations, and we postpone it to Appendix A.5.

Pulling back: Now we can apply (R.SO) with completely positive and trace nonincreasing superoperator $\mathcal{F}_\beta(\rho)$ on p' to (9.15) and obtain:

$$\vdash_{qTP} \left\{ \left(\mathcal{I}_p \otimes \mathcal{F}_\beta^* \right)(D) \right\} P_1 \| \cdots \| P_n \left\{ \left(\mathcal{I}_p \otimes \mathcal{F}_\beta^* \right)(E) \right\}.$$

Then by Fact 9.1, it holds equivalently that

$$\left\{ \frac{1}{\prod_i d_i} \left(\bigotimes_{i=1}^{n} \mathcal{E}_i^* \right) (|\beta\rangle_p \langle\beta|) \otimes I_{p'} \right\} P_1 \| \cdots \| P_n \left\{ \frac{1}{\prod_i d_i} |\beta\rangle_p \langle\beta| \otimes I_{p'} \right\}. \tag{9.20}$$

Therefore, applying rules (R.TI) and (R.Lin) to (9.20) yields:

$$\left\{ \left(\bigotimes_{i=1}^{n} \mathcal{E}_i^* \right) (|\beta\rangle_p \langle\beta|) \right\} P_1 \| \cdots \| P_n \left\{ |\beta\rangle_p \langle\beta| \right\}$$

as we desired. This completes the proof of Claim 9.1.

Step 2: Our second step is to generalise Claim 9.1 to the case of $B = |\beta\rangle \langle\beta|$ with a general quantum state $|\beta\rangle$.

Claim 9.2. *For any pure state $|\beta\rangle$, we have:*

$$\vdash_{qTP} \{ \mathcal{E}^*(|\beta\rangle \langle\beta|) \} P_1 \| \cdots \| P_n \{ |\beta\rangle \langle\beta| \}.$$

Proof of Claim 9.2. For each $i \in [n]$, assume $\Phi_i = \{|1\rangle_i, |2\rangle_i, \cdots\}$ is an orthonormal basis of $\mathcal{H}_i$. We first define a sequence $\{P_k\}_{k \geq 1}$ of projectors on $\mathcal{H}_p$, the state Hilbert space of the whole program, as follows:

$$P_k = P_{1k} \otimes P_{2k} \otimes \cdots \otimes P_{nk},$$

where:

$$\forall i \in [n]: \quad \begin{cases} P_{ik} = I_i, & \text{if } k > \dim \mathcal{H}_i, \\ P_{ik} = \sum_{j \leq k} |j\rangle_i \langle j|, & \text{otherwise.} \end{cases}$$

We further define:

$$|\beta_k\rangle = P_k |\beta\rangle.$$

It is obvious that for all i, k, P_{ik} has a finite rank. Therefore, the reduced density operator of $|\beta_k\rangle$ on each $\mathcal{H}_i$ also has a finite rank and the norm of $|\beta_k\rangle$ is less than or equal to 1. Thus we can use Claim 9.1 to derive that

$$\vdash_{qTP} \{\mathcal{E}^*(|\beta_k\rangle\langle\beta_k|)\} P_1 \| \cdots \| P_n \{|\beta_k\rangle\langle\beta_k|\}. \tag{9.21}$$

Moreover, we observe:

Fact 9.2.

$$|\beta_k\rangle\langle\beta_k| \xrightarrow{w.o.t.} |\beta\rangle\langle\beta|, \qquad \mathcal{E}^*(|\beta_k\rangle\langle\beta_k|) \xrightarrow{w.o.t.} \mathcal{E}^*(|\beta\rangle\langle\beta|). \tag{9.22}$$

For readability, we omit the proof of this fact here, but the reader can find it in Appendix A.5.

Now we can apply rule (R.Lim) to Eq. (9.21) and then use Fact 9.2 to derive:

$$\vdash_{qTP} \{\mathcal{E}^*(|\beta\rangle\langle\beta|)\} P_1 \| \cdots \| P_n \{|\beta\rangle\langle\beta|\}$$

as we desired. This completes the proof of Claim 9.2.

Step 3: Our final step is to deal with a general quantum predicate B.

Claim 9.3. *For any quantum predicate B, we have:*

$$\vdash_{qTP} \{\mathcal{E}^*(B)\} P_1 \| \cdots \| P_n \{B\}.$$

Proof of Claim 9.3. For any quantum predicate B, we can always diagonalise it as follows (spectral decomposition):

$$B = \sum_i \lambda_i |\beta_i\rangle\langle\beta_i|$$

with $|\beta_i\rangle$ being a pure state and $0 \leq \lambda_i \leq 1$ for all i. Let us set:

$$B_k = \sum_{i \leq k} \lambda_i |\beta_i\rangle\langle\beta_i|$$

for every $k \geq 0$. Then with Lemma 9.2, we see that for each i,

$$\vdash_{qTP} \{\mathcal{E}^*(|\beta_i\rangle\langle\beta_i|)\} P_1 \| \cdots \| P_n \{|\beta_i\rangle\langle\beta_i|\}. \tag{9.23}$$

Applying rule (R.CC) to (9.23) yields:

$$\vdash_{qTP} \left\{ \sum_{i \leq k} \lambda_i \mathcal{E}^*(|\beta_i\rangle\langle\beta_i|) \right\} P_1 \| \cdots \| P_n \left\{ \sum_{i \leq k} \lambda_i |\beta_i\rangle\langle\beta_i| \right\},$$

or simply,

$$\vdash_{qTP} \{A_k\} P_1 \| \cdots \| P_n \{B_k\}, \tag{9.24}$$

where:

$$A_k = \sum_{i \leq k} \lambda_i \mathcal{E}^*(|\beta_i\rangle\langle\beta_i|) = \mathcal{E}^*(B_k).$$

Note that $\{B_k\}$ is an increasing sequence with respect to Löwner order. Then we have $B_k \xrightarrow{w.o.t.} B$, and $A_k \xrightarrow{w.o.t.} \mathcal{E}^*(B)$. Therefore, applying rule (R.Lim) to (9.24) yields

$$\vdash_{qTP} \{\mathbb{C}^*(B)\} P_1 \| \cdots \| P_n \{B\},$$

and we complete the entire proof. $\qquad\qquad\square$

$$(\text{R.PC.SP}) \quad \frac{P_i : \text{Abort}(C_i) \quad P_i : \text{Term}(D_i) \quad \{D_i + A_i\} P_i \{B_i\} \quad (i = 1, ..., n)}{\{I - \bigotimes_{i=1}^{n}(I_i - C_i) + \bigotimes_{i=1}^{n} A_i\} P_1 \| \cdots \| P_n \{\bigotimes_{i=1}^{n} B_i\}}$$

$$(\text{R.A.P}) \quad \frac{P_i : \text{Abort}(A_i) \ (i = 1, \cdots, n)}{P_1 \| \cdots \| P_m : \text{Abort}\left(I - \bigotimes_{i=1}^{n}(I_i - A_i)\right)}$$

$$(\text{R.T.P}) \quad \frac{P_i : \text{Term}(A_i) \ (i = 1, \cdots, n)}{P_1 \| \cdots \| P_m : \text{Term}\left(I - \bigotimes_{i=1}^{m}(I_i - A_i)\right)}$$

FIGURE 9.9 Rules for partial correctness of disjoint parallel programs. In these rules, I_i is the identity operator on $\mathcal{H}_{P_i}$ for each i, and $I = \bigotimes_{i=1}^{n} I_i$ the identity operator on $\bigotimes_{i=1}^{n} \mathcal{H}_i$.

Partial correctness: Now we turn to deal with partial correctness. Different from the usual, partial correctness in the case of disjoint parallel quantum programs is harder to handle than total correctness. We have to strengthen the rules (R.PC.P) to (R.PC.SP). Moreover, in order to prove partial correctness of disjoint parallel quantum programs, we need to introduce some rules for reasoning about their abortion and termination (see Definition 6.11). They are presented in Fig. 9.9. Rule (R.A.P) is designed for reasoning about the *abortion of parallel program* $P_1 \| ... \| P_n$ from the abortion of its components $P_1, ..., P_n$, and rule (R.T.P) is given for proving the *termination of parallel programs*. It is worth comparing rule (R.PC.P) with its *strengthened* version (R.PC.SP) carefully. The precondition $\bigotimes_{i=1}^{n} A_i$ of the conclusion of rule (R.PC.P) is weakened in rule (R.PC.SP). The price is that certain abortion and termination conditions are added into the premise. It is particularly interesting to see that a cut of D_i between $P_i : \text{Term}(D_i)$ and $\{D_i + A_i\} P_i \{B_i\}$ happens in the premise of (R.PC.SP), and thus D_i does not appear in the conclusion. It is also interesting to note that the postcondition of the conclusion of rule (R.PC.SP) is the same as that of (R.PC.P) and thus is a product quantum predicate, but the precondition can be entangled.

Let the proof systems qPD (quantum Hoare logic for partial correctness defined in Fig. 5.6) be extended with the parallel composition rule (R.PC.SP) for tensor products of quantum predicates and some appropriate auxiliary rules:

$$qPPA = qPD \cup \{(\text{R.PC.SP}), (\text{R.A.P}), (\text{R.T.P})\}$$
$$\cup \{(\text{R.CC1}), (\text{R.CC2}), (\text{R.SO}), (\text{R.TI}), (\text{R.Lim})\}.$$

Then $qPPA$ is (relatively) complete for partial correctness of disjoint parallel quantum programs:

Theorem 9.3 (Completeness for partial correctness). *For any disjoint quantum programs $P_1, ..., P_n$ and quantum predicates A, B:*

$$\models_{par} \{A\} P_1 \| \cdots \| P_n \{B\} \Leftrightarrow \vdash_{qPPA} \{A\} P_1 \| \cdots \| P_n \{B\}.$$

Proof. The proof of this theorem is similar to that of Theorem 9.2, but the calculation is much more involved. For readability, we postpone the detailed proof to Appendix A.5. □

Remark 9.3. 1. The rule (R.A.P) in the proof system qPPA is actually a special case of (R.PC.SP) with $A_i = [\![P_i]\!]^*(B_i)$ and $D_i = I_i - [\![P_i]\!]^*(I_i)$.
2. Note that assertions $P_i : \text{Abort}(C_i)$ and $P_i : \text{Term}(D_i)$ appear in the premise of rule (R.PC.SP). As pointed out at the end of Definition 6.11, the first assertion can be verified in qPD, and the second can be verified in qTD but not in qPD. So, $qPPA$ is only complete relative to a theory about termination assertions $P : \text{Term}(D)$, which is a subtheory of qTD.

9.3.8 Completeness of the entanglement transformation method

In this subsection, we present a proof system for disjoint parallel quantum programs using the method of entanglement transformation, and prove its (relative) completeness.

Partial correctness: Let us start from the partial correctness and define the following proof system:

$$qPPE = qPD \cup \{(\text{R.PC.SP}), (\text{R.S2E.P}), (\text{R.CC1}), (\text{R.CC2}), (\text{R.Lim})\}.$$

The proof system $qPPE$ is also an extension of quantum Hoare logic qPD for partial correctness. But the verification of disjoint parallel quantum programs using $qPPE$ is fundamentally different from that using $qPPA$ defined in the above subsection. Whence the precondition or postcondition for a disjoint parallel quantum program are entangled, as discussed in Section 9.3.6, we can use rule (R.S2E) to transform the verification problem to verification of the same program but with a separable precondition and postcondition, which can be dealt with by (R.PC.SP) together with (R.CC.1) and (R.CC2). It turns out that this method is also complete; that is, we have:

Theorem 9.4 (Completeness for partial correctness). *The proof system qPPE is (relatively) complete for partial correctness of disjoint parallel quantum programs.*

Proof. We only need to prove that for any disjoint quantum programs $P_1, \ldots, P_n$ and quantum predicates A, B:

$$\models_{par} \{A\}P_1\| \cdots \|P_n\{B\} \Rightarrow \vdash_{qPPE} \{A\}P_1\| \cdots \|P_n\{B\}.$$

Assume that $\models_{par} \{A\}P_1\| \cdots \|P_n\{B\}$. We write $\mathcal{E} = [\![P_1\| \cdots \|P_n]\!]$ for the semantic function of $P_1\| \cdots \|P_n$. Then by Lemma 7.1 we have $A \sqsubseteq \mathcal{E}^*(B) + I - \mathcal{E}^*(I)$, and by rule (R.Or) it suffices to show that

$$\vdash_{qPP} \{\mathcal{E}^*(B) + I - \mathcal{E}^*(I)\}P_1\| \cdots \|P_n\{B\}. \tag{9.25}$$

Here, $\mathcal{E}^*$ stands for the dual of $\mathcal{E}$. In what follows, we prove Eq. (9.25) in four steps, gradually from a special form of B to a general B. Note that since $P_1, \ldots, P_n$ are disjoint, we have $\mathcal{E} = \bigotimes_{i=1}^n \mathcal{E}_i$, where for each $i = 1, \ldots, n$, $\mathcal{E}_i$ is the semantic function of P_i.

1. Let $B = \bigotimes_{i=1}^n B_i$ be a product predicate, where B_i acts on $\mathcal{H}_i$. Then from the completeness of qPD for quantum **while**-programs, we obtain for each i,

$$\vdash_{qPD} \{\mathcal{E}_i^*(B_i) + I_i - \mathcal{E}_i^*(I_i)\}P_i\{B_i\}$$

where I_i stands for the identity operator on the state space of P_i. Furthermore, we know both $\models P_i : \text{Abort}(I_i - \mathcal{E}_i^*(I_i))$ and $\models P_i : \text{Term}(I_i - \mathcal{E}_i^*(I_i))$ by definition. Thus, it follows that

$$\vdash_{qPPE} \left\{ I - \bigotimes_{i=1}^n \mathcal{E}_i^*(I_i) + \bigotimes_{i=1}^n \mathcal{E}_i^*(B_i) \right\} P_1\| \cdots \|P_n \left\{ \bigotimes_{i=1}^n B_i \right\}$$

from (R.PC.SP). Then we obtain Eq. (9.25) from the fact that $\mathcal{E}^*(B) = \bigotimes_{i=1}^n \mathcal{E}_i^*(B_i)$ and $\mathcal{E}^*(I) = \bigotimes_{i=1}^n \mathcal{E}_i^*(I_i)$.
2. Let $B = \sum_{j=1}^m p_j \left(\bigotimes_{i=1}^n B_{ji} \right)$ be a separable predicate, where $p_j \geq 0$ and $\sum_{j=1}^m p_j \leq 1$. Then we have:

$$\mathcal{E}^*(B) = \sum_{j=1}^m p_j \left(\bigotimes_{i=1}^n \mathcal{E}_i^*(B_{ji}) \right),$$

and Eq. (9.25) follows from Step 1 and rules (R.CC.1) and (R.CC.2).
3. Let B be a quantum predicate supported on a finite dimensional subspace of $\bigotimes_{i=1}^n \mathcal{H}_i$. Then from Theorem 9.1, there exists $\epsilon \in (0, 1]$ such that $(1 - \epsilon)I + \epsilon B$ is separable. Then from Step 2, we obtain:

$$\vdash_{qPPE} \{I - \epsilon\mathcal{E}^*(I) + \epsilon\mathcal{E}^*(B)\}P_1\| \cdots \|P_n\{(1 - \epsilon)I + \epsilon B\},$$

and Eq. (9.25) follows from (R.S2E), since

$$I - \epsilon\mathcal{E}^*(I) + \epsilon\mathcal{E}^*(B) = (1 - \epsilon)I + \epsilon(I - \mathcal{E}^*(I) + \mathcal{E}^*(B)).$$

4. Finally, let B be a general quantum predicate in $\bigotimes_{i=1}^n \mathcal{H}_i$. For any integers $k \geq 1$ and $1 \leq i \leq n$, let $k_i = \min\{k, \dim(\mathcal{H}_i)\}$ and $\mathcal{H}_{i,k}$ be a subspace of $\mathcal{H}_i$ such that $\dim(\mathcal{H}_{i,k}) = k_i$ and $\mathcal{H}_{i,1} \sqsubseteq \mathcal{H}_{i,2} \sqsubseteq \ldots$. Let $\mathcal{P}_k$ be the (finite dimensional) projection onto the space $\bigotimes_{i=1}^n \mathcal{H}_{i,k}$. Then obviously, we have $\mathcal{P}_k(B) \xrightarrow{w.o.t.} B$ and $\mathcal{E}^*(\mathcal{P}_k(B)) \xrightarrow{w.o.t.} \mathcal{E}^*(B)$, and Eq. (9.25) follows from Step 3 and rule (R.Lim). □

Total correctness: To deal with total correctness using entanglement transformation, rule (R.S2E) needs to be slightly modified as:

$$(\text{R.S2E}^*) \quad \frac{P : \text{Abort}(I - C) \qquad \{(1 - \epsilon)C + \epsilon A\} P \{(1 - \epsilon)I + \epsilon B\}}{\{A\} P \{B\}}$$

It is clear that the only difference between rules (R.S2E*) and (R.S2E) is the abortion condition added in the premise of the former.

Now we define the following extension of quantum Hoare logic qTD for total correctness:

$$qTPE = qTD \cup \{(R.PC.P), (R.S2E), (R.CC), (R.Lim)\}.$$

It is easy to check that rule (R.S2E*) and thus $qTPE$ are sound. Furthermore, we have:

Theorem 9.5 (Completeness of total correctness). *The proof system $qTPE$ is (relatively) complete for total correctness of disjoint parallel quantum programs.*

The proof of this theorem is similar to that of Theorem 9.4.

Remark 9.4. It is worth noting that rule (R.S2E*) can be localised in the precondition to:

$$(\text{R.S2E}') \quad \frac{P_i : \text{Abort}(I_i - C_i) \qquad \{(1-\epsilon)\bigotimes_{i=1}^{n} C_i + \epsilon A\} P_1 \| \cdots \| P_n \{(1-\epsilon)I + \epsilon B\}}{\{A\} P_1 \| \cdots \| P_n \{B\}}$$

so that the (relative) completeness is still true.

9.4 Syntax of parallel quantum programs with shared variables

Disjoint parallel quantum programs were carefully studied in the previous sections. The remainder of this chapter is devoted to deal with a class of more general parallel quantum programs, namely parallel quantum programs with shared variables. In this section, we first introduce their syntax.

The syntax of parallel quantum programs with shared variables is given by removing the constraint of disjoint variables in Definition 9.1 and introducing atomic regions.

Definition 9.7. 1. Component quantum programs are generated by the grammar for quantum **while**-programs given in Eq. (5.3) together with the following clause for atomic regions:

$$P ::= \langle P_0 \rangle$$

where P_0 is loop-free and contains no further atomic regions.

2. Parallel quantum programs (with shared variables) are generated by the grammar given in Eq. (5.3) together with the following clause for parallel composition:

$$P ::= P_1 \| \cdots \| P_n \equiv \|_{i=1}^{n} P_i$$

where $n > 1$, and $P_1, ..., P_n$ are component quantum programs.

The syntax of parallel quantum programs defined above is similar to that of classical parallel programs. In particular, as in the classical case, *atomic regions* are introduced to prevent interference from other components in their computation. A *normal* subprogram of program P is defined to be a subprogram of P that does not occur within any atomic region of P.

The set of quantum variables in a parallel quantum program is defined as follows: $var(\langle P \rangle) = var(P)$, and if $P \equiv P_1 \| \cdots \| P_n$ then

$$var(P) = \bigcup_{i=1}^{n} var(P_i).$$

Furthermore, the state Hilbert space of a parallel quantum program P is $\mathcal{H}_P = \mathcal{H}_{var(P)}$. It is worth pointing out that in general for a parallel quantum program $P \equiv P_1 \| \cdots \| P_n$ with shared variables,

$$\mathcal{H}_P \neq \bigotimes_{i=1}^{n} \mathcal{H}_{P_i}$$

because it is not required that $var(P_1), \cdots, var(P_n)$ are disjoint.

$$(AR) \quad \frac{\langle P, \rho \rangle \to^* \langle \downarrow, \rho' \rangle}{\langle \langle P \rangle, \rho \rangle \to \langle \downarrow, \rho' \rangle}$$

FIGURE 9.10　Transition rule for atomic regions.

9.5　Semantics of parallel quantum programs with shared variables

In this section, we further define the operational and denotational semantics of parallel quantum programs with shared variables. Superficially, they are straightforward generalisations of the corresponding notions in classical programming. But as we already saw in Section 9.2, even for disjoint parallel quantum programs, nondeterminism induced by quantum measurements and its intertwining with parallelism; in particular when some infinite computations of loops are involved, make the semantics much harder to deal with than in the classical case. We will see shortly that shared quantum variables bring a new dimension of complexity.

Definition 9.8. The operational semantics of parallel quantum programs is defined by the transitions rules in Figs 5.1 and 9.3 and rule (AR) in Fig. 9.10 for atomic regions.

The rule (AR) means that any terminating computation of P is reduced to a single-step computation of atomic region $\langle P \rangle$. Such a reduction guarantees that a computation of $\langle P \rangle$ may not be interfered by other components in a parallel composition. Then the rule (PC) in Fig. 9.3 applies to both disjoint and shared-variable parallelism.

Based on the operational semantics defined above, the denotational semantics of parallel quantum programs with shared variables can be defined in a way similar to but more involved than Definition 9.5. First, for a program P and an input ρ, we recall from Eq. (9.2) that $\mathcal{V}(P, \rho)$ is the set of values $val(\pi)$, where π ranges over all computations of P starting in ρ. We further define the upper closure of $\mathcal{V}(P, \rho)$:

$$\overline{\mathcal{V}(P, \rho)} = \left\{ \bigsqcup_k \rho_k : \{\rho_k\} \text{ is an increasing chain in } (\mathcal{V}(P, \rho), \sqsubseteq) \right\},$$

where $\sqsubseteq$ is the Löwner order, and $\bigsqcup_k \rho_k$ stands for the least upper bound of $\{\rho_k\}$ in CPO $(\mathcal{D}(\mathcal{H}_P), \sqsubseteq)$, which always exists (see Section 5.3.2). Then we have:

Definition 9.9 (Denotational semantics). The semantic function of a parallel program P (with shared variables) is the mapping $[\![P]\!] : \mathcal{D}(\mathcal{H}_P) \to 2^{\mathcal{D}(\mathcal{H}_P)}$ defined by

$$[\![P]\!](\rho) = \left\{ \text{maximal elements of } \left(\overline{\mathcal{V}(P, \rho)}, \sqsubseteq \right) \right\}$$

for any $\rho \in \mathcal{D}(\mathcal{H}_P)$.

Let us carefully explain the design decision behind the above definition. First, it follows from rule (AR) that the semantics of an atomic region $\langle P \rangle$ is the same as that of P as a **while**-program; that is, for any input ρ:

$$[\![\langle P \rangle]\!](\rho) = [\![P]\!](\rho).$$

Second, we notice a difference between Definition 9.5 for disjoint parallelism and Definition 9.9 for shared-variable parallelism: in the latter, $[\![P]\!](\rho)$ consists of the maximal elements of $\overline{\mathcal{V}(P, \rho)}$, rather than simply $\mathcal{V}(P, \rho)$ as in the former. Indeed, it is easy to show that $\left(\overline{\mathcal{V}(P, \rho)}, \sqsubseteq \right)$ is inductive; that is, it contains an upper bound of every increasing chain in it. Then we see that $[\![P]\!](\rho)$ is nonempty by Zorn's lemma in set theory. In particular, if $(\mathcal{V}(P, \rho), \sqsubseteq)$ has a maximal element, then it must be in $[\![P]\!](\rho)$. In general, however, for a parallel program P with shared variables, $\mathcal{V}(P, \rho)$ may have no maximal element, as shown in the following:

Example 9.8. Consider parallel program:

$$P \equiv \textbf{while } M[q] = 1 \textbf{ do } q := U[q] \parallel q := V[q]$$

where:

- two processes share a variable q, which is a qutrit with state Hilbert space $\mathcal{H}_q = span\ \{|0\rangle, |1\rangle, |2\rangle\}$;
- measurement $M = \{M_0, M_1\}$ with $M_0 = |2\rangle\langle 2|$ and $M_1 = |0\rangle\langle 0| + |1\rangle\langle 1|$;
- unitary operators:

$$U = |+\rangle\langle +| + e^{i\pi c}|-\rangle\langle -| + |2\rangle\langle 2|, \qquad V = |1\rangle\langle 0| + |2\rangle\langle 1| + |0\rangle\langle 2|.$$

Here, $|\pm\rangle = \frac{1}{\sqrt{2}}(|0\rangle \pm |1\rangle)$.

For input pure state $|0\rangle$, we can calculate $val(\pi)$ for a computation π of P in the following cases:

Case 1. The second component $q := V[q]$ is executed first, and then the **while**-loop (i.e. the first component) is executed. In this case, the state is first changed from $|0\rangle$ to $|1\rangle$, and it is $U^n|1\rangle \in span\ \{|0\rangle, |1\rangle\}$ immediately after the nth iteration of U in the loop body. So, the program never terminates, and $val(\pi) = 0$.

Case 2. The **while**-loop is executed first and the second component is never executed. In this case, the program does not terminate and $val(\pi) = 0$.

Case 3. The **while**-loop is executed first, and then the second component is executed during the nth iteration. In this case, either V occurs before U, and it holds that

$$val(\pi) = M_0 U V U^{n-1}|0\rangle\langle 0|U^{\dagger n-1}V^{\dagger}U^{\dagger}M_0^{\dagger}$$
$$= |\langle 2|UVU^{n-1}|0\rangle|^2 \cdot |2\rangle\langle 2| = |\langle 1|U^{n-1}|0\rangle|^2 \cdot |2\rangle\langle 2|,$$

or U occurs before V, and

$$val(\pi) = M_0 V U^n|0\rangle\langle 0|U^{\dagger n}M_0^{\dagger} = |\langle 2|VU^n|0\rangle|^2 \cdot |2\rangle\langle 2| = |\langle 1|U^n|0\rangle|^2 \cdot |2\rangle\langle 2|.$$

Note that

$$|\langle 1|U^n|0\rangle|^2 = \left|\frac{1 - e^{i\pi nc}}{2}\right|^2 = \frac{1 - \cos \pi nc}{2}.$$

Then we obtain:

$$\mathcal{V}(P, |0\rangle\langle 0|) = \{0\} \cup \left\{\frac{1 - \cos \pi nc}{2} \cdot |2\rangle\langle 2| : n = 0, 1, 2, ...\right\}.$$

If we choose parameter c being an irrational number, then by Kronecker's theorem in number theory we assert that the set

$$\left\{\frac{1 - \cos \pi nc}{2} : n = 0, 1, 2, ...\right\}$$

of coefficients is dense in the unit interval $[0, 1]$, but the supremum 1 is not attainable. Therefore, $\mathcal{V}(P, |0\rangle\langle 0|)$ has no maximal element with respect to the Löwner order $\sqsubseteq$. Furthermore, it holds that $\overline{\mathcal{V}(P, |0\rangle\langle 0|)} = \{a \cdot |2\rangle\langle 2| : a \in [0, 1]\}$, and thus $[\![P]\!](|0\rangle\langle 0|) = |2\rangle\langle 2|$.

To conclude this subsection, we present an example showing the difference between the behaviours of a quantum program and its atomic version in parallel with another quantum program involving a quantum measurement on a shared variable.

Example 9.9. Let p, q be qubit variables,

$$P_1 \equiv p := H[p];\ p := H[p], \qquad P_2 \equiv \text{if } M[p] = 0 \rightarrow \text{skip}$$
$$\square \qquad\qquad 1 \rightarrow q := X[q]$$
$$\textbf{fi}$$

and $P_1' \equiv \langle P_1 \rangle$, where H, X are the Hadamard and Pauli gates, respectively and M the measurement in the computational basis. Consider the EPR (Einstein–Podolsky–Rosen) pair $|\psi\rangle = \frac{1}{\sqrt{2}}(|00\rangle + |11\rangle)$ as an input, where the first qubit is p and the second is q.

1. One of the computations of parallel composition $P_1' \| P_2$ is

$$\pi_1 = \langle P_1' \| P_2, |\psi\rangle\rangle \to_1 \langle \downarrow \| P_2, |\psi\rangle\rangle$$

$$\to_2 \left\{ \langle \downarrow \| \mathbf{skip}, \tfrac{1}{\sqrt{2}}|00\rangle\rangle, \langle \downarrow \| q := X[q], \tfrac{1}{\sqrt{2}}|11\rangle\rangle \right\}$$

$$\to_2 \left\{ \langle \downarrow, \tfrac{1}{\sqrt{2}}|00\rangle\rangle, \langle \downarrow, \tfrac{1}{\sqrt{2}}|10\rangle\rangle \right\}$$

Indeed, for all other computations π of $P_1' \| P_2$ starting in $|\psi\rangle$, we have:

$$val(\pi) = val(\pi_1) = \frac{1}{2}(|00\rangle\langle 00| + |10\rangle\langle 10|) \triangleq \rho_1,$$

and thus $[\![P_1' \| P_2]\!](|\psi\rangle) = \{\rho_1\}$.

2. $P_1 \| P_2$ has a computation starting in $|\psi\rangle$ that is quite different from π_1:

$$\pi_2 = \langle P_1 \| P_2, |\psi\rangle\rangle \to_1 \left\{ \langle p := H[p] \| P_2, \tfrac{1}{\sqrt{2}}(|+0\rangle + |-1\rangle)\rangle \right\}$$

$$\to_2 \begin{cases} \langle p := H[p] \| \mathbf{skip}, \tfrac{1}{2}(|00\rangle + |01\rangle)\rangle, \\ \langle p := H[p] \| q := X[q], \tfrac{1}{2}(|10\rangle - |11\rangle)\rangle \end{cases}$$

$$\to_2 \begin{cases} \langle p := H[p] \| \downarrow, \tfrac{1}{2}(|00\rangle + |01\rangle)\rangle, \\ \langle p := H[p] \| \downarrow, \tfrac{1}{2}(|11\rangle - |10\rangle)\rangle \end{cases}$$

$$\to_1 \left\{ \langle \downarrow, \tfrac{1}{2}(|+0\rangle + |+1\rangle)\rangle, \langle \downarrow, \tfrac{1}{2}(|-1\rangle - |-0\rangle)\rangle \right\}.$$

We have:

$$val(\pi_1) \neq val(\pi_2) = \frac{1}{4}(|00\rangle\langle 00| + |00\rangle\langle 11| + |01\rangle\langle 01| + |01\rangle\langle 10|$$

$$+ |10\rangle\langle 01| + |10\rangle\langle 10| + |11\rangle\langle 00| + |11\rangle\langle 11|) \triangleq \rho_2$$

and $[\![P_1 \| P_2]\!](|\psi\rangle) = \{\rho_1, \rho_2\}$.

The above example indicates that the determinism of the denotational semantics of disjoint parallel quantum programs (Lemma 9.2) is no longer true for parallel quantum programs with shared variables.

9.6 Reasoning about parallel quantum programs with shared variables

Our aim of this section is to introduce some useful rules for reasoning about correctness of parallel quantum programs with shared variables.

First of all, let us formally define the notion of correctness for parallel quantum programs with shared variables based on their denotational semantics introduced in the previous section. As pointed out at the beginning of Section 9.3, the definition of correctness of quantum **while**-programs (Definition 6.8) can be directly adopted for disjoint parallel quantum programs. However, Example 9.9 shows that for a parallel quantum program P with shared variables and an input ρ, $[\![P]\!](\rho)$ may have more than one element. Therefore, the notion of correctness of quantum **while**-programs is not directly applicable to parallel quantum programs with shared variables. But a simple modification of it works.

Definition 9.10 (Partial and total correctness). Let P be a parallel quantum program (with shared variables) and A, B quantum predicates in $\mathcal{H}_P$. Then the correctness formula $\{A\}P\{B\}$ is true in the sense of total correctness (respectively, partial correctness), written

$$\models_{tot} \{A\}P\{B\} \quad (resp. \models_{par} \{A\}P\{B\}),$$

$$(\text{R.At}) \quad \frac{\{A\}P\{B\}}{\{A\}\langle P\rangle\{B\}}$$

FIGURE 9.11   Rule for atomic regions.

if for each input $\rho \in \mathcal{D}(\mathcal{H}_P)$, it holds that

$$\text{tr}(A\rho) \leq \text{tr}(B\rho') \quad (\textit{resp. } \text{tr}(A\rho) \leq \text{tr}(B\rho') + [\text{tr}(\rho) - \text{tr}(\rho')])$$

for all $\rho' \in [\![P]\!](\rho)$.

In Section 9.3, we were able to develop a (relatively) complete logical system for disjoint parallel quantum programs by finding an appropriate quantum generalisation of a special case of rule (R.PC) in Fig. 9.1 (i.e. Hoare's parallel rule) together with several auxiliary rules. Unfortunately, the idea used in Section 9.3 does not work here because the third major challenge pointed out at the beginning of this chapter – combining quantum predicates in the overlap of state Hilbert spaces – will emerge in the case of shared variables. Let us gradually introduce a new idea to partially avoid this hurdle.

9.6.1   A rule for component quantum programs

As a basis for dealing with parallel quantum programs, we first consider component quantum programs. The proof techniques for classical component programs can be generalised to the quantum case without any difficulty. More precisely, partial and total correctness of component quantum programs can be verified with the proof system qPD and qTD for quantum **while**-programs plus the rule (R.AT) in Fig. 9.11 for atomic regions.

9.6.2   Proof outlines

The most difficult issue in reasoning about parallel programs with shared variables is interference between their different components. The notion of proof outline was introduced in classical programming theory so that the proofs of programs can be organised in a structured way. More importantly, it provides an appropriate way to describe interference freedom between the component programs – a crucial premise in inference rule (R.PC) for a parallel program with shared variables. So in this subsection, we generalise the notion of proof outline to quantum **while**-programs so that it can be used in next subsection to present our inference rules for parallel quantum programs with shared variables.

Definition 9.11. Let P be a quantum **while**-program. A proof outline for partial correctness of P is a formula

$$\{A\}P^*\{B\}$$

formed by the formation axioms and rules in Fig. 9.12, where P^* results from P by interspersing quantum predicates.

Obviously, (Ax.Sk$'$), (Ax.In$'$), (Ax.UT$'$) are the same as (Ax.Sk), (Ax.In), and (Ax.UT), respectively, in Fig. 5.6. But (R.SC$'$), (R.IF$'$), (R.LP$'$), and (R.Or$'$) in Fig. 9.12 are obtained from their counterparts in Fig. 5.6 by interspersing intermediate quantum predicates in appropriate places; for example, in rule (R.IF$'$), a predicate A_{m_i} is interspersed into the branch corresponding to measurement outcome m_i. In particular, keyword "**inv**" is introduced in rule (R.LP$'$) to indicate loop invariants (see Example 8.2 for a discussion about invariants of quantum **while**-loops). Furthermore, rule (R.Del) is introduced to delete redundant intermediate predicates.

The notion of proof outline for total correctness of quantum **while**-programs can be defined in a similar way; but we omit it here because in the rest of this section, for simplicity of presentation, we only consider partial correctness of parallel quantum programs. The proof techniques introduced in this section can be easily generalised to the case of total correctness by adding ranking functions (see Section 6.5; in particular, Definition 6.10).

We will mainly use a special form of proof outlines defined in the following:

Definition 9.12. A proof outline $\{A\}P^*\{B\}$ of quantum **while**-program P is called standard if every subprogram Q of P is proceded by exactly one quantum predicate, denoted $pre(Q)$, in P^*.

The following proposition shows that the notion of standard proof outline is general enough for our purpose.

(Ax.Sk') $\{A\}\textbf{Skip}\{A\}$ (Ax.In') $\left\{\sum_i |i\rangle_q \langle 0|A|0\rangle_q \langle i|\right\} q := |0\rangle\{A\}$

(Ax.UT') $\{U^\dagger AU\}\overline{q} := U\,[\overline{q}]\,\{A\}$ (R.SC') $\dfrac{\{A\}P_1^*\{B\} \quad \{B\}P_2^*\{C\}}{\{A\}P_1^*; \{B\}P_2^*\{C\}}$

(R.IF') $\dfrac{\left\{A_{m_i}\right\} P_{m_i}^* \{B\} \ (i=1,...,k)}{\begin{array}{l}\left\{\sum_i^k M_{m_i}^\dagger A_{m_i} M_{m_i}\right\} \textbf{ if } M[\overline{q}] = m_1 \to \left\{A_{m_1}\right\} P_{m_1}^* \\ \qquad\qquad .... \\ \qquad\qquad \square\ M[\overline{q}] = m_k \to \left\{A_{m_k}\right\} P_{m_k}^* \\ \qquad \textbf{fi}\ \{B\}\end{array}}$

(R.LP') $\dfrac{\{B\}P^* \left\{M_0^\dagger AM_0 + M_1^\dagger BM_1\right\}}{\left\{\textbf{inv}: M_0^\dagger AM_0 + M_1^\dagger BM_1\right\} \textbf{ while } M[\overline{q}] = 1 \textbf{ do } \{B\}\ P^*\ \left\{M_0^\dagger AM_0 + M_1^\dagger BM_1\right\} \textbf{ od } \{A\}}$

(R.Or') $\dfrac{A \sqsubseteq A' \quad \{A'\}P^*\{B'\} \quad B' \sqsubseteq B}{\{A\}\{A'\}P\{B'\}\{B\}}$ (R.Del) $\dfrac{\{A\}P^*\{B\}}{\{A\}P^{**}\{B\}}$

FIGURE 9.12 Formation axioms and rules for partial correctness of quantum **while**-programs. In (R.IF'), $\{m_1, ..., m_k\}$ is the set of all possible outcomes of measurement M. In (R.Del), P^{**} is obtained by deleting some quantum predicates from P^*, expect those labelled with "**inv**".

Proposition 9.1. *For any quantum **while**-program P, we have:*

1. *If $\{A\}P^*\{B\}$ is a proof outline for partial correctness, then $\vdash_{qPD} \{A\}P\{B\}$.*
2. *If $\vdash_{qPD} \{A\}P\{B\}$, then there is a standard proof outline $\{A\}P^*\{B\}$ for partial correctness.*

Proof. This proposition can be easily proved by induction on the lengths of proof and formation; in particular, employing rule (R.Del). □

The notion of proof outline enables us to present a soundness of quantum Hoare logic stronger than the soundness part of Theorem 6.1. It indicates that soundness is well maintained in each step of the proofs of quantum **while**-programs. To this end, we need an auxiliary notation defined in the following:

Definition 9.13. Let P be a quantum **while**-program and T a subprogram of P. Then $at(T, P)$ is inductively defined as follows:

1. If $T \equiv P$, then $at(T, P) \equiv P$;
2. If $P \equiv P_1; P_2$, then

$$at(T, P) \equiv \begin{cases} at(T, P_1); P_2 & \text{when } T \text{ is a subprogram of } P_1, \\ at(T, P) \equiv at(T, P_2) & \text{when } T \text{ is a subprogram of } P_2; \end{cases}$$

3. If $P \equiv \textbf{if } (\square m \cdot M[\overline{q}] = m \to P_m) \textbf{ fi}$, then for each m, whenever T is a subprogram of P_m, we define $at(T, P) \equiv at(T, P_m)$;
4. If $P \equiv \textbf{while } M[\overline{q}] = 1 \textbf{ do } P' \textbf{ od}$ and T is a subprogram of P', then $at(T, P) \equiv at(T, P'); P$.

Intuitively, $at(T, P)$ is (a syntactic expression of) the remainder of program P that is to be executed when the program control reaches subprogram T. For a simple presentation, here we slightly abuse the notation $at(T, P)$ because the same subprogram T can appear in different parts of P. So, $at(T, P)$ is actually defined for a fixed occurrence of T within P.

Now we are ready to present the strong soundness theorem for quantum **while**-programs.

Theorem 9.6 (Strong soundness for quantum **while**-programs). *Let $\{A\}P^*\{B\}$ be a standard proof outline for partial correctness of quantum **while**-program P. If*

$$\langle P, \rho\rangle \to^* \{|\langle P_i, \rho_i\rangle|\},$$

then:

1. *for each i, $P_i \equiv at(T_i, P)$ for some subprogram T_i of P or $P_i \equiv \downarrow$; and*

$$(\text{R.At}')\quad \frac{\{A\}P^*\{B\}}{\{A\}\langle P\rangle\{B\}}$$

FIGURE 9.13 Rule for atomic regions.

2. *it holds that*

$$tr(A\rho) \le \sum_i tr(B_i\rho_i),\tag{9.26}$$

where

$$B_i = \begin{cases} B & \text{if } P_i \equiv \downarrow, \\ pre(T_i) & \text{if } P_i \equiv at(T_i, P). \end{cases}$$

Proof. See Appendix A.5.4. □

The soundness for quantum **while**-programs given in Theorem 6.1 can be easily derived from the above theorem. Of course, the above theorem is a generalisation of the strong soundness for classical **while**-programs (see [28], Theorem 3.3). But it is worthy to notice a major difference between the classical and quantum cases: due to the branching caused by quantum measurements, in the right-hand side of inequality (9.26) of the above theorem, we have to take a summation over a configuration ensemble $\{|\langle P_i, \rho_i\rangle|\}$ rather than considering a single configuration $\langle P_i, \rho_i\rangle$.

Proof outlines for partial correctness of component quantum programs are generated by the rules in Fig. 9.12 together with the rule (R.At') in Fig. 9.13. A proof outline of a component program P is standard if every normal subprogram Q is preceded by exactly one quantum predicate $pre(Q)$. The notation $at(T, P)$ is defined in the same way as in Definition 9.13, but only for normal subprograms T of P. The strong soundness theorem for quantum **while**-programs (Theorem 9.6) can be easily generalised to the case of component quantum programs.

9.6.3 Interference freedom

With the preparation given in the previous subsection, we now consider how we can reason about correctness of parallel quantum programs with shared variables. Let us start from the following example showing noncompositionality in the sense that correctness of a parallel quantum program is not solely determined by correctness of its component programs.

Example 9.10. Let q be a quantum variable of type **Bool** (Boolean) or **Int** (Integers). Consider the following two programs:

$$P_1 \equiv q := U[q], \qquad P_1' \equiv q := V[q]; q := W[q]$$

where U, V, W are unitary operators on $\mathcal{H}_q$ such that $U = WV$. It is obvious that P_1 and P_1' are equivalent in the following sense: for any quantum predicates A, B in $\mathcal{H}_q$,

$$\models_{par}\{A\}P_1\{B\} \Leftrightarrow \models_{par}\{A\}P_1'\{B\}.$$

Now let us further consider their parallel composition with the simple initialisation program:

$$P_2 \equiv q := |0\rangle.$$

We show that $P_1 \| P_2$ and $P_1' \| P_2$ are not equivalent; that is,

$$\models_{par}\{A\}P_1\|P_2\{B\} \Leftrightarrow \models_{par}\{A\}P_1'\|P_2\{B\}$$

is not always true. Let us define the deformation index of unitary operator U as

$$D(U) = \inf_\rho \frac{\langle 0|U\rho U^\dagger|0\rangle}{\langle 0|\rho|0\rangle}.$$

Then we have:

$$\models_{par}\{\lambda \cdot |0\rangle\langle 0|\}P_1\|P_2\{|0\rangle\langle 0|\} \text{ if and only if } \lambda \le \min\left[D(U), |\langle 0|U|0\rangle|^2\right];\tag{9.27}$$

$$\models_{par} \{\lambda \cdot |0\rangle\langle 0|\} P_1' \| P_2 \{|0\rangle\langle 0|\} \text{ if and only if}$$

$$\lambda \leq \min \left[D(U), D(V) \cdot |\langle 0|W|0\rangle|^2, |\langle 0|U|0\rangle|^2 \right]. \tag{9.28}$$

It is easy to see that the partial correctness in (9.27) is true but the one in (9.28) is false when q is a qubit, $\lambda = 1$, $U = I$ (the identity), and $V = W = H$ is the Hadamard gate.

The above example clearly illustrates that as in the case of classical parallel programs, we have to take into account interference between the component programs of a parallel quantum program. Moreover, appearance of parameter λ in Eqs (9.27) and (9.28) indicates that interference between quantum programs is subtler than that between classical programs. It motivates us to introduce a parameterised notion of interference freedom for quantum programs. Let us first consider interference between a quantum predicate and a proof outline.

Definition 9.14. Let $0 \leq \lambda \leq 1$, and let A be a quantum predicate and $\{B\}P^*\{C\}$ a standard proof outline for partial correctness of quantum component program P. We say that A is λ-interference free with $\{B\}P^*\{C\}$ if:

1. for any atomic region, normal initialisation or unitary transformation Q in P, it holds that

$$\models_{par} \{\lambda A + (1-\lambda)pre(Q)\} Q \{\lambda A + (1-\lambda)post(Q)\} \tag{9.29}$$

where $post(Q)$ is the quantum predicate immediately after Q in $\{B\}P^*\{C\}$;

2. for any normal case statement $Q \equiv \textbf{if } (\square\ M[q] = m \rightarrow Q_m) \textbf{ fi}$ in P, it holds that

$$\models_{par} \{\lambda A + (1-\lambda)pre(Q)\} \textbf{ if } \left(\square M[q] = m \rightarrow \{\lambda A + (1-\lambda)post_m(Q)\}\ Q_m\right)$$
$$\textbf{fi } \{\lambda A + (1-\lambda)post(Q)\} \tag{9.30}$$

where $post_m(Q)$ is the quantum predicate immediately after the mth branch of Q in $\{B\}P^*\{C\}$.

Remark 9.5. The reader might be wondering about why $post(Q)$ and $post_m(Q)$ appear in Eqs (9.29) and (9.30). This looks very different from the classical case. When defining interference freedom of A with $\{B\}P^*\{C\}$ for a classical program P, we only require that

$$\models_{par} \{A \wedge pre(Q)\} Q \{A\} \tag{9.31}$$

for each basic statement Q in P (see [28], Definition 8.1). Actually, the difference between the classical and quantum cases is not as big as what we think at the first glance. In the classical case, condition (9.31) can be combined with

$$\models_{par} \{pre(Q)\} Q \{post(Q)\},$$

which holds automatically, to yield:

$$\models_{par} \{A \wedge pre(Q)\} Q \{A \wedge post(Q)\}. \tag{9.32}$$

If conjunctive $\wedge$ in Eq. (9.32) is replaced by a convex combination (with probabilities λ and $1-\lambda$), then we obtain Eqs (9.29) and (9.30).

The above definition can be straightforwardly generalised to the notion of interference freedom between a family of proof outlines, where noninterference between each quantum predicate in one proof outline and another proof outline is required.

Definition 9.15. Let $\{A_i\}P_i^*\{B_i\}$ be a standard proof outline for partial correctness of component quantum program P_i for each $1 \leq i \leq n$.

1. If $\Lambda = \{\lambda_{ij}\}_{i \neq j}$ is a family of real numbers in the unit interval, then we say that $\{A_i\}P^*\{B_i\}$ $(i = 1, ..., n)$ are Λ-interference free whenever for any $i \neq j$, each quantum predicate C in $\{A_i\}P_i^*\{B_i\}$ is λ_{ij}-interference free with $\{A_j\}P_j^*\{B_j\}$.

2. In particular, $\{A_i\}P^*\{B_i\}$ $(i = 1, ..., n)$ are said to be λ-interference free if they are Λ-interference free for $\Lambda = \{\lambda_{ij}\}_{i \neq j}$ with $\lambda_{ij} \equiv \lambda$ (the same parameter) for all $i \neq j$.

Obviously, the interference defined above is a logical notion. It is fundamentally different from the important notion of interference in quantum physics. On the other hand, keeping in mind that quantum predicates in the above definitions are interpreted as physical observables, we believe that there must be certain interesting connection between these two notions of interference to be understood.

$$\text{(R.PC.L)} \quad \frac{\text{Standard proof outlines } \{A_i\}\, P_i^*\, \{B_i\}\, (i = 1, ..., n) \text{ are } \Lambda\text{-interference free}}{\{\sum_{i=1}^{n} p_i A_i\}\, P_1 \| \cdots \| P_n\, \{\sum_{i=1}^{n} p_i B_i\}}$$

FIGURE 9.14 Rule for parallel quantum programs with shared variables. Here, $\{p_i\}_{i=1}^{n}$ is a probability distribution, and $\Lambda = \{\lambda_{ij}\}_{i \neq j}$ satisfies: $\sum_{i \neq j} \frac{p_i}{\lambda_{ij}} \leq 1$ for every j.

9.6.4 A rule for parallel composition of quantum programs with shared variables

The notion of interference freedom introduced above provides us with a key ingredient in defining a quantum extension of inference rule (R.PC) for parallelism with shared variables. Another key ingredient would be a quantum generalisation of the logical conjuction used in combining the preconditions and postconditions. As discussed at the beginning of this chapter, tensor product is not appropriate for this purpose, but probabilistic (convex) combination can serve as a kind of approximation of conjunction. This idea leads to rule (R.PC.L) in Fig. 9.14.

It is worth carefully comparing rule (R.PC.L) with (R.PC.P) for disjoint parallel quantum programs. First, Λ-interference freedom in (R.PC.L) is not necessary in (R.PC.P), since disjointness implies interference freedom. Second, conjunctions $\bigwedge_i A_i$ and $\bigwedge_i B_i$ of preconditions and postconditions in rule (R.PC) for classical parallel programs are replaced by tensor products $\bigotimes_i A_i$ and $\bigotimes_i B_i$ in (R.PC.P). But in (R.PC.L), programs $P_1, ..., P_n$ are allowed to share variables, the tensor products of preconditions and postconditions are then not always well-defined. So, we choose to use probabilistic combinations $\sum_i p_i A_i$ and $\sum_i p_i B_i$. Obviously, probabilistic combination is not a perfect quantum generalisation of conjunction.

Let us first give a simple example to illustrate how to use rule (R.PC.L) in reasoning about shared-variable parallel quantum programs.

Example 9.11. Let q_1, q_2, r be three qubit variables, and let P_i be a quantum programs with variables q_i and r:

$$P_i \equiv q_i := |0\rangle); \quad q_i := H[q_i]; \quad q_i, r := \mathrm{CNOT}[q_i, r]$$

for $i = 1, 2$, where CNOT is the control-NOT gate with q_i as the control qubit and r as the data qubit, and H is the Hadamard gate. Note that P_1 and P_2 have a shared variable r. We consider their parallel composition $P_1 \| P_2$. Using rule (R.PC.L), we can derive its correctness formula:

$$\vdash_{par} \left\{ \frac{\sqrt{2}}{2} |\psi\rangle\langle\psi| \right\} P_1 \| P_2 \{|\psi\rangle\langle\psi|\}, \tag{9.33}$$

where the pure state $|\psi\rangle$ in the precondition and postcondition is given as follows:

$$|\psi\rangle = \frac{\sqrt{2}+1}{4}[|000\rangle + |001\rangle] + \frac{\sqrt{2}-1}{4}[|110\rangle + |111\rangle] + \frac{1}{4}[|010\rangle + |011\rangle + |100\rangle + |101\rangle],$$

with the order of register: q_1, q_2, r. First, we have the proof outlines of P_i:

$$\left\{ \frac{\sqrt{2}}{2} |\psi\rangle\langle\psi| \right\} q_i := |0\rangle \{|\psi\rangle\langle\psi|\} q_i := H[q_i] \{|\psi\rangle\langle\psi|\} q_i, r := \mathrm{CNOT}[q_i, r] \{|\psi\rangle\langle\psi|\}$$

for $i = 1, 2$, respectively. Moreover, one can verify that these two proof outlines are 0.5-interference free because

$$\vdash_{qPD} \left\{ \frac{2+\sqrt{2}}{4} |\psi\rangle\langle\psi| \right\} q_i := |0\rangle \{|\psi\rangle\langle\psi|\}.$$

Then (9.33) is derived from (R.PC.L) with $p_0 = 0.5$, $p_1 = 0.5$.

One may show that with the postcondition $|\psi\rangle\langle\psi|$, the maximal factor c which guarantees validity of the correctness formula

$$\models_{par} \{c|\psi\rangle\langle\psi|\} P_1 \| P_2 \{|\psi\rangle\langle\psi|\}$$

is $c_{max} = \frac{3+2\sqrt{2}}{8} \approx 0.728$. The factor $\frac{\sqrt{2}}{2} \approx 0.707$ we derived in (9.33) is very close to c_{max}, but a formal derivation of c_{max} is much more involved and omitted here.

Remark 9.6. For some more sophisticated applications, a combination of (R.PC.P) and (P.PC.L) can achieve a better quantum approximation of the conjunctions in (R.PC). We first find maximal subfamilies, say $\mathcal{P}_j$ of $P_1, ..., P_n$ of which the elements are disjoint. Then we can apply (R.PC.P) to each of these subfamily to derive:

$$\vdash_{par} \{C_i\} \|_{P_i \in \mathcal{P}_j} P_i \{D_j\} \tag{9.34}$$

where

$$C_j = \bigotimes_{P_i \in \mathcal{P}_j} A_i, \qquad D_j = \bigotimes_{P_i \in \mathcal{P}_j} B_i.$$

Furthermore, a probabilistic combination of (9.34) can be derived as

$$\vdash_{par} \left\{ \sum_j p_j C_j \right\} P_1 \| \cdots \| P_n \left\{ \sum_j p_j D_j \right\}.$$

We believe that this idea is strong enough to derive a large class of useful correctness properties of parallel quantum programs with shared variables. The reason is that in many-body physics, an overwhelming majority of systems of physics interest can be described by local Hamiltonian: $H = \sum_j H_j$, where each H_j is k-local, meaning that it acts over at most k components of the system. It is clear that the above idea can be used to prove correctness of parallel quantum programs with their preconditions and postconditions being local Hamiltonians.

Theorem 9.6 can be generalised from quantum **while**-programs to parallel quantum program, showing the strong soundness of inference rule (R.PC.L) (combined with the other rules introduced in this chapter):

Theorem 9.7 (Strong soundness for parallel quantum programs with convex combination of quantum predicates). *Let $\{A_i\} P_i^* \{B_i\}$ be a standard proof outline for partial correctness of component quantum program P_i $(i = 1, ..., n)$ and*

$$\langle P_1 \| \cdots \| P_n, \rho \rangle \rightarrow^* \{|\langle P_{1s} \| \cdots \| P_{ns}, \rho_s \rangle|\}.$$

Then:

1. *for each $1 \leq i \leq n$ and for every s, $P_{is} \equiv at(T_{is}, P_i)$ for some normal subprogram T_{is} of P_i or $P_{is} \equiv \downarrow$; and*
2. *for any probability distribution $\{p_i\}_{i=1}^n$, if $\{A_i\} P_i^* \{B_i\}$ $(i = 1, ..., n)$ are Λ-interference free for some $\Lambda = \{\lambda_{ij}\}_{i \neq j}$ satisfying*

$$\sum_{i \neq j} \frac{p_i}{\lambda_{ij}} \leq 1 \text{ for } j = 1, ..., n; \tag{9.35}$$

in particular, if they are λ-interference free for some $\lambda \geq 1 - \min_{i=1}^n p_i$, then we have:

$$tr\left[\left(\sum_{i=1}^n p_i A_i \right) \rho \right] \leq \sum_s tr\left[\left(\sum_{i=1}^n p_i B_{is} \right) \rho_s \right]$$

where

$$B_{is} = \begin{cases} B_i & \text{if } P_{is} \equiv \downarrow, \\ pre(T_{is}) & \text{if } P_{is} \equiv at(T_{is}, P_i). \end{cases}$$

Proof. See Appendix A.5.5. $\qquad\qquad\qquad\qquad\qquad\qquad\qquad\qquad\qquad\qquad\qquad\qquad \square$

At this moment, we are only able to conceive rule (R.PC.L) as a quantum generalisation of the rule (R.PC) for classical parallel programs with shared variables. In classical computing, as proved in [326], rule (R.PC) together with a rule for auxiliary variables and Hoare logic for sequential programs gives rise to a (relatively) complete logical system for reasoning

$$\text{(R.PC.J)} \quad \frac{\begin{array}{c}\text{Standard proof outlines } \{A_i\}\, P_i^*\, \{B_i\}\, (i = 1, ..., n) \text{ are } \Lambda\text{-interference free} \\ A \text{ is a join of } \{A_i\}, \text{ and } B \text{ is a join of } \{B_i\}\end{array}}{\{A\} P_1 \| \cdots \| P_n \{B\}}$$

FIGURE 9.15   Rule for parallel quantum programs with shared variables.

about parallel programs with shared variables. However, it is not the case for rule (R.PC.L) in parallel quantum programming, because not every (largely entangled) precondition (resp. postcondition) of $P_1 \| \cdots \| P_n$ can be written in the form of $\sum_{i=1}^{n} p_i A_i$ (resp. $\sum_{i=1}^{n} p_i B_i$) with all A_i and B_i being separable. As will be further discussed in the next section, the problem of fining a (relatively) complete proof system for shared-variable parallel quantum programs is still widely open.

9.7   Discussions

In the previous sections, we have defined the syntax and operational and denotational semantics of parallel quantum programs and presents several useful inference rules for reasoning about their correctness. In particular, it is proved that our inference rules form a (relatively) complete proof system for disjoint parallel quantum programs. However, this is certainly merely one of the first steps toward a comprehensive theory of parallel quantum programming and leaves a series of fundamental problems unsolved. In this section, we discuss some of them.

1. (Relatively) complete axiomatisation: Perhaps, the most important and difficult open problem at this stage is to develop a (relatively) *complete* logical system for verification of parallel quantum programs with shared variables.

- *Stronger rule for parallel composition*: As pointed out in the last section, inference rule (R.PC.L) can be used to prove some useful correctness properties of such quantum programs, but it seems far from being the rule for parallel composition needed in a (relatively) complete logical system for these quantum programs. A possible candidate for the rule that we are seeking should be based on the notions of *join* and *margin* of operators: let $\mathcal{H} = \bigotimes_{i=1}^{n} \mathcal{H}_i$ and $\mathcal{J}$ be a family of subsets of $\{1, ..., n\}$. For each $J \in \mathcal{J}$, given a positive operator A_J on $\mathcal{H}_J = \bigotimes_{j \in J} \mathcal{H}_j$. If positive operator A on $\mathcal{H}$ satisfies: $A_J = tr_{J^c} A$ for every $J \in \mathcal{J}$, where $J^c = \{1, ..., n\} \setminus J$, then A is called a join of $\{A_J\}_{J \in \mathcal{J}}$, and each A_J is called the margin of A on $\mathcal{H}_J$. With the notion of join, we can conceive that the inference rule needed for parallel composition of quantum programs with shared variables should be some variant of rule (R.PC.J) given in Fig. 9.15.

- *Auxiliary variables*: As is well-known in the theory of classical parallel programming (see [28], Chapters 7 and 8, and [160], Chapter 7), to achieve a (relatively) complete logical system for reasoning about parallel programs, except finding a strong enough rule for parallel composition, one must introduce *auxiliary variables* to record the control flow of a program, which, at the same time, should not influence the control flow inside the program. We presented several rules in Section 6.7 for introducing auxiliary variables, and they were employed to establish (relative) completeness of our proof system for disjoint parallel quantum programs. However, there they were used to deal with entanglement and not for recording control flows. It seems that auxiliary variables recording control flows are also needed in parallel quantum programming. At this moment, however, we do not have a clear idea about how such auxiliary variables can be introduced in the case of parallel quantum programs with shared variables.

- *Infinite-dimension*: The issue of infinite-dimensional state Hilbert spaces naturally arises when developing a logical system for parallel quantum programs with infinite data types like integers and reals. As we saw in Section 9.3, this issue was properly resolved with auxiliary rule (R.Lim) defined in terms of weak convergence of operators in the case of disjoint parallel quantum programs. But it is still unknown whether the same idea works or not for shared variables; in particular, how it can be used in combination with a parallel composition rule like (R.PC.J) considered above?

In summary, it seems that a *full* solution to the above three issues and achieving a (relatively) complete proof system for parallel quantum programs are still far beyond the current reach.

2. Mechanisation: A theorem prover for quantum Hoare logic was implemented in Isabelle/HOL and Coq for verification of quantum **while**-programs [281,450]. It would be desirable to further formalise the syntax, semantics and proof rules presented in this chapter and to extend the theorem prover so that it can be used for verification of parallel quantum programs. Mechanisation of the current proof rules seems feasible. In the future, however, if we are able to find a stronger rule of the form (R.PC.J) discussed above, implementing an automatic tool for verification of parallel quantum programs based on such a rule will be difficult. It may even rely on a future breakthrough in finding an algorithmic solution to the following long-standing open problem (listed in [383] as one of the ten most prominent mathematical challenges in quantum chemistry; see also [253] and references therein):

Quantum marginal problem: Given a family $\mathcal{J}$ of subsets of $\{1, ..., n\}$, and for each $J \in \mathcal{J}$, given a density operator (mixed state) ρ_J in $\mathcal{H}_J$. Is there a join (global state) of $\{\rho_j\}_{J \in \mathcal{J}}$ in $\mathcal{H}$?

3. Applications: As pointed out in [294], parallelism at various levels will be an important consideration for quantum computing; in particular, proper architectural support for parallel implementation of quantum gates may be pivotal for harnessing the power of NISQ (Noisy Intermediate Scale Quantum) devices. Our target applications of the results presented in this chapter are of course verification and analysis of parallel quantum programs and perhaps also reasoning about concurrency in operating systems of quantum computers. On the other hand, as will be discussed in Section 13.9, some ideas in quantum programming can be applied to quantum physics. Along this line, it would be interesting to see whether our results can also be used for reasoning about many-body quantum systems (see Remark 9.6 for a brief discussion about a link between our parallel composition rule (R.PC.L) and local Hamiltonians).

4. Extensions: As a first step in the studies of parallel quantum programming, this chapter mainly tried to find appropriate quantum generalisation of the Owicki–Gries and Lamport method. An interesting problem for future research is how to extend moderner verification techniques beyond the Owicki–Gries and Lamport paradigm for parallel quantum programs; for example:

- *Compositional techniques*: The verification technique presented in this chapter is noncompositional as is the Owicki–Gries and Lamport method. It is desirable to develop some compositional verification techniques that can reduce verification of a large program to independent verification of its subprograms for parallel quantum programs, e.g. quantum extension of Jone's rely-guarantee paradigm for shared variable parallelism [233] and Misra and Chandy's assumption-commitment paradigm for synchronous message passing [86].

- *Separation logic and modular reasoning*: Concurrent separation logic [76,321] is a modern logic for reasoning about parallelism and concurrency. One of its central idea is to use separating conjunctions $\star_{i=1}^n A_i$, $\star_{i=1}^n B_i$ of preconditions and postconditions to replace the ordinary conjunctions $\bigwedge_{i=1}^n A_i$, $\bigwedge_{i=1}^n B_i$ in the parallel composition rule (R.PC). In particular, the new parallel composition rule with separating conjunctions supports modular reasoning about threads and processes. It will be a great challenge to realise this idea in the presence of quantum correlations that are fundamentally different from their classical counterparts, although some quantum extensions of separation logic were already introduced in [270,451]. Indeed, we are even not sure this is possible or not.

- *Message passing*: Shared variables and message passing are two major mechanics of process interaction in parallel and distributed programming. This chapter focuses on the model of parallel quantum programming with shared variables. The message passing mechanism in distributed quantum programming will be discussed in the next chapter.

- *Reasoning about weak memory models*: The memory model for parallelism of quantum programs assumed in this chapter is the same as in the original Owicki–Gries and Lamport method, namely sequential consistency. Recently, the Owicki–Gries and Lamport method has been generalised to deal with various weak memory models; see for example [264]. How to define and reason about parallel quantum programs with weak memory models?

9.8 Bibliographic remarks and further readings

The theoretical research on parallel quantum programming was initiated in the draft paper [437], in which a series of results about classical parallel programs presented in Chapters 7 and 8 of [28] are generalised to the quantum case. The part of [437] for disjoint parallel quantum programs was published as [438]. The exposition of this chapter largely follows [437,438].

Some more practical researches on parallel quantum programming have recently been reported in a series of papers. For example, an extension of the Message Passing Interface (MPI) was introduced by Häner, Steiger, Hoefler, and Troyer [197] to enable high-performance implementations of quantum algorithms. A parallel extension of Microsoft's quantum programming language Q# was defined by Häner, Kliuchnikov, Roetteler, Soeken, and Vaschillo [198] to facilitate space–time tradeoff in quantum computing. The multiprogramming mechanism has also been introduced into quantum computing in [118,283,320].

Chapter 10

Distributed quantum programs

Distributed systems: A distributed system consists of a collection of physically distributed components that operate upon separate (their own) memories, and communicate and synchronise via message passing through channels between them. The message communications can be roughly classified into the following two categories:

- *Asynchronous communication*: messages are sent regardless the state of the receivers of those messages, i.e., it might even be the case that a sent message does not arrive, or will never be received by any receiver at all.
- *Synchronous communication*: message communication only takes place when both the sender is ready to send a message and the receiver of that message is known and ready to receive that message, after which that message is exchanged (this is often called "handshake" or "rendezvous").

Process algebras: Many different programming models and languages have been proposed in traditional computer science for abstract descriptions of distributed systems. In this chapter, we choose to focus on a particularly elegant formal model of concurrent and distributed systems, namely process algebras. Various process algebras have been introduced since later 1970s and early 1980s. The most popular process algebras include Milner's CCS (Calculus of Communicating Systems) [301,302] and pi-calculus [303,304], and Hoare's CSP (Communicating Sequential Processes) [210,211]. They provide primitives for explicit and high-level descriptions of interactions, communications, and synchronisations between a collection of independent processes. In particular, as the name suggested, they provide algebraic laws for reasoning about equivalence between systems based on the central notion of bisimulation.

Distributed quantum systems: A distributed quantum system is a distributed system with some of its components being quantum (sub)systems. The communications between its components can be:

- *Classical communication*: classical message (data, information) is sent through a classical channel; or
- *Quantum communication*: a quantum state is sent through a quantum channel.

But it is particularly worth noting that, except quantum communication, quantum state passing from a sender to a receiver can also be realised by the sender and receiver's local (quantum) operations and classical communications between them (this scheme is often called LOCC), if certain entanglement between them exists, as exemplified by quantum teleportation introduced in Section 4.6.

Currently, there are mainly two kinds of distributed quantum systems in practice:

- *Quantum communication systems*: It has been well understood from the early days of quantum information research that quantum communication systems have the advantage over their classical counterparts that their security and ability to detect the presence of eavesdropping are provable based the basic principles of quantum mechanics. Now quantum communication and cryptographic systems have already become commercial products.
- *Distributed quantum computing*: As already pointed out at the beginning of Chapter 9, since large-scale quantum computers are out of the reach of current technology, parallel and distributed quantum computing have been proposed for realising large-capacity quantum computing. Indeed, both parallel and distributed architectures were adopted in the IBM Quantum roadmap announced in 2022. Some distributed quantum programming models have also been introduced, including QMPI [197], an quantum extension of MPI (Message Passing Interface).

Similar to its classical counterpart, a quantum network (in particular, quantum internet) can be seen as a combination of quantum communication and distributed quantum computing. Several proposals for implementing quantum networks and quantum network programming have been presented in the last few years [114,406].

Quantum process algebras: To provide formal techniques for modelling, analysis, and verification of quantum communication and distributed quantum computing systems, process algebras have been generalised to the quantum setting around 2005. For example, a language CQP (Communicating Quantum Processes) was defined in [169] as a quantum extension of the pi-calculus by adding primitives for measurements and transformations of quantum states and allowing transmission of qubits, and a language QPAlg (Quantum Process Algebra) was defined in [235] by adding primitives expressing unitary transformations and quantum measurements, as well as communications of quantum states, to a classical process algebra

Foundations of Quantum Programming. https://doi.org/10.1016/B978-0-44-315942-8.00022-8

similar to CCS. Another quantum extension qCCS was introduced in [147,148,429]. In particular, the notion of bisimulation has been generalised to these quantum process algebras for reasoning about equivalence of quantum systems.

In this chapter, we introduce a process algebra-based model of distributed quantum programming, qCCS, which is a quantum extension of Milner's CCS.

10.1 Quantum process algebra qCCS

CCS (Calculus of Communicating Systems) is one of the most popular process algebras introduced by Milner [301,302] around 1980. Its syntax is defined based on the following primitives:

 (i) indivisible actions for modelling communications between processes; and
 (ii) combinators of processes, including nondeterministic choice, parallel composition, and channel restriction.

Processes are formally represented as expressions constructed from these primitives. Their operational semantics is defined in terms of transitions between processes labelled by actions. Based on it, a key notion of bisimulation is introduced for establishing semantic equivalence between processes. Then a series of algebraic laws can be developed for reasoning about correctness of systems (i.e. equivalence between specifications and implementation).

qCCS is a quantum extension of CCS, perhaps more precisely, an adaptation of CCS in the quantum world. In this section, we define the syntax and operational semantics of qCCS and present a series of examples. The bisimulation semantics of qCCS will be carefully discussed in Section 10.2. Furthermore, the notion of approximate bisimulation will be introduced in Section 10.3 for characterisation of approximate equivalence between quantum processes.

As always done in the previous parts of this book, we mainly consider a purely quantum version of qCCS in which only quantum variables and quantum communications are involved. In Section 10.4, we will briefly discuss how to add classical variables and classical communications into qCCS.

10.1.1 Syntax

The purely quantum version of qCCS is an algebra of pure quantum processes in which communications by moving quantum states physically are allowed and computations are modelled by superoperators, but no classical data is explicitly involved. So, the alphabet of qCCS consists of:

- a set $qChan$ of names for quantum channels, ranged over by c, d, ...;
- τ, the name of silent action;
- a set $qVar$ of quantum variables, ranged over by $p, q, r, ...$ For each quantum variable $q \in qVar$, imagine that we have a quantum system named by q, with Hilbert space $\mathcal{H}_q$ as its state space. We say that two variables q and r have the same type if $\mathcal{H}_q = \mathcal{H}_r$ (in the sense of isomorphism). For any $X \subseteq qVar$, we define

$$\mathcal{H}_X = \bigotimes_{q \in X} \mathcal{H}_q.$$

In particular, if $X = qVar$, it is written as $\mathcal{H}_{all}$.
- a set of process constant schemes, ranged over by metavariables $A, B, ...$ For each scheme A, a nonnegative arity $ar(A)$ is assigned to it. Let $\overline{q} = q_1, ..., q_{ar(A)}$ be a sequence of distinct quantum variables. Then $A(\overline{q})$ is called a process constant.

Now we can define the syntax of qCCS. Let us write $\mathcal{P}$ for the set of quantum processes. For each quantum process $P \in \mathcal{P}$, we write $qv(P)$ for the set of free quantum variables in P.

Definition 10.1. Quantum processes are inductively defined by the following formation rules:

1. $\mathbf{nil} \in \mathcal{P}$ and $qv(\mathbf{nil}) = \emptyset$;
2. each process constant $A(\overline{q}) \in \mathcal{P}$ and $qv(A(\overline{q})) = \{\overline{q}\}$;
3. if $P \in \mathcal{P}$, then:
 a. $\tau.P \in \mathcal{P}$ and $qv(\tau.P) = qv(P)$;
 b. $\mathcal{E}[\overline{q}].P \in \mathcal{P}$ and $qv(\mathcal{E}[\overline{q}].P) = qv(P) \cup \{\overline{q}\}$, where $\mathcal{E}$ is a quantum operation (i.e. superoperator) on $\mathcal{H}_{\overline{q}}$;
 c. $c?q.P \in \mathcal{P}$ and $qv(c?q.P) = qv(P) \setminus \{q\}$;
 d. $c!q.P \in \mathcal{P}$ provided $q \notin qv(P)$, and $qv(c!q.P) = qv(P) \cup \{q\}$;
 e. $P \backslash L \in \mathcal{P}$ and $qv(P \backslash L) = qv(P)$, where $L \subseteq qChan$;

4. if $P, Q \in \mathcal{P}$, then:

    a. $P + Q \in \mathcal{P}$ and $qv(P + Q) = qv(P) \cup qv(Q)$;

    b. $P \| Q \in \mathcal{P}$ provided $qv(P) \cap qv(Q) = \emptyset$, and $qv(P \| Q) = qv(P) \cup qv(Q)$.

The syntax of qCCS can be summarised using the standard BNF (Backus–Naur form) grammar as follows:

$$P ::= \mathbf{nil} \mid A(\overline{q}) \mid \tau.P \mid \mathcal{E}[\overline{q}].P \mid c?q.P \mid c!q.P \mid P\backslash L \mid P + P \mid P\|P.$$

The above definition needs some intuitive explanations:

- **nil** stands for the empty process doing nothing.
- $\tau.P$ is a process that first performs a silent, internal action τ, and then behaves as process P.
- $\mathcal{E}[\overline{q}].P$ is a process that first performs a quantum operation on quantum register $\overline{q}$, and then behaves as process P. The quantum operation $\mathcal{E}$ can be thought of as a sequential quantum computation performed locally on $\overline{q}$. This point will be further discussed in Section 10.2.5.
- $c?q.P$ is a process that communicates with another process in the following way: it receives a quantum state, say ρ, from channel c and then behaves as process P with quantum variables q being in state ρ.
- If $q \notin qv(P)$, then $c!q.P$ is a process that first sends the state of quantum variable q through channel c to another process and then behaves as process P. The condition $q \notin qv(P)$ is imposed here to avoid a violation of the nocloning principle of quantum information – an unknown quantum state cannot be perfectly cloned (see Section 2.4.1). Indeed, if $q \in qv(P)$, then a copy of the state of q is sent out, and another copy of it is left in P. This is not allowed by the nocloning principle.
- $P \backslash L$ is a process that behaves as process P except that communications through any channel in L are forbidden.
- $P + Q$ is a nondeterministic choice of P and Q; that is, it is a process that behaves either like P or like Q, as soon as one of P and Q is chosen the other is discarded.
- $P\|Q$ is the parallel composition of P and Q. If $qv(P) \cap qv(Q) = \emptyset$, then $P\|Q$ stands for a system in which P and Q may proceed independently but may also communicate with each other through quantum channels existing between them. The condition $qv(P) \cap qv(Q) = \emptyset$ is required here also for avoiding a violation of the nocloning principle. If $q \in qv(P) \cap qv(Q)$, then we consider the communication between processes $R = c?q.(P\|Q)$ and $S = c!q.\mathbf{nil}$. In $R\|S$, the state of q is sent from S to R through channel c, and then a copy of the state of q is used in P, and another copy of it is used in Q. Again, this is not allowed by the nocloning principle.
- For each process constant scheme A, a defining equation of the form

$$A(\overline{q}) \stackrel{def}{=} P \tag{10.1}$$

will be assumed, where P is a process with $qv(P) \subseteq \{\overline{q}\}$. Eq. (10.1) means that process $A(\overline{q})$ behaves as process P; that is, the behaviour of $A(\overline{q})$ is (recursively) defined by P. It is worth noting that we assign a set of free quantum variables $\overline{q}$ to process constant A in advance in order to fulfil the conditions required by the nocloning principle discussed above. The process constant schemes provide us with a mechanism for recursive definition in qCCS.

Example 10.1. A recursive definition of process constant scheme A of the form:

$$A(q) \stackrel{def}{=} c!r.A(q)$$

is not legitimate in qCCS since if $r = q$ then $r \in qv(A(q))$ and $c!q.A(q)$ is not a process, and if $r \neq q$ then $qv(c!r.A(q)) \not\subseteq \{q\}$. However,

$$A(q) \stackrel{def}{=} c?r.c!r.A(q)$$

is a legitimate defining equation of A.

The above explanations of the processes defined in Definition 10.1 will be reflected in the operational semantics of qCCS defined in the next subsection.

Bound variables and α-conversion: As in classical programming theory, we need to deal with free variables and bound variables separately. From the above discussions, we see that there are only two kinds of binding in our language for quantum processes:

1. the restriction $\backslash L$ binds all channel names in L, and

2. the input prefix $c?q$ binds quantum variable q.

The point 2 was clearly shown in the definition of the free variables in $c?q.P$ (see clause 3.c of Definition 10.1). We will use symbol $\equiv_\alpha$ to denote α-convertibility on processes defined by replacing bound (quantum) variables in the standard way; that is, $P \equiv_\alpha Q$ if they are syntactically equal except the differences in the names of bound variables in them.

Substitutions: The substitution of quantum variables in qCCS has to be treated in a very careful way due to the fact that arbitrary cloning of quantum information is forbidden.

Definition 10.2. A substitution of quantum variables is a one-to-one mapping f from $qVar$ into itself satisfying

1. q and $f(q)$ have the same type for all $q \in qVar$; and
2. $f|_{qVar \setminus X} = Id_{qVar \setminus X}$ for some finite subset X of $qVar$, where Id_Y stands for the identity function on Y, and $f|Y$ is the restriction of f on Y.

It is common that two different classical variables can be substituted by the same variable. But in qCCS a substitution is required to be an injection. Such a requirement comes from our intention that different variables are references to different quantum systems. Since quantum variable $f(q)$ will be used to substitute quantum variable q, it is reasonable to require that the q-system and the $f(q)$-system have the same state space.

Let $P \in \mathcal{P}$ and f be a substitution. Then $P[f]$ denotes the process obtained from P by substituting $f(q)$ for each free occurrence of q in P, simultaneously for all q. To give a precise definition of $P[f]$, we need to introduce the notions of application of a substitution on quantum states and on superoperators. If f is a one-to-one mapping from $qVar$ into itself, then:

- f induces naturally an isomorphism from $\mathcal{H}_{all} = \mathcal{H}_{qVar}$ onto $\mathcal{H}_{f(qVar)}$. For simplicity, it is also denoted by f. Precisely, the isomorphism $f : \mathcal{H}_{all} \to \mathcal{H}_{f(qVar)}$ is defined by

$$f\left(\bigotimes_{q \in qVar} |\varphi_q\rangle_q\right) = \bigotimes_{q \in qVar} |\varphi_q\rangle_{f(q)}$$

for any $|\varphi_q\rangle \in \mathcal{H}_q$, $q \in qVar$. Applying f to a state which is not a tensor product of states in $\mathcal{H}_q$ ($q \in qVar$) may be carried out simply by linearity.

- Furthermore, it induces a bijection between density operators $f : \mathcal{D}(\mathcal{H}_{all}) \to \mathcal{D}(\mathcal{H}_{f(qVar)})$. For any $\rho = \sum_i p_i |\varphi_i\rangle\langle\varphi_i| \in \mathcal{D}(\mathcal{H}_{all})$, where $|\varphi_i\rangle \in \mathcal{H}_{all}$ for all i, we have:

$$f(\rho) = \sum_i p_i |f(\varphi_i)\rangle\langle f(\varphi_i)|.$$

In particular, if $f(p) = q$, $f(q) = p$ and $f(r) = r$ for all $r \neq p, q$, then $f(\rho)$ is often written as $\rho\{q/p\}$.

- For any superoperator $\mathcal{E}$ on $\mathcal{H}_X$, we define superoperator $\mathcal{E}[f]$ on $\mathcal{H}_{f(X)}$ by

$$\mathcal{E}[f] = f|_X \circ \mathcal{E} \circ (f|_X)^{-1}$$

where $f|_X$ is the restriction of f on X, which is obviously a bijection from X onto $f(X)$.

$$
\begin{array}{ccc}
\mathcal{D}(\mathcal{H}_X) & \xrightarrow{\mathcal{E}} & \mathcal{D}(\mathcal{H}_X) \\[1em]
(f|_X)^{-1} \uparrow & & \downarrow f|_X \\[1em]
\mathcal{D}(\mathcal{H}_{f(X)}) & \xrightarrow[\mathcal{E}[f]]{} & \mathcal{D}(\mathcal{H}_{f(X)})
\end{array}
$$

Now we are able to define substitution of quantum variables in a quantum process formally.

Definition 10.3. For any $P \in \mathcal{P}$ and substitution f, $P[f]$ is inductively defined as follows:

1. if P is a process constant $A(q_1, ..., q_n)$ then $P[f] = A(f(q_1), ..., f(q_n))$;
2. if $P = \mathbf{nil}$ then $P[f] = \mathbf{nil}$;
3. if $P = \tau.P'$ then $P[f] = \tau.P'[f]$;

4. if $P = \mathcal{E}[\overline{q}].P'$ then $P[f] = (\mathcal{E}[f])[f(\overline{q})].P'[f]$;
5. if $P = c?p.P'$ then $P[f] = c?q.P'\{q/p\}[f_q]$, where $q \notin qv(c?p.P') \cup qv(P'[f])$, and f_q is the substitution with

$$\begin{cases} f_q(q) = q, \\ f_q(f^{-1}(q)) = f(q), \\ f_q(r) = f(r) \text{ for all } r \neq q, f^{-1}(q); \end{cases}$$

6. if $P = c!q.P'$ then $P[f] = c!f(q).P'[f]$;
7. if $P = P_1 + P_2$ then $P[f] = P_1[f] + P_2[f]$;
8. if $P = P_1 \| P_2$ then $P[f] = P_1[f] \| P_2[f]$;
9. if $P = P' \backslash L$ then $P[f] = P'[f] \backslash L$.

In particular, let $\overline{q} = q_1, ..., q_n$ and $\overline{r} = r_1, ..., r_n$. If $f(q_i) = r_i$ ($1 \leq i \leq n$) and $f(q) = q$ for all $q \notin \overline{q}$, we write $P\{\overline{r}/\overline{q}\}$ or $P\{r_1/q_1, ..., r_n/q_n\}$ for $P[f]$.

Example 10.2. The requirement that a substitution f is one-to-one is necessary when we consider the substitution of a output prefix or a parallel composition. For example, if $f(p) = f(q) = p$, and

$$P_1 = c!p.d!q.\mathbf{nil}, \qquad P_2 = c!p.\mathbf{nil} \| d!q.\mathbf{nil},$$

then the following two expressions

$$P_1[f] = c!p.d!p.\mathbf{nil}, \qquad P_2[f] = c!p.\mathbf{nil} \| d!p.\mathbf{nil}$$

are not processes in qCCS.

It is reasonable to expect that $(P[f])[f^{-1}] \equiv_\alpha P$. But this is not always the case. Indeed, it is not true when there is a variable conflict where $f(q) \in qv(P) \backslash \{q\}$ for some $q \in qv(P)$. If this variable conflict does not happen, then $P[f]$ is said to be well-defined. In what follows. We always assume that $P[f]$ is well-defined whenever it occurs.

10.1.2 Operational semantics

In this subsection, we define the operational semantics of qCCS. As usual, it will be given in terms of transitions between configurations, labelled by actions.

Configurations: A configuration is defined to be a pair $\langle P, \rho \rangle$, where $P \in \mathcal{P}$ is a process, and $\rho \in \mathcal{D}(\mathcal{H}_{all})$ specifies the current state of quantum variables. The density operator ρ in a configuration $\langle P, \rho \rangle$ is called the environment of the configuration. Intuitively, ρ is an instantiation (or valuation) of quantum variables. It should be noted that the instantiations of variables in a classical process algebra can be made independently from each other, but quantum systems represented by different variables may be correlated because ρ is allowed to be an entangled state. The set of configurations is written qCon.

Actions: We write Act for the set of actions; that is, $Act = \{\tau\} \cup Act_{op} \cup Act_{com}$, where τ is the silent action, and

- Act_{op} is the set of quantum operations $\mathcal{E}[\overline{q}]$ in which $\overline{q}$ is a sequence of quantum variables and $\mathcal{E}$ is a superoperator on $\mathcal{H}_{\overline{q}}$; and
- Act_{com} is the set of quantum communication actions, including inputs $c?q$ and output $c!q$ in which $c \in qChan$ and $q \in qVar$.

The set Act will be ranged over by metavariables $\alpha, \beta, ...$ We need the following notations for actions:

- For each $\alpha \in Act$, we use $cn(\alpha)$ to denote the channel name in action α; that is, $cn(c?q) = cn(c!q) = c$, but $cn(\tau)$ and $cn(\mathcal{E}[\overline{q}])$ are not defined.
- We write $fv(\alpha)$ for the set of free variables in α; that is, $fv(c!q) = \{q\}, fv(\mathcal{E}[\overline{q}]) = \{\overline{q}\}, fv(\tau) = fv(c?q) = \emptyset$.
- We define $bv(\alpha)$ to be the bound variable in α; that is, $bv(c?q) = q$, and $bv(\tau), bv(\mathcal{E}[\overline{q}])$ and $bv(c!q)$ are not defined.

To define the semantics of qCCS, we also need the following notations. We use transition

$$\langle P, \rho \rangle \xrightarrow{\alpha} \langle Q, \sigma \rangle$$

$$\textbf{Tau}: \quad \langle \tau.P, \rho \rangle \xrightarrow{\tau} \langle P, \rho \rangle$$

$$\textbf{Oper}: \quad \langle \mathcal{E}[\overline{q}].P, \rho \rangle \xrightarrow{\mathcal{E}[\overline{q}]} \langle P, \mathcal{E}_{\overline{q}}(\rho) \rangle$$

$$\textbf{Input}: \quad \langle c?q.P, \rho \rangle \xrightarrow{c?r} \langle P\{r/q\}, \rho \rangle \quad \text{for each } r \notin qv(c?q.P)$$

$$\textbf{Output}: \quad \langle c!q.P, \rho \rangle \xrightarrow{c!q} \langle P, \rho \rangle$$

$$\textbf{Choice}: \quad \frac{\langle P, \rho \rangle \xrightarrow{\alpha} \langle P', \rho' \rangle}{\langle P + Q, \rho \rangle \xrightarrow{\alpha} \langle P', \rho' \rangle}$$

$$\textbf{Intl1}: \quad \frac{\langle P, \rho \rangle \xrightarrow{c?q} \langle P', \rho' \rangle}{\langle P \| Q, \rho \rangle \xrightarrow{c?q} \langle P' \| Q, \rho' \rangle} \quad \text{if } q \notin qv(Q)$$

$$\textbf{Intl2}: \quad \frac{\langle P, \rho \rangle \xrightarrow{\alpha} \langle P', \rho' \rangle}{\langle P \| Q, \rho \rangle \xrightarrow{\alpha} \langle P' \| Q, \rho' \rangle} \quad \text{if } \alpha \text{ is not an input action}$$

$$\textbf{Comm}: \quad \frac{\langle P, \rho \rangle \xrightarrow{c?q} \langle P', \rho \rangle \quad \langle Q, \rho \rangle \xrightarrow{c!q} \langle Q', \rho \rangle}{\langle P \| Q, \rho \rangle \xrightarrow{\tau} \langle P' \| Q', \rho \rangle}$$

$$\textbf{Res}: \quad \frac{\langle P, \rho \rangle \xrightarrow{\alpha} \langle P', \rho' \rangle}{\langle P \backslash L, \rho \rangle \xrightarrow{\alpha} \langle P' \backslash L, \rho' \rangle} \quad \text{if } cn(\alpha) \notin L$$

$$\textbf{Def}: \quad \frac{\langle P\{\overline{r}/\overline{q}\}, \rho \rangle \xrightarrow{\alpha} \langle P', \rho' \rangle}{\langle A(\overline{r}), \rho \rangle \xrightarrow{\alpha} \langle P', \rho' \rangle} \quad \text{if } A(\overline{q}) \stackrel{def}{=} P$$

FIGURE 10.1 Transition rules for quantum processes. The symmetric forms of the **Choice**, **Intl1**, **Intl2** and **Comm** rules are omitted here.

to mean that process P in the environment ρ performs action α and then becomes process Q and the environment is changed to σ. For any finite set $X \subseteq qVar$ and superoperator $\mathcal{E}$ on $\mathcal{H}_X$, we recall that the cylindric extension of $\mathcal{E}$ on $\mathcal{H}_{all}$ is defined to be

$$\mathcal{E}_X \stackrel{def}{=} \mathcal{E} \otimes \mathcal{I}_{qVar \backslash X} \tag{10.2}$$

where $\mathcal{I}_{qVar \backslash X}$ is the identity operator on $\mathcal{H}_{qVar \backslash X}$.

Definition 10.4. The operational semantics of quantum processes is defined as a labelled transition system $(qCon, Act, \rightarrow)$, where the transition relation $\rightarrow$ is defined by the transition rules given in Fig. 10.1.

Some of the transition rules in Fig. 10.1 are self-explanatory, but others need certain intuitive explanations:

- The operator $\mathcal{E}_{\overline{q}}(\cdot)$ in the **Oper** rule is the cylindrical extension of $\mathcal{E}$ on $\mathcal{H}_{all}$ as defined by Eq. (10.2).

- In the output transition $\langle c!q.P, \rho \rangle \xrightarrow{c!q} \langle P, \rho \rangle$, the q-system is sent out through channel c. Note that the current state of the q-system is specified in ρ. But ρ is not necessary to be a separable state, and it is possible that the q-system is entangled with the r-system for some $r \in qVar \backslash \{q\}$. Moreover, the entanglement between the q-system and the r-systems ($r \in qVar \backslash \{q\}$) is preserved after the action $c!q$.

- The input transition $\langle c?q.P, \rho \rangle \xrightarrow{c?r} \langle P\{r/q\}, \rho \rangle$ means that the r-system is received from channel c and then it is put into the (free) occurrences of q in P. It is worth noting that there may be more than one free occurrences of a single variable q in P because it is not required that $qv(P_1) \cap qv(P_2) = \emptyset$ in a summation $P \equiv P_1 + P_2$. It should be noted that in $c?q.P$ the variable q is bound and it does not represent concretely the q-system. Instead it is merely a reference to the place where the received system will go. Thus, $c?q.P$ can perform action $c?r$ with $r \neq q$. The side condition $r \notin qv(c?p.P)$ for the input transition is introduced to avoid variable name conflict, and it also makes that $P\{r/q\}$ is well-defined.

- It is particularly worth noting that during performing both the input and output actions, the state of the environment is not changed. Whenever an input action and an output action are performed simultaneously, then passing quantum systems happens in a communication described by the **Comm** rule. It is realised in a "call-by-name (of quantum variables)" scheme and does not change the state of the environment. Since the communication is considered to be internal to the composite process $P \| Q$, the transition $\langle P \| Q, \rho \rangle \xrightarrow{\tau} \langle P' \| Q', \rho \rangle$ in the conclusion of the **Comm** is labelled by the silent action τ, which is not observable from the external.

- From Definition 10.1.4.b, we note that it is required that $fv(P') \cap fv(Q') = \emptyset$ to guarantee that the **Comm** rule is reasonable. However, we do not need to impose this condition into the **Comm** rule because it is a consequence of the

other rules. The verification of this condition is postponed to the end of Lemma 10.2. The same happens to the **Intl1** and **Intl2** rules.
- The **Res** rule means that if the channel in an input or output action α is in L, then process $P \setminus L$ is not allowed to perform α.
- The **Def** rule defines the semantics of recursive definition $A(\overline{q}) \overset{def}{=} P$, meaning that $A(\overline{r})$ can do whatever $P\{\overline{r}/\overline{q}\}$ does. Here, note that variables $\overline{q}$ are substituted by arbitrary variables $\overline{r}$ with the same types as $\overline{q}$.

10.1.3 Examples

To illustrate the transition rules introduced in the last subsection, we give some simple examples. In the first example, we use the language of qCCS to describe how quantum systems are passed between processes:

Example 10.3. Let us consider the following processes:

$$P_1 = c?r.P_1', \qquad P_2 = c!q.P_2'$$

and $P = (P_1 \| P_2) \setminus c$, where $q \notin qv(P_1)$. Then for any state ρ, using the **Comm** and **Res** rules, we see that the only possible transition of P is

$$\langle P, \rho \rangle \overset{\tau}{\to} \langle (P_1'\{q/r\} \| P_2') \setminus c, \rho \rangle. \tag{10.3}$$

Note that in transition (10.3) the q-system is passed from P_2 to P_1 but the state ρ of the environment is not changed. This is reasonable because ρ does not contain any position information of the quantum systems under consideration; more precisely, in a configuration $\langle Q, \rho \rangle$, for each quantum variable p, ρ only describes the state of the p-system, but it does not indicate any subprocess of Q by which the p-system is possessed.

The next two examples show how a unitary transformation is performed after a communication between processes:

Example 10.4. Let P_2 be as in Example 10.3 and

$$Q_1 = c?r.H[r].Q_1', \qquad Q = (Q_1 \| P_2) \setminus c,$$

and $\rho = |0\rangle_q \langle 0| \otimes \rho'$, where $\rho' \in \mathcal{D}(\mathcal{H}_{qVar \setminus \{q\}})$ and $q \notin qv(Q_1)$, then

$$\langle Q, \rho \rangle \overset{\tau}{\to} \langle (H[q].Q_1'\{q/r\} \| P_2') \setminus c, \rho \rangle$$
$$\overset{H[q]}{\to} \langle (Q_1'\{q/r\} \| P_2') \setminus c, |+\rangle_q \langle +| \otimes \rho' \rangle. \tag{10.4}$$

At the beginning of transition (10.4), the state of the q-system is $|0\rangle$. Then the q-system is passed from P_2 to Q_1 and the Hadamard transformation H is performed on it at Q_1. The state of the q-system becomes $|+\rangle = \frac{1}{\sqrt{2}}(|0\rangle + |1\rangle)$ after the transition.

Example 10.5. Suppose that P_2 is as in Example 10.3,

$$R_1 = c?r.CNOT[r,s].R_1', \qquad R = (R_1 \| P_2) \setminus c$$

and $\sigma = |+\rangle_q \langle +| \otimes |0\rangle_s \langle 0| \otimes \sigma'$, where $\sigma' \in \mathcal{D}(\mathcal{H}_{qVar \setminus \{q,s\}})$ and $q \notin qv(R_1)$. Then

$$\langle R, \sigma \rangle \overset{\tau}{\to} \langle (CNOT[q,s].R_1'\{q/r\} \| P_2') \setminus c, \sigma \rangle$$
$$\overset{CNOT[q,s]}{\to} \langle (R_1'\{q/r\} \| P_2') \setminus c, |\beta_{00}\rangle_{qs} \langle \beta_{00}| \otimes \sigma' \rangle \tag{10.5}$$

where $|\beta_{00}\rangle = \frac{1}{\sqrt{2}}(|00\rangle + |11\rangle)$ is the EPR pair.

In transition (10.5), the q-system is passed from P_2 to R_1, and then the *CNOT* operator is applied to it and the s-system together. It is worth noting that the state of the qs-system is separable before the transition, but an entanglement between the q-system and the s-system is created at the end of the transition.

Next let us consider a quantum measurement performed after a communication between two quantum processes.

Example 10.6. Let P_2 be as in Example 10.3 and

$$S_1 = c?r.CNOT[r, s].\mathcal{M}_{0,1}[s].S_1', \qquad S = (S_1 \| P_2)\backslash c,$$

where $\mathcal{M}_{0,1}$ is the quantum operation realised by the measurement of a single qubit in the computational basis $|0\rangle$, $|1\rangle$, with the measurement result ignored; that is,

$$\mathcal{M}_{0,1}(\rho) = P_0 \rho P_0 + P_1 \rho P_1$$

for each $\rho \in \mathcal{D}(\mathcal{H}_2)$, where $P_0 = |0\rangle\langle 0|$ and $P_1 = |1\rangle\langle 1|$. Then for the initial state σ given in Example 10.5,

$$\langle S, \sigma\rangle \xrightarrow{\tau} \langle(CNOT[q, s].\mathcal{M}_{0,1}[s].S_1'\{q/r\}\| P_2')\backslash c, \sigma\rangle$$
$$\xrightarrow{CNOT[q,s]} \langle(\mathcal{M}_{0,1}[s].S_1'\{q/r\}\| P_2')\backslash c, |\beta_{00}\rangle_{qs}\langle\beta_{00}| \otimes \sigma'\rangle \qquad (10.6)$$
$$\xrightarrow{\mathcal{M}_{0,1}[s]} \langle(S_1'\{q/r\}\| P_2')\backslash c, \frac{1}{2}(|00\rangle_{qs}\langle 00| + |11\rangle_{qs}\langle 11|) \otimes \sigma'\rangle.$$

In transition (10.6), the measurement in the computational basis $|0\rangle$, $|1\rangle$ is performed on the s-system. We can see that the q-system and the s-system are always in the same state in the last configuration. This is because they are entangled before the measurement. Indeed, the most interesting thing to observe in Examples 10.5 and 10.6 is how entangled systems behave during computation and communication.

The communication channels in qCCS (named by elements of $qChan$) are implicitly assumed to be noiseless. However, the next example shows that we can formally describe noisy quantum channels in qCCS by combining noiseless communications and quantum operations on the passed systems.

Example 10.7 (Quantum noisy channels). (1) We imagine a simple scenario where Alice sends quantum information to Bob through a noisy channel. Usually, a quantum noisy channel is represented by a superoperator $\mathcal{E}$ (see Section 2.6 and [318], Chapters 8 and 12). Thus, Alice and Bob may be described as processes:

$$P = c_1!q.P', \qquad Q = c_2?s.Q'$$

respectively, and the channel is described as a nullary process constant scheme C of which the defining equation is

$$C \stackrel{def}{=} c_1?r.\mathcal{E}[r].c_2!r.C.$$

Consider process $S = (P\|C\|Q)\backslash\{c_1, c_2\}$. If the information that Alice wants to send is expressed by a quantum state ρ of the q-system, then for any $\rho' \in \mathcal{D}(\mathcal{H}_{qVar\backslash\{q\}})$, we have:

$$\langle S, \rho \otimes \rho'\rangle \xrightarrow{\tau} \langle(P'\|\mathcal{E}[q].c_2!q.C\|Q)\backslash\{c_1, c_2\}, \rho \otimes \rho'\rangle$$
$$\xrightarrow{\mathcal{E}[q]} \langle(P'\|c_2!q.C\|Q)\backslash\{c_1, c_2\}, \mathcal{E}(\rho) \otimes \rho'\rangle$$
$$\xrightarrow{\tau} \langle(P'\|C\|Q'\{q/s\})\backslash\{c_1, c_2\}, \mathcal{E}(\rho) \otimes \rho'\rangle.$$

Here, note that $qv(C)$ does not contain r; otherwise C is not a process. Thus, we have $C\{q/r\} = C$.

(2) Now suppose that a system-environment model of the quantum noisy channel $\mathcal{E}$ is given by

$$\mathcal{E}(\rho) = tr_E\left[PU(\rho \otimes |e_0\rangle\langle e_0|)U^\dagger P\right]$$

for all density operator ρ on $\mathcal{H}_q$, where E is an environment system with Hilbert space $\mathcal{H}_E$, U is a unitary transformation on $\mathcal{H}_q \otimes \mathcal{H}_E$, P is a projector onto some closed subspace of $\mathcal{H}_q \otimes \mathcal{H}_E$, and $|e_0\rangle$ is a fixed state in $\mathcal{H}_E$ (see Theorem 2.3(2)). Let $\mathcal{E}_U$, $\mathcal{E}_P$ and $\mathcal{E}_{tr_E}$ be superoperators on $\mathcal{H}_q \otimes \mathcal{H}_E$ defined as follows:

$$\mathcal{E}_U(\sigma) = U\sigma U^\dagger,$$
$$\mathcal{E}_P(\sigma) = P\sigma P,$$
$$\mathcal{E}_{tr_E}(\sigma) = \sum_k \langle e_k|\sigma|e_k\rangle \otimes |e_0\rangle\langle e_0|$$

for all $\sigma \in \mathcal{D}(\mathcal{H}_q \otimes \mathcal{H}_E)$, where $\{|e_k\rangle\}$ is an orthonormal basis of $\mathcal{H}_E$. We define process constant scheme C' by

$$C'(E) \stackrel{def}{=} c_1?r.\mathcal{E}_U[r, E].\mathcal{E}_P[r, E].\mathcal{E}_{tr_E}[r, E].c_2!r.C'(E).$$

Consider process $S' = (P \| C'(E) \| Q) \backslash \{c_1, c_2\}$. Then for all $\rho \in \mathcal{D}(\mathcal{H}_q)$ and $\rho'' \in \mathcal{D}(\mathcal{H}_{qVar \backslash \{q, E\}})$, the transitions of S' are given as follows:

$$\langle S', \rho \otimes |e_0\rangle \langle e_0| \otimes \rho'' \rangle \stackrel{\tau}{\rightarrow} \langle (P' \| \mathcal{E}_U[q, E].\mathcal{E}_P[q, E].\mathcal{E}_{tr_E}[q, E].c_2!q.C'(E)$$
$$\| Q) \backslash \{c_1, c_2\}, \rho \otimes |e_0\rangle \langle e_0| \otimes \rho'' \rangle$$
$$\stackrel{\mathcal{E}_U[q,E]}{\rightarrow} \langle (P' \| \mathcal{E}_P[q, E].\mathcal{E}_{tr_E}[q, E].c_2!q.C'(E) \| Q) \backslash \{c_1, c_2\}, U(\rho \otimes |e_0\rangle \langle e_0|)U^\dagger \otimes \rho'' \rangle$$
$$\stackrel{\mathcal{E}_P[q,E]}{\rightarrow} \langle (P' \| \mathcal{E}_{tr_E}[q, E].c_2!q.C'(E) \| Q) \backslash \{c_1, c_2\}, PU(\rho \otimes |e_0\rangle \langle e_0|)U^\dagger P \otimes \rho'' \rangle$$
$$\stackrel{\mathcal{E}_{tr_E}[q,E]}{\rightarrow} \langle (P' \| c_2!q.C'(E) \| Q) \backslash \{c_1, c_2\}, \mathcal{E}(\rho) \otimes |e_0\rangle \langle e_0| \otimes \rho'' \rangle$$
$$\stackrel{\tau}{\rightarrow} \langle (P' \| C'(E) \| Q'\{q/s\}) \backslash \{c_1, c_2\}, \mathcal{E}(\rho) \otimes |e_0\rangle \langle e_0| \otimes \rho'' \rangle.$$

It is desirable to have a physical device, called quantum-copying machine, which can produce two copies of an unknown input quantum state at their output. However, recall from the nocloning theorem (Theorem 2.2) that such an ideal quantum-copying machine does not exist. On the other hand, Buzek and Hillery [82] designed an approximate quantum copier. The procedure of such a copier can be described as follows. Suppose that an agent Q wants to copy a (unknown) quantum state, Q sends the state to a copier P through channel c, and P receives it and puts it at place r (called the original mode). First, P has to ask for a new place from another agent R as the copy mode. Then P performs a copying operation on the original and copy modes together, which is represented by a unitary transformation U, independent of the input state. Finally, P will send two (approximate) copies of the original state back to Q through channel c. The following example gives a formal description of the approximate copier in the language of qCCS.

Example 10.8 (Approximate quantum copier). The copier P and agents Q, R may be described as follows:

$$P = c?r.d?s.U[r, s].c!r.c!s.P, \quad Q = c!q.c?u.c?v.Q', \quad R = d!q_0.\textbf{nil},$$

and the whole system can be written as process $S = (P \| Q \| R) \backslash \{c, d\}$. Note that P is a nullary process constant scheme and $r, s \notin qv(P)$. Let $\rho = |\varphi\rangle_q \langle \varphi| \otimes |0\rangle_{q_0} \langle 0| \otimes \sigma$, where $\sigma \in \mathcal{D}(\mathcal{H}_{qVar \backslash \{q, q_0\}})$, $|\varphi\rangle$ is the state to be copied, and the initial state of the copy mode is assumed to be $|0\rangle$. Assume that

$$U|\varphi\rangle_q |0\rangle_{q_0} = |\varphi'\rangle_q |\varphi'\rangle_{q_0}. \tag{10.7}$$

Then the copying process is described by the following transitions:

$$\langle S, \rho \rangle \stackrel{\tau}{\rightarrow} \langle (d?s.U[q, s].c!q.c!s.P \| c?u.c?v.Q' \| R) \backslash \{c, d\}, \rho \rangle$$
$$\stackrel{\tau}{\rightarrow} \langle (U[q, q_0].c!q.c!q_0.P \| c?u.c?v.Q' \| \textbf{nil}) \backslash \{c, d\}, \rho \rangle$$
$$\stackrel{U[q,q_0]}{\rightarrow} \langle (c!q.c!q_0.P \| c?u.c?v.Q' \| \textbf{nil}) \backslash \{c, d\}, \rho' \rangle$$
$$\stackrel{\tau}{\rightarrow} \langle (c!q_0.P \| c?v.Q'\{q/u\} \| \textbf{nil}) \backslash \{c, d\}, \rho' \rangle$$
$$\stackrel{\tau}{\rightarrow} \langle P \| Q'\{q/u\}\{q_0/v\} \| \textbf{nil}) \backslash \{c, d\}, \rho' \rangle,$$

where $\rho' = |\varphi'\rangle_q \langle \varphi'| \otimes |\varphi'\rangle_{q_0} \langle \varphi'| \otimes \sigma$.

The nocloning theorem excludes the possibility that for all $|\varphi\rangle \in \mathcal{H}_q$, $|\varphi'\rangle = |\varphi\rangle$ in Eq. (10.7). But it is shown in [82] that there exists a (universal) copier P which approximately copies the input state $|\varphi\rangle$ such that the quality of the output state $|\varphi'\rangle$, measured by the norm of the difference between $|\varphi\rangle$ and $|\varphi'\rangle$, does not depend on $|\varphi\rangle$.

10.1.4 Properties of transitions

Now we establish some basic properties of the transition relation defined in Section 10.1.2. Their proofs can be carried out by induction on the depth of inference. More precisely, according to Definition 10.4, every transition $\langle P, \rho \rangle \xrightarrow{\alpha} \langle P, \rho' \rangle$ in the operational semantics of quantum processes is derived by applying a finite number of transition rules from Fig. 10.1. Note that there are two transitions in the premise of the **Comm** rule. Then the derivation of a transition can be thought of as a tree (but not simply a sequence) with each of its nodes associated with a transition. Consequently, the proof of a property about the transition under consideration can be done by induction on the depth (i.e. height) of its derivation tree. This is a standard proof technique widely used in semantics of programming languages. The proofs of most of the results in this section are routine, but some need very careful analysis. To help the reader master the proof technique, we will present the detailed proof of Lemma 10.2. But for readability, the proofs of other results will be postponed to Appendix A.6.1.

First, we observe how does the environment (i.e. the state of all quantum variables) of a configuration change in a transition.

Lemma 10.1. 1. *If $\langle P, \rho \rangle \xrightarrow{\mathcal{E}[\overline{q}]} \langle P', \rho' \rangle$, then*
   a. $\rho' = \mathcal{E}_{\overline{q}}(\rho)$*; and*
   b. $\langle P, \sigma \rangle \xrightarrow{\mathcal{E}[\overline{q}]} \langle P', \mathcal{E}_{\overline{q}}(\sigma) \rangle$ *holds for all $\sigma \in \mathcal{D}(\mathcal{H}_{all})$.*
2. *If $\langle P, \rho \rangle \xrightarrow{\alpha} \langle P', \rho' \rangle$ and α is not of the form $\mathcal{E}[\overline{q}]$, then*
   a. $\rho = \rho'$*; and*
   b. $\langle P, \sigma \rangle \xrightarrow{\alpha} \langle P', \sigma \rangle$ *holds for all $\sigma \in \mathcal{D}(\mathcal{H}_{all})$. Thus, we can simply write $P \xrightarrow{\alpha} P'$.*

The above lemma indicates that only a quantum operation can change the environment of a configuration; other actions (i.e. silent action, input, output, and communication) cannot. The proof of this lemma is routine, and left as an exercise for the reader.

Next we see how the variables in an action are related to the free variables of a process performing this action and those of the process immediately after it.

Lemma 10.2. *If $\langle P, \rho \rangle \xrightarrow{\alpha} \langle P', \rho' \rangle$, then*
1. $fv(\alpha) \subseteq qv(P) \setminus qv(P')$*; and*
2. $qv(P') \subseteq qv(P) \cup \{bv(\alpha)\}$*.*

Proof. The proof is carried out by induction on the depth of inference. The induction hypothesis assumes that the conclusion is true whenever the depth of a derivation tree of $\langle P, \rho \rangle \xrightarrow{\alpha} \langle P', \rho' \rangle$ is smaller than k. Now suppose that $\langle P, \rho \rangle \xrightarrow{\alpha} \langle P', \rho' \rangle$ has a derivation tree of depth k. We consider how the last step is derived; that is, what is the last rule used in the derivation tree. Then we need to consider the following cases:

Case 1. The last rule is **Intl2**. Let $P = P_1 \| Q$, $\langle P_1, \rho \rangle \xrightarrow{\alpha} \langle P_1', \rho' \rangle$ and $P' = P_1' \| Q$. Then the induction hypothesis implies that $fv(\alpha) \subseteq qv(P_1) \setminus qv(P_1')$ and $qv(P_1') \subseteq qv(P_1) \cup \{bv(\alpha)\}$. It follows immediately that

$$qv(P') = qv(P_1') \cup qv(Q) \subseteq qv(P_1) \cup \{bv(\alpha)\} \cup qv(Q)$$
$$= qv(P) \cup \{bv(\alpha)\}.$$

On the other hand, we have

$$qv(P_1) \setminus qv(P_1') \subseteq qv(P_1) \cup qv(Q) \setminus qv(P_1') \cup qv(Q)$$
$$= qv(P) \setminus qv(P')$$

because $qv(P_1) \cap qv(Q) = \emptyset$. This implies $fv(\alpha) \subseteq qv(P) \setminus qv(P')$.

Case 2. The last rule is **Comm**. Suppose that $P = P_1 \| Q$,

$$\langle P_1, \rho \rangle \xrightarrow{c?q} \langle P_1', \rho \rangle, \qquad \langle Q, \rho \rangle \xrightarrow{c!q} \langle Q', \rho \rangle$$

and $P' = P_1' \| Q'$. Then $\alpha = \tau$ and $qv(\alpha) = \emptyset \subseteq qv(P) \setminus qv(P')$. In addition, the induction hypothesis leads to

$$qv(P') = qv(P_1') \cup qv(Q') \subseteq qv(P_1) \cup \{q\} \cup qv(Q).$$

We also have $q \in qv(Q) \setminus qv(Q') \subseteq qv(Q)$. Thus,

$$qv(P') \subseteq qv(P_1) \cup qv(Q) = qv(P) = qv(P) \cup \{bv(\alpha)\}.$$

Other cases are similar, and thus we complete the proof. □

This lemma enables us to verify that the **Intl1**, **Intl2**, and **Comm** rules are well-defined. For instance, let us consider **Comm**. If

$$\langle P, \rho \rangle \xrightarrow{c?q} \langle P', \rho \rangle \text{ and } \langle Q, \rho \rangle \xrightarrow{c!q} \langle Q', \rho \rangle,$$

then using the above lemma we obtain $qv(P') \subseteq qv(P) \cup \{q\}$, $qv(Q') \subseteq qv(Q)$ and $q \notin qv(Q')$. If $P \| Q \in \mathcal{P}$ is a process, this obviously leads to $qv(P') \cap qv(Q') = \emptyset$ because $qv(P) \cap qv(Q) = \emptyset$. The other two rules can be dealt with in a similar way.

The next lemma shows that the variable in an input can be changed in a transition provided a corresponding modification of the process after the transition is made. This is because variable q in an input action $c?q$ is a bound variable (rather than a free variable).

Lemma 10.3. *If $\langle P, \rho \rangle \xrightarrow{c?q} \langle P', \rho \rangle$ and $r \notin qv(P)$, then $\langle P, \rho \rangle \xrightarrow{c?r} \langle P'', \rho \rangle$ for some $P'' \equiv_\alpha P'\{r/q\}$.*

Exercise 10.1. Prove Lemma 10.3.

The following two lemmas carefully examine interference of substitution and transition on each other. Let f be a substitution (see Definition 10.2). We define its extension on actions by

$$f(\tau) = \tau, \quad f(\mathcal{E}[\overline{q}]) = \mathcal{E}[f][f(\overline{q})], \quad f(c?q) = c?q, \quad f(c!q) = c!f(q).$$

Lemma 10.4. *If $\langle P, \rho \rangle \xrightarrow{\alpha} \langle P', \rho' \rangle$ and $f(bv(\alpha)) = bv(\alpha)$, then*

$$\langle P[f], f(\rho) \rangle \xrightarrow{f(\alpha)} \langle P'', f(\rho') \rangle$$

for some $P'' \equiv_\alpha P'[f]$.

Proof. See Appendix A.6.1. □

As a (partial) inverse of the above lemma, we have:

Lemma 10.5. *If $\langle P[f], f(\rho) \rangle \xrightarrow{\alpha} \langle Q, \sigma \rangle$ and $f(bv(\alpha)) = bv(\alpha)$, then for some β, P' and ρ', it holds that $\langle P, \rho \rangle \xrightarrow{\beta} \langle P', \rho' \rangle$, $Q \equiv_\alpha P'[f]$, $\sigma = f(\rho')$ and $\alpha = f(\beta)$.*

Proof. See Appendix A.6.1. □

Finally, we exhibit a certain invariance of transitions under α-conversion.

Lemma 10.6. *Let $P_1 \equiv_\alpha P_2$. Then*

1. *if $\langle P_1, \rho \rangle \xrightarrow{\alpha} \langle P_1', \rho' \rangle$ and α is not an input, then $\langle P_2, \rho \rangle \xrightarrow{\alpha} \langle P_2', \rho' \rangle$ for some $P_2' \equiv_\alpha P_1'$;*

2. *if $\langle P_1, \rho \rangle \xrightarrow{c?q} \langle P_1', \rho \rangle$, then for any $r \notin qv(P_2)$, $\langle P_2, \rho \rangle \xrightarrow{c?r} \langle P_2', \rho \rangle$ for some $P_2' \equiv_\alpha P_1'\{r/q\}$.*

Exercise 10.2. Prove Lemma 10.6.

10.2 Bisimulations between quantum processes

Bisimulation is a central notion in classical process algebras. It is a powerful tool for specifying and reasoning about equivalence of communicating and computing systems. Intuitively, two systems are bisimilar if they behave in the same way in the sense that one system can simulate the other and vice versa, and they cannot be distinguished from each other by an external observer. There are mainly two variants of bisimulations, namely *strong bisimulation* and *weak bisimulation*. The former is used in the situations where the silent action τ is treated exactly like any other actions and thus can be recognised by an external observer, and the latter is defined with the assumption that the silent action τ cannot be recognised by an external observer.

In this section, we introduce the notion of bisimulation for quantum processes defined in the previous section. We will mainly consider strong bisimulation because the basic idea of weak bisimulation is similar to that of strong bisimulation although the treatment of weak bisimulations in applications is much subtler.

10.2.1 Basic definitions

We first define the notion of strong bisimulation between configurations.

Definition 10.5. A symmetric relation $\mathcal{R} \subseteq qCon \times qCon$ is called a strong bisimulation if for any $\langle P, \rho \rangle, \langle Q, \sigma \rangle \in qCon$, $\langle P, \rho \rangle \mathcal{R} \langle Q, \sigma \rangle$ implies:

1. whenever $\langle P, \rho \rangle \xrightarrow{\alpha} \langle P', \rho' \rangle$ and α is not an input, then for some Q' and σ', it holds that $\langle Q, \sigma \rangle \xrightarrow{\alpha} \langle Q', \sigma' \rangle$ and $\langle P', \rho' \rangle \mathcal{R} \langle Q', \sigma' \rangle$;
2. whenever $\langle P, \rho \rangle \xrightarrow{c?q} \langle P', \rho \rangle$ and $q \notin qv(P) \cup qv(Q)$, then for some Q', it holds that $\langle Q, \sigma \rangle \xrightarrow{c?q} \langle Q', \sigma \rangle$ and $\langle P'\{r/q\}, \rho \rangle \mathcal{R} \langle Q'\{r/q\}, \sigma \rangle$ for all $r \notin qv(P') \cup qv(Q') \setminus \{q\}$.

Intuitively, clause 1 in the above definition (together with the symmetry of $\mathcal{R}$) means that two configurations $\langle P, \rho \rangle$ and $\langle Q, \sigma \rangle$ can simulate each other; that is, if one of them can perform an action α, then the other can do the same. It should be noted that strong bisimulation $\mathcal{R}$ is defined in a recursive way, since it is required that the two configurations $\langle P', \rho' \rangle$ and $\langle Q', \sigma' \rangle$ after the action satisfy the relation $\mathcal{R}$ too. Input actions are treated separately in clause 2. Since q in c?q is a bound variable, it can be substituted by other variables r. Here, we require $r \notin qv(P') \cup qv(Q') \setminus \{q\}$. If we would not impose this requirement, then two previously different quantum states may become the same state after substitution $\{r/q\}$. This is forbidden by the nocloning principle of quantum information.

Then strong bisimilarity between two configurations can be defined as the weakest (i.e. largest) strong bisimulation between them.

Definition 10.6. For any $\langle P, \rho \rangle, \langle Q, \sigma \rangle \in qCon$, we say that $\langle P, \rho \rangle$ and $\langle Q, \sigma \rangle$ are strongly bisimilar, written

$$\langle P, \rho \rangle \sim \langle Q, \sigma \rangle,$$

if $\langle P, \rho \rangle \mathcal{R} \langle Q, \sigma \rangle$ for some strong bisimulation $\mathcal{R}$. In other words, the strong bisimilarity on $qCon$ is the greatest strong bisimulation:

$$\sim = \bigcup \{\mathcal{R} : \mathcal{R} \text{ is a strong bisimulation}\}.$$

The following lemma gives a recursive characterisation of strong bisimilarity between configurations. It is often useful in establishing strong bisimilarity between processes in applications.

Lemma 10.7. *For any $\langle P, \rho \rangle, \langle Q, \sigma \rangle \in qCon$, $\langle P, \rho \rangle \sim \langle Q, \sigma \rangle$ if and only if:*

1. *whenever $\langle P, \rho \rangle \xrightarrow{\alpha} \langle P', \rho' \rangle$ and α is not an input, then for some Q' and σ', it holds that $\langle Q, \sigma \rangle \xrightarrow{\alpha} \langle Q', \sigma' \rangle$ and $\langle P', \rho' \rangle \sim \langle Q', \sigma' \rangle$;*
2. *whenever $\langle P, \rho \rangle \xrightarrow{c?q} \langle P', \rho \rangle$ and $q \notin qv(P) \cup qv(Q)$, then for some Q', it holds that $\langle Q, \sigma \rangle \xrightarrow{c?q} \langle Q', \sigma \rangle$ and $\langle P'\{r/q\}, \rho \rangle \sim \langle Q'\{r/q\}, \sigma \rangle$ for all $r \notin qv(P') \cup qv(Q') \setminus \{q\}$,*

and the symmetric forms of clauses 1 and 2.

Proof. ($\Rightarrow$) If $\langle P, \rho \rangle \sim \langle Q, \sigma \rangle$, then there exists a strong bisimulation $\mathcal{R}$ such that $\langle P, \rho \rangle \mathcal{R} \langle Q, \sigma \rangle$. By definition, clauses 1 and 2 in Definition 10.5 and their symmetric forms are thus satisfied. Since $\mathcal{R} \subseteq \sim$, clauses 1 and 2 in this lemma and their symmetric forms are satisfied too.

($\Leftarrow$) We define relation:

$$\mathcal{R} = \{((\langle P, \rho \rangle, \langle Q, \sigma \rangle) : \text{configurations } \langle P, \rho \rangle \text{ and } \langle Q, \sigma \rangle \text{ satisfy}$$
$$\text{conditions 1 and 2 in this lemma and their symmetric forms}\}. \tag{10.8}$$

It is routine to prove that $\mathcal{R}$ is a strong bisimulation. Therefore, if $\langle P, \rho \rangle$ and $\langle Q, \sigma \rangle)$ satisfy clauses 1, 2 and their symmetric forms, then $((\langle P, \rho \rangle, \langle Q, \sigma \rangle) \in \mathcal{R}$. By definition, we have $\langle P, \rho \rangle \sim \langle Q, \sigma \rangle$. $\square$

Now strong bisimilarity between two processes may be defined by comparing them in the same environment.

Definition 10.7. For any quantum processes $P, Q \in \mathcal{P}$, we say that P and Q are strongly bisimilar, written $P \sim Q$, if $\langle P, \rho \rangle \sim \langle Q, \rho \rangle$ for all $\rho \in \mathcal{D}(\mathcal{H})$.

The next proposition shows that α-convertibility is stronger than strong bisimilarity, and thus strong bisimilarity is preserved by α-conversion.

Proposition 10.1. *If $P_1 \equiv_\alpha P_2$, then $P_1 \sim P_2$.*

Proof. It is easy to show that relation

$$\mathcal{R} = \{(\langle P_1, \rho \rangle, \langle P_2, \rho \rangle) : P_1 \equiv_\alpha P_2\} \qquad (10.9)$$

is a strong bisimulation by using Lemma 10.6. □

Exercise 10.3. Prove the relations $\mathcal{R}$ in Eqs (10.8) and (10.9) are both strong bisimulations.

Proof technique of 'strong bisimulation up to': It is often difficult to prove that a relation $\mathcal{R}$ is a bisimulation directly. To ease this difficulty, the 'up to' technique has been developed and widely used in classical process algebras. We now generalise this powerful proof technique to quantum processes.

Let us first consider bisimulations up to substitution. For any relation $\mathcal{R} \subseteq qCon \times qCon$, its extension with substitution is defined as

$$sub(\mathcal{R}) = \{(\langle P[f], f(\rho) \rangle, \langle Q[f], f(\sigma) \rangle) :$$
$$\langle P, \rho \rangle \mathcal{R} \langle Q, \sigma \rangle \text{ and } f \text{ is a substitution}\}.$$

Then Definition 10.5 can be generalised to the following:

Definition 10.8. A symmetric relation $\mathcal{R} \subseteq qCon \times qCon$ is called a strong bisimulation up to substitution if for any $\langle P, \rho \rangle, \langle Q, \sigma \rangle \in qCon$, $\langle P, \rho \rangle \mathcal{R} \langle Q, \sigma \rangle$ implies:

1. whenever $\langle P, \rho \rangle \xrightarrow{\alpha} \langle P', \rho' \rangle$ and α is not an input, then for some $\langle Q', \sigma' \rangle$, it holds that $\langle Q, \sigma \rangle \xrightarrow{\alpha} \langle Q', \sigma' \rangle$ and $\langle P', \rho' \rangle sub(\mathcal{R}) \langle Q', \sigma' \rangle$; and
2. whenever $\langle P, \rho \rangle \xrightarrow{c?q} \langle P', \rho \rangle$ and $q \notin qv(P) \cup qv(Q)$, then for some Q', it holds that $\langle Q, \sigma \rangle \xrightarrow{c?q} \langle Q', \sigma \rangle$ and for all $r \notin qv(P') \cup qv(Q') \setminus \{q\}$, $\langle P'\{r/q\}, \rho \rangle sub(\mathcal{R}) \langle Q'\{r/q\}, \sigma \rangle$.

Obviously, it holds that $\mathcal{R} \subseteq sub(\mathcal{R})$. So, bisimulation up to substitution is a notion weaker than bisimulation itself. Furthermore, we have the following:

Lemma 10.8. *If $\mathcal{R}$ is a strong bisimulation up to substitution then $\mathcal{R} \subseteq \sim$.*

Exercise 10.4. Prove Lemma 10.8.

Similarly, we can define the notion of strong bisimulation up to $\sim$.

Definition 10.9. A symmetric relation $\mathcal{R} \subseteq qCon \times qCon$ is called a strong bisimulation up to $\sim$ if for any $\langle P, \rho \rangle, \langle Q, \sigma \rangle \in qCon$, $\langle P, \rho \rangle \mathcal{R} \langle Q, \sigma \rangle$ implies:

1. whenever $\langle P, \rho \rangle \xrightarrow{\alpha} \langle P', \rho' \rangle$ and α is not an input, then for some $\langle Q', \sigma' \rangle$, it holds that $\langle Q, \sigma \rangle \xrightarrow{\alpha} \langle Q', \sigma' \rangle$ and $\langle P', \rho' \rangle \sim \mathcal{R} \sim \langle Q', \sigma' \rangle$; and
2. whenever $\langle P, \rho \rangle \xrightarrow{c?q} \langle P', \rho \rangle$ and $q \notin qv(P) \cup qv(Q)$, then for some Q', it holds that $\langle Q, \sigma \rangle \xrightarrow{c?q} \langle Q', \sigma \rangle$ and for all $r \notin qv(P') \cup qv(Q') \setminus \{q\}$, $\langle P'\{r/q\}, \rho \rangle \sim \mathcal{R} \sim \langle Q'\{r/q\}, \sigma \rangle$.

It is clear that bisimulation up to $\sim$ is also a notion weaker than bisimulation, and we also have:

Lemma 10.9. *If $\mathcal{R}$ is a strong bisimulation up to $\sim$ then $\mathcal{R} \subseteq \sim$.*

Exercise 10.5. Prove Lemma 10.9. Hint: Lemma 10.8 is needed this proof.

The above two lemmas provide a basis for the proof technique of "strong bisimulation up tp": to prove $\langle P, \rho \rangle \sim \langle Q, \sigma \rangle$, it suffices to find a bisimulation $\mathcal{R}$ up to substitution or $\sim$ such that $(\langle P, \rho \rangle, \langle Q, \sigma \rangle) \in \mathcal{R}$. This proof technique will be needed in proving Proposition 10.5 and Theorem 10.2.

10.2.2 Algebraic laws

In this subsection, we establish a series of algebraic laws that can be used in reasoning about equivalence between quantum processes in the sense of strong bisimilarity. The basic idea in proving these laws is as follows. To prove strong bisimilarity $P \sim Q$, we only need to construct a strong bisimulation that contains pairs $(\langle P, \rho \rangle, \langle Q, \rho \rangle)$ of configurations for all environment ρ. Some proofs of the results in this subsection are routine, but others are quite involved. We will present the detailed proof of Proposition 10.2 in order to help the reader master the proof technique. For readability, however, the proofs of other results will be left to Appendix A.6.2.

The first proposition shows that up to strong bisimilarity, quantum processes enjoy commutativity, associativity, idempotent law and unit element under nondeterministic choice, parallel composition, and channel restriction.

Proposition 10.2. *For any $P, Q, R \in \mathcal{P}$, and $K, L \subseteq qChan$, we have:*

1. $P + Q \sim Q + P$;
2. $P + (Q + R) \sim (P + Q) + R$;
3. $P + P \sim P$;
4. $P + \mathbf{nil} \sim P$;
5. $P \| Q \sim Q \| P$;
6. $P \| (Q \| R) \sim (P \| Q) \| R$;
7. $P \| \mathbf{nil} \sim P$;
8. $P \backslash L \sim P$ *if* $cn(P) \cap L = \emptyset$, *where* $cn(P)$ *is the set of free channel names in* P;
9. $(P \backslash K) \backslash L \sim P \backslash (K \cup L)$.

Proof. The clauses 1–4 may be proved by using Lemma 10.7, and the clauses 5–9 may be proved by constructing appropriate strong bisimulation. Here, we only prove clause 6 as an example. Put

$$\mathcal{R} = \{ (\langle P \| (Q \| R), \rho \rangle, \langle (P \| Q) \| R, \rho \rangle) : P, Q, R \in \mathcal{P} \text{ and } \rho \in \mathcal{D}(\mathcal{H}) \}$$

It suffices to show that $\mathcal{R}$ is a strong bisimulation. Suppose that

$$\langle P \| (Q \| R), \rho \rangle \xrightarrow{\alpha} \langle S, \rho' \rangle. \tag{10.10}$$

We only consider the following two cases, and the others are easy or similar.

Case 1. The transition (10.10) is derived from $\langle Q, \rho \rangle \xrightarrow{c?q} \langle Q', \rho \rangle$ and $\langle R, \rho \rangle \xrightarrow{c!q} \langle R', \rho \rangle$ by **Comm**. Then $\alpha = \tau$, $\rho' = \rho$ and $S = P \| (Q' \| R')$. It follows from Lemma 10.2 that $q \in qv(R)$. This leads to $q \notin qv(P \| Q) = qv(P) \cup qv(Q)$ because $(P \| Q) \| R \in \mathcal{P}$. Consequently, we may apply the **Intl1** rule to assert that

$$\langle P \| Q, \rho \rangle \xrightarrow{c?q} \langle P \| Q', \rho \rangle$$

and furthermore by the **Comm** rule we obtain

$$\langle (P \| Q) \| R, \rho \rangle \xrightarrow{\tau} \langle (P \| Q') \| R', \rho \rangle.$$

Now it suffices to note that $\langle S, \rho \rangle \mathcal{R} \langle (P \| Q') \| R', \rho \rangle$.

Case 2. $\alpha = c?x$, $x \notin qv(P \| (Q \| R)) \cup qv((P \| Q) \| R) = qv(P) \cup qv(Q) \cup qv(R)$ and the transition (10.10) is derived from $\langle P, \rho \rangle \xrightarrow{c?q} \langle P', \rho \rangle$ by **Intl1**. Then $\rho' = \rho$ and $S = P' \| (Q \| R)$. Since $q \notin qv(Q)$, it follows from the **Intl1** rule that $\langle P \| Q, \rho \rangle \xrightarrow{c?q} \langle P' \| Q, \rho \rangle$. We also have $q \notin qv(R)$. Then using the **Intl1** rule once again we obtain

$$\langle (P \| Q) \| R, \rho \rangle \xrightarrow{c?q} \langle (P' \| Q) \| R, \rho \rangle.$$

Finally, we note that for each $r \notin qv(P' \| (Q \| R)) \cup qv((P' \| Q) \| R) \backslash \{q\}$, it holds that $S\{r/q\} = P'\{r/q\} \| (Q \| R)$ and

$$((P' \| Q) \| R)\{r/q\} = (P'\{r/q\} \| Q) \| R.$$

Then it follows that

$$\langle S\{r/q\}, \rho \rangle \mathcal{R} \langle ((P' \| Q) \| R)\{r/q\}, \rho \rangle. \qquad \square$$

The next proposition presents an expansion law for a typical distributed system expressed as a parallel composition with certain channel restriction. The right-hand side of the law describes the immediate actions of such a distributed system (up to strong bisimilarity), and it can be thought of as a summarisation of the transition rules **Intel1**, **Intl2**, and **Comm** (under the channel restriction).

Proposition 10.3 (Expansion law). *For any $P, Q \in \mathcal{P}$, we have:*

$$(P\|Q)\backslash L \sim \sum\{\alpha.(P'\|Q)\backslash L : P \xrightarrow{\alpha} P' \text{ and } cn(\alpha) \notin L\}$$
$$+ \sum\{\alpha.(P\|Q')\backslash L : Q \xrightarrow{\alpha} Q' \text{ and } cn(\alpha) \notin L\}$$
$$+ \sum\{\tau.(P'\|Q')\backslash L : P \xrightarrow{c?q} P' \text{ and } Q \xrightarrow{c!q} Q', \text{ or } P \xrightarrow{c!q} P' \text{ and } Q \xrightarrow{c?q} Q'\}.$$

Proof. Write S for the process in the right-hand side. Then it is routine to show that $\langle (P\|Q)\backslash L, \rho \rangle \sim \langle S, \rho \rangle$ for all $\rho \in \mathcal{D}(\mathcal{H})$. □

Exercise 10.6. Complete the proof of Proposition 10.3.

10.2.3 Congruence

In this subsection, we show that strong bisimilarity is a congruence relation with respect to all combinators in qCCS; that is, it is preserved by these combinators. This congruence property enables us to prove strong bisimilarity between two large processes from strong bisimilarity between their components. A combination of the congruence property and the algebraic laws developed in the last subsection provides us with a powerful technique for reasoning about equivalence of distributed and communicating quantum systems.

First, the following proposition indicates that strong bisimilarity is preserved by substitution of quantum variables.

Proposition 10.4. *For any $P, Q \in \mathcal{P}$ and for any substitution f, $P \sim Q$ if and only if $P[f] \sim Q[f]$.*

Proof. The proof of this proposition requires careful manipulation of variables; see Appendix A.6.2 for the details. □

Next we can prove that strong bisimilarity is preserved by recursive definition, prefixes (silent action τ, quantum operation $\mathcal{E}[\overline{q}]$, output $c!q$ and input $c?q$), nondeterministic choice, parallel composition, and channel restriction.

Theorem 10.1. 1. *If $A \stackrel{def}{=} P$ then $A \sim P$.*
2. *If $P \sim Q$, then we have:*
  a. $\tau.P \sim \tau.Q$;
  b. $\mathcal{E}[\overline{q}].P \sim \mathcal{E}[\overline{q}].Q$;
  c. $c!q.P \sim c!q.Q$;
  d. $c?q.P \sim c?q.Q$;
  e. $P + R \sim Q + R$;
  f. $P\|R \sim Q\|R$;
  g. $P\backslash L \sim Q\backslash L$.

Proof. The proofs of 1, 2.a–c, and 2.e are routine applications of Lemma 10.7, and 2.d may be proved by using Lemma 10.7 and Proposition 10.4. For 2.g, we only need to show that

$$\mathcal{R} = \{((\langle P\backslash L, \rho \rangle, \langle Q\backslash L, \sigma \rangle)) : \langle P, \rho \rangle \sim \langle Q, \sigma \rangle\}$$

is a strong bisimulation, and the routine details are omitted.

The proof of 2.f is not straightforward as others. Indeed, it is tricky to construct a strong bisimulation equating $P\|R$ and $Q\|R$. The major difficulty arises from interference between sequential quantum computation and communicating quantum systems. The key technique used in the proof is inserting a properly chosen quantum operation into an existing sequence of quantum operations. Furthermore, the proof requires a very careful analysis of interplay between quantum variables, sequential applications of superoperators, and communication of quantum systems as well as subtle treatment of substitution of quantum variables. We leave the involved proof details to Appendix A.6.2. □

10.2.4 Recursion

Theorem 10.1.1 shows that strong bisimilarity is preserved by recursive definition with process constants. In this subsection, we generalise this result to a more general recursive scheme. To this end, we assume a set of process variable schemes, ranged over by $\mathbf{X}, \mathbf{Y}, \ldots$. For each process variable scheme $\mathbf{X}$, a nonnegative arity $ar(\mathbf{X})$ is assigned to it. If $\overline{q} = q_1, \ldots, q_{ar(\mathbf{X})}$ is a tuple of distinct quantum variables, $\mathbf{X}(\overline{q})$ is called a process variable. Then the syntax of qCCS can be expanded as in the following:

Definition 10.10. Quantum process expressions are defined by adding the following clause into Definition 10.1 (and replacing the word "process" by the phrase "process expression"):

- each process variable $\mathbf{X}(\overline{q})$ is a process expression and its free quantum variables are $qv(\mathbf{X}(\overline{q})) = \{\overline{q}\}$.

We use metavariables $\mathbf{E}, \mathbf{F}, \ldots$ to range over process expressions.

Suppose that $\mathbf{E}$ is a process expression, and $\{\mathbf{X}_i(\overline{q}_i) : i \leq m\}$ is a family of process variables. If $\{P_i : i \leq m\}$ is a family of processes such that $qv(P_i) \subseteq \{\overline{q}_i\}$ for all $i \leq m$, then we write

$$\mathbf{E}\left\{\mathbf{X}_i(\overline{q}_i) := P_i, i \leq m\right\}$$

for the process obtained by replacing simultaneously $\mathbf{X}_i\{\overline{r}_i\}$ in $\mathbf{E}$ with $P_i\{\overline{r}/\overline{q}\}$ for all $i \leq m$.

The notion of strong bisimilarity for quantum processes can be naturally generalised to quantum process expressions.

Definition 10.11. Let $\mathbf{E}$ and $\mathbf{F}$ be process expressions containing at most process variable schemes $\mathbf{X}_i$ $(i \leq m)$. If for all families $\{P_i\}$ of processes with $qv(P_i) \subseteq \{\overline{q}_i\}, i \leq m$,

$$\mathbf{E}\left\{\mathbf{X}_i(\overline{q}_i) := P_i, i \leq m\right\} \sim \mathbf{F}\left\{\mathbf{X}_i(\overline{q}_i) := P_i, i \leq m\right\},$$

then we say that $\mathbf{E}$ and $\mathbf{F}$ are strongly bisimilar and write $\mathbf{E} \sim \mathbf{F}$.

The following proposition shows that a more general recursive definition than that in Theorem 10.1.1 preserves strong bisimilarity too.

Proposition 10.5. *Let $\{A_i : i \leq m\}$ and $\{B_i : i \leq m\}$ be two families of process constant schemes, and let $\{\mathbf{E}_i : i \leq m\}$ and $\{\mathbf{F}_i : i \leq m\}$ contain at most process variable schemes $\mathbf{X}_i$ $(i \leq m)$. If for all $i \leq m$, we have: $\mathbf{E}_i \sim \mathbf{F}_i$, and*

$$A_i(\overline{q}_i) \stackrel{def}{=} \mathbf{E}_i\left\{\mathbf{X}_j(\overline{q}_j) := A_j(\overline{q}_j), j \leq m\right\},$$
$$B_i(\overline{q}_i) \stackrel{def}{=} \mathbf{F}_i\left\{\mathbf{X}_j(\overline{q}_j) := B_j(\overline{q}_j), j \leq m\right\},$$

then $A_i(\overline{q}_i) \sim B_i(\overline{q}_i)$ for all $i \leq m$.

Proof. For simplicity, we write $\mathbf{E}(A)$ for $\mathbf{E}\{\mathbf{X}(\overline{q}) := A(\overline{q})\}$ for any process expression $\mathbf{E}$, process variable scheme $\mathbf{X}$ and process constant scheme A. We only present the proof for the simplest case where $A(\overline{q}) \stackrel{def}{=} \mathbf{E}(A)$, $B(\overline{q}) \stackrel{def}{=} \mathbf{F}(B)$, and $\mathbf{E} \sim \mathbf{F}$, and it can be generalised to the general case without any essential difficulty. We set

$$\mathcal{R} = \{(\langle \mathbf{G}(A), \rho\rangle, \langle \mathbf{G}(B), \rho\rangle) : \mathbf{G} \text{ contains at most}$$
$$\text{the process variable scheme } \mathbf{X} \text{ and } \rho \in \mathcal{D}(\mathcal{H})\}.$$

With Lemma 10.9, it suffices to show that $\mathcal{R}$ is a strong bisimulation up to $\sim$. Suppose that

$$\langle \mathbf{G}(A), \rho\rangle \stackrel{\alpha}{\rightarrow} \langle P, \rho'\rangle. \tag{10.11}$$

Then it suffices to prove the following two claims:

Claim 1. If α is not an input, then for some Q, $\langle \mathbf{G}(B), \rho\rangle \stackrel{\alpha}{\rightarrow} \langle Q, \rho'\rangle$, and $\langle P, \rho'\rangle \sim \langle P_1, \rho'\rangle \mathcal{R} \langle Q_1, \rho'\rangle \sim \langle Q, \rho'\rangle$ for some P_1, Q_1;

Claim 2. If $\alpha = c?q$ and $q \notin qv(\mathbf{G}(A)) \cup qv(\mathbf{G}(B))$, then for some Q, $\langle \mathbf{G}(B), \rho\rangle \stackrel{c?q}{\rightarrow} \langle Q, \rho\rangle$, and for all $r \notin qv(P) \cup qv(Q) \setminus \{q\}$,

$$\langle P\{r/q\}, \rho' = \rho\rangle \sim \langle P_1, \rho\rangle \mathcal{R} \langle Q_1, \rho\rangle \sim \langle Q\{r/q\}, \rho\rangle.$$

for some P_1, Q_1.

Note that the above claims are a little bit stronger than the two conditions in Definition 10.9, where the environments of the configurations involved in $\sim \mathcal{R} \sim$ are not required to be the same.

The proof of these two claims is very involved. For readability, we postpone it to Appendix A.6.3. ☐

To conclude this section, we consider the solutions to recursive equations with respect to strong bisimilarity. A process variable scheme $\mathbf{X}$ is said to be weakly guarded in a process expression $\mathbf{E}$ if every occurrence of $\mathbf{X}$ in $\mathbf{E}$ is within a subexpression of the form $\alpha.\mathbf{F}$. The following lemma describes the transitions of weakly guarded process expressions:

Lemma 10.10. *If* $\mathbf{X}_i$ *($i \leq m$) are weakly guarded in* $\mathbf{E}$*, and*

$$\langle \mathbf{E}\{\mathbf{X}_i(\widetilde{q}_i) := P_i, i \leq m\}, \rho \rangle \to \langle P', \rho' \rangle,$$

then for some $\mathbf{E}'$*, we have:*

1. $P' = \mathbf{E}'\{\mathbf{X}_i(\widetilde{q}_i) := P_i, i \leq m\}$*; and*
2. $\langle \mathbf{E}\{\mathbf{X}_i(\widetilde{q}_i) := Q_i, i \leq m\}, \rho \rangle \to \langle \mathbf{E}'\{\mathbf{X}_i(\widetilde{q}_i) := Q_i, i \leq m\}, \rho' \rangle.$

Proof. Induction on the structure of $\mathbf{E}$. ☐

Under the assumption of weakly guarded process variables, the following theorem shows uniqueness of solutions of recursive equations up to strong bisimilarity.

Theorem 10.2. *Suppose that quantum process expressions* $\mathbf{E}_i$ *($i \leq m$) contain at most process variable schemes* $\mathbf{X}_i$ *($i \leq m$), and each* $\mathbf{X}_i$ *is weakly guarded in each* $\mathbf{E}_j$ *($i, j \leq m$). If processes* P_i *and* Q_i *($i \leq m$) satisfy that, for all* $i \leq m$, $qv(P_i), qv(Q_i) \subseteq \{\overline{q}_i\}$*, and*

$$P_i \sim \mathbf{E}_i \left\{ \mathbf{X_j}(\overline{q}_j) := P_j, j \leq m \right\},$$
$$Q_i \sim \mathbf{E}_i \left\{ \mathbf{X_j}(\overline{q}_j) := Q_j, j \leq m \right\},$$

then $P_i \sim Q_i$ *for all* $i \leq m$.

Proof. For simplicity, we write $\mathbf{G}(\widetilde{P})$ for $\mathbf{G}\{\mathbf{X}_i(\overline{q}_i) := P_i, 1 \leq i \leq m\}$ and $\mathbf{G}(\widetilde{Q})$ for $\mathbf{G}\{\mathbf{X}_i(\overline{q}_i) := Q_i, 1 \leq i \leq m\}$. Let

$$\mathcal{R} = \{(\langle \mathbf{G}(\widetilde{P}), \rho \rangle, \langle \mathbf{G}(\widetilde{Q}), \rho \rangle) : \mathbf{G} \text{ contains at most } \mathbf{X}_i$$
$$(1 \leq i \leq m) \text{ and } \rho \in \mathcal{D}(\mathcal{H})\} \cup Id_{qCon},$$

where Id_{qCon} is the identity relation on configurations. Our purpose is to show that $\mathcal{R}$ is a strong bisimulation up to $\sim$. Assume that

$$\langle \mathbf{G}(\widetilde{P}), \rho \rangle \xrightarrow{\alpha} \langle P, \rho' \rangle. \tag{10.12}$$

It suffices to prove the following two claims:

Claim 1. If α is not an input, then for some Q, $\langle \mathbf{G}(\widetilde{Q}), \rho \rangle \xrightarrow{\alpha} \langle Q, \rho' \rangle$, and $\langle P, \rho' \rangle \sim \langle P_1, \rho' \rangle \mathcal{R} \langle Q_1, \rho' \rangle \sim \langle Q, \rho' \rangle$ for some P_1, Q_1;

Claim 2. If $\alpha = c?q$ and $q \notin qv(\mathbf{G}(\widetilde{P})) \cup qv(\mathbf{G}(\widetilde{Q}))$, then for some Q, $\langle \mathbf{G}(\widetilde{Q}), \rho \rangle \xrightarrow{c?q} \langle Q, \rho \rangle$, and for all $r \notin qv(P) \cup qv(Q) \setminus \{q\}$, it holds that

$$\langle P\{r/q\}, \rho' = \rho \rangle \sim \langle P_1, \rho \rangle \mathcal{R} \langle Q_1, \rho \rangle \sim \langle Q\{r/q\}, \rho \rangle$$

for some P_1, Q_1.

For readability, we leave the tedious proof of these claims to Appendix A.6.3. ☐

The above theorem is very useful for reasoning about equivalence of complex quantum processes. To prove two processes are strongly bisimilar, we only need to show that they satisfy the same recursive equation.

$$\text{Oper-Red}: \quad \frac{\mathcal{E} = (\mathcal{E}^{(n)} \otimes \mathcal{I}_{\overline{q}\backslash\overline{q}_n}) \circ ... \circ (\mathcal{E}^{(2)} \otimes \mathcal{I}_{\overline{q}\backslash\overline{q}_2}) \circ (\mathcal{E}^{(1)} \otimes \mathcal{I}_{\overline{q}\backslash\overline{q}_1})}{\mathcal{E}^{(1)}[\overline{q}_1]\mathcal{E}^{(2)}[\overline{q}_2]...\mathcal{E}^{(n)}[\overline{q}_n] \to \mathcal{E}[\overline{q}]}$$

$$\text{String-Struct}: \quad \frac{t \to t'}{t_1 t t_2 \to t_1 t' t_2}$$

FIGURE 10.2 Reduction rules for strings of actions. In rule (**Oper-Red**), $\overline{q}_i$ is a finite subset of $qVar$, $\mathcal{E}^{(i)}$ is a superoperator on $\mathcal{H}_{\overline{q}_i}$ for all $1 \le i \le n$, and $\overline{q} = \bigcup_{i=1}^{n} \overline{q}_i$. In rule (**String-Struct**), $t, t', t_1, t_2 \in Act^*$ are any strings of actions.

$$\text{Act-Red}: \quad \frac{\alpha_1...\alpha_m \to \beta_1...\beta_n}{\alpha_1....\alpha_m.P \to \beta_1....\beta_n.P}$$

$$\text{Pre-Struct}: \quad \frac{P \to P'}{\alpha.P \to \alpha.P'}$$

$$\text{Sum-Struct}: \quad \frac{P \to P'}{P + Q \to P' + Q}$$

$$\text{Par-Struct}: \quad \frac{P \to P'}{P\|Q \to P'\|Q}$$

$$\text{Res-Struct}: \quad \frac{P \to P'}{P\backslash L \to P'\backslash L}$$

$$\text{Ref}: \quad P \to P$$

$$\text{Trans}: \quad \frac{P \to Q \quad Q \to R}{P \to R}$$

FIGURE 10.3 Reduction rules for processes. Here, the symmetric forms of the **Sum-Struct** and **Par-Struct** rules are omitted.

10.2.5 Strong reduction-bisimilarity

As we discussed before, quantum operations describe sequential computation in quantum processes. It is required in the definition of strong bisimulation (Definition 10.5) that two bisimilar processes must perform exactly the same sequences of quantum operations. This condition is obviously overdiscriminative because two different sequences of quantum operations may have the same effect. To overcome this objection, we need to introduce the notion of operation reduction.

We define operation reduction in two steps. First, reduction between strings of actions is defined by the two rules given in Fig. 10.2. Then operation reduction between processes is a natural extension of reduction between strings of actions, and it is defined by the structural rules presented in Fig. 10.3. Almost all of the rules in Figs 10.2 and 10.3 are self-explanatory. We only need to point out that the premise $\alpha_1...\alpha_m \to \beta_1...\beta_n$ of the (**Act-Red**) rule for reduction between processes in Fig. 10.3 is a reduction between strings of actions, and should be deduced by the rules in Fig. 10.2.

The following proposition presents two basic properties of operation reduction between quantum processes.

Lemma 10.11. 1. *For any $P \in \mathcal{P}$, there exists a unique process, written $\lceil P \rceil$, such that $P \to \lceil P \rceil$, and $\lceil P \rceil \to Q$ does not hold for all $Q \in \mathcal{P}$ except $\lceil P \rceil$ itself.*
2. *If $P \to P'$, then $P' \to \lceil P \rceil$.*

Proof. Routine by induction on the structure of P. $\qquad\square$

By incorporating operation reduction introduced above into strong bisimilarity, we can define the notion of strong reduction-bisimilarity. Intuitively, it is defined by ignoring different decompositions of a quantum operation in the quantum processes under consideration. Formally, we have:

Definition 10.12. Strong reduction-bisimilarity $\overset{*}{\sim}$ is defined to be the transitive closure of $\simeq$, i.e.,

$$\overset{*}{\sim} = \bigcup_{n=1}^{\infty} \simeq^n,$$

where for any $P, Q \in \mathcal{P}$, $P \simeq Q$ if there are $P_1, P_2, Q_1,$ and Q_2 such that $P \sim P_1 \to P_2$, $Q \sim Q_1 \to Q_2$, and $P_2 \sim Q_2$.

$$
\begin{array}{ccccc}
P & \sim & P_1 & \to & P_2 \\[6pt]
\simeq & & & & \sim \\[6pt]
Q & \sim & Q_1 & \to & Q_2
\end{array}
$$

Strong reduction-bisimilarity provides us with a framework in which we can observe interaction between sequential quantum computation and communication in distributed quantum systems. Some basic algebraic properties of strong reduction-bisimilarity are presented in the following:

Theorem 10.3. 1. *If $P \sim Q$ then $P \overset{*}{\sim} Q$.*
2. *If $P \to P'$ then $P \overset{*}{\sim} P'$. In particular, if $\overline{q} = \bigcup_{i=1}^{n} \overline{q}_n$ and*

$$\mathcal{E} = (\mathcal{E}^{(n)} \otimes \mathcal{I}_{\overline{q} \setminus \overline{q}_n}) \circ ... \circ (\mathcal{E}^{(2)} \otimes \mathcal{I}_{\overline{q} \setminus \overline{q}_2}) \circ (\mathcal{E}^{(1)} \otimes \mathcal{I}_{\overline{q} \setminus \overline{q}_1}),$$

then we have:
   a. $\mathcal{E}^{(1)}[\overline{q}_1].\mathcal{E}^{(2)}[\overline{q}_2]....\mathcal{E}^{(n)}[\overline{q}_n].P \overset{*}{\sim} \mathcal{E}[\overline{q}].P;$
   b. $A(\overline{q}) \overset{*}{\sim} \mathcal{E}[\overline{q}].A(\overline{q})$ *when process constant scheme A is defined by*

$$A(\overline{q}) \overset{def}{=} \mathcal{E}^{(1)}[\overline{q}_1].\mathcal{E}^{(2)}[\overline{q}_2]....\mathcal{E}^{(n)}[\overline{q}_n].A(\overline{q}).$$

3. $\overset{*}{\sim}$ *is an equivalence relation.*
4. *If $P \overset{*}{\sim} Q$ then*
   a. $\alpha.P \overset{*}{\sim} \alpha.Q;$
   b. $P + R \overset{*}{\sim} Q + R;$
   c. $P \| R \overset{*}{\sim} Q \| R;$ *and*
   d. $P \setminus L \overset{*}{\sim} Q \setminus L.$

Proof. Clauses 1, 2, and 3 are immediately from Definition 10.12, and clause 4 can be easily proved by using Theorem 10.1. □

10.2.6 Weak bisimulations

In the previous subsections, we developed a theory of strong bisimulations between quantum processes, where each action of one process must be matched by the same action of the other, even for the silent action τ. As mentioned at the beginning of this section, we can define a notion of weak bisimulation in which we only require that each τ action be matched by zero or more τ actions. Formally, we have:

Definition 10.13. A symmetric relation $\mathcal{R} \subseteq qCon \times qCon$ is called a weak bisimulation if for any $\langle P, \rho \rangle, \langle Q, \sigma \rangle \in qCon$, $\langle P, \rho \rangle \mathcal{R} \langle Q, \sigma \rangle$ implies conditions 1 for action $\alpha = $ a quantum operation $\mathcal{E}[\overline{q}]$ or an output $c!q$ and 2 in Definition 10.5, together with

3. whenever $\langle P, \rho \rangle \overset{\tau}{\to} \langle P', \rho' \rangle$, then for some Q' and σ', it holds that $\langle Q, \sigma \rangle \overset{\tau}{\to}^* \langle Q', \sigma' \rangle$ and $\langle P', \rho' \rangle \mathcal{R} \langle Q', \sigma' \rangle$, where $\overset{\tau}{\to}^*$ stands for the reflexive and transitive closure of $\overset{\tau}{\to}$; that is, $\langle Q, \sigma \rangle \overset{\tau}{\to}^* \langle Q', \sigma' \rangle$ if and only if

$$\langle Q, \sigma \rangle \overset{\tau}{\to} \langle Q_1, \sigma_1 \rangle \overset{\tau}{\to} ... \overset{\tau}{\to} \langle Q_n, \sigma_n \rangle = \langle Q', \sigma' \rangle$$

for some integer $n \geq 0$ and configurations $\langle Q_1, \sigma_1 \rangle, ..., \langle Q_n, \sigma_n \rangle$.

Weak bisimulations are more appropriate than strong bisimulations in many applications where τ is considered as an internal action and thus cannot be detected by an external observer. A theory of weak bisimulations between quantum processes can be developed in a way similar to that presented in the previous subsections. We omit it here, but encourage the reader to work out its details as an exercise. Moreover, we can define weak reduction-bisimilarity by combining operation reduction and weak bisimilarity.

10.3 Approximate bisimulations between quantum processes

The reader should be noted that in a strong or weak bisimulation, a quantum operation $\mathcal{E}[\overline{q}]$ performed by one process must be matched by exactly the same operation performed by the other. In many practical applications, such perfect match may not make sense because quantum operations form a continuum and their minor changes can violate bisimilarity between two quantum processes. In particular, it is hard to realise when the quantum operations are implemented with the current

NISQ (Noisy Intermediate-Scale Quantum) devices. This observation motivates us to introduce an approximate variant of bisimulations where a quantum operation $\mathcal{E}[\overline{q}]$ is allowed to be matched by another quantum operation $\mathcal{F}[\overline{q}]$ close to it. In this section, we only consider approximate strong bisimulations because approximate weak bisimulations can be handled in a similar way.

To define the notion of approximate strong bisimulation, the first thing we need to do is to choose an appropriate distance that measures the closeness between two quantum operations $\mathcal{E}$ and $\mathcal{F}$. In this section, we employ the diamond distance $D_\diamond(\mathcal{E}, \mathcal{F})$ defined in Section 2.6. The reason is that a process is often entangled with other processes in a distributed system. Second, to make that approximate strong bisimulations enjoy certain robustness, we introduce the following:

Definition 10.14. Let λ be a nonnegative real number, and let $\mathcal{R}$ be a binary relation between quantum processes. If for any $P \in \mathcal{P}$ and $\rho, \sigma \in \mathcal{D}(\mathcal{H})$, $D(\rho, \sigma) \leq \lambda$ implies $\langle P, \rho\rangle\mathcal{R}\langle P, \sigma\rangle$, where $D(\cdot, \cdot)$ stands for trace distance (see Eq. (2.16)), then $\mathcal{R}$ is said to be λ-closed.

Now we are able to define approximate strong bisimulations and approximate strong bisimilarity between configurations.

Definition 10.15. A symmetric, λ-closed relation $\mathcal{R} \subseteq qCon \times qCon$ is called a strong λ-bisimulation if for any $\langle P, \rho\rangle, \langle Q, \sigma\rangle \in qCon$, $\langle P, \rho\rangle\mathcal{R}\langle Q, \sigma\rangle$ implies conditions 1 for action $\alpha =$ silent action τ or an output $c!q$ and 2 in Definition 10.5, together with

3. whenever $\langle P, \rho\rangle \xrightarrow{\mathcal{E}[\overline{q}]} \langle P', \rho'\rangle$, then for some $\mathcal{F}$, Q' and σ', it holds that $\langle Q, \sigma\rangle \xrightarrow{\mathcal{F}[\overline{q}]} \langle Q', \sigma'\rangle$, $\langle P', \rho'\rangle\mathcal{R}\langle Q', \sigma'\rangle$, and $D_\diamond(\mathcal{E}, \mathcal{F}) \leq \lambda$.

Definition 10.16. For any $\langle P, \rho\rangle, \langle Q, \sigma\rangle \in qCon$, we say that $\langle P, \rho\rangle$ and $\langle Q, \sigma\rangle$ are strongly λ-bisimilar, written $\langle P, \rho\rangle \sim_\lambda \langle Q, \sigma\rangle$, if $\langle P, \rho\rangle\mathcal{R}\langle Q, \sigma\rangle$ for some strong λ-bisimulation $\mathcal{R}$. In other words, strong λ-bisimilarity on Con is defined by

$$\sim_\lambda = \bigcup\{\mathcal{R} : \mathcal{R} \text{ is a strong } \lambda-\text{bisimulation}\}.$$

Similar to Lemma 10.7, we have the following recursive characterisation of λ-bisimilarity between configurations.

Lemma 10.12. *For any $\langle P, \rho\rangle, \langle Q, \sigma\rangle \in qCon$, $\langle P, \rho\rangle \sim_\lambda \langle Q, \sigma\rangle$ if and only if the following hold: conditions 1 for $\alpha =$ silent action τ or an output $c!q$ and 2 in Lemma 10.7 with $\sim$ replaced by $\sim_\lambda$,*

3. *whenever $\langle P, \rho\rangle \xrightarrow{\mathcal{E}[\overline{q}]} \langle P', \rho'\rangle$, then for some $\mathcal{F}$ and Q' and σ', it holds that $\langle Q, \sigma\rangle \xrightarrow{\mathcal{F}[\overline{q}]} \langle Q', \sigma'\rangle$, $\langle P', \rho'\rangle \sim_\lambda \langle Q', \sigma'\rangle$, and $D_\diamond(\mathcal{E}, \mathcal{F}) \leq \lambda$,*

and the symmetric forms of them.

Proof. Similar to the proof of Lemma 10.7. □

The following lemma presents a quantitative form of the fact that the composition of two strong bisimulations is a strong bisimulation.

Lemma 10.13. **1.** *If R_i is a strong λ_i-bisimulation $(i = 1, 2)$, then $\mathcal{R}_1 \circ \mathcal{R}_2$ is a strong $(\lambda_1 + \lambda_2)$-bisimulation.*
2. *(Transitivity of approximate strong bisimilarity) If $\langle P_1, \rho_1\rangle \sim_{\lambda_1} \langle P_2, \rho_2\rangle$ and $\langle P_2, \rho_2\rangle \sim_{\lambda_2} \langle P_3, \rho_3\rangle$, then $\langle P_1, \rho_1\rangle \sim_{\lambda_1+\lambda_2} \langle P_3, \rho_3\rangle$.*

Proof. Obviously, clause 2 is a corollary of clause 1. So, we only need to prove clause 1. Let us first show that $\mathcal{R}_1 \circ \mathcal{R}_2$ is $(\lambda_1 + \lambda_2)$-closed. If $D(\rho, \sigma) \leq \lambda_1 + \lambda_2$, then there must be some δ such that $D(\rho, \delta) \leq \lambda_1$ and $D(\delta, \sigma) \leq \lambda_2$. Since $\mathcal{R}_i$ is λ_i-closed for $i = 1, 2$, it holds that $\langle P, \rho\rangle\mathcal{R}_1\langle P, \delta\rangle$ and $\langle P, \delta\rangle\mathcal{R}_2\langle P, \sigma\rangle$. This implies $\langle P, \rho\rangle\mathcal{R}_1 \circ \mathcal{R}_2\langle P, \sigma\rangle$.

Now suppose that $\langle P, \rho\rangle\mathcal{R}_1 \circ \mathcal{R}_2\langle Q, \sigma\rangle$. Then $\langle P, \rho\rangle\mathcal{R}_1\langle R, \delta\rangle \mathcal{R}_2\langle Q, \sigma\rangle$ for some R and δ. We only need to consider the following case: if $\langle P, \rho\rangle \xrightarrow{\mathcal{E}[\overline{q}]} \langle P', \rho'\rangle$, then for some $\mathcal{G}$, R' and δ', $\langle R, \delta\rangle \xrightarrow{\mathcal{G}[\overline{q}]} \langle R', \delta'\rangle$, $\langle P', \rho'\rangle\mathcal{R}_1\langle R', \delta'\rangle$ and $D_\diamond(\mathcal{E}, \mathcal{G}) \leq \lambda_1$, and furthermore, for some $\mathcal{F}$, Q' and σ', $\langle Q, \sigma\rangle \xrightarrow{\mathcal{F}[X]} \langle Q', \sigma'\rangle$, $\langle R', \delta'\rangle\mathcal{R}_2\langle Q', \sigma'\rangle$ and $D_\diamond(\mathcal{G}, \mathcal{F}) \leq \lambda_2$. Then $\langle P', \rho'\rangle\mathcal{R}_1 \circ \mathcal{R}_2\langle Q', \sigma'\rangle$ and

$$D_\diamond(\mathcal{E}, \mathcal{F}) \leq D_\diamond(\mathcal{E}, \mathcal{G}) + D_\diamond(\mathcal{G}, \mathcal{F}) \leq \lambda_1 + \lambda_2. \qquad \square$$

Similar to Definition 10.7, we can define λ-strong bisimilarity between quantum processes based on λ-strong bisimilarity between configurations. Furthermore, it can be equivalently characterised by a distance between quantum processes.

Definition 10.17. Let $P, Q \in \mathcal{P}$ be two quantum processes. Then:

1. We say that P and Q are strongly λ-bisimilar, written $P \sim_\lambda Q$, if $\langle P, \rho \rangle \sim_\lambda \langle Q, \rho \rangle$ for all $\rho \in \mathcal{D}(\mathcal{H})$.

2. The strong bisimulation distance between P and Q is defined by

$$D_{sb}(P, Q) = \inf\{\lambda \geq 0 : P \sim_\lambda Q\}.$$

The following theorem shows that all of the process constructors in qCCS are all nonexpansive according to pseudo-metric D_{sb}. Essentially, it is a quantitative form of congruence of strong bisimilarity and thus a generalisation of Theorem 10.1.

Theorem 10.4. 1. *Strong bisimulation distance D_{sb} is a pseudo-metric on $\mathcal{P}$.*

2. *For any quantum processes P, Q, we have:*

    a. $D_{sb}(\alpha.P, \alpha.Q) \leq D_{sb}(P, Q)$ *if α is τ, an output or an input;*

    b. $D_{sb}(\mathcal{E}[\overline{q}].P, \mathcal{F}[\overline{r}].Q) \leq \max\{\eta_{\overline{q},\overline{r}}, D_\diamond(\mathcal{E}, \mathcal{F}) + D_{sb}(P, Q)\}$, *where*

$$\eta_{\overline{q},\overline{r}} = \begin{cases} 0, & \text{if } \overline{q} = \overline{r}, \\ \infty, & \text{otherwise}; \end{cases}$$

    c. $D_{sb}(P + R, Q + R) \leq D_{sb}(P, Q)$;

    d. $D_{sb}(P \| R, Q \| R) \leq D_{sb}(P, Q)$ *if all superoperators occurring in P, Q, and R are trace-preserving;*

    e. $D_{sb}(P \backslash L, Q \backslash L) \leq D_{sb}(P, Q)$.

Proof. To prove clause 1, we only need to check the triangle inequality

$$D_{sb}(P, R) \leq D_{sb}(P, Q) + D_{sb}(Q, R)$$

for any quantum processes P, Q, and R. It suffices to show that for any $\lambda_1, \lambda_2 > 0$, if $D_{sb}(P, Q) < \lambda_1$ and $D_{sb}(Q, R) < \lambda_2$, then $D_{sb}(P, R) < \lambda_1 + \lambda_2$. In fact, it follows from $D_{sb}(P, Q) < \lambda_1$ and $D_{sb}(Q, R) < \lambda_2$ that for some $\mu_1 < \lambda_1$ and $\mu_2 < \lambda_2$, we have $P \sim_{\mu_1} Q \sim_{\mu_2} R$. Thus, for all ρ, $\langle P, \rho \rangle \sim_{\mu_1} \langle Q, \rho \rangle \sim_{\mu_2} \langle R, \rho \rangle$, and there are strong μ_1-bisimulation $\mathcal{R}_1$ and strong μ_2-bisimulation $\mathcal{R}_2$ such that $\langle P, \rho \rangle \mathcal{R}_1 \langle Q, \rho \rangle \mathcal{R}_2 \langle R, \rho \rangle$. This leads to $\langle P, \rho \rangle \mathcal{R}_1 \circ \mathcal{R}_2 \langle R, \rho \rangle$. The above lemma asserts that $\mathcal{R}_1 \circ \mathcal{R}_2$ is a strong $(\mu_1 + \mu_2)$-bisimulation, and thus $\langle P, \rho \rangle \sim_{\mu_1 + \mu_2} \langle R, \rho \rangle$. Hence, $P \sim_{\mu_1 + \mu_2} R$, and $D_{sb}(P, R) \leq \mu_1 + \mu_2 < \lambda_1 + \lambda_2$.

Clause 2.a is immediate from Lemma 10.12. The proofs of 2.c and 2.e are easy.

Now we prove clause 2.b. It is obvious for the case of $X \neq Y$. Now assume $\overline{q} = \overline{r}$. If $D_\diamond(\mathcal{E}, \mathcal{F}) < \lambda$ and $D_{sb}(P, Q) < \mu$, then there is $\mu' < \mu$ such that $P \sim_{\mu'} Q$; that is, $\langle P, \sigma \rangle \sim_{\mu'} \langle Q, \sigma \rangle$ for all σ. For each ρ, we have

$$\langle \mathcal{E}[\overline{q}].P, \rho \rangle \overset{\mathcal{E}[\overline{q}]}{\to} \langle P, \mathcal{E}_{\overline{q}}(\rho) \rangle \text{ and } \langle \mathcal{F}[\overline{q}].Q, \rho \rangle \overset{\mathcal{F}[\overline{r}]}{\to} \langle Q, \mathcal{F}_{\overline{q}}(\rho) \rangle.$$

Note that

$$D(\mathcal{E}_{\overline{q}}(\rho), \mathcal{F}_{\overline{q}}(\rho)) = D(\mathcal{E}(\rho), \mathcal{F}(\rho)) \leq D_\diamond(\mathcal{E}, \mathcal{F}) < \lambda$$

and $\sim_\lambda$ is λ-closed. Then

$$\langle P, \mathcal{E}_{\overline{q}}(\rho) \rangle \sim_{\mu'} \langle Q, \mathcal{E}_{\overline{q}}(\rho) \rangle \sim_\lambda \langle Q, \mathcal{F}_{\overline{q}}(\rho) \rangle,$$

and $\langle P, \mathcal{E}_{\overline{q}}(\rho) \rangle \sim_{\lambda + \mu'} \langle Q, \mathcal{F}_{\overline{q}}(\rho) \rangle$. From Lemma 10.12 we see that $\langle \mathcal{E}[\overline{q}].P, \rho \rangle \sim_{\lambda + \mu'} \langle \mathcal{F}[\overline{r}].Q, \rho \rangle$. Hence

$$D_{sb}(\mathcal{E}[\overline{q}].P, \mathcal{F}[\overline{q}].Q) \leq \lambda + \mu' < \lambda + \mu.$$

This completes the proof by noting that λ and μ are arbitrary.

Finally, we prove clause 2.d. For arbitrary $\lambda > 0$, if $D_{sb}(P, Q) < \lambda$, then there is $\mu < \lambda$ such that $P \sim_\mu Q$; that is, $\langle P, \rho \rangle \sim_\mu \langle Q, \rho \rangle$ for all ρ. Our purpose is to show that $D_{sb}(P \| R, Q \| R) \leq \lambda$. To do this, we only need to find a strong μ-bisimulation $\mathcal{R}_\mu$ containing $(\langle P \| R, \rho \rangle, \langle Q \| R, \rho \rangle)$ for all ρ. This can be carried out by a modification of the technique used in the proof of Theorem 10.1.2.f. We put the technical details into the Appendix A.6.4. $\square$

An approximate version of strong reduction-bisimilarity can also be defined in a natural way:

Definition 10.18. Let $P, Q \in \mathcal{P}$ be two quantum processes. Then:

1. We say that P and Q are strongly λ-reduction-bisimilar, written $P \overset{*}{\sim}_\lambda Q$, if there are $n \geq 0$, $\lambda_1, ..., \lambda_n \geq 0$ and $R_1, R_1', ..., R_n, R_n' \in \mathcal{P}$ such that $\sum_{i=1}^n \lambda_i \leq \lambda$ and

$$P \overset{*}{\sim} R_1 \sim_{\lambda_1} R_1' \overset{*}{\sim} ... \overset{*}{\sim} R_n \sim_{\lambda_n} R_n' \overset{*}{\sim} Q.$$

2. The strong reduction-bisimulation distance between P and Q is defined by

$$D_{srb}(P, Q) = \inf\{\lambda \geq 0 : P \overset{*}{\sim}_\lambda Q\}$$

Similar to Theorem 10.4, we have:

Theorem 10.5. 1. *Strong reduction-bisimulation distance D_{srb} is a pseudo-metric on $\mathcal{P}$.*
2. *For any quantum processes P, Q, we have:*
    a. $D_{srb}(\alpha.P, \alpha.Q) \leq D_{srb}(P, Q)$ *if α is τ, an output or an input;*
    b. $D_{srb}(\mathcal{E}[\overline{q}].P, \mathcal{F}[\overline{r}].Q) \leq \max\{\eta_{\overline{q},\overline{r}}, D_\diamond(\mathcal{E}, \mathcal{F}) + D_{srb}(P, Q)\}$, *where $\eta_{\overline{q},\overline{r}}$ is as in Theorem 10.4.2.b;*
    c. $D_{srb}(P + R, Q + R) \leq D_{srb}(P, Q)$;
    d. $D_{srb}(P\|R, Q\|R) \leq D_{srb}(P, Q)$ *if all superoperators occurring in P, Q, and R are trace-preserving;*
    e. $D_{srb}(P\backslash L, Q\backslash L) \leq D_{srb}(P, Q)$.

Proof. 1. To show the triangle inequality:

$$D_{srb}(P, Q) + D_{srb}(Q, R) \geq D_{srb}(P, R),$$

it suffices to note that for any $\lambda, \mu \geq 0$, $P \overset{*}{\sim}_\lambda Q$ and $Q \overset{*}{\sim}_\mu R$ implies $P \overset{*}{\sim}_{\lambda+\mu} R$. This is immediate from the definition of strong λ-reduction-bisimilarity.

2. We choose to prove 2.b, and the proofs of the other items are similar. Assume that $X = Y$. For any $\lambda \geq 0$, if $P \overset{*}{\sim}_\lambda Q$, then we have

$$P \overset{*}{\sim} R_1 \sim_{\lambda_1} R_1' \overset{*}{\sim} ... \overset{*}{\sim} R_n \sim_{\lambda_n} R_n' \overset{*}{\sim} Q$$

for some $R_1, R_1', ..., R_n, R_n'$ and $\lambda_1, ..., \lambda_n$ with $\sum_{i=1}^n \lambda_i \leq \lambda$. Then it follows from Theorems 10.3.4 and 10.4.2 that

$$\mathcal{E}[\overline{q}].P \overset{*}{\sim} \mathcal{E}[\overline{q}].R_1 \sim_{D(\mathcal{E}, \mathcal{F})+\lambda_1} \mathcal{F}[\overline{q}].R_1' \overset{*}{\sim} ...$$
$$\overset{*}{\sim} \mathcal{F}[\overline{q}].R_n \sim_{\lambda_n} \mathcal{F}[\overline{q}].R_n' \overset{*}{\sim} \mathcal{F}[\overline{q}].Q$$

On the other hand, we have

$$(D_\diamond(\mathcal{E}, \mathcal{F}) + \lambda_1) + \lambda_2 + ... + \lambda_n \leq D_\diamond(\mathcal{E}, \mathcal{F}) + \lambda.$$

Thus, $\mathcal{E}[\overline{q}].P \overset{*}{\sim}_{D(\mathcal{E}, \mathcal{F})+\lambda} \mathcal{F}[\overline{q}].Q$. Therefore,

$$D_{srb}(\mathcal{E}[\overline{q}].P, \mathcal{F}[\overline{q}].Q) \leq \inf\{D_\diamond(\mathcal{E}, \mathcal{F}) + \lambda : P \overset{*}{\sim}_\lambda Q\}$$
$$= D_\diamond(\mathcal{E}, \mathcal{F}) + D_{srb}(P, Q). \qquad \square$$

Approximate bisimulation can be used to describe implementation of a quantum process by some (usually finitely many) special quantum gates. A quantum process $P \in \mathcal{P}$ is said to be finite if it contains no process constants. We write $\mathcal{P}_{fin}$ for the set of finite quantum processes. For any set Ω of quantum gates, we write $\mathcal{P}_{fin}[\Omega]$ for the set of finite quantum processes in which only gates from Ω and measurements in the computational bases are used as quantum operations (see clause 3.b in Definition 10.1). By combining Theorems 10.3.2.a and 10.5.2 we obtain:

Corollary 10.1. *If Ω is an approximately universal set of quantum gates (e.g., the Hadamard gate, phase gate, CNOT, and $\pi/8$ gate (or the Toffoli gate)) (see Definition 3.8 and Theorem 3.2), then $\mathcal{P}_{fin}[\Omega]$ is dense in $\mathcal{P}_{fin}$ according to pseudo-metric D_{srb}.*

To conclude this section, we propose an interesting problem for future research. One of the most spectacular results in fault-tolerant quantum computation is the threshold theorem (see [318], Chapter 10), which means that it is possible to efficiently perform an arbitrarily large quantum computation provided the noise in individual quantum gates is below a certain constant. This theorem considers only the case of sequential quantum computation. Its generalisation in parallel and distributed quantum computation would be a challenge. The notion of approximate bisimulation provides us with a formal tool for observing robustness of distributed quantum computation against inaccuracy in the implementation of its elementary gates, and we guess that it can be used to establish a distributed generalisation of the (fault-tolerance) threshold theorem.

10.4 Adding classical variables

For clearer understanding, in the previous sections we have been focusing on a purely quantum process algebra qCCS in which no classical communication is involved. However, in most of the real-world applications, classical and quantum communications (and computation) occur simultaneously. So, in this section, we expand the language of qCCS by adding classical variables, and study a classical-quantum hybrid process algebra, called cqCCS.

10.4.1 Syntax

Let us first define the syntax of our expanded cqCCS. Its alphabet consists of:

1. a set *cVar* of classical variables, ranged over by $x, y, \ldots$;
2. a set of function symbols for classical data, including constants;
3. a set of predicate symbols for classical data;
4. a set *qVar* of quantum variables, ranged over by $q, r, \ldots$;
5. a set of quantum operation symbols, ranged over by $\mathcal{E}, \ldots$;
6. a set of quantum measurement symbols, ranged over by $M, \ldots$;
7. a set *cChan* of (names of) classical communication channels, ranged over by $c, d, \ldots$;
8. a set *qChan* of (names of) quantum communication channels, ranged over by $\mathsf{c}, \mathsf{d}, \ldots$;
9. a set of process constant schemes, ranged over by $A, B, \ldots$.

We assume that the reader is familiar with first-order logic. Then (classical) expressions (i.e. terms) and first-order logical formulas can be generated from classical variables, function symbols, and predicate symbols. They are used to specify classical data. We write *Exp* and *Wff* for the sets of these expressions and logical formulas, ranged over by $e, \ldots$ and $b, \ldots$, respectively. Each of quantum operation symbols $\mathcal{E}$ or quantum measurement symbols M is associated with a positive integer $ar(E)$ or $ar(M)$, called its arity. Each of process constant scheme A is associated with two nonnegative integers $car(A)$ and $qar(A)$.

We write *Proc* for the set of classical-quantum hybrid processes (cq-processes for short). For each $P \in Proc$, the sets of free classical variables and free quantum variables in P are denoted $cv(P)$, $qv(P)$, respectively.

Definition 10.19. Processes in cqCCS (i.e. cq-processes) are inductively defined by the following formation rules:

1. **nil** $\in Proc$, $cv(\mathbf{nil}) = \emptyset$ and $qv(\mathbf{nil}) = \emptyset$;
2. $A(\overline{x}; \overline{q}) \in Proc$, $cv(A(\overline{x}; \overline{q})) = \{\overline{x}\}$ and $qv(A(\overline{x}; \overline{q})) = \{\overline{q}\}$;
3. if $P \in Proc$, then:
   a. $\tau.P \in Proc$, $cv(\tau.P) = cv(P)$ and $qv(\tau.P) = qv(P)$;
   b. $c?x.P \in Proc$, $cv(c?x.P) = cv(P) \setminus \{x\}$ and $qv(c?x.P) = qv(P)$;
   c. $c!e.P \in Proc$, $cv(c!e.P) = cv(P) \cup var(e)$ [the variables in e] and $qv(c!e.P) = qv(P)$;
   d. $\mathsf{c}?q.P \in Proc$, $cv(\mathsf{c}?q.P) = cv(P)$ and $qv(\mathsf{c}?q.P) = qv(P) \setminus \{q\}$;
   e. $\mathsf{c}!q.P \in Proc$ provided $q \notin qv(P)$, $cv(\mathsf{c}!q.P) = cv(P)$ and $qv(\mathsf{c}!q.P) = qv(P) \cup \{q\}$;
   f. $\mathcal{E}[\overline{q}].P \in Proc$, $cv(\mathcal{E}[\overline{q}].P) = cv(P)$ and $qv(\mathcal{E}[\overline{q}].P) = qv(P) \cup \{\overline{q}\}$;
   g. $M[\overline{q} : x].P \in Proc$, $cv(M[\overline{q} : x].P) = cv(P) \cup \{x\}$ and $qv(M[\overline{q} : x].P) = qv(P) \cup \{\overline{q}\}$;
   h. $P \setminus L \in Proc$, $cv(P \setminus L) = cv(P)$ and $qv(P \setminus L) = qv(P)$;
   i. **if** b **then** $P \in Proc$, $cv(\mathbf{if}\ b\ \mathbf{then}\ P) = cv(P) \cup var(b)$ [the variables in b] and $qv(\mathbf{if}\ b\ \mathbf{then}\ P) = qv(P)$;
4. if $P, Q \in Proc$, then:
   a. $P + Q \in Proc$, $cv(P + Q) = cv(P) \cup cv(Q)$ and $qv(P + Q) = qv(P) \cup qv(Q)$;
   b. $P \| Q \in Proc$ provided $qv(P) \cap qv(Q) = \emptyset$, $cv(P \| Q) = cv(P) \cup cv(Q)$ and $qv(P \| Q) = qv(P) \cup qv(Q)$.

The above definition is an extension of Definition 10.1. We only need to explain those process constructs that are introduced in the former but not appeared in the latter:

- In qCCS, a process constant is defined in the form $A(\overline{q})$ equipped with only quantum variables $\overline{q}$. In cqCCS, however, a process constant appears as $A(\overline{x}; \overline{q})$ with both classical variables $\overline{x}$ and quantum variables $\overline{q}$. Accordingly, for each process constant scheme A, a defining equation of the form

$$A(\overline{x}, \overline{q}) \stackrel{def}{=} P \tag{10.13}$$

is assumed, where $P \in Proc$ is a cq-process with $cv(P) \subseteq \{\overline{x}\}$ and $qv(P) \subseteq \{\overline{q}\}$.
- Clauses 3.b and 3.c in the above definition are designed for specifying classical communications. Process $c?x.P$ receives a classical datum, say d, from classical channel c and then behaves as P with all free occurrences of x substituted by d, written $P\{d/x\}$. Process $c!e.P$ sends the value of classical expression e through classical channel c and then behaves as P.
- $M[\overline{q} : x].P$ is a process that first performs measurement M on quantum variables $\overline{q}$, stores the outcome in classical variable x, and then behaves as process P. The prefix $M[\overline{q} : x]$ serves as a bridge from the quantum part of the process to its classical part.
- b in the conditional **if** b **then** P stands for a classical Boolean expression. Whenever it is evaluated to be true, then the conditional behaves as P; otherwise, the conditional terminates. It is worth noting that the conditional construct provides a bridge from the classical part of a process back to its quantum part; that is, classical information b is used to control a quantum process P.

By simply combining the notion of substitution in classical first-order logic and Definition 10.3, we can introduce substitution $P[f]$ of a cq-process $P \in Proc$ with f consisting of a mapping from $cVar$ into the set of classical expressions and a one-to-one mapping from $qVar$ into itself.

10.4.2 Operational semantics

The operational semantics of cqCCS can be defined by generalising that of qCCS. Note that both prefix of the form $M[\overline{q} : x]$ and parallel composition of the form $P \| Q$ appear in cqCCS. So, as discussed in Section 9.2, we need to deal with the nondeterminism caused by quantum measurements and the nondeterminism introduced by parallelism at the same time. Following the idea used there, the operational semantics of cqCCS must be defined as a transition relation between configuration ensembles rather than configurations as in qCCS. A configuration in cqCCS is a triple $\langle P, v, \rho \rangle$, where $P \in Proc$ is a cq-process, v is a valuation of classical variables, and $\rho \in \mathcal{D}(\mathcal{H}_{qVar})$ is a state of all quantum variables. We write $cqCon$ for the set of all configurations in cqCCS. Furthermore, a configuration ensemble in cqCCS is a multiset

$$\mathcal{A} = \{|\langle P_i, v_i, \rho_i \rangle|\}$$

of configurations with $\sum_i \text{tr}(\rho_i) \leq 1$. We always identify a singleton $\{|\langle P, v, \rho \rangle|\}$ with configuration $\langle P, v, \rho \rangle$. In addition, the set of actions in qCCS should be enlarged to $Act = \{\tau\} \cup Act_{op} \cup Act_{com}$ with Act_{com} including not only quantum communications of the form $c?q$ and $c!q$, but also classical communications $c?d$ and $c!d$, where $c \in cChan$, and d is a classical datum.

Definition 10.20. The operational semantics of cq-processes is a transition relation between configuration ensembles labelled by actions. It is defined by the transition rules given in Figs 10.4, 10.5, and 10.6.

10.4.3 Examples

In Section 4.6, we learned several basic quantum communication protocols. In this subsection, we show how they can be formally modelled in our classical-quantum process algebra cqCCS.

Quantum teleportation is a protocol that allows the sender Alice to transmit an unknown state of a qubit to the receiver Bob by sending only two bits of classical information if an entanglement between them is provided. The following example gives a formal description of this protocol as a process in cqCCS.

$$\textbf{Tau}: \quad \langle \tau.P, v, \rho \rangle \xrightarrow{\tau} \langle P, v, \rho \rangle$$

$$\textbf{Oper}: \quad \langle \mathcal{E}[\overline{q}].P, v, \rho \rangle \xrightarrow{\mathcal{E}[\overline{q}]} \langle P, v, \mathcal{E}_{\overline{q}}(\rho) \rangle$$

$$\textbf{C-Input}: \quad \langle c?x.P, v, \rho \rangle \xrightarrow{c?d} \langle P\{d/x\}, v[d \leftarrow x], \rho \rangle \quad \text{for each } d \text{ in the domain of } x$$

$$\textbf{C-Output}: \quad \langle c!e.P, v, \rho \rangle \xrightarrow{c!d} \langle P, v, \rho \rangle \quad \text{where } d = v(e) \text{ [the value of } e \text{ under valuation } v]$$

$$\textbf{Q-Input}: \quad \langle c?q.P, v, \rho \rangle \xrightarrow{c?r} \langle P\{r/q\}, v, \rho \rangle \quad \text{for each } r \notin qv(c?q.P)$$

$$\textbf{Q-Output}: \quad \frac{}{\langle c!q.P, v, \rho \rangle \xrightarrow{c!q} \langle P, v, \rho \rangle}$$

$$\textbf{Meas}: \quad \langle M[\overline{q} : x].P, v, \rho \rangle \xrightarrow{\tau} \{| \langle P, v[m \leftarrow x], M_m \rho M_m^{\dagger} \rangle |\} \quad \text{if } M = \{M_m\}$$

$$\textbf{Def}: \quad \frac{\langle P\{\overline{y}/\overline{x}; \overline{r}/\overline{q}\}, v, \rho \rangle \xrightarrow{\alpha} \mathcal{A}}{\langle A(\overline{y}; \overline{r}), v, \rho \rangle \xrightarrow{\alpha} \mathcal{A}} \quad \text{if } A(\overline{x}; \overline{q}) \overset{def}{=} P$$

FIGURE 10.4 Transition rules for cq-processes (I).

$$\textbf{Choice}: \quad \frac{\langle P, v, \rho \rangle \xrightarrow{\alpha} \mathcal{A}}{\langle P + Q, v, \rho \rangle \xrightarrow{\alpha} \mathcal{A}}$$

$$\textbf{Intl1}: \quad \frac{\langle P, v, \rho \rangle \xrightarrow{c?q} \langle P', v, \rho' \rangle}{\langle P \| Q, v, \rho \rangle \xrightarrow{c?q} \langle P' \| Q, v, \rho' \rangle} \quad \text{if } q \notin qv(Q)$$

$$\textbf{Intl2}: \quad \frac{\langle P, v, \rho \rangle \xrightarrow{\alpha} \{| \langle P_i, v_i, \rho_i \rangle |\}}{\langle P \| Q, v, \rho \rangle \xrightarrow{\alpha} \{| \langle P_i \| Q, v_i, \rho_i \rangle |\}} \quad \text{if } \alpha \text{ is not an input action}$$

$$\textbf{Comm}: \quad \frac{\langle P, v, \rho \rangle \xrightarrow{c?q} \langle P', v, \rho \rangle \quad \langle Q, v, \rho \rangle \xrightarrow{c!q} \langle Q', v, \rho \rangle}{\langle P \| Q, v, \rho \rangle \xrightarrow{\tau} \langle P' \| Q', v, \rho \rangle}$$

$$\textbf{Res}: \quad \frac{\langle P, v, \rho \rangle \xrightarrow{\alpha} \{| \langle P_i, v_i, \rho_i \rangle |\}}{\langle P \backslash L, v, \rho \rangle \xrightarrow{\alpha} \{| \langle P_i \backslash L, v_i, \rho_i \rangle |\}} \quad \text{if } cn(\alpha) \notin L$$

$$\textbf{Cond}: \quad \frac{\langle P, v, \rho \rangle \xrightarrow{\alpha} \mathcal{A}}{\langle \textbf{if } b \textbf{ then } P, v, \rho \rangle \xrightarrow{\alpha} \mathcal{A}} \quad \text{if } v(b) \text{ [the value of } b \text{ under valuation } v] = \text{true}$$

FIGURE 10.5 Transition rules for cq-processes (II). The symmetric forms of the **Choice**, **Intl1**, **Intl2**, and **Comm** rules are omitted here.

$$(\text{MS1}) \quad \frac{\langle P, v, \rho \rangle \rightarrow \mathcal{A}}{\{| \langle P, v, \rho \rangle |\} \rightarrow \mathcal{A}}$$

$$(\text{MS2}) \quad \frac{\{\mathcal{A}_i\}_{i \in I} \text{ is a partition of } \mathcal{A} \qquad I = I_0 \cup I_1}{\mathcal{A}_i \nrightarrow \text{ for every } i \in I_0 \qquad \mathcal{A}_i \rightarrow \mathcal{B}_i \text{ for every } i \in I_1}$$
$$\mathcal{A} \rightarrow \left(\bigcup_{i \in I_0} \mathcal{A}_i \right) \cup \left(\bigcup_{i \in I_1} \mathcal{B}_i \right)$$

FIGURE 10.6 Rules for ensembles. In (MS2), $\cup$ and $\bigcup$ for ensembles stand for union of multisets.

Example 10.9. Let c be a classical channel, X and Z Pauli gates, and M the measurement in the computational basis. We set

$$Alice := CNOT[q_0, q_1].H[q_0].M[q_0 : x_0].c!x_0.M[q_1 : x_1].c!x_1.\textbf{nil},$$
$$Bob := c?x_0.c?x_1.\textbf{if } x_0 = 0 \wedge x_1 = 0 \textbf{ then nil}$$
$$+ \textbf{if } x_0 = 0 \wedge x_1 = 1 \textbf{ then } X[q_2].\textbf{nil}$$
$$+ \textbf{if } x_0 = 1 \wedge x_1 = 0 \textbf{ then } Z[q_2].\textbf{nil}$$
$$+ \textbf{if } x_0 = 1 \wedge x_1 = 1 \textbf{ then } X[q_2].Z[q_2].\textbf{nil}.$$

Then the protocol of quantum teleportation can be written as the process:

$$Teleportation = (Alice \| Bob) \backslash c.$$

Exercise 10.7. Work out all execution paths of the quantum teleportation protocol; that is, transitions starting from configuration $(Teleportation, v, |\psi\rangle_{q_0}|\beta_{00}\rangle_{q_1q_2})$, where $v(x_0) = v(x_1) = 0$.

Superdense coding allows Alice to transmit two bits of classical information to Bob by sending only one qubit if a maximal entanglement exists between them a priori. The next example shows how this protocol can be written in the language of cqCCS defined in the previous subsections.

Example 10.10. Let c be a quantum channel, X and Z Pauli gates, M the measurement in the Bell states, and y a classical variable for two-bit data. We set

$$Alice := \textbf{if } x_0 = 0 \wedge x_1 = 0 \textbf{ then } c!q_1.\textbf{nil}$$
$$+ \textbf{if } x_0 = 0 \wedge x_1 = 1 \textbf{ then } Z[q_1].c!q_1.\textbf{nil}$$
$$+ \textbf{if } x_0 = 1 \wedge x_1 = 0 \textbf{ then } X[q_1].c!q_1.\textbf{nil}$$
$$+ \textbf{if } x_0 = 1 \wedge x_1 = 1 \textbf{ then } X[q_1].Z[q_1].c!q_1.\textbf{nil},$$
$$Bob := c?q_1.M[q_1q_2 : y].\textbf{nil}.$$

The protocol of superdense coding can be formally modelled as the process:

$$SDCoding = (Alice \| Bob) \setminus c.$$

Exercise 10.8. Work out all execution transitions starting from configuration $(SDCoding, v, |\beta_{00}\rangle_{q_1q_2})$, where $v(x_0) = i_0$, $v(x_1) = i_1$ and $v(y) = 00$.

10.4.4 Bisimulations

In this subsection, we generalise the notion of bisimulation defined in qCCS into cqCCS. Note that the operational semantics of qCCS is defined as a transition relation between configurations, but that of cqCCS is a transition relation between configuration ensembles. On the other hand, a bisimulation in qCCS is defined as a binary relation between configurations. So, we first need to find a way of lifting a relation between configurations to a relation between configuration ensembles. Indeed, this can be done by mimicking the idea used for lifting a relation between two sets to a relation between probability distributions over them, which has been successfully used in probabilistic process algebras.

Definition 10.21. Let $\mathcal{R} \subseteq cqCon \times cqCon$ be a binary relation between configurations in cqCCS. Then its lifting to configuration ensembles $\mathcal{R}^{\uparrow}$ is defined as follows: for any two ensembles $\mathcal{A} = \{|\langle P_i, v_i, \rho_i\rangle|\}$ and $\mathcal{B} = \{|\langle Q_j, w_j, \sigma_i\rangle|\}$, $\mathcal{A}\mathcal{R}^{\uparrow}\mathcal{B}$ if and only if there is a weight function $\mu : \{i\} \times \{j\} \to [0, 1]$ such that

1. $\langle P_i, v_i, \rho_i\rangle\mathcal{R}\langle Q_j, w_j, \sigma_j\rangle$ for all i, j with $\mu(i, j) > 0$;
2. $\sum_j \mu(i, j) = \text{tr}(\rho_i)$ for every i, and $\sum_i \mu(i, j) = \text{tr}(\sigma_j)$ for every j.

With the lifting technique, Definition 10.5 can be straightforwardly generalised into cqCCS.

Definition 10.22. A symmetric relation $\mathcal{R} \subseteq cqCon \times cqCon$ is called a strong bisimulation if for any $\langle P, v, \rho\rangle, \langle Q, w, \sigma\rangle \in cqCon$, $\langle P, v, \rho\rangle\mathcal{R}\langle Q, w, \sigma\rangle$ implies:

1. whenever $\langle P, v, \rho\rangle \xrightarrow{\alpha} \mathcal{A}$ and α is neither a classical input nor a quantum input, then for some $\mathcal{B}$, it holds that $\langle Q, w, \sigma\rangle \xrightarrow{\alpha} \mathcal{B}$ and $\mathcal{A}\mathcal{R}^{\uparrow}\mathcal{B}$;
2. whenever $\langle P, v, \rho\rangle \xrightarrow{c?d} \langle P', v', \rho\rangle$, then for some $x \notin cv(P) \cup cv(Q)$, it holds that $P \equiv P\{d/x\}$, $v' = v[d \leftarrow x]$, $\langle Q, w, \sigma\rangle \xrightarrow{c?d} \langle Q\{d/x\}, w[d \leftarrow x], \sigma\rangle$ and $\langle P', v, \rho\rangle\mathcal{R}\langle Q\{d/x\}, w[d \leftarrow x], \sigma\rangle$;
3. whenever $\langle P, v, \rho\rangle \xrightarrow{c?q} \langle P', v, \rho\rangle$ and $q \notin qv(P) \cup qv(Q)$, then for some Q', it holds that $\langle Q, w, \sigma\rangle \xrightarrow{c?q} \langle Q', w, \sigma\rangle$ and $\langle P'\{r/q\}, v, \rho\rangle\mathcal{R}\langle Q'\{r/q\}, w, \sigma\rangle$ for all $r \notin qv(P') \cup qv(Q') \setminus \{q\}$.

Based on the above definition, we can further define the notions of weak bisimulation, reduction-bisimulation, and approximate bisimulation for cq-processes. Furthermore, the main results in Sections 10.2 and 10.3 can be generalised into cqCCS, but we omit them here because the basic ideas are similar to the case of qCCS but the details are quite involved. The reader can find these details in [148,149] if she/he is interested in them.

10.5   Bibliographic remarks and further readings

Early work on quantum process algebras mainly includes: (1) CQP (Communicating Quantum Processes) proposed by Gay and Nagarajan [169]; (2) QPAlg (Quantum Process Algebra) by Jorrand and Lalire [235,265]; and (3) process algebra with logarithmic cost quantum random access machine for specifying and reasoning about quantum security protocols by Adão and Mateus [10].

This chapter focuses on qCCS, a quantum extension of CCS. A certain familiarity with classical process algebras, in particular CCS, is helpful for understanding the materials presented in this chapter. An excellent textbook for CCS is [302]. Sections 10.1 to 10.3 of this chapter are mainly based on [429]. The materials in Section 10.4 are taken from Feng et al. [148,149] with some minor modifications.

Further developments of qCCS and cqCCS include symbolic bisimulations [145], open bisimulations [124] and ground bisimulations [345] for cq-processes. Some ideas needed in the transition from bisimulations between probabilistic processes to bisimulations between quantum processes was discussed by Deng [123]. They have been applied in equivalence checking of quantum communication protocols by Ardeshir-Larijani et al. [32–34] and in security verification of quantum cryptographic protocols by Gay, Nagarajan and Papanikolaou [172] and Kubota et al. [257–259], including QKD (Quantum Key Distribution) by Feng et al. [154].

Quantum process algebra CQP [169] has also been further developed in several directions; for example, probabilistic branching bisimilarity [119], model checking [120] and type checking [170] of quantum processes, and application in analysis of quantum error-correction code [122] and quantum cryptographic protocols [121].

Recently, a Hoare-style logic for reasoning about distributed quantum programs written in a CSP-like language was proposed by Feng et al. [151]. It is essentially a quantum generalisation of Apt's proof system for the verification of CSP programs [27].

Finally, it should be pointed out that although theoretical research on communicating and distributed quantum systems started 15 years ago, practical distributed quantum programming techniques only emerged very recently. The work of QMPI (Quantum Message Passing Interface) [197] was already mentioned at the end of last chapter. A compilation framework for efficient communication in distributed quantum programs was proposed by Wu et al. [411].

Part V

Quantum control flows

All quantum programs considered in the previous parts only have classical control flows. In this part, we introduce quantum control flows into quantum programs. As discussed in Section 1.2, the introduction of quantum control flows leads to a new paradigm of quantum programming – superposition-of-programs – where programs can be executed in superposition. As we will see in the examples presented below, this programming paradigm provides a new view for thinking and reasoning about quantum algorithms.

Quantum control flows are introduced gradually in two chapters:

- In classical programming, case statement is the basic program construct for the description of control flows. Accordingly, as the first step toward a theory of quantum control flows, we define the notion of quantum case statement in Chapter 11. Its formal semantics is carefully studied there. Furthermore, the notion of quantum choice is derived.
- In Chapter 12, we study quantum control flows in much more involved program constructs, namely recursions (and loops). Due to the potentially infinite behaviours of recursions, their semantics cannot be defined in the basic framework of quantum mechanics introduced in Chapter 2. Instead, we need second quantisation – a fundamental mathematical tool in quantum field theory – to formally define the semantics of recursions with quantum control flows.

Chapter 11

Quantum case statements

Quantum programs in the superposition-of-data paradigm have been systematically investigated in Chapters 5 to 10. In particular, in Chapter 5, we studied quantum **while**-programs and recursive quantum programs, and showed how can some quantum algorithms be conveniently written as this kind of quantum programs. The control flow of a quantum **while**-program is generated by the case statements and **while**-loops within it, and the control flow of a recursive quantum program is further produced by procedure calls. Since the information that determines the control flow of a quantum **while**-program or a recursive quantum program is classical rather than quantum, such a control flow was properly named as a classical control flow (in a quantum program).

The aim of this chapter and the next is to introduce quantum programs in the superposition-of-programs paradigm; in other words, quantum programs with quantum control flows. As we know, the control flow of a program is determined by those program constructs within it like case statement, loop and recursion. Interestingly, the notions of case statement, loop and recursion in classical programming split into two different versions in the quantum setting:

1. *Case statement, loop and recursion with classical control* that have been studied in detail in Chapters 5 to 8;
2. *Quantum case statement, loop and recursion* – case statement, loop and recursion with *quantum control* – to be discussed in this and next chapters.

As we will see later, a large class of quantum algorithms can be much more conveniently programmed in a programming language with quantum control. In particular, superposition-of-programs paradigm provides a new view and intuition for specifying and reasoning about quantum algorithms.

This chapter focuses on quantum case statements and one of their natural derivatives, namely quantum choices. Loop and recursion with quantum control flow will be discussed in the next chapter. This chapter is organised as follows:

- In Section 11.1, the notion of quantum case statement is carefully motivated through the example of quantum walk on a graph. The control flow of a quantum case statement is then analysed, and the technical difficulty in defining the semantics of quantum case statement is unveiled.
- A new quantum programming language QuGCL is defined in Section 11.2 to support programming with quantum case statement.
- Section 11.3 prepares several key ingredients needed in defining the denotational semantics of QuGCL, including guarded composition of various quantum operations. The denotational semantics of QuGCL is then presented in Section 11.4.
- In Section 11.5, the notion of quantum choice is defined based on quantum case statement.
- A family of algebraic laws for QuGCL programs are presented in Section 11.6. They can be used in verification, transformation, and compilation of programs with quantum case statements.
- A series of examples are presented in Section 11.8 to illustrate the expressive power of the language QuGCL.
- The possible variants and generalisations of quantum case statement are discussed in Section 11.9.
- The proofs of some lemmas, propositions, and theorems in Sections 11.3 to 11.6 are tedious. For readability, they are deferred to Appendix A.7.

11.1 Case statements: from classical to quantum

Let us start from an intuitive discussion about the following two questions:

- Why should we introduce the new notion of quantum case statement?
- How does it differ from the case statement in the quantum programs considered in Chapter 5?

We answer these questions and thus motivate the notion of quantum case statement in three steps:

1. ***Case statement in classical programming***: Recall that a conditional statement in classical programming is written as

$$\textbf{if } b \textbf{ then } S_1 \textbf{ else } S_0 \textbf{ fi} \tag{11.1}$$

Foundations of Quantum Programming. https://doi.org/10.1016/B978-0-44-315942-8.00024-1

where b is a Boolean expression. When b is true, subprogram S_1 will be executed; otherwise, S_0 will be executed. More generally, a case statement in classical programming is a collection of guarded commands written as

$$\mathbf{if}\ (\square i \cdot G_i \rightarrow S_i)\ \mathbf{fi} \tag{11.2}$$

where for each $1 \leq i \leq n$, the subprogram S_i is guarded by the Boolean expression G_i, and S_i will be executed only when G_i is true.

2. *Classical case statement in quantum programming*: A notion of classical case statement in quantum programming was defined in Chapter 5 based on a quantum measurement. Let $\overline{q}$ be a family of quantum variables and $M = \{M_m\}$ a measurement on $\overline{q}$. For each possible measurement outcome m, let S_m be a quantum program. Then a case statement can be written as follows:

$$\mathbf{if}\ (\square m \cdot M[\overline{q}] = m \rightarrow S_m)\ \mathbf{fi} \tag{11.3}$$

The statement (11.3) selects a command to execute next according to the outcome of measurement M:

- if the outcome is m, then the corresponding command S_m will be executed.

In particular, whenever M is a yes–no measurement; that is, it has only two possible outcome 1 (yes) and 0 (no), then case statement (11.3) is a generalisation of conditional statement (11.1), and it can be appropriately termed as classical conditional statement in quantum programming. As indicated by Exercise 5.5, quantum **while**-loop (5.5) can be seen as a recursive program declared by such a conditional statement.

3. *Quantum case statement*: Except (11.3), there is actually another kind of case statement, which is very useful in quantum programming. This new notion of case statement can be defined by extending a key idea from the definition of the shift operator of a quantum walk on a graph. Recall from Example 4.2 that the shift operator is an operator on $\mathcal{H}_d \otimes \mathcal{H}_p$ defined as follows:

$$S|i, v\rangle = |i, v_i\rangle$$

for each direction $1 \leq i \leq n$ and each vertex $v \in V$, where v_i is the ith neighbour of v, and $\mathcal{H}_d$, $\mathcal{H}_p$ are the direction "coin" space and the position space, respectively.

This shift operator can be viewed in a slightly different way: for each $1 \leq i \leq n$, we define the shift S_i in the direction i as an operator on $\mathcal{H}_p$:

$$S_i|v\rangle = |v_i\rangle$$

for any $v \in V$. Then we are able to combine these operators S_i ($1 \leq i \leq n$) along the "coin" to form the whole shift operator S:

$$S|i, v\rangle = |i\rangle S_i|v\rangle \tag{11.4}$$

for any $1 \leq i \leq n$ and $v \in V$. It is worth noticing that operators S and S_i ($1 \leq i \leq n$) are defined in different Hilbert spaces: S is on $\mathcal{H}_d \otimes \mathcal{H}_p$, whereas all S_i are on $\mathcal{H}_p$.

Let us carefully observe the behaviour of shift operator S. The operators $S_1, ..., S_n$ can be seen as a collection of programs independent to each other. Then S can be seen as a kind of case statement of $S_1, ..., S_n$ because S selects one of them for execution. But Eq. (11.4) clearly indicates that this case statement is different from (11.3):

- the selection in Eq. (11.4) is made according to the basis state $|i\rangle$ of the "coin space", which is quantum information rather than classical information.

Thus, we can appropriately call S a *quantum case statement*. At this stage, the reader might still not be convinced that the behaviours of case statement (11.3) and a quantum case statement are really different, despite the fact that measurement outcomes m are classical information, and basis states $|i\rangle$ are quantum information. The essential difference between them will become clearer later when we consider the control flow of a quantum case statement.

The above idea can be significantly extended. Let $S_1, S_2, ..., S_n$ be a collection of general quantum programs whose state spaces are the same Hilbert space $\mathcal{H}$. We introduce an external quantum system, called the "coin" system. It is allowed to be a single system or a composite system, so denoted by a quantum register $\overline{q}$ consisting of a family of new quantum variables that do not appear in $S_1, S_2, ..., S_n$. Assume that the state space of system $\overline{q}$ is an n-dimensional Hilbert space $\mathcal{H}_q$ and $\{|i\rangle\}_{i=1}^{n}$ is an orthonormal basis of it. Then a quantum case statement S can be defined by combining programs

$S_1, S_2, ..., S_n$ along the basis $\{|i\rangle\}$:

$$
\begin{aligned}
S \equiv \mathbf{qif}\, [\overline{q}] : \quad &|1\rangle \rightarrow S_1 \\
\square \quad &|2\rangle \rightarrow S_2 \\
&...... \\
\square \quad &|n\rangle \rightarrow S_n \\
\mathbf{fiq} &
\end{aligned}
\tag{11.5}
$$

or more compactly

$$
S \equiv \mathbf{qif}\, [\overline{q}](\square i \cdot |i\rangle \rightarrow S_i)\, \mathbf{fiq}
$$

Quantum control flows: Now let us look at the control flow of quantum case statement (11.5) – the order of its execution. The control flow of S can be clearly seen through its semantics. Following Eq. (11.4), it is reasonable to conceive that the semantics $[\![S]\!]$ of S should be defined on the tensor product $\mathcal{H}_{\overline{q}} \otimes \mathcal{H}$ by

$$
[\![S]\!](|i\rangle|\varphi\rangle) = |i\rangle \left([\![S_i]\!]|\varphi\rangle \right)
\tag{11.6}
$$

for every $1 \leq i \leq n$ and $|\varphi\rangle \in \mathcal{H}$, where $[\![S_i]\!]$ is the semantics of S_i. Then the control flow of program S is determined by "coin" variables $\overline{q}$. For each $1 \leq i \leq n$, S_i is guarded by the basis state $|i\rangle$. In other words, the execution of program (11.5) is controlled by "coin" $\overline{q}$:

- when $\overline{q}$ is in state $|i\rangle$, the corresponding subprogram S_i will be executed.

The really interesting thing here is that $\overline{q}$ is a quantum "coin" rather than a classical "coin", and thus it can be not only in the basis states $|i\rangle$ but also in a superposition of them. A superposition of these basis states yields a quantum control flow – *superposition of control flows*:

$$
[\![S]\!]\left(\sum_{i=1}^{n} \alpha_i |i\rangle |\varphi_i\rangle \right) = \sum_{i=1}^{n} \alpha_i |i\rangle \left([\![S_i]\!]|\varphi_i\rangle \right)
\tag{11.7}
$$

for all $|\varphi_i\rangle \in \mathcal{H}$ and complex numbers α_i $(1 \leq i \leq n)$. Intuitively, in Eq. (11.7), for every $1 \leq i \leq n$, subprogram S_i is executed with probability amplitude α_i. This is very different from the classical case statement (11.3) of quantum programs where different guards "$M[\overline{q}] = m_1$",..., "$M[\overline{q}] = m_n$" cannot be superposed.

Technical difficulty in defining semantics of quantum case statements: At the first glance, it seems that the defining equation of shift operator in a quantum walk can be smoothly generalised to Eq. (11.6) to define the denotational semantics of a general quantum case statement. But there is actually a major (and subtle) difficulty in Eq. (11.6). For the case where no quantum measurement occurs in any S_i $(1 \leq i \leq n)$, the operational semantics of each S_i is simply given as a sequence of unitary operators, and Eq. (11.6) is not problematic at all. Whenever some S_i contains quantum measurements, however, its semantic structure becomes a tree of linear operators with branching happening at each point where a measurement is performed. Then Eq. (11.6) becomes meaningless within the framework of quantum mechanics, and defining the semantics of quantum case statement S requires to properly combine a collection of trees of quantum operations such that the relevant quantum mechanical principles are still obeyed. This problem will be circumvented in Sections 11.3 and 11.4 by introducing a semiclassical semantics in terms of operator-valued functions.

Exercise 11.1. Why Eq. (11.6) cannot properly define the semantics of quantum case statement (11.5) when a quantum measurement appears in some of S_i $(1 \leq i \leq n)$? Give some example(s) to illustrate your argument.

11.2 QuGCL: a language with quantum case statements

The notion of quantum case statement was carefully motivated in the previous section. Now we start to study programming with quantum case statement. First of all, we formally define a programming language QuGCL with the program construct of quantum case statement. It can be seen as a quantum counterpart of Dijkstra's GCL (Guarded Command Language) [132]. The alphabet of QuGCL is given as follows:

- As in Chapter 5, we assume a countable set *qVar* of quantum variables ranged over by $q, q_1, q_2, ...$ For each quantum variable $q \in qVar$, its type is a Hilbert space $\mathcal{H}_q$, which is the state space of the quantum system denoted by q. For a quantum register $\overline{q} = q_1, q_2, ..., q_n$ of distinct quantum variables, we write:

$$\mathcal{H}_{\overline{q}} = \bigotimes_{i=1}^{n} \mathcal{H}_{q_i}.$$

- For simplicity of the presentation, QuGCL is designed as a purely quantum programming language, but we include a countably infinite set *Var* of classical variables ranged over by x, y, ... so that we can use them to record the outcomes of quantum measurements. However, classical computation described by, for example, the assignment statement $x := e$ in a classical programming language, is excluded. For each classical variable $x \in Var$, its type is assumed to be a nonempty set D_x; that is, x takes values from D_x. In applications, if x is used to store the outcome of a quantum measurement M, then all possible outcomes of M should be in D_x.
- The sets of classical and quantum variables are required to disjoint: $qVar \cap Var = \emptyset$.

Using the alphabet presented above, we can define programs in QuGCL. For each QuGCL program S, we write $var(S)$ for the set of its classical variables, $qvar(P)$ for its quantum variables and $cvar(P)$ for its "coin" variables.

Definition 11.1. QuGCL programs are inductively defined as follows:

1. **abort** and **skip** are programs, and

$$var(\textbf{abort}) = var(\textbf{skip}) = \emptyset,$$
$$qvar(\textbf{abort}) = qvar(\textbf{skip}) = \emptyset,$$
$$cvar(\textbf{abort}) = cvar(\textbf{skip}) = \emptyset.$$

2. If $\overline{q}$ is a quantum register, and U is a unitary operator on $\mathcal{H}_{\overline{q}}$, then

$$\overline{q} := U[\overline{q}]$$

is a program, and

$$var(\overline{q} := U[\overline{q}]) = \emptyset, \quad qvar(\overline{q} := U[\overline{q}]) = \overline{q}, \quad cvar(\overline{q} := U[\overline{q}]) = \emptyset.$$

3. If S_1 and S_2 are programs such that $var(S_1) \cap var(S_2) = \emptyset$, then $S_1; S_2$ is a program, and

$$var(S_1; S_2) = var(S_1) \cup var(S_2),$$
$$qvar(S_1; S_2) = qvar(S_1) \cup qvar(S_2),$$
$$cvar(S_1; S_2) = cvar(S_1) \cup cvar(S_2).$$

4. If $\overline{q}$ is a quantum register, x is a classical variable, $M = \{M_m\}$ is a quantum measurement in $\mathcal{H}_{\overline{q}}$ such that all possible outcomes of M are in D_x, and $\{S_m\}$ is a family of programs indexed by the outcomes m of measurement M such that $x \notin \bigcup_m var(S_m)$, then the classical case statement of S_m's guarded by measurement outcomes m's:

$$S \equiv \textbf{if } (\square m \cdot M[\overline{q} : x] = m \rightarrow S_m) \textbf{ fi} \tag{11.8}$$

is a program, and

$$var(S) = \{x\} \cup \left(\bigcup_m var(S_m) \right),$$
$$qvar(S) = \overline{q} \cup \left(\bigcup_m qvar(S_m) \right),$$
$$cvar(S) = \bigcup_m cvar(S_m).$$

5. If $\overline{q}$ is a quantum register, $\{|i\rangle\}$ is an orthonormal basis of $\mathcal{H}_{\overline{q}}$, and $\{S_i\}$ is a family of programs indexed by the basis states $|i\rangle$'s such that

$$\overline{q} \cap \left(\bigcup_i qvar(S_i) \right) = \emptyset,$$

then the quantum case statement of S_i's guarded by basis states $|i\rangle$'s:

$$S \equiv \mathbf{qif}\,[\overline{q}]\,(\Box i \cdot |i\rangle \rightarrow S_i)\;\mathbf{fiq} \tag{11.9}$$

is a program, and

$$var(S) = \bigcup_i var(S_i),$$

$$qvar(S) = \overline{q} \cup \left(\bigcup_i qvar(S_i) \right),$$

$$cvar(S) = \overline{q} \cup \left(\bigcup_i cvar(S_i) \right).$$

The above definition looks quite complicated with quantum programs and their classical, quantum and "coin" variables being defined simultaneously. But the syntax of QuGCL can be simply summarised as follows:

$$S := \mathbf{abort} \mid \mathbf{skip} \mid \overline{q} := U[\overline{q}] \mid S_1; S_2$$
$$\mid \mathbf{if}\,(\Box m \cdot M[\overline{q} : x] = m \rightarrow S_m)\;\mathbf{fi} \qquad \text{(classical case statement)}$$
$$\mid \mathbf{qif}\,[\overline{q}]\,(\Box i \cdot |i\rangle \rightarrow S_i)\;\mathbf{fiq} \qquad \text{(quantum case statement)}$$

The meanings of **skip**, unitary transformation and sequential composition in QuGCL are the same as in the quantum **while**-language defined in Chapter 5. As in Dijkstra's GCL, **abort** is the undefined instruction that can do anything and even does not need to terminate. The intuitive meaning of quantum case statement (11.9) was already carefully explained in Section 11.1. But several delicate points in the design of the language QuGCL deserve further explanations:

- The requirement $var(S_1) \cap var(S_2) = \emptyset$ in the sequential composition $S_1; S_2$ means that the outcomes of measurements performed at different points are stored in different classical variables. Such a requirement is mainly for technical convenience, and it will considerably simplify the presentation.
- The statements (11.8) and (11.3) are essentially the same, and the only difference between them is that a classical variable x is added in (11.8) to record the measurement outcome. It is required in statement (11.8) that $x \notin \bigcup_m var(S_m)$. This means that the classical variables already used to record the outcomes of the measurements in S_m's are not allowed to store the outcome of a new measurement. This technical requirement is cumbersome, but it can significantly simplify the presentation of the semantics of QuGCL. On the other hand, it is not required that the measured quantum variables $\overline{q}$ do not occur in S_m. So, measurement M can be performed not only on an external system but also on some quantum variables within S_m.
- It should be emphasised that in the quantum case statement (11.9) the variables in $\overline{q}$ are not allowed to appear in any S_i's. This indicates that the "coin system" $\overline{q}$ is *external* to programs S_i's. This requirement is so important that it will be emphasised again and again in this chapter and the next. The reason for this requirement will become clear when we consider the semantics of quantum case statement in the following two sections.
- Obviously, all "coins" are quantum variables: $cvar(S) \subseteq qvar(S)$ for all programs S. It will be needed in defining a kind of equivalence between quantum programs to distinguish the set $cvar(S)$ of "coin" variables from other quantum variables in S.

To conclude this section, let us see a simple example showing how a large quantum gate employed in several important quantum algorithms [22,80], namely quantum random-access gate, can be conveniently programmed in QuGCL.

Example 11.1. Let $n \geq 1$ be an integer. Then quantum random-access gates RAG_n on $n + 2$ qubits is defined in the computational basis by

$$\text{RAG}_n |i, b, x_1, ..., x_n\rangle = |i, x_i, x_1, ..., x_{i-1}, b, x_{i+1}, ..., x_n\rangle \tag{11.10}$$

for all $1 \leq i \leq n$ and $b, x_1, ..., x_n \in \{0, 1\}$. It can be written as a quantum case statement in QuGCL:

$$\text{RAG}_n = \mathbf{qif}\,\Box_{i=1}^{n}\,|i\rangle \rightarrow \text{SWAP}[q_0, q_i]\;\mathbf{fiq}. \tag{11.11}$$

It should be pointed out that compared with the defining Eq. (11.10), program (11.11) provides a clearer intuition that RAG_n is a (quantum) alternation of n SWAP gates.

11.3 Guarded compositions of quantum operations

The syntax of quantum programming language QuGCL was defined in the last section. Now we consider how to define the semantics of QuGCL. It is clear that the main issue in defining the semantics of QuGCL is the treatment of quantum case statement because the semantics of the other program constructs either are trivial or were already well-defined in Chapter 5. As was pointed out in Section 11.1, a major difficulty in defining the semantics of a quantum case statement emerges in the case where quantum measurements occur in some of its branch subprograms. So, in this section, we prepare the key mathematical tool – guarded composition of quantum operations – for overcoming this difficulty.

11.3.1 Guarded composition of unitary operators

To ease the understanding of a general definition of guarded composition, we start with a special case of the guarded composition of unitary operators, which is a straightforward generalisation of the quantum walk shift operator S in Eq. (11.4). In this easy case, no quantum measurements are involved.

Definition 11.2. For each $1 \leq i \leq n$, let U_i be a unitary operator on Hilbert space $\mathcal{H}$. Let $\mathcal{H}_q$ be an auxiliary Hilbert space, called the "coin space", with $\{|i\rangle\}$ as an orthonormal basis. Then we define a linear operator U on $\mathcal{H}_q \otimes \mathcal{H}$ by

$$U(|i\rangle|\psi\rangle) = |i\rangle U_i |\psi\rangle \tag{11.12}$$

for any $|\psi\rangle \in \mathcal{H}$ and for any $1 \leq i \leq n$. By linearity we have:

$$U\left(\sum_i \alpha_i |i\rangle|\psi_i\rangle\right) = \sum_i \alpha_i |i\rangle U_i |\psi_i\rangle \tag{11.13}$$

for any $|\psi_i\rangle \in \mathcal{H}$ and complex numbers α_i. The operator U is called the guarded composition of U_i ($1 \leq i \leq n$) along the basis $\{|i\rangle\}$ and written as

$$U \equiv \bigoplus_{i=1}^{n} (|i\rangle \to U_i) \ or \ simply \ U \equiv \bigoplus_{i=1}^{n} U_i$$

It is easy to check that the guarded composition U is an unitary operator on $\mathcal{H}_q \otimes \mathcal{H}$. In particular, quantum "coin" q should be considered as a system external to the principal system that has $\mathcal{H}$ as its state space; otherwise the state space of the system composed by the "coin" and the principal system is not $\mathcal{H}_q \otimes \mathcal{H}$, and defining Eqs (11.12) and (11.13) are inappropriate.

Actually, the guarded composition of unitary operators is nothing new; it is just a quantum multiplexor (QMUX) introduced in Section 3.1.4.

Example 11.2. A QMUX U with k select qubits and d-qubit-wide data bus can be represented by a block-diagonal matrix:

$$U = diag(U_0, U_1, ..., U_{2^k-1}) = \begin{pmatrix} U_0 & & & \\ & U_1 & & \\ & & ... & \\ & & & U_{2^k-1} \end{pmatrix}.$$

Multiplexing $U_0, U_1, ..., U_{2^k-1}$ with k select qubits is exactly the guarded composition

$$\bigoplus_{i=0}^{2^k-1} (|i\rangle \to U_i) \tag{11.14}$$

along the computational basis $\{|i\rangle\}$ of k qubits. Eq. (11.14) clearly indicates that multiplexor U is a quantum alternation of U_i ($0 \leq i \leq 2^k - 1$).

The guarded composition U of U_i's in Definition 11.2 certainly depends on the chosen orthogonal basis $\{|i\rangle\}$ of the "coin" space $\mathcal{H}_q$. For any two different orthonormal basis $\{|i\rangle\}$ and $\{|\varphi_i\rangle\}$ of the "coin space" $\mathcal{H}_q$, there exists an unitary operator U_q such that $|\varphi_i\rangle = U_q|i\rangle$ for all i. Furthermore, a routine calculation yields:

Lemma 11.1. *The two compositions along different bases $\{|i\rangle\}$ and $\{|\varphi_i\rangle\}$ are related to each other by*

$$\bigoplus_i (|\varphi_i\rangle \to U_i) = (U_q \otimes I_{\mathcal{H}}) \bigoplus_i (|i\rangle \to U_i) \left(U_q^\dagger \otimes I_{\mathcal{H}}\right)$$

where $I_{\mathcal{H}}$ is the identity operator on $\mathcal{H}$.

The above lemma shows that the guarded composition along one orthonormal basis $\{|\varphi_i\rangle\}$ can be expressed in terms of the guarded composition along any other orthonormal basis $\{|i\rangle\}$. Therefore, the choice of orthonormal basis of the "coin space" is not essential for the definition of guarded composition.

11.3.2 Operator-valued functions

A general form of guarded composition of quantum operations cannot be defined by a straightforward generalisation of Definition 11.2. Instead, we need an auxiliary notion of operator-valued function. For any Hilbert space $\mathcal{H}$, we write $\mathcal{L}(\mathcal{H})$ for the space of (bounded linear) operators on $\mathcal{H}$.

Definition 11.3. Let Δ be a nonempty set. Then a function $F : \Delta \to \mathcal{L}(\mathcal{H})$ is called an operator-valued function in $\mathcal{H}$ over Δ if

$$\sum_{\delta \in \Delta} F(\delta)^\dagger \cdot F(\delta) \sqsubseteq I_{\mathcal{H}}, \tag{11.15}$$

where $I_{\mathcal{H}}$ is the identity operator on $\mathcal{H}$, and $\sqsubseteq$ stands for the Löwner order (see Definition 2.13). In particular, F is said to be full when inequality (11.15) becomes equality.

The simplest examples of operator-valued function are unitary operators and quantum measurements.

Example 11.3. 1. A unitary operator U on Hilbert space $\mathcal{H}$ can be seen as a full operator-valued function over a singleton $\Delta = \{\epsilon\}$. This function maps the only element ϵ of Δ to U.
2. A quantum measurement $M = \{M_m\}$ in Hilbert space $\mathcal{H}$ can be seen as a full operator-valued function over the set $\Delta = \{m\}$ of its possible outcomes. This function maps each outcome m to the corresponding measurement operator M_m.

It is interesting to compare part 2 of the above example with Example 2.9.2 where a quantum operation is induced from a quantum measurement by ignoring the measurement outcomes. However, in the above example the measurement outcomes are explicitly recorded in the index set $\Delta = \{m\}$.

More generally than the above example, a quantum operation defines a family of operator-valued functions. Let $\mathcal{E}$ be a quantum operation on Hilbert space $\mathcal{H}$. Then $\mathcal{E}$ has the Kraus operator-sum representation:

$$\mathcal{E} = \sum_i E_i \circ E_i^\dagger,$$

meaning:

$$\mathcal{E}(\rho) = \sum_i E_i \rho E_i^\dagger$$

for all density operators ρ on $\mathcal{H}$ (see Theorem 2.3). For such a representation, we set $\Delta = \{i\}$ for the set of indexes, and define an operator-valued function over Δ by

$$F(i) = E_i$$

for every i. Since operator-sum representation of $\mathcal{E}$ is not unique, by the above procedure $\mathcal{E}$ defines possibly more than a single operator-valued function.

Definition 11.4. The set $\mathbb{F}(\mathcal{E})$ of operator-valued functions generated by a quantum operation $\mathcal{E}$ consists of the operator-valued functions defined by all different Kraus operator-sum representations of $\mathcal{E}$.

Conversely, an operator-valued function determines uniquely a quantum operation.

Definition 11.5. Let F be an operator-valued function in Hilbert space $\mathcal{H}$ over set Δ. Then F defines a quantum operation $\mathcal{E}(F)$ on $\mathcal{H}$ as follows:

$$\mathcal{E}(F) = \sum_{\delta \in \Delta} F(\delta) \circ F(\delta)^{\dagger};$$

that is,

$$\mathcal{E}(F)(\rho) = \sum_{\delta \in \Delta} F(\delta) \rho F(\delta)^{\dagger}$$

for every density operator ρ on $\mathcal{H}$.

To further clarify the relationship between operator-valued functions and quantum operations, for a family $\mathbb{F}$ of operator-valued functions, we write:

$$\mathcal{E}(\mathbb{F}) = \{\mathcal{E}(F) : F \in \mathbb{F}\}.$$

It is obvious that $\mathcal{E}(\mathbb{F}(\mathcal{E})) = \{\mathcal{E}\}$ for each quantum operation $\mathcal{E}$. On the other hand, for any operator-valued function F over $\Delta = \{\delta_1, ..., \delta_k\}$, it follows from Lemma 6.4 (i.e. Theorem 8.2 in [318]) that $\mathbb{F}(\mathcal{E}(F))$ consists of all operator-valued functions G over some set $\Gamma = \{\gamma_1, ..., \gamma_l\}$ such that

$$G(\gamma_i) = \sum_{j=1}^{n} u_{ij} \cdot F(\delta_j)$$

for each $1 \leq i \leq n$, where $n = \max(k, l)$, $U = (u_{ij})$ is an $n \times n$ unitary matrix, $F(\delta_i) = G(\gamma_j) = 0_{\mathcal{H}}$ for all $k + 1 \leq i \leq n$ and $l + 1 \leq j \leq n$, and $0_{\mathcal{H}}$ is the zero operator on $\mathcal{H}$.

11.3.3 Guarded composition of operator-valued functions

Now we are going to define the guarded composition of operator-valued functions, which will serve as a step-stone in defining the guarded composition of quantum operations. Before doing so, we need to introduce a notation. Let Δ_i be a nonempty set for every $1 \leq i \leq n$. Then we write:

$$\bigoplus_{i=1}^{n} \Delta_i = \left\{\oplus_{i=1}^{n} \delta_i : \delta_i \in \Delta_i \text{ for every } 1 \leq i \leq n\right\}. \tag{11.16}$$

Here, $\oplus_{i=1}^{n} \delta_i$ is simply a notation indicating a formal, syntactic combination of δ_i $(1 \leq i \leq n)$. The intuitive meaning behind this notation will be explained when δ_i are used to denote the states of classical variables in the next section.

Definition 11.6. For each $1 \leq i \leq n$, let F_i be an operator-valued function in Hilbert space $\mathcal{H}$ over set Δ_i. Let $\mathcal{H}_q$ be a "coin" Hilbert space with $\{|i\rangle\}$ as an orthonormal basis. Then the guarded composition

$$F \triangleq \bigoplus_{i=1}^{n} (|i\rangle \to F_i) \text{ or simply } F \triangleq \bigoplus_{i=1}^{n} F_i$$

of F_i $(1 \leq i \leq n)$ along the basis $\{|i\rangle\}$ is an operator-valued function

$$F : \bigoplus_{i=1}^{n} \Delta_i \to \mathcal{L}(\mathcal{H}_q \otimes \mathcal{H})$$

in $\mathcal{H}_q \otimes \mathcal{H}$ over $\bigoplus_{i=1}^{n} \Delta_i$. It is defined in the following three steps:

1. For any $\delta_i \in \Delta_i$ $(1 \leq i \leq n)$,

$$F\left(\oplus_{i=1}^{n} \delta_i\right)$$

is an operator on $\mathcal{H}_q \otimes \mathcal{H}$.

2. For each $|\Psi\rangle \in \mathcal{H}_q \otimes \mathcal{H}$, there is a unique tuple $(|\psi_1\rangle, ..., |\psi_n\rangle)$ such that $|\psi_1\rangle, ..., |\psi_n\rangle \in \mathcal{H}$ and $|\Psi\rangle$ can be written as

$$|\Psi\rangle = \sum_{i=1}^{n} |i\rangle |\psi_i\rangle,$$

and then we define:

$$F\left(\oplus_{i=1}^{n} \delta_i\right) |\Psi\rangle = \sum_{i=1}^{n} \left(\prod_{k \neq i} \lambda_{k\delta_k}\right) |i\rangle \left(F_i(\delta_i)|\psi_i\rangle\right). \tag{11.17}$$

3. For any $\delta_k \in \Delta_k$ $(1 \leq k \leq n)$, the coefficients are given as

$$\lambda_{k\delta_k} = \sqrt{\frac{\operatorname{tr}\left(F_k(\delta_k)^\dagger F_k(\delta_k)\right)}{\sum_{\tau_k \in \Delta_k} \operatorname{tr}\left(F_k(\tau_k)^\dagger F_k(\tau_k)\right)}}. \tag{11.18}$$

In particular, if F_k is full and $d = \dim \mathcal{H} < \infty$, then

$$\lambda_{k\delta_k} = \sqrt{\frac{\operatorname{tr}\left(F_k(\delta_k)^\dagger F_k(\delta_k)\right)}{d}}.$$

The above definition is very involved. In particular, at the first glance it is not easy to see where the product of $\lambda_{k\delta_k}$ in Eq. (11.17) comes from. A simple answer to this question is that the product is chosen for normalisation of probability amplitudes. This point can be clearly seen from the proof of Lemma 11.3 (presented in Appendix A.7). Intuitively, the square $\lambda_{k\delta_k}^2$ of the coefficients defined in Eq. (11.18) can be understood as a kind of conditional probability. Actually, some different choices of coefficients in Eqs (11.17) and (11.18) are possible; a further discussion on this issue is given in Section 11.9.1.

One thing worthing a special attention is that the state space of guarded composition F in the above definition is $\mathcal{H}_q \otimes \mathcal{H}$, and thus quantum "coin" q must be treated as a system external to the principal system with state space $\mathcal{H}$.

It is easy to see that whenever Δ_i is a singleton for all $1 \leq i \leq n$, then all $\lambda_{k\delta_k} = 1$, and Eq. (11.17) degenerates to (11.13). So, the above definition is a generalisation of guarded composition of unitary operators introduced in Definition 11.2.

The following lemma shows that the guarded composition of operator-valued functions is well-defined.

Lemma 11.2. *The guarded composition $\bigoplus_{i=1}^{n} (|i\rangle \rightarrow F_i)$ is an operator-valued function in $\mathcal{H}_q \otimes \mathcal{H}$ over $\bigoplus_{i=1}^{n} \Delta_i$. In particular, if all F_i $(1 \leq i \leq n)$ are full, then so is F.*

For readability, the proof of this lemma is postponed to Appendix A.7.1. The reader is encouraged to work out a proof as an exercise.

Similar to Lemma 11.1, the choice of orthonormal basis of the "coin space" in the guarded composition of operator-valued function is not essential. For any two orthonormal bases $\{|i\rangle\}$ and $\{|\varphi_i\rangle\}$ of the "coin space" $\mathcal{H}_q$, let U_q be the unitary operator such that $|\varphi_i\rangle = U_q|i\rangle$ for all i. Then we have:

Lemma 11.3. *The two compositions along different bases $\{|i\rangle\}$ and $\{|\varphi_i\rangle\}$ are related to each other by*

$$\bigoplus_{i=1}^{n} (|\varphi_i\rangle \rightarrow F_i) = (U_q \otimes I_\mathcal{H}) \cdot \bigoplus_{i=1}^{n} (|i\rangle \rightarrow F_i) \cdot \left(U_q^\dagger \otimes I_\mathcal{H}\right);$$

that is,

$$\bigoplus_{i=1}^{n} (|\varphi_i\rangle \rightarrow F_i) \left(\oplus_{i=1}^{n} \delta_i\right) = (U_q \otimes I_\mathcal{H}) \left[\bigoplus_{i=1}^{n} (|i\rangle \rightarrow F_i) \left(\oplus_{i=1}^{n} \delta_i\right)\right] \left(U_q^\dagger \otimes I_\mathcal{H}\right)$$

for any $\delta_1 \in \Delta_1, ..., \delta_n \in \Delta_n$.

We now give an example to illustrate Definition 11.6. This example shows how to compose two quantum measurements via a quantum "coin", which is a qubit.

Example 11.4. Consider a guarded composition of two simplest quantum measurements:

- $M^{(0)}$ is the measurement on a qubit (the principal qubit) p in the computational basis $|0\rangle, |1\rangle$, i.e. $M^{(0)} = \{M_0^{(0)}, M_1^{(0)}\}$, where

$$M_0^{(0)} = |0\rangle\langle 0|, \quad M_1^{(0)} = |1\rangle\langle 1|;$$

- $M^{(1)}$ is the measurement of the same qubit but in a different basis:

$$|\pm\rangle = \frac{1}{\sqrt{2}}(|0\rangle \pm |1\rangle),$$

i.e. $M^{(1)} = \{M_+^{(1)}, M_-^{(1)}\}$, where

$$M_+^{(1)} = |+\rangle\langle +|, \quad M_-^{(1)} = |-\rangle\langle -|.$$

Then the guarded composition of $M^{(0)}$ and $M^{(1)}$ along the computational basis of another qubit (the "coin qubit") q is the measurement

$$M = M^{(0)} \oplus M^{(1)} = \{M_{0+}, M_{0-}, M_{1+}, M_{1-}\}$$

on two qubits q and p, where ij is an abbreviation of $i \oplus j$, and

$$M_{ij}\left(|0\rangle_q|\psi_0\rangle_p + |1\rangle_q|\psi_1\rangle_p\right) = \frac{1}{\sqrt{2}}\left(|0\rangle_q M_i^{(0)}|\psi_0\rangle_p + |1\rangle_q M_j^{(1)}|\psi_1\rangle_p\right)$$

for any states $|\psi_0\rangle, |\psi_1\rangle$ of the principal qubit p and $i \in \{0, 1\}$, $j \in \{+, -\}$. Furthermore, for each state $|\Psi\rangle$ of two qubits q, p and for any $i \in \{0, 1\}$, $j \in \{+, -\}$, a routine calculation yields that the probability that the outcome is ij when performing the guarded composition M of $M^{(0)}$ and $M^{(1)}$ on the two qubit system q, p in state $|\Psi\rangle$ is

$$p(i, j||\Psi\rangle, M) = \frac{1}{2}\left[p\left(i|_q\langle 0|\Psi\rangle, M^{(0)}\right) + p\left(j|_q\langle 1|\Psi\rangle, M^{(1)}\right)\right],$$

where:

1. if $|\Psi\rangle = |0\rangle_q|\psi_0\rangle_p + |1\rangle_q|\psi_1\rangle_p$, then

$$_q\langle k|\Psi\rangle = |\psi_k\rangle$$

   is the "conditional" state of the principal qubit p given that the two qubit system q, p is in state $|\Psi\rangle$ and the "coin" qubit q is in the basis state $|k\rangle$ for $k = 0, 1$;
2. $p\left(i|_q\langle 0|\Psi\rangle, M^{(0)}\right)$ is the probability that the outcome is i when performing measurement $M^{(0)}$ on qubit p in state $_q\langle 0|\Psi\rangle$;
3. $p\left(j|_q\langle 1|\Psi\rangle, M^{(1)}\right)$ is the probability that the outcome is j when performing measurement $M^{(1)}$ on qubit p in state $_q\langle 1|\Psi\rangle$.

11.3.4 Guarded composition of quantum operations

In the last subsection, we learned how to compose a family of operator-valued functions employing an external quantum "coin". Now the guarded composition of a family of quantum operations can be defined through the guarded composition of the operator-valued functions generated from them.

Definition 11.7. For each $1 \le i \le n$, let $\mathcal{E}_i$ be a quantum operation (i.e. superoperator) on Hilbert space $\mathcal{H}$. Let $\mathcal{H}_q$ be a "coin" Hilbert space with $\{|i\rangle\}$ as an orthonormal basis. Then the guarded composition of $\mathcal{E}_i$ ($1 \le i \le n$) along the basis $\{|i\rangle\}$ is defined to be the family of quantum operations on $\mathcal{H}_q \otimes \mathcal{H}$:

$$\bigoplus_{i=1}^{n}(|i\rangle \to \mathcal{E}_i) = \left\{\mathcal{E}\left(\bigoplus_{i=1}^{n}(|i\rangle \to F_i)\right) : F_i \in \mathbb{F}(\mathcal{E}_i) \text{ for every } 1 \le i \le n\right\},$$

where:

1. $\mathbb{F}(\mathcal{F})$ stands for the set of operator-valued functions generated by quantum operation $\mathcal{F}$ (see Definition 11.4);
2. $\mathcal{E}(F)$ is the quantum operation defined by an operator-valued function F (see Definition 11.5).

Similar to the cases in Definitions 11.2 and 11.6, the guarded composition $\bigoplus_{i=1}^{n}(|i\rangle \to \mathcal{E}_i)$ is a quantum operation on space $\mathcal{H}_q \otimes \mathcal{H}$, and thus quantum "coin" q is external to the principal system with state space $\mathcal{H}$.

It is easy to see that if $n = 1$ then the above guarded composition of quantum operations consists of only $\mathcal{E}_1$. For $n > 1$, however, it is usually not a singleton, as shown by the following example. For any unitary operator U on a Hilbert space $\mathcal{H}$, we write $\mathcal{E}_U = U \circ U^\dagger$ for the quantum operation defined by U; that is, $\mathcal{E}_U(\rho) = U\rho U^\dagger$ for all density operators ρ in $\mathcal{H}$ (see Example 2.8).

Example 11.5. Suppose that U_0 and U_1 are two unitary operators on a Hilbert space $\mathcal{H}$. Let U be the composition of U_0 and U_1 guarded by the computational basis $|0\rangle, |1\rangle$ of a qubit:

$$U = U_0 \oplus U_1.$$

Then $\mathcal{E}_U$ is an element of the guarded composition

$$\mathcal{E} = \mathcal{E}_{U_0} \oplus \mathcal{E}_{U_1}$$

of superoperators $\mathcal{E}_{U_0}$ and $\mathcal{E}_{U_1}$. But $\mathcal{E}$ contains more than one element. Indeed, it holds that

$$\mathcal{E} = \left\{ \mathcal{E}_{U_\theta} = U_\theta \circ U_\theta^\dagger : 0 \leq \theta < 2\pi \right\},$$

where

$$U_\theta = U_0 \oplus e^{i\theta} U_1.$$

Note that the nonuniqueness of the members of the guarded composition $\mathcal{E}$ is caused by the relative phase θ between U_0 and U_1.

We now examine the choice of basis of the "coin space" in the guarded composition of quantum operations. To this end, we need the following two notations:

- For any two quantum operations $\mathcal{E}_1$ and $\mathcal{E}_2$ in a Hilbert space $\mathcal{H}$, their sequential composition $\mathcal{E}_2 \circ \mathcal{E}_1$ is the quantum operation on $\mathcal{H}$ defined by

$$(\mathcal{E}_2 \circ \mathcal{E}_1)(\rho) = \mathcal{E}_2(\mathcal{E}_1(\rho))$$

for any density operator ρ on $\mathcal{H}$.
- More generally, for any quantum operation $\mathcal{E}$ and any set Ω of quantum operations on Hilbert space $\mathcal{H}$, we define the sequential compositions of Ω and $\mathcal{E}$ by

$$\mathcal{E} \circ \Omega = \{\mathcal{E} \circ \mathcal{F} : \mathcal{F} \in \Omega\} \quad \text{and} \quad \Omega \circ \mathcal{E} = \{\mathcal{F} \circ \mathcal{E} : \mathcal{F} \in \Omega\}.$$

The following lemma can be easily derived from Lemma 11.3, and it shows that the choice of orthonormal basis of the "coin space" is not essential for the guarded composition of quantum operations. For any two orthonormal bases $\{|i\rangle\}$ and $\{|\varphi_i\rangle\}$ of the "coin space" $\mathcal{H}_q$, let U_q be the unitary operator such that $|\varphi_i\rangle = U_q|i\rangle$ for all i. Then we have:

Lemma 11.4. *The two compositions along different bases $\{|i\rangle\}$ and $\{|\varphi_i\rangle\}$ are related to each other by*

$$\bigoplus_{i=1}^{n}(|\varphi_i\rangle \to \mathcal{E}_i) = \left[\mathcal{E}_{U_q^\dagger \otimes I_\mathcal{H}} \circ \bigoplus_{i=1}^{n}(|i\rangle \to \mathcal{E}_i) \right] \circ \mathcal{E}_{U_q \otimes I_\mathcal{H}},$$

where $\mathcal{E}_{U_q \otimes I_\mathcal{H}}$ and $\mathcal{E}_{U_q^\dagger \otimes I_\mathcal{H}}$ are the quantum operations on $\mathcal{H}_q \otimes \mathcal{H}$ defined by unitary operators $U_q \otimes I_\mathcal{H}$ and $U_q^\dagger \otimes I_\mathcal{H}$, respectively.

Exercise 11.2. Prove Lemmas 11.1, 11.3, and 11.4.

11.4 Semantics of QuGCL programs

With the preparation in Section 11.3, we are ready to define the semantics of the quantum programming language QuGCL presented in Section 11.2. Before doing it, we introduce several notations needed in this section.

- Let $\mathcal{H}$ and $\mathcal{H}'$ be two Hilbert spaces, and let E be an operator on $\mathcal{H}$. Then the cylindrical extension of E on $\mathcal{H} \otimes \mathcal{H}'$ is defined to be the operator $E \otimes I_{\mathcal{H}'}$, where $I_{\mathcal{H}'}$ is the identity operator on $\mathcal{H}'$. For simplicity, we will write E for $E \otimes I_{\mathcal{H}'}$ whenever confusion does not happen.
- Let F be an operator-valued function in $\mathcal{H}$ over Δ. Then the cylindrical extension of F in $\mathcal{H} \otimes \mathcal{H}'$ is the operator-valued function $\overline{F}$ in $\mathcal{H} \otimes \mathcal{H}'$ over Δ defined by

$$\overline{F}(\delta) = F(\delta) \otimes I_{\mathcal{H}'}$$

  for every $\delta \in \Delta$. For simplicity, we often write F for $\overline{F}$ whenever confusion can be excluded from the context.
- Let $\mathcal{E} = \sum_i E_i \circ E_i^\dagger$ be a quantum operation on $\mathcal{H}$. Then the cylindrical extension of $\mathcal{E}$ in $\mathcal{H} \otimes \mathcal{H}'$ is defined to be the quantum operation:

$$\overline{\mathcal{E}} = \sum_i (E_i \otimes I_{\mathcal{H}'}) \circ \left(E_i^\dagger \otimes I_{\mathcal{H}'} \right).$$

For simplicity, $\mathcal{E}$ will be used to denote its extension $\overline{\mathcal{E}}$ when no confusion occurs. In particular, if E is an operator on $\mathcal{H}$, and ρ is a density operator on $\mathcal{H} \otimes \mathcal{H}'$, then $E\rho E^\dagger$ should be understood as $(E \otimes I_{\mathcal{H}'}) \rho \left(E^\dagger \otimes I_{\mathcal{H}'} \right)$.

11.4.1 Classical states

The first step in defining the semantics of QuGCL is to define the states of classical variables in QuGCL. As already stated in Section 11.2, classical variables in QuGCL will be only used to record the outcomes of quantum measurements.

Definition 11.8. Classical states and their domains are inductively defined as follows:

1. ϵ is a classical state, called the empty state, and $dom(\epsilon) = \emptyset$;
2. If $x \in Var$ is a classical variable, and $a \in D_x$ is an element of the domain of x, then $[x \leftarrow a]$ is a classical state, and $dom([x \leftarrow a]) = \{x\}$;
3. If both δ_1 and δ_2 are classical states, and $dom(\delta_1) \cap dom(\delta_2) = \emptyset$, then $\delta_1\delta_2$ is a classical state, and $dom(\delta_1\delta_2) = dom(\delta_1) \cup dom(\delta_2)$;
4. If δ_i is a classical state for every $1 \leq i \leq n$, then $\oplus_{i=1}^n \delta_i$ is a classical state, and

$$dom \left(\oplus_{i=1}^n \delta_i \right) = \bigcup_{i=1}^n dom(\delta_i).$$

Intuitively, a classical state δ defined by clauses 1 to 3 in the above definition can be seen as a (partial) assignment to classical variables; more precisely, δ is an element of cartesian product $\prod_{x \in dom(\delta)} D_x$; that is, a choice function:

$$\delta : dom(\delta) \rightarrow \bigcup_{x \in dom(\delta)} D_x$$

such that $\delta(x) \in D_x$ for every $x \in dom(\delta)$. The state $\oplus_{i=1}^n \delta_i$ defined by clause 4 is a formal combination of states δ_i $(1 \leq i \leq n)$. It will be used in defining the semantics of quantum case statement, which is a guarded composition of operator-valued functions. From Eq. (11.16) and Definition 11.6 we can see why such a combination is required. More concretely, we have:

- The empty state ϵ is the empty function. Since $\prod_{x \in \emptyset} D_x = \{\epsilon\}$, ϵ is the only possible state with empty domain.
- The state $[x \leftarrow a]$ assigns value a to variable x but the values of the other variables are undefined.
- The composed state $\delta_1\delta_2$ can be seen as the assignment to variables in $dom(\delta_1) \cup dom(\delta_2)$ given by

$$(\delta_1\delta_2)(x) = \begin{cases} \delta_1(x) & \text{if } x \in dom(\delta_1), \\ \delta_2(x) & \text{if } x \in dom(\delta_2). \end{cases} \tag{11.19}$$

Eq. (11.19) is well-defined since it is required that $dom(\delta_1) \cap dom(\delta_2) = \emptyset$. In particular, $\epsilon\delta = \delta\epsilon = \delta$ for any state δ, and if $x \notin dom(\delta)$ then $\delta[x \leftarrow a]$ is the assignment to variables in $dom(\delta) \cup \{x\}$ given by

$$\delta[x \leftarrow a](y) = \begin{cases} \delta(y) & \text{if } y \in dom(\delta), \\ a & \text{if } y = x. \end{cases}$$

Hence, $[x_1 \leftarrow a_1] \cdots [x_k \leftarrow a_k]$ is a classical state that assigns value a_j to variable x_j for every $1 \le j \le k$. It will be abbreviated to

$$[x_1 \leftarrow a_1, \cdots, x_k \leftarrow a_k]$$

in the sequel.

- The state $\oplus_{i=1}^{n}\delta_i$ can be thought of as a kind of nondeterministic choice of δ_i ($1 \le i \le n$). As will be seen in the next subsection (in particular, clause 5 of Definition 11.9), a classical state $\delta = [x_1 \leftarrow a_1, \cdots, x_k \leftarrow a_k]$ is actually generated by a sequence of measurements $M_1, ..., M_k$ with their outcomes $a_1, ..., a_k$ stored in variables $x_1, ..., x_k$, respectively. However, for quantum measurements $M_1, ..., M_k$, other outcomes $a'_1, ..., a'_k$ are possible, and then we may have many other classical states $\delta' = [x_1 \leftarrow a'_1, \cdots, x_k \leftarrow a'_k]$. So, a state of the form $\oplus_{i=1}^{n}\delta_i$ is needed to record a collection of all different outcomes of measurement sequence $M_1, ..., M_k$.

11.4.2 Semi-classical semantics

Now we can define the semiclassical semantics of QuGCL, which will serve as a stepping stone for defining its purely quantum semantics. For each QuGCL program S, we write $\Delta(S)$ for the set of all possible states of its classical variables.

- The semiclassical denotational semantics $\|S\|$ of S will be defined as an operator-valued function in $\mathcal{H}_{qvar(S)}$ over $\Delta(S)$, where $\mathcal{H}_{qvar(S)}$ is the state Hilbert space of quantum variables occurring in S.

In particular, if $qvar(S) = \emptyset$; for example $S = \textbf{abort}$ or $\textbf{skip}$, then $\mathcal{H}_{qvar(S)}$ is a one-dimensional space $\mathcal{H}_\emptyset$, and an operator on $\mathcal{H}_\emptyset$ can be identified with a complex number; for instance the zero operator is number 0 and the identity operator is number 1. For any set $V \subseteq qVar$ of quantum variables, we write I_V for the identity operator on Hilbert space $\mathcal{H}_V = \bigotimes_{q \in V} \mathcal{H}_q$.

Definition 11.9. The classical states $\Delta(S)$ and semiclassical semantic function $\|S\|$ of a QuGCL program S are inductively defined as follows:

1. $\Delta(\textbf{abort}) = \{\epsilon\}$, and $\|\textbf{abort}\|(\epsilon) = 0$;
2. $\Delta(\textbf{skip}) = \{\epsilon\}$, and $\|\textbf{skip}\|(\epsilon) = 1$;
3. If $S \equiv \overline{q} := U[\overline{q}]$, then $\Delta(S) = \{\epsilon\}$, and $\|S\|(\epsilon) = U_{\overline{q}}$, where $U_{\overline{q}}$ is the unitary operator U acting on $\mathcal{H}_{\overline{q}}$;
4. If $S \equiv S_1; S_2$, then

$$\Delta(S) = \Delta(S_1); \Delta(S_2) = \{\delta_1\delta_2 : \delta_1 \in \Delta(S_1), \delta_2 \in \Delta(S_2)\}, \qquad (11.20)$$

$$\|S\|(\delta_1\delta_2) = \left(\|S_2\|(\delta_2) \otimes I_{V \setminus qvar(S_2)}\right) \cdot \left(\|S_1\|(\delta_1) \otimes I_{V \setminus qvar(S_1)}\right)$$

where $V = qvar(S_1) \cup qvar(S_2)$;

5. If S is a classical case statement:

$$S \equiv \textbf{if } (\square m \cdot M[\overline{q} : x] = m \rightarrow S_m) \textbf{ fi},$$

where quantum measurement $M = \{M_m\}$, then

$$\Delta(S) = \bigcup_m \{\delta[x \leftarrow m] : \delta \in \Delta(S_m)\},$$

$$\|S\|(\delta[x \leftarrow m]) = \left(\|S_m\|(\delta) \otimes I_{V \setminus qvar(S_m)}\right) \cdot \left(M_m \otimes I_{V \setminus \overline{q}}\right)$$

for every $\delta \in \Delta(S_m)$ and for every outcome m, where

$$V = \overline{q} \cup \left(\bigcup_m qvar(S_m)\right);$$

6. If S is a quantum case statement:

$$S \equiv \mathbf{qif}\,[\overline{q}]\,(\square i \cdot |i\rangle \to S_i)\;\mathbf{fiq},$$

then

$$\Delta(S) = \bigoplus_i \Delta(S_i), \tag{11.21}$$

$$\|S\| = \bigoplus_i \left(|i\rangle \to \|S_i\|\right), \tag{11.22}$$

where operation $\bigoplus$ in Eq. (11.21) is defined by Eq. (11.16), and $\bigoplus$ in Eq. (11.22) stands for the guarded composition of operator-valued functions (see Definition 11.6).

Since it is required in Definition 11.1 that $var(S_1) \cap var(S_2) = \emptyset$ in the sequential composition $S_1; S_2$, we have $dom(\delta_1) \cap dom(\delta_2) = \emptyset$ for any $\delta_1 \in \Delta(S_1)$ and $\delta_2 \in \Delta(S_2)$. Thus, Eq. (11.20) is well-defined.

Intuitively, the semiclassical semantics of quantum programs can be imagined as follows:

- If a quantum program S does not contain any quantum case statement, then its semantic structure is a tree with its nodes labelled by basic commands and its edges by linear operators. This tree grows up from the root in the following way:
  - if the current node is labelled by a unitary transformation U, then a single edge stems from the node and it is labelled by U; and
  - if the current node is labelled by a measurement $M = \{M_m\}$, then for each possible outcome m, an edge stems from the node and it is labelled by the corresponding measurement operator M_m.

  Obviously, branching in the semantic tree comes from the different possible outcomes of a measurement in S. Each classical state $\delta \in \Delta(S)$ is corresponding to a branch in the semantic tree of S, and it denotes a possible path of execution. Furthermore, the value of semantic function $\|S\|$ in state δ is the (sequential) composition of the operators labelling the edges of δ. This can be clearly seen from clauses 1–5 of the above definition.
- The semantic structure of a quantum program S with quantum case statements is much more complicated. It can be seen as a tree with superpositions of nodes that generate superpositions of branches. The value of semantic function $\|S\|$ in a superposition of branches is then defined as the guarded composition of the values in these branches.

11.4.3 Purely quantum semantics

The purely quantum semantics of a quantum program written in QuGCL can be naturally defined as the quantum operation induced by its semiclassical semantic function (see Definition 11.5).

Definition 11.10. For each QuGCL program S, its purely quantum denotational semantics is the quantum operation $[\![S]\!]$ on $\mathcal{H}_{qvar(S)}$ defined as follows:

$$[\![S]\!] = \mathcal{E}(\|S\|) = \sum_{\delta \in \Delta(S)} \|S\|(\delta) \circ \|S\|(\delta)^{\dagger}, \tag{11.23}$$

where $\|S\|$ is the semiclassical semantic function of S.

The following proposition presents an explicit representation of the purely quantum semantics of a QuGCL program in terms of its subprograms. This representation is easier to use in applications than the above abstract definition.

Proposition 11.1. **1.** $[\![\mathbf{abort}]\!] = 0$;

2. $[\![\mathbf{skip}]\!] = 1$;

3. $[\![S_1; S_2]\!] = [\![S_1]\!]; [\![S_2]\!]$;

4. $[\![\overline{q} := U[\overline{q}]]\!] = U_{\overline{q}} \circ U_{\overline{q}}^{\dagger}$;

5.

$$\left[\!\!\left[\mathbf{if}\;(\square m \cdot M[\overline{q} : x] = m \to S_m)\;\mathbf{fi}\right]\!\!\right] = \sum_m \left[\left(M_m \circ M_m^{\dagger}\right); [\![S_m]\!]\right].$$

Here, $[\![S_m]\!]$ *should be seen as a cylindrical extension on $\mathcal{H}_V$ from $\mathcal{H}_{qvar(S_m)}$, $M_m \circ M_m^\dagger$ is seen as a cylindrical extension on $\mathcal{H}_V$ from $\mathcal{H}_{\overline{q}}$, and*

$$V = \overline{q} \cup \left(\bigcup_m qvar(S_m) \right);$$

6.

$$[\![\mathbf{qif}\,[\overline{q}]\,(\square i \cdot |i\rangle \rightarrow S_i)\,\mathbf{fiq}]\!] \in \bigoplus_i \left(|i\rangle \rightarrow [\![S_i]\!] \right). \tag{11.24}$$

Here $[\![S_i]\!]$ *should be understood as a cylindrical extension on $\mathcal{H}_V$ from $\mathcal{H}_{qvar(S_i)}$ for every $1 \leq i \leq n$, and*

$$V = \overline{q} \cup \left(\bigcup_i qvar(S_i) \right).$$

Essentially, clauses 2–5 in the above proposition are the same as the corresponding clauses in Proposition 5.1. But clause 6 has no counterpart in Proposition 5.1. The proof of this proposition is deferred to Appendix A.7.2. Actually, the proof is not difficult although it is tedious. The reader is encouraged to try to prove this proposition in order to gain a better understanding of Definitions 11.9 and 11.10.

The above proposition shows that the purely quantum denotational semantics is *almost compositional*, but it is *not completely compositional* because the symbol "$\in$" appears in Eq. (11.24). The symbol "$\in$" can be understood as a *refinement relation*. It is worth noting that in general the symbol "$\in$" in (11.24) cannot be replaced by equality. This is exactly the reason that the purely quantum semantics of a program has to be derived through its semiclassical semantics but cannot be defined directly by a structural induction.

It should be stressed that the symbol "$\in$" in Eq. (11.24) does not mean that the purely quantum semantics of quantum case statement is not well-defined. In fact, it is uniquely defined by Eqs (11.22) and (11.23) as a quantum operation. The right-hand side of Eq. (11.24) is not the semantics of any program. It is the guarded composition of the semantics of programs S_i. Since it is the guarded composition of a family of quantum operations, it can be a set consisting of more than one quantum operation, as shown in Example 11.5. The semantics of the quantum case statement is one member of the set of quantum operations in the right-hand side of Eq. (11.24).

Exercise 11.3. Find an example to show that Eq. (11.24) is not true when the symbol "$\in$" is replaced by equality.

Equivalence between quantum programs can be introduced based on their purely quantum denotational semantics. Roughly speaking, two programs are equivalent if the outputs computed by them are the same for the same input. Formally, we have:

Definition 11.11. Let P and Q be two QuGCL programs. Then:

1. We say that P and Q are equivalent and write $P = Q$ if

$$[\![P]\!] \otimes \mathcal{I}_{Q \setminus P} = [\![Q]\!] \otimes \mathcal{I}_{P \setminus Q},$$

where $\mathcal{I}_{Q \setminus P}$ is the identity quantum operation on $\mathcal{H}_{qvar(Q) \setminus qvar(P)}$ and $\mathcal{I}_{P \setminus Q}$ the identity quantum operation on $\mathcal{H}_{qvar(P) \setminus qvar(Q)}$.

2. The "coin-free" equivalence $P =_{CF} Q$ holds if

$$\mathrm{tr}_{\mathcal{H}_{cvar(P) \cup cvar(Q)}} \left([\![P]\!] \otimes \mathcal{I}_{Q \setminus P} \right) = \mathrm{tr}_{\mathcal{H}_{cvar(P) \cup cvar(Q)}} \left([\![Q]\!] \otimes \mathcal{I}_{P \setminus Q} \right).$$

The symbol "tr" in the above equation denotes partial trace. The partial trace on density operators was introduced in Definition 2.22. Furthermore, the notion of partial trace can be generalised to quantum operations: for any quantum operation $\mathcal{E}$ on $\mathcal{H}_1 \otimes \mathcal{H}_2$, $\mathrm{tr}_{\mathcal{H}_1}(\mathcal{E})$ is a quantum operation from $\mathcal{H}_1 \otimes \mathcal{H}_2$ to $\mathcal{H}_2$ defined by

$$\mathrm{tr}_{\mathcal{H}_1}(\mathcal{E})(\rho) = \mathrm{tr}_{\mathcal{H}_1}(\mathcal{E}(\rho))$$

for all density operators ρ on $\mathcal{H}_1 \otimes \mathcal{H}_2$.

Obviously, $P = Q$ implies $P =_{CF} Q$. The "coin-free" equivalence means that "coin" variables are only used to produce quantum control flows of programs (or to realise superposition of programs, as will be discussed in the next section). The computational outcome of a program P is stored in the "principal" state space $\mathcal{H}_{qvar(P)\setminus cvar(P)}$. For the special case of $qvar(P) = qvar(Q)$, we have:

- $P = Q$ if and only if $[\![P]\!] = [\![Q]\!]$; and
- $P =_{CF} Q$ if and only if $\text{tr}_{\mathcal{H}_{cvar(P)}}[\![P]\!] = \text{tr}_{\mathcal{H}_{cvar(P)}}[\![Q]\!]$.

The notions of equivalence given in the above definition provide a basis for quantum program transformation and optimisation where the transformed program is required to be equivalent to the source program. A set of algebraic laws that can help to establish equivalence between QuGCL programs will be presented in Section 11.6.

11.4.4 Weakest precondition semantics

The notion of quantum weakest precondition was introduced in Section 6.1.1, and the weakest precondition semantics of quantum **while**-programs were presented in Section 6.3. Here, we give the weakest precondition semantics of QuGCL programs. They can be derived from Proposition 11.1 together with Proposition 6.1. As in classical programming and in the case of quantum **while**-programs, weakest precondition semantics provides us with a way for analysing QuGCL programs backwards.

Proposition 11.2. 1. $wp.\textbf{abort} = 0$;

2. $wp.\textbf{skip} = 1$;

3. $wp.(S_1; S_2) = wp.S_2; wp.S_1$;

4. $wp.U[\overline{q}] = U_{\overline{q}}^{\dagger} \circ U_{\overline{q}}$;

5.

$$wp.\textbf{if} \ (\square m \cdot M[\overline{q}:x] = m \to S_m) \ \textbf{fi} = \sum_m \left[wp.S_m; \left(M_m^{\dagger} \circ M_m \right) \right];$$

6. $wp.\textbf{qif}\,[\overline{q}]\,(\square i \cdot |i\rangle \to S_i) \ \textbf{fiq} \in \square_i \,(|i\rangle \to wp.S_i)$.

Some cylindrical extensions of quantum operations are used but unspecified in the above proposition because they can be recognised from the context. In the right-hand sides of the equations in clauses 3 and 5, the symbol ";" stands for composition of quantum operations. Again, the symbol "$\in$" in the above clause 6 cannot be replaced by equality because the right-hand side of clause 6 is a set that may contain more than one quantum operation.

We can define the refinement relation between quantum QuGCL programs in terms of their weakest precondition semantics. To this end, we first generalise the Löwner order to the case of quantum operations: for any two quantum operations $\mathcal{E}$ and $\mathcal{F}$ on Hilbert space $\mathcal{H}$,

- $\mathcal{E} \sqsubseteq \mathcal{F}$ if and only if $\mathcal{E}(\rho) \sqsubseteq \mathcal{F}(\rho)$ for all density operators ρ on $\mathcal{H}$.

Definition 11.12. Let P and Q be two QuGCL programs. Then we say that P is refined by Q and write $P \sqsubseteq Q$ if

$$wp.P \otimes \mathcal{I}_{Q\setminus P} \sqsubseteq wp.Q \otimes \mathcal{I}_{P\setminus Q},$$

where $\mathcal{I}_{Q\setminus P}$ and $\mathcal{I}_{P\setminus Q}$ are the same as in Definition 11.11.

Intuitively, $P \sqsubseteq Q$ means that P is improved by Q because the precondition of P is weakened to the precondition of Q. It is easy to see that $P \sqsubseteq Q$ and $Q \sqsubseteq P$ implies $P \equiv Q$. The notion of "coin-free" refinement can be defined in a way similar to Definition 11.11.2.

The refinement techniques have been successfully developed in classical programming so that specifications (of users' requirements) can be refined step by step using various refinement laws and finally transferred to codes that can be executed on machines; see [37] and [311] for a systematic exposition of refinement techniques. These techniques were extended to probabilistic programming in [417] and quantum programming with classical control flows [424]. Here, we are not going to further consider how can refinement techniques be used in quantum programming with quantum control flows, but leave it as a topic for future research.

11.4.5 An example

To close out this section, we present a simple example that helps us to understand the semantic notions introduced above.

Example 11.6. Let q be a qubit variable and x, y two classical variables. Consider the QuGCL program

$$P \equiv \mathbf{qif}\ |0\rangle \to H[q];$$
$$\mathbf{if}\ M^{(0)}[q:x] = 0 \to X[q];$$
$$\square \qquad\qquad 1 \to Y[q]$$
$$\mathbf{fi}$$
$$\square\ |1\rangle \to S[q];$$
$$\mathbf{if}\ M^{(1)}[q:x] = 0 \to Y[q]$$
$$\square \qquad\qquad 1 \to Z[q]$$
$$\mathbf{fi};$$
$$X[q];$$
$$\mathbf{if}\ M^{(0)}[q:y] = 0 \to Z[q]$$
$$\square \qquad\qquad 1 \to X[q]$$
$$\mathbf{fi}$$
$$\mathbf{fiq}$$

where $M^{(0)}$, $M^{(1)}$ are the measurements on a qubit in computational basis $|0\rangle, |1\rangle$ and basis $|\pm\rangle$, respectively (see Example 11.4), H is the Hadamard gate, X, Y, Z are the Pauli matrices, and S is the phase gate (see Examples 3.1 and 3.2). The program P is a quantum case statement between two subprograms P_0 and P_1 with the "coin" omitted. The first subprogram P_0 is the Hadamard gate followed by the measurement in the computational basis, where whenever the outcome is 0, then the gate X follows; whenever the outcome is 1, then the gate Y follows. The second subprogram P_1 is the gate S followed by the measurement in basis $|\pm\rangle$, the gate X, and the measurement in the computational basis.

1. For simplicity, we write a for classical state $[x \leftarrow a]$ of program P_0 and bc for classical state $[x \leftarrow b, y \leftarrow c]$ of program P_1 for any $a, c \in \{0, 1\}$ and $b \in \{+, -\}$. Then the semiclassical semantic functions of P_0 and P_1 are given as follows:

$$\begin{cases} \llbracket P_0 \rrbracket(0) = X \cdot |0\rangle\langle 0| \cdot H = \frac{1}{\sqrt{2}}\begin{pmatrix} 0 & 0 \\ 1 & 1 \end{pmatrix}, \\[2mm] \llbracket P_0 \rrbracket(1) = Y \cdot |1\rangle\langle 1| \cdot H = \frac{i}{\sqrt{2}}\begin{pmatrix} -1 & 1 \\ 0 & 0 \end{pmatrix}, \\[2mm] \llbracket P_1 \rrbracket(+0) = Z \cdot |0\rangle\langle 0| \cdot X \cdot Y \cdot |+\rangle\langle +| \cdot S = \frac{1}{2}\begin{pmatrix} i & -1 \\ 0 & 0 \end{pmatrix}, \\[2mm] \llbracket P_1 \rrbracket(+1) = X \cdot |1\rangle\langle 1| \cdot X \cdot Y \cdot |+\rangle\langle +| \cdot S = \frac{1}{2}\begin{pmatrix} -i & 1 \\ 0 & 0 \end{pmatrix}, \\[2mm] \llbracket P_1 \rrbracket(-0) = Z \cdot |0\rangle\langle 0| \cdot X \cdot Z \cdot |-\rangle\langle -| \cdot S = \frac{1}{2}\begin{pmatrix} 1 & -i \\ 0 & 0 \end{pmatrix}, \\[2mm] \llbracket P_1 \rrbracket(-1) = X \cdot |1\rangle\langle 1| \cdot X \cdot Z \cdot |-\rangle\langle -| \cdot S = \frac{1}{2}\begin{pmatrix} 1 & -i \\ 0 & 0 \end{pmatrix}. \end{cases}$$

The semiclassical semantic function of P is an operator-valued function in the state space of two qubits over classical states

$$\Delta(P) = \{a \oplus bc : a, c \in \{0, 1\}\ and\ b \in \{+, -\}\}.$$

It follows from Eq. (11.17) that

$$\llbracket P \rrbracket(a \oplus bc)(|0\rangle|\varphi\rangle) = \lambda_{1(bc)}|0\rangle\left(\llbracket P_0 \rrbracket(a)|\varphi\rangle\right),$$
$$\llbracket P \rrbracket(a \oplus bc)(|1\rangle|\varphi\rangle) = \lambda_{0a}|1\rangle\left(\llbracket P_1 \rrbracket(bc)|\varphi\rangle\right),$$

where $\lambda_{0a} = \frac{1}{\sqrt{2}}$ and $\lambda_{1(bc)} = \frac{1}{2}$ for $a, c \in \{0, 1\}$ and $b \in \{+, -\}$. Using

$$\|P\|(a \oplus bc) = \sum_{i,j \in 0,1} (\|P\|(a \oplus bc)|ij\rangle)\langle ij|,$$

we can compute:

$$\|P\|(0 \oplus +0) = \frac{1}{2\sqrt{2}} \begin{pmatrix} 0 & 1 & 0 & 0 \\ 0 & 1 & 0 & 0 \\ 0 & 0 & i & 0 \\ 0 & 0 & -1 & 0 \end{pmatrix},$$

$$\|P\|(0 \oplus +1) = \frac{1}{2\sqrt{2}} \begin{pmatrix} 0 & 1 & 0 & 0 \\ 0 & 1 & 0 & 0 \\ 0 & 0 & -i & 0 \\ 0 & 0 & 1 & 0 \end{pmatrix},$$

$$\|P\|(0 \oplus -0) = \|P\|(0 \oplus -1) = \frac{1}{2\sqrt{2}} \begin{pmatrix} 0 & 1 & 0 & 0 \\ 0 & 1 & 0 & 0 \\ 0 & 0 & 1 & 0 \\ 0 & 0 & -i & 0 \end{pmatrix},$$

$$\|P\|(1 \oplus +0) = \frac{1}{2\sqrt{2}} \begin{pmatrix} -1 & 0 & 0 & 0 \\ 1 & 0 & 0 & 0 \\ 0 & 0 & i & 0 \\ 0 & 0 & -1 & 0 \end{pmatrix},$$

$$\|P\|(1 \oplus +1) = \frac{1}{2\sqrt{2}} \begin{pmatrix} -1 & 0 & 0 & 0 \\ 1 & 0 & 0 & 0 \\ 0 & 0 & -i & 0 \\ 0 & 0 & 1 & 0 \end{pmatrix},$$

$$\|P\|(1 \oplus -0) = \|P\|(1 \oplus -1) = \frac{1}{2\sqrt{2}} \begin{pmatrix} 1 & 0 & 0 & 0 \\ 1 & 0 & 0 & 0 \\ 0 & 0 & 1 & 0 \\ 0 & 0 & -i & 0 \end{pmatrix}.$$

2. The purely quantum semantics of program P is the quantum operation:

$$[\![P]\!] = \sum_{a,c \in \{0,1\} \text{ and } b \in \{+,-\}} E_{abc} \circ E_{abc}^\dagger,$$

where $E_{abc} = \|P\|(a \oplus bc)$.

3. It follows from Proposition 6.1 that the weakest precondition semantics of P is the quantum operation:

$$wp.P = \sum_{a,c \in \{0,1\} \text{ and } b \in \{+,-\}} E_{abc}^\dagger \circ E_{abc}.$$

Exercise 11.4. Use the above example to convince yourself that Eq. (11.6) is not suitable for defining the semantics of a quantum case statement of which some branch contains measurements.

11.5   Quantum choice

In the previous three sections, we introduced the syntax and semantics of quantum programming language QuGCL with the new program construct of quantum case statement. A notion of quantum choice can be defined in terms of quantum case statement. This notion is very helpful both as a syntactic sugar in coding and for simplification of the presentation. But more importantly, it is of independent significance conceptually.

11.5.1   Choices: from classical to quantum via probabilistic

As pointed out in Section 11.1, the notion of quantum case statement stemmed from the construction of quantum walks. The initial idea of quantum choice also comes from the definition of quantum walks. To motivate the notion of quantum choice, let us go through a conceptual transition from nondeterministic choice to probabilistic choice and then to quantum choice.

1. **Classical choice**: We first observe that nondeterminism arises from case statement (11.2) as a consequence of the "overlapping" of the guards $G_1, G_2, ..., G_n$; that is, if more than one guards G_i are true at the same time, the case statement needs to select one from the corresponding commands S_i for execution. In particular, if $G_1 = G_2 = \cdots = G_n = \textbf{true}$, then the case statement becomes a demonic choice:

$$\square_{i=1}^n \, S_i \tag{11.25}$$

where the alternatives S_i are chosen unpredictably.

2. **Probabilistic choice**: To formalise randomised algorithms, research on probabilistic programming started in 1980's with the introduction of probabilistic choice:

$$\square_{i=1}^n \, S_i \, @ \, p_i \tag{11.26}$$

where $\{p_i\}$ is a probability distribution; that is, $p_i \geq 0$ for all i, and $\sum_{i=1}^n p_i = 1$. The probabilistic choice (11.26) randomly chooses the command S_i with probability p_i for every i, and thus it can be seen as a refinement (or resolution) of the demonic choice (11.25).

3. **Quantum choice**: Recall from Examples 4.1 and 4.2 that the single-step operator of a quantum walk is a "coin tossing operator" followed by a shift operator, which, as indicated in Section 11.1, can be seen as a quantum case statement. Simply following this idea, a general form of quantum choice can be easily defined based on the notion of quantum case statement.

Definition 11.13. Let S be a program such that $\overline{q} = qvar(S)$, and let S_i be programs for all i. Assume that quantum variables $\overline{q}$ are external to all S_i; that is,

$$\overline{q} \cap \left(\bigcup_i qvar(S_i) \right) = \emptyset.$$

If $\{|i\rangle\}$ is an orthonormal basis of $\mathcal{H}_{\overline{q}}$ – the state Hilbert space of the "coin" system denoted by $\overline{q}$, then the quantum choice of S_i's with "coin-tossing" program S along the basis $\{|i\rangle\}$ is defined as

$$[S]\left(\bigoplus_i |i\rangle \to S_i \right) \triangleq S; \textbf{qif } [\overline{q}] \, (\square i \cdot |i\rangle \to S_i) \textbf{ fiq}. \tag{11.27}$$

In particular, if $n = 2$, then the quantum choice will be abbreviated to $S_0 \, {}_S\oplus \, S_1$.

The above definition is not easy to understand in an abstract way. For a better understanding of it, the reader should revisit Examples 4.1 and 4.2 with the idea of this definition in mind. At this point, she/he can also move to read Example 11.8 below.

Since a quantum choice is defined in terms of quantum case statements, the semantics of the former can be directly derived from that of the latter.

Obviously, if the "coin-tossing program" S do nothing; that is, its semantics is the identity operator on $\mathcal{H}_{\overline{q}}$, for example $S = \textbf{skip}$, then quantum choice "$[S]\,(\bigoplus_i |i\rangle \to S_i)$" degenerates to quantum case statement "$\textbf{qif } [\overline{q}]\,(\square i \cdot |i\rangle \to S_i) \textbf{ fiq}$". In general, however, we should carefully distinguish a quantum choice from a quantum case statement.

It is interesting to compare quantum choice (11.27) with probabilistic choice (11.26). As said before, a probabilistic choice is a resolution of nondeterminism. In a probabilistic choice, we can simply say that the choice is made according to a certain probability distribution, and does not necessarily to specify how this distribution is generated. However, when defining a quantum choice, a "device" that can actually perform the choice, namely a "quantum coin", has to be explicitly introduced. So, a quantum choice can be further seen as a resolution of nondeterminism in the choice of (quantum) "devices" that generate the probability distribution of a probabilistic choice. A mathematical formulation of this idea will be given in the next subsection.

11.5.2 Quantum implementation of probabilistic choice

The relationship between probabilistic choice and quantum choice was briefly discussed after Definition 11.13. Now we examine this relationship in a more precise way. To this end, we first expand the syntax and semantics of QuGCL to include probabilistic choice.

Definition 11.14. Let S_i be a QuGCL program for each $1 \leq i \leq n$, and let $\{p_i\}_{i=1}^n$ be a subprobability distribution; that is, $p_i > 0$ for each $1 \leq i \leq n$ and $\sum_{i=1}^n p_i \leq 1$. Then

1. The probabilistic choice of $S_1, ..., S_n$ according to $\{p_i\}_{i=1}^n$ is

$$\sum_{i=1}^n S_i @ p_i.$$

2. The quantum variables of the choice are:

$$qvar\left(\sum_{i=1}^n S_i @ p_i\right) = \bigcup_{i=1}^n qvar(S_i).$$

3. The purely quantum denotational semantics of the choice is:

$$\left[\!\!\left[\sum_{i=1}^n S_i @ p_i\right]\!\!\right] = \sum_{i=1}^n p_i \cdot [\![S_i]\!]. \tag{11.28}$$

Intuitively, program $\sum_{i=1}^n S_i @ p_i$ chooses S_i to execute with probability p_i for every $1 \leq i \leq n$, and it aborts with probability $1 - \sum_{i=1}^n p_i$. The right-hand side of Eq. (11.28) is the probabilistic combination of quantum operations $[\![S_i]\!]$ according to distribution $\{p_i\}$; that is,

$$\left(\sum_{i=1}^n p_i \cdot [\![S_i]\!]\right)(\rho) = \sum_{i=1}^n p_i \cdot [\![S_i]\!](\rho)$$

for all density operators ρ. It is obvious that $\sum_{i=1}^n p_i \cdot [\![S_i]\!]$ is a quantum operation too.

A clear description about the relationship between probabilistic choice and quantum choice requires us to further expand the syntax and semantics of QuGCL by introducing local quantum variables.

Definition 11.15. Let S be a QuGCL program, $\overline{q}$ a quantum register and ρ a density operator on $\mathcal{H}_{\overline{q}}$. Then

1. The block command defined by S restricted to $\overline{q} = \rho$ is:

$$\textbf{begin local } \overline{q} := \rho; \ S \ \textbf{end}. \tag{11.29}$$

2. The quantum variables of the block command are:

$$qvar\left(\textbf{begin local } \overline{q} := \rho; \ S \ \textbf{end}\right) = qvar(S) \setminus \overline{q}.$$

3. The purely quantum denotational semantics of the block command is give as follows:

$$[\![\textbf{begin local } \overline{q} := \rho; \ S \ \textbf{end}]\!] (\sigma) = \text{tr}_{\mathcal{H}_{\overline{q}}}([\![S]\!](\sigma \otimes \rho))$$

for any density operator σ on $\mathcal{H}_{qvar(S)\setminus\overline{q}}$. Here, symbol "tr" stands for partial trace (see Definition 2.22).

The above definition is essentially a restatement of Definition 5.13. The only difference between them is that in block (11.29), $\overline{q}$ has to be initialised before program S using the statement $\overline{q} = \rho$, since initialisation is not included in the syntax of QuGCL.

Let us consider a simple example that can help us to understand the above two definitions.

Example 11.7 (Continuation of Example 11.4; Probabilistic mixture of measurements). Let $M^{(0)}$ and $M^{(1)}$ be the measurements on a qubit in the computational basis and in the basis $|\pm\rangle$, respectively. We consider a random choice between $M^{(0)}$ and $M^{(1)}$.

- If we perform measurement $M^{(0)}$ on qubit p in state $|\psi\rangle$ and discard the outcomes of measurement, then we get

$$\rho_0 = M_0^{(0)}|\psi\rangle\langle\psi|M_0^{(0)} + M_1^{(0)}|\psi\rangle\langle\psi|M_1^{(0)};$$

- If we perform measurement $M^{(1)}$ on $|\psi\rangle$ and discard the outcomes, then we get

$$\rho_1 = M_+^{(1)}|\psi\rangle\langle\psi|M_+^{(1)} + M_-^{(1)}|\psi\rangle\langle\psi|M_-^{(1)}.$$

Here, measurement operators $M_0^{(0)}$, $M_1^{(0)}$, $M_+^{(1)}$, $M_-^{(1)}$ are as in Example 11.4. We now take the unitary matrix

$$U = \begin{pmatrix} \sqrt{s} & \sqrt{r} \\ \sqrt{r} & -\sqrt{s} \end{pmatrix}$$

where $s, r \geq 0$ and $s + r = 1$, and introduce a "coin" qubit q. Let

$$P_i \equiv \textbf{if } M^{(i)}[p:x] = 0 \to \textbf{skip}$$
$$\square \qquad\qquad\qquad 1 \to \textbf{skip}$$
$$\textbf{fi}$$

for $i = 0, 1$, and put the quantum choice of P_0 and P_1 according the "coin tossing operator" U into a block with the "coin" qubit q as a local variable:

$$P \equiv \textbf{begin local } q := |0\rangle;\ P_0 \ _{U[q]}\oplus P_1 \ \textbf{end}$$

Then for any $|\psi\rangle \in \mathcal{H}_p$, $i \in \{0, 1\}$ and $j \in \{+, -\}$, we have:

$$[\![P]\!](|\psi\rangle\langle\psi|) = \text{tr}_{\mathcal{H}_q}\left(\sum_{i\in\{0,1\}\text{ and }j\in\{+,-\}} |\psi_{ij}\rangle\langle\psi_{ij}|\right)$$

$$= 2\left(\sum_{i\in\{0,1\}} \frac{s}{2}M_i^{(0)}|\psi\rangle\langle\psi|M_i^{(0)} + \sum_{j\in\{+,-\}} \frac{r}{2}M_j^{(1)}|\psi\rangle\langle\psi|M_j^{(1)}\right)$$

$$= s\rho_0 + r\rho_1,$$

where:

$$|\psi_{ij}\rangle \overset{\triangle}{=} M_{ij}(U|0\rangle|\psi\rangle) = \sqrt{\frac{s}{2}}|0\rangle M_i^{(0)}|\psi\rangle + \sqrt{\frac{r}{2}}|1\rangle M_j^{(1)}|\psi\rangle,$$

and measurement operators M_{ij} are as in Example 11.4. So, program P can be seen as a probabilistic mixture of measurements $M^{(0)}$ and $M^{(1)}$, with respective probabilities s, r.

Now we are ready to precisely characterise the relationship between probabilistic choice and quantum choice. Roughly speaking, if the "coin" variables are immediately treated as local variables, then a quantum choice degenerates to a probabilistic choice.

Theorem 11.1. *Let* $qVar(S) = \bar{q}$. *Then we have:*

$$\textbf{begin local } \bar{q} := \rho;\ [S]\left(\bigoplus_{i=1}^n |i\rangle \to S_i\right)\ \textbf{end} = \sum_{i=1}^n S_i @ p_i \qquad (11.30)$$

where probability $p_i = \langle i|[\![S]\!](\rho)|i\rangle$ *for every* $1 \leq i \leq n$.

For readability, the tedious proof of the above theorem is deferred to Appendix A.7.3. The inverse of this theorem is also true. For any probability distribution $\{p_i\}_{i=1}^n$, we can find an $n \times n$ unitary operator U such that

$$p_i = |U_{i0}|^2 \ (1 \leq i \leq n).$$

So, it follows immediately from the above theorem that a probabilistic choice $\sum_{i=1}^n S_i @ p_i$ can always be implemented by a quantum choice:

$$\textbf{begin local } \overline{q} := |0\rangle; [U[\overline{q}]] \left(\bigoplus_{i=1}^n |i\rangle \to S_i \right) \textbf{ end}$$

where $\overline{q}$ is a family of new quantum variables with an n-dimensional state space. As said in Subsection 11.5.1, probabilistic choice (11.26) can be thought of as a refinement of nondeterministic choice (11.25). Since for a given probability distribution $\{p_i\}$, there are more than one "coin program" S to implement the probabilistic choice $\sum_{i=1}^n S_i @ p_i$ in Eq. (11.30), a quantum choice can be further seen as a refinement of a probabilistic choice where a specific "device" (quantum "coin") is explicitly given for generating the probability distribution $\{p_i\}$.

11.6 Algebraic laws

Algebraic approach has been employed in classical programming that establishes various algebraic laws for programs so that calculation of programs becomes possible by using these laws. In particular, algebraic laws are useful for verification, transformation, and compilation of programs. In this section, we present a family of basic algebraic laws for quantum case statement and quantum choice. For readability, all of the proofs of these laws are postponed to Appendix A.7.4.

The laws given in the following theorem show that quantum case statement is idempotent, commutative and associative, and sequential composition is distributive over quantum case statement from the right.

Theorem 11.2 (Laws for quantum case statement). **1.** *Idempotent Law: If $S_i = S$ for all i, then*

$$\textbf{qif } (\square i \cdot |i\rangle \to S_i) \textbf{ fiq} = S.$$

2. *Commutative Law: For any permutation τ of $\{1, ..., n\}$, we have:*

$$\textbf{qif } [\overline{q}] \left(\square_{i=1}^n i \cdot |i\rangle \to S_{\tau(i)} \right) \textbf{ fiq}$$
$$= U_{\tau^{-1}}[\overline{q}]; \textbf{qif } [\overline{q}] \left(\square_{i=1}^n i \cdot |i\rangle \to S_i \right) \textbf{ fiq}; U_\tau[\overline{q}],$$

where:
a. τ^{-1} *is the inverse of τ, i.e. $\tau^{-1}(i) = j$ if and only if $\tau(j) = i$ for $i, j \in \{1, ..., n\}$; and*
b. U_τ (*respectively, $U_{\tau^{-1}}$*) *is the unitary operator permutating the basis $\{|i\rangle\}$ of $\mathcal{H}_{\overline{q}}$ with τ (respectively, τ^{-1}); that is,*

$$U_\tau(|i\rangle) = |\tau(i)\rangle \ (resp. \ U_{\tau^{-1}}(|i\rangle) = |\tau^{-1}(i)\rangle)$$

for every $1 \leq i \leq n$.
3. *Associative Law:*

$$\textbf{qif } (\square i \cdot |i\rangle \to \textbf{qif } (\square j_i \cdot |j_i\rangle \to S_{ij_i}) \textbf{ fiq}) \textbf{ fiq}$$
$$= \textbf{qif } (\overline{\alpha}) (\square i, j_i \cdot |i, j_i\rangle \to S_{ij_i}) \textbf{ fiq}$$

for some family $\overline{\alpha}$ of parameters, where the right-hand side is a parameterised quantum case statement that will be defined in Section 11.9.1 below.
4. *Distributive Law: If $\overline{q} \cap qvar(Q) = \emptyset$, then*

$$\textbf{qif } [\overline{q}] (\square i \cdot |i\rangle \to S_i) \textbf{ fiq}; Q =_{CF} \textbf{qif } (\overline{\alpha})[\overline{q}] (\square i \cdot |i\rangle \to (S_i; Q)) \textbf{ fiq}$$

for some family $\overline{\alpha}$ of parameters, where the right-hand side is a parameterised quantum case statement, and symbol "$=_{CF}$" stands for "coin-free" equivalence (see Definition 11.11). In particular, if we further assume that Q contains no measurements, then

$$\textbf{qif } [\overline{q}] (\square i \cdot |i\rangle \to S_i) \textbf{ fiq}; Q = \textbf{qif } [\overline{q}] (\square i \cdot |i\rangle \to (S_i; Q)) \textbf{ fiq}.$$

A quantum choice is defined as a "coin" program followed by a quantum case statement. A natural question would be: is it possible to move the "coin" program to the end of a quantum case statement? The following theorem positively answers this question under the condition that encapsulation in a block with local variables is allowed.

Theorem 11.3. *For any programs S_i and unitary operator U, we have:*

$$[U[\bar{q}]]\left(\bigoplus_{i=1}^n |i\rangle \to S_i\right) = \mathbf{qif}\ (\Box i \cdot U_{\bar{q}}^{\dagger}|i\rangle \to S_i)\ \mathbf{fiq};\ U[\bar{q}]. \tag{11.31}$$

More generally, for any programs S_i and S with $\bar{q} = qvar(S)$, there are new quantum variables $\bar{r}$, a pure state $|\varphi_0\rangle \in \mathcal{H}_{\bar{r}}$, an orthonormal basis $\{|\psi_{ij}\rangle\}$ of $\mathcal{H}_{\bar{q}} \otimes \mathcal{H}_{\bar{r}}$, programs Q_{ij}, and a unitary operator U on $\mathcal{H}_{\bar{q}} \otimes \mathcal{H}_{\bar{r}}$ such that

$$[S]\left(\bigoplus_{i=1}^n |i\rangle \to S_i\right) = \mathbf{begin\ local}\ \bar{r} := |\varphi_0\rangle;$$
$$\mathbf{qif}\ (\Box i, j \cdot |\psi_{ij}\rangle \to Q_{ij})\ \mathbf{fiq}; \tag{11.32}$$
$$U[\bar{q}, \bar{r}]$$
$$\mathbf{end}.$$

The next theorem is the counterpart of Theorem 11.2 for quantum choice, showing that quantum choice is also idempotent, commutative and associative, and sequential composition is distributive over quantum choice from the right.

Theorem 11.4 (Laws for quantum choice). **1.** *Idempotent Law: If $qvar(Q) = \bar{q}$, $tr[\![Q]\!](\rho) = 1$ and $S_i = S$ for all $1 \leq i \leq n$, then*

$$\mathbf{begin\ local}\ \bar{q} := \rho; [Q]\left(\bigoplus_{i=1}^n |i\rangle \to S_i\right)\ \mathbf{end} = S.$$

2. *Commutative Law: For any permutation τ of $\{1, ..., n\}$, we have:*

$$[S]\left(\bigoplus_{i=1}^n |i\rangle \to S_{\tau(i)}\right) = [S; U_\tau[\bar{q}]]\left(\bigoplus_{i=1}^n |i\rangle \to S_i\right); U_{\tau^{-1}}[\bar{q}],$$

where $qvar(S) = \bar{q}$, and U_τ, $U_{\tau^{-1}}$ are the same as in Theorem 11.2.2.
3. *Associative Law: Let*

$$\Gamma = \{(i, j_i) : 1 \leq i \leq m\ \text{and}\ 1 \leq j_i \leq n_i\} = \bigcup_{i=1}^m (\{i\} \times \{1, ..., n_i\})$$

and

$$R = [S]\left(\bigoplus_{i=1}^n |i\rangle \to Q_i\right).$$

Then

$$[S]\left(\bigoplus_{i=1}^m |i\rangle \to [Q_i]\left(\bigoplus_{j_i=1}^{n_i} |j_i\rangle \to R_{ij_i}\right)\right) = [R(\bar{\alpha})]\left(\bigoplus_{(i,j_i)\in\Gamma} |i, j_i\rangle \to R_{ij_i}\right),$$

for some family $\bar{\alpha}$ of parameters, where the right-hand side is a parameterised quantum choice defined in Section 11.9.1 below.
4. *Distributive Law: If $qvar(S) \cap qvar(Q) = \emptyset$, then*

$$[S]\left(\bigoplus_{i=1}^n |i\rangle \to S_i\right); Q =_{CF} [S(\bar{\alpha})]\left(\bigoplus_{i=1}^n |i\rangle \to (S_i; Q)\right)$$

for some family $\overline{\alpha}$ of parameters, where the right-hand side is a parameterised quantum choice. Here, symbol "$=_{CF}$" stands for "coin-free" equivalence (see Definition 11.11). In particular, if we further assume that Q contains no measurements, then

$$[S]\left(\bigoplus_{i=1}^{n}|i\rangle \to S_i\right); Q = [S]\left(\bigoplus_{i=1}^{n}|i\rangle \to (S_i; Q)\right).$$

A series of techniques for loop transformation, optimisation, and parallelisation have been proposed for classical optimising compilers [44]. In a sense, quantum case statements and quantum choices can be thought of as quantum counterparts of classical for-loops. So, we conclude this section by leaving the following:

Problem 11.1. Develop techniques for transformation, optimisation, and parallelisation of (nested) quantum case statements and quantum choices.

11.7   A new paradigm of quantum programming – superposition-of-programs

A *programming paradigm* is a way or style of building the structure and elements of programs, and has significant implications for the execution model of the programming language.

The programming language QuGCL with quantum case statement and quantum choice studied in the previous sections supports a new quantum programming paradigm – *superposition-of-programs*. The basic idea of superposition-of-programs was already briefly discussed in Section 1.2.2. Now, after introducing the formal definitions of quantum case statement and quantum choice, this idea becomes much clearer. In this section, we further elaborate this quantum programming paradigm.

Essentially, the superposition-of-programs paradigm provides us with a new view of designing and reasoning about quantum algorithms. Actually, programmers can think of quantum choice (11.27) as a superposition of programs. More precisely,

- Quantum choice (11.27) first runs "coin-tossing" program S to create a superposition of the respective execution paths of programs S_i $(1 \leq i \leq n)$; and then it enters a quantum case statement of $S_1, ..., S_n$.
- During the execution of the quantum case statement, each S_i is running along its own path within the whole superposition of execution paths of $S_1, ..., S_n$.

This view will be more clearly manifested by a series of examples in the next section.

Superposition of programs can be thought of as a higher-level superposition than *superposition of data*. The idea of superposition of data is well-understood by the quantum computation community, and the studies of quantum programming in the previous chapters have been carried out around this idea. However, the studies of superposition of programs are still at the very beginning, and this chapter and the next represent the first step toward this new quantum programming paradigm.

Quantum case statement and quantum choice are two important ingredients in the realisation of the quantum programming paradigm of superposition-of-programs. But only quantum case statement was introduced as a primitive program construct in the syntax of QuGCL because quantum choice may be easily defined as a derived program construct from quantum case statement. In the next chapter, the notion of quantum recursion with quantum control flow will be introduced in order to further realise the superposition-of-programs paradigm.

11.8   Illustrative examples

A theory of the quantum programming paradigm of superposition-of-programs; i.e. programming with quantum case statement and quantum choice, has been developed in the previous sections, using quantum programming language QuGCL. In this section, we give some examples to show how can some quantum algorithms be conveniently written as programs in the language QuGCL. In particular, through these examples, we expect that the reader will become familiar with the new view of superposition-of-programs in thinking and reasoning about quantum computation.

11.8.1   Quantum walks

The design of the language QuGCL, in particular the definition of quantum case statement and quantum choice, was inspired by the construction of some simplest quantum walks. A large number of variants and generalisations of quantum walks have been introduced in the last two decades. Quantum walks have been widely used in the development of quantum algorithms including quantum simulation. Various extended quantum walks in the literature can be easily written as QuGCL programs. Here, we only present several simple examples.

Example 11.8. Recall from Example 4.1 that the Hadamard walk is a quantum generalisation of one-dimensional random walk. Let p, c be the quantum variables for position and coin, respectively. The type of variable p is the infinite-dimensional Hilbert space

$$\mathcal{H}_p = span\{|n\rangle : n \in \mathbb{Z} \ (integers)\} = \left\{ \sum_{n=-\infty}^{\infty} \alpha_n |n\rangle : \sum_{n=-\infty}^{\infty} |\alpha_n|^2 < \infty \right\},$$

and the type of c is the 2-dimensional Hilbert space $\mathcal{H}_c = span\{|L\rangle, |R\rangle\}$, where L, R stand for Left and Right, respectively. The state space of the Hadamard walk is $\mathcal{H} = \mathcal{H}_c \otimes \mathcal{H}_p$. Let $I_{\mathcal{H}_p}$ be the identity operator on $\mathcal{H}_p$, H the 2×2 Hadamard matrix and T_L, T_R the left- and right-translations, respectively; that is,

$$T_L|n\rangle = |n-1\rangle, \qquad T_R|n\rangle = |n+1\rangle$$

for every $n \in \mathbb{Z}$. Then a single step of the Hadamard walk can be described by the unitary operator

$$W = (|L\rangle\langle L| \otimes T_L + |R\rangle\langle R| \otimes T_R) \left(H \otimes I_{\mathcal{H}_p} \right). \tag{11.33}$$

It can also be written as the QuGCL program:

$$T_L[p]_{H[c]} \oplus T_R[p] \equiv H[c]; \ \textbf{qif } [c] \ |L\rangle \rightarrow T_L[p]$$
$$\square \qquad |R\rangle \rightarrow T_R[p]$$
$$\textbf{fiq.}$$

This program is the quantum choice of the left-translation T_L and the right-translation T_R according to the "coin" program $H[c]$. The Hadamard walk repeatedly runs this program.

The following are several variants of this walk considered in the recent physics literature.

1. A simple variant of the above Hadamard walk is the unidirectional quantum walk, where the walker either moves to the right or stays in the previous position. So, the left-translation T_L should be replaced by the program **skip** whose semantics is the identity operator $I_{\mathcal{H}_p}$, and a single step of the new quantum walk can be written as the QuGCL program:

$$\textbf{skip}_{H[c]} \oplus T_R[p].$$

It is a quantum choice of **skip** and the right-translation T_R.

2. A feature of the Hadamard walk and its unidirectional variant is that the "coin tossing operator" H is independent of the position and time. A new kind of quantum walk was proposed, where the "coin tossing" operator depends on both position n and time t:

$$C(n, t) = \frac{1}{\sqrt{2}} \begin{pmatrix} c(n, t) & s(n, t) \\ s^*(n, t) & -e^{i\theta} c(n, t) \end{pmatrix}.$$

Then for a given time t, step t of the walk can be written as the QuGCL program:

$$W_t \equiv \textbf{qif } [p](\square n \cdot |n\rangle \rightarrow C(n, t)[c]) \ \textbf{fiq};$$
$$\textbf{qif } [c] \ |L\rangle \rightarrow T_L[p]$$
$$\square \qquad |R\rangle \rightarrow T_R[p]$$
$$\textbf{fiq.}$$

The program W_t is a sequential composition of two quantum case statements. In the first quantum case statement, "coin-tossing" program $C(n, t)$ is selected to execute on quantum coin variable c according to position $|n\rangle$, and a superposition of different positions is allowed. Furthermore, since W_t may be different for different time points t, the first T steps can be written as the program:

$$W_1; W_2; ...; W_T.$$

3. Another simple generalisation of the Hadamard walk is the quantum walk with three "coin" states. The "coin" space of this walk is a 3-dimensional Hilbert space $\mathcal{H}_c = span\{|L\rangle, |0\rangle, |R\rangle\}$, where L and R are used to indicate moving to the

left and to the right, respectively, as before, but 0 means staying at the previous position. The "coin tossing" operator is the unitary

$$U = \frac{1}{3}\begin{pmatrix} -1 & 2 & 2 \\ 2 & -1 & 2 \\ 2 & 2 & -1 \end{pmatrix}.$$

Then a single step of the walk can be written as the QuGCL program:

$$[U[c]]\,(|L\rangle \to T_L[p] \oplus |0\rangle \to \textbf{skip} \oplus |R\rangle \to T_R[p]).$$

This is the quantum choice of **skip**, the left- and right-translations according to the "coin" program $U[c]$.

The quantum walks in the above example have only a single walker as well as a single "coin". In the following two examples, we consider some more complicated quantum walks in which multiple walkers participate and multiple "coins" are equipped to control the walkers.

Example 11.9. We consider a one-dimensional quantum walk driven by multiple "coins". In this walk, there is still a single walker, but it is controlled by M different "coins". Each of these "coins" has its own state space, but the "coin tossing" operator for all of them are the same, namely the 2×2 Hadamard matrix. Now let variable p, Hilbert spaces $\mathcal{H}_p$, $\mathcal{H}_c$ and operators T_L, T_R, H are the same as in Example 11.8, and let $c_1, ..., c_M$ be the quantum variables for the M "coins". Then the state space of the walk is

$$\mathcal{H} = \bigotimes_{m=1}^{M} \mathcal{H}_{c_m} \otimes \mathcal{H}_p,$$

where $\mathcal{H}_{c_m} = \mathcal{H}_c$ for all $1 \leq m \leq M$. We write

$$W_m \equiv \left(T_L[p]_{H[c_1]} \oplus T_R[p]\right); ...; \left(T_L[p]_{H[c_m]} \oplus T_R[p]\right)$$

for $1 \leq m \leq M$. If we cycle among the M "coins", starting from the "coin" c_1, then the first T steps of the walk can be written in the language QuGCL as follows:

$$W_M; ...; W_M; W_r$$

where W_M is iterated for $d = \lfloor T/M \rfloor$ times, and $r = T - Md$ is the remainder of T divided by M. This program is a sequential composition of T quantum choices of the left- and right translations controlled by different "coins".

Example 11.10. We consider a quantum walk consisting of two walkers on a line sharing "coins". The two walkers have different state spaces, and each of them has its own "coin". So, the state Hilbert space of the whole quantum walk is $\mathcal{H}_c \otimes \mathcal{H}_c \otimes \mathcal{H}_p \otimes \mathcal{H}_p$. If the two walkers are completely independent, then the step operator of this walk is $W \otimes W$, where W is defined by Eq. (11.33). But more interesting is the case where a two-qubit unitary operator U is introduced to entangle the two "coins". This case can be thought of as that the two walkers are sharing "coins". A step of this quantum walk can be written as a QuGCL program as follows:

$$U[c_1, c_2]; \left(T_L[q_1]_{H[c_1]} \oplus T_R[q_1]\right); \left(T_L[q_2]_{H[c_2]} \oplus T_R[q_2]\right)$$

where q_1, q_2 are the position variables and c_1, c_2 the "coin" variables of the two walkers, respectively. Here, the two walkers both use the Hadamard operator H for "coin-tossing".

Obviously, a generalisation to the case with more than two walkers can also be easily programmed in QuGCL.

11.8.2 Quantum phase estimation

Not only quantum walk-based algorithm can be conveniently programmed in the language QuGCL. In this subsection, we show how to program quantum phase estimation algorithm in QuGCL. More importantly, writing it as a program using quantum case statement and quantum choice can clearly reveal the intuition behind its design.

Recall from Section 4.3.1, given a unitary operator U and its eigenvector $|u\rangle$. The goal of this algorithm is to estimate the phase φ of the eigenvalue $e^{2\pi i \varphi}$ corresponding to $|u\rangle$. The algorithm is described in Fig. 11.1. Here, for each $j = 0, 1, ..., t -$

- **Procedure:**

1. $|0\rangle^{\otimes t}|u\rangle \xrightarrow{H^{\otimes} \text{ on the first } t \text{ qubits}} \dfrac{1}{\sqrt{2^t}}\sum\limits_{j=0}^{2^t-1}|j\rangle|u\rangle$

2. $\xrightarrow{\text{oracles}} \dfrac{1}{\sqrt{2^t}}\sum\limits_{j=0}^{2^t-1}|j\rangle U^j|u\rangle = \dfrac{1}{\sqrt{2^t}}\sum\limits_{j=0}^{2^t-1}e^{2\pi ij\varphi}|j\rangle|u\rangle$

3. $\xrightarrow{FT^\dagger} \dfrac{1}{\sqrt{2^t}}\sum\limits_{j=0}^{2^t-1}e^{2\pi ij\varphi}\left(\dfrac{1}{\sqrt{2^t}}\sum\limits_{k=0}^{2^t-1}e^{-2\pi ijk/2^t}|k\rangle\right)|u\rangle$

4. $\xrightarrow{\text{measure the first } t \text{ qubits}} |m\rangle|u\rangle,$

FIGURE 11.1 Quantum phase estimation.

- **Program:**

1. $\mathbf{skip}_{H[c_1]} \oplus S_1;$

   ......

2. $\mathbf{skip}_{H[c_t]} \oplus S_t;$

3. $q_t := H[q_t];$

4. $T_t;$

5. $q_{t-1} := H[q_{t-1}];$

6. $T_{t-1};$

7. $q_{t-2} := H[q_{t-2}];$

   ......

8. $T_2;$

9. $q_1 := H[q_1];$

10. $\mathbf{if}\ (\square\ M[q_1, ..., q_t : x] = m \rightarrow \mathbf{skip})\ \mathbf{fi}$

FIGURE 11.2 Quantum phase estimation program.

1, an oracle performs controlled-U^{2^j} operator, and $FT^\dagger$ stand for the inverse quantum Fourier transform. Essentially, steps 1 and 2 are designed to produce different bits of phase $\varphi = 0.\varphi_1\varphi_2...\varphi_t...$ by performing different exponents of U. These two steps were described as circuit (4.12). Steps 3 and 4 are then used to extract the value of φ by performing the inverse Fourier transform $FT^\dagger$ and a measurement. The key insight in steps 1 and 2 is that different exponents $U^0, U^1, U^2, ..., U^{2^t-1}$ can be performed simultaneously employing quantum parallelism, which is the main reason that quantum computation can outperform classical computation here. However, this point cannot be easily seen from circuit (4.12).

Now we use qubit variables $q_1, ..., q_t$ as well as a quantum variable p of which the type is the Hilbert space of unitary operator U. Let $\overline{q}$ stand for sequence $q_1, ..., q_t$. Then steps 1 and 2 in Fig. 11.1 can be written as the following subprogram:

$$H^{\otimes t}[\overline{q}];\ \mathbf{qif}\left(\square_{x=0}^{2^t-1}|x\rangle \rightarrow U^x[p]\right)\mathbf{fiq}$$
$$= [H^{\otimes t}[\overline{q}]]\left(\bigoplus_{x=0}^{2^n-1}|x\rangle \rightarrow U^x[p]\right). \tag{11.34}$$

The quantum parallel execution of $U^0, U^1, U^2, ..., U^{2^t-1}$ is clearly shown in program (11.34).

Let us further introduce a classical variable to record the outcomes of a measurement. Then quantum phase estimation can be written as the QuGCL program in Fig. 11.2, where:

- for $1 \leq k \leq t$,

$$S_k \equiv q := U[q]; ...; q := U[q]$$

   (the sequential composition of 2^{k-1} copies of unitary transformation U);
- for $2 \leq k \leq t$, the subprogram T_k is given in Fig. 11.3, and the operator $R_k^\dagger$ in T_k is given by

- **Subprogram:**

  1. **qif** $[q_t]$ $|0\rangle \to$ **skip**
  2. $\square$ $\qquad$ $|1\rangle \to R_k^\dagger[q_{k-1}]$
  3. **fiq**;
  4. **qif** $[q_{t-1}]$ $|0\rangle \to$ **skip**
  5. $\square$ $\qquad$ $|1\rangle \to R_{k-1}^\dagger[q_{k-1}]$
  6. **fiq**;

  $\qquad$ ......

  7. **qif** $[q_{k+1}]$ $|0\rangle \to$ **skip**
  9. $\square$ $\qquad$ $|1\rangle \to R_2^\dagger[q_{k-1}]$
  10. **fiq**

FIGURE 11.3 Subprogram T_k.

$$R_k^\dagger = \begin{pmatrix} 1 & 0 \\ 0 & e^{-2\pi i/2^k} \end{pmatrix};$$

- $M = \{M_m : m \in \{0,1\}^t\}$ is the measurement on t qubits in the computational basis; that is, $M_m = |m\rangle\langle m|$ for every $m \in \{0,1\}^t$.

It can be seen from Eq. (4.8) that the part of lines 3–9 in the phase estimation program (Fig. 11.2) is actually the inverse quantum Fourier transform. Since the language QuGCL does not include any initialisation statement, $|0\rangle^t|u\rangle$ in Fig. 11.1 can only be seen as an input to the program.

Exercise 11.5. How subprogram (11.34) is compiled or refined in Figs. 11.2 and 11.3?

11.8.3 Linear combination of unitary operators

A new approach to quantum simulation was proposed by Childs and Wiebe [93] based on the LCU – Linear Combination $\sum_i \alpha_i U_i$ of Unitary operators U_i. The implementation of LCU represents a basic idea for designing quantum algorithms and has found successful applications in solving many other problems.

For simplicity, let us only consider the following basic algorithm:

- For any unitary operators U_0, U_1 and for any real number $\kappa > 0$, the algorithm can implement an operator proportional to $\kappa U_0 + U_1$ (with failure probability at most $\|U_0 - U_1\|^2 \kappa/(\kappa+1)^2$).

The general LCU scheme can then be realised by recursively applying the above basic algorithm.

Concretely, the above basic algorithm is executed in the following three steps:

1. Perform unitary operator

$$V_\kappa = \begin{pmatrix} \sqrt{\dfrac{k}{k+1}} & -\dfrac{1}{\sqrt{k+1}} \\ \dfrac{1}{\sqrt{k+1}} & \sqrt{\dfrac{k}{k+1}} \end{pmatrix}$$

   on an ancilla qubit;
2. Perform a zero-controlled U_0 gate and a one-controlled U_1 gate on the state $|\psi\rangle$ of the principal system using the ancilla as the control;
3. Apply V_k^+ to the ancilla qubit and measure it in the computational basis.

The state is transformed as follows:

$$|0\rangle|\psi\rangle \to \left(\sqrt{\frac{k}{k+1}}|0\rangle + \frac{1}{\sqrt{k+1}}|1\rangle \right) |\psi\rangle$$

$$\to \sqrt{\frac{k}{k+1}}|0\rangle U_0|\psi\rangle + \frac{1}{\sqrt{k+1}}|1\rangle U_1|\psi\rangle$$

$$\to \frac{1}{k+1}|0\rangle (kU_0 + U_1)|\psi\rangle + \frac{\sqrt{k}}{k+1}|1\rangle (U_1 - U_0)|\psi\rangle.$$

The first two steps are crucial for the algorithm. Using quantum choice defined in this chapter, they can be conveniently written as the following program:

$$[V_k]\,(|0\rangle \to U_0 \oplus |1\rangle \to U_1) \tag{11.35}$$

More importantly, program (11.35) gives us a good intuition behind the algorithm design:

- V_k is a quantum coin that generate $|0\rangle$ with probability $\frac{k}{k+1}$ and $|1\rangle$ with probability $\frac{1}{k+1}$, and (11.35) is a quantum choice between U_0 and U_1 with "coin-tossing" V_k, or a superposition of U_0 and U_1.

This intuition extends to the general scheme of LCU.

11.9 Discussions

In the previous sections, the two program constructs of quantum case statement and quantum choice have been thoroughly studied, and they were used to program quantum walk-based algorithms, quantum phase estimation and LCU (Linear Combination of Unitaries). It was mentioned in Section 11.3.3 that a choice of coefficients different from that in Definition 11.6 is possible, which implies the possibility of a different semantics of quantum case statement. This section is devoted to discuss several variants of quantum case statement and quantum choice. These variants can only appear in the quantum setting and have no counterparts in classical programming. They are both conceptually interesting and useful in applications. Indeed, some of these variants were already used in the statements of several algebraic laws in Section 11.6.

11.9.1 Coefficients in guarded compositions

The coefficients in the right-hand side of the defining Eq. (11.17) of guarded composition of operator-valued functions are chosen in a very special way with a physical interpretation in terms of conditional probability. This subsection shows that other choices of these coefficients are possible.

Guarded composition of unitaries: Let us first consider the simplest case: the guarded composition

$$U \triangleq \bigoplus_{k=1}^{n} (|k\rangle \to U_k)$$

of unitary operators U_k $(1 \le k \le n)$ on a Hilbert space $\mathcal{H}$ along an orthonormal basis $\{|k\rangle\}$ of a "coin" Hilbert space $\mathcal{H}_c$. If for each $1 \le k \le n$, we add a relative phase θ_k into the defining Eq. (11.12) of U:

$$U\,(|k\rangle|\psi\rangle) = e^{i\theta_k}|k\rangle U_k|\psi\rangle \tag{11.36}$$

for all $|\psi\rangle \in \mathcal{H}$, then Eq. (11.13) is changed to

$$U\left(\sum_k \alpha_k|k\rangle|\psi_k\rangle\right) = \sum_k \alpha_k e^{i\theta_k}|k\rangle U_k|\psi_k\rangle. \tag{11.37}$$

Note that phases θ_k in Eq. (11.36) can be different for different basis states $|k\rangle$. It is easy to see that the new operator U defined by Eq. (11.36) or (11.37) is still unitary.

Guarded composition of operator-valued functions: The idea of adding relative phases also applies to the guarded composition of operator-valued functions. Consider

$$F \triangleq \bigoplus_{k=1}^{n} (|k\rangle \to F_k)$$

where $\{|k\rangle\}$ is an orthonormal basis of $\mathcal{H}_c$, and F_k is an operator-valued function in $\mathcal{H}$ over Δ_k for every $1 \le k \le n$. We arbitrarily choose a sequence $\theta_1, ..., \theta_n$ of real numbers and change the defining Eq. (11.17) of F to

$$F(\oplus_{k=1}^n \delta_k)|\Psi\rangle = \sum_{k=1}^n e^{i\theta_k} \left(\prod_{l \ne k} \lambda_{l\delta_l} \right) |k\rangle \, (F_k(\delta_k)|\psi_k\rangle) \tag{11.38}$$

for any state

$$|\Psi\rangle = \sum_{k=1}^n |k\rangle|\psi_k\rangle \in \mathcal{H}_c \otimes \mathcal{H},$$

where $\lambda_{l\delta_l}$'s are the same as in Definition 11.6. Then it is clear that F defined by Eq. (11.38) is still an operator-valued function. Indeed, this conclusion is true for a much more general definition of guarded composition of operator-valued functions. Let F_k be an operator-valued function in $\mathcal{H}$ over Δ_k for each $1 \le k \le n$, and let

$$\overline{\alpha} = \left\{ \alpha^{(k)}_{\delta_1,...,\delta_{k-1},\delta_{k+1},...,\delta_n} : 1 \le k \le n, \; \delta_l \in \Delta_l \; (l = 1, ..., k-1, k+1, ..., n) \right\} \tag{11.39}$$

be a family of complex numbers satisfying the normalisation condition:

$$\sum_{\delta_1 \in \Delta_1,...,\delta_{k-1} \in \Delta_{k-1}, \delta_{k+1} \in \Delta_{k+1},...,\delta_n \in \Delta_n} \left| \alpha^{(k)}_{\delta_1,...,\delta_{k-1},\delta_{k+1},...,\delta_n} \right|^2 = 1 \tag{11.40}$$

for every $1 \le k \le n$. Then we can define the $\overline{\alpha}$-guarded composition

$$F \overset{\triangle}{=} (\overline{\alpha}) \bigoplus_{k=1}^n (|i\rangle \to F_k)$$

of F_k $(1 \le k \le n)$ along an orthonormal basis $\{|k\rangle\}$ of $\mathcal{H}_c$ by

$$F \left(\oplus_{k=1}^n \delta_k \right) \left(\sum_{k=1}^n |k\rangle|\psi_k\rangle \right) = \sum_{k=1}^n \alpha^{(k)}_{\delta_1,...,\delta_{k-1},\delta_{k+1},...,\delta_n} |k\rangle \, (F_k(\delta_k)|\psi_k\rangle) \tag{11.41}$$

for any $|\psi_1\rangle, ..., |\psi_n\rangle \in \mathcal{H}$ and for any $\delta_k \in \Delta_k$ $(1 \le k \le n)$. Note that coefficient

$$\alpha^{(k)}_{\delta_1,...,\delta_{k-1},\delta_{k+1},...,\delta_n}$$

does not contain parameter δ_k. This independence together with condition (11.40) guarantees that the $\overline{\alpha}$-guarded composition is an operator-valued function, as can be seen from the proof of Lemma 11.2 presented in Appendix A.7.1.

Example 11.11. 1. Definition 11.6 is a special case of $\overline{\alpha}$-guarded composition because if for any $1 \le i \le n$ and $\delta_k \in \Delta_k$ $(k = 1, ..., i-1, i+1, ..., n)$, we set

$$\alpha^i_{\delta_1,...,\delta_{i-1},\delta_{i+1},...,\delta_n} = \prod_{k \ne i} \lambda_{k\delta_k},$$

where $\lambda_{k\delta_k}$'s are given by Eq. (11.18), then Eq. (11.41) degenerates to (11.17).
2. Another possible choice of $\overline{\alpha}$ is

$$\alpha^i_{\delta_1,...,\delta_{i-1},\delta_{i+1},...,\delta_n} = \frac{1}{\sqrt{\prod_{k \ne i} |\Delta_k|}}$$

for all $1 \le i \le n$ and $\delta_k \in \Delta_k$ $(k = 1, ..., i-1, i+1, ..., n)$. Obviously, for this family $\overline{\alpha}$ of coefficients, the $\overline{\alpha}$-guarded composition cannot be obtained by modifying Definition 11.6 with relative phases.

Quantum case statement and quantum choice: Now we are able to introduce parameterised quantum case statement and quantum choice, with their semantics defined in terms of guarded composition of operator-valued functions.

Definition 11.16. 1. Let $\bar{q}$, $\{|i\rangle\}$ and $\{S_i\}$ be as in Definition 11.1 (4). Furthermore, let the classical states $\Delta(S_i) = \Delta_i$ for every i, and let $\bar{\alpha}$ be a family of parameters satisfying condition (11.40), as in Eq. (11.39). Then the $\bar{\alpha}$-quantum case statement of $S_1, ..., S_n$ guarded by basis states $|i\rangle$'s is

$$S \equiv \mathbf{qif}\,(\bar{\alpha})[\bar{q}]\,(\Box i \cdot |i\rangle \to S_i)\,\mathbf{fiq} \tag{11.42}$$

and its semiclassical semantics is

$$\|S\| = (\bar{\alpha}) \bigoplus_{i=1}^{n} \left(|i\rangle \to \|S_i\| \right).$$

2. Let S, $\{|i\rangle\}$ and S_i's be as in Definition 11.13, and let $\bar{\alpha}$ be as above. Then the $\bar{\alpha}$-quantum choice of S_i's according to S along the basis $\{|i\rangle\}$ is defined as

$$[S(\bar{\alpha})]\left(\bigoplus_i |i\rangle \to S_i \right) \equiv S; \mathbf{qif}\,(\bar{\alpha})[\bar{q}]\,(\Box i \cdot |i\rangle \to S_i)\,\mathbf{fiq}.$$

The symbol $[\bar{q}]$ in quantum case statement (11.42) can be dropped whenever quantum variables $\bar{q}$ can be recognised from the context. At the first glance, it seems unreasonable that the parameters $\bar{\alpha}$ in the syntax (11.42) of $\bar{\alpha}$-quantum case statement are indexed by the classical states of S_i. But this is not problematic at all because the classical states of S_i are completely determined by the syntax of S_i.

The purely quantum denotational semantics of the $\bar{\alpha}$-quantum case statement can be obtained from its semiclassical semantics according to Definition 11.10, and the semantics of $\bar{\alpha}$-quantum choice can be derived from the semantics of $\bar{\alpha}$-quantum case statement. The notions of parameterised quantum case statement and quantum choice were already used in the presentation of several theorems in Section 11.6.

Problem 11.2. Prove or disprove the following statement: for any $\bar{\alpha}$, there exists unitary operator U such that

$$\mathbf{qif}\,(\bar{\alpha})[\bar{q}]\,(\Box i \cdot |i\rangle \to S_i)\,\mathbf{fiq} = [U[\bar{q}]]\left(\bigoplus_i |i\rangle \to S_i \right).$$

What happens when $U[\bar{q}]$ is replaced by a general quantum program (of which the semantics can be a general quantum operation rather than a unitary)?

11.9.2 Quantum case statements guarded by subspaces

A major difference between case statement (11.2) of classical programs and quantum case statement (11.9) can be revealed by a comparison between their guards: the guards G_i in the former are propositions about the program variables, whereas the guards $|i\rangle$ in the latter are basis states of the "coin" space $\mathcal{H}_c$. However, this difference is not as big as we imagine at the first glance. In the Birkhoff–von Neumann quantum logic (see Section 7.3, or [66,115]), a proposition about a quantum system is expressed by a closed subspace of the state Hilbert space of the system. This observation leads us to a way to define quantum case statement guarded by propositions about the "coin" system instead of basis states of the "coin" space.

Definition 11.17. Let $\bar{q}$ be a sequence of quantum variables and $\{S_i\}$ be a family of quantum programs such that

$$\bar{q} \cap \left(\bigcup_i qvar(S_i) \right) = \emptyset.$$

Suppose that $\{X_i\}$ is a family of propositions about the "coin" system $\bar{q}$, i.e. closed subspaces of the "coin" space $\mathcal{H}_{\bar{q}}$, satisfying the following two conditions:

1. X_i's are pairwise orthogonal, i.e. $X_{i_1} \perp X_{i_2}$ provided $i_1 \neq i_2$;

2. $\bigoplus_i X_i \overset{\triangle}{=} span\left(\bigcup_i X_i \right) = \mathcal{H}_{\bar{q}}$.

Then

1. The quantum case statement of S_i's guarded by subspaces X_i's:

$$S \equiv \textbf{qif } [\overline{q}] \, (\Box i \cdot X_i \to S_i) \textbf{ fiq} \tag{11.43}$$

is a program.

2. The quantum variables of S are:

$$qvar(S) = \overline{q} \cup \left(\bigcup_i qvar(S_i) \right).$$

3. The purely quantum denotational semantics of the quantum case statement is the set:

$$\llbracket S \rrbracket = \left\{ \llbracket \textbf{qif } [\overline{q}] \, (\Box i, j_i \cdot |\varphi_{ij_i}\rangle \to S_{ij_i}) \textbf{ fiq} \rrbracket \right\}, \tag{11.44}$$

where $\{|\varphi_{ij_i}\rangle\}$ ranges over all orthonormal bases of X_i for each i, and $S_{ij_i} = S_i$ for every i, j_i.

Intuitively, $\{X_i\}$ in quantum case statement (11.43) can be thought of as a partition of the whole state Hilbert space $\mathcal{H}_{\overline{q}}$. For simplicity, the variables $\overline{q}$ in Eq. (11.43) can be dropped if they can be recognised from the context. It is clear that the (disjoint) union $\bigcup_i \{|\varphi_{ij_i}\rangle\}$ of the bases of subspaces X_i's in Eq. (11.44) is an orthonormal basis of the whole "coin" space $\mathcal{H}_c$. From the right hand side of Eq. (11.44), we note that the purely quantum semantics of program (11.43) guarded by subspaces is a set of quantum operations rather than a single quantum operation. So, quantum case statement (11.43) is a nondeterministic program, and its nondeterminism comes from different choices of the bases of guard subspaces. Furthermore, a quantum case statement guarded by basis states of these subspaces is a refinement of quantum case statement (11.43). On the other hand, if $\{|i\rangle\}$ is an orthonormal basis of $\mathcal{H}_{\overline{q}}$, and for each i, X_i is the one-dimensional subspace span$\{|i\rangle\}$, then the above definition degenerates to the quantum case statement (11.9) guarded by basis states $|i\rangle$.

The notion of equivalence for quantum programs in Definition 11.11 can be easily generalised to the case of nondeterministic quantum programs (i.e. programs with a set of quantum operations rather than a single quantum operation as its semantics) provided we make the following conventions:

- If Ω is a set of quantum operations and $\mathcal{F}$ a quantum operation, then

$$\Omega \otimes \mathcal{F} = \{\mathcal{E} \otimes \mathcal{F} : \mathcal{E} \in \Omega\};$$

- We identify a single quantum operation with the set containing only this quantum operation.

Some basic properties of quantum case statement guarded by subspaces are given in the following:

Proposition 11.3. 1. *If for every i, S_i does not contain any measurement, then for any orthonormal basis $\{|\varphi_{ij_i}\rangle\}$ of X_i ($1 \leq i \leq n$), we have:*

$$\textbf{qif } (\Box i \cdot X_i \to S_i) \textbf{ fiq} = \textbf{qif } (\Box i, j_i \cdot |\varphi_{ij_i}\rangle \to S_{ij_i}) \textbf{ fiq}$$

where $S_{ij_i} = S_i$ for every i, j_i. In particular, if for every i, U_i is an unitary operator in $\mathcal{H}_{\overline{q}}$, then

$$\textbf{qif } [\overline{p}] \, (\Box i \cdot X_i \to U_i[\overline{q}]) \textbf{ fiq} = U[\overline{p}, \overline{q}]$$

where

$$U = \sum_i \left(I_{X_i} \otimes U_i \right)$$

is an unitary operator on $\mathcal{H}_{\overline{p} \cup \overline{q}}$.

2. *Let U be a unitary operator on $\mathcal{H}_{\overline{q}}$. If for every i, X_i is an invariant subspace of U, i.e.*

$$U(X_i) = \{U|\psi\rangle : |\psi\rangle \in X_i\} \subseteq X_i,$$

then

$$U[\overline{q}]; \textbf{qif } [\overline{q}] \, (\Box i \cdot X_i \to S_i) \textbf{ fiq}; U^\dagger[\overline{q}] = \textbf{qif } [\overline{q}] \, (\Box i \cdot X_i \to S_i) \textbf{ fiq}.$$

Exercise 11.6. Prove Proposition 11.3

We conclude this section by pointing out that a generalised notion of quantum choice can be defined based on either parameterised quantum case statement or quantum case statement guarded by subspaces, and the algebraic laws established in Section 11.6 can be easily generalised for parameterised quantum case statement and quantum choice as well as those guarded by subspaces. The details are omitted here, but the reader can try to figure out them as an exercise.

11.10   Bibliographic remarks and further readings

This chapter is mainly based on the draft paper [434]; an earlier version of [434] appeared as [433]. The work reported in [433,434] was inspired by earlier research on quantum random works [11,16,24]. The examples presented in Section 11.8.1 were taken from recent physics literature: the unidirectional quantum walk was examined in [309]; the quantum walk with "coin tossing operator" depending on time and position was employed in [262] to implement quantum measurement; the quantum walk with three coin states was considered in [223], the one-dimensional quantum walk driven by multiple coins was defined in [78]; the quantum walk consisting of two walkers on a line sharing coins was introduced in [413].

- **GCL and its extensions**: (1) The programming language QuGCL studied in this chapter is a quantum counterpart of Dijkstra's GCL (Guarded Command Language). The language GCL was originally defined in [132], but one can find an elegant and systematic presentation of GCL in [311]. The language pGCL for probabilistic programming was defined by introducing probabilistic choice into GCL; for a systematic exposition of probabilistic programming with probabilistic choice, we refer to [297]. A comparison between quantum choice and probabilistic choice was given in Section 11.5.
  (2) Another quantum extension qGCL of GCL was defined in Sanders and Zuliani's pioneering paper [361]; see also [455]. qGCL was obtained by adding three primitives for quantum computation – initialisation, unitary transformation, quantum measurement – into the probabilistic language pGCL. Note that the control flows of qGCL programs are always classical. QuGCL can also be seen as an extension of qGCL obtained by adding quantum case statement (with quantum control flow).

- **Quantum control flow**: Quantum programs with quantum control flow was first considered by Altenkirch and Grattage [19,21]. But the way of defining quantum control flow in this chapter is very different from that used in [19,266]. A careful discussion about the difference between the approach in [19] and ours can be found in [433,434]. Our approach was mainly inspired by the following line of research: a superposition of evolutions (rather than that of states) of a quantum system was considered by physicists Aharonov, Anandan, Popescu, and Vaidman [15] as early as in 1990, and they proposed to introduce an external system in order to implement the superposition. The idea of using such an external "coin" system was rediscovered by Aharonov, Ambainis, Bach, Kempe, Nayak, Vazirani, Vishwanath, and Watrous in defining quantum walks [11,24]. The fact that the shift operator S of a quantum walk can be seen as a quantum case statement and the single-step operator W as a quantum choice was noticed in [433,434] by introducing the single-direction shift operators S_i's. It then motivated the design decision of quantum case statement and quantum choice as well as the quantum programming paradigm of superposition-of-programs. In particular, whenever no measurements are involved, then the semantics of a quantum case statement can be defined in terms of the guarded composition of unitary operators. However, defining the semantics of a quantum case statement in its full generality requires the notion of guarded composition of quantum operations introduced in [433,434].

- **More related computer science literature**: (1) As pointed out in Section 11.3.1, guarded composition of unitary operators is essentially quantum multiplexor introduced by Shende, Bullock, and Markov [374] and discussed in Section 3.6. It was called by Kitaev, Shen, and Vyalyi as a measuring operator in [248].
  (2) The quantum programming language Scaffold [4] supports quantum control primitives with the restriction that the code comprising the body of each module must be purely quantum (and unitary). Hence, its semantics only requires guarded composition of unitary operators defined in Section 11.3.1.
  (3) Some very interesting discussions about quantum case statements were given by Bǎdescu and Panangaden [39]; in particular, they observed that quantum case statements are not monotone with respect to the Löwner order and thus not compatible with the semantics of recursion defined in [367].
  (4) A notable recent work is a model of quantum control machine proposed by Yuan, Villanyi, and Carbin [448] that supports quantum control flows and superposition of programs.

- **Related physics literature**: (1) In recent years, more and more papers concerning superposition of quantum gates or more general quantum operations (i.e. quantum channels) have been published in the physics literature. For example, Zhou et al. [453] proposed an architecture-independent technique for adding control to arbitrary unknown quantum operations and demonstrated in a photonic system. This problem was further considered by Araújo et al. [30] and Friis et al. [163]. Quantum conditional operations were proposed by Bisio, Dall'Arno, and Perinotti [67]. Routed quantum circuits were introduced by Vanrietvelde, Kristjánsson, and Barrett [398].

(2) The interesting idea of superposition of causal structures in quantum computation was first introduced by Chiribella et al. [94,95]. It has been developed and generalised by a series of papers (e.g. [18,31,108]) and implemented in a series of experiments (e.g. [182,343,359]).

Chapter 12

Quantum recursion

Recursion is one of the central ideas of computer science. Most modern programming languages support recursion or at least a special form of recursion such as **while**-loop. A quantum extension of **while**-loop was already introduced in Section 5.1. A more general notion of recursion in quantum programming was defined in Section 5.5. It was appropriately called *classical recursion of quantum programs* because its control flow is determined by the involved case statements of the form (5.4) and **while**-loops of the form (5.5) and thus is doomed-to-be classical, as discussed in Section 5.1.

In the last chapter, we studied quantum case statements and quantum choices of which the control flows are genuinely quantum because they are governed by quantum "coins". This chapter further defines the notion of quantum recursion based on quantum case statement and quantum choice. The control flow of such a quantum recursive program is then quantum rather than classical. As we will see later, the treatment of quantum recursion with quantum control is much harder than classical recursion in quantum programming. The introduction of quantum recursion with quantum control enriches the quantum programming paradigm of superposition-of-programs.

The chapter is organised as follows.

- The syntax of quantum recursive programs is defined in Section 12.1. Recursive quantum walks are introduced in Section 12.2 as examples for carefully motivating the notion of quantum recursion. It should be emphasised that Section 12.1 provides us with a language in which a precise formulation of recursive quantum walks is possible.
- It requires mathematical tools from second quantisation – a theoretical framework in which we are able to depict quantum systems with variable number of particles – to define the semantics of quantum recursive programs. Since it is used only in this chapter, second quantisation was not included in the preliminaries chapter on quantum mechanics (Chapter 2). Instead, we introduce the basics of second quantisation; in particular, Fock spaces and operators in them, in Section 12.3.
- We define the semantics of quantum recursion in two steps. The first step is carried out in Section 12.4 where quantum recursive equations are solved in the free Fock space, which is mathematically convenient to manipulate but does not represent a realistic system in physics. The second step is completed in Section 12.5 where the solutions of recursive equations are symmetrised so that they can apply in the physically meaningful framework, namely the symmetric and antisymmetric Fock spaces of bosons and fermions, respectively. Furthermore, the principal system semantics of a quantum recursive program is defined in Section 12.6 by tracing out auxiliary "quantum coins" from its symmetrised semantics.
- Recursive quantum walks are reconsidered in Section 12.7 to illustrate various semantic notions introduced in this chapter. A special class of quantum recursions, namely quantum **while**-loops with quantum control flows are carefully examined in Section 12.8.

12.1 Syntax of quantum recursive programs

In this section, we formally define the syntax of quantum recursive programs. To give the reader a clearer picture, we choose not to include quantum measurements in the declarations of quantum recursions. It is not difficult to add quantum measurements into the theory of quantum recursive programs by combining the ideas used in this chapter and the last one, but the presentation will be much more complicated.

Program schemes: Let us start by exhibiting the alphabet of the language of quantum recursive programs. In the last chapter, any quantum variable can serve as a "coin" in defining a quantum case statement. For convenience, in this chapter we explicitly separate quantum "coins" from other quantum variables; that is, we assume two sets of quantum variables:

- principal system variables, ranged over by $p, q, ...$;
- "coin" variables, ranged over by $c, d, ...$

These two sets are required to be disjoint. We also assume a set of procedure identifiers, ranged over by $X, X_1, X_2, ...$ A modification of quantum programming language QuGCL presented in the last chapter is defined by the next:

Foundations of Quantum Programming. https://doi.org/10.1016/B978-0-44-315942-8.00025-3

Definition 12.1. Program schemes are defined by the following syntax:

$$P ::= X \mid \textbf{abort} \mid \textbf{skip} \mid P_1; P_2 \mid U[\overline{c}, \overline{q}] \mid \textbf{qif}\,[c](\square i \cdot |i\rangle \to P_i)\,\textbf{fiq}$$

Obviously, the above definition is obtained from Definition 11.1 by adding procedure identifiers and excluding measurements (and thus classical variables for recording the outcomes of measurements). More explicitly,

- X is a procedure identifier.
- **abort**, **skip**, and sequential composition $P_1; P_2$ are as in Definition 11.1.
- Unitary transformation $U[\overline{c}, \overline{q}]$ is the same as before except that "coins" and principal system variables are separated; that is, $\overline{c}$ is a sequence of "coin" variables, $\overline{q}$ is a sequence of principal system variables, and U is a unitary operator on the state Hilbert space of the system consisting of $\overline{c}$ and $\overline{q}$. We will always put "coin" variables before principal system variables. Both of $\overline{c}$ and $\overline{q}$ are allowed to be empty. When $\overline{c}$ is empty, we simply write $U[\overline{q}]$ for $U[\overline{c}, \overline{q}]$ and it describes the evolution of the principal system $\overline{q}$; when $\overline{q}$ is empty, we simply write $U[\overline{c}]$ for $U[\overline{c}, \overline{q}]$ and it describes the evolution of the "coins" $\overline{c}$. If both $\overline{c}$ and $\overline{q}$ are not empty, then $U[\overline{c}, \overline{q}]$ describes the interaction between "coins" $\overline{c}$ and the principal system $\overline{q}$.
- Quantum case statement $\textbf{qif}\,[c](\square i \cdot |i\rangle \to P_i)\,\textbf{fiq}$ is as Definition 11.1. Here, for simplicity we only use a single "coin" c rather than a sequence of "coins". Once again, we emphasise that "coin" c is required not to occur in any subprogram P_i because according to its physical interpretation, it is always external to the principal system.

Recall from Section 11.5, quantum choice can be defined in terms of quantum case statement and sequential composition:

$$[P(c)] \bigoplus_i (|i\rangle \to P_i) \overset{\triangle}{=} P; \textbf{qif}\,[c]\,(\square i \cdot |i\rangle \to P_i)\,\textbf{fiq}$$

where P contains only quantum variable c. In particular, if the "coin" is a qubit, then a quantum choice can be abbreviated as

$$P_0 \oplus_P P_1.$$

Quantum program schemes without procedure identifiers are actually a special class of quantum programs considered in the last chapter. So, their semantics can be directly derived from Definition 11.9. For convenience of the reader, we explicitly display their semantics in the following definition. The principal system of a quantum program P is the composition of the systems denoted by principal system variables appearing in P. We write $\mathcal{H}$ for the state Hilbert space of the principal system.

Definition 12.2. The semantics $[\![P]\!]$ of a program P (i.e. a program scheme without procedure identifiers) is inductively defined as follows:

1. If $P = \textbf{abort}$, then $[\![P]\!] = 0$ (the zero operator on $\mathcal{H}$), and if $P = \textbf{skip}$, then $[\![P]\!] = I$ (the identity operator on $\mathcal{H}$);
2. If P is an unitary transformation $U[\overline{c}, \overline{q}]$, then $[\![P]\!]$ is the unitary operator U (on the state Hilbert space of the system consisting of $\overline{c}$ and $\overline{q}$);
3. If $P = P_1; P_2$, then $[\![P]\!] = [\![P_2]\!] \cdot [\![P_1]\!]$;
4. If $P = \textbf{qif}\,[c](\square i \cdot |i\rangle \to P_i)\,\textbf{fiq}$, then

$$[\![P]\!] = \square\,(c, |i\rangle \to [\![P_i]\!]) \overset{\triangle}{=} \sum_i \left(|i\rangle_c \langle i| \otimes [\![P_i]\!]\right). \tag{12.1}$$

The above definition is a special case of Definition 11.9 where the semiclassical semantics of QuGCL programs were defined. However, the reader may notice that in the above definition we use $[\![P]\!]$ to denote the semantics of a program P, and in the last chapter $\|P\|$ is employed to denote the semiclassical semantics of P and $[\![P]\!]$ denotes the purely quantum semantics of P. We choose to write $[\![P]\!]$ for the semantics of P in the above definition because in this chapter programs contain no measurements, so their semiclassical semantics and purely quantum semantics are essentially the same. Obviously, $[\![P]\!]$ in the above definition is an operator on the state Hilbert space of the system consisting of both the principle system of P and the "coins" in P; i.e. $\mathcal{H}_C \otimes \mathcal{H}$, where $\mathcal{H}_C$ is the state space of the "coins" in P. Since **abort** may appear in P, $[\![P]\!]$ is not necessarily to be a unitary. Using the terminology in the last chapter, $[\![P]\!]$ can be seen as an operator-valued function in $\mathcal{H}_C \otimes \mathcal{H}$ over a singleton $\Delta = \{\epsilon\}$.

Quantum recursive programs: Finally, we can define the syntax of quantum recursive programs. If a program scheme P contains at most the procedure identifiers $X_1, ..., X_m$, then we write

$$P = P[X_1, ..., X_m].$$

Definition 12.3. 1. Let $X_1, ..., X_m$ be different procedure identifiers. A declaration for $X_1, ..., X_m$ is a system of equations:

$$D: \begin{cases} X_1 \Leftarrow P_1, \\ ...... \\ X_m \Leftarrow P_m, \end{cases}$$

where for every $1 \le i \le m$, $P_i = P_i[X_1, ..., X_m]$ is a program scheme containing at most procedure identifiers $X_1, ..., X_m$.

2. A recursive program consists of a program scheme $P = P[X_1, ..., X_m]$, called the main statement, and a declaration D for $X_1, ..., X_m$ such that all "coin" variables in P do not appear in D; that is, they do not appear in the procedure bodies $P_1, ..., P_m$.

The requirement in the above definition that the "coins" in the main statement P and those in the declaration D are distinct is obviously necessary because a "coin" used to define a quantum case statement is always considered to be external to its principal system.

Perhaps, the reader already noticed that the above definition looks almost the same as Definitions 5.15 and 5.16. But there is actually an essential difference between them: in the above definition, program schemes $P_1, ..., P_m$ in the declaration D and the main statement P can contain quantum case statements, whereas only case statements of the form (5.4) (and **while**-loops of the form (5.5)) are present in Definitions 5.15 and 5.16. Therefore, as said repeatedly, a recursive program defined here has quantum control flow, but a recursive program considered in Section 5.5 has only classical control flow. For this reason, the former is termed as a *quantum recursive program* and the latter a *recursive quantum program*. As we saw in Section 5.5, the techniques in classical programming theory can be straightforwardly generalised to define the semantics of recursive quantum programs. On the other hand, if a quantum program containing quantum case statements is not recursively defined, its semantics can be defined using the techniques developed in the last chapter; in particular, Definition 12.2 is a simplified version of Definition 11.9. However, new techniques are required in order to define the semantics of quantum recursive programs, as will be clearly seen at the end of the next section.

12.2 Motivating examples: recursive quantum walks

The syntax of quantum recursive programs was introduced in the last section. The aim of this section is two-fold:

1. present some motivating examples of quantum recursive programs;
2. give a hint to answering the question: how to define the semantics of quantum recursive programs?

This aim will be achieved by considering a class of examples, called recursive quantum walks, which are a variant of quantum walks introduced in Section 4.5. Actually, recursive quantum walks can only be properly presented with the help of the syntax given in the last section.

12.2.1 Specification of recursive quantum walks

A one-dimensional quantum walk, called Hadamard walk, was defined in Example 4.1. For simplicity, in this section we focus on the recursive Hadamard walk – a modification of Hadamard walk. Recursive quantum walks on a graph can be defined by modifying Example 4.2 in a similar way.

Recall from Examples 4.2 and 11.8 that the state Hilbert space of the Hadamard walk is $\mathcal{H}_d \otimes \mathcal{H}_p$, where

- $\mathcal{H}_d = \text{span}\{|L\rangle, |R\rangle\}$ is the "direction coin" space, and L, R are used to indicate the direction Left and Right, respectively;
- $\mathcal{H}_p = \text{span}\{|n\rangle : n \in \mathbb{Z}\}$ is the position space, and n indicates the position marked by integer n.

The single-step operator W of the Hadamard walk is a quantum choice, which is the sequential composition of a "coin-tossing" Hadamard operator H on the "direction coin" d and translation operator T on the position variable p. The translation T is a quantum case statement that selects left or right translations according to the basis states $|L\rangle, |R\rangle$ of the "coin" d:

- If d is in state $|L\rangle$ then the walker moves one position left;
- If d is in state $|R\rangle$ then it moves one position right.

Of course, d can also be in a superposition of $|L\rangle$ and $|R\rangle$, and thus a superposition of left and right translations happens, which produces a quantum control flow. Formally,

$$W = T_L[p] \oplus_{H[d]} T_R[p] = H[d]; \mathbf{qif}\ [d]\ |L\rangle \to T_L[p]$$
$$\square \quad\ \ |R\rangle \to T_R[p]$$
$$\mathbf{fiq}$$

where T_L and T_R are the left and right translation operators, respectively, on the position space $\mathcal{H}_p$. The Hadamard walk is then defined in a simple way of recursion with the single-step operator W, namely *repeated applications* of W.

Now we modify slightly the Hadamard walk using a little bit more complicated form of recursion.

Example 12.1. 1. The unidirectionally recursive Hadamard walk first runs the "coin-tossing" Hadamard operator $H[d]$ and then a quantum case statement:

- If the "direction coin" d is in state $|L\rangle$ then the walker moves one position left;
- If d is in state $|R\rangle$ then it moves one position right, followed by **a procedure behaving as the recursive walk itself**.

Using the syntax presented in the last section, the unidirectionally recursive Hadamard walk can be precisely defined to be a recursive program X declared by the following equation:

$$X \Leftarrow T_L[p] \oplus_{H[d]} (T_R[p]; X) \tag{12.2}$$

where d, p are the direction and position variables, respectively.

2. The bidirectionally recursive Hadamard walk first runs the "coin-tossing" Hadamard operator $H[d]$ and then a quantum case statement:

- If the "direction coin" d is in state $|L\rangle$ then the walker moves one position left, followed by **a procedure behaving as the recursive walk itself**;
- If d is in state $|R\rangle$ then it moves one position right, also followed by **a procedure behaving as the recursive walk itself**.

More precisely, the walk can be defined to be the program X declared by the following recursive equation:

$$X \Leftarrow (T_L[p]; X) \oplus_{H[d]} (T_R[p]; X). \tag{12.3}$$

3. A variant of the bidirectionally recursive Hadamard walk is the program X (or Y) declared by the following system of recursive equations:

$$\begin{cases} X \Leftarrow T_L[p] \oplus_{H[d]} (T_R[p]; Y), \\ Y \Leftarrow (T_L[p]; X) \oplus_{H[d]} T_R[p]. \end{cases} \tag{12.4}$$

The main difference between recursive Eqs (12.3) and (12.4) is that in the former procedure identifier X is calling itself, but in the latter X is calling Y and at the same time Y is calling X.

4. Note that we used the same "coin" d in the two equations of (12.4). If two different "coins" d and e are used, then we have another variant of the bidirectionally recursive Hadamard walk specified by

$$\begin{cases} X \Leftarrow T_L[p] \oplus_{H[d]} (T_R[p]; Y), \\ Y \Leftarrow (T_L[p]; X) \oplus_{H[e]} T_R[p]. \end{cases} \tag{12.5}$$

5. We can define a recursive quantum walk in another way if quantum case statement with three branches is employed:

$$X \Leftarrow U[d]; \mathbf{qif}\ [d]\ |L\rangle \to T_L[p]$$
$$\square \quad\ \ |R\rangle \to T_R[p]$$
$$\square \quad\ \ |I\rangle \to X$$
$$\mathbf{fiq}$$

where d is not a qubit but a qutrit, i.e. a quantum system with 3-dimensional state Hilbert space $\mathcal{H}_d = span\{|L\rangle, |R\rangle, |I\rangle\}$, L, R stand for the directions Left and Right, respectively, and I for Iteration, and U is a 3×3 unitary matrix, e.g. the 3-dimensional Fourier transform:

$$F_3 = \begin{pmatrix} 1 & 1 & 1 \\ 1 & e^{\frac{2}{3}\pi i} & e^{\frac{4}{3}\pi i} \\ 1 & e^{\frac{4}{3}\pi i} & e^{\frac{2}{3}\pi i} \end{pmatrix}.$$

Transitions of recursive quantum walks: Now let us have a glimpse of the behaviours of recursive quantum walks. We employ an idea similar to that used in Section 5.2. We use $\downarrow$ to denote the empty program or termination. A configuration is defined to be a pair

$$\langle S, |\psi\rangle\rangle$$

with S being a program or the empty program $\downarrow$, and $|\psi\rangle$ a pure state of the quantum system. It should be pointed out that since no measurements are involved here, we only need to consider a pure state in a configuration but not a mixed state as in the previous chapters. Then the behaviour of a program can be visualised by a sequence of transitions between superpositions of configurations. Note that in Section 5.2 the computation of a program is a sequence of transitions between configurations. Here, however, we have to consider transitions between superpositions of configurations. Naturally, these superpositions of configurations are generated by quantum control flow of the program.

We only consider the unidirectionally recursive quantum walk X declared by Eq. (12.2) as an example. The reader is encouraged to work out the first few transitions of other walks in the above example in order to better understand how quantum recursive calls happen. Assume that it is initialised in state $|L\rangle_d|0\rangle_p$; that is, the "coin" is in direction L and the walker is at position 0. Then we have:

$$
\begin{aligned}
\langle X, |L\rangle_d|0\rangle_p\rangle &\xrightarrow{(a)} \frac{1}{\sqrt{2}}\langle \downarrow, |L\rangle_d|-1\rangle_p\rangle + \frac{1}{\sqrt{2}}\langle X, |R\rangle_d|1\rangle_p\rangle \\
&\xrightarrow{(b)} \frac{1}{\sqrt{2}}\langle \downarrow, |L\rangle_d|-1\rangle_p\rangle + \frac{1}{2}\langle \downarrow, |R\rangle_d|L\rangle_{d_1}|0\rangle_p\rangle + \frac{1}{2}\langle X, |R\rangle_d|R\rangle_{d_1}|2\rangle_p\rangle \\
&\to \quad \ldots\ldots \\
&\to \sum_{i=0}^{n} \frac{1}{\sqrt{2^{i+1}}}\langle \downarrow, |R\rangle_{d_0}\ldots|R\rangle_{d_{i-1}}|L\rangle_{d_i}|i-1\rangle_p\rangle \\
&\quad + \frac{1}{\sqrt{2^{n+1}}}\langle X, |R\rangle_{d_0}\ldots|R\rangle_{d_{n-1}}|R\rangle_{d_n}|n+1\rangle_p\rangle
\end{aligned}
\tag{12.6}
$$

Here, $d_0 = d$, and new quantum "coins" $d_1, d_2, \ldots$ that are identical to the original "coin" d are introduced in order to avoid the conflict of variables for "coins". To see why these distinct "coins" $d_1, d_2, \ldots$ have to be introduced, we recall from Sections 11.1 and 11.2 that the "coins" $\overline{q}$ in a quantum case statement **qif** $[\overline{q}]$ $(\square i \cdot |i\rangle \to S_i)$ **fiq** is required to be external to subprograms S_i. Therefore, in Eq. (12.2) "coin" d is external to procedure X. Now let us see what happens in Eq. (12.6).

- First, the term after the arrow $\xrightarrow{(a)}$ is obtained by replacing the symbol X in the term before $\xrightarrow{(a)}$ with $T_L[p] \oplus_{H[d]}$ $(T_R[p]; X)$. So, in the term after $\xrightarrow{(a)}$, d is external to X.

- To obtain the term after $\xrightarrow{(b)}$, we replace the symbol X in the term after $\xrightarrow{(a)}$ by $T_L[p] \oplus_{H[d_1]} (T_R[p]; X)$. Here, d_1 must be different from d; otherwise in the term after $\xrightarrow{(a)}$, $d = d_1$ occurs (although implicitly) in X, and thus a contradiction.

Repeating this argument illustrates that $d_0 = d, d_1, d_2, \ldots$ should be different to each other.

Exercise 12.1. Show the first few steps of recursive quantum walks defined by Eqs (12.4) and (12.5) initialised in $|L\rangle_d|0\rangle_p$. Observe the difference between the behaviours of the two walks. Notice that such a difference is impossible for classical random walks where it does not matter to use two different "coins" with the same probability distribution.

Interference in recursive quantum walks: The above recursive quantum walks are good examples of quantum recursion, but their behaviours are not very interesting from the viewpoint of quantum physics. As pointed out in Section 4.5, the major difference between the behaviours of classical random walks and quantum walks is caused by quantum interference

– two separate paths leading to the same point may be out of phase and cancel one another. It is clear from Eq. (12.6) that quantum interference does not happen in the unidirectionally recursive quantum walk. Similarly, no quantum interference occurs in the other recursive quantum walks defined in the above example. The following is a much more interesting recursive quantum walk that shows a new phenomenon of quantum interference. As can be seen in Eq. (4.17), the paths that are cancelled in a (nonrecursive) quantum walk are finite. However, it is possible that infinite paths are cancelled in a recursive quantum walk.

Example 12.2. Let $n \geq 2$. A variant of bidirectionally recursive quantum walk can be defined as the program X declared by the following recursive equation:

$$X \Leftarrow \left(T_L[p] \oplus_{H[d]} T_R[p]\right)^n ; \left((T_L[p]; X) \oplus_{H[d]} (T_R[p]; X)\right) \tag{12.7}$$

Here, we use S^n to denote the sequential composition of n copies of a program S.

Now let us look at the behaviour of this walk. We assume that the walk is initialised in state $|L\rangle_d |0\rangle_p$. Then the first three steps of the walk are given as follows:

$$
\begin{aligned}
\langle X, |L\rangle_d |0\rangle_p \rangle &\to \frac{1}{\sqrt{2}} [\langle X_1, |L\rangle_d |-1\rangle_p \rangle + \langle X_1, |R\rangle_d |1\rangle_p \rangle] \\
&\to \frac{1}{2} [\langle X_2, |L\rangle_d |-2\rangle_p \rangle + \langle X_2, |R\rangle_d |0\rangle_p \rangle + \langle X_2, |L\rangle_d |0\rangle_p \rangle - \langle X_2, |R\rangle_d |2\rangle_p \rangle] \\
&\to \frac{1}{2\sqrt{2}} [\langle X_3, |L\rangle_d |-3\rangle_p \rangle + \langle X_3, |R\rangle_d |-1\rangle_p \rangle + \langle X_3, |L\rangle_d |-1\rangle_p \rangle \\
&\quad - \langle X_3, |R\rangle_d |1\rangle_p \rangle + \langle X_3, |L\rangle_d |-1\rangle_p \rangle + \langle X_3, |R\rangle_d |1\rangle_p \rangle \\
&\quad - \langle X_3, |L\rangle_d |1\rangle_p \rangle + \langle X_3, |R\rangle_d |3\rangle_p \rangle] \\
&= \frac{1}{2\sqrt{2}} [\langle X_3, |L\rangle_d |-3\rangle_p \rangle + \langle X_3, |R\rangle_d |-1\rangle_p \rangle + 2\langle X_3, |L\rangle_d |-1\rangle_p \rangle \\
&\quad - \langle X_3, |L\rangle_d |1\rangle_p \rangle + \langle X_3, |R\rangle_d |3\rangle_p \rangle]
\end{aligned}
\tag{12.8}
$$

where

$$X_i = \left(T_L[p] \oplus_{H[d]} T_R[p]\right)^{n-i} ; \left((T_L[p]; X) \oplus_{H[d]} (T_R[p]; X)\right)$$

for $i = 1, 2, 3$. We observe that in the last step of Eq. (12.8) two configurations

$$-\langle X_3, |R\rangle_d |1\rangle_p \rangle, \quad \langle X_3, |R\rangle_d |1\rangle_p \rangle$$

cancel one another. It is clear that both of them can generate infinite paths because they contain the recursive walk X itself. Comparing Eq. (12.8) with (12.6), the reader may wonder why no new "coins" were introduced in (12.8). Actually, only the part $\left(T_L[p] \oplus_{H[d]} T_R[p]\right)^n$ in the right-hand side of Eq. (12.7) is executed and no recursive calls happen in the three steps given in Eq. (12.8). Of course, fresh "coins" will be needed in the later steps where X is recursively called in order to avoid variable conflicts.

The behaviour of the recursive program specified by the following equation:

$$X \Leftarrow \left((T_L[p]; X) \oplus_{H[d]} (T_R[p]; X)\right) ; \left(T_L[p] \oplus_{H[d]} T_R[p]\right)^n \tag{12.9}$$

is even more puzzling. Note that Eq. (12.9) is obtained from Eq. (12.7) by changing the order of the two subprograms in its right-hand side.

Exercise 12.2. Examine the behaviour of the walk X declared by Eq. (12.9) starting at $|L\rangle_d |0\rangle_p$.

12.2.2 How to solve recursive quantum equations?

We have already seen from Eqs (12.6) and (12.8) the first steps of the recursive quantum walks. But a precise description of their behaviours amounts to solving recursive Eqs (12.2), (12.3), (12.4), (12.5), and (12.7), respectively. In the theory of classical programming languages, syntactic approximation is employed to define the semantics of recursive programs. It was also successfully used in Section 5.5 to define the semantics of recursive quantum programs (without quantum control flows). Naturally, we like to see whether syntactic approximation can be applied to quantum recursive programs too. To begin with, let us recall this technique by considering a simple recursive program declared by a single equation

$$X \Leftarrow F(X).$$

Let

$$\begin{cases} X^{(0)} = \textbf{abort}, \\ X^{(n+1)} = F[X^{(n)}/X] \text{ for } n \geq 0, \end{cases}$$

where $F[X^{(n)}/X]$ is the result of substitution of X in $F(X)$ by $X^{(n)}$. The program $X^{(n)}$ is called the nth syntactic approximation of X. Roughly speaking, the syntactic approximations $X^{(n)}$ ($n = 0, 1, 2, ...$) describe the initial fragments of the behaviour of the recursive program X. Then the semantics $[\![X]\!]$ of X is defined to be the limit of the semantics $[\![X^{(n)}]\!]$ of its syntactic approximations $X^{(n)}$:

$$[\![X]\!] = \lim_{n \to \infty} \left[\!\left[X^{(n)}\right]\!\right].$$

Now we try to apply this method to the unidirectionally recursive Hadamard walk and construct its syntactic approximations as follows:

$$X^{(0)} = \textbf{abort},$$
$$X^{(1)} = T_L[p] \oplus_{H[d]} (T_R[p]; \textbf{abort}),$$
$$X^{(2)} = T_L[p] \oplus_{H[d]} (T_R[p]; T_L[p] \oplus_{H[d_1]} (T_R[p]; \textbf{abort})), \tag{12.10}$$
$$X^{(3)} = T_L[p] \oplus_{H[d]} (T_R[p]; T_L[p] \oplus_{H[d_1]} (T_R[p]; T_L[p] \oplus_{H[d_2]} (T_R[p]; \textbf{abort}))),$$
$$\ldots\ldots\ldots$$

However, a serious problem arises in constructing these approximations:

- We have to continuously introduce new "coin" variables in order to avoid variable conflict; that is, for every $n = 1, 2, ...$, we have to introduce a new "coin" variable d_n in the $(n + 1)$th syntactic approximation because as emphasised many times before, "coins" $d, d_1, ..., d_{n-1}$ should be considered external to the inner most system that contains d_n. Therefore, variables $d, d_1, d_2, ..., d_n$, ... denote distinct "coins". On the other hand, they must be thought of as identical particles in the sense that their physical properties are the same. Moreover, the number of the "coin" particles that are needed in running the recursive Hadamard walk is usually unknown beforehand because we do not know when the walk terminates.

Obviously, a solution to this problem requires a mathematical framework in which we can deal with quantum systems where the number of particles of the same type – the "coins" – may vary. It is worth noting that this problem appears only in the quantum case but not in the theory of classical programming languages because it is caused by employing an external "coin" system in defining a quantum case statement.

12.3 Second quantisation

At the end of the last section, we observed that solving a quantum recursive equation requires a mathematical model of a quantum system consisting of a variable number of identical particles. It is clear that such a model is out of the scope of basic quantum mechanics described in Chapter 2, where we only considered a composite quantum system with a fixed number of subsystems that are not necessarily identical (see Postulate of quantum mechanics 4 in Section 2.4). Fortunately, physicists had developed a formalism for describing quantum systems with variable particle number, namely second quantisation, more than eighty years ago. For convenience of the reader, we give a brief introduction to the second quantisation method in this section. This introduction focuses on the mathematical formulation of second quantisation needed in the sequent sections; for physical interpretations, the reader can consult textbook [293].

12.3.1 Multiple-particle states

We first consider a quantum system of a fixed number of particles. It is assumed that these particles have the same state Hilbert space, but they are not necessarily identical particles. Let $\mathcal{H}$ be the state Hilbert space of a single particle. For any $n \geq 1$, we can define the tensor product $\mathcal{H}^{\otimes n}$ of n copies of $\mathcal{H}$ by Definition 2.18. For any family $|\psi_1\rangle, ..., |\psi_n\rangle$ of single-particle states in $\mathcal{H}$, Postulate of quantum mechanics 4 asserts that we have a state

$$|\psi_1\rangle \otimes \cdots \otimes |\psi_n\rangle = |\psi_1 \otimes \cdots \otimes \psi_n\rangle$$

of n independent particles, in which the ith particle is in state $|\psi_i\rangle$ for every $1 \leq i \leq n$. Then $\mathcal{H}^{\otimes n}$ consists of the linear combinations of vectors $|\psi_1 \otimes \cdots \otimes \psi_n\rangle$:

$$\mathcal{H}^{\otimes n} = \text{span}\{|\psi_1 \otimes \cdots \otimes \psi_n\rangle : |\psi_1\rangle, ..., |\psi_n\rangle \in \mathcal{H}\}$$
$$= \left\{ \sum_{i=1}^{m} \alpha_i |\psi_{i1} \otimes \cdots \otimes \psi_{in}\rangle : m \geq 0, \alpha_i \in \mathbb{C}, |\psi_{i1}\rangle, ..., |\psi_{in}\rangle \in \mathcal{H} \right\}.$$

Recall from Section 2.4 that $\mathcal{H}^{\otimes n}$ is a Hilbert space too. More explicitly, the basic operations of vectors in $\mathcal{H}^{\otimes n}$ are defined by the following equations together with linearity:

1. Addition:

$$|\psi_1 \otimes \cdots \otimes \psi_i \otimes \cdots \otimes \psi_n\rangle + |\psi_1 \otimes \cdots \otimes \psi_i' \otimes \cdots \otimes \psi_n\rangle$$
$$= |\psi_1 \otimes \cdots \otimes (\psi_i + \psi_i') \otimes \cdots \otimes \psi_n\rangle;$$

2. Scalar product:

$$\lambda |\psi_1 \otimes \cdots \otimes \psi_i \otimes \cdots \otimes \psi_n\rangle = |\psi_1 \otimes \cdots \otimes (\lambda \psi_i) \otimes \cdots \otimes \psi_n\rangle;$$

3. Inner product:

$$\langle \psi_1 \otimes \cdots \otimes \psi_n | \varphi_1 \otimes \cdots \otimes \varphi_n \rangle = \prod_{i=1}^{n} \langle \psi_i | \varphi_i \rangle.$$

Exercise 12.3. Show that if $\mathcal{B}$ is a basis of $\mathcal{H}$, then

$$\{|\psi_1 \otimes \cdots \otimes \psi_n\rangle : |\psi_1\rangle, ..., |\psi_n\rangle \in \mathcal{B}\}$$

is a basis of $\mathcal{H}^{\otimes n}$.

Permutation operators: Now we turn to consider a quantum system of multiple identical particles that possess the same intrinsic properties. Let us start by introducing several operators for describing the symmetry of identical particles. For each permutation π of $1, ..., n$, i.e. a bijection from $\{1, ..., n\}$ onto itself that maps i to $\pi(i)$ for every $1 \leq i \leq n$, we can define the permutation operator P_π on the space $\mathcal{H}^{\otimes n}$ by

$$P_\pi |\psi_1 \otimes \cdots \otimes \psi_n\rangle = |\psi_{\pi(1)} \otimes \cdots \otimes \psi_{\pi(n)}\rangle$$

together with linearity. Several basic properties of permutation operators are given in the following:

Proposition 12.1. **1.** P_π *is a unitary operator.*
2. $P_{\pi_1} P_{\pi_2} = P_{\pi_1 \pi_2}$, *where $\pi_1 \pi_2$ is the composition of π_1 and π_2.*
3. $P_\pi^\dagger = P_{\pi^{-1}}$, *where $P_\pi^\dagger$ stands for the conjugate transpose (i.e. inverse) of P_π, and π^{-1} is the inverse of π.*

Furthermore, symmetrisation and antisymmetrisation operators can be defined in terms of permutation operators:

Definition 12.4. The symmetrisation and antisymmetrisation operators on $\mathcal{H}^{\otimes n}$ are defined by

$$S_+ = \frac{1}{n!} \sum_\pi P_\pi,$$

$$S_- = \frac{1}{n!} \sum_\pi (-1)^\pi P_\pi,$$

where π traverse over all permutations of $1, ..., n$, and $(-1)^\pi$ is the signature of the permutation π; that is,

$$(-1)^\pi = \begin{cases} 1 & \text{if } \pi \text{ is even,} \\ -1 & \text{if } \pi \text{ is odd.} \end{cases}$$

We list several useful properties of symmetrisation and antisymmetrisation in the following:

Proposition 12.2. 1. $P_\pi S_+ = S_+ P_\pi = S_+$.
2. $P_\pi S_- = S_- P_\pi = (-1)^\pi S_-$.
3. $S_+^2 = S_+ = S_+^\dagger$.
4. $S_-^2 = S_- = S_-^\dagger$.
5. $S_+ S_- = S_- S_+ = 0$.

Exercise 12.4. Prove Propositions 12.1 and 12.2.

Symmetric and antisymmetric states: Of course, quantum mechanics described in Section 2 can be used to cope with a quantum system of multiple particles. However, it is not complete when these particles are identical, and it must be supplemented by the following:

- **The principle of symmetrisation**: The states of n identical particles are either completely symmetric or completely antisymmetric with the permutation of the n particles.

  - The symmetric particles are called *bosons*;
  - The antisymmetric particles are called *fermions*.

At the beginning of this subsection, we saw that $\mathcal{H}^{\otimes n}$ is the state Hilbert space of n particle if all of them have the same state space $\mathcal{H}$. According to the above principle, it is not the case that every vector in $\mathcal{H}^{\otimes n}$ can be used to model a state of n identical particles. However, for each state $|\Psi\rangle$ in $\mathcal{H}^{\otimes n}$, we can construct the following two states by symmetrisation or antisymmetrisation:

- a symmetric (bosonic) state: $S_+ |\Psi\rangle$;
- an antisymmetric (a fermionic) state: $S_- |\Psi\rangle$.

In particular, the symmetric and antisymmetric states corresponding to the product of one-particle states $|\psi_1\rangle, ..., |\psi_n\rangle$ are written as

$$|\psi_1, \cdots, \psi_n\rangle_v = S_v |\psi_1 \otimes \cdots \otimes \psi_n\rangle_v$$

where v is $+$ or $-$. With this notation, the principle of symmetrisation can be restated as follows:

- For the bosons, the order of states $|\psi_i\rangle$ in $|\psi_1, \cdots, \psi_n\rangle_+$ is insignificant.
- For the fermions, $|\psi_1, \cdots, \psi_n\rangle_-$ changes sign under permutations of two states:

$$|\psi_1, \cdots, \psi_i, \cdots, \psi_j, \cdots, \psi_n\rangle_- = -|\psi_1, \cdots, \psi_j, \cdots, \psi_i, \cdots, \psi_n\rangle_-. \tag{12.11}$$

An immediate corollary of Eq. (12.11) is the following:

- **Pauli's exclusion principle**: If two states $|\psi_i\rangle$ and $|\psi_j\rangle$ are identical, then $|\psi_1, \cdots, \psi_i, \cdots, \psi_j, \cdots, \psi_n\rangle_-$ vanishes – two fermions can never be found in the same individual quantum state.

In summary, the principle of symmetrisation implies that the state space of a system of n identical particles is not total of $\mathcal{H}^{\otimes n}$, but rather one of the following two subspaces:

Definition 12.5. 1. The n-fold symmetric tensor product of $\mathcal{H}$:

$$\mathcal{H}_+^{\otimes n} = S_+ \left(\mathcal{H}^{\otimes n} \right)$$
$$= \text{the closed subspace of } \mathcal{H}^{\otimes n} \text{ generated by the symmetric}$$
$$\text{tensor products } |\psi_1, \cdots, \psi_n\rangle_+ \text{ with } |\psi_1\rangle, ..., |\psi_n\rangle \in \mathcal{H}$$

2. The n-fold antisymmetric tensor product of $\mathcal{H}$:

$$\mathcal{H}_-^{\otimes n} = S_- \left(\mathcal{H}^{\otimes n} \right)$$
$$= \text{the closed subspace of } \mathcal{H}^{\otimes n} \text{ generated by the antisymmetric}$$
$$\text{tensor products } |\psi_1, \cdots, \psi_n\rangle_- \text{ with } |\psi_1\rangle, ..., |\psi_n\rangle \in \mathcal{H}$$

The addition, scalar product and inner product in $\mathcal{H}_v^{\otimes n}$ ($v = +, -$) are directly inherited from $\mathcal{H}^{\otimes n}$. In particular, the following proposition provides a convenient way to compute the inner products in $\mathcal{H}_\pm^{\otimes n}$:

Proposition 12.3. *The inner product of symmetric and antisymmetric tensor products:*

$$_+\langle \psi_1, \cdots, \psi_n | \varphi_1, \cdots, \varphi_n \rangle_+ = \frac{1}{n!} per\left(\langle \psi_i | \varphi_j \rangle \right)_{ij},$$

$$_-\langle \psi_1, \cdots, \psi_n | \varphi_1, \cdots, \varphi_n \rangle_- = \frac{1}{n!} det\left(\langle \psi_i | \varphi_j \rangle \right)_{ij},$$

where det and per stand for the determinant of matrix and the permutation (i.e. the determinant without the minus signs), respectively.

Exercise 12.5. 1. Compute the dimensions of the symmetric and antisymmetric tensor product spaces $\mathcal{H}_\pm^{\otimes n}$.
2. Prove Proposition 12.3.

12.3.2 Fock spaces

Quantum systems of a fixed number of identical particles were studied in the last subsection. Now let us see how to describe a quantum system with variable number of particles. A natural idea is that the state Hilbert space of such a system is the direct sum of the state spaces of different numbers of particles. To realise this idea, let us first introduce the notion of direct sum of Hilbert spaces.

Definition 12.6. Let $\mathcal{H}_1, \mathcal{H}_2, ...$ be an infinite sequence of Hilbert spaces. Then their direct sum is defined to be the vector space:

$$\bigoplus_{i=1}^{\infty} \mathcal{H}_i = \left\{ (|\psi_1\rangle, |\psi_2\rangle, ...) : |\psi_i\rangle \in \mathcal{H}_i \ (i = 1, 2, ...) \text{ with } \sum_{i=1}^{\infty} \||\psi_i\|^2 < \infty \right\}$$

in which we define:

- Addition:

$$(|\psi_1\rangle, |\psi_2\rangle, ...) + (|\varphi_1\rangle, |\varphi_2\rangle, ...) = (|\psi_1\rangle + |\varphi_1\rangle, |\psi_2\rangle + |\varphi_2\rangle, ...);$$

- Scalar multiplication:

$$\alpha(|\psi_1\rangle, |\psi_2\rangle, ...) = (\alpha|\psi_1\rangle, \alpha|\psi_2\rangle, ...);$$

- Inner product:

$$\langle (\psi_1, \psi_2, ...) | (\varphi_1, \varphi_2, ...) \rangle = \sum_{i=1}^{\infty} \langle \psi_i | \varphi_i \rangle.$$

Exercise 12.6. Show that $\bigoplus_{i=1}^{\infty} \mathcal{H}_i$ is a Hilbert space.

Let $\mathcal{H}$ be the state Hilbert space of one particle. If we introduce the vacuum state $|\mathbf{0}\rangle$, then the 0-fold tensor product of $\mathcal{H}$ can be defined as the one-dimensional space

$$\mathcal{H}^{\otimes 0} = \mathcal{H}_\pm^{\otimes 0} = span\{|\mathbf{0}\rangle\}.$$

Now we are ready to describe the state space of a quantum system with variable number of identical particles.

Definition 12.7. 1. The free Fock space over $\mathcal{H}$ is defined to be the direct sum of the n-fold tensor products of $\mathcal{H}$:

$$\mathcal{F}(\mathcal{H}) = \bigoplus_{n=0}^{\infty} \mathcal{H}^{\otimes n}.$$

2. The symmetric (bosonic) Fock space and the antisymmetric (fermionic) Fock space over $\mathcal{H}$ are defined by

$$\mathcal{F}_v(\mathcal{H}) = \bigoplus_{n=0}^{\infty} \mathcal{H}_v^{\otimes n}$$

where $v = +$ for bosons or $v = -$ for fermions.

The principle of symmetrisation tells us that only the symmetric or antisymmetric Fock space is meaningful in physics, but here we also introduce the free Fock space since it is a useful mathematical tool that is sometimes easier to deal with than the symmetric and antisymmetric Fock spaces, as we will see in the next section.

To understand the Fock spaces better, let us look more carefully at the states in them and operations on them:

1. A state in $\mathcal{F}_v(\mathcal{H})$ is of the form:

$$|\Psi\rangle = \sum_{n=0}^{\infty} |\Psi(n)\rangle \triangleq (|\Psi(0)\rangle, |\Psi(1)\rangle, \cdots, |\Psi(n)\rangle, \cdots)$$

where $|\Psi(n)\rangle \in \mathcal{H}_v^{\otimes n}$ is a state of n particles for all $n = 0, 1, 2, ...,$ and

$$\sum_{n=0}^{\infty} \langle \Psi(n)|\Psi(n)\rangle < \infty.$$

2. Basic operations on $\mathcal{F}_v(\mathcal{H})$:

   • Addition:

$$\left(\sum_{n=0}^{\infty} |\Psi(n)\rangle \right) + \left(\sum_{n=0}^{\infty} |\Phi(n)\rangle \right) = \sum_{n=0}^{\infty} (|\Psi(n)\rangle + |\Phi(n)\rangle);$$

   • Scalar product:

$$\alpha \left(\sum_{n=0}^{\infty} |\Psi(n)\rangle \right) = \sum_{n=0}^{\infty} \alpha|\Psi(n)\rangle;$$

   • Inner product:

$$\left\langle \sum_{n=0}^{\infty} \Psi(n) \Big| \sum_{n=0}^{\infty} \Phi(n) \right\rangle = \sum_{n=0}^{\infty} \langle \Psi(n)|\Phi(n)\rangle.$$

3. Basis of $\mathcal{F}_v(\mathcal{H})$: The symmetric or antisymmetric product states $|\psi_1, ..., \psi_n\rangle_v$ ($n \geq 0$ and $|\psi_1\rangle, ..., |\psi_n\rangle \in \mathcal{H}$) form a basis of Fock space $\mathcal{F}_v(\mathcal{H})$; that is,

$$\mathcal{F}_v(\mathcal{H}) = \text{span}\{|\psi_1, \cdots, \psi_n\rangle_v : n = 0, 1, 2, ... \text{ and } |\psi_1\rangle, ..., |\psi_n\rangle \in \mathcal{H}\}$$

   where $|\psi_1, \cdots, \psi_n\rangle_v$ is the vacuum state $|\mathbf{0}\rangle$ if $n = 0$.
4. We identify state $(0, ..., 0, |\Psi(n)\rangle, 0, ..., 0)$ in $\mathcal{F}_v(\mathcal{H})$ with the state $|\Psi(n)\rangle$ in $\mathcal{H}_v^{\otimes n}$. Then $\mathcal{H}_v^{\otimes n}$ can be seen as a subspace of $\mathcal{F}_v(\mathcal{H})$. Moreover, for different particle numbers $m \neq n$, $\mathcal{H}_v^{\otimes m}$ and $\mathcal{H}_v^{\otimes n}$ are orthogonal because $\langle \Psi(m)|\Psi(n)\rangle = 0$.

Operators on Fock spaces: We already learned that a state of a quantum system with variable number of identical particles can be represented by a vector in the Fock spaces. Now we move forward to prepare the mathematical tools for the description of observables and evolution of such a quantum system. We first define operators on the direct sum of Hilbert spaces.

Definition 12.8. For each $i \geq 1$, let A_i be a bounded operator on $\mathcal{H}_i$ such that the sequence $\|A_i\|$ ($i = 1, 2, ...$) of norms (see Definition 2.11) is bounded; that is, $\|A_i\| \leq C$ ($i = 1, 2, ...$) for some constant C. Then we define operator

$$A = (A_1, A_2, ...)$$

on $\bigoplus_{i=1}^{\infty} \mathcal{H}_i$ as follows:

$$A(|\psi_1\rangle, |\psi_2\rangle, ...) = (A_1|\psi_1\rangle, A_2|\psi_2\rangle, ...) \tag{12.12}$$

for every $(|\psi_1\rangle, |\psi_2\rangle, ...) \in \bigoplus_{i=1}^{\infty} \mathcal{H}_i$.

Similarly, we can define operator $A = (A_1, ..., A_n)$ on the direct sum $\bigoplus_{i=1}^{n} \mathcal{H}_i$ for a finite number n. For simplicity of presentation, we often write:

$$\sum_{i=1}^{\infty} A_i = (A_1, A_2, ...) \text{ and } \sum_{i=1}^{n} A_i = (A_1, ..., A_n).$$

Exercise 12.7. Show that A defined by Eq. (12.12) is a bounded operator on $\bigoplus_{i=1}^{\infty} \mathcal{H}_i$ and

$$\|A\| \leq \sup_{i=1}^{\infty} \|A_i\|.$$

Now we can use the above idea to define operators on Fock spaces. For each $n \geq 1$, let $\mathbf{A}(n)$ be an operator on $\mathcal{H}^{\otimes n}$. Then operator

$$\mathbf{A} = \sum_{n=0}^{\infty} \mathbf{A}(n) \tag{12.13}$$

can be defined on the free Fock space $\mathcal{F}(\mathcal{H})$ by Definition 12.8:

$$\mathbf{A}|\Psi\rangle = \mathbf{A}\left(\sum_{n=0}^{\infty} |\Psi(n)\rangle\right) = \sum_{n=0}^{\infty} \mathbf{A}(n)|\Psi(n)\rangle$$

for any

$$|\Psi\rangle = \sum_{n=0}^{\infty} |\Psi(n)\rangle$$

in $\mathcal{F}(\mathcal{H})$, where $\mathbf{A}|\mathbf{0}\rangle = 0$; that is, the vacuum state is considered to be an eigenvector of operator $\mathbf{A}$ with eigenvalue 0. Obviously, for all $n \geq 0$, $\mathcal{H}_v^{\otimes n}$ is invariant under $\mathbf{A}$; that is, $\mathbf{A}(\mathcal{H}_v^{\otimes n}) \subseteq \mathcal{H}_v^{\otimes n}$.

A general operator in the form of (12.13) does not necessarily preserve symmetry (respectively, antisymmetry) of bosons (respectively, fermions). To define an operator on the bosonic or fermionic Fock space, we need to consider its symmetry.

Definition 12.9. If for each $n \geq 0$ and for each permutation π of $1, ..., n$, P_π and $\mathbf{A}(n)$ commute; that is,

$$P_\pi \mathbf{A}(n) = \mathbf{A}(n) P_\pi,$$

then operator $\mathbf{A} = \sum_{n=0}^{\infty} \mathbf{A}(n)$ is said to be symmetric.

It is easy to see that both the symmetric Fock space $\mathcal{F}_+(\mathcal{H})$ and the antisymmetric Fock space $\mathcal{F}_-(\mathcal{H})$ are closed under a symmetric operator $\mathbf{A} = \sum_{n=0}^{\infty} \mathbf{A}(n)$:

$$\mathbf{A}(\mathcal{F}_v(\mathcal{H})) \subseteq \mathcal{F}_v(\mathcal{H})$$

for $v = +, -$. In other words, a symmetric operator $\mathbf{A}$ maps a bosonic (or fermonic) state $|\Psi\rangle$ to a bosonic (respectively, fermonic) state $\mathbf{A}|\Psi\rangle$.

Exercise 12.8. Is the following statement correct: if an operator $\mathbf{A}$ on $\mathcal{F}(\mathcal{H})$ satisfies that $\mathbf{A}(\mathcal{F}_+(\mathcal{H})) \subseteq \mathcal{F}_+(\mathcal{H})$ (or $\mathbf{A}(\mathcal{F}_-(\mathcal{H})) \subseteq \mathcal{F}_-(\mathcal{H})$), then $\mathbf{A}$ is symmetric? Prove your conclusion.

We can further introduce the symmetrisation functional $\mathbb{S}$ that maps every operator $\mathbf{A} = \sum_{n=0}^{\infty} \mathbf{A}(n)$ to a symmetric operator:

$$\mathbb{S}(\mathbf{A}) = \sum_{n=0}^{\infty} \mathbb{S}(\mathbf{A}(n)) \tag{12.14}$$

where for each $n \geq 0$,

$$\mathbb{S}(\mathbf{A}(n)) = \frac{1}{n!} \sum_{\pi} P_\pi \mathbf{A}(n) P_\pi^{-1} \tag{12.15}$$

with π traversing over all permutations of $1, ..., n$, where P_π^{-1} is the inverse of P_π. Thus, each operator $\mathbf{A}$ on the free Fock space can be transformed by the symmetrisation functional $\mathbb{S}$ to an operator $\mathbf{S}(\mathbf{A})$ that can be properly applied on the bosonic or fermonic Fock spaces.

12.3.3   Observables in Fock spaces

In the last subsection, Fock spaces were introduced as the state Hilbert spaces of quantum systems with variable particle number. We also studied various operators on the Fock spaces. Now we see how to describe the observables of these systems.

Many-body observables: To warm up, let us start from the observables of a fixed number $n \geq 1$ of particles. By the basic postulates of quantum mechanics, in general, an observable of a quantum system with n particles can be expressed by a Hermitian operator on $\mathcal{H}^{\otimes n}$. Here, we like to carefully look at a very special class of observables in the state space $\mathcal{H}^{\otimes n}$ of n particles.

First, let us consider the simplest case where only one of the n particles is observed. Assume that O is a single-particle observable in $\mathcal{H}$. Then for each $1 \leq i \leq n$, the action $O^{[i]}$ of O on the ith factor of $\mathcal{H}^{\otimes n}$ can be defined by

$$O^{[i]}|\psi_1 \otimes \cdots \psi_i \otimes \cdots \otimes \psi_n\rangle = |\psi_1 \otimes \cdots \otimes (O\psi_i) \otimes \cdots \otimes \psi_n\rangle$$

together with linearity; that is,

$$O^{[i]} = I^{\otimes(i-1)} \otimes O \otimes I^{\otimes(n-i)},$$

where I is the identity operator on $\mathcal{H}$. Obviously, for a fixed i, the operator $O^{[i]}$ is not symmetric. Combining these actions $O^{[i]}$ on different particles i, we have:

Definition 12.10. The one-body observable corresponding to O is

$$O_1(n) = \sum_{i=1}^{n} O^{[i]}.$$

Secondly, we consider an observable on two of the n particles. Assume that O is an observable in the two-particle space $\mathcal{H} \otimes \mathcal{H}$. Then for any $1 \leq i < j \leq n$, we can define $O^{[ij]}$ on $\mathcal{H}^{\otimes n}$ as the operator which acts as O on the ith and jth factors of $\mathcal{H}^{\otimes n}$ and trivially on others; that is,

$$O^{[ij]} = I^{\otimes(i-1)} \otimes O \otimes I^{\otimes(j-i-1)} \otimes O \otimes I^{\otimes(n-j)}.$$

If observable O is allowed to apply to any two of these n particles, we have:

Definition 12.11. The two-body observable for the system of n particles corresponding to O is defined as

$$O_2(n) = \sum_{1 \leq i < j \leq n} O^{[ij]}.$$

Exercise 12.9. Show that if O is invariant under exchange of two particles: $O^{[ij]} = O^{[ji]}$ for all $1 \leq i, j \leq n$, then

$$O_2(n) = \frac{1}{2} \sum_{i \neq j} O^{[ij]}.$$

Furthermore, we can define k-body observables $O_k(n)$ for $2 < k \leq n$ in a way similar to Definitions 12.10 and 12.11.

Observables in Fock spaces: Let us now move on to study observables with variable number of particles. First, we notice that Eq. (12.13) provides us with a natural way to define observables in Fock spaces; more precisely, if for each $n \geq 1$, the operator $\mathbf{A}(n)$ in Eq. (12.13) is an observable of n particles, then

$$\mathbf{A} = \sum_{n=0}^{\infty} \mathbf{A}(n)$$

is called an extensive observable in the free Fock space $\mathcal{F}(\mathcal{H})$. In particular, if $\mathbf{A}$ is symmetric, then it is also an observable in both the symmetric and antisymmetric Fock spaces.

The following proposition gives a convenient method for computing the mean value of an extensive observable.

Proposition 12.4. *The mean value of* $\mathbf{A} = \sum_{n=0}^{\infty} \mathbf{A}(n)$ *in state* $|\Psi\rangle = \sum_{n=0}^{\infty} |\Psi(n)\rangle$ *is*

$$\langle \Psi | \mathbf{A} | \Psi \rangle = \sum_{n=0}^{\infty} \langle \Psi(n) | \mathbf{A}(n) | \Psi(n) \rangle$$

$$= \sum_{n=0}^{\infty} \langle \Psi(n) | \Psi(n) \rangle \cdot \frac{\langle \Psi(n) | \mathbf{A}(n) | \Psi(n) \rangle}{\langle \Psi(n) | \Psi(n) \rangle}$$

where:

1. $\langle \Psi(n) | \Psi(n) \rangle$ *is the probability to find n particles in the state* $|\Psi\rangle$;
2.

$$\frac{\langle \Psi(n) | \mathbf{A}(n) | \Psi(n) \rangle}{\langle \Psi(n) | \Psi(n) \rangle}$$

is the mean value of $\mathbf{A}(n)$ *for the system of n particles.*

Second, we consider a special classes of observables in the Fock spaces, which are direct extensions of the many-body observables $O_k(n)$ introduced in the previous paragraph. As an application of the above procedure, for a given $k \geq 1$, the k-body observables in the free Fock space can be defined as follows:

$$\mathbf{O}_k = \sum_{n \geq k} O_k(n),$$

where for all $n \geq k$, $O_k(n)$ is the k-body observable in $\mathcal{H}^{\otimes n}$ (see Definitions 12.10 and 12.11). Furthermore, note that $\mathbf{O}_k$ is symmetric; for example, one-body observables $O_1(n)$ commute with the permutations:

$$O_1(n) | \psi_1, ..., \psi_n \rangle_{\pm} = \sum_{j=1}^{n} | \psi_1, ..., \psi_{j-1}, O\psi_j, \psi_{j+1}, ..., \psi_n \rangle_{\pm}.$$

A similar equation holds for $k \geq 2$. Therefore, $\mathbf{O}_k$ can be directly used in the symmetric and antisymmetric Fock spaces.

A particularly important observable in Fock spaces is defined in the following:

Definition 12.12. The particle number operator N in $\mathcal{F}_{\pm}(\mathcal{H})$ is defined by

$$\mathbf{N} \left(\sum_{n=0}^{\infty} |\Psi(n)\rangle \right) = \sum_{n=0}^{\infty} n |\Psi(n)\rangle.$$

As suggested by its name, for each $n \geq 0$, the particle number operator $\mathbf{N}$ gives the number n explicitly in front of the n-particle component $|\Psi(n)\rangle$ of a state $|\Psi\rangle$ in the Fock spaces. Several basic properties of the particle number operator are given in the following two propositions:

Proposition 12.5. 1. *For each* $n = 0, 1, 2...,$ $\mathcal{H}_{\pm}^{\otimes n}$ *is the eigen-subspace of* $\mathbf{N}$ *with eigenvalue n.*
2. *The mean value of* $\mathbf{N}$ *in state* $|\Psi\rangle = \sum_{n=0}^{\infty} |\Psi(n)\rangle$ *is*

$$\langle \Psi | \mathbf{N} | \Psi \rangle = \sum_{n=0}^{\infty} n \langle \Psi(n) | \Psi(n) \rangle.$$

Proposition 12.6. *Extensive observables* $\mathbf{A}$ *and particle number operator* $\mathbf{N}$ *commute:* $\mathbf{AN} = \mathbf{NA}$.

Exercise 12.10. Prove Propositions 12.5 and 12.6.

12.3.4   Evolution in Fock spaces

We now turn to consider the dynamics of a quantum system with variable particle number. Such a quantum system can evolve in two different ways:

1. the evolution does not change the number of particles; and
2. the evolution changes the number of particles.

In this subsection, we focus on the first kind of evolution, and the second will be discussed in the next subsection. Obviously, Eq. (12.13) also gives us a method to define an evolution of the first kind. More precisely, if for every $n \geq 0$, the dynamics of n particles is modelled by operator $\mathbf{A}(n)$, then $\mathbf{A} = \sum_{n=0}^{\infty} \mathbf{A}(n)$ describes an evolution in the Fock spaces that does not change the number of particles.

Let us more carefully examine a special evolution of this kind. Assume that the (discrete-time) evolution of one particle is represented by unitary operator U. Then the evolution of n particles without mutual interactions can be described by operator

$$\mathbf{U}(n) = U^{\otimes n}$$

on the space $\mathcal{H}^{\otimes n}$:

$$\mathbf{U}(n)|\psi_1 \otimes \ldots \otimes \psi_n\rangle = |U\psi_1 \otimes \ldots \otimes U\psi_n\rangle \tag{12.16}$$

for all $|\psi_1\rangle, \ldots, |\psi_n\rangle$ in $\mathcal{H}$. Here, the same unitary U applies to all of the n particles simultaneously. It is easy to verify that $\mathbf{U}(n)$ commutes with the permutations:

$$\mathbf{U}(n)|\psi_1, \ldots, \psi_n\rangle_{\pm} = |U\psi_1, \ldots, U\psi_n\rangle_{\pm}.$$

Then using Eq. (12.13), we can define a symmetric operator on the Fock spaces $\mathcal{F}_{\pm}(\mathcal{H})$:

$$\mathbf{U} = \sum_{n=0}^{\infty} \mathbf{U}(n). \tag{12.17}$$

Clearly, it depicts the evolution of a quantum system with variable number of particles but without mutual interaction between the particles.

12.3.5   Creation and annihilation of particles

In the previous subsection, we learned how to describe the first kind of evolutions in the Fock spaces, where the number of particles is not changed; for example, the operator $\mathbf{U}$ defined by Eq. (12.17) maps states of n particles to states of particles of the same number. In this subsection, we study the second kind of evolutions in the Fock spaces that can change the number of particles. Obviously, this kind of evolutions cannot be treated within the basic framework of quantum mechanics presented in Chapter 2. Nevertheless, the transitions between states of different particle numbers can be described by two basic operators – creation and annihilation.

Definition 12.13. For each one-particle state $|\psi\rangle$ in $\mathcal{H}$, the creation operator $a^{\dagger}(\psi)$ on $\mathcal{F}_{\pm}(\mathcal{H})$, associated with a given $|\psi\rangle$, is defined by

$$a^{\dagger}(\psi)|\psi_1, \ldots, \psi_n\rangle_v = \sqrt{n+1}|\psi, \psi_1, \ldots, \psi_n\rangle_v \tag{12.18}$$

for any $n \geq 0$ and all $|\psi_1\rangle, \ldots, |\psi_n\rangle$ in $\mathcal{H}$, together with linearity.

From its defining Eq. (12.18), we see that the operator $a^{\dagger}(\psi)$ adds a particle in the individual state $|\psi\rangle$ to the system of n particles without modifying their respective states; in particular, the symmetry or antisymmetry of the state is preserved in this transition. The coefficient $\sqrt{n+1}$ is added in the right-hand side of Eq. (12.18) mainly for the sake of coefficient normalisation.

Definition 12.14. For each one-particle state $|\psi\rangle$ in $\mathcal{H}$, the annihilation operator $a(\psi)$ on $\mathcal{F}_{\pm}(\mathcal{H})$ is defined to be the Hermitian conjugate of $a^{\dagger}(\psi)$:

$$a(\psi) = (a^{\dagger}(\psi))^{\dagger}$$

that is,

$$\left(a^\dagger(\psi)|\varphi_1, ..., \varphi_n\rangle_v, |\psi_1, ..., \psi_n\rangle_v\right) = (|\varphi_1, ..., \varphi_n\rangle_v, a(\psi)|\psi_1, ..., \psi_n\rangle_v) \tag{12.19}$$

for all $|\varphi_1\rangle, ..., |\varphi_n\rangle, |\psi_1\rangle, ..., |\psi_n\rangle \in \mathcal{H}$ and for every $n \geq 0$.

The following proposition gives a representation of annihilation operators.

Proposition 12.7.

$$a(\psi)|\mathbf{0}\rangle = 0,$$

$$a(\psi)|\psi_1, \cdots, \psi_n\rangle_\pm = \frac{1}{\sqrt{n}} \sum_{i=1}^{n} (v)^i \langle\psi|\psi_i\rangle|\psi_1, \cdots, \psi_{i-1}, \psi_{i+1}, \cdots, \psi_n\rangle_\pm.$$

It can be clearly seen from the above proposition that annihilation operator $a(\psi)$ decreases the number of particles by one unit, while preserving the symmetry of the state.

Exercise 12.11. Prove Proposition 12.7. Hint: directly use the defining Eq. (12.19) of $a(\psi)$.

12.4   Solving recursive equations in the free Fock space

As convinced by an example of recursive quantum walk at the end of Section 12.2, we have to deal with a quantum system with variable number of identical particles in order to model the behaviour of quantum "coins" employed in the execution of a quantum recessive program. So, a mathematical framework for this purpose, namely second quantisation, was introduced in the last section. Indeed, second quantisation provides us with all of the necessary tools for defining the semantics of quantum recursion. The purpose of this section and the next one is to carefully define the semantics of quantum recursive programs. It will be done in two steps. In this section, we show how to solve recursive equations in the free Fock spaces without considering symmetry or antisymmetry of the particles that are used to implement the quantum "coins".

12.4.1   A domain of operators on the free Fock space

Similar to the cases of recursive classical programs and classical recursion of quantum programs studied in Section 5.5, we first need to set the stage – a domain in which we can accommodate the solutions of quantum recursive equations. In this subsection, we study such a domain as an abstract mathematical object, leaving its applications to semantics of recursive quantum programs aside. This focus can give us a better understanding of the structure of the domain.

State space of the system: We consider a large system consisting of a principal system and a set C of quantum "coins". For each $c \in C$, let $\mathcal{H}_c$ be the state Hilbert space of "coin" c and $\mathcal{F}(\mathcal{H}_c)$ the free Fock space over $\mathcal{H}_c$. We write

$$\mathcal{G}(\mathcal{H}_C) \stackrel{\triangle}{=} \bigotimes_{c\in C} \mathcal{F}(\mathcal{H}_c)$$

for the tensor product of the free Fock spaces of all "coins". We also assume that $\mathcal{H}$ is the state Hilbert space of the principal system. Then the state space of the quantum system combining the principal system with variable numbers of "coins" is $\mathcal{G}(\mathcal{H}_C) \otimes \mathcal{H}$.

Let ω be the set of nonnegative integers. Then ω^C is the set of C-indexed tuples of nonnegative integers: $\bar{n} = \{n_c\}_{c\in C}$ with $n_c \in \omega$ for all $c \in C$. It is easy to see that

$$\mathcal{G}(\mathcal{H}_C) \otimes \mathcal{H} = \bigoplus_{\bar{n}\in\omega^C} \left[\left(\bigotimes_{c\in C} \mathcal{H}_c^{\otimes n_c}\right) \otimes \mathcal{H}\right]$$

Flat order between operators: Furthermore, let $\mathcal{O}(\mathcal{G}(\mathcal{H}_C) \otimes \mathcal{H})$ be the set of all operators of the form

$$\mathbf{A} = \sum_{\bar{n}\in\omega^C} \mathbf{A}(\bar{n}),$$

where $\mathbf{A}(\overline{n})$ is an operator on $\left(\bigotimes_{c \in C} \mathcal{H}_c^{\otimes n_c}\right) \otimes \mathcal{H}$ for each $\overline{n} \in \omega^C$. Then $\mathcal{O}(\mathcal{G}(\mathcal{H}_C) \otimes \mathcal{H})$ will serve as the space of the solutions of quantum recursive equations.

To present the partial order in $\mathcal{O}(\mathcal{G}(\mathcal{H}_C) \otimes \mathcal{H})$ needed for solving quantum recursive equations, we first define a partial order $\leq$ in ω^C as follows:

- $\overline{n} \leq \overline{m}$ if and only if $n_c \leq m_c$ for all $c \in C$.

A subset $\Omega \subseteq \omega^C$ is said to be *below-closed* if $\overline{n} \in \Omega$ and $\overline{m} \leq \overline{n}$ imply $\overline{m} \in \Omega$.

Definition 12.15. The flat order $\sqsubseteq$ on $\mathcal{O}(\mathcal{G}(\mathcal{H}_C) \otimes \mathcal{H})$ is defined as follows: for any operator $\mathbf{A} = \sum_{\overline{n} \in \omega^C} \mathbf{A}(\overline{n})$ and $\mathbf{B} = \sum_{\overline{n} \in \omega^C} \mathbf{B}(\overline{n})$ on $\mathcal{O}(\mathcal{G}(\mathcal{H}_C) \otimes \mathcal{H})$,

- $\mathbf{A} \sqsubseteq \mathbf{B}$ if and only if there exists a below-closed subset $\Omega \subseteq \omega^C$ such that
  - $\mathbf{A}(\overline{n}) = \mathbf{B}(\overline{n})$ for all $\overline{n} \in \Omega$; and
  - $\mathbf{A}(\overline{n}) = 0$ for all $\overline{n} \in \omega^C \setminus \Omega$.

As said above, the flat order can be simply understood as an abstract mathematical object. But our intention behind it has to be explained with its application to the semantics of quantum recursive programs. A quantum excursive program P is executed by repeated substitutions, in each of which new "coins" should be added in order to avoid variable conflict, as shown in the example at the end of Section 12.2. For each $\overline{n} \in \omega^C$, n_c is used to record the number of copies of "coin" c employed in the computation of program P. So, $\overline{n} \leq \overline{m}$ indicates that the (copies) of "coins" denoted by $\overline{m}$ are more than that denoted by $\overline{n}$. Obviously, the more "coins" are used in the execution of P, the more "content" is computed. Thus, if $\mathbf{A}$ and $\mathbf{B}$ are the partial computational results of P at two different stages of execution, then $\mathbf{A} \sqsubseteq \mathbf{B}$ means that the computed "content" at the stage of $\mathbf{B}$ is more than that at the stage of $\mathbf{A}$. This explanation will become clearer after reading Proposition 12.8.

The following is a key lemma in this chapter that unveils the lattice-theoretic structure of operators on the free Fock space.

Lemma 12.1. $(\mathcal{O}(\mathcal{G}(\mathcal{H}_C) \otimes \mathcal{H}), \sqsubseteq)$ *is a complete partial order (CPO) (see Definition 5.10).*

Proof. First, $\sqsubseteq$ is reflexive because ω^C itself is below-closed. To show that $\sqsubseteq$ is transitive, we assume that $\mathbf{A} \sqsubseteq \mathbf{B}$ and $\mathbf{B} \sqsubseteq \mathbf{C}$. Then there exist below-closed subsets $\Omega, \Gamma \subseteq \omega^C$ such that

1. $\mathbf{A}(\overline{n}) = \mathbf{B}(\overline{n})$ for all $\overline{n} \in \Omega$ and $\mathbf{A}(\overline{n}) = 0$ for all $\overline{n} \in \omega^C \setminus \Omega$;
2. $\mathbf{B}(\overline{n}) = \mathbf{C}(\overline{n})$ for all $\overline{n} \in \Gamma$ and $\mathbf{B}(\overline{n}) = 0$ for all $\overline{n} \in \omega^C \setminus \Gamma$.

Clearly, $\Omega \cap \Gamma$ is below-closed too, and $\mathbf{A}(\overline{n}) = \mathbf{B}(\overline{n}) = \mathbf{C}(\overline{n})$ for all $\overline{n} \in \Omega \cap \Gamma$. On the other hand, if

$$\overline{n} \in \omega^C \setminus (\Omega \cap \Gamma) = (\omega^C \setminus \Omega) \cup [\Omega \cap (\omega^C \setminus \Gamma)],$$

then:

- either $\overline{n} \in \omega^C \setminus \Omega$ and it follows from the above clause 1 that $\mathbf{A}(\overline{n}) = 0$;
- or $\overline{n} \in \Omega \cap (\omega^C \setminus \Gamma)$ and by combining the above clauses 1 and 2 we obtain $\mathbf{A}(\overline{n}) = \mathbf{B}(\overline{n}) = 0$.

Therefore, $\mathbf{A} \sqsubseteq \mathbf{C}$. Similarly, we can prove that $\sqsubseteq$ is antisymmetric. So, $(\mathcal{O}(\mathcal{G}(\mathcal{H}_C) \otimes \mathcal{H}), \sqsubseteq)$ is a partial order.

Obviously, the operator $\mathbf{A} = \sum_{\overline{n} \in \omega^C} \mathbf{A}(\overline{n})$ with $\mathbf{A}(\overline{n}) = 0$ (the zero operator on $\left(\bigotimes_{c \in C} \mathcal{H}_c^{\otimes n_c}\right) \otimes \mathcal{H}$) for all $\overline{n} \in \omega^C$ is the least element of $(\mathcal{O}(\mathcal{G}(\mathcal{H}_C) \otimes \mathcal{H}), \sqsubseteq)$. Now it suffices to show that any chain $\{\mathbf{A}_i\}$ in $(\mathcal{O}(\mathcal{G}(\mathcal{H}_C) \otimes \mathcal{H}), \sqsubseteq)$ has the least upper bound. For each i, we put

$$\Delta_i = \{\overline{n} \in \omega^C : \mathbf{A}_i(\overline{n}) \neq 0\},$$
$$\Delta_i \downarrow = \{\overline{m} \in \omega^C : \overline{m} \leq \overline{n} \text{ for some } \overline{n} \in \Delta_i\}.$$

Here $\Delta_i \downarrow$ is the below-completion of Δ_i. Furthermore, we define operator $\mathbf{A} = \sum_{\overline{n} \in \omega^C} \mathbf{A}(\overline{n})$ as follows:

$$\mathbf{A}(\overline{n}) = \begin{cases} \mathbf{A}_i(\overline{n}) & \text{if } \overline{n} \in \Delta_i \downarrow \text{ for some } i, \\ 0 & \text{if } \overline{n} \notin \bigcup_i (\Delta_i \downarrow). \end{cases}$$

Claim 1: $\mathbf{A}$ is well-defined; that is, if $\overline{n} \in \Delta_i \downarrow$ and $\overline{n} \in \Delta_j \downarrow$, then $\mathbf{A}_i(\overline{n}) = \mathbf{A}_j(\overline{n})$. In fact, since $\{\mathbf{A}_i\}$ is a chain, we have $\mathbf{A}_i \sqsubseteq \mathbf{A}_j$ or $\mathbf{A}_j \sqsubseteq \mathbf{A}_i$. We only consider the case of $\mathbf{A}_i \sqsubseteq \mathbf{A}_j$ (the case of $\mathbf{A}_j \sqsubseteq \mathbf{A}_i$ can be proved by duality). Then there exists a below-closed subset $\Omega \subseteq \omega^C$ such that $\mathbf{A}_i(\overline{n}) = \mathbf{A}_j(\overline{n})$ for all $\overline{n} \in \Omega$ and $\mathbf{A}_i(\overline{n}) = 0$ for all $\overline{n} \in \omega^C \setminus \Omega$. It follows from $\overline{n} \in \Delta_i \downarrow$ that $\overline{n} \leq \overline{m}$ for some $\overline{m}$ with $\mathbf{A}_i(\overline{m}) \neq 0$. Since $\overline{m} \notin \omega^C \setminus \Omega$, i.e. $\overline{m} \in \Omega$, we have $\overline{n} \in \Omega$ because Ω is below-closed. So, $\mathbf{A}_i(\overline{n}) = \mathbf{A}_j(\overline{n})$.

  Claim 2: $\mathbf{A} = \bigsqcup_i \mathbf{A}_i$. In fact, for each i, $\Delta_i \downarrow$ is below-closed, and $\mathbf{A}_i(\overline{n}) = \mathbf{A}(\overline{n})$ for all $\overline{n} \in \Delta_i \downarrow$ and $\mathbf{A}_i(\overline{n}) = 0$ for all $\overline{n} \in \omega^C \setminus (\Delta_i \downarrow)$. So, $\mathbf{A}_i \sqsubseteq \mathbf{A}$, and $\mathbf{A}$ is an upper bound of $\{\mathbf{A}_i\}$. Now assume that $\mathbf{B}$ is an upper bound of $\{\mathbf{A}_i\}$: for all i, $\mathbf{A}_i \sqsubseteq \mathbf{B}$; that is, there exists below-closed $\Omega_i \subseteq \omega^C$ such that $\mathbf{A}_i(\overline{n}) = \mathbf{B}(\overline{n})$ for all $\overline{n} \in \Omega_i$ and $\mathbf{A}_i(\overline{n}) = 0$ for all $\overline{n} \in \omega^C \setminus \Omega_i$. By the definition of Δ_i and below-closeness of Ω_i, we know that $\Delta_i \downarrow \subseteq \Omega_i$. We take

$$\Omega = \bigcup_i (\Delta_i \downarrow).$$

Clearly, Ω is below-closed, and if $\overline{n} \in \omega^C \setminus \Omega$, then $\mathbf{A}(\overline{n}) = 0$. On the other hand, if $\overline{n} \in \Omega$, then for some i, we have $\overline{n} \in \Delta_i \downarrow$, and it follows that $\overline{n} \in \Omega_i$ and $\mathbf{A}(\overline{n}) = \mathbf{A}_i(\overline{n}) = \mathbf{B}(\overline{n})$. Therefore, $\mathbf{A} \sqsubseteq \mathbf{B}$.   □

  Algebraic operations of operators: The above lemma presented the lattice-theoretical structure of $\mathcal{O}(\mathcal{G}(\mathcal{H}_C) \otimes \mathcal{H})$. Now we further define two algebraic operations in $\mathcal{O}(\mathcal{G}(\mathcal{H}_C) \otimes \mathcal{H})$, namely product and guarded composition. These two operations will be used to define the semantics of sequential compositions and quantum case statements in quantum program schemes.

Definition 12.16. For any operators $\mathbf{A} = \sum_{\overline{n} \in \omega^C} \mathbf{A}(\overline{n})$ and $\mathbf{B} = \sum_{\overline{n} \in \omega^C} \mathbf{B}(\overline{n})$ on $\mathcal{O}(\mathcal{G}(\mathcal{H}_C) \otimes \mathcal{H})$, their product is defined as

$$\mathbf{A} \cdot \mathbf{B} = \sum_{\overline{n} \in \omega^C} (\mathbf{A}(\overline{n}) \cdot \mathbf{B}(\overline{n})), \tag{12.20}$$

which is also on $\mathcal{O}(\mathcal{G}(\mathcal{H}_C) \otimes \mathcal{H})$.

  The above definition is a component-wise extension of ordinary operator product: for each $\overline{n} \in \omega^C$, $\mathbf{A}(\overline{n}) \cdot \mathbf{B}(\overline{n})$ is the product of operators $\mathbf{A}(\overline{n})$ and $\mathbf{B}(\overline{n})$ on $\left(\bigotimes_{c \in C} \mathcal{H}_c^{n_c} \right) \otimes \mathcal{H}$.

  The guarded composition of operators on the free Fock space can be defined by simply extending Eq. (12.1) in the same way.

Definition 12.17. Let $c \in C$ and $\{|i\rangle\}$ be an orthonormal basis of $\mathcal{H}_c$, and let $\mathbf{A}_i = \sum_{\overline{n} \in \omega^C} \mathbf{A}_i(\overline{n})$ be an operator on $\mathcal{O}(\mathcal{G}(\mathcal{H}_C) \otimes \mathcal{H})$ for each i. Then the guarded composition of $\mathbf{A}_i$'s along with the basis $\{|i\rangle\}$ is

$$\square(c, |i\rangle \to \mathbf{A}_i) = \sum_{\overline{n} \in \omega^C} \left(\sum_i (|i\rangle_c \langle i| \otimes \mathbf{A}_i(\overline{n})) \right). \tag{12.21}$$

  Note that for each $\overline{n} \in \omega^C$, $\sum_i (|i\rangle_c \langle i| \otimes \mathbf{A}_i(n))$ is an operator on

$$\mathcal{H}_c^{\otimes(n_c+1)} \otimes \left(\bigotimes_{d \in C \setminus \{c\}} \mathcal{H}_d^{n_d} \right) \otimes \mathcal{H},$$

and thus $\square(c, |i\rangle \to \mathbf{A}_i) \in \mathcal{O}(\mathcal{G}(\mathcal{H}_C) \otimes \mathcal{H})$.

  The following lemma shows that both product and guarded composition of operators on the free Fock space are continuous with respect to the flat order (see Definition 5.11).

Lemma 12.2. *Let $\{\mathbf{A}_j\}$ and $\{\mathbf{B}_j\}$ be chains in $(\mathcal{O}(\mathcal{G}(\mathcal{H}_C) \otimes \mathcal{H}), \sqsubseteq)$, and so do $\{\mathbf{A}_{ij}\}$ for each i. Then*

1. $\bigsqcup_j (\mathbf{A}_j \cdot \mathbf{B}_j) = \left(\bigsqcup_j \mathbf{A}_j \right) \cdot \left(\bigsqcup_j \mathbf{B}_j \right).$
2. $\bigsqcup_j \square(c, |i\rangle \to \mathbf{A}_{ij}) = \square\left(c, |i\rangle \to \left(\bigsqcup_j \mathbf{A}_{ij} \right) \right).$

Proof. We only prove part 2. The proof of part 1 is similar. For each i, we assume that

$$\bigsqcup_j \mathbf{A}_{ij} = \mathbf{A}_i = \sum_{\overline{n} \in \omega^C} \mathbf{A}_i(\overline{n}).$$

By the construction of least upper bound in $(\mathcal{O}(\mathcal{G}(\mathcal{H}_C) \otimes \mathcal{H}), \sqsubseteq)$ given in the proof of Lemma 12.1, we can write

$$\mathbf{A}_{ij} = \sum_{\overline{n} \in \Omega_{ij}} \mathbf{A}_i(\overline{n})$$

for some $\Omega_{ij} \subseteq \omega^C$ with $\bigcup_j \Omega_{ij} = \omega^C$ for every i. By appending zero operators to the end of shorter summations, we may further ensure that index sets Ω_{ij}'s for all i are the same, say Ω_j. Then by the defining Eq. (12.21) we obtain:

$$\bigsqcup_j \square\left(c, |i\rangle \to \mathbf{A}_{ij}\right) = \bigsqcup_j \sum_{\overline{n} \in \Omega_j} \left(\sum_i (|i\rangle_c \langle i| \otimes \mathbf{A}_i(\overline{n}))\right)$$

$$= \sum_{\overline{n} \in \omega^C} \left(\sum_i (|i\rangle_c \langle i| \otimes \mathbf{A}_i(\overline{n}))\right) = \square(c, |i\rangle \to \mathbf{A}_i). \qquad \square$$

12.4.2 Semantic functionals of program schemes

The semantics of quantum programs (i.e. program schemes without procedure identifiers) was already defined in Definition 12.2. With the preparation in the last subsection, now we are able to define the semantics of general quantum program schemes.

Let $P = P[X_1, ..., X_m]$ be a program scheme with procedure identifiers $X_1, ..., X_m$. We write C for the set of "coins" occurring in P. For each $c \in C$, let $\mathcal{H}_c$ be the state Hilbert space of quantum "coin" c. By the principal system of P we mean the composition of the systems denoted by principal variables appearing in P. Let $\mathcal{H}$ be the state Hilbert space of the principal system. Then the semantics of P can be defined as a functional in the domain $\mathcal{O}(\mathcal{G}(\mathcal{H}_C) \otimes \mathcal{H})$ described in the last subsection.

Definition 12.18. The semantic functional of program scheme $P = P[X_1, ..., X_m]$ is a mapping

$$\llbracket P \rrbracket : \mathcal{O}\left(\mathcal{G}(\mathcal{H}_C) \otimes \mathcal{H}\right)^m \to \mathcal{O}\left(\mathcal{G}(\mathcal{H}_C) \otimes \mathcal{H}\right).$$

For any operators $\mathbf{A}_1, ..., \mathbf{A}_m \in \mathcal{O}(\mathcal{G}(\mathcal{H}_C) \otimes \mathcal{H})$, $\llbracket P \rrbracket(\mathbf{A}_1, ..., \mathbf{A}_m)$ is inductively defined as follows:

1. If $P = \textbf{abort}$, then $\llbracket P \rrbracket(\mathbf{A}_1, ..., \mathbf{A}_m)$ is the zero operator

$$\mathbf{A} = \sum_{\overline{n} \in \omega^C} \mathbf{A}(\overline{n})$$

with $\mathbf{A}(\overline{n}) = 0$ (the zero operator on $\left(\bigotimes_{c \in C} \mathcal{H}_c^{\otimes n_c}\right) \otimes \mathcal{H}$) for all $\overline{n} \in \omega^C$;

2. If $P = \textbf{skip}$, then $\llbracket P \rrbracket(\mathbf{A}_1, ..., \mathbf{A}_m)$ is the identity operator

$$\mathbf{A} = \sum_{\overline{n} \in \omega^C} \mathbf{A}(\overline{n})$$

with $\mathbf{A}(\overline{n}) = I$ (the identity operator on $\left(\bigotimes_{c \in C} \mathcal{H}_c^{\otimes n_c}\right) \otimes \mathcal{H}$) for all $\overline{n} \in \omega^C$ with $n_c \neq 0$ for every $c \in C$;

3. If $P = U[\overline{c}, \overline{q}]$, then $\llbracket P \rrbracket(\mathbf{A}_1, ..., \mathbf{A}_m)$ is the cylindrical extension of U:

$$\mathbf{A} = \sum_{\overline{n} \in \omega^C} \mathbf{A}(\overline{n})$$

with

$$\mathbf{A}(\overline{n}) = I_1 \otimes I_2(\overline{n}) \otimes U \otimes I_3$$

where:
   a. I_1 is the identity operator on the state Hilbert space of those "coins" that are not in $\overline{c}$;
   b. $I_2(\overline{n})$ is the identity operator on $\bigotimes_{c \in \overline{c}} \mathcal{H}_c^{\otimes(n_c - 1)}$; and

    c. I_3 is the identity operator on the state Hilbert space of those principal variables that are not in $\overline{q}$ for all $n \geq 1$;

4. If $P = X_j$ $(1 \leq j \leq m)$, then $[\![P]\!](\mathbf{A}_1, ..., \mathbf{A}_m) = \mathbf{A}_j$;

5. If $P = P_1; P_2$, then

$$[\![P]\!](\mathbf{A}_1, ..., \mathbf{A}_m) = [\![P_2]\!](\mathbf{A}_1, ..., \mathbf{A}_m) \cdot [\![P_1]\!](\mathbf{A}_1, ..., \mathbf{A}_m)$$

(see the defining Eq. (12.20) of product of operators on the free Fock space);

6. If $P = \mathbf{qif}\ [c](\square i \cdot |i\rangle) \to P_i)\ \mathbf{fiq}$, then

$$[\![P]\!](\mathbf{A}_1, ..., \mathbf{A}_m) = \square\left(c, |i\rangle \to [\![P_i]\!](\mathbf{A}_1, ..., \mathbf{A}_m)\right)$$

(see the defining Eq. (12.21) of guarded composition of operators on the free Fock space).

It is easy to see that whenever $m = 0$; that is, P contains no procedure identifiers, then the above definition degenerates to Definition 12.2.

Continuity of semantic functionals: As we learned from classical programming theory and in Section 5.5, continuity of the functions involved in a recursive equation is usually crucial for the existence of solutions of the equation. So, we now examine continuity of the semantic functionals defined above. To this end, the cartesian power $\mathcal{O}(\mathcal{G}(\mathcal{H}_C) \otimes \mathcal{H})^m$ is naturally equipped with the order $\sqsubseteq$ defined component-wise from the flat order in the CPO $(\mathcal{O}(\mathcal{G}(\mathcal{H}_C) \otimes \mathcal{H}), \sqsubseteq)$: for any $\mathbf{A}_1, ..., \mathbf{A}_m, \mathbf{B}_1, ..., \mathbf{B}_m \in \mathcal{O}(\mathcal{G}(\mathcal{H}_C) \otimes \mathcal{H})$,

- $(\mathbf{A}_1, ..., \mathbf{A}_m) \sqsubseteq (\mathbf{B}_1, ..., \mathbf{B}_m)$ if and only if for every $1 \leq i \leq m$, $\mathbf{A}_i \sqsubseteq \mathbf{B}_i$.

The second occurrence of symbol "$\sqsubseteq$" in the above statement stands for the flat order in $\mathcal{O}(\mathcal{G}(\mathcal{H}_C) \otimes \mathcal{H})$. Then $(\mathcal{O}(\mathcal{G}(\mathcal{H}_C) \otimes \mathcal{H})^m, \sqsubseteq)$ is a CPO too. Furthermore, we have:

Theorem 12.1 (Continuity of semantic functionals). *For any program scheme $P = P[X_1, ..., X_m]$, the semantic functional*

$$[\![P]\!] : \left(\mathcal{O}(\mathcal{G}(\mathcal{H}_C) \otimes \mathcal{H})^m, \sqsubseteq\right) \to (\mathcal{O}(\mathcal{G}(\mathcal{H}_C) \otimes \mathcal{H}), \sqsubseteq)$$

is continuous.

Proof. It can be easily proved by induction on the structure of P using Lemma 12.2. $\qquad\square$

Creation functionals: There is an essential difference between quantum recursive programs defined in this chapter and recursive quantum programs (without quantum control flows) studied in Section 5.5. The semantics of recursive quantum programs can be defined in a way that is very similar to the way in which we deal with recursion in classical programming theory. More explicitly, it can be properly characterised as a fixed point of semantic functionals. However, semantic functionals are not complete for describing the behaviour of quantum recursive programs considered here. They must be combined with the notion of creation functional defined in the following:

Definition 12.19. For each "coin" $c \in C$, the creation functional

$$\mathbb{K}_c : \mathcal{O}(\mathcal{G}(\mathcal{H}_C) \otimes \mathcal{H}) \to \mathcal{O}(\mathcal{G}(\mathcal{H}_C) \otimes \mathcal{H})$$

is defined as follows: for any $\mathbf{A} = \sum_{\overline{n} \in \omega^C} \mathbf{A}(\overline{n}) \in \mathcal{O}(\mathcal{G}(\mathcal{H}_C) \otimes \mathcal{H})$,

$$\mathbb{K}_c(\mathbf{A}) = \sum_{\overline{n} \in \omega^C} (I_c \otimes \mathbf{A}(\overline{n}))$$

where I_c is the identity operator on $\mathcal{H}_c$.

We observe that $\mathbf{A}(\overline{n})$ is an operator on $\left(\bigotimes_{d \in C} \mathcal{H}_d^{\otimes n_d}\right) \otimes \mathcal{H}$, whereas $I_c \otimes \mathbf{A}(\overline{n})$ is an operator on

$$\mathcal{H}_c^{\otimes(n_c+1)} \otimes \left(\bigotimes_{d \in C \setminus \{c\}} \mathcal{H}_d^{\otimes n_d}\right) \otimes \mathcal{H}.$$

In a sense, the creation functional can be seen as a counterpart of creation operator (Definition 12.13) in the domain $\mathcal{O}(\mathcal{G}(\mathcal{H}_C) \otimes \mathcal{H})$. Intuitively, the creation functional $\mathbb{K}_c$ moves all copies of $\mathcal{H}_c$ one position to the right so that ith copy becomes $(i+1)$th copy for all $i = 0, 1, 2, ...$ Thus, a new position is created at the left end for a new copy of $\mathcal{H}_c$. For other "coins" d, however, $\mathbb{K}_c$ does not move any copy of $\mathcal{H}_d$.

It is clear that for any two "coins" c, d, the corresponding creation functionals $\mathbb{K}_c$ and $\mathbb{K}_d$ commute; that is,

$$\mathbb{K}_a \circ \mathbb{K}_d = \mathbb{K}_d \circ \mathbb{K}_c.$$

Note that the set C of "coins" in a program scheme P is finite. Suppose that $C = \{c_1, c_2, ..., c_k\}$. Then we can define the creation functional

$$\mathbb{K}_C = \mathbb{K}_{c_1} \circ \mathbb{K}_{c_2} \circ ... \circ \mathbb{K}_{c_k}.$$

For the special case where the set C of "coins" is empty, $\mathbb{K}_C$ is the identity functional; that is, $\mathbb{K}_C(\mathbf{A}) = \mathbf{A}$ for all $\mathbf{A}$.

Continuity of the creation functionals with respect to the flat order between operators on the free Fock space is shown in the following:

Lemma 12.3 (Continuity of creation functionals). *For each $c \in C$, the creation functionals*

$$\mathbb{K}_c \text{ and } \mathbb{K}_C : (\mathcal{O}(\mathcal{G}(\mathcal{H}_C) \otimes \mathcal{H}), \sqsubseteq) \to (\mathcal{O}(\mathcal{G}(\mathcal{H}_C) \otimes \mathcal{H}), \sqsubseteq)$$

are continuous.

Proof. Straightforward by definition. $\qquad\qquad\qquad\qquad\qquad\qquad\qquad\qquad\qquad\qquad\qquad\qquad$ □

Finally, combining continuity of semantic functionals and the creation functionals (Theorem 12.1 and Lemma 12.3), we obtain:

Corollary 12.1. *Let $P = P[X_1, ..., X_m]$ be a program scheme and C the set of "coins" occurring in P. We define the functional*

$$\mathbb{K}_C^m \circ [\![P]\!] : (\mathcal{O}(\mathcal{G}(\mathcal{H}_C) \otimes \mathcal{H})^m, \sqsubseteq) \to (\mathcal{O}(\mathcal{G}(\mathcal{H}_C) \otimes \mathcal{H}), \sqsubseteq)$$

by

$$(\mathbb{K}_C^m \circ [\![P]\!]) (\mathbf{A}_1, ..., \mathbf{A}_m) = [\![P]\!] (\mathbb{K}_C(\mathbf{A}_1), ..., \mathbb{K}_C(\mathbf{A}_m))$$

for any $\mathbf{A}_1, ..., \mathbf{A}_m \in \mathcal{O}(\mathcal{G}(\mathcal{H}_C) \otimes \mathcal{H})$. Then $\mathbb{K}_C^m \circ [\![P]\!]$ is continuous.

12.4.3 Fixed point semantics

Now we have all the ingredients needed to define the denotational semantics of quantum recursive programs using the standard fixed point technique. Let us consider a quantum recursive program P declared by the system of equations:

$$D : \begin{cases} X_1 \Leftarrow P_1, \\ \quad ...... \\ X_m \Leftarrow P_m, \end{cases} \tag{12.22}$$

where $P_i = P_i[X_1, ..., X_m]$ is a quantum program scheme containing at most procedure identifiers $X_1, ..., X_m$ for every $1 \le i \le m$. Using the functional $[\![\cdot]\!]$ and $\mathbb{K}_C$ defined in the last subsection, the system D of recursive equations naturally induces a semantic functional:

$$[\![D]\!] : \mathcal{O}(\mathcal{G}(\mathcal{H}_C) \otimes \mathcal{H})^m \to \mathcal{O}(\mathcal{G}(\mathcal{H}_C) \otimes \mathcal{H})^m$$

defined as follows:

$$[\![D]\!] (\mathbf{A}_1, ..., \mathbf{A}_m) = \left((\mathbb{K}_C^m \circ [\![P_1]\!]) (\mathbf{A}_1, ..., \mathbf{A}_m), ..., (\mathbb{K}_C^m \circ [\![P_m]\!]) (\mathbf{A}_1, ..., \mathbf{A}_m) \right) \tag{12.23}$$

for all $\mathbf{A}_1, ..., \mathbf{A}_m \in \mathcal{O}(\mathcal{G}(\mathcal{H}_C) \otimes \mathcal{H})$, where C is the set of "coins" appearing in D; that is, in one of $P_1, ..., P_m$. It follows from Corollary 12.1 that

$$[\![D]\!] : (\mathcal{O}(\mathcal{G}(\mathcal{H}_C) \otimes \mathcal{H})^m, \sqsubseteq) \to (\mathcal{O}(\mathcal{G}(\mathcal{H}_C) \otimes \mathcal{H})^m, \sqsubseteq)$$

is continuous. Then the Knaster–Tarski Fixed Point Theorem (see Theorem 5.1) asserts that $[\![D]\!]$ has the least fixed point $\mu[\![D]\!]$, which is exactly what we need to define the semantics of P.

Definition 12.20. The fixed point (denotational) semantics of the quantum recursive program P declared by D is

$$\llbracket P \rrbracket_{fix} = \llbracket P \rrbracket (\mu \llbracket D \rrbracket);$$

that is, if $\mu \llbracket D \rrbracket = (\mathbf{A}_1^*, ..., \mathbf{A}_m^*) \in \mathcal{O}\left(\mathcal{G}(\mathcal{H}_C) \otimes \mathcal{H}\right)^m$, then

$$\llbracket P \rrbracket_{fix} = \llbracket P \rrbracket \left(\mathbf{A}_1^*, ..., \mathbf{A}_m^*\right)$$

(see Definition 12.18).

12.4.4 Syntactic approximation

The fixed point semantics of quantum recursive programs was described in the last subsection. We now turn to consider the syntactic approximation technique for defining the semantics of quantum recursive programs. As one may expect, the semantics defined in this subsection will be proved to be equivalent to the fixed point semantics.

Substitution of quantum programs: As discussed at the end of Section 12.2, a problem that was not present in the classical programming theory is that we have to carefully avoid the conflict of quantum "coin" variables when defining the notion of substitution. To overcome it, we assume that each "coin" variable $c \in C$ has infinitely many copies $c_0, c_1, c_2, ...$ with $c_0 = c$. The variables $c_1, c_2, ...$ are used to represent a sequence of particles that are all identical to the particle $c_0 = c$. Then the notion of quantum program scheme defined in Section 12.1 will be used in a slightly broader way: a quantum program scheme may contain not only a "coin" c but also some of its copies $c_1, c_2, ...$ Such a quantum program scheme is called a generalised quantum program scheme. If such a generalised quantum program scheme contains no procedure identifiers, then it is called a generalised quantum program. With these assumptions, we can introduce the notion of substitution.

Definition 12.21. Let $P = P[X_1, ..., X_m]$ be a generalised quantum program scheme that contains at most procedure identifiers $X_1, ..., X_m$, and let $Q_1, ..., Q_m$ be generalised quantum programs (without any procedure identifier). Then the simultaneous substitution

$$P[Q_1/X_1, ..., Q_m/X_m]$$

of $X_1, ..., X_m$ by $Q_1, ..., Q_m$ in P is inductively defined as follows:

1. If $P = \mathbf{abort}, \mathbf{skip}$ or an unitary transformation, then

$$P[Q_1/X_1, ..., Q_m/X_m] = P;$$

2. If $P = X_i$ $(1 \leq i \leq m)$, then

$$P[Q_1/X_1, ..., Q_m/X_m] = Q_i;$$

3. If $P = P_1; P_2$, then

$$P[Q_1/X_1, ..., Q_m/X_m] = P_1[Q_1/X_1, ..., Q_m/X_m]; P_2[Q_1/X_1, ..., Q_m/X_m];$$

4. If $P = \mathbf{qif} [c](\square i \cdot |i\rangle \rightarrow P_i)$ $\mathbf{fiq}$, then

$$P[Q_1/X_1, ..., Q_m/X_m] = \mathbf{qif} [c]\left(\square i \cdot |i\rangle \rightarrow P_i'\right) \mathbf{fiq}$$

where for every i, P_i' is obtained through replacing the jth copy c_j of c in $P_i[Q_1/X_1, ..., Q_m/X_m]$ by the $(j + 1)$th copy c_{j+1} of c for all j.

Note that in clause 4 of the above definition, since P is a generalised quantum program scheme, the "coin" c may not be an original "coin" but some copy d_k of an original "coin" $d \in C$. In this case, the jth copy of c is actually the $(k + j)$th copy of d: $c_j = (d_k)_j = d_{k+j}$ for $j \geq -d$.

Semantics of substituted programs: The semantics of a generalised quantum program P can be given using Definition 12.2 in the way where a "coin" c and its copies $c_1, c_2, ...$ are treated as distinct variables to each other. For each "coin" c, let n_c be the greatest index n such that the copy c_n appears in P. Then the semantics $[\![P]\!]$ of P is an operator on $\left(\bigotimes_{c \in C} \mathcal{H}_c^{\otimes n_c}\right) \otimes \mathcal{H}$. Furthermore, it can be identified with its cylindrical extension in $\mathcal{O}\left(\mathcal{G}(\mathcal{H}_C) \otimes \mathcal{H}\right)$:

$$\sum_{\overline{m} \in \omega^C} \left(I(\overline{m}) \otimes [\![P]\!]\right),$$

where for each $\overline{m} \in \omega^C$, $I(\overline{m})$ is the identity operator on $\bigotimes_{c \in C} \mathcal{H}_c^{\otimes m_c}$. Based on this observation, the semantics of substitution defined above is characterised by the following:

Lemma 12.4. *For any (generalised) quantum program scheme $P = P[X_1, ..., X_m]$ and (generalised) quantum programs $Q_1, ..., Q_m$, we have:*

$$[\![P[Q_1/X_1, ..., Q_m/X_m]]\!] = \left(\mathbb{K}_C^m \circ [\![P]\!]\right)\left([\![Q_1]\!], ..., [\![Q_m]\!]\right)$$
$$= [\![P]\!]\left(\mathbb{K}_C([\![Q_1]\!]), ..., \mathbb{K}_C([\![Q_m]\!])\right),$$

where $\mathbb{K}_C$ is the creation functional with C being the set of "coins" in P.

Proof. We prove the lemma by induction on the structure of P.

Case 1. $P = $ **abort**, **skip** or an unitary transformation. Obvious.

Case 2. $P = X_j \ (1 \leq j \leq m)$. Then

$$P[Q_1/X_1, ..., Q_m/X_m] = Q_m.$$

On the other hand, since the set of "coins" in P is empty,

$$\mathbb{K}_C\left([\![Q_i]\!]\right) = [\![Q_i]\!]$$

for all $1 \leq i \leq m$. Thus, by clause 4 of Definition 12.18 we obtain:

$$[\![P[Q_1/X_1, ..., Q_m/X_m]]\!] = [\![Q_m]\!]$$
$$= [\![P]\!]\left([\![Q_1]\!], ..., [\![Q_m]\!]\right)$$
$$= [\![P]\!]\left(\mathbb{K}_C([\![Q_1]\!]), ..., \mathbb{K}_C([\![Q_m]\!])\right).$$

Case 3. $P = P_1; P_2$. Then by clause 3 of Definition 12.2, clause 5 of Definition 12.18 and the induction hypothesis, we have:

$$[\![P[Q_1/X_1, ..., Q_m/X_m]]\!] = [\![P_1[Q_1/X_1, ..., Q_m/X_m]; P_2[Q_1/X_1, ..., Q_m/X_m]]\!]$$
$$= [\![P_2[Q_1/X_1, ..., Q_m/X_m]]\!] \cdot [\![P_1[Q_1/X_1, ..., Q_m/X_m]]\!]$$
$$= [\![P_2]\!]\left(\mathbb{K}_C([\![Q_1]\!]), ..., \mathbb{K}_C([\![Q_m]\!])\right) \cdot [\![P_1]\!]\left(\mathbb{K}_C([\![Q_1]\!]), ..., \mathbb{K}_C([\![Q_m]\!])\right)$$
$$= [\![P_1; P_2]\!]\left(\mathbb{K}_C([\![Q_1]\!]), ..., \mathbb{K}_C([\![Q_m]\!])\right)$$
$$= [\![P]\!]\left(\mathbb{K}_C([\![Q_1]\!]), ..., \mathbb{K}_C([\![Q_m]\!])\right).$$

Case 4. $P = $ **qif** $[c](\square i \cdot |i\rangle \to P_i)$ **fiq**. Then

$$P[Q_1/X_1, ..., Q_m/X_m] = \textbf{qif}\,[c]\left(\square i \cdot |i\rangle \to P_i'\right)\,\textbf{fiq},$$

where P_i' is obtained according to clause 4 of Definition 12.21. For each i, by the induction hypothesis we obtain:

$$[\![P_i[Q_1/X_1, ..., Q_m/X_m]]\!] = [\![P_i]\!]\left(\mathbb{K}_{C \setminus \{c\}}([\![Q_1]\!]), ..., \mathbb{K}_{C \setminus \{c\}}([\![Q_m]\!])\right)$$

because the "coin" c does not appear in P_i'. Furthermore, it follows that

$$[\![P_i']\!] = \mathbb{K}_c([\![P_i[Q_1/X_1, ..., Q_m/X_m]]\!])$$
$$= \mathbb{K}_c([\![P_i]\!]\left(\mathbb{K}_{C \setminus \{c\}}([\![Q_1]\!]), ..., \mathbb{K}_{C \setminus \{c\}}([\![Q_m]\!])\right))$$
$$= [\![P_i]\!]\left((\mathbb{K}_c \circ \mathbb{K}_{C \setminus \{c\}})([\![Q_1]\!]), ..., (\mathbb{K}_c \circ \mathbb{K}_{C \setminus \{c\}})([\![Q_m]\!])\right)$$

$$= [\![P_i]\!]\left(\mathbb{K}_C([\![Q_1]\!]), ..., \mathbb{K}_C([\![Q_m]\!])\right).$$

Therefore, by clause 4 of Definition 12.2, clause 6 of Definition 12.18 and Eq. (12.21), we have:

$$\begin{aligned}
[\![P[Q_1/X_1, ..., Q_m/X_m]]\!] &= \sum_i \left(|i\rangle\langle i| \otimes [\![P_i']\!]\right) \\
&= \square\left(c, |i\rangle \to [\![P_i]\!]\left(\mathbb{K}_C([\![Q_1]\!]), ..., \mathbb{K}_C([\![Q_m]\!])\right)\right) \\
&= [\![P]\!]\left(\mathbb{K}_C([\![Q_1]\!]), ..., \mathbb{K}_C([\![Q_m]\!])\right).
\end{aligned}$$ $\qquad\square$

Essentially, the above lemma shows that the semantic functional of a generalised quantum program scheme is compositional modulo the creation functional.

Syntactic approximation: Now the notion of syntactic approximation can be properly defined for quantum recursive programs based on Definition 12.21.

Definition 12.22. 1. Let $X_1, ..., X_m$ be procedure identifiers declared by the system D of recursive Eqs (12.22). Then for each $1 \leq k \leq m$, the nth syntactic approximation $X_k^{(n)}$ of X_k is inductively defined as follows:

$$\begin{cases}
X_k^{(0)} = \textbf{abort}, \\
X_k^{(n+1)} = P_k\left[X_1^{(n)}/X_1, ..., X_m^{(n)}/X_m\right] \text{ for } n \geq 0.
\end{cases}$$

2. Let $P = P[X_1, ..., X_m]$ be a quantum recursive program declared by the system D of Eqs (12.22). Then for each $n \geq 0$, its nth syntactic approximation $P^{(n)}$ is inductively defined as follows:

$$\begin{cases}
P^{(0)} = \textbf{abort}, \\
P^{(n+1)} = P\left[X_1^{(n)}/X_1, ..., X_m^{(n)}/X_m\right] \text{ for } n \geq 0.
\end{cases}$$

Syntactic approximation actually gives an operational semantics of quantum recursive programs. As in the theory of classical programming, substitution represents an application of the socalled *copy rule*:

- At runtime, a procedure call is treated like the procedure body inserted at the place of call.

Of course, simplifications may happen within $X_k^{(n)}$ by operations of linear operators; for example,

$$CNOT[q_1, q_2]; X[q_2]; CNOT[q_1, q_2]$$

can be replaced by $X[q_2]$, where q_1, q_2 are principal system variables, *CNOT* is the controlled-NOT gate and X is the NOT gate. To simplify the presentation, we choose not to explicitly describe these simplifications.

The major difference between the classical case and the quantum case is that in the latter we need to continuously introduce new "coin" variables to avoid variable conflict when we unfold a quantum recursive program using its syntactic approximations: for each $n \geq 0$, a new copy of each "coin" in P_k is created in the substitution

$$X_k^{(n+1)} = P_k\left[X_1^{(n)}/X_1, ..., X_m^{(n)}/X_m\right]$$

(see clause 4 of Definition 12.21). Thus, a quantum recursive program should be understood as a quantum system with variable particle number and described in the second quantisation formalism.

Recursions as limits: Note that for all $1 \leq k \leq m$ and $n \geq 0$, the syntactic approximation $X_k^{(n)}$ is a generalised quantum program containing no procedure identifiers. Thus, its semantics $\left[\!\!\left[X_k^{(n)}\right]\!\!\right]$ can be given by a slightly extended version of Definition 12.2:

- a "coin" c and its copies $c_1, c_2, ...$ are allowed to appear in the same (generalised) program and they are considered as distinct variables.

As before, the principal system is the composite system of the subsystems denoted by principal variables appearing in $P_1, ..., P_m$ and its state Hilbert space is denoted by $\mathcal{H}$. Assume that C is the set of "coin" variables appearing in $P_1, ..., P_m$.

For each $c \in C$, we write $\mathcal{H}_c$ for the state Hilbert space of quantum "coin" c. Then it is easy to see that $\left[\!\left[X_k^{(n)}\right]\!\right]$ is an operator on

$$\bigoplus_{j=0}^{n}\left(\mathcal{H}_C^{\otimes n_j} \otimes \mathcal{H}\right)$$

where $\mathcal{H}_C = \bigotimes_{c \in C} \mathcal{H}_c$. So, we can imagine that $\left[\!\left[X_k^{(n)}\right]\!\right] \in \mathcal{O}\left(\mathcal{G}(\mathcal{H}_C) \otimes \mathcal{H}\right)$. Furthermore, we have:

Lemma 12.5. *For each $1 \le k \le m$, $\left\{\left[\!\left[X_k^{(n)}\right]\!\right]\right\}_{n=0}^{\infty}$ is an increasing chain with respect to the flat order, and thus*

$$\left[\!\left[X_k^{(\infty)}\right]\!\right] = \lim_{n \to \infty}\left[\!\left[X_k^{(n)}\right]\!\right] \triangleq \bigsqcup_{n=0}^{\infty}\left[\!\left[X_k^{(n)}\right]\!\right] \tag{12.24}$$

exists in $(\mathcal{O}\left(\mathcal{G}(\mathcal{H}_C) \otimes \mathcal{H}\right), \sqsubseteq)$.

Proof. We show that

$$\left[\!\left[X_k^{(n)}\right]\!\right] \sqsubseteq \left[\!\left[X_k^{(n+1)}\right]\!\right]$$

by induction on n. The case of $n = 0$ is trivial because

$$\left[\!\left[X_k^{(0)}\right]\!\right] = [\![\textbf{abort}]\!] = 0.$$

In general, by the induction hypothesis on $n - 1$ and Corollary 12.1, we have:

$$\begin{aligned}\left[\!\left[X_k^{(n)}\right]\!\right] &= [\![P_k]\!]\left(\mathbb{K}_C([\![X_1^{(n-1)}]\!]), ..., \mathbb{K}_C([\![X_m^{(n-1)}]\!])\right) \\ &\sqsubseteq [\![P_k]\!]\left(\mathbb{K}_C([\![X_1^{(n)}]\!]), ..., \mathbb{K}_C([\![X_m^{(n)}]\!])\right) \\ &= \left[\!\left[X_k^{(n+1)}\right]\!\right],\end{aligned}$$

where C is the set of "coins" in D. Then existence of the least upper bound (12.24) follows immediately from Lemma 12.1. $\qquad\square$

We now are ready to define the operational semantics of quantum recursive programs in terms of substitution.

Definition 12.23. Let P be a quantum recursive program declared by the system D of Eqs (12.22). Then its operational semantics is

$$[\![P]\!]_{op} = [\![P]\!]\left([\![X_1^{(\infty)}]\!], ..., [\![X_m^{(\infty)}]\!]\right).$$

The operator $[\![P]\!]_{op}$ is called the operational semantics for the reason that it is defined based on the copy rule. But it is actually not an operational semantics in the strict sense because the notion of limit is involved in $[\![X_i^{(\infty)}]\!]$ ($1 \le i \le m$).

The operational semantics of quantum recursive program P defined above can be characterised by the limit of its syntactic approximations (with respect to its declaration D).

Proposition 12.8. *It holds in the domain $(\mathcal{O}(\mathcal{G}(\mathcal{H}_C) \otimes \mathcal{H}), \sqsubseteq)$ that*

$$[\![P]\!]_{op} = \bigsqcup_{n=0}^{\infty}\left[\!\left[P^{(n)}\right]\!\right].$$

Proof. It follows from Lemma 12.4 that

$$\bigsqcup_{n=0}^{\infty}\left[\!\left[P^{(n)}\right]\!\right] = \bigsqcup_{n=0}^{\infty}\left[\!\left[P[X_1^{(n)}/X_1, ..., X_m^{(n)}/X_m]\right]\!\right]$$

$$= \bigsqcup_{n=0}^{\infty} [\![P]\!] \left(\mathbb{K}_C([\![X_1^{(n)}]\!]), ..., \mathbb{K}_C([\![X_m^{(n)}]\!]) \right)$$

where $\mathbb{K}_C$ is the creation functional with respect to the "coins" C in P. However, all the "coins" C in P do not appear in $X_1^{(n)}, ..., X_m^{(n)}$ (see the condition in Definition 12.3). So,

$$\mathbb{K}_C \left([\![X_k^{(n)}]\!] \right) = [\![X_k^{(n)}]\!]$$

for every $1 \le k \le m$, and by Theorem 12.1 we obtain:

$$\bigsqcup_{n=0}^{\infty} [\![P^{(n)}]\!] = \bigsqcup_{n=0}^{\infty} [\![P]\!] \left([\![X_1^{(n)}]\!], ..., [\![X_m^{(n)}]\!] \right)$$

$$= [\![P]\!] \left(\bigsqcup_{n=0}^{\infty} [\![X_1^{(n)}]\!], ..., \bigsqcup_{n=0}^{\infty} [\![X_m^{(n)}]\!] \right)$$

$$= [\![P]\!] \left([\![X_1^{\infty}]\!], ..., [\![X_m^{\infty}]\!] \right)$$

$$= [\![P]\!]_{op}. \qquad \square$$

Intuitively, for each $n \ge 0$, $[\![P^{(n)}]\!]$ denotes the partial computational result of recursive program P up to the nth step. Thus, the above proposition shows that the complete computational result can be approximated by partial computational results.

Equivalence of two semantics: Finally, the equivalence between fixed point-based denotational and substitution-based operational semantics of recursive programs is established in the following:

Theorem 12.2 (Equivalence of denotational semantics and operational semantics). *For any quantum recursive program P, we have:*

$$[\![P]\!]_{fix} = [\![P]\!]_{op}.$$

Proof. By Definitions 12.20 and 12.23, it suffices to show that $\left([\![X_1^{(\infty)}]\!], ..., [\![X_m^{(\infty)}]\!] \right)$ is the least fixed point of semantic functional $[\![D]\!]$, where D is the declaration of procedure identifiers in P. With Theorem 12.1 and Lemmas 12.3 and 12.4, we obtain:

$$\left[\!\left[X_k^{(\infty)}\right]\!\right] = \bigsqcup_{n=0}^{\infty} \left[\!\left[X_k^{(n)}\right]\!\right]$$

$$= \bigsqcup_{n=0}^{\infty} \left[\!\left[P_k[X_1^{(n)}/X_1, ..., X_m^{(n)}/X_m] \right]\!\right]$$

$$= \bigsqcup_{n=0}^{\infty} [\![P_k]\!] \left(\mathbb{K}_C([\![X_1^{(n)}]\!]), ..., \mathbb{K}_C([\![X_m^{(n)}]\!]) \right)$$

$$= [\![P_k]\!] \left(\mathbb{K}_C \left(\bigsqcup_{n=0}^{\infty} [\![X_1^{(n)}]\!] \right), ..., \mathbb{K}_C \left(\bigsqcup_{n=0}^{\infty} [\![X_m^{(n)}]\!] \right) \right)$$

$$= [\![P_k]\!] \left(\mathbb{K}_C([\![X_1^{(\infty)}]\!]), ..., \mathbb{K}_C([\![X_m^{(\infty)}]\!]) \right)$$

for every $1 \le k \le m$, where C is the set of "coins" in D. So, $\left([\![X_1^{(\infty)}]\!], ..., [\![X_m^{(\infty)}]\!] \right)$ is a fixed point of $[\![D]\!]$. On the other hand, if $(\mathbf{A}_1, ..., \mathbf{A}_m) \in \mathcal{O}(\mathcal{G}(\mathcal{H}_C) \otimes \mathcal{H})^m$ is a fixed point of $[\![D]\!]$, then we can prove that for every $n \ge 0$,

$$\left([\![X_1^{(n)}]\!], ..., [\![X_m^{(n)}]\!] \right) \sqsubseteq (\mathbf{A}_1, ..., \mathbf{A}_m)$$

by induction on n. Indeed, the case of $n = 0$ is obvious. In general, using the induction hypothesis on $n - 1$, Corollary 12.1 and Lemma 12.4 we obtain:

$$
\begin{aligned}
(\mathbf{A}_1, ..., \mathbf{A}_m) &= [\![D]\!](\mathbf{A}_1, ..., \mathbf{A}_m) \\
&= \left(\left(\mathbb{K}_C^m \circ [\![P_1]\!] \right)(\mathbf{A}_1, ..., \mathbf{A}_m), ..., \left(\mathbb{K}_C^m \circ [\![P_m]\!] \right)(\mathbf{A}_1, ..., \mathbf{A}_m) \right) \\
&\sqsupseteq \left(\left(\mathbb{K}_C^m \circ [\![P_1]\!] \right)\left([\![X_1^{(n-1)}]\!], ..., [\![X_m^{(n-1)}]\!] \right), ..., \left(\mathbb{K}_C^m \circ [\![P_m]\!] \right)\left([\![X_1^{(n-1)}]\!], ..., [\![X_m^{(n-1)}]\!] \right) \right) \\
&= \left([\![X_1^{(n)}]\!], ..., [\![X_m^{(n)}]\!] \right).
\end{aligned}
$$

Therefore, it holds that

$$
\left([\![X_1^{(\infty)}]\!], ..., [\![X_m^{(\infty)}]\!] \right) = \bigsqcup_{n=0}^{\infty} \left([\![X_1^{(n)}]\!], ..., [\![X_m^{(n)}]\!] \right) \sqsubseteq (\mathbf{A}_1, ..., \mathbf{A}_m),
$$

and $\left([\![X_1^{(\infty)}]\!], ..., [\![X_m^{(\infty)}]\!] \right)$ is the least fixed point of $[\![D]\!]$. □

In light of this theorem, we will simply write $[\![P]\!]$ for both the denotational (fixed point) and operational semantics of a recursive program P. But we should carefully distinguish the semantics $[\![P]\!] \in \mathcal{O}(\mathcal{G}(\mathcal{H}_C) \otimes \mathcal{H})$ of a recursive program $P = P[X_1, ..., X_m]$ declared by a system of equations about $X_1, ..., X_m$ from the semantic functional

$$
[\![P]\!] : \mathcal{O}(\mathcal{G}(\mathcal{H}_C) \otimes \mathcal{H})^m \to \mathcal{O}(\mathcal{G}(\mathcal{H}_C) \otimes \mathcal{H})
$$

of program scheme $P = P[X_1, ..., X_m]$. Usually, such a difference can be recognised from the context.

12.5 Recovering symmetry and antisymmetry

The last section developed the techniques for solving quantum recursive equations in the free Fock space. However, the solutions found in the free Fock space are still not what we really need because they may not preserve symmetry or antisymmetry and thus cannot directly apply to the symmetric Fock space for bosons or the antisymmetric Fock space for fermions. In this section, we introduce the technique of symmetrisation that allows us to transform every solution in the free Fock space to a solution in the bosonic or fermionic Fock spaces.

12.5.1 Symmetrisation functional

Domain of symmetric operators: Let us first isolate a special subdomain of $\mathcal{O}(\mathcal{G}(\mathcal{H}_C) \otimes \mathcal{H})$, namely the domain of symmetric operators. As in Section 12.4.1, let $\mathcal{H}$ be the state Hilbert space of the principal system and C the set of "coins", and

$$
\mathcal{G}(\mathcal{H}_C) \otimes \mathcal{H} = \left(\bigotimes_{c \in C} \mathcal{F}(\mathcal{H}_c) \right) \otimes \mathcal{H} = \bigoplus_{\overline{n} \in \omega^C} \left[\left(\bigotimes_{c \in C} \mathcal{H}_c^{\otimes n_c} \right) \otimes \mathcal{H} \right],
$$

where ω is the set of nonnegative integers, and for each $c \in C$, $\mathcal{F}(\mathcal{H}_c)$ is the free Fock space over the state Hilbert space $\mathcal{H}_c$ of "coin" c. As a simple generalisation of Definition 12.9, we have:

Definition 12.24. For any operator $\mathbf{A} = \sum_{\overline{n} \in \omega^C} \mathbf{A}(\overline{n}) \in \mathcal{O}(\mathcal{G}(\mathcal{H}_C) \otimes \mathcal{H})$, we say that $\mathbf{A}$ is symmetric if for each $\overline{n} \in \omega^C$, for each $c \in C$ and for each permutation π of $0, 1, ..., n_c - 1$, P_π and $\mathbf{A}(\overline{n})$ commute; that is,

$$
P_\pi \mathbf{A}(\overline{n}) = \mathbf{A}(\overline{n}) P_\pi.
$$

Note that in the above definition P_π actually stands for its cylindrical extension

$$
P_\pi \otimes \left(\bigotimes_{d \in C \setminus \{c\}} I_d \right) \otimes I
$$

on $\left(\bigotimes_{d \in C} \mathcal{H}_d^{\otimes n_d} \right) \otimes \mathcal{H}$, where I_d is the identity operator on $\mathcal{H}_d^{\otimes n_d}$ for every $d \in C \setminus \{c\}$, and I is the identity operator on $\mathcal{H}$.

We write $\mathcal{SO}(\mathcal{G}(\mathcal{H}_C) \otimes \mathcal{H})$ for the set of all symmetric operators $\mathbf{A} \in \mathcal{O}(\mathcal{G}(\mathcal{H}_C) \otimes \mathcal{H})$. Its lattice-theoretic structure is presented in the following:

Lemma 12.6. $(\mathcal{SO}(\mathcal{G}(\mathcal{H}_C) \otimes \mathcal{H}), \sqsubseteq)$ *is a complete subpartial order of CPO* $(\mathcal{O}(\mathcal{G}(\mathcal{H}_C) \otimes \mathcal{H}), \sqsubseteq)$.

Proof. It suffices to observe that symmetry of operators is preserved by the least upper bound in $(\mathcal{O}(\mathcal{G}(\mathcal{H}_C) \otimes \mathcal{H}), \sqsubseteq)$; that is, if $\mathbf{A}_i$ is symmetric, so is $\bigsqcup_i \mathbf{A}_i$, as constructed in the proof of Lemma 12.1. $\square$

Symmetrisation functional: Now we can straightforwardly generalise the symmetrisation functional in a single Fock space defined by Eqs (12.14) and (12.15) into the space $\mathcal{O}(\mathcal{G}(\mathcal{H}_C) \otimes \mathcal{H})$.

Definition 12.25. 1. For each $\overline{n} \in \omega^C$, the symmetrisation functional $\mathbb{S}$ over operators on the space $\left(\bigotimes_{c \in C} \mathcal{H}_c^{\otimes n_c} \right) \otimes \mathcal{H}$ is defined by

$$\mathbb{S}(\mathbf{A}) = \left(\prod_{c \in C} \frac{1}{n_c!} \right) \cdot \sum_{\{\pi_c\}} \left[\left(\bigotimes_{c \in C} P_{\pi_c} \right) \mathbf{A} \left(\bigotimes_{c \in C} P_{\pi_c}^{-1} \right) \right]$$

for every operator $\mathbf{A}$ on $\left(\bigotimes_{c \in C} \mathcal{H}_c^{\otimes n_c} \right) \otimes \mathcal{H}$, where $\{\pi_c\}$ traverses over all C-indexed families with π_c being a permutation of $0, 1, ..., n_c - 1$ for every $c \in C$.

2. The symmetrisation functional can be extended to $\mathcal{O}(\mathcal{G}(\mathcal{H}_C) \otimes \mathcal{H})$ in a natural way:

$$\mathbb{S}(\mathbf{A}) = \sum_{\overline{n} \in \omega^C} \mathbb{S}(\mathbf{A}(\overline{n}))$$

for any $\mathbf{A} = \sum_{\overline{n} \in \omega^C} \mathbf{A}(\overline{n}) \in \mathcal{O}(\mathcal{G}(\mathcal{H}_C) \otimes \mathcal{H})$.

Obviously, $\mathbb{S}(\mathbf{A}) \in \mathcal{SO}(\mathcal{G}(\mathcal{H}_C) \otimes \mathcal{H})$. Clause 1 of the above definition is essentially the same as Eq. (12.15) but applied to a more complicated space $\left(\bigotimes_{c \in C} \mathcal{H}_c^{\otimes n_c} \right) \otimes \mathcal{H}$. Clause 2 is then a component-wise generalisation of clause 1. Furthermore, the following lemma establishes continuity of the symmetrisation functional with respect to the flat order.

Lemma 12.7. *The symmetrisation functional*

$$\mathbb{S} : (\mathcal{O}(\mathcal{G}(\mathcal{H}_C) \otimes \mathcal{H}), \sqsubseteq) \to (\mathcal{SO}(\mathcal{G}(\mathcal{H}_C) \otimes \mathcal{H}), \sqsubseteq)$$

is continuous.

Proof. What we need to prove is that

$$\mathbb{S}\left(\bigsqcup_i \mathbf{A}_i \right) = \bigsqcup_i \mathbb{S}(\mathbf{A}_i)$$

for any chain $\{\mathbf{A}_i\}$ in $(\mathcal{O}(\mathcal{G}(\mathcal{H}_C) \otimes \mathcal{H}), \sqsubseteq)$. Assume that $\mathbf{A} = \bigsqcup_i \mathbf{A}_i$. Then by the proof of Lemma 12.1, we can write

$$\mathbf{A} = \sum_{\overline{n} \in \omega} \mathbf{A}(\overline{n}) \text{ and } \mathbf{A}_i = \sum_{\overline{n} \in \Omega_i} \mathbf{A}(\overline{n})$$

for some Ω_i with $\bigcup_i \Omega_i = \omega^C$. So, it holds that

$$\bigsqcup_i \mathbb{S}(\mathbf{A}_i) = \bigsqcup_i \sum_{\overline{n} \in \Omega_i} \mathbb{S}(\mathbf{A}(\overline{n})) = \sum_{\overline{n} \in \omega^C} \mathbb{S}(\mathbf{A}(\overline{n})) = \mathbb{S}(\mathbf{A}). \qquad \square$$

12.5.2   Symmetrisation of semantics of quantum recursion

With the preparation in the previous subsection, now we can directly apply the symmetrisation functional to the solutions of quantum recursive equations in the free Fock space to give the semantics of quantum recursive programs in the symmetric or antisymmetric Fock space.

Definition 12.26. Let $P = P[X_1, ..., X_m]$ be a quantum recursive program declared by the system D of Eqs (12.22). Then its symmetric semantics $\llbracket P \rrbracket_{sym}$ is the symmetrisation of its semantics $\llbracket P \rrbracket$ in the free Fock space:

$$\llbracket P \rrbracket_{sym} = \mathbb{S}(\llbracket P \rrbracket)$$

where $\mathbb{S}$ is the symmetrisation functional,

$$\llbracket P \rrbracket = \llbracket P \rrbracket_{fix} = \llbracket P \rrbracket_{op} \in \mathcal{O}(\mathcal{G}(\mathcal{H}_C) \otimes \mathcal{H})$$

(see Theorem 12.2), C is the set of "coins" in D, and $\mathcal{H}$ is the state Hilbert space of the principal system of D.

Intuitively, for each "coin" $c \in C$, we use $v_c = +$ or $-$ to indicate that c is a boson or a fermion, respectively. Moreover, we write v for the sequence $\{v_c\}_{c \in C}$. Then

$$\mathcal{G}_v(\mathcal{H}_C) \overset{\triangle}{=} \bigotimes_{c \in C} \mathcal{F}_{v_c}(\mathcal{H}_c) \subsetneq \mathcal{G}(\mathcal{H}_C).$$

According to the principle of symmetrisation, a physically meaningful input to program P should be a state $|\Psi\rangle$ in $\mathcal{G}_v(\mathcal{H}_C) \otimes \mathcal{H}$. However, the output $\llbracket P \rrbracket(|\Psi\rangle)$ is not necessarily in $\mathcal{G}_v(\mathcal{H}_C) \otimes \mathcal{H}$ and thus might not be meaningful. Nevertheless, it holds that

$$\llbracket P \rrbracket_{sym}(|\Psi\rangle) = \mathbb{S}(\llbracket P \rrbracket)(|\Psi\rangle) \in \mathcal{G}_v(\mathcal{H}_C) \otimes \mathcal{H}.$$

As a symmetrisation of Proposition 12.8, we have a characterisation of symmetric semantics in terms of syntactic approximations:

Proposition 12.9. $\llbracket P \rrbracket_{sym} = \bigsqcup_{n=0}^{\infty} \mathbb{S}\left(\llbracket P^{(n)} \rrbracket\right).$

Proof. It follows from Proposition 12.8 and Lemma 12.7 (continuity of the symmetrisation functional) that

$$\llbracket P \rrbracket_{sym} = \mathbb{S}(\llbracket P \rrbracket) = \mathbb{S}\left(\bigsqcup_{n=0}^{\infty} \llbracket P^{(n)} \rrbracket\right) = \bigsqcup_{n=0}^{\infty} \mathbb{S}\left(\llbracket P^{(n)} \rrbracket\right). \qquad \square$$

12.6 Principal system semantics of quantum recursion

In the last section, the symmetric semantics of quantum recursive programs was defined by symmetrising their semantics in the free Fock space. Let P be a quantum recursive program with $\mathcal{H}$ being the state Hilbert space of its principal variables and C being the set of its "coins". Then semantics $\llbracket P \rrbracket$ is an operator on space $\mathcal{G}(\mathcal{H}_C) \otimes \mathcal{H}$, where $\mathcal{G}(\mathcal{H}_C) = \bigotimes_{c \in C} \mathcal{F}(\mathcal{H}_c)$, and for each $c \in C$, $\mathcal{H}_c$ is the state Hilbert space of "coin" c, $\mathcal{F}(\mathcal{H}_c)$ is the free Fock space over $\mathcal{H}_c$. Furthermore, we put

$$\mathcal{G}_v(\mathcal{H}_C) = \bigotimes_{c \in C} \mathcal{F}_{v_c}(\mathcal{H}_c)$$

where v is the sequence $\{v_c\}_{c \in C}$, and for each $c \in C$, $v_c = +$ or $-$ if "coin" c is implemented by a boson or a fermion, respectively. Then symmetric semantics $\llbracket P \rrbracket_{sym}$ is an operator on $\mathcal{G}_v(\mathcal{H}_C) \otimes \mathcal{H}$. As we know from the discussions in the previous sections, quantum "coins" in C (and their copies) are only introduced to help the execution of program P but do not actually participate in the computation. What really concerns us is the computation done by the principal system. More precisely, we consider the computation of P with input $|\psi\rangle \in \mathcal{H}$ of principal variables. Assume that the "coins" are initialised in state $|\Psi\rangle \in \mathcal{G}_v(\mathcal{H}_C)$. Then the computation of the program P starts in state $|\Psi\rangle \otimes |\psi\rangle$. At the end, the computational result of P will be stored in the Hilbert space $\mathcal{H}$ of the principal system. This observation leads to the following:

Definition 12.27. Given a state $|\Psi\rangle \in \mathcal{G}_v(\mathcal{H}_C)$. The principal system semantics of program P with respect to "coin" initialisation $|\Psi\rangle$ is the mapping $\llbracket P, \Psi \rrbracket$ from pure states in $\mathcal{H}$ to partial density operators, i.e. positive operators with trace ≤ 1 (see Section 5.2), in $\mathcal{H}$:

$$\llbracket P, \Psi \rrbracket(|\psi\rangle) = tr_{\mathcal{G}_v(\mathcal{H}_C)}(|\Phi\rangle\langle\Phi|)$$

for each pure state $|\psi\rangle$ in $\mathcal{H}$, where

$$|\Phi\rangle = [\![P]\!]_{sym}(|\Psi\rangle \otimes |\psi\rangle),$$

$[\![P]\!]_{sym}$ is the symmetric semantics of P, and $tr_{\mathcal{G}_v(\mathcal{H}_C)}$ is the partial trace over $\mathcal{G}_v(\mathcal{H}_C)$ (see Definition 2.22).

As a corollary of Proposition 12.9, we have the following characterisation of the principal system semantics in terms of syntactic approximation:

Proposition 12.10. *For any quantum recursive program P, any initial "coin" state $|\Psi\rangle$ and any principal system state $|\psi\rangle$,*

$$[\![P, \Psi]\!](|\psi\rangle) = \bigsqcup_{n=0}^{\infty} tr_{\bigotimes_{c \in C} \mathcal{H}_{vc}^{\otimes n}} (|\Phi_n\rangle\langle\Phi_n|)$$

where C is the set of "coins" in P,

$$|\Phi_n\rangle = \mathbb{S}\left([\![P^{(n)}]\!] (|\Psi\rangle \otimes |\psi\rangle) \right)$$

and $P^{(n)}$ is the nth syntactic approximation of P for every $n \geq 0$.

Exercise 12.12. Prove the above proposition.

12.7 Illustrative examples: revisit recursive quantum walks

A general theory of quantum recursive programs has been developed in the previous sections. To illustrate the ideas proposed there, let us reconsider two simple recursive quantum walks defined in Section 12.2.

Example 12.3 (Unidirectionally recursive Hadamard walk). Recall from Example 12.1 that the unidirectionally recursive Hadamard walk is defined as quantum recursive program X declared by

$$X \Leftarrow T_L[p] \oplus_{H[d]} (T_R[p]; X).$$

1. For each $n \geq 0$, the semantics of the nth approximation of the walk is

$$[\![X^{(n)}]\!] = \sum_{i=0}^{n-1} \left[\left(\bigotimes_{j=0}^{i-1} |R\rangle_{d_j}\langle R| \otimes |L\rangle_{d_i}\langle L| \right) \mathbf{H}(i) \otimes T_L T_R^i \right] \tag{12.25}$$

where $d_0 = d$, $\mathbf{H}(i)$ is the operator on $\mathcal{H}_d^{\otimes i}$ defined from the Hadamard operator H by Eq. (12.16). This can be easily shown by induction on n, starting from the first three approximations displayed in Eq. (12.10). Therefore, the semantics of the unidirectionally recursive Hadamard walk in the free Fock space $\mathcal{F}(\mathcal{H}_d) \otimes \mathcal{H}_p$ is the operator:

$$\begin{aligned}
[\![X]\!] &= \lim_{n \to \infty} [\![X^{(n)}]\!] \\
&= \sum_{i=0}^{\infty} \left[\left(\bigotimes_{j=0}^{i-1} |R\rangle_{d_j}\langle R| \otimes |L\rangle_{d_i}\langle L| \right) \mathbf{H}(i) \otimes T_L T_R^i \right] \\
&= \left[\sum_{i=0}^{\infty} \left(\bigotimes_{j=0}^{i-1} |R\rangle_{d_j}\langle R| \otimes |L\rangle_{d_i}\langle L| \right) \otimes T_L T_R^i \right] (\mathbf{H} \otimes I)
\end{aligned} \tag{12.26}$$

where $\mathcal{H}_d = span\{|L\rangle, |R\rangle\}$, $\mathcal{H}_p = span\{|n\rangle : n \in \mathbb{Z}\}$, I is the identity operator on the position Hilbert space $\mathcal{H}_p$, $\mathbf{H}(i)$ is as in Eq. (12.25), and

$$\mathbf{H} = \sum_{i=0}^{\infty} \mathbf{H}(i)$$

is the extension of H in the free Fock space $\mathcal{F}(\mathcal{H}_d)$ over the direction Hilbert space $\mathcal{H}_d$.

2. For each $i \geq 0$, we compute the symmetrisation:

$$\mathbb{S}\left(\bigotimes_{j=0}^{i-1} |R\rangle_{d_j} \langle R| \otimes |L\rangle_{d_i} \langle L| \right)$$

$$= \frac{1}{(i+1)!} \sum_{\pi} P_{\pi} \left(\bigotimes_{j=0}^{i-1} |R\rangle_{d_j} \langle R| \otimes |L\rangle_{d_i} \langle L| \right) P_{\pi}^{-1}$$

(where π traverses over all permutations of $0, 1, ..., i$)

$$= \frac{1}{i+1} \sum_{j=0}^{i} (|R\rangle_{d_0} \langle R| \otimes ... \otimes |R\rangle_{d_{j-1}} \langle R| \otimes |L\rangle_{d_j} \langle L|$$

$$\otimes |R\rangle_{d_{j+1}} \langle R| \otimes ... \otimes |R\rangle_{d_i} \langle R|)$$

$$\stackrel{\triangle}{=} G_i.$$

Therefore, the symmetric semantics of the unidirectionally recursive Hadamard walk is

$$\mathbb{S}(\llbracket X \rrbracket) = \left(\sum_{i=0}^{\infty} G_i \otimes T_L T_R^i \right) (\mathbf{H} \otimes I).$$

Example 12.4 (Bidirectionally recursive Hadamard walk). Let us consider the semantics of the bidirectionally recursive Hadamard walk. Recall from Example 12.1 that it is declared by equations:

$$\begin{cases} X \Leftarrow T_L[p] \oplus_{H[d]} (T_R[p]; Y), \\ Y \Leftarrow (T_L[p]; X) \oplus_{H[d]} T_R[p]. \end{cases} \tag{12.27}$$

To simplify the presentation, we first introduce several notations. For any string $\Sigma = \sigma_0 \sigma_1 ... \sigma_{n-1}$ of symbols L and R, its dual is defined to be

$$\overline{\Sigma} = \overline{\sigma_0} \overline{\sigma_1} ... \overline{\sigma_{n-1}}$$

where $\overline{L} = R$ and $\overline{R} = L$. We write the pure state

$$|\Sigma\rangle = |\sigma_0\rangle_{d_0} \otimes |\sigma_1\rangle_{d_1} \otimes ... \otimes |\sigma_{n-1}\rangle_{d_{n-1}}$$

in the space $\mathcal{H}_d^{\otimes n}$. Then its density operator representation is

$$\rho_{\Sigma} = |\Sigma\rangle\langle\Sigma| = \bigotimes_{j=0}^{n-1} |\sigma_j\rangle_{d_j} \langle \sigma_j|.$$

Moreover, we write the composition of left and right translations:

$$T_{\Sigma} = T_{\sigma_{n-1}} ... T_{\sigma_1} T_{\sigma_0}.$$

1. The semantics of procedures X and Y in the free Fock space are

$$\llbracket X \rrbracket = \left[\sum_{n=0}^{\infty} \left(\rho_{\Sigma_n} \otimes T_n \right) \right] (\mathbf{H} \otimes I_p),$$

$$\llbracket Y \rrbracket = \left[\sum_{n=0}^{\infty} \left(\rho_{\overline{\Sigma_n}} \otimes T_n' \right) \right] (\mathbf{H} \otimes I_p), \tag{12.28}$$

where **H** is as in Example 12.3, and

$$\Sigma_n = \begin{cases} (RL)^k L & \text{if } n = 2k+1, \\ (RL)^k RR & \text{if } n = 2k+2, \end{cases}$$

$$T_n = T_{\Sigma_n} = \begin{cases} T_L & \text{if } n \text{ is odd}, \\ T_R^2 & \text{if } n \text{ is even}, \end{cases}$$

$$T_n' = T_{\overline{\Sigma_n}} = \begin{cases} T_R & \text{if } n \text{ is odd}, \\ T_L^2 & \text{if } n \text{ is even}. \end{cases}$$

It is clear from Eqs (12.26) and (12.28) that the behaviours of unidirectionally and bidirectionally recursive Hadamard walks are very different: the former can go to any one of the positions $-1, 0, 1, 2, \ldots$, but in the latter walk X can only go to the positions -1 and 2, and Y can only go to the positions 1 and -2.

2. The symmetric semantics of the bidirectionally recursive Hadamard walk specified by Eq. (12.27) is:

$$[\![X]\!] = \left[\sum_{n=0}^{\infty} (\gamma_n \otimes T_n)\right] (\mathbf{H} \otimes I_p),$$

$$[\![Y]\!] = \left[\sum_{n=0}^{\infty} (\delta_n \otimes T_n)\right] (\mathbf{H} \otimes I_p)$$

where:

$$\gamma_{2k+1} = \frac{1}{\binom{2k+1}{k}} \sum_{\Gamma} \rho_\Gamma,$$

$$\delta_{2k+1} = \frac{1}{\binom{2k+1}{k}} \sum_{\Delta} \rho_\Delta$$

with Γ ranging over all strings of $(k+1)$ L's and k R's and Δ ranging over all strings of k L's and $(k+1)$ R's, and

$$\gamma_{2k+2} = \frac{1}{\binom{2k+2}{k}} \sum_{\Gamma} \rho_\Gamma,$$

$$\sigma_{2k+2} = \frac{1}{\binom{2k+2}{k}} \sum_{\Delta} \rho_\Delta$$

with Γ ranging over all strings of k L's and $(k+2)$ R's and Δ ranging over all strings of $(k+2)$ L's and k R's.

3. Finally, we consider the principal system semantics of the bidirectionally recursive Hadamard walk. Suppose that it starts from the position 0.

   a. If the "coins" are bosons initialised in state

$$|\Psi\rangle = |L, L, \ldots, L\rangle_+ = |L\rangle_{d_0} \otimes |L\rangle_{d_1} \otimes \ldots \otimes |L\rangle_{d_{n-1}},$$

then we have

$$[\![X]\!]_{sym}(|\Psi\rangle \otimes |0\rangle) = \begin{cases} \frac{1}{\sqrt{2^n}\binom{2k+1}{k}} \sum_{\Gamma} |\Gamma\rangle \otimes |-1\rangle & \text{if } n = 2k+1, \\ \frac{1}{\sqrt{2^n}\binom{2k+2}{k}} \sum_{\Delta} |\Delta\rangle \otimes |2\rangle & \text{if } n = 2k+2, \end{cases}$$

where Γ traverses over all strings of $(k+1)$ L's and k R's, and Δ traverses over all strings of k L's and $(k+2)$ R's. Therefore, the principal system semantics with the "coin" initialisation $|\Psi\rangle$ is:

$$[\![X, \Psi]\!](|0\rangle) = \begin{cases} \frac{1}{2^n}|-1\rangle\langle-1| & \text{if } n \text{ is odd}, \\ \frac{1}{2^n}|2\rangle\langle2| & \text{if } n \text{ is even}. \end{cases}$$

b. For each single-particle state $|\psi\rangle$ in $\mathcal{H}_d$, the corresponding coherent state of bosons in the symmetric Fock space $\mathcal{F}_+(\mathcal{H}_d)$ over $\mathcal{H}_d$ is defined as

$$|\psi\rangle_{coh} = \exp\left(-\frac{1}{2}\langle\psi|\psi\rangle\right) \sum_{n=0}^{\infty} \frac{[a^{\dagger}(\psi)]^n}{n!}|\mathbf{0}\rangle$$

where $|\mathbf{0}\rangle$ is the vacuum state and $a^{\dagger}(\cdot)$ the creation operator. If the "coins" are initialised in the coherent state $|L\rangle_{coh}$ of bosons corresponding to $|L\rangle$, then we have:

$$[\![X]\!]_{sym}(|L\rangle_{coh} \otimes |0\rangle)$$

$$= \frac{1}{\sqrt{e}}\left(\sum_{k=0}^{\infty} \frac{1}{\sqrt{2^{2k+1}\binom{2k+1}{k}}} \sum_{\Gamma_k} |\Gamma_k\rangle\right) \otimes |-1\rangle$$

$$+ \frac{1}{\sqrt{e}} \sum_{k=0}^{\infty} \left(\frac{1}{\sqrt{2^{2k+2}\binom{2k+2}{k}}} \sum_{\Delta_k} |\Delta_k\rangle\right) \otimes |2\rangle,$$

where Γ_k ranges over all strings of $(k+1)$ L's and k R's, and Δ_k ranges over all strings of k L's and $(k+2)$ R's. So, the principal system semantics with "coin" initialisation $|L\rangle_{coh}$ is:

$$[\![X, L_{coh}]\!](|0\rangle) = \frac{1}{\sqrt{e}}\left(\sum_{k=0}^{\infty} \frac{1}{2^{2k+1}}|-1\rangle\langle-1| + \sum_{k=0}^{\infty} \frac{1}{2^{2k+2}}|2\rangle\langle2|\right)$$

$$= \frac{1}{\sqrt{e}}\left(\frac{2}{3}|-1\rangle\langle-1| + \frac{1}{3}|2\rangle\langle2|\right).$$

It is interesting to compare termination in subclauses a and b of clause 3 in the above example. In case a, the "coins" start in an n-particle state, so the quantum recursive program X terminates within n steps; that is, termination probability within n steps is $p_T^{(\leq n)} = 1$. But in case b, the "coins" start in a coherent state, and program X does not terminate within a finite number of steps although it almost surely terminates; that is, $p_T^{(\leq n)} < 1$ for all n and $\lim_{n\to\infty} p_T^{(\leq n)} = 1$.

To conclude this section, we point out that only the behaviour of the two simplest among the recursive quantum walks defined in Section 12.2 were examined above. The analysis of the others, in particular the recursive quantum walks defined by Eqs (12.7) and (12.9), seems very difficult, and are left as a topic for further studies.

12.8 Quantum while-loops (with quantum control)

The general form of quantum recursion was carefully studied in previous sections. In this section, as an application of the theory developed before, we consider a special class of quantum recursive programs, namely quantum loops with quantum control flows.

Arguably, **while**-loop is the simplest and most popular form of recursion used in various programming languages. Recall that in classical programming, the **while**-loop:

$$\text{while } b \text{ do } S \text{ od} \tag{12.29}$$

can be seen as the recursive program X declared by the equation:

$$X \Leftarrow \text{if } b \text{ then } S; X \text{ else skip fi} \tag{12.30}$$

where b is a Boolean expression.

Quantum while-loops with classical control: In Chapter 5, we defined a measurement-based **while**-loop:

$$\text{while } M[\overline{q}] = 1 \text{ do } P \text{ od} \tag{12.31}$$

as a quantum extension of loop (12.29), where M is a quantum measurement. As pointed out before, the control flow of this loop is classical before it is determined by the outcomes of measurement M.

It cab be easily shown that loop (12.31) is the solution of recursive equation with classical case statement in quantum programming:

$$X \Leftarrow \textbf{if } M[\overline{q}] = 0 \rightarrow \textbf{skip}$$
$$\square \qquad 1 \rightarrow P; X \qquad (12.32)$$
$$\textbf{fi}$$

Quantum while-loops with quantum control: In Chapter 11, we pointed out that in the quantum setting, the notion of case statement splits into two different versions: (a) the one used in Eq. (12.32); and (b) quantum case statement with quantum control. Furthermore, the notion of quantum choice was defined based on quantum case statement. Now we can define a kind of quantum **while**-loop by using quantum case statement and quantum choice in the place of classical case statement **if**...**then**...**else**...**fi** in Eq. (12.30) or (12.32). Inherited from quantum case statement and quantum choice, the control flow of this new quantum loop is genuinely quantum.

Example 12.5 (Quantum **while**-loops with quantum control). **1.** The first form of quantum **while**-loop with quantum control:

$$\textbf{qwhile } [c] = |1\rangle \textbf{ do } U[q] \textbf{ od} \qquad (12.33)$$

is defined to be the quantum recursive program X declared by

$$X \Leftarrow \textbf{qif}[c] \; |0\rangle \rightarrow \textbf{skip}$$
$$\square \qquad |1\rangle \rightarrow U[q]; X \qquad (12.34)$$
$$\textbf{fiq}$$

where c is a quantum "coin" variable denoting a qubit, q is a principal quantum variable, and U is a unitary operator on the state Hilbert space $\mathcal{H}_q$ of system q.

2. The second form of quantum **while**-loop with quantum control:

$$\textbf{qwhile } V[c] = |1\rangle \textbf{ do } U[q] \textbf{ od} \qquad (12.35)$$

is defined to be the quantum recursive program X declared by

$$X \Leftarrow \textbf{skip} \oplus_{V[c]} (U[q]; X)$$
$$\equiv V[c]; \textbf{qif}[c] \; |0\rangle \rightarrow \textbf{skip}$$
$$\square \qquad |1\rangle \rightarrow U[q]; X \qquad (12.36)$$
$$\textbf{fiq}$$

Note that the quantum recursive Eq. (12.36) is obtained by replacing the quantum case statement **qif**...**fiq** in Eq. (12.34) by the quantum choice $\oplus_{V[c]}$.

3. Actually, quantum loops (12.33) and (12.35) are not very interesting because there is not any interaction between the quantum "coin" c and the principal quantum system q in them. This situation is corresponding to the trivial case of classical loop (12.30) where the loop guard b is irrelevant to the loop body S. The classical loop (12.30) becomes truly interesting only when the loop guard b and the loop body S share some program variables. Likewise, a much more interesting form of quantum **while**-loop with quantum control is

$$\textbf{qwhile } W[c; q] = |1\rangle \textbf{ do } U[q] \textbf{ od} \qquad (12.37)$$

which is defined to be the program X declared by the quantum recursive equation

$$X \Leftarrow W[c, q]; \textbf{qif}[c] \; |0\rangle \rightarrow \textbf{skip}$$
$$\square \qquad |1\rangle \rightarrow U[q]; X$$
$$\textbf{fiq}$$

where W is a unitary operator on the state Hilbert space $\mathcal{H}_c \otimes \mathcal{H}_q$ of the composed system of the quantum "coin" c and the principal system q. The operator W describes the interaction between the "coin" c and the principal system q. It is obvious that the loop (12.37) degenerates to the loop (12.35) whenever $W = V \otimes I$, where I is the identity operator on $\mathcal{H}_q$.

It is very interesting to compare quantum loops in the above example with the measurement-based **while**-loop (12.31). First of all, we stress once again that the control flow of the former is defined by a quantum "coin" and thus it is quantum; in contrast, the control flow of the latter is determined by the outcomes of a measurement and thus it is classical. In order to further understand the difference between loops (12.31) and (12.37), let us have a close look at the semantics of loop (12.37).

1. A routine calculation shows that the semantics of the loop (12.37) in the free Fock space is the operator:

$$\llbracket X \rrbracket = \sum_{k=1}^{\infty} (|1\rangle_{c_0} \langle 1| \otimes (|1\rangle_{c_1} \langle 1| \otimes \dots (|1\rangle_{c_{k-2}} \langle 1| \otimes (|0\rangle_{c_{k-1}} \langle 0| \otimes U^{k-1}[q])$$

$$W[c_{k-1}, q])W[c_{k-2}, q]\dots)W[c_1, q])W[c_0, q]$$

$$= \sum_{k=1}^{\infty} \left[\left(\bigotimes_{j=0}^{k-2} |1\rangle_{c_j} \langle 1| \otimes |0\rangle_{c_{k-1}} \langle 0| \otimes U^{k-1}[q] \right) \prod_{j=0}^{k-1} W[c_j, q] \right].$$

2. Furthermore, the symmetric semantics of the loop is:

$$\llbracket X \rrbracket_{sym} = \sum_{k=1}^{\infty} \left[\left(\mathbf{A}(k) \otimes U^{k-1}[q] \right) \prod_{j=0}^{k-1} W[c_j, q] \right],$$

where:

$$\mathbf{A}(k) = \frac{1}{k} \sum_{j=0}^{k-1} |1\rangle_{c_0} \langle 1| \otimes \dots \otimes |1\rangle_{c_{j-1}} \langle 1| \otimes |0\rangle_{c_j} \langle 0|$$

$$\otimes |1\rangle_{c_{j+1}} \langle 1| \otimes \dots \otimes |1\rangle_{c_{k-1}} \langle 1|.$$

3. Now we consider the principal semantics of loop (12.37) in a special case. Let q be a qubit, $U = H$ (the Hadamard gate) and $W = CNOT$ (the controlled-NOT). If the "coins" are initialised in the n-boson state

$$|\Psi_n\rangle = |0, 1, \dots, 1\rangle_+ = \frac{1}{n} \sum_{j=0}^{n-1} |1\rangle_{c_0} \dots |1\rangle_{c_{j-1}} |0\rangle_{c_j} |1\rangle_{c_{j+1}} \dots |1\rangle_{c_{n-1}}$$

and the principal system q starts in state $|-\rangle = \frac{1}{\sqrt{2}}(|0\rangle - |1\rangle)$, then we have:

$$|\Phi_n\rangle \triangleq \llbracket X \rrbracket_{sym}(|\Psi_n\rangle \otimes |-\rangle) = (-1)^n \frac{1}{n} |\Psi_n\rangle \otimes |\psi_n\rangle$$

where

$$|\psi_n\rangle = \begin{cases} |+\rangle & \text{if } n \text{ is even}, \\ |-\rangle & \text{if } n \text{ is odd}. \end{cases}$$

Consequently, the principal system semantics is

$$\llbracket X, \Psi_n \rrbracket(|-\rangle) = tr_{\mathcal{F}_T(\mathcal{H}_v)}(|\Phi_n\rangle \langle \Phi_n|) = \frac{1}{n^3} |\psi_n\rangle \langle \psi_n|.$$

We conclude this chapter by leaving a series of problems for further studies.

Problem 12.1. 1. Although in this chapter we presented several examples of quantum recursion, it is still not well understood what kind of computational problems can be solved more conveniently by using quantum recursion.

2. Another important question is: what kind of physical systems can be used to implement quantum recursion where new "coins" must be continuously created?

Problem 12.2. We even do not fully understand how should a quantum recursion use its "coins" in its computational process. In the definition of the principal system semantics of a recursive program (Definition 12.27), a state $|\Psi\rangle$ in the Fock space of "coins" is given *a priori*. This means that the states of a "coin" and its copies are given once for all. Another possibility is that the states of the copies of a "coin" are created step by step. As an example, let us consider the recursive program X declared by

$$X \Leftarrow a_c^\dagger(|0\rangle); R_y[c, p]; \mathbf{qif}\ [c]\ |0\rangle \to \mathbf{skip}$$
$$\square\ |1\rangle \to T_R[p]; X$$
$$\mathbf{fiq}$$

where $a^\dagger$ is the creation operator, c is a "coin" variable with state space $\mathcal{H}_c = span\{|0\rangle, |1\rangle\}$, the variable p and operator T_R are as in the Hadamard walk,

$$R_y[c, p] = \sum_{n=0}^{\infty}\left[R_y\left(\frac{\pi}{2^{n+1}}\right) \otimes |n\rangle_p\langle n|\right]$$

and $R_y(\theta)$ is the rotation of a qubit about the y-axis in the Bloch sphere (see Example 3.3). Intuitively, $R_y[c, p]$ is a controlled rotation where position of p is used to determine the rotated angle. It is worth noting that this program X is a quantum loop defined in Eq. (12.37) but modified by adding a creation operator at the beginning. Its initial behaviour starting at position 0 with the "coin" c being in the vacuum state $|0\rangle$ is visualised by the following transitions:

$$|\mathbf{0}\rangle|0\rangle_p \xrightarrow{a_d^\dagger(|0\rangle)} |0\rangle|0\rangle_p \xrightarrow{R_x[d,p]} \frac{1}{\sqrt{2}}(|0\rangle + |1\rangle)|0\rangle_p$$
$$\xrightarrow{\mathbf{qif...fiq}} \frac{1}{\sqrt{2}}\left[\langle E, |0\rangle|0\rangle_p\rangle + \langle X, |1\rangle|1\rangle_p\rangle\right].$$

The first configuration at the end of the above equation terminates, but the second continues the computation as follows:

$$|1\rangle|1\rangle_p \xrightarrow{a_d^\dagger(|0\rangle)} |0, 1\rangle_v|0\rangle_p \xrightarrow{R_x[d,p]} \cdots.$$

It is clear from the above example that the computation of a recursive program with the creation operator is very different from that without it. A careful study of quantum recursions that allow the creation operator appears in their syntax is certainly interesting.

Problem 12.3. The theory of quantum recursive programs in this chapter was developed in the language of Fock spaces. Second quantisation method can be equivalently presented using the occupation number representation (see [293], Section 2.1.7; also see Definition 12.12 for a related notion – the particle number operator). Give an occupation number restatement of the theory of quantum recursion.

Problem 12.4. (Floyd-)Hoare logic for quantum programs with classical control flows was presented in Chapter 6. How to develop a (Floyd-)Hoare logic for quantum programs with quantum control flows defined in the last and this chapter?

12.9 Bibliographic remarks and further readings

Quantum recursion with classical control flow (in the superposition-of-data paradigm) was discussed in Section 5.5. This chapter can be seen as the counterpart of Section 5.5 in the superposition-of-programs paradigm, dealing with quantum recursion with quantum control flow. The exposition of this chapter is based on the draft paper [420].

Quantum recursion studied both in Section 5.5 and in this chapter is quantum generalisation of classical recursion in imperative programming. Two good references for the theory of classical recursive programs are [28] (Chapters 4 and 5) and [288] (Chapter 5). The book [292] contains many examples of recursive programs. It is very interesting to examine the quantum counterparts of these examples.

It should be pointed out that no parameters are introduced in quantum recursion considered in this chapter (as well as that in Section 5.5). A new scheme of quantum recursive programming with parameters was proposed recently in [436].

Its control flow is quantum because quantum case statements are used there. In particular, it was shown that a series of quantum programs can be elegantly programmed in this scheme of quantum recursion.

The lambda calculus is a suitable formalism for coping with recursion and high-order computation, and it provides a solid basis for functional programming. Both the lambda calculus and functional programming have been extended into the quantum setting (see Section 13.3 below and the references cited there). But so far, only quantum recursion with classical control has been considered in functional quantum programming.

The main mathematical tool employed in this chapter is second quantisation method. The materials about second quantisation in Section 12.3 are standard and can be found in many textbooks of advanced quantum mechanics. Our presentation in Section 12.3 largely follows [36,293,366].

Part VI

Prospects

Chapter 13

Prospects

In the previous chapters, we have systematically studied foundations of quantum programming along the line from superposition-of-data to superposition-of-programs, and classical parallelism and quantum parallelism are examined together. We saw from the previous chapters that various methodologies and techniques in classical programming can be extended or adapted to program quantum computers. On the other hand, the subject of quantum programming is not a simple and straightforward generalisation of its classical counterpart, and we have to deal with a bunch of completely new phenomena that arise in the quantum realm but would not arise in classical programming. These problems come from the "weird" nature of quantum systems; for example, nocloning of quantum data, noncommutativity of observables, entanglement between different variables and processes, coexistence of classical and quantum control flows. They make quantum programming being a rich and exciting subject.

This final chapter presents an overview of further developments and prospects of quantum programming. More explicitly, its aim is two-fold:

- We briefly discuss some important approaches to quantum programming or related issues that are not treated in the main body of this book.
- We point out some topics for future research that are, as I believe, important for the further developments of the subject, but not mentioned in the previous chapters.

13.1 Quantum machines and quantum programs

Understanding the notions of algorithm, program, and computational machine and their relationship was the starting point of computer science. All of these fundamental notions have been generalised into the framework of quantum computation. The main body of this book has been devoted to a systematic exposition of theoretical foundations of quantum programming. We also studied several models of quantum computational machines in Chapter 3, including quantum circuits, quantum Turing machines, and quantum random access stored-program machines. In this section, we briefly discuss the relationship between quantum programs and quantum computational models, including those studied in Chapter 3 and several others.

Quantum programs and quantum Turing machines: Benioff [51] constructed a quantum mechanical model of a Turing machine. His construction is the first quantum mechanical description of computer, but it is not a real quantum computer because the machine may exist in an intrinsically quantum state between computation steps, but at the end of each computation step the tape of the machine always goes back to one of its classical states. The first truly quantum Turing machine was described by Deutsch [127] in 1985. In his machine, the tape is able to exist in quantum states too. A thorough exposition of the quantum Turing machine is given in [59]. Our exposition of quantum Turing machines in Section 3.2 largely follows [59]. Yao [415] showed that quantum circuit model is equivalent to a quantum Turing machine in the sense that they can simulate each other in polynomial time.

The relationship between programs and Turing machines in classical computation is well-understood; see for example [65,234]. But up to now, not much research on the relationship between quantum programs and quantum Turing machines has been done, except some interesting discussions by Bernstein and Vazirani in [59] and Miszczak [306,307]. For example, a fundamental issue that is still not properly understood is *programs as data* in quantum computation. It seems that this issue has very different implications in the paradigm of superposition-of-data studied in Parts II–IV of this book and in the paradigm of superposition-of-programs studied in Part V. Obviously, a good vehicle for examining this issue is an appropriate extension of random access stored-program machines (RASPs for short). But quantum RASPs studied in Section 3.3 can only accommodate superposition-of-data, and it is still an open problem to find a proper definition of quantum RASPs allowing superposition-of-programs.

Quantum programs and nonstandard models of quantum computation: Quantum circuits, quantum Turing machines, and quantum RASPs are quantum generalisations of their classical counterparts. However, several novel models of quantum computation that have no evident classical analogues have been proposed too. If some of them can be realised

Foundations of Quantum Programming. https://doi.org/10.1016/B978-0-44-315942-8.00027-7

for practical use, then programming methodologies and techniques for them will be fundamentally different from those developed in this book.

1. *Adiabatic quantum computation*: This model was proposed by Farhi, Goldstone, Gutmann, and Sipser [144]. It is a continuous-time model of quantum computation in which the evolution of the quantum register is governed by a hamiltonian that varies slowly. The state of the system is prepared at the beginning in the ground state of the initial hamiltonian. The solution of a computational problem is then encoded in the ground state of the final hamiltonian. The adiabatic theorem in quantum physics guarantees that the final state of the system will differ from the ground state of the final hamiltonian by a negligible amount provided the hamiltonian of the system evolves slowly enough. Thus the solution can be obtained with a high probability by measuring the final state. Adiabatic computing was shown by Aharonov et al. [14] to be polynomially equivalent to conventional quantum computing in the circuit model, and it can be seen as a special form of quantum annealing [249].

2. *Measurement-based quantum computation*: In the quantum Turing machine and quantum circuits, measurements are mainly used at the end to extract computational outcomes from quantum states. However, Raussendorf and Briegel [348] proposed a one-way quantum computer and Nielsen [319] and Leung [272] introduced teleportation quantum computation, both of them suggest that measurements can play a much more important role in quantum computation. In a one-way quantum computer, universal computation can be realised by one-qubit measurements together with a special entangled state, called a cluster state, of a large number of qubits. Teleportation quantum computation is based on Gottesman and Chuang's idea of teleporting quantum gates [184] and allows us to realise universal quantum computation using only projective measurement, quantum memory, and preparation of the $|0\rangle$ state.

3. *Topological quantum computation*: A crucial challenge in constructing large quantum computers is quantum decoherence. Topological quantum computation was proposed by Kitaev [247] as a model of quantum computation in which a revolutionary strategy is adopted to build significantly more stable quantum computers. This model employs two-dimensional quasi-particles, called anyons, whose world lines form braids, which are used to construct logic gates of quantum computers. The key point is that small perturbations do not change the topological properties of these braids. This makes quantum decoherence simply irrelevant for topological quantum computers.

Only very few papers have been devoted to the studies of programming in these nonstandard models of quantum computation. Rieffel et al. [354] developed some techniques for programming quantum annealers. Danos, Kashefi, and Panangaden [116,117] proposed a calculus for formally reasoning about (programs in) measurement-based quantum computation. A measurement-based quantum programming language MCBeth was recently defined in [142]. Compilation for topological quantum computation was considered by Kliuchnikov, Bocharov, and Svore [252].

Research in this direction will be vital once the physical implementation of some of these models becomes possible. On the other hand, it will be challenging due to the fundamental differences between these nonstandard models and the standard models on which quantum programming methodology has been developed. For example, the mathematical description of topological quantum computation is given in terms of topological quantum field theory, knot theory, and lower-dimensional topology. The studies of programming methodology for topological quantum computers (e.g. fixed point semantics of recursive programs) might even bring exciting open problems to these mainstream areas of mathematics.

13.2 Implementation of quantum programming languages

The main body of this book is devoted to the exposition of high-level concepts and models of quantum programming. From a practical viewpoint, however, implementing quantum programming languages and designing quantum compilers are crucial for the successful applications of quantum computing. The implementation issue of quantum programming languages was already briefly mentioned in Section 1.1.1. In this section, we do some further discussions.

Some research in this direction had already been reported in the early literature; for example, Svore, Aho, Cross, et al. [385] proposed a layered quantum software architecture, which is a four-phase design flow mapping a high-level language quantum program onto a quantum device through an intermediate quantum assembly language. Zuliani [456] designed a compiler for the language qGCL in which compilation is realised by algebraic transformation from a qGCL program into a normal form that can be directly executed by a target machine. Nagarajan, Papanikolaou, and Williams [316] defined a hybrid classical-quantum computer architecture – the Sequential Quantum Random Access Memory machine (SQRAM) – based on Knill's QRAM, presented a set of templates for quantum assembly code, and developed a compiler for a subset of Selinger's QPL. A translation between the quantum extension of **while**-language defined in Chapter 5 and a quantum extension of classical flowchart language was given in [427]. A series of compilation techniques have been developed through the projects of languages Quipper [187], LIQUi|> [405], Scaffold [4,230], and QuaFL [269].

In particular, a significant progress in synthesis and optimisation of quantum circuits has been made; see for examples [25,69,70,175,251,357,442,445]. All of the above studies are based on the popular circuit model of quantum computation. Nevertheless, as mentioned in the last section, Danos, Kashefi, and Panangaden [116] presented an elegant low-level language based on a novel and promising physical implementation model of quantum computation, namely measurement-based one-way quantum computer.

In the last 10 years, as the rapid progress in physical realisation of quantum hardware, quantum program implementation, compilation, and optimisation have been intensively researched. There are already too many literatures in this area to describe them all in a single section. Here, we only mention a few of them. IBM's Qiskit [221] provides a convenient Pythonic quantum circuit construction framework based on their own quantum instruction set OpenQSAM [113]. It supports classical control flows and can run on IBM's hardware backends. Microsoft's Q# [386] supports many high-level language features and has its independent compiler and simulator, and compiled Q# programs can be executed on several real quantum hardwares. Quantinuum's t|ket> [347] is a hardware platform-agnostic quantum software development framework, providing state-of-the-art performance in circuit compilation. isQ [193] is a software stack for quantum programming in an imperative programming language with many useful high-level features, e.g. classical control flow and recursion. isQ programs can be compiled into several different kinds of intermediate representation and assemblies, including QIR [346], OpenQASM 3.0 [113], and QCIS (specially tailored for the superconducting quantum hardware at the University of Science and Technology of China).

Up to now, the majority of research on quantum programming language implementation has been devoted to quantum circuit compilation and optimisation. Only very few works (e.g. [456]) have been reported in the literature on transformations and optimisation of high-level language constructs. Whence quantum hardware can execute more complex quantum programs like measurement-based case statements (5.4), quantum **while**-loops (5.5) and their nested forms, their compilation, optimisation, and parallelisation will become an important issue (see example, Chapter 9 of [17] and [38] for the counterpart issue in classical computing). In particular, we need to examine whether the techniques successfully applied in classical compiler optimisation, e.g. loop fusion and loop interchange, can be used for quantum programs. An interesting comparison of static and dynamic code generation for quantum computing was made in [261] through a case study. On the other hand, the analysis techniques developed in Chapter 8 may help in, for example, data-flow analysis and redundancy elimination of quantum programs. Particularly for quantum computing, an important topic for future research is the compilation of quantum programs with quantum control defined in Chapters 11 and 12 (see [358] for a preliminary work).

13.3   Functional quantum programming

This book focuses on imperative quantum programming, but functional quantum programming has been an active research area in the last decade.

The lambda calculus is a formalism of high-order functions and it is a logical basis of some important classical functional programming languages such as LISP, Scheme, ML, and Haskell. The research on functional quantum programming started with an attempt to define a quantum extension of lambda calculus made by Maymin [296] and van Tonder [397]. In a series of papers [369,370,372], Selinger, and Valiron systematically developed quantum lambda calculus with well-defined operational semantics, strong type system, and a practical type inference algorithm. As already mentioned in Section 1.1.1, a denotational semantics of quantum lambda calculus was recently properly defined by Hasuo and Hoshino [202] and Pagani, Selinger, and Valiron [329]. The nocloning property of quantum data makes quantum lambda calculus closely related to linear lambda calculus developed by the linear logic community. Quantum lambda calculus was used by Selinger and Valiron [371] to provide a fully abstract model for the linear fragment of a quantum functional programming language, which is obtained by adding higher-order functions into Selinger's quantum flowchart language QFC [367].

One of the earliest proposals for functional quantum programming was made by Mu and Bird [314]. They introduced a monadic style of quantum programming and coded the Deutsch–Josza algorithm in Haskell. A line of systematic research on functional quantum programming had been persuaded by Altenkirch and Grattage [19]. As mentioned in Section 1.1.1, they proposed a functional language QML for quantum computation. An implementation of QML in Haskell was presented by Grattage [186] as a compiler. An equational theory for QML was developed by Altenkirch, Grattage, Vizzoto, and Sabry [20]. Notably, QML is the first quantum programming language with quantum control, but it was defined in a way very different from that presented in Chapters 11 and 12. The recent highlight of functional quantum programming is the implementation of languages Quipper [187,188] and LIQUi|> [405]: the former is an embedded language using Haskell as its host language, and the later is embedded in F#.

The control flow of all quantum lambda calculus defined in the literature as well as functional quantum programming languages (except QML) is classical. So, an interesting topic for further research is to incorporate quantum control (case statement, choice, and recursion) introduced in Chapters 11 and 12 into quantum lambda calculus and functional quantum programming.

13.4 Categorical semantics of quantum programs

In this book, semantics of quantum programming languages have been defined in the standard Hilbert space formalism of quantum mechanics. Abramsky and Coecke [5,6] proposed a category-theoretic axiomatisation of quantum mechanics. This novel axiomatisation has been successfully used to address a series of problems in quantum foundations and quantum information. In particular, it provides effective methods for high-level description and verification of quantum communication protocols, including teleportation, logic-gate teleportation, and entanglement swapping. Furthermore, a logic of strongly compact closed categories with biproducts in the form of proof-net calculus was developed by Abramsky and Duncan [7] as a categorical quantum logic. It is particularly suitable for high-level reasoning about quantum processes.

A powerful tool for graphical representation of quantum computation, namely the ZX calculus [101,246], stemmed from categorical quantum mechanics. It has been successfully applied in various areas; in particular, optimisation of quantum circuits [136] and the t|ket> compiler [112] as well as verification of quantum error-correction code [137].

Heunen and Jacobs [205] investigated quantum logic from the perspective of categorical logic, and they showed that kernel subobjects in dagger kernel categories precisely capture orthomodular structure. Jacobs [226] introduced the block construct for quantum programming languages in a categorical manner. More recently, he [227] proposed a categorical axiomatisation of quantitative logic for quantum systems where quantum measurements are defined in terms of instruments that may have a side-effect on the observed system. He further used it to define a dynamic logic with test operators that is very useful for reasoning about quantum programs and protocols.

Some categories of operator algebras (e.g. W^*-algebras) have also been constructed for defining semantics of quantum programming languages [97].

Further applications of category-theoretic techniques to quantum programming will certainly be a fruitful direction of research. In particular, it is desirable to have a categorical characterisation of quantum case statement and quantum choice defined in Chapter 11 and quantum recursion based on second quantisation defined in Chapter 12.

13.5 From concurrent quantum programs to quantum concurrency

As discussed in Chapters 9 and 10, the studies of concurrent quantum programs, including parallel and distributed quantum programs, have been conducted mainly along the following two lines:

- Despite convincing demonstration of quantum computing hardwares, it is still beyond the ability of the current technology to scale them to the level of practical applications. So, it was conceived to use the physical resources of two or more small capacity quantum computers to form a large capacity quantum computing system, and various experiments in the physical implementation of parallel and distributed quantum computing have been reported in recent years. Concurrency is then an unavoidable issue in programming such parallel and distributed quantum computing systems. A basic theoretical model of parallel quantum programming (with shared variables/memories) was presented in Chapter 9. Two more practical models of parallel and distributed quantum programming, namely QParallel and QMPI, were introduced by Häner, Kliuchnikov, Roetteler, Soeken, and Vaschillo [198] and Häner, Steiger, Hoefler, and Troyer [197], respectively.
- Process algebras are popular formal models for the description of interactions, communications, and synchronisation between processes. To provide formal techniques for modelling, analysis, and verification of quantum communication and cryptographic protocols, several quantum generalisations of process algebras have been proposed, including Gay and Nagarajan's CQP [169,170], Jorrand and Lalire's QPAlg [235,265]. In particular, qCCS introduced in Chapter 10 is a natural quantum extension [147,148,429] of classical value-passing CCS. The central notion of bisimulation between processes and its several variants, e.g. symbolic bisimulation [145], branching bisimulation [265] and approximate bisimulations/bisimulation metrics [149,429], have been generalised to various quantum process algebras. Quantum process algebras have been used in verification of correctness and security of quantum cryptographic protocols, quantum error-correction codes, and linear optical quantum computing [32,33,121,122,161,162,174,257,259,416].

Understanding the combined bizarre behaviour of concurrent and quantum systems is extremely hard. Almost all existing work in this direction can be appropriately termed as *concurrent quantum programming* but not *quantum concurrent programming*; for example, a *concurrent quantum program* is defined by Yu et al. [444] as a collection of quantum processes together with a kind of *classical* fairness that is used to schedule the execution of the involved processes. However, the behaviour of a *quantum concurrent program* is much more complicated. We need to very carefully define its execution model because a series of new problems arises in the quantum setting:

1. *Interleaving* abstraction has been widely used in the analysis of classical concurrent programs. But entanglement between different quantum processes forces us to restrict its applications. Superposition-of-programs defined in Chapters 11 and 12 adds another dimension of difficulty to this problem; for example, how can the summation operator in quantum process algebras be replaced by a quantum choice?

2. Research in physics reveals that certain new *synchronisation* mechanisms are possible in the quantum regime; for example, entanglement can be used to overcome certain classical limit in synchronisation [176]. An interesting question is: how to incorporate such new synchronisation mechanisms into quantum concurrent programming?

3. We still do not know how to define a notion of fairness that can better embody both the quantum feature of the participating processes and the entanglement between them. A possible way to do this is further generalising the idea of "quantum coins" and employing some ideas from quantum games [139,300] to control the processes in a quantum concurrent program.

13.6 Entanglement in quantum programming

It has been realised from the very beginning of quantum computing research that entanglement is one of the most important resources that enable a quantum computer to outperform its classical counterpart. The effect of entanglement in parallel quantum programs was carefully examined in Chapter 9, and that in distributed quantum programs was implicitly (but not explicitly) considered in Chapter 10. Here, we introduce several pieces of other work on entanglement that has direct or potential connections to quantum programming.

The role of entanglement in sequential quantum computation has been carefully analysed by several researchers; see for example [237]. Abstract interpretation techniques were employed by Jorrand and Perdrix [236] and Honda [214] to analyse entanglement evolution in quantum programming written in a language similar to the quantum **while**-language defined in Chapter 5. The compiler [230] of quantum programming language Scaffold [4] facilitates a conservative analysis of entanglement. It was observed in [430] that information leakage can be caused by an entanglement, and thus the Trojan Horse may exploit an entanglement between itself and a user with sensitive information as a covert channel. This presents a challenge to programming language-based information-flow security in quantum computing.

Certainly, entanglement is more essential in parallel and distributed quantum computation than in sequential quantum computation [81,98]. Except those discussed in Chapters 9 and 10, an algebraic language for specifying distributed quantum computing circuits and entanglement resources was defined in [425]. It was also noticed in [147–149,429] that entanglement brings extra difficulties to defining bisimulations preserved by parallel composition in quantum process algebras. Conversely, quantum process algebras provide us with a formal framework for further examining the role of entanglement in concurrent quantum computation. In the last section, we already mentioned the possible influence of entanglement on interleaving abstraction in the execution models of quantum concurrent programs.

I expect that research on entanglement in quantum programming, especially in the mode of parallel, concurrent and distributed computing, will be fruitful.

13.7 Model-checking quantum systems

Analysis and verification techniques for quantum programs (with classical control) were studied in Chapters 6 and 8. A nature extension of this line of research is model-checking quantum programs and communication protocols. Actually, several model-checking techniques have been developed in the last decade not only for quantum programs but also for general quantum systems.

The earlier work mainly targeted at checking quantum communication protocols. Gay, Nagarajan, and Papanikolaou [171,330] used the probabilistic model-checker PRISM [263] to verify the correctness of several quantum protocols including BB84 [52]. Furthermore, they [173] developed an automatic tool QMC (Quantum Model-Checker). QMC uses the stabiliser formalism [318] for the modelling of systems, and the properties to be checked by QMC are expressed in Baltazar, Chadha, Mateus, and Sernadas's quantum computation tree logic [42,43,295].

However, to develop model-checking techniques for general quantum systems, including quantum programs, at least the following two problems must be carefully addressed:

- We need to clearly define a conceptual framework in which we can properly reason about quantum systems, including (1) *formal models of quantum systems*, and (2) *specification languages suited to formalise the properties of quantum systems to be checked*.
- The state spaces of the classical systems that model-checking techniques can be applied to are usually finite or countably infinite. But the state spaces of quantum systems are inherently continuous even when they are finite-dimensional, so we

have to explore mathematical structures of the state spaces so that it suffices to examine only a finite number of (or at most countably infinitely many) representative elements, e.g. those in an orthonormal basis.

The models of quantum systems considered in the current literature on quantum model-checking are either quantum automata or quantum Markov chains and Markov decision processes. The actions in a quantum automaton are described by unitary transformations. Quantum Markov models can be seen as a generalisation of quantum automata where actions are depicted by general quantum operations (or superoperators).

Since some key issues in model-checking can be reduced to the reachability problem, reachability analysis of quantum Markov chains presented in Section 8.4.4 provides a basis of quantum model-checking. The issue of checking linear-time properties of quantum systems was considered in [431], where a linear-time property is defined to be an infinite sequence of sets of atomic propositions modelled by closed subspaces of the state Hilbert spaces. But model-checking more general temporal properties are still totally untouched. Indeed, we even do not know how to properly define a general temporal logic for quantum systems, although this problem has been studied by physicists for quite a long time (see [228] for example). A particularly interesting issue is to define an appropriate temporal logic for specifying and reasoning about quantum trajectories [77] and develop algorithms for checking consistent histories of quantum systems [189].

Another kind of quantum Markov chains were introduced by Gudder [192] and Feng et al. [157], which can be more appropriately termed as superoperator valued Markov chains because they are defined by replacing transition probabilities in a classical Markov chain with superoperators. Feng et al. [157] further noticed that superoperator valued Markov chains are especially convenient for a higher-level description of quantum programs and protocols and developed model-checking techniques for them, where a logic called QCTL (quantum computation tree logic, different from that in [42]) was defined by replacing probabilities in PCTL (probabilistic computation tree logic) with superoperators. A model-checker based on [157] was implemented by Feng, Hahn, Turrini, and Zhang [150]. Furthermore, reachability problem for recursive superoperator valued Markov chains was studied by Feng et al. [156].

The book [428] gives a systematic exposition of the existing results in the field of model-checking quantum systems.

13.8 Programming techniques for quantum machine learning

Quantum machine learning [62] and variational quantum algorithms [84] have been widely identified as one of the earliest practical applications of quantum computing, and arguably will be one of the major applications in the NISQ era. Examples include learning algorithms stimulated by the HHL (Harrow–Hassidim–Lloyd) algorithm for systems of linear equations [2,286,287,349], quantum neural networks [50,104], and variational eigen-solver (VQE) [337]. Similar to classical machine learning, a basic model of these quantum algorithms is parameterised quantum circuits, and gradient-based methods are then employed to train them. In particular, automatic differentiation techniques that have been extensively used in classical machine learning for efficient computation of gradients have been generalised into the quantum setting [57,365].

By noticing the benefit of introducing program control flows into neural networks, a new programming paradigm, called differential programming [3,96,167], has been developed in recent years. One of its main advantages is that programs become parameterised and the parameters in them can be optimised by gradient-based methods. This paradigm has quickly been generalised into quantum computing. Zhu, Hung, Chakrabarti, and Wu [454] defined a parameterised version of quantum **while**-language studied in Chapter 5, and developed automatic differentiation techniques as well as a series of code-transformation rules for parameterised quantum programs with bounded **while**-loops. The main results of [454] were extended by Fang et al. [143] to unbounded loops by introducing a randomised estimator for derivatives to handle the infinite sum in the differentiation of unbounded loops.

Another approach to programming variational quantum algorithms was proposed in [232], where by observing that variational quantum algorithms are always hybrid classical-quantum algorithms, a language that can manipulate both classical and quantum data was designed for programming them. The classical part of the language is a probabilistic variant of lambda calculus, and the quantum part is a first-order type system. A denotational semantics of the language was rigorously defined. But a key issue of supporting gradient-based optimisation of parameters in variational quantum algorithms in this language was not addressed yet.

13.9 Quantum programming applied to physics

Of course, the subject of quantum programming has been developed mainly with the purpose of programming future quantum computers. However, some ideas, methodologies, and techniques in quantum programming may also be applied to quantum physics and quantum engineering.

The hypothesis that *the universe is a quantum computer* has been proposed by several leading physicists [285,394]. If you agree with this view, I would like to argue that *God (or the nature) is a quantum programmer*. Furthermore, I believe that translating various ideas from programming theory to quantum physics will produce some novel insights. For example, the notion of quantum weakest precondition defined in Section 6.1 may provide with us a new way for backward analysis of physical systems. Recently, Hoare logic has been extended to reason about dynamical systems with continuous evolution described by differential equations [72,340]. It is interesting to develop a logic based on this work and quantum Hoare logic presented in Chapter 6 that can be used to reason about continuous-time quantum systems governed by Schrödinger equation.

As pointed out by Dowling and Milburn [134], we are currently in the midst of a second quantum revolution – *transition from quantum theory to quantum engineering*. The aim of quantum theory is to find fundamental rules that govern the physical systems already existing in the nature. Instead, quantum engineering intends to design and implement new systems (machines, devices, etc) that do not exist before to accomplish some desirable tasks, based on quantum theory.

Experiences in today's engineering indicate that it is not guaranteed that a human designer completely understands the behaviours of the systems she/he designed, and a bug in her/his design may cause some serious problems and even disasters. So, correctness, safety, and reliability of complex engineering systems have been a key issue in various engineering fields. Certainly, it will be even more serious in quantum engineering than in today's engineering because it is much harder for a system designer to understand the behaviours of quantum systems. The verification and analysis techniques for quantum programs may be adapted to design and implement automatic tools for correctness and safety verification of quantum engineering systems. Moreover, (a continuous-time extension of) model-checking techniques for quantum systems discussed in Section 13.7 are obviously useful in quantum engineering. It is sure that this line of research combined with quantum simulation [99,284] will be fruitful.

Appendix A

Omitted proofs in the main text

A.1   Omitted proofs in Chapter 5

Several lemmas about the domains of partial density operators and quantum operations were presented without proofs in Section 5.3.2. For completeness, we give their proofs in this section.

Spectral decomposition: The proof of Lemma 5.2 requires the notion of square root of a positive operator, which in turn requires the spectral decomposition theorem for Hermitian operators in an infinite-dimensional Hilbert space $\mathcal{H}$. Recall from Definition 2.16 that an operator $M \in \mathcal{L}(\mathcal{H})$ is Hermitian if $M^\dagger = M$. As defined in Section 2.2, a projector P_X is associated with each closed subspace X of $\mathcal{H}$. A spectral family in $\mathcal{H}$ is a family

$$\{E_\lambda\}_{-\infty < \lambda < +\infty}$$

of projectors indexed by real numbers λ satisfying the following conditions:

1. $E_{\lambda_1} \sqsubseteq E_{\lambda_2}$ whenever $\lambda_1 \leq \lambda_2$;
2. $E_\lambda = \lim_{\mu \to \lambda+} E_\mu$ for each λ; and
3. $\lim_{\lambda \to -\infty} E_\lambda = 0_\mathcal{H}$ and $\lim_{\lambda \to +\infty} E_\lambda = I_\mathcal{H}$.

Theorem A.1 (Spectral decomposition; [344], Theorem III.6.3). *If M is a Hermitian operator with $spec(M) \subseteq [a, b]$, then there is a spectral family $\{E_\lambda\}$ such that*

$$M = \int_a^b \lambda d E_\lambda,$$

where the integral in the right-hand side is defined to be an operator satisfying the following condition: for any $\epsilon > 0$, there exists $\delta > 0$ such that for any $n \geq 1$ and $x_0, x_1, ..., x_{n-1}, x_n, y_1, ..., y_{n-1}, y_n$ with

$$a = x_0 \leq y_1 \leq x_1 \leq ... \leq y_{n-1} \leq x_{n-1} \leq y_n \leq x_n = b,$$

it holds that

$$d\left(\int_a^b \lambda d E_\lambda, \sum_{i=1}^n y_i (E_{x_i} - E_{x_{i-1}})\right) < \epsilon$$

whenever $\max_{i=1}^n (x_i - x_{i-1}) < \delta$. Here, $d(\cdot, \cdot)$ stands for the distance between operators (see Definition 2.14).

Now we are able to define the square root of a positive operator A. Since A is a Hermitian operator, it enjoys a spectral decomposition:

$$A = \int \lambda d E_\lambda.$$

Then its square root is defined to be

$$\sqrt{A} = \int \sqrt{\lambda} d E_\lambda.$$

With the above preliminaries, we can give:

Proof of Lemma 5.2. First, for any positive operator A, we get:

$$|\langle \varphi | A | \psi \rangle|^2 = \left|\left(\sqrt{A}|\varphi\rangle, \sqrt{A}|\psi\rangle\right)\right|^2 \leq \langle \varphi | A | \varphi \rangle \langle \psi | A | \psi \rangle \tag{A.1}$$

by the Cauchy–Schwarz inequality (see [318], page 68).

Now let $\{\rho_n\}$ be an increasing sequence in $(\mathcal{D}(\mathcal{H}), \sqsubseteq)$. For any $|\psi\rangle \in \mathcal{H}$, put $A = \rho_n - \rho_m$ and $|\varphi\rangle = A|\psi\rangle$. Then

$$\langle\psi|A|\psi\rangle \leq \langle\psi|\rho_n|\psi\rangle \leq \|\psi\|^2 \cdot tr(\rho_n) \leq \|\psi\|^2,$$

and similarly we have $\langle\varphi|A|\varphi\rangle \leq \|\varphi\|^2$. Thus, it follows from Eq. (A.1) that

$$|\langle\varphi|A|\psi\rangle|^2 \leq \|\psi\|^2 \cdot \|\varphi\|^2.$$

Furthermore, we obtain:

$$
\begin{aligned}
\|A\|^4 &= \sup_{|\psi\rangle \neq 0} \frac{\|A|\psi\rangle\|^4}{\|\psi\|^4} \\
&= \sup_{|\psi\rangle \neq 0} \frac{\langle\varphi|A|\psi\rangle^2}{\|\psi\|^4} \\
&\leq \sup_{|\psi\rangle \neq 0} \frac{\|\varphi\|^2}{\|\psi\|^2} \\
&= \sup_{|\psi\rangle \neq 0} \frac{\|A|\psi\rangle\|^2}{\|\psi\|^2} = \|A\|^2
\end{aligned}
$$

and $\|A\| \leq 1$. This leads to

$$
\begin{aligned}
\langle\varphi|A|\varphi\rangle &= \left(A\sqrt{A}|\psi\rangle, A\sqrt{A}|\psi\rangle\right) \\
&= \left\|A\sqrt{A}|\psi\rangle\right\|^2 \\
&\leq \|A\|^2 \cdot \left\|\sqrt{A}|\psi\rangle\right\|^2 \\
&= \left(\sqrt{A}|\psi\rangle, \sqrt{A}|\psi\rangle\right) \\
&= \langle\psi|A|\psi\rangle.
\end{aligned}
$$

Using Eq. (A.1) once again we get:

$$
\begin{aligned}
\||\rho_n|\psi\rangle - \rho_m|\psi\rangle\|^4 &= |\langle\varphi|A|\psi\rangle|^2 \\
&\leq \langle\psi|A|\psi\rangle^2 = |\langle\psi|\rho_n|\psi\rangle - \langle\psi|\rho_m|\psi\rangle|^2.
\end{aligned}
\tag{A.2}
$$

Note that $\{\langle\psi|\rho_n|\psi\rangle\}$ is an increasing sequence of real numbers bounded by $\|\psi\|^2$, and thus it is a Cauchy sequence. This together with Eq. (A.2) implies that $\{\rho_n|\psi\rangle\}$ is a Cauchy sequence in $\mathcal{H}$. So, we can define:

$$\left(\lim_{n\to\infty} \rho_n\right)|\psi\rangle = \lim_{n\to\infty} \rho_n|\psi\rangle.$$

Furthermore, for any complex numbers $\lambda_1, \lambda_2 \in \mathbb{C}$ and $|\psi_1\rangle, |\psi_2\rangle \in \mathcal{H}$, it holds that

$$
\begin{aligned}
\left(\lim_{n\to\infty} \rho_n\right)(\lambda_1|\psi_1\rangle + \lambda_2|\psi_2\rangle) &= \lim_{n\to\infty} \rho_n(\lambda_1|\psi_1\rangle + \lambda_2|\psi_2\rangle) \\
&= \lim_{n\to\infty} (\lambda_1\rho_n|\psi_1\rangle + \lambda_2\rho_n|\psi_2\rangle) \\
&= \lambda_1 \lim_{n\to\infty} \rho_n|\psi_1\rangle + \lambda_2 \lim_{n\to\infty} \rho_n|\psi_2\rangle \\
&= \lambda_1 \left(\lim_{n\to\infty} \rho_n\right)|\psi_1\rangle + \lambda_2 \left(\lim_{n\to\infty} \rho_n\right)|\psi_2\rangle,
\end{aligned}
$$

and $\lim_{n\to\infty} \rho_n$ is a linear operator. For any $|\psi\rangle \in \mathcal{H}$, we have:

$$\langle\psi|\lim_{n\to\infty} \rho_n|\psi\rangle = \left(|\psi\rangle, \lim_{n\to\infty} \rho_n|\psi\rangle\right) = \lim_{n\to\infty} \langle\psi|\rho_n|\psi\rangle \geq 0.$$

Thus, $\lim_{n\to\infty}\rho_n$ is positive. Let $\{|\psi_i\rangle\}$ be an orthonormal basis of $\mathcal{H}$. Then

$$
\begin{aligned}
tr\left(\lim_{n\to\infty}\rho_n\right) &= \sum_i \langle\psi_i|\lim_{n\to\infty}\rho_n|\psi_i\rangle \\
&= \sum_i\left(|\psi_i\rangle,\lim_{n\to\infty}\rho_n|\psi_i\rangle\right) \\
&= \lim_{n\to\infty}\sum_i\langle\psi_i|\rho_n|\psi_i\rangle \\
&= \lim_{n\to\infty}tr(\rho_n)\le 1,
\end{aligned}
$$

and $\lim_{n\to\infty}\rho_n\in\mathcal{D}(\mathcal{H})$. So, it suffices to show that

$$
\lim_{n\to\infty}\rho_n=\bigsqcup_{n=0}^{\infty}\rho_n;
$$

that is,

1. $\rho_m\sqsubseteq\lim_{n\to\infty}\rho_n$ for all $m\ge 0$; and
2. if $\rho_m\sqsubseteq\rho$ for all $m\ge 0$, then $\lim_{n\to\infty}\rho_n\sqsubseteq\rho$.

Note that for any positive operators B and C, $B\sqsubseteq C$ if and only if $\langle\psi|B|\psi\rangle\le\langle\psi|C|\psi\rangle$ for all $|\psi\rangle\in\mathcal{H}$. Then both (i) and (ii) follow immediately from

$$
\langle\psi|\lim_{n\to\infty}\rho_n|\psi\rangle=\lim_{n\to\infty}\langle\psi|\rho_n|\psi\rangle.
$$

This completes the proof of Lemma 5.2. $\qquad\square$

The proof of Lemma 5.3 can be easily done based on Lemma 5.2.

Proof of Lemma 5.3. Suppose that $\mathcal{E}$ is a quantum operation with Kraus representation $\mathcal{E}=\sum_i E_i\circ E_i^\dagger$ (see Theorem 2.3), and $\{\rho_n\}$ is an increasing sequence in $\mathcal{D}(\mathcal{H})$. Then by Lemma 5.2 we obtain:

$$
\begin{aligned}
\mathcal{E}\left(\bigsqcup_n\rho_n\right) &= \mathcal{E}\left(\lim_{n\to\infty}\rho_n\right) \\
&= \sum_i E_i\left(\lim_{n\to\infty}\rho_n\right)E_i^\dagger \\
&= \lim_{n\to\infty}\sum_i E_i\rho_n E_i^\dagger \\
&= \lim_{n\to\infty}\mathcal{E}(\rho_n) \\
&= \bigsqcup_n\mathcal{E}(\rho_n). \qquad\square
\end{aligned}
$$

Finally, we can prove Lemma 5.4.

Proof of Lemma 5.4. Let $\{\mathcal{E}_n\}$ be an increasing sequence in $(QO(\mathcal{H}),\sqsubseteq)$. Then for any $\rho\in\mathcal{D}(\mathcal{H})$, $\{\mathcal{E}_n(\rho)\}$ is an increasing sequence in $(\mathcal{D}(\mathcal{H}),\sqsubseteq)$. With Lemma 5.2 we can define:

$$
\left(\bigsqcup_n\mathcal{E}_n\right)(\rho)=\bigsqcup_n\mathcal{E}_n(\rho)=\lim_{n\to\infty}\mathcal{E}_n(\rho),
$$

and it holds that

$$
tr\left(\left(\bigsqcup_n\mathcal{E}_n\right)(\rho)\right)=tr\left(\lim_{n\to\infty}\mathcal{E}_n(\rho)\right)=\lim_{n\to\infty}tr(\mathcal{E}_n(\rho))\le 1
$$

because $tr(\cdot)$ is continuous. Furthermore, $\bigsqcup_n \mathcal{E}_n$ can be defined on the whole of $\mathcal{L}(\mathcal{H})$ by linearity. The defining equation of $\bigsqcup_n \mathcal{E}_n$ implies:

1. $\mathcal{E}_m \sqsubseteq \bigsqcup_n \mathcal{E}_n$ for all $m \geq 0$;
2. if $\mathcal{E}_m \sqsubseteq \mathcal{F}$ for all $m \geq 0$ then $\bigsqcup_n \mathcal{E}_n \sqsubseteq \mathcal{F}$.

So, it suffices to show that $\bigsqcup_n \mathcal{E}_n$ is completely positive. Suppose that $\mathcal{H}_R$ is an extra Hilbert space. For any $C \in \mathcal{L}(\mathcal{H}_R)$ and $D \in \mathcal{L}(\mathcal{H})$, we have:

$$
\left(\mathcal{I}_R \otimes \bigsqcup_n \mathcal{E}_n \right)(C \otimes D) = C \otimes \left(\bigsqcup_n \mathcal{E}_n \right)(D)
$$

$$
= C \otimes \lim_{n \to \infty} \mathcal{E}_n(D)
$$

$$
= \lim_{n \to \infty} (C \otimes \mathcal{E}_n(D))
$$

$$
= \lim_{n \to \infty} (\mathcal{I}_R \otimes \mathcal{E}_n)(C \otimes D).
$$

Then for any $A \in \mathcal{L}(\mathcal{H}_R \otimes \mathcal{H})$ we get:

$$
\left(\mathcal{I}_R \otimes \bigsqcup_n \mathcal{E}_n \right)(A) = \lim_{n \to \infty} (\mathcal{I}_R \otimes \mathcal{E}_n)(A)
$$

by linearity. Thus, if A is positive, then $(\mathcal{I}_R \otimes \mathcal{E}_n)(A)$ is positive for all n, and $\left(\mathcal{I}_R \otimes \bigsqcup_n \mathcal{E}_n \right)(A)$ is positive. $\square$

A.2 Omitted proofs in Chapter 6

Let us first recall from [350] the notions of weak and strong convergence in functional analysis, which are needed when the state Hilbert space of a quantum program is infinite-dimensional.

Definition A.1. Let $\{A_n\}$ be a sequence of operators on a separable Hilbert space $\mathcal{H}$. Then:

1. $\{A_n\}$ weakly converges to an operator A, written: $A_n \xrightarrow{w.o.t.} A$, if for all $|\psi\rangle, |\phi\rangle \in \mathcal{H}$,

$$
\lim_{n \to \infty} \langle \psi | A_n | \phi \rangle = \langle \psi | A | \phi \rangle.
$$

2. $\{A_n\}$ strongly converges to an operator A, written: $A_n \xrightarrow{s.o.t.} A$, if for all $|\psi\rangle \in \mathcal{H}$,

$$
\lim_{n \to \infty} \| (A_n - A)|\psi\rangle \| = 0.
$$

Lemma A.1. $A_n \xrightarrow{s.o.t.} A$ implies $A_n \xrightarrow{w.o.t.} A$.

The next lemma gives a characterisation of weak convergence of operators (and thus, quantum predicates) in terms of convergence of traces, which are complex numbers.

Lemma A.2. *For quantum predicates $\{A_n\}$ and A in $\mathcal{H}$, $A_n \xrightarrow{w.o.t.} A$ if and only if for all $\rho \in \mathcal{D}(\mathcal{H})$,*

$$
\lim_{n \to \infty} \mathrm{tr}(A_n \rho) = \mathrm{tr}(A\rho). \tag{A.3}
$$

Proof. ($\Leftarrow$) For $|\psi\rangle \in \mathcal{H}$, we have $\rho = |\psi\rangle\langle\psi| / \||\psi\rangle\|^2 \in \mathcal{D}(\mathcal{H})$. Then (A.3) implies:

$$
\lim_{n \to \infty} \mathrm{tr}\left((A_n - A) \frac{|\psi\rangle\langle\psi|}{\||\psi\rangle\|^2} \right) = 0 \quad \Rightarrow \quad \lim_{n \to \infty} (A_n|\psi\rangle, |\psi\rangle) = (A|\psi\rangle, |\psi\rangle),
$$

which leads to the definition of weak operator convergence.

($\Rightarrow$) For any $\epsilon > 0$ and $\rho \in \mathcal{D}(\mathcal{H})$, we assume the spectral decomposition:

$$
\rho = \sum_{i=1}^{\infty} \lambda_i |\psi_i\rangle\langle\psi_i|.
$$

Then there exists integer N such that for all $k \geq N$,

$$\mathrm{tr}\left(\sum_{i \geq N} \lambda_i |\psi_i\rangle\langle\psi_i|\right) = \sum_{i \geq N} \lambda_i \leq \epsilon$$

because $\sum_{i=1}^{\infty} \lambda \leq 1$. On the other hand, as $A_n \xrightarrow{w.o.t.} A$, there exists integer M such that for all $m \geq M$:

$$\forall i < N, \quad |\mathrm{tr}(A_m|\psi_i\rangle\langle\psi_i|) - \mathrm{tr}(A|\psi_i\rangle\langle\psi_i|)| \leq \epsilon.$$

Since A_m, A arc quantum predicates; that is, $0 \sqsubseteq A_m$, $A \sqsubseteq I$, we have $\|A_m - A\|_1 \leq 2$. Thus by the Cauchy–Schwarz inequality, we obtain:

$$|\mathrm{tr}(A_m\rho) - \mathrm{tr}(A\rho)| = \left|\mathrm{tr}\left((A_m - A)\sum_{i<N}\lambda_i|\psi_i\rangle\langle\psi_i|\right) + \mathrm{tr}\left((A_m - A)\sum_{i \geq N}\lambda_i|\psi_i\rangle\langle\psi_i|\right)\right|$$

$$\leq \sum_{i<N}\lambda_i \max_{i<N}|\mathrm{tr}((A_m - A)|\psi_i\rangle\langle\psi_i|)| + \|A_m - A\|_1 \mathrm{tr}\left(\sum_{i \geq N}\lambda_i|\psi_i\rangle\langle\psi_i|\right)$$

$$\leq \epsilon + 2\epsilon = 3\epsilon \qquad \square$$

Now we are ready to present:

Proof of Lemma 6.8.5. We only prove soundness of (R.Lim) for partial correctness. The case of total correctness is similar. For any $\rho \in \mathcal{D}(\mathcal{H}_{all})$ and for each n, according to the assumption $\models_{par} \{A_n\} P\{B_n\}$, we have:

$$\mathrm{tr}(A_n\rho) \leq \mathrm{tr}\left(B_n[\![P]\!](\rho)\right) + [\mathrm{tr}(\rho) - \mathrm{tr}([\![P]\!](\rho))],$$

and we can take $n \to \infty$ to obtain:

$$\lim_{n\to\infty} \mathrm{tr}(A_n\rho) \leq \lim_{n\to\infty} \mathrm{tr}\left(B_n[\![P]\!](\rho)\right) + [\mathrm{tr}(\rho) - \mathrm{tr}([\![P]\!](\rho))].$$

On the other hand, it is assumed that $A_n \xrightarrow{w.o.t.} A$ and $B_n \xrightarrow{w.o.t.} B$. So, it follows from Lemma A.2 that

$$\mathrm{tr}(A\rho) \leq \mathrm{tr}(B[\![P]\!](\rho)) + \mathrm{tr}(\rho) - \mathrm{tr}([\![P]\!](\rho)).$$

Thus, $\models_{par} \{A\} P\{B\}$. $\qquad \square$

A.3 Omitted proofs in Chapter 7

A.3.1 Technical preparations

In the proofs of various results of Chapter 7 that will be presented in the subsequent subsections, we need a series of technical results about quantum states, subspaces of Hilbert spaces, and quantum operations. We collect and prove them in this subsection so that they can be directly used there.

Restriction of quantum states: We first prove some technical results needed in proving Lemmas 7.3(1) and 7.5(1). To this end, let us recall the following:

Definition A.2. 1. Let $\rho \in \mathcal{D}(\mathcal{H})$ and $X \in S(\mathcal{H})$. Then we define:

$$\rho \in X \text{ iff } \mathrm{supp}(\rho) \subseteq X.$$

2. Let $\rho \in \mathcal{D}(\mathcal{H}_1 \otimes \mathcal{H}_2)$. Then its restriction on $\mathcal{H}_1$ is defined as

$$\rho \downarrow \mathcal{H}_1 = \mathrm{tr}_{\mathcal{H}_2}(\rho).$$

Then we can present the required technical results as the following three lemmas:

Lemma A.3. *Let $\rho \in \mathcal{D}(\mathcal{H}_1 \otimes \mathcal{H}_2)$ and $X \in \mathcal{S}(\mathcal{H}_1)$. Then: $\rho \downarrow \mathcal{H}_1 \in X$ iff $\rho \in X \otimes \mathcal{H}_2$.*

Proof. Let $\{|i\rangle\}$ be an orthonormal basis of $\mathcal{H}_2$. Then we have: for any $|\Psi\rangle \in \mathcal{H}_1 \otimes \mathcal{H}_2$,

- *Claim*: $|\Psi\rangle \in X \otimes \mathcal{H}_2$ iff for all i, $\langle i|\Psi\rangle \in X$.

In fact, if $|\Psi\rangle \in X \otimes \mathcal{H}_2$, then we can write $|\Psi\rangle = \sum_i \alpha_i |\psi_i\rangle|i\rangle$ such that $|\psi_i\rangle \in X$ for all i. Thus, for each i', $\langle i'|\Psi\rangle = \alpha'_i|\psi_{i'}\rangle \in X$. Conversely, if $\langle i|\Psi\rangle \in X$ for all i, then we can write $|\Psi\rangle = \sum_{i'} \alpha_{i'}|\psi_{i'}\rangle|i'\rangle$ with $|\psi_{i'}\rangle \in \mathcal{H}_2$ and $\alpha_{i'} \neq 0$ for all i', and $\langle i|\Psi\rangle = \alpha_i|\psi_i\rangle \in X$, which implies $|\psi_i\rangle \in X$. Consequently, $|\Psi\rangle \in X \otimes \mathcal{H}_2$.

Now we assume the spectral decomposition $\rho = \sum_j p_j |\Psi_j\rangle\langle\Psi_j|$ with $p_j > 0$ for all j. Then it holds that $\mathrm{supp}(\rho) = \bigvee_j |\Psi_j\rangle\langle\Psi_j|$, and

$$\mathrm{supp}(\rho \downarrow \mathcal{H}_1) = \mathrm{supp}(\mathrm{tr}_{\mathcal{H}_2}\rho) = \mathrm{supp}\left(\sum_i \langle i|\rho|i\rangle\right) = \bigvee_i \mathrm{supp}\langle i|\rho|i\rangle$$

$$= \bigvee_i \mathrm{supp}\left(\sum_j p_i \langle i|\Psi_j\rangle\langle\Psi_j|i\rangle\right) = \bigvee_{i,j} \langle i|\Psi_j\rangle\langle\Psi_j|i\rangle$$

where (and in the sequel) $\bigvee$ stands for the join of closed subspaces (see Eq. (7.12) for its definition). Therefore, by the above claim, we obtain:

$$\mathrm{supp}(\rho \downarrow \mathcal{H}_1) \subseteq X \Leftrightarrow \text{ for all } i, j, \langle i|\Psi_j\rangle \in X$$
$$\Leftrightarrow \text{ for all } j, |\Psi_j\rangle \in X \otimes \mathcal{H}_2$$
$$\Leftrightarrow \mathrm{supp}(\rho) \subseteq X \otimes \mathcal{H}_2. \qquad \square$$

Lemma A.4. *Let $\rho_i \in \mathcal{D}(\mathcal{H}_1 \otimes \mathcal{H}_2)$ and $p_i \geq 0$ for each i, and $\sum_i p_i \leq 1$. Then*

$$\left(\sum_i p_i \rho_i\right) \downarrow \mathcal{H}_1 = \sum_i p_i (\rho_i \downarrow \mathcal{H}_1).$$

Proof. Routine by definition and some basic properties of partial trace. $\qquad \square$

Lemma A.5. *Let $\rho, \sigma, \sigma' \in \mathcal{D}(\mathcal{H}_1 \otimes \mathcal{H}_2)$. If $\sigma \perp \sigma'$ does not holds and $\rho \downarrow \mathcal{H}_1 = \sigma \downarrow \mathcal{H}_1$, then there exists ρ' such that $\rho \perp \rho'$ does not holds and $\rho' \downarrow \mathcal{H}_1 = \sigma' \downarrow \mathcal{H}_1$.*

Proof. We choose $\rho' = (\sigma' \downarrow \mathcal{H}_1) \otimes I_{\mathcal{H}_2}/\dim(\mathcal{H}_2)$. It is easy to verify that ρ' satisfies the stated conditions. $\qquad \square$

Restriction of subspaces of Hilbert spaces: Now we present some technical results needed in proving Lemma 7.3.2. They will also be used in proving some results in Section 8.5.

Definition A.3. Let $X \in \mathcal{S}(\mathcal{H}_1 \otimes \mathcal{H}_2)$. Then its restriction on $\mathcal{H}_1$ is defined as

$$X \downarrow \mathcal{H}_1 = \mathrm{supp}[\mathrm{tr}_{\mathcal{H}_2}(P_X)]$$

where P_X is the projection operator onto X.

Some basic properties of the restriction of subspaces of Hilbert spaces are given in the following:

Lemma A.6. *Let $X_i \in \mathcal{S}(\mathcal{H}_1 \otimes \mathcal{H}_2)$ for all i. Then*

$$\left(\bigvee_i X_i\right) \downarrow \mathcal{H}_1 = \bigvee_i (X_i \downarrow \mathcal{H}_1), \qquad \left(\bigcap_i X_i\right) \downarrow \mathcal{H}_1 \subseteq \bigcap_i (X_i \downarrow \mathcal{H}_1). \tag{A.4}$$

Proof. The second part (the inclusion) of (A.4) is obvious. To verify the first part (the equality) of (A.4), let us first prove that for any Hermitian operator A on $\mathcal{H}_1 \otimes \mathcal{H}_2$:

$$\text{supp}\left[\text{tr}_{\mathcal{H}_2}(\text{supp}A)\right] = \text{supp}\left(\text{tr}_{\mathcal{H}_2}A\right). \tag{A.5}$$

We can assume that $A = \sum_i \lambda_i |\Psi_i\rangle\langle\Psi_i|$, where $\lambda_i \neq 0$ for each i, and $\{|\Psi_i\rangle\}$ are a family of states in $\mathcal{H}_1 \otimes \mathcal{H}_2$ which are orthogonal to each other. Then $\text{supp}A = \sum_i |\Psi_i\rangle\langle\Psi_i|$ and

$$\text{tr}_{\mathcal{H}_2}(\text{supp}A) = \sum_j \sum_i \langle j|\Psi_i\rangle\langle\Psi_i|j\rangle, \qquad \text{tr}_{\mathcal{H}_2}(A) = \sum_j \sum_i \lambda_i \langle j|\Psi_i\rangle\langle\Psi_i|j\rangle$$

where $\{|j\rangle\}$ is an orthonormal basis of $\mathcal{H}_2$. Note that $\text{supp}(\lambda A) = \text{supp}A$ provided $\lambda \neq 0$. Therefore, we have:

$$\text{supp}\left[\text{tr}_{\mathcal{H}_2}(\text{supp}A)\right] = \bigvee_j \bigvee_i \text{supp}(\langle j|\Psi_i\rangle\langle\Psi_i|j\rangle) = \text{supp}\left(\text{tr}_{\mathcal{H}_2}A\right).$$

Now we obtain:

$$\begin{aligned}
\left(\bigvee_i P_i\right) \downarrow \mathcal{H}_1 &= \text{supp}\left[\text{tr}_{\mathcal{H}_2}\left(\bigvee_i P_i\right)\right] \\
&= \text{supp}\left[\text{tr}_{\mathcal{H}_2}\text{supp}\left(\sum_i P_i\right)\right] \\
&= \text{supp}\left[\text{tr}_{\mathcal{H}_2}\left(\sum_i P_i\right)\right] \qquad \text{By Eq. (A.5)} \\
&= \text{supp}\left[\sum_i \text{tr}_{\mathcal{H}_2}(P_i)\right] \\
&= \bigvee_i \text{supp}\left[\text{tr}_{\mathcal{H}_2}(P_i)\right] \\
&= \bigvee_i (P_i \downarrow \mathcal{H}_1).
\end{aligned}$$

$\square$

Images and preimages of quantum operations: Several key notions in Chapter 7 are defined based on the notions of image and preimage of quantum operations, and many results there are proved using some properties of them. These properties will also be used in proving some results in Section 8.4. So, we collect and prove the properties here.

Definition A.4. Let $\mathcal{E}$ be a quantum operation on Hilbert space $\mathcal{H}$ and $X \in S(\mathcal{H})$. Then:

1. The image of X under $\mathcal{E}$ is defined as

$$\mathcal{E}(X) = \bigvee_{|\psi\rangle \in X} \text{supp}[\mathcal{E}(|\psi\rangle\langle\psi|)]. \tag{A.6}$$

2. The preimage of X under $\mathcal{E}$ is defined as

$$\begin{aligned}
\mathcal{E}^{-1}(X) &= \{|\psi\rangle \in \mathcal{H} : \text{supp}(\mathcal{E}(|\psi\rangle\langle\psi|)) \subseteq X\} \\
&= \bigvee\{Y \in S(\mathcal{H}) : \mathcal{E}(Y) \subseteq X\}.
\end{aligned} \tag{A.7}$$

It is easy to see that $\mathcal{E}(X)$ is the subspace of $\mathcal{H}$ spanned by the images under $\mathcal{E}$ of all states in X. Moreover, $\mathcal{E}^{-1}(X)$ is clearly well-defined as a subspace of $\mathcal{H}$; that is, the right-hand side of (A.7) is indeed a subspace. Actually, it is the maximal subspace Y satisfying that $\mathcal{E}(Y) \subseteq X$.

The needed properties of images and preimages of quantum operations are presented in the following two lemmas:

Lemma A.7. 1. $\mathcal{E}(\text{supp}(\rho)) = \text{supp}(\mathcal{E}(\rho))$.

2. $\mathcal{E}\left(\bigcap_i X_i\right) \subseteq \bigcap_i \mathcal{E}(X_i)$, $\mathcal{E}\left(\bigvee_i X_i\right) = \bigvee_i \mathcal{E}(X_i)$.

3. *Let $\mathcal{E}$ have the Kraus operator-sum representation $\mathcal{E} = \sum_i E_i \circ E_i^\dagger$. Then*

$$\mathcal{E}(X) = \text{span}\,\{E_i|\psi\rangle : i \in I \text{ and } |\psi\rangle \in X\}.$$

4. $\mathcal{E}(X^\perp) \subseteq \mathcal{E}(X)^\perp$. *In particular, if $\mathcal{E}(\mathcal{H}) = \mathcal{H}$, then $\mathcal{E}(X^\perp) = \mathcal{E}(X)^\perp$.*

5. $\mathcal{E}(X \to Y) \subseteq \mathcal{E}(X) \to \mathcal{E}(Y)$, *where $\to$ stands for the Sasaki implication (see Section 7.3.2).*

6. $\mathcal{E}^{-1}(X) = \left(\mathcal{E}^*\left(X^\perp\right)\right)^\perp$, *where $\mathcal{E}^*$ is the (Schrödinger–Heisenberg) dual of $\mathcal{E}$.*

7. $\mathcal{E}^{-1}\left(\bigcap_i X_i\right) = \bigcap_i \mathcal{E}^{-1}(X_i)$, $\mathcal{E}^{-1}\left(\bigvee_i X_i\right) \supseteq \bigvee_i \mathcal{E}^{-1}(X_i)$.

Proof. The proofs of clauses 1–3 are left for the reader as exercises.

4. Since $\mathcal{E}$ is linear, it holds that

$$\mathcal{E}(P_{X^\perp}) + \mathcal{E}(P_X) = \mathcal{E}(P_{X^\perp} + P_X) = \mathcal{E}(I)$$

and $\mathcal{E}(P_{X^\perp}) = \mathcal{E}(I) - \mathcal{E}(P_X)$. Note that $\mathcal{E}$ is trace-nonincreasing. We have $\mathcal{E}(I) \sqsubseteq I$. Therefore, $\mathcal{E}(P_{X^\perp}) \sqsubseteq I - \mathcal{E}(P_X)$. This means that $\mathcal{E}(X^\perp) \subseteq \mathcal{E}(X)^\perp$.

5. By the definition of Sasaki implication, we know that $X \to Y = X^\perp \vee (X \cap Y)$. Therefore, we have:

$$\begin{aligned}
\mathcal{E}(X \to Y) &= \mathcal{E}(X^\perp \vee (X \cap Y)) \\
&= \mathcal{E}(X^\perp) \vee \mathcal{E}(X \cap Y) \\
&\subseteq \mathcal{E}(X^\perp) \vee (\mathcal{E}(X) \cap \mathcal{E}(Y)) \\
&\subseteq \mathcal{E}(X)^\perp \vee (\mathcal{E}(X) \cap \mathcal{E}(Y)) \qquad \text{(By clause 4)} \\
&= \mathcal{E}(X) \to \mathcal{E}(Y).
\end{aligned}$$

6. By duality between $\mathcal{E}$ and $\mathcal{E}^*$, we have:

$$X^\perp \subseteq \mathcal{E}^*(Z^\perp) \Leftrightarrow \mathcal{E}(Z) \subseteq X.$$

Therefore, it holds that

$$\begin{aligned}
\mathcal{E}^*(X^\perp) &= \bigwedge \left\{Y : X^\perp \subseteq \mathcal{E}^*(Y)\right\} \\
&= \bigwedge \left\{Z^\perp : X^\perp \subseteq \mathcal{E}^*(Z^\perp)\right\} \\
&= \bigwedge \left\{Z^\perp : \mathcal{E}(Z) \subseteq X\right\}.
\end{aligned}$$

Consequently, we obtain:

$$\begin{aligned}
\left(\mathcal{E}^*(X^\perp)\right)^\perp &= \left(\bigwedge \left\{Z^\perp : \mathcal{E}(Z) \subseteq X\right\}\right)^\perp \\
&= \bigvee \{Z : \mathcal{E}(Z) \subseteq X\} = \mathcal{E}^{-1}(X).
\end{aligned}$$

7. The second conclusion is obvious. Let us prove the first conclusion. For any ρ,

$$\begin{aligned}
\rho \in \mathcal{E}^{-1}\left(\bigcap_i X_i\right) \text{ iff } \quad & \mathcal{E}(\rho) \in \bigcap_i X_i \\
\text{iff} \quad & \forall i, \mathcal{E}(\rho) \in X_i \\
\text{iff} \quad & \forall i, \rho \in \mathcal{E}^{-1}(X_i) \\
\text{iff} \quad & \rho \in \bigcap_i \mathcal{E}^{-1}(X_i).
\end{aligned}$$

$\square$

Lemma A.8. *Let $X \in S(\mathcal{H}_1 \otimes \mathcal{H}_2)$ and $\mathcal{E}$ be a quantum operation on $\mathcal{H}_1$. Then*

$$\mathcal{E}(X \downarrow \mathcal{H}_1) = \mathcal{E}(X) \downarrow \mathcal{H}_1, \qquad \mathcal{E}^{-1}(X \downarrow \mathcal{H}_1) = \mathcal{E}^{-1}(X) \downarrow \mathcal{H}_1.$$

Proof. Easy by the linearity of both $\mathcal{E}$ and partial trace $\text{tr}_{\mathcal{H}_2}$.

$\square$

A.3.2   Proofs of the lemmas in Section 7.4.2

In this subsection, we present the proofs of some lemmas that were omitted in Section 7.4.2.

Proof of Lemma 7.3. Assume that $var(\tau) \subseteq V \subseteq Var$. We want to prove:

1. $\rho \downarrow V = \rho' \downarrow V$ implies $[\![\tau]\!]_{\mathbb{I}}(\rho) \downarrow V = [\![\tau]\!]_{\mathbb{I}}(\rho') \downarrow V$;
2. $X \downarrow V = X' \downarrow V$ implies $[\![\tau]\!]_{\mathbb{I}}^*(X) \downarrow V = [\![\tau]\!]_{\mathbb{I}}^*(X') \downarrow V$.

Let us first prove clause 1. We proceed by induction on the length of τ.

(1) If $\tau = \mathcal{E}(\overline{q})$, then $[\![\tau]\!]_{\mathbb{I}}(\rho) = \left(\mathcal{E}^{\mathbb{I}} \otimes \mathcal{I}_{Var\setminus \overline{q}}\right)(\rho)$. Assume that $\{|k\rangle\}$ is an orthonormal basis of $\mathcal{H}_{Var\setminus V}$, and $\mathcal{E}^{\mathbb{I}} = \sum_i E_i \circ E_i^\dagger$ (in the Klause operator-sum representation). Then we have:

$$
\begin{aligned}
[\![\tau]\!]_{\mathbb{I}}(\rho) \downarrow V &= \mathrm{tr}_{Var\setminus V}\left[\left(\mathcal{E}^{\mathbb{I}} \otimes \mathcal{I}_{Var\setminus \overline{q}}\right)(\rho)\right] \\
&= \sum_k \langle k| \sum_i (E_i \otimes I_{Var\setminus \overline{q}})\rho (E_i^\dagger \otimes I_{Var\setminus \overline{q}})|k\rangle \\
&= \sum_i \sum_k \left(E_i \otimes \langle k| \otimes I_{V\setminus \overline{q}}\right)\rho \left(E_i^\dagger \otimes |k\rangle \otimes I_{V\setminus \overline{q}}\right) \\
&= \sum_i \left(E_i \otimes I_{V\setminus \overline{q}}\right)\sum_k \langle k|\rho|k\rangle \left(E_i^\dagger \otimes I_{V\setminus \overline{q}}\right) \\
&= \sum_i \left(E_i \otimes I_{V\setminus \overline{q}}\right)(\rho \downarrow V)\left(E_i^\dagger \otimes I_{V\setminus \overline{q}}\right)
\end{aligned}
$$

because $(Var \setminus V) \cap \overline{q} = \emptyset$. Similarly, we have:

$$
[\![\tau]\!]_{\mathbb{I}}(\rho') \downarrow V = \sum_i \left(E_i \otimes I_{V\setminus \overline{q}}\right)(\rho' \downarrow V)\left(E_i^\dagger \otimes I_{V\setminus \overline{q}}\right).
$$

Therefore, from the assumption $\rho \downarrow V = \rho' \downarrow V$, it follows that $[\![\tau]\!]_{\mathbb{I}}(\rho) \downarrow V = [\![\tau]\!]_{\mathbb{I}}(\rho') \downarrow V$.

(2) If $\tau = \tau_1 \tau_2$, then $V \supseteq var(\tau) \supseteq var(\tau_1)$, and by the assumption $\rho \downarrow V = \rho' \downarrow V$ and the induction hypothesis on τ_1 we obtain $[\![\tau_1]\!]_{\mathbb{I}}(\rho) \downarrow V = [\![\tau_1]\!]_{\mathbb{I}}(\rho') \downarrow V$. Furthermore, by the induction hypothesis on τ_2, we obtain:

$$
[\![\tau]\!]_{\mathbb{I}}(\rho) \downarrow V = [\![\tau_2]\!]_{\mathbb{I}}([\![\tau_1]\!]_{\mathbb{I}}(\rho)) \downarrow V = [\![\tau_2]\!]_{\mathbb{I}}([\![\tau_1]\!]_{\mathbb{I}}(\rho')) \downarrow V = [\![\tau]\!]_{\mathbb{I}}(\rho') \downarrow V.
$$

(3) The case of $\tau = \tau_1 \otimes \tau_2$ is similar to (2).

(4) If $\tau = \sum_i p_i \tau_i$, then for each i, $var(\tau_i) \subseteq var(\tau) \subseteq V$, and by the induction hypothesis, we have:

$$
[\![\tau_i]\!]_{\mathbb{I}}(\rho) \downarrow V = [\![\tau_i]\!]_{\mathbb{I}}(\rho') \downarrow V.
$$

Therefore, by Lemma A.4, we obtain:

$$
\begin{aligned}
[\![\tau]\!]_{\mathbb{I}}(\rho) \downarrow V &= \left(\sum_i p_i [\![\tau_i]\!]_{\mathbb{I}}(\rho)\right) \downarrow V \\
&= \sum_i p_i \left([\![\tau_i]\!]_{\mathbb{I}}(\rho) \downarrow V\right) \\
&= \sum_i p_i \left([\![\tau_i]\!]_{\mathbb{I}}(\rho') \downarrow V\right) \\
&= \left(\sum_i p_i [\![\tau_i]\!]_{\mathbb{I}}(\rho')\right) \downarrow V = [\![\tau]\!]_{\mathbb{I}}(\rho') \downarrow V.
\end{aligned}
$$

The proof of clause 2 is similar to the proof of clause 1 given above, but we need to use Lemma A.6 in proving clause 2 for the case of $\tau = \mathcal{E}(\overline{q})$, and

$$
\mathrm{supp}\left(\sum_i A_i\right) = \bigvee_i \mathrm{supp} A_i
$$

with positive operators A_i for the case of $\tau = \sum_i p_i \tau_i$.   □

Proof of Lemma 7.4. We proceed by induction on the length of τ to show that

$$[\![\tau]\!]_{\mathbb{I}}(\rho) \in X \Leftrightarrow \rho \in \left([\![\tau]\!]_{\mathbb{I}}^*(X^\perp)\right)^\perp.$$

(1) If $\tau = \mathcal{E}(\overline{q})$, then $[\![\tau]\!]_{\mathbb{I}} = \mathcal{F}$ where $\mathcal{F} = \mathcal{E}^{\mathbb{I}} \otimes \mathcal{I}_{Var \setminus \overline{q}}$. We reason:

$$\begin{aligned}
[\![\tau]\!]_{\mathbb{I}}(\rho) \in X &\Leftrightarrow \operatorname{supp}(\mathcal{F}(\rho)) \subseteq X \\
&\Leftrightarrow tr(P_{X^\perp}\mathcal{F}(\rho)) = 0 \\
&\Leftrightarrow tr(\mathcal{F}^*(P_{X^\perp})\rho) = 0 \\
&\Leftrightarrow \operatorname{supp}(\rho) \subseteq \left(\mathcal{F}^*(X^\perp)\right)^\perp \\
&\Leftrightarrow \rho \in \left([\![\tau]\!]_{\mathbb{I}}^*(X^\perp)\right)^\perp
\end{aligned}$$

(2) If $\tau = \tau_1 \tau_2$, then by the induction hypothesis we have

$$\begin{aligned}
[\![\tau]\!]_{\mathbb{I}}(\rho) = [\![\tau_2]\!]_{\mathbb{I}}([\![\tau_1]\!]_{\mathbb{I}}(\rho)) \in X &\Leftrightarrow [\![\tau_1]\!]_{\mathbb{I}}(\rho) \in \left([\![\tau_2]\!]_{\mathbb{I}}^*(X^\perp)\right)^\perp \\
&\Leftrightarrow \rho \in \left([\![\tau_1]\!]_{\mathbb{I}}^*\left([\![\tau_2]\!]_{\mathbb{I}}^*(X^\perp)\right)\right)^\perp \\
&\Leftrightarrow \rho \in \left([\![\tau]\!]_{\mathbb{I}}^*(X^\perp)\right)^\perp
\end{aligned}$$

(3) If $\tau = \tau_1 \otimes \tau_2$, the proof is similar to (2).
(4) If $\tau = \sum_i p_i \tau_i$ with $p_i > 0$ for all i, then

$$[\![\tau]\!]_{\mathbb{I}}(\rho) = \sum_i p_i [\![\tau_i]\!]_{\mathbb{I}}(\rho) \in X \Leftrightarrow \text{for all } i, [\![\tau_i]\!]_{\mathbb{I}}(\rho) \in X$$

$$\Leftrightarrow \text{for all } i, \rho \in \left([\![\tau_i]\!]_{\mathbb{I}}^*(X^\perp)\right)^\perp \quad \text{(By the induction hypothesis)}$$

$$\Leftrightarrow \rho \in \bigcap_i \left([\![\tau_i]\!]_{\mathbb{I}}^*(X^\perp)\right)^\perp = \left(\bigvee_i [\![\tau_i]\!]_{\mathbb{I}}^*(X^\perp)\right)^\perp = \left([\![\tau]\!]_{\mathbb{I}}^*(X^\perp)\right)^\perp.$$

Finally, the simple form when τ is unitary follows from the fact that in this special case, we have $[\![\tau]\!]_{\mathbb{I}}^*(X^\perp) = ([\![\tau]\!]_{\mathbb{I}}^*(X))^\perp$.   □

Proof of Lemma 7.5. Lemma 7.5 consists of two parts. Part 2 (Renaming) is trivial. We only prove part 1 (Restriction):

$$\rho \downarrow free(\beta) = \rho' \downarrow free(\beta) \Rightarrow (\mathbb{I}, \rho) \models \beta \text{ iff } (\mathbb{I}, \rho') \models \beta.$$

Let us proceed by induction on the length of β.

(i) If $\beta = P(\tau)$, then $free(\beta) = var(\tau)$, and by the assumption $\rho \downarrow free(\beta) = \rho' \downarrow free(\beta)$ and Lemma 7.3 we obtain $[\![\tau]\!]_{\mathbb{I}}(\rho) \downarrow free(\beta) = [\![\tau]\!]_{\mathbb{I}}(\rho') \downarrow free(\beta)$. Therefore,

$$\begin{aligned}
(\mathbb{I}, \rho) \models \beta &\Leftrightarrow [\![\tau]\!]_{\mathbb{I}}(\rho) \downarrow free(\beta) \in P^{\mathbb{I}} \\
&\Leftrightarrow [\![\tau]\!]_{\mathbb{I}}(\rho') \downarrow free(\beta) \in P^{\mathbb{I}} \\
&\Leftrightarrow (\mathbb{I}, \rho') \models \beta.
\end{aligned}$$

(ii) If $\beta = \neg\beta'$, then $free(\beta) = free(\beta')$. We want to prove that $(\mathbb{I}, \rho) \models \beta$ implies $(\mathbb{I}, \rho') \models \beta$. This can be done by contradiction. Let us assume that $(\mathbb{I}, \rho') \not\models \beta$. Then there exists σ' such that $\rho' \perp \sigma'$ does not hold and $(\mathbb{I}, \sigma') \models \beta'$. Consequently, by the assumption $\rho \downarrow free(\beta) = \rho' \downarrow free(\beta)$ and Lemma A.5 we know that there exists σ such that $\rho \perp \sigma$ does not hold and $\sigma \downarrow free(\beta') = \sigma' \downarrow free(\beta')$. Therefore, by the induction hypothesis we obtain $(\mathbb{I}, \sigma) \models \beta'$, which implies $(\mathbb{I}, \rho) \not\models \beta$.

(iii) If $\beta = \beta_1 \wedge \beta_2$, then $free(\beta) = free(\beta_1) \cup free(\beta_2)$, and the assumption $\rho \downarrow free(\beta) = \rho' \downarrow free(\beta)$ implies $\rho \downarrow free(\beta_i) = \rho' \downarrow free(\beta_i)$ for $i = 1, 2$. Thus, by the induction hypothesis we have:

$$
\begin{aligned}
(\mathbb{I}, \rho) \models \beta &\Leftrightarrow (\mathbb{I}, \rho) \models \beta_1 \text{ and } (\mathbb{I}, \rho) \models \beta_2 \\
&\Leftrightarrow (\mathbb{I}, \rho') \models \beta_1 \text{ and } (\mathbb{I}, \rho') \models \beta_2 \\
&\Leftrightarrow (\mathbb{I}, \rho') \models \beta.
\end{aligned}
$$

(iv) If $\beta = \tau^*(\beta')$, then $free(\beta) = var(\tau) \cup free(\beta')$. So, $var(\tau) \subseteq free(\beta)$, and by Lemma 7.3 we have $[\![\tau]\!]_{\mathbb{I}}(\rho)) \downarrow free(\beta) = [\![\tau]\!]_{\mathbb{I}}(\rho')) \downarrow free(\beta)$. Note that $free(\beta') \subseteq free(\beta)$. It holds that $[\![\tau]\!]_{\mathbb{I}}(\rho)) \downarrow free(\beta') = [\![\tau]\!]_{\mathbb{I}}(\rho')) \downarrow free(\beta')$. Then by the induction hypothesis on β', we obtain:

$$
(\mathbb{I}, \rho) \models \beta \Leftrightarrow (\mathbb{I}, [\![\tau]\!]_{\mathbb{I}}(\rho)) \models \beta' \Leftrightarrow (\mathbb{I}, [\![\tau]\!]_{\mathbb{I}}(\rho')) \models \beta' \Leftrightarrow (\mathbb{I}, \rho') \models \beta.
$$

(v) If $\beta = (\forall \overline{q})\beta'$, then $free(\beta) = free(\beta') \setminus \overline{q}$. Suppose that $(\mathbb{I}, \rho) \models \beta$. Then for all any quantum term τ with $var(\tau) \subseteq \overline{q}$,

$$
(\mathbb{I}, [\![\tau]\!]_{\mathbb{I}}(\rho)) \models \beta'. \tag{A.8}
$$

Our aim is to show that $(\mathbb{I}, \rho') \models \beta$; that is, for any τ' with $var(\tau') \subseteq \overline{q}$,

$$
(\mathbb{I}, [\![\tau']\!]_{\mathbb{I}}(\rho')) \models \beta'. \tag{A.9}
$$

First, from the assumption that $\rho \downarrow free(\beta) = \rho' \downarrow free(\beta)$ we obtain that $\rho \downarrow (free(\beta') \setminus \overline{q}) = \rho' \downarrow (free(\beta') \setminus \overline{q})$. Then by the assumption that $\mathbb{I}$ is term-expressive, we assert that there exists a sequence $\{\tau_n\}$ of quantum terms such that $var(\tau_n) \subseteq \overline{q}$ for all n, the sequence $\{[\![\tau_n]\!]_{\mathbb{I}}(\rho)\}$ is nondecreasing, and

$$
\lim_{n \to \infty} [\![\tau_n]\!]_{\mathbb{I}}(\rho) = [\![\tau']\!]_{\mathbb{I}}(\rho'). \tag{A.10}
$$

On the other hand, it follows from (A.8) that $(\mathbb{I}, [\![\tau_n]\!]_{\mathbb{I}}(\rho)) \models \beta'$ for all n.

Finally, we obtain (A.9) by combining (A.10) and Lemma 7.6.3, and thus the proof is completed. $\qquad\square$

Proof of Lemma 7.6. This proof can be carried out by induction on the length of β with some routine (but lengthy) calculations. The only thing that needs us to pay attention is the following fact: in proving clause 3 (for the limit of quantum states) in the induction basis case of $\beta = P(\tau)$, we have:

$$
\lim_{n \to \infty} [\![\tau]\!]_{\mathbb{I}}(\rho_n) = [\![\tau]\!]_{\mathbb{I}}(\lim_{n \to \infty} \rho_n) \tag{A.11}
$$

and the interpretation $P^{\mathbb{I}}$ of quantum predicate symbol P is a *closed* space. Eq. (A.11) can be proved by induction on the length of quantum term τ. $\qquad\square$

Proof of Lemma 7.7. We need to prove:

$$
(\mathbb{I}, \rho) \models \beta \text{ if and only if } \rho \in [\![\beta]\!]_{\mathbb{I}}.
$$

The "only if" part is obvious. We now prove the "if" part. Assume the spectral decomposition $\rho = \sum_i p_i |\psi_i\rangle\langle\psi_i|$ with $p_i > 0$ for all i. If $\rho \in [\![\beta]\!]_{\mathbb{I}}$, then $\text{span}\{|\psi_i\rangle\} = \text{supp}\rho \subseteq [\![\beta]\!]_{\mathbb{I}}$. Thus, for each i, we have:

$$
|\psi_i\rangle \in [\![\beta]\!]_{\mathbb{I}} = \bigvee_{(\mathbb{I}, \sigma) \models \beta} \text{supp}\sigma;
$$

that is, there exists σ_i such that $(\mathbb{I}, \sigma_i) \models \beta$ and $|\psi_i\rangle \in \text{supp}\sigma_i$. It follows from Lemma 7.6.1 that $(\mathbb{I}, |\psi_i\rangle) \models \beta$ for all i. Furthermore, by Lemma 7.6.2 we obtain $(\mathbb{I}, \rho) \models \beta$. $\qquad\square$

Proof of Theorem 7.4. We proceed by induction on the length of β.

(1) If $\beta = P(\tau)$, then we have:

$$
\begin{aligned}
(\mathbb{I}, \rho) \models \beta &\Leftrightarrow [\![\tau]\!]_{\mathbb{I}}(\rho) \downarrow var(\tau) \in P^{\mathbb{I}} \\
&\Leftrightarrow [\![\tau]\!]_{\mathbb{I}}(\rho) \in P^{\mathbb{I}} \otimes \mathcal{H}_{Var \setminus var(\tau)} \qquad\qquad \text{(By Lemma A.3)} \\
&\Leftrightarrow \rho \in [\![\tau]\!]_{\mathbb{I}}^*(P^{\mathbb{I}} \otimes \mathcal{H}_{Var \setminus \bar{q}}) = [\![\tau]\!]_{\mathbb{I}}^*(P^{\mathbb{I}}) \otimes \mathcal{H}_{Var \setminus \bar{q}} = [\![\beta]\!]_{\mathbb{I}} \qquad \text{(By Lemma 7.4)}
\end{aligned}
$$

(2) If $\beta = \neg\beta'$, then

$$
\begin{aligned}
(\mathbb{I}, \rho) \models \beta &\Leftrightarrow \text{ for all } \rho', \ (\mathbb{I}, \rho') \models \beta' \text{ implies } \rho' \perp \rho \\
&\Leftrightarrow \text{ for all } \rho', \ \rho' \in [\![\beta']\!]_{\mathbb{I}} \text{ implies } \rho' \perp \rho \qquad \text{(By the induction hypothesis)} \\
&\Leftrightarrow \rho \in ([\![\beta']\!]_{\mathbb{I}})^{\perp} = [\![\beta]\!]_{\mathbb{I}}.
\end{aligned}
$$

(3) If $\beta = \beta_1 \wedge \beta_2$, then

$$
\begin{aligned}
(\mathbb{I}, \rho) \models \beta &\Leftrightarrow (\mathbb{I}, \rho) \models \beta_1 \text{ and } (\mathbb{I}, \rho) \models \beta_2 \\
&\Leftrightarrow \rho \in [\![\beta_1]\!]_{\mathbb{I}} \text{ and } \rho \in [\![\beta_2]\!]_{\mathbb{I}} \qquad \text{(By the induction hypothesis)} \\
&\Leftrightarrow \text{supp}(\rho) \subseteq [\![\beta_1]\!]_{\mathbb{I}} \text{ and } \text{supp}(\rho) \subseteq [\![\beta_2]\!]_{\mathbb{I}} \\
&\Leftrightarrow \text{supp}(\rho) \subseteq [\![\beta_1]\!]_{\mathbb{I}} \cap [\![\beta_2]\!]_{\mathbb{I}} = [\![\beta]\!]_{\mathbb{I}} \\
&\Leftrightarrow \rho \in [\![\beta]\!]_{\mathbb{I}}.
\end{aligned}
$$

(4) If $\beta = \tau^*(\beta')$, then

$$
\begin{aligned}
(\mathbb{I}, \rho) \models \beta &\Leftrightarrow (\mathbb{I}, [\![\tau]\!]_{\mathbb{I}}(\rho)) \models \beta' \\
&\Leftrightarrow [\![\tau]\!]_{\mathbb{I}}(\rho) \in [\![\beta']\!]_{\mathbb{I}} \qquad \text{(By the induction hypothesis)} \\
&\Leftrightarrow \rho \in [\![\tau]\!]_{\mathbb{I}}^*([\![\beta']\!]_{\mathbb{I}}) = [\![\beta]\!]_{\mathbb{I}} \qquad \text{(By Lemma 7.4)}
\end{aligned}
$$

(5) If $\beta = (\forall \bar{q})\beta'$, then

$$
\begin{aligned}
(\mathbb{I}, \rho) \models \beta &\Leftrightarrow \text{ for all } \tau \text{ with } var(\tau) \subseteq \bar{q}, (\mathbb{I}, \rho) \models \tau^*(\beta') \\
&\Leftrightarrow \text{ for all } \tau \text{ with } var(\tau) \subseteq \bar{q}, \text{supp}\rho \subseteq [\![\mathbb{I}]\!]^*([\![\beta']\!]_{\mathbb{I}}) \qquad \text{(By (4) proved above)} \\
&\Leftrightarrow \text{supp}\rho \subseteq \bigcap_{var(\tau) \subseteq \bar{q}} [\![\mathbb{I}]\!]^*([\![\beta']\!]_{\mathbb{I}}). \qquad\qquad\qquad\qquad\qquad (A.12)
\end{aligned}
$$

Therefore, we have:

$$
[\![\beta]\!] = \bigvee_{(\mathbb{I},\rho) \models \beta} \text{supp}\rho = \bigcap_{var(\tau) \subseteq \bar{q}} [\![\mathbb{I}]\!]^*([\![\beta']\!]_{\mathbb{I}}).
$$

Note that the second equality in the above equation comes from the following fact: we can always find a density operator ρ such that the inclusion in Eq. (A.12) becomes equality. $\square$

A.3.3   Substitutions and term-adjoint formulas

It was pointed out in Subsection 7.4.2 that a term-adjoint formula of the form $\tau^*(\beta)$ is introduced for a role in our $\mathcal{QL}$ as the one of substitution in classical first-order logic. But their definitions look very different. In this appendix, we show when their semantics coincide. To this end, we introduce the following definition which is similar to substitution in classical logic.

Definition A.5. Let β be a formula without term-adjoint subformulas and τ a term with $var(\tau) \subseteq free(\beta)$. Then the (simultaneous) substitution of variables $var(\tau)$ by term τ in β, written $\beta[\tau]$, is inductively defined as follows:

1. $\beta = P(\tau')$, then $\beta[\tau] = P(\tau\tau')$;
2. If $\beta = \neg\beta'$, then $\beta[\tau] = \neg\beta'[\tau]$;

3. If $\beta = \beta_1 \wedge \beta_2$, then $\beta[\tau] = \beta_1[\tau] \wedge \beta_2[\tau]$;

4. If $\beta = (\forall \overline{q})\beta'$, then $\beta[\tau] = (\forall \overline{q})\beta'[\tau]$.

It should be noted that the assumption $var(\tau) \subseteq free(\beta)$ implies that $\overline{q} \cap var(\tau) = \emptyset$ in clause 4 of the above definition. It is particularly interesting to see that the simultaneous substitution $\beta[\tau]$ of variables $var(\tau)$ in β is carried out in the possible presence of entanglement between them.

The following lemma shows that in the case of unitary term τ, the term-adjoint formula $\tau^*(\beta)$ and substitution $\beta[\tau]$ are actually equivalent.

Lemma A.9 (Substitution). *If τ is a unitary term, then for any formula β we have: $\tau^*(\beta) \equiv \beta[\tau]$.*

Indeed, whenever β does not contain negation $\neg$ and universal quantifier $\forall$, the above lemma holds also for nonunitary term τ.

Proof. What we need to prove is that for any interpretation $\mathbb{I}$ and quantum state ρ, it holds that $(\mathbb{I}, \rho) \models \beta[\tau]$ iff $(\mathbb{I}, [\![\tau]\!]_{\mathbb{I}}(\rho)) \models \beta$. In other words,

$$[\![\beta[\tau]]\!]_{\mathbb{I}} = ([\![\tau]\!]_{\mathbb{I}})^{-1} ([\![\beta]\!]_{\mathbb{I}}).$$

We prove this lemma by induction on the length of β. First of all, we note that $\beta[\tau]$ is defined only when $var(\tau) \subseteq free(\beta)$.

(1) If $\beta = P(\tau')$, then $\beta[\tau] = P(\tau\tau')$, and $var(\tau) \subseteq free(\beta)$ implies $var(\tau\tau') = var(\tau')$. So, it holds that

$$
\begin{aligned}
(\mathbb{I}, \rho) \models \beta[\tau] &\Leftrightarrow [\![\tau\tau']\!]_{\mathbb{I}}(\rho) \downarrow var(\tau\tau') \in P^{\mathbb{I}} \\
&\Leftrightarrow [\![\tau']\!]_{\mathbb{I}}([\![\tau]\!]_{\mathbb{I}}(\rho)) \downarrow var(\tau') \in P^{\mathbb{I}} \\
&\Leftrightarrow (\mathbb{I}, [\![\tau]\!]_{\mathbb{I}}(\rho)) \models \beta.
\end{aligned}
$$

(2) If $\beta = \neg\beta'$, then $\beta[\tau] = \neg\beta'[\tau]$. We first prove that $(\mathbb{I}, [\![\tau]\!]_{\mathbb{I}}(\rho)) \models \beta$ implies $(\mathbb{I}, \rho) \models \beta[\tau]$; that is, for all ρ', $(\mathbb{I}, \rho') \models \beta'[\tau]$ implies $\rho' \perp \rho$. Indeed, by the induction hypothesis on β', we have $(\mathbb{I}, [\![\tau]\!]_{\mathbb{I}}(\rho')) \models \beta'$. Thus, by the assumption $(\mathbb{I}, [\![\tau]\!]_{\mathbb{I}}(\rho)) \models \beta$; that is, for all σ, $(\mathbb{I}, \sigma) \models \beta'$ implies $\sigma \perp [\![\tau]\!]_{\mathbb{I}}(\rho)$, we obtain $[\![\tau]\!]_{\mathbb{I}}(\rho') \perp [\![\tau]\!]_{\mathbb{I}}(\rho)$. Consequently, it holds that $\rho' \perp \rho$ because τ is a unitary term.

Conversely, we prove that $(\mathbb{I}, \rho) \models \beta[\tau]$ implies $(\mathbb{I}, [\![\tau]\!]_{\mathbb{I}}(\rho)) \models \beta$; that is, for any σ, $(\mathbb{I}, \sigma) \models \beta'$ implies $\sigma \perp [\![\tau]\!]_{\mathbb{I}}(\rho)$. In fact, since τ is a unitary term, there must be ρ' such that $\sigma = [\![\tau]\!]_{\mathbb{I}}(\rho')$. Then by the induction hypothesis, we obtain $(\mathbb{I}, \rho') \models \beta'[\tau]$, which, together with the assumption $(\mathbb{I}, \rho) \models \beta[\tau]$, implies $\rho' \perp \rho$. Thus, by the unitarity of τ, we assert that $\sigma = [\![\tau]\!]_{\mathbb{I}}(\rho') \perp [\![\tau]\!]_{\mathbb{I}}(\rho)$.

(3) If $\beta = \beta_1 \wedge \beta_2$, then $\beta[\tau] = \beta_1[\tau] \wedge \beta_2[\tau]$, and the induction hypothesis yields:

$$
\begin{aligned}
(\mathbb{I}, \rho) \models \beta[\tau] &\Leftrightarrow (\mathbb{I}, \rho) \models \beta_1[\tau] \text{ and } (\mathbb{I}, \rho) \models \beta_2[\tau] \\
&\Leftrightarrow (\mathbb{I}, [\![\tau]\!]_{\mathbb{I}}(\rho)) \models \beta_1 \text{ and } (\mathbb{I}, [\![\tau]\!]_{\mathbb{I}}(\rho)) \models \beta_2 \\
&\Leftrightarrow (\mathbb{I}, [\![\tau]\!]_{\mathbb{I}}(\rho)) \models \beta.
\end{aligned}
$$

(4) If $\beta = (\forall \overline{q})\beta'$, then $\beta[\tau] = (\forall \overline{q})\beta'[\tau]$ and $var(\tau) \subseteq free(\beta) = free(\beta') \setminus \overline{q}$, which implies $var(\beta'[\tau]) = var(\beta')$. Thus, we have:

$$
\begin{aligned}
(\mathbb{I}, \rho) \models \beta[\tau] &\Leftrightarrow \text{for all } \tau' \text{ with } var(\tau') \subseteq \overline{q}, (\mathbb{I}, \rho) \models \tau'^*(\beta'[\tau]) \\
&\Leftrightarrow \text{for all } \tau' \text{ with } var(\tau') \subseteq \overline{q}, (\mathbb{I}, \rho) \models \beta'[\tau][\tau'] = \beta'[\tau'][\tau] \\
&\Leftrightarrow \text{for all } \tau' \text{ with } var(\tau') \subseteq \overline{q}, (\mathbb{I}, [\![\tau]\!]_{\mathbb{I}}^*(\rho)) \models \beta'[\tau'] \\
&\Leftrightarrow (\mathbb{I}, [\![\tau]\!]_{\mathbb{I}}^*(\rho)) \models (\forall \overline{q})\beta' = \beta \\
&\Leftrightarrow (\mathbb{I}, \rho) \models \tau^*(\beta).
\end{aligned}
$$

Note that in the above reasoning, the second biimplication was derived by using the fact that $var(\tau) \cap \overline{q} = \emptyset$ and thus $var(\tau') \cap var(\tau) = \emptyset$. $\qquad\square$

A.3.4   Proof of the soundness of logic $\mathcal{QL}$ (Theorem 7.5)

We first recall that logic $\mathcal{QL}$ has two layers. The first layer is the first-order equational logic $QT_=$. Its soundness (Lemma 7.8) can be proved by checking the soundness of the inference rules given in Fig. 7.5. We omit the details because they are all routine. Based on this, we can prove Theorem 7.5.

It suffices to show that all axioms presented in Fig. 7.6 are valid, and all inference rules there preserve validity.

The validity of axiom ($\mathcal{QL}$1) comes immediately from Theorem 7.3.

($\mathcal{QL}$2) and ($\mathcal{QL}$3): If $QT \vdash \tau_1 = \tau_2$, then it follows from Lemma 7.8 that for any interpretation $\mathbb{I}$ and state ρ, $[\![\tau_1]\!]_{\mathbb{I}}(\rho) = [\![\tau_2]\!]_{\mathbb{I}}(\rho)$. Thus, we have:

$$(\mathbb{I}, \rho) \models P(\tau_1) \Rightarrow [\![\tau_1]\!]_{\mathbb{I}}(\rho) \in P^{\mathbb{I}} \Rightarrow [\![\tau_2]\!]_{\mathbb{I}}(\rho) \in P^{\mathbb{I}} \Rightarrow (\mathbb{I}, \rho) \models P(\tau_2),$$
$$(\mathbb{I}, \rho) \models \tau_1^*(\beta) \Rightarrow (\mathbb{I}, [\![\tau_1]\!]_{\mathbb{I}}(\rho)) \models \beta \Rightarrow (\mathbb{I}, [\![\tau_2]\!]_{\mathbb{I}}(\rho)) \models \beta \Rightarrow (\mathbb{I}, \rho) \models \tau_2^*(\beta).$$

($\mathcal{QL}$4): For any interpretation $\mathbb{I}$ and state ρ, we have:

$$(\mathbb{I}, \rho) \models P(\tau_i) \text{ for all } i \Rightarrow [\![\tau_i]\!]_{\mathbb{I}}(\rho) \in P^{\mathbb{I}} \text{ for all } i$$
$$\Rightarrow \mathrm{supp}[\![\tau_i]\!]_{\mathbb{I}}(\rho) \subseteq P^{\mathbb{I}} \text{ for all } i$$
$$\Rightarrow \mathrm{supp}\left(\left[\!\left[\sum_i p_i \tau_i\right]\!\right]_{\mathbb{I}}(\rho)\right) = \mathrm{supp}\left(\sum_i p_i [\![\tau_i]\!]_{\mathbb{I}}(\rho)\right) = \bigvee_i \mathrm{supp}[\![\tau_i]\!]_{\mathbb{I}}(\rho) \subseteq P^{\mathbb{I}}$$
$$\Rightarrow \left[\!\left[\sum_i p_i \tau_i\right]\!\right]_{\mathbb{I}}(\rho) \in P^{\mathbb{I}} \Rightarrow (\mathbb{I}, \rho) \models P(\sum_i p_i \tau_i).$$

($\mathcal{QL}$5): For any interpretation $\mathbb{I}$ and state ρ, we have $[\![\tau_1 \tau_2]\!]_{\mathbb{I}}(\rho) = [\![\tau_2]\!]_{\mathbb{I}}([\![\tau_1]\!]_{\mathbb{I}}(\rho))$ and

$$(\mathbb{I}, \rho) \models \tau_1^*(\tau_2^*(\beta)) \Leftrightarrow (\mathbb{I}, [\![\tau_1]\!]_{\mathbb{I}}(\rho)) \models \tau_2^*(\beta) \Leftrightarrow (\mathbb{I}, [\![\tau_2]\!]_{\mathbb{I}}([\![\tau_1]\!]_{\mathbb{I}}(\rho))) \models \beta$$
$$\Leftrightarrow (\mathbb{I}, [\![\tau_1 \tau_2]\!]_{\mathbb{I}}(\rho)) \models \beta \Leftrightarrow (\mathbb{I}, \rho) \models (\tau_1 \tau_2)^*(\beta).$$

($\mathcal{QL}$6): For any interpretation $\mathbb{I}$ and state ρ, we have:

$$(\mathbb{I}, \rho) \models \tau^*(\beta) \Rightarrow (\mathbb{I}, [\![\tau]\!]_{\mathbb{I}}(\rho)) \models \beta$$
$$\Rightarrow (\mathbb{I}, [\![\tau]\!]_{\mathbb{I}}(\rho)) \models \beta' \quad \text{(By the assumption } \beta \vdash \beta')$$
$$\Rightarrow (\mathbb{I}, \rho) \models \tau^*(\beta').$$

($\mathcal{QL}$7): For any interpretation $\mathbb{I}$ and state ρ, we have:

$$(\mathbb{I}, \rho) \models \tau_1^*(P(\tau_2)) \Leftrightarrow (\mathbb{I}, [\![\tau_1]\!]_{\mathbb{I}}(\rho)) \models P(\tau_2)$$
$$\Leftrightarrow (\mathbb{I}, [\![\tau_2]\!]_{\mathbb{I}}([\![\tau_1]\!]_{\mathbb{I}}(\rho)) \in P^{\mathbb{I}}$$
$$\Leftrightarrow (\mathbb{I}, [\![\tau_1 \tau_2]\!]_{\mathbb{I}}(\rho)) \in P^{\mathbb{I}}$$
$$\Leftrightarrow (\mathbb{I}, \rho) \models P(\tau_1 \tau_2).$$

($\mathcal{QL}$8): For any interpretation $\mathbb{I}$ and state ρ, we have:

$$(\mathbb{I}, \rho) \models \tau^*(\neg\beta) \Leftrightarrow (\mathbb{I}, [\![\tau]\!]_{\mathbb{I}}(\rho)) \models \neg\beta \tag{A.13}$$
$$\Leftrightarrow \text{for all } \rho', (\mathbb{I}, \rho') \models \beta \text{ implies } \rho' \perp [\![\tau]\!]_{\mathbb{I}}(\rho),$$
$$(\mathbb{I}, \rho) \models \neg\tau^*(\beta) \Leftrightarrow \text{for all } \sigma, (\mathbb{I}, \sigma) \models \tau^*(\beta) \text{ implies } \sigma \perp \rho. \tag{A.14}$$

We first prove $(\mathbb{I}, \rho) \models \tau^*(\neg\beta) \Rightarrow (\mathbb{I}, \rho) \models \neg\tau^*(\beta)$. For any σ, if $(\mathbb{I}, \sigma) \models \tau^*(\beta)$, then $(\mathbb{I}, [\![\tau]\!]_{\mathbb{I}}(\sigma)) \models \beta$. By (A.13), we obtain $[\![\tau]\!]_{\mathbb{I}}(\sigma) \perp [\![\tau]\!]_{\mathbb{I}}(\rho)$. Since τ is unitary, it holds that $\sigma \perp \rho$.

Conversely, we can prove $(\mathbb{I}, \rho) \models \neg\tau^*(\beta) \Rightarrow (\mathbb{I}, \rho) \models \tau^*(\neg\beta)$. For any ρ', if $(\mathbb{I}, \rho') \models \beta$, then by the unitarity of τ, we have $\rho' = [\![\tau]\!]_{\mathbb{I}}(\sigma)$ for some σ. Thus, $(\mathbb{I}, \sigma) \models \tau^*(\beta)$, and by (A.14) we obtain $\sigma \perp \rho$, which, together with the unitary of τ, leads to $\rho' \perp [\![\tau]\!]_{\mathbb{I}}(\rho)$.

($\mathcal{QL}$9): For any interpretation $\mathbb{I}$ and state ρ, we have:

$$(\mathbb{I}, \rho) \models \tau^*(\beta_1 \wedge \beta_2) \Leftrightarrow (\mathbb{I}, [\![\tau]\!]_{\mathbb{I}}(\rho)) \models \beta_1 \wedge \beta_2$$
$$\Leftrightarrow (\mathbb{I}, [\![\tau]\!]_{\mathbb{I}}(\rho)) \models \beta_1 \text{ and } (\mathbb{I}, [\![\tau]\!]_{\mathbb{I}}(\rho)) \models \beta_2$$
$$\Leftrightarrow (\mathbb{I}, \rho) \models \tau^*(\beta_1) \text{ and } (\mathbb{I}, \rho) \models \tau^*(\beta_2)$$
$$\Leftrightarrow (\mathbb{I}, \rho) \models \tau^*(\beta_1) \wedge \tau^*(\beta_2).$$

($\mathcal{QL}$10): By Theorem 7.4.3 and 4, we obtain:

$$[\![(\tau_1 \otimes \tau_2)^*(\beta_1 \wedge \beta_2)]\!]_{\mathbb{I}} = [\![\tau_1 \otimes \tau_2]\!]_{\mathbb{I}}^* \left([\![\beta_1 \wedge \beta_2]\!]_{\mathbb{I}}\right)$$
$$= \left([\![\tau_1]\!]_{\mathbb{I}}^* \otimes [\![\tau_2]\!]_{\mathbb{I}}^*\right) \left([\![\beta_1]\!]_{\mathbb{I}} \cap [\![\beta_2]\!]_{\mathbb{I}}\right)$$
$$= [\![\tau_1]\!]_{\mathbb{I}}^* \left([\![\beta_1]\!]_{\mathbb{I}}\right) \cap [\![\tau_2]\!]_{\mathbb{I}}^* \left([\![\beta_2]\!]_{\mathbb{I}}\right)$$
$$= [\![\tau_1^*(\beta_1)]\!]_{\mathbb{I}} \cap [\![\tau_2^*(\beta_2)]\!]_{\mathbb{I}}$$
$$= [\![\tau_1^*(\beta_1) \wedge \tau_2^*(\beta_2)]\!]_{\mathbb{I}}.$$

Note that here, the third equality is implied by the condition $var(\tau_1) \cap var(\tau_2) = \emptyset$, and the fourth is derived from the condition $free(\beta_i) \subseteq var(\tau_i)$ for $i = 1, 2$.

($\mathcal{QL}$11): From the condition $\tau^*(\beta) \models \gamma$, we obtain $[\![\tau^*(\beta)]\!]_{\mathbb{I}} \subseteq [\![\gamma]\!]_{\mathbb{I}}$. Since τ is unitary, it follows from Theorem 7.4.4 that

$$[\![\beta]\!]_{\mathbb{I}} = [\![\tau^{-1}]\!]_{\mathbb{I}}^* \left([\![\tau]\!]_{\mathbb{I}}^*([\![\beta]\!]_{\mathbb{I}})\right) = [\![\tau^{-1}]\!]_{\mathbb{I}}^* \left([\![\tau^*(\beta)]\!]_{\mathbb{I}}\right) \subseteq [\![\tau^{-1}]\!]_{\mathbb{I}}^*([\![\gamma]\!]_{\mathbb{I}}) = [\![(\tau^{-1})^*(\gamma)]\!]_{\mathbb{I}}.$$

($\mathcal{QL}$12): The proof is similar to ($\mathcal{QL}$11).

($\mathcal{QL}$13): Using Theorem 7.4, we compute:

$$[\![\tau^*((\forall \overline{q} \beta))]\!]_{\mathbb{I}} = [\![\tau]\!]_{\mathbb{I}}^*([\![(\forall \overline{q} \beta)]\!]_{\mathbb{I}}$$
$$= [\![\tau]\!]_{\mathbb{I}}^* \left(\bigcap_{var(\sigma) \subseteq \overline{q}} [\![\sigma]\!]_{\mathbb{I}}^*([\![\beta]\!]_{\mathbb{I}}) \right)$$
$$= \bigcap_{var(\sigma) \subseteq \overline{q}} [\![\tau]\!]_{\mathbb{I}}^*([\![\sigma]\!]_{\mathbb{I}}^*([\![\beta]\!]_{\mathbb{I}}))$$
$$= \bigcap_{var(\sigma) \subseteq \overline{q}} [\![\sigma]\!]_{\mathbb{I}}^*([\![\tau]\!]_{\mathbb{I}}^*([\![\beta]\!]_{\mathbb{I}}))$$
$$= [\![(\forall \overline{q}) \tau^*(\beta)]\!]_{\mathbb{I}}.$$

Here, the third and fourth equalities are derived from the condition that τ is unitary, and $var(\tau) \cap var(\sigma) = \emptyset$.

($\mathcal{QL}$14): It follows immediately from Definition 7.11.5.

($\mathcal{QL}$15): In the case of $\overline{q} \cap free(\beta) = \emptyset$, the conclusion is obvious because $(\forall \overline{q})\beta \equiv \beta$. Now we assume that $free(\Sigma) \subseteq free(\beta) \setminus \overline{q}$. First, it follows from $\Sigma \models \beta$ that

$$\bigcap_{\gamma \in \Sigma} [\![\gamma]\!]_{\mathbb{I}} \subseteq [\![\beta]\!]_{\mathbb{I}}.$$

Then for any quantum term τ with $var(\tau) \subseteq \overline{q}$, we have $var(\tau) \cap free(\Sigma) = \emptyset$ and

$$\bigcap_{\gamma \in \Sigma} [\![\gamma]\!]_{\mathbb{I}} = [\![\tau]\!]_{\mathbb{I}}^* \left(\bigcap_{\gamma \in \Sigma} [\![\gamma]\!]_{\mathbb{I}} \right) \subseteq [\![\tau]\!]_{\mathbb{I}}^*([\![\beta]\!]_{\mathbb{I}}).$$

Therefore, it holds that

$$\bigcap_{\gamma \in \Sigma} [\![\gamma]\!]_{\mathbb{I}} \subseteq \bigcap_{var(\tau) \subseteq \overline{q}} [\![\tau]\!]_{\mathbb{I}}^*([\![\beta]\!]_{\mathbb{I}}) = [\![(\forall \overline{q})\beta]\!]_{\mathbb{I}}$$

and $\Sigma \models (\forall \overline{q})\beta$.

A.3.5 Proof of the soundness of adaptation rules (Theorem 7.8)

Let us first present the following technical lemma that is needed in the proofs of the adaptation rules. Its proof is routine and thus omitted.

Lemma A.10. 1. *If $free(\delta) \cap var(S) = \emptyset$, then for any interpretation $\mathbb{I}$, we have $[\![S]\!]_\mathbb{I}([\![\delta]\!]_\mathbb{I}) = [\![\delta]\!]_\mathbb{I}$.*
2. *If $var(\tau) \cap var(S) = \emptyset$, then for any interpretation $\mathbb{I}$ and for any $X \in S(\mathcal{H})$, we have $[\![S]\!]_\mathbb{I}([\![\tau]\!]_\mathbb{I}^*(X)) = [\![\tau]\!]_\mathbb{I}^*([\![S]\!]_\mathbb{I}(X))$.*

We now prove the soundness of the adaptation rules.

(Invariance): If $\mathbb{I} \models_{par} \{\beta\}S\{\gamma\}$, then we have $[\![S]\!]_\mathbb{I}([\![\beta]\!]_\mathbb{I}) \subseteq [\![\gamma]\!]_\mathbb{I}$, and with Lemma A.10.1 it follows that

$$[\![S]\!]_\mathbb{I}([\![\beta \wedge \delta]\!]_\mathbb{I}) = [\![S]\!]_\mathbb{I}([\![\beta]\!]_\mathbb{I} \cap [\![\delta]\!]_\mathbb{I})$$
$$\subseteq [\![S]\!]_\mathbb{I}([\![\beta]\!]_\mathbb{I}) \cap [\![S]\!]_\mathbb{I}([\![\delta]\!]_\mathbb{I})$$
$$\subseteq [\![\gamma]\!]_\mathbb{I} \cap [\![\delta]\!]_\mathbb{I} = [\![\gamma \wedge \delta]\!]_\mathbb{I}.$$

Therefore, $\mathbb{I} \models_{par} \{\beta \wedge \delta\}S\{\gamma \wedge \delta\}$.

(Substitution): If $\mathbb{I} \models_{par} \{\beta\}S\{\gamma\}$, then it holds that $[\![S]\!]_\mathbb{I}([\![\beta]\!]_\mathbb{I}) \subseteq [\![\gamma]\!]_\mathbb{I}$, and with Lemma A.10.2 we obtain:

$$[\![S]\!]_\mathbb{I}([\![\tau^*(\beta)]\!]_\mathbb{I}) = [\![S]\!]_\mathbb{I}([\![\tau]\!]_\mathbb{I}^*([\![\beta]\!]_\mathbb{I}))$$
$$= [\![\tau]\!]_\mathbb{I}^*([\![S]\!]_\mathbb{I}([\![\beta]\!]_\mathbb{I}))$$
$$\subseteq [\![\tau]\!]_\mathbb{I}^*([\![\gamma]\!]_\mathbb{I}) = [\![\tau^*(\gamma)]\!]_\mathbb{I}.$$

(Conjunction): Assume that $\models_\mathbb{I} \{\beta_i\}S\{\gamma_i\}$ $(i = 1, 2)$. Then we have $[\![S]\!]_\mathbb{I}([\![\beta_i]\!]_\mathbb{I}) \subseteq [\![\gamma_i]\!]_\mathbb{I}$ $(i = 1, 2)$ and

$$[\![S]\!]_\mathbb{I}([\![\beta_1 \wedge \beta_2]\!]_\mathbb{I}) = [\![S]\!]_\mathbb{I}([\![\beta_1]\!]_\mathbb{I} \cap [\![\beta_2]\!]_\mathbb{I})$$
$$\subseteq [\![S]\!]_\mathbb{I}([\![\beta_1]\!]_\mathbb{I}) \cap [\![S]\!]_\mathbb{I}([\![\beta_2]\!]_\mathbb{I})$$
$$\subseteq [\![\gamma_1]\!]_\mathbb{I} \cap [\![\gamma_2]\!]_\mathbb{I} = [\![\gamma_1 \wedge \gamma_2]\!]_\mathbb{I}.$$

So, it holds that $\models_\mathbb{I} \{\beta_1 \wedge \beta_2\}S\{\gamma_1 \wedge \gamma_2\}$.

(Disjunction): Assume that $\models_\mathbb{I} \{\beta_i\}S\{\gamma\}$ $(i = 1, 2)$. Then we have $[\![S]\!]_\mathbb{I}([\![\beta_i]\!]_\mathbb{I}) \subseteq [\![\gamma]\!]_\mathbb{I}$ $(i = 1, 2)$. Using Proposition 5.2.1(iv) in [421], we obtain:

$$[\![S]\!]_\mathbb{I}([\![\beta_1 \vee \beta_2]\!]_\mathbb{I}) = [\![S]\!]_\mathbb{I}([\![\beta_1]\!]_\mathbb{I} \vee [\![\beta_2]\!]_\mathbb{I})$$
$$[\![S]\!]_\mathbb{I}([\![\beta_1]\!]_\mathbb{I}) \vee [\![S]\!]_\mathbb{I}([\![\beta_2]\!]_\mathbb{I})$$
$$\subseteq [\![\gamma]\!]_\mathbb{I}.$$

So, it holds that $\models_\mathbb{I} \{\beta_1 \wedge \beta_2\}S\{\gamma\}$.

($\exists$-Introduction): Assume that $\models_\mathbb{I} \{\beta\}S\{\gamma\}$. Then $[\![S]\!]_\mathbb{I}([\![\beta]\!]_\mathbb{I}) \subseteq [\![\gamma]\!]_\mathbb{I}$. If S terminates in $\mathbb{I}$, then $[\![S]\!]_\mathbb{I}(I) = I$, and with Lemma A.7.3 we obtain:

$$[\![S]\!]_\mathbb{I}\left([\![\beta]\!]_\mathbb{I}^\perp\right) = ([\![S]\!]_\mathbb{I}([\![\beta]\!]_\mathbb{I}))^\perp \supseteq [\![\gamma]\!]_\mathbb{I}^\perp,$$
$$[\![\tau]\!]_\mathbb{I}^*\left([\![S]\!]_\mathbb{I}\left([\![\beta]\!]_\mathbb{I}^\perp\right)\right) \supseteq [\![\tau]\!]_\mathbb{I}^*\left([\![\gamma]\!]_\mathbb{I}^\perp\right).$$

Furthermore, if $\overline{q} \cap [var(S) \cup free(\gamma)] = \emptyset$, then for any τ with $var(\tau) \subseteq \overline{q}$, we have $var(\tau) \cap var(S) = \emptyset$, $var(\tau) \cap free(\gamma) = \emptyset$, and

$$[\![S]\!]_\mathbb{I}\left[\left([\![\tau]\!]_\mathbb{I}^*\left([\![\beta]\!]_\mathbb{I}^\perp\right)\right)^\perp\right] \subseteq \left[[\![S]\!]_\mathbb{I}\left([\![\tau]\!]_\mathbb{I}^*\left([\![\beta]\!]_\mathbb{I}^\perp\right)\right)\right]^\perp \quad \text{(By Lemma A.7.3)}$$
$$= \left[[\![\tau]\!]_\mathbb{I}^*\left([\![S]\!]_\mathbb{I}\left([\![\beta]\!]_\mathbb{I}^\perp\right)\right)\right]^\perp \quad \text{(Since } var(\tau) \cap var(S) = \emptyset\text{)}$$
$$\subseteq \left([\![\tau]\!]_\mathbb{I}^*\left([\![\gamma]\!]_\mathbb{I}^\perp\right)\right)^\perp$$
$$= ([\![\tau]\!]_\mathbb{I}^*([\![\gamma]\!]_\mathbb{I}))^{\perp\perp} \quad \text{(By Lemma A.7.3)}$$

$$= [\![\tau]\!]_{\mathbb{I}}^*([\![\gamma]\!]_{\mathbb{I}})$$
$$= [\![\gamma]\!]_{\mathbb{I}}. \qquad \text{(Since } var(\tau) \cap free(\gamma) = \emptyset)$$

Therefore, we have:

$$
\begin{aligned}
[\![S]\!]_{\mathbb{I}}([\![(\exists \overline{q})\beta]\!]_{\mathbb{I}}) &= [\![S]\!]_{\mathbb{I}}\left[\bigvee_{var(\tau)\subseteq \overline{q}}\left([\![\tau]\!]_{\mathbb{I}}^*\left([\![\beta]\!]_{\mathbb{I}}^\perp\right)\right)^\perp\right]\\
&= \bigvee_{var(\tau)\subseteq \overline{q}}[\![S]\!]_{\mathbb{I}}\left[\left([\![\tau]\!]_{\mathbb{I}}^*\left([\![\beta]\!]_{\mathbb{I}}^\perp\right)\right)^\perp\right] \qquad \text{(By Lemma A.7.2)}\\
&\subseteq [\![\gamma]\!]_{\mathbb{I}}
\end{aligned}
$$

and $\models_{\mathbb{I}} \{(\exists \overline{q})\beta\}S\{\gamma\}$.

(**Hoare adaptation**): Several key laws in Birkhoff–von Neumann quantum logic are used in this proof in an essential way, including the ortho-modularity (see Theorem 7.2). Assume that $\models_{par} \{\beta\}S\{\gamma\}$, $var(S) \subseteq \overline{p}$ and $\overline{q} = free(\beta) \cup free(\gamma) \setminus [free(\delta) \cup \overline{p}]$. We want to prove

$$\models_{par} \{(\exists \overline{q})[\beta \wedge (\forall \overline{p})(\gamma \to \delta)]\}S\{\delta\}. \tag{A.15}$$

First, we have: for any interpretation $\mathbb{I}$,

$$
\begin{aligned}
[\![S]\!]_{\mathbb{I}}([\![(\exists \overline{q})[\beta \wedge (\forall \overline{p})(\gamma \to \delta)]]\!]_{\mathbb{I}}) &= [\![S]\!]_{\mathbb{I}}\left(\bigvee_{var(\tau)\subseteq \overline{q}}[\![\tau]\!]_{\mathbb{I}}^*\left([\![\beta]\!]_{\mathbb{I}} \cap [\![(\forall \overline{p})(\gamma \to \delta)]\!]_{\mathbb{I}}\right)\right)\\
&= \bigvee_{var(\tau)\subseteq \overline{q}}[\![S]\!]_{\mathbb{I}}\left([\![\tau]\!]_{\mathbb{I}}^*([\![\beta]\!]_{\mathbb{I}} \cap [\![(\forall \overline{p})(\gamma \to \delta)]\!]_{\mathbb{I}})\right)
\end{aligned}
$$

where the last equality is derived using Lemma A.7.2. Therefore, it suffices to show that for any quantum term τ with $var(\tau) \subseteq \overline{q}$,

$$[\![S]\!]_{\mathbb{I}}\left([\![\tau]\!]_{\mathbb{I}}^*([\![\beta]\!]_{\mathbb{I}} \cap [\![(\forall \overline{p})(\gamma \to \delta)]\!]_{\mathbb{I}})\right) \subseteq [\![\delta]\!]_{\mathbb{I}}.$$

We observe:

$$[\![S]\!]_{\mathbb{I}}\left([\![\tau]\!]_{\mathbb{I}}^*([\![\beta]\!]_{\mathbb{I}} \cap [\![(\forall \overline{p})(\gamma \to \delta)]\!]_{\mathbb{I}})\right) = [\![\tau]\!]_{\mathbb{I}}^*\left([\![S]\!]_{\mathbb{I}}([\![\beta]\!]_{\mathbb{I}} \cap [\![(\forall \overline{p})(\gamma \to \delta)]\!]_{\mathbb{I}})\right) \tag{A.16}$$
$$\subseteq [\![\tau]\!]_{\mathbb{I}}^*\left([\![S]\!]_{\mathbb{I}}([\![\beta]\!]_{\mathbb{I}}) \cap [\![S]\!]_{\mathbb{I}}([\![(\forall \overline{p})(\gamma \to \delta)]\!]_{\mathbb{I}})\right) \tag{A.17}$$
$$\subseteq [\![\tau]\!]_{\mathbb{I}}^*\left([\![\gamma]\!]_{\mathbb{I}} \cap [\![S]\!]_{\mathbb{I}}([\![(\forall \overline{p})(\gamma \to \delta)]\!]_{\mathbb{I}})\right) \tag{A.18}$$

Here, (A.16) is true because $var(S) \cap var(\tau) = \emptyset$, which is implied by the assumption that $var(S) \subseteq \overline{p}$ and $var(\tau) \subseteq \overline{q} = free(\beta) \cup free(\gamma) \setminus [free(\delta) \cup \overline{p}]$; (A.17) is obtained using Lemma A.7.2; and (A.18) is derived from the assumption $\models_{par} \{\beta\}S\{\gamma\}$, i.e. $[\![S]\!]_{\mathbb{I}}([\![\beta]\!]_{\mathbb{I}}) \subseteq [\![\gamma]\!]_{\mathbb{I}}$.

Let us assume that S is term representable in $\mathbb{I}$. Then there exists a quantum term σ_0 such that $var(\sigma_0) \subseteq var(S)$ and $[\![S]\!]_{\mathbb{I}}([\![\sigma_0]\!]_{\mathbb{I}}(X)) = X$ for all X. Furthermore, we have:

$$
\begin{aligned}
[\![S]\!]_{\mathbb{I}}([\![(\forall \overline{p})(\gamma \to \delta)]\!]_{\mathbb{I}}) &= [\![S]\!]_{\mathbb{I}}\left(\bigcap_{var(\sigma)\subseteq \overline{p}}[\![\sigma]\!]_{\mathbb{I}}^*([\![\gamma \to \delta]\!]_{\mathbb{I}})\right)\\
&\subseteq [\![S]\!]_{\mathbb{I}}\left([\![\sigma_0]\!]_{\mathbb{I}}^*([\![\gamma \to \delta]\!]_{\mathbb{I}})\right)\\
&= [\![S]\!]_{\mathbb{I}}\left([\![\sigma_0]\!]_{\mathbb{I}}^*([\![\gamma]\!]_{\mathbb{I}} \to [\![\delta]\!]_{\mathbb{I}})\right)\\
&\subseteq [\![S]\!]_{\mathbb{I}}\left([\![\sigma_0]\!]_{\mathbb{I}}^*([\![\gamma]\!]_{\mathbb{I}})\right) \to [\![S]\!]_{\mathbb{I}}\left([\![\sigma_0]\!]_{\mathbb{I}}^*([\![\delta]\!]_{\mathbb{I}})\right).
\end{aligned}
$$

Here, the last inclusion is derived by Lemma A.7.4. It follows that

$$
\begin{aligned}
&\llbracket \gamma \rrbracket_{\mathbb{I}} \cap \llbracket S \rrbracket_{\mathbb{I}}(\llbracket (\forall \overline{p})(\gamma \to \delta) \rrbracket_{\mathbb{I}}) \\
&= \llbracket S \rrbracket_{\mathbb{I}}\left(\llbracket \sigma_0 \rrbracket_{\mathbb{I}}^*(\llbracket \gamma \rrbracket_{\mathbb{I}})\right) \cap \llbracket S \rrbracket_{\mathbb{I}}(\llbracket (\forall \overline{p})(\gamma \to \delta) \rrbracket_{\mathbb{I}}) \\
&\subseteq \llbracket S \rrbracket_{\mathbb{I}}\left(\llbracket \sigma_0 \rrbracket_{\mathbb{I}}^*(\llbracket \gamma \rrbracket_{\mathbb{I}})\right) \cap \left[\llbracket S \rrbracket_{\mathbb{I}}\left(\llbracket \sigma_0 \rrbracket_{\mathbb{I}}^*(\llbracket \gamma \rrbracket_{\mathbb{I}})\right) \to \llbracket S \rrbracket_{\mathbb{I}}\left(\llbracket \sigma_0 \rrbracket_{\mathbb{I}}^*(\llbracket \delta \rrbracket_{\mathbb{I}})\right)\right] \\
&\subseteq \llbracket S \rrbracket_{\mathbb{I}}\left(\llbracket \sigma_0 \rrbracket_{\mathbb{I}}^*(\llbracket \delta \rrbracket_{\mathbb{I}})\right) = \llbracket \delta \rrbracket_{\mathbb{I}}.
\end{aligned}
\tag{A.19}
$$

Note that the second inclusion in (A.19) is derived by the fact that the Sasaki implication $\to$ satisfies $a \wedge (a \to b) \le b$, which is in turn guaranteed by the ortho-modularity (see Theorem 7.2). Substituting (A.19) into (A.18), we obtain:

$$
\llbracket S \rrbracket_{\mathbb{I}}\left(\llbracket \tau \rrbracket_{\mathbb{I}}^*(\llbracket \beta \rrbracket_{\mathbb{I}} \cap \llbracket (\forall \overline{p})(\gamma \to \delta) \rrbracket_{\mathbb{I}})\right) \subseteq \llbracket \tau \rrbracket_{\mathbb{I}}^*(\llbracket \delta \rrbracket_{\mathbb{I}}) = \llbracket \delta \rrbracket_{\mathbb{I}}
$$

because $var(\tau) \subseteq \overline{q} = free(\beta) \cup free(\gamma) \setminus [free(\delta) \cup \overline{p}]$ and thus $var(\tau) \cap free(\delta) = \emptyset$. Thus, we complete the proof.

A.3.6 Proof of negation normal forms (Theorem 7.9)

To prove the theorem, we proceed by induction on the length of F.

(1) If F is an atomic formula, it is obviously true.

(2) If $F \equiv F_1 \otimes F_2$, then by induction hypothesis, for $i = 1, 2$, we can assume that $F_i = \lambda_i G_i$, where $\lambda_i > 0$, and G_i is a negation normal form. Obviously, $G_1 \otimes G_2$ is a negation normal form, and it holds that $F = (\lambda_1 \lambda_2)(G_1 \otimes G_2)$.

(3) If $F \equiv K(\mathcal{F}) \equiv \sum_i K_i^\dagger F_i K_i$, then by the induction hypothesis, we can assume that each $F_i = \lambda_i G_i$, where $\lambda_i > 0$, and G_i is a negation normal form. Let $\lambda = \max_i \lambda_i$. We introduce a new Kraus operator symbol $L = \{L_i\}$ and interpret it by $L_i^{\mathbb{I}} = \sqrt{\frac{\lambda_i}{\lambda}} K_i^{\mathbb{I}}$ for every i. Then

$$
\sum_i \left(L_i^{\mathbb{I}}\right)^\dagger L_i^{\mathbb{I}} = \sum_i \frac{\lambda_i}{\lambda} \left(K_i^{\mathbb{I}}\right)^\dagger K_i^{\mathbb{I}} \subseteq \sum_i \left(K_i^{\mathbb{I}}\right)^\dagger K_i^{\mathbb{I}} \subseteq I
$$

and $G \equiv L(\mathcal{G}) = \sum_i L_i^\dagger G_i L_i$ is a negation normal form, where $\mathcal{G} = \{G_i\}$. Moreover, we have $F = \lambda G$.

(4) If $F \equiv \neg F'$, then let us consider the following subcases:

(4.1) Whenever F' is an atomic formula, it is obviously true.

(4.2) Whenever $F' \equiv \neg F''$, then by the induction hypothesis we have $F'' = \lambda G$ for some $\lambda > 0$ and negation normal form G. Thus, $F = F'' = \lambda G$.

(4.3) Whenever $F' \equiv F_1 \otimes F_2$, then by the induction hypothesis, we assert that $\neg F_1 = \mu_1 H_1$, $F_2 = \lambda_2 G_2$ and $\neg F_2 = \mu_2 H_2$ for some $\mu_1, \mu_2, \lambda_2 > 0$ and negation normal forms H_1, H_2, G_2. Then we introduce a Kraus operator symbol $K = \{K_1, K_2\}$ interpreted by

$$
K_1^{\mathbb{I}} = \sqrt{\frac{\mu_2}{\mu_2 + \mu_1 \lambda_2}}(I_1 \otimes I_2), \qquad K_2^{\mathbb{I}} = \sqrt{\frac{\mu_1 \lambda_2}{\mu_2 + \mu_1 \lambda_2}}(I_1 \otimes I_2).
$$

Let $D_1 = I_1(q_1, ..., q_k) \otimes H_2$, $D_2 = H_1 \otimes B_2$, where I_i is the identity operator on $\mathcal{H}_{type(F_i)}$ $(i = 1, 2)$, and $type(F_1) = \{q_1, ..., q_k\}$. Then

$$
F = (\mu_2 + \mu_1 \lambda_2)(K_1^\dagger D_1 K_1 + K_2^\dagger D_2 K_2)
$$

as desired.

(4.4) Whenever $F' \equiv K(\mathcal{F}) \equiv \sum_{i=1}^m K_i^\dagger F_i K_i$, then by the induction hypothesis, for each i we have $\neg F_i = \lambda_i G_i$ for some $\lambda_i > 0$ and negation normal form G_i. Since $\sum_{i=1}^m K_i^\dagger K_i \sqsubseteq I$, it holds that

$$
0 \sqsubseteq I - \sum_{i=1}^m K_i^\dagger K_i
$$

where 0, I are the zero and identity operators on $\mathcal{H}_{type(F)}$, respectively. Put $\lambda = \max_{i=1}^{m} \lambda_i$ and introduce a new Kraus operator symbol $L = \{L_0, L_1\}$ interpreted by

$$L_0^{\mathbb{I}} = \sqrt{\frac{1}{1+\lambda}\left(I - \sum_{i=1}^{m} K_i^\dagger K_i\right)}, \qquad L_i = \sqrt{\frac{\lambda_i}{1+\lambda}} K_i \quad (i = 1, ..., m).$$

Then

$$F = (1+\lambda)\left[L_0^\dagger I(q_1, ..., q_n)L_0 + \sum_{i=1}^{m} L_i^\dagger G_i L_i\right]$$

as desired, where $type(A) = \{q_1, ..., q_n\}$.

A.4 Omitted proofs in Chapter 8

A.4.1 Proofs of the lemmas in Section 8.4

Several technical lemmas were used in Section 8.4. For convenience of the reader, here we collect their proofs.

Proof of Lemma 8.13. We first give a series of lemmas that will serve as key steps in the proof of Lemma 8.13. Recall that $\mathcal{E}$ is a quantum operation and $M = \{M_0, M_1\}$ a quantum measurement. The quantum operations $\mathcal{E}_0, \mathcal{E}_1$ are defined by the measurement operators M_0, M_1, respectively; that is,

$$\mathcal{E}_i(\rho) = M_i \rho M_i^\dagger$$

for all density operators ρ and $i = 0, 1$. We write $\mathcal{G} = \mathcal{E} \circ \mathcal{E}_1$.

Lemma A.11. *The quantum operation $\mathcal{G} + \mathcal{E}_0$ is trace-preserving:*

$$tr\left[(\mathcal{G} + \mathcal{E}_0)(\rho)\right] = tr(\rho) \tag{A.20}$$

for all partial density operators ρ.

Proof. It suffices to see that

$$\sum_i (E_i M_1)^\dagger E_i M_1 + M_0^\dagger M_0 = M_1^\dagger \left(\sum_i E_i^\dagger E_i\right) M_1 + M_0^\dagger M_0$$

$$= M_1^\dagger M_1 + M_0^\dagger M_0 = I. \qquad \square$$

The next lemma shows that every complex matrix can be represented by four positive matrices.

Lemma A.12. *For any matrix A, there are positive matrices B_1, B_2, B_3, B_4 such that*

1. $A = (B_1 - B_2) + i(B_3 - B_4)$; *and*
2. $tr\left(B_i^2\right) \leq tr\left(A^\dagger A\right)$ $(i = 1, 2, 3, 4)$.

Proof. We can take Hermitian operators

$$\left(A + A^\dagger\right)/2 = B_1 - B_2, \qquad -i\left(A - A^\dagger\right)/2 = B_3 - B_4,$$

where B_1, B_2 are positive operators with orthogonal supports, and B_3, B_4 are also positive operators with orthogonal supports. Then it holds that

$$\sqrt{tr\left(B_1^2\right)} = \sqrt{tr\left(B_1^\dagger B_1\right)}$$

$$\leq \sqrt{tr\left(B_1^\dagger B_1 + B_2^\dagger B_2\right)}$$

$$= \left\| \left(\left(A + A^\dagger \right) /2 \otimes I \right) |\Phi\rangle \right\|$$
$$\leq \left(\left\| (A \otimes I)|\Phi\rangle \right\| + \left\| \left(A^\dagger \otimes I \right) |\Phi\rangle \right\| \right) /2$$
$$= \sqrt{\mathrm{tr}\left(A^\dagger A \right)}.$$

It is similar to prove that $\mathrm{tr}\left(B_i{}^2 \right) \leq \mathrm{tr}\left(A^\dagger A \right)$ for $i = 2, 3, 4$. $\qquad \square$

Let R be the matrix representation of quantum operation $\mathcal{G}$; see its defining Eq. (8.44). Then a bound of the powers of R is given in the following:

Lemma A.13. *For any integer $n \geq 0$, and for any state $|\alpha\rangle$ in $\mathcal{H} \otimes \mathcal{H}$, we have:*

$$\left\| R^n |\alpha\rangle \right\| \leq 4\sqrt{d} \| |\alpha\rangle \|$$

where $d = \dim \mathcal{H}$ is the dimension of Hilbert space $\mathcal{H}$.

Proof. Suppose that $|\alpha\rangle = \sum_{i,j} a_{ij} |ij\rangle$. Then we can write:

$$|\alpha\rangle = (A \otimes I)|\Phi\rangle$$

where $A = (a_{ij})$ is a $d \times d$ matrix. A routine calculation yields:

$$\| |\alpha\rangle \| = \sqrt{\mathrm{tr}\left(A^\dagger A \right)}.$$

We write:

$$A = (B_1 - B_2) + i(B_3 - B_4)$$

according to Lemma A.12. The idea behind this decomposition is that the trace-preserving property of Eq. (A.20) only applies to positive operators. Put

$$|\beta_i\rangle = (B_i \otimes I)|\Phi\rangle$$

for $i = 1, 2, 3, 4$. Using the triangle inequality, we obtain:

$$\left\| R^n |\alpha\rangle \right\| \leq \sum_{i=1}^4 \left\| R^n |\beta_i\rangle \right\| = \sum_{i=1}^4 \left\| \left(\mathcal{G}^n(B_i) \otimes I \right) |\Phi\rangle \right\|.$$

Note that

$$\left\| \left(\mathcal{G}^n(B_i) \otimes I \right) |\Phi\rangle \right\| = \sqrt{\mathrm{tr}\left(\mathcal{G}^n(B_i) \right)^2}, \tag{A.21}$$

$$\mathrm{tr}\left(B_i^2 \right) \leq (\mathrm{tr} B_i)^2. \tag{A.22}$$

Moreover, we know from Lemma A.11 that

$$\mathrm{tr}\left[\mathcal{G}^n(B_i) \right] \leq \mathrm{tr}\left[(\mathcal{G} + \mathcal{E}_0)^n (B_i) \right] = \mathrm{tr} B_i. \tag{A.23}$$

Combining Eqs (A.21), (A.22), and (A.23) yields

$$\sqrt{\mathrm{tr}(\mathcal{G}^n(B_i))^2} \leq \sqrt{(\mathrm{tr}\mathcal{G}^n(B_i))^2} \leq \sqrt{(\mathrm{tr} B_i)^2}.$$

Furthermore, by the Cauchy-inequality we have

$$(\mathrm{tr} B_i)^2 \leq d \cdot \left(\mathrm{tr} B_i^2 \right).$$

Therefore, it follows from Lemma A.12 that

$$\| R^n |\alpha\rangle \| \leq \sum_{i=1}^{4} \sqrt{d \cdot \mathrm{tr}\left(B_i^2\right)} \leq 4\sqrt{d \cdot \mathrm{tr}\left(A^\dagger A\right)} = 4\sqrt{d}\||\alpha\rangle\|. \qquad \Box$$

Now we are ready to prove Lemma 8.13. We prove part 1 by refutation. If there is some eigenvalue λ of R with $|\lambda| > 1$, suppose the corresponding normalised eigenvector is $|x\rangle$: $R|x\rangle = \lambda|x\rangle$. Choose integer n such that $|\lambda|^n > 4\sqrt{d}$. Then

$$\| R^n |x\rangle \| = \|\lambda^n |x\rangle\| = |\lambda|^n > 4\sqrt{d}\||x\rangle\|.$$

This contradicts to Lemma A.13.

Part 2 can also be proved by refutation. Without any loss of generality, we assume that $|\lambda_1| = 1$ with $k_1 > 1$ in the Jordan decomposition of R:

$$R = SJ(R)S^{-1}.$$

Suppose that $\{|i\rangle\}_{i=1}^{d^2}$ is the orthonormal basis of $\mathcal{H} \otimes \mathcal{H}$ compatible with the numbering of the columns and rows of R. Take an unnormalised vector $|y\rangle = S|k_1\rangle$, where $|k_1\rangle$ is the k_1th state in the basis $\{|i\rangle\}_{i=1}^{d^2}$. Since S is nonsingular, there are real numbers $L, r > 0$ such that

$$r \cdot \||x\rangle\| \leq \|S|x\rangle\| \leq L \cdot \||x\rangle\|$$

for any vector $|x\rangle$ in $\mathcal{H} \otimes \mathcal{H}$. By definition, it holds that $\||y\rangle\| \leq L$. We can choose integer n such that $nr > L \cdot 4\sqrt{d}$ because $r > 0$. Then a routine calculation yields:

$$R^n |y\rangle = L \cdot \sum_{t=0}^{k_1-1} \binom{n}{t} \lambda_1^{n-t} |k_1 - t\rangle.$$

Consequently, we have:

$$\| R^n |y\rangle \| \geq r \cdot \sum_{t=1}^{k_1} \binom{n}{t} |\lambda_1|^{n-t}$$

$$\geq nr > L \cdot 4\sqrt{d} \geq 4\sqrt{d}\||y\rangle\|.$$

This contradicts to Lemma A.13 again, and we complete the proof. $\qquad \Box$

Proof of Lemma 8.16. Recall that $J(N)$ is the matrix obtained from the Jordon normal form $J(R)$ of R through replacing the 1-dimensional Jordan blocks corresponding to the eigenvalues with module 1 by number 0. Without any loss of generality, we assume that the eigenvalues of R satisfy:

$$1 = |\lambda_1| = \cdots = |\lambda_s| > |\lambda_{s+1}| \geq \cdots \geq |\lambda_l|.$$

Then

$$J(R) = \begin{pmatrix} U & 0 \\ 0 & J_1 \end{pmatrix}$$

where $U = diag\,(\lambda_1, \cdots, \lambda_s)$ is an $s \times s$ diagonal unitary, and

$$J_1 = diag\left(J_{k_{s+1}}(\lambda_{s+1}), \cdots, J_{k_l}(\lambda_l)\right).$$

Moreover, we have:

$$J(N) = \begin{pmatrix} 0 & 0 \\ 0 & J_1 \end{pmatrix}.$$

The convergence of

$$\sum_{n=0}^{\infty} \left(\mathcal{E}_0 \circ \mathcal{G}^n \right)$$

follows immediately from Lemma 5.4, and it in turn implies the convergence of $\sum_{n=0}^{\infty} N_0 R^n$. It is clear that

$$\sum_{n=0}^{\infty} N_0 R^n = \sum_{n=0}^{\infty} N_0 S J(R)^n S^{-1}.$$

Since S is nonsingular, we see that

$$\sum_{n=0}^{\infty} N_0 S J(R)^n$$

converges. This implies that

$$\lim_{n \to \infty} N_0 S J(R)^n = 0.$$

Now we write:

$$N_0 S = \begin{pmatrix} Q & P \\ V & T \end{pmatrix},$$

where Q is an $s \times s$ matrix, T is a $(d^2 - s) \times (d^2 - s)$ matrix, and $d = \dim \mathcal{H}$ is the dimension of the state space $\mathcal{H}$. Then

$$N_0 S J(R)^n = \begin{pmatrix} Q U^n & P J_1{}^n \\ V U^n & T J_1{}^n \end{pmatrix},$$

and it follows that $\lim_{n \to \infty} Q U^n = 0$ and $\lim_{n \to \infty} V U^n = 0$. So, we have:

$$tr\left(Q^\dagger Q \right) = \lim_{n \to \infty} \mathrm{tr}(Q U^n)^\dagger Q U^n = 0,$$
$$tr\left(V^\dagger V \right) = \lim_{n \to \infty} \mathrm{tr}\left(V U^n \right)^\dagger V U^n = 0.$$

This yields $Q = 0$ and $V = 0$, and it follows immediately that $N_0 R^n = N_0 N^n$. $\qquad\square$

Proof of Lemma 8.21.2. We are going to show that any two BSCCs X, Y of a quantum Markov chain are orthogonal provided $\dim X \neq \dim Y$. This proof requires a technical preparation. An operator A (not necessarily a partial density operator as in Definition 8.31.1) on $\mathcal{H}$ is called a fixed point of quantum operation $\mathcal{E}$ if $\mathcal{E}(A) = A$. The following lemma shows that fixed points can be preserved by the positive matrix decomposition given in Lemma A.12.

Lemma A.14. *Let $\mathcal{E}$ be a quantum operation on $\mathcal{H}$ and A a fixed point of $\mathcal{E}$. If we have:*
1. $A = (X_+ - X_-) + i(Y_+ - Y_-)$;
2. X_+, X_-, Y_+, Y_- *are all positive matrices; and*
3. $supp(X_+) \perp supp(X_-)$ *and* $supp(Y_+) \perp supp(Y_-)$,

then X_+, X_-, Y_+, Y_- are all fixed points of $\mathcal{E}$.

Lemma A.14 is taken from Wolf [409].

Exercise A.1. Prove Lemma A.14.

Now we are ready to prove Lemma 8.21.2. Suppose without any loss of generality that $\dim X < \dim Y$. By Theorem 8.16, we know that there are two minimal fixed point states ρ and σ with $supp(\rho) = X$ and $supp(\sigma) = Y$. Note that for any $\lambda > 0$, $\rho - \lambda \sigma$ is also a fixed point of $\mathcal{E}$. We can take λ sufficiently large such that

$$\rho - \lambda \sigma = \Delta_+ - \Delta_-$$

with $\Delta_\pm$ being positive, $supp(\Delta_-) = supp(\sigma)$, and $supp(\Delta_+) \perp supp(\Delta_-)$. Let P be the projection onto Y. It follows from Lemma A.14 that both Δ_+ and Δ_- are fixed points of $\mathcal{E}$. Then

$$P\rho P = \lambda P\sigma P + P\Delta_+ P - P\Delta_- P = \lambda\sigma - \Delta_-$$

is a fixed point state of $\mathcal{E}$ too. Note that $supp(P\rho P) \subseteq Y$, σ is the minimal fixed point state and $supp(\sigma) = Y$. Therefore, we have $P\rho P = p\sigma$ for some $p \geq 0$. Now if $p > 0$, then by Proposition 8.3.3 we obtain:

$$Y = supp(\sigma) = supp(P\rho P) = span\{P|\psi\rangle : |\psi\rangle \in X\}.$$

This implies $\dim Y \leq \dim X$, contradicting our assumption. Thus we have $P\rho P = 0$, which implies $X \perp Y$. $\qquad\square$

Proof of Lemma 8.23. Roughly speaking, this lemma asserts that a fixed point state of $\mathcal{E}$ can be decomposed into two orthogonal fixed point states. The proof technique for Lemma 8.21.2 showing that two BSCCs are orthogonal can be used in the proof of this lemma. First, we note that for any $\lambda > 0$, $\rho - \lambda\sigma$ is also a fixed point of $\mathcal{E}$, and thus we can take λ sufficiently large such that

$$\rho - \lambda\sigma = \Delta_+ - \Delta_-$$

with $\Delta_\pm$ being positive, $supp(\Delta_-) = supp(\sigma)$, and $supp(\Delta_+)$ is the orthogonal complement of $supp(\Delta_-)$ in $supp(\rho)$. By Lemma A.14, both Δ_+ and Δ_- are fixed points of $\mathcal{E}$. Let $\eta = \Delta_+$. We have:

$$supp(\rho) = supp(\rho - \lambda\sigma) = supp(\Delta_+) \oplus supp(\Delta_-) = supp(\eta) \oplus supp(\sigma). \qquad\square$$

Proof of Lemma 8.24. For part 1, we are required to figure out the complexity for computing the asymptotic average $\mathcal{E}_\infty(\rho)$ of a density operator ρ. To this end, we first present a lemma about the matrix representation of the asymptotic average of a quantum operation.

Lemma A.15. *Let $M = SJS^{-1}$ be the Jordan decomposition of M where*

$$J = \bigoplus_{k=1}^{K} J_k(\lambda_k) = diag\left(J_1(\lambda_1), ..., J_K(\lambda_K)\right),$$

and $J_k(\lambda_k)$ is the Jordan block corresponding to the eigenvalue λ_k. Define

$$J_\infty = \bigoplus_{k \text{ s.t. } \lambda_k = 1} J_k(\lambda_k)$$

and $M_\infty = SJ_\infty S^{-1}$. Then M_∞ is the matrix representation of $\mathcal{E}_\infty$.

Exercise A.2. Prove Lemma A.15.

Now we can prove part 1 of Lemma 8.24. We know from [106] that the time complexity of Jordan decomposition for a $d \times d$ matrix is $O(d^4)$. So, we can compute the matrix representation M_∞ of $\mathcal{E}_\infty$ in time $O(d^8)$. Furthermore, $\mathcal{E}_\infty(\rho)$ can be computed using the correspondence:

$$(\mathcal{E}_\infty(\rho) \otimes I_\mathcal{H})|\Psi\rangle = M_\infty(\rho \otimes I_\mathcal{H})|\Psi\rangle$$

where $|\Psi\rangle = \sum_{i=1}^{d} |i\rangle|i\rangle$ is the (unnormalised) maximally entangled state in $\mathcal{H} \otimes \mathcal{H}$.

For part 2, we need to settle the complexity for finding the density operator basis of the set of fixed points of $\mathcal{E}$; i.e. {matrices $A : \mathcal{E}(A) = A$}. We first notice that this density operator basis can be computed in the following three steps:

(a) Compute the matrix representation M of $\mathcal{E}$. The time complexity is $O(md^4)$, where $m \leq d^2$ is the number of operators E_i in the Kraus representation $\mathcal{E} = \sum_i E_i \circ E_i^\dagger$.

(b) Find a basis $\mathcal{B}$ for the null space of the matrix $M - I_{\mathcal{H} \otimes \mathcal{H}}$, and transform them into matrix forms. This can be done by Gaussian elimination with complexity being $O((d^2)^3) = O(d^6)$.

(c) For each basis matrix A in $\mathcal{B}$, compute positive matrices X_+, X_-, Y_+, Y_- such that $supp(X_+) \perp supp(X_-)$, $supp(Y_+) \perp supp(Y_-)$, and

$$A = X_+ - X_- + i(Y_+ - Y_-).$$

Let Q be the set of nonzero elements in $\{X_+, X_-, Y_+, Y_-\}$. Then by Lemma A.14, every element of Q is a fixed point state of $\mathcal{E}$. Replace A by elements of Q after normalisation. Then the resultant $\mathcal{B}$ is the required density operator basis. At last, we make the elements in $\mathcal{B}$ linearly independent. This can be done by removing the redundant elements in $\mathcal{B}$ using Gaussian elimination. The computational complexity of this step is $O(d^6)$.

So, we see that the total complexity for computing the density operator basis of $\{$matrices $A : \mathcal{E}(A) = A\}$ is $O(d^6)$. $\qquad\square$

A.4.2 Proofs of the lemmas in Section 8.5

We first prove a group of lemmas about restriction and extension of projections presented in Section 8.5.2.

Proof of Lemma 8.30. Part 1 is exactly Lemma A.6 and proved in Appendix A.3.1. The proof of part 2 is similar to that of part 1 and left for the reader as an exercise. Part 4 is obvious.

To prove part 3, let $\{|j\rangle\}$, $\{|k\rangle\}$ be orthonormal bases of $\mathcal{H}_2$ and $\mathcal{H}_3$, respectively. Then

$$
\begin{aligned}
[P \downarrow (\mathcal{H}_1 \otimes \mathcal{H}_2)] \downarrow \mathcal{H}_1 &= \mathrm{supp}\left[\mathrm{tr}_{\mathcal{H}_2}\left(P \downarrow (\mathcal{H}_1 \otimes \mathcal{H}_2)\right)\right] \\
&= \mathrm{supp}\left[\mathrm{tr}_{\mathcal{H}_2}\left(\mathrm{supp}\left(\mathrm{tr}_{\mathcal{H}_3} P\right)\right)\right] \\
&= \mathrm{supp}\left[\sum_j \langle j|\mathrm{supp}\left(\mathrm{tr}_{\mathcal{H}_3} P\right)|j\rangle\right] \\
&= \mathrm{supp}\left[\sum_j \langle j|\mathrm{supp}\sum_k \langle k|P|k\rangle|j\rangle\right] \\
&= \mathrm{supp}\sum_{j,k} \langle j|\langle k|P|k\rangle|j\rangle \\
&= \mathrm{supp}\left[\mathrm{tr}_{\mathcal{H}_2 \otimes \mathcal{H}_3}(P)\right] = P \downarrow \mathcal{H}_1
\end{aligned}
$$

because $\{|j,k\rangle\}$ is an orthonormal basis of $\mathcal{H}_2 \otimes \mathcal{H}_3$. $\qquad\square$

Proof of Lemma 8.31. Part 1 is obvious. To prove part 2, for any $|\Psi\rangle \in P$, we want to show that $|\Psi\rangle \in (P \downarrow \mathcal{H}_1) \uparrow (\mathcal{H}_1 \otimes \mathcal{H}_2) = (P \downarrow \mathcal{H}_1) \otimes \mathcal{H}_2$. First, we can choose an orthonormal basis $\{|i\rangle\}_{i=1}^n$ of $\mathcal{H}_2$ and write

$$|\Psi\rangle = \sum_{i=1}^m \alpha_i |\varphi_i\rangle|i\rangle$$

for some $m \leq n$, complex numbers $\alpha_i \neq 0$ and $|\varphi_i\rangle \in \mathcal{H}_1$. Thus, it suffices to show that $|\varphi_i\rangle \in P \downarrow \mathcal{H}_1$ for all $1 \leq i \leq m$. In fact, it is easy to compute

$$\mathrm{tr}_{\mathcal{H}_2}|\Psi\rangle\langle\Psi| = \sum_{i=1}^m |\alpha_i|^2 |\varphi_i\rangle\langle\varphi_i|.$$

Then it follows from $|\Psi\rangle \in P$ that

$$\bigvee_{i=1}^m |\varphi_i\rangle\langle\varphi_i| = \mathrm{supp}\left(\mathrm{tr}_{\mathcal{H}_2}|\Psi\rangle\langle\Psi|\right) \subseteq \mathrm{supp}\left(\mathrm{tr}_{\mathcal{H}_2} P\right) = P \downarrow \mathcal{H}_1.$$

Part 3 ($\Leftarrow$) follows immediately from part 2. To prove part 3 ($\Rightarrow$), assume $Q \downarrow \mathcal{H}_1 \sqsubseteq P$, then using part 2, we obtain:

$$Q \sqsubseteq (Q \downarrow \mathcal{H}_1) \uparrow (\mathcal{H}_1 \otimes \mathcal{H}_2) \sqsubseteq P \uparrow (\mathcal{H}_1 \otimes \mathcal{H}_2). \qquad\square$$

Proof of Lemma 8.32. Part 2 is obvious. To prove part 1, we compute:

$$\mathcal{E}(P \downarrow \mathcal{H}_1) = \mathcal{E}\left(\mathrm{supptr}_{\mathcal{H}_2} P\right) = \bigvee_{|\psi\rangle \in \mathrm{supp}(\mathrm{tr}_{\mathcal{H}_2} P)} \mathrm{supp}\,\mathcal{E}(|\psi\rangle\langle\psi|)$$

$$= \mathrm{supp}\left(\sum_{|\psi\rangle \in \mathrm{supp}(\mathrm{tr}_{\mathcal{H}_2} P)} \mathcal{E}(|\psi\rangle\langle\psi|)\right)$$

$$= \mathrm{supp}\left(\sum_{|\Psi\rangle \in P} \mathrm{tr}_{\mathcal{H}_2}((\mathcal{E} \otimes \mathcal{I}_2)(|\Psi\rangle\langle\Psi|))\right)$$

$$= \mathrm{supp}\left(\mathrm{tr}_{\mathcal{H}_2}\left[\sum_{|\Psi\rangle \in P}((\mathcal{E} \otimes \mathcal{I}_2)(|\Psi\rangle\langle\Psi|))\right]\right)$$

$$= \mathrm{supp}\left(\mathrm{tr}_{\mathcal{H}_2}\left[\bigvee_{|\Psi\rangle \in P} \mathrm{supp}((\mathcal{E} \otimes \mathcal{I}_2)(|\Psi\rangle\langle\Psi|))\right]\right)$$

$$= (\mathcal{E} \otimes \mathcal{I}_2)(P) \downarrow \mathcal{H}_1. \qquad \square$$

Now we present the proofs of the lemmas given in Section 8.5.3.

Proof of Lemma 8.33. First, we note that $\mathbb{P} = (P_V)_{V \in S}$ with $P_V = \emptyset$ for every $V \in S$ is the least element of both $\mathcal{LS}(S)$ and $\mathcal{LS}_n(S)$. Second, assume that $\mathbb{P}_0 \sqsubseteq \mathbb{P}_1 \sqsubseteq \cdots \sqsubseteq \mathbb{P}_i \sqsubseteq \cdots$ where $\mathbb{P}_i = (P_{iV})_{V \in S}$. We set $P_V = \bigvee_{i=0}^\infty P_{iv}$. Then it is easy to see that $\mathbb{P} = (P_V)_{V \in S} = \bigvee_{i=0}^\infty \mathbb{P}_i \in \mathcal{LS}(S)$. Furthermore, if all $\mathbb{P}_i \in \mathcal{LS}_n(S)$, then for any $V_1, V_2 \in S$, we have:

$$P_{V_1} \downarrow (V_1 \cap V_2) = \left(\bigvee_{i=0}^\infty P_{iV_1}\right) \downarrow (V_1 \cap V_2)$$

$$= \bigvee_{i=0}^\infty \left[P_{iV_1} \downarrow (V_1 \cap V_2)\right] \qquad \text{(By Lemma 8.30.1)}$$

$$= \bigvee_{i=0}^\infty \left[P_{iV_2} \downarrow (V_1 \cap V_2)\right] \qquad \text{(By consistency of every } \mathbb{P}_i)$$

$$= \cdots = P_{V_2} \downarrow (V_1 \cap V_2).$$

Therefore, $\mathbb{P} \in \mathcal{LS}_n(S)$. $\qquad \square$

Proof of Lemma 8.34. For any $V' \in T$ with $W \subseteq V'$, we have $W \subseteq V \cap V'$ and

$$P_{V'} \downarrow W = \left[P_{V'} \downarrow (V \cap V')\right] \downarrow W \qquad \text{(By Lemma 8.30.3)}$$

$$= \left[P_V \downarrow (V \cap V')\right] \downarrow W \qquad \text{(By consistency of } \mathbb{P})$$

$$= P_V \downarrow W.$$

Thus, it follows that

$$Q_W = \bigvee_{V' \in T : W \subseteq V'} (P_{V'} \downarrow W) = P_V \downarrow W. \qquad \square$$

Proof of Lemma 8.35. For any $\mathbb{P} = (P_V)_{V \in S} \in \mathcal{LS}_n(S)$, let $\alpha_{T \to S}(\mathbb{P}) = \mathbb{Q} = (Q_W)_{W \in T}$. What we need to prove is that for any $W_1, W_2 \in S$:

$$Q_{W_1} \downarrow (W_1 \cap W_2) = Q_{W_2} \downarrow (W_1 \cap W_2).$$

Since $S \trianglelefteq T$, we assert that for $i = 1, 2$, there exists $V_i \in T$ such that $W_i \subseteq V_i$. By Lemma 8.34 we obtain $Q_{W_i} = P_{V_i} \downarrow W_i$. Then $W_1 \cap W_2 \subseteq V_1 \cap V_2$ and

$$
\begin{aligned}
Q_{W_1} \downarrow (W_1 \cap W_2) &= \left(P_{V_1} \downarrow W_1\right) \downarrow (W_1 \cap W_2) \\
&= P_{V_1} \downarrow (W_1 \cap W_2) && \text{(By Lemma A.6.2)} \\
&= \left[P_{V_1} \downarrow (V_1 \cap V_2)\right] \downarrow (W_1 \cap W_2) && \text{(By Lemma A.6.2)} \\
&= \left[P_{V_2} \downarrow (V_1 \cap V_2)\right] \downarrow (W_1 \cap W_2) && \text{(By consistency of } \mathbb{P} \in \mathcal{LS}_n(S)) \\
&= \cdots = Q_{W_2} \downarrow (W_1 \cap W_2).
\end{aligned}
$$

$\square$

Proof of Lemma 8.36. For any $\mathbb{P} = (P_V)_{V \in T} \in \mathcal{LS}(T)$, let $\alpha_{T \to S}(\mathbb{P}) = \mathbb{Q} = (Q_W)_{W \in S} \in \mathcal{LS}(S)$. Then for every $W \in S$:

$$
Q_W = \bigvee_{V \in T : W \subseteq V} (P_V \downarrow W).
$$

Furthermore, let $\alpha_{S \to R}(\mathbb{Q}) = \mathbb{Y} = (Y_X)_{X \in R} \in \mathcal{LS}(R)$ and $\alpha_{T \to R}(\mathbb{P}) = \mathbb{Z} = (Z_X)_{X \in R} \in \mathcal{LS}(R)$. Then

$$
\begin{aligned}
Y_X &= \bigvee_{W \in S : X \subseteq W} (Q_W \downarrow X) \\
&= \bigvee_{W \in S : X \subseteq W} \left[\left(\bigvee_{V \in T : W \subseteq V} (P_V \downarrow W)\right) \downarrow X\right] \\
&= \bigvee_{W \in S : X \subseteq W} \bigvee_{V \in T : W \subseteq V} [(P_V \downarrow W) \downarrow X] && \text{(By Lemma 8.30.1)} \\
&= \bigvee_{W \in S : X \subseteq W} \bigvee_{V \in T : W \subseteq V} (P_V \downarrow X) && \text{(By Lemma 8.30.3)} \\
&\sqsubseteq \bigvee_{V \in T : X \subseteq V} (P_V \downarrow X) = Z_X.
\end{aligned}
$$

Now assume that $\mathbb{P} = (P_V)_{V \in T} \in \mathcal{LS}_n(T)$. For any $V \in T$ and $X \in R$ with $X \subseteq V$, since $R \trianglelefteq S$, there exists $W \in S$ such that $X \subseteq W$. Furthermore, since $S \trianglelefteq T$, there exists $V' \in T$ such that $W \subseteq V'$. Then $X \subseteq V \cap V'$ and by Lemma 8.30.3 and the consistency in Definition 8.42.2 we obtain:

$$
P_V \downarrow X = \left(P_V \downarrow V \cap V'\right) \downarrow X = \left(P_{V'} \downarrow V \cap V'\right) \downarrow X = P_{V'} \downarrow X.
$$

Therefore, it holds that

$$
Z_X = \bigvee_{V \in T : X \subseteq V} (P_V \downarrow X) = \bigvee_{W \in S : X \subseteq W} \bigvee_{V' \in T : W \subseteq V'} (P_V' \downarrow X) = Y_X.
$$

$\square$

A.5 Omitted proofs in Chapter 9

A.5.1 Proof of the lemmas in Section 9.2

We first prove a diamond property for disjoint parallel quantum programs.

Lemma A.16. *The operational semantics of disjoint parallel quantum programs enjoys the diamond property:*

- *if $\mathcal{A} \to \mathcal{A}_1$, $\mathcal{A} \to \mathcal{A}_2$ and $\mathcal{A}_1 \neq \mathcal{A}_2$, then there exists $\mathcal{B}$ such that $\mathcal{A}_1 \to \mathcal{B}$ and $\mathcal{A}_2 \to \mathcal{B}$.*

Proof. Assume that $\mathcal{A}$ comes from certain transitions of a parallel composition of n programs. Then all programs in $\mathcal{A}$ are parallel compositions of n programs (except the terminating ones $\downarrow$). Suppose that $\mathcal{A} \to \mathcal{A}_1$ results from a transition of the ith component of some program

$$
P \equiv \langle P_1 \| \cdots \| P_i \| \cdots \| P_n, \rho \rangle \in \mathcal{A};
$$

that is, $\langle P_i, \rho \rangle \to \{|\langle Q_{ik}, \sigma_k \rangle|\}$ and $\mathcal{A}_1 = (\mathcal{A} \setminus \{P\}) \cup \mathcal{B}_1$, where:

$$\mathcal{B}_1 = \{|\langle P_1 \| \cdots \| P_{i-1} \| Q_{ik} \| P_{i+1} \| \cdots \| P_n, \sigma_k \rangle|\}.$$

Note that here, only rules (PC) and (MS1) are used to derive the transition. The conclusion can be easily generalised to the case where rule (MS2) is employed. Also, suppose that $\mathcal{A} \to \mathcal{A}_2$ results from a transition of the jth component of some program

$$R \equiv \langle R_1 \| \cdots \| R_i \| \cdots \| R_n, \delta \rangle \in \mathcal{A};$$

that is, $\langle R_j, \delta \rangle \to \{|\langle S_{jl}, \theta_l \rangle|\}$ and $\mathcal{A}_2 = (\mathcal{A} \setminus \{R\}) \cup \mathcal{B}_2$, where:

$$\mathcal{B}_2 = \{|\langle R_1 \| \cdots \| R_{j-1} \| S_{jl} \| R_{j+1} \| \cdots \| R_n, \theta_l \rangle|\}.$$

Case 1. P and R are two different elements of multiset $\mathcal{A}$. Put

$$\mathcal{B} = (\mathcal{A} \setminus \{P, R\}) \cup \mathcal{B}_1 \cup \mathcal{B}_2.$$

Then it is easy to derive $\mathcal{A}_1 \to \mathcal{B}$ and $\mathcal{A}_2 \to \mathcal{B}$ by transitional rules (PC) and (MS).

Case 2. P and R are the same element of multiset $\mathcal{A}$. Then it must be that $i \neq j$ because $\mathcal{A}_1 \neq \mathcal{A}_2$. Note that each element of $\mathcal{B}_1$ is of the form

$$\langle P_1 \| \cdots \| P_{i-1} \| Q_{ik} \| P_{i+1} \| \cdots \| P_n, \sigma_k \rangle,$$

and each element of $\mathcal{B}_2$ is of the form

$$\langle P_1 \| \cdots \| P_{j-1} \| R_{jl} \| P_{j+1} \| \cdots \| P_n, \delta_l \rangle.$$

Here, σ_k is obtained from applying certain operators in P_i to ρ, and δ_l is obtained from applying some operators in P_j to ρ. Now we can make the transition of the jth component in $\mathcal{B}_1$ and the transition of the ith component in $\mathcal{B}_2$. After that, an element in $\mathcal{B}_1$ becomes some configuration(s) of the form

$$\langle P_1 \| \cdots \| P_{i-1} \| Q_{ik} \| P_{i+1} \| \cdots \| P_{j-1} \| R_{jl} \| P_{j+1} \| \cdots \| P_n, \theta_{kl} \rangle \tag{A.24}$$

where θ_{kl} is obtained from applying the operators that generated δ_l to σ_k, and an element in $\mathcal{A}_2$ becomes some configuration(s) of the form

$$\langle P_1 \| \cdots \| P_{i-1} \| Q_{ik} \| P_{i+1} \| \cdots \| P_{j-1} \| R_{jl} \| P_{j+1} \| \cdots \| P_n, \eta_{kl} \rangle \tag{A.25}$$

where η_{kl} is obtained from applying the operators that generated σ_k to δ_l. We use $\mathcal{B}_1'$, $\mathcal{B}_2'$ to denote the sets of elements given in Eqs. (A.24), (A.25), respectively. Note that $var(P_i) \cap var(P_j) = \emptyset$. So, an operator on $\mathcal{H}_{P_i}$ and an operator on $\mathcal{H}_{P_j}$ always commute. Therefore, $\mathcal{B}_1' = \mathcal{B}_2'$, and we complete the proof by setting $\mathcal{B} = \mathcal{B}_1' (= \mathcal{B}_2')$. $\square$

A confluence property follows from the above diamond property.

Lemma A.17. *If $\langle P, \rho \rangle \to \mathcal{A}_1 \to \cdots \to \mathcal{A}_k \to \cdots$ and $\langle P, \rho \rangle \to \mathcal{B}_1 \to \cdots \to \mathcal{B}_k \to \cdots$, then there are $C_1, \cdots, C_k \cdots$ such that*

$$\langle P, \rho \rangle \to^* C_1 \to^* \cdots \to^* C_k \to^* \cdots$$

and $\mathcal{A}_k \to^* C_k$ and $\mathcal{B}_k \to^* C_k$ for every k.

Proof. We proceed by induction on k to find C_k. For the case of $k = 1$, it follows immediately from the diamond property (Lemma A.16) that C_1 exists. Now assume that we have

$$\langle P, \rho \rangle \to^* C_1 \to^* \cdots \to^* C_k,$$

$\mathcal{A}_k \to^m C_k$ and $\mathcal{B}_k \to^r C_k$. Then repeatedly using the diamond property we can find $\mathcal{A}_{k+1}'$ such that $\mathcal{A}_{k+1} \to^m \mathcal{A}_{k+1}'$ and $C_k \to \mathcal{A}_{k+1}'$. Similarly, we have $\mathcal{B}_{k+1}'$ such that $C_k \to \mathcal{B}_{k+1}'$ and $\mathcal{B}_{k+1} \to^r \mathcal{B}_{k+1}'$. Consequently, we can use the diamond property once again and find C_{k+1} such that $\mathcal{A}_{k+1}' \to C_{k+1}$ and $\mathcal{B}_{k+1}' \to C_{k+1}$. Obviously, it holds that $C_k \to^* C_{k+1}$, $\mathcal{A}_{k+1} \to^* C_{k+1}$ and $\mathcal{B}_{k+1} \to^* C_{k+1}$. $\square$

Now we are ready to prove Lemma 9.2 by refutation.

Proof of Lemma 9.2. Assume that $[\![P]\!](\rho)$ has two different elements $val(\pi_1) \neq val(\pi_2)$. We consider the following two cases:

Case 1. One of π_1 and π_2 is finite. Suppose that, say, π_1 is longer than π_2. Then π_1 is finite, and using Lemma A.17 we can show that π_1 can be extended. Thus, π_1 is not a computation, a contradiction.

Case 2. Both $\pi_1 = \langle P, \rho \rangle \to \mathcal{A}_1 \to \cdots \to \mathcal{A}_k \to \cdots$ and $\pi_2 = \langle P, \rho \rangle \to \mathcal{B}_1 \to \cdots \to \mathcal{B}_k \to \cdots$ are infinite. Then by Lemma A.17 we have a computation:

$$\pi = \langle P, \rho \rangle \to \mathcal{C}_1 \to^* \cdots \to^* \mathcal{C}_k \to^* \cdots$$

such that $\mathcal{A}_k \to^* \mathcal{C}_k$ and $\mathcal{B}_k \to^* \mathcal{C}_k$ for every k. It follows that $val(\mathcal{A}_k) \leq val(\mathcal{C}_k)$ and $val(\mathcal{B}_k) \leq val(\mathcal{C}_k)$ for all k. Furthermore, we have:

$$val(\pi_1) = \lim_{k \to \infty} val(\mathcal{A}_k) \leq \lim_{k \to \infty} val(\mathcal{C}_k) = val(\pi)$$

and $val(\pi_2) \leq val(\pi)$. Since $val(\pi_1) \neq val(\pi_2)$, we have either $val(\pi_1) < val(\pi)$ or $val(\pi_2) < val(\pi)$. This contradicts to the assumption that both $val(\pi_1)$ and $val(\pi_2)$ are maximal elements of $\mathcal{V}(P, \rho)$ in Definition 9.5. $\square$

Proof of Lemma 9.3. The proof is carried out in the following two steps:

1. For any input ρ, by Definition 9.3 we see that π is a computation of $P_1 \| \cdots \| P_n$ starting in ρ if and only if it is a computation of $P_{i_1} \| \cdots \| P_{i_n}$ starting in ρ. Then by Definition 9.5 it follows that

$$[\![P_1 \| \cdots \| P_n]\!](\rho) = [\![P_{i_1} \| \cdots \| P_{i_n}]\!](\rho).$$

2. For each computation

$$\pi = \langle P_1; \cdots; P_n, \rho \rangle \to \mathcal{A}_1 \to \cdots \to \mathcal{A}_k \to \cdots$$

of $P_1; \cdots; P_n$ starting in ρ, we note that each configuration in $\mathcal{A}_k$ must be of the form $\langle Q; P_l; \cdots; P_n, \sigma \rangle$ for some $1 \leq l \leq n$. Then we can replace it by the configuration

$$\langle \downarrow \| \cdots \| \downarrow \| Q \| P_l \| \cdots \| P_n, \sigma \rangle$$

and thus obtain configuration ensemble $\mathcal{A}'_k$. It is easy to see that

$$\pi' = \langle P_1 \| \cdots \| P_n, \rho \rangle \to \cdots \mathcal{A}'_1 \to \cdots \to \mathcal{A}'_k \to \cdots$$

is a computation of $P_1 \| \cdots \| P_n$ and $val(\pi') = val(\pi)$. Therefore, we have:

$$\mathcal{V}(P_1; \cdots; P_n, \rho) \subseteq \mathcal{V}(P_1 \| \cdots \| P_n, \rho).$$

By Lemma 9.2 (Determinism) we know that $[\![P_1 \| \cdots \| P_n]\!](\rho)$ is the greatest element of $(\mathcal{V}(P_1 \| \cdots \| P_n, \rho), \sqsubseteq)$. Then it follows from Definition 9.5 that

$$[\![P_1; \cdots; P_n]\!](\rho) \sqsubseteq [\![P_1 \| \cdots \| P_n]\!](\rho).$$

To prove the reverse of the above inequality, we note that for any quantum **while**-program P and any computation $\langle P, \rho \rangle \to \mathcal{B}_1 \to \cdots \to \mathcal{B}_k \to \cdots$, sequence $\{val(\mathcal{B}_k)\}$ is increasing with respect to $\sqsubseteq$. Then for any other quantum **while**-program P', we have:

$$[\![P]\!](\rho) \sqsubseteq [\![P; P']\!](\rho). \tag{A.26}$$

Furthermore, we can prove:

$$[\![P_1; \cdots; P_n]\!](\rho) \sqsubseteq [\![(P_1; P'_1); \cdots; (P_n; P'_n)]\!](\rho)$$

by induction on n. Indeed, the induction hypothesis for $n - 1$ implies:

$$[\![P_1; \cdots; P_n]\!](\rho) = [\![P_n]\!]([\![P_1; \cdots; P_{n-1}]\!](\rho))$$

$$\sqsubseteq [\![P_n]\!]([\![(P_1; P_1'); \cdots ; (P_{n-1}; P_{n-1}')]\!](\rho))$$
$$\sqsubseteq [\![P_n; P_n']\!]([\![(P_1; P_1'); \cdots ; (P_{n-1}; P_{n-1}')]\!](\rho))$$
$$= [\![(P_1; P_1'); \cdots ; (P_n; P_n')]\!](\rho).$$

Now, for any computation

$$\pi = \langle P_1 \| \cdots \| P_n, \rho\rangle \to \mathcal{A}_1 \to \cdots \to \mathcal{A}_k \to \cdots$$

of $P_1 \| \cdots \| P_n$, and for any $k \geq 1$, we observe that $\mathcal{A}_k$ is obtained from $\langle P_1 \| \cdots \| P_n, \rho\rangle$ by a finite number of transitions, each of which is performed by one of $P_1, \cdots, P_n$. Since $P_1, \cdots, P_n$ are disjoint, an operator on $\mathcal{H}_{P_i}$ always commutes with any operator on $\mathcal{H}_{P_j}$ provided $i \neq j$. Thus, these transitions can be reordered in order to satisfy the following requirements:

a. P_i is (semantically) equivalent to $Q_i; P_i'$ for every $i = 1, ..., n$;
b. the first group of transitions are done by Q_1, the second by Q_2, and so on.

Using inequality (A.26), we obtain:

$$val(\mathcal{A}_k) \sqsubseteq [\![Q_1; \cdots ; Q_n]\!](\rho)$$
$$\sqsubseteq [\![(Q_1; P_1'); \cdots ; (Q_n; P_n')]\!](\rho) = [\![P_1; \cdots ; P_n]\!](\rho)$$

and it follows that

$$val(\pi) = \lim_{k \to \infty} val(\mathcal{A}_k) \sqsubseteq [\![P_1; \cdots ; P_n]\!](\rho).$$

Therefore, $[\![P_1; \cdots ; P_n]\!](\rho)$ is an upper bound of $\mathcal{V}(P_1 \| \cdots \| P_n, \rho)$, and

$$[\![P_1 \| \cdots \| P_n]\!](\rho) \sqsubseteq [\![P_1; \cdots ; P_n]\!](\rho). \qquad \square$$

A.5.2 Proofs of facts in Section 9.3

Proof of Fact 9.1. Let us first prove Eq. (9.18). We directly compute:

$$(\mathcal{I}_p \otimes \mathcal{F}_\beta^*)(E) = \sum_{\forall i \in [n]: k_i \in \mathcal{J}_i} \left(\bigotimes_{i=1}^{n} |k_i\rangle_{i'}\right) {}_{p'}\langle\bar\beta| \left[\bigotimes_{i=1}^{n}(|\Psi_i\rangle\langle\Psi_i|)\right] |\bar\beta\rangle_{p'} \left(\bigotimes_{i=1}^{n} {}_{i'}\langle k_i|\right)$$

$$= \sum_{\substack{\forall i \in [n]: \\ k_i \in \mathcal{J}_i,\, l_i, l_i', j_i, j_i' \in [d_i]}} \alpha_{l_1, \cdots, l_n} \alpha_{l_1', \cdots, l_n'}^{*} \left(\bigotimes_{i=1}^{n} |k_i\rangle_{i'}\right) \left(\bigotimes_{i=1}^{n} {}_{i'}\langle l_i|\right) \times$$

$$\frac{1}{\prod_i d_i} \left[\bigotimes_{i=1}^{n}(|j_i\rangle_i\langle j_i'| \otimes |j_i\rangle_{i'}\langle j_i'|)\right] \left(\bigotimes_{i=1}^{n} |l_i'\rangle_{i'}\right) \left(\bigotimes_{i=1}^{n} {}_{i'}\langle k_i|\right)$$

$$= \sum_{\substack{\forall i \in [n]: \\ k_i \in \mathcal{J}_i,\, l_i, l_i' \in [d_i]}} \alpha_{l_1, \cdots, l_n} \alpha_{l_1', \cdots, l_n'}^{*} \frac{1}{\prod_i d_i} \left(\bigotimes_{i=1}^{n} |k_i\rangle_{i'}\right) \left[\bigotimes_{i=1}^{n}(|l_i\rangle_i\langle l_i'|)\right] \left(\bigotimes_{i=1}^{n} {}_{i'}\langle k_i|\right)$$

$$= \left\{\frac{1}{\prod_i d_i} \sum_{\substack{\forall i \in [n]: \\ l_i, l_i' \in [d_i]}} \alpha_{l_1, \cdots, l_n} \alpha_{l_1', \cdots, l_n'}^{*} \left[\bigotimes_{i=1}^{n}(|l_i\rangle_i\langle l_i'|)\right]\right\}$$

$$\otimes \left\{\sum_{\substack{\forall i \in [n]: \\ k_i \in \mathcal{J}_i}} \left(\bigotimes_{i=1}^{n} |k_i\rangle_{i'}\right) \left(\bigotimes_{i=1}^{n} {}_{i'}\langle k_i|\right)\right\}$$

$$= \frac{1}{\prod_i d_i} |\beta\rangle_p \langle\beta| \otimes I_{p'}.$$

Eq. (9.19) is proved by the following computation:

$$
(\mathcal{I}_p \otimes \mathcal{F}_\beta^*)(D) = \sum_{\forall i \in [n]: k_i \in \mathcal{J}_i} \left(\bigotimes_{i=1}^n |k_i\rangle_{i'} \right) {}_{p'}\langle \bar{\beta}| \left[\bigotimes_{i=1}^n (\mathcal{E}_i^* \otimes \mathcal{I}_{i'})(|\Psi_i\rangle\langle\Psi_i|) \right] |\bar{\beta}\rangle_{p'} \left(\bigotimes_{i=1}^n {}_{i'}\langle k_i| \right)
$$

$$
= \sum_{\substack{\forall\, i \in [n]: \\ k_i \in \mathcal{J}_i,\, l_i, l_i', j_i, j_i' \in [d_i]}} \alpha_{l_1,\cdots,l_n} \alpha^*_{l_1',\cdots,l_n'} \left(\bigotimes_{i=1}^n |k_i\rangle_{i'} \right) \left(\bigotimes_{i=1}^n {}_{i'}\langle l_i| \right) \times
$$

$$
\left[\frac{1}{\prod_i d_i} \bigotimes_{i=1}^n (\mathcal{E}_i^*(|j_i\rangle_i\langle j_i'|) \otimes |j_i\rangle_{i'}\langle j_i'|) \right] \left(\bigotimes_{i=1}^n |l_i'\rangle_{i'} \right) \left(\bigotimes_{i=1}^n {}_{i'}\langle k_i| \right)
$$

$$
= \sum_{\substack{\forall\, i \in [n]: \\ k_i \in \mathcal{J}_i,\, l_i, l_i' \in [d_i]}} \alpha_{l_1,\cdots,l_n} \alpha^*_{l_1',\cdots,l_n'} \left(\bigotimes_{i=1}^n |k_i\rangle_{i'} \right) \left[\frac{1}{\prod_i d_i} \bigotimes_{i=1}^n \mathcal{E}_i^*(|l_i\rangle_i\langle l_i'|) \right] \left(\bigotimes_{i=1}^n {}_{i'}\langle k_i| \right)
$$

$$
= \left\{ \frac{1}{\prod_i d_i} \sum_{\substack{\forall\, i \in [n]: \\ l_i, l_i' \in [d_i]}} \alpha_{l_1,\cdots,l_n} \alpha^*_{l_1',\cdots,l_n'} \left[\left(\bigotimes_{i=1}^n \mathcal{E}_i^* \right) \left(\bigotimes_{i=1}^n |l_i\rangle_i\langle l_i'| \right) \right] \right\} \otimes \left\{ \sum_{\substack{\forall\, i \in [n]: \\ k_i \in \mathcal{J}_i}} \left(\bigotimes_{i=1}^n (|k_i\rangle_{i'}\langle k_i|) \right) \right\}
$$

$$
= \frac{1}{\prod_i d_i} \left(\bigotimes_{i=1}^n \mathcal{E}_i^* \right) \left\{ \sum_{\substack{\forall\, i \in [n]: \\ l_i, l_i' \in [d_i]}} \alpha_{l_1,\cdots,l_n} \alpha^*_{l_1',\cdots,l_n'} \left[\bigotimes_{i=1}^n |l_i\rangle_i\langle l_i'| \right] \right\} \otimes \left\{ \sum_{\substack{\forall\, i \in [n]: \\ k_i \in \mathcal{J}_i}} \left(\bigotimes_{i=1}^n (|k_i\rangle_{i'}\langle k_i|) \right) \right\}
$$

$$
= \frac{1}{\prod_i d_i} \left(\bigotimes_{i=1}^n \mathcal{E}_i^* \right) (|\beta\rangle_p\langle\beta|) \otimes I_{p'}. \qquad \square
$$

Before proving Fact 9.2, we present some properties about convergence of operators. The following lemma shows that for quantum predicates, convergence according to the Löwner order and strong convergence coincide.

Lemma A.18. *Let $\{A_n\}$ be an increasing (respectively, decreasing) sequence of quantum predicates with respect to Löwner order and $A = \bigsqcup_{n=0}^\infty A_n$ (respectively, $\bigsqcap_{n=0}^\infty A_n$). Then $\{A_n\}$ strongly converges to A: $A_n \xrightarrow{s.o.t.} A$*

Proof. It suffices that note that for any $|\psi\rangle \in \mathcal{H}$, we have $\lim_{n\to\infty} \|A_n|\psi\rangle - A|\psi\rangle\| = 0$. $\qquad \square$

The next lemma shows that the dual of a quantum operation is continuous with respect to weak convergence of operators.

Lemma A.19. *For quantum predicates $\{A_n\}$, A and quantum operation $\mathcal{E}$, if $A_n \xrightarrow{w.o.t.} A$, then $\mathcal{E}^*(A_n) \xrightarrow{w.o.t.} \mathcal{E}^*(A)$.*

Proof. For any $\rho \in \mathcal{D}(\mathcal{H})$, with Lemma A.2 we observe:

$$
\lim_{n\to\infty} \mathrm{tr}\left(\mathcal{E}^*(A_n)\rho\right) = \lim_{n\to\infty} \mathrm{tr}\left(A_n\mathcal{E}(\rho)\right) = \mathrm{tr}(A\mathcal{E}(\rho)) = \mathrm{tr}\left(\mathcal{E}^*(A)\rho\right)
$$

which implies $\mathcal{E}^*(A_n) \xrightarrow{w.o.t.} \mathcal{E}^*(A)$. $\qquad \square$

Now we are ready to present:

Proof of Fact 9.2. We first note that for each i, $P_{ik} \xrightarrow{s.o.t.} I_i$ because for any $|\psi\rangle \in \mathcal{H}_i$, $\lim_{n\to\infty} \|P_{ik}|\psi\rangle - I_i|\psi\rangle\| = 0$. Then by Theorem 1 in [260] we have:

$$
P_{1k} \otimes P_{2k} \otimes \cdots \otimes P_{nk} \xrightarrow{s.o.t.} I_1 \otimes I_2 \cdots \otimes I_n,
$$

or equivalently,

$$
P_k \xrightarrow{s.o.t.} I.
$$

According to the definition of $|\beta_k\rangle$, we see that

$$|\beta_k\rangle \xrightarrow{\|\cdot\|} |\beta\rangle,$$

and therefore,

$$|\beta_k\rangle\langle\beta_k| \xrightarrow{s.o.t.} |\beta\rangle\langle\beta| \quad \Rightarrow \quad |\beta_k\rangle\langle\beta_k| \xrightarrow{w.o.t.} |\beta\rangle\langle\beta|.$$

To see this, we notice that for any $|\psi\rangle \in \mathcal{H}$, it follows from the Cauchy–Schwarz inequality and Lemma A.1 that

$$
\begin{aligned}
\lim_{k\to\infty} \||\beta_k\rangle\langle\beta_k|\psi\rangle - |\beta\rangle\langle\beta|\psi\rangle\| &= \lim_{k\to\infty} \||\beta_k\rangle((\langle\beta_k| - \langle\beta|)|\psi\rangle + (|\beta_k\rangle - |\beta\rangle)\langle\beta|\psi\rangle\| \\
&\leq \lim_{k\to\infty} \||\beta_k\rangle\|\|\psi\rangle\|\||\beta_k\rangle - |\beta\rangle\| + |\langle\beta|\psi\rangle|\||\beta_k\rangle - |\beta\rangle\| \\
&= 0
\end{aligned}
$$

Furthermore, using Lemma A.19 we obtain:

$$\mathcal{E}^*(|\beta_k\rangle\langle\beta_k|) \xrightarrow{w.o.t.} \mathcal{E}^*(|\beta\rangle\langle\beta|). \qquad \square$$

A.5.3 Proof of Theorem 9.3

We first prove soundness of qPPA. It suffices to show that rule (R.PC.SP) is sound for partial correctness because soundness of the other rules in qPP have been proved before.

Proof. For each i, it follows from assumptions $\models P_i : \text{Abort}(C_i)$, $\models P_i : \text{Term}(D_i)$ and $\models_{par} \{D_i + A_i\} P_i \{B_i\}$ that

$$C_i \sqsubseteq I_i - \llbracket P_i \rrbracket^*(I_i), \quad I_i - \llbracket P_i \rrbracket^*(I_i) \sqsubseteq D_i, \quad D_i + A_i \sqsubseteq I_i - \llbracket P_i \rrbracket^*(I_i) + \llbracket P_i \rrbracket^*(B_i).$$

Consequently, we obtain:

$$\llbracket P_i \rrbracket^*(I_i) \sqsubseteq I_i - C_i, \quad A_i \sqsubseteq \llbracket P_i \rrbracket^*(B_i).$$

Note that the semantic function for disjoint parallel program $P \equiv P_1 \| \cdots \| P_n$ is $\llbracket P \rrbracket = \bigotimes_{i=1}^n \llbracket P_i \rrbracket$. Then it is straightforward to see that

$$
\begin{aligned}
I - \bigotimes_{i=1}^n (I_i - C_i) + \bigotimes_{i=1}^n A_i &\sqsubseteq I - \bigotimes_{i=1}^n \llbracket P_i \rrbracket^*(I_i) + \bigotimes_{i=1}^n \llbracket P_i \rrbracket^*(B_i) \\
&= I - \llbracket P \rrbracket^*(I) + \llbracket P \rrbracket^* \left(\bigotimes_{i=1}^n B_i \right)
\end{aligned}
$$

which actually means:

$$\models_{par} \left\{ I - \bigotimes_{i=1}^n (I_i - C_i) + \bigotimes_{i=1}^n A_i \right\} P_1 \| \cdots \| P_n \left\{ \bigotimes_{i=1}^n B_i \right\}. \qquad \square$$

Remark A.1. In Remark 9.3, we pointed out that if nested parallelism is allowed, then rule (R.T.P) must be added in order to preserve the completeness of proof system qPP. The soundness of (R.T.P) is proved as follows. For each i, it follows from the assumption $\models P_i : \text{Term}(A_i)$ that

$$I_i - \llbracket P_i \rrbracket^*(I_i) \sqsubseteq A_i, i.e. \ I_i - A_i \sqsubseteq \llbracket P_i \rrbracket^*(I_i).$$

Since $P \equiv P_1 \| \cdots \| P_n$ is a disjoint parallel program, we have $\llbracket P \rrbracket = \bigotimes_{i=1}^n \llbracket P_i \rrbracket$ and

$$I - \llbracket P \rrbracket^*(I) = I - \bigotimes_{i=1}^m \llbracket P_i \rrbracket^*(I_i) \sqsubseteq I - \bigotimes_{i=1}^m (I_i - A_i),$$

which means:

$$\models P_1 \| \cdots \| P_n : \text{Term}\left(I - \bigotimes_{i=1}^{m}(I_i - A_i)\right).$$

Now we turn to prove completeness of qPPA. The idea is similar to the proof of Theorem 9.2. So, we use the notations defined there. Assume that

$$\models_{par} \{A\}P_1 \| \cdots \| P_n\{B\}.$$

We write $\mathcal{E} = [\![P_1 \| \cdots \| P_n]\!]$ for the semantic function of the parallel program, and for each $i = 1, ..., n$, let $\mathcal{E}_i$ be the semantic function of program P_i. Then by Lemma 7.1 we have:

$$A \sqsubseteq I - \mathcal{E}^*(I) + \mathcal{E}^*(B)$$

where I is the identity operator on $\mathcal{H}_p$, the state Hilbert space of whole parallel program, and by rule (R.Or) it suffices to show that

$$\vdash_{qPP} \{I - \mathcal{E}^*(I) + \mathcal{E}^*(B)\}P_1 \| \cdots \| P_n\{B\}. \tag{A.27}$$

We will complete the proof of Eq. (A.27) in four steps. Our first step is to consider a special form of $B = |\beta\rangle\langle\beta|$ with certain constraint on $|\beta\rangle$.

Claim A.1. *For any vector $|\beta\rangle$ such that its norm less than or equal to 1 and for each i, its reduced density operator on $\mathcal{H}_i$ is of finite rank, we have:*

$$\vdash_{qPP} \{I - \mathcal{E}^*(I) + \mathcal{E}^*(|\beta\rangle\langle\beta|)\}P_1 \| \cdots \| P_n\{|\beta\rangle\langle\beta|\}.$$

Proof of Claim A.1. We use the notations defined in the proof of Claim 9.1. For each program P_i, completeness of qPD ensures that

$$\vdash_{qPD} \{I_i \otimes I_{i'} - (\mathcal{E}_i^* \otimes \mathcal{I}_{i'})(I_i \otimes I_{i'}) + (\mathcal{E}_i^* \otimes \mathcal{I}_{i'})(|\Psi_i\rangle\langle\Psi_i|)\}P_i\{|\Psi_i\rangle\langle\Psi_i|\},$$

where $\mathcal{I}_{i'}$ is the identity superoperator on $\mathcal{H}_{i'}$. On the other hand, it is easy to check that

$$\models P_i : \text{Abort}\left(I_i \otimes I_{i'} - (\mathcal{E}_i^* \otimes \mathcal{I}_{i'})(I_i \otimes I_{i'})\right),$$
$$\models P_i : \text{Term}\left(I_i \otimes I_{i'} - (\mathcal{E}_i^* \otimes \mathcal{I}_{i'})(I_i \otimes I_{i'})\right).$$

Then we can use rule (R.PC.SP) to derive:

$$\vdash_{qPP} \left\{I_p \otimes I_{p'} - \bigotimes_{i=1}^{n}\left[I_i \otimes I_{i'} - \left(I_i \otimes I_{i'} - (\mathcal{E}_i^* \otimes \mathcal{I}_{i'})(I_i \otimes I_{i'})\right)\right] + \bigotimes_{i=1}^{n}(\mathcal{E}_i^* \otimes \mathcal{I}_{i'})(|\Psi_i\rangle\langle\Psi_i|)\right\}$$

$$P_1 \| \cdots \| P_n \left\{\bigotimes_{i=1}^{n}(|\Psi_i\rangle\langle\Psi_i|)\right\},$$

or simply,

$$\vdash_{qPP} \{D'\}P_1 \| \cdots \| P_n\{E\}$$

with the notation:

$$D' = I_{pp'} - \bigotimes_{i=1}^{n}\left[(\mathcal{E}_i^* \otimes \mathcal{I}_{i'})(I_i \otimes I_{i'})\right] + D$$
$$= I_p \otimes I_{p'} - \mathcal{E}^*(I_p) \otimes I_{p'} + D.$$

Notice that $\mathcal{F}_\beta^*(I_{p'}) = I_{p'}$. Then the following fact immediately follows from Fact 9.1 and linearity.

Fact A.1.

$$(\mathcal{I}_p \otimes \mathcal{F}_\beta^*)(D') = \left(I_p - \mathcal{E}^*(I_p) + \frac{1}{\prod_{i=1}^{n}d_i}\mathcal{E}^*(|\beta\rangle_p\langle\beta|)\right) \otimes I_{p'}.$$

Furthermore, applying rule (R.SO) with quantum operation $\mathcal{F}_\beta$, we obtain:

$$\vdash_{qPP} \left\{ \left(\mathcal{I}_p \otimes \mathcal{F}_\beta^* \right) (D') \right\} P_1 \| \cdots \| P_n \left\{ \left(\mathcal{I}_p \otimes \mathcal{F}_\beta^* \right) (E') \right\},$$

which, together with Facts 9.1 and A.1 and rule (R.TI), implies:

$$\vdash_{qPP} \left\{ I_p - \mathcal{E}^*(I_p) + \frac{1}{\prod_{i=1}^n d_i} \mathcal{E}^*(|\beta\rangle_p \langle\beta|) \right\} P_1 \| \cdots \| P_n \left\{ \frac{1}{\prod_{i=1}^n d_i} |\beta\rangle_p \langle\beta| \right\}.$$

For each i, it is obvious that

$$\models P_i : \text{Term}\left(I_i - \mathcal{E}_i^*(I_i) \right). \tag{A.28}$$

Thus, using rule (R.T.P) we obtain:

$$\vdash_{qPP} P_1 \| \cdots \| P_n : \text{Term}\left(I - \mathcal{E}^*(I) \right). \tag{A.29}$$

Therefore, applying rule (R.CC2) with $p = \prod_{i=1}^n d_i$ we have:

$$\vdash_{qPP} \left\{ I - \mathcal{E}^*(I) + \mathcal{E}^*(|\beta\rangle\langle\beta|) \right\} P_1 \| \cdots \| P_n \{ |\beta\rangle\langle\beta| \}$$

as is desired. $\qquad\qquad\square$

Our second step is to generalise the conclusion of Claim A.1 to the case of $B = |\beta\rangle\langle\beta|$ with a general vector $|\beta\rangle$.

Claim A.2. *For any pure state $|\beta\rangle$, we have:*

$$\vdash_{qPP} \{ I - \mathcal{E}^*(I) + \mathcal{E}^*(|\beta\rangle\langle\beta|) \} P_1 \| \cdots \| P_n \{ |\beta\rangle\langle\beta| \}.$$

Proof of Claim A.2. We use the notations introduced in the proof of Claim 9.1. First, we can use Claim A.1 to assert that

$$\vdash_{qPP} \{ I - \mathcal{E}^*(I) + \mathbb{C}^*(|\beta_k\rangle\langle\beta_k|) \} P_1 \| \cdots \| P_n \{ |\beta_k\rangle\langle\beta_k| \}. \tag{A.30}$$

Moreover, as shown in the proof of Lemma 9.1, it holds that

$$|\beta_k\rangle\langle\beta_k| \xrightarrow{w.o.t.} |\beta\rangle\langle\beta|.$$

Thus, with Lemma A.19, it follows immediately that

$$I - \mathcal{E}^*(I) + \mathbb{C}^*(|\beta_k\rangle\langle\beta_k|) \xrightarrow{w.o.t.} I - \mathcal{E}^*(I) + \mathbb{C}^*(|\beta\rangle\langle\beta|)$$

Now, applying rule (R.Lim), we obtain:

$$\vdash_{qPP} \{ I - \mathcal{E}^*(I) + \mathbb{C}^*(|\beta\rangle\langle\beta|) \} P_1 \| \cdots \| P_n \{ |\beta\rangle\langle\beta| \}$$

as is desired. $\qquad\qquad\square$

Next we further generalise the conclusion of Claim A.2 to a more general quantum predicate B, using the spectral decomposition of B.

Claim A.3. *For any quantum predicate B with finite rank, we have:*

$$\vdash_{qPP} \{ I - \mathcal{E}^*(I) + \mathcal{E}^*(B) \} P_1 \| \cdots \| P_n \{ B \}.$$

Proof of Claim A.3. We assume that postcondition B has a finite rank $d_B < \infty$. Then B can be diagonalised as follows:

$$B = \sum_{i=1}^{d_B} p_i |\beta_i\rangle\langle\beta_i|$$

with $p_i \geq 0$ and $|\beta_i\rangle$ being pure states for all $i \in [d_B]$. Now for each i, according to Claim A.2, we have:

$$\vdash_{qPP} \{I - \mathcal{E}^*(I) + \mathbb{C}^*(|\beta_i\rangle\langle\beta_i|)\} P_1 \| \cdots \| P_n \{|\beta_i\rangle\langle\beta_i|\}. \tag{A.31}$$

We consider the following two cases:

- **Case 1**: $\sum_{i=1}^{d_B} p_i \leq 1$. The completeness of qPD implies:

$$\vdash_{qPD} \{I_i - \mathcal{E}_i^*(I_i)\} P_i \{0\}, \text{ i.e. } \vdash_{qPD} P_i : \text{Abort}(I_i - \mathcal{E}_i^*(I_i)).$$

Then using rule (R.A.P), we obtain:

$$\vdash_{qPP} P_1 \| \cdots \| P_n : \text{Abort}(I - \mathcal{E}^*(I)).$$

Therefore, combining the above equation with Eq. (A.31) for all $i \in [d_B]$ and rule (R.CC1) yields:

$$\vdash_{qPP} \left\{ \sum_{i \in [d_B]} p_i \left(I - \mathcal{E}^*(I) + \mathcal{E}^*(|\beta_i\rangle\langle\beta_i|)\right) + \left(1 - \sum_{i \in [d_B]} p_i\right)(I - \mathcal{E}^*(I)) \right\}$$
$$P_1 \| \cdots \| P_n \left\{ \sum_{i \in [d_B]} p_i |\beta_i\rangle\langle\beta_i| \right\},$$

or equivalently,

$$\vdash_{qPP} \{I - \mathcal{E}^*(I) + \mathcal{E}^*(B)\} P_1 \| \cdots \| P_n \{B\}.$$

- **Case 2**: $\sum_{i=1}^{d_B} p_i > 1$. Combining Eq. (A.29) with Eq. (A.31) for all $i \in [d_B]$ and rule (R.CC2), we have:

$$\vdash_{qPP} \left\{ \sum_{i \in [d_B]} p_i \left(I - \mathcal{E}^*(I) + \mathcal{E}^*(|\beta_i\rangle\langle\beta_i|)\right) - \left(\sum_{i \in [d_B]} p_i - 1\right)(I - \mathcal{E}^*(I)) \right\}$$
$$P_1 \| \cdots \| P_n \left\{ \sum_{i \in [d_B]} p_i |\beta_i\rangle\langle\beta_i| \right\},$$

or equivalently,

$$\vdash_{qPP} \{I - \mathcal{E}^*(I) + \mathcal{E}^*(B)\} P_1 \| \cdots \| P_n \{B\}. \qquad \square$$

Finally, we can complete the proof by showing the following:

Claim A.4. *For any quantum predicate B, we have:*

$$\vdash_{qPP} \{I - \mathcal{E}^*(I) + \mathcal{E}^*(B)\} P_1 \| \cdots \| P_n \{B\}.$$

Proof of Claim A.4. For any quantum predicate B, we can always diagonalise it as follows:

$$B = \sum_i \lambda_i |\beta_i\rangle\langle\beta_i|$$

with $0 \leq \lambda_i \leq 1$ for all i (spectral decomposition). Let us set

$$B_k = \sum_{i \leq k} \lambda_i |\beta_i\rangle\langle\beta_i|$$

for each $k \geq 0$. According to Claim A.3, we know that for all k,

$$\vdash_{qPP} \{I - \mathcal{E}^*(I) + \mathcal{E}^*(B_k)\} P_1 \| \cdots \| P_n \{B_k\}. \tag{A.32}$$

On the other hand, $\{B_k\}$ is an increasing sequence with respect to Löwner order. So, by Lemma A.18 we have:

$$B_k \xrightarrow{w.o.t.} B.$$

Furthermore, we can use Lemma A.19 to deduce that

$$I - \mathcal{E}^*(I) + \mathcal{E}^*(B_k) \xrightarrow{w.o.t.} I - \mathcal{E}^*(I) + \mathcal{E}^*(B).$$

Therefore, applying rule (R.Lim) to Eq. (A.32), we obtain:

$$\vdash_{qTP} \{I - \mathcal{E}^*(I) + \mathbb{C}^*(B)\} P_1 \| \cdots \| P_n \{B\}. \qquad \square$$

A.5.4 Proof of Theorem 9.6

Suppose that

$$\langle P, \rho \rangle \to^n \{|\langle P_i, \rho_i \rangle|\}.$$

We proceed by induction on the length n of computation.

▶ Induction basis: For $n = 0$, $\{|\langle P_i, \rho_i \rangle|\}$ is a singleton $\{|\langle P_1, \rho_1 \rangle|\}$ with $P_1 \equiv P$ and $\rho_1 \equiv \rho$. Then we can choose $T_1 \equiv P$ and it holds that $P_1 \equiv at(T_1, P)$. Note that in the proof outline $\{A\} P^* \{B\}$, we have $A \sqsubseteq pre(P) = B_1$. Thus,

$$tr(A\rho) \leq tr(B_1 \rho_1) = \sum_i tr(B_i \rho_i).$$

▶ Induction step: Now we assume that

$$\langle P, \rho \rangle \to^{n-1} \mathcal{A} \to \mathcal{A}'$$

and the conclusion is true for length $n - 1$. Here, we only consider the simple case where the last step is derived by rule (MS1) with $\mathcal{A} = \{|\langle P_i, \rho_i \rangle|\}$ and $\mathcal{A}_\downarrow = \{\langle P, \rho \rangle \in \mathcal{A} : P \not\equiv \downarrow\}$ being a singleton $\{|\langle P_{i_0}, \rho_{i_0} \rangle|\}$. (A general case with $\mathcal{A}_\downarrow$ having more than one element follows from the fact that rule (MS2) preserves the inequality in clause (2) of Theorem 6.1.) Then we can assume that

$$\mathcal{A}' = \{|\langle P_i, \rho_i \rangle| i \neq i_0|\} \cup \{|\langle Q_j, \sigma_j \rangle|\}$$

where $\langle P_{i_0}, \rho_{i_0} \rangle \to \{|\langle Q_j, \sigma_j \rangle|\}$ is derived by one of the rules used in Definition 9.2 except (MS1) and (MS2). Thus, we need to consider the following cases:

Case 1. The last step uses rule (IF'). Then P_{i_0} can be written in the following form:

$$P_{i_0} \equiv \mathbf{if} \ (\square m \cdot M[\overline{q}] = m \to R_m) \ \mathbf{fi},$$

and for each j, $Q_j \equiv R_m \equiv at(R_m, P)$ and $\sigma_j = M_m \rho_{i_0} M_m^\dagger$ for some m. On the other hand, a segment of the proof outline $\{A\} P^* \{B\}$ must be derived by the following inference:

$$\frac{\{A_m\} R_m^* \{C\} \text{ for every } m}{\left\{ \sum_m M_m^\dagger A_m M_m \right\} \ \mathbf{if} \ \left(\square m \cdot M[\overline{q}] = m \to \{A_m\} R_m^*\right) \ \mathbf{fi} \{C\}}$$

and $B_{i_0} = pre\left(P_{i_0}\right) \sqsubseteq \sum_m M_m^\dagger A_m M_m$, $A_m = pre(R_m)$. Therefore,

$$tr\left(B_{i_0} \rho_{i_0}\right) \leq tr\left(\sum_m M_m^\dagger A_m M_m \rho_{i_0}\right)$$

$$= \sum_m tr\left(M_m^\dagger A_m M_m \rho_{i_0}\right)$$

$$= \sum_m tr\left(A_m M_m \rho_{i_0} M_m^\dagger\right)$$

$$= \sum_j tr\left(pre\left(Q_j\right)\sigma_j\right).$$

By the induction hypothesis, we obtain:

$$tr(A\rho) \le \sum_{i \ne i_0} tr\left(B_i \rho_i\right) + tr\left(B_{i_0}\rho_{i_0}\right)$$

$$\le \sum_{i \ne i_0} tr\left(B_i \rho_i\right) + \sum_j tr\left(pre\left(Q_j\right)\sigma_j\right).$$

So, the conclusion is true in this case.

Case 2. The last step uses rule (L′). Then P_{i_0} must be in the following form:

$$P_{i_0} \equiv \textbf{while } M[\overline{q}] = 1 \textbf{ do } R \textbf{ od}$$

and $\{|\langle Q_j, \sigma_j\rangle|\} = \{|\langle Q_0, \sigma_0\rangle, \langle Q_1, \sigma_1\rangle|\}$ with $Q_0 \equiv \textbf{skip}$, $\sigma_0 = M_0\rho_{i_0}M_0^\dagger$, $Q_1 \equiv R; P_{i_0}$ and $\sigma_1 = M_1\rho_{i_0}M_1^\dagger$. A segment of $\{A\}P^*\{B\}$ must be derived by the following inference:

$$\frac{\{D\}R^*\{M_0CM_0^\dagger + M_1DM_1^\dagger\}}{\begin{array}{l}\{M_0CM_0^\dagger + M_1DM_1^\dagger\} \textbf{ while } M[\overline{q}] = 0 \textbf{ do } \{C\} \textbf{ skip } \{C\} \\ \qquad\qquad = 1 \textbf{ do } R^*\{M_0CM_0^\dagger + M_1DM_1^\dagger\} \\ \textbf{od } \{C\}\end{array}}$$

and $B_{i_0} \sqsubseteq M_0CM_0^\dagger + M_1DM_1^\dagger$. Then $Q_0 \equiv at(\textbf{skip}, P)$, $pre(Q_0) = C$, $Q_1 \equiv at(R, P)$ and $pre(Q_1) = D$. It follows that

$$tr\left(B_{i_0}\rho_{i_0}\right) \le tr\left[\left(M_0CM_0^\dagger + M_1DM_1^\dagger\right)\rho_{i_0}\right]$$

$$= tr\left(M_0CM_0^\dagger\rho_{i_0}\right) + tr\left(M_1DM_1^\dagger\rho_{i_0}\right)$$

$$= tr\left(CM_0^\dagger\rho_{i_0}M_0\right) + tr\left(DM_1^\dagger\rho_{i_0}M_1\right)$$

$$= tr\left(pre(Q_0)\sigma_0\right) + tr\left(pre(Q_1)\sigma_1\right).$$

Furthermore, by the induction hypothesis, we have:

$$tr(A\rho) \le \sum_{i \ne i_0} tr\left(B_i \rho_i\right) + tr\left(B_{i_0}\rho_{i_0}\right)$$

$$\le \sum_{i \ne i_0} tr\left(B_i \rho_i\right) + \sum_j tr\left(pre\left(Q_j\right)\sigma_j\right).$$

Thus, the conclusion is true in this case.

Case 3. The last step uses rule (Sk), (In) or (UT). Similar but easier.

A.5.5 Proof of Theorem 9.7

We prove the conclusion by induction on the length l of transition sequence:

$$\langle P_1\| \cdots \| P_n, \rho\rangle \rightarrow^l \{|\langle P_{1s}\| \cdots \| P_{ns}, \rho_s\rangle|\}.$$

The conclusion is obviously true in the induction basis case of $l = 0$. Now we assume that

$$\langle P_1\| \cdots \| P_n, \rho\rangle \rightarrow^l \{|\langle P'_{1k}\| \cdots \| P'_{nk}, \rho'_k\rangle|\} \rightarrow \{|\langle P_{1s}\| \cdots \| P_{ns}, \rho_s\rangle|\}$$

and the last step is a transition performed by the rth component ($1 \le r \le n$):

$$\langle P'_{rk}, \rho'_k\rangle \rightarrow \left\{|\langle Q^{(h)}_{rk}, \rho^{(h)}_k\rangle|\right\} \tag{A.33}$$

for each k. Then

$$\{|\langle P_{1s} \| \cdots \| P_{ns}, \rho_s \rangle|\} = \bigcup_k \left\{ |\langle P'_{1k} \| \cdots \| P'_{(r-1)k} \| Q^{(h)}_{rk} \| P'_{(r+1)k} \| \cdots \| P'_{nk}, \rho^{(h)}_k \rangle|\right\}. \tag{A.34}$$

By the induction hypothesis for the first l steps, we obtain:

$$tr\left[\left(\sum_{i=1}^{n} p_i A_i\right)\rho\right] \le \sum_k tr\left[\left(\sum_{i=1}^{n} p_i B'_{ik}\right)\rho'_k\right] \tag{A.35}$$

where

$$B'_{ik} = \begin{cases} B_i & \text{if } P'_{ik} \equiv \downarrow, \\ pre(T'_{ik}) & \text{if } P'_{ik} \equiv at(T'_{ik}, P_i). \end{cases}$$

We set

$$B^{(h)}_{rk} = \begin{cases} B_r & \text{if } Q^{(h)}_{rk} \equiv \downarrow, \\ pre(S^{(h)}_{rk}) & \text{if } Q^{(h)}_{rk} \equiv at(S^{(h)}_{rk}, P_r). \end{cases}$$

Then for each k, by an argument similar to the case of Theorem 9.6 on transition (A.33), we can prove that

$$tr\left(B'_{rk}\rho'_k\right) \le \sum_h tr\left(B^{(h)}_{rk}\rho^{(h)}_k\right). \tag{A.36}$$

On the other hand, $\{A_i\}P^*_i\{B_i\}$ $(i=1,...,n)$ are Λ-interference free. Then for every $i \ne r$, it follows from transition (A.33) that

$$tr\left[\left(\lambda_{ir} B'_{ik} + (1 - \lambda_{ik}) B'_{rk}\right)\rho'_k\right] \le \sum_h tr\left[\left(\lambda_{ir} B'_{ik} + (1 - \lambda_{ir}) B^{(h)}_{rk}\right)\rho^{(h)}_k\right]. \tag{A.37}$$

Note that $\sum_{i=1}^{n} p_i = 1$, thus condition (9.35) implies:

$$p_r - \sum_{i \ne r} \frac{p_i (1 - \lambda_{ir})}{\lambda_{ir}} \ge 0.$$

Therefore, we have:

$$tr\left[\left(\sum_{i=1}^{n} p_i A_i\right)\rho\right] \le \sum_k tr\left[\left(\sum_{i=1}^{n} p_i B'_{ik}\right)\rho'_k\right] \tag{A.38}$$

$$= \sum_k tr\left[\left(\sum_{i \ne r}^{n} p_i B'_{ik} + p_r B'_{rk}\right)\rho'_k\right] \tag{A.39}$$

$$= \sum_k tr\left\{\left[\sum_{i \ne r}^{n} \frac{p_i}{\lambda_{ir}}\left(\lambda_{ir} B'_{ik} + (1 - \lambda_{ir}) B'_{rk}\right) + \left(p_r - \sum_{i \ne r} \frac{p_i (1 - \lambda_{ir})}{\lambda_{ir}}\right) B'_{rk}\right]\rho'_k\right\} \tag{A.40}$$

$$\le \sum_k \left\{\sum_{i \ne r}^{n} \frac{p_i}{\lambda_{ir}} \sum_h tr\left[\left(\lambda_{ir} B'_{ik} + (1 - \lambda_{ir}) B^{(h)}_{rk}\right)\rho^{(h)}_k\right] + \left(p_r - \sum_{i \ne r} \frac{p_i (1 - \lambda_{ir})}{\lambda_{ir}}\right) \sum_h B^{(h)}_{rk}\rho^{(h)}_k\right\} \tag{A.41}$$

$$= \sum_{k,h} tr\left[\left(\sum_{i \ne r}^{n} p_i B'_{ik} + p_r B^{(h)}_{rk}\right)\rho^{(h)}_k\right] \tag{A.42}$$

$$= \sum_s tr\left[\left(\sum_{i=1}^{n} p_i B_{is}\right)\rho_s\right]. \tag{A.43}$$

Here, (A.38) comes from Eq. (A.35), the first and second part of (A.41) from (A.37), (A.36), respectively, and (A.43) from (A.34).

A.6 Omitted proofs in Chapter 10

A.6.1 Proofs of the lemmas in Section 10.1.4

Proof of Lemma 10.4. We prove the conclusion by induction on the depth of inference for deriving $\langle P, \rho \rangle \overset{\alpha}{\to} \langle P', \rho' \rangle$. Based on the induction hypothesis, we consider different cases where the last rule is used in the derivation tree. The cases that the last rule is **Tau, Output, Choice, Intl2** or **Res** are easy, and the cases that the last rule is **Oper** or **Comm** are similar to those in the proof of Lemma 10.5 below. So, we only consider the following three cases:

Case 1. The last rule is **Input**. Let $p = c?q.Q$. Then $P[f] = c?r.Q\{r/q\}[f_r]$, where $r \notin qv(c?q.Q) \cup qv(Q[f])$, $f_r(q) = r$ and $f_r(u) = u$ for all $u \neq q$. Suppose that

$$\langle P, \rho \rangle \overset{\alpha = c?s}{\to} \langle P' = Q\{s/q\}, \rho' = \rho \rangle,$$

where $s \notin qv(c?q.Q)$. We now need the following:

Claim. $s \notin qv(c?q.Q)$ *implies* $s \notin qv(c?r.Q\{r/q\}[f_r])$.

We prove this claim by contradiction. If $s \in qv(c?r.Q\{r/q\}[f_r])$, then $s \in qv(Q\{r/q\}[f_r])$ and $s \neq r$. It follows that

$$qv(Q\{r/q\}[f_r]) \subseteq f(qv(c?q.Q)) \cup \{r\}$$

because $f_r(r) = r$ and $f_r(u) = u$ for all $u \neq q$. Thus, we have $s \in f(qv(c?q.Q))$ since $s \neq r$, and there exists $v \in qv(c?q.Q)$ such that $s = f(v)$. Note that $s = bv(\alpha)$ and $f(bv(\alpha)) = bv(\alpha)$. This leads to $f(s) = s = f(v)$. Since f is one-to-one, it holds that $s = v \in qv(c?q.Q)$. This contradicts the assumption of the claim, and thus the claim is proved.

By the above claim and the **Input** rule, we obtain:

$$\langle P[f], f(\rho) \rangle \overset{c?s = \alpha}{\to} \langle Q\{r/q\}[f_r]\{s/r\}, f(\rho) \rangle.$$

Finally, we have to show that

$$Q\{r/q\}[f_r]\{s/r\} \equiv_\alpha Q\{s/q\}[f] = P'[f].$$

In fact, q is substituted by r in $Q\{r/q\}$, and $f_r(r) = r$. Then q is substituted by s in $Q\{r/q\}[f_r]\{s/r\}$. This is also true in $Q\{s/q\}[f]$ because $f(s) = s$. If $u \in qv(Q)$ and $u \neq q$, then u becomes $f_r(u) = f(u)$ in $Q\{r/q\}[f_r]$. Note that $f(u) \neq r$. Otherwise, $f_r(u) = r = f_r(r)$ and $u = r$ because f_r is one-to-one. This contradicts to $r \notin qv(c?q.Q)$. Therefore, u is substituted by $f(u)$ in $Q\{r/q\}[f_r]\{s/r\}$. The same happens in $Q\{s/q\}[f]$.

Case 2. The last rule is **Intl1**. Suppose that $P = P_1 \| P_2$ and

$$\frac{\langle P_1, \rho \rangle \overset{c?q}{\to} \langle P_1', \rho' \rangle}{\langle P, \rho \rangle \overset{\alpha = c?q}{\to} \langle P' = P_1' \| P_2, \rho' \rangle} \quad q \notin qv(Q)$$

Since $f(bv(\alpha)) = bv(\alpha)$, it follows from the induction hypothesis that

$$\langle P_1 f, f(\rho) \rangle \overset{c?q}{\to} \langle Q_1, f(\rho) \rangle$$

with $Q_1 \equiv_\alpha P_1'[f]$. We assert that $q \notin qv(P_2[f])$. If not so, then there exists $u \in qv(P_2)$ such that $q = f(u)$. Note that $q = bv(\alpha)$ and $f(q) = q$. It holds that $f(q) = f(u)$ and $q = u \in qv(P_2)$ because f is one-to-one. This is a contradiction. Thus, we can use the **Intl1** rule to derive

$$\langle Pf = P_1 f \| P_2 f, f(\rho) \rangle \overset{\alpha = c?q}{\to} \langle Q_1 \| P_2 f, f(\rho) \rangle,$$

and $Q_1 \| P_2[f] \equiv_\alpha (P_1' \| P_2)[f] = P'[f]$.

Case 3. The last rule is **Comm**. Let $P = P_1 \| P_2$ and

$$\frac{\langle P_1, \rho \rangle \overset{c?q}{\to} \langle P_1', \rho \rangle \qquad \langle P_2, \rho \rangle \overset{c!q}{\to} \langle P_2', \rho \rangle}{\langle P, \rho \rangle \overset{\tau}{\to} \langle P_1' \| P_2', \rho \rangle}$$

Then by the induction hypothesis, we have:

$$\langle P_2[f], f(\rho) \rangle \overset{c!f(q)}{\to} \langle P_2'[f], f(\rho) \rangle.$$

This together with Lemma 10.2 implies $f(q) \in qv(P_2[f])$. On the other hand, we can find $y \notin qv(P_1)$ with $f(r) = r$ because f is almost everywhere the identity in the sense that $f(u) = u$ for all except a finite number of variables u. Then using Lemma 10.3 we obtain $\langle P_1, \rho \rangle \overset{c?r}{\to} \langle Q_1, \rho \rangle$ with $Q_1 \equiv_\alpha P_1'\{r/q\}$. Now it follows from the induction hypothesis that

$$\langle P_1[f], f(\rho) \rangle \overset{c?r}{\to} \langle Q_1', f(\rho) \rangle$$

for some $Q_1' \equiv_\alpha Q_1[f]$. Since $f(q) \in qv(P_2[f])$ and $qv(P_1[f]) \cap qv(P_2[f]) = \emptyset$, it holds that $f(q) \notin qv(P_1[f])$, and with Lemma 10.3 we are able to assert that

$$\langle P_1[f], f(\rho) \rangle \overset{c?f(q)}{\to} \langle Q_1'', f(\rho) \rangle$$

with $Q_1'' \equiv_\alpha Q_1'\{f(q)/r\}$. Then by applying the **Comm** rule, we have:

$$\langle P[f] = P_1[f] \| P_2[f], f(\rho) \rangle \overset{\tau}{\to} \langle Q_1'' \| P_2', f(\rho) \rangle.$$

Now it holds that

$$Q_1'' \equiv_\alpha Q_1'\{f(q)/r\} \equiv_\alpha Q_1[f]\{f(q)/r\} \equiv_\alpha P_1'\{r/q\}[f]\{f(q)/r\} \equiv_\alpha P_1'[f].$$

The last α-conversion is verified as follows: q becomes r in $P_1'\{r/q\}$, and it is still r in $P_1'\{r/q\}[f]$ because $f(r) = r$. Then q is substituted by $f(q)$ in $P_1'\{r/q\}[f]\{f(q)/r\}$. For any $u \in qv(P_1') \setminus \{q\}$, u is not changed in $P_1'\{r/q\}$, and it becomes $f(u)$ in $P_1'\{r/q\}[f]$. If $f(u) \neq r$, then u is substituted by $f(u)$ in $P_1'\{r/q\}[f]\{f(q)/r\}$. So, it suffices to show that $f(u) \neq r$. If not so, then $f(u) = r = f(r)$ and $u = r$ because f is one-to-one. Using Lemma 10.2 we assert that $qv(P_1') \subseteq qv(P_1) \cup \{q\}$ since $\langle P_1, \rho \rangle \overset{c?q}{\to} \langle P_1', \rho \rangle$. This leads to $u \in qv(P_1') \setminus \{q\} \subseteq qv(P_1)$. However, $r \notin qv(P_1)$. This is a contradiction. $\square$

Proof of Lemma 10.5. We proceed by induction on the depth of inference for deriving $\langle P[f], f(\rho) \rangle \overset{\alpha}{\to} \langle Q, \sigma \rangle$. We only consider the following three cases:

Case 1. The last rule is **Oper**. Then $P = \mathcal{E}[\overline{q}].R$, $P[f] = \mathcal{E}[f][f(\overline{q})].R[f]$ and

$$\langle P[f], f(\rho) \rangle \overset{\mathcal{E}[f][f(\overline{q})]}{\to} \langle R[f], (\mathcal{E}[f])_{f(\overline{q})}(f(\rho)) \rangle.$$

On the other hand, we have $\langle P, \rho \rangle \overset{\mathcal{E}[\overline{q}]}{\to} \langle R, \mathcal{E}_{\overline{q}}(\rho) \rangle$. It suffices to show that $f(\mathcal{E}_{\overline{q}}(\rho)) = (\mathcal{E}[f])_{f(\overline{q})}(f(\rho))$. In fact,

$$\begin{aligned}
(\mathcal{E}[f])_{f(\overline{q})} &= \mathcal{E}[f] \otimes \mathcal{I}_{qVar \setminus f(\overline{q})} \\
&= (f|_{\overline{q}} \circ \mathcal{E} \circ (f|_{\overline{q}})^{-1}) \otimes \mathcal{I}_{qVar \setminus f(\overline{q})} \\
&= f \circ (\mathcal{E} \otimes \mathcal{I}_{qVar \setminus X}) \circ f^{-1} \\
&= f \circ \mathcal{E}_{\overline{q}} \circ f^{-1}.
\end{aligned}$$

Thus, we obtain

$$(\mathcal{E}[f])_{f(\overline{q})}(f(\rho)) = (f \circ \mathcal{E}_{\overline{q}} \circ f^{-1})(f(\rho)) = f(\mathcal{E}_{\overline{q}}(\rho)).$$

Case 2. The last rule is **Input**. Then $P = c?q.R$, $P[f] = c?r.R\{r/q\}[f_r]$, where $r \notin qv(c?q.R) \cup qv(R[f])$, $f_r(q) = r$ and $f_r(u) = u$ for all $u \neq q$, and

$$\langle P[f], f(\rho) \rangle \overset{\alpha = c?s}{\to} \langle R\{r/q\}f_r\{s/r\}, f(\rho) \rangle$$

where $s \notin qv(\text{c}?r.R\{r/q\}[f_r])$. We first prove the following:

    Claim: $s \notin qv(\text{c}?r.R\{r/q\}[f_r])$ implies $s \notin qv(\text{c}?q.R)$

    In fact, if $s \in qv(\text{c}?q.R)$, then $s \in qv(R)$ and $s \neq q$. This leads to $s \in qv(R\{r/q\})$. Since $s = bv(\alpha)$, we have $s = f(s) = f_r(s) \in qv(R\{r/q\}[f_r])$. Note that $r \notin qv(\text{c}?q.R)$. Then $s \neq r$, and $s \in qv(\text{c}?r.R\{r/q\}[f_r])$.

    Now using the **Input** rule we have $\langle P, \rho \rangle \xrightarrow{\text{c}?s} \langle R\{s/q\}, \rho \rangle$, and it suffices to note that $R\{r/q\}[f_r]\{s/r\} = R\{s/q\}[f]$.

    Case 3. The last rule is **Comm**. Suppose that $P = P_1 \| P_2$ and we have

$$\frac{\langle P_1[f], f(\rho) \rangle \xrightarrow{\text{c}?q} \langle Q_1, f(\rho) \rangle \qquad \langle P_2[f], f(\rho) \rangle \xrightarrow{\text{c}!q} \langle Q_2, f(\rho) \rangle}{\langle P[f] = P_1[f] \| P_2[f], f(\rho) \rangle \xrightarrow{\tau} \langle Q_1 \| Q_2, f(\rho) \rangle}$$

Then by the induction hypothesis we obtain $\langle P_2, \rho \rangle \xrightarrow{\text{c}!r} \langle P_2', \rho \rangle$, $f(r) = q$ and $Q_2 \equiv_\alpha P_2'[f]$ for some r and P_2'.

    We can find variable $s \notin qv(P_1[f])$ such that $f(s) = s$ because f is almost everywhere the identity. Thus by Lemma 10.3 we assert that $\langle P_1[f], f(\rho) \rangle \xrightarrow{\text{c}!s} \langle Q_1', f(\rho) \rangle$ for some $Q_1' \equiv_\alpha Q_1\{s/q\}$. Now using the induction hypothesis we have $\langle P_1, \rho \rangle \xrightarrow{\text{c}!s} \langle P_1', \rho \rangle$ for some P_1' with $Q_1' \equiv_\alpha P_1'[f]$. From Lemma 10.2 we see that $y \in qv(P_2)$, which implies $r \notin qv(P_1)$. Then using Lemma 10.3 once again we obtain $\langle P_1, \rho \rangle \xrightarrow{\text{c}?r} \langle P_1'', \rho \rangle$ for some $P_1'' \equiv_\alpha P_1'\{r/s\}$. Therefore, it is derived by the **Comm** rule that $\langle P, \rho \rangle \xrightarrow{\tau} \langle P_1'' \| P_2', \rho \rangle$. What remains is to show that

$$Q_1 \| Q_2 \equiv_\alpha (P_1'' \| P_2')[f] = P_1''[f] \| P_2'[f].$$

Note that we already have $Q_2 \equiv_\alpha P_2'[f]$. On the other hand, since $P_1'' \equiv_\alpha P_1'\{r/s\}$, $Q_1' \equiv_\alpha P_1'[f]$ and $Q_1' \equiv_\alpha Q_1\{s/q\}$, it follows that

$$P_1''[f] \equiv_\alpha P_1'\{r/s\}[f] \equiv_\alpha P_1'[f]\{q/s\}$$
$$\equiv_\alpha Q_1'\{q/s\} \equiv_\alpha Q_1\{s/q\}\{q/s\} \equiv_\alpha Q_1$$

because $q = f(r)$. $\qquad\qquad\qquad\qquad\qquad\qquad\qquad\qquad\qquad\qquad\qquad\qquad\qquad\qquad$ $\square$

A.6.2   Proofs of the results in Section 10.2.3

Proof of Proposition 10.4. ($\Rightarrow$) We first show that $P \sim Q$ implies $P[f] \sim Q[f]$. Put

$$\mathcal{R} = \{(\langle P', \rho \rangle, \langle Q', \sigma \rangle) : P' \equiv_\alpha P[f], Q' \equiv_\alpha Q[f] \text{ and } \langle P, f^{-1}(\rho) \rangle \sim \langle Q, f^{-1}(\sigma) \rangle\}.$$

It suffices to show that $\mathcal{R}$ is a strong bisimulation.

    Suppose that $P' \equiv_\alpha P[f]$, $Q' \equiv_\alpha Q[f]$ and $\langle P, f^{-1}(\rho) \rangle \sim \langle Q, f^{-1}(\sigma) \rangle$. If $\langle P', \rho \rangle \xrightarrow{\text{c}?q} \langle R, \rho \rangle$ and $q \notin qv(P') \cup qv(Q')$, we can choose $r \notin qv(P') \cup qv(Q') \cup qv(R)$ such that $f(r) = r$ because f is almost everywhere the identity, and $qv(P')$, $qv(Q')$ and $qv(R)$ are all finite. Since $r \notin qv(P')$, and $P' \equiv_\alpha P[f]$ implies $qv(P[f]) = qv(P')$, we have $q \notin qv(P[f])$. Then it follows from Lemma 10.6 that $\langle P[f], \rho \rangle \xrightarrow{\text{c}?r} \langle R_1, \rho \rangle$ for some $R_1 \equiv_\alpha R\{r/q\}$. Now we can use Lemma 10.5 to derive that

$$\langle P, f^{-1}(\rho) \rangle \xrightarrow{\text{c}?r} \langle R_2, f^{-1}(\rho) \rangle$$

for some R_2 with $R_1 \equiv_\alpha R_2[f]$ because $f(r) = r$. Note that $r \notin qv(P) \cup qv(Q)$. Otherwise, we have

$$r = f(r) \in qv(P[f]) \cup qv(Q[f]) = qv(P') \cup qv(Q'),$$

which contradicts to the assumption about r. Thus, $\langle P, f^{-1}(\rho) \rangle \sim \langle Q, f^{-1}(\sigma) \rangle$, together with Lemma 10.7, leads to

$$\langle Q, f^{-1}(\sigma) \rangle \xrightarrow{\text{c}?r} \langle S_2, f^{-1}(\sigma) \rangle$$

for some S_2 such that

$$\langle R_2\{s/r\}, f^{-1}(\rho) \rangle \sim \langle S_2\{s/r\}, f^{-1}(\sigma) \rangle$$

for all $s \notin qv(R_2) \cup qv(S_2) \setminus \{r\}$. Then, using Lemma 10.4 we obtain $\langle Q[f], \sigma \rangle \xrightarrow{c?r} \langle S_1, \sigma \rangle$ for some $S_1 \equiv_\alpha S_2[f]$, and an application of Lemma 10.6 yields $\langle Q', \sigma \rangle \xrightarrow{c?q} \langle S, \sigma \rangle$ for some $S \equiv_\alpha S_1\{q/r\}$ because $f(r) = r$ and $q \notin qv(Q')$. So, what we still need to prove is that

$$\langle R\{u/s\}, \rho \rangle \mathcal{R} \langle S\{u/s\}, \sigma \rangle$$

for each $u \notin qv(R) \cup qv(S) \setminus \{x\}$. This comes immediately from the following three items:

(i) Since $R_1 \equiv_\alpha R\{r/q\}$, it holds that $q \notin qv(R_1)$. Note that $r \notin qv(R)$. This implies

$$R \equiv_\alpha R\{r/q\}\{q/r\} \equiv_\alpha R_1\{q/r\} \equiv_\alpha R_2[f]\{q/r\}$$

because $R_1 \equiv_\alpha R_2[f]$. Then

$$R\{u/q\} \equiv_\alpha R_2[f]\{q/r\}\{u/q\} \equiv_\alpha R_2[f]\{u/r\}$$

since $q \notin qv(R_1) = qv(R_2[f])$. Furthermore, we obtain

$$R\{u/q\} \equiv_\alpha R_2[f]\{u/r\} \equiv_\alpha R_2\{f^{-1}(u)/r\}[f]$$

because $f(r) = r$, f is one-to-one, and $f(v) \neq r$ when $v \neq r$.

(ii) Similarly, we have $S\{u/q\} \equiv_\alpha S_2\{f^{-1}(u)/r\}[f]$.

(iii) $f^{-1}(u) \notin qv(R_2) \cup qv(S_2) \setminus \{r\}$. Otherwise, we have $u \in qv(R_2[f]) \cup qv(S_2[f])$ and $r \neq u$ because $f(r) = r$. Since $R_2[f] \equiv_\alpha R\{r/q\}$ and $S_2[f] \equiv_\alpha S\{r/q\}$, it holds that $u \in qv(R\{r/q\}) \cup qv(S\{r/q\})$. This implies that $u \neq q$ and $u \in qv(R) \cup qv(S)$, or $q \in qv(R) \cup qv(S)$ and $u = r$. However, we already know that $r \neq u$. Then it must be the case that $u \neq q$ and $u \in qv(R) \cup qv(S)$, which contradicts to the assumption about u.

For the case that $\langle P, \rho \rangle \xrightarrow{\alpha} \langle R, \rho' \rangle$ and α is τ or of the form $c!x$, the argument is similar and much easier. Thus, we complete proof of the conclusion that $P \sim Q$ implies $P[f] \sim Q[f]$.

($\Leftarrow$) Conversely, we show that $P[f] \sim Q[f]$ implies $P \sim Q$. Note that f^{-1} is also a substitution. Then it holds that $(P[f])[f^{-1}] \sim (Q[f])[f^{-1}]$. Since $P \equiv_\alpha (P[f])[f^{-1}]$ and $Q \equiv_\alpha (Q[f])[f^{-1}]$, we obtain $P \sim (P[f])[f^{-1}]$ and $Q \sim (Q[f])[f^{-1}]$ by using Proposition 10.1, and it follows that $P \sim Q$. $\square$

Proof of Theorem 10.1. The basic idea of the proof of Theorem 10.1.2.f was given in Section 10.2.3. Now we complete its details. Define $\mathcal{R}$ to be a binary relation between configurations, consisting of the pairs:

$$(\langle P \| R, \mathcal{F}_{Y_n}^{(n)} \mathcal{E}_{X_n}^{(n)} \mathcal{F}_{Y_{n-1}}^{(n-1)} \mathcal{E}_{X_{n-1}}^{(n-1)} ... \mathcal{F}_{Y_1}^{(1)} \mathcal{E}_{X_1}^{(1)} \mathcal{F}_{Y_0}^{(0)}(\rho) \rangle,$$
$$\langle Q \| R, \mathcal{F}_{Y_n}^{(n)} \mathcal{E}_{X_n}^{(n)} \mathcal{F}_{Y_{n-1}}^{(n-1)} \mathcal{E}_{X_{n-1}}^{(n-1)} ... \mathcal{F}_{Y_1}^{(1)} \mathcal{E}_{X_1}^{(1)} \mathcal{F}_{Y_0}^{(0)}(\sigma) \rangle),$$

where $n \geq 0$, $R \in \mathcal{P}$, X_i ($1 \leq i \leq n$) and Y_i ($0 \leq i \leq n$) are finite subsets of Var, $\mathcal{E}_{X_i}^{(i)}$ is a superoperator on $\mathcal{H}_{X_i}$ for each $1 \leq i \leq n$, and $\mathcal{F}_{Y_i}^{(i)}$ is a superoperator on $\mathcal{H}_{Y_i}$ for each $0 \leq i \leq n$, and

$$\langle P, \mathcal{E}_{X_n}^{(n)} \mathcal{E}_{X_{n-1}}^{(n-1)} ... \mathcal{E}_{X_1}^{(1)}(\rho) \rangle \sim \langle Q, \mathcal{E}_{X_n}^{(n)} \mathcal{E}_{X_{n-1}}^{(n-1)} ... \mathcal{E}_{X_1}^{(1)}(\sigma) \rangle.$$

The idea behind the definition of $\mathcal{R}$ is that we can insert an arbitrary quantum operation $\mathcal{F}_{Y_i}^{(i)}$ between two existing previously quantum operation $\mathcal{E}_{X_i}^{(i)}$ and $\mathcal{E}_{X_{i+1}}^{(i+1)}$ for any $1 \leq i \leq n-1$, and we can also insert an arbitrary quantum operation $\mathcal{F}_{Y_n}^{(n)}$ after the last operation $\mathcal{E}_{X_n}^{(n)}$ and insert $\mathcal{F}_{Y_0}^{(0)}$ before the first operation $\mathcal{E}_{X_1}^{(1)}$. The technique of insertion is unnecessary in the classical value-passing CCS from which sequential computation is abstracted by assuming value expressions (see [302], page 55). However, it is indispensable in qCCS where one has to consider interference between sequential quantum computation and communicating quantum systems.

For simplicity, we write $\mathcal{A} = \mathcal{E}_{X_n}^{(n)} \mathcal{E}_{X_{n-1}}^{(n-1)} ... \mathcal{E}_{X_1}^{(1)}$ and

$$\mathcal{B} = \mathcal{F}_{Y_n}^{(n)} \mathcal{E}_{X_n}^{(n)} \mathcal{F}_{Y_{n-1}}^{(n-1)} \mathcal{E}_{X_{n-1}}^{(n-1)} ... \mathcal{F}_{Y_1}^{(1)} \mathcal{E}_{X_1}^{(1)} \mathcal{F}_{Y_0}^{(0)}.$$

If $P \sim Q$, then for each ρ, $\langle P, \rho \rangle \sim \langle Q, \rho \rangle$, and it implies $\langle P \| R, \rho \rangle \mathcal{R} \langle Q \| R, \rho \rangle$ by taking $n = 0$ and $\mathcal{F}_{Y_0}^{(0)} = \mathcal{I}_{\mathcal{H}_{Y_0}}$ in $\mathcal{B}$. Therefore, it suffices to show that $\mathcal{R}$ is a strong bisimulation. To this end, suppose that $\langle P, \mathcal{A}(\rho) \rangle \sim \langle Q, \mathcal{A}(\sigma) \rangle$ and

$$\langle P \| R, \mathcal{B}(\rho) \rangle \xrightarrow{\alpha} \langle S, \rho' \rangle. \tag{A.44}$$

Our aim is to find a transition of $\langle Q \| R, \mathcal{B}(\rho) \rangle$ which matches transition (A.44) according to Definition 10.5. We consider the following four cases:

Case 1. $\alpha = \tau$. We have $\rho' = \mathcal{B}(\rho)$, and this case is divided into the following four subcases:

Subcase 1.1. The transition (A.44) is derived by **Intl2** from $\langle P, \mathcal{B}(\rho) \rangle \xrightarrow{\tau} \langle P', \mathcal{B}(\rho) \rangle$. Then $S = P' \| R$. By Lemma 10.1 we obtain $\langle P, \mathcal{A}(\rho) \rangle \xrightarrow{\tau} \langle P', \mathcal{A}(\rho) \rangle$. Since $\langle P, \mathcal{A}(\rho) \rangle \sim \langle Q, \mathcal{A}(\sigma) \rangle$, it holds that $\langle Q, \mathcal{A}(\sigma) \rangle \xrightarrow{\tau} \langle Q', \mathcal{A}(\sigma) \rangle$ for some Q' with $\langle P', \mathcal{A}(\rho) \rangle \sim \langle Q', \mathcal{A}(\sigma) \rangle$. Applying Lemma 10.1 once again we have $\langle Q, \mathcal{B}(\sigma) \rangle \xrightarrow{\tau} \langle Q', \mathcal{B}(\sigma) \rangle$, and the **Intl2** rule allows us to assert that

$$\langle Q \| R, \mathcal{B}(\sigma) \rangle \xrightarrow{\tau} \langle Q' \| R, \mathcal{B}(\sigma) \rangle.$$

It is easy to see that $\langle S, \rho' \rangle \mathcal{R} \langle Q' \| R, \mathcal{B}(\sigma) \rangle$ from the definition of $\mathcal{R}$.

Subcase 1.2. The transition (A.44) is derived by **Intl2** from $\langle R, \mathcal{B}(\rho) \rangle \xrightarrow{\tau} \langle R', \mathcal{B}(\rho) \rangle$. Then $S = P \| R'$, and from Lemma 10.1 and the **Intl2** rule it follows that $\langle R, \mathcal{B}(\sigma) \rangle \xrightarrow{\tau} \langle R', \mathcal{B}(\sigma) \rangle$ and

$$\langle Q \| R, \mathcal{B}(\sigma) \rangle \xrightarrow{\tau} \langle Q \| R', \mathcal{B}(\sigma) \rangle.$$

In addition, we have $\langle S, \rho' \rangle \mathcal{R} \langle Q \| R', \mathcal{B}(\sigma) \rangle$ because $\langle P, \mathcal{A}(\rho) \rangle \sim \langle Q, \mathcal{A}(\sigma) \rangle$.

Subcase 1.3. The transition (A.44) is derived by **Comm** from $\langle P, \mathcal{B}(\rho) \rangle \xrightarrow{c?q} \langle P', \mathcal{B}(\rho) \rangle$ and $\langle R, \mathcal{B}(\rho) \rangle \xrightarrow{c!q} \langle R', \mathcal{B}(\rho) \rangle$. First, we have $\langle P, \mathcal{A}(\rho) \rangle \xrightarrow{c?q} \langle P', \mathcal{A}(\rho) \rangle$ and $\langle R, \mathcal{B}(\sigma) \rangle \xrightarrow{c!q} \langle R', \mathcal{B}(\sigma) \rangle$ by using Lemma 10.1. With Lemma 10.2 we see $q \in qv(R)$. Note that $qv(P) \cap qv(R) = qv(Q) \cap qv(R) = \emptyset$. Thus, $q \notin qv(P) \cup qv(Q)$. Since $\langle P, \mathcal{A}(\rho) \rangle \sim \langle Q, \mathcal{A}(\sigma) \rangle$, it follows that $\langle Q, \mathcal{A}(\sigma) \rangle \xrightarrow{c?q} \langle Q', \mathcal{A}(\sigma) \rangle$ for some Q' with $\langle P', \mathcal{A}(\rho) \rangle \sim \langle Q', \mathcal{A}(\sigma) \rangle$. By Lemma 10.1 and the **Comm** rule we obtain $\langle Q, \mathcal{B}(\sigma) \rangle \xrightarrow{c?q} \langle Q', \mathcal{B}(\sigma) \rangle$ and

$$\langle Q \| R, \mathcal{B}(\sigma) \rangle \xrightarrow{\tau} \langle Q' \| R', \mathcal{B}(\sigma) \rangle.$$

Moreover, it holds that $\langle S, \rho' \rangle \mathcal{R} \langle Q' \| R', \mathcal{B}(\sigma) \rangle$.

Subcase 1.4. The transition (A.44) is derived by **Comm** from $\langle P, \mathcal{B}(\rho) \rangle \xrightarrow{c!q} \langle P', \mathcal{B}(\rho) \rangle$ and $\langle R, \mathcal{B}(\rho) \rangle \xrightarrow{c?q} \langle R', \mathcal{B}(\rho) \rangle$. Similar to Subcase 1.3.

Case 2. $\alpha = \mathcal{G}[\bar{s}]$, where $\bar{s}$ is a finite subset of $qVar$, and $\mathcal{G}$ is a superoperator on $\mathcal{H}_{\bar{s}}$. We have $\rho' = \mathcal{G}_{\bar{s}} \mathcal{B}(\rho)$, and this case is divided into the following two subcases:

Subcase 2.1. The transition (A.44) is derived by **Intl2** from $\langle P, \mathcal{B}(\rho) \rangle \xrightarrow{\mathcal{G}[\bar{s}]} \langle P', \mathcal{G}_{\bar{s}} \mathcal{B}(\rho) \rangle$. Then $S = P' \| R$. It follows from Lemma 10.1 that $\langle P, \mathcal{A}(\rho) \rangle \xrightarrow{\mathcal{G}[\bar{s}]} \langle P', \mathcal{G}_{\bar{s}} \mathcal{A}(\rho) \rangle$, and $\langle Q, \mathcal{A}(\sigma) \rangle \xrightarrow{\mathcal{G}[\bar{s}]} \langle Q', \mathcal{G}_{\bar{s}} \mathcal{A}(\sigma) \rangle$ for some Q' with $\langle P', \mathcal{G}_{\bar{s}} \mathcal{A}(\rho) \rangle \sim \langle Q', \mathcal{G}_{\bar{s}} \mathcal{A}(\sigma) \rangle$ because $\langle P, \mathcal{A}(\rho) \rangle \sim \langle Q, \mathcal{A}(\sigma) \rangle$. Hence, using Lemma 10.1 once again we obtain $\langle Q, \mathcal{B}(\sigma) \rangle \xrightarrow{\mathcal{G}[\bar{s}]} \langle Q', \mathcal{G}_{\bar{s}} \mathcal{B}(\sigma) \rangle$. Consequently, using the **Intl2** rule leads to

$$\langle Q \| R, \mathcal{B}(\sigma) \rangle \xrightarrow{\mathcal{G}[\bar{s}]} \langle Q' \| R, \mathcal{G}_{\bar{s}} \mathcal{B}(\sigma) \rangle.$$

Comparing carefully $\mathcal{G}_{\bar{s}} \mathcal{A}$ and $\mathcal{G}_{\bar{s}} \mathcal{B}$, we see that $\mathcal{G}_{\bar{s}} \mathcal{B}$ results from inserting

$$\mathcal{F}_{Y_{n+1}}^{(n+1)} = \mathcal{I}_{\mathcal{H}_{Y_{n+1}}} = \mathcal{I}_{\mathcal{H}}, \mathcal{F}_{Y_n}^{(n)}, \mathcal{F}_{Y_{n-1}}^{(n-1)}, ..., \mathcal{F}_{Y_1}^{(1)}, \mathcal{F}_{Y_0}^{(0)}$$

at appropriate positions in $\mathcal{G}_Z \mathcal{A}$, where Y_{n+1} is an arbitrary finite subset of $qVar$. This implies $\langle S, \rho' \rangle \mathcal{R} \langle Q' \| R, \mathcal{G}_{\bar{s}} \mathcal{B}(\sigma) \rangle$.

Subcase 2.2. The transition (A.44) is derived by **Intl2** from $\langle R, \mathcal{B}(\rho) \rangle \xrightarrow{\mathcal{G}[\bar{s}]} \langle R', \mathcal{G}_{\bar{s}} \mathcal{B}(\rho) \rangle$. Then $S = P \| R'$, and $\langle R, \mathcal{B}(\sigma) \rangle \xrightarrow{\mathcal{G}[\bar{s}]} \langle R', \mathcal{G}_{\bar{s}} \mathcal{B}(\sigma) \rangle$ follows immediately by using Lemma 10.1. Hence, it holds that

$$\langle Q \| R, \mathcal{B}(\sigma) \rangle \xrightarrow{\mathcal{G}[\bar{s}]} \langle Q \| R', \mathcal{G}_{\bar{s}} \mathcal{B}(\sigma) \rangle.$$

Let

$$\mathcal{K}_{Y_n \cup \bar{s}}^{(n)} = (\mathcal{F}_{Y_n}^{(n)} \otimes \mathcal{I}_{\mathcal{H}_{\bar{s} \setminus Y_n}}) \circ (\mathcal{G}_{\bar{s}} \otimes \mathcal{I}_{\mathcal{H}_{Y_n \setminus \bar{s}}}).$$

Then $\mathcal{K}_{Y_n \cup \overline{s}}^{(n)}$ is a superoperator on $\mathcal{H}_{Y_n \cup \overline{s}}$, and $\mathcal{G}_{\overline{s}}\mathcal{B}$ is obtained by inserting appropriately

$$\mathcal{K}_{Y_n \cup \overline{s}}^{(n)}, \mathcal{F}_{Y_{n-1}}^{(n-1)}, ..., \mathcal{F}_{Y_1}^{(1)}, \mathcal{F}_{Y_0}^{(0)}$$

in $\mathcal{A}$. Now it follows that $\langle S, \rho' \rangle \mathcal{R} \langle Q \| R, \mathcal{G}_{\overline{s}}\mathcal{B}(\sigma) \rangle$ from $\langle P, \mathcal{A}(\rho) \rangle \sim \langle Q, \mathcal{A}(\sigma) \rangle$.

At the first glance, one may think that the full generality of $\mathcal{A}$ is not necessary because in the above two subcases we only add a quantum operation at the beginning of a sequence of quantum operations. However, this is not the case. It should be noted that our proof is carried by induction on the depth of inference (A.44), and quantum operation inserted at the beginning of a sequence will be moved to the middle of a larger sequence in the later steps.

Case 3. $\alpha = c!q$. We need to consider the following two subcases:

Subcase 3.1. The transition (A.44) is derived by **Intl2** from $\langle P, \mathcal{B}(\rho) \rangle \xrightarrow{c!q} \langle P', \mathcal{B}(\rho) \rangle$. Similar to Subcase 1.1.

Subcase 3.2. The transition (A.44) is derived by **Intl2** from $\langle R, \mathcal{B}(\rho) \rangle \xrightarrow{c!q} \langle R', \mathcal{B}(\rho) \rangle$. Similar to Subcase 1.2.

Case 4. $\alpha = c?q$ and $q \notin qv(P \| R) \cup qv(Q \| R) = qv(P) \cup qv(Q) \cup qv(R)$. We have $\rho' = \mathcal{B}(\rho)$, and this case is divided into the following two subcases:

Subcase 4.1. The transition (A.44) is derived by **Intl1** from $\langle P, \mathcal{B}(\rho) \rangle \xrightarrow{c?q} \langle P', \mathcal{B}(\rho) \rangle$. Then $S = P' \| R$, and using Lemma 10.1 we obtain $\langle P, \mathcal{A}(\rho) \rangle \xrightarrow{c?q} \langle P', \mathcal{A}(\rho) \rangle$. From $\langle P, \mathcal{A}(\rho) \rangle \sim \langle Q, \mathcal{A}(\sigma) \rangle$ and $q \notin qv(P) \cup qv(Q)$, it follows that $\langle Q, \mathcal{A}(\sigma) \rangle \xrightarrow{c?q} \langle Q', \mathcal{A}(\sigma) \rangle$ for some Q' with for all $r \notin qv(P') \cup qv(Q') \setminus \{q\}$, and

$$\langle P'\{r/q\}, \mathcal{A}(\rho) \rangle \sim \langle Q'\{r/q\}, \mathcal{A}(\sigma) \rangle.$$

Furthermore, we have $\langle Q, \mathcal{B}(\sigma) \rangle \xrightarrow{c?q} \langle Q', \mathcal{B}(\sigma) \rangle$ by using Lemma 10.1 once again. Note that $q \notin qv(R)$. Thus, applying the **Intl1** rule yields $\langle Q \| R, \mathcal{B}(\sigma) \rangle \xrightarrow{c?q} \langle Q' \| R, \mathcal{B}(\sigma) \rangle$. What remains is to verify that

$$\langle (P' \| R)\{s/q\}, \mathcal{B}(\rho) \rangle \mathcal{R} \langle (Q' \| R)\{s/q\}, \mathcal{B}(\sigma) \rangle$$

for all $s \notin qv(P' \| R) \cup qv(Q' \| R) \setminus \{q\}$. To this end, we only need to note that

$$(P' \| R)\{s/q\} = P'\{s/q\} \| R\{s/q\},$$
$$(Q' \| R)\{s/q\} = Q'\{s/q\} \| R\{s/q\},$$

and $s \notin qv(P' \| R) \cup qv(Q' \| R) \setminus \{q\}$ implies $s \notin qv(P') \cup qv(Q') \setminus \{q\}$.

Subcase 4.2. The transition (A.44) is derived by **Intl1** from $\langle R, \mathcal{B}(\rho) \rangle \xrightarrow{c?q} \langle R', \mathcal{B}(\rho) \rangle$. Then $S = P \| R'$, and $\langle R, \mathcal{B}(\sigma) \rangle \xrightarrow{c?q} \langle R', \mathcal{B}(\sigma) \rangle$ follows from Lemma 10.1. Consequently, we may obtain

$$\langle Q \| R, \mathcal{B}(\sigma) \rangle \xrightarrow{c?q} \langle Q \| R', \mathcal{B}(\sigma) \rangle$$

by using the **Intl1** rule, because $q \notin qv(Q)$. So, we only need to show that

$$\langle (P \| R')\{r/q\}, \mathcal{B}(\rho) \rangle \mathcal{R} \langle (Q \| R')\{r/q\}, \mathcal{B}(\sigma) \rangle$$

for all $r \notin qv(P \| R') \cup qv(Q \| R') \setminus \{q\}$. Note that $q \notin qv(P) \cup qv(Q)$. Thus, it holds that $(P \| R')\{r/q\} = P \| R'\{r/q\}$ and $(Q \| R')\{r/q\} = Q \| R'\{r/q\}$, and the conclusion follows immediately from the definition of $\mathcal{R}$. $\square$

A.6.3 Proofs of the results in Section 10.2.4

Proof of Proposition 10.5. A outline of the proof of Proposition 10.5 was given in Section 10.2.4. Now we complete the proof by proving Claims 1 and 2 stated there. We proceed by induction on the depth of inference (10.11). For simplicity, we only consider the following five cases, and the others are similar or easy and thus omitted.

Case 1. $\mathbf{G} = \mathbf{X}(\overline{r})$, $\alpha = c?u$ and $u \notin qv(\mathbf{G}(A)) \cup fv(\mathbf{G}(B))$. Then $\mathbf{G}(A) = A(\overline{r})$, $\mathbf{G}(B) = B(\overline{r})$, $u \notin \{\overline{r}\}$, and $\rho' = \rho$. We want to find some Q such that

$$\langle \mathbf{G}(B) = B(\overline{r}), \rho \rangle \xrightarrow{c?u} \langle Q, \rho \rangle,$$

and for all $s \notin qv(P) \cup qv(Q) \setminus \{u\}$, $\langle P\{s/u\}, \rho \rangle \sim \mathcal{R} \sim \langle Q\{s/u\}, \rho \rangle$.

First, we choose some $v_0 \notin \{\overline{r}\}$. Then for each $s \notin qv(P) \cup qv(Q) \setminus \{u\}$, from (10.11) and Lemma 10.1.2 we obtain

$$\langle \mathbf{G}(A), \rho\{v_0/s\} \rangle \overset{c?u}{\to} \langle P, \rho\{v_0/z\} \rangle. \tag{A.45}$$

Since $A(\overline{q}) \overset{def}{=} \mathbf{E}(A)$, transition (A.45) must be derived by the **Def** rule from

$$\langle \mathbf{E}(A)\{\overline{r}/\overline{q}\}, \rho\{v_0/s\} \rangle \overset{c?u}{\to} \langle P, \rho\{v_0/s\} \rangle. \tag{A.46}$$

On the other hand, we have $qv(\mathbf{E}(A)) \subseteq \{\overline{q}\}$. Thus, $qv(\mathbf{E}(A)\{\overline{r}/\overline{q}\}) \subseteq \{\overline{r}\}$ and $u \notin qv(\mathbf{E}(A)\{\overline{r}/\overline{q}\})$. Note that $\mathbf{E}(A)\{\overline{r}/\overline{q}\} = \mathbf{E}\{\overline{r}/\overline{q}\}(A)$, and the depth of inference (A.46) is smaller than that of inference (A.45), which is equal to the depth of inference (10.11). So, the induction hypothesis leads to, for some R,

$$\langle \mathbf{E}(B)\{\overline{r}/\overline{q}\} = \mathbf{E}\{\overline{r}/\overline{q}\}(B), \rho\{v_0/s\} \rangle \overset{c?u}{\to} \langle R, \rho\{v_0/s\} \rangle \tag{A.47}$$

and for all $v \notin qv(P) \cup qv(R) \setminus \{u\}$,

$$\langle P\{v/u\}, \rho\{v_0/s\} \rangle \sim \mathcal{R} \sim \langle R\{v/u\}, \rho\{v_0/s\} \rangle. \tag{A.48}$$

It follows from $\mathbf{E} \sim \mathbf{F}$ that $\mathbf{E}(B) \sim \mathbf{F}(B)$. Furthermore, it is easy to show that $\mathbf{E}(B)\{\overline{r}/\overline{q}\} \sim \mathbf{F}(B)\{\overline{r}/\overline{q}\}$. Since $B(\overline{q}) \overset{def}{=} \mathbf{F}(B)$, it holds that $u \notin qv(\mathbf{F}(B)\{\overline{r}/\overline{q}\}) \subseteq \{\overline{r}\}$. Consequently, for some Q,

$$\langle \mathbf{F}(B)\{\overline{r}/\overline{q}\}, \rho\{v_0/s\} \rangle \overset{c?u}{\to} \langle Q, \rho\{v_0/s\} \rangle \tag{A.49}$$

and for all $v \notin qv(R) \cup qv(Q) \setminus \{u\}$,

$$\langle Q\{v/u\}, \rho\{v_0/s\} \rangle \sim \langle R\{v/u\}, \rho\{v_0/s\} \rangle. \tag{A.50}$$

Using the **Def** rule, we obtain

$$\langle B(\overline{r}), \rho\{v_0/s\} \rangle \overset{c?u}{\to} \langle Q, \rho\{v_0/s\} \rangle$$

from (A.49), and Lemma 10.1.2 yields $\langle B(\overline{r}), \rho \rangle \overset{c?u}{\to} \langle Q, \rho \rangle$.

Now we have to show that

$$\langle P\{s/u\}, \rho \rangle \sim \mathcal{R} \sim \langle Q\{s/u\}, \rho \rangle$$

for all $s \notin qv(P) \cup qv(Q) \setminus \{u\}$. In fact, from (10.11), (A.47), (A.49), and Lemma 10.2.2 we see that $qv(P) \subseteq qv(\mathbf{G}(A)) \cup \{u\}$, $qv(R) \subseteq qv(\mathbf{E}(B)) \cup \{u\}$, and $qv(Q) \subseteq qv(\mathbf{F}(B)) \cup \{u\}$. Then $qv(P), qv(R), qv(Q) \subseteq \{\widetilde{y}\} \cup \{u\}$, and $v_0 \notin \{\overline{r}\}$ implies $v_0 \notin qv(P) \cup qv(R) \cup qv(Q) \setminus \{u\}$. Furthermore, it follows from (A.48) and (A.50) that

$$\langle P\{v_0/u\}, \rho\{v_0/s\} \rangle \sim \mathcal{R} \sim \langle R\{v_0/u\}, \rho\{v_0/s\} \rangle \sim \langle Q\{v_0/u\}, \rho\{v_0/s\} \rangle.$$

With the observation $\mathbf{G}(A)[f] = \mathbf{G}[f](A)$ for all substitutions f, we see that $sub(\mathcal{R}) = \mathcal{R}$. Therefore, we obtain

$$\langle P\{s/u\}, \rho \rangle = \langle P\{v_0/u\}\{s/v_0\}, \rho\{v_0/s\}\{s/v_0\} \rangle$$
$$\sim \mathcal{R} \sim \langle Q\{v_0/u\}\{s/v_0\}, \rho\{v_0/s\}\{s/v_0\} \rangle = \langle Q\{s/u\}, \rho \rangle.$$

Case 2. $\mathbf{G} = \mathcal{E}[\overline{q}].\mathbf{G}_1$. Then $\mathbf{G}(A) = \mathcal{E}[\overline{q}].\mathbf{G}_1(A)$, $\mathbf{G}(B) = \mathcal{E}[\overline{q}].\mathbf{G}_1(B)$, $\alpha = \mathcal{E}[\overline{q}]$, $P = \mathbf{G}_1(A)$ and $\rho' = \mathcal{E}_{\overline{q}}(\rho)$. We have

$$\langle \mathbf{G}(B), \rho \rangle \overset{\alpha = \mathcal{E}[\overline{q}]}{\to} \langle \mathbf{G}_1(B), \mathcal{E}_{\overline{q}}(\rho) \rangle$$

and $\langle P, \rho' \rangle \mathcal{R} \langle \mathbf{G}_1(B), \mathcal{E}_{\overline{q}}(\rho) \rangle$.

Case 3. $\mathbf{G} = c?q.\mathbf{G}_1$. Then transition (10.11) must be as follows:

$$\langle \mathbf{G}(A) = c?q.\mathbf{G}_1(A), \rho \rangle \overset{\alpha = c?r}{\to} \langle P = \mathbf{G}_1(A)\{r/q\}, \rho' = \rho \rangle$$

where $r \notin qv(\mathbf{G}_1(A)) \setminus \{q\}$. In this case, we have the assumption that $r \notin qv(\mathbf{G}(A)) \cup qv(\mathbf{G}(B))$. Since $\mathbf{G}(B) = c?q.\mathbf{G}_1(B)$, we obtain

$$\langle \mathbf{G}(B), \rho \rangle \xrightarrow{c?r} \langle \mathbf{G}_1(B)\{r/q\}, \rho \rangle$$

by the **Input** rule. Moreover, for any $s \notin qv(P) \cup qv(\mathbf{G}_1(B)\{r/q\}) \setminus \{r\}$, we have

$$P\{s/r\} = \mathbf{G}_1(A)\{r/q\}\{s/r\} = \mathbf{G}_1(A)\{s/q\} = \mathbf{G}_1\{s/q\}(A),$$
$$\mathbf{G}_1(B)\{r/q\}\{s/r\} = \mathbf{G}_1(B)\{s/q\} = \mathbf{G}_1\{s/q\}(B).$$

So, it follows that $\langle P\{s/r\}, \rho' \rangle \mathcal{R} \langle \mathbf{G}_1(B)\{r/q\}\{s/r\}, \rho \rangle$.

Case 4. $\mathbf{G} = \mathbf{G}_1 \| \mathbf{G}_2$, $\alpha = c?q$, $q \notin qv(\mathbf{G}_1(A)) \cup qv(\mathbf{G}_2(A))$ and transition (10.11) is derived by the **Intl1** from $\langle \mathbf{G}_1(A), \rho \rangle \xrightarrow{c?x} \langle P_1, \rho \rangle$. Then $\mathbf{G}(A) = \mathbf{G}_1(A) \| \mathbf{G}_2(A)$, $P = P_1 \| \mathbf{G}_2(A)$ and $\rho' = \rho$. By the induction hypothesis we have, for some Q_1, $\langle \mathbf{G}_1(B), \rho \rangle \xrightarrow{c?q} \langle Q_1, \rho \rangle$, and for all $r \notin qv(P_1) \cup qv(Q_1) \setminus \{q\}$,

$$\langle P_1\{r/q\}, \rho \rangle \sim \langle P_1', \rho \rangle \mathcal{R} \langle Q_1', \rho \rangle \sim \langle Q_1\{r/q\}, \rho \rangle$$

for some P_1', Q_1'. It is clear that $q \notin qv(\mathbf{G}_2(B))$. Thus, we obtain

$$\langle \mathbf{G}(B) = \mathbf{G}_1(B) \| \mathbf{G}_2(B), \rho \rangle \xrightarrow{c?q} \langle Q_1 \| \mathbf{G}_2(B), \rho \rangle$$

by the **Intl1** rule. For any $s \notin qv(P) \cup qv(Q_1 \| \mathbf{G}_2(B)) \setminus \{q\}$, we have $s \notin qv(P_1) \cup qv(Q_1) \setminus \{q\}$, and

$$\langle P_1\{s/q\}, \rho \rangle \sim \langle P_1', \rho \rangle \mathcal{R} \langle Q_1', \rho \rangle \sim \langle Q_1'\{s/q\}, \rho \rangle.$$

This, together with Proposition 10.1.2.f, leads to

$$\langle P\{s/q\}, \rho \rangle = \langle P_1\{s/q\} \| \mathbf{G}_2(A), \rho \rangle \sim \langle P_1' \| \mathbf{G}_2(A), \rho \rangle \mathcal{R}$$
$$\langle Q_1' \| \mathbf{G}_2(B), \rho \rangle \sim \langle Q_1\{s/q\} \| \mathbf{G}_2(B) = (Q_1 \| \mathbf{G}_2(B))\{s/q\}, \rho \rangle.$$

Case 5. $\mathbf{G} = \mathbf{G}_1 \| \mathbf{G}_2$, $\alpha = \tau$ and transition (10.11) is derived by the **Comm** rule from $\langle \mathbf{G}_1(A), \rho \rangle \xrightarrow{c?q} \langle P_1, \rho \rangle$ and $\langle \mathbf{G}_2(A), \rho \rangle \xrightarrow{c!q} \langle P_2, \rho \rangle$. Then $\rho' = \rho$ and $P = P_1 \| P_2$. With the induction hypothesis we have, for some Q_1, Q_2, $\langle \mathbf{G}_1(B), \rho \rangle \xrightarrow{c?q} \langle Q_1, \rho \rangle$ and $\langle \mathbf{G}_2(B), \rho \rangle \xrightarrow{c!q} \langle Q_2, \rho \rangle$,

$$\langle P_1, \rho \rangle \sim \langle P_1', \rho \rangle \mathcal{R} \langle Q_1', \rho \rangle \sim \langle Q_1, \rho \rangle$$

for some P_1', Q_1', and

$$\langle P_2, \rho \rangle \sim \langle P_2', \rho \rangle \mathcal{R} \langle Q_2', \rho \rangle \sim \langle Q_2, \rho \rangle$$

for some P_2', Q_2'. Then

$$\langle \mathbf{G}(B) = \mathbf{G}_1(B) \| \mathbf{G}_2(B), \rho \rangle \xrightarrow{\tau} \langle Q_1 \| Q_2, \rho \rangle,$$

and by Proposition 10.1.2.f it follows that

$$\langle P, \rho \rangle \sim \langle P_1' \| P_2', \rho \rangle \mathcal{R} \langle Q_1' \| Q_2', \rho \rangle \sim \langle Q_1 \| Q_2, \rho \rangle. \qquad \square$$

Proof of Theorem 10.2. A outline of the proof of Theorem 10.2 was given in Section 10.2.4. To complete the proof, we only need to prove Claims 1 and 2 stated there. Let us proceed by induction on the depth of inference (10.12). We only consider the following case as an example:

Case 1. $\mathbf{G} = \mathbf{Y}(\bar{r})$, $\alpha = c?q$ and $q \notin qv(\mathbf{G}(\widetilde{P})) \cup qv(\mathbf{G}(\widetilde{Q}))$. Then $\mathbf{Y} = \mathbf{X}_i$ for some $i \leq m$, $\mathbf{G}(\widetilde{P}) = P_i\{\bar{r}/\bar{q}_i\}$, $\mathbf{G}(\widetilde{Q}) = Q_i\{\bar{r}/\bar{q}_i\}$, and $\rho = \rho'$. We choose some quantum variable

$$u \notin \bigcup_{i=1}^{m}(fv(P_i) \cup qv(Q_i) \cup qv(\mathbf{E}_i)) \cup \{\bar{r}\}.$$

Then $u \notin qv(\mathbf{G}(\widetilde{P}))$, and $\langle P_i\{\overline{r}/\overline{q}_i\}, \rho\rangle \overset{c?u}{\to} \langle P', \rho\rangle$ for some $P' \equiv_\alpha P\{u/q\}$. Since $P_i \sim \mathbf{E}_i(\widetilde{P})$, we obtain

$$P_i\{\overline{r}/\overline{q}_i\} \sim \mathbf{E}_i(\widetilde{P})\{\overline{r}/\overline{q}_i\} = \mathbf{E}_i\{\overline{r}/\overline{q}_i\}(\widetilde{P}).$$

It holds that

$$u \notin qv(P_i\{\overline{r}/\overline{q}_i\}) \cup qv(\mathbf{E}_i\{\overline{r}/\overline{q}_i\}(\widetilde{P})).$$

So, we have

$$\langle \mathbf{E}_i\{\overline{r}/\overline{q}_i\}(\widetilde{P}), \rho\rangle \overset{c?u}{\to} \langle P'', \rho\rangle$$

for some P'', and

$$\langle P'\{s/u\}, \rho\rangle \sim \langle P''\{s/u\}, \rho\rangle \tag{A.51}$$

for all $s \notin qv(P') \cup qv(P'') \setminus \{u\}$. By Lemma 10.10 we obtain for some $\mathbf{E}'$, $P'' = \mathbf{E}'(\widetilde{P})$ and

$$\langle \mathbf{E}_i(\widetilde{Q})\{\overline{r}/\overline{q}_i\} = \mathbf{E}_i\{\overline{r}/\overline{q}_i\}(\widetilde{Q}), \rho\rangle \overset{c?u}{\to} \langle \mathbf{E}'(\widetilde{Q}), \rho\rangle.$$

Note that $\mathbf{G}(\widetilde{Q}) \sim \mathbf{E}_i(\widetilde{Q})\{\overline{r}/\overline{q}_i\}$, and

$$u \notin qv(\mathbf{G}(\widetilde{Q})) \cup qv(\mathbf{E}_i(\widetilde{Q})\{\overline{r}/\overline{q}_i\}).$$

Then for some Q', $\langle \mathbf{G}(\widetilde{Q}), \rho\rangle \overset{c?u}{\to} \langle Q', \rho\rangle$, and

$$\langle \mathbf{E}'(\widetilde{Q})\{s/u\}, \rho\rangle \sim \langle Q'\{s/u\}, \rho\rangle \tag{A.52}$$

for all $s \notin qv(\mathbf{E}'(\widetilde{Q})) \cup qv(Q') \setminus \{u\}$. Since $q \notin qv(\mathbf{G}(\widetilde{Q}))$, we have $\langle \mathbf{G}(\widetilde{Q}), \rho\rangle \overset{c?q}{\to} \langle Q, \rho\rangle$, where $Q \equiv_\alpha Q'\{q/u\}$.

It follows from Lemma 10.2 that $qv(P) \subseteq qv(P_i\{\overline{r}/\overline{q}_i\}) \cup \{q\}$. Then $u \notin qv(P) \setminus \{q\}$. Since $P' \equiv_\alpha P\{u/q\}$, it holds that $P \equiv_\alpha P'\{q/u\}$. We now choose

$$v_0 \notin \bigcup_{i=1}^{m}(qv(P_i) \cup qv(Q_i) \cup qv(\mathbf{E}_i)) \cup \{\overline{r}\} \cup qv(P) \cup qv(Q).$$

It is obvious that $qv(P') \subseteq qv(P) \cup \{u\}$. On the other hand, we see that $qv(P'') \subseteq qv(\mathbf{E}_i\{\overline{r}/\overline{q}_i\}(\widetilde{P}))$ by Lemma 10.2. Thus, $v_0 \notin qv(P') \cup qv(P'') \setminus \{u\}$, and from (A.51) we obtain $\langle P'\{v_0/u\}, \rho\rangle \sim \langle P''\{v_0/u\}, \rho\rangle$. Furthermore, it follows that $\langle P', \rho\{u/v_0\}\rangle \sim \langle P'', \rho\{u/v_0\}\rangle$ and

$$\langle P'\{q/u\}, \rho\{u/v_0\}\{q/u\} = \rho\{q/v_0\}\rangle \sim \langle P''\{q/u\}, \rho\{q/v_0\}\rangle.$$

Then using Proposition 10.1 we obtain

$$\begin{aligned} \langle P, \rho\{q/v_0\}\rangle &\sim \langle P''\{q/u\} = \mathbf{E}'(\widetilde{P})\{q/u\} \\ &= \mathbf{E}'\{q/u\}(\widetilde{P}), \rho\{q/v_0\}\rangle \\ \mathcal{R}\langle \mathbf{E}'\{q/u\}(\widetilde{Q}) &= \mathbf{E}'(\widetilde{Q})\{q/u\}, \rho\{q/v_0\}. \end{aligned}$$

Again, we see that

$$qv(\mathbf{E}'(\widetilde{Q})) \subseteq qv(\mathbf{E}_i(\widetilde{Q})\{\overline{r}/\overline{q}_i\}) \cup \{u\}$$

and $qv(Q') \subseteq qv(Q_i\{\overline{r}/\overline{q}_i\})$ by Lemma 10.2. Hence, $v_0 \notin qv(\mathbf{E}'(\widetilde{Q})) \cup qv(Q') \setminus \{u\}$. This, together with (A.52), implies $\langle \mathbf{E}'(\widetilde{Q})\{v_0/u\}, \rho\rangle \sim \langle Q'\{v_0/u\}, \rho\rangle$. Furthermore, we obtain:

$$\begin{aligned} \langle \mathbf{E}'\{q/u\} &= \mathbf{E}'\{v_0/u\}\{q/v_0\}, \rho\{q/v_0\}\rangle \\ &\sim \langle Q'\{q/u\} = Q'\{v_0/u\}\{q/v_0\}, \rho\{q/v_0\}\rangle \\ &\sim \langle Q, \rho\{q/v_0\}\rangle \end{aligned}$$

because $Q \equiv_\alpha Q'\{q/u\}$.

Now it suffices to show that for all $r \notin qv(P) \cup qv(Q) \setminus \{q\}$, we have

$$\langle P\{r/q\}, \rho \rangle \sim \langle P', \rho \rangle \mathcal{R} \langle Q', \rho \rangle \sim \langle Q\{r/q\}, \rho \rangle$$

for some P', Q'. This can be carried out in a way similar to that at the end of Case 1 in the proof of Proposition 10.5. $\square$

A.6.4 Proof of Theorem 10.4.2.d

We can construct $\mathcal{R}_\mu$ by modifying $\mathcal{R}$ in the proof of Theorem 10.1.2.f (see Appendix A.6.2). Let $\mathcal{R}_\mu = \mathcal{B}_\mu \cup \mathcal{R}'_\mu$, where

$$\mathcal{B}_\mu = \{(\langle P, \rho \rangle, \langle P, \sigma \rangle) : D(\rho, \sigma) \leq \mu\},$$

and $\mathcal{R}'_\mu$ consists of the pairs:

$$(\langle P \| R, \mathcal{F}_{Y_n}^{(n)} \mathcal{E}_{X_n}^{(n)} \mathcal{F}_{Y_{n-1}}^{(n-1)} \mathcal{E}_{X_{n-1}}^{(n-1)} ... \mathcal{F}_{Y_1}^{(1)} \mathcal{E}_{X_1}^{(1)} \mathcal{F}_{Y_0}^{(0)}(\rho) \rangle,$$
$$\langle Q \| R, \mathcal{F}_{Y_n}^{(n)} \mathcal{E}_{X_n}^{\prime(n)} \mathcal{F}_{Y_{n-1}}^{(n-1)} \mathcal{E}_{X_{n-1}}^{\prime(n-1)} ... \mathcal{F}_{Y_1}^{(1)} \mathcal{E}_{X_1}^{\prime(1)} \mathcal{F}_{Y_0}^{(0)}(\sigma) \rangle),$$

in which it holds that

$$\langle P, \mathcal{E}_{X_n}^{(n)} \mathcal{E}_{X_{n-1}}^{(n-1)} ... \mathcal{E}_{X_1}^{(1)}(\rho) \rangle \sim_\mu \langle Q, \mathcal{E}_{X_n}^{\prime(n)} \mathcal{E}_{X_{n-1}}^{\prime(n-1)} ... \mathcal{E}_{X_1}^{\prime(1)}(\sigma) \rangle.$$

The difference between $\mathcal{R}$ in the proof of Theorem 10.1.2.f and $\mathcal{R}'_\mu$ is that, in $\mathcal{R}'_\mu$, $\mathcal{E}_{X_i}^{(i)}$ and $\mathcal{E}_{X_i}^{\prime(i)}$ are allowed to be different $(i \leq n)$. Now it suffices to show that $\mathcal{R}_\mu$ is a strong μ-bisimulation. It is obvious that $\mathcal{R}_\mu$ is μ-closed.

Suppose that $\langle P, \rho \rangle \mathcal{B}_\mu \langle P, \sigma \rangle$ and $\langle P, \rho \rangle \xrightarrow{\alpha} \langle P', \rho' \rangle$. If $\alpha \notin Act_{op}$, then $\rho' = \rho$, and with Lemma 10.1 we have $\langle P, \sigma \rangle \xrightarrow{\alpha} \langle P', \sigma \rangle$ and $\langle P', \rho' \rangle \mathcal{B}_\mu \langle P', \sigma \rangle$ (for the case that $\alpha = c?x$ and $x \notin fv(P)$, it holds that $\langle P'\{y/x\}, \rho' \rangle \mathcal{B}_\mu \langle P'\{y/x\}, \sigma \rangle$ for all $y \notin fv(P') \setminus \{x\}$). If $\alpha = \mathcal{E}[X]$, then $\rho' = \mathcal{E}_X(\rho)$, and by Lemma 10.1 we obtain $\langle P, \sigma \rangle \xrightarrow{\alpha} \langle P', \mathcal{E}_X(\sigma) \rangle$. Furthermore, it is easy to show that $D(\rho', \mathcal{E}_X(\sigma)) \leq D(\rho, \sigma) \leq \mu$ and $\langle P', \rho' \rangle \mathcal{B}_\mu \langle P', \mathcal{E}_X(\sigma) \rangle$.

Finally, we use the symbols $\mathcal{A}$ and $\mathcal{B}$ in the same way as in the proof of Theorem 10.1.2.f, and let $\mathcal{A}'$ and $\mathcal{B}'$ be obtained by replacing $\mathcal{E}_{X_i}^{(i)}$ with $\mathcal{E}_{X_i}^{\prime(i)}$ $(i \leq n)$ in $\mathcal{A}$ and $\mathcal{B}$, respectively. Suppose that $\langle P, \mathcal{A}(\rho) \rangle \sim_\mu \langle Q, \mathcal{A}'(\sigma) \rangle$ and $\langle P \| R, \mathcal{B}(\rho) \rangle \xrightarrow{\alpha} \langle S, \rho' \rangle$. We only consider the case that $\alpha = \mathcal{G}[Z]$ and the transition is derived by **Intl2** from $\langle P, \mathcal{B}(\rho) \rangle \xrightarrow{\mathcal{G}[Z]} \langle P', \mathcal{G}_Z \mathcal{B}(\rho) \rangle$ (and the other cases are the same as in the proof of Theorem 10.1.2.f). It holds that $S = P' \| R$ and $\rho' = \mathcal{G}_Z \mathcal{B}(\rho)$. An application of Lemma 10.1 leads to

$$\langle P, \mathcal{A}(\rho) \rangle \xrightarrow{\mathcal{G}[Z]} \langle P', \mathcal{G}_Z \mathcal{A}(\rho) \rangle.$$

Since $\langle P, \mathcal{A}(\rho) \rangle \sim_\mu \langle Q, \mathcal{A}'(\rho) \rangle$, there are $\mathcal{G}'$ and Q' such that

$$\langle Q, \mathcal{A}'(\sigma) \rangle \xrightarrow{\mathcal{G}'[Z]} \langle Q', \mathcal{G}'_Z \mathcal{A}'(\sigma) \rangle \sim_\mu \langle P', \mathcal{G}_Z \mathcal{A}(\rho) \rangle$$

and $D_\diamond(\mathcal{G}, \mathcal{G}') \leq \mu$. Then, using Lemma 10.1 once again, we obtain

$$\langle Q, \mathcal{B}'(\sigma) \rangle \xrightarrow{\mathcal{G}'[Z]} \langle Q', \mathcal{G}'_Z \mathcal{B}'(\sigma) \rangle,$$

and it follows that

$$\langle Q \| R, \mathcal{B}'(\sigma) \rangle \xrightarrow{\mathcal{G}'[Z]} \langle Q' \| R, \mathcal{G}'_Z \mathcal{B}'(\sigma) \rangle.$$

It is easy to see that $\langle S, \rho' \rangle \mathcal{R}'_\mu \langle Q' \| R, \mathcal{G}'_Z \mathcal{B}'(\sigma) \rangle$ from the definition of $\mathcal{R}'_\mu$. $\square$

A.7 Omitted proofs in Chapter 11

The proofs of the main results in Chapter 11 all include tedious calculations. So, for readability, they have been stated in Chapter 11 without proofs. For completeness, here we present their detailed proofs.

A.7.1   Proof of Lemma 11.2

Let F be the operator-valued function given in Definition 11.6. We write:

$$\overline{F} \triangleq \sum_{\delta_1 \in \Delta_1, \ldots, \delta_n \in \Delta_n} F(\oplus_{i=1}^n \delta_i)^\dagger \cdot F(\oplus_{i=1}^n \delta_i).$$

Let us start with an auxiliary equality. For any $|\Phi\rangle, |\Psi\rangle \in \mathcal{H}_c \otimes \mathcal{H}$, we can write

$$|\Phi\rangle = \sum_{i=1}^n |i\rangle |\varphi_i\rangle \text{ and } |\Psi\rangle = \sum_{i=1}^n |i\rangle |\psi_i\rangle$$

where $|\varphi_i\rangle, |\psi_i\rangle \in \mathcal{H}$ for each $1 \le i \le n$. Then we have:

$$
\begin{aligned}
\langle \Phi | \overline{F} | \Psi \rangle &= \sum_{\delta_1, \ldots, \delta_n} \langle \Phi | F(\oplus_{i=1}^n \delta_i)^\dagger \cdot F(\oplus_{i=1}^n \delta_i) | \Psi \rangle \\
&= \sum_{\delta_1, \ldots, \delta_n} \sum_{i,i'=1}^n \left(\prod_{k \ne i} \lambda_{k\delta_k}^* \right) \left(\prod_{k \ne i'} \lambda_{k\delta_k} \right) \langle i | i' \rangle \langle \varphi_i | F_i(\delta_i)^\dagger F_{i'}(\delta_{i'}) | \psi_{i'} \rangle \\
&= \sum_{\delta_1, \ldots, \delta_n} \sum_{i=1}^n \left(\prod_{k \ne i} |\lambda_{k\delta_k}|^2 \right) \langle \varphi_i | F_i(\delta_i)^\dagger F_i(\delta_i) | \psi_i \rangle \\
&= \sum_{i=1}^n \left[\sum_{\delta_1, \ldots, \delta_{i-1}, \delta_{i+1}, \ldots, \delta_n} \left(\prod_{k \ne i} |\lambda_{k\delta_k}|^2 \right) \cdot \sum_{\delta_i} \langle \varphi_i | F_i(\delta_i)^\dagger F_i(\delta_i) | \psi_i \rangle \right] \\
&= \sum_{i=1}^n \sum_{\delta_i} \langle \varphi_i | F_i(\delta_i)^\dagger F_i(\delta_i) | \psi_i \rangle \\
&= \sum_{i=1}^n \langle \varphi_i | \sum_{\delta_i} F_i(\delta_i)^\dagger F_i(\delta_i) | \psi_i \rangle
\end{aligned}
\tag{A.53}
$$

because for each k, we have:

$$\sum_{\delta_k} |\lambda_{k\delta_k}|^2 = 1,$$

and thus

$$\sum_{\delta_1, \ldots, \delta_{i-1}, \delta_{i+1}, \ldots, \delta_n} \left(\prod_{k \ne i} |\lambda_{k\delta_k}|^2 \right) = \prod_{k \ne i} \left(\sum_{\delta_k} |\lambda_{k\delta_k}|^2 \right) = 1. \tag{A.54}$$

Now we are ready to prove our conclusions by using Eq. (A.53).

1. We first prove that $\overline{F} \sqsubseteq I_{\mathcal{H}_c \otimes \mathcal{H}}$; that is, F is an operator-valued function in $\mathcal{H}_c \otimes \mathcal{H}$ over $\oplus_{i=1}^n \Delta_n$. It suffices to show that

$$\langle \Phi | \overline{F} | \Phi \rangle \le \langle \Phi | \Phi \rangle$$

for each $|\Phi\rangle \in \mathcal{H}_c \otimes \mathcal{H}$. In fact, for each $1 \le i \le n$, since F_i is an operator-valued function, we have:

$$\sum_{\delta_i} F_i(\delta_i)^\dagger F_i(\delta_i) \sqsubseteq I_{\mathcal{H}}.$$

Therefore, it holds that

$$\langle \varphi_i | \sum_{\delta_i} F_i(\delta_i)^\dagger F_i(\delta_i) | \varphi_i \rangle \le \langle \varphi_i | \varphi_i \rangle.$$

Then it follows immediately from Eq. (A.53) that

$$\langle \Phi | \overline{F} | \Phi \rangle \leq \sum_{i=1}^{n} \langle \varphi_i | \varphi_i \rangle = \langle \Phi | \Phi \rangle.$$

So, F is an operator-valued function.

2. Secondly, we prove that F is full for the case where all F_i ($1 \leq i \leq n$) are full. It requires us to show that $\overline{F} = I_{\mathcal{H}_c \otimes \mathcal{H}}$. In fact, for every $1 \leq i \leq n$, we have:

$$\sum_{\delta_i} F_i(\delta_i)^\dagger F_i(\delta_i) = I_{\mathcal{H}}$$

because F_i is full. Thus, it follows from Eq. (A.53) that

$$\langle \Phi | \overline{F} | \Psi \rangle = \sum_{i=1}^{n} \langle \varphi_i | \psi_i \rangle = \langle \Phi | \Psi \rangle$$

for any $|\Phi\rangle, |\Psi\rangle \in \mathcal{H}_c \otimes \mathcal{H}$. So, it holds that $\overline{F} = I_{\mathcal{H}_c \otimes \mathcal{H}}$ by arbitrariness of $|\Phi\rangle$ and $\Psi\rangle$, and F is full.

A.7.2   Proof of Proposition 11.1

Clauses 1–4 are obvious, and we only prove 5 and 6.

(1) To prove clause 5, let

$$S \equiv \mathbf{if}\ (\square m \cdot M[\overline{q} : x] = m \to S_m)\ \mathbf{fi}.$$

Then by Definitions 11.9 and 11.10, for any partial density operator ρ in $\mathcal{H}_{qvar(S)}$, we have:

$$\begin{aligned}
[\![S]\!](\rho) &= \sum_{m} \sum_{\delta \in \Delta(S_m)} [\![S]\!](\delta[x \leftarrow m]) \rho [\![S]\!](\delta[x \leftarrow m])^\dagger \\
&= \sum_{m} \sum_{\delta \in \Delta(S_m)} \left([\![S_m]\!](\delta) \otimes I_{qvar(S) \setminus qvar(S_m)} \right) \left(M_m \otimes I_{qvar(S) \setminus \overline{q}} \right) \\
&\qquad\qquad \rho \left(M_m^\dagger \otimes I_{qvar(S) \setminus \overline{q}} \right) \left([\![S_m]\!](\delta)^\dagger \otimes I_{qvar(S) \setminus qvar(S_m)} \right) \\
&= \sum_{m} \sum_{\delta \in \Delta(S_m)} \left([\![S_m]\!](\delta) \otimes I_{qvar(S) \setminus qvar(S_m)} \right) \left(M_m \rho M_m^\dagger \right) \\
&\qquad\qquad \left([\![S_m]\!](\delta)^\dagger \otimes I_{qvar(S) \setminus qvar(S_m)} \right) \\
&= \sum_{m} [\![S_m]\!] \left(M_m \rho M_m^\dagger \right) \\
&= \left(\sum_{m} \left[(M_m \circ M_m^\dagger); [\![S_m]\!] \right] \right) (\rho).
\end{aligned}$$

(2) Now we prove clause 6. For simplicity of the presentation, we write:

$$S \equiv \mathbf{qif}\ [\overline{q}](\square i \cdot |i\rangle \to S_i)\ \mathbf{fiq}.$$

By Definition 11.9, we obtain:

$$[\![S]\!] = \bigoplus_i (|i\rangle \to [\![S_i]\!]).$$

Note that $\lfloor\!\lfloor S_i\rfloor\!\rfloor \in \mathbb{F}(\lfloor\!\lfloor S_i\rfloor\!\rfloor)$ for every $1 \leq i \leq n$, where $\mathbb{F}(\mathcal{E})$ stands for the set of operator-valued functions generated by quantum operation $\mathcal{E}$ (see Definition 11.4). Therefore, it follows from Definition 11.10 that

$$\llbracket S\rrbracket = \mathcal{E}(\lfloor\!\lfloor S\rfloor\!\rfloor) \in \left\{\mathcal{E}\left(\bigoplus_i (|i\rangle \to F_i)\right) : F_i \in \mathbb{F}(\lfloor\!\lfloor S_i\rfloor\!\rfloor) \text{ for every } i\right\}$$

$$= \bigoplus_i (|i\rangle \to \llbracket S_i\rrbracket).$$

A.7.3 Proof of Theorem 11.1

To simplify the presentation, we write:

$$R \equiv \mathbf{qif}\,[\overline{q}](\square i \cdot |i\rangle \to S_i)\,\mathbf{fiq}.$$

To prove the equivalence of two QuGCL programs, we have to show that their purely quantum semantics are the same. However, purely quantum semantics is defined in terms of semiclassical semantics (see Definition 11.10). So, we need to work at the level of semiclassical semantics first, and then lift it to the purely quantum semantics. Assume that the semiclassical semantics $\lfloor\!\lfloor S_i\rfloor\!\rfloor$ is the operator-valued function over Δ_i such that

$$\lfloor\!\lfloor S_i\rfloor\!\rfloor(\delta_i) = E_{i\delta_i}$$

for each $\delta_i \in \Delta_i$. Let states $|\psi\rangle \in \mathcal{H}_{\bigcup_{i=1}^n qvar(S_i)}$ and $|\varphi\rangle \in \mathcal{H}_{\overline{q}}$. We can write $|\varphi\rangle = \sum_{i=1}^n \alpha_i |i\rangle$ for some complex numbers α_i $(1 \leq i \leq n)$. Then for any $\delta_i \in \Delta_i$ $(1 \leq i \leq n)$, we have:

$$|\Psi_{\delta_1\ldots\delta_n}\rangle \overset{\triangle}{=} \lfloor\!\lfloor R\rfloor\!\rfloor(\oplus_{i=1}^n \delta_i)(|\varphi\rangle|\psi\rangle)$$

$$= \lfloor\!\lfloor R\rfloor\!\rfloor(\oplus_{i=1}^n \delta_i)\left(\sum_{i=1}^n \alpha_i|i\rangle|\psi\rangle\right)$$

$$= \sum_{i=1}^n \alpha_i\left(\prod_{k\neq i}\lambda_{k\delta_k}\right)|i\rangle(E_{i\sigma_i}|\psi\rangle)$$

where $\lambda_{i\delta_i}$'s are defined as in Eq. (11.18). We continue to compute:

$$|\Psi_{\delta_1\ldots\delta_n}\rangle\langle\Psi_{\delta_1\ldots\delta_n}| = \sum_{i,j=1}^n\left[\alpha_i\alpha_j^*\left(\prod_{k\neq i}\lambda_{k\delta_k}\right)\left(\prod_{k\neq j}\lambda_{k\delta_k}\right)|i\rangle\langle j| \otimes E_{i\delta_i}|\psi\rangle\langle\psi|E_{j\delta_j}^\dagger\right],$$

and it follows that

$$tr_{\mathcal{H}_{\overline{q}}}|\Psi_{\delta_1\ldots\delta_n}\rangle\langle\Psi_{\delta_1\ldots\delta_n}| = \sum_{i=1}^n |\alpha_i|^2\left(\prod_{k\neq i}\lambda_{k\delta_k}\right)^2 E_{i\delta_i}|\psi\rangle\langle\psi|E_{i\delta_i}^\dagger.$$

Using Eq. (A.54), we obtain:

$$tr_{\mathcal{H}_{\overline{q}}}\llbracket R\rrbracket(|\varphi\psi\rangle\langle\varphi\psi|) = tr_{\mathcal{H}_{\overline{q}}}\left(\sum_{\delta_1,\ldots,\delta_n}|\Psi_{\delta_1\ldots\delta_n}\rangle\langle\Psi_{\delta_1\ldots\delta_n}|\right)$$

$$= \sum_{\delta_1,\ldots,\delta_n} tr_{\mathcal{H}_{\overline{q}}}|\Psi_{\delta_1\ldots\delta_n}\rangle\langle\Psi_{\delta_1\ldots\delta_n}| \qquad (A.55)$$

$$= \sum_{i=1}^{n} |\alpha_i|^2 \left[\sum_{\delta_1,\dots,\delta_{i-1},\delta_{i+1},\dots,\delta_n} \left(\prod_{k\neq i} \lambda_{k\delta_k} \right)^2 \right] \cdot \left[\sum_{\delta_i} E_{i\delta_i} |\psi\rangle\langle\psi| E_{i\delta_i}^\dagger \right]$$

$$= \sum_{i=1}^{n} |\alpha_i|^2 [\![S_i]\!](|\psi\rangle\langle\psi|).$$

Now we do spectral decomposition for $[\![S]\!](\rho)$, which is a density operator, and assume that

$$[\![S]\!](\rho) = \sum_l s_l |\varphi_l\rangle\langle\varphi_l|.$$

We further write $|\varphi_l\rangle = \sum_i \alpha_{li}|i\rangle$ for every l. For any density operator σ in $\mathcal{H}_{\bigcup_{i=1}^{n} qvar(S_i)}$, we can write σ in the form of $\sigma = \sum_m r_m |\psi_m\rangle\langle\psi_m|$. Then using Eq. (A.55), we get:

$$[\![\textbf{begin local } \overline{q} := \rho; [S] \left(\bigoplus_{i=1}^{n} |i\rangle \to S_i \right) \textbf{ end}]\!](\sigma)$$

$$= tr_{\mathcal{H}_{\overline{q}}}[\![S; R]\!](\sigma \otimes \rho) = tr_{\mathcal{H}_{\overline{q}}}[\![R]\!](\sigma \otimes [\![S]\!](\rho))$$

$$= tr_{\mathcal{H}_{\overline{q}}}[\![R]\!]\left(\sum_{m,l} r_m s_l |\psi_m\varphi_l\rangle\langle\psi_m\varphi_l| \right)$$

$$= \sum_{m,l} r_m s_l \, tr_{\mathcal{H}_{\overline{q}}}[\![R]\!](|\psi_m\varphi_l\rangle\langle\psi_m\varphi_l|)$$

$$= \sum_{m,l} r_m s_l \sum_{i=1}^{n} |\alpha_{li}|^2 [\![S_i]\!](|\psi_m\rangle\langle\psi_m|)$$

$$= \sum_{l} \sum_{i=1}^{n} s_l |\alpha_{li}|^2 [\![S_i]\!]\left(\sum_m r_m |\psi_m\rangle\langle\psi_m| \right)$$

$$= \sum_{l} \sum_{i=1}^{n} s_l |\alpha_{li}|^2 [\![S_i]\!](\sigma)$$

$$= \sum_{i=1}^{n} \left(\sum_l s_l |\alpha_{li}|^2 \right) [\![S_i]\!](\sigma) = \left[\!\left[\sum_{i=1}^{n} S_i @ p_i \right]\!\right](\sigma),$$

where:

$$p_i = \sum_l s_l |\alpha_{li}|^2 = \sum_l s_l \langle i|\varphi_l\rangle\langle\varphi_l|i\rangle$$

$$= \langle i| \left(\sum_l s_l |\varphi_l\rangle\langle\varphi_l| \right) |i\rangle = \langle i|[\![S]\!](\rho)|i\rangle.$$

A.7.4 Proofs of the theorems in Section 11.6

The proof of Theorem 11.2 is similar to but simpler than the proof of Theorem 11.4 given below. So, we omit it.

Proof of Theorem 11.3. We first prove the easier part, namely Eq. (11.31). Let LHS and RHS stand for the left and right hand side of Eq. (11.31), respectively. What we want to prove is $[\![LHS]\!] = [\![RHS]\!]$. But as explained in the proof of Theorem 11.1, we need to work with the semiclassical semantics, and show that $\|LHS\| = \|RHS\|$. Assume that $\|S_i\|$ is the operator-valued function over Δ_i such that

$$\|S_i\|(\delta_i) = F_{i\delta_i}$$

for each $\delta_i \in \Delta_i$ $(1 \leq i \leq n)$. We write:

$$S \equiv \mathbf{qif} \, (\square i \cdot U_{\overline{q}}^{\dagger} |i\rangle \to S_i) \, \mathbf{fiq}.$$

Then for any state $|\psi\rangle = \sum_{i=1}^{n} |i\rangle |\psi_i\rangle$, where $|\psi_i\rangle \in \mathcal{H}_V$ $(1 \leq i \leq n)$, and $V = \bigcup_{i=1}^{n} qvar(S_i)$, we have:

$$\llbracket S \rrbracket (\oplus_{i=1}^{n} \delta_i) |\psi\rangle = \llbracket S \rrbracket (\oplus_{i=1}^{n} \delta_i) \left[\sum_{i=1}^{n} \left(\sum_{j=1}^{n} U_{ij} (U_{\overline{q}}^{\dagger} |j\rangle) \right) |\psi_i\rangle \right]$$

$$= \llbracket S \rrbracket (\oplus_{i=1}^{n} \delta_i) \left[\sum_{j=1}^{n} (U_{\overline{q}}^{\dagger} |j\rangle) \left(\sum_{i=1}^{n} U_{ij} |\psi_i\rangle \right) \right]$$

$$= \sum_{j=1}^{n} \left(\prod_{k \neq j} \lambda_{k\delta_k} \right) (U_{\overline{q}}^{\dagger} |j\rangle) F_{j\delta_j} \left(\sum_{i=1}^{n} U_{ij} |\psi_i\rangle \right),$$

where $\lambda_{k\delta_k}$'s are defined by Eq. (11.18). Then it holds that

$$\llbracket RHS \rrbracket (\oplus_{i=1}^{n} \delta_i) |\psi\rangle = U_{\overline{q}} (\llbracket S \rrbracket (\oplus_{i=1}^{n} \delta_i) |\psi\rangle)$$

$$= \sum_{j=1}^{n} \left(\prod_{k \neq j} \lambda_{k\delta_k} \right) |j\rangle F_{j\delta_j} \left(\sum_{i=1}^{n} U_{ij} |\psi_i\rangle \right)$$

$$= \llbracket S \rrbracket (\oplus_{i=1}^{n} \delta_i) \left[\sum_{j=1}^{n} |j\rangle \left(\sum_{i=1}^{n} U_{ij} |\psi_i\rangle \right) \right]$$

$$= \llbracket S \rrbracket (\oplus_{i=1}^{n} \delta_i) \left[\sum_{i=1}^{n} \left(\sum_{j=1}^{n} U_{ij} |j\rangle \right) |\psi_i\rangle \right]$$

$$= \llbracket S \rrbracket (\oplus_{i=1}^{n} \delta_i) \left(\sum_{i=1}^{n} (U_{\overline{q}} |i\rangle) |\psi_i\rangle \right)$$

$$= \llbracket LHS \rrbracket (\oplus_{i=1}^{n} \delta_i) |\psi\rangle.$$

So, we complete the proof of Eq. (11.31).

Now we turn to prove the harder part, namely Eq. (11.32). The basic idea is to use Eq. (11.31) that we just proved above to prove the more general Eq. (11.32). What we need to do is to turn the general "coin" program S in Eq. (11.32) into a special "coin" program, which is a unitary transformation. The technique that we used before to deal with quantum operations is always the Kraus operator-sum representation. Here, however, we have to employ the system-environment model of quantum operations (see Theorem 2.3). Since $\llbracket S \rrbracket$ is a quantum operation on $\mathcal{H}_{\overline{q}}$, there must be a family of quantum variables $\overline{r}$, a pure state $|\varphi_0\rangle \in \mathcal{H}_{\overline{r}}$, a unitary operator U on $\mathcal{H}_{\overline{q}} \otimes \mathcal{H}_{\overline{r}}$, and a projection operator K onto some closed subspace $\mathcal{K}$ of $\mathcal{H}_{\overline{r}}$ such that

$$\llbracket S \rrbracket (\rho) = tr_{\mathcal{H}_{\overline{r}}} (KU(\rho \otimes |\varphi_0\rangle \langle \varphi_0|) U^{\dagger} K) \tag{A.56}$$

for all density operators ρ on $\mathcal{H}_{\overline{q}}$. We choose an orthonormal basis of $\mathcal{K}$ and then extend it to an orthonormal basis $\{|j\rangle\}$ of $\mathcal{H}_{\overline{r}}$. Define pure states $|\psi_{ij}\rangle = U^{\dagger} |ij\rangle$ for all i, j and programs

$$Q_{ij} \equiv \begin{cases} S_i & \text{if } |j\rangle \in \mathcal{K}, \\ \mathbf{abort} & \text{if } |j\rangle \notin \mathcal{K}. \end{cases}$$

Then by a routine calculation we have:

$$\llbracket \mathbf{qif} \, (\square i, j \cdot |ij\rangle \to Q_{ij}) \, \mathbf{fiq} \rrbracket (\sigma) = \llbracket \mathbf{qif} \, (\square i \cdot |i\rangle \to S_i) \, \mathbf{fiq} \rrbracket (K\sigma K) \tag{A.57}$$

for any $\sigma \in \mathcal{H}_{\overline{q} \cup \overline{r} \cup V}$, where

$$V = \bigcup_{i=1}^{n} qvar(S_i).$$

We now write RHS for the right hand side of Eq. (11.32). Then we have:

$$[\![RHS]\!](\rho) = tr_{\mathcal{H}_{\overline{r}}} \left([\![\mathbf{qif}\, (\Box i, j \cdot U^\dagger |ij\rangle \to Q_{ij})\, \mathbf{fiq};\, U[\overline{q}, \overline{r}]]\!](\rho \otimes |\varphi_0\rangle\langle\varphi_0|) \right)$$

$$= tr_{\mathcal{H}_{\overline{r}}} \left(\left[\!\!\left[[U[\overline{q}, \overline{r}]] \left(\bigoplus_{i,j} |ij\rangle \to Q_{ij} \right) \right]\!\!\right] (\rho \otimes |\varphi_0\rangle\langle\varphi_0|) \right)$$

$$= tr_{\mathcal{H}_{\overline{r}}} \left([\![\mathbf{qif}\, (\Box i, j \cdot |ij\rangle \to Q_{ij})\, \mathbf{fiq}]\!](U(\rho \otimes |\varphi_0\rangle\langle\varphi_0|)U^\dagger) \right)$$

$$= tr_{\mathcal{H}_{\overline{r}}} [\![\mathbf{qif}\, (\Box i \cdot |i\rangle \to S_i)\, \mathbf{fiq}]\!](KU(\rho \otimes |\varphi_0\rangle\langle\varphi_0|)U^\dagger K)$$

$$= [\![\mathbf{qif}\, (\Box i \cdot |i\rangle \to S_i)\, \mathbf{fiq}]\!](tr_{\mathcal{H}_{\overline{r}}}(KU(\rho \otimes |\varphi_0\rangle\langle\varphi_0|)U^\dagger K))$$

$$= [\![\mathbf{qif}\, (\Box i \cdot |i\rangle \to S_i)\, \mathbf{fiq}]\!]([\![S]\!](\rho))$$

$$= \left[\!\!\left[[S] \left(\bigoplus_i |i\rangle \to S_i \right) \right]\!\!\right] (\rho)$$

for all density operators ρ on $\mathcal{H}_{\overline{q}}$. Here, the second equality is obtained by using Eq. (11.31), the fourth equality comes from (A.57), the fifth equality holds because

$$\overline{r} \cap qvar(\mathbf{qif}\, (\Box i \cdot |i\rangle \to S_i)\, \mathbf{fiq}) = \emptyset,$$

and the sixth equality follows from Eq. (A.56). Therefore, Eq. (11.32) is proved. $\qquad\square$

Proof of Theorem 11.4. (1) Clause 1 is immediate from Theorem 11.1.
 (2) To prove clause 2, we write:

$$Q \equiv \mathbf{qif}\, [\overline{q}](\Box i \cdot |i\rangle \to S_i)\, \mathbf{fiq},$$
$$R \equiv \mathbf{qif}\, [\overline{q}](\Box i \cdot |i\rangle \to S_{\tau(i)})\, \mathbf{fiq}.$$

By definition, we have $LHS = S; R$ and

$$RHS = S; U_\tau[\overline{q}]; Q; U_{\tau^{-1}}[\overline{q}].$$

So, it suffices to show that $R \equiv U_\tau[\overline{q}]; Q; U_{\tau^{-1}}[\overline{q}]$. Again, we first need to deal with the semiclassical semantics of the two sides of this equality. Assume that $\|S_i\|$ is the operator-valued function over Δ_i with

$$\|S_i\|(\delta_i) = E_{i\delta_i}$$

for each $\delta_i \in \Delta_i$ $(1 \le i \le n)$. For each state $|\Psi\rangle \in \mathcal{H}_{\overline{q} \cup \bigcup_{i=1}^{n} qvar(S_i)}$, we can write

$$|\Psi\rangle = \sum_{i=1}^{n} |i\rangle|\psi_i\rangle$$

for some $|\psi_i\rangle \in \mathcal{H}_{\bigcup_{i=1}^{n} qvar(S_i)}$ $(1 \le i \le n)$. Then for any $\delta_1 \in \Delta_{\tau(1)}, ..., \delta_n \in \Delta_{\tau(n)}$, it holds that

$$|\Psi_{\delta_1 \ldots \delta_n}\rangle \stackrel{\triangle}{=} \|R\|(\oplus_{i=1}^{n} \delta_i)(|\Psi\rangle)$$

$$= \sum_{i=1}^{n} \left(\prod_{k \ne i} \mu_{k\delta_k} \right) |i\rangle (E_{\tau(i)\delta_i}|\psi_i\rangle),$$

where:

$$\mu_{k\delta_k} = \sqrt{\frac{tr\, E^{\dagger}_{\tau(k)\delta_k} E_{\tau(k)\delta_k}}{\sum_{\theta_k \in \Sigma_{\tau(k)}} tr\, E^{\dagger}_{\tau(k)\theta_k} E_{\tau(k)\theta_k}}} = \lambda_{\tau(k)\delta_k} \tag{A.58}$$

for every k and δ_k, and $\lambda_{i\sigma_i}$'s are defined by Eq. (11.18). On the other hand, we first observe:

$$|\Psi'\rangle \overset{\triangle}{=} (U_\tau)_{\overline{q}}(|\Psi\rangle) = \sum_{i=1}^{n} |\tau(i)\rangle |\psi_i\rangle = \sum_{j=1}^{n} |j\rangle |\psi_{\tau^{-1}(j)}\rangle.$$

Then for any $\delta_1 \in \Delta_1, ..., \delta_n \in \Delta_n$, it holds that

$$|\Psi''_{\delta_1...\delta_n}\rangle \overset{\triangle}{=} \llbracket Q \rrbracket \left(\bigoplus_{i=1}^{n} \delta_i \right) (|\Psi'\rangle)$$

$$= \sum_{j=1}^{n} \left(\prod_{l \neq j} \lambda_{l\delta_{\tau^{-1}(l)}} \right) |j\rangle (E_{j\delta_{\tau^{-1}(j)}} |\psi_{\tau^{-1}(j)}\rangle)$$

$$= \sum_{i=1}^{n} \left(\prod_{k \neq i} \lambda_{\tau(k)\delta_k} \right) |\tau(i)\rangle (E_{\tau(i)\delta_i} |\psi_i\rangle).$$

Furthermore, we have:

$$(U_{\tau^{-1}})_{\overline{q}}(|\Psi''_{\delta_1...\delta_n}\rangle) = \sum_{i=1}^{n} \left(\prod_{k \neq i} \lambda_{\tau(k)\delta_k} \right) |i\rangle (E_{\tau(i)\delta_i} |\psi_i\rangle).$$

Consequently, we can compute the purely quantum semantics:

$$\llbracket U_\tau[\overline{q}]; Q; U_{\tau^{-1}}[\overline{q}] \rrbracket (|\Psi\rangle\langle\Psi|) = \llbracket Q; U_{\tau^{-1}}[\overline{q}] (|\Psi'\rangle\langle\Psi'|) \rrbracket$$

$$= (U_{\tau^{-1}})_{\overline{q}} \left(\sum_{\delta_1,...,\delta_n} |\Psi''_{\delta_1...\delta_n}\rangle\langle\Psi''_{\delta_1...\delta_n}| \right) (U_\tau)_{\overline{q}} \tag{A.59}$$

$$= \sum_{\delta_1,...,\delta_n} |\Psi_{\delta_1...\delta_n}\rangle\langle\Psi_{\delta_1...\delta_n}| = \llbracket R \rrbracket (\Psi)\langle\Psi|).$$

Here, the third equality comes from Eq. (A.58) and the fact that τ is one-onto-one, and thus $\tau^{-1}(j)$ traverses over $1, ..., n$ as j does. Therefore, it follows from Eq. (A.59) and spectral decomposition that

$$\llbracket R \rrbracket (\rho) = \llbracket U_\tau[\overline{q}]; Q; U_{\tau^{-1}}[\overline{q}] \rrbracket (\rho)$$

for any density operator ρ on $\mathcal{H}_{\overline{q} \cup \bigcup_{i=1}^{n} qvar(S_i)}$, and we complete the proof of clause 2.

(3) To prove clause 3, we write:

$$X_i \equiv \mathbf{qif}\, (\square j_i \cdot |j_i\rangle \to R_{ij_i})\, \mathbf{fiq},$$

$$Y_i \equiv [Q_i] \left(\bigoplus_{j_i=1}^{n_i} |j_i\rangle \to R_{ij_i} \right)$$

for every $1 \leq i \leq m$, and we further put:

$$X \equiv \mathbf{qif}\, (\square i \cdot |i\rangle \to Y_i)\, \mathbf{fiq},$$

$$T \equiv \mathbf{qif}\, (\square i \cdot |i\rangle \to Q_i)\, \mathbf{fiq},$$

$$Z \equiv \mathbf{qif}\, (\overline{\alpha})(\square i, j_i \in \Delta \cdot |i, j_i\rangle \to R_{ij_i})\, \mathbf{fiq}.$$

Then by the definition of quantum choice we have $LHS = S; X$ and $RHS = S; T; Z$. So, it suffices to show that $X \equiv T; Z$. To do this, we consider the semiclassical semantics of the involved programs. For each $1 \leq i \leq m$, and for each $1 \leq j_i \leq n_i$, we assume:

- $\llbracket Q_i \rrbracket$ is the operator-valued function over Δ_i such that

$$\llbracket Q_i \rrbracket(\delta_i) = F_{i\delta_i}$$

for every $\delta_i \in \Delta_i$; and
- $\llbracket R_{ij_i} \rrbracket$ is the operator-valued function over Σ_{ij_i} such that

$$\llbracket R_{ij_i} \rrbracket(\sigma_{ij_i}) = E_{(ij_i)\sigma_{ij_i}}$$

for every $\sigma_{ij_i} \in \Sigma_{ij_i}$.

We also assume that state $|\Psi\rangle = \sum_{i=1}^{m} |i\rangle |\Psi_i\rangle$ where each $|\Psi_i\rangle$ is further decomposed into

$$|\Psi_i\rangle = \sum_{j_i=1}^{n_i} |j_i\rangle |\psi_{ij_i}\rangle$$

with $|\psi_{ij_i}\rangle \in \mathcal{H}_{\bigcup_{j_i=1}^{n_i} qvar(R_{ij_i})}$ for every $1 \leq i \leq m$ and $1 \leq j_i \leq n_i$. To simplify the presentation, we use the abbreviation $\overline{\sigma}_i = \oplus_{j_i=1}^{n_i} \sigma_{ij_i}$. Now we compute the semiclassical semantics of program Y_i:

$$
\begin{aligned}
\llbracket Y_i \rrbracket(\delta_i \overline{\sigma}_i)|\Psi_i\rangle &= \llbracket X_i \rrbracket(\overline{\sigma}_i)(\llbracket Q_i \rrbracket(\delta_i)|\Psi_i\rangle) \\
&= \llbracket X_i \rrbracket(\overline{\sigma}_i)\left(\sum_{j_i=1}^{n_i} \left(F_{i\delta_i}|j_i\rangle \right) |\psi_{ij_i}\rangle \right) \\
&= \llbracket X_i \rrbracket(\overline{\sigma}_i)\left[\sum_{j_i=1}^{n_i} \left(\sum_{l_i=1}^{n_i} \langle l_i|F_{i\delta_i}|j_i\rangle |l_i\rangle \right) |\psi_{ij_i}\rangle \right] \\
&= \llbracket X_i \rrbracket(\overline{\sigma}_i)\left[\sum_{l_i=1}^{n_i} |l_i\rangle \left(\sum_{j_i=1}^{n_i} \langle l_i|F_{i\delta_i}|j_i\rangle |\psi_{ij_i}\rangle \right) \right] \\
&= \sum_{l_i=1}^{n_i} \left[\Lambda_{il_i} \cdot |l_i\rangle \left(\sum_{j_i=1}^{n_i} \langle l_i|F_{i\delta_i}|j_i\rangle E_{(il_i)\sigma_{il_i}} |\psi_{ij_i}\rangle \right) \right]
\end{aligned}
\tag{A.60}
$$

where the coefficients:

$$\Lambda_{il_i} = \prod_{l \neq l_i} \lambda_{(il)\sigma_{il}},$$

$$\lambda_{(il)\sigma_{il}} = \sqrt{\frac{tr E_{(il)\sigma_{il}}^{\dagger} E_{(il)\sigma_{il}}}{\sum_{k=1}^{n_i} tr E_{(ik)\sigma_{ik}}^{\dagger} E_{(ik)\sigma_{ik}}}}$$

for each $1 \leq l \leq n_i$. Then using Eq. (A.60), we can further compute the semiclassical semantics of program X:

$$
\begin{aligned}
\llbracket X \rrbracket(\oplus_{i=1}^{m}(\delta_i \overline{\sigma}_i))|\Psi\rangle &= \sum_{i=1}^{m} \left(\Gamma_i \cdot |i\rangle \llbracket Y_i \rrbracket(\delta_i \overline{\sigma}_i)|\Psi_i\rangle \right) \\
&= \sum_{i=1}^{m} \sum_{l_i=1}^{n_i} \left[\Gamma_i \cdot \Lambda_{il_i} \cdot |il_i\rangle \left(\sum_{j_i=1}^{n_i} \langle l_i|F_{i\delta_i}|j_i\rangle E_{(il_i)\sigma_{il_i}} |\psi_{ij_i}\rangle \right) \right]
\end{aligned}
\tag{A.61}
$$

where:

$$\Gamma_i = \prod_{h \neq i} \gamma_{h\overline{\sigma}_h},$$

$$\gamma_{i\overline{\sigma}_i} = \sqrt{\frac{tr \lfloor\!\lfloor Y_i \rfloor\!\rfloor (\delta_i \overline{\sigma}_i)^{\dagger} \lfloor\!\lfloor Y_i \rfloor\!\rfloor (\delta_i \overline{\sigma}_i)}{\sum_{h=1}^{m} tr \lfloor\!\lfloor Y_h \rfloor\!\rfloor (\delta_h \overline{\sigma}_h)^{\dagger} \lfloor\!\lfloor Y_h \rfloor\!\rfloor (\delta_h \overline{\sigma}_h)}} \tag{A.62}$$

for every $1 \leq i \leq m$. On the other hand, we can compute the semiclassical semantics of program T:

$$\lfloor\!\lfloor T \rfloor\!\rfloor (\oplus_{i=1}^{m} \delta_i) |\Psi\rangle = \lfloor\!\lfloor T \rfloor\!\rfloor (\oplus_{i=1}^{m} \delta_i) \left(\sum_{i=1}^{m} |i\rangle |\Psi_i\rangle \right)$$

$$= \sum_{i=1}^{m} \left(\Theta_i \cdot |i\rangle F_{i\delta_i} |\Psi_i\rangle \right)$$

$$= \sum_{i=1}^{m} \left[\Theta_i \cdot |i\rangle \left(\sum_{j_i=1}^{n_i} (F_{i\delta_i} |j_i\rangle) |\psi_{ij_i}\rangle \right) \right]$$

$$= \sum_{i=1}^{m} \left[\Theta_i \cdot |i\rangle \left(\sum_{j_i=1}^{n_i} \left(\sum_{l_i=1}^{n_i} \langle l_i | F_{i\delta_i} |j_i\rangle |l_i\rangle \right) |\psi_{ij_i}\rangle \right) \right]$$

$$= \sum_{i=1}^{m} \sum_{l_i=1}^{n_i} \left[\Theta_i \cdot |il_i\rangle \left(\sum_{j_i=1}^{n_i} \langle l_i | F_{i\delta_i} |j_i\rangle |\psi_{ij_i}\rangle \right) \right]$$

where:

$$\Theta_i = \prod_{h \neq i} \theta_{h\delta_h},$$

$$\theta_{i\delta_i} = \sqrt{\frac{tr F_{i\delta_i}^{\dagger} E_{i\delta_i}}{\sum_{h=1}^{m} tr F_{h\delta_h}^{\dagger} F_{h\delta_h}}}$$

for every $1 \leq i \leq m$. Consequently, we obtain the semiclassical semantics of program $T; Z$:

$$\lfloor\!\lfloor T; Z \rfloor\!\rfloor \left((\oplus_{i=1}^{m} \delta_i) (\oplus_{i=1}^{m} \overline{\sigma}_i) \right) |\Psi\rangle = \lfloor\!\lfloor Z \rfloor\!\rfloor (\oplus_{i=1}^{m} \overline{\sigma}_i) \left(\lfloor\!\lfloor T \rfloor\!\rfloor (\oplus_{i=1}^{m} \delta_i) |\Psi\rangle \right)$$

$$= \lfloor\!\lfloor Z \rfloor\!\rfloor \left(\oplus_{i=1}^{m} \oplus_{l_i=1}^{n_i} \sigma_{ij_i} \right) \left(\sum_{i=1}^{m} \sum_{l_i=1}^{n_i} \left[\Theta_i \cdot |il_i\rangle \left(\sum_{j_i=1}^{n_i} \langle l_i | F_{i\delta_i} |j_i\rangle |\psi_{ij_i}\rangle \right) \right] \right) \tag{A.63}$$

$$= \sum_{i=1}^{m} \sum_{l_i=1}^{n_i} \left[\alpha_{\{\sigma_{jk_j}\}_{(j,k_j) \neq (i,l_i)}}^{il_i} \cdot \Theta_i \cdot |il_i\rangle \left(\sum_{j_i=1}^{n_i} \langle l_i | F_{i\delta_i} |j_i\rangle E_{(il_i)\sigma_{il_i}} |\psi_{ij_i}\rangle \right) \right].$$

By comparing Eqs (A.61) and (A.63), we see that it suffices to take

$$\alpha_{\{\sigma_{jk_j}\}_{(j,k_j) \neq (i,l_i)}}^{il_i} = \frac{\Gamma_i \cdot \Delta_{il_i}}{\Theta_i} \tag{A.64}$$

for all i, l_i and $\{\sigma_{jk_j}\}_{(j,k_j) \neq (i,l_i)}$. What remains to prove is the normalisation condition:

$$\sum_{\{\sigma_{jk_j}\}_{(j,k_j) \neq (i,l_i)}} \left| \alpha_{\{\sigma_{jk_j}\}_{(j,k_j) \neq (i,l_i)}}^{il_i} \right|^2 = 1. \tag{A.65}$$

To do this, we first compute coefficients $\gamma_{i\overline{\sigma}_i}$. Let $\{|\varphi\rangle\}$ be an orthonormal basis of $\mathcal{H}_{\bigcup_{j_i=1}^{n_i} qvar(R_{ij_i})}$. Then we have:

$$G_{\varphi j_i} \stackrel{\triangle}{=} \llbracket Y_i \rrbracket(\delta_i \overline{\sigma}_i)|\varphi\rangle|j_i\rangle = \sum_{l_i=1}^{n_i} \Lambda_{il_i} \cdot \langle l_i|F_{i\delta_i}|j_i\rangle E_{(il_i)\sigma_{il_i}}|\varphi\rangle|l_i\rangle.$$

It follows that

$$G_{\varphi j_i}^\dagger G_{\varphi j_i} = \sum_{l_i, l_i'=1}^{n_i} \Lambda_{il_i} \cdot \Lambda_{il_i'} \langle j_i|F_{i\delta_i}^\dagger|l_i\rangle\langle l_i'|F_{i\delta_i}|j_i\rangle\langle\varphi|E_{(il_i)\sigma_{il_i}}^\dagger E_{(il_i')\sigma_{il_i'}}|\varphi\rangle\langle l_i|l_i'\rangle$$

$$= \sum_{l_i=1}^{n_i} \Lambda_{il_i}^2 \cdot \langle j_i|F_{i\delta_i}^\dagger|l_i\rangle\langle l_i|F_{i\delta_i}|j_i\rangle\langle\varphi|E_{(il_i)\sigma_{il_i}}^\dagger E_{(il_i)\sigma_{il_i}}|\varphi\rangle.$$

Furthermore, we obtain:

$$tr\llbracket Y_i \rrbracket(\delta_i\overline{\sigma}_i)^\dagger \llbracket Y_i \rrbracket(\delta_i\overline{\sigma}_i) = \sum_{\varphi, j_i} G_{\varphi j_i}^\dagger G_{\varphi j_i}$$

$$= \sum_{l_i=1}^{n_i} \Lambda_{il_i}^2 \cdot \left(\sum_{j_i}\langle j_i|F_{i\delta_i}^\dagger|l_i\rangle\langle l_i|F_{i\delta_i}|j_i\rangle\right)\left(\sum_{\varphi}\langle\varphi|E_{(il_i)\sigma_{il_i}}^\dagger E_{(il_i)\sigma_{il_i}}|\varphi\rangle\right) \qquad (A.66)$$

$$= \sum_{l_i=1}^{n_i} \Lambda_{il_i}^2 \cdot tr(F_{i\delta_i}^\dagger|l_i\rangle\langle l_i|F_{i\delta_i})tr(E_{(il_i)\sigma_{il_i}}^\dagger E_{(il_i)\sigma_{il_i}}).$$

Now a routine but tedious calculation yields Eq. (A.65) through substituting Eq. (A.66) into (A.62) and then substituting Eqs (A.62) and (A.64) into (A.65).

(4) Finally, we prove clause 4. To prove the first equality, we write:

$$X \equiv \mathbf{qif} \, (\square i \cdot |i\rangle \to S_i) \, \mathbf{fiq},$$
$$Y \equiv \mathbf{qif} \, (\overline{\alpha})(\square i \cdot |i\rangle \to (S_i; Q)) \, \mathbf{fiq}.$$

Then by definition we have $LHS = S; X; Q$ and $RHS = S; Y$. So, it suffices to show that $X; Q =_{CF} Y$. Suppose that

$$\llbracket S_i \rrbracket(\sigma_i) = E_{i\sigma_i}$$

for every $\sigma_i \in \Delta(S_i)$ and $\llbracket Q \rrbracket(\delta) = F_\delta$ for every $\delta \in \Delta(Q)$, and suppose that

$$|\Psi\rangle = \sum_{i=1}^{n} |i\rangle|\psi_i\rangle$$

where $|\psi_i\rangle \in \mathcal{H}_{\bigcup_i qvar(S_i)}$ for all i. Then it holds that

$$\llbracket X; Q \rrbracket((\oplus_{i=1}^{n}\sigma_i)\delta)|\Psi\rangle = \llbracket Q \rrbracket(\delta)(\llbracket X \rrbracket(\oplus_{i=1}^{n}\sigma_i)|\Psi\rangle)$$

$$= F_\delta\left(\sum_{i=1}^{n} \Lambda_i|i\rangle(E_{i\sigma_i}|\psi_i\rangle)\right)$$

$$= \sum_{i=1}^{n} \Lambda_i \cdot |i\rangle(F_\delta E_{i\sigma_i}|\psi_i\rangle)$$

because $qvar(S) \cap qvar(Q) = \emptyset$, where:

$$\Lambda_i = \prod_{k \neq i} \lambda_{k\sigma_k}.$$

$$\lambda_{i\sigma_i} = \sqrt{\frac{tr\, E_{i\sigma_i}^\dagger E_{i\sigma_i}}{\sum_{k=1}^n tr\, E_{k\sigma_k}^\dagger E_{k\sigma_k}}}. \tag{A.67}$$

Furthermore, we have:

$$tr_{\mathcal{H}_{qvar(S)}}(\llbracket X; Q \rrbracket(|\Psi\rangle\langle\Psi|))$$

$$= tr_{\mathcal{H}_{qvar(S)}}\left[\sum_{\{\sigma_i\},\delta}\sum_{i,j}\Lambda_i\Lambda_j \cdot |i\rangle\langle j|(F_\delta E_{i\sigma_i}|\psi_i\rangle\langle\psi_j|E_{j\sigma_j}^\dagger F_\delta^\dagger)\right] \tag{A.68}$$

$$= \sum_{\{\sigma_i\},\delta}\sum_i \Lambda_i^2 \cdot F_\delta E_{i\sigma_i}|\psi_i\rangle\langle\psi_i|E_{i\sigma_i}^\dagger F_\delta^\dagger.$$

On the other hand, we can compute the semiclassical semantics of Y:

$$\llbracket Y \rrbracket(\oplus_{i=1}^n \sigma_i\delta_i)|\Psi\rangle = \sum_{i=1}^n \alpha_{\{\sigma_k,\delta_k\}_{k\neq i}}^{(i)} \cdot |i\rangle(\llbracket S_i; Q \rrbracket(\sigma_i\delta_i)|\psi_i\rangle)$$

$$= \sum_{i=1}^n \alpha_{\{\sigma_k,\delta_k\}_{k\neq i}}^{(i)} \cdot |i\rangle(F_{\delta_i}E_{\sigma_i}|\psi_i\rangle).$$

Furthermore, we obtain:

$$tr_{\mathcal{H}_{qvar(S)}}(\llbracket Y \rrbracket(|\Psi\rangle\langle\Psi|))$$

$$= tr_{\mathcal{H}_{qvar(S)}}\left[\sum_{\{\sigma_i,\delta_i\}}\sum_{i,j}\alpha_{\{\sigma_k,\delta_k\}_{k\neq i}}^{(i)}(\alpha_{\{\sigma_l,\delta_l\}_{l\neq j}}^{(j)})^* \cdot |i\rangle\langle j|(F_{\delta_i}E_{i\sigma_i}|\psi_i\rangle\langle\psi_j|E_{j\sigma_j}^\dagger F_{\delta_j}^\dagger)\right] \tag{A.69}$$

$$= \sum_{\{\sigma_i\},\delta}\sum_i \left|\alpha_{\{\sigma_k,\delta_k\}_{k\neq i}}^{(i)}\right|^2 \cdot F_{\delta_i}E_{i\sigma_i}|\psi_i\rangle\langle\psi_i|E_{i\sigma_i}^\dagger F_{\delta_i}^\dagger.$$

Comparing Eqs (A.68) and (A.69), we see that

$$tr_{\mathcal{H}_{qvar(S)}}(\llbracket X; Q \rrbracket(|\Psi\rangle\langle\Psi|)) = tr_{\mathcal{H}_{qvar(S)}}(\llbracket Y \rrbracket(|\Psi\rangle\langle\Psi|))$$

if we take

$$\alpha_{\{\sigma_k,\delta_k\}_{k\neq i}}^{(i)} = \frac{\Lambda_i}{\sqrt{|\Delta(Q)|}}$$

for all i, $\{\sigma_k\}$ and $\{\delta_k\}$. Since

$$qvar(S) \subseteq cvar(X; Q) \cup cvar(Y),$$

it follows that

$$tr_{\mathcal{H}_{cvar(X;Q)\cup cvar(Y)}}(\llbracket X; Q \rrbracket(|\Psi\rangle\langle\Psi|)) = tr_{\mathcal{H}_{cvar(X;Q)\cup cvar(Y)}}(\llbracket Y \rrbracket(|\Psi\rangle\langle\Psi|)).$$

Therefore, we can assert that

$$tr_{\mathcal{H}_{cvar(X;Q)\cup cvar(Y)}}(\llbracket X; Q \rrbracket(\rho)) = tr_{\mathcal{H}_{cvar(X;Q)\cup cvar(Y)}}(\llbracket Y \rrbracket(\rho))$$

for all density operator ρ by spectral decomposition. Thus, we have $X; Q \equiv_{CF} Y$, and the proof of the first equality of clause 4 is completed.

For the special case where Q contains no measurements, $\Delta(Q)$ is a singleton, say $\{\delta\}$. We write:

$$Z \equiv \mathbf{qif}\,(\Box i \cdot |i\rangle \to (P_i; Q))\,\mathbf{fiq}.$$

Then

$$\lfloor Z \rfloor (\oplus_{i=1}^{n} \sigma_i \delta) |\Psi\rangle = \sum_{i=1}^{n} \left(\prod_{k \neq i} \theta_{k\sigma_k} \right) \cdot |i\rangle (F_\delta E_{\sigma_i} |\psi_i\rangle),$$

where:

$$\theta_{i\sigma_i} = \sqrt{\frac{tr E_{i\sigma_i}^{\dagger} F_\delta^{\dagger} F_\delta E_{i\sigma_i}}{\sum_{k=1}^{n} tr E_{k\sigma_k}^{\dagger} F_\delta^{\dagger} F_\delta E_{k\sigma_k}}} = \lambda_{i\sigma_i},$$

and $\lambda_{i\sigma_i}$ is given by Eq. (A.67), because $F_\delta^{\dagger} F_\delta$ is the identity operator. Consequently, $\lfloor X; Q \rfloor = \lfloor Z \rfloor$, and we complete the proof of the second equality of clause 4. $\square$

References

[1] S. Aaronson, Quantum lower bound for recursive Fourier sampling, arXiv:quant-ph/0209060.

[2] S. Aaronson, Read the fine print, Nature Physics 11 (2015) 291–293.

[3] M. Abadi, G.D. Plotkin, A simple differentiable programming language, Proceedings of the ACM on Programming Languages 4 (POPL) (2020) 38.

[4] A.J. Abhari, A. Faruque, M. Dousti, L. Svec, O. Catu, A. Chakrabati, C.-F. Chiang, S. Vanderwilt, J. Black, F. Chong, M. Martonosi, M. Suchara, K. Brown, M. Pedram, T. Brun, Scaffold: Quantum Programming Language, Technical Report TR-934-12, Dept. of Computer Science, Princeton University, 2012.

[5] S. Abramsky, High-level methods for quantum computation and information, in: Proceedings of the 19th Annual IEEE Symposium on Logic in Computer Science (LICS 2004), IEEE Computer Society, 2004, pp. 410–414.

[6] S. Abramsky, B. Coecke, A categorical semantics of quantum protocols, in: Proceedings of the 19th Annual IEEE Symposium on Logic in Computer Science (LICS), 2004, pp. 415–425.

[7] S. Abramsky, R. Duncan, A categorical quantum logic, Mathematical Structures in Computer Science 16 (2006) 469–489.

[8] S. Abramsky, E. Haghverdi, P. Scott, Geometry of interaction and linear combinatory algebras, Mathematical Structures in Computer Science 12 (2002) 625–665.

[9] R. Adams, QPEL: quantum program and effect language, in: Proceedings of the 11th Workshop on Quantum Physics and Logic (QPL), in: EPTCS, vol. 172, 2014, pp. 133–153.

[10] P. Adão, P. Mateus, A process algebra for reasoning about quantum security, Electronic Notes in Theoretical Computer Science 170 (6) (2007) 3–21.

[11] D. Aharonov, A. Ambainis, J. Kempe, U. Vazirani, Quantum walks on graphs, in: Proceedings of the 33rd ACM Symposium on Theory of Computing (STOC), 2001, pp. 50–59.

[12] A.V. Aho, J.E. Hopcroft, The Design and Analysis of Computer Algorithms, Pearson Education, 1974.

[13] D. Aharonov, M. Ganz, L. Magnin, Dining philosophers, leader election and ring size problems, in the quantum setting, arXiv:1707.01187, 2017.

[14] D. Aharonov, W. van Dam, J. Kempe, Z. Landau, S. Lloyd, O. Regev, Adiabatic quantum computation is equivalent to standard quantum computation, in: Proceedings of the 45th Symposium on Foundations of Computer Science (FOCS 2004), 2004, pp. 42–51.

[15] Y. Aharonov, J. Anandan, S. Popescu, L. Vaidman, Superpositions of time evolutions of a quantum system and quantum time-translation machine, Physical Review Letters 64 (1990) 2965–2968.

[16] Y. Aharonov, L. Davidovich, N. Zagury, Quantum random walks, Physical Review A 48 (1993) 1687–1690.

[17] A.V. Aho, M.S. Lam, R. Sethi, J.D. Ullman, Compilers: Principles, Techniques, and Tools, second edition, Addison-Wesley, 2007.

[18] J.-M.A. Allen, J. Barrett, D.C. Horsman, C.M. Lee, R.W. Spekkens, Quantum common causes and quantum causal models, Physical Review X 7 (2017) 031021.

[19] T. Altenkirch, J. Grattage, A functional quantum programming language, in: Proc. of the 20th Annual IEEE Symposium on Logic in Computer Science (LICS), 2005, pp. 249–258.

[20] T. Altenkirch, J. Grattage, J.K. Vizzotto, A. Sabry, An algebra of pure quantum programming, Electronic Notes in Theoretical Computer Science 170 (2007) 23–47.

[21] T. Altenkirch, A.S. Green, The quantum IO monad, in: I. Mackie, S. Gay (Eds.), Semantic Techniques in Quantum Computation, Cambridge University Press, 2010, pp. 173–205.

[22] A. Ambainis, Quantum walk algorithm for element distinctness, SIAM Journal on Computing 37 (2007) 210–239.

[23] A. Ambainis, Quantum walks and their algorithmic applications, International Journal of Quantum Information 1 (2004) 507–518.

[24] A. Ambainis, E. Bach, A. Nayak, A. Vishwanath, J. Watrous, One-dimensional quantum walks, in: Proceedings of the 33rd ACM Symposium on Theory of Computing (STOC), 2001, pp. 37–49.

[25] M. Amy, D. Maslov, M. Mosca, M. Rötteler, A meet-in-the-middle algorithm for fast synthesis of depth-optimal quantum circuits, IEEE Transactions on Computer-Aided Design of Integrated Circuits and Systems 32 (2013) 818–830.

[26] P. Andrés-Martínez, C. Heunen, Weakly measured while loops: peeking at quantum states, Quantum Science and Technology 7 (2022) 025007.

[27] K.R. Apt, Correctness proofs of distributed termination algorithms, ACM Transactions on Programming Languages and Systems 8 (1986) 388–405.

[28] K.R. Apt, F.S. de Boer, E.-R. Olderog, Verification of Sequential and Concurrent Programs, Springer, London, 2009.

[29] K.R. Apt, E.-R. Olderog, Fifty years of Hoare's logic, Formal Aspects of Computing 31 (2019) 751–807.

[30] M. Araújo, A. Feix, F. Costa, C. Brukner, Quantum circuits cannot control unknown operations, New Journal of Physics 16 (2004) 093026.

[31] M. Araújo, F. Costa, C. Brukner, Computational advantage from quantum-controlled ordering of gates, Physical Review Letters 113 (2014) 250402.

[32] E. Ardeshir-Larijani, S.J. Gay, R. Nagarajan, Equivalence checking of quantum protocols, in: Proceedings of the 19th International Conference on Tools and Algorithms for the Construction and Analysis of Systems (TACAS 2013), 2013, pp. 478–492.

[33] E. Ardeshir-Larijani, S.J. Gay, R. Nagarajan, Verification of concurrent quantum protocols by equivalence checking, in: Proceedings of the 20th International Conference on Tools and Algorithms for the Construction and Analysis of Systems (TACAS 2014), 2014, pp. 500–514.

[34] E. Ardeshir-Larijani, S.J. Gay, R. Nagarajan, Automated equivalence checking of concurrent quantum systems, ACM Transactions on Computational Logic 19 (2018) 28.

[35] M. Avanzini, G. Moser, R. Pechoux, S. Perdrix, V. Zamdzhiev, Quantum expectation transformers for cost analysis, in: Proceedings of the 37th Annual ACM/IEEE Symposium on Logic in Computer Science (LICS), 2022, 10.

[36] S. Attal, Fock spaces, http://math.univ-lyon1.fr/~attal/Mescours/fock.pdf.

[37] R.-J. Back, J. von Wright, Refinement Calculus: A Systematic Introduction, Springer, New York, 1998.

[38] D.F. Bacon, S.L. Graham, O.J. Sharp, Compiler transformations for high-performance computing, ACM Computing Surveys 26 (1994) 345–420.

[39] C. Bădescu, P. Panangaden, Quantum alternation: prospects and problems, in: Proceedings of the 12th International Workshop on Quantum Physics and Logic (QPL), in: EPTCS, vol. 195, 2015, pp. 33–42.

[40] C. Baier, J.-P. Katoen, Principles of Model Checking, MIT Press, Cambridge, Massachusetts, 2008.

[41] A. Baltag, S. Smets, LQP: the dynamic logic of quantum information, Mathematical Structures in Computer Science 16 (2006) 491–525.

[42] P. Baltazar, R. Chadha, P. Mateus, Quantum computation tree logic – model checking and complete calculus, International Journal of Quantum Information 6 (2008) 219–236.

[43] P. Baltazar, R. Chadha, P. Mateus, A. Sernadas, Towards model-checking quantum security protocols, in: Proceedings of the 1st Workshop on Quantum Security (QSec07), 2007, p. 14.

[44] U. Banerjee, Loop Transformations for Restructuring Compilers: the Foundations, Kluwer, Boston, 1993.

[45] J. Bang-Jensen, G. Gutin, Digraphs: Theory, Algorithms and Applications, Springer, Berlin, 2007.

[46] M. Barbosa, G. Barthe, X. Fan, B. Grégoire, S.-H. Hung, J. Katz, P.-Y. Strub, X.D. Wu, L. Zhou, EasyPQC: verifying post-quantum cryptography, in: Proceedings of the 2021 ACM SIGSAC Conference on Computer and Communications Security (CCS), 2021, pp. 2564–2586.

[47] A. Barenco, C.H. Bennett, R. Cleve, D.P. DiVincenzo, N. Margolus, P. Shor, T. Sleator, J.A. Smolin, H. Weinfurter, Elementary gates for quantum computation, Physical Review A 52 (1995) 3457–3467.

[48] G. Barthe, J. Hsu, M.S. Ying, N.K. Yu, L. Zhou, Relational proofs for quantum programs, Proceedings of the ACM on Programming Languages 4 (POPL) (2020) 21.

[49] F. Bauer-Marquart, S. Leue, C. Schilling, symQV: automated symbolic verification of quantum programs, in: Proceedings of the 25th International Symposium on Formal Methods (FM), 2023, pp. 181–198.

[50] K. Beer, D. Bondarenko, T. Farrelly, T.J. Osborne, R. Salzmann, D. Scheiermann, R. Wolf, Training deep quantum neural networks, Nature Communications 11 (2020) 808.

[51] P.A. Benioff, The computer as a physical system: a microscopic quantum mechanical Hamiltonian model of computer s as represented by Turing machines, Journal of Statistical Physics 22 (1980) 563–591.

[52] C.H. Bennett, G. Brassard, Quantum cryptography: public key distribution and coin tossing, in: Proceedings of International Conference on Computers, Systems and Signal Processing, 1984, pp. 175–179.

[53] C.H. Bennett, G. Brassard, C. Crépeau, R. Jozsa, A. Peres, W.K. Wootters, Teleporting an unknown quantum state via dual classical and Einstein-Podolsky-Rosen channels, Physical Review Letters 70 (1993) 1895–1899.

[54] C.H. Bennett, D.P. DiVincenzo, C.A. Fuchs, T. Mor, E. Rains, P.W. Shor, J.A. Smolin, Quantum nonlocality without entanglement, Physical Review A 59 (1999) 1070.

[55] C.H. Bennett, S. Wiesner, Communication via one- and two-particle operators on Einstein-Podolsky-Rosen states, Physical Review Letters 69 (1992) 2881–2884.

[56] N. Benton, Simple relational correctness proofs for static analyses and program transformations, in: Proceedings of the 31st ACM Symposium on Principles of Programming Languages (POPL), 2004, pp. 14–25.

[57] V. Bergholm, J. Izaac, M. Schuld, C. Gogolin, M.S. Alam, S. Ahmed, J.M. Arrazola, C. Blank, A. Delgado, S. Jahangiri, K. McKiernan, J.J. Meyer, Z. Niu, A. Szava, N. Killoran, PennyLane: automatic differentiation of hybrid quantum-classical computations, arXiv:1811.04968.

[58] E. Bernstein, U. Vazirani, Quantum complexity theory, in: Proc. of the 25th Annual ACM Symposium on Theory of Computing (STOC), 1993, pp. 11–20.

[59] E. Bernstein, U. Vazirani, Quantum complexity theory, SIAM Journal on Computing 26 (1997) 1411–1473.

[60] S. Bettelli, T. Calarco, L. Serafini, Toward an architecture for quantum programming, The European Physical Journal D 25 (2003) 181–200.

[61] R. Bhatia, Matrix Analysis, Springer, Berlin, 1991.

[62] J. Biamonte, P. Wittek, N. Pancotti, P. Rebentrost, N. Wiebe, S. Lloyd, Quantum machine learning, Nature 549 (2017) (2017) 195–202.

[63] B. Bichsel, M. Baader, T. Gehr, M. Vechev, Silq: a high-level quantum language with safe uncomputation and intuitive semantics, in: Proceedings of the 41st ACM Conference on Programming Language Design and Implementation (PLDI), 2020, pp. 286–300.

[64] B. Bichsel, M. Baader, A. Paradis, M. Vechev, Abstract: analysis of quantum circuits via abstract stabilizer simulation, arXiv:2304.00921.

[65] R. Bird, Programs and Machines: An Introduction to the Theory of Computation, John Wiley & Sons, 1976.

[66] G. Birkhoff, J. von Neumann, The logic of quantum mechanics, Annals of Mathematics 37 (1936) 823–843.

[67] A. Bisio, M. Dall'Arno, P. Perinotti, Quantum conditional operations, Physical Review A 94 (2016) 022340.

[68] R.F. Blute, P. Panangaden, R.A.G. Seely, Holomorphic models of exponential types in linear logic, in: Proceedings of the 9th Conference on Mathematical Foundations of Programming Semantics (MFPS), in: LNCS, vol. 802, Springer, 1994, pp. 474–512.

[69] A. Bocharov, M. Rötteler, K.M. Svore, Efficient synthesis of universal repeat-until-success circuits, Physical Review Letters 114 (2015) 080502.

[70] A. Bocharov, K.M. Svore, Resource-optimal single-qubit quantum circuits, Physical Review Letters 109 (2012) 190501.

[71] A. Bordg, H. Lachnitt, Y.J. He, Certified quantum computation in Isabelle/HOL, Journal of Automated Reasoning 65 (2021) 691–709.

[72] R.J. Boulton, R. Hardy, U. Martin, Hoare logic for single-input single-output continuous-time control systems, in: Proceeding of the 6th International Workshop on Hybrid Systems: Computation and Control (HSCC 2003), in: LNCS, vol. 2623, Springer, 2003, pp. 113–125.

[73] S.L. Braunstein, C.M. Caves, R. Jozsa, N. Linden, S. Popescu, R. Schack, Separability of very noisy mixed states and implications for NMR quantum computing, Physical Review Letters 83 (1999) 1054.

[74] S. Bravyi, D. Gosset, R. König, Quantum advantage with shallow circuits, Science 362 (2018) 308–311.

[75] H.-P. Breuer, F. Petruccione, The Theory of Open Quantum Systems, Oxford University Press, Oxford, 2002.

[76] S. Brookes, P.W. O'Hearn, Concurrent separation logic, ACM SIGLOC News 3 (3) (2016) 47–65.

[77] T. Brun, A simple model of quantum trajectories, American Journal of Physics 70 (2002) 719–737.

[78] T.A. Brun, H.A. Carteret, A. Ambainis, Quantum walks driven by many coins, Physical Review A 67 (2003) 052317.

[79] O. Brunet, P. Jorrand, Dynamic quantum logic for quantum programs, International Journal of Quantum Information 2 (2004) 45–54.

[80] H. Buhrman, B. Loff, S. Patro, F. Speelman, Memory compression with quantum random-access gates, in: Proceedings of the 17th Conference on the Theory of Quantum Computation, Communication and Cryptography (TQC), 2022, pp. 10:1–10:19.

[81] H. Buhrman, H. Röhrig, Distributed quantum computing, in: Proceedings of the 28th International Symposium on Mathematical Foundations of Computer Science (MFCS 2003), in: LNCS, vol. 2747, Springer, 2003, pp. 1–20.

[82] V. Bužek, M. Hillery, Quantum copying: beyond the no-cloning theorem, Physical Review A 54 (1996) 1844–1852.

[83] F.A. Calderon-Vargas, T. Proctor, K. Rudinger, M. Sarovar, Quantum circuit debugging and sensitivity analysis via local inversions, Quantum 7 (2023) 921.

[84] M. Cerezo, A. Arrasmith, R. Babbush, S.C. Benjamin, S. Endo, K. Fujii, J.R. McClean, K. Mitarai, X. Yuan, L. Cincio, P.J. Coles, Variational quantum algorithms, Nature Reviews Physics 3 (2021) 625–644.

[85] R. Chadha, P. Mateus, A. Sernadas, Reasoning about imperative quantum programs, Electronic Notes in Theoretical Computer Science 158 (2006) 19–39.

[86] K.M. Chandy, J. Misra, Parallel Program Design: A Foundation, Addison-Wesley, 1988.

[87] C. Chareton, S. Bardin, F. Bobot, V. Perrelle, B. Valiron, An automated deductive verification framework for circuit-building quantum programs, in: Proceedings of the 30th European Symposium on Programming (ESOP), 2021, pp. 148–177.

[88] C. Chareton, S. Bardin, D. Lee, B. Valiron, R. Vilmart, Z.W. Xu, Formal methods for quantum programs: a survey, arXiv:2109.06493.

[89] K. Chatterjee, H.F. Fu, P. Novotný, R. Hasheminezhad, Algorithmic analysis of qualitative and quantitative termination problems for affine probabilistic programs, in: Proceedings of the 43rd Annual ACM Symposium on Principles of Programming Languages (POPL), 2016, pp. 327–342.

[90] Y.-F. Chen, K.-M. Chung, O. Lengál, J.-A. Lin, W.-L. Tsai, D.-D. Yen, An automata-based framework for verification and bug hunting in quantum circuits, Proceedings of the ACM on Programming Languages 7 (PLDI) (2023) 156, 1218–1243.

[91] A.M. Childs, Universal computation by quantum walk, Physical Review Letters 102 (2009) 180501.

[92] A.M. Childs, R. Cleve, E. Deotto, E. Farhi, S. Gutmann, D.A. Spielman, Exponential algorithmic speedup by quantum walk, in: Proceedings of the 35th ACM Symposium on Theory of Computing (STOC), 2003, pp. 59–68.

[93] A.M. Childs, N. Wiebe, Hamiltonian simulation using linear combinations of unitary operations, Quantum Information & Computation 12 (2012) 901–924.

[94] G. Chiribella, Perfect discrimination of no-signalling channels via quantum superposition of causal structures, Physical Review A 86 (2012) 040301.

[95] G. Chiribella, G.M. D'Ariano, P. Perinotti, B. Valiron, Quantum computations without definite causal structure, Physical Review A 88 (2013) 022318.

[96] L. Chizat, E. Oyallon, F. Bach, On lazy training in differentiable programming, in: Advances in Neural Information Processing Systems (NeurIPS), 2019, pp. 2933–2943.

[97] K. Cho, Semantics for a quantum programming language by operator algebras, in: Proceedings 11th Workshop on Quantum Physics and Logic (QPL), in: EPTCS, vol. 172, 2014, pp. 165–190.

[98] J.I. Cirac, A.K. Ekert, S.F. Huelga, C. Macchiavello, Distributed quantum computation over noisy channels, Physical Review A 59 (1999) 4249–4254.

[99] J.I. Cirac, P. Zoller, Goals and opportunities in quantum simulation, Nature Physics 8 (2012) 264–266.

[100] R. Cleve, J. Watrous, Fast parallel circuits for the quantum Fourier transform, in: Proceedings of the 41st IEEE Annual Symposium on Foundations of Computer Science (FOCS), 2000, pp. 526–536.

[101] B. Coecke, R. Duncan, Interacting quantum observables, in: Proceedings of the 37th International Colloquium on Automata, Languages and Programming (ICALP), in: LNCS, vol. 5126, Springer, 2008, pp. 298–310.

[102] M.A. Colón, S. Sankaranarayanan, H.B. Sipma, Linear invariant generation using non-linear constraint solving, in: Proceedings of the 15th International Conference on Computer Aided Verification (CAV), in: LNCS, vol. 2725, Springer, 2003, pp. 420–433.

[103] M. Colón, H. Sipma, Synthesis of linear ranking functions, in: Proceedings of the 7th International Conference on Tools and Algorithms for the Construction and Analysis of Systems (TACAS), in: LNCS, vol. 2031, Springer, 2001, pp. 67–81.

[104] I. Cong, S. Choi, M.D. Lukin, Quantum convolutional neural networks, Nature Physics 15 (2019) 1273–1278.

[105] D. Copsey, M. Oskin, F. Impens, T. Metodiev, A. Cross, F.T. Chong, I.L. Chuang, J. Kubiatowicz, Toward a scalable, silicon-based quantum computing architecture, IEEE Journal of Selected Topics in Quantum Electronics 9 (2003) 1552–1569.

[106] T.H. Cormen, C.E. Leiserson, R.L. Rivest, C. Stein, Introduction to Algorithms, third edition, The MIT Press, 2009.

[107] H. Corrigan-Gibbs, D.J. Wu, D. Boneh, Quantum operating systems, in: Proceedings of the 16th Workshop on Hot Topics in Operating Systems (HotOS), 2017, pp. 76–81.

[108] F. Costa, S. Shrapnel, Quantum causal modelling, New Journal of Physics 18 (2016) 063032.

[109] P. Cousot, Principles of Abstract Interpretation, The MIT Press, Cambridge, Massachusetts, 2021.

[110] P. Cousot, R. Cousot, Abstract interpretation: a unified lattice model for static analysis of programs by construction or approximation of fixpoints, in: Proceedings of the 4th ACM Symposium on Principles of Programming Languages (POPL), 1977, pp. 238–252.

[111] P. Cousot, N. Halbwachs, Automatic discovery of linear restraints among variables of a program, in: Proceedings of the 5th ACM Symposium on Principles of Programming Languages (POPL), 1978, pp. 84–96.

[112] A. Cowtan, S. Dilkes, R. Duncan, W. Simmons, S. Sivarajah, Phase gadget synthesis for shallow circuits, Electronic Proceedings in Theoretical Computer Science 318 (2020) 213–228.

[113] A. Cross, A. Javadi-Abhari, T. Alexander, N. de Beaudrap, L.S. Bishop, S. Heidel, C.A. Ryan, P. Sivarajah, J. Smolin, J.M. Gambetta, B.R. Johnson, OpenQASM 3: a broader and deeper quantum assembly language, ACM Transactions on Quantum Computing 3 (2022) 12, 1–50.

[114] A. Dahlberg, B. van der Vecht, C. Delle Donne, M. Skrzypczyk, I. te Raa, W. Kozlowski, S. Wehner, NetQASM – a low-level instruction set architecture for hybrid quantum-classical programs in a quantum internet, Quantum Science and Technology 7 (2022) 035023.

[115] M. Dalla Chiara, R. Giuntini, R. Greechie, Reasoning in Quantum Theory: Sharp and Unsharp Quantum Logics, Kluwer, Dordrecht, 2004.

[116] V. Danos, E. Kashefi, P. Panangaden, The measurement calculus, Journal of the ACM 54 (2007) 8.

[117] V. Danos, E. Kashefi, P. Panangaden, S. Perdrix, Extended measurement calculus, in: I. Mackie, S. Gay (Eds.), Semantic Techniques in Quantum Computation, Cambridge University Press, 2010, pp. 235–310.

[118] P. Das, S.S. Tannu, P.J. Nair, M. Qureshi, A case for multi-programming quantum computers, in: Proceedings of the 52nd Annual IEEE/ACM International Symposium on Microarchitecture (MICRO), 2019, pp. 291–303.

[119] T.A.S. Davidson, Formal Verification Techniques Using Quantum Process Calculus, PhD Thesis, University of Warwick, 2012.

[120] T.A.S. Davidson, S.J. Gay, H. Mlnarik, R. Nagarajan, N. Papanikolaou, Model checking for communicating quantum processes, International Journal of Unconventional Computing 8 (2012) 73–98.

[121] T.A.S. Davidson, S.J. Gay, R. Nagarajan, Formal analysis of quantum systems using process calculus, Electronic Proceedings in Theoretical Computer Science 59 (2011) 104–110.

[122] T.A.S. Davidson, S.J. Gay, R. Nagarajan, I.V. Puthoor, Analysis of a quantum error correcting code using quantum process calculus, Electronic Proceedings in Theoretical Computer Science 95 (2012) 67–80.

[123] Y.X. Deng, Bisimulations for probabilistic and quantum processes, in: Proceedings of the 29th International Conference on Concurrency Theory (CONCUR), vol. 2, 2018, pp. 1–14.

[124] Y.X. Deng, Y. Feng, Open bisimulation for quantum processes, in: Proceedings of IFIP Theoretical Computer Science (TCS), in: LNCS, vol. 7604, Springer, 2012, pp. 119–133.

[125] Y.X. Deng, Y. Feng, Formal semantics of a classical-quantum language, Theoretical Computer Science 913 (2022) 73–93.

[126] H. Derksen, J. Weyman, Quiver representations, Notices of the American Mathematical Society 52 (2005) 200–206.

[127] D. Deutsch, Quantum theory, the Church-Turing principle and the universal quantum computer, Proceedings of The Royal Society of London A 400 (1985) 97–117.

[128] D. Deutsch, Quantum theory, the Church-Turing principle and the universal quantum computer, Proceedings of the Royal Society A 444 (1985) 97–117.

[129] D. Deutsch, R. Jozsa, Rapid solutions of problems by quantum computation, Proceedings of the Royal Society of London A 439 (1992) 553–558.

[130] D. Dieks, Communication by EPR devices, Physics Letters A 92 (6) (1982) 271–272.

[131] E. D'Hondt, P. Panangaden, Quantum weakest preconditions, Mathematical Structures in Computer Science 16 (2006) 429–451.

[132] E.W. Dijkstra, Guarded commands, nondeterminacy and formal derivation of programs, Communications of the ACM 18 (1975) 453–457.

[133] E.W. Dijkstra, A Discipline of Programming, Prentice-Hall, 1976.

[134] J.P. Dowling, G.J. Milburn, Quantum technology: the second quantum revolution, Philosophical Transactions of the Royal Society London A 361 (2003) 1655–1674.

[135] R.Y. Duan, S. Severini, A. Winter, Zero-error communication via quantum channels, noncommutative graphs, and a quantum Lovász number, IEEE Transactions on Information Theory 59 (2013) 1164–1174.

[136] R. Duncan, A. Kissinger, S. Perdrix, J. van de Wetering, Graph-theoretic simplification of quantum circuits with the ZX-calculus, Quantum 4 (2020) 279.

[137] R. Duncan, M. Lucas, Verifying the Steane code with quantomatic, Electronic Proceedings in Theoretical Computer Science 171 (2014) 33–49.

[138] A. Dvurečenskij, Gleason's Theorem and Its Applications, Kluwer, 1993.

[139] J. Eisert, M. Wilkens, M. Lewenstein, Quantum games and quantum strategies, Physical Review Letters 83 (1999) 3077–3080.

[140] J. Esparza, S. Schwoon, A BDD-based model checker for recursive programs, in: Proceedings of the 13th International Conference on Computer Aided Verification (CAV), in: LNCS, vol. 2102, Springer, 2001, pp. 324–336.

[141] K. Etessami, M. Yannakakis, Recursive Markov chains, stochastic grammars, and monotone systems of nonlinear equations, Journal of the ACM 56 (2009) 1.

[142] A. Evans, S. Omonije, R. Soulé, R. Rand, MCBeth: a measurement based quantum programming language, arXiv:2204.10784.

[143] W. Fang, M.S. Ying, X.D. Wu, Differentiable quantum programming with unbounded loops, ACM Transactions on Software Engineering and Methodology (2023).

[144] E. Farhi, J. Goldstone, S. Gutmann, M. Sipser, Quantum computation by adiabatic evolution, arXiv:quant-ph/0001106.

[145] Y. Feng, Y.X. Deng, M.S. Ying, Symbolic bisimulation for quantum processes, ACM Transactions on Computational Logic 15 (2014) 14.

[146] Y. Feng, R.Y. Duan, Z.F. Ji, M.S. Ying, Proof rules for the correctness of quantum programs, Theoretical Computer Science 386 (2007) 151–166.

[147] Y. Feng, R.Y. Duan, Z.F. Ji, M.S. Ying, Probabilistic bisimulations for quantum processes, Information and Computation 205 (2007) 1608–1639.

[148] Y. Feng, R.Y. Duan, M.S. Ying, Bisimulation for quantum processes, in: Proceedings of the 38th ACM Symposium on Principles of Programming Languages (POPL), 2011, pp. 523–534.

[149] Y. Feng, R.Y. Duan, M.S. Ying, Bisimulation for quantum processes, ACM Transactions on Programming Languages and Systems 34 (2012) 17.

[150] Y. Feng, E.M. Hahn, A. Turrini, L.J. Zhang, QPMC: a model checker for quantum programs and protocols, in: Proceedings of the 20th International Symposium on Formal Methods (FM 2015), in: LNCS, vol. 9109, Springer, 2015, pp. 265–272.

[151] Y. Feng, S.J. Li, Abstract interpretation, Hoare logic, and incorrectness logic for quantum programs, Information and Computation 294 (2023).

[152] Y. Feng, S.J. Li, M.S. Ying, Verification of distributed quantum programs, ACM Transactions on Computational Logic 23 (2022) 19, 1–40.

[153] Y. Feng, Y.T. Xu, Verification of nondeterministic quantum programs, in: Proceedings of the 28th ACM International Conference on Architectural Support for Programming Languages and Operating Systems (ASPLOS), 2023, pp. 789–805.

[154] Y. Feng, M.S. Ying, Toward automatic verification of quantum cryptographic protocols, in: Proceedings of 26th International Conference on Concurrency Theory (CONCUR), 2015, pp. 441–455.

[155] Y. Feng, M.S. Ying, Quantum Hoare logic with classical variables, ACM Transactions on Quantum Computing 2 (2021) 16.

[156] Y. Feng, N.K. Yu, M.S. Ying, Reachability analysis of recursive quantum Markov chains, in: Proceedings of the 38th International Symposium on Mathematical Foundations of Computer Science (MFCS), 2013, pp. 385–396.

[157] Y. Feng, N.K. Yu, M.S. Ying, Model checking quantum Markov chains, Journal of Computer and System Sciences 79 (2013) 1181–1198.

[158] R.W. Floyd, Assigning meanings to programs, in: Proceedings of the Symposium on Mathematical Aspects of Computer Science, 1967, pp. 19–33.

[159] F.G. Foster, On the stochastic matrices associated with certain queuing processes, The Annals of Mathematical Statistics 24 (1953) 355–360.

[160] N. Francez, Program Verication, Addison-Wesley, 1992.

[161] S. Franke-Arnold, S.J. Gay, I.V. Puthoor, Quantum process calculus for linear optical quantum computing, in: Proceedings of the 5th International Conference on Reversible Computation (RC), in: LNCS, vol. 7948, Springer, 2013, pp. 234–246.

[162] S. Franke-Arnold, S.J. Gay, I.V. Puthoor, Verification of linear optical quantum computing using quantum process calculus, Electronic Proceedings in Theoretical Computer Science 160 (2014) 111–129, EXPRESS/SOS.

[163] N. Friis, V. Dunjko, W. Dür, H.J. Briegel, Implementing quantum control for unknown subroutines, Physical Review A 89 (2014) 030303.

[164] P. Fu, K. Kishida, P. Selinger, Linear dependent type theory for quantum programming languages: extended abstract, in: Proceedings of the 35th Annual ACM/IEEE Symposium on Logic in Computer Science (LICS), 2020, pp. 440–453.

[165] X. Fu, et al., eQASM: an executable quantum instruction set architecture, in: 2019 IEEE International Symposium on High Performance Computer Architecture, 2019, pp. 224–237.

[166] X. Fu, J.T. Yu, X. Su, et al., Quingo: a programming framework for heterogeneous quantum-classical computing with NISQ features, ACM Transactions on Quantum Computing 2 (2021) 19.

[167] A.L. Gaunt, M. Brockschmidt, N. Kushman, D. Tarlow, Differentiable programs with neural libraries, in: Proceedings of the 34th International Conference on Machine Learning (ICML), 2017, pp. 1213–1222.

[168] S.J. Gay, Quantum programming languages: survey and bibliography, Mathematical Structures in Computer Science 16 (2006) 581–600.

[169] S.J. Gay, R. Nagarajan, Communicating quantum processes, in: Proceedings of the 32nd ACM Symposium on Principles of Programming Languages (POPL), 2005, pp. 145–157.

[170] S.J. Gay, R. Nagarajan, Types and typechecking for communicating quantum processes, Mathematical Structures in Computer Science 16 (2006) 375–406.

[171] S.J. Gay, R. Nagarajan, N. Papanikolaou, Probabilistic model-checking of quantum protocols, in: Proceedings of the 2nd International Workshop on Developments in Computational Models (DCM'06), 2006.

[172] S.J. Gay, R. Nagarajan, N. Papanikolaou, Specification and verification of quantum protocols, in: S.J. Gay, I. Mackie (Eds.), Semantic Techniques in Quantum Computation, Cambridge University Press, 2010, pp. 414–472.

[173] S.J. Gay, N. Papanikolaou, R. Nagarajan, QMC: a model checker for quantum systems, in: Proceedings of the 20th International Conference on Computer Aided Verification (CAV), in: LNCS, vol. 5123, Springer, 2008, pp. 543–547.

[174] S.J. Gay, I.V. Puthoor, Application of quantum process calculus to higher dimensional quantum protocols, Electronic Proceedings in Theoretical Computer Science 158 (2014) 15–28, QPL.

[175] B. Giles, P. Selinger, Exact synthesis of multiqubit Clifford+T circuits, Physical Review A 87 (2013) 032332.

[176] V. Giovannetti, S. Lloyd, L. Maccone, Quantum-enhanced positioning and clock synchronisation, Nature 412 (2001) 417–419.

[177] J.-Y. Girard, Geometry of interaction I: interpretation of system F, in: Logic Colloquium 88, North-Holland, 1989, pp. 221–260.

[178] N. Gisin, G. Ribordy, W. Tittel, H. Zbinden, Quantum cryptography, Reviews of Modern Physics 74 (2002) 145.

[179] A.M. Gleason, Measures on the closed subspaces of a Hilbert space, Journal of Mathematics and Mechanics 6 (1957) 885–893.

[180] M. Golovkins, Quantum pushdown automata, in: Proceedings of the 27th Conference on Current Trends in Theory and Practice of Informatics (SOFSEM), in: LNCS, vol. 1963, Springer, 2000, pp. 336–346.

[181] Google Quantum AI, Cirq: an open source framework for programming quantum computers, https://quantumai.google/cirq.

[182] K. Goswami, C. Giarmatzi, M. Kewming, F. Costa, C. Branciard, J. Romero, A.G. White, Indefinite causal order in a quantum switch, Physical Review Letters 121 (2018) 090503.

[183] D. Gottesman, Theory of fault-tolerant quantum computation, Physical Review A 57 (1998) 127–137.

[184] D. Gottesman, I. Chuang, Quantum teleportation as a universal computational primitive, Nature 402 (1999) 390–393.

[185] M. Grant, S. Boyd, CVX: Matlab software for disciplined convex programming, version 2.0 beta, http://cvxr.com/cvx, September 2013.

[186] J. Grattage, An overview of QML with a concrete implementation in Haskell, Electronic Notes in Theoretical Computer Science 270 (2011) 165–174.

[187] A.S. Green, P.L. Lumsdaine, N.J. Ross, P. Selinger, B. Valiron, Quipper: a scalable quantum programming language, in: Proceedings of the 34th ACM Conference on Programming Language Design and Implementation (PLDI), 2013, pp. 333–342.

[188] A.S. Green, P.L. Lumsdaine, N.J. Ross, P. Selinger, B. Valiron, An introduction to quantum programming in Quipper, arXiv:1304.5485.

[189] R.B. Griffiths, Consistent histories and quantum reasoning, Physical Review A 54 (1996) 2759–2774.

[190] L.K. Grover, Fixed-point quantum search, Physical Review Letters 95 (2005) 150501.

[191] S. Gudder, Lattice properties of quantum effects, Journal of Mathematical Physics 37 (1996) 2637–2642.

[192] S. Gudder, Quantum Markov chains, Journal of Mathematical Physics 49 (2008) 072105.

[193] J.Z. Guo, H.Z. Lou, J.T. Yu, R.L. Li, W. Fang, J.Y. Liu, P.X. Long, S.G. Ying, M.S. Ying, isQ: an integrated software stack for quantum programming, IEEE Transactions on Quantum Engineering (2023).

[194] A. Gupta, A. Rybalchenko, InvGen: an efficient invariant generator, in: Proceedings of the 21st International Conference on Computer Aided Verification (CAV), 2009, pp. 634–640.

[195] L. Gurvits, H. Barnum, Separable balls around the maximally mixed multipartite quantum states, Physical Review A 68 (2003) 042312.

[196] T. Häner, V. Kliuchnikov, M. Roetteler, M. Soeken, A. Vaschillo, QParallel: explicit parallelism for programming quantum computers, arXiv: 2210.03680.

[197] T. Häner, D.S. Steiger, T. Hoefler, M. Troyer, Distributed quantum computing with QMPI, in: Proceedings of the International Conference for High Performance Computing, Networking, Storage and Analysis (SC), vol. 16, 2021, pp. 1–13.

[198] T. Häner, V. Kliuchnikov, M. Roetteler, M. Soeken, A. Vaschillo, QParallel: explicit parallelism for programming quantum computers, arXiv: 2210.03680.

[199] A.W. Harrow, A. Hassidim, S. Lloyd, Quantum algorithm for linear systems of equations, Physical Review Letters 103 (2009) 150502.

[200] S. Hart, M. Sharir, A. Pnueli, Termination of probabilistic concurrent programs, ACM Transactions on Programming Languages and Systems 5 (1983) 356–380.

[201] J.D. Hartog, E.P. de Vink, Verifying probabilistic programs using a Hoare like logic, International Journal of Foundations of Computer Science 13 (2003) 315–340.

[202] I. Hasuo, N. Hoshino, Semantics of higher-order quantum computation via geometry of interaction, in: Proceedings of the 26th Annual IEEE Symposium on Logic in Computer Science (LICS), 2011, pp. 237–246.

[203] B. Hayes, Programming your quantum computer, American Scientist 102 (2014) 22–25.

[204] B. Heim, M. Soeken, S. Marshall, C. Granade, M. Roetteler, A. Geller, M. Troyer, K. Svore, Quantum programming languages, Nature Reviews Physics 2 (2020) 709–722.

[205] C. Heunen, B. Jacobs, Quantum logic in dagger kernel categories, in: Proceedings of Quantum Physics and Logic (QPL), 2009.

[206] K. Hietala, A Verified Software Toolchain for Quantum Programming, PhD Thesis, University of Maryland, 2022.

[207] K. Hietala, R. Rand, S.-H. Hung, X.D. Wu, M. Hicks, A verified optimizer for quantum circuits, Proceedings of the ACM on Programming Languages 5 (POPL) (2021) 37, 1–29.

[208] C.A.R. Hoare, An axiomatic basis for computer programming, Communications of the ACM 12 (1969) 576–580.

[209] C.A.R. Hoare, Procedures and parameters: an axiomatic approach, in: Symposium on Semantics of Algorithmic Languages, in: Lecture Notes in Mathematics, vol. 188, Springer, 1971, pp. 102–116.

[210] C.A.R. Hoare, Communicating sequential processes, Communications of the ACM 21 (1978) 666–677.

[211] C.A.R. Hoare, Communicating Sequential Processes, Prentice Hall, 1985.

[212] T. Hoare, R. Milner (Eds.), Grand Challenges in Computing Research, 2004, by organised, CPHC BCS, IEE EPSRC, etc., http://www.ukcrc.org. uk/grand-challenges/index.cfm.

[213] S. Honarvar, M.R. Mousavi, R. Nagarajan, Property-based testing of quantum programs in Q#, in: Proceedings of the IEEE/ACM 42nd International Conference on Software Engineering Workshops (ICSEW), 2020, pp. 430–435.

[214] K. Honda, Analysis of quantum entanglement in quantum programs using stabiliser formalism, Electronic Proceedings in Theoretical Computer Science 195 (QPL) (2015) 262–272.

[215] R.A. Horn, C.R. Johnson, Matrix Analysis, Cambridge University Press, 1986.

[216] R. Horodecki, P. Horodecki, M. Horodecki, K. Horodecki, Quantum entanglement, Reviews of Modern Physics 81 (2009) 865–942.

[217] P. Hoyer, J. Neerbek, Y. Shi, Quantum complexities of ordered searching, sorting and element distinctness, in: Proceedings of the 28th International Colloquium on Automata, Languages, and Programming (ICALP), 2001, pp. 62–73.

[218] Y.P. Huang, M. Martonosi, Statistical assertions for validating patterns and finding bugs in quantum programs, in: Proceedings of the 46th International Symposium on Computer Architecture (ISCA), 2019, pp. 541–553.

[219] S.-H. Hung, K. Hietala, S.P. Zhu, M.S. Ying, M. Hicks, X.D. Wu, Quantitative robustness analysis of quantum programs, Proceedings of the ACM on Programming Languages 3 (POPL) (2019) 31, 1–29.

[220] IBM Q Team, IBM quantum experience, https://www.ibm.com/quantum-computing/, 2018.

[221] IBM Q Team, Qiskit: an open-source sdk for working with quantum computers at the level of pulses, circuits, and algorithms, https://github.com/Qiskit.

[222] IBM Research, Expanding the IBM quantum roadmap to anticipate the future of quantum-centric supercomputing, https://research.ibm.com/blog/ibm-quantum-roadmap-2025.

[223] N. Inui, N. Konno, E. Segawa, One-dimensional three-state quantum walk, Physical Review E 72 (2005) 056112.

[224] S. Ishtiaq, P.W. O'Hearn, BI as an assertion language for mutable data structure, in: Proceedings of the 28th ACM Symposium on Principles of Programming Languages (POPL), 2001, pp. 14–26.

[225] D. Ittah, T. Häner, V. Kliuchnikov, T. Hoefler, Enabling dataflow optimization for quantum programs, arXiv:2101.11030.

[226] B. Jacobs, On block structures in quantum computation, Electronic Notes in Theoretical Computer Science 298 (2013) 233–255.

[227] B. Jacobs, New directions in categorical logic, for classical, probabilistic and quantum logic, Logical Methods in Computer Science 11 (3) (2015).

[228] C.J. Isham, N. Linden, Quantum temporal logic and decoherence functionals in the histories approach to generalized quantum theory, Journal of Mathematical Physics 35 (1994) 5452.

[229] K.E. Iverson, Notation as a tool of thought, Communications of the ACM 23 (8) (1980) 444–465.

[230] A. JavadiAbhari, S. Patil, D. Kudrow, J. Heckey, A. Lvov, F.T. Chong, M. Martonosi, ScaffCC: scalable compilation and analysis of quantum programs, Parallel Computing 45 (2015) 2–17.

[231] Z.F. Ji, J.X. Chen, Z.H. Wei, M.S. Ying, The LU-LC conjecture is false, Quantum Information & Computation 10 (2010) 97–108.

[232] X.D. Jia, A. Kornell, B. Lindenhovius, M. Mislove, V. Zamdzhiev, Semantics for variational quantum programming, Proceedings of the ACM on Programming Languages 6 (POPL) (2022) 26, 1–31.

[233] C.B. Jones, Tentative steps towards a development method for interfering programs, ACM Transactions on Programming Languages and Systems 5 (1983) 596–619.

[234] N.D. Jones, Computability and Complexity: From a Programming Perspective, MIT Press, 1997.

[235] P. Jorrand, M. Lalire, Toward a quantum process algebra, in: Proceedings of the 1st ACM Conference on Computing Frontier, 2004, pp. 111–119.

[236] P. Jorrand, S. Perdrix, Abstract interpretation techniques for quantum computation, in: I. Mackie, S. Gay (Eds.), Semantic Techniques in Quantum Computation, Cambridge University Press, 2010, pp. 206–234.

[237] R. Jozsa, N. Linden, On the role of entanglement in quantum-computational speed-up, Proceedings - Royal Society. Mathematical, Physical and Engineering Sciences 459 (2003) 2011–2032.

[238] M.F. Kaashoek, Parallelism and operating systems, in: Proceedings of the SOSP History Day, vol. 10, 2015, pp. 1–35.

[239] R. Kadison, Order properties of bounded self-adjoint operators, Proceedings of the American Mathematical Society 34 (1951) 505–510.

[240] Y. Kakutani, A logic for formal verification of quantum programs, in: Proceedings of the 13th Asian Computing Science Conference (ASIAN), in: LNCS, vol. 5913, Springer, 2009, pp. 79–93.

[241] E. Kashefi, Quantum domain theory – definitions and applications, arXiv:quant-ph/0306077.

[242] J.-P. Katoen, A. McIver, L. Meinicke, C.C. Morgan, Linear-invariant generation for probabilistic programs – automated support for proof-based methods, in: Proc. 17th International Symposium on Static Analysis (SAS), in: LNCS, vol. 6337, Springer, 2010, pp. 390–406.

[243] S. Katz, Z. Manna, Logical analysis of programs, Communications of the ACM 19 (1976) 188–206.

[244] H.J. Keisler, Probability quantifiers, in: J. Barwise, S. Feferman (Eds.), Model Theoretic Logics, Springer, 1985, pp. 509–556.

[245] J.C. King, A Program Verifier, PhD thesis, Department of Computer Science, Carnegie-Mellon University, 1969.

[246] A. Kissinger, J. van de Wetering, PyZX: large scale automated diagrammatic reasoning, Electronic Proceedings in Theoretical Computer Science 318 (2020) 229–241.

[247] A. Kitaev, Fault-tolerant quantum computation by anyons, arXiv:quantph/9707021.

[248] A. Kitaev, A.H. Shen, M.N. Vyalyi, Classical and Quantum Computation, American Mathematical Society, Providence, 2002.

[249] T. Kadowaki, H. Nishimori, Quantum annealing in the transverse Ising model, Physical Review E 58 (1998) 5355.

[250] T. Kleymann, Hoare logic and auxiliary variables, Formal Aspects of Computing 11 (1999) 541–566.

[251] V. Kliuchnikov, D. Maslov, M. Mosca, Fast and efficient exact synthesis of single qubit unitaries generated by Clifford and T gates, Quantum Information & Computation 13 (2013) 607–630.

[252] V. Kliuchnikov, A. Bocharov, K.M. Svore, Asymptotically optimal topological quantum compiling, Physical Review Letters 112 (2014) 140504.

[253] A.A. Klyachko, Quantum marginal problem and N-representability, Journal of Physics. Conference Series 36 (2006) 72–86.

[254] E.H. Knill, Conventions for Quantum Pseudo-code, Technical Report, Los Alamos National Laboratory, 1996.

[255] A. Kondacs, J. Watrous, On the power of quantum finite state automata, in: Proceedings of the 38th Symposium on Foundation of Computer Science (FOCS), 1997, pp. 66–75.

[256] K. Kraus, States, Effects and Operations: Fundamental Notions of Quantum Theory, Springer, 1983.

[257] T. Kubota, Verification of Quantum Cryptographic Protocols using Quantum Process Algebras, PhD Thesis, Department of Computer Science, University of Tokyo, 2014.

[258] T. Kubota, Y. Kakutani, G. Kato, Y. Kawano, H. Sakurada, Application of a process calculus to security proofs of quantum protocols, in: Proceedings of Foundations of Computer Science in WORLDCOMP, 2012, pp. 141–147.

[259] T. Kubota, Y. Kakutani, G. Kato, Y. Kawano, H. Sakurada, Semi-automated verification of security proofs of quantum cryptographic protocols, Journal of Symbolic Computation (2015).

[260] C.S. Kubrusly, P.C.M. Vieira, Convergence and decomposition for tensor products of Hilbert space operators, Operators and Matrices 2 (2008) 407–416.

[261] D. Kudrow, K. Bier, Z. Deng, D. Franklin, Y. Tomita, K.R. Brown, F.T. Chong, Quantum rotation: a case study in static and dynamic machine-code generation for quantum computer, in: Proceedings of the 40th ACM/IEEE International Symposium on Computer Architecture (ISCA), 2013, pp. 166–176.

[262] P. Kurzyński, A. Wójcik, Quantum walk as a generalized measure device, Physical Review Letters 110 (2013) 200404.

[263] M. Kwiatkowska, G. Norman, P. Parker, Probabilistic symbolic model-checking with PRISM: a hybrid approach, International Journal on Software Tools for Technology Transfer 6 (2004) 128–142.

[264] O. Lahav, V. Vafeiadis, Owicki-Gries reasoning for weak memory models, in: Proceedings of the 42nd International Colloquium on Automata, Languages, and Programming (ICALP), 2015, pp. 311–323.

[265] M. Lalire, Relations among quantum processes: bisimilarity and congruence, Mathematical Structures in Computer Science 16 (2006) 407–428.

[266] M. Lampis, K.G. Ginis, M.A. Papakyriakou, N.S. Papaspyrou, Quantum data and control made easier, Electronic Notes in Theoretical Computer Science 210 (2008) 85–105.

[267] L. Lamport, Proving the correctness of multiprocess programs, IEEE Transactions on Software Engineering 3 (1977) 125–143.

[268] A. Lapets, M. Rötteler, Abstract resource cost derivation for logical quantum circuit description, in: Proceedings of the ACM Workshop on Functional Programming Concepts in Domain-Specific Languages (FPCDSL), 2013, pp. 35–42.

[269] A. Lapets, M.P. da Silva, M. Thome, A. Adler, J. Beal, M. Rötteler, QuaFL: a typed DSL for quantum programming, in: Proceedings of the ACM Workshop on Functional Programming Concepts in Domain-Specific Languages (FPCDSL), 2013, pp. 19–27.

[270] X.-B. Le, S.-W. Lin, J. Sun, D. Sanán, A quantum interpretation of separating conjunction for local reasoning of quantum programs based on separation logic, Proceedings of the ACM on Programming Languages 6 (POPL) (2022) 36, 1–27.

[271] M. Lewis, S. Soudjani, P. Zuliani, Formal verification of quantum programs: theory, tools and challenges, ACM Transactions on Quantum Computing (2023).

[272] D.W. Leung, Quantum computation by measurements, International Journal of Quantum Information 2 (2004) 33–43.

[273] G.S. Li, L. Zhou, N.K. Yu, Y.F. Ding, M.S. Ying, Y. Xie, Projection-based runtime assertions for testing and debugging quantum programs, Proceedings of the ACM on Programming Languages 4 (OOPSLA) (2020) 150, 1–29.

[274] Y.J. Li, D. Unruh, Quantum relational Hoare logic with expectations, in: Proceedings of the 48th International Colloquium on Automata, Languages, and Programming (ICALP), vol. 136, 2021, pp. 1–20.

[275] Y.J. Li, M.S. Ying, (Un)decidable problems about reachability of quantum systems, in: Proceedings of the 25th International Conference on Concurrency Theory (CONCUR), 2014, pp. 482–496.

[276] Y.J. Li, M.S. Ying, Algorithmic analysis of termination problems for quantum programs, Proceedings of the ACM on Programming Languages 2 (POPL) (2018) 35, 1–29.

[277] Y.J. Li, N.K. Yu, M.S. Ying, Termination of nondeterministic quantum programs, Acta Informatica 51 (2014) 1–24.

[278] C. Lin, L. Snyder, Principles of Parallel Programming, Pearson, 2008.

[279] J. Liu, G. Byrd, H. Zhou, Quantum circuits for dynamic runtime assertions in quantum computation, in: Proceedings of the 25th International Conference on Architectural Support for Programming Languages and Operating Systems (ASPLOS), 2020, pp. 1017–1030.

[280] J. Liu, H. Zhou, Systematic approaches for precise and approximate quantum state runtime assertion, in: Proceedings of the 27th IEEE International Symposium on High-Performance Computer Architecture (HPCA), 2021, pp. 179–193.

[281] J.Y. Liu, B.H. Zhan, S.L. Wang, S.G. Ying, T. Liu, Y.J. Li, M.S. Ying, N.J. Zhan, Formal verification of quantum algorithms using quantum Hoare logic, in: Proceedings of the 31st International Conference on Computer Aided Verification (CAV), 2019, pp. 187–207.

[282] J.Y. Liu, L. Zhou, G. Barthe, M.S. Ying, Quantum weakest preconditions for reasoning about expected runtimes of quantum programs, in: Proceedings of the 37th Annual ACM/IEEE Symposium on Logic in Computer Science (LICS), vol. 4, 2022, pp. 1–13.

[283] L. Liu, X. Dou, Qucloud: a new qubit mapping mechanism for multi-programming quantum computing in cloud environment, in: Proceedings of the 2021 IEEE International Symposium on High-Performance Computer Architecture (HPCA), 2021, pp. 167–178.

[284] S. Lloyd, Universal quantum simulators, Science 273 (1996) 1073–1078.

[285] S. Lloyd, A theory of quantum gravity based on quantum computation, arXiv:quant-ph/0501135.

[286] S. Lloyd, M. Mohseni, P. Rebentrost, Quantum principal component analysis, Nature Physics 10 (2014) 631–633.

[287] S. Lloyd, M. Mohseni, P. Rebentrost, Quantum algorithms for supervised and unsupervised machine learning, arXiv:1307.0411v2.

[288] J. Loeckx, K. Sieber, The Foundations of Program Verification, second edition, John Wiley & Sons, Chichester, 1987.

[289] N.B. Lovett, S. Cooper, M. Everitt, M. Trevers, V. Kendon, Universal quantum computation using the discrete-time quantum walk, Physical Review A 81 (2010) 042330.

[290] I. Mackie, S. Gay (Eds.), Semantic Techniques in Quantum Computation, Cambridge University Press, 2010.

[291] F. Magniez, M. Santha, M. Szegedy, Quantum algorithms for the triangle problem, SIAM Journal on Computing 37 (2007) 413–427.

[292] Z. Manna, Mathematical Theory of Computation, McGraw-Hill, 1974.

[293] Ph.A. Martin, F. Rothen, Many-Body Problems and Quantum Field Theory: An Introduction, Springer, Berlin, 2004.

[294] M. Martonosi, M. Röetteler, Next steps in quantum computing: computer science's role, Computing Community Consortium (2018).

[295] P. Mateus, J. Ramos, A. Sernadas, C. Sernadas, Temporal logics for reasoning about quantum systems, in: I. Mackie, S. Gay (Eds.), Semantic Techniques in Quantum Computation, Cambridge University Press, 2010, pp. 389–413.

[296] P. Maymin, Extending the lambda calculus to express randomized and quantumized algorithms, arXiv:quant-ph/9612052.

[297] A. McIver, C. Morgan, Abstraction, Refinement and Proof for Probabilistic Systems, Springer, New York, 2005.

[298] T.S. Metodi, F.T. Chong, Quantum Computing for Computer Architects, Synthesis Lectures in Computer Architecture No. 1, second edition, Morgan & Claypool Publishers, 2011.

[299] G. Meuli, M. Soeken, M. Roetteler, T. Häner, Enabling accuracy-aware quantum compilers using symbolic resource estimation, Proceedings of the ACM on Programming Languages 4 (OOPSLA) (2020) 130, 1–26.

[300] D.A. Meyer, Quantum strategies, Physical Review Letters 82 (1999) 1052–1055.

[301] R. Milner, A Calculus of Communicating Systems, Springer, 1980.

[302] R. Milner, Communication and Concurrency, Prentice Hall, 1989.

[303] R. Milner, Communicating and Mobile Systems: the Pi-Calculus, Springer, 1999.

[304] R. Milner, J. Parrow, D. Walker, A calculus of mobile processes, I and II, Information and Computation 100 (1992) 1–77.

[305] A. Miné, Tutorial on static inference of numeric invariants by abstract interpretation, Foundations and Trends in Programming Languages 4 (2017) 120–372.

[306] J.A. Miszczak, Models of quantum computation and quantum programming languages, Bulletin of the Polish Academy of Science: Technical Sciences 59 (2011) 305–324.

[307] J.A. Miszczak, High-Level Structures for Quantum Computing, Morgan & Claypool Publishers, 2012.

[308] C. Monroe, J. Kim, Scaling the ion trap quantum processor, Science 339 (2013) 1164–1169.

[309] M. Montero, Unidirectional quantum walks: evolution and exit times, Physical Review A 88 (2013) 012333.

[310] C. Moore, M. Nilsson, Parallel quantum computation and quantum codes, SIAM Journal on Computing 31 (2001) 799–815.

[311] C. Morgan, Programming from Specifications, Prentice Hall, Hertfordshire, 1988.

[312] C. Moore, M. Nilsson, Parallel quantum computation and quantum codes, SIAM Journal on Computing 31 (2001) 799–815.

[313] C. Moore, J.P. Crutchfield, Quantum automata and quantum grammars, Theoretical Computer Science 237 (2000) 275–306.

[314] S.-C. Mu, R. Bird, Functional quantum programming, in: Proceedings of the 2nd Asian Workshop on Programming Languages and Systems (APLAS), 2001, pp. 75–88.

[315] J.M. Myers, Can a universal quantum computer be fully quantum?, Physical Review Letters 78 (1997) 1823.

[316] R. Nagarajan, N. Papanikolaou, D. Williams, Simulating and compiling code for the sequential quantum random access machine, Electronic Notes in Theoretical Computer Science 170 (2007) 101–124.

[317] M. Nakanishi, Quantum pushdown automata with garbage tape, International Journal of Foundations of Computer Science 29 (2018) 425–446.

[318] M.A. Nielsen, I.L. Chuang, Quantum Computation and Quantum Information, Cambridge University Press, 2000.

[319] M.A. Nielsen, Quantum computation by measurement and quantum memory, Physical Letters A 308 (2003) 96–100.

[320] S. Niu, A. Todri-Sanial, Enabling multi-programming mechanism for quantum computing in the NISQ era, Quantum 7 (2023) 925.

[321] P.W. O'Hearn, Separation logic, Communications of the ACM 62 (2019) 86–95.

[322] P.W. O'Hearn, Incorrectness logic, Proceedings of the ACM on Programming Languages 4 (POPL) (2020) 10:1–10:32.

[323] P.W. O'Hearn, D. Pym, The logic of bunched implications, The Bulletin of Symbolic Logic 5 (1999) 215–244.

[324] F. Olmedo, A. Díaz-Caro, Runtime analysis of quantum programs: a formal approach, in: International Workshop on Programming Languages for Quantum Computing (PLanQC), 2020.

[325] B. Ömer, Structured Quantum Programming, Ph.D. thesis, Technical University of Vienna, 2003.

[326] S. Owicki, A consistent and complete deductive system for the verification of parallel programs, in: Proceedings of the 8th ACM Symposium on Theory of Computation (STOC), 1976, pp. 73–86.

[327] S. Owicki, D. Gries, An axiomatic proof technique for parallel programs I, Acta Informatica 6 (1976) 319–340.

[328] M. Ozawa, Quantum nondemolition monitoring of universal quantum computers, Physical Review Letters 80 (1998) 631.

[329] M. Pagani, P. Selinger, B. Valiron, Applying quantitative semantics to higher-order quantum computing, in: Proceedings of the 41st ACM Symposium on Principles of Programming Languages (POPL), 2014, pp. 647–658.

[330] N.K. Papanikolaou, Model Checking Quantum Protocols, Ph.D. Thesis, Department of Computer Science, University of Warwick, 2008.

[331] A.K. Pati, S.L. Braunstein, Impossibility of deleting an unknown quantum state, Nature 404 (2000) 164.

[332] J. Paykin, R. Rand, S. Zdancewic, QWIRE: a core language for quantum circuits, in: Proceedings of the 44th ACM Symposium on Principles of Programming Languages (POPL), 2017, pp. 846–858.

[333] Y.X. Peng, K. Hietala, R.Z. Tao, L.Y. Li, R. Rand, M. Hicks, X.D. Wu, A formally certified end-to-end implementation of Shor's factorization algorithm, arXiv:2204.07112.

[334] Y.X. Peng, M.S. Ying, X.D. Wu, Algebraic reasoning of quantum programs via non-idempotent Kleene algebra, in: Proceedings of the 43rd ACM International Conference on Programming Language Definition and Implementation (PLDI), 2022, pp. 657–670.

[335] S. Perdrix, Quantum entanglement analysis based on abstract interpretation, in: Proceedings of the International Static Analysis Symposium (SAS), 2008, pp. 270–282.

[336] A. Peres, W.K. Wootters, Optimal detection of quantum information, Physical Review Letters 66 (1991) 1119.

[337] A. Peruzzo, J. McClean, P. Shadbolt, M.H. Yung, X.Q. Zhou, P.J. Love, A. Aspuru-Guzik, J.L. O'Brien, A variational eigenvalue solver on a photonic quantum processor, Nature Communications 5 (2014) 4213.

[338] S. Pirandola, J. Eisert, C. Weedbrook, A. Furusawa, S.L. Braunstein, Advances in quantum teleportation, Nature Photonics 9 (2015) 641–652.

[339] S. Pirandola, U.L. Andersen, L. Banchi, M. Berta, D. Bunandar, R. Colbeck, D. Englund, T. Gehring, C. Lupo, C. Ottaviani, J.L. Pereira, M. Razavi, J. Shamsul Shaari, M. Tomamichel, V.C. Usenko, G. Vallone, P. Villoresi, P. Wallden, Advances in quantum cryptography, Advances in Optics and Photonics 12 (2020) 1012–1236.

[340] A. Platzer, Differential dynamic logic for hybrid systems, Journal of Automated Reasoning 41 (2008) 143–189.

[341] M.B. Plenio, S.S. Virmani, An introduction to entanglement theory, in: E. Andersson, P. Öhberg (Eds.), Quantum Information and Coherence, Springer, 2014, pp. 173–209.

[342] J. Preskill, Quantum computing in the NISQ era and beyond, Quantum 2 (2018) 79.

[343] L.M. Procopio, A. Moqanaki, M. Araújo, F. Costa, I.A. Calafell, E.G. Dowd, D.R. Hamel, L.A. Rozema, C. Brukner, P. Walther, Experimental superposition of orders of quantum gates, Nature Communications 6 (2015) 7913.

[344] E. Prugovečki, Quantum Mechanics in Hilbert Space, Academic Press, New York, 1981.

[345] X.D. Qin, Y.X. Deng, W.J. Du, Verifying quantum communication protocols with ground bisimulation, in: Proceedings of the 26th International Conference on Tools and Algorithms for the Construction and Analysis of Systems (TACAS 2020), 2020, pp. 21–38.

[346] QIR Alliance, https://github.com/qir-alliance.

[347] Quantinuum – Cambridge Quantum Computing, Pytket user manual, https://cqcl.github.io/pytket/manual/index.html.

[348] R. Raussendorf, H.J. Briegel, A one-way quantum computer, Physical Review Letters 86 (2001) 5188–5191.

[349] P. Rebentrost, M. Mohseni, S. Lloyd, Quantum support vector machine for big data classification, Physical Review Letters 113 (2014) 130501.

[350] M. Reed, B. Simon, Methods of Modern Mathematical Physics I: Functional Analysis, Academic Press, 1998.

[351] M. Rennela, Towards a quantum domain theory: order-enrichment and fixpoints in W*-algebras, in: Proceedings of the 30th Conference on the Mathematical Foundations of Programming Semantics (MFPS), 2014.

[352] J.C. Reynolds, Separation logic: a logic for shared mutable data structures, in: Proceedings of the 17th Annual IEEE Symposium on Logic in Computer Science (LICS), 2002, pp. 55–74.

[353] T. Reps, S. Horwitz, M. Sagiv, Precise interprocedural dataflow analysis via graph reachability, in: Proceedings of the 22nd ACM Symposium on Principles of Programming Languages (POPL), 1995, pp. 49–61.

[354] E.G. Rieffel, D. Venturelli, B. O'Gorman, M.B. Do, E.M. Prystay, V.N. Smelyanskiy, A case study in programming a quantum annealer for hard operational planning problems, Quantum Information Processing 14 (2015) 1–36.

[355] S.S. Robert, J.C. Michael, W.J. Zeng, A practical quantum instruction set architecture, arXiv:1608.03355.

[356] M. Roetteler, M. Naehrig, K.M. Svore, K. Lauter, Quantum resource estimates for computing elliptic curve discrete logarithms, in: Proceedings of the International Conference on the Theory and Application of Cryptology and Information Security, 2017, pp. 241–270.

[357] N.J. Ross, P. Selinger, Optimal ancilla-free Clifford+T approximation of z-rotations, arXiv:1403.2975.

[358] Y. Rouselakis, N.S. Papaspyrou, Y. Tsiouris, E.N. Todoran, Compilation to quantum circuits for a language with quantum data and control, in: Proceedings of the 2013 Federated Conference on Computer Science and Information Systems (FedCSIS), 2013, pp. 1537–1544.

[359] G. Rubino, L.A. Rozema, A. Feix, M. Araújo, J.M. Zeuner, L.M. Procopia, Č. Brunkner, P. Walther, Experimental verification of an indefinite causal order, Science Advances 3 (2017) e1602589.

[360] R. Rüdiger, Quantum programming languages: an introductory overview, The Computer Journal 50 (2007) 134–150.

[361] J.W. Sanders, P. Zuliani, Quantum programming, in: Proceedings of 5th International Conference on Mathematics of Program Construction (MPC), in: LNCS, vol. 1837, Springer, 2000, pp. 88–99.

[362] S. Sankaranarayanan, H.B. Sipma, Z. Manna, Non-linear loop invariant generation using Gröbner bases, in: Proceedings of the 31st ACM Symposium on Principles of Programming Languages (POPL), 2004, pp. 318–329.

[363] M. Santha, Quantum walk based search algorithms, in: Proceeding of the 5th International Conference on Theory and Applications of Models of Computation (TAMC 2008), in: LNCS, vol. 4978, Springer, 2008, pp. 31–46.

[364] D. Schlingemann, Local equivalence of graph states, in: O. Krueger, R.F. Werner (Eds.), Some Open Problems in Quantum Information Theory, arXiv:quant-ph/0504166, 2005, See also https://qig.itp.uni-hannover.de/qiproblems/Open_Problems.

[365] M. Schuld, V. Bergholm, C. Gogolin, J. Izaac, N. Killoran, Evaluating analytic gradients on quantum hardware, Physical Review A 99 (2019) 032331.

[366] F. Schwabl, Advanced Quantum Mechanics, fourth edition, Springer, 2008.

[367] P. Selinger, Towards a quantum programming language, Mathematical Structures in Computer Science 14 (2004) 527–586.

[368] P. Selinger, A brief survey of quantum programming languages, in: Proceedings of the 7th International Symposium on Functional and Logic Programming, in: LNCS, vol. 2998, Springer, 2004, pp. 1–6.

[369] P. Selinger, Toward a semantics for higher-order quantum computation, in: Proceedings of the 2nd International Workshop on Quantum Programming Languages (QPL), in: TUCS General Publications, vol. 33, 2004, pp. 127–143.

[370] P. Selinger, B. Valiron, A lambda calculus for quantum computation with classical control, Mathematical Structures in Computer Science 16 (2006) 527–552.

[371] P. Selinger, B. Valiron, On a fully abstract model for a quantum linear functional language, Electronic Notes in Theoretical Computer Science 210 (2008) 123–137.

[372] P. Selinger, B. Valiron, Quantum lambda calculus, in: S. Gay, I. Mackie (Eds.), Semantic Techniques in Quantum Computation, Cambridge University Press, 2010, pp. 135–172.

[373] R. Sethi, Programming Languages: Concepts and Constructs, Addison-Wesley, 2002.

[374] V.V. Shende, S.S. Bullock, I.L. Markov, Synthesis of quantum-logic circuits, IEEE Transactions on CAD of Integrated Circuits and Systems 25 (2006) 1000–1010.

[375] M. Sharir, A. Pnueli, S. Hart, Verification of probabilistic programs, SIAM Journal on Computing 13 (1984) 292–314.

[376] N. Shenvi, J. Kempe, K.B. Whaley, Quantum random-walk search algorithm, Physical Review A 67 (2003) 052307.

[377] P.W. Shor, Algorithms for quantum computation: discrete logarithms and factoring, in: Proceedings of the 35th IEEE Annual Symposium on Foundations of Computer Science (FOCS), 1994, pp. 124–134.

[378] P.W. Shor, Why haven't more quantum algorithms been discovered, Journal of the ACM 50 (2003) 87–90.

[379] K. Singhal, S. Marshall, K. Hietala, R. Rand, Toward a type-theoretic interpretation of Q#, in: International Workshop on Programming Languages for Quantum Computing (PLanQC), 2021.

[380] R.S. Smith, M.J. Curtis, W.J. Zeng, A practical quantum instruction set architecture, arXiv:1608.03355v2, 2017.

[381] Stanford Invariant Generator, http://theory.stanford.edu/~srirams/Software/sting.html.

[382] S. Staton, Algebraic effects, linearity, and quantum programming languages, in: Proceedings of the 42nd ACM Symposium on Principles of Programming Languages (POPL), 2015, pp. 395–406.

[383] F.H. Stillinger, et al., Mathematical Challenges from Theoretical/Computational Chemistry, National Academy Press, 1995.

[384] M. Suzuki, General theory of fractal path integrals with applications to many-body theories and statistical physics, Journal of Mathematical Physics 32 (1991) 400–407.

[385] K.M. Svore, A.V. Aho, A.W. Cross, I.L. Chuang, I.L. Markov, A layered software architecture for quantum computing design tools, IEEE Computer 39 (2006) 74–83.

[386] K. Svore, A. Geller, M. Troyer, J. Azariah, C. Granade, B. Heim, V. Kliuchnikov, M. Mykhailova, A. Paz, M. Roetteler, Q#: enabling scalable quantum computing and development with a high-level DSL, in: Proceedings of the Real World Domain Specific Languages Workshop (RWDSL), 2018, 7.

[387] A. Tafliovich, E.C.R. Hehner, Quantum predicative programming, in: Proceedings of the 8th International Conference on Mathematics of Program Construction (MPC), in: LNCS, vol. 4014, Springer, 2006, pp. 433–454.

[388] A. Tafliovich, E.C.R. Hehner, Programming with quantum communication, Electronic Notes in Theoretical Computer Science 253 (2009) 99–118.

[389] G. Takeuti, Quantum set theory, in: E. Beltrametti, B.C. van Fraassen (Eds.), Current Issues in Quantum Logics, Plenum, New York, 1981, pp. 303–322.

[390] S. Tani, H. Kobayashi, K. Matsumoto, Exact quantum algorithms for the leader election problem, ACM Transactions on Computation Theory 4 (2012) 1.

[391] R.Z. Tao, Y.N. Shi, J.A. Yao, X.P. Li, A. Javadi-Abhari, A.W. Cross, F.T. Chong, R.H. Gu, Giallar: push-button verification for the qiskit quantum compiler, in: Proceedings of the 43rd ACM International Conference on Programming Language Design and Implementation (PLDI), 2022, pp. 641–656.

[392] R.Z. Tao, Y.N. Shi, J.A. Yao, J. Hui, F.T. Chong, R.H. Gu, Gleipnir: toward practical error analysis for quantum programs, in: Proceedings of the 42nd ACM International Conference on Programming Language Design and Implementation (PLDI), 2021, pp. 48–64.

[393] K. Temme, T.J. Osborne, K.G. Vollbrecht, D. Poulin, F. Verstraete, Quantum Metropolis sampling, Nature 471 (2011) 87–90.

[394] G. 't Hooft, The cellular automaton interpretation of quantum mechanics – a view on the quantum nature of our universe, compulsory or impossible?, arXiv:1405.1548v2.

[395] D. Unruh, Quantum relational Hoare logic, Proceedings of the ACM on Programming Languages 3 (POPL) (2019) 33, 1–31.

[396] D. Unruh, Quantum Hoare logic with ghost variables, in: Proceedings of the 34th Annual ACM/IEEE Symposium on Logic in Computer Science (LICS), 2019.

[397] A. van Tonder, A lambda calculus for quantum computation, SIAM Journal on Computing 33 (2004) 1109–1135.

[398] A. Vanrietvelde, H. Kristjánsson, J. Barrett, Routed quantum circuits, Quantum 5 (2021) 503.

[399] V.S. Varadarajan, Geometry of Quantum Theory, Springer, New York, 1985.

[400] S.E. Venegas-Andraca, Quantum walks: a comprehensive review, Quantum Information Processing 11 (2012) 1015–1106.

[401] F. Voichick, L.Y. Li, R. Rand, M. Hicks, Qunity: a unified language for quantum and classical computing, Proceedings of the ACM on Programming Languages 7 (POPL) (2023) 32, 921–951.

[402] J.Y. Wang, Q. Zhang, G.H. Xu, M. Kim, QDiff: differential testing of quantum software stacks, in: Proceedings of the 36th IEEE/ACM International Conference on Automated Software Engineering (ASE), 2021, pp. 692–704.

[403] Q.S. Wang, R.L. Li, M.S. Ying, Equivalence checking of sequential quantum circuits, IEEE Transactions on Computer-Aided Design of Integrated Circuits and Systems 41 (2022) 3143–3156.

[404] Q.S. Wang, M.S. Ying, Quantum random access stored-program machines, Journal of Computer and System Sciences 131 (2023) 13–63.

[405] D. Wecker, K.M. Svore, LIQUi|>: a software design architecture and domain-specific language for quantum computing, http://research.microsoft.com/pubs/209634/1402.4467.pdf.

[406] S. Wehner, D. Elkouss, R. Hanson, Quantum Internet: a vision for the road ahead, Science 362 (6412) (2018).

[407] G. Winskel, The Formal Semantics of Programming Languages: An Introduction, MIT Press, 1993.

[408] W.M. Witzel, W.D. Craft, R. Carr, D. Kapur, Verifying quantum phase estimation (QPE) using prove-it, arXiv:2304.02183.

[409] M.M. Wolf, Quantum Channels and Operators: Guided Tour, unpublished lecture notes, 2012.

[410] W. Wootters, W. Zurek, A single quantum cannot be cloned, Nature 299 (1982) 802–803.

[411] A.B. Wu, H.Z. Zhang, G.S. Li, A. Shabani, Y. Xie, Y.F. Ding, AutoComm: a framework for enabling efficient communication in distributed quantum programs, in: Proceeding of 55th IEEE/ACM International Symposium on Microarchitecture (MICRO), 2022, pp. 1027–1041.

[412] M.K. Xu, Z.K. Li, O. Padon, S.N. Lin, J. Pointing, A. Hirth, H. Ma, J. Palsberg, A. Aiken, U.A. Acar, Z.H. Jia, Quartz: superoptimization of quantum circuits, in: Proceedings of the 43rd ACM International Conference on Programming Language Design and Implementation (PLDI), 2022, pp. 625–640.

[413] P. Xue, B.C. Sanders, Two quantum walkers sharing coins, Physical Review A 85 (2011) 022307.

[414] P. Yan, H.R. Jiang, N.K. Yu, On incorrectness logic for quantum programs, Proceedings of the ACM on Programming Languages 6 (OOPSLA) (2022) 1–28.

[415] A.C. Yao, Quantum circuit complexity, in: Proceedings of the 34th Annual IEEE Symposium on Foundations of Computer Science (FOCS), 1993, pp. 352–361.

[416] K. Yasuda, T. Kubota, Y. Kakutani, Observational equivalence using schedulers for quantum processes, Electronic Proceedings in Theoretical Computer Science 172 (QPL) (2014) 191–203.

[417] M.S. Ying, Reasoning about probabilistic sequential programs in a probabilistic logic, Acta Informatica 39 (2003) 315–389.

[418] M.S. Ying, Foundations of quantum programming, in: Kazunori Ueda (Ed.), Proceedings of the 8th Asian Symposium on Programming Languages and Systems (APLAS), in: LNCS, vol. 6461, Springer, 2010, pp. 16–20.

[419] M.S. Ying, Floyd–Hoare logic for quantum programs, ACM Transactions on Programming Languages and Systems 39 (2011) 19.

[420] M.S. Ying, Quantum recursion and second quantisation, arXiv:1405.4443.

[421] M.S. Ying, Toward automatic verification of quantum programs, Formal Aspects of Computing 31 (2019) 3–25.

[422] M.S. Ying, Birkhoff–von Neumann quantum logic as an assertion language for quantum programs, arXiv:2205.01959, 2022.

[423] M.S. Ying, J.X. Chen, Y. Feng, R.Y. Duan, Commutativity of quantum weakest preconditions, Information Processing Letters 104 (2007) 152–158.

[424] M.S. Ying, R.Y. Duan, Y. Feng, Z.F. Ji, Predicate transformer semantics of quantum programs, in: I. Mackie, S. Gay (Eds.), Semantic Techniques in Quantum Computation, Cambridge University Press, 2010, pp. 311–360.

[425] M.S. Ying, Y. Feng, An algebraic language for distributed quantum computing, IEEE Transactions on Computers 58 (2009) 728–743.

[426] M.S. Ying, Y. Feng, Quantum loop programs, Acta Informatica 47 (2010) 221–250.

[427] M.S. Ying, Y. Feng, A flowchart language for quantum programming, IEEE Transactions on Software Engineering 37 (2011) 466–485.

[428] M.S. Ying, Y. Feng, Model Checking Quantum Systems: Principles and Algorithms, Cambridge University Press, 2021.

[429] M.S. Ying, Y. Feng, R.Y. Duan, Z.F. Ji, An algebra of quantum processes, ACM Transactions on Computational Logic 10 (2009) 19.

[430] M.S. Ying, Y. Feng, N.K. Yu, Quantum information-flow security: noninterference and access control, in: Proceedings of the IEEE 26th Computer Security Foundations Symposium (CSF'2013), 2013, pp. 130–144.

[431] M.S. Ying, Y.J. Li, N.K. Yu, Y. Feng, Model-checking linear-time properties of quantum systems, ACM Transactions on Computational Logic 15 (2014) 22.

[432] M.S. Ying, S.G. Ying, X.D. Wu, Invariants of quantum programs: characterisations and generation, in: Proceedings of the 44th ACM Symposium on Principles of Programming Languages (POPL), 2017, pp. 818–832.

[433] M.S. Ying, N.K. Yu, Y. Feng, Defining quantum control flows of programs, arXiv:1209.4379.

[434] M.S. Ying, N.K. Yu, Y. Feng, Alternation in quantum programming: from superposition of data to superposition of programs, arXiv:1402.5172.

[435] M.S. Ying, N.K. Yu, Y. Feng, R.Y. Duan, Verification of quantum programs, Science of Computer Programming 78 (2013) 1679–1700.

[436] M.S. Ying, Z.C. Zhang, Quantum recursive programming with quantum case statements, arXiv:2311.01725.

[437] M.S. Ying, L. Zhou, Y.J. Li, Reasoning about parallel quantum programs, arXiv:1810.11334, 2018.

[438] M.S. Ying, L. Zhou, Y.J. Li, Y. Feng, A proof system for disjoint parallel quantum programs, Theoretical Computer Science 897 (2022) 164–184.

[439] S.G. Ying, Y. Feng, N.K. Yu, M.S. Ying, Reachability analysis of quantum Markov chains, in: Proceedings of the 24th International Conference on Concurrency Theory (CONCUR), 2013, pp. 334–348.

[440] S.G. Ying, M.S. Ying, Reachability analysis of quantum Markov decision processes, Information and Computation 263 (2018) 31–51.

[441] N.K. Yu, Structured theorem for quantum programs and its applications, ACM Transactions on Software Engineering and Methodology 32 (2023) 103, 1–35.

[442] N.K. Yu, R.Y. Duan, M.S. Ying, Five two-qubit gates are necessary for implementing Toffoli gate, Physical Review A 88 (2013) 010304.

[443] N.K. Yu, J. Palsberg, Quantum abstract interpretation, in: Proceedings of the 42nd ACM International Conference on Programming Language Design and Implementation (PLDI), 2021, pp. 542–558.

[444] N.K. Yu, M.S. Ying, Reachability and termination analysis of concurrent quantum programs, in: Proceedings of the 23th International Conference on Concurrency Theory (CONCUR), 2012, pp. 69–83.

[445] N.K. Yu, M.S. Ying, Optimal simulation of Deutsch gates and the Fredkin gate, Physical Review A 91 (2015) 032302.

[446] C. Yuan, C. McNally, M. Carbin, Twist: sound reasoning for purity and entanglement in quantum programs, Proceedings of the ACM on Programming Languages 6 (POPL) (2022) 30, 1–32.

[447] C. Yuan, M. Carbin, Tower: data structures in quantum superposition, Proceedings of the ACM on Programming Languages 6 (OOPSLA) (2022) 134, 259–288.

[448] C. Yuan, A. Villanyi, M. Carbin, Quantum control machine: the limits of quantum programs as data, arXiv:2304.15000.

[449] J.J. Zhao, Quantum software engineering: landscapes and horizons, arXiv:2007.07047.

[450] L. Zhou, G. Barthe, P.-Y. Strub, J.Y. Liu, M.S. Ying, CoqQ: foundational verification of quantum programs, Proceedings of the ACM on Programming Languages 7 (POPL) (2023) 833–865.

[451] L. Zhou, G. Barthe, J. Hsu, M.S. Ying, N.K. Yu, A quantum interpretation of bunched logic & quantum separation logic, in: Proceedings of the 36th ACM/IEEE Symposium on Logic in Computer Science (LICS), 2021, pp. 1–14.

[452] L. Zhou, N.K. Yu, M.S. Ying, An applied quantum Hoare logic, in: Proceedings of the 40th ACM International Conference on Programming Language Design and Implementation (PLDI), 2019, pp. 1149–1162.

[453] X.Q. Zhou, T.C. Ralph, P. Kalasuwan, M. Zhang, A. Peruzzo, B.P. Lanyon, J.L. O'Brien, Adding control to arbitrary unkown quantum operations, Nature Communications 2 (2011) 413, 1–8.

[454] S.P. Zhu, S.-H. Hung, S. Chakrabarti, X.D. Wu, On the principles of differentiable quantum programming languages, in: Proceedings of the 41st ACM International Conference on Programming Language Design and Implementation (PLDI), 2020, pp. 272–285.

[455] P. Zuliani, Quantum Programming, D.Phil. Thesis, University of Oxford, 2001.

[456] P. Zuliani, Compiling quantum programs, Acta Informatica 41 (2005) 435–473.

[457] P. Zuliani, Quantum programming with mixed states, in: Proceedings of the 3rd International Workshop on Quantum Programming Languages (QPL), 2005.

[458] P. Zuliani, Reasoning about faulty quantum programs, Acta Informatica 46 (2009) 403–432.

[459] K. Życzkowski, P. Horodecki, A. Sanpera, M. Lewenstein, Volume of the set of separable states, Physical Review A 58 (1998) 883–892.

Index

Printed in the United States
by Baker & Taylor Publisher Services